Pro Spring 2.5

Jan Machacek, Aleksa Vukotic,
Anirvan Chakraborty, and Jessica Ditt

Apress®

Pro Spring 2.5

ISBN-13 (pbk): 978-1-59059-921-1

ISBN-10 (pbk): 1-59059-921-7

ISBN-13 (electronic): 978-1-4302-0506-7

Printed and bound in the United States of America 9 8 7 6 5 4 3 2 1

SpringSource is the company behind Spring, the de facto standard in enterprise Java. SpringSource is a leading provider of enterprise Java infrastructure software, and delivers enterprise class software, support and services to help organizations utilize Spring. The open source–based Spring Portfolio is a comprehensive enterprise application framework designed on long-standing themes of simplicity and power. With more than five million downloads to date, Spring has become an integral part of the enterprise application infrastructure at organizations worldwide. For more information, visit `www.springsource.com`.

Lead Editors: Steve Anglin and Tom Welsh
Technical Reviewer: Rick Evans
Editorial Board: Clay Andres, Steve Anglin, Ewan Buckingham, Tony Campbell, Gary Cornell, Jonathan Gennick, Kevin Goff, Matthew Moodie, Joseph Ottinger, Jeffrey Pepper, Frank Pohlmann, Ben Renow-Clarke, Dominic Shakeshaft, Matt Wade, Tom Welsh
Project Manager: Sofia Marchant
Copy Editors: Heather Lang, Damon Larson
Associate Production Director: Kari Brooks-Copony
Production Editor: Kelly Winquist
Compositor: Kinetic Publishing Services
Proofreader: April Eddy
Indexer: Broccoli Information Management
Cover Designer: Kurt Krames
Manufacturing Director: Tom Debolski

Distributed to the book trade worldwide by Springer-Verlag New York, Inc., 233 Spring Street, 6th Floor, New York, NY 10013. Phone 1-800-SPRINGER, fax 201-348-4505, e-mail `orders-ny@springer-sbm.com`, or visit `http://www.springeronline.com`.

For information on translations, please contact Apress directly at 2855 Telegraph Avenue, Suite 600, Berkeley, CA 94705. Phone 510-549-5930, fax 510-549-5939, e-mail `info@apress.com`, or visit `http://www.apress.com`.

Apress and friends of ED books may be purchased in bulk for academic, corporate, or promotional use. eBook versions and licenses are also available for most titles. For more information, reference our Special Bulk Sales–eBook Licensing web page at `http://www.apress.com/info/bulksales`.

The source code for this book is available to readers at `http://www.apress.com`. You will need to answer questions pertaining to this book in order to successfully download the code.

To Marc, who still thinks that beans grow on trees
—Jan

To my parents, Andja and Slobodan, who have guided me through life and encouraged me to follow my own path
—Aleksa

To my parents, Sujata and Kalyan, for their unconditional love and support
—Anirvan

To Ioannis, for the vital nudges when I needed them most (and so much more), and to my family, just for being my family
—Jessica

Contents at a Glance

PART 4 ■ ■ ■ Java EE 5

Contents

PART 2 Data Access

Foreword

It was with a heavy heart that I made the decision not to participate in writing *Pro Spring 2.5*. I am deeply thankful that Jan was around to pick up this book and run with it. *Pro Spring* has been a big part of my life for over three years, and I didn't relinquish the reins lightly. When Juergen and I set out working on Spring Framework 2.0, I knew that I wouldn't have the time to participate in the writing process and write the software at the same time. Fortunately, Jan was there to step into the breach.

Jan and Apress had additionally planned to release *Pro Spring 2.0*, but Juergen and I inadvertently made it impossible for them to keep up by making many changes to the Spring Framework. I vividly remember cringing when updating all the JSP form tags, knowing that I was creating yet more work for Jan.

With the 2.5 release just on the horizon, Jan made the sensible choice to forego a 2.0 edition and head straight for 2.5. This was a wise move. The Spring Framework 2.5 release reflects the state of the art in both the Spring Framework and in enterprise Java frameworks as a whole. A guide book to this critical tool is necessary reading for any conscientious Java developer.

I recall, back in the early days of running Cake Solutions, when we decided we needed to hire another programmer. We were very inexperienced at hiring in general, and hiring programmers is fraught with problems. We knew that we wanted to get a graduate, but we never imagined that we would get someone as accomplished as Jan.

I remember, in his first week, he wrote a complete desktop mailing package from scratch—and it worked. Over the last five years, Jan has been at the center of most of the projects run at Cake, many of which are large-scale Java products based on the Spring Framework. His knowledge of Spring comes from an immense amount of practical experience: he has been in the trenches with Spring since version 1.0 and has delivered successful systems on top of it.

To his credit, Jan realized that writing *Pro Spring 2.5* was too big a job for just one man, so he roped in the rest of the Cake Solutions team to help him. This prospect excited me greatly— a team of real programmers, with real experience in Spring, passing along that knowledge. There is no doubt that many will find this book to be an indispensable reference.

And so, although I am disappointed at being unable to work on this book myself, I am glad that Jan was there to deliver what so many people have been asking for, an updated version of *Pro Spring*.
Enjoy,

Rob Harrop
Principal Software Engineer and Lead Engineer
of the SpringSource Application Platform

About the Authors

JAN MACHACEK is the chief software architect at Cake Solutions, which places him at the center of all architectural decisions in all projects. Apart from the architecture, Jan is often called on to help with some of the most complex and challenging areas of the implementation. Since joining Cake, Jan has proven his expertise in Java not only by taking on a wide variety of complex projects but also through his collection of published works. In his free time, Jan is a keen cyclist and a member of the Manchester Wheelers' Club. He tries his best in various time trials and road races.

Jan authored Chapters 1–4, 6, 9, 11, 14, 16, and 22.

ALEKSA VUKOTIC is a software architect at Cake Solutions. He oversees the architecture as well as the implementation of most of Cake's projects. He has extensive experience with most Java EE technologies, particularly Spring MVC and Security. He also has the knack, which means he can solve virtually any technical problem. He is an excellent tutor and is in charge of directing a team of Cake Solutions developers, helping the team in solving the most complex problems. As well as his interest in Java and .NET platforms, Aleksa enjoys sports, music, and nights out. Aleksa works with Jan on all of the major projects at Cake Solutions.

Aleksa authored Chapters 5, 8, 10, 15, 17, and 21.

ANIRVAN CHAKRABORTY is a senior developer at Cake Solutions. His extensive experience with the Spring Framework and attention to detail puts him in charge of the implementation of some of the challenging aspects of Cake Solutions's projects. Anirvan takes great pride in his code and always makes sure the code can be used as an example to others. When he does not have his head buried in Java EE and Linux, he enjoys good food and drink with his friends. He is also an ardent follower of the sport of cricket and enjoys reading detective novels.

Anirvan authored Chapters 7, 13, 19, and 20.

JESSICA DITT has been a developer at London-based Avenue A | Razorfish since early 2008. Prior to that, she was part of the Cake Solutions team for 2.5 years. She has been working on numerous enterprise-level projects, all of which were written using the Spring Framework and Spring Web Flow. Jessica has acquired significant expertise in efficient indexing using Lucene and has efficiently addressed Java EE application scalability issues using Gigaspaces. Out of the office, Jessica is a keen volleyball player and enjoys spending time in the gym.

Jessica authored Chapters 12 and 18.

About the Technical Reviewer

RICK EVANS is an independent contractor based in the UK with many years of experience working in the health, financial, and retail sectors. Over the years, Rick has committed on a number of open source projects, including Spring and Spring.NET. A polished teacher and mentor, Rick often speaks professionally about technology and delivers training on a wide range of enterprise technologies and disciplines.

Acknowledgments

When writing a book, a substantial amount of work goes on behind the scenes, and authors are backed by an excellent team of editors, proofreaders, and technical reviewers. This book was no exception, and we would like to thank everyone who worked on the book. Our thanks goes to Rick, the technical reviewer, who has done enormous amounts of work to ensure that this book is of the highest quality. The great editorial team at Apress also deserves our thanks: most importantly, Sofia Marchant; our editor, Tom Welsh; Heather Lang; Kelly Winquist; and many others. Without their help, we would not have been able to complete this book. I would also like to thank Rob Harrop for agreeing to write the Foreword. Finally, we all wish to thank the managing director of Cake Solutions, Guy Remond; he gave some of Cake Solutions's time to us to work on the book.

Introduction

Recently, the Java world has witnessed a dramatic shift away from so-called "heavyweight" architectures such as Enterprise JavaBeans (EJB) toward lighter weight frameworks such as Spring. Complex and container-dependent services, such as CMP, and transaction management systems have been replaced with simpler alternatives such as Hibernate and aspect-oriented programming (AOP). At the core, Spring provides a comprehensive, lightweight container based on the principle of Inversion of Control (IoC), on which you can build your own applications. On top of this container, Spring provides a myriad of useful services, bringing together a large range of highly competent open source projects into a single cohesive framework.

The quality of the Spring Framework has seen it replacing traditional Java EE architectures in many cases; as a result, more and more developers see the need for comprehensive Spring skills. Despite Spring having quite an extensive suite of documentation and examples, we feel that many developers are still struggling to understand how to use Spring and, more importantly, how to use it effectively. Because of this, we decided to write a new edition of *Pro Spring*.

At first, we thought we would just update a few chapters and call it *Pro Spring 2.5*. However, we quickly realized that Spring 2.5 brought so many new features and improvements that, although we kept the old *Pro Spring* name, this is a completely new book.

Through this book, you will learn how to use Spring to build better web and stand-alone applications and how to sift through the many choices available to you through the framework. Our aim is to provide you with all the knowledge you need to use Spring *effectively* in your own applications and to give you insight into what is happening behind the scenes in Spring.

For example, you will

- Learn the fundamentals of IoC in the context of AOP.
- Become aware of the seamlessness and power of Spring by referencing the easy-to-understand sample applications we provide.
- Learn how to replace common EJB features with Spring alternatives, including Spring's comprehensive AOP-based transaction management framework.
- Effectively manage your Spring components and applications using Spring's built-in JMX engine.
- Learn how to add scheduling to your Spring application with Quartz.

After reading this book, you will be equipped with all the knowledge you need to build applications effectively using Spring and its related open source projects.

PART 1

Getting Started with Spring

In this part of the book, we will introduce the Spring Framework, starting with the steps needed to download the binary and source distributions. We will next explain the Inversion of Control (IoC) pattern and aspect-oriented programming (AOP). IoC and AOP lie at the heart of the Spring Framework. Toward the end of Part 1, we will show you, in full detail, various ways to configure Spring-managed beans. Finally, we will round off Part 1 with a look at some of the most important Spring design patterns.

CHAPTER 1

Introducing Spring

When we think of the community of Java developers, we are reminded of the hordes of gold rush prospectors of the late 1840s, frantically panning the rivers of North America looking for fragments of gold. As Java developers, our rivers run rife with open source projects, but, like the prospectors, finding a useful project can be time consuming and arduous. And yet, more and more developers are turning to open source tools and code. Open source brings innovative code and few restrictions on its usage, allowing developers to focus on the core of the applications they build.

A common gripe about many open source Java projects is that they exist merely to fill a gap in the implementation of the latest buzzword-heavy technology or pattern. Another problem is that some projects lose all their momentum: code that looked very promising in version 0.1 never reaches version 0.2, much less 1.0. Having said that, many high-quality, user-friendly projects meet and address a real need for real applications. In the course of this book, you will meet a carefully chosen subset of these projects. You will get to know one in particular rather well—Spring.

Spring has come a long way since the early code written by Rod Johnson in his book *Expert One-to-One J2EE Design and Development* (Wrox, October 2002). It has seen contributions from the most respected Java developers in the world and reached version 2.5.

Throughout this book, you will see many applications of different open source technologies, all of which are unified under the Spring Framework. When working with Spring, an application developer can use a large variety of open source tools, without needing to write reams of infrastructure code and without coupling his application too closely to any particular tool. This chapter is a gentle introduction to the Spring Framework. If you are already familiar with Spring, you might want to skip this chapter and go straight to Chapter 2, which deals with the setup and introduces the "Hello, World" application in Spring.

Our main aims in this book are to provide as comprehensive a reference to the Spring Framework as we can and, at the same time, give plenty of practical, application-focused advice without it seeming like a clone of the documentation. To help with this, we build a full application using Spring throughout the book to illustrate how to use Spring technologies.

What Is Spring?

The first thing we need to explain is the name Spring. We will use "Spring" in most of the text of this book, but we may not always mean the same thing. Sometimes, we will mean the Spring Framework and sometimes the Spring project. We believe the distinction will always be clear and that you will not have any trouble understanding our meaning.

The core of the Spring Framework is based on the principle of Inversion of Control (IoC). Applications that follow the IoC principle use configuration that describes the dependencies between its components. It is then up to the IoC framework to satisfy the configured dependencies. The "inversion" means that the application does not control its structure; it is up to the IoC framework to do that.

Consider an example where an instance of class `Foo` depends on an instance of class `Bar` to perform some kind of processing. Traditionally, `Foo` creates an instance of `Bar` using the new operator or obtains one from some kind of factory class. Using the IoC technique, an instance of `Bar` (or a subclass) is provided to `Foo` at runtime by some external process. This injection of dependencies at runtime has sometimes led to IoC being given the much more descriptive name dependency injection (DI). The precise nature of the dependencies managed by DI is discussed in Chapter 3.

Spring's DI implementation puts focus on loose coupling: the components of your application should assume as little as possible about other components. The easiest way to achieve loose coupling in Java is to code to interfaces. Imagine your application's code as a system of components: in a web application, you will have components that handle the HTTP requests and then use the components that contain the business logic of the application. The business logic components, in turn, use the data access objects (DAOs) to persist the data to a database. The important concept is that each component does not know what concrete implementation it is using; it only sees an interface. Because each component of the application is aware only of the interfaces of the other components, we can switch the implementation of the components (or entire groups or layers of components) without affecting the components that use the changed components. Spring's DI core uses the information from your application's configuration files to satisfy the dependencies between its components. The easiest way to allow Spring to set the dependencies is to follow the JavaBean naming conventions in your components, but it is not a strict requirement (for a quick introduction to JavaBeans, go to Chapter 3).

When you use DI, you allow dependency configuration to be externalized from your code. JavaBeans provide a standard mechanism for creating Java resources that are configurable in a standard way. In Chapter 3, you will see how Spring uses the JavaBean specification to form the core of its DI configuration model; in fact, any Spring-managed resource is referred to as a bean. If you are unfamiliar with JavaBeans, take a look at the quick primer at the beginning of Chapter 3.

Interfaces and DI are mutually beneficial. We are sure that everyone reading this book will agree that designing and coding an application to interfaces makes for a flexible application that is much more amenable to unit testing. But the complexity of writing code that manages the dependencies between the components of an application designed using interfaces is quite high and places an additional coding burden on developers. By using DI, you reduce the amount of extra code you need for an interface-based design to almost zero. Likewise, by using interfaces, you can get the most out of DI because your beans can utilize any interface implementation to satisfy their dependency.

In the context of DI, Spring acts more like a container than a framework—providing instances of your application classes with all the dependencies they need—but it does so in a much less intrusive way than, say, the EJB container that allows you to create persistent entity beans. Most importantly, Spring will manage the dependencies between the components of your application automatically. All you have to do is create a configuration file that describes the dependencies; Spring will take care of the rest. Using Spring for DI requires nothing more than following the JavaBeans naming conventions within your classes (a requirement that, as you will see in Chapter 4, you can bypass using Spring's method injection support)—there are no special classes from which to inherit or proprietary naming schemes to follow. If anything, the only change you make in an application that uses DI is to expose more properties on your JavaBeans, thus allowing more dependencies to be injected at runtime.

■ **Note** A container builds the environment in which all other software components live. Spring is a container, because it creates the components of your application and the components are children of the container.

A framework is a collection of components that you can use to build your applications. Spring is a framework, because it provides components to build common parts of applications, such as data access support, MVC support, and many others.

Although we leave a full discussion of DI until Chapter 3, it is worth taking a look at the benefits of using DI rather than a more traditional approach:

Reduce glue code: One of the biggest plus points of DI is its ability to reduce dramatically the amount of code you have to write to glue the different components of your application together. Often, this code is trivial—where creating a dependency involves simply creating a new instance of a class. However, the glue code can get quite complex when you need to look up dependencies in a JNDI repository or when the dependencies cannot be invoked directly, as is the case with remote resources. In these cases, DI can really simplify the glue code by providing automatic JNDI lookup and automatic proxying of remote resources.

Externalize dependencies: You can externalize the configuration of dependencies, which allows you to reconfigure easily without needing to recompile your application. This gives you two interesting benefits. First, as you will see in Chapter 4, DI in Spring gives you the ideal mechanism for externalizing all the configuration options of your application for free. Second, this externalization of dependencies makes it much simpler to swap one implementation of a dependency for another. Consider the case where you have a DAO component that performs data operations against a PostgreSQL database and you want to upgrade to Oracle. Using DI, you can simply reconfigure the appropriate dependency on your business objects to use the Oracle implementation rather than the PostgreSQL one.

Manage dependencies in a single place: In the traditional approach to dependency management, you create instances of your dependencies where they are needed—within the dependent class. Even worse, in typical large applications, you usually use a factory or locator to find the dependent components. That means that your code depends on the factory or locator as well as the actual dependency. In all but the most trivial of applications, you will have dependencies spread across the classes in your application, and changing them can prove problematic. When you use DI, all the information about dependencies is the responsibility of a single component (the Spring IoC container), making the management of dependencies much simpler and less error prone.

Improve testability: When you design your classes for DI, you make it possible to replace dependencies easily. This comes in especially handy when you are testing your application. Consider a business object that performs some complex processing; for part of this, it uses a DAO object to access data stored in a relational database. You are not interested in testing the DAO; you simply want to test the business object with various sets of data. In a traditional approach, where the service object is responsible for obtaining an instance of the DAO itself, you have a hard time testing this, because you are unable to replace the DAO implementation easily with a dummy implementation that returns your test data. Instead, you need to make sure that your test database contains the correct data and uses the full DAO implementation for your tests. Using DI, you can create a mock implementation of the DAO that returns the test data, and then you can pass this to your service object for testing. This mechanism can be extended for testing any tier of your application and is especially useful for testing web components, where you can create fake implementations of `HttpServletRequest` and `HttpServletResponse`.

Foster good application design: Designing for DI means, in general, designing against interfaces. A typical injection-oriented application is designed so that all major components are defined as interfaces, and then concrete implementations of these interfaces are created and wired together using the DI container. This kind of design was possible in Java before the advent of DI and DI-based containers such as Spring, but by using Spring, you get a whole host of DI features for free, and you can concentrate on building your application logic, not a framework to support it.

As you can see from this list, DI provides a lot of benefits, but it is not without its drawbacks too. In particular, DI can make seeing just what implementation of a particular dependency is being hooked into which objects difficult, especially for someone not intimately familiar with the code. Typically, this is only a problem when developers are inexperienced with DI; after becoming more experienced, developers find that the centralized view of an application given by Spring DI lets them see the whole picture. For the most part, the massive benefits far outweigh this small drawback, but you should consider this when planning your application.

Beyond Dependency Injection

The Spring core alone, with its advanced DI capabilities, is a worthy tool, but where Spring really excels is in its myriad of additional features, all elegantly designed and built using the principles of DI. Spring provides tools to help build every layer of an application, from helper application programming interfaces (APIs) for data access right through to advanced model-view-controller (MVC) capabilities. What is great about these features is that, although Spring often provides its own approach, you can easily integrate them with other tools, making them all first-class members of the Spring family.

Aspect-Oriented Programming with Spring

Aspect-oriented programming (AOP) is one of the technologies of the moment in the programming space. AOP lets you implement crosscutting logic—that is, logic that applies to many parts of your application—in a single place, and then have that logic automatically applied right across the application. AOP is enjoying an immense amount of time in the limelight at the moment; however, behind all the hype is a truly useful technology that has a place in any Java developer's toolbox.

There are two main kinds of AOP implementation. Static AOP, such as AspectJ (`www.aspectj.org`), provides a compile-time solution for building AOP-based logic and adding it to an application. Dynamic AOP, such as that in Spring, allows crosscutting logic to be applied arbitrarily to any other code at runtime. Finally, in Spring 2.5, you can use load-time dynamic weaving, which applies the crosscutting logic when the class loader loads the class. Both kinds of AOP have their places, and indeed, Spring provides features to integrate with AspectJ. This is covered in more detail in Chapters 5 and 6.

There are many applications for AOP. The typical one given in many traditional examples involves performing some kind of tracing, but AOP has found many more ambitious uses, even within the Spring Framework itself, particularly in transaction management. Spring AOP is covered in depth in Chapters 5–7, where we show you typical uses of AOP within the Spring Framework and your own application. We also look into the issue of performance and consider some areas where traditional technologies can work better than AOP.

Accessing Data in Spring

Data access and persistence seem to be the most often discussed topics in the Java world. It seems that you cannot visit a community site such as `www.theserverside.com` without being bombarded with articles and blog entries describing the latest, greatest data access tool.

Spring provides excellent integration with a choice selection of these data access tools. Moreover, Spring makes the use of JDBC, a viable option for many projects thanks to its simplified wrapper APIs around the standard JDBC API. As of Spring version 1.1, you have support for JDBC, Hibernate, iBATIS, and Java Data Objects (JDO).

The JDBC support in Spring makes building an application on top of JDBC realistic, even for complex applications. The support for Hibernate, iBATIS, and JDO makes their already simple APIs even simpler, thus easing the burden on developers. When using the Spring APIs to access data via any tool, you can take advantage of Spring's excellent transaction support. A full discussion of this support can be found in Chapter 15.

One of Spring's nicest features is the ability to mix and match data access technologies easily within an application. For instance, you may be running an application with Oracle, using Hibernate for much of your data access logic. However, if you want to take advantage of Oracle-specific features, it is simple to implement that particular part of your data access tier using Spring's JDBC APIs.

Simplifying and Integrating with Java EE

There has been a lot of discussion recently about the complexity of various Java EE APIs, especially those of EJB. It is evident from the EJB 3.0 specification that this discussion has been taken on board by the expert group, and EJB 3.0 brought some simplifications and many new features. Even with the simplifications over EJB 2.0, using Spring's simplified support for many Java EE technologies is still more convenient. For instance, Spring provides a selection of classes for building and accessing EJB resources. These classes cut out a lot of the grunt work from both tasks and provide a more DI-oriented API for EJBs.

For any resources stored in a JNDI-accessible location, Spring allows you to do away with the complex lookup code and have JNDI-managed resources injected as dependencies into other objects at runtime. As a side effect of this, your application code becomes decoupled from JNDI, giving you more scope for code reuse in the future.

As of version 1.0.2, Spring does not support JMS access. However, the CVS repository already contains a large array of classes that are to be introduced in 1.1. Using these classes simplifies all interaction with Java Message Service (JMS) destinations and should reduce a lot of the boilerplate code you need to write in order to use JMS from your Spring applications.

Chapters 11–13 explain how Spring works with the most important Java EE application components; Chapter 14 addresses application integration issues; and Chapter 20 deals with management of Java EE applications.

Job Scheduling Support

Many advanced applications require some kind of scheduling capability. Whether for sending updates to customers or doing housekeeping tasks, the ability to schedule code to run at a predefined time is an invaluable tool for developers.

Spring supports two scheduling mechanisms: one uses the `Timer` class, which has been available since Java 1.3; and the other uses the Quartz scheduling engine. Scheduling based on the `Timer` class is quite primitive and is limited to fixed periods defined in milliseconds. With Quartz, on the other hand, you can build complex schedules using the Unix cron format to define when tasks should be run.

Spring's scheduling support is covered in full in Chapter 11.

Mail Support

Sending e-mail is a typical requirement for many different kinds of applications and is given first-class treatment within the Spring Framework. Spring provides a simplified API for sending e-mail messages that fits nicely with its DI capabilities. It supports pluggable implementations of the mail API and comes complete with two implementations: one uses JavaMail, and the other uses Jason Hunter's `MailMessage` class from the `com.oreilly.servlet` package available from `http://servlets.com/cos`.

Spring lets you create a prototype message in the DI container and use this as the base for all messages sent from your application. This allows for easy customization of mail parameters such as the subject and sender address. However, there is no support for customizing the message body outside of the code. In Chapter 12, we look at Spring's mail support in detail and discuss a solution that combines templating engines such as Velocity and FreeMarker and Spring, allowing mail content to be externalized from the Java code.

In addition to simple mail-sending code, we will show how to use Spring events to implement fully asynchronous messaging infrastructure. We will make use of the Spring Java Management Extensions (JMX) features to show how to create an efficient management console for the mail queues.

Dynamic Languages

Dynamic languages in Spring allow you to implement components of your application in languages other than Java (Spring 2.5 supports BeanShell, JRuby, and Groovy). This allows you to externalize part of your application's code so that it can be easily updated by administrators and power users. You could do this even without Spring, but the support built into Spring means that the rest of your application will not be aware that a component is implemented in another language; it will appear to be an ordinary Spring bean.

Many large applications have to deal with complex business processes. This would not be too difficult to handle in Java, but in most cases, these processes change over time, and users want to be able to make the changes themselves. This is where a domain-specific language implementation comes in.

In Chapter 14, you will see how to use the dynamic language support in Spring 2.5 and how to use it to implement a simple domain-specific language.

Remoting Support

Accessing or exposing remote components in Java has never been simple. Using Spring, you can take advantage of extensive support for a wide range of remoting techniques that help you expose and access remote services quickly.

Spring supports a variety of remote access mechanisms, including Java RMI, JAX-RPC, Caucho Hessian, and Caucho Burlap. In addition to these remoting protocols, Spring 1.1 introduced its own HTTP-based protocol that is based on standard Java serialization. By applying Spring's dynamic proxying capabilities, you can have a proxy to a remote resource injected as a dependency into one of your components, thus removing the need to couple your application to a specific remoting implementation and also reducing the amount of code you need to write for your application.

As well as making it easy to access remote components, Spring provides excellent support for exposing a Spring-managed resource as a remote service. This lets you export your service using any of the remoting mechanisms mentioned earlier, without needing any implementation-specific code in your application.

Integrating applications written in different programming languages, and possibly running on different platforms, is one of the most compelling reasons for using remote services. In Chapter 14, we will show how to use remoting between Java applications and a C# Windows rich client application making full use of a Spring service running on a Unix system.

Managing Transactions

Spring provides an excellent abstraction layer for transaction management, allowing for programmatic and declarative transaction control. By using the Spring abstraction layer for transactions, you can easily change the underlying transaction protocol and resource managers. You can start with simple, local, resource-specific transactions and move to global, multiresource transactions without having to change your code. Transactions are covered in full detail in Chapter 15.

The Spring MVC Framework

Although Spring can be used in almost any application, from a service-only application, through web and rich-client ones, it provides a rich array of classes for creating web-based applications. Using Spring, you have maximum flexibility when you are choosing how to implement your web front end.

For a web application of any complexity, it makes sense to use a framework with a paradigm that clearly separates the processing logic from the views. To achieve this, you can use the Spring Struts support or use Spring's own excellent MVC framework. To implement complex page flows, you can use Spring Web Flow. You can use a large array of different view technologies, from JavaServer Pages (JSP) and Apache's Jakarta Velocity to Apache POI (to generate Microsoft Excel output) and iText (to create output in Adobe PDF format). The Spring MVC framework is quite comprehensive and provides support classes that address the majority of your requirements. For the rest, you can easily extend the MVC framework to add in your own functionality.

The view support in Spring MVC is extensive and steadily improving. As well as standard support for JSP, which is greatly bolstered by the Spring tag libraries, you can take advantage of fully integrated support for Jakarta Velocity, FreeMarker, Jakarta Tiles (separate from Struts), and XSLT. Moreover, you will find a set of base view classes that make it simple to add Excel and PDF output to your applications.

We cover the Spring MVC implementation in Chapter 16.

Spring Web Flow

Web Flow represents a new way of developing web applications, especially ones that rely on fairly complex transitions between the pages. Web Flow greatly simplifies the implementation of such systems. Because it is a Spring project, it integrates closely with the Spring MVC framework. Just like Spring MVC, Web Flow can use any type of view technology.

We discuss Web Flow in detail in Chapter 18.

AJAX

AJAX is not only a buzzword of Web 2.0 but also an important technique for creating rich web applications. Put simply, it allows web applications to interact with servers without causing unnecessary page reloads. You may argue that it has little to do with the Spring Framework, but if you need to build highly interactive Web 2.0 applications, you cannot escape it. We will show you how to write the necessary code to add AJAX functionality to your Spring web applications. Because Spring does not provide any framework-level infrastructure to deal with the implementation of AJAX web applications, we will show some important design and performance choices you have to make in your web applications.

Chapter 18 covers AJAX applications in much more detail.

Internationalization

Internationalization is an important aspect of any large application; Spring has extensive support for creating multilanguage applications, and we will show you how to deal with the complexities of this task. The issues facing the developers of multilanguage applications are twofold: first, they must write code without any textual information hard-coded; second, they must design the application in a way that will allow for easy translation in the future.

This issue is further highlighted in situations where developers have to deal with exceptions: in most cases, the message of the exception will be in one language—the language of the developer. We will show you how to overcome this limitation.

All aspects of internationalization are covered in Chapter 17.

Simplified Exception Handling

One area where Spring really helps to reduce the amount of repetitive, boilerplate code you need to write is exception handling. The Spring philosophy is that checked exceptions are overused in Java and that a framework should not force you to catch any exception from which you are unlikely to be able to recover—a point of view that we agree with wholeheartedly.

In reality, many frameworks reduce the impact of having to write code to handle checked exceptions. However, many of these frameworks take the approach of sticking with checked exceptions but artificially reducing the granularity of the exception class hierarchy. One thing you will notice with Spring is that, because of the convenience afforded to the developer by using unchecked exceptions, the exception hierarchy is remarkably granular. Throughout this book, you will see how Spring's exception-handling mechanisms can reduce the amount of code you have to write, while improving your ability to identify, classify, and diagnose application errors.

The Spring Project

Among the most attractive things about the Spring project are the level of activity currently present in the community and the amount of cross-pollination with other projects, such as CGLIB, Apache Geronimo, and AspectJ. One of the most often touted benefits of open source is that if a project on which you rely folds tomorrow, you would be left with the code. But let's face it—you do not want to be left with a codebase the size of Spring to support and improve. For this reason, it is comforting to know how well established and active the Spring community is and how many successful applications are using the Spring Framework at their core.

Origins of Spring

As mentioned previously, the origins of Spring can be traced back to the book *Expert One-to-One J2EE Design and Development* by Rod Johnson (Wrox, 2002). In this book, Rod presented his Interface 21 Framework, which he had developed to use in his own applications. Released into the open source world, this framework formed the foundation of Spring as we know it today. Spring proceeded quickly through the early beta and release candidate stages, and the first official 1.0 release was made available March 24, 2004. Since then, Spring has several major releases and is currently in its 2.5 release (at the time of this writing).

The Spring Community

The Spring community is one of the best in any open source project we have encountered. The mailing lists and forums are always active, and progress on new features is usually rapid. The development team is dedicated to making Spring the most successful of all the Java application frameworks, and this shows in the quality of the code that is produced. Much of the ongoing development in Spring consists of reworking existing code to be faster, smaller, neater, or all three.

Spring benefits from excellent relationships with other open source projects, which is a good thing when you consider how much the full Spring distribution relies on integration with other products. From a user's perspective, one of the best things about Spring is the excellent documentation and test suite that come with it. Documentation is provided for almost all Spring features, making it easier for new users to pick up the framework. The test suite is impressively comprehensive, because the development team writes tests for everything. If they find a bug, they fix it by first writing a test that highlights the bug and getting the test to pass.

What does all this mean to you? Well, it means that you can be confident in the quality of the Spring Framework and know that, for the foreseeable future, the Spring development team intends to go on improving what is already an excellent framework.

Spring for Microsoft .NET

The main Spring Framework is 100 percent Java-based. However, due to the success of the Java version, developers in the .NET world started to feel a little bit left out, so Mark Pollack and Rod Johnson started the Spring .NET project. The two projects have completely different development teams, so the .NET project should have minimal impact on the development of the Java version of the Spring Framework. In fact, the authors believe that this is excellent news. Contrary to popular belief in the Java world, .NET is not a load of garbage produced by the Beast—a fact that we can attest to after delivering several successful .NET applications to our clients.

This project opens up whole new avenues for cross-pollination, especially since .NET already has the lead in some areas, such as source-level metadata, and should help to create better product on both platforms. Another side effect of this project is that it makes the move between platforms much easier for developers, because you can use Spring on both sides. This is all the more true since other projects, such as Hibernate and iBATIS, now have .NET equivalents. You can find more information on Spring .NET at `www.springframework.net`.

The Spring IDE

In all but the simplest Spring applications, the application's configuration files become fairly large and complex; it is convenient to use some kind of integrated development environment (IDE) to help you write the code.

The Spring IDE project is another offshoot of the main Spring project, and it functions as a plug-in for the Eclipse platform. Using Spring IDE, you can get full source highlighting and code insight functionality for your Spring configuration files. You can also reduce the number of errors that can creep into your configuration files, thus speeding up the development cycle. In addition to Spring IDE in Eclipse, you can use IntelliJ IDEA for your Java and Spring development. The Spring support in IntelliJ IDEA 7.0 is indeed excellent.

The Spring Security (Formerly Acegi)

The Spring Security module evolved directly from Acegi, which was a security system built on top of Spring. It provides the full spectrum of security services required for Spring-based applications, including multiple authentication back ends, single sign-on support, and caching. We do not cover Acegi in any detail in this book, but you can find more details at `http://acegisecurity.sourceforge.net/`. Support for Acegi is provided through the Spring forums at `http://forum.springframework.org`.

Alternatives to Spring

Going back to our previous comments on the number of open source projects, you should not be surprised to learn that Spring is not the only framework offering DI or full end-to-end support for building applications. In fact, there are almost too many projects to mention. In the spirit of being open, we include a brief discussion of some of these frameworks here, but we believe that none of them offer quite as comprehensive a solution as Spring.

PicoContainer

PicoContainer (`www.picocontainer.org`) is an exceptionally small (100kB) DI container that allows you to use DI for your application without introducing any dependencies other than PicoContainer itself. Because PicoContainer is nothing more than a DI container, you may find that as your application grows, you need to introduce another framework, such as Spring, in which case you would have been better off using Spring from the start. If all you need is a tiny DI container, PicoContainer is a good choice. But since Spring packages the DI container separate from the rest of the framework, you can just as easily use that and keep your options open.

NanoContainer

NanoContainer (`www.nanocontainer.org`) is an extension to PicoContainer for managing trees of individual PicoContainer containers. Because Spring provides all the same functionality in the standard DI container, NanoContainer is not really a major improvement over Spring. Where NanoContainer becomes interesting is in its support for scripting languages that interact with it. However, Spring comes with full support for scripting languages as well.

Keel Framework

The Keel Framework (`www.keelframework.org`) is more of a metaframework, in that most of its capabilities come from other frameworks that are all brought together under a single roof. For instance, DI functionality comes from the Apache Avalon container, while web functionality comes from Struts or a similar framework. Keel has many implementations of the same components and links them all together into a cohesive structure, allowing you to swap out implementations with minimal impact on your application. Despite its wide feature set, Keel does not seem to have enjoyed the same level of acceptance as Spring. Although we have investigated Keel only briefly, we feel that this is partially to do with the level of accessibility. Spring is immediately accessible to developers of all levels, whereas Keel seems to be more complex. Having said that, Keel's feature set is impressive, and it is certainly a direct competitor for Spring.

Google Guice

The Guice (pronounced "juice") framework focuses purely on dependency injection. As such, it is not a direct competition for the Spring Framework; in fact, you can use Spring-managed beans in Guice. Apart from the focus of the framework, the main difference between Guice and Spring is the approach to the configuration of the applications. Guice uses automatic wiring or annotation-based configuration. Automatic wiring means that the framework examines the components it is aware of and will try to guess the dependencies between them. The guess is based on the dependency's type and name. As even the creators of Guice admit (and we wholeheartedly agree), automatic wiring is not suitable for large enterprise applications. For complex applications, Guice authors recommend using annotation-based configuration. Because Guice uses annotations, it does not need any complex configuration files like Spring.

Unfortunately, by adding annotations, you limit the code you write only to Guice. Even with this drawback, Guice is an excellent framework, and its big advantage is that it can be used in cooperation with Spring.

The Sample Code

Throughout the text, we will use two main approaches to sample code. To demonstrate fine and very specific points, we will create single-purpose small applications. To demonstrate complex code, we will create applications that may share code across multiple chapters. You can download the code from Source Code section of the Apress web site (`http://www.apress.com`).

Summary

In this chapter, we presented you with a high-level view of the Spring Framework complete with discussions of all the major features, and we pointed you to the sections of this book where those features are discussed in detail. We also had a very brief look at some of the concepts that we will be dealing with throughout this book. After reading this chapter, you should have an idea of what Spring can do for you; all that remains is to see how it can do it.

In the next chapter, we explain everything you need to know to get up and running with a basic Spring application. We show you how to obtain the Spring Framework and discuss the packaging options, the test suite, and the documentation. Also, Chapter 2 introduces some basic Spring code, including the time-honored "Hello, World" example in all its DI-based glory. On that note, let's press on!

CHAPTER 2

Getting Started

When trying out a new framework, the first step is usually the most complex one. The documentation and numerous blogs on the Spring Framework already assume you know how to find your way around Spring applications. While sounding really impressive, sentences like "Spring favors programming to interfaces" or "Spring promotes lose coupling" do not mean much.

In this chapter, we will walk you through the first steps involved in creating a simple Spring application. We will first take a look at how to obtain the latest Spring distribution. Then we will take the plunge and write a simple "Hello, World" application. Once you have mastered that, we will take a more detailed look at all the code that comes with the Spring distribution. We will explain which libraries you typically need for a console application, a web application, a rich client application, and an enterprise application. Finally, we will take a look at how you can obtain the latest (and latest stable) Spring source code from CVS and how to build your own release of Spring.

Obtaining the Spring Framework

Our first step will be to download the Spring Framework distribution. The Spring Framework is now part of the Spring portfolio, which includes projects that are closely associated with the framework. The portfolio includes Spring Web Flow (see Chapter 18), Spring Security (formerly Acegi Security for Spring), Spring Web Services (see Chapter 15), Spring Batch, and Spring Integration.

There are many other exciting projects, among the most notable are Spring Dynamic Modules for OSGi, Spring Rich Client, Spring IDE, and many others; all are available at `www.springframework.org/projects`.

For now, though, we only need the Spring Framework, which you can download at `www.springframework.org/download`. The link will take you to the SourceForge download page, where you should download the `spring-framework-2.5.1-with-dependencies.zip` archive.

Checking Out Spring from CVS

Spring is under constant development with many new features being added almost daily. If you want to get a grip on new features before they make their way into a release, then obtaining the latest source code from CVS is the best way of going about it.

To check out the latest version of the Spring code, install CVS, which you can download from `www.cvshome.org`, and run the following command:

```
cvs -d:pserver:anonymous@springframework.cvs.sourceforge.net:➥
/cvsroot/springframework login
```

When prompted for your password, simply press Enter to send a blank password. Next, enter the following command to check out the HEAD of the CVS repository, which contains the latest changes that have been committed:

```
cvs -z3 -d:pserver:anonymous@springframework.cvs.sourceforge.net:➥
/cvsroot/springframework co -P spring
```

This command gives you the absolute latest version of the code, including two separate source trees: one contains the main source for Spring including any new features considered stable enough to be in the main tree; and the other, the sandbox, contains code still classified as work in progress. New code in the main tree is likely to make it into the next release, but code in the sandbox might not. Be aware that any new code is subject to change without notice; for this reason, avoid basing any of your new applications around unreleased code.

Older versions of Spring are stored in CVS tagged by their version number, so you can download any version of Spring directly from CVS. If you are unsure of the tags to use, you can find them by browsing the CVS repository online at `http://springframework.cvs.sourceforge.net/springframework/`.

Building Spring from Source Code

Let's take a look at how we can compile the framework from the source code. Even though it is possible to compile the HEAD version from CVS, we recommend that you compile one of the final releases. In the following example, we will take the latest version of Spring available at the time of this writing, version 2.5.2. The CVS tag for the source is `release-2-5-1`; you will need to run the commands in Listing 2-1 to check out the tag.

Listing 2-1. *Commands to Check Out the 2.5.1 Release of Spring*

```
cvs -d:pserver:anonymous@springframework.cvs.sourceforge.net:➥
/cvsroot/springframework login
cvs -z3 -d:pserver:anonymous@springframework.cvs.sourceforge.net:➥
/cvsroot/springframework co -r release-2-5-2 -P spring
```

Assuming that you have Apache Ant installed, that you have set the `$ANT_HOME` environment variable, and that the `$PATH` includes `$ANT_HOME/bin`, you can run `ant alljars`. This will build all source code and produce the Spring JAR files. The JAR files will be created in the `dist` directory, whose full structure is shown in Listing 2-2.

Listing 2-2. *Showing the Compiled Modules*

```
janm@janm-ff:~/spring/dist$ find -iname \*.jar | sort -r
./weaving/spring-tomcat-weaver.jar
./weaving/spring-aspects.jar
./weaving/spring-agent.jar
./weaving-sources/spring-tomcat-weaver-sources.jar
./weaving-sources/spring-aspects-sources.jar
./weaving-sources/spring-agent-sources.jar
./spring-sources.jar
./spring.jar
./modules/spring-webmvc-struts.jar
./modules/spring-webmvc-portlet.jar
./modules/spring-webmvc.jar
./modules/spring-web.jar
./modules/spring-tx.jar
./modules/spring-test.jar
./modules/spring-orm.jar
```

```
./modules/spring-jms.jar
./modules/spring-jdbc.jar
./modules/spring-core.jar
./modules/spring-context-support.jar
./modules/spring-context.jar
./modules/spring-beans.jar
./modules/spring-aop.jar
./module-sources/spring-web-sources.jar
./module-sources/spring-webmvc-struts-sources.jar
./module-sources/spring-webmvc-sources.jar
./module-sources/spring-webmvc-portlet-sources.jar
./module-sources/spring-tx-sources.jar
./module-sources/spring-test-sources.jar
./module-sources/spring-orm-sources.jar
./module-sources/spring-jms-sources.jar
./module-sources/spring-jdbc-sources.jar
./module-sources/spring-core-sources.jar
./module-sources/spring-context-support-sources.jar
./module-sources/spring-context-sources.jar
./module-sources/spring-beans-sources.jar
./module-sources/spring-aop-sources.jar
```

These JAR files are the same ones you can get in the Spring binary distribution; in the next section, we will take a more detailed look at the packages.

Verifying Your Spring Distribution

With every distribution, you get the full source code for the test suite, along with the Ant script you need to run the tests and produce the test report. If you think your distribution has a bug, first run the test suite to see if the bug is highlighted in one of the tests. Although many open source projects claim that most bugs are in user code and not in their code, Spring can back this up with a test suite that consists of thousands of tests. Don't just take our word for it; you can run all Spring tests by running `ant tests` at the command line.

We do not recommend that you build Spring from source code and use the compiled code in your day-to-day development. It is much easier and much more convenient to use automated tools such as Maven 2 to determine which version of Spring, and other libraries, your application needs to compile, test, and run.

Spring Packaging

When you unzip the full Spring distribution or compile the source distribution, the `dist` subdirectory contains the full Spring distribution. However, there are many different JARs and, even more confusingly, `spring.jar`. The reason for this split is that some applications may not require the entire Spring Framework. The decision whether to use various smaller JARs or the entire `spring.jar` depends on the type of application you are writing and on its environment.

Most applications work absolutely fine with the entire `spring.jar` on the classpath. However, if you deploy your application in an application server that already contains other versions of the Spring Framework libraries, you may come across versioning conflicts. Another situation where you may not want to include the entire `spring.jar` in your application is if you wish to use only parts of the Spring's code. Table 2-1 summarizes all the Spring JARs that are included in the default distribution.

Table 2-1. *Spring JAR Files*

JAR File	Description
`spring-aop.jar`	This JAR contains all the classes you need to use Spring's AOP features within your application. You also need to include this JAR in your application if you plan to use other features in Spring that use AOP, such as declarative transaction management.
`spring-beans.jar`	This archive contains all of Spring's dependency injection. It contains the bean factories and supporting classes. In most cases, you will need to add `spring-context.jar`, which contains code needed to build the application context.
`spring-context.jar`	This JAR contains code needed to build the Spring application context; it packages the main `ApplicationConext` interface and its implementations together with code for instrumentation, JNDI, scheduling, themes, and validation.
`spring-context-support.jar`	This package contains utility Spring code—this means caching, instrumentation, e-mail and scheduling support, and the very interesting scripting languages support.
`spring-core.jar`	This contains the core files of the Spring Framework: it deals with annotations, enumerations, task execution, resource loading, and other utilities and exceptions you may find useful even outside the context of the Spring Framework.
`spring-jdbc.jar`	This package contains code for the JDBC support classes, namely the `JdbcTemplate` and `JdbcDaoSupport` classes; we discuss JDBC support in Chapter 7.
`spring-jms.jar`	This JAR contains code for JMS; see Chapter 15 for examples of transactional message queues.
`spring-orm.jar`	This archive contains the files needed for object-relational mapping (ORM) tools. Including this package on your classpath will give you Spring support for Hibernate 3, iBATIS, JDO, JPA, and TopLink.
`spring-test.jar`	This package contains support code to write unit and integration tests using the Spring Framework. It supports the JUnit 3, JUnit 4, and TestNG testing frameworks. In addition, you can use classes from the `org.springframework.mock` package, which represent mock implementations of JNDI and web classes.
`spring-tx.jar`	This one contains support for core data access exceptions and transaction technologies. These two areas are closely bound together, because the transactions generally work with some data access code.
`spring-web.jar`	This JAR contains code for the Spring web application support (utilities, binders, multipart resolvers). For more details, see Chapter 16.
`spring-webmvc-portlet.jar`	This JAR contains code needed to build portlet-based (rather than servlet-based) web applications. If you have an application server that supports the Portlet API (JSR 168), you can use this package.
`spring-webmvc-struts.jar`	This package contains code needed to use Spring with the Jakarta Struts Framework.
`spring-webmvc.jar`	This package contains the Spring MVC code; you will find much more detail about Spring MVC in Chapter 17.

As we said before, each of these JARs contains fragments of the entire Spring distribution. However, `spring.jar` is still not the entire distribution of Spring. The `spring.jar` library does not include the code in the `spring-mvc-*.jar` files.

Spring Dependencies

If we leave the `dist` directory and go to the `lib` directory, you will notice that it contains a large number of libraries. These dependencies are necessary to build and test the entire Spring Framework distribution, but not all of the dependencies will be needed in your applications. Table 2-2 lists the Spring 2.5 dependencies, including their short descriptions.

Table 2-2. *Spring Dependencies*

Dependency Group	JAR Files	Description
ant	ant.jar, ant-junit.jar, ant-launcher.jar	Spring uses Apache Ant as its build tool, as well as for many tasks such as generating documentation and running tests. Ant is not used at all at runtime, so you do not need to include this JAR file in your distribution.
aopalliance	aopalliance.jar	The AOP Alliance (http://aopalliance.sourceforge.net/) is a combined, open source collaboration between many projects to provide a standard set of interfaces for AOP in Java. Spring's AOP implementation is based on the standard AOP Alliance APIs. You only need this JAR file if you plan to use Spring's AOP or AOP-based features.
axis	axis.jar, saaj.jar, wsdl4j.jar	Spring uses the Apache Axis project to support the JAX-RPC capabilities in Spring remoting. You only need these files if you are using JAX-RPC remoting.
caucho	burlap-2.1.7.jar, hessian-3.0.13.jar	Spring remoting provides support for a wide variety of different protocols, including Caucho's Burlap and Hessian. You only need the JARs in this group if you are using the corresponding protocols in your application.
cglib	cglib-full-2.0.2.jar	CGLIB is used to generate dynamic proxy classes for use in both the core DI and AOP implementations. You almost always need to include CGLIB with your application, because it is used to implement a wide range of Spring's functionality.
cos	cos.jar	COS stands for com.oreilly.servlet, which is a collection of useful classes for working with servlets and web-based applications. Spring uses COS in two areas: for handling file uploads and sending e-mail. In both cases, COS is just an implementation choice, so you only need to include cos.jar if you choose to use COS over one of the other implementations.
dom4j	dom4j.jar	You must have dom4j when you are using Hibernate, so you need to include this JAR file if you plan to use Hibernate for ORM in your application.
easymock	easymock.jar, easymockclassextension.jar	EasyMock is used in the Spring test suite, so you only need to use this JAR for building and running the test suite; you do not need to distribute this with your application.

Continued

Table 2-2. *Continued*

Dependency Group	JAR Files	Description
freemarker	freemaker.jar	Spring provides wrapper classes around the FreeMarker templating engine and also provides support for using FreeMarker templates as views for your web applications. This is required whenever you are using FreeMarker.
hibernate	ehcache.jar, hibernate3.jar, odmg.jar	These JAR files are required when you are using Spring's Hibernate integration and support classes. If you are using a different ORM tool, such as iBATIS, you can leave these JARs out of your application. When you are using Hibernate, you must also include the CGLIB JAR file in your application.
hsqldb	hsqldb.jar	The hsqldb.jar file is used by the Spring sample applications.
ibatis	ibatis-common.jar, ibatis-sqlmap.jar, ibatis-sqlmap-2.jar	These files are required when you are using Spring's iBATIS integration classes, but you can leave them out of your application if you are using JDBC or another ORM tool such as Hibernate or JDO.
itext	itext-1.3.1.jar	Spring uses iText to provide PDF support in the web tier. Only include this JAR if your web applications need to generate PDF output.
j2ee	activation.jar, connector-api.jar, ejb.jar, jaxrpc.jar, jdbc2_0-stdext.jar, jms.jar, jstl.jar, jta.jar, mail.jar, servlet.jar, xml-apis.jar	As you can see, there is a large array of different Java EE-related JAR files. You need the activation.jar and mail.jar files if you want to use the JavaMail implementation of Spring's mail support. You need connector-api.jar to use the JCA connector for Hibernate, ejb.jar to use Spring's EJB support, and jms.jar to use Spring's JMS support. For web applications, you need servlet.jar, and you need jstl.jar if you want to use Spring's JSTL support. The jaxrpc.jar file is required for JAX-RPC support in Spring remoting, and jta.jar is used for JTA transaction support. The remaining two jars, jdbc2_0-stdext.jar and xml-apis.jar, are needed for JDBC and XML configuration support, respectively—but only when you are using a version 1.3 JVM.
jakarta	jakarta-commons commons-attributes-api.jar, commons-attributes-compiler.jar, commons-beanutils.jar, commons-collections.jar, commons-dbcp.jar, commons-digester.jar, commons-discovery.jar, commons-fileupload.jar, commons-lang.jar, commons-logging.jar, commons-pool.jar, commons-validator.jar	Many of the components from the Jakarta Commons project are used by Spring. You need the commons-attribute-api.jar if you want to use source-level metadata in your application, plus you need the compiler JAR file to compile the attributes into your application. The beanutils, collections, digester, discovery, and validator JAR files are used by Struts, and Hibernate uses collections as well. dbcp is used by Spring's JDBC support when you are using DBCP connection pools, and pooling is required by some of the sample applications.

Dependency Group	JAR Files	Description
jakarta (*Continued*)		fileupload is required if you want to use the corresponding Spring wrapper to handle file uploads in your web applications. Finally, logging is used throughout Spring, so you need to include it in every Spring-based application.
jakarta-taglibs	standard.jar	This is the Jakarta JSTL implementation, and it is used by some of the Spring sample applications.
jboss	jboss-common-jdbc-wrapper.jar	This is required when you are using Spring's JDBC classes in an application running on the JBoss application server.
jdo	jdo.jar	This is required for Spring's JDO support.
jdom	jdom.jar	JDOM is required when you are using iBATIS 1.3 with Spring. The version of iBATIS covered in this chapter is 2.0.
jotm	jotm.jar, xapool.jar	The jotm.jar file is required if you plan to use JOTM in conjunction with Spring's transaction abstraction layer. You only need xapool.jar if you plan to use XAPool for connection pooling in your application.
junit	junit.jar	JUnit is not required at all at runtime; it is only used for building and running the test suite.
log4j	log4j-1.2.14.jar	This is required when you want to use Spring to configure log4j logging.
poi	poi-2.5.1.jar	This adds support for Microsoft Excel output to Spring's MVC framework.
quartz	quartz.jar	This is used for Spring Quartz-based scheduling support.
regexp	jakarta-oro-2.0.7.jar	This is required when you are using regular expressions to specify point cuts in AOP. You can find more details on this in Chapter 6.
struts	struts-1.1.jar	The Struts JAR is required whenever you want to use Struts in conjunction with Spring to build a web application.
velocity	velocity-1.4.jar, velocity-tools-generic-1.1.jar	Spring provides wrapper classes around Velocity to make it DI enabled and to reduce the amount of code you need to write to use Velocity in your application. In addition to this, Spring provides classes to support the use of Velocity as the view provider in the web tier. If you are using any of these features, you need to include the Velocity JAR files in your distribution.
xdoclet	xjavadoc-1.0.jar	Commons Attributes uses this to parse your source code files and extract the attribute information. Include this JAR file if you are using Spring's Commons Attributes support.

We found that the best way to create applications is to start with the minimal set of dependencies and only add another JAR if necessary. The main reason for this is neither speed nor size but the possibility of conflict when two dependent libraries rely on different versions of the same library. In this case, most developers take the latest (or later) version and try to get the application to compile. If that works and the tests verify that the application is working correctly, they assume that the conflict is resolved. This approach usually works, and until there is more widespread support for OSGi modules, we have no other choice. Welcome to JAR hell!

Spring Sample Applications

An area where many open source, and indeed commercial, products fail is in providing enough well documented sample code to make it easy for people to get started. Thankfully, Spring comes with a complete set of nifty sample applications that demonstrate a wide selection of the features in Spring. A point to note is that the sample applications are treated as first-class citizens of the framework by the development team, and they are constantly being improved and worked on by the team. For this reason, you generally find that, after you get what you can from the test suite, the samples are a great place to get started when you are looking at new features.

The PetClinic Application

PetClinic is an interesting sample application that was built to showcase Spring's data access support. In it, you find a web-based application for querying and updating the database of a fictional veterinary office. The interesting thing about this application is that it comes with a selection of interchangeable data access implementations that highlight how easy it is to decouple your application from the data access logic when you are using Spring.

The Hibernate data access implementation really shows off Spring's Hibernate support by implementing each of the eight data access methods with a single line. The JDBC implementation is equally interesting. First, much of the JDBC logic is contained in an abstract base class. This class provides hook methods for subclasses when you need to use provider-specific SQL features—in the PetClinic case, this happens with the automatic generation of primary keys. Second, when you are looking at the base class, it is interesting to see how much of the repetitive error-handling code that is prevalent when you are using JDBC is removed. Third, it is very interesting to see how data access is handled in a much more object-oriented way.

This project also contains a very solid example of how to build a web application using Spring's MVC support, so if you are planning to use Spring MVC for one of your own applications, make sure you take a look at this sample first.

We cover JDBC support in Chapter 9, Hibernate in Chapter 11, and Spring MVC in Chapter 17.

The PetPortal Application

This application offers sample implementation of the Portlet MVC support in Spring using the favorite pet shop scenario. It is a simplified jPetStore application; it demonstrates wizard-style controllers and validators, file upload handling, and redirection to external web sites.

The jPetStore Application

The jPetStore application is based on the jPetStore sample created by Clinton Begin for iBATIS. As far as sample applications go, this one is huge. It contains a full DAO layer, created using Spring and iBATIS, with implementations for Oracle, Microsoft SQL Server, MySQL, and PostgreSQL. The business tier is fully Spring managed and, coupled with the DAO layer, it presents a good example of Spring-managed transactions.

Also included with this application is a solid example of how to use both Spring MVC and Struts. This application also highlights how to use Spring remoting using JAX-RPC.

Spring MVC is covered in Chapters 17, iBATIS in Chapter 10, and Spring remoting in Chapter 15.

The Tiles Example Application

Tiles is one of our favorite open source tools, because it reduces a lot of the drudge work when you are building user interfaces for the Web, and it really helps separate individual UI elements into reusable fragments. Because of this, the Tiles support in Spring is especially welcome, and this sample application makes getting started with Tiles in your own sample application easy.

We cover Tiles in detail in Chapter 17.

The ImageDB Application

This is one of our favorite sample applications, because it shows off loads of useful Spring features. Specifically, you see how to load and store large binary objects (LOBs) in a database, how to handle file uploads, and how to schedule jobs using the Quartz job scheduler. As if that weren't enough, you also see how to use Velocity as the view technology in the web tier.

We cover LOBs in Chapters 9 and 11, file uploads in Chapter 17, job scheduling in Chapter 12, and Velocity support in Chapter 17.

The JasperRepots Application

Reports are one of the most dreaded programming tasks; this application shows how to use the JasperReports framework to ease the development of PDF and Excel reports without a single line of Java web code. We discuss the reporting support in Chapter 17.

JCA-10 Application

The aim of the sample is to show how to use the support of JCA CCI 1.0 in Spring. It uses the sample JCA connector of the Java EE SDK version 1.3 modified to be used with Hypersonic and to execute SQL requests directly on the CCI interaction specification. The connector of the sample only supports local transactions and works in a stand-alone mode.

To use it in a managed mode, you must package the JAR in `spring-cciblackbox-tx.rar` and deploy it on your JCA 1.0–compliant application server (for example, JBoss 4).

The Countries Application

This is an intriguing example that demonstrates some of the more advanced features of Spring MVC. It looks at using `HandlerInterceptors` to provide common preprocessing for your controllers as well as utilizing Excel and PDF output for the view technology. This example is quite small and is certainly worth a look if you are planning to use Excel or PDF within your application. We cover `HandlerInterceptors` as well as Excel and PDF integration in Chapter 16.

Setting Up Spring and Your IDE

Now that you have the full Spring distribution, it is time to look at how you set it up in your favorite IDE. While you can use command-line tools (such as `ant` and `maven`) to build your applications, working in an IDE is much more comfortable. Also, having the Spring libraries set up is useful, so you can step into their code. We will use IntelliJ IDEA, though other IDEs are just as easy to set up.

Regardless of your choice of IDE, let's first examine the directory structure of the applications we will show in this book. Figure 2-1 shows the directory structure of the sample application for this chapter.

```
▼ ch02 (/Users/janm/Writing/prospring2/bookcode/ch02)
  ▼ src
    ▼ main
      ▼ java
        ▼ com.apress.prospring2.ch02
          ▶ closelycoupled
          ▶ decoupled
          ▶ spring
            TypicalHelloWorld
      ▼ resources
        ▶ META-INF
          beans.properties
          msf.properties
    ▼ test
      ▼ java
          com.apress.prospring.ch02
        resources
    ch02.iml
▼ Libraries
  ▶ < 1.5 > (/System/Library/Frameworks/JavaVM.framework/Home)
  ▶ spring-2.5
```

Figure 2-1. *Directory structure of the sample application*

The directory structure shows that we have one `src` directory that contains code for the main code and test code. Each of the `test` and `main` source directories further has the `java` and `resources` subdirectories. All Java code goes into the `java` directory; all other files that are not Java source code, but make up part of the application, go to the `resources` directory. Next, we have the `lib` directory at the same level as the entire project. We do not just leave all JAR files in the `lib` directory; instead, we create subdirectories with some descriptive names. For the application in this chapter, we will only need the `lib/org/springframework/spring.jar` library. Figure 2-2 shows how we have set up the module in IntelliJ IDEA—you can clearly see the source and test source directories.

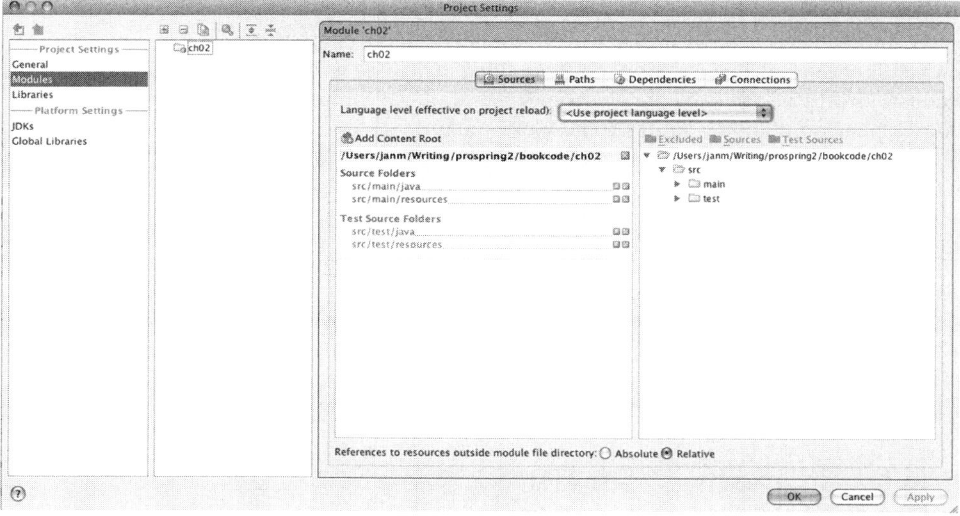

Figure 2-2. *IntelliJ IDEA module setup*

This would be enough to start writing plain Java code, but we know that we are going to write some Spring code! To prepare for that, we need to add the libraries we are going to need: `spring.jar` and `commons-logging-1.1.jar`. Figure 2-3 shows these libraries set up in IntelliJ IDEA.

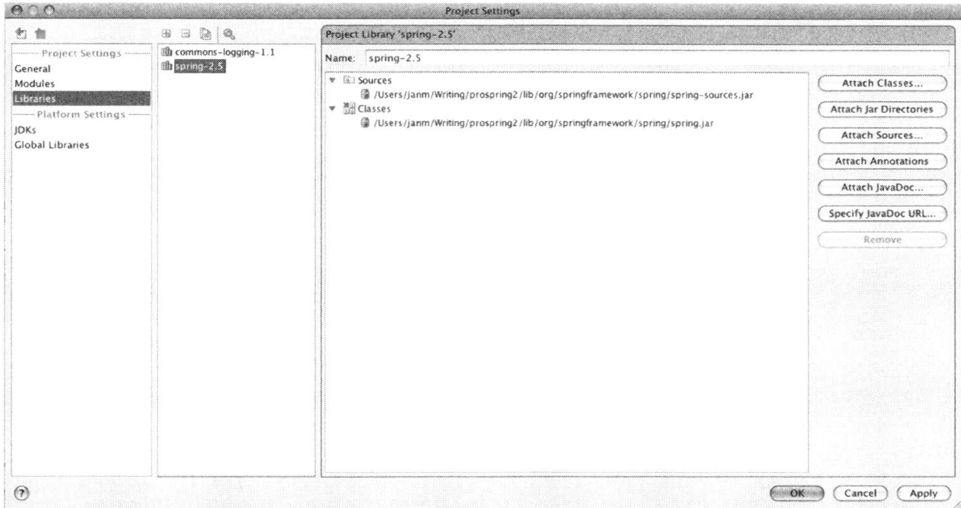

Figure 2-3. *Library setup in IntelliJ IDEA*

In Figure 2-3, you can see that we have added the `spring.jar` library and its dependency, `commons-logging-1.1`. We have also attached the `spring-sources.jar`, which contains the source code compiled into `spring.jar`. Finally, Figure 2-4 shows that we have added the two libraries as module dependencies.

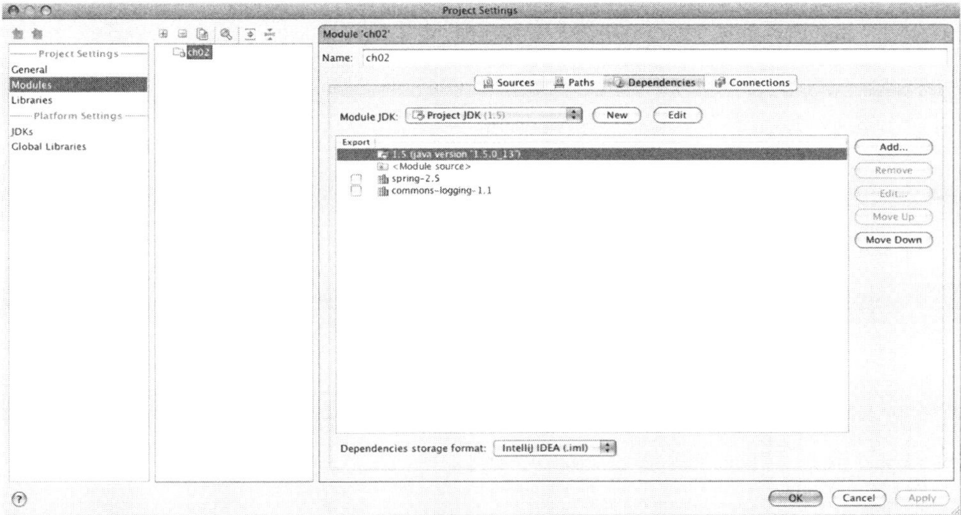

Figure 2-4. *Module dependencies*

Once you have all this set up, you are ready to follow the source code we are going to show in this chapter. Alternatively, you can open the sample application project, which includes code for all chapters.

Hello, World

Let us put all worries about different versions of dependent libraries and even the JARs that make up the Spring distribution aside and write a "Hello, World" application. Throughout this chapter, we will improve this application using traditional programming and then refactor the application to use the Spring Framework. Listing 2-3 shows a typical "Hello, World" application.

Listing 2-3. *Typical "Hello, World"*

```
public class TypicalHelloWorld {

    public static void main(String[] args) {
        System.out.println("Hello, world.");
    }

}
```

The code is trivial but also completely impossible to extend or modify. If we wanted to print the message to standard error stream, we would need to modify the source code and recompile. It would be nice if we had one piece of code that provided the message and other code that took care of outputting the message. Our first attempt could be the code in Listing 2-4.

Listing 2-4. *Attempt to Make the "Hello, World" Application More Generic*

```
final class MessageSource {
    private final String message;

    public MessageSource(String message) {
        this.message = message;
    }

    public String getMessage() {
        return message;
    }
}

class MessageDestination {

    public void write(PrintStream out, String message) {
        out.println(message);
    }

}

public class CloselyCoupledHelloWorld {

    public static void main(String[] args) {
        MessageSource source = new MessageSource("Hello, world");
        MessageDestination destination = new MessageDestination();
        destination.write(System.out, source.getMessage());
    }

}
```

This code looks more generic and more configurable but is actually even worse than the original code in Listing 2-3: it is still too closely coupled but is more complicated. We can achieve significant improvement if we make the `MessageSource` and `MessageDestination` interfaces and change the `MessageDestination`'s `write` method so that it does not require the `PrintStream` argument. Figure 2-5 shows a UML diagram of the changed solution.

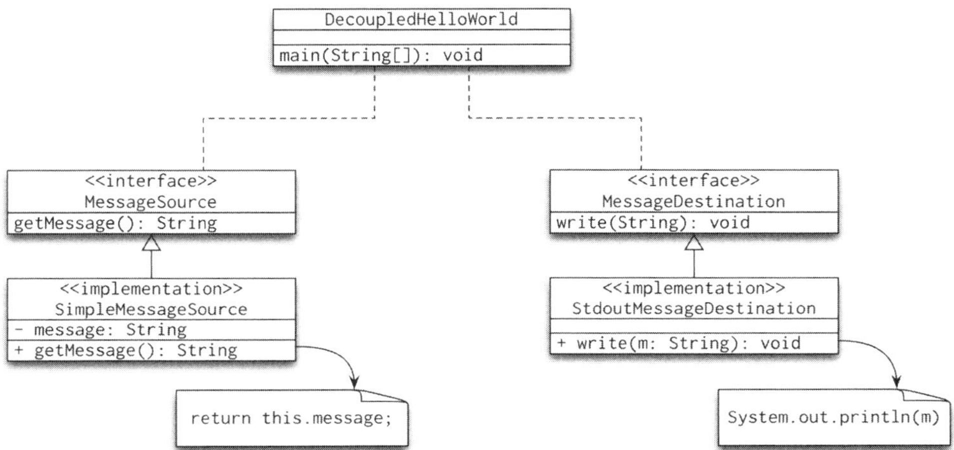

Figure 2-5. *UML class diagram of the refactored application*

Now, this approach is much better. The `DecoupledHelloWorld` class directly uses only the interfaces; each interface has only one implementation. However, the `DecoupledHelloWorld` still needs to create the instances of the interfaces (see Listing 2-5).

Listing 2-5. *Still Closely Coupled Implementation of "Hello, World"*

```
public class DecoupledHelloWorld {

    public static void main(String[] args) {
        MessageSource source = new SimpleMessageSource("Hello, world");
        MessageDestination destination = new StdoutMessageDestination();

        destination.write(source.getMessage());
    }

}
```

The problematic lines are in bold: even though the rest of the code uses the interfaces, the `DecoupledHelloWorld` application is directly aware of the implementations. It would be better if we could use some kind of factory. This factory would could use arbitrarily complex configuration rules and ultimately return properly configured instances of the `MessageSource` and `MessageDestination` implementations. Review the UML diagram in Figure 2-6, which illustrates the factory.

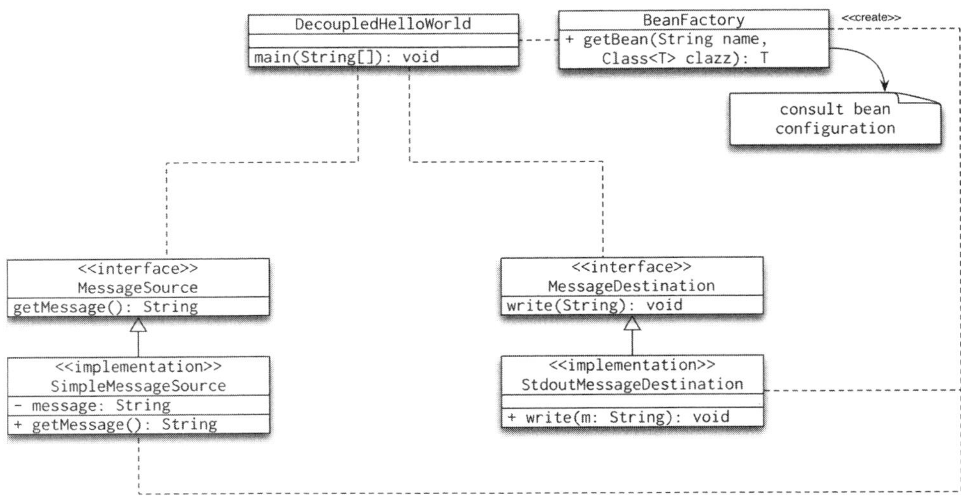

Figure 2-6. *UML class diagram of the decoupled "Hello, World" with a factory*

Now, `DecoupledHelloWorld` only uses the factory, and the factory manages the creation of the appropriate beans and returns them to `DefaultHelloWorld`. The name argument in the `getBean` method uniquely identifies the bean. Therefore, the factory takes care of the life cycle of the beans it manages. Take a look at Listing 2-6; it shows a possible implementation of the `BeanFactory`, which uses a properties file to determine the classes of beans it needs to instantiate.

Listing 2-6. *Implementation and Use of the BeanFactory Class*

com.apress.prospring2.ch02.decoupled.beanfactory.BeanFactory

```
public class BeanFactory {
    private Map<String, String> beanDefinitions;

    public BeanFactory(String beanDefinitionsSource) {
        readBeanDefinitions(beanDefinitionsSource);
    }

    private void readBeanDefinitions(String beanDefinitionsSource) {
        Properties props = new Properties();
        InputStream is = BeanFactory.class.getResourceAsStream(
            beanDefinitionsSource);
        if (is == null) {
           throw new RuntimeException("Could not load properties file " +
               beanDefinitionsSource);
        }
        try {
            props.load(is);
            is.close();
            this.beanDefinitions = new HashMap<String, String>();
            for (Map.Entry<Object, Object> entry : props.entrySet()) {
                this.beanDefinitions.put(entry.getKey().toString(),
                    entry.getValue().toString());
            }
        } catch (IOException e) {
```

```
            throw new RuntimeException("Could not read the properties file " +
                beanDefinitionsSource);
        }
    }

    public Object getBean(String name) {
        String className = this.beanDefinitions.get(name);
        if (className == null) return null;
        try {
            return Class.forName(className).newInstance();
        } catch (Exception e) {
            throw new RuntimeException("Could not create bean " + name);
        }
    }

}
```

com.apress.prospring2.ch02.decoupled.demo.FactoryDecoupledHelloWorld

```
public class FactoryDecoupledHelloWorld {

    public static void main(String[] args) {
        BeanFactory bf =
            new BeanFactory("/META-INF/plain/helloworld-context.properties");

        MessageSource source = (MessageSource) bf.getBean("source");
        MessageDestination destination =
            (MessageDestination) bf.getBean("destination");

        destination.write(source.getMessage());
    }
}
```

META-INF/plain/helloworld-context.properties

```
source=com.apress.prospring2.ch02.decoupled.source.SimpleMessageSource
destination=com.apress.prospring2.ch02.decoupled.destination.➥
StdoutMessageDestination
```

This design is flexible enough, but there is one drawback: the `BeanFactory` class is directly tied to using Java properties files as the source of the bean configuration data.

It would be better if there were another interface that maintained the life cycles of all beans, some kind of `BeanRegistry`. Then, we would have `BeanDefinitionReader` implementations that understand particular format of the bean definition file. The readers would read the file and register all beans found in the file. The factory would then use the registry to obtain bean definitions (regardless of where the definitions came from) and create the required beans. But wait! We would be wasting our time, because this is exactly what Spring does!

Putting Spring Into "Hello, World"

Finally, we get to a point where we can take a look at using Spring in our "Hello, World" application. We have improved it in the previous listings, but we have ended up writing a lot of code to do that. Listing 2-7 shows how we can achieve the same result with just one Java source file, one properties file, and the Spring Framework.

Listing 2-7. *Using Spring to Simplify the Sample Code*

```
import org.springframework.beans.factory.support.BeanDefinitionReader;
import org.springframework.beans.factory.support.DefaultListableBeanFactory;
import org.springframework.beans.factory.support.PropertiesBeanDefinitionReader;
import org.springframework.core.io.ClassPathResource;
import com.apress.prospring2.ch02.decoupled.MessageSource;
import com.apress.prospring2.ch02.decoupled.MessageDestination;

public class FirstSpringHelloWorld {

    public static void main(String[] args) {
        DefaultListableBeanFactory bf = new DefaultListableBeanFactory();
        BeanDefinitionReader reader = new PropertiesBeanDefinitionReader(bf);
        reader.loadBeanDefinitions(
           new ClassPathResource("/META-INF/spring/helloworld-context.properties"));

        MessageSource source = (MessageSource) bf.getBean("source");
        MessageDestination destination =
           (MessageDestination) bf.getBean("destination");

        destination.write(source.getMessage());
    }

}
```

This code works just like the code we would eventually get to using our refactoring techniques: it creates a `BeanFactory` as an instance of `DefaultListableBeanFactory`. The `DefaultListableBeanFactory` class also implements `BeanDefinitionRegistry`. Next, we create `BeanDefinitionReader`, in our case `PropertiesBeanDefinitionReader`, giving it reference to the `BeanDefinitionRegistry` instance. On the next line, we call the `loadBeanDefinitions` method, and we give it a `Resource` implementation called `ClassPathResource`. Once the `loadBeanDefinitions` method finishes, the `BeanDefinitionRegistry` is set up, and the `BeanFactory` can use it to give us instances of the defined beans. We do just that with the two calls of the `getBean` method. We only need to give it the bean name. Finally, we use the returned beans to get the `"Hello, world"` message.

Before we can run this application, we need to create the `/META-INF/spring/helloworld-context.properties` file. Listing 2-8 shows this file.

Listing 2-8. *The helloworld-context.properties File*

```
source.(class)=com.apress.prospring2.ch02.decoupled.source.SimpleMessageSource
destination.(class)=com.apress.prospring2.ch02.decoupled.destination.➥
StdoutMessageDestination
```

As you can see, the format of this file is almost exactly the same as the format we have chosen for our non-Spring application. When you now compile and run the `FirstSpringHelloWorld` application, you will see the familiar `"Hello, world"` message.

Dependency Injection

The code you have seen until now does not use the DI pattern. It uses dependency lookup. We will explore the dependency injection pattern in far more detail in the next chapter, but for now, consider that the code in `FirstSpringHelloWorld` had to know the names of the `MessageSource` and `MessageDestination` beans. It had to look them up and then use them. This clouds the implementation, because in addition to the problem we are trying to solve, we need to know details about the setup of the application. It would be much better if the `MessageSource` and `MessageDestination` interfaces somehow got automatically set. To get you started, we will show you how to create a MessageService, which uses MessageSource and MessageDestination beans, but we will use Spring to inject the MessageSource and MessageDestination beans into the MessageService bean. Listing 2-9 shows the implementation of MessageService.

Listing 2-9. *MessageService Implementation*

```
public interface MessageService {

    void execute();

}

public class DefaultMessageService implements MessageService {
    private MessageSource source;
    private MessageDestination destination;

    public void execute() {
        this.destination.write(this.source.getMessage());
    }

    public void setSource(MessageSource source) {
        this.source = source;
    }

    public void setDestination(MessageDestination destination) {
        this.destination = destination;
    }
}
```

We intend to use the implementation of the MessageService, the DefaultMessageService, in the main method in the DISpringHelloWorld example. If you look at the code in Listing 2-10, you will see that we only get the service bean, but we do not control the creation and life cycle of the service bean—we leave that to Spring.

Listing 2-10. *The Dependency Injection Spring Application*

```
public class DISpringHelloWorld {

    public static void main(String[] args) {
        DefaultListableBeanFactory bf = new DefaultListableBeanFactory();
        BeanDefinitionReader reader = new PropertiesBeanDefinitionReader(bf);
        reader.loadBeanDefinitions(
          new ClassPathResource("/META-INF/spring/helloworld2-context.properties"));

        MessageService service = (MessageService) bf.getBean("service");
        service.execute();
    }

}
```

The last piece of puzzle is the helloworld2-context.properties file. Somehow, this file must contain enough information to tell Spring that to create an instance of bean named service, it must first create instances of the source and destination beans and then inject them (e.g., invoke the setSource and setDestination methods) on the service bean. Listing 2-11 shows just how easy it is to do that.

Listing 2-11. *The helloworld2-context.properties file*

```
source.(class)=com.apress.prospring2.ch02.decoupled.source.SimpleMessageSource
destination.(class)=com.apress.prospring2.ch02.decoupled.destination.➥
StdoutMessageDestination
service.(class)=com.apress.prospring2.ch02.spring.DefaultMessageService    # 1
service.source(ref)=source    # 2
service.destination(ref)=destination    # 3
```

Line number one defines a bean named service as an instance of `DefaultMessageService`. The dependency injection instructions are on the lines numbered two and three. When we then call `getBean("service")` in the `main` method, Spring will use this information to create the three beans and return the fully constructed instance of the `DefaultMessageService`.

There is much more to dependency injection in Spring, and we give far more detail in the following chapters, but this is a good starting point for further experiments. The most difficult part to grasp for Spring newbies is that the objects seem to live in thin air; it is usually difficult to give up control over construction of objects and let the framework handle it.

The Impact of Spring

If you design your application in a similar way to the design we have taken in the last section of this chapter, the impact of using the Spring Framework will be absolutely minimal. Spring heavily promotes coding to interfaces—your code should be split into interfaces and their implementations. The interfaces form the beans that other beans can use, as you have seen in `MessageSource`, `MessageDestination`, and more crucially, `MessageService`. The implementations then take full advantage of the dependency injection, but at no point do the various implementations of the interfaces need to be aware of each other. This gives the ultimate flexibility and testability of the applications you will create.

Even more importantly, the code in the interfaces and implementations is plain Java code; the implementations are not aware of the fact that they are running in a dependency injection context.

Summary

In this chapter, we have presented you with all the background information you need to get up and running with Spring. We showed you how to obtain both the Spring release distribution and the current development version directly from CVS. We described how Spring is packaged and the dependencies you need for each of Spring's features. Using this information, you can make informed decisions about which of the Spring JAR files your application needs and which dependencies you need to distribute with your application. Spring's documentation, sample applications, and test suite provide Spring users with an ideal base from which to start their Spring development, so we took some time to investigate what is available in the Spring distribution. Finally, we presented an example of how, using Spring DI, it is possible to make the traditional "Hello, World" application a loosely coupled, extendable message-rendering application.

The important thing to realize is that we only scratched the surface of Spring DI in this chapter, and we barely made a dent in Spring as a whole. In the next chapter, we take an in-depth look at the sample application that we will be building, paying particular attention to how we can use Spring to solve common design issues and how we have made our application simpler and more manageable using Spring.

CHAPTER 3

Introducing Inversion of Control

In Chapter 1, during the first discussion of Inversion of Control (IoC), you might recall that we mentioned that Martin Fowler renamed the Inversion of Control pattern to the more descriptive dependency injection (DI). However, this is not strictly true; in reality, DI is a specialized form of IoC, although you will often find that the two terms are used interchangeably. In this chapter, we take a much more detailed look at IoC and DI, formalizing the relationship between the two concepts and looking in great detail at how Spring fits into the picture.

After defining both and looking at Spring's relationship with them, we will explore the concepts that are essential to Spring's implementation of DI. This chapter only covers the basics of Spring's DI implementation; we discuss more advanced DI features in Chapter 4 and look at DI in the context of application design Chapter 8. More specifically, this chapter will cover IoC concepts, IoC in Spring, and IoC configuration in Spring `BeanFactories`.

First, we'll discuss the various kinds of IoC including DI and dependency lookup. We'll look at the differences between the various IoC approaches and present the pros and cons of each.

Next, we'll look at IoC capabilities available in Spring and how these capabilities are implemented, in particular, at DI and the setter- and constructor-based approaches Spring offers. This part of the chapter also provides the first full discussion of the `BeanFactory` interface, which is central to the whole Spring framework.

The final part of this chapter focuses on using the annotation- and XML-based configuration approach for the `BeanFactory` configuration. We'll start out with a discussion of DI configuration and move on to look at additional services provided by the `BeanFactory`, such as bean inheritance, life cycle management, and automatic wiring.

IoC and DI

At its core, IoC, and therefore DI, aims to offer a simpler mechanism for provisioning component dependencies (often referred to as an object's collaborators) and managing these dependencies throughout their life cycles. A component that requires certain dependencies is often referred to as the dependent object or, in the case of IoC, the target. This is a rather grand way of saying that IoC provides services through which a component can access its dependencies and services for interacting with the dependencies throughout their lives. In general, IoC can be decomposed into two subtypes: DI and dependency lookup. These subtypes are further decomposed into concrete implementations of the IoC services. From this definition, you can clearly see that when we are talking about DI we are always talking about IoC, but when we are talking about IoC, we are not always talking about DI.

Types of IoC

You may be wondering why there are two different types of IoC and why these types are split further into different implementations. There seems to be no clear answer to these questions; certainly the different types provide a level of flexibility, but to us, it seems that IoC is more of a mixture of old and new ideas; the two different types of IoC represent this.

Dependency lookup is the more traditional approach, and at first glance, it seems more familiar to Java programmers. DI is a newer, less well established approach that, although apparently counterintuitive at first, is actually much more flexible and usable than dependency lookup.

With dependency-lookup–style IoC, a component must acquire a reference to a dependency, whereas with DI, the dependencies are literally injected into the component by the IoC container. Dependency lookup comes in two types: dependency pull (see Listing 3-1) and contextualized dependency lookup (CDL). DI also has two common flavors: constructor DI and setter DI.

Listing 3-1. *Example of the Dependency Pull Approach*

```
package com.apress.prospring2.ch03.ioc;

import com.apress.prospring2.ch02.spring.MessageService;
import org.springframework.beans.factory.BeanFactory;
import org.springframework.beans.factory.support.BeanDefinitionReader;
import org.springframework.beans.factory.support.DefaultListableBeanFactory;
import org.springframework.beans.factory.support.PropertiesBeanDefinitionReader;
import org.springframework.core.io.ClassPathResource;

public class DependencyPullDemo {

    public static void main(String[] args) {
        BeanFactory bf = getBeanFactory();

        MessageService service = (MessageService) bf.getBean("service");
        service.execute();
    }

    private static BeanFactory getBeanFactory() {
        DefaultListableBeanFactory bf = new DefaultListableBeanFactory();
        BeanDefinitionReader reader = new PropertiesBeanDefinitionReader(bf);
        reader.loadBeanDefinitions(new ClassPathResource(
             "/META-INF/spring/ioc-pull-context.properties"));
        return bf;
    }
}
```

Figure 3-1 shows the UML sequence diagram for the dependency lookup.

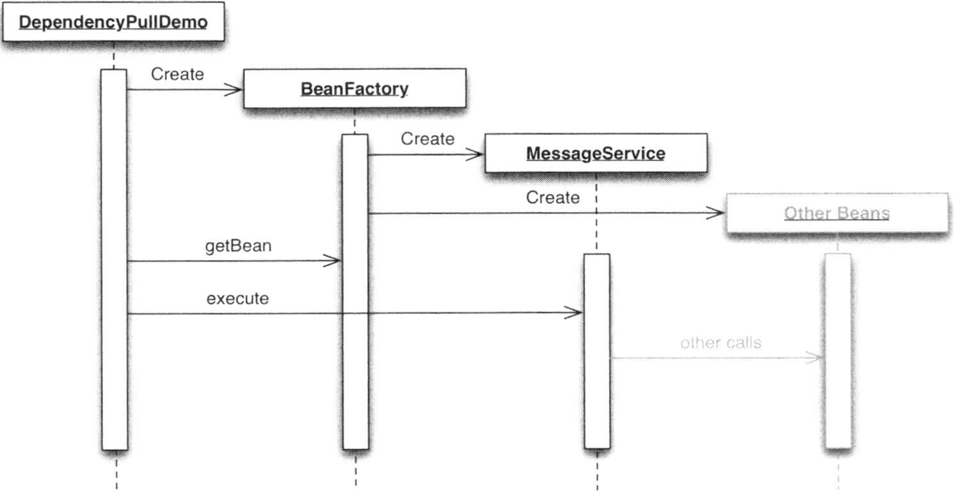

Figure 3-1. *Dependency lookup UML sequence diagram*

This kind of IoC is not only prevalent in Java EE-based applications, which make extensive use of JNDI lookups to obtain dependencies from a registry, but it is also pivotal to working with Spring in many environments.

Contextualized Dependency Lookup

Contextualized dependency lookup (CDL) is similar, in some respects, to dependency pull, but in CDL, lookup is performed against the container that is managing the resource, not from some central registry, and it is usually performed at some set point. CDL works by having the component implement an interface similar to the one in Listing 3-2.

Listing 3-2. *Contextualized Dependency Lookup Component Marker Interface*

```
public interface ManagedComponent {

    void lookup(BeanFactory container);

}
```

By implementing this interface, a component is signaling to the container that it wishes to obtain a dependency. When the container is ready to pass dependencies to a component, it calls `lookup()` on each component in turn. The component can then look up its dependencies using the `BeanFactory` interface (see Listing 3-3).

Listing 3-3. *Contextualized Dependency Lookup Example*

```
public class ContextualizedDependencyLookupDemo {
    private static Set<ManagedComponent> components =
        new HashSet<ManagedComponent>();

    private static class MessageServiceComponent implements ManagedComponent {
        private MessageService service;

        public void lookup(BeanFactory container) {
            this.service = (MessageService)container.getBean("service");
        }

        public void run() {
            this.service.execute();
        }
    }

    public static void main(String[] args) {
        BeanFactory bf = getBeanFactory();
        MessageServiceComponent msc = new MessageServiceComponent();
        registerComponent(msc);
        allowComponentsToLookup(bf);
        msc.run();
    }

    private static void allowComponentsToLookup(BeanFactory bf) {
        for (ManagedComponent component : components) {
            component.lookup(bf);
        }
    }

    private static void registerComponent(ManagedComponent managedComponent) {
        components.add(managedComponent);
    }

    private static BeanFactory getBeanFactory() {
        DefaultListableBeanFactory bf = new DefaultListableBeanFactory();
        BeanDefinitionReader reader = new PropertiesBeanDefinitionReader(bf);
        reader.loadBeanDefinitions(new ClassPathResource(
            "/META-INF/spring/ioc-pull-context.properties"));
        return bf;
    }

}
```

The code in bold shows the `MessageServiceComponent` managed component. The `ContextualizedDependencyLookupDemo` acts as the container. The container prepares the dependencies, and when it finishes all necessary work, it calls the `lookup()` method on all components. Figure 3-2 shows the UML sequence diagram of the CDL.

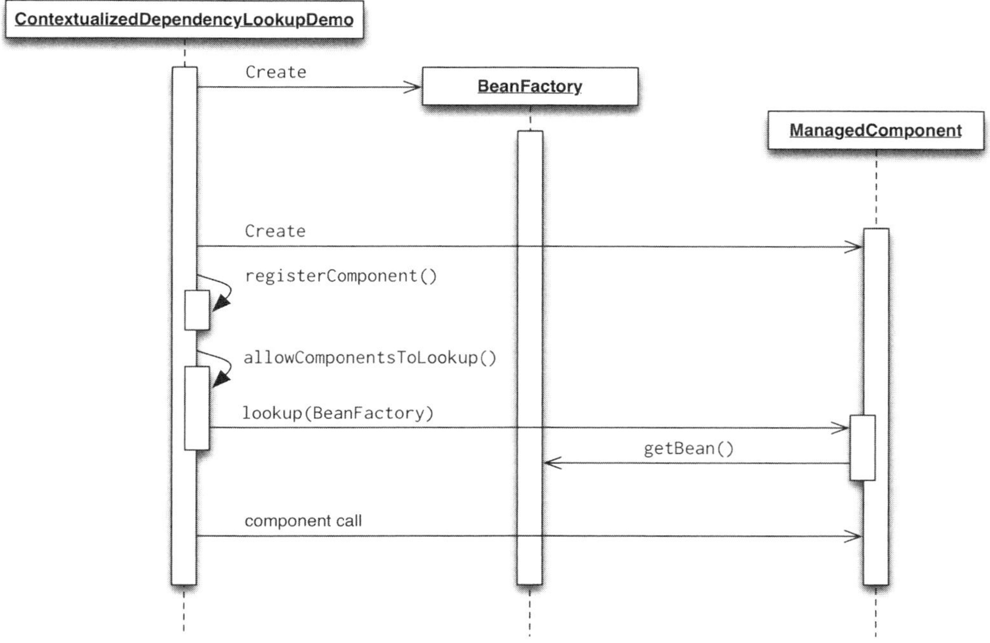

Figure 3-2. *Contextualized dependency lookup UML sequence diagram*

We see that the `ContextualizedDependencyLookupDemo` acts as a container that manages (and in this example, uses) the `ManagedComponent` instances.

Constructor DI

In constructor DI, a component's dependencies are provided to it in its constructor(s). The component declares a constructor or a set of constructors, taking as arguments its dependencies, and the IoC container passes the dependencies to the component when it instantiates it, as shown in Listing 3-4.

Listing 3-4. *Component Dependency Injection Example*

```
public class CtorDependencyInjectionDemo {

    private static class DependentComponent {
        private MessageService service;

        private DependentComponent(MessageService service) {
            Assert.notNull(service, "The 'service' argument must not be null.");
            this.service = service;
        }

        public void run() {
            this.service.execute();
        }
    }
```

```
    public static void main(String[] args) {
        BeanFactory bf = getBeanFactory();

        MessageService service = (MessageService) bf.getBean("service");

        DependentComponent dc = new DependentComponent(service);
        dc.run();
    }

    private static BeanFactory getBeanFactory() { /* code as before */ }

}
```

Here, we see that the `DependentComponent`'s constructor takes a single `MessageService` argument. It also checks that the argument is not `null`; if this check were not there, we could write `new DependentComponent(null)`, which is clearly incorrect, because it would cause a `NullPointerException` in the `run()` method.

Setter DI

In setter DI, the IoC container injects a component's dependencies into the component via JavaBean-style setter methods. A component's setters expose the set of the dependencies the IoC container can manage. Listing 3-5 shows a typical setter-DI–based component.

Listing 3-5. *Setter Dependency Injection Example*

```
public class SetterDependencyInjectionDemo {

    private static class DependentComponent {
        private MessageService service;

        private DependentComponent() {
        }

        public void setService(MessageService service) {
            this.service = service;
        }

        public void run() {
            this.service.execute();
        }
    }

    public static void main(String[] args) {
        BeanFactory bf = getBeanFactory();

        MessageService service = (MessageService) bf.getBean("service");

        DependentComponent dc = new DependentComponent();
        dc.setService(service);
        dc.run();
    }

    private static BeanFactory getBeanFactory() { /* code as before */ }

}
```

Unlike the constructor injection, we can create an instance of the `DependentComponent` without having the dependency. We are free to invoke the setter at any point in the application. We can also call the setter more than once, which allows us to swap the dependency at runtime.

Injection vs. Lookup

Choosing which style of IoC to use—injection or lookup—is not usually a difficult decision. In many cases, the type of IoC you use is mandated by the container you are using. For instance, if you are using EJB 2.0, you must use lookup-style IoC to obtain the EJB from the Java EE container. EJB 3.0 introduces DI through its `@Inject` annotation. In Spring, aside from initial bean lookups, your components and their dependencies are always wired together using injection-style IoC.

■ **Note** When you are using Spring, you can access EJB resources without needing to perform an explicit lookup. Spring can act as an adapter between lookup- and injection-style IoC systems, thus allowing you to manage all resources using injection.

The real question is this: given the choice, which method should you use, injection or lookup? The answer to this is most definitely injection. If you look at the code in Listings 3-4 and 3-5, you can clearly see that using injection has zero impact on your components' code. The dependency pull code, on the other hand, must actively obtain a reference to the registry and interact with it to obtain the dependencies; using CDL requires your classes to implement a specific interface and look up all dependencies programatically. When you are using injection, the most your classes have to do is allow dependencies to be injected using either constructors or setters.

Using injection, you are free to use your classes completely decoupled from the IoC container, manually supplying dependent objects with their collaborators, whereas with lookup, your classes are always dependent on classes and interfaces defined by the container. Another drawback with lookup is that it becomes very difficult to test your classes in isolation from the container. Using injection, testing your components is trivial, because you can simply provide the dependencies yourself using the appropriate constructor or setter.

Lookup-based solutions are, by necessity, more complex than injection-based ones. Although complexity is nothing to be afraid of, we question the validity of adding unneeded complexity to a process as core to your application as dependency management.

All of these reasons aside, the biggest reason to choose injection over lookup is that it makes your life easier. You write substantially less code when you are using injection, and the code that you do write is simple and can, in general, be automated by a good IDE. You will notice that all of the code in the injection samples is passive, in that it doesn't actively try to accomplish a task; the most exciting thing you see in injection code is objects getting stored in a field—not much can go wrong there! Passive code is much simpler to maintain than active code, because there is very little that can go wrong. Consider the following code taken from Listing 3-3:

```
public void lookup(BeanFactory container) {
    this.service = (MessageService)container.getBean("service");
}
```

In this code, plenty could go wrong: the dependency key could change; the container instance could be null; or the returned dependency might be the incorrect type. Naturally, the last two cases would result in a `NullPointerException` or a `ClassCastException`, but you would find out only when you run the application; you could not discover this in an automated test. We say this code has a lot of moving parts, because plenty of things can break. Using lookup might decouple the components of your application, but it adds complexity in the additional code required to couple these components back together to perform any useful tasks.

Setter Injection vs. Constructor Injection

Now that we have established which method of IoC is preferable, we still need to choose whether to use setter injection or constructor injection. Constructor injection is particularly useful when you absolutely must have an instance of the dependency class before your component is used. Many containers, Spring included, provide a mechanism for ensuring that all dependencies are defined when you use setter injection, but by using constructor injection, you assert the requirement for the dependency in a container-agnostic manner.

Setter injection is useful in a variety of different cases. If you want the component to expose its dependencies to the container but provide its own defaults, setter injection is usually the best way to accomplish this. Another benefit of setter injection is that it allows dependencies to be declared on an interface, although this is not as useful as you might first think. Consider a typical business interface with one business method, `defineMeaningOfLife()`. If, in addition to this method, you define a setter for injection such as `setEncylopedia()`, you are mandating that all implementations must use or at least be aware of the encyclopedia dependency. You do not need to define this setter at all—any decent IoC container, Spring included, can work with the component in terms of the business interface but still provide the dependencies of the implementing class. An example of this may clarify this matter slightly. Consider the business interface in Listing 3-6.

Listing 3-6. *The Oracle Interface*

```
public interface Oracle {

    String defineMeaningOfLife();
}
```

Notice that the business interface does not define any setters for DI. This interface could be implemented as shown in Listing 3-7.

Listing 3-7. *Implementation of the Oracle Interface*

```
public class BookwormOracle implements Oracle {
    private Encyclopedia encyclopedia;

    public String defineMeaningOfLife() {
        Long ageOfUniverse = this.encyclopedia.findLong("AgeOfUniverse");
        Long constantOfLife = this.encyclopedia.findLong("ConstantOfLife");
        return String.valueOf(ageOfUniverse / constantOfLife);
    }

    public void setEncyclopedia(Encyclopedia encyclopedia) {
        this.encyclopedia = encyclopedia;
    }
}
```

As you can see, the `BookwormOracle` class not only implements the `Oracle` interface but also defines the setter for DI. Spring is more than comfortable dealing with a structure like this—there is absolutely no need to define the dependencies on the business interface. The ability to use interfaces to define dependencies is an often-touted benefit of setter injection, but in actuality, you should strive to use setters solely for injection out of your business interfaces.

Defining the dependency setter methods on the interface makes it harder to reimplement that interface in the future, perhaps when the implementation technoloy changes. Take an e-mail sending interface, the `Emailer`, with the `send(MailMessage)` method. We could take the naïve approach and define `setSmtpHost(String)`, `setSmtpPassword(String)`, and `setSmtpUsername(String)` in the `Emailer` interface, thus forcing every implementation to include these methods. If the only implementation of the `Emailer` interface is the `SmtpEmailer`, then all fits together perfectly. However, if you then start using a JNDI-bound `javax.mail.Session`, you no longer need the SMTP server details, yet your `JNDIEmailer` must implement the `setSmtpHost(String)`, `setSmtpPassword(String)`, and `setSmtpUsername(String)` methods. To avoid having to implement unnecessary methods, the interfaces should be as clean as possible, completely hiding the implementation details.

Setter injection also allows you to swap dependencies for a different implementation on the fly without creating a new instance of the parent component (Chapter 20 shows how Spring makes use of this in its JMX support). Perhaps the biggest benefit of setter injection is that it is the least intrusive of the injection mechanisms. If you are defining constructors for injection on a class that would otherwise just have the default constructor, you are affecting all code that uses that class in a non-IoC environment. Extra setters that are defined on a class for IoC purposes do not affect the ability of other classes to interact with it.

In general, setter injection is the best choice, because it has the least effect on your code's usability in non-IoC settings. Constructor injection is a good choice when you want to ensure that dependencies are being passed to a component, but bear in mind that many containers provide their own mechanism for doing this with setter injection. Most of the code in this book's sample application uses setter injection, although there are a few examples of constructor injection.

IoC in Spring

As we mentioned earlier, IoC is a big part of what Spring does, and the core of Spring's implementation is based on DI, although dependency lookup features are provided as well. When Spring automatically provides collaborators to a dependent object, it does so using DI. In a Spring-based application, it is always preferable to use dependency injection to pass collaborators to dependent objects rather than have the dependent objects obtain the collaborators via lookup. Although DI is the preferred mechanism for wiring together collaborators and dependent objects, you need dependency lookup to access the dependent objects. In many environments, Spring cannot automatically wire up *all* of your application components using DI, and you must use dependency lookup to access the initial set of components. When you are building web applications using Spring's MVC support, Spring can avoid this by gluing your entire application together automatically. Wherever possible, you should use DI with Spring; otherwise, you can fall back on the dependency lookup capabilities. You will see examples of both in action during the course of this chapter, and we will point them out when they first arise.

An interesting feature of Spring's IoC container is that it has the ability to act as an adaptor between its own dependency injection container and external dependency lookup containers. We look at this in more detail in Chapter 4.

Spring supports both constructor and setter injection and bolsters the standard IoC feature set with a whole host of useful additions to make your life easier.

The rest of this chapter introduces the basics of Spring's DI container complete with plenty of examples.

DI with Spring

Spring's support for DI is comprehensive and, as you will see in Chapter 4, goes beyond the standard IoC feature set we have discussed so far. The rest of this chapter addresses the basics of Spring's DI container, looking at both setter and constructor injection, along with a detailed look at how DI is configured in Spring.

Beans and BeanFactories

The core of Spring's DI container is the `BeanFactory`. A `BeanFactory` is responsible for managing components and their dependencies. In Spring, the term "bean" is used to refer to any component managed by the container. Typically, your beans adhere, on some level, to the JavaBeans specification, but this is not required, especially if you plan to use constructor injection to wire your beans together.

Your application interacts with the Spring DI container via the `BeanFactory` interface. At some point, your application must create an instance of a class that implements the `BeanFactory` interface and configure it with bean and dependency information. After this is complete, your application can access the beans via the `BeanFactory` and get on with its processing. In some cases, all of this setup is handled automatically, but in many cases, you need to code the setup yourself. All of the examples in this chapter require manual setup of the `BeanFactory` implementation.

Although a `BeanFactory` can be configured programmatically, it is more common to see it configured externally using some kind of configuration file. Internally, bean configuration is represented by instances of classes that implement the `BeanDefinition` interface. The bean configuration stores not only information about a bean itself but also about the beans that it depends on. For any `BeanFactory` class that also implements the `BeanDefinitionRegistry` interface, you can read the `BeanDefinition` data from a configuration file, using either `PropertiesBeanDefinitionReader` or `XmlBeanDefinitionReader`. The two main `BeanFactory` implementations that come with Spring implement `BeanDefinitionRegistry`.

So you can identify your beans within the `BeanFactory`, each bean is assigned a name. Each bean has at least one name but can have any number of them. Any names after the first are considered aliases for the same bean. You use bean names to retrieve a bean from the `BeanFactory` and to establish dependency relationships—that is, bean X depends on bean Y.

BeanFactory Implementations

The description of the `BeanFactory` might make using it seem overly complex, but in practice, this is not the case. In fact, we discussed all of the concepts in the previous section and in the simple example in Chapter 2. Listing 3-8 shows a sample application that uses the `Oracle` interface.

Listing 3-8. *Using the BeanFactory*

```
public class BeanFactoryDemo {

    public static void main(String[] args) {
        DefaultListableBeanFactory bf = new DefaultListableBeanFactory();
        BeanDefinitionReader reader = new PropertiesBeanDefinitionReader(bf);
        reader.loadBeanDefinitions(
            new ClassPathResource(
                "/META-INF/spring/beanfactorydemo1-context.properties"));

        Oracle oracle = (Oracle) bf.getBean("oracle");
        System.out.println("Meaning of life is " + oracle.defineMeaningOfLife());
    }

}
```

In this example, you can see that we are using the `DefaultListableBeanFactory`—one of the two main `BeanFactory` implementations supplied with Spring—and that we are reading in the `BeanDefinition` information from a properties file using the `PropertiesBeanDefinitionReader`. Once the `BeanFactory` implementations is created and configured, we retrieve the `MessageRenderer` bean using its name, `renderer`, which is configured in the properties file (see Listing 3-9).

Listing 3-9. *The beanfactorydemo1-context.properties File*

```
oracle.(class)=com.apress.prospring2.ch03.di.BookwormOracle
encyclopedia.(class)=com.apress.prospring2.ch03.di.HardcodedEncyclopedia
oracle.encyclopedia(ref)=encyclopedia
```

In addition to the `PropertiesBeanDefinitionReader`, Spring also provides `XmlBeanDefinitionReader`, which allows you to manage your bean configuration using XML rather than properties. The properties files are only usable for small, simple applications. They quickly become unusable when you are dealing with a large number of beans. For this reason, it is preferable to use the XML configuration format for all but the most trivial of applications. This leads nicely to a discussion of the second of the two main `BeanFactory` implementations: `XmlBeanFactory`.

The `XmlBeanFactory` is derived from `DefaultListableBeanFactory` and simply extends it to perform automatic configuration using the `XmlBeanDefinitionReader`. We can use this to write the code in Listing 3-10.

Listing 3-10. *Using the XmlBeanFactory*

```
public class XmlBeanFactoryDemo {

    public static void main(String[] args) {
        XmlBeanFactory bf = new XmlBeanFactory(
            new ClassPathResource("/META-INF/spring/beanfactorydemo1-context.xml"));

        Oracle oracle = (Oracle) bf.getBean("oracle");
        System.out.println("Meaning of life is " + oracle.defineMeaningOfLife());
    }

}
```

For the rest of this book, including the sample application, we will be using the XML configuration format exclusively. You are free to investigate the properties format yourself— you will find plenty of examples throughout the Spring codebase.

Of course, you are free to define your own `BeanFactory` implementations, although be aware that doing so is quite involved; you need to implement a lot more interfaces than just `BeanFactory` to get the same level of functionality you have with the supplied `BeanFactory` implementations. If all you want to do is define a new configuration mechanism, create your definition reader and wrap this in a simple `BeanFactory` implementation derived from `DefaultListableBeanFactory`. By "new configuration mechanism," we mean one using formats other than properties and XML; for example, you can implement a `BeanDefinitionReader` that uses a relational database as the source of the configuration data. There is a way to allow Spring to handle custom namespaces in the XML configuration files; go to Chapter 7 for more details.

XML Bean Definition

The key to getting set up with any Spring-based application is creating the `BeanFactory` configuration file for your application. A basic configuration without any bean definitions looks similar to the code in Listing 3-11.

Listing 3-11. *Empty Bean Definition XML*

```
<?xml version="1.0" encoding="UTF-8"?>
<beans xmlns="http://www.springframework.org/schema/beans"
       xmlns:xsi="http://www.w3.org/2001/XMLSchema-instance"
       xsi:schemaLocation="
```

```
                http://www.springframework.org/schema/beans
                http://www.springframework.org/schema/beans/spring-beans.xsd">

</beans>
```

Each bean is defined using a `<bean>` tag under the root of the `<beans>` tag. The `<bean>` tag typically has two attributes: `id` and `class`. The `id` attribute is used to give the bean its default name, and the `class` attribute specifies the type of the bean. Listing 3-12 shows the XML file that defines the beans implementing the `Oracle` and `Encyclopedia` interfaces.

Listing 3-12. *XML Configuration File for the Code in Listing 3-10*

```
<?xml version="1.0" encoding="UTF-8"?>
<beans xmlns="http://www.springframework.org/schema/beans"
       xmlns:xsi="http://www.w3.org/2001/XMLSchema-instance"
       xsi:schemaLocation="
                http://www.springframework.org/schema/beans
                http://www.springframework.org/schema/beans/spring-beans.xsd">

    <bean id="oracle" class="com.apress.prospring2.ch03.di.BookwormOracle">
        <property name="encyclopedia">
            <bean class="com.apress.prospring2.ch03.di.HardcodedEncyclopedia"/>
        </property>
    </bean>

</beans>
```

You can see that we have defined the bean with `id` `oracle` as an instance of the `BookwormOracle` and that its `encyclopedia` property is an anonymous bean, which means that no other component can use the `encyclopedia` dependency of the `oracle` bean. If we wanted to allow other beans to use the `encyclopedia` bean, we would have to move it from the inner anonymous bean to a top-level bean (see Listing 3-13).

Listing 3-13. *Using the Encyclopedia Bean As a Top-Level Bean*

```
<?xml version="1.0" encoding="UTF-8"?>
<beans xmlns="http://www.springframework.org/schema/beans"
       xmlns:xsi="http://www.w3.org/2001/XMLSchema-instance"
       xsi:schemaLocation="
                http://www.springframework.org/schema/beans
                http://www.springframework.org/schema/beans/spring-beans.xsd">

    <bean id="encyclopedia"
            class="com.apress.prospring2.ch03.di.HardcodedEncyclopedia"/>

    <bean id="oracle" class="com.apress.prospring2.ch03.di.BookwormOracle">
        <property name="encyclopedia" ref="encyclopedia"/>
    </bean>

</beans>
```

The choice of whether the dependent beans are inner anonymous or top-level beans is entirely up to us. In any case, Spring will need to maintain the instance of the bean.

Using Constructor Injection

In the previous example, the Encyclopedia implementation, HardcodedEncyclopedia, contained hard-coded values for its entries. In the Spring configuration file, you can easily create a configurable Encyclopedia that allows the message to be defined externally (see Listing 3-14).

Listing 3-14. *The ConfigurableEncyclopedia Class*

```
public class ConfigurableEncyclopedia implements Encyclopedia {
    private Map<String, Long> entries;

    public ConfigurableEncyclopedia(Map<String, Long> entries) {
        Assert.notNull(entries, "The 'entries' argument cannot be null.");
        this.entries = entries;
    }

    public Long findLong(String entry) {
        return this.entries.get(entry);
    }
}
```

As you can see, creating an instance of ConfigurableEncyclopedia without providing a value for the entries is impossible (and giving null will throw an IllegalArgumentException). This behavior is exactly what we want, and this class is ideally suited for use with constructor injection. Listing 3-15 shows how you can redefine the encyclopedia bean definition to create an instance of ConfigurableEncyclopedia, injecting the entries using constructor injection.

Listing 3-15. *Creating an Instance of the ConfigurableEncyclopedia*

```
<?xml version="1.0" encoding="UTF-8"?>
<beans xmlns="http://www.springframework.org/schema/beans"
       xmlns:xsi="http://www.w3.org/2001/XMLSchema-instance"
       xmlns:util="http://www.springframework.org/schema/util"
       xsi:schemaLocation="
                http://www.springframework.org/schema/beans
                http://www.springframework.org/schema/beans/spring-beans.xsd
                http://www.springframework.org/schema/util
                http://www.springframework.org/schema/util/spring-util.xsd">

    <bean id="encyclopedia"
         class="com.apress.prospring2.ch03.di.ConfigurableEncyclopedia">
        <constructor-arg>
            <util:map>
                <entry key="AgeOfUniverse" value="13700000000"/>
                <entry key="ConstantOfLife" value="326190476"/>
            </util:map>
        </constructor-arg>
    </bean>

    <bean id="oracle" class="com.apress.prospring2.ch03.di.BookwormOracle">
        <property name="encyclopedia" ref="encyclopedia"/>
    </bean>

</beans>
```

In Listing 13-5, we used a <constructor-arg> tag. We have made the example slightly more complicated by passing a Map<String, Long> to the constructor. We use the util:map element to create an inner anonymous bean of type Map that we then pass to the ConfigurableEncyclopedia(Map<String, Long>) constructor. Do not worry if you do not recognise the util:map element; we will explain this in much more detail in Chapter 7. Still, the code in Listing 3-15 clearly demonstrates that Spring beans really can be instances of any class you can use in Java.

When you have more than one constructor argument or your class has more than one constructor, typically, you need to give each <constructor-arg> tag an index attribute to specify the index of the argument, starting at zero, in the constructor signature. It is always best to use the index attribute whenever you are dealing with constructors that have multiple arguments to avoid confusion between the parameters and ensure that Spring picks the correct constructor.

Avoiding Constructor Confusion

In some cases, Spring finds it impossible to tell which constructor you want it to use for constructor injection. This usually arises when you have two constructors with the same number of arguments and the types used in the arguments are represented in exactly the same way. Consider the code in Listing 3-16.

Listing 3-16. *Constructor Confusion*

```
public class ConstructorConfusionDemo {
    private String someValue;

    public ConstructorConfusionDemo(String someValue) {
        System.out.println("ConstructorConfusionDemo(String) called");
        this.someValue = someValue;
    }

    public ConstructorConfusionDemo(int someValue) {
        System.out.println("ConstructorConfusionDemo(int) called");
        this.someValue = "Number: " + Integer.toString(someValue);
    }

    public static void main(String[] args) {
        BeanFactory factory = new XmlBeanFactory(
                new ClassPathResource(
                    "/META-INF/spring/beanfactorydemo3-context.xml"));

        ConstructorConfusionDemo cc =
            (ConstructorConfusionDemo)factory.getBean("constructorConfusion");
        System.out.println(cc);
    }

    public String toString() {
        return someValue;
    }

}
```

Here, you can clearly see what this code does—it simply retrieves a bean of type ConstructorConfusionDemo from the BeanFactory and writes the value to stdout. Now, look at the configuration code in Listing 3-17.

Listing 3-17. *Confused Constructors*

```
<?xml version="1.0" encoding="UTF-8"?>
<beans xmlns="http://www.springframework.org/schema/beans"
       xmlns:xsi="http://www.w3.org/2001/XMLSchema-instance"
       xsi:schemaLocation="
                http://www.springframework.org/schema/beans
                http://www.springframework.org/schema/beans/spring-beans.xsd">

    <bean id="constructorConfusion"
        class="com.apress.prospring2.ch03.beanfactory.ConstructorConfusionDemo">
        <constructor-arg value="1"/>
    </bean>

</beans>
```

Which of the constructors is called in this case? Running the example yields the following output:

```
ConstructorConfusionDemo(String) called
1

Process finished with exit code 0
```

This shows that the constructor with the `String` argument was called. This is not the desired effect, since we want to prefix any integer values passed in using constructor injection with `Number:`, as shown in the `int` constructor. To get around this, we need to make a small modification to the configuration, shown in Listing 3-18.

Listing 3-18. *Overcoming Constructor Confusion*

```
<?xml version="1.0" encoding="UTF-8"?>
<beans xmlns="http://www.springframework.org/schema/beans"
       xmlns:xsi="http://www.w3.org/2001/XMLSchema-instance"
       xsi:schemaLocation="
                http://www.springframework.org/schema/beans
                http://www.springframework.org/schema/beans/spring-beans.xsd">

    <bean id="constructorConfusion"
        class="com.apress.prospring2.ch03.beanfactory.ConstructorConfusionDemo">
        <constructor-arg value="1" type="int"/>
    </bean>

</beans>
```

Notice now that the `<constructor-arg>` tag has an additional attribute, `type`, that specifies the type of argument that Spring should look for. Running the example again with the corrected configuration yields the correct output:

```
ConstructorConfusionDemo(int) called
Number: 1

Process finished with exit code 0
```

Injection Parameters

In the two previous examples, you saw how to inject other components and values into a bean using both setter injection and constructor injection. Spring supports a myriad of options for injection parameters, allowing you to inject not only other components and simple values but also Java collections, externally defined properties, and even beans in another factory. You can set all of these injection parameter types for both setter injection and constructor injection by using the corresponding tag under the `<property>` and `<constructor-args>` tags, respectively.

Injecting Simple Values

Injecting simple values into your beans is easy. To do so, simply specify the value in the configuration tag using the `value` attribute; alternatively. you can specify the value inside a `<value>` tag. By default, the `value` attribute and `<value>` tag can not only read `String` values but can also convert these values to any primitive or primitive wrapper class. Listing 3-19 shows a simple bean that has a variety of properties exposed for injection.

Listing 3-19. *Injecting Simple Values*

```
public class InjectSimpleDemo {
    private String name;
    private int age;
    private float height;
    private boolean isProgrammer;
    private Long ageInSeconds;

    public static void main(String[] args) {
        XmlBeanFactory factory = new XmlBeanFactory(
            new ClassPathResource("/META-INF/spring/injectdemo1-context.xml"));
        InjectSimpleDemo simple =
            (InjectSimpleDemo)factory.getBean("injectSimpleDemo");
        System.out.println(simple);
    }

    public void setAgeInSeconds(Long ageInSeconds) {
        this.ageInSeconds = ageInSeconds;
    }

    public void setIsProgrammer(boolean isProgrammer) {
        this.isProgrammer = isProgrammer;
    }

    public void setAge(int age) {
        this.age = age;
    }

    public void setHeight(float height) {
        this.height = height;
    }

    public void setName(String name) {
        this.name = name;
    }

    @Override
    public String toString() {
```

```
        return String.format("Name: %s\nAge: %d\nAge in Seconds: %d\n" +
                 "Height: %g\nIs Programmer?: %b",
                this.name, this.age, this.ageInSeconds,
                this.height, this.isProgrammer);
    }
}
```

In addition to the properties, the InjectSimple class also defines the main() method that creates an XmlBeanFactory and retrieves an InjectSimple bean from Spring. The property values of this bean are then written to stdout. The configuration for this bean is shown in Listing 3-20.

Listing 3-20. *Configuring Simple Value Injection*

```
<?xml version="1.0" encoding="UTF-8"?>
<beans xmlns="http://www.springframework.org/schema/beans"
       xmlns:xsi="http://www.w3.org/2001/XMLSchema-instance"
       xsi:schemaLocation="
                http://www.springframework.org/schema/beans
                http://www.springframework.org/schema/beans/spring-beans.xsd">

    <bean id="injectSimpleDemo"
         class="com.apress.prospring2.ch03.beanfactory.InjectSimpleDemo">
        <property name="name" value="John Smith"/>
        <property name="age" value="35"/>
        <property name="height" value="1.79"/>
        <property name="isProgrammer" value="true"/>
        <property name="ageInSeconds" value="1103760000"/>
    </bean>

</beans>
```

You can see from Listings 3-18 and 3-19 that it is possible to define properties on your bean that accept String values, primitive values, or primitive wrapper values and inject values for these properties using the value attribute. Here is the output created by running this example, which is just what was expected:

```
Name: John Smith
Age: 35
Age in Seconds: 1103760000
Height: 1.79000
Is Programmer?: true

Process finished with exit code 0
```

In Chapter 4, you will see how to expand the range of types that can be injected using the value attribute and <value> tag.

In addition to the standard <property> tag, you can use the p namespace to set the properties of the beans. The p namespace allows you to configure the dependencies as attributes of the <bean> tag. Listing 3-21 shows the configuration of the injectSimpleDemo bean from Listing 3-20 using the p namespace.

Listing 3-21. *Configuration Using the p Namespace*

```
<?xml version="1.0" encoding="UTF-8"?>
<beans xmlns="http://www.springframework.org/schema/beans"
```

```
       xmlns:xsi="http://www.w3.org/2001/XMLSchema-instance"
       xmlns:p="http://www.springframework.org/schema/p"
       xsi:schemaLocation="
             http://www.springframework.org/schema/beans
             http://www.springframework.org/schema/beans/spring-beans.xsd">

    <bean id="injectSimpleDemo"
          class="com.apress.prospring2.ch03.beanfactory.InjectSimpleDemo"
          p:age="35" p:ageInSeconds="1103760000"
          p:height="1.79" p:isProgrammer="false"/>

</beans>
```

Running the InjectSimpleDemo with the configuration file from Listing 3-21 produces the same output. The only advantage of using the p namespace is that you have less code to write, especially if you need to configure only a small number of properties. You may notice that the p namespace usage in Listing 3-21 allows you to inject only simple values, not references—we will discuss injecting references using the p namespace in the next section.

Injecting Beans in the Same Factory

As you have already seen, you can inject one bean into another using the ref attribute; you can also use the <ref> tag. To configure Spring to inject one bean into another, you first need to configure two beans: one to be injected and one to be the target of the injection. Once this is done, you simply configure the injection using the ref attribute on the target bean. Listing 3-22 shows the configuration for the oracle bean again.

Listing 3-22. *Configuring Bean Injection*

```
<?xml version="1.0" encoding="UTF-8"?>
<beans xmlns="http://www.springframework.org/schema/beans"
       xmlns:xsi="http://www.w3.org/2001/XMLSchema-instance"
       xmlns:util="http://www.springframework.org/schema/util"
       xsi:schemaLocation="
             http://www.springframework.org/schema/beans
             http://www.springframework.org/schema/beans/spring-beans.xsd
             http://www.springframework.org/schema/util
             http://www.springframework.org/schema/util/spring-util.xsd">

    <bean id="encyclopedia"
        class="com.apress.prospring2.ch03.di.ConfigurableEncyclopedia">
        <constructor-arg>
            <util:map>
                <entry key="AgeOfUniverse" value="13700000000"/>
                <entry key="ConstantOfLife" value="326190476"/>
            </util:map>
        </constructor-arg>
    </bean>

    <bean id="oracle" class="com.apress.prospring2.ch03.di.BookwormOracle">
        <property name="encyclopedia" ref="encyclopedia"/>
    </bean>

</beans>
```

An important point to note is that the type being injected does not have to be the exact type defined on the target; the types just need to be compatible. Being compatible means, for example, that if the declared type on the target is an interface, the injected type must implement this interface. If the declared type is a class, the injected type must either be the same type or a subtype. In this example, the BookwormOracle class defines the setEncyclopedia(Encyclopedia) method to receive an instance of Encyclopedia, which is an interface, and the injected type is ConfigurableEncyclopedia, a class that implements Encyclopedia. This is a point that causes confusion for some developers, but it is really quite simple. Injection is subject to the same typing rules as any Java code, so as long as you are familiar with how Java typing works, understanding typing in injection is easy.

Apart from using the <property> tag, you can also use the p namespace to inject other beans. The style of code to inject bean references is similar to the properties configuration syntax. As an example, the code in Listing 3-23 shows the configuration file from Listing 3-22 using the p namespace.

Listing 3-23. *Configuring Bean Injection Using the p Namespace*

```
<?xml version="1.0" encoding="UTF-8"?>
<beans xmlns="http://www.springframework.org/schema/beans"
       xmlns:xsi="http://www.w3.org/2001/XMLSchema-instance"
       xmlns:util="http://www.springframework.org/schema/util"
       xmlns:p="http://www.springframework.org/schema/p"
       xsi:schemaLocation="
                http://www.springframework.org/schema/beans
                http://www.springframework.org/schema/beans/spring-beans.xsd
                http://www.springframework.org/schema/util
                http://www.springframework.org/schema/util/spring-util.xsd">

    <bean id="encyclopedia"
          name="knowitall"
          class="com.apress.prospring2.ch03.di.ConfigurableEncyclopedia">
        <constructor-arg>
            <util:map>
                <entry key="AgeOfUniverse" value="13700000000"/>
                <entry key="ConstantOfLife" value="326190476"/>
            </util:map>
        </constructor-arg>
    </bean>

    <bean id="oracle" class="com.apress.prospring2.ch03.di.BookwormOracle"
            p:encyclopedia-ref="knowitall"/>

</beans>
```

The code is very similar to the code from Listing 3-21; the only notable difference is that we had to append -ref to the encyclopedia property name in the oracle bean to indicate that the BeanFactory should use the bean with the id (or name) knowitall rather than use the value (String)"knowitall" as the property value.

In the previous examples, the id of the bean to inject was specified using the ref attribute of the <property> tag. As you will see later, in the section titled "Understanding Bean Naming," you can give a bean more than one name so that you can refer to it using a variety of aliases. When you use the ref attribute, the <property> tag looks at the bean's id and any of its aliases. Listing 3-24 shows an alternative configuration for the previous example using an alternative name for the injected bean.

Listing 3-24. *Injecting Using Bean Aliases*

```
<?xml version="1.0" encoding="UTF-8"?>
<beans xmlns="http://www.springframework.org/schema/beans"
       xmlns:xsi="http://www.w3.org/2001/XMLSchema-instance"
       xmlns:util="http://www.springframework.org/schema/util"
       xsi:schemaLocation="
                http://www.springframework.org/schema/beans
                http://www.springframework.org/schema/beans/spring-beans.xsd
                http://www.springframework.org/schema/util
                http://www.springframework.org/schema/util/spring-util.xsd">

    <bean id="encyclopedia"
          name="knowitall"
          class="com.apress.prospring2.ch03.di.ConfigurableEncyclopedia">
        <constructor-arg>
            <util:map>
                <entry key="AgeOfUniverse" value="13700000000"/>
                <entry key="ConstantOfLife" value="326190476"/>
            </util:map>
        </constructor-arg>
    </bean>

    <bean id="oracle" class="com.apress.prospring2.ch03.di.BookwormOracle">
        <property name="encyclopedia" ref="knowitall"/>
    </bean>

</beans>
```

In this example, the `encyclopedia` bean is given an alias using the `name` attribute, and then it is injected into the `oracle` bean by using this alias in conjunction with the `bean` attribute of the `<property>` tag. Don't worry too much about the naming semantics at this point—we discuss this in much more detail later in the chapter.

Injection and BeanFactory Nesting

So far, the beans we have been injecting have been located in the same bean factory as the beans they are injected into. However, Spring supports a hierarchical structure for `BeanFactories` so that one factory is considered the parent of another. By allowing `BeanFactories` to be nested, Spring allows you to split your configuration into different files—a godsend on larger projects with lots of beans.

When nesting `BeanFactories`, Spring allows beans in the child factory to reference beans in the parent factory. The only drawback is that this can be done only in configuration. It is impossible to call `getBean()` on the child `BeanFactory` to access a bean in the parent `BeanFactory`.

`BeanFactory` nesting using the `XmlBeanFactory` is very simple. To nest one `XmlBeanFactory` inside another, simply pass the parent `XmlBeanFactory` as a constructor argument to the child `XmlBeanFactory`. This is shown in Listing 3-25.

Listing 3-25. *Nesting XmlBeanFactories*

```
XmlBeanFactory parent = new XmlBeanFactory(
    new ClassPathResource("/META-INF/spring/injectdemo1-context.xml"));
XmlBeanFactory child = new XmlBeanFactory(
   new ClassPathResource("/META-INF/spring/injectdemo2-context.xml"),
   parent);
```

Inside the configuration file for the child BeanFactory, referencing a bean in the parent BeanFactory works exactly like referencing a bean in the child BeanFactory, unless you have a bean in the child BeanFactory that shares the same name. In that case, you can no longer use the convenient ref attribute of the <property> tag but must start using the <ref parent=""/> tag. Listing 3-26 shows how to write the XML configuration file with reference to the parent bean.

Listing 3-26. *Child BeanFactory Configuration*

```
<?xml version="1.0" encoding="UTF-8"?>
<beans xmlns="http://www.springframework.org/schema/beans"
       xmlns:xsi="http://www.w3.org/2001/XMLSchema-instance"
       xsi:schemaLocation="
                http://www.springframework.org/schema/beans
                http://www.springframework.org/schema/beans/spring-beans.xsd">

    <bean id="name" class="java.lang.String">
        <constructor-arg value="Johnny Smith"/>
    </bean>

    <bean id="injectSimpleChild"
         class="com.apress.prospring2.ch03.beanfactory.InjectSimpleDemo">
        <property name="name" ref="name"/>
        <property name="age" value="2"/>
        <property name="height" value="0.8"/>
        <property name="isProgrammer" value="false"/>
        <property name="ageInSeconds" value="63072000"/>
    </bean>

    <bean id="injectSimpleChild2"
        class="com.apress.prospring2.ch03.beanfactory.InjectSimpleDemo">
        <property name="name">
            <ref parent="name"/>
        </property>
        <property name="age" value="2"/>
        <property name="height" value="0.8"/>
        <property name="isProgrammer" value="false"/>
        <property name="ageInSeconds" value="63072000"/>
    </bean>

</beans>
```

Notice that we have two beans, injectSimpleChild and injectSimpleChild2. Both beans use the name bean to set the value of their name property. However, the injectSimpleChild bean uses the local name bean, while injectSimpleChild2 uses the name bean from the parent BeanFactory. If we tried using this configuration file on its own, it would fail, because there is no parent bean factory. We can verify this by modifying the line that creates the child BeanFactory as follows:

```
XmlBeanFactory child = new XmlBeanFactory(new ClassPathResource(
    "/META-INF/spring/injectdemo3-context.xml"));
```

When we run the application, the child BeanFactory has no reference to the parent BeanFactory, and the application will fail with a BeanCreationException:

```
Exception in thread "main" org.springframework.beans.factory.BeanCreationException:
    Error creating bean with name 'injectSimpleChild2' defined in class path
    resource [META-INF/spring/injectdemo3-context.xml]: Cannot resolve reference to
    bean 'name' while setting bean property 'name';
    ...
Caused by: org.springframework.beans.factory.BeanCreationException:
    Error creating bean with name 'injectSimpleChild2' defined in class path
    resource [META-INF/spring/injectdemo3-context.xml]:
    Can't resolve reference to bean 'name' in parent factory: ➥
    no parent factory available
  ...

Process finished with exit code 1
```

To run the example, we must complete the parent BeanFactory configuration file (see Listing 3-27).

Listing 3-27. *Parent BeanFactory Configuration*

```
<?xml version="1.0" encoding="UTF-8"?>
<beans xmlns="http://www.springframework.org/schema/beans"
       xmlns:xsi="http://www.w3.org/2001/XMLSchema-instance"
       xsi:schemaLocation="
                http://www.springframework.org/schema/beans
                http://www.springframework.org/schema/beans/spring-beans.xsd">

    <bean id="name" class="java.lang.String">
        <constructor-arg value="John Smith"/>
    </bean>

    <bean id="injectSimpleParent"
         class="com.apress.prospring2.ch03.beanfactory.InjectSimpleDemo">
        <property name="name" ref="name"/>
        <property name="age" value="2"/>
        <property name="height" value="0.8"/>
        <property name="isProgrammer" value="false"/>
        <property name="ageInSeconds" value="63072000"/>
    </bean>

</beans>
```

When we run the application now, the child BeanFactory can access all beans in the parent BeanFactory. Thus, the <ref parent="name"/> tag in the child BeanFactory configuration for the injectSimpleChild2 bean will be able to find the bean with the ID name and set the value of the name property to "John Smith".

Using Collections for Injection

Often, your beans need access to collections of objects rather than just individual beans or values. Therefore, it should come as no surprise that Spring allows you to inject a collection of objects into one of your beans. Using the collection is simple: you choose either <list>, <map>, <set>, or <props> to represent a List, Map, Set, or Properties instance. Then, you pass in the individual items just as you would with any other injection. The <props> tag allows for only strings to be passed in as the value, because the Properties class only permits String elements. When using <list>, <map>, or <set>, you can use any tag you'd use when injecting into a property, even another collection tag.

This allows you to pass in a `List` of `Map` objects, a `Map` of `Set` objects, or even a `List` of `Map` objects of `Set` objects of `List` objects! Listing 3-28 shows a class that can have all four collection types injected into it.

Listing 3-28. *Collection Injection Example*

```
public class CollectionsDemo {
    private Map map;
    private Properties props;
    private Set set;
    private List list;

    public static void main(String[] args) {
        BeanFactory factory = new XmlBeanFactory(
            new ClassPathResource(
                 "/META-INF/spring/collectionsdemo1-context.xml");
        CollectionsDemo instance =
            (CollectionsDemo)factory.getBean("collectionsDemo");
        instance.displayInfo();
    }

    public void setList(List list) {
        this.list = list;
    }

    public void setSet(Set set) {
        this.set = set;
    }

    public void setMap(Map map) {
        this.map = map;
    }

    public void setProps(Properties props) {
        this.props = props;
    }

    public void displayInfo() {

        // display the Map
        Iterator i = map.keySet().iterator();

        System.out.println("Map contents:\n");
        while (i.hasNext()) {
            Object key = i.next();
            System.out.println("Key: " + key + " - Value: " + map.get(key));
        }

        // display the properties
        i = props.keySet().iterator();
        System.out.println("\nProperties contents:\n");
        while (i.hasNext()) {
            String key = i.next().toString();
            System.out.println("Key: " + key + " - Value: "
                    + props.getProperty(key));
        }
```

```
        // display the set
        i = set.iterator();
        System.out.println("\nSet contents:\n");
        while (i.hasNext()) {
            System.out.println("Value: " + i.next());
        }

        // display the list
        i = list.iterator();
        System.out.println("\nList contents:\n");
        while (i.hasNext()) {
            System.out.println("Value: " + i.next());
        }
    }

}
```

That is quite a lot of code, but it actually does very little. The `main()` method retrieves a `CollectionsDemo` bean from Spring and calls the `displayInfo()` method. This method just outputs the contents of the `List`, `Map`, `Properties`, and `Set` instances that will be injected from Spring. In Listing 3-29, you can see the verbose configuration required to inject values for each of the properties on the `CollectionInjection` class.

Listing 3-29. *Verbose Configuration for the CollectionsDemo*

```
<?xml version="1.0" encoding="UTF-8"?>
<beans xmlns="http://www.springframework.org/schema/beans"
       xmlns:xsi="http://www.w3.org/2001/XMLSchema-instance"
       xsi:schemaLocation="
                http://www.springframework.org/schema/beans
                http://www.springframework.org/schema/beans/spring-beans.xsd">

    <bean id="collectionsDemo"
        class="com.apress.prospring2.ch03.beanfactory.CollectionsDemo">
        <property name="map">
            <map>
                <entry key="someValue">
                    <value>Hello World!</value>
                </entry>
                <entry key="someBean">
                    <ref local="oracle"/>
                </entry>
            </map>
        </property>
        <property name="props">
            <props>
                <prop key="firstName">
                    Jan
                </prop>
                <prop key="secondName">
                    Machacek
                </prop>
            </props>
        </property>
        <property name="set">
            <set>
                <value>Hello World!</value>
```

```
                <ref local="oracle"/>
            </set>
        </property>
        <property name="list">
            <list>
                <value>Hello World!</value>
                <ref local="oracle"/>
            </list>
        </property>
    </bean>

    <bean id="oracle" class="com.apress.prospring2.ch03.di.BookwormOracle"/>

</beans>
```

In this code, you can see that we have injected values into all four setters exposed on the ConstructorInjection class. For the map property, we have injected a Map instance using the <map> tag. Notice that each entry is specified using an <entry> tag, and each has a String key and an entry value. This entry value can be any value you can inject into a property separately; this example shows the use of the <value> and <ref> tags to add a String value and a bean reference to the Map. For the props property, we use the <props> tag to create an instance of java.util.Properties and populate it using <prop> tags. Notice that, although the <prop> tag is keyed in a similar manner to the <entry> tag, you can only specify a String value for each property that goes in the Properties instance.

As a handy trick, you can use Spring's built-in PropertyEditor support to simplify declaration of properties. You can write

```
<property name="props">
    <value>
        firstName=Jan
        lastName=Machacek
    </value>
</property>
```

instead of using the rather verbose nested <props> and <prop> tags.

Both the <list> and <set> tags work in exactly the same way: you specify each element using any of the individual value tags such as <value> and <ref> that are used to inject a single value into a property. In Listing 3-29, you can see that we have added a String value and a bean reference to both the List and the Set.

Here is the output generated by Listing 3-29; as expected, it simply lists the elements added to the collections in the configuration file:

```
Map contents:

Key: someValue - Value: Hello World!
Key: someBean - Value: com.apress.prospring2.ch03.di.BookwormOracle@1a4bd4

Properties contents:

Key: secondName - Value: Machacek
Key: firstName - Value: Jan

Set contents:

Value: Hello World!
Value: com.apress.prospring2.ch03.di.BookwormOracle@1a4bd4
```

```
List contents:

Value: Hello World!
Value: com.apress.prospring2.ch03.di.BookwormOracle@1a4bd4

Process finished with exit code 0
```

Remember, with the <list>, <map>, and <set> elements, you can employ any of the tags used to set the value of noncollection properties to specify the value of one of the entries in the collection. This is quite a powerful concept, because you are not limited just to injecting collections of primitive values; you can also inject collections of beans or other collections.

Using this functionality makes modularizing your application and providing different, user-selectable implementations of key pieces of application logic much easier. Consider a download manager application: it should be able to handle the HTTP, FTP, TFTP, SFTP, and many other protocols. Figure 3-3 shows the UML diagram of the core components of the application.

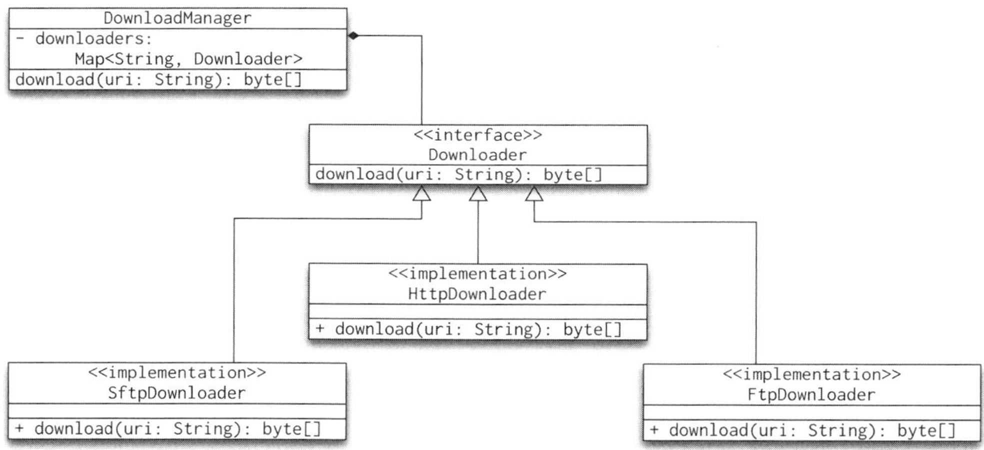

Figure 3-3. *UML class diagram of the download manager*

You can see that the Downloader interface has as many implementations as necessary, and each implementation deals with the details of the transfer protocol. The DownloadManager class has a Map<String, Downloader> whose keys are the scheme names (http, ftp, tftp, and so on) and whose values are instances of the Downloader interface. The DownloadManager's download(String) method examines the URI and picks the appropriate Downloader implementation from the map. It then calls its download method, passing the URI. This design of the download manager application allows us to plug in additional protocol handlers; the only change is the implementation of the Downloader interface and modification of the DownloadManager bean configuration.

Understanding Bean Naming

Spring supports a quite complex bean naming structure that allows you the flexibility to handle many different situations. Every bean must have at least one name that is unique within the containing BeanFactory. Spring follows a simple resolution process to determine what name is used for the bean. If you give the <bean> tag an id attribute, the value of that attribute is used as the name. If no id attribute is specified, Spring looks for a name attribute and, if one is defined, it uses the first name defined in the name attribute (we say the first name because it is possible to define multiple names within the name attribute; this is covered in more detail shortly). If neither the id nor the name attribute is specified, Spring uses the bean's class name as the name, provided, of course, that no other bean is using the same name (in which case, a unique name will be generated). Listing 3-30 shows a sample configuration that uses all three naming schemes.

Listing 3-30. *Bean Naming*

```
<bean id="string1" class="java.lang.String"/>
<bean name="string2" class="java.lang.String"/>
<bean class="java.lang.String"/>
```

Each of these approaches is equally valid from a technical point of view, but which is the best choice for your application? To start with, avoid using the automatic name-by-class behavior. This doesn't allow you much flexibility to define multiple beans of the same type, and it is much better to define your own names. That way, if Spring changes the default behavior in the future, your application continues to work. When choosing whether to use id or name, always use id to specify the bean's default name. The id attribute in the XML is declared as an XML identity in the schema for the Spring configuration file. This means that not only can the XML parser perform validation on your file, but any good XML editor should be able to do the same, thus reducing the number of errors as a result of mistyped bean names. Essentially, this allows your XML editor to validate that the bean you are referencing in the local attribute of a <ref> tag actually exists.

The only drawback of using the id attribute is that you are limited to characters that are allowed within XML element IDs. If you find that you cannot use a character you want in your name, you can specify that name using the name attribute, which does not have to adhere to the XML naming rules. That said, you should still consider giving your bean a name using id, and you can define the desirable name using name aliasing as discussed in the next section.

Bean Name Aliasing

Spring allows a bean to have more than one name. You can achieve this by specifying a comma- or semicolon-separated list of names in the name attribute of the bean's <bean> tag. You can do this in place of, or in conjunction with, using the id attribute. Listing 3-31 shows a simple <bean> configuration that defines multiple names for a single bean.

Listing 3-31. *Configuring Multiple Bean Names*

```
<?xml version="1.0" encoding="UTF-8"?>
<beans xmlns="http://www.springframework.org/schema/beans"
       xmlns:xsi="http://www.w3.org/2001/XMLSchema-instance"
       xsi:schemaLocation="
                http://www.springframework.org/schema/beans
                http://www.springframework.org/schema/beans/spring-beans.xsd">

    <bean id="name1" name="name2,name3,name4" class="java.lang.String"/>

</beans>
```

As you can see, we have defined four names: one using the id attribute, and the other three as a comma-separated list in the name attribute. Alternatively, you can use the <alias> tag, specifying one or more aliases for any given bean name (see Listing 3-32).

Listing 3-32. *Use of the <alias> Tag*

```
<?xml version="1.0" encoding="UTF-8"?>
<beans xmlns="http://www.springframework.org/schema/beans"
       xmlns:xsi="http://www.w3.org/2001/XMLSchema-instance"
       xsi:schemaLocation="
                http://www.springframework.org/schema/beans
                http://www.springframework.org/schema/beans/spring-beans.xsd">

    <bean id="name1" name="name2,name3,name4" class="java.lang.String"/>
    <alias name="name2" alias="namex1"/>
    <alias name="name1" alias="namex2"/>

</beans>
```

Notice that we have used one of the existing aliases of the bean `id="name1"`; therefore, we now have beans `name1`, `name2`, `name3`, `name4`, `namex1`, and `namex2` representing the same instance of `String`. Listing 3-33 shows a sample Java routine that grabs the same bean from the `BeanFactory` six times using the different names and verifies that the beans are the same.

Listing 3-33. *Accessing Beans Using Aliases*

```
public class AliasDemo {
    public static void main(String[] args) {
        BeanFactory factory = new XmlBeanFactory(
            new ClassPathResource(
                "/META-INF/spring/aliasdemo-context.xml"));

        String s1 = (String)factory.getBean("name1");
        String s2 = (String)factory.getBean("name2");
        String s3 = (String)factory.getBean("name3");
        String s4 = (String)factory.getBean("name4");
        String s5 = (String)factory.getBean("namex1");
        String s6 = (String)factory.getBean("namex2");

        System.out.println((s1 == s2));
        System.out.println((s2 == s3));
        System.out.println((s3 == s4));
        System.out.println((s4 == s5));
        System.out.println((s5 == s6));
    }

}
```

This code prints `true` five times to `stdout` for the configuration contained in Listing 3-33, verifying that the beans accessed using different names are, in fact, the same bean.

You can retrieve a list of the bean's aliases by calling `BeanFactory.getAliases(String)` and passing in any one of the bean's names. The number of names returned in the list is always one less than the total number of names assigned to the bean, because Spring considers one of the names to be the default. Which name is the default depends on how you configured the bean. If you specified a name using the `id` attribute, that name is always the default. If you did not use the `id` attribute, the first name in the list passed to the `name` attribute will be used.

Bean name aliasing is a strange beast, because it is not something you tend to use when building a new application. If you are going to have many other beans inject another bean, they may as well use the same name to access that bean. However, as your application goes into production and maintenance work gets carried out, modifications made, and so on, bean name aliasing becomes more useful.

Consider the following scenario. You have an application in which 50 different beans, configured using Spring, all require an implementation of the Foo interface: 25 of the beans use the StandardFoo implementation with the bean name standardFoo, and the other 25 use the SuperFoo implementation with the superFoo bean name. Six months after you put the application into production, you decide to move the first 25 beans to the SuperFoo implementation. To do this, you have three options.

The first is to change the implementation class of the standardFoo bean to SuperFoo. The drawback of this approach is that you have two instances of the SuperFoo class lying around when you really only need one. In addition, you now have two beans to make changes to when the configuration changes.

The second option is to update the injection configuration for the 25 beans that are changing, which changes the beans' names from standardFoo to superFoo. This approach is not the most elegant way to proceed—you could perform a find and replace, but rolling back your changes when management isn't happy means retrieving an old version of your configuration from your version control system.

The third, and most ideal, approach is to remove (or comment out) the definition for the standardFoo bean and make standardFoo an alias to the superFoo bean. This change requires minimal effort and restoring the system to its previous configuration is just as simple.

Bean Instantiation Modes

By default, all beans in Spring are singletons. This means that Spring maintains a single instance of the bean, all dependent objects use the same instance, and all calls to BeanFactory.getBean() return the same instance. We demonstrated this in the previous example shown in Listing 3-33, where we were able to use identity comparison (==) rather than the equals() comparison to check if the beans were the same.

The term "singleton" is used in Java to refer to two distinct concepts: an object that has a single instance within the application, and the singleton design pattern. We refer to the first concept as singleton and to the singleton pattern as Singleton. The Singleton design pattern was popularized in the seminal *Design Patterns: Elements of Reusable Object Oriented Software* by Erich Gamma, Richard Helm, Ralph Johnson, and John M. Vlissides (Addison-Wesley, 1995). The problem arises when people confuse the need for singleton instances with the need to apply the singleton pattern. Listing 3-34 shows a typical implementation of the singleton pattern in Java.

Listing 3-34. *The Singleton Design Pattern*

```
public class Singleton {
    private static Singleton instance = new Singleton();

    private Singleton() {

    }

    public static Singleton getInstance() {
        return instance;
    }
}
```

This pattern achieves its goal of allowing you to maintain and access a single instance of a class throughout your application, but it does so at the expense of increased coupling. Your application code must always have explicit knowledge of the Singleton class in order to obtain the instance—completely removing the ability to code to interfaces. In reality, the singleton pattern is actually two patterns in one. The first, and desired, pattern involves maintenance of a single instance of an object. The second, and less desirable, is a pattern for object lookup that completely removes the possibility of using interfaces. Using the singleton pattern also makes it very difficult to swap out implementations arbitrarily, because most objects that require the `Singleton` instance directly access the `Singleton` object. This can cause all kinds of headaches when you are trying to unit test your application, because you are unable to replace the `Singleton` with a mock for testing purposes.

Fortunately, with Spring, you can take advantage of the singleton instantiation model without having to work around the Singleton design pattern. All beans in Spring are, by default, created as singleton instances, and Spring uses the same instances to fulfill all requests for that bean. Of course, Spring is not limited to use of the `singleton` instance; it can still create a new instance of the bean to satisfy every dependency and every call to `getBean()`. It does all of this without any impact on your application code, and for this reason, we like to refer to Spring as being *instantiation mode agnostic*. This is a very powerful concept. If you start off with an object that is a singleton but discover that it is not really suited to multithread access, you can change it to a nonsingleton without affecting any of your application code. Spring offers many different nonsingleton instantiation modes; Table 3-1 lists all of them.

Table 3-1. *Nonsingleton Instantiation Modes*

Mode	Description
`prototype`	Every call to the `getBean()` method returns a new instance of the bean.
`request`	Every call to the `getBean()` method in a web application will return a unique instance of the bean for every HTTP request. This behavior is only implemented in the `WebApplicationContext` and its subinterfaces.
`session`	Calls to the `getBean()` method will return a unique instance of the bean for every HTTP `Session`. Just like `request`, this scope is only available in `WebApplicationContext` and its subinterfaces.
`global session`	The `getBean()` calls will return a unique instance of the bean for the global HTTP session in a portlet context. Just like `request` and `session` scopes, this instantiation mode is only supported in `WebApplicationContext` and its subinterfaces.

We will make full use of the instantiation modes in Chapter 17, but you can see already that the nonsingleton bean scopes give you fine control over the life cycle of the beans in your application. Before we write web applications in Spring, we will take a look at the `singleton` and `prototype` instantiation modes. Listing 3-35 shows one singleton and one prototype bean.

Listing 3-35. *Singleton and Prototype Beans*

```
<?xml version="1.0" encoding="UTF-8"?>
<beans xmlns="http://www.springframework.org/schema/beans"
       xmlns:xsi="http://www.w3.org/2001/XMLSchema-instance"
       xsi:schemaLocation="
                http://www.springframework.org/schema/beans
                http://www.springframework.org/schema/beans/spring-beans.xsd">

    <bean id="singleMe" class="java.lang.String" scope="singleton">
        <constructor-arg type="java.lang.String" value="Singleton -- Jan Machacek"/>
    </bean>

    <bean id="prototypeMe" class="java.lang.String" scope="prototype">
        <constructor-arg type="java.lang.String" value="Prototype -- Jan Machacek"/>
    </bean>

</beans>
```

You can see that we have two `java.lang.String` beans: one as `prototype` and one as `singleton`. When we run the code in Listing 3-36, we will see that Spring manages a single instance of the `singleMe` bean and creates a new instance for every call to `getBean()` for `prototypeMe`.

Listing 3-36. *Using Singletons and Prototypes*

```
public class ScopeDemo {

    private static void compare(final BeanFactory factory, final String beanName) {
        String b1 = (String)factory.getBean(beanName);
        String b2 = (String)factory.getBean(beanName);
        System.out.println("Bean b1=" + b1 + ", b2=" + b2);
        System.out.println("Same?  " + (b1 == b2));
        System.out.println("Equal? " + (b1.equals(b2)));
    }

    public static void main(String[] args) {
        BeanFactory factory = new XmlBeanFactory(
            new ClassPathResource(
                "/META-INF/spring/beanscopedemo1-context.xml"));
        compare(factory, "singleMe");
        compare(factory, "prototypeMe");
    }

}
```

Notice that we call the `getBean()` method regardless of the bean instantiation mode, and Spring takes care of returning the appropriate bean instance. When we run this application, it confirms that the bean instantiation modes work as expected.

```
Bean b1=Singleton -- Jan Machacek, b2=Singleton -- Jan Machacek
Same?  true
Equal? true
Bean b1=Prototype -- Jan Machacek, b2=Prototype -- Jan Machacek
Same?  false
Equal? true

Process finished with exit code 0
```

If we tried to change the bean scope to `request`, `session`, or `globalSession`, we would receive an `IllegalStateException`, because our `BeanFactory` is not running in a web application context and therefore cannot access the HTTP request.

Choosing an Instantiation Mode

In most scenarios, it is quite easy to see which instantiation mode is suitable. Typically, we find that singleton is the default mode for our beans. In general, singletons should be used in the following scenarios:

- *Shared object with no state*: When you have an object that maintains no state and has many dependent objects, use singletons. Because you do not need synchronization if there is no state, you do not really need to create a new instance of the bean each time a dependent object needs to use it for some processing.
- *Shared object with read-only state*: This is similar to the previous point, but you have some read-only state, for example a read-only property. In this case, you still do not need synchronization, so creating an instance to satisfy each request for the bean is just adding additional overhead.
- *Shared object with shared state*: If you have a bean that has state that must be shared, singleton is the ideal choice. In this case, ensure that your synchronization for state writes is as granular as possible.
- *High throughput objects with writable state*: If you have a bean that is used a great deal in your application, you may find that keeping a singleton and synchronizing all write access to the bean state allows for better performance than constantly creating hundreds of instances of the bean. When using this approach, try to keep the synchronization as granular as possible without sacrificing consistency. You will find that this approach is particularly useful when your application creates a large number of instances over a long period of time, when your shared object has only a small amount of writable state, or when the instantiation of a new instance is expensive.

You should consider using nonsingletons in the following scenarios:

- *Object with writable state*: If you have a bean that has a lot of writable state, you may find that the cost of synchronization is greater than the cost of creating a new instance to handle each request from a dependent object.
- *Object with private state*: In some cases, your dependent objects need a bean that has private state so that they can conduct their processing separately from other objects that depend on that bean. In this case, a singleton is clearly not suitable.

The main asset you gain from Spring's instantiation management is that your applications can immediately benefit from the lower memory usage associated with singletons, with very little effort on your part. If you find later that a singleton does not meet the needs of your application, modifying your configuration to use nonsingleton mode is an easy task.

Resolving Dependencies

During normal operation, Spring is able to resolve dependencies by simply looking at your configuration file. In this way, Spring can ensure that each bean is configured in the correct order so that each bean has its dependencies correctly configured. If Spring just created the beans and configured them in any order, a bean could be created and configured before its dependencies, which is obviously not what you want; doing so would cause all sorts of problems within your application.

Unfortunately, Spring is not aware of any dependencies that exist between beans in your code. For instance, assume we have two legacy classes, `A` and `B`, that use the `Shared` class to store some configuration details and that class `A` needs to be fully instantiated before class `B`. Listing 3-37 shows the example legacy code.

Listing 3-37. *Legacy Code of Classes A, B, and Shared*

```
// Shared.java
public final class Shared {
    private static Object value = null;
    private Shared() {
```

```
    }

    public synchronized static void setValue(Object o) {
        value = o;
    }

    public static Object getValue() {
        return value;
    }
}

// A.java
public class A {

    public A() {
        Shared.setValue("Undetermined");
    }

    @Override
    public String toString() {
        final StringBuilder sb = new StringBuilder();
        sb.append("A");
        sb.append("{}");
        sb.append("Shared.getValue()=").append(Shared.getValue()).append("}");
        return sb.toString();
    }
}

// B.java
public class B {

    public B() {
        Shared.setValue("Completed");
    }

    @Override
    public String toString() {
        final StringBuilder sb = new StringBuilder();
        sb.append("B");
        sb.append("{}");
        sb.append("Shared.getValue()=").append(Shared.getValue()).append("}");
        return sb.toString();
    }
}
```

We can use Spring to manage the instances of classes `A` and `B` as beans `a` and `b`. However, the functionality of the application depends on the order in which we ask Spring to instantiate the beans. Consider the code in Listing 3-38, which shows the `BeanFactory` configuration.

Listing 3-38. *BeanFactory Configuration for Beans a and b*

```
<?xml version="1.0" encoding="UTF-8"?>
<beans xmlns="http://www.springframework.org/schema/beans"
       xmlns:xsi="http://www.w3.org/2001/XMLSchema-instance"
       xsi:schemaLocation="
                http://www.springframework.org/schema/beans
                http://www.springframework.org/schema/beans/spring-beans.xsd">
```

```
    <bean id="b" class="com.apress.prospring2.ch03.beandependency.B"/>
    <bean id="a" class="com.apress.prospring2.ch03.beandependency.A"/>

</beans>
```

Now, if we call getBean("b") before getBean("a"), we will break the constraint stating that bean b depends on bean a (see Listing 3-39).

Listing 3-39. *Dependency-Breaking Sample Application*

```
public class DependencyDemo {

    public static void main(String[] args) {
        XmlBeanFactory bf = new XmlBeanFactory(
            new ClassPathResource(
                "/META-INF/spring/beandependencydemo1-context.xml"));

        B b = (B) bf.getBean("b");
        A a = (A) bf.getBean("a");
        System.out.println(a);
        System.out.println(b);
    }

}
```

Running the application will show that the dependency constraint is indeed broken (because we called getBean("b") before getBean("a")):

```
A{}Shared.getValue()=Undetermined}
B{}Shared.getValue()=Undetermined}

Process finished with exit code 0
```

We can fix this using the depends-on attribute in the bean definition:

```
<bean id="b" class="com.apress.prospring2.ch03.beandependency.B" depends-on="a"/>
```

When we run the application with the modified BeanFactory configuration file, the output will show that Spring creates bean a before creating bean b:

```
A{}Shared.getValue()=Completed}
B{}Shared.getValue()=Completed}

Process finished with exit code 0
```

Notice that, in the example, we could make the dependency constraint work even without using the depends-on attribute simply by calling getBean("a") before getBean("b"). However, if you are using Spring to inject beans a and b into some other beans, there is no guarantee in which order Spring will choose to instantiate the beans, making the depends-on attribute the only way to control the dependency between beans a and b.

Automatically Wiring Your Beans

In all the examples so far, we have had to define explicitly, via the configuration file, how individual beans are wired together. If you don't like having to wire all your components together, you can have Spring attempt to do so automatically. By default, automatic wiring is disabled. To enable it, you specify which method of automatic wiring you wish to use using the `autowire` attribute of the bean you wish to automatically wire.

Spring supports four modes for automatic wiring: `byName`, `byType`, `constructor`, and `autodetect`. When using `byName` wiring, Spring attempts to wire each property to a bean of the same name. So, if the target bean has a property named `foo` and a `foo` bean is defined in the `BeanFactory`, the `foo` bean is assigned to the `foo` property of the target.

When using `byType` automatic wiring, Spring attempts to wire each of the properties on the target bean automatically using a bean of the same type in the `BeanFactory`. So if you have a property of type `String` on the target bean and a bean of type `String` in the `BeanFactory`, Spring wires the `String` bean to the target bean's `String` property. If you have more than one bean of the same type, in this case `String`, in the same `BeanFactory`, Spring is unable to decide which one to use for the automatic wiring and throws an exception.

The `constructor` wiring mode functions just like `byType` wiring, except that it uses constructors rather than setters to perform the injection. Spring attempts to match the greatest numbers of arguments it can in the constructor. So, if your bean has two constructors, one that accepts a `String` and one that accepts a `String` and an `Integer`, and you have both a `String` and an `Integer` bean in your `BeanFactory`, Spring uses the two-argument constructor.

The final mode, `autodetect`, instructs Spring to choose between the `constructor` and `byType` modes automatically. If your bean has a default (no arguments) constructor, Spring uses `byType`; otherwise, it uses `constructor`.

Listing 3-40 shows a simple configuration that automatically wires four beans of the same type using each of the different modes.

Listing 3-40. *BeanFactory Configuration File for the Automatic Wiring Demonstration*

```
<?xml version="1.0" encoding="UTF-8"?>
<beans xmlns="http://www.springframework.org/schema/beans"
       xmlns:xsi="http://www.w3.org/2001/XMLSchema-instance"
       xsi:schemaLocation="
                http://www.springframework.org/schema/beans
                http://www.springframework.org/schema/beans/spring-beans.xsd">

    <bean id="foo" class="com.apress.prospring2.ch03.autowiring.Foo"/>
    <bean id="bar" class="com.apress.prospring2.ch03.autowiring.Bar"/>

    <bean id="byName" autowire="byName"
        class="com.apress.prospring2.ch03.autowiring.Target"/>
    <bean id="byType" autowire="byType"
        class="com.apress.prospring2.ch03.autowiring.Target"/>
    <bean id="constructor" autowire="constructor"
        class="com.apress.prospring2.ch03.autowiring.Target"/>
    <bean id="autodetect" autowire="autodetect"
        class="com.apress.prospring2.ch03.autowiring.Target"/>

</beans>
```

This configuration should look very familiar to you now. Notice that each of the `Target` beans has a different value for the `autowire` attribute. Listing 3-41 shows a simple Java application that retrieves each of the `Target` beans from the `BeanFactory`.

Listing 3-41. *Automatic Wiring Demonstration*

```
public class Target {
    private Foo foo;
    private Foo foo2;
    private Bar bar;

    public Target() {
        System.out.println("Target()");
    }

    public Target(Foo foo) {
        System.out.println("Target(Foo)");
        this.foo = foo;
    }

    public Target(Foo foo, Bar bar) {
        System.out.println("Target(Foo, Bar)");
        this.foo = foo;
        this.bar = bar;
    }

    public void setDependency(Bar bar) {
        System.out.println("Target.setDependency(Bar)");
        this.bar = bar;
    }

    public void setFoo(Foo foo) {
        System.out.println("Target.setFoo(Foo)");
        this.foo = foo;
    }

    public void setFoo2(Foo foo2) {
        System.out.println("Target.setFoo2(Foo)");
        this.foo2 = foo2;
    }

    public void setBar(Bar bar) {
        System.out.println("Target.setBar(Bar)");
        this.bar = bar;
    }

    @Override
    public String toString() {
        final StringBuilder sb = new StringBuilder();
        sb.append("Target");
        sb.append("{foo=").append(foo);
        sb.append(", foo2=").append(foo2);
        sb.append(", bar=").append(bar);
        sb.append('}');
        return sb.toString();
    }
}
```

In this code, you can see that the Target class has three constructors: a no-argument constructor, a constructor that accepts a Foo instance, and a constructor that accepts a Foo and a Bar instance. In addition to these constructors, the Target bean has three properties: two of type Foo and one of type Bar. Each of these properties and constructors writes a message to stdout when it is called. The main method simply retrieves each of the Target beans declared in the BeanFactory, triggering the automatic wiring process. Here is the output from running this example:

```
byName:
Target()
Target.setBar(Bar)
Target.setFoo(Foo)
Target{foo=com.apress.prospring2.ch03.autowiring.Foo, foo2=null, ➥
bar=com.apress.prospring2.ch03.autowiring.Bar}

byType:
Target()
Target.setBar(Bar)
Target.setDependency(Bar)
Target.setFoo(Foo)
Target.setFoo2(Foo)
Target{foo=com.apress.prospring2.ch03.autowiring.Foo, ➥
foo2=com.apress.prospring2.ch03.autowiring.Foo, ➥
bar=com.apress.prospring2.ch03.autowiring.Bar}

constructor:
Target(Foo, Bar)
Target{foo=com.apress.prospring2.ch03.autowiring.Foo, foo2=null, ➥
bar=com.apress.prospring2.ch03.autowiring.Bar}

autodetect:
Target()
Target.setBar(Bar)
Target.setDependency(Bar)
Target.setFoo(Foo)
Target.setFoo2(Foo)
Target{foo=com.apress.prospring2.ch03.autowiring.Foo, ➥
foo2=com.apress.prospring2.ch03.autowiring.Foo, ➥
bar=com.apress.prospring2.ch03.autowiring.Bar}


Process finished with exit code 0
```

From the output, you can see that when Spring uses byName, the only property that is set is the foo property, because this is the only property with a corresponding bean entry in the configuration file. When using byType, Spring sets the value of all three properties. The foo and foo2 properties are set by the foo bean, and the myBarProperty is set by the bar bean. When using constructor, Spring uses the two-argument constructor, because Spring can provide beans for both arguments and does not need to fall back to another constructor. In this case, autodetect functions just like byType, because we defined a default constructor. If we had not done this, autodetect would have functioned just like constructor.

In addition to explicit configuration, you can use the @Autowired annotation, which instructs the AutowiredAnnotationBeanPostProcessor to automatically wire your beans' dependencies exposed by fields, setters, or constructors. We will take a look at the bean post processors and AutowiredAnnotationBeanPostProcessor in Chapter 4, but as a teaser, take a look at Listing 3-42.

Listing 3-42. *Automatic Wiring Using @Autowired*

```
public class AnnotatedTarget {
    @Autowired
    private Foo foo;
    @Autowired
    private Foo foo2;
    @Autowired
    private Bar bar;

    @Override
    public String toString() {
        final StringBuilder sb = new StringBuilder();
        sb.append("AnnotatedTarget");
        sb.append("{foo=").append(foo);
        sb.append(", foo2=").append(foo2);
        sb.append(", bar=").append(bar);
        sb.append('}');
        return sb.toString();
    }
}
```

When to Use Automatic Wiring

In most cases, the answer to the question of whether you should use automatic wiring is definitely "No!" Automatic wiring can save you time in small applications, but in many cases, it leads to bad practices and is inflexible in large applications. Using byName seems like a good idea, but it may lead you to give your classes artificial property names so that you can take advantage of the automatic wiring functionality. The whole idea behind Spring is that you can create your classes how you like and have Spring work for you, not the other way around. You may be tempted to use byType until you realize that you can only have one bean for each type in your BeanFactory—a restriction that is problematic when you need to maintain beans with different configurations of the same type. The same argument applies to the use of constructor wiring, which follows the same semantics as byType. The autodetect wiring strategy is simply byType and constructor bundled together.

In some cases, automatic wiring can save you time, but defining your wiring explicitly does not really take much extra effort, and you benefit from explicit semantics and full flexibility on property naming and on how many instances of the same type you manage. For any nontrivial application, steer clear of automatic wiring at all costs.

Unit testing is the exception to the rule of avoiding automatic wiring. We cover testing in detail in Chapter 22, and we make extensive use of the @Autowired annotation to tell Spring integration test support code to automatically wire the beans under test.

Checking Dependencies

When creating bean instances and wiring together dependencies, Spring does not, by default, check to see that every property on a bean has a value. In many cases, you do not need Spring to perform this check, but if you have a bean that absolutely must have a value for all of its properties, you can ask Spring to check this for you.

As the Spring documentation points out, value checking is not always effective. You may provide a default value for some properties, or you may just want to assert that only one particular property must have a value; the dependency checking capabilities of Spring do not take these features into consideration. That said, having Spring perform this check for you can be quite useful in certain circumstances. In many cases, doing so allows you to remove checks from your code and have Spring perform them just once at startup.

Besides the default (no checking), Spring has three modes for dependency checking: `simple`, `objects`, and `all`. The `simple` mode checks to see whether all properties that are either collections or built-in types have values. In this mode, Spring does not check to see whether or not properties of any other types are set. This mode can be quite useful for checking whether all the configuration parameters for a bean are set, because they are typically either built-in values or collections of built-in values.

The `objects` mode checks any property not covered by the `simple` mode, but it does not check properties that are covered by `simple`. So if you have a bean that has two properties, one of type `int` and the other of type `Foo`, `objects` checks whether a value is specified for the `Foo` property but does not check for the `int` property.

The `all` mode checks all properties, essentially performing the checks of both the `simple` and `objects` mode. Listing 3-43 shows a `simple` class that has two properties: one `int` property and one property of the same type as the class itself.

Listing 3-43. *Dependency Check Target Bean*

```
public class SimpleBean {
    private int someInt;
    private SimpleBean nestedSimpleBean;

    public void setSomeInt(int someInt) {
        this.someInt = someInt;
    }

    public void setNestedSimpleBean(SimpleBean nestedSimpleBean) {
        this.nestedSimpleBean = nestedSimpleBean;
    }

    @Override
    public String toString() {
        final StringBuilder sb = new StringBuilder();
        sb.append("SimpleBean");
        sb.append("{someInt=").append(someInt);
        sb.append(", nestedSimpleBean=").append(nestedSimpleBean);
        sb.append('}');
        return sb.toString();
    }
}
```

The sample application's `main()` method creates an `XmlBeanFactory` using the configuration file in Listing 3-44 and gets beans `target1`, `target2`, and `target3`.

Listing 3-44. *Configuration File for Dependency Checking*

```
<?xml version="1.0" encoding="UTF-8"?>
<beans xmlns="http://www.springframework.org/schema/beans"
       xmlns:xsi="http://www.w3.org/2001/XMLSchema-instance"
       xsi:schemaLocation="
                http://www.springframework.org/schema/beans
                http://www.springframework.org/schema/beans/spring-beans.xsd">

    <bean id="target1" class="com.apress.prospring2.ch03.dependencycheck.SimpleBean"
            dependency-check="simple">
        <property name="someInt" value="1"/>
    </bean>
```

```
    <bean id="target2" class="com.apress.prospring2.ch03.dependencycheck.SimpleBean"
        dependency-check="objects">
        <property name="nestedSimpleBean" ref="nestedSimpleBean"/>
    </bean>

    <bean id="target3" class="com.apress.prospring2.ch03.dependencycheck.SimpleBean"
        dependency-check="all">
        <property name="nestedSimpleBean" ref="nestedSimpleBean"/>
        <property name="someInt" value="1"/>
    </bean>

    <bean id="nestedSimpleBean"
        class="com.apress.prospring2.ch03.dependencycheck.SimpleBean"/>

</beans>
```

As you can see from this configuration, each of the beans being retrieved from the `BeanFactory` has a different setting for the `dependency-check` attribute. The configuration currently ensures that all properties that need to be populated as per the `dependency-check` attribute have values, and as a result, the Java application runs without error. Try commenting out some of the `<property>` tags and see what happens: some IDEs will show the error (see Figure 3-4), and when you run the sample application, Spring throws an unsatisfied dependency exception (`org.springframework.beans.factory.UnsatisfiedDependencyException`), indicating which property should have a value that does not have one.

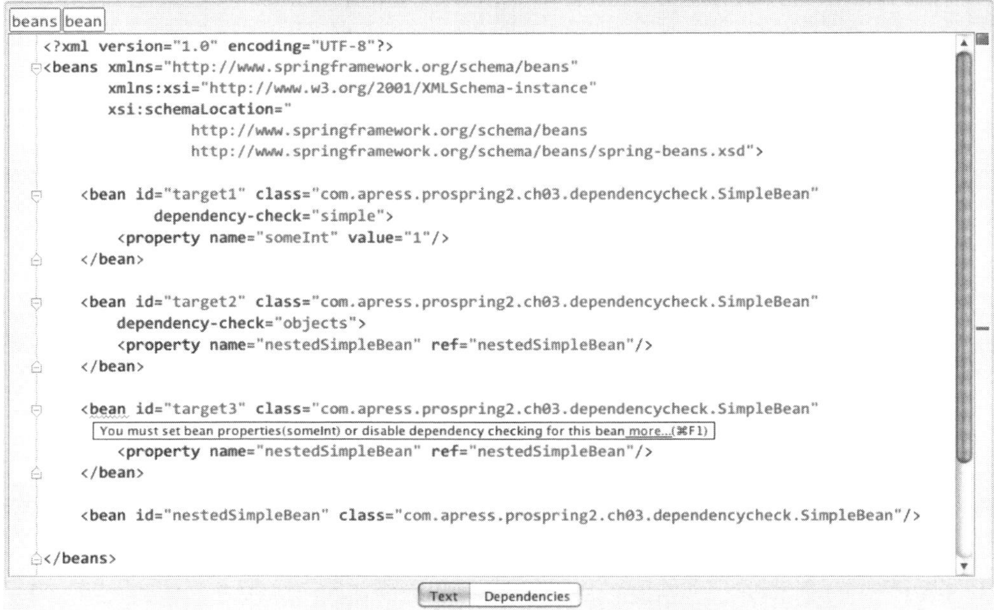

Figure 3-4. *Dependency check validation in IntelliJ IDEA*

Bean Inheritance

In some cases, you many need multiple definitions of beans that are the same type or implement a shared interface. This can become problematic if you want these beans to share some configuration settings but differ in others. The process of keeping the shared configuration settings in sync is quite error-prone, and on large projects, doing so can be time consuming. To get around this, Spring allows you to create a <bean> definition that inherits its property settings from another bean in the same BeanFactory. You can override the values of any properties on the child bean as required, which allows you to have full control, but the parent bean can provide each of your beans with a base configuration. Listing 3-45 shows a simple configuration with two beans with String name and int age properties.

Listing 3-45. *Bean Inheritance Configuration*

```
<?xml version="1.0" encoding="UTF-8"?>
<beans xmlns="http://www.springframework.org/schema/beans"
       xmlns:xsi="http://www.w3.org/2001/XMLSchema-instance"
       xsi:schemaLocation="
                http://www.springframework.org/schema/beans
                http://www.springframework.org/schema/beans/spring-beans.xsd">

    <bean id="parent" class="com.apress.prospring2.ch03.inheritance.SimpleBean"
        abstract="true">
        <property name="name" value="Jan Machacek"/>
    </bean>

    <bean id="bean1" class="com.apress.prospring2.ch03.inheritance.SimpleBean"
        parent="parent">
        <property name="age" value="28"/>
    </bean>

    <bean id="bean2" class="com.apress.prospring2.ch03.inheritance.SimpleBean"
        parent="parent"/>

</beans>
```

In this code, you can see that the parent bean is declared as abstract=true, which means that Spring can't instantiate it, but it can use it as the superbean of another bean. An example of that is in the <bean> tag for the bean1 bean. It has an extra attribute, parent, which indicates that Spring should consider the parent bean the parent of the bean. Because the bean1 bean has its own value for the age property, Spring passes this value to the bean. However, bean1 has no value for the name property, so Spring uses the value given to the parent bean. Similarly, bean2 does not include a value for the age property; therefore, it will remain at its default value ((int)0). Listing 3-46 shows the code for the SimpleBean class used in a previous configuration.

Listing 3-46. *SimpleBean Class*

```
public class SimpleBean {
    private String name;
    private int age;

    public void setName(String name) {
        this.name = name;
    }

    public void setAge(int age) {
        this.age = age;
    }
```

```
    @Override
    public String toString() {
        final StringBuilder sb = new StringBuilder();
        sb.append("SimpleBean");
        sb.append("{name='").append(name).append('\'');
        sb.append(", age=").append(age);
        sb.append('}');
        return sb.toString();
    }
}
```

As you can see, the `main()` method of the `SimpleBean` class grabs both the `bean1` and `bean2` beans from the `BeanFactory` and writes the contents of their properties to `stdout`. Here is the output from this example:

```
SimpleBean{name='Jan Machacek', age=28}
SimpleBean{name='Jan Machacek', age=0}

Process finished with exit code 0
```

As expected, the `bean1` bean inherited the value for its `name` property from the `parent` bean but was able to provide its own value for the `age` property. Bean `bean2` did not supply a value for `age`, which remains at its default value.

Considerations for Using Bean Inheritance

Child beans inherit both constructor arguments and property values from the parent beans, so you can use both styles of injection with bean inheritance. This level of flexibility makes bean inheritance a powerful tool for building applications with more than a handful of bean definitions. If you are declaring a lot of beans of the same value with shared property values, avoid the temptation to use copy and paste to share the values; instead, set up an inheritance hierarchy in your configuration.

When you are using inheritance, remember that bean inheritance does not have to match a Java inheritance hierarchy. It is perfectly acceptable to use bean inheritance on five beans of the same type. Think of bean inheritance as being more like a templating feature than an inheritance feature. Be aware, however, that if you are changing the type of the child bean, that type must be compatible with the type of the parent bean.

Summary

In this chapter, we covered a lot of ground with both the Spring core and IoC in general. We showed you examples of the different types of IoC and presented a discussion of the pros and cons of using each mechanism in your applications. We looked at which IoC mechanisms Spring provides and when, and when not, to use each within your applications. While exploring IoC, we introduced the Spring `BeanFactory`, which is the core component for Spring's IoC capabilities, and more specifically, we focused on the `XmlBeanFactory` that allows external configuration of Spring using XML.

This chapter also introduced you to the basics of Spring's IoC feature set including setter injection, constructor injection, automatic wiring, and bean inheritance. In the discussion of configuration, we demonstrated how you can configure your bean properties with a wide variety of different values, including other beans, using the `XmlBeanFactory`.

This chapter only scratches the surface of Spring and Spring's IoC container. In the next chapter, we look at some IoC-related features specific to Spring, and we take a more detailed look at other functionality available in the Spring core.

CHAPTER 4

Beyond the Basics

In the previous chapter, we took a detailed look at the concept of Inversion of Control (IoC) and how it fits into the Spring Framework. However, as we said at the end of the last chapter, we have only really scratched the surface of what the Spring core can do.

Spring provides a wide array of services that supplement and extend the basic IoC capabilities provided by the `BeanFactory` and associated implementations. A number of projects provide IoC containers, but none so far provides the same comprehensive feature set Spring provides. In this chapter, we are going to look in detail at some additional IoC–related features offered in Spring along with other functionality offered by the Spring core.

First, we'll look at managing the bean life cycle. So far, all the beans you have seen have been fairly simple and completely decoupled from the Spring container. In this section, we look at some strategies you can employ to enable your beans to receive notifications from the Spring container at various points throughout their life cycles. You can do this by either implementing specific interfaces laid out by Spring or specifying methods that Spring can call via reflection.

We'll also explain how to make your beans Spring aware. In some cases, you want a bean to be able to interact with the `BeanFactory` that configured it. For this reason, Spring offers two interfaces, `BeanNameAware` and `BeanFactoryAware`, that allow your bean to obtain its own name and a reference to its `BeanFactory`, respectively. This section of the chapter looks at implementing these interfaces and some practical considerations for using them in your application.

Next, we'll practice using method injection. As of release 1.1, Spring provides a new mechanism for managing dependencies when working with beans of different life cycles (singletons and non-singletons). In addition to this, Spring provides functionality to allow you to replace any method of any bean with a new implementation, without touching the original code.

We'll also cover the `FactoryBean` interface, which as its name implies, is intended to be implemented by any bean that acts as a factory for other beans. The `FactoryBean` interface provides a mechanism by which you can easily integrate your own factories with the Spring `BeanFactory`.

After that, we'll work with the JavaBeans `PropertyEditor` interface. This standard interface provided in the java.beans package is used to convert property values to and from `String` representations. Spring uses `PropertyEditor` interfaces extensively, mainly to read values specified in the `BeanFactory` configuration and convert them into the correct types. In this section of the chapter, we discuss the set of `PropertyEditor` interfaces supplied with Spring and how you can use them within your application. We also take a look at implementing a custom `PropertyEditor`.

Spring 2.5 allows you to create a new annotation-based configuration of the beans, which we'll also cover in this chapter. This is in addition to configuration using the XML (using both old-school DTD or new schema-based) or—for very simple situations—using the properties files.

Finally, you'll learn about the Spring `ApplicationContext` interface, an extension of the `BeanFactory` intended for use in full applications. The `ApplicationContext` interface provides a useful set of additional functionality, including internationalized message provision, resource loading, and event publishing. `ApplicationContext` also enables a much simpler configuration, and in many cases, such as when you are building web applications, you can create and configure an `ApplicationContext` automatically. In this chapter, we take a detailed look at the `ApplicationContext` interface and the features it offers. We also jump ahead of ourselves a little and look at how the `ApplicationContext` simplifies the use of Spring when building web applications.

Spring's Impact on Application Portability

All of the features discussed in this chapter are specific to Spring, and in many cases, are not available in other IoC containers. Although many IoC containers offer life cycle management functionality, they probably do so through a different set of interfaces than Spring. If the portability of your application between different IoC containers is truly important, you might want to avoid using some of the features that couple your application to Spring.

Remember, however, that by setting a constraint—so that your application is portable between IoC containers—you are losing out on the wealth of functionality Spring offers. Because you are likely to be making a strategic choice to use Spring, it makes sense to use it to the best of its ability.

Be careful not to create a requirement for portability out of thin air. In many cases, the end users of your application do not care if the application can run on three different IoC containers, they just want it to run. In our experience, trying to build an application on the lowest common denominator of features available in your chosen technology is often a mistake. Doing so often puts your application at a disadvantage right from the get-go. In *Expert One-on-One: J2EE Development without EJB* (Wrox, 2004), Rod Johnson and Jürgen Höller describe these types of requirements as phantom requirements and provide a much more detailed discussion of phantom requirements and how they can affect your project. However, if your application *requires* IoC container portability, do not see this as a drawback—it is a true requirement, and therefore, one your application should fulfill.

Because Spring advocates lightweight components, you will rarely need to tie your code closely to the Spring Framework. We recommend that you write your beans in a truly container-agnostic way and implement `FactoryBean` or `BeanPostProcessor`, which will perform any custom processing necessary to make the bean easily usable in Spring. Consider a situation where you require a certain dependency to be set on a bean. Your bean can implement the `InitializingBean` interface and check that the dependency is set in the `afterPropertiesSet()` method, but that ties your bean to the Spring Framework. In this situation, you should consider using constructor DI and check that the argument representing the dependency passed to the constructor is not `null`. This will make your bean truly container-independent *and* give you full control over its dependencies.

Bean Life Cycle Management

An important part of any IoC container, Spring included, is that beans can be constructed in such a way that they receive notifications at certain points in their life cycles. This enables your beans to perform relevant processing at certain points throughout their lives. The number of possible notifications is huge, but in general, two life cycle events are particularly relevant to a bean: postinitialization and predestruction.

In the context of Spring, the postinitialization event is raised as soon as Spring finishes setting all the property values on the bean and finishes any dependency checks that you configured it to perform. The predestruction event is fired just before Spring destroys the bean instance. Both of these life cycle events are only fired for beans that are singletons. Spring doesn't manage the life cycles of beans that are configured as nonsingletons.

Spring provides two mechanisms a bean can use to hook into each of these events and perform some additional interface-based or method-based processing. Using the interface-based mechanism, your bean implements an interface specific to the type of notification it wishes to receive, and Spring notifies the bean via a callback method defined in the interface. For the method-based mechanism,

Spring allows you to specify, in your `BeanFactory` configuration, the name of a method to call when the bean is initialized and the name of a method to call when the bean is destroyed.

In the case of both events, the mechanisms achieve exactly the same goal. The interface mechanism is used extensively throughout Spring so that you don't have to remember to specify the initialization or destruction each time you use one of Spring's components. However, in your own beans, you may be better served using the method-based mechanism, because your beans do not need to implement any Spring-specific interfaces. Although we stated that portability often isn't as important a requirement as many texts lead you to believe, this does not mean you should sacrifice portability when a perfectly good alternative exists. That said, if you are coupling your application to Spring in other ways, using the interface method allows you to specify the callback once and then forget about it. If you are defining a lot of beans of the same type that need to take advantage of the life cycle notifications, using the interface mechanism is the perfect way to avoid needing to repeat yourself—an extra coding burden that can lead to hard-to-diagnose errors and an application that is problematic to maintain.

Overall, the choice of which mechanism you use for receiving life cycle notifications depends on your application requirements. If you are concerned about portability or you are just defining one or two beans of a particular type that need the callbacks, use the method-based mechanism. If you are not too concerned about portability or you are defining many beans of the same type that need the life cycle notifications, using the interface-based mechanism is the best way to ensure that your beans always receive the notifications they are expecting. If you plan to use a bean across many different Spring projects, then you almost certainly want the functionality of that bean to be as self-contained as possible, so you should definitely use the interface-based mechanism.

Hooking into Bean Creation

By being aware of when it is initialized, a bean can check to see whether all its required dependencies are satisfied. Although Spring can check dependencies for you, its approach is pretty much an all-or-nothing, and it doesn't offer any opportunities for applying additional logic to the dependency resolution procedure. Consider a bean that has four dependencies declared as setters, two of which are required and one of which has a suitable default in the event that no dependency is provided. Using an initialization callback, your bean can check for the dependencies it requires, throwing an exception or providing a default as needed.

If you are using setter injection, a bean cannot perform these checks in its no-argument constructor, because at this point, Spring has not had an opportunity to provide values for the dependencies it can satisfy. The initialization callback in Spring is called *after* Spring finishes providing the dependencies that it can and performs any dependency checks that you ask it to.

You are not limited to using the initialization callback just to check dependencies; you can do anything you want in the callback, but it is most useful for the purpose we have described. In many cases, the initialization callback is also the place to trigger any actions that your bean must take automatically in response to its configuration. For instance, if you build a bean to run scheduled tasks, the initialization callback provides the ideal place to start the scheduler—after all, the configuration data is set on the bean.

■ **Note** You will not have to write a bean to run scheduled tasks, because this is something Spring can do automatically through its integration with the Quartz scheduling engine. We cover this in more detail in Chapter 12.

Specifying an Initialization Method

As we mentioned previously, one way to receive the initialization callback is to designate a method on your bean as an initialization method and tell Spring to use this method as an initialization method. As discussed previously, this callback mechanism is useful when you have only a few beans of the same type or when you want to keep your application decoupled from Spring. Another reason for using this mechanism is to enable your Spring application to work with beans that were built previously or were provided by third-party vendors.

Specifying a callback method is simply a case of specifying the name in the `init-method` attribute of a bean's `<bean>` tag. Listing 4-1 shows a basic bean with two dependencies.

Listing 4-1. *The SimpleBean Class*

```
public class SimpleBean {
    private static final String DEFAULT_NAME = "Jan Machacek";
    private String name;
    private int age = 0;

    public void init() {
        System.out.println("initializing bean");
        if (this.name == null) {
            System.out.println("No name specified, using default.");
            this.name = DEFAULT_NAME;
        }
        if (this.age == 0) {
            throw new IllegalArgumentException("You must set the [age] property " +➥
                "bean of type [" + getClass().getName() + "]");
        }
    }

    public String getName() {
        return name;
    }

    public void setName(String name) {
        this.name = name;
    }

    public int getAge() {
        return age;
    }

    public void setAge(int age) {
        this.age = age;
    }

    @Override
    public String toString() {
        final StringBuilder sb = new StringBuilder();
        sb.append("SimpleBean");
        sb.append("{name='").append(name).append('\'');
        sb.append(", age=").append(age);
        sb.append('}');
        return sb.toString();
    }
}
```

Notice that we have defined a method, `init()`, to act as the initialization callback. The `init()` method checks to see if the `name` property has been set, and if it has not, it uses the default value stored in the `DEFAULT_VALUE` constant. The `init()` method also checks to see if the `age` property is set and throws an `IllegalArgumentException` if it is not.

The main() method of the SimpleBeanDemo class attempts to obtain three beans from the BeanFactory, all of type SimpleBean, using its own getBean() method. Notice that in the getBean() method, if the bean is obtained successfully, its details are written to stdout. If an exception is thrown in the init() method, as will occur in this case if the age property is not set, Spring wraps that exception in a BeanCreationException. The getBean() method catches these exceptions and writes a message to stdout informing us of the error.

Listing 4-2 shows a BeanFactory configuration that defines the beans used in Listing 4-1.

Listing 4-2. *Configuring the Simple Beans*

```
<?xml version="1.0" encoding="UTF-8"?>
<beans xmlns="http://www.springframework.org/schema/beans"
       xmlns:xsi="http://www.w3.org/2001/XMLSchema-instance"
       xsi:schemaLocation="
                http://www.springframework.org/schema/beans
                http://www.springframework.org/schema/beans/spring-beans.xsd">

    <bean id="simple1" class="com.apress.prospring2.ch04.lifecycle.SimpleBean"
            init-method="init">
        <property name="age" value="29"/>
        <property name="name" value="Dr. Jekyll"/>
    </bean>
    <bean id="simple2" class="com.apress.prospring2.ch04.lifecycle.SimpleBean"
            init-method="init">
        <property name="age" value="29"/>
    </bean>
    <bean id="simple3" class="com.apress.prospring2.ch04.lifecycle.SimpleBean"
            init-method="init">
        <property name="name" value="Mr. Hyde"/>
    </bean>

</beans>
```

As you can see, the <bean> tag for each of the three beans has an init-method attribute that tells Spring that it should invoke the init() method as soon as it finishes configuring the bean. The simple1 bean has values for both the name and age properties, so it passes through the init() method with absolutely no changes. The simple2 bean has no value for the name property, meaning that in the init() method, the name property is given the default value. Finally, the simple3 bean has no value for the age property. The logic defined in the init() method treats this as an error, so an IllegalArgumentException is thrown. Running this example yields the following output:

```
initializing bean
SimpleBean{name='Dr. Jekyll', age=29}
initializing bean
No name specified, using default.
SimpleBean{name='Jan Machacek', age=29}
initializing bean
Exception in thread "main" org.springframework.beans.factory.BeanCreationException: ➥
Error creating bean with name 'simple3' defined in class path resource ➥
[META-INF/spring/lifecycledemo-context.xml]: Invocation of init method failed; ➥
nested exception is ➥
java.lang.IllegalArgumentException: You must set the [age] property bean of type ➥
[com.apress.prospring2.ch04.lifecycle.SimpleBean]
...
```

From this output, you can see that simple1 was configured correctly with the values that we specified in the configuration file. For simple2, the default value for the name property was used, because no value was specified in the configuration. Finally, for simple3, no bean instance was created because the init() method raised an error, because we did not set the age property.

As you can see, using the initialization method is an ideal way to ensure that your beans are configured correctly. By using this mechanism, you can take full advantage of the benefits of IoC without losing any of the control you get from manually defining dependencies. The only constraint on your initialization method is that it cannot accept any arguments. You can define any return type, although that type is ignored by Spring. You can even use a static method as long as it accepts no arguments.

The benefits of this mechanism are negated when using a static initialization method, because you cannot access any of the bean's state to validate it. If your bean is using static state as a mechanism for saving memory and you are using a static initialization method to validate this state, you should consider moving the static state to instance state and using a nonstatic initialization method. If you use Spring's singleton management capabilities, the end effect is the same, but you have a bean that is much simpler to test and the additional ability to create multiple instances of the bean with their own state when necessary. Of course, there are instances in which you need to use static state shared across multiple instances of a bean, in which case, you can always use a static initialization method.

Implementing the InitializingBean Interface

The InitializingBean interface defined in Spring allows you to define, inside your bean code, that you want the bean to receive notification that Spring has finished configuring it. Just like when you are using an initialization method, this gives you the opportunity to check the bean configuration to ensure that it is valid, providing any default values along the way.

The InitializingBean interface defines a single method, afterPropertiesSet(), that serves the same purpose as the init() method in Listing 4-1. Listing 4-3 shows a reimplementation of the previous example using the InitializingBean interface in place of the initialization method.

Listing 4-3. *Using the InitializingBean Interface*

```
public class SimpleBeanIB implements InitializingBean {
    private static final String DEFAULT_NAME = "Jan Machacek";
    private String name;
    private int age = 0;

    public String getName() {
        return name;
    }

    public void setName(String name) {
        this.name = name;
    }

    public int getAge() {
        return age;
    }

    public void setAge(int age) {
        this.age = age;
    }

    @Override
```

```
    public String toString() {
        final StringBuilder sb = new StringBuilder();
        sb.append("SimpleBean");
        sb.append("{name='").append(name).append('\'');
        sb.append(", age=").append(age);
        sb.append('}');
        return sb.toString();
    }

    public void afterPropertiesSet() throws Exception {
        System.out.println("initializing bean");
        if (this.name == null) {
            System.out.println("No name specified, using default.");
            this.name = DEFAULT_NAME;
        }
        if (this.age == 0) {
            throw new IllegalArgumentException("You must set the [age] property " +
                "bean of type [" + getClass().getName() + "]");
        }
    }
}
```

As you can see, not much in this example has changed. Aside from the obvious class name change, the only difference is that this class implements `InitializingBean` and the initialization logic has moved into the `InitializingBean.afterPropertiesSet()` method.

In Listing 4-4, you can see the configuration for this example.

Listing 4-4. *Configuration Using InitializingBean*

```
<?xml version="1.0" encoding="UTF-8"?>
<beans xmlns="http://www.springframework.org/schema/beans"
       xmlns:xsi="http://www.w3.org/2001/XMLSchema-instance"
       xsi:schemaLocation="
                http://www.springframework.org/schema/beans
                http://www.springframework.org/schema/beans/spring-beans.xsd">

    <bean id="simple1" class="com.apress.prospring2.ch04.lifecycle.SimpleBeanIB">
        <property name="age" value="29"/>
        <property name="name" value="Dr. Jekyll"/>
    </bean>
    <bean id="simple2" class="com.apress.prospring2.ch04.lifecycle.SimpleBeanIB">
        <property name="age" value="29"/>
    </bean>
    <bean id="simple3" class="com.apress.prospring2.ch04.lifecycle.SimpleBeanIB">
        <property name="name" value="Mr. Hyde"/>
    </bean>

</beans>
```

Again, there's not much difference between the configuration code in Listing 4-4 and the configuration code from Listing 4-2. The noticeable difference is the omission of the `init-method` attribute. Because the `SimpleBeanIB` class implements the `InitializingBean` interface, Spring knows which method to call as the initialization callback, thus removing the need for any additional configuration. The output from this example is shown here:

```
initializing bean
SimpleBean{name='Dr. Jekyll', age=29}
initializing bean
No name specified, using default.
SimpleBean{name='Jan Machacek', age=29}
initializing bean
Exception in thread "main" org.springframework.beans.factory.BeanCreationException: ➥
Error creating bean with name 'simple3' defined in class path resource ➥
[META-INF/spring/lifecycledemo2-context.xml]: Invocation of init method failed; ➥
nested exception is java.lang.IllegalArgumentException: ➥
You must set the [age] property bean of type ➥
[com.apress.prospring2.ch04.lifecycle.SimpleBeanIB]
```

There is no difference in the output of the two examples; both work in exactly the same way. As we discussed earlier, both approaches have their benefits and drawbacks. Using an initialization method, you have the benefit of keeping your application decoupled from Spring, but you have to remember to configure the initialization method for every bean that needs it. Using `InitializingBean`, you have the benefit of being able to specify the initialization callback once for all instances of your bean class, but you have to couple your application to do so. In the end, you should let the requirements of your application drive the decision about which approach to use. If portability is an issue, use the initialization method; otherwise, use the `InitializingBean` interface to reduce the amount of configuration your application needs and the chance of errors creeping into your application due to misconfiguration.

Order of Resolution

You can use both an initialization method and the `InitializingBean` on the same bean instance. In this case, Spring invokes `InitializingBean.afterPropertiesSet()` first, followed by your initialization method. This two-stage initialization can be useful if you have an existing bean that performs some initialization in a specific method, but you need to add some more initialization code when you use Spring. However, a better approach is to call your bean's initialization method from `afterPropertiesSet()`. This way, if Spring changes the initialization order in a future release, your code continues to work as it should.

The afterPropertiesSet Method and Class Hierarchies

A useful pattern to consider when creating beans that implement the `InitializingBean` interface and are expected to have subclasses is the template method pattern. Using this pattern, you can ensure that the subclasses will be able to add their own initialization—in a strictly controlled way. Consider the code in Listing 4-5.

Listing 4-5. *The Initialization Template Method*

```
public abstract class SimpleBeanSupport implements InitializingBean {
    private String value;

    /**
     * Subclasses may override this method to perform additional initialization.
     * This method gets invoked after the initialization of the
     * {@link SimpleBeanSupport} completes.
     * @throws Exception If the subclass initialization fails.
     */
    protected void initSimple() throws Exception {
```

```
        // do nothing
    }

    public final void afterPropertiesSet() throws Exception {
        Assert.notNull(this.value, "The [value] property of [" +
            getClass().getName() + "] must be set.");
        initSimple();
    }

    public final void setValue(String value) {
        this.value = value;
    }

    protected final String getValue() {
        return this.value;
    }
}

public class SoutSimpleBean extends SimpleBeanSupport {
    private String person;

    protected void initSimple() throws Exception {
        Assert.notNull(this.person, "The [person] property of [" +
           getClass().getName() + "] must be set.");
    }

    public void setPerson(String person) {
        this.person = person;
    }

    @Override
    public String toString() {
        return String.format("%s says \"%s\"", this.person, getValue());
    }
}
```

Let's take a detailed look at the code we've just written: the abstract class `SimpleBeanSupport` implements the `InitializingBean` interface, but the implementation of the `afterPropertiesSet` method is marked as `final`. That means that the initialization code cannot be changed in any way. This ensures that the subclasses cannot change the basic initialization code. However, we would still like the subclasses to be able to specify *additional* initialization, if they need it. We have, therefore, created the `initSimple()` method that the subclasses can override, but this method is guaranteed to be executed after the code in the superclass. You can see the application of the initialization template method pattern in the `SystemoutSimpleBean`. It provides additional code to initialize itself by overriding the `initSimple()` method.

Given the application context file shown in Listing 4-6, the application simply prints this:

```
Winston Churchill says "This report, by its very length, defends itself against ➥
the risk of being read."
```

Listing 4-6. *ApplicationContext Configuration File for the Initialization Template Method*

```
<?xml version="1.0" encoding="UTF-8"?>
<beans xmlns="http://www.springframework.org/schema/beans"
       xmlns:xsi="http://www.w3.org/2001/XMLSchema-instance"
       xsi:schemaLocation="
```

```
            http://www.springframework.org/schema/beans
            http://www.springframework.org/schema/beans/spring-beans.xsd">

    <bean id="simple1" class="com.apress.prospring2.ch04.lifecycle.SoutSimpleBean">
        <property name="person" value="Winston Churchill"/>
        <property name="value"
            value="This report, by its very length, defends itself against the risk➥
               of being read."/>
    </bean>

</beans>
```

Hooking into Bean Destruction

When using a BeanFactory implementation that implements the ConfigurableListableBeanFactory interface (such as XmlBeanFactory), you can signal the BeanFactory that you want to destroy all singleton instances with a call to destroySingletons(). Typically, you provide this signal when your application shuts down, and doing so allows you to clean up any resources that your beans might be holding open, thus allowing your application to shut down gracefully. This callback also provides the perfect place to flush any data you are storing in memory to persistent storage and to allow your beans to end any long-running processes they may have started.

To allow your beans to receive notification that destroySingletons() has been called, you have two options, both similar to the mechanisms available for receiving an initialization callback. The destruction callback is often used in conjunction with the initialization callback. In many cases, you create and configure a resource in the initialization callback and release the resource in the destruction callback.

Executing a Method When a Bean Is Destroyed

To designate a method to be called when a bean is destroyed, you simply specify the name of the method in the destroy-method attribute of the bean's <bean> tag. Spring calls it just before it destroys the singleton instance of the bean. Listing 4-7 shows a simple class that implements InitializingBean, and in the afterPropertiesSet() method, it creates an instance of FileInputStream and stores this in a private field.

Listing 4-7. *Using a destroy-method Callback*

```
public class DestructiveBean implements InitializingBean {
public class DestructiveBean {
    private InputStream is = null;
    private String filePath = null;

    public void afterPropertiesSet() throws Exception {
        System.out.println("Initializing Bean");

        Assert.notNull(this.filePath, "The [filePath] property of [" +
          getClass().getName() + "] must be set.");

        new File(this.filePath).createNewFile();
        this.is = new FileInputStream(this.filePath);
    }

    public void destroy() {
        System.out.println("Destroying Bean");
```

```
        if (this.is != null) {
            try {
                this.is.close();
                this.is = null;
                new File(this.filePath).delete();
            } catch (IOException ex) {
                System.err.println("WARN: An IOException occured"
                        + " while trying to close the InputStream");
            }
        }
    }

    public void setFilePath(String filePath) {
        this.filePath = filePath;
    }
}
```

This code also defines a `destroy()` method, in which the `FileInputStream` is closed and set to `null`, releasing the resource without relying on the garbage collection. The `main()` method in Listing 4-8 retrieves a bean of type `DestructiveBean` from the `XmlBeanFactory` and invokes `ConfigurableListableBeanFactory.destroySingletons()`, instructing Spring to destroy all the singletons it is managing. Both the initialization and destruction callbacks write a message to `stdout` informing us that they have been called.

Listing 4-8. *Sample Application for the destroySingletons() Call*

```
public class DestructiveBeanDemo {

    public static void main(String[] args) {
        System.out.println(factory.getBean("destructive"));
        factory.destroySingletons();
        System.out.println("Almost done!");
        new BufferedInputStream(System.in).read();
    }

}
```

Listing 4-9 completes the example with the `BeanFactory` configuration file for the `destructiveBean` bean.

Listing 4-9. *Configuring a destroy-method Callback*

```
<?xml version="1.0" encoding="UTF-8"?>
<beans xmlns="http://www.springframework.org/schema/beans"
       xmlns:xsi="http://www.w3.org/2001/XMLSchema-instance"
       xsi:schemaLocation="
                http://www.springframework.org/schema/beans
                http://www.springframework.org/schema/beans/spring-beans.xsd">

    <bean id="destructive"
        class="com.apress.prospring2.ch04.lifecycle.DestructiveBean"
            destroy-method="destroy">
        <property name="filePath" value="/tmp/prospring25"/>
    </bean>

</beans>
```

Notice that we have specified the destroy() method as the destruction callback using the destroy-method attribute. Running this example yields the following output:

```
$ ls -l /tmp/
total 0
[Run the application from the IDE]
Mar 17, 2008 3:40:24 PM org.springframework.beans.factory.xml.➥
XmlBeanDefinitionReader loadBeanDefinitions
INFO: Loading XML bean definitions from class path resource ➥
[META-INF/spring/lifecycledemo4-context.xml]
Initializing Bean
DestructiveBean{is=java.io.FileInputStream@61cd2, filePath='/tmp/prospring25'}
$ ls -l /tmp/
total 0
-rw-r--r--  1 janm  wheel      0 17 Mar 15:40 prospring25

<Enter>
Destroying Bean
Almost done!
Mar 17, 2008 3:41:23 PM org.springframework.beans.factory.support.➥
DefaultSingletonBeanRegistry destroySingletons
INFO: Destroying singletons in org.springframework.beans.factory.xml.➥
XmlBeanFactory@edbe39: defining beans [destructive]; root of factory hierarchy

$ ls -l /tmp
total 0

<Enter>
Process finished with exit code 0
```

Spring first invokes the initialization callback, and the DestructiveBean instance creates the FileInputStream instance and stores it. Next, during the call to destroySingletons(), Spring iterates over the set of singletons it is managing, in this case just one, and invokes any destruction callbacks that are specified. This is where the DestructiveBean instance closes the FileInputStream.

Implementing the DisposableBean Interface

As with initialization callbacks, Spring provides an interface, in this case DisposableBean, that you can implement in your beans as an alternative mechanism for receiving destruction callbacks. The DisposableBean interface defines a single method, destroy(), that is called just before the bean is destroyed. Using this mechanism is orthogonal to using the InitializingBean interface to receive initialization callbacks. Listing 4-10 shows a modified implementation of the DestructiveBean class that implements the DisposableBean interface.

Listing 4-10. *Implementing DisposableBean*

```
public class DestructiveBeanI implements InitializingBean, DisposableBean {
    private InputStream is = null;
    private String filePath = null;

    public void afterPropertiesSet() throws Exception {
        System.out.println("Initializing Bean");

        Assert.notNull(this.filePath, "The [filePath] property of [" +
           getClass().getName() + "] must be set.");
```

```
        new File(this.filePath).createNewFile();
        this.is = new FileInputStream(this.filePath);
    }

    public void destroy() {
        System.out.println("Destroying Bean");

        if (this.is != null) {
            try {
                this.is.close();
                this.is = null;
                new File(this.filePath).delete();
            } catch (IOException ex) {
                System.err.println("WARN: An IOException occured"
                        + " while trying to close the InputStream");
            }
        }
    }

    public void setFilePath(String filePath) {
        this.filePath = filePath;
    }

    @Override
    public String toString() {
        final StringBuilder sb = new StringBuilder();
        sb.append("DestructiveBean");
        sb.append("{is=").append(is);
        sb.append(", filePath='").append(filePath).append('\'');
        sb.append('}');
        return sb.toString();
    }
}
```

Again, there is not much difference between the code that uses the callback method mechanism and the code that uses the callback interface mechanism. In Listing 4-10, we even used the same method names. Listing 4-11 shows an amended configuration for this example.

Listing 4-11. *Configuration Using the DisposableBean Interface*

```
<?xml version="1.0" encoding="UTF-8"?>
<beans xmlns="http://www.springframework.org/schema/beans"
       xmlns:xsi="http://www.w3.org/2001/XMLSchema-instance"
       xsi:schemaLocation="
                http://www.springframework.org/schema/beans
                http://www.springframework.org/schema/beans/spring-beans.xsd">

    <bean id="destructive"
        class="com.apress.prospring2.ch04.lifecycle.DestructiveBean">
        <property name="filePath" value="/tmp/prospring25"/>
    </bean>

</beans>
```

As you can see, aside from the different class name, the only difference is the omission of the `destroy-method` attribute. Using the configuration file to run the code in Listing 4-8 yields the following output:

```
Mar 17, 2008 3:51:54 PM org.springframework.beans.factory.xml.➥
XmlBeanDefinitionReader loadBeanDefinitions
INFO: Loading XML bean definitions from class path resource ➥
[META-INF/spring/lifecycledemo5-context.xml]
Initializing Bean
DestructiveBean{is=java.io.FileInputStream@639bf1, filePath='/tmp/prospring25'}
<Enter>

Mar 17, 2008 3:51:56 PM org.springframework.beans.factory.support.➥
DefaultSingletonBeanRegistry destroySingletons
Destroying Bean
Almost done!
INFO: Destroying singletons in org.springframework.beans.factory.xml.➥
XmlBeanFactory@14627a: defining beans [destructive]; root of factory hierarchy
<Enter>

Process finished with exit code 0
```

Again, the output from the two different mechanisms is exactly the same. The destruction callback is an ideal mechanism for ensuring that your applications shut down gracefully and do not leave resources open or in an inconsistent state. However, you still have to decide whether to use the destruction method callback or the `DisposableBean` interface. Again, let the requirements of your application drive your decision in this respect; use the method callback where portability is an issue; otherwise, use the `DisposableBean` interface to reduce the amount of configuration required.

Using a Shutdown Hook

The only drawback of the destruction callbacks in Spring is that they are not fired automatically; you need to remember to call `destroySingletons()` before your application is closed. When your application runs as a servlet, you can simply call `destroySingletons()` in the servlet's `destroy()` method. However, in a stand-alone application, things are not quite so simple, especially if your application has multiple exit points. Fortunately, Java allows you to create a shutdown hook, a thread that is executed just before the application shuts down. This is the perfect way to invoke the `destroySingletons()` method of your `BeanFactory`. The easiest way to take advantage of this mechanism is to create a class that implements the `Runnable` interface and have the `run()` method call `destroySingletons()`. This is shown in Listing 4-12.

Listing 4-12. *Implementing a Shutdown Hook*

```
public class ShutdownHook implements Runnable {
    private ConfigurableListableBeanFactory beanFactory;

    public ShutdownHook(ConfigurableListableBeanFactory beanFactory) {
        Assert.notNull(beanFactory, "The 'beanFactory' argument must not be null.");
        this.beanFactory = beanFactory;
    }

    public void run() {
        this.beanFactory.destroySingletons();
    }
}
```

Using this class, you can create an instance of `Thread` and register this `Thread` as a shutdown hook using `Runtime.addShutdownHook()`, as shown in Listing 4-13.

Listing 4-13. *Registering a Shutdown Hook*

```
public class ShutdownHookDemo {

    public static void main(String[] args) throws IOException {
        XmlBeanFactory factory = new XmlBeanFactory(
            new ClassPathResource("/META-INF/spring/lifecycledemo5-context.xml"));
        Runtime.getRuntime().addShutdownHook(new Thread(new ShutdownHook(factory)));
        new BufferedInputStream(System.in).read();
    }

}
```

Notice that we obtain a reference to the current `Runtime` using `Runtime.getRuntime()` and call `addShutdownHook()` on this reference. Running this example results in the following output:

```
INFO [main] XmlBeanDefinitionReader.loadBeanDefinitions(308) | ➥
Loading XML bean definitions from class path resource ➥
[META-INF/spring/lifecycledemo5-context.xml]
<Enter>

INFO [Thread-0] DefaultSingletonBeanRegistry.destroySingletons(340) | ➥
Destroying singletons in org.springframework.beans.factory.xml.➥
XmlBeanFactory@79a49f: defining beans [destructive]; root of factory hierarchy
```

As you can see, the `destroySingletons()` method is invoked, even though we didn't write any code to explicitly invoke it as the application was shutting down.

Making Your Beans Spring Aware

One of the biggest selling points of DI over dependency lookup as a mechanism for achieving IoC is that your beans do not need to be aware of the implementation of the container that is managing them. To a bean that uses constructor injection, the Spring container is the same as the container provided by PicoContainer. However, in certain circumstances, you may need a bean that is using DI to obtain its dependencies so it can interact with the container for some other reason. An example of this may be a bean that needs access to the `BeanFactory` to automatically configure a shutdown hook for you. In other cases, a bean may wish to know its name so it can perform some additional processing based on this name.

■ **Caution** Giving the bean name some kind of business meaning is generally a bad idea and can lead to configuration problems where bean names have to be artificially manipulated to support their business meaning.

However, we have found that being able to have a bean find out its name at runtime is really useful for logging. Consider a situation where you have many beans of the same type running under different configurations. The bean name can be included in log messages to help you differentiate between the one generating errors and the ones that are working fine when something goes wrong.

Using the BeanNameAware Interface

The `BeanNameAware` interface, which can be implemented by a bean that wants to obtain its own name, has a single method: `setBeanName(String)`. Spring calls the `setBeanName()` method after it has finished configuring your bean but before any life cycle callbacks (to initialize or destroy) are called. In most cases, the implementation of the setBeanName() interface is just a single line that stores the value passed in by the container in a field for use later on. Listing 4-14 shows a simple bean that obtains its name using BeanNameAware and later uses this bean name when writing log messages.

Listing 4-14. *Implementing BeanNameAware*

```
public class LoggingBean implements BeanNameAware {
    private static final Log logger = LogFactory.getLog(LoggingBean.class);
    private String name;

    public void setBeanName(String name) {
        this.name = name;
    }

    public void run() {
        if (logger.isInfoEnabled()) {
            logger.info("Bean name " + this.name);
        }
    }
}
```

This implementation is fairly trivial. Remember that BeanNameAware.setBeanName() is called before the first instance of the bean is returned to your application via a call to BeanFactory.getBean(), so there is no need to check to see if the bean name is available in the someOperation() method. Listing 4-15 shows a simple configuration for this example.

Listing 4-15. *Configuring the LoggingBean Example*

```
<?xml version="1.0" encoding="UTF-8"?>
<beans xmlns="http://www.springframework.org/schema/beans"
       xmlns:xsi="http://www.w3.org/2001/XMLSchema-instance"
       xsi:schemaLocation="
                http://www.springframework.org/schema/beans
                http://www.springframework.org/schema/beans/spring-beans.xsd">

    <bean id="logging" class="com.apress.prospring2.ch04.interaction.LoggingBean"/>

</beans>
```

No special configuration is required to take advantage of the BeanNameAware interface. In Listing 4-16, you can see a simple example application that retrieves the LoggingBean instance from the BeanFactory and calls the run() method.

Listing 4-16. *The LoggingBeanDemo Class*

```
public class LoggingBeanDemo {
    public static void main(String[] args) {
        XmlBeanFactory factory = new XmlBeanFactory(
            new ClassPathResource("/META-INF/spring/interactiondemo-context.xml")
        );
        LoggingBean lb = (LoggingBean)factory.getBean("logging");
        lb.run();
    }
}
```

This example generates the following log output—notice the inclusion of the bean name in the log message for the call to run():

```
INFO [main] LoggingBean.run(20) | Bean name is'logging'.
```

Using the BeanNameAware interface is really quite simple and handy when you are improving the quality of your log messages. Avoid being tempted to give your bean names business meaning just because you can access them; by doing so, you are coupling your classes to Spring as well as a particular configuration for a feature that brings negligible benefit. If your beans need some kind of name internally, have them implement an interface such as Nameable with a method setName() and give each bean a name using DI. This way, you can keep the names you use for configuration concise, and you won't need to manipulate your configuration unnecessarily to give your beans names with business meaning.

Using the BeanFactoryAware Interface

Using the BeanFactoryAware method, it is possible for your beans to get a reference to the BeanFactory that configured them. The main reason this interface was created was to allow a bean to access other beans programmatically, using getBean(). You should, however, avoid this practice and use DI to provide your beans with their collaborators. If you use the lookup-based getBean() approach to obtain dependencies when you can use DI, you are adding unnecessary complexity to your beans and coupling them to the Spring Framework without good reason.

Of course, the BeanFactory isn't just used to look up beans; it performs a great many other tasks. As you saw previously, one of these tasks is to destroy all singletons, notifying each of them in turn before doing so. In the previous section, you saw how to create a shutdown hook to ensure that the BeanFactory is instructed to destroy all singletons before the application shuts down. By using the BeanFactoryAware interface, you can build a bean that can be configured in a BeanFactory to create and configure a shutdown hook bean automatically. Listing 4-17 shows the code for this bean.

Listing 4-17. *The ShutdownHookBean Class*

```
public class ShutdownHookBean implements BeanFactoryAware, Runnable {
    private static final Log logger = LogFactory.getLog(ShutdownHookBean.class);
    private ConfigurableListableBeanFactory beanFactory;

    public void setBeanFactory(BeanFactory beanFactory) throws BeansException {
        if (beanFactory instanceof DefaultListableBeanFactory) {
            this.beanFactory = (ConfigurableListableBeanFactory)beanFactory;
            Runtime.getRuntime().addShutdownHook(new Thread(this));
        }
    }

    public void run() {
        if (this.beanFactory != null) {
            logger.info("Destroying singletons.");
            this.beanFactory.destroySingletons();
        }
    }
}
```

Most of this code should seem familiar to you by now. The BeanFactoryAware interface defines a single method, setBeanFactory(BeanFactory), which Spring calls to pass your bean a reference to its BeanFactory. In Listing 4-17, the ShutdownHookBean class checks to see if the BeanFactory is of type ConfigurableListableBeanFactory, meaning it has a destroySingletons() method; if it does, it saves the reference to a field. You can also see that if the BeanFactory is a ConfigurableListableBeanFactory, the bean registers itself as a shutdown hook with the current Runtime instance. Listing 4-18 shows how to configure this bean to work with the DestructiveBeanWithInterface bean used in the previous section.

Listing 4-18. *Configuring the ShutdownHookBean Class*

```
<?xml version="1.0" encoding="UTF-8"?>
<beans xmlns="http://www.springframework.org/schema/beans"
       xmlns:xsi="http://www.w3.org/2001/XMLSchema-instance"
       xsi:schemaLocation="
                http://www.springframework.org/schema/beans
                http://www.springframework.org/schema/beans/spring-beans.xsd">

    <bean id="logging" class="com.apress.prospring2.ch04.interaction.LoggingBean"/>

    <bean class="com.apress.prospring2.ch04.interaction.ShutdownHookBean"/>

</beans>
```

Notice that no special configuration is required. Listing 4-19 shows a simple example application that uses the ShutdownHookBean to manage the destruction of singleton beans.

Listing 4-19. *Using ShutdownHookBean*

```
public class ShutdownHookBeanDemo {
    public static void main(String[] args) {
        XmlBeanFactory factory = new XmlBeanFactory(
            new ClassPathResource("/META-INF/spring/interactiondemo2-context.xml")
        );

        factory.preInstantiateSingletons();
        LoggingBean lb = (LoggingBean)factory.getBean("logging");
        lb.run();
    }
}
```

This code should seem quite familiar to you, but note that we have included a call to ConfigurableListableBeanFactory.preInstantiateSingletons(). By default, Spring lazily instantiates singleton beans as they are needed. This is a problem for the ShutdownHookBean, because it needs to be instantiated to register itself as a shutdown hook. Invoking preInstantiateSingletons() causes Spring to run through all its singleton bean definitions and create the instances, invoking any callback methods as appropriate. Running this example yields the following output, as expected:

```
INFO [main] XmlBeanDefinitionReader.loadBeanDefinitions(308) | ➥
Loading XML bean definitions from class path resource ➥
[META-INF/spring/interactiondemo2-context.xml]
INFO [main] DefaultListableBeanFactory.preInstantiateSingletons(385) | ➥
Pre-instantiating singletons in org.springframework.beans.factory.xml.➥
XmlBeanFactory@57ae58: defining beans ➥
[logging,com.apress.prospring2.ch04.interaction.ShutdownHookBean#0]; ➥
root of factory hierarchy
INFO [main] LoggingBean.run(20) | Bean name is'logging'.
```

```
INFO [Thread-0] ShutdownHookBean.run(27) | Destroying singletons.
INFO [Thread-0] DefaultSingletonBeanRegistry.destroySingletons(340) | ➥
Destroying singletons in org.springframework.beans.factory.xml.➥
XmlBeanFactory@57ae58: defining beans ➥
[logging,com.apress.prospring2.ch04.interaction.ShutdownHookBean#0]; ➥
root of factory hierarchy
```

As you can see, even though no calls to `destroySingletons()` are in the main application, the `ShutdownHookBean` is registered as a shutdown hook and calls `destroySingletons()` just before the application shuts down.

Using Method Injection

A new IoC-oriented feature introduced with Spring 1.1 is method injection, which allows greater flexibility for interactions between collaborators. Spring's method injection capabilities come in two loosely related forms, lookup method injection and method replacement. Lookup method injection provides a new mechanism by which a bean can obtain one of its dependencies, and method replacement allows you to replace the implementation of any method on a bean arbitrarily, without having to change the original source code.

To provide these two features, Spring uses the dynamic bytecode enhancement capabilities of CGLIB. If you want to use lookup method injection or method replacement in your application, make sure you have the CGLIB JAR file on your classpath. Since version 1.1, Spring has included a fully packaged CGLIB JAR file, which includes the ASM bytecode manipulation library as well.

Lookup Method Injection

Lookup method injection was added to Spring to overcome the problems encountered when a bean depends on another bean with a different life cycle—specifically, when a singleton depends on a nonsingleton. In this situation, both setter and constructor injection result in the singleton maintaining a single instance of what should be a nonsingleton bean. In some cases, you will want to have the singleton bean obtain a new instance of the nonsingleton every time it requires the bean in question.

Typically, you can achieve this by having the singleton bean implement `BeanFactoryAware`. Then, using the `BeanFactory` instance, the singleton bean can look up a new instance of the nonsingleton dependency every time it needs it. Lookup method injection allows the singleton bean to declare that it requires a nonsingleton dependency and receive a new instance of the nonsingleton bean each time it needs to interact with it, without needing to implement any Spring-specific interfaces.

In lookup method injection, your singleton declares a method, the lookup method, which returns an instance of the nonsingleton bean. When you obtain a reference to the singleton in your application, you are actually receiving a reference to a dynamically created subclass on which Spring has implemented the lookup method. A typical implementation involves defining the lookup method, and thus the bean class, as abstract. This prevents any strange errors from creeping in when you forget to configure the method injection, and you are working directly against the bean class with the empty method implementation instead of the Spring-enhanced subclass. This topic is quite complex and is best shown by example.

In this example, we create one nonsingleton bean and two singleton beans; all beans implement the same interface. One of the singletons obtains an instance of the nonsingleton bean using traditional setter injection; the other uses method injection. Listing 4-20 shows the `MyHelper` bean, which is the nonsingleton bean in our example.

Listing 4-20. *The MyHelper Bean*

```
public class MyHelper {

    public void doSomethingHelpful() {
        // do it!
    }
}
```

This bean is decidedly unexciting, but it serves the purposes of this example perfectly. In Listing 4-21, you can see the DemoBean interface, which is implemented by both of the singleton beans.

Listing 4-21. *The DemoBean Interface*

```
public interface DemoBean {

    MyHelper getMyHelper();
    void someOperation();
}
```

This interface has two methods: getMyHelper() and someOperation(). The sample application uses the getMyHelper() method to get a reference to the MyHelper instance and, in the case of the method lookup bean, to perform the actual method lookup. The someOperation() method is a simple method that depends on the MyHelper class to do its processing.

Listing 4-22 shows the StandardLookupDemoBean class, which uses setter injection to obtain an instance of the MyHelper class.

Listing 4-22. *The StandardLookupDemoBean Class*

```
public class StandardLookupDemoBean implements DemoBean {
    private MyHelper helper;

    public void setMyHelper(MyHelper helper) {
        this.helper = helper;
    }

    public MyHelper getMyHelper() {
        return this.helper;
    }

    public void someOperation() {
        helper.doSomethingHelpful();
    }
}
```

This code should all look familiar, but notice that the someOperation() method uses the stored instance of MyHelper to complete its processing. In Listing 4-23, you can see the AbstractLookupDemoBean class, which uses method injection to obtain an instance of the MyHelper class.

Listing 4-23. *The AbstractLookupDemoBean Class*

```
package com.apress.prospring2.ch04.mi;

public abstract class AbstractLookupDemoBean implements DemoBean {

    public abstract MyHelper getMyHelper();
```

```
    public void someOperation() {
        getMyHelper().doSomethingHelpful();
    }
}
```

Notice that the getMyHelper() method is declared as abstract, and that this method is called by the someOperation() method to obtain a MyHelper instance. In Listing 4-24, you can see the configuration code required for this example.

Listing 4-24. *Configuring Method Lookup Injection*

```
<?xml version="1.0" encoding="UTF-8"?>
<beans xmlns="http://www.springframework.org/schema/beans"
       xmlns:xsi="http://www.w3.org/2001/XMLSchema-instance"
       xsi:schemaLocation="
                http://www.springframework.org/schema/beans
                http://www.springframework.org/schema/beans/spring-beans.xsd">

    <bean id="helper" class="com.apress.prospring2.ch04.mi.MyHelper"
        scope="prototype"/>

    <bean id="abstractLookupBean"
        class="com.apress.prospring2.ch04.mi.AbstractLookupDemoBean">
        <lookup-method name="getMyHelper" bean="helper"/>
    </bean>

    <bean id="standardLookupBean"
        class="com.apress.prospring2.ch04.mi.StandardLookupDemoBean">
        <property name="myHelper" ref="helper"/>
    </bean>

</beans>
```

The configuration for the helper and standardLookupBean beans should look familiar to you by now. For the abstractLookupBean, you need to configure the lookup method using the <lookup-method> tag. The name attribute of the <lookup-method> tag tells Spring the name of the method on the bean that it should override. This method must not accept any arguments, and the return type should be that of the bean you want to return from the method. The bean attribute tells Spring which bean the lookup method should return.

The final piece of code for this example is the demo appliation in Listing 4-25.

Listing 4-25. *The LookupDemo Class*

```
public class LookupDemo {

    public static void main(String[] args) {
        XmlBeanFactory factory = new XmlBeanFactory(
                new ClassPathResource("/META-INF/spring/midemo-context.xml")
        );
        stressTest(factory, "abstractLookupBean");
        stressTest(factory, "standardLookupBean");
    }

    private static void stressTest(XmlBeanFactory factory, String beanName) {
        DemoBean bean = (DemoBean)factory.getBean(beanName);
        MyHelper helper1 = bean.getMyHelper();
        MyHelper helper2 = bean.getMyHelper();
```

```
        System.out.println("Testing " + beanName);
        System.out.println("Helper Instances the Same?: " + (helper1 == helper2));

        StopWatch stopWatch = new StopWatch();
        stopWatch.start("lookupDemo");

        for (int i = 0; i < 100000; i++) {
            MyHelper helper = bean.getMyHelper();
            helper.doSomethingHelpful();
        }

        stopWatch.stop();

        System.out.println("100000 gets took " + stopWatch.getTotalTimeMillis() +
            " ms");

    }

}
```

In this code, you can see that we retrieve the abstractLookupBean and the standardLookupBean from the BeanFactory and in the stressTest() method. The first part of the stressTest() method creates two local variables of MyHelper and assigns them each a value by calling getMyHelper() on the bean passed to it. Using these two variables, it writes a message to stdout indicating whether or not the two references point to the same object. For the abstractLookupBean class, a new instance of MyHelper should be retrieved for each call to getMyHelper(), so the references should not be the same. For standardLookupBean, a single instance of MyHelper is passed to the bean by setter injection, and this instance is stored and returned for every call to getMyHelper(), so the two references should be the same.

■ **Note** The StopWatch class used in the previous example is a utility class available with Spring. You'll find StopWatch very useful when you need to perform simple performance tests and when you are testing your applications.

The final part of the stressTest() method runs a simple performance test to see which of the beans is faster. Clearly, the standardLookupBean should be faster, because it returns the same instance each time, but seeing the difference is interesting. Here is the output we received from this example:

```
Testing abstractLookupBean
Helper Instances the Same?: false
100000 gets took 323 ms
Testing standardLookupBean
Helper Instances the Same?: true
100000 gets took 1 ms
```

The helper instances are, as expected, the same when we use standardLookupBean and different when we use abstractLookupBean. The performance difference is noticeable when we use the standardLookupBean. The obvious reason for this difference is the fact that we have set the helper bean's scope to prototype and that every call to the getMyHelper() method in abstractDemoBean returns a new instance of the helper bean. However, this was a requirement to start with, which means that we cannot change the scope of the helper bean to singleton. The second reason why the abstractLookupBean is significantly slower than the standardLookupBean is because the bean is a CGLIB proxy to the AbstractLookupDemoBean class (see Figure 4-1).

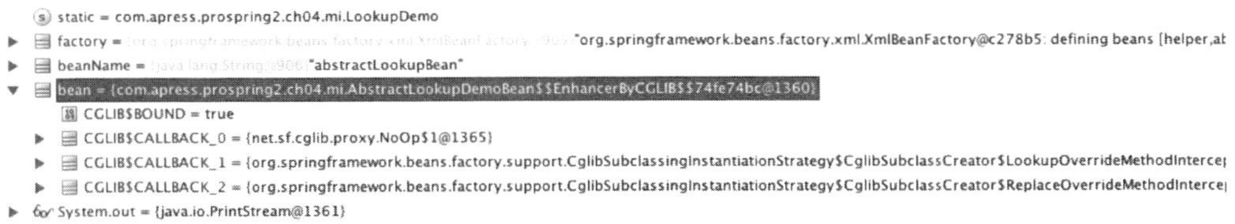

```
static = com.apress.prospring2.ch04.mi.LookupDemo
▶ factory = "org.springframework.beans.factory.xml.XmlBeanFactory@c278b5: defining beans [helper,at
▶ beanName = "abstractLookupBean"
▼ bean = {com.apress.prospring2.ch04.mi.AbstractLookupDemoBean$$EnhancerByCGLIB$$74fe74bc@1360}
    CGLIB$BOUND = true
  ▶ CGLIB$CALLBACK_0 = {net.sf.cglib.proxy.NoOp$1@1365}
  ▶ CGLIB$CALLBACK_1 = {org.springframework.beans.factory.support.CglibSubclassingInstantiationStrategy$CglibSubclassCreator$LookupOverrideMethodIntercep
  ▶ CGLIB$CALLBACK_2 = {org.springframework.beans.factory.support.CglibSubclassingInstantiationStrategy$CglibSubclassCreator$ReplaceOverrideMethodIntercep
▶ System.out = {java.io.PrintStream@1361}
```

Figure 4-1. *Debugger view of the CGLIB proxy*

The proxy intercepts all calls to the `getMyHelper()` method and returns the `helper` bean; the nature of the intercepts causes the slowness.

Considerations for Method Lookup Injection

Method lookup injection is intended for use when you want to work with two beans of different life cycles. Avoid the temptation to use method lookup injection when the beans share the same life cycle, especially if they are singletons. Listing 4-24 shows a noticeable difference in performance between using method injection to obtain new instances of a dependency and using standard DI to obtain a single instance of a dependency. Also, make sure you don't use method lookup injection needlessly, even when you have beans of different life cycles.

Consider a situation in which you have three singletons that share a dependency in common. You want each singleton to have its own instance of the dependency, so you create the dependency as a nonsingleton, but you are happy with each singleton using the same instance of the collaborator throughout its life. In this case, setter injection is the ideal solution; method lookup injection just adds unnecessary overhead.

As we mentioned before, method lookup injection was created so you could avoid having lots of beans that implemented `BeanFactoryAware` and performed lookups manually using `getBean()`. So how does performing manual lookups with `BeanFactoryAware` compare to method lookup injection from a performance perspective? Listing 4-26 shows another implementation of the `DemoBean` interface that also implements `BeanFactoryAware` and uses the `getBean()` method to look up its nonsingleton dependency manually.

Listing 4-26. *The BeanFactoryAwareLookupDemoBean Class*

```
public class BeanFactoryAwareLookupDemoBean implements DemoBean, BeanFactoryAware {
    private BeanFactory beanFactory;

    public MyHelper getMyHelper() {
        return (MyHelper) this.beanFactory.getBean("helper");
    }

    public void someOperation() {
        getMyHelper().doSomethingHelpful();
    }

    public void setBeanFactory(BeanFactory beanFactory) throws BeansException {
        this.beanFactory = beanFactory;
    }
}
```

As you can see, the `getMyHelper()` method performs a lookup each time it is called, returning a new instance of the `helper` bean each time. We have added another call to `stressTest(factory, "factoryLookupBean");` to the code in Listing 4-25 and received this result:

```
Testing abstractLookupBean
Helper Instances the Same?: false
100000 gets took 318 ms
Testing standardLookupBean
Helper Instances the Same?: true
100000 gets took 1 ms
Testing factoryLookupBean
Helper Instances the Same?: false
100000 gets took 187 ms
```

As you can see, the manual lookup approach is approximately 60 percent faster. However, unless performance is absolutely paramount, we recommend that you use the `<lookup-method>` approach, which does not tie your beans' code to the Spring Framework. The alternative is to closely couple your beans to the Spring Framework by implementing the `BeanFactoryAware` interface and performing the lookup manually. Using method lookup injection, you can keep your beans decoupled from Spring without major performance loss, and you can keep the configuration of the beans completely separate from the Java code.

When you are using method lookup injection, there are a few design guidelines that you should bear in mind when building your classes. In the earlier examples, we declared the lookup method in an interface. The only reason we did this was to avoid duplicating the `stressTest()` method twice for two different bean types. As we mentioned earlier, generally, you do not need to pollute a business interface with unnecessary definitions that are used solely for IoC purposes. Another point to bear in mind is that although you aren't required to make your lookup method abstract; doing so prevents you from forgetting to configure the lookup method and using a blank implementation by accident.

Method Replacement

Although the Spring documentation classifies method replacement as a form of injection, it is very different from what you have seen so far. So far, we have used injection purely to supply beans with their collaborators. Using method replacement, you can replace the implementation of any method on any beans arbitrarily without having to change the source of the bean you are modifying.

Internally, you achieve this by creating a subclass of the bean class dynamically. You use CGLIB and redirect calls to the method you want to replace to another bean that implements the `MethodReplacer` interface.

In Listing 4-27 you can see a simple bean that declares two overloads of a `formatMessage()` method.

Listing 4-27. *The ReplacementTarget Class*

```
package com.apress.prospring2.ch04.mi;

public class ReplacementTarget {

    public String formatMessage(String msg) {
        StringBuilder sb = new StringBuilder();
        sb.append("<h1>").append(msg).append("</h1>");
        return sb.toString();
    }

    public String formatMessage(Object msg) {
        StringBuilder sb = new StringBuilder();
        sb.append("<h1>").append(msg).append("</h1>");
        return sb.toString();
```

```
    }
}
```

You can replace any of the methods on the ReplacementTarget class using Spring's method replacement functionality. In this example, we show you how to replace the formatMessage(String method), and we also compare the performance of the replaced method with that of the original.

To replace a method, you first need to create an implementation of the MethodReplacer class; this is shown in Listing 4-28.

Listing 4-28. *Implementing MethodReplacer*

```
public class FormatMessageReplacer implements MethodReplacer {

    public Object reimplement(Object obj, Method method, Object[] args)
        throws Throwable {
        String msg = (String) args[0];
        return "<h2>" + msg + "</h2>";
    }
}
```

The MethodReplacer interface has a single method, reimplement(), that you must implement. Three arguments are passed to reimplement(): the bean on which the original method was invoked, a Method instance that represents the method that is being overridden, and the array of arguments passed to the method. The reimplement() method should return the result of your reimplemented logic and, obviously, the type of the return value should be compatible with the return type of the method you are replacing. In Listing 4-28, the FormatMessageReplacer replaces calls to all methods, regardless of their signatures. We can do this because we instruct Spring to only replace the formatMessage(String) method. Listing 4-29 shows a BeanFactory that defines two beans of type ReplacementTarget—one has the formatMessage(String) method replaced, and the other does not.

Listing 4-29. *Configuring Method Replacement*

```
<?xml version="1.0" encoding="UTF-8"?>
<beans xmlns="http://www.springframework.org/schema/beans"
       xmlns:xsi="http://www.w3.org/2001/XMLSchema-instance"
       xsi:schemaLocation="
                http://www.springframework.org/schema/beans
                http://www.springframework.org/schema/beans/spring-beans.xsd">

    <bean id="methodReplacer"
        class="com.apress.prospring2.ch04.mi.FormatMessageReplacer"/>
    <bean id="replacementTarget"
        class="com.apress.prospring2.ch04.mi.ReplacementTarget">
        <replaced-method name="formatMessage" replacer="methodReplacer">
            <arg-type match="java.lang.String"/>
        </replaced-method>
    </bean>
    <bean id="standardTarget"
        class="com.apress.prospring2.ch04.mi.ReplacementTarget"/>

</beans>
```

As you can see from Listing 4-29, the MethodReplacer implementation is declared as a bean in the BeanFactory. We then used the <replaced-method> tag to replace the formatMessage(String) method on the replacementTargetBean. The name attribute of the <replaced-method> tag specifies the name of the method to replace and the replacer attribute is used to specify the name of the MethodReplacer bean that we want to replace the method implementation. In cases where there are overloaded methods such as in the ReplacementTarget class, you can use the <arg-type> tag to specify the method signature to match. The <arg-type> supports pattern matching, so String is matched to java.lang.String and to java.lang.StringBuffer.

Listing 4-30 shows a simple demonstration application that retrieves both the standardTarget and replacementTarget beans from the BeanFactory, executes their formatMessage(String) methods, and runs a simple performance test to see which is faster.

Listing 4-30. *Method Replacement in Action*

```
public class MethodReplacementDemo {

    static interface StressTestCallback {
        void run(ReplacementTarget target);
    }

    public static void main(String[] args) {
        XmlBeanFactory factory = new XmlBeanFactory(
                new ClassPathResource("/META-INF/spring/midemo3-context.xml")
        );
        StressTestCallback stringCallback = new StressTestCallback() {
            private final String msg = "Hello";

            public void run(ReplacementTarget target) {
                target.formatMessage(msg);
            }

            @Override
            public String toString() {
                return "formatMessage(String)";
            }
        };
        StressTestCallback objectCallback = new StressTestCallback() {
            private final Object msg = new Object();

            public void run(ReplacementTarget target) {
                target.formatMessage(msg);
            }

            @Override
            public String toString() {
                return "formatMessage(Object)";
            }
        };
        stressTest(factory, "replacementTarget", stringCallback);
        stressTest(factory, "standardTarget", stringCallback);
        stressTest(factory, "standardTarget", objectCallback);
        stressTest(factory, "standardTarget", objectCallback);
    }

    private static void stressTest(XmlBeanFactory factory, String beanName,
        StressTestCallback callback) {
        ReplacementTarget target = (ReplacementTarget)factory.getBean(beanName);
        callback.run(target);
```

```
        StopWatch stopWatch = new StopWatch();
        stopWatch.start("perfTest");
        for (int i = 0; i < 1000000; i++) {
            callback.run(target);
        }
        stopWatch.stop();
        System.out.println("1000000 invocations of formatMessage("
                + callback + ") on "
                + beanName + " took: "
                + stopWatch.getTotalTimeMillis() + " ms");
    }

}
```

You should be very familiar with this code by now, so we won't go into any detail on it. On our machine, running this example yields the following output:

```
1000000 invocations of formatMessage(formatMessage(String))
    on replacementTarget took: 1033 ms
1000000 invocations of formatMessage(formatMessage(String))
    on standardTarget took: 241 ms
1000000 invocations of formatMessage(formatMessage(Object))
    on replacementTarget took: 330 ms
1000000 invocations of formatMessage(formatMessage(Object))
    on standardTarget took: 320 ms
```

As expected, the output from the `replacementTarget` bean reflects the overridden implementation the `MethodReplacer` provides, and the dynamically replaced method is over four times slower than the statically defined method. Calling a nonreplaced method on a bean with at least one replaced method is only slightly slower than calling the same method on a bean with no replaced methods. We verify this by calling the `formatMessage(Object)` method on both the `standardTarget` and `replacementTarget` beans: the performance call to the `formatMessage(Object)` method on the `replacementTarget` bean is slightly slower.

When to Use Method Replacement

We will resist the temptation to say, "Never use method replacement." Instead, we'll tell you that method replacement can prove quite useful in a variety of circumstances, especially when you only want to override a particular method for a single bean rather than all beans of the same type. That said, we still prefer to use standard Java mechanisms for overriding methods rather than depending on runtime bytecode enhancement.

If you are going to use method replacement as part of your application, we recommend that you use one `MethodReplacer` per method or group of overloaded methods. Avoid the temptation to use a single `MethodReplacer` for lots of unrelated methods; this results in lots of unnecessary `String` comparisons while your code works out which method it is supposed to reimplement. We have found that performing simple checks to ensure that the `MethodReplacer` is working with the correct method is useful and doesn't add too much overhead to your code. If you are really concerned about performance, you can simply add a `boolean` property to your `MethodReplacer`, which allows you to turn the check on and off using DI.

Using FactoryBean

One of the problems that you will face when using Spring is how to create and inject dependencies that cannot be created simply by using the new operator. To overcome this problem, Spring provides the FactoryBean interface that acts as an adaptor for objects that cannot be created and managed using the standard Spring semantics. Typically, you use a FactoryBean to create beans you cannot use the new operator to create, such as those you access through static factory methods, although this is not always the case. Simply put, a FactoryBean is a bean that acts as a factory for other beans. FactoryBean implementations are configured within your BeanFactory like any normal bean. However, when Spring uses the FactoryBean to satisfy a dependency or lookup request, it does not return the FactoryBean; instead, it invokes the FactoryBean.getObject() method and returns the result of that invocation.

FactoryBean implementations are used to great effect in Spring, most notably in the creation of transactional proxies, which we cover in Chapter 16, in the automatic retrieval of resources from a JNDI context, and many other situations. However, FactoryBean implementations are not useful just for building the internals of Spring; you'll find them very useful when you build your own applications, because they allow you to manage many more resources using IoC than you would otherwise be able to.

The MessageDigestFactoryBean

Often, the projects that we work on require some kind of cryptographic processing; typically, this involves generating a message digest or hash of a user's password to be stored in a database. In Java, the MessageDigest class provides functionality for creating a digest of any arbitrary data. MessageDigest itself is abstract, and you obtain concrete implementations by calling MessageDigest.getInstance() and passing in the name of the digest algorithm you want to use. For instance, if we want to use the MD5 algorithm to create a digest, we use the following code to create the MessageDigest instance:

```
MessageDigest md5 = MessageDigest.getInstance("MD5");
```

If we want to use Spring to manage the creation of the MessageDigest object, the best way we can do so without a FactoryBean is to create a property algorithmName on our bean and use an initialization callback to call MessageDigest.getInstance(). Using a FactoryBean, we can encapsulate this logic inside a bean. Once we do so, any beans that require a MessageDigest instance can simply declare a property, messageDigest and use the FactoryBean to obtain the instance. Listing 4-31 shows an implementation of FactoryBean that does just this.

Listing 4-31. *The MessageDigestFactoryBean Class*

```
public class MessageDigestFactoryBean implements FactoryBean, InitializingBean {
    private static final String DEFAULT_ALGORITHM = "MD5";

    private String algorithm = DEFAULT_ALGORITHM;
    private MessageDigest messageDigest;

    public Object getObject() throws Exception {
        return this.messageDigest.clone();
    }

    public Class getObjectType() {
        return MessageDigest.class;
    }

    public boolean isSingleton() {
```

```
        return true;
    }

    public void setAlgorithm(String algorithm) {
        this.algorithm = algorithm;
    }

    public void afterPropertiesSet() throws Exception {
        this.messageDigest = MessageDigest.getInstance(this.algorithm);
    }
}
```

The FactoryBean interface declares three methods: getObject(), getObjectType(), and isSingleton(). Spring calls the getObject() method to retrieve the Object created by the FactoryBean. This is the actual Object that is passed to other beans that use the FactoryBean as a collaborator. In Listing 4-31, you can see that the MessageDigestFactoryBean passes a clone of the stored MessageDigest instance that is created in the InitializingBean.afterPropertiesSet() callback.

The getObjectType() method allows you to tell Spring what type of Object your FactoryBean will return. The returned type can be null if you do not know the type in advance, but if you specify a type, Spring can use it for automatic wiring purposes. We return MessageDigest as our type, because we do not know what concrete type will be returned—not that it matters because all beans will define their dependencies using MessageDigest anyway.

The isSingleton() property allows you to inform Spring whether the FactoryBean is managing a singleton instance or not. Remember that by setting the scope="singleton" of the FactoryBean's <bean> tag, you tell Spring about the singleton status of the FactoryBean itself, not the Objects it is returning.

Now, let's see how the FactoryBean is employed in an application. In Listing 4-32, you can see a simple application that obtains the MessageDigest instances from the BeanFactory.

Listing 4-32. *The MessageDigestDemo Class*

```
public class MessageDigestDemo {

    public static void main(String[] args) {
        XmlBeanFactory factory = new XmlBeanFactory(
                new ClassPathResource("/META-INF/spring/factorydemo-context.xml")
        );
        MessageDigest d1 = (MessageDigest)factory.getBean("sha");
        MessageDigest d2 = (MessageDigest)factory.getBean("md5");
        calculateDigest("Hello, world", d1);
        calculateDigest("Hello, world", d2);
    }

    private static void calculateDigest(String message, MessageDigest digest) {
        System.out.print("Digest using " + digest.getAlgorithm() + ": ");
        digest.reset();
        final byte[] bytes = digest.digest(message.getBytes());
        for (byte b : bytes) {
            System.out.print(String.format("%02x", b));
        }
        System.out.println("");
    }

}
```

Listing 4-33 shows a simple BeanFactory configuration that defines two MessageDigestFactoryBean implementations: one for the SHA1 algorithm and the other using the MD5 algorithm.

Listing 4-33. *Configuring Factory Beans*

```
<?xml version="1.0" encoding="UTF-8"?>
<beans xmlns="http://www.springframework.org/schema/beans"
       xmlns:xsi="http://www.w3.org/2001/XMLSchema-instance"
       xsi:schemaLocation="
                http://www.springframework.org/schema/beans
                http://www.springframework.org/schema/beans/spring-beans.xsd">

    <bean id="sha"
     class="com.apress.prospring2.ch04.factoy.MessageDigestFactoryBean">
        <property name="algorithm" value="SHA1"/>
    </bean>

    <bean id="md5"
        class="com.apress.prospring2.ch04.factoy.MessageDigestFactoryBean"/>

</beans>
```

We have configured the two MessageDigestFactoryBean implementations. Not only that, when we call the getBean() method on the BeanFactory implementation, Spring will use the MessageDigestFactoryBean.getObject() and return a MessageDigest instance. Therefore, running the example from Listing 4-32 shows this:

```
Digest using SHA1: e02aa1b106d5c7c6a98def2b13005d5b84fd8dc8
Digest using MD5: bc6e6f16b8a077ef5fbc8d59d0b931b9
```

A FactoryBean is the perfect solution when you are working with classes that cannot be created using the new operator and that you still want to use as Spring beans. If you work with objects that are created using a factory method and you want to use these classes in a Spring application, create a FactoryBean to act as an adaptor, allowing your classes to take full advantage of Spring's IoC capabilities.

Accessing a FactoryBean Directly

Given that Spring automatically satisfies any references to a FactoryBean by the objects produced by that FactoryBean, you may be wondering if you can actually access the FactoryBean directly. The answer is, "Yes."

Accessing the FactoryBean is actually very simple: you prefix the bean name with an ampersand in the call to getBean(), as shown in Listing 4-34.

Listing 4-34. *Accessing FactoryBeans Directly*

```
public class MessageDigestFactoryDemo {

    public static void main(String[] args) throws Exception {
        XmlBeanFactory factory = new XmlBeanFactory(
                new ClassPathResource("/META-INF/spring/factorydemo-context.xml")
        );
        MessageDigestFactoryBean factoryBean =
             (MessageDigestFactoryBean)factory.getBean("&sha");
```

```
        MessageDigest d1 = (MessageDigest)factory.getBean("sha");
        MessageDigest d2 = (MessageDigest)factoryBean.getObject();
        System.out.println("Equal MessageDigests created? "
                + (d1.getAlgorithm().equals(d2.getAlgorithm())));
    }

}
```

This feature is used in a few places in the Spring code, but your application should really have no reason to use it. The FactoryBean interface is intended to be used as a piece of supporting infrastructure to allow you to use more of your application's classes in an IoC setting. Avoid accessing the FactoryBean directly and invoking getObject() manually; if you do not, you are making extra work for yourself and are unnecessarily coupling your application to a specific implementation detail that could quite easily change in the future.

The BeanFactoryPostProcessor

The concept of the BeanFactoryPostProcessor is similar to the BeanPostProcessor: the BeanFactoryPostProcessor executes after Spring has finished constructing the BeanFactory but before the BeanFactory constructs the beans.

■ Note Actually, Spring can detect the BeanFactoryPostProcessor beans and instantiate them before instantiating any other bean in the BeanFactory.

Using the BeanFactoryPostProcessor, we can adapt the beans' values according to the BeanFactory's environment. Table 4-1 summarizes the BeanFactoryPostProcessors included in the default Spring distribution.

Table 4-1. *BeanFactory Post-Processors in Spring*

Post-Processor	Description
AspectJWeavingEnabler	This post-processor registers AspectJ's ClassPreProcessorAgentAdapter to be used in Spring's LoadTimeWeaver (for more information about load-time weaving, go to Chapter 6).
CustomAutowireConfigurer	This one allows you to specify annotations, in addition to @Qualifier, to indicate that a bean is a candidate for automatic wiring.
CustomEditorConfigurer	This registers the PropertyEditor implementations that Spring will use in attempts to convert string values in the configuration files to types required by the beans.
CustomScopeConfigurer	Use this post-processor to configure custom scopes (in addition to singleton, prototype, request, session, and globalSession) in the configuration file. Set the scopes property to a Map containing the scope name as key and the implementation of the Scope interface as value.

Continued

Table 4-1. *Continued*

Post-Processor	Description
`PreferencesPlaceholderConfigurer`	This post-processor will replace the values in beans' properties using JDK 1.4's Preferences API. The Preferences API states that it will try to resolve a value first from user preferences (`Preferences.userRoot()`), then system preferences (`Preferences.systemRoot()`), and finally from a preferences file.
`PropertyOverrideConfigurer`	This post-processor will replace values of beans' properties from values loaded from the specified properties file. It will search the properties file for a property constructed from the bean name and property: for property `a` of bean `x`, it will look for `x.a` in the properties file. If the property does not exist, the post-processor will leave the value found in the configuration file.
`PropertyPlaceholderConfigurer`	This post-processor will replace values of properties with values loaded from the configured properties file, if the values follow certain formatting rules (by default, `${property-name}`).
`ServletContextPropertyPlaceholderConfigurer`	This post-processor extends `PropertyPlaceholderConfigurer`; therefore, it replaces beans' properties if they follow the specified naming convention. In addition to its superclass, this processor will load values from `context-param` entries of the servlet that is hosting the application.

As an example, we will use a `BeanFactoryPostProcessor` that loads values for certain bean properties from a properties file. Let's take the code in Listing 4-35, which shows configuration for a bean with three `String` properties: `connectionString`, `username`, and `password`.

Listing 4-35. *SimpleBean Configuration*

```
<?xml version="1.0" encoding="UTF-8"?>
<beans xmlns="http://www.springframework.org/schema/beans"
       xmlns:xsi="http://www.w3.org/2001/XMLSchema-instance"
       xsi:schemaLocation="
                http://www.springframework.org/schema/beans
                http://www.springframework.org/schema/beans/spring-beans.xsd">

    <bean id="simpleBean" class="com.apress.prospring2.ch04.bfpp.SimpleBean">
        <property name="connectionString" value="${simpleBean.connectionString}"/>
        <property name="password" value="${simpleBean.password}"/>
        <property name="username" value="username"/>
    </bean>

</beans>
```

If we run a sample application from Listing 4-36, it will simply print out the values we set to the properties.

Listing 4-36. *Sample Application for the BeanFactoryPostProcessor*

```
public class PropertyConfigurerDemo {

    public static void main(String[] args) {
        ConfigurableListableBeanFactory beanFactory = new XmlBeanFactory(
                new ClassPathResource("/META-INF/spring/bfpp-context.xml")
        );

        System.out.println(beanFactory.getBean("simpleBean"));
    }

}
```

If the SimpleBean's toString() method prints out the values of its properties, we will see the following:

```
SimpleBean{password='${simpleBean.password}', username='username', ➥
connectionString='${simpleBean.connectionString}'}
```

Let's now add a bean of type PropertyPlaceholderConfigurer, which is an implementation of the BeanFactoryPostProcessor interface, to the BeanFactory configuration file (see Listing 4-37).

Listing 4-37. *Modified BeanFactory Configuration File*

```
<?xml version="1.0" encoding="UTF-8"?>
<beans xmlns="http://www.springframework.org/schema/beans"
       xmlns:xsi="http://www.w3.org/2001/XMLSchema-instance"
       xsi:schemaLocation="
                http://www.springframework.org/schema/beans
                http://www.springframework.org/schema/beans/spring-beans.xsd">

    <bean id="bfpp"
       class="org.springframework.beans.factory.config.➥
             PropertyPlaceholderConfigurer">
        <property name="location" value="classpath:/META-INF/bfpp.properties"/>
    </bean>

    <bean id="simpleBean" class="com.apress.prospring2.ch04.bfpp.SimpleBean">
        <property name="connectionString" value="${simpleBean.connectionString}"/>
        <property name="password" value="${simpleBean.password}"/>
        <property name="username" value="username"/>
    </bean>

</beans>
```

If we run the sample application again, it will print the same output. The XmlBeanFactory does not automatically register the BeanFactoryPostProcessor beans. We must do this manually and modify the PropertyConfigurerDemo class to use the bfpp bean in Listing 4-38.

Listing 4-38. *Usage of the BeanFactoryPostProcessor Bean*

```
public class PropertyConfigurerDemo {

    public static void main(String[] args) {
        ConfigurableListableBeanFactory beanFactory = new XmlBeanFactory(
                new ClassPathResource("/META-INF/spring/bfpp-context.xml")
```

```
        );
        BeanFactoryPostProcessor bfpp =
           (BeanFactoryPostProcessor)beanFactory.getBean("bfpp");
        bfpp.postProcessBeanFactory(beanFactory);

        System.out.println(beanFactory.getBean("simpleBean"));
    }

}
```

Assuming we have the /META-INF/bfpp.properties file with definitions for simpleBean.connectionString=Hello and simpleBean.password=won't tell, the sample application will now print this:

```
SimpleBean{password='won't tell!', username='username', connectionString='hello'}
```

We created the ConfigurableListableBeanFactory instance and obtained the BeanFactoryPostProcessor implementation. We called the post-processor's postProcessBeanFactory, passing the ConfigurableListableBeanFactory as its argument. The post-processor replaced the values of the properties of all relevant beans. Therefore, when we called the getBean("simpleBean"), the BeanFactory returned an instance of SimpleBean with its connectionString and password properties set by the post-processor.

Implementing a BeanFactoryPostProcessor

To explore the BeanFactoryPostProcessor further, we will implement a simple post-processor that removes potentially obscene property values (it is all too easy to leave something like "bollocks" in a bean definition; you certainly don't want the users to see this in production). Listing 4-39 shows the bean definition we would like to clean up.

Listing 4-39. *Potentially Dangerous Bean Definition*

```
<?xml version="1.0" encoding="UTF-8"?>
<beans xmlns="http://www.springframework.org/schema/beans"
       xmlns:xsi="http://www.w3.org/2001/XMLSchema-instance"
       xsi:schemaLocation="
                http://www.springframework.org/schema/beans
                http://www.springframework.org/schema/beans/spring-beans.xsd">

    <bean id="simpleBean" class="com.apress.prospring2.ch04.bfpp.SimpleBean">
        <property name="connectionString" value="bollocks"/>
        <property name="password" value="winky"/>
        <property name="username" value="bum"/>
    </bean>

</beans>
```

We are going to write a post-processor that will examine all bean definitions and change inappropriate property values. The task is quite simple: we will go through definitions of all beans in the BeanFactory, and for each bean, we will check its properties. Even though this seems simple, the bean definitions are not trivial to deal with. We cover BeanDefinition in much more detail in Chapter 7; here, we will simply use it. Listing 4-40 shows the post-processor implementation.

Listing 4-40. *The ObscenityRemovingBeanFactoryPostProcessor Implementation*

```
public class ObscenityRemovingBeanFactoryPostProcessor
    implements BeanFactoryPostProcessor {

    private Set<String> obscenities;

    public ObscenityRemovingBeanFactoryPostProcessor() {
        this.obscenities = new HashSet<String>();
    }

    public void postProcessBeanFactory(ConfigurableListableBeanFactory beanFactory)
        throws BeansException {

        String[] beanNames = beanFactory.getBeanDefinitionNames();
        for (String beanName : beanNames) {
            BeanDefinition bd = beanFactory.getBeanDefinition(beanName);
            StringValueResolver valueResolver = new StringValueResolver() {
                public String resolveStringValue(String strVal) {
                    if (isObscene(strVal)) return "****";
                    return strVal;
                }
            };
            BeanDefinitionVisitor visitor =
                new BeanDefinitionVisitor(valueResolver);
            visitor.visitBeanDefinition(bd);
        }
    }

    private boolean isObscene(Object value) {
        String potentialObscenity = value.toString().toUpperCase();
        return this.obscenities.contains(potentialObscenity);
    }

    public void setObscenities(Set<String> obscenities) {
        this.obscenities.clear();
        for (String obscenity : obscenities) {
            this.obscenities.add(obscenity.toUpperCase());
        }
    }
}
```

The code in bold shows the crucial portions of the post-processor: first, we get names of all beans in this `BeanFactory`, and we get each bean's definition. The `BeanDefinition` is a complex object that holds all information necessary to construct the bean. To examine the `BeanDefinition`'s details, we should use the `BeanDefinitionVisitor`. The visitor provides a version-independent façade for the internal classes and interfaces Spring Framework uses. The `BeanDefinitionVisitor.visitBeanDefinition` method visits all aspects of the definition (parent bean name, bean class name, factory bean name, and many more). The `BeanDefinitionVisitor` uses the `StringValueResolver` to calculate the final value of the string values passed to the definition (alternatively, you can subclass the `BeanDefinitionVisitor` and override its `resolveStringValue` method). We took the first approach and implemented the `StringValueResolver`. Our implementation checks that the value is not in our set of obscenities; if it is, we replace it with `"****"`. Listing 4-41 shows the `BeanFactory` configuration file that includes the `BeanFactoryPostProcessor`.

Listing 4-41. *Updated BeanFactory Configuration*

```
<?xml version="1.0" encoding="UTF-8"?>
<beans xmlns="http://www.springframework.org/schema/beans"
       xmlns:xsi="http://www.w3.org/2001/XMLSchema-instance"
       xsi:schemaLocation="
                http://www.springframework.org/schema/beans
                http://www.springframework.org/schema/beans/spring-beans.xsd">

    <bean id="bfpp"
         class="com.apress.prospring2.ch04.bfpp.➥
            ObscenityRemovingBeanFactoryPostProcessor">
        <property name="obscenities">
            <set>
                <value>bollocks</value>
                <value>winky</value>
                <value>bum</value>
                <value>Microsoft</value>
            </set>
        </property>
    </bean>

    <bean id="simpleBean" class="com.apress.prospring2.ch04.bfpp.SimpleBean">
        <property name="connectionString" value="bollocks"/>
        <property name="password" value="winky"/>
        <property name="username" value="bum"/>
    </bean>

</beans>
```

The sample application in Listing 4-42 uses the configuration file and demonstrates that the post-processor works and cleans up our foul-mouthed bean.

Listing 4-42. *Sample Application for the BeanFactoryPostProcessor*

```
public class ObscenityCleaningDemo {

    public static void main(String[] args) {
        ConfigurableListableBeanFactory beanFactory = new XmlBeanFactory(
                new ClassPathResource("/META-INF/spring/bfpp-context.xml")
        );
        BeanFactoryPostProcessor bfpp =
            (BeanFactoryPostProcessor)beanFactory.getBean("bfpp");
        bfpp.postProcessBeanFactory(beanFactory);

        SimpleBean simpleBean = (SimpleBean) beanFactory.getBean("simpleBean");
        System.out.println(simpleBean);
    }

}
```

When we run this application, Spring loads the bean definitions from the configuration file. We then get the `BeanFactoryPostProcessor` instance and call its `postProcessBeanFactory` method. This call modifies the `BeanDefinition` instances in the `BeanFactory`, so when we then call `getBean("simpleBean")`, Spring constructs the bean using the cleaned up definition. Therefore, the application prints out this:

```
SimpleBean{password='****', username='****', connectionString='****'}
```

You can register new beans in the post-processor, but you cannot add a new `BeanDefinition`. To demonstrate this, we modify our post-processor to include a singleton that maintains the set of all obscenities removed (see Listing 4-43).

Listing 4-43. *Modified ObscenityRemovingBeanFactoryPostProcessor*

```
public class ObscenityRemovingBeanFactoryPostProcessor
    implements BeanFactoryPostProcessor, BeanNameAware {

    private Set<String> obscenities;
    private Set<String> obscenitiesRemoved;
    private String name;

    public ObscenityRemovingBeanFactoryPostProcessor() {
        this.obscenities = new HashSet<String>();
        this.obscenitiesRemoved = new HashSet<String>();
    }

    public void postProcessBeanFactory(ConfigurableListableBeanFactory beanFactory)
         throws BeansException {
        String[] beanNames = beanFactory.getBeanDefinitionNames();
        for (String beanName : beanNames) {
            if (beanName.equals(this.name)) continue;

            BeanDefinition bd = beanFactory.getBeanDefinition(beanName);
            StringValueResolver valueResolver = new StringValueResolver() {
                public String resolveStringValue(String strVal) {
                    if (isObscene(strVal)) {
                        obscenitiesRemoved.add(strVal);
                        return "****";
                    }
                    return strVal;
                }
            };
            BeanDefinitionVisitor visitor=
                new BeanDefinitionVisitor(valueResolver);
            visitor.visitBeanDefinition(bd);
        }
        beanFactory.registerSingleton("obscenitiesRemoved",
           this.obscenitiesRemoved);
    }

    private boolean isObscene(Object value) {
        String potentialObscenity = value.toString().toUpperCase();
        return this.obscenities.contains(potentialObscenity);
    }

    public void setObscenities(Set<String> obscenities) {
        this.obscenities.clear();
        for (String obscenity : obscenities) {
            this.obscenities.add(obscenity.toUpperCase());
        }
    }
```

```
    public void setBeanName(String name) {
        this.name = name;
    }
}
```

There are two modifications in the post-processor: first, we make it bean-name aware (BeanNameAware) and check that we are not changing BeanDefinition for this bean. After all, the ObscenityRemovingBeanFactoryPostProcessor is an ordinary bean. Next, we maintain a set of all replacements we have made and register that set as a singleton bean with the "obscenitiesRemoved" name. If we add System.out.println(beanFactory.getBean("obscenitiesRemoved")); to the sample application, it will print this:

```
SimpleBean{password='****', username='****', connectionString='****'}
[bum, bollocks, winky]
```

In the next section, we will look at how the CustomEditorConfigurer works with the PropertyEditors to convert the String values in bean configuration to the types required by the beans.

JavaBeans PropertyEditor

For those of you not entirely familiar with JavaBeans concepts, the PropertyEditor class converts a property's value to and from its native type representation into a String. Originally, this was conceived as a way to allow property values to be entered, as String values, into an editor and transform them into the correct types. However, because PropertyEditors are inherently lightweight classes, they have found uses in many different settings, including Spring.

Because a good portion of property values in a Spring-based application start life in the BeanFactory configuration file, they are essentially strings. However, the property that these values are set on may not be String-typed. So, to save you from having to create a load of String-typed properties artificially, Spring allows you to define PropertyEditor classes to manage the conversion of String-based property values into the correct types.

The Built-in PropertyEditors

Spring comes with several built-in PropertyEditor implementations that are preregistered with the BeanFactory. Listing 4-44 shows a simple bean that declares seven properties, one for each of the types supported by the built-in PropertyEditors.

Listing 4-44. *Using the Built-in PropertyEditors*

```
public class PropertyEditorBean {
    private Class cls;
    private File file;
    private URL url;
    private Locale locale;
    private Properties properties;
    private String[] strings;
    private byte[] bytes;
    private Pattern pattern;

    public void setPattern(Pattern pattern) {
        System.out.println("Setting pattern: " + pattern);
        this.pattern = pattern;
    }
```

```
    public void setClass(Class cls) {
        System.out.println("Setting class: " + cls.getName());
        this.cls = cls;
    }

    public void setFile(File file) {
        System.out.println("Setting file: " + file.getName());
        this.file = file;
    }

    public void setLocale(Locale locale) {
        System.out.println("Setting locale: " + locale.getDisplayName());
        this.locale = locale;
    }

    public void setProperties(Properties properties) {
        System.out.println("Loaded " + properties.size() + " properties");
        this.properties = properties;
    }

    public void setStrings(String[] strings) {
        System.out.println("Loaded " + strings.length + " Strings");
        this.strings = strings;
    }

    public void setUrl(URL url) {
        System.out.println("Setting URL: " + url.toExternalForm());
        this.url = url;
    }

    public void setBytes(byte[] bytes) {
        System.out.println("Adding " + bytes.length + " bytes");
        this.bytes = bytes;
    }

    public static void main(String[] args) {
        BeanFactory factory = new XmlBeanFactory(
                new ClassPathResource("/META-INF/spring/pedemo-context.xml")
        );
        PropertyEditorBean bean = (PropertyEditorBean) factory
                .getBean("builtInSample");
    }
}
```

In Listing 4-45, you can see a simple `BeanFactory` configuration specifying values for all of the properties in Listing 4-44.

Listing 4-45. *Configuration Using PropertyEditors*

```
<?xml version="1.0" encoding="UTF-8"?>
<beans xmlns="http://www.springframework.org/schema/beans"
       xmlns:xsi="http://www.w3.org/2001/XMLSchema-instance"
       xsi:schemaLocation="
                http://www.springframework.org/schema/beans
                http://www.springframework.org/schema/beans/spring-beans.xsd">
```

```
    <bean id="builtInSample"
        class="com.apress.prospring2.ch04.pe.PropertyEditorBean">
        <property name="bytes" value="Hello, World"/>
        <property name="class" value="java.lang.String"/>
        <property name="file" value="/tmp"/>
        <property name="locale" value="en_GB"/>
        <property name="pattern" value="^(.*)$"/>
        <property name="properties">
            <value>
                a=b
                c=d
            </value>
        </property>
        <property name="strings" value="Aleksa,Ani,Jessica,Jan"/>
        <property name="url" value="http://www.cakesolutions.net"/>
    </bean>

</beans>
```

Although all the properties on the PropertyEditorBean are not String values, the values for the properties are specified as simple strings. Running this example yields the following output:

```
Adding 12 bytes
Setting class: java.lang.String
Setting file: tmp
Setting locale: English (United Kingdom)
Setting pattern: ^(.*)$
Loaded 2 properties
Loaded 4 Strings
Setting URL: http://www.cakesolutions.net
```

Spring has, using the built-in PropertyEditors, converted the String representations of the various properties to the correct types. Table 4-2 summarizes the built-in PropertyEditor implementations available in Spring.

Table 4-2. *Spring PropertyEditor Implementations*

PropertyEditor	Registered By Default?	Description
ByteArrayPropertyEditor	Yes	This PropertyEditor converts a String value into an array of bytes.
ClassEditor	Yes	The ClassEditor converts from a fully qualified class name into a Class instance. When using this PropertyEditor, be careful not to include any extraneous spaces on either side of the class name when using XmlBeanFactory, because this results in a ClassNotFoundException.
CustomBooleanEditor	No	This customizable editor for Boolean values is intended to be used in UI-centric code, where it can parse different String representations of Boolean values; for example, “Yes”/“No” or “Ano”/“Ne”.
CustomCollectionEditor	No	This PropertyEditor can be used to create any type of the Java Collections framework or an array.

PropertyEditor	Registered By Default?	Description
CustomDateEditor	No	Just like the CustomBooleanEditor, this PropertyEditor is typically used in the controller's initBinder method to enable the application to parse dates entered in a locale-specific format to a java.util.Date.
CustomNumberEditor	No	This PropertyEditor converts a String into an Integer, a Long, a BigDecimal, or any other Number subclass.
FileEditor	Yes	The FileEditor converts a String file path into a File instance. Spring does not check to see if the file (or directory) exists.
InputStreamEditor	Yes	This editor will convert a String into an InputStream. Note that this PropertyEditor is a not reflective; it can only convert String to InputStream, not the other way around. Internally, the conversion is achieved by instantiating a temporary ResourceEditor for a Resource.
LocaleEditor	Yes	The LocaleEditor converts the String representation of a locale, such as en-GB, into a java.util.Locale instance.
PatternEditor	Yes	This ResourceEditor converts a regular expression (passed in as a String) into a java.util.regex.Pattern instance.
PropertiesEditor	Yes	PropertiesEditor converts a String in the format key1=value1\n key2=value2\n key*n*=value*n* into an instance of java.util.Properties with the corresponding properties configured.
StringArrayPropertyEditor	Yes	The StringArrayPropertyEditor class converts a comma-separated list of String elements into a String array.
StringTrimmerEditor	No	The StringTrimmerEditor can be used to trim nonempty Strings and to transform each empty String into null.
URLEditor	Yes	The URLEditor converts a String representation of a URL into an instance of java.net.URL.

This set of PropertyEditors provides a good base for working with Spring and makes configuring your application with common components, such as files and URLs, much simpler.

Creating a Custom PropertyEditor

Although the built-in PropertyEditors cover some of the standard cases of property type conversion, a time may come when you need to create your own PropertyEditor to support a class or a set of classes you are using in your application.

Spring has full support for registering a custom PropertyEditor; the only downside is that the java.beans.PropertyEditor interface has a lot of methods, many of which are irrelevant to the task at hand—converting property types. Thankfully, Spring provides the PropertyEditorSupport class, which your own PropertyEditors can extend, leaving you to implement only a single method: setAsText().

In a recent application we built using Spring, we wanted to externalize the complex numbers we used in the application. At first glance, we thought the way to do this was to expose the complex numbers as String-typed properties, and then, in an initialization callback, use a utility class to convert the String values into the complex number objects. However, by employing a custom PropertyEditor, we discovered that we could expose Complex type properties and have the PropertyEditor perform the compilation as the property values are set. Let's begin by looking at our simplified Complex class in Listing 4-46.

Listing 4-46. *The Simple Implementation of the Complex Class*

```
public final class Complex {
    private double re;
    private double im;

    public Complex(Double re, Double im) {
        if (re != null) this.re = re;
        if (im != null) this.im = im;
    }

    public double getRe() {
        return re;
    }

    public double getIm() {
        return im;
    }

    public Complex add(Complex rhs) {
        return new Complex(this.re + rhs.re, this.im + rhs.im);
    }

    @Override
    public String toString() {
        final StringBuilder sb = new StringBuilder();
        sb.append("(").append(this.re);
        if (this.im > 0) sb.append("+");
        sb.append(this.im).append(")");
        return sb.toString();
    }
}
```

The implementation is straightforward, but we have removed most of the complex algebra methods for simplicity. The interesting part is the PropertyEditor that allows us to convert String instances to Complex instances (see Listing 4-47).

Listing 4-47. *The ComplexPropertyEditor Class*

```
public class ComplexPropertyEditor extends PropertyEditorSupport {
    private static final String MINUS_SIGN = "-";
    private static final String COMPLEX_UNIT = "j";
    private static final Pattern COMPLEX_PATTERN =
        Pattern.compile("([+\\-])?([0-9.]+)([j]?)", Pattern.CASE_INSENSITIVE);

    public void setAsText(String s) throws IllegalArgumentException {
        Matcher matcher = COMPLEX_PATTERN.matcher(s);
        Double re = null;
        Double im = null;
```

```
        while (matcher.find()) {
            if (COMPLEX_UNIT.equalsIgnoreCase(matcher.group(3))) {
                im = getValue(matcher);
            } else {
                re = getValue(matcher);
            }
        }
        if (re == null && im == null) {
            throw new IllegalArgumentException(
                "Cannot convert value " + s + " to " + Complex.class.getName());
        } else {
            setValue(new Complex(re, im));
        }
    }

    private double getValue(Matcher matcher) {
        double d;
        d = Double.parseDouble(matcher.group(2));
        if (MINUS_SIGN.equals(matcher.group(1))) d = -d;
        return d;
    }
}
```

As you can see, the code in the `PropertyEditor` is not too difficult and simply parses the input text, constructs the `Complex` instance, and sets the value of the underlying property.

In Listing 4-48, you can see a simple bean that sums the complex numbers and displays the result.

Listing 4-48. *The CustomEditorExample Bean*

```
public class CustomEditorDemo {
    private Complex[] values;

    public static void main(String[] args) {
        ConfigurableListableBeanFactory factory = new XmlBeanFactory(
                new ClassPathResource("/META-INF/spring/pedemo2-context.xml")
        );

        factory.addPropertyEditorRegistrar(new PropertyEditorRegistrar() {
            public void registerCustomEditors(PropertyEditorRegistry registry) {
                registry.registerCustomEditor(Complex.class,
                    new ComplexPropertyEditor());
            }
        });
        CustomEditorDemo bean =
                (CustomEditorDemo) factory.getBean("exampleBean");

        System.out.println(bean.sum());
    }

    private Complex sum() {
        Complex result = new Complex(0d, 0d);
        for (Complex value : this.values) {
            result = result.add(value);
        }
        return result;
    }
```

```
    public void setValues(Complex[] values) {
        this.values = values;
    }

}
```

The most complex part of using a custom PropertyEditor is the registration process. You can register your PropertyEditor with Spring in one of two ways. The first is by calling ConfigurableBeanFactory.addPropertyEditorRegistrar() and passing the implementation of PropertyEditorRegistrar. Then, you can register the PropertyEditor implementations in the PropertyEditorRegistrar.registerCustomEditors method.

The second, and preferred, mechanism is to define a bean of type CustomEditorConfigurer in your BeanFactory configuration, specifying the editors in a Map-typed property of that bean. In addition to using a Map of custom PropertyEditors, you can use a list of beans of type PropertyEditorRegistrar. The main benefit of using the implementation of the PropertyEditorRegistrar is the MVC framework, where you can use your PropertyEditorRegistrar bean's registerCustomEditors in the initBinder method. For more information about Spring MVC, go to Chapter 17.

The CustomEditorConfigurer is an example of a BeanFactoryPostProcessor, a class that can make changes to a BeanFactory's configuration before the application uses it. Other common bean factory post-processors are PropertyPlaceholderConfigurer and PropertyOverrideConfigurer. You can find more information about these classes in the Spring documentation. The only drawback of using a BeanFactoryPostProcessor with a BeanFactory is that post-processors are not applied automatically. However, as you will see shortly, this is not a problem you encounter when using the ApplicationContext, which is one of the reasons ApplicationContext is preferred over BeanFactory for most applications.

Listing 4-49 shows a BeanFactory configuration that configures a CustomEditorConfigurer and the ComplexPropertyEditor.

Listing 4-49. *Using CustomEditorConfigurer*

```
<?xml version="1.0" encoding="UTF-8"?>
<beans xmlns="http://www.springframework.org/schema/beans"
       xmlns:xsi="http://www.w3.org/2001/XMLSchema-instance"
       xsi:schemaLocation="
                http://www.springframework.org/schema/beans
                http://www.springframework.org/schema/beans/spring-beans.xsd">

    <bean id="customEditorConfigurer"
        class="org.springframework.beans.factory.config.CustomEditorConfigurer">
        <property name="customEditors">
            <map>
                <entry key="com.apress.prospring2.ch04.pe.Complex">
                    <bean class="com.apress.prospring2.ch04.pe.➥
                        ComplexPropertyEditor"/>
                </entry>
            </map>
        </property>
    </bean>

    <bean id="exampleBean" class="com.apress.prospring2.ch04.pe.CustomEditorDemo">
        <property name="values">
            <list>
                <value>10</value>
                <value>-10j</value>
                <value>10+30j</value>
```

```
            </list>
        </property>
    </bean>

</beans>
```

You should notice three points in this configuration. The first is that the custom PropertyEditors are injected into the CustomEditorConfigurer class using the Map-typed customEditors property. The second point is that each entry in the Map represents a single PropertyEditor with the key of the entry being the name of the class for which the PropertyEditor is used. As you can see, the key for the PatternPropertyEditor is com.apress.prospring2.ch04.pe.Complex, which signifies that this is the class for which the editor should be used. The final point of interest here is that we used an anonymous bean declaration as the value of the single Map entry. No other bean needs to access this bean, so it needs no name, and as a result, you can declare it inside of the <entry> tag.

Listing 4-50 shows the code for the CustomEditorExample class that is registered as a bean in Listing 4-49.

Listing 4-50. *The CustomEditorExample Class*

```
public class CustomEditorDemo {
    private Complex[] values;

    public static void main(String[] args) {
        ConfigurableListableBeanFactory factory = new XmlBeanFactory(
                new ClassPathResource("/META-INF/spring/pedemo2-context.xml")
        );

        CustomEditorConfigurer configurer =
           (CustomEditorConfigurer)factory.getBean("customEditorConfigurer");
        configurer.postProcessBeanFactory(factory);

        CustomEditorDemo bean =
                (CustomEditorDemo) factory.getBean("exampleBean");

        System.out.println(bean.sum());
    }

    private Complex sum() {
        Complex result = new Complex(0d, 0d);
        for (Complex value : this.values) {
            result = result.add(value);
        }
        return result;
    }

    public void setValues(Complex[] values) {
        this.values = values;
    }

}
```

Most of this code is fairly intuitive; and in both cases, the value printed out is (20.0+20.0j). The only point of interest in the second example is the call to CustomEditorConfigurer.postProcessBeanFactory(), which passes in the BeanFactory instance. This is where the custom editors are registered in Spring; you should call this before you attempt to access any beans that need to use the custom PropertyEditors. Read on to see how we can avoid this fairly clumsy call!

Choosing a Registration Process

Even though we have shown the programmatic registration process, we believe that in all cases, the declarative process is better suited to the needs of most, if not all, applications. When using the programmatic process, adding a new `PropertyEditor` means changing the application code, whereas with the declarative mechanism, you can simply update the configuration. Using the declarative mechanism also encourages you to define your editors as beans, which means you can configure them using DI.

When using a `BeanFactory`, you require roughly the same amount of Java code for each mechanism as when you are registering a single `PropertyEditor`. When using an `ApplicationContext`, you require no Java code whatsoever to use the declarative mechanism, which strengthens the argument against using the programmatic mechanism.

Before moving on, let's recap. By using custom `PropertyEditor` implementations, you can avoid exposing a lot of unnecessary `String`-typed properties on your beans. However, they are not always the ideal solution. We chose the complex number editor to demonstrate this.

In general, you can use a `PropertyEditor` when the entire identity and configuration of the `Object` can be represented as a `String`, or where the configuration can be changed or derived from the identity.

The BeanPostProcessor

Sometimes, you may find yourself in a position where you need to perform some additional processing immediately before and after Spring instantiates the bean. The processing can be as simple as modifying the bean or as complex as returning a completely different object! The `BeanPostProcessor` interface has two methods: `postProcessBeforeInitialization`, which is called before Spring calls any bean initialization hooks (such as `InitializingBean.afterPropertiesSet` or the `init-method`), and `postProcessAfterInitialization`, which Spring calls after the initialization hooks succeed.

To demonstrate the simple case, let's reimplement bean initialization and destruction using annotations. Listing 4-51 shows a simple bean with methods annotated with the JSR 250 annotations.

Listing 4-51. *Annotated Bean Example*

```
public class SimpleBean {

    @PostConstruct
    public void initialize() {
        System.out.println("Initializing bean " + getClass());
    }

    @PreDestroy
    public void cleanUp() {
        System.out.println("Cleaning up bean " + getClass());
    }

}
```

We would like Spring to use these annotations automatically, so we do not want to specify the `init-method` or `destroy-method` attributes in the `<bean>` definition in the `BeanFactory` configuration. However, we can use `InitDestroyAnnotationBeanPostProcessor`, an implementation of `BeanPostProcessor` that invokes all methods on the target bean with the configured initialization annotation. Because it also implements the `DestructionAwareBeanPostProcessor`, it invokes all methods on the target bean annotated with the destruction annotation. Listing 4-52 shows the `SimpleBean` and the `InitDestroyBeanPostProcessor` bean definitions.

Listing 4-52. *BeanFactory Configuration File*

```
<?xml version="1.0" encoding="UTF-8"?>
<beans xmlns="http://www.springframework.org/schema/beans"
       xmlns:xsi="http://www.w3.org/2001/XMLSchema-instance"
       xsi:schemaLocation="
                http://www.springframework.org/schema/beans
                http://www.springframework.org/schema/beans/spring-beans.xsd">

    <bean id="simpleBean" class="com.apress.prospring2.ch04.bpp.SimpleBean"/>
    <bean id="bpp"
        class="org.springframework.beans.factory.annotation.➥
             InitDestroyAnnotationBeanPostProcessor">
        <property name="initAnnotationType" value="javax.annotation.PostConstruct"/>
        <property name="destroyAnnotationType" value="javax.annotation.PreDestroy"/>
    </bean>

</beans>
```

You can see that we have declared the `simpleBean` bean without `init-method` or `destroy-method`. We have also declared the `InitDestroyAnnotationBeanPostProcessor` and set its `initAnnotationType` and `destroyAnnotationType` to the JSR 250 annotations. This code may look complicated, but it means that we can specify any type of annotation; we do not have to use JSR 250 annotations. Finally, the example application in Listing 4-53 demonstrates that the `BeanPostProcessor` really initializes and destroys the bean.

Listing 4-53. *Sample Application for the InitDestroyAnnotationBeanPostProcessor*

```
public class SimpleBeanDemo {

    public static void main(String[] args) {
        ConfigurableListableBeanFactory beanFactory = new XmlBeanFactory(
                new ClassPathResource("/META-INF/spring/bpp-context.xml")
        );
        BeanPostProcessor bpp = (BeanPostProcessor)beanFactory.getBean("bpp");
        beanFactory.addBeanPostProcessor(bpp);

        SimpleBean sb = (SimpleBean)beanFactory.getBean("simpleBean");
        System.out.println(sb);

        beanFactory.destroySingletons();
    }

}
```

When we run the application, it prints out the following output:

```
INFO [main] XmlBeanDefinitionReader.loadBeanDefinitions(308) | ➥
Loading XML bean definitions from class path resource ➥
[META-INF/spring/bpp-context.xml]
Initializing bean class com.apress.prospring2.ch04.bpp.SimpleBean
com.apress.prospring2.ch04.bpp.SimpleBean@c16c2c0
INFO [main] DefaultSingletonBeanRegistry.destroySingletons(340) | ➥
Destroying singletons in org.springframework.beans.factory.xml.➥
XmlBeanFactory@2a4bd173: defining beans [simpleBean,bpp]; root of factory hierarchy
Cleaning up bean class com.apress.prospring2.ch04.bpp.SimpleBean
```

This proves that the `BeanPostProcessor` calls the `simpleBean`'s annotated methods at the correct point in the application life cycle.

This was a simple usage of `BeanPostProcessor`: it modifies an existing bean, but it does not change it in any fundamental way. In Chapter 5 and Chapter 14, you will see that there are bean post-processors that completely change the type of the bean—really! Figure 4-2 shows that the type of the `textSource` bean returned from the `BeanFactory` is `Messenger`, but Listing 4-54 shows that the type of the `textSource` bean is `GroovyScriptFactory`. The `ScriptFactoryPostProcessor` turns, in this instance, the `GroovyScriptFactory` beans into beans of a type that are implemented in the Groovy script.

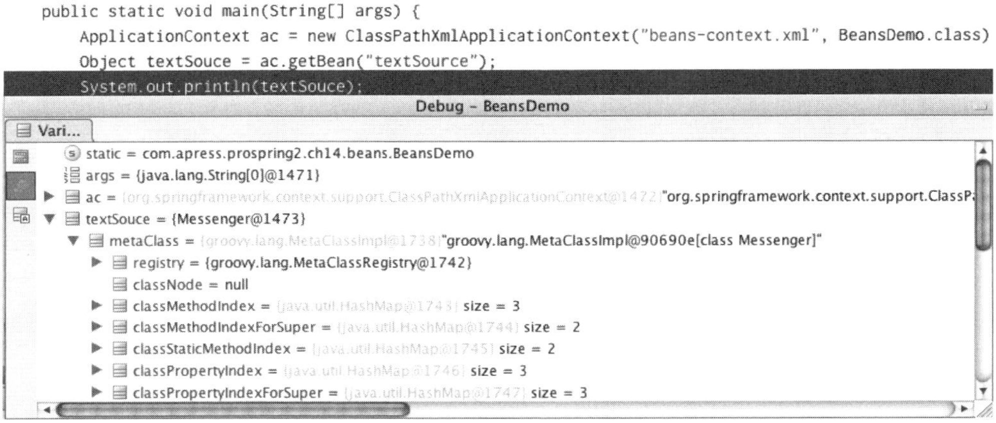

```
public static void main(String[] args) {
    ApplicationContext ac = new ClassPathXmlApplicationContext("beans-context.xml", BeansDemo.class)
    Object textSouce = ac.getBean("textSource");
    System.out.println(textSouce);
```

```
Debug - BeansDemo
Vari...
static = com.apress.prospring2.ch14.beans.BeansDemo
args = {java.lang.String[0]@1471}
ac = "org.springframework.context.support.ClassP
textSouce = {Messenger@1473}
  metaClass = "groovy.lang.MetaClassImpl@90690e[class Messenger]"
    registry = {groovy.lang.MetaClassRegistry@1742}
    classNode = null
    classMethodIndex = size = 3
    classMethodIndexForSuper = size = 2
    classStaticMethodIndex = size = 2
    classPropertyIndex = size = 3
    classPropertyIndexForSuper = size = 3
```

Figure 4-2. *BeanPostProcessor returning a different bean type*

Listing 4-54. *Definition of the textSource Bean*

```
<bean id="textSource"
    class="org.springframework.scripting.groovy.GroovyScriptFactory">
    <constructor-arg>
        <value>inline:
            class Messenger
                implements com.apress.prospring2.ch14.beans.TextSource {
                public String getMessage() { return &quot;Hello&quot; }
            }
        </value>
    </constructor-arg>
</bean>
```

Do not worry about the Groovy script; we simply wanted to explain what `BeanPostProcessors` can do in detail. We cover the dynamic language `BeanPostProcessor` implementations in Chapter 14.

Implementing a BeanPostProcessor

Let's create a simple `BeanPostProcessor` that can timestamp our beans. The aim is to set the `Date` fields annotated with the `@Timestamp` annotation from Listing 4-55.

Listing 4-55. *@Timestamp Annotation*

```
@Retention(RetentionPolicy.RUNTIME)
@Target(ElementType.FIELD)
public @interface Timestamp {
}
```

Listing 4-56 shows the new `creationDate` field in the `SimpleBean` class from Listing 4-51.

Listing 4-56. *Modified SimpleBean with the @Timestamp Field*

```
public class SimpleBean {
    @Timestamp
    Date creationDate;

    @PostConstruct
    public void initialize() {
        System.out.println("Initializing bean " + getClass());
    }

    @PreDestroy
    public void cleanUp() {
        System.out.println("Cleaning up bean " + getClass());
    }

    @Override
    public String toString() {
        return "Bean was created at " + this.creationDate;
    }

}
```

We now have a field annotated with `@Timestamp`; we now need to write a `BeanPostProcessor` that checks every bean and sets its annotated `Date` fields to the current `Date`. Listing 4-57 shows our implementation of the `TimestampingBeanPostProcessor` that does just that.

Listing 4-57. *TimestampingBeanPostProcessor*

```
public class TimestampingBeanPostProcessor implements BeanPostProcessor {

    public Object postProcessBeforeInitialization(final Object bean,
        final String beanName) throws BeansException {

        ReflectionUtils.doWithFields(bean.getClass(),
            new ReflectionUtils.FieldCallback() {
                public void doWith(Field field) throws IllegalArgumentException,
                    IllegalAccessException {
                    field.set(bean, new Date());
                }
            }, new ReflectionUtils.FieldFilter() {
            public boolean matches(Field field) {
                return field.getType() == Date.class &&
                        field.getAnnotation(Timestamp.class) != null;
            }
        });
        return bean;
    }
```

```
    public Object postProcessAfterInitialization(Object bean, String beanName)
        throws BeansException {
        return bean;
    }
}
```

We have only implemented the `postProcessBeforeInitialization`, because we wanted to record the timestamp when Spring begins the bean instantiation. Even though the reflection code is not simple, its function is. It scans all fields of all beans and sets those that have the `@Timestamp` annotation and are of the `Date` type. We need to modify the `BeanFactory` configuration file and the example application to register the `TimestampingBeanPostProcessor` bean. Listing 4-58 shows the addition to the `BeanFactory` configuration file.

Listing 4-58. *The TimestampingBeanPostProcessor Bean*

```
<bean id="bpp2"
     class="com.apress.prospring2.ch04.bpp.TimestampingBeanPostProcessor"/>
```

The modification to the sample application is very simple too; Listing 4-59 shows that we get the `bpp2` bean and use it in the call to the `addBeanPostProcessor` call.

Listing 4-59. *Modified Sample Application*

```
public class SimpleBeanDemo {

    public static void main(String[] args) {
        ConfigurableListableBeanFactory beanFactory = new XmlBeanFactory(
                new ClassPathResource("/META-INF/spring/bpp-context.xml")
        );
        BeanPostProcessor bpp = (BeanPostProcessor)beanFactory.getBean("bpp");
        BeanPostProcessor bpp2 = (BeanPostProcessor)beanFactory.getBean("bpp2");
        beanFactory.addBeanPostProcessor(bpp);
        beanFactory.addBeanPostProcessor(bpp2);

        SimpleBean sb = (SimpleBean)beanFactory.getBean("simpleBean");
        System.out.println(sb);

        beanFactory.destroySingletons();
    }

}
```

Running the modified example application produces output that shows that the `TimestampingBeanPostProcessor` works:

```
INFO [main] XmlBeanDefinitionReader.loadBeanDefinitions(308) | ➥
Loading XML bean definitions from class path resource ➥
[META-INF/spring/bpp-context.xml]
Initializing bean class com.apress.prospring2.ch04.bpp.SimpleBean
Bean was created at Fri Mar 28 11:00:02 GMT 2008
INFO [main] DefaultSingletonBeanRegistry.destroySingletons(340) | ➥
Destroying singletons in org.springframework.beans.factory.xml.➥
XmlBeanFactory@f292738: defining beans [simpleBean,bpp,bpp2]; ➥
root of factory hierarchy
Cleaning up bean class com.apress.prospring2.ch04.bpp.SimpleBean
```

It also shows that Spring combines all BeanPostProcessors to create the final instance of the bean: in this case, it has used the TimestampingBeanPostProcessor and the InitDestroyAnnotationBeanPostProcessor. The approach we have taken is the simplest one, but it requires that the target field is not private. It would be better to allow the BeanPostProcessor to also call methods with the @Timestamp annotation and one argument of type java.util.Date, but doing so would only make the post-processor code more complex.

If we are implementing a BeanPostProcessor similar to the ScriptFactoryPostProcessor—in other words, a BeanPostProcessor that changes the type of the bean—we should not simply implement the BeanPostProcessor interface and return a different type of bean from its postProcessBeforeInitialization or postProcessAfterInitialization methods. The reason is that if the bean that is the target of the post processing is a dependency of another bean, Spring is unable to determine its post-processed type, which means that it cannot use the post-processed bean in by-type automatic wiring.

As an example, let's create a simple Dependency class with no additional properties and modify the SimpleBean (see Listing 4-60).

Listing 4-60. *SimpleBean with the @Autowired, @PostConstruct, and @PreDestroy Annotations*

```
public class SimpleBean {
    @Timestamp
    Date creationDate;

    @Autowired
    String dependency;

    @PostConstruct
    public void initialize() {
        System.out.println("Initializing bean " + getClass());
    }

    @PreDestroy
    public void cleanUp() {
        System.out.println("Cleaning up bean " + getClass());
    }

    @Override
    public String toString() {
        return "Bean was created at " + this.creationDate + " with " +
            this.dependency;
    }
}
```

Here, we can see that we have declared automatically wired field String dependency. If we implement only the BeanPostProcessor interface to change the type of the Dependency bean to String, the automatic wiring will fail. The output of running the sample application proves this:

```
INFO [main] XmlBeanDefinitionReader.loadBeanDefinitions(308) | ➥
Loading XML bean definitions from class path resource ➥
[META-INF/spring/bpp2-context.xml]
Exception in thread "main" org.springframework.beans.factory.BeanCreationException: ➥
Error creating bean with name 'simpleBean': Autowiring of fields failed; ➥
nested exception is org.springframework.beans.factory.BeanCreationException:➥
Could not autowire field: ➥
java.lang.String com.apress.prospring2.ch04.bpp.SimpleBean.dependency;
...
```

Clearly, Spring did not know that a BeanPostProcessor will turn Dependency into String. Spring provides a BeanPostProcessor subinterface, SmartInstantiationAwareBeanPostProcessor, that can deal with this situation. However, this interface is intended for internal use within the framework and may change between even minor revisions of Spring. As users of the Spring Framework, we should use the InstantiationAwareBeanPostProcessorAdapter, which implements SmartInstantiationAwareBeanPostProcessor but provides a stable signature. Let's use that post-processor adapter to implement a BeanPostProcessor that can predict the type of the post-processed bean (see Listing 4-61).

Listing 4-61. *Using InstantiationAwareBeanPostProcessorAdapter*

```
public class TypedDependencyBeanPostProcessor extends
    InstantiationAwareBeanPostProcessorAdapter {

    public Class predictBeanType(Class beanClass, String beanName) {
        if (beanClass.equals(Dependency.class)) {
            return String.class;
        }
        return beanClass;
    }

    public Object postProcessBeforeInitialization(final Object bean,
        final String beanName)
        throws BeansException {
        if (bean.getClass().equals(Dependency.class)) {
            return "Hello, world";
        }
        return bean;
    }

    public Object postProcessAfterInitialization(Object bean, String beanName)
        throws BeansException {
        return bean;
    }
}
```

The BeanPostProcessor implementation is very simple: we turn all Dependency objects into String objects, but we also predict that we'll do just that in the predictBeanType method. Running the sample application now shows that Spring can automatically wire our String property:

```
INFO [main] XmlBeanDefinitionReader.loadBeanDefinitions(308) | ➥
Loading XML bean definitions from class path resource ➥
[META-INF/spring/bpp2-context.xml]
Initializing bean class com.apress.prospring2.ch04.bpp.SimpleBean
Bean was created at Fri Mar 28 11:44:59 GMT 2008 with Hello, world
INFO [main] DefaultSingletonBeanRegistry.destroySingletons(340) | ➥
Destroying singletons in org.springframework.beans.factory.xml.➥
XmlBeanFactory@6e681db8: defining beans ...
Cleaning up bean class com.apress.prospring2.ch04.bpp.SimpleBean
```

When to Use BeanPostProcessor

Clearly, you can do a lot with a BeanPostProcessor; in fact, you could be tempted to post-process every bean in your application. While there is no harm in post-processing that changes the bean definition (such as adding initialization and destruction methods), you need to be much more careful with post-processing that changes the type or behavior of beans—doing this makes the dependencies in the application less clear.

The Spring Framework uses the first type of post-processors to set annotated dependencies, and provide initialization and destruction methods. It uses the second type of post-processing to deal with the dynamic language beans and to turn `@Aspect`-annotated beans into real aspects.

We have found that good situations when to use `BeanPostProcessor` implementations are those when you need an instance of a bean that you then transform into another type of bean. We have taken this approach in the Service Orchestration Spring Module, where we turn beans annotated with the `@State` definition into `StateDefinition` beans.

The Spring ApplicationContext

So far, all interaction with Spring has been via the `BeanFactory` interface and its subinterfaces. Although using the `BeanFactory` interface is a good way of interacting with Spring in the sample applications, it lacks the features you need in normal applications. Recall that, in some of the previous examples, we had to call control methods on the `BeanFactory`, such as `preInstantiateSingletons()`, or we had to invoke a `BeanFactoryPostProcessor` manually, as in the case of the `CustomEditorConfigurer`. This is where the `ApplicationContext` comes in.

`ApplicationContext` is an extension of `BeanFactory`: it provides all the same functionality, but it reduces the amount of code you need to interact with it and adds new features into the pot for good measure. When using an `ApplicationContext`, you can control bean instantiation declaratively on a bean-by-bean basis, and any `BeanPostProcessors` and `BeanFactoryPostProcessors` registered in the `ApplicationContext` are executed automatically for you.

The main function of the `ApplicationContext` is to provide a much richer framework on which to build your applications. An `ApplicationContext` is much more aware of the beans that you configure within it than a bean factory is, and in the case of many of the Spring infrastructure classes and interfaces, such as `BeanFactoryPostProcessor`, the `ApplicationContext` interacts with them on your behalf, reducing the amount of code you need to write to use Spring.

The biggest benefit of using `ApplicationContext` is that it allows you to configure and manage Spring and Spring-managed resources in a completely declarative way. This means that wherever possible, Spring provides support classes to load an `ApplicationContext` into your application automatically, thus removing the need for you to write any code to access the `ApplicationContext`. In practice, this feature is currently only available when you are building web applications with Spring, so Spring also provides implementations of `ApplicationContext` you can create yourself.

In addition to providing a model that is focused more on declarative configuration, the `ApplicationContext` supports the following features not present in a `BeanFactory`:

- Internationalization
- Event publication
- Resource management and access
- Additional life cycle interfaces
- Improved automatic configuration of infrastructure components

So should you use `ApplicationContext` or `BeanFactory`? Unless you are looking for a really lightweight IoC solution for your application, you should almost certainly use `ApplicationContext`. The additional support functionality provided by `ApplicationContext` really makes your life easier, reducing the amount of code you need to write and providing some useful additional features. When you are building a web application with Spring, having an `ApplicationContext` (actually a `WebApplicationContext`) provided for you automatically makes choosing `ApplicationContext` over `BeanFactory` a real no-brainer.

Implementations of ApplicationContext

Like `BeanFactory`, `ApplicationContext` is an interface, and you are free to provide your own implementations. Of course, creating an `ApplicationContext` is no trivial feat, so Spring provides three implementations intended for use in production applications. All three implementations use the same configuration format as the `XmlBeanFactory`. In fact, as you will see, they offer more complete support for the format than `XmlBeanFactory`.

For stand-alone applications where the `ApplicationContext` cannot be loaded automatically, you can choose from either `FileSystemXmlApplicationContext` or `ClasspathXmlApplicationContext`. These names are self-explanatory, and functionally, these classes are quite similar. With `FileSystemXmlApplicationContext`, you can load the configuration from anywhere in the file system provided your application has permissions. Using `ClasspathXmlApplicationContext`, you can load from anywhere on the classpath; this is useful if you want to package the configuration with a bunch of classes inside a JAR file.

The `XmlWebApplicationContext` is intended solely for use in a web application environment, and as you will see in Chapter 17, by using either `ContextLoaderListener` or `ContextLoaderServlet`, you can load the `ApplicationContext` configuration automatically for your web application.

For the rest of this chapter, we will be using the `ClasspathXmlApplicationContext` to run the examples. Also notice the location of the `ApplicationContext` configuration files: `/META-INF/spring/*-context.xml`. Storing the files in this location allows you to load all Spring `ApplicationContext` configuration files in one call, using Ant-style wildcards.

Using ApplicationContextAware

Earlier in the chapter, you saw how a bean can obtain a reference to its `BeanFactory` by implementing the `BeanFactoryAware` interface. In the same way, a bean can obtain a reference to its `ApplicationContext` by implementing `ApplicationContextAware`. Listing 4-62 shows a bean that implements this interface.

Listing 4-62. *Implementing ApplicationContextAware*

```
public class ContextAwareDemo implements ApplicationContextAware {
    private ApplicationContext ctx;

    public void setApplicationContext(ApplicationContext applicationContext)
            throws BeansException {
        ctx = applicationContext;
    }

    public static void main(String[] args) {
        ApplicationContext ctx = new ClassPathXmlApplicationContext(
                "/META-INF/spring/acdemo1-context.xml");

        ContextAwareDemo demo = (ContextAwareDemo) ctx.getBean("contextAware");
        demo.displayAppContext();
    }

    public void displayAppContext() {
        System.out.println(ctx);
    }

}
```

The ApplicationContextAware interface declares a single method, setApplicationContext(), and implementing the interface is very much like implementing BeanFactoryAware. In the main() method, we create an instance of FileSystemXmlApplicationContext, and from this, we obtain an instance of the ContextAwareDemo bean. Listing 4-63 shows the configuration for this example.

Listing 4-63. *Configuration for ContextAwareDemo Class*

```
<?xml version="1.0" encoding="UTF-8"?>
<beans xmlns="http://www.springframework.org/schema/beans"
       xmlns:xsi="http://www.w3.org/2001/XMLSchema-instance"
       xsi:schemaLocation="
                http://www.springframework.org/schema/beans
                http://www.springframework.org/schema/beans/spring-beans.xsd">

    <bean id="contextAware"
       class="com.apress.prospring2.ch04.context.ContextAwareDemo"/>

</beans>
```

Notice that although we are using ApplicationContext and not BeanFactory, the configuration format is exactly the same, meaning that using ApplicationContext is no more difficult than using BeanFactory. Running this example gives the following output:

```
org.springframework.context.support.ClassPathXmlApplicationContext@50502819: ➥
display name ➥
[org.springframework.context.support.ClassPathXmlApplicationContext@50502819]; ➥
startup date [Mon Mar 31 19:41:21 BST 2008]; root of context hierarchy
```

The ContextAwareDemo is able to obtain a reference to its ApplicationContext and display its details. The comments about the use of the BeanFactoryAware interface also apply to this interface.

Controlling Bean Initialization

Recall that, in an earlier example, we built a ShutdownHookBean class that automatically registered a shutdown hook Thread with the JVM to dispose of all singletons in the BeanFactory. You might also remember that to ensure that the ShutdownHookBean was instantiated, we had to call the preInstantiateSingletons() method of the BeanFactory. This is slightly annoying, because it means that an application has to have prior knowledge of the configuration; it also means that all singletons, not just the one we want, are instantiated in advance.

When using ApplicationContext, there is a solution to this problem: the lazy-init attribute. By setting the lazy-init attribute on a bean's <bean> tag to false, you are telling the ApplicationContext that you want to create the bean in advance and the ApplicationContext should not wait until it is first requested. Listing 4-64 shows a revised configuration for the shutdown hook bean example.

Listing 4-64. *Using lazy-init*

```
<?xml version="1.0" encoding="UTF-8"?>
<beans xmlns="http://www.springframework.org/schema/beans"
       xmlns:xsi="http://www.w3.org/2001/XMLSchema-instance"
       xsi:schemaLocation="
                http://www.springframework.org/schema/beans
                http://www.springframework.org/schema/beans/spring-beans.xsd">
```

```
    <bean id="destructiveBean"
       class="com.apress.prospring2.ch04.lifecycle.DestructiveBeanI">
        <property name="filePath" value="/tmp/prospring"/>
    </bean>

    <bean id="shutdownHook"
          lazy-init="false"
          class="com.apress.prospring2.ch04.interaction.ShutdownHookBean"/>

</beans>
```

Notice that, for the `shutdownHook` bean, we set the `lazy-init` attribute to `false`. Although `lazy-init` is `false` by default in many of the Spring implementations of `ApplicationContext`, there is no harm in making it explicit—this way, the `ApplicationContext` implementation won't affect your bean. In Listing 4-65, you can see a revised driver application for this example, which omits the call to `preInstantiateSingletons()`.

Listing 4-65. *The LazyInitDemo Class*

```
public class LazyInitDemo {

    public static void main(String[] args) {
        ApplicationContext ctx = new ClassPathXmlApplicationContext(
                "/META-INF/spring/acdemo2-context.xml");

        ctx.getBean("destructiveBean");
    }

}
```

Running this example results in the same output as before but without the need to call `preInstantiateSingletons()`:

```
INFO [main] AbstractApplicationContext.prepareRefresh(400) | Refreshing ➥
org.springframework.context.support.ClassPathXmlApplicationContext@53077fc9: ➥
display name [org.springframework.context.support.➥
ClassPathXmlApplicationContext@53077fc9]; ➥
startup date [Mon Mar 31 19:46:52 BST 2008]; root of context hierarchy
INFO [main] XmlBeanDefinitionReader.loadBeanDefinitions(308) | ➥
Loading XML bean definitions from class path resource ➥
[META-INF/spring/acdemo2-context.xml]
INFO [main] AbstractApplicationContext.obtainFreshBeanFactory(415) | ➥
Bean factory for application context ➥
[org.springframework.context.support.ClassPathXmlApplicationContext@53077fc9]: ➥
org.springframework.beans.factory.support.DefaultListableBeanFactory@395fd251
INFO [main] DefaultListableBeanFactory.preInstantiateSingletons(385) | ➥
Pre-instantiating singletons in org.springframework.beans.factory.support.➥
DefaultListableBeanFactory@395fd251: defining beans ...
Initializing Bean
INFO [Thread-0] ShutdownHookBean.run(27) | Destroying singletons.
INFO [Thread-0] DefaultSingletonBeanRegistry.destroySingletons(340) | ➥
Destroying singletons in ➥
org.springframework.beans.factory.support.DefaultListableBeanFactory@395fd251: ➥
defining beans [destructiveBean,shutdownHook]; root of factory hierarchy
Destroying Bean
```

Using the ShutdownHookBean is clearly beneficial, because it lets you have fine-grained control over when each bean in your application is created without having to modify any of the application code.

Using Annotation-Based Configuration

So far, we have configured our beans in the XML configuration files. Starting with Spring 2.0, you can use annotations to configure your beans. By annotating your classes, you state their typical usage or stereotype. Table 4-3 summarizes the annotations in Spring 2.5.

Table 4-3. *Stereotype Annotations in Spring 2.5*

Annotation	Description
`@Component`	This is the basic stereotype; classes annotated with `@Component` will become Spring beans.
`@Controller`	Spring will use any class annotated with the `@Controller` annotation as a `Controller` in Spring MVC support.
`@Repository`	Classes with the `@Repository` annotation represent a repository (e.g., a data access object).
`@Service`	The `@Service` annotation marks classes that implement a part of the business logic of the application.

When Spring discovers one of these annotations, it creates the appropriate bean. By "appropriate," we mean the bean Spring creates has behavior that matches the stereotype. Classes annotated with the `@Controller` annotation become Spring MVC controllers; classes with the `@Repository` annotation get automatic exception translation; `@Service`- and `@Component`-annotated classes do not change the default behavior of the bean but may carry additional semantics in the future versions of Spring.

Automatically Detecting Annotated Classes

Without being able to automatically detect the annotated classes, you would not find annotations very usable. Take a look at the code in Listing 4-66, which shows a class with the `@Component` annotation.

Listing 4-66. *SimplestBean Class with the @Component Annotation*

```
@Component
public class SimplestBean {

    @Override
    public String toString() {
        final StringBuilder sb = new StringBuilder();
        sb.append("SimplestBean");
        sb.append("{}");
        return sb.toString();
    }
}
```

Because we have the `@Component` annotation, we would like Spring (the `ApplicationContext`, to be more exact) to automatically pick up this class and turn it into a Spring-managed bean so that we can ultimately use it in an application similar to one in Listing 4-67.

Listing 4-67. *Sample Application for the Annotation-Based Configuration*

```
public class AnnotationDemo1 {

    public static void main(String[] args) {
        ApplicationContext ac = new ClassPathXmlApplicationContext(
                "/META-INF/spring/annotationdemo1-context.xml"
        );
        System.out.println(ac.getBean("simplestBean"));
    }

}
```

We can obviously define the `simplestBean` bean in the configuration file, but we would like to avoid writing any configuration at all for the `simplestBean`. Unfortunately, there is no way to automatically discover all classes on the classpath. Therefore, we cannot just make the `ApplicationContext` implementations scan every class on the classpath and check whether they have the appropriate annotation.

■ **Note** Even if we could scan the entire classpath and discover the annotated classes, doing so would not be a good idea. Loading all classes on the classpath could take far too long. Even worse, there could be annotated classes that we simply do not want to use.

However, we can scan a particular package (and its subpackages) for annotated classes; to do that, we simply use the `<context:component-scan />` element in the `ApplicationContext` XML configuration file. Listing 4-68 shows the `ApplicationContext` XML configuration file for the sample application.

Listing 4-68. *ApplicationContext XML Configuration File*

```
<?xml version="1.0" encoding="UTF-8"?>
<beans xmlns="http://www.springframework.org/schema/beans"
       xmlns:context="http://www.springframework.org/schema/context"
       xmlns:xsi="http://www.w3.org/2001/XMLSchema-instance"
       xsi:schemaLocation="
               http://www.springframework.org/schema/beans
               http://www.springframework.org/schema/beans/spring-beans.xsd
               http://www.springframework.org/schema/context
               http://www.springframework.org/schema/context/spring-context.xsd">

    <context:component-scan base-package="com.apress.prospring2.ch04.annotations"/>

</beans>
```

Notice the declaration of the context namespace and the `<context:component-scan . . ./>` element. When we now run the sample application from Listing 4-67, it will print out this:

```
SimplestBean{}
```

This output proves that Spring has discovered the `SimplestBean` class, because we annotated it with the `@Component` annotation; it also proves that the class created a bean with the ID `simpleBean`. Let's now take a look at how you can customize the automatic discovery process: quite possibly, you'll want to assign an `id` to the beans, exclude a particular package from the automatic discovery, or use different annotations altogether.

Controlling the Automatic Detection Process

By default, Spring picks up classes annotated with the `@Component` annotation (or any other annotation that is itself annotated with the `@Component` annotation). If you want to add to this default behavior, you can use filters to include or exclude candidate classes. You can also use the `use-default-filters="false"` attribute in the `<component-scan . . ./>` element to turn off the annotation-based scanning behavior.

Whether or not you use the default scanning strategy, there are four filter types, and you need to write an expression that matches the type of the filter you use. Table 4-4 lists all filter types in Spring and provides some sample expressions.

Table 4-4. *Spring Filter Types*

Type	Description	Expression example
`annotation`	Set another type of annotation you will use to mark the classes you want Spring to scan.	`com.apress.prospring2.ch04.annotations.Magic`
`assignable`	Specify a full class name to which the candidate class should be assignable.	`com.apress.prospring2.ch04.annotations.ComponentMarker`
`regex`	Specify a regular expression that the candidate class name should match.	`com\.apress\.prospring2\.ch04\.annotation\.*`
`aspectj`	Use a pointcut-style expression to specify the class names of the candidate classes.	`com.apress..annotations.*Service*`

The example expressions in Table 4-4 are self-explanatory for annotation, assignable, and regular expression types. You may be wondering how we can use pointcut-style expression: there is nothing stopping you from writing `* void com.apress..annotations.*Service()`, which represents a method, not a class. Spring uses only the class name element of the expression during the component scan. Listing 4-69 shows a modified sample application that lists all beans in the `ApplicationContext`.

Listing 4-69. *Sample Application That Lists All Defined Beans*

```
public class AnnotationDemo2 {

    public static void main(String[] args) {
        ApplicationContext ac = new ClassPathXmlApplicationContext(
                "/META-INF/spring/annotationdemo2-context.xml"
        );
        String[] beanNames = ac.getBeanDefinitionNames();
        for (String beanName : beanNames) {
            System.out.println(beanName + ": " + ac.getBean(beanName));
        }
    }

}
```

Together with the XML configuration file in Listing 4-70, we can use this application to demonstrate the different configuration settings for component scanning.

Listing 4-70. *ApplicationContext XML Configuration File*

```
<?xml version="1.0" encoding="UTF-8"?>
<beans xmlns="http://www.springframework.org/schema/beans"
       xmlns:context="http://www.springframework.org/schema/context"
       xmlns:xsi="http://www.w3.org/2001/XMLSchema-instance"
```

```
        xsi:schemaLocation="
                http://www.springframework.org/schema/beans
                http://www.springframework.org/schema/beans/spring-beans.xsd
                http://www.springframework.org/schema/context
                http://www.springframework.org/schema/context/spring-context.xsd">

    <context:component-scan base-package="com.apress.prospring2.ch04.annotations">
        <context:include-filter type="annotation"
            expression="com.apress.prospring2.ch04.annotations.Magic"/>
        <context:include-filter type="assignable"
           expression="com.apress.prospring2.ch04.annotations.ComponentMarker"/>
        <context:include-filter type="aspectj"
            expression="* void com.apress..annotations.*Service*(..)"/>
    </context:component-scan>

</beans>
```

You can see that we have added three more filters: the annotation filter specifies that, in addition to the standard annotations, classes with the @Magic annotation should be considered bean candidates. Next, we have the assignable type, and in this example, we have chosen to create beans from classes that implement the ComponentMarker interface. As the name implies, it is a marker interface with no methods. Finally, we show that you can also use a pointcut expression and that even though you have a method-level pointcut here, Spring will only take its class name. To fully demonstrate the component scanning, we have added the CandidateService class (which matches the aspectj type expression), the MarkedBean that implements the ComponentMarker interface (which matches the assignable type expression), and the MarkedBean with the @Magic annotation (which matches the annotation type expression). When we run the application, it will print the following:

```
candidateService: CandidateService{}
markedBean: MarkedBean{}
simplestBean: SimplestBean{}
```

In addition to controlling which classes Spring will pick up as candidates for beans, you may also want to control the name Spring will choose for the beans. By default, Spring bases the bean name on the class name. The simplest way to control the naming is to provide a value in the annotations. Listing 4-71 shows the change we have made to the SimplestBean.

Listing 4-71. *SimplestBean Class with Modified @Component Annotation*

```
@Component("mostComplicatedBean")
public class SimplestBean {

    @Override
    public String toString() {
        final StringBuilder sb = new StringBuilder();
        sb.append("SimplestBean");
        sb.append("{}");
        return sb.toString();
    }
}
```

Spring will pick up the bean id from the value in the @Component annotation; therefore, the application would now print mostComplexBean: SimplestBean{} instead of simplestBean: SimplestBean{}. Controlling the bean names for beans that were picked up using not annotations, but one of the three remaining strategies is more complex: you need to implement the BeanNameGenerator interface and set it in the name-generator attribute of the <component-scan . . ./> element.

Finally, you may want to be able to control the scope of the automatically created beans. The easiest way to do so is to use the @Scope annotation and specify the name of the scope. You can use any of the scope names registered in Spring, from the basic singleton and prototype to request, session, and globalSession in web and portal applications. Alternatively, you can implement the ScopeResolver interface and specify it in the scope-resolver attribute of the <component-scan . . ./> element. To deal with the beans with request, session, and globalSession scopes, we can specify the type of the proxy Spring will return when it returns an instance of the bean using the scoped-proxy attribute in the <component-scan . . ./> element. Table 4-5 shows the possible values and their descriptions.

Table 4-5. *Values for the scoped-proxy Attribute*

Value	Description
no	Spring will always create a new instance of the dependency.
interface	Spring will create a JDK dynamic proxy using the Proxy.newProxyInstance() call, and use the returned proxy as the dependency.
targetClass	Spring will create a proxy of the same type as the dependency.

When to Use Component Scanning

Although automatic component scanning is a useful tool, XML configuration files give you better control of your application setup. There is one notable exception—the web tier. We found the @Controller annotation (together with @RequestMapping, @SessionAttributes, and many others explained in detail in Chapter 17) an excellent choice for fast MVC development. And, you are very unlikely to have two controllers performing the same functionality, unlike in the rest of the application, where you may have several implementations of a business logic interface.

In addition to MVC development, using annotations and component scanning is an excellent choice for the @AspectJ support in Spring: you will see in Chapters 5 and 6 that you can configure your application to automatically find all @AspectJ-annotated classes and automatically create the appropriate AOP proxies.

Internationalization with MessageSource

One area in which Spring really excels is in support for internationalization (i18n). Using the MessageSource interface, your application can access String resources, called messages, stored in a variety of different languages. For each language you want to support in your application, you maintain a list of messages that are keyed to correspond to messages in other languages. For instance, if I wanted to display "The quick brown fox jumped over the lazy dog" in English and in Czech, I would create two messages, both keyed as msg; the one in English would say, "The quick brown fox jumped over the lazy dog," and the one in Czech would say, "Příšerně žlut'oučký kůň úpěl d'ábelské ódy."

Although you don't need to use ApplicationContext to use MessageSource, the ApplicationContext interface actually extends MessageSource and provides special support for loading messages and making them available in your environment. Automatic loading of messages is available in any environment, but automatic access is only provided in certain Spring-managed scenarios, such as when you are using Spring's MVC framework to build a web application. Although any class can implement ApplicationContextAware, and thus access the automatically loaded messages, we suggest a better solution later in this chapter in the section entitled "Using MessageSource in Stand-Alone Applications."

Before we continue, if you are unfamiliar with internalization support in Java, we suggest that you at least check out the Javadocs for the Locale and ResourceBundle classes.

Using ApplicationContext and MessageSource

Aside from ApplicationContext, Spring provides three MessageSource implementations: ResourceBundleMessageSource, ReloadableResourceMessageSource, and StaticMessageSource. The StaticMessageSource is not really meant to be used in a production application, because you can't configure it externally, and this is generally one of the main requirements when you are adding internationalization capabilities to your application. The ResourceBundleMessageSource loads messages using a Java ResourceBundle. ReloadableResourceMessageSource is essentially the same, except it supports scheduled reloading of the underlying source files.

All of the implementations, ApplicationContext included, implement another interface called HierarchicalMessageSource, which allows for many MessageSource instances to be nested and is key to the way ApplicationContext works with message sources.

To take advantage of ApplicationContext's support for MessageSource, you must define a bean in your configuration of type MessageSource and with the name messageSource. ApplicationContext takes this MessageSource and nests it within its default MessageSource, allowing you to access the messages using the ApplicationContext. This can be hard to visualize, so take a look at the following example; Listing 4-72 shows a simple application that accesses a set of messages for both the English and Czech languages.

Listing 4-72. *Exploring MessageSource Usage*

```
public class MessageSourceDemo {
    public static void main(String[] args) {
        ApplicationContext ctx = new ClassPathXmlApplicationContext(
                "/META-INF/spring/acdemo3-context.xml");

        Locale english = Locale.ENGLISH;
        Locale czech = new Locale("cs", "CZ");

        System.out.println(ctx.getMessage("msg", null, english));
        System.out.println(ctx.getMessage("msg", null, Locale.UK));
        System.out.println(ctx.getMessage("msg", null, czech));
        System.out.println(ctx.getMessage("hello", null, Locale.UK));

        System.out.println(ctx.getMessage("nameMsg", new Object[] { "Jan",
                "Machacek" }, english));
    }

}
```

Don't worry about the calls to getMessage() just yet; we return to those shortly. For now, just know that they retrieve a keyed message for the locale specified. In Listing 4-73, you can see the configuration used by this application.

Listing 4-73. *Configuring a MessageSource Bean*

```
<?xml version="1.0" encoding="UTF-8"?>
<beans xmlns="http://www.springframework.org/schema/beans"
       xmlns:xsi="http://www.w3.org/2001/XMLSchema-instance"
       xsi:schemaLocation="
                http://www.springframework.org/schema/beans
                http://www.springframework.org/schema/beans/spring-beans.xsd">

    <bean id="messageSource"
        class="org.springframework.context.support.ResourceBundleMessageSource">
        <property name="basenames">
```

```
            <list>
                <value>messages</value>
            </list>
        </property>
    </bean>
</beans>
```

Here, we are defining a `ResourceBundleMessageSource` bean with the name `messageSource` as required and configuring it with a set of names to form the base of its file set. A Java `ResourceBundle`, which is used by the `ResourceBundleMessageSource`, works on a set of properties files that are identified by base names. When looking for a message for a particular `Locale`, the `ResourceBundle` looks for a file that is named as a combination of the base name and the `Locale` name. For instance, if the base name is `foo` and we are looking for a message in the `en-GB` (British English) locale, the `ResourceBundle` looks for a file called `foo_en_GB.properties`. If this file does not exist, it will attempt to find `foo_en.properties`, and if even this file does not exist, it will attempt to load `foo.properties`. Notice that we have not used the `basename` property, but the `basenames` property. The `basename` property is actually a special case in which there is only one entry in the `basenames` property.

To test the application, we need to create the resource bundles. We are going to create `messages_cs_CZ.properties`, `messages_en_GB.properties`, and `messages_en.properties`. Listing 4-74 shows the contents of all these files.

Listing 4-74. *The messages*.properties Files*

```
# messages_cs_CZ.properties
msg=Příšerně žluťoučký kůň úpěl ďábelské ódy
nameMsg=Jmenuji se {0}
hello=Nazdar

# messages_en_GB.properties
msg=The quick brown fox jumps over the lazy dog
nameMsg=My name is {0}

# messages_en.properties
msg=Jackdaws love my big sphinx of quartz
nameMsg=My name is {0}
hello=Hello
```

Running this application (with the appropriate `ResourceBundle` files created and present in the classpath) yields the following output:

```
Jackdaws love my big sphinx of quartz
The quick brown fox jumps over the lazy dog
Příšerně žluťoučký kůň úpěl ďábelské ódy
My name is Jan Machacek
```

The example shows the fallback at work: the bundle has the `msg` and `nameMsg` keys for all three locales, but the `hello` key exists only for locales `cz_CZ` and `en`. The call to `getMessage("hello", null, Locale.UK)` will not find the key in `messages_en_GB.properties`, but it will fall back to `messages_en.properties`, where the key exists. This allows you to write the common messages for locales that share the same language in a common file and only cover the differences in the specific locale resource files. Now, this example raises even more questions. First, what does "Příšerně žluťoučký kůň úpěl ďábelské ódy" mean? What did those calls to `getMessage()` mean? Why did we use `ApplicationContext.getMessage()` rather than access the `ResourceBundleMessageSource` bean directly? We'll answer each of these questions in the following sections.

Příšerně žluťoučký kůň úpěl ďábelské ódy

The English translation of the Czech phrase in the output from Listing 4-74 is, "A too yellow horse moaned devil odes." The sentence does not contain all the ASCII characters, but it contains all the accented Czech characters.

The getMessage() Method

The `MessageSource` interface defines three overloads for the `getMessage()` method. These are described in Table 4-6.

Table 4-6. *Overloads for MessageSource.getMessage()*

Method Signature	Description
`getMessage(String, Object[], Locale)`	This is the standard `getMessage()` method. The `String` argument is the key of the message corresponding to the key in the properties file. The final argument, `Locale`, tells `ResourceBundleMessageSource` which properties file to look in. Even though the first and second calls to `getMessage()` in the example used the same key, they returned different messages that correspond to the `Locale` that was passed in to `getMessage()`.
`getMessage(String, Object[], String, Locale)`	This overload works in the same way as `getMessage(String, Object[], Locale)`, except for the second `String` argument, which allows you to pass in a default value in case a message for the supplied key is not available for the supplied `Locale`.
`getMessage(MessageSourceResolvable, Locale)`	This overload is a special case. We discuss it in further detail in the section entitled "The MessageSourceResolvable Interface."

In Listing 4-46, the first call to `getMessage()` used `msg` as the key, and this corresponded to the following entry in the properties file for the `en` locale: `msg=The quick brown fox jumped over the lazy dog`. The `Object[]` array argument is used for replacements in the message. In the third call to `getMessage()` in Listing 4-46, we passed in an array of two strings. The message that was keyed as `nameMsg` was `My name is {0} {1}`. The numbers in braces are placeholders, and each is replaced with the corresponding entry in the argument array

Error Reporting and Handling in Applications

Friendly error reporting is an important consideration for today's applications. If you are developing an application that will be localized to different languages, you must be careful about the exceptions you throw. Listing 4-75 makes perfect sense in English but will not be useful in Czech.

Listing 4-75. *Nonlocalizable Error Reporting*

```
public class ErrorReporter {

    public void evaluate(double[] values) {
        if (values.length % 2 != 0)
            throw new SourceDataInvalidException(
                "The number of samples must be divisible by 2.");
        for (int i = 0; i < values.length; i++) {
            double value = values[i];
```

```
            if (value < 0)
                throw new ArgumentDomainException(
                    "Element " + i + " was less than 0.");
            Math.log(value);
        }
    }
}

public class SourceDataInvalidException extends NestedRuntimeException {
    private static final long serialVersionUID = -4844180669945134483L;

    public SourceDataInvalidException(String message) {
        super(message);
    }
}

public class ArgumentDomainException extends NestedRuntimeException {
    private static final long serialVersionUID = 4589477591557787475L;

    public ArgumentDomainException(String message) {
        super(message);
    }
}
```

Let's ignore the purpose of the calculation for the moment and take a look at how we could use it in a sample application in Listing 4-76.

Listing 4-76. *ErrorReportingDemo Sample Application*

```
public class ErrorReportingDemo {

    private static void run(ApplicationContext context, Locale locale,
        ErrorReporter reporter, double[] values) {
        try {
            reporter.evaluate(values);
            System.out.println("Success");
        } catch (SourceDataInvalidException ex) {
            System.out.println(ex);
        } catch (ArgumentDomainException ex) {
            System.out.println(ex);
        }
    }

    public static void main(String[] args) {
        ApplicationContext ctx = new ClassPathXmlApplicationContext(
                "/META-INF/spring/acdemo4-context.xml");
        ErrorReporter reporter = (ErrorReporter) ctx.getBean("errorReporter");
        Locale en_GB = new Locale("en", "GB");
        Locale cs_CZ = new Locale("cs", "CZ");
        run(ctx, en_GB, reporter, new double[] { 1 } );
        run(ctx, en_GB, reporter, new double[] { 1, -2 } );
        run(ctx, en_GB, reporter, new double[] { 1, 3 } );
        run(ctx, cs_CZ, reporter, new double[] { 1 } );
        run(ctx, cs_CZ, reporter, new double[] { 1, -2 } );
        run(ctx, cs_CZ, reporter, new double[] { 1, 3 } );
    }

}
```

When we run this application, it will use the ApplicationContext configuration file shown in Listing 4-77. It simply gets the errorReporter bean and calls its evaluate method. If the call throws an exception, the sample application catches it and prints the message.

Listing 4-77. *ApplicationContext Configuration File*

```
<?xml version="1.0" encoding="UTF-8"?>
<beans xmlns="http://www.springframework.org/schema/beans"
       xmlns:xsi="http://www.w3.org/2001/XMLSchema-instance"
       xsi:schemaLocation="
                http://www.springframework.org/schema/beans
                http://www.springframework.org/schema/beans/spring-beans.xsd">
    <bean id="errorReporter"
        class="com.apress.prospring2.ch04.context.ErrorReporter"/>
</beans>
```

The application works and the error messages are indeed friendly, but it is impossible to translate them. We cannot even try simple string substitution in an attempt to translate the messages, because the ArgumentDomainException's message contains a variable value.

To make the application localizable, we need to change the ErrorReporter and the NestedRuntimeException subclasses. First, we need to include the failing value as a property of the exception. Listing 4-78 shows these modifications.

Listing 4-78. *Modified ArgumentDomainException and SourceDataInvalidException*

```
public class ArgumentDomainException extends NestedRuntimeException {
    private static final long serialVersionUID = 4589477591557787475L;
    private double argument;

    public ArgumentDomainException(String msg, double argument) {
        super(msg);
        this.argument = argument;
    }

    public double getArgument() {
        return argument;
    }
}

public class SourceDataInvalidException extends NestedRuntimeException {
    private static final long serialVersionUID = -4844180669945134483L;
    private int length;

    public SourceDataInvalidException(String msg, int length) {
        super(msg);
        this.length = length;
    }

    public int getLength() {
        return length;
    }
}
```

The ErrorReporter class needs to pass the failing values to the exceptions' constructors. We can tackle the internalization issue at the same time: instead of using a message, we can use a message key. Listing 4-79 shows the modification to the ErrorReporter class.

Listing 4-79. *Internalizable ErrorReporter*

```
public class ErrorReporter {

    public void evaluate(double[] values) {
        if (values.length % 2 != 0)
            throw new SourceDataInvalidException(
                "@Lcom.apress.prospring2.ch04.context.sourcedatainvalid",
                    values.length);
        for (int i = 0; i < values.length; i++) {
            double value = values[i];
            if (value < 0)
                throw new ArgumentDomainException(
                    "@Lcom.apress.prospring2.ch04.context.argumentdomain",
                        value);
            Math.log(value);
        }
    }

}
```

Notice that we have changed the error messages to resemble message keys; moreover, each exception now carries the necessary details as its fields. This allows us to create a resource bundle and try out the code shown in Listing 4-80.

Listing 4-80. *Internalizatiable ErrorReportingDemo*

```
public class BetterErrorReportingDemo {

    private static void run(ApplicationContext context, Locale locale,
        ErrorReporter reporter, double[] values) {
        try {
            reporter.evaluate(values);
            System.out.println("Success");
        } catch (SourceDataInvalidException ex) {
            System.out.println(context.getMessage(ex.getMessage(),
                new Object[] { ex.getLength() }, locale ));
        } catch (ArgumentDomainException ex) {
            System.out.println(context.getMessage(ex.getMessage(),
                new Object[] { ex.getArgument() }, locale ));
        }
    }

    public static void main(String[] args) {
        ApplicationContext ctx = new ClassPathXmlApplicationContext(
                "/META-INF/spring/acdemo5-context.xml");
        ErrorReporter reporter = (ErrorReporter) ctx.getBean("errorReporter");
        Locale en_GB = new Locale("en", "GB");
        Locale cs_CZ = new Locale("cs", "CZ");
        run(ctx, en_GB, reporter, new double[] { 1 } );
        run(ctx, en_GB, reporter, new double[] { 1, -2 } );
        run(ctx, en_GB, reporter, new double[] { 1, 3 } );
        run(ctx, cs_CZ, reporter, new double[] { 1 } );
        run(ctx, cs_CZ, reporter, new double[] { 1, -2 } );
        run(ctx, cs_CZ, reporter, new double[] { 1, 3 } );
    }

}
```

We will reuse the messages resource bundle we have created in the previous example; we only need to add the key definitions. Finally, we need to add the `messageSource` bean to the `ApplicationContext` configuration file (see Listing 4-81).

Listing 4-81. *ApplicationContext Configuration File for the BetterErrorReportingDemo*

```
<?xml version="1.0" encoding="UTF-8"?>
<beans xmlns="http://www.springframework.org/schema/beans"
       xmlns:xsi="http://www.w3.org/2001/XMLSchema-instance"
       xsi:schemaLocation="
             http://www.springframework.org/schema/beans
             http://www.springframework.org/schema/beans/spring-beans.xsd">

    <bean id="messageSource"
        class="org.springframework.context.support.ResourceBundleMessageSource">
       <property name="basenames">
           <list>
               <value>messages</value>
           </list>
        </property>
    </bean>

    <bean id="errorReporter"
        class="com.apress.prospring2.ch04.context.ErrorReporter"/>
</beans>
```

The final point to notice about the new code is that we have prefixed the error keys with `@L`. We found that doing this is quite useful, because we can then extract all keys from the Java sources by running `find . -name \*.java -exec grep -o @L[^\\\"]* {} \;` in the project directory. The output from running this command in `bookcode/ch04/src/main/java` follows:

```
@Lcom.apress.prospring2.ch04.context.sourcedatainvalid
@Lcom.apress.prospring2.ch04.context.argumentdomain
```

We can now copy the messages, paste them to the appropriate resource bundle, and translate them without having to manually search through the source code for all the messages.

Why Use ApplicationContext As a MessageSource?

To answer this question, we need to jump a little ahead of ourselves and look at the web application support in Spring. The general answer to this question is that you shouldn't use the `ApplicationContext` as a `MessageSource` when doing so unnecessarily couples your bean to the `ApplicationContext` (this is discussed in more detail in the next section). You should use the `ApplicationContext` when you are building a web application using Spring MVC or Spring Web Flow. We will focus on Spring MVC in this chapter, but similar rules apply to Spring Web Flow.

The core interface in Spring MVC is `Controller`. Unlike frameworks like Struts that require that you implement your controllers by inheriting from a concrete class, Spring simply requires that you implement the `Controller` interface. Having said that, Spring provides a collection of useful base classes that you will, more often than not, use to implement your own controllers. All of these base classes are themselves subclasses (directly or indirectly) of the `ApplicationObjectSupport` class.

Remember that, in a web application setting, the `ApplicationContext` is loaded automatically. `ApplicationObjectSupport` accesses this `ApplicationContext`, wraps it in a `MessageSourceAccessor` object, and makes that available to your controller via the protected `getMessageSourceAccessor()` method. `MessageSourceAccessor` provides a wide array of convenience methods for working with

MessageSource instances. This form of automatic injection is quite beneficial; it removes the need for all of your controllers to expose a messageSource property.

However, the fact that ApplicationSource extends MessageSource is not the best reason for using ApplicationContext as a MessageSource in your web application. The main reason to use ApplicationContext rather than a manually defined MessageSource bean is that Spring does, where possible, expose ApplicationContext as a MessageSource to the view tier. This means that when you are using Spring's JSP tag library, the <spring:message> tag automatically reads messages from the ApplicationContext, and when you are using JSTL, the <fmt:message> tag does the same.

All of these benefits mean that using the MessageSource support in ApplicationContext is better when you are building a web application than managing an instance of MessageSource separately. This is especially true when you consider that all you need to do to take advantage of this feature is configure a MessageSource bean with the name messageSource.

Using MessageSource in Stand-Alone Applications

When you are using MessageSources in stand-alone applications where Spring offers no additional support other than to nest the messageSource bean automatically in the ApplicationContext, making the MessageSource instances available using DI is best. You can opt to make your beans aware of the application context (ApplicationContextAware), but doing so precludes their use in a BeanFactory context. Add to this the fact that you complicate testing without any discernible benefit, and clearly, you should stick to using DI to access MessageSource objects in a stand-alone setting.

The MessageSourceResolvable Interface

You can use an Object that implements MessageSourceResolvable in place of a key and a set of arguments when you are looking up a message from a MessageSource. This interface is most widely used in the Spring validation libraries to link Error objects to their internationalized error messages. You will see an example of how to use MessageSourceResolvable in Chapter 17 when we look at error handling in the Spring MVC library.

Using Application Events

Another feature of the ApplicationContext not present in the BeanFactory is the ability to publish and receive events using the ApplicationContext as a broker. An event is class derived from ApplicationEvent, which itself derives from the java.util.EventObject. Any bean can listen for events by implementing the ApplicationListener interface; the ApplicationContext automatically registers any bean that implements this interface as a listener when it is configured. Events are published using the ApplicationContext.publishEvent() method, so the publishing class must have knowledge of the ApplicationContext. In a web application, this is simple because many of your classes are derived from Spring Framework classes that allow access to the ApplicationContext through a protected method. In a stand-alone application, you can have your publishing bean implement ApplicationContextAware to enable it to publish events.

Listing 4-82 shows an example of a basic event class.

Listing 4-82. *Creating an Event Class*

```
public class MessageEvent extends ApplicationEvent {
    private static final long serialVersionUID = -6786033091498612636L;
    private String message;
```

```
    public MessageEvent(Object source, String message) {
        super(source);
        this.message = message;
    }

    public String getMessage() {
        return message;
    }
}
```

This code is quite basic; the only point of note is that the ApplicationEvent has a single constructor that accepts a reference to the source of the event. This is reflected in the constructor for MessageEvent. In Listing 4-83, you can see the code for the listener.

Listing 4-83. *The MessageEventListener Class*

```
public class MessageEventListener implements ApplicationListener {
    public void onApplicationEvent(ApplicationEvent event) {
        if (event instanceof MessageEvent) {
            MessageEvent messageEvent = (MessageEvent)event;
            System.out.println("Received " + messageEvent.getMessage() +
                    " from " + messageEvent.getSource());
        }
    }
}
```

The ApplicationListener interface defines a single method, onApplicationEvent, that is called by Spring when an event is raised. The MessageEventListener is only interested in events of type MessageEvent, so it checks to see whether the event raised is of that type, and if so, it writes the message to stdout. Publishing events is simple; it is just a matter of creating an instance of the event class and passing it to the ApplicationContext.publishEvent() method, as shown in Listing 4-84.

Listing 4-84. *Publishing an Event*

```
public class EventPublisherDemo implements ApplicationContextAware {

    private ApplicationContext ctx;

    public static void main(String[] args) {
        ApplicationContext ctx = new ClassPathXmlApplicationContext(
                "/META-INF/spring/eventsdemo1-context.xml");

        EventPublisherDemo pub = (EventPublisherDemo) ctx.getBean("publisher");
        pub.publish("Hello World!");
        pub.publish("The quick brown fox jumped over the lazy dog");
    }

    public void setApplicationContext(ApplicationContext applicationContext)
            throws BeansException {
        this.ctx = applicationContext;

    }

    public void publish(String message) {
        ctx.publishEvent(new MessageEvent(this, message));
    }

}
```

Here, you can see that the EventPublisherDemo class retrieves an instance of itself from the ApplicationContext, and using the publish() method, publishes two MessageEvent instances to the ApplicationContext. The EventPublisherDemo bean instance accesses the ApplicationContext by implementing ApplicationContextAware. Listing 4-85 shows the configuration for this example.

Listing 4-85. *Configuring ApplicationListener Beans*

```
<?xml version="1.0" encoding="UTF-8"?>
<beans xmlns="http://www.springframework.org/schema/beans"
       xmlns:xsi="http://www.w3.org/2001/XMLSchema-instance"
       xsi:schemaLocation="
                http://www.springframework.org/schema/beans
                http://www.springframework.org/schema/beans/spring-beans.xsd">

    <bean id="publisher"
        class="com.apress.prospring2.ch04.event.EventPublisherDemo"/>
    <bean class="com.apress.prospring2.ch04.event.MessageEventListener"/>

</beans>
```

Notice that you do not need a special configuration to register the MessageEventListener with the ApplicationContext; it is picked up automatically by Spring. Running this example results in the following output:

```
Received Hello World! from com.apress.prospring2.ch04.event.EventPublisherDemo@...
Received The quick brown fox jumped over the lazy dog from ➥
com.apress.prospring2.ch04.event.EventPublisherDemo@144f3ba2
```

Considerations for Event Usage

In many applications, certain components need to be notified of certain events. Often, you do this by writing code to notify each component explicitly or by using a messaging technology such as JMS. The drawback of writing code to notify each component individually is that you are coupling those components to the publisher, in many cases unnecessarily.

Consider a situation where you cache product details in your application to avoid trips to the database. Another component allows product details to be modified and persisted to the database. To avoid making the cache invalid, the update component explicitly notifies the cache that the user details have changed. In this example, the update component is coupled to a component that, really, has nothing to do with its business responsibility. A better solution would be to have the update component publish an event every time a product's details are modified and have interested components, such as the cache, listen for that event. This strategy has the benefit of keeping the components decoupled, which makes it simple to remove the cache if need be or to add another listener that is interested in knowing when a product's details change. If you are interested in declarative caching, take a look at the Cache Spring Modules project, which provides declarative and annotation-based cache management using many different cache providers (OSCache, Ehcache, etc.).

Using JMS in this case would be overkill, because the process of invalidating the product's entry in the cache is quick and is not business critical. The use of the Spring event infrastructure adds very little overhead to your application.

Typically, we use events for reactionary logic that executes quickly and is not part of the main application logic. In the previous example, the invalidation of a product in cache happens in reaction to updating product details, it executes quickly (or it should), and it is not part of the main function of the application. For processes that are long running and form part of the main business logic, we prefer to use JMS or similar messaging systems, such as Microsoft Message Queing (MSMQ). In a recent project, we built an e-commerce system with some complex order fulfillment logic. For this, we chose to use JMS, because it is more suited to long-running processes, and as the system grows, we can factor the JMS-driven order processing onto a separate machine if necessary.

Accessing Resources

Often, an application needs to access a variety of resources in different forms. You might need to access some configuration data stored in a file in the file system, some image data stored in a JAR file on the classpath, or maybe some data on a server elsewhere. Spring provides a unified mechanism for accessing resources in a protocol-independent way. This means that your application can access a file resource in the same way, whether it is stored in the file system, the classpath, or on a remote server.

At the core of Spring's resource support is the `Resource` interface. The `Resource` interface defines seven self-explanatory methods: `exists()`, `getDescription()`, `getFile()`, `getFileName()`, `getInputStream()`, `getURL()`, and `isOpen()`. In addition to these seven methods, there is one that is not quite so self-explanatory: `createRelative()`. The `createRelative()` method creates a new `Resource` instance using a path that is relative to the instance on which it is invoked. You can provide your own `Resource` implementations (explaining how to do so is outside the scope of this chapter), but in most cases, you'll use one of the built-in implementations for accessing file, classpath, or URL resources.

Internally, Spring uses another interface, `ResourceLoader`, and the default implementation, `DefaultResourceLoader`, to locate and create `Resource` instances. However, you generally won't interact with `DefaultResourceLoader`. Instead, you will be using another `ResourceLoader` implementation—`ApplicationContext`.

Listing 4-86 shows a sample application that accesses three resources using `ApplicationContext`.

Listing 4-86. *Accessing Resources Using ApplicationContext*

```
public class ResourceDemo {

    public static void main(String[] args) throws Exception{
        ApplicationContext ctx = new ClassPathXmlApplicationContext(
            "/META-INF/spring/resourcesdemo1-context.xml");

        Resource res1 = ctx.getResource("file:///tmp");
        displayInfo(res1);
        Resource res2 = ctx.getResource("classpath:com/apress/prospring2/ch04/pe/" +
            "Complex.class");
        displayInfo(res2);
        Resource res3 = ctx.getResource("http://www.google.co.uk");
        displayInfo(res3);
    }

    private static void displayInfo(Resource res) throws Exception{
        System.out.println(res.getClass());
        System.out.println(res.getURL().getContent());
        System.out.println("");
    }

}
```

You should note that the configuration file used in this example is unimportant. Notice that in each call to `getResource()`, we pass in a URI for each resource. You will recognize the common `file:` and `http:` protocols that we pass in for `res1` and `res3`. The `classpath:` protocol we use for `res2` is

Spring-specific and indicates that the ResourceLoader should look in the classpath for the resource. Running this example results in the following output:

```
class org.springframework.core.io.UrlResource
sun.net.www.content.text.PlainTextInputStream@39a4036f

class org.springframework.core.io.ClassPathResource
java.io.BufferedInputStream@185c2a25

class org.springframework.core.io.UrlResource
sun.net.www.protocol.http.HttpURLConnection$HttpInputStream@3c0a30fd
```

Notice that for both the file: and http: protocols, Spring returns a UrlResource instance. Spring does include a FileSystemResource class, but the DefaultResourceLoader does not use this class at all. Once a Resource instance is obtained, you are free to access the contents as you see fit, using getFile(), getInputStream(), or getURL(). In some cases, such as when you are using the http: protocol, the call to getFile() results in a FileNotFoundException. For this reason, we recommend that you use getInputStream() to access resource contents, because it is likely to function for all possible resource types.

Summary

In this chapter, you have seen a wide range of Spring-specific features that complement the core IoC capabilities. You saw how to hook into the life cycle of a bean and make it aware of the Spring environment. We demonstrated how to use method injection to overcome the problem of dealing with beans with incompatible life cycles, and we introduced the FactoryBean implemenation as a solution for IoC-enabling a set of classes that would be difficult to construct without using the factory pattern. We also looked at how you can use a PropertyEditor to simplify application configuration and remove the need for artificial String-typed properties. Finally, we finished with an in-depth look at the additional features offered by the ApplicationContext including internalization, event publication, and resource access.

In this chapter, we have explored the object-oriented approach to building applications; we have shown that you can create flexible applications whose components are not closely coupled together. In the next two chapters, we will leave the comfortable world of object-oriented programming and take a look at aspect-oriented programming and support for AOP in Spring.

CHAPTER 5

Introducing Spring AOP

Over the last few years, aspect-oriented programming (AOP) has become a hot topic in the Java world, and many articles, discussions, and implementations of AOP have become available for Java programmers. AOP is often referred to as a tool for implementing crosscutting concerns, which means that you use AOP for modularizing individual pieces of logic, known as concerns, and you apply these concerns to many parts of an application. Logging and security are typical examples of crosscutting concerns that are present in many applications. Consider an application that logs the start and end of every method for debugging purposes. You will probably refactor the logging code into a special class, but you still have to call methods on that class twice per method in your application in order to perform the logging. Using AOP, you can simply specify that you want the methods on your logging class to be invoked before and after each method call in your application.

To use AOP, you should understand how it complements, rather than competes with, object-oriented programming (OOP). OOP is very good at solving a wide variety of problems that we as programmers encounter. However, if you take the logging example again, you can plainly see that OOP is lacking when it comes to implementing crosscutting logic on a large scale. Using AOP on its own to develop an entire application is practically impossible, given that AOP functions on top of OOP. Likewise, although developing entire applications using OOP is certainly possible, you can work smarter by employing AOP to solve particular problems that involve crosscutting logic.

We are going to cover AOP in this chapter and the next. In this chapter, we cover Spring AOP in isolation from much of the rest of the framework.

First, we cover the basics of AOP as a technology in this chapter. Most of the concepts covered in the "AOP Concepts" section are not specific to Spring and can be found in any AOP implementation. If you are already familiar with another AOP implementation, feel free to skip over this section.

Next, we'll explain the two distinct types of AOP: static and dynamic. In static AOP, like AspectJ's AOP (`http://eclipse.org/aspectj/`), the crosscutting logic is applied to your code at compile time, and you cannot change it without modifying the code and recompiling. With dynamic AOP, like Spring's AOP, crosscutting logic is applied dynamically, at runtime. This allows you to make changes in the distribution of crosscutting without recompiling the application. These types of AOP are complementary, and when used together, they form a powerful combination in your applications.

Note Static and dynamic AOP are distinct from the static and dynamic crosscutting concepts. The differentiation between static and dynamic crosscutting is largely academic and is of no relevance to Spring AOP. For more information on this topic and on AOP as a whole, we recommend that you read *AspectJ in Action: Practical Aspect-Oriented Programming* by Ramnivas Laddad (Manning, 2003).

Once you understand the types of AOP, we'll get down to the details of Spring's AOP implementation. Spring AOP is only a subset of the full AOP feature set found in other implementations like AspectJ.

In this section, we take a high-level look at which features are present in Spring, how they are implemented, and why some features are excluded from the Spring implementation.

Proxies are a huge part of how Spring AOP works, and you must understand them to get the most out of Spring AOP. So next, we'll look at the two different kinds of proxies: JDK dynamic proxy and CGLIB proxy. In particular, we look at the different scenarios in which Spring uses each proxy, the performance of the two proxy types, and some simple guidelines to follow in your application to get the most from Spring AOP.

Finally, we'll look at some practical examples of AOP usage. We start off with a simple "Hello, World" example to ease you into Spring's AOP code; then we continue with a detailed description of the different AOP features that are available in Spring, complete with examples.

In Chapter 6, we take a much more framework-oriented view of Spring AOP, including how to configure AOP using `@AspectJ` annotations as well as XML Spring configuration.

AOP Concepts

As with most technologies, AOP comes with its own specific set of concepts and terms, and you should understand what these terms mean before we explain how to use AOP in an application. The following list explains the core concepts of AOP:

- *Joinpoint*: A joinpoint is a well-defined point during the execution of your application. Typical examples of joinpoints include a call to a method, the method invocation itself, class initialization, and object instantiation. Joinpoints are a core concept of AOP and define the points in your application at which you can insert additional logic using AOP.
- *Advice*: The code that is executed at a particular joinpoint is called the advice. There are many different types of advice, including before advice, which executes before the joinpoint, and after advice, which executes after it.
- *Pointcuts*: A pointcut is a collection of joinpoints that you use to define when advice should be executed. By creating pointcuts, you gain fine-grained control over how you apply advice to the components in your application. As mentioned previously, a typical joinpoint is a method invocation. A typical pointcut is the collection of all method invocations in a particular class. Often, you can compose pointcuts in complex relationships to further constrain when advice is executed. We discuss pointcut composition in more detail in the next chapter.
- *Aspects*: An aspect is the combination of advice and pointcuts. This combination results in a definition of the logic that should be included in the application and where it should execute.
- *Weaving*: This is the process of actually inserting aspects into the application code at the appropriate point. For compile-time AOP solutions, this is, unsurprisingly, done at compile time, usually as an extra step in the build process. Likewise, for runtime AOP solutions, the weaving process is executed dynamically at runtime.
- *Target*: An object whose execution flow is modified by some AOP process is referred to as the target object. Often, you see the target object referred to as the advised object.
- *Introduction*: Introduction is the process by which you can modify the structure of an object by introducing additional methods or fields to it. You can use introduction to make any object implement a specific interface without needing the object's class to implement that interface explicitly.

Don't worry if you find these concepts confusing; they will all become clear when you see some examples. Also be aware that you are shielded from many of these concepts in Spring AOP, and some are not relevant due to Spring's choice of implementation. We will discuss each of these features in the context of Spring as we progress through the chapter.

Types of AOP

As we mentioned earlier, there are two distinct types of AOP: static and dynamic. The difference between them is really the point at which the weaving process occurs and how this process is achieved.

Static AOP

Many of the first AOP implementations were static. In static AOP, the weaving process forms another step in the build process for an application. In Java terms, you achieve the weaving process in a static AOP implementation by modifying the actual bytecode of your application, changing and extending the application code as necessary. Clearly, this is a well-performing way of achieving the weaving process, because the end result is just Java bytecode, and you do not need any special tricks at runtime to determine when advice should be executed.

The drawback of this mechanism is that any modifications you make to the aspects, even if you simply want to add another joinpoint, require you to recompile the entire application.

AspectJ is an excellent example of a static AOP implementation.

Dynamic AOP

Dynamic AOP implementations like Spring AOP differ from static AOP implementations in that the weaving process is performed dynamically at runtime. The way that this is achieved is implementation dependent, but as you will see, Spring's approach is to create proxies for all advised objects, allowing for advice to be invoked as required. The slight drawback of dynamic AOP is that, typically, it does not perform as well as static AOP, but its performance is steadily improving. The major benefit of dynamic AOP implementations is the ease with which you can modify the entire aspect set of an application without needing to recompile the main application code.

Choosing an AOP Type

Choosing whether to use static or dynamic AOP is actually quite a hard decision. There is no reason for you to choose either implementation exclusively, because both have their benefits. Spring 1.1 introduced integration with AspectJ, allowing you to use both types of AOP with ease. We cover this feature in more detail in Chapter 6. In general, static AOP implementations have been around longer, and they tend to have more feature-rich implementations, with a greater number of available joinpoints. Indeed, Spring supports only a subset of the features available with AspectJ. Typically, if performance is absolutely critical or you need an AOP feature that is not implemented in Spring, then you will want to use AspectJ. In most other cases, Spring AOP is better. Remember that many AOP-based features are already available in Spring, such as declarative transaction management. Reimplementing these using AspectJ is a waste of time and effort, especially since Spring has tried-and-tested implementations ready for you to use.

Most importantly, let the requirements of your application drive your choice of AOP implementation, and don't restrict yourself to a single implementation if a combination of implementations would better suit your application. In general, we have found that Spring AOP is less complex than AspectJ, so it tends to be our first choice. If we find that Spring AOP won't do what we want it to do, or we discover during application tuning that performance is poor, then we move to AspectJ instead.

AOP in Spring

You can think of Spring's AOP implementation as coming in two logical parts. The first part is the AOP core, which provides fully decoupled, purely programmatic AOP functionality. The second part of the AOP implementation is the set of framework services that make AOP easier to use in your applications. On top of this, other components of Spring, such as the transaction manager and EJB helper classes, provide AOP-based services to simplify the development of your application. In this chapter, we focus solely on the basics of the AOP core. The framework services and the advanced functionality of the core are covered in Chapter 6.

Spring AOP is really a subset of the full AOP feature set, implementing only a handful of the constructs available in implementations like AspectJ. Don't be fooled into thinking Spring AOP is not useful, however. Indeed, one of the most powerful aspects of Spring AOP is that it is so simple to use because it is unencumbered with extra features that you often do not need. The implementation of only a subset of the AOP feature set is a specific design goal of Spring, allowing Spring to focus on simple access to the most common features of AOP. To make sure that you are not left without the AOP features that you need, in the 1.1 release Spring's designers added full integration with AspectJ.

The AOP Alliance

The AOP Alliance (`http://aopalliance.sourceforge.net/`) is a joint effort between representatives of many open source AOP projects, including Spring, to define a standard set of interfaces for AOP implementations. The AOP Alliance is very conservative, resisting the temptation to over-constrain AOP while it is still growing, and as a result, they have only defined interfaces for a subset of AOP features. Wherever applicable, Spring uses the AOP Alliance interfaces rather than defining its own. This allows you to reuse certain advice across multiple AOP implementations that support the AOP Alliance interfaces.

"Hello, World" in AOP

Before we dive into discussing the Spring AOP implementation in detail, we want to present a simple example to provide some context for these discussions. In this example, we take a simple class that outputs the message "World", and then using AOP, we transform an instance of this class at runtime to output "Hello, World!" instead. Listing 5-1 shows the basic `MessageWriter` class.

Listing 5-1. *The MessageWriter Class*

```
package com.apress.prospring.ch05.simple;

public class MessageWriter {

    public void writeMessage() {
        System.out.print("World");
    }
}
```

The `MessageWriter` class is nothing special; it has just one method that writes the message "World" to `stdout`. We want to advise—that is, add some advice to—this class so that the `writeMessage()` method actually writes "Hello World!" instead.

To do this, we need to execute some code before the method body executes to write "Hello", and some code after the method body executes to write "!". In AOP terms, what we need is an around advice—that is, advice that executes around a joinpoint. In this case, the joinpoint is the invocation of the `writeMessage()` method. Listing 5-2 shows the implementation of the around advice, the `MessageDecorator` class.

Listing 5-2. *Implementing Around Advice*

```
package com.apress.prospring2.ch05.simple;

import org.aopalliance.intercept.MethodInterceptor;
```

```
import org.aopalliance.intercept.MethodInvocation;

public class MessageDecorator implements MethodInterceptor {

    public Object invoke(MethodInvocation invocation) throws Throwable {
        System.out.print("Hello ");
        Object retVal = invocation.proceed();
        System.out.println("!");
        return retVal;
    }
}
```

The `MethodInterceptor` interface is the AOP Alliance standard interface for implementing around advice for method invocation joinpoints. The `MethodInvocation` object represents the method invocation that is being advised, and using this object, we control when the method invocation is actually allowed to proceed. Because this is around advice, we are essentially capable of performing some actions before the method is invoked and some actions after it is invoked but before it returns. In Listing 5-2, we simply write `Hello` to `stdout`, invoke the method with a call to `MethodInvocation.proceed()`, and then write ! to `stdout`.

The final step in this sample is to weave the `MessageDecorator` advice into the code. To do this, we create an instance of `MessageWriter`, the target, and then create a proxy of this instance, instructing the proxy factory to weave in the `MessageDecorator` advice. This is shown in Listing 5-3.

Listing 5-3. *Weaving the MessageDecorator Advice*

```
package com.apress.prospring2.ch05.simple;

import org.springframework.aop.framework.ProxyFactory;

public class HelloWorldWeaver {

    public static void main(String[] args) {
        MessageWriter target = new MessageWriter();

        // create the proxy
        ProxyFactory pf = new ProxyFactory();

        pf.addAdvice(new MessageDecorator());
        pf.setTarget(target);

        MessageWriter proxy = (MessageWriter) pf.getProxy();

        // write the messages
        target.writeMessage();
        System.out.println("");
        proxy.writeMessage();
    }
}
```

The important part here is that we use the `ProxyFactory` class to create the proxy of the target object, weaving in the advice at the same time. We pass the `MessageDecorator` advice to the `ProxyFactory` with a call to `addAdvice()` and specify the target for weaving with a call to `setTarget()`. Once the target is set and some advice is added to the `ProxyFactory`, we generate the proxy with a call to `getProxy()`. Finally, we call `writeMessage()` on both the original target object and the proxy object. Here are the results of running this example:

```
World
Hello World!
```

As you can see, calling `writeMessage()` on the untouched target object resulted in a standard method invocation, and no extra content was written to `stdout`. However, the invocation of the proxy caused the code in the `MessageDecorator` to execute, creating the desired output `Hello World!` From this example, you can see that the advised class had no dependencies on Spring or the AOP Alliance interfaces; the beauty of Spring AOP, and indeed AOP in general, is that you can advise almost any class, even if that class was created without AOP in mind. The only restriction, in Spring AOP at least, is that you can't advise final classes, because they cannot be overridden and therefore cannot be proxied.

Spring AOP Architecture

The core architecture of Spring AOP is based around proxies. When you want to create an advised instance of a class, you must use the `ProxyFactory` class to create a proxy of an instance of that class, first providing the `ProxyFactory` with all the aspects that you want to be woven into the proxy. Using `ProxyFactory` is a purely programmatic approach to creating AOP proxies. For the most part, you don't need to use this in your application; instead, you can rely on the `ProxyFactoryBean` class to provide declarative proxy creation. However, it is important to understand how proxy creation works. For the rest of this chapter, we will use the programmatic approach to proxy creation. In the next chapter, we discuss using `ProxyFactoryBean` when creating proxies.

Internally, Spring has two proxy implementations: JDK dynamic proxy and CGLIB proxy. In previous releases of Spring, there was not much difference between the two proxy types, and CGLIB proxies were only used when you wanted to proxy classes rather than interfaces or when you explicitly specified them. As of the 1.1 release of Spring, the CGLIB proxy is noticeably faster than JDK dynamic proxies in most cases. This is especially true when you are running on a release 1.3 virtual machine, which suffers from poor reflection performance. Understanding proxies and how they are used internally is key to getting the best performance out of your application. We discuss proxies in great detail later in the chapter, in the section titled "All About Proxies."

Joinpoints in Spring

One of the more noticeable simplifications in Spring AOP is that it only supports one joinpoint type: method invocation. At first glance, this might seem like a severe limitation if you are familiar with other AOP implementations like AspectJ, which supports many more joinpoints, but in fact, it actually makes Spring more accessible.

The method invocation joinpoint is by far the most useful joinpoint available, and using it, you can achieve many of the tasks that make AOP useful in day-to-day programming. Remember that if you need to advise some code at a joinpoint other than a method invocation, you can always use Spring and AspectJ together.

Aspects in Spring

In Spring AOP, an aspect is represented by an instance of a class that implements the `Advisor` interface. Spring provides a selection of convenience `Advisor` implementations that you can use in your applications, thus removing the need for you to create lots of different `Advisor` implementations for your example. There are two subinterfaces of `Advisor`: `IntroductionAdvisor` and `PointcutAdvisor`. The `PointcutAdvisor` interface is implemented by all `Advisors` that use pointcuts to control the applicability of advice to joinpoints.

In Spring, introductions are treated as special kinds of advice. Using the `IntroductionAdvisor` interface, you can control those classes to which an introduction applies. We cover this in more detail in the next chapter.

We discuss the different `PointcutAdvisor` implementations in detail later in this chapter in the section titled "Advisors and Pointcuts in Spring."

The ProxyFactory Class

The `ProxyFactory` class controls the weaving and proxy creation process in Spring AOP. Before you can actually create a proxy, you must specify the advised or target object. You can do this, as you saw earlier, using the `setTarget()` method. Internally, `ProxyFactory` delegates the proxy creation process to an instance of `DefaultAopProxyFactory`, which in turn delegates to either `Cglib2AopProxy` or `JdkDynamicAopProxy`, depending on the settings of your application. We discuss proxy creation in more detail later in this chapter.

Using the `ProxyFactory` class, you control which aspects you want to weave into the proxy. As mentioned earlier, you can weave only an aspect—that is, advice combined with a pointcut—into advised code. However, in some cases you want advice to apply to the invocation of all methods in a class, not just a selection. For this reason, the `ProxyFactory` class provides the `addAdvice()` method that you saw in Listing 6-3. Internally, `addAdvice()` wraps the advice you pass it in an instance of `DefaultPointcutAdvisor`, which is the standard implementation of `PointcutAdvisor`, and configures it with a pointcut that includes all methods by default. When you want more control over the `Advisor` that is created, or when you want to add an introduction to the proxy, create the `Advisor` yourself and use the `addAdvisor()` method of the `ProxyFactory()`.

You can use the same `ProxyFactory` instance to create many different proxies, each with different aspects. To help with this, `ProxyFactory` has `removeAdvice()` and `removeAdvisor()` methods, which allow you to remove any advice or `Advisor` from the `ProxyFactory` that you previously passed to it. To check whether or not a `ProxyFactory` has particular advice attached to it, call `adviceIncluded()`, passing in the advice object for which you want to check.

Be aware that `ProxyFactory` defines quite a few methods that have been deprecated in favor of other methods such as `addAdvice()`. You can find full details of these methods in the Javadoc. Avoid using the deprecated methods, because they will likely be removed in future versions of Spring, and each has an alternative. If you stick with the methods used in this book, you will be OK.

Creating Advice in Spring

Spring supports five different flavors of advice, described in Table 5-1.

Table 5-1. *Advice Types in Spring*

Advice Name	Interface	Description
Before	`org.springframework.aop.MethodBeforeAdvice`	Using before advice, you can perform custom processing before a joinpoint executes. Because a joinpoint in Spring is always a method invocation, this essentially allows you to perform preprocessing before the method executes. Before advice has full access to the target of the method invocation as well as the arguments passed to the method, but it has no control over the execution of the method itself.

Continued

Table 5-1. *Continued*

Advice Name	Interface	Description
After returning	`org.springframework.aop.AfterReturningAdvice`	After returning advice is executed after the method invocation at the joinpoint has finished executing and has returned a value. The after returning advice has access to the target of the method invocation, the arguments passed to the method, and the return value as well. Because the method has already executed when the after returning advice is invoked, it has no control over the method invocation at all.
Around	`org.aopalliance.intercept.MethodInterceptor`	In Spring, around advice is modeled using the AOP Alliance standard of a method interceptor. Your advice is allowed to execute before and after the method invocation, and you can control the point at which the method invocation is allowed to proceed. You can choose to bypass the method altogether if you want, providing your own implementation of the logic.
Throws	`org.springframework.aop.ThrowsAdvice`	Throws advice is executed after a method invocation returns but only if that invocation threw an exception. It is possible for throws advice to catch only specific exceptions, and if you choose to do so, you can access the method that threw the exception, the arguments passed into the invocation, and the target of the invocation.
Introduction	`org.springframework.aop.IntroductionInterceptor`	Spring models introductions as special types of interceptors. Using an introduction interceptor, you can specify the implementation for methods that are being introduced by the advice. Introductions are covered in more detail in the next chapter.

We have found that these advice types, coupled with the method invocation joinpoint, allow us to perform about 90 percent of the tasks we want to perform with AOP. For the other 10 percent, which we use only rarely, we fall back on AspectJ.

Interfaces for Advice

From our previous discussion of the `ProxyFactory` class, recall that advice is added to a proxy either directly using the `addAdvice()` method or indirectly using an `Advisor`, with the `addAdvisor()` method. In previous releases of Spring, we had an `addXXX()` method for each type of advice (these methods are still present, albeit deprecated). Originally, each advice interface was separate from the others, but more recently, a well-defined hierarchy has been created for advice interfaces. This hierarchy is based on the AOP Alliance interfaces and is shown in detail in Figure 5-1.

This kind of hierarchy not only has the benefit of being sound OO design, but it also means that you can deal with advice types generically, as in using a single `addAdvice()` method on the `ProxyFactory`, and you can add new advice types easily without having to modify the `ProxyFactory` class.

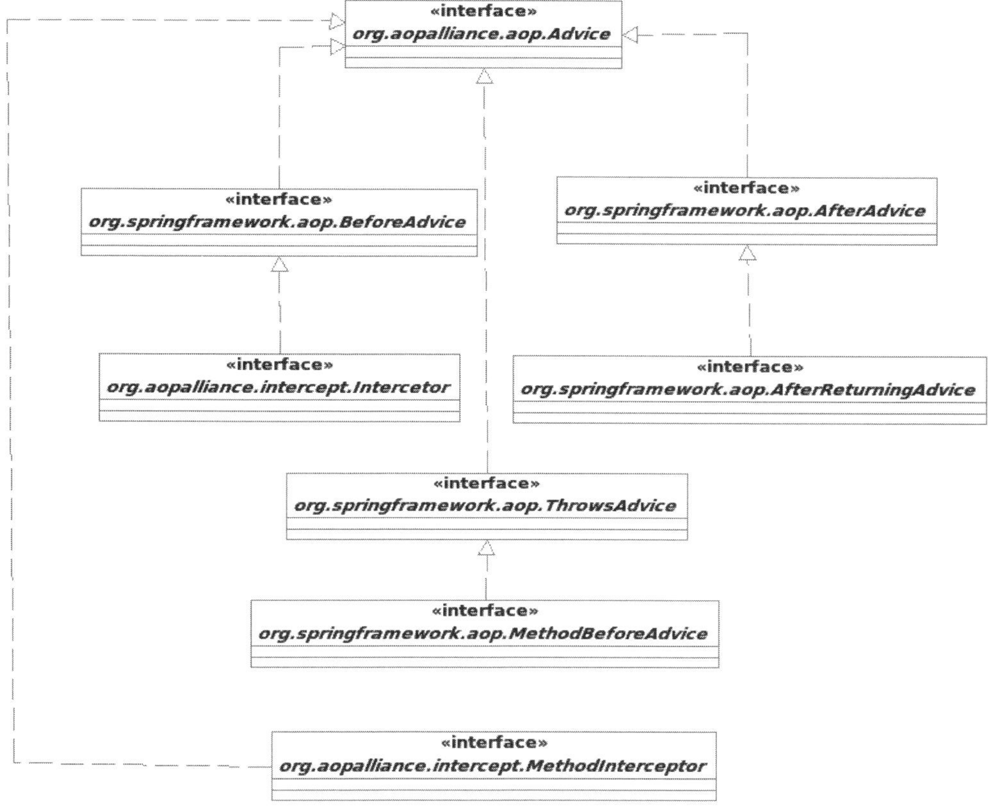

Figure 5-1. *Interfaces for Spring advice types*

Creating Before Advice

Before advice is one of the most useful advice types available in Spring. Before advice can modify the arguments passed to a method and can prevent the method from executing by raising an exception. In the next chapter, you will see before advice used frequently when we look at how AOP is used in the SpringBlog application. In this section, we show you two examples of using before advice: a simple example that writes a message to `stdout` containing the name of the method before the method executes and a simple security advice that you can use to restrict access to methods on an object.

In Listing 5-4, you can see the code for the `SimpleBeforeAdvice` class.

Listing 5-4. *The SimpleBeforeAdvice Class*

```
package com.apress.prospring2.ch05.simple;

import java.lang.reflect.Method;

import org.springframework.aop.MethodBeforeAdvice;
import org.springframework.aop.framework.ProxyFactory;

public class SimpleBeforeAdvice implements MethodBeforeAdvice {
```

```
    public static void main(String[] args) {
        MessageWriter target = new MessageWriter();

        // create the proxy
        ProxyFactory pf = new ProxyFactory();

        pf.addAdvice(new SimpleBeforeAdvice());
        pf.setTarget(target);

        MessageWriter proxy = (MessageWriter) pf.getProxy();

        // write the messages
        proxy.writeMessage();
    }

    public void before(Method method, Object[] args, Object target)
            throws Throwable {
        System.out.println("Before method: " + method.getName());
    }

}
```

In this code, you can see that we have advised an instance of the `MessageWriter` class that we created earlier with an instance of the `SimpleBeforeAdvice` class. The `MethodBeforeAdvice` interface, which is implemented by `SimpleBeforeAdvice`, defines a single method, `before()`, which the AOP framework calls before the method at the joinpoint is invoked. Remember that, for now, we are using the default pointcut provided by the `addAdvice()` method, which matches all methods in a class. The `before()` method is passed three arguments: the method that is to be invoked, the arguments that will be passed to that method, and the `Object` that is the target of the invocation. The `SimpleBeforeAdvice` class uses the `Method` argument of the `before()` method to write a message to `stdout` containing the name of the method to be invoked. Running this example gives us the following output:

```
Before method: writeMessage
World
```

As you can see, the output from the call to `writeMessage()` is shown, but just before it, you can see the output generated by the `SimpleBeforeAdvice`.

Securing Method Access Using Before Advice

The previous example was fairly trivial and didn't really show the power of AOP. In this section, we are going to build before advice that checks user credentials before allowing the method invocation to proceed. If the user credentials are invalid, an exception is thrown by the advice, thus preventing the method from executing. The example in this section is simplistic. It allows users to authenticate with any password, and it also allows only a single, hard-coded user access to the secured methods. However, it does illustrate how easy it is to use AOP to implement a crosscutting concern such as security.

Listing 5-5 shows the `SecureBean` class. This is the class that we will be securing using AOP.

Listing 5-5. *The SecureBean Class*

```
package com.apress.prospring2.ch05.security;

public class SecureBean {
```

```
    public void writeSecureMessage() {
        System.out.println("Every time I learn something new, "
                + "it pushes some old stuff out of my brain");
    }
}
```

The SecureBean class imparts a small pearl of wisdom from Homer Simpson, wisdom that we don't want everyone to see. Because this example requires users to authenticate, we are somehow going to need to store their details. Listing 5-6 shows the UserInfo class we use to store a user's credentials.

Listing 5-6. *The UserInfo Class*

```
package com.apress.prospring2.ch05.security;

public class UserInfo {
    private String username;
    private String password;

    public UserInfo(String username, String password) {
        this.username = username;
        this.password = password;
    }

    public String getPassword() {
        return password;
    }

    public String getUsername() {
        return username;
    }
}
```

There is nothing of particular interest in this class; it simply holds data about the user so that we can do something useful with it. Listing 5-7 shows the SecurityManager class, which is responsible for authenticating users and storing their credentials for later retrieval.

Listing 5-7. *The SecurityManager Class*

```
package com.apress.prospring2.ch05.security;

public class SecurityManager {

    private static ThreadLocal<UserInfo> threadLocal = new ThreadLocal<UserInfo>();

    public void login(String username, String password) {
        // assumes that all credentials
        // are valid for a login
        threadLocal.set(new UserInfo(username, password));
    }

    public void logout() {
        threadLocal.set(null);
    }
```

```
    public UserInfo getLoggedOnUser() {
        return threadLocal.get();
    }
}
```

The application uses the `SecurityManager` class to authenticate a user and, later, to retrieve the details of the currently authenticated user. The application authenticates a user using the `login()` method. In a real application, the `login()` method would probably check the supplied application against a database or Lightweight Directory Access Protocol (LDAP) directory, but here, we assume all users are allowed to authenticate. The `login()` method creates a `UserInfo` object for the user and stores it on the current thread using a `ThreadLocal`. The `logout()` method sets any value that might be stored in the `ThreadLocal` to `null`. Finally, the `getLoggedOnUser()` method returns the `UserInfo` object for the currently authenticated user. This method returns `null` if no user is authenticated.

To check whether or not a user is authenticated and, if so, whether or not the user is permitted to access the methods on `SecureBean`, we need to create advice that executes before the method and checks the `UserInfo` object returned by `SecurityManager.getLoggedOnUser()` against the set of credentials for allowed users. The code for this advice, `SecurityAdvice`, is shown in Listing 5-8.

Listing 5-8. *The SecurityAdvice Class*

```
package com.apress.prospring2.ch05.security;

import java.lang.reflect.Method;

import org.springframework.aop.MethodBeforeAdvice;

public class SecurityAdvice implements MethodBeforeAdvice {

    private SecurityManager securityManager;

    public SecurityAdvice() {
        this.securityManager = new SecurityManager();
    }

    public void before(Method method, Object[] args, Object target)
            throws Throwable {
        UserInfo user = securityManager.getLoggedOnUser();

        if (user == null) {
            System.out.println("No user authenticated");
            throw new SecurityException(
                    "You must log in before attempting to invoke the method: "
                            + method.getName());
        } else if ("janm".equals(user.getUsername())) {
            System.out.println("Logged in user is janm - OKAY!");
        } else {
            System.out.println("Logged in user is " + user.getUsername()
                    + " NOT GOOD :(");
            throw new SecurityException("User " + user.getUsername()
                    + " is not allowed access to method " + method.getName());
        }

    }
}
```

The SecurityAdvice class creates an instance of SecurityManager in its constructor and stores this instance in a field. You should note that the application and the SecurityAdvice don't need to share the same SecurityManager instance, because all data is stored with the current thread using ThreadLocal. In the before() method, we perform a simple check to see if the user name of the authenticated user is janm. If so, we allow the user access; otherwise, an exception is raised. Also notice that we check for a null UserInfo object, which indicates that the current user is not authenticated.

In Listing 5-9, you can see a sample application that uses the SecurityAdvice class to secure the SecureBean class.

Listing 5-9. *The SecurityExample Class*

```
package com.apress.prospring2.ch05.security;

import org.springframework.aop.framework.ProxyFactory;

public class SecurityExample {

    public static void main(String[] args) {
        // get the security manager
        SecurityManager mgr = new SecurityManager();

        // get the bean
        SecureBean bean = getSecureBean();

        // try as janm
        mgr.login("janm", "*****");
        bean.writeSecureMessage();
        mgr.logout();

        // try as aleksav
        try {
            mgr.login("aleksav", "****");
            bean.writeSecureMessage();
        } catch(SecurityException ex) {
            System.out.println("Exception Caught: " + ex.getMessage());
        } finally {
            mgr.logout();
        }

        // try with no credentials
        try {
            bean.writeSecureMessage();
        } catch(SecurityException ex) {
            System.out.println("Exception Caught: " + ex.getMessage());
        }

    }

    private static SecureBean getSecureBean() {
        // create the target
        SecureBean target = new SecureBean();

        // create the advice
        SecurityAdvice advice = new SecurityAdvice();
```

```
        // get the proxy
        ProxyFactory factory = new ProxyFactory();
        factory.setTarget(target);
        factory.addAdvice(advice);

        return (SecureBean)factory.getProxy();

    }
}
```

In the getSecureBean() method, we create a proxy of the SecureBean class that is advised using an instance of SecurityAdvice. This proxy is returned to the caller. When the caller invokes any method on this proxy, the call is first routed to the instance of SecurityAdvice for a security check. In the main() method, we test three different scenarios, invoking the SecureBean.writeSecureMessage() method with two different sets of user credentials and then no user credentials at all. Because the SecurityAdvice only allows method calls to proceed if the currently authenticated user is janm, we expect that the only successful scenario in Listing 5-9 is the first of these scenarios. Running this example gives the following output:

```
Logged in user is janm - OKAY!
Every time I learn something new, it pushes some old stuff out of my brain
Logged in user is aleksav NOT GOOD :(
Exception Caught: User aleksav is not allowed access to method writeSecureMessage
No user authenticated
Exception Caught: You must log in before attempting to invoke the method: ➥
writeSecureMessage
```

As you can see, only the first invocation of SecureBean.writeSecureMessage() was allowed to proceed. The remaining invocations were prevented by the SecurityException thrown by the SecurityAdvice.

This example is simple, but it does highlight the usefulness of the before advice. Security is a typical example of before advice, but we also find it useful when a scenario demands the modification of arguments going into the method. In Chapter 6, we show you how to use before advice to create an obscenity filter.

Creating After Returning Advice

As its name implies, after returning advice is executed after the method invocation at the joinpoint returns. Given that the method has already executed, you can't change the arguments that are passed to it. Although you can read these, you can neither change the execution path nor prevent the method from executing. These restrictions are expected; what you might not expect, however, is that you cannot modify the return value in the after returning advice; you are restricted to performing some additional processing. Although after returning advice cannot modify the return value of a method invocation, it can throw an exception that can be sent up the stack instead of the return value.

In this section, we look at two examples of using after returning advice in an application. The first example simply writes a message to stdout after the method has been invoked. The second example shows how you can use after returning advice to add additional error checking to a method. Consider a class KeyGenerator that generates keys for cryptographic purposes. Many cryptographic algorithms suffer from the problem that a small number of keys in the keyspace are considered weak. A weak key is any key whose characteristics make it significantly easier to derive the original message without knowing the key. For the DES algorithm, there are a total of 2^{56} possible keys. From this keyspace, four keys are considered weak and another twelve are considered semiweak. Although the chance of one of these keys being generated randomly is ridiculously small (1 in 2^{52}), testing for the keys is so simple that it seems lax not to do so. In the second example of this section, we build an after returning advice that checks for weak keys generated by the `KeyGenerator` and raises an exception if one is found.

■ **Note** For more information on weak keys and cryptography at large, we recommend that you read *Applied Cryptography* by Bruce Schneier (Wiley, 1995).

In Listing 5-10, you can see the `SimpleAfterReturningAdvice` class, which demonstrates the use of after returning advice by writing a message to `stdout` after a method has returned.

Listing 5-10. *The SimpleAfterReturningAdvice Class*

```
package com.apress.prospring2.ch05.simple;

import java.lang.reflect.Method;

import org.springframework.aop.AfterReturningAdvice;
import org.springframework.aop.framework.ProxyFactory;

public class SimpleAfterReturningAdvice implements AfterReturningAdvice {

    public static void main(String[] args) {
        MessageWriter target = new MessageWriter();

        // create the proxy
        ProxyFactory pf = new ProxyFactory();

        pf.addAdvice(new SimpleAfterReturningAdvice());
        pf.setTarget(target);

        MessageWriter proxy = (MessageWriter) pf.getProxy();

        // write the messages
        proxy.writeMessage();
    }

    public void afterReturning(Object returnValue, Method method, Object[] args,
            Object target) throws Throwable {
        System.out.println("");
        System.out.println("After method: " + method.getName());
    }
}
```

This example is really not that different from the `SimpleBeforeAdvice` class that you saw earlier. Notice that the `AfterReturningAdvice` interface declares a single method, `afterReturning()`, which is passed the return value of method invocation, a reference to the method that was invoked, the arguments that were passed to the method, and the target of the invocation. Running this example results in the following output:

```
World
After method: writeMessage
```

The output is very similar to that of the before advice example except that, as expected, the message written by the advice appears after the message written by the `writeMessage()` method.

A good use of after returning advice is to perform some additional error checking when it is possible for a method to return an invalid value. In the scenario we described earlier, it is possible for a cryptographic key generator to generate a key that is considered weak for a particular algorithm. Ideally, the key generator would check for these weak keys, but since the chance of these keys arising is often very small, many generators do not check. By using after returning advice, we can advise the method that generates the key and performs this additional check. Listing 5-11 shows an extremely primitive key generator.

Listing 5-11. *The KeyGenerator Class*

```
package com.apress.prospring2.ch05.crypto;

import java.util.Random;

public class KeyGenerator {

    public static final long WEAK_KEY = 0xFFFFFFF0000000L;
    public static final long STRONG_KEY = 0xACDF03F590AE56L;

    private Random rand = new Random();

    public long getKey() {
        int x = rand.nextInt(3);

        if(x == 1) {
            return WEAK_KEY;
        } else {
            return STRONG_KEY;
        }
    }
}
```

It is plain to see that this key generator is ridiculously insecure, but we didn't want you to have to wait around for years while a real key generator produced a weak key, so we created this generator, which has a one-in-three chance of producing a weak key. In Listing 5-12, you can see the `WeakKeyCheckAdvice` that checks to see if the result of the `getKey()` method is a weak key.

Listing 5-12. *Checking for Weak Keys*

```
package com.apress.prospring2.ch05.crypto;

import java.lang.reflect.Method;

import org.springframework.aop.AfterReturningAdvice;

public class WeakKeyCheckAdvice implements AfterReturningAdvice {

    public void afterReturning(Object returnValue, Method method,
            Object[] args, Object target) throws Throwable {

        if ((target instanceof KeyGenerator)
                && ("getKey".equals(method.getName()))) {
            long key = (Long) returnValue;
```

```
            if (key == KeyGenerator.WEAK_KEY) {
                throw new SecurityException(
                        "Key Generator generated a weak key. Try again");
            }
        }
    }
}
```

In the afterReturning() method, we check first to see if the method that was executed at the joinpoint was the getKey() method. If so, we then check the result value to see if it was the weak key. If we find that the result of the getKey() method was a weak key, we throw a SecurityException to inform the calling code of this. Listing 5-13 shows a simple application that demonstrates the use of this advice.

Listing 5-13. *Testing the WeakKeyCheckAdvice Class*

```
package com.apress.prospring2.ch05.crypto;

import org.springframework.aop.framework.ProxyFactory;

public class AfterAdviceExample {

    public static void main(String[] args) {
        KeyGenerator keyGen = getKeyGenerator();

        for(int x = 0; x < 10; x++) {
            try {
                long key = keyGen.getKey();
                System.out.println("Key: " + key);
            } catch(SecurityException ex) {
                System.out.println("Weak Key Generated!");
            }
        }

    }

    private static KeyGenerator getKeyGenerator() {

        KeyGenerator target = new KeyGenerator();

        ProxyFactory factory = new ProxyFactory();
        factory.setTarget(target);
        factory.addAdvice(new WeakKeyCheckAdvice());

        return (KeyGenerator)factory.getProxy();
    }
}
```

After creating an advised proxy of a KeyGenerator target, the AfterAdviceExample class attempts to generate ten keys. If a SecurityException is thrown during a single generation, a message is written to stdout informing the user that a weak key was generated; otherwise, the generated key is displayed. A single run of this on our machine generated the following output:

```
Weak Key Generated!
Key: 48658904092028502
Key: 48658904092028502
Key: 48658904092028502
Key: 48658904092028502
Key: 48658904092028502
Weak Key Generated!
Weak Key Generated!
Key: 48658904092028502
Weak Key Generated!
```

As you can see, the KeyGenerator class sometimes generates weak keys, as expected, and the WeakKeyCheckAdvice ensures that a SecurityException is raised whenever a weak key is encountered.

Creating Around Advice

Around advice functions like a combination of before and after advice, with one big difference—you can modify the return value. Not only that, you can also prevent the method from actually executing. This means that using around advice, you can essentially replace the entire implementation of a method with new code. Around advice in Spring is modeled as an interceptor using the MethodInterceptor interface. There are many uses for around advice, and you will find that many features of Spring use method interceptors, such as the remote proxy support and the transaction management features. Method interception is also a good mechanism for profiling the execution of your application, and it forms the basis of the example in this section.

We are not going to build a simple example for method interception; instead, we refer to the first example in Listing 5-2, which shows how to use a basic method interceptor to write out a message on either side of a method invocation. Notice from this earlier example that the invoke() method of the MethodInterceptor class does not provide the same set of arguments as the MethodBeforeAdvice and AfterReturningAdvice—that is, the method is not passed the target of the invocation, the method that was invoked, or the arguments used. However, you can get access to this data using the MethodInvocation object that is passed to invoke(). You will see a demonstration of this in the following example.

For this example, we want to achieve some way to advise a class so that we get basic information about the runtime performance of its methods. Specifically, we want to know how long the method took to execute. To achieve this, we can use the StopWatch class included in Spring, and we clearly need a MethodInterceptor, because we need to start the StopWatch before the method invocation and stop it right afterward.

Listing 5-14 shows the WorkerBean class that we are going to profile using the StopWatch class and an around advice.

Listing 5-14. *The WorkerBean Class*

```
package com.apress.prospring2.ch05.profiling;

public class WorkerBean {

    public void doSomeWork(int noOfTimes) {
        for(int x = 0; x < noOfTimes; x++) {
            work();
        }
    }
```

```
    private void work() {
        System.out.print("");
    }
}
```

This is a very simple class. The `doSomeWork()` method accepts a single argument, `noOfTimes`, and calls the `work()` method exactly the number of times specified by this method. The `work()` method simply has a dummy call to `System.out.print()`, which passes in an empty `String`. This prevents the compiler from optimizing out the `work()` method and thus the call to `work()`.

In Listing 5-15, you can see the `ProfilingInterceptor` class that uses the `StopWatch` class to profile method invocation times. We use this interceptor to profile the `WorkerBean` class shown in Listing 5-14.

Listing 5-15. *The ProfilingInterceptor Class*

```
package com.apress.prospring2.ch05.profiling;

import java.lang.reflect.Method;

import org.aopalliance.intercept.MethodInterceptor;
import org.aopalliance.intercept.MethodInvocation;
import org.springframework.util.StopWatch;

public class ProfilingInterceptor implements MethodInterceptor {

    public Object invoke(MethodInvocation invocation) throws Throwable {
        // start the stop watch
        StopWatch sw = new StopWatch();
        sw.start(invocation.getMethod().getName());

        Object returnValue = invocation.proceed();

        sw.stop();
        dumpInfo(invocation, sw.getTotalTimeMillis());
        return returnValue;
    }

    private void dumpInfo(MethodInvocation invocation, long ms) {
        Method m = invocation.getMethod();
        Object target = invocation.getThis();
        Object[] args = invocation.getArguments();

        System.out.println("Executed method: " + m.getName());
        System.out.println("On object of type: " + target.getClass().getName());

        System.out.println("With arguments:");
        for (int x = 0; x < args.length; x++) {
            System.out.print("    > " + args[x]);
        }
        System.out.print("\n");

        System.out.println("Took: " + ms + " ms");
    }
}
```

In the invoke() method, which is the only method in the MethodInterceptor interface, we create an instance of StopWatch and start it running immediately, allowing the method invocation to proceed with a call to MethodInvocation.proceed(). As soon as the method invocation has ended and the return value has been captured, we stop the StopWatch and pass the total number of milliseconds taken, along with the MethodInvocation object, to the dumpInfo() method. Finally, we return the Object returned by MethodInvocation.proceed() so that the caller obtains the correct return value. In this case, we did not want to disrupt the call stack in any way; we were simply acting as an eavesdropper on the method invocation. If we had wanted to, we could have changed the call stack completely, redirecting the method call to another object or a remote service, or we could simply have reimplemented the method logic inside the interceptor and returned a different return value.

The dumpInfo() method writes some information about the method call to stdout, along with the time taken for the method to execute. In the first three lines of dumpInfo(), you can see how you can use the MethodInvocation object to determine the method that was invoked, the original target of the invocation, and the arguments used.

Listing 5-16 shows the ProfilingExample class that first advises an instance of WorkerBean with a ProfilingInterceptor and then profiles the doSomeWork() method.

Listing 5-16. *The ProfilingExample Class*

```
package com.apress.prospring2.ch05.profiling;

import org.springframework.aop.framework.ProxyFactory;

public class ProfilingExample {

    public static void main(String[] args) {
        WorkerBean bean = getWorkerBean();
        bean.doSomeWork(10000000);
    }

    private static WorkerBean getWorkerBean() {
        WorkerBean target = new WorkerBean();

        ProxyFactory factory = new ProxyFactory();
        factory.setTarget(target);
        factory.addAdvice(new ProfilingInterceptor());

        return (WorkerBean)factory.getProxy();
    }
}
```

You should be more than familiar with this code by now. Running this example on our machine produces the following output:

```
Executed method: doSomeWork
On object of type: com.apress.prospring.ch05.profiling.WorkerBean
With arguments:
    > 10000000
Took: 1898 ms
```

From this output, you can see which method was executed, what the class of the target was, what arguments were passed in, and how long the invocation took.

Creating Throws Advice

Throws advice is similar to after returning advice in that it executes after the joinpoint, which is always a method invocation, but throws advice only executes if the method threw an exception. Throws advice is also similar to after returning advice in that it has little control over program execution. If you are using a throws advice, you can't choose to ignore the exception that was raised and return a value for the method instead. The only modification you can make to the program flow is to change the type of exception that is thrown. This is actually quite a powerful idea and can make application development much simpler. Consider a situation where you have an API that throws an array of poorly defined exceptions. Using throws advice, you can advise all classes in that API and reclassify the exception hierarchy into something more manageable and descriptive. Of course, you can also use throws advice to provide centralized error logging across your application, thus reducing the amount of error logging code that is spread across your application.

As you saw from the diagram in Figure 5-1, throws advice is implemented by the `ThrowsAdvice` interface. Unlike the interfaces you have seen so far, `ThrowsAdvice` does not define any methods; instead, it is simply a marker interface used by Spring. The reason for this is that Spring allows typed throws advice, which allows you to define exactly which `Exception` types your throws advice should catch. Spring achieves this by detecting methods with certain signatures using reflection. Spring looks for two distinct method signatures. This is best demonstrated with an example. Listing 5-17 shows a simple bean with two methods that throw exceptions of different types.

Listing 5-17. *The ErrorBean Class*

```
package com.apress.prospring2.ch05.simple;

public class ErrorBean {

    public void errorProneMethod() throws Exception {
        throw new Exception("Foo");
    }

    public void otherErrorProneMethod() throws IllegalArgumentException {
        throw new IllegalArgumentException("Bar");
    }
}
```

In Listing 5-18, you can see the `SimpleThrowsAdvice` class that demonstrates both of the method signatures that Spring looks for on a throws advice.

Listing 5-18. *The SimpleThrowsAdvice Class*

```
package com.apress.prospring2.ch05.simple;

import java.lang.reflect.Method;

import org.springframework.aop.ThrowsAdvice;
import org.springframework.aop.framework.ProxyFactory;

public class SimpleThrowsAdvice implements ThrowsAdvice {

    public static void main(String[] args) throws Exception {
        ErrorBean errorBean = new ErrorBean();
```

```
        ProxyFactory pf = new ProxyFactory();
        pf.setTarget(errorBean);
        pf.addAdvice(new SimpleThrowsAdvice());

        ErrorBean proxy = (ErrorBean) pf.getProxy();

        try {
            proxy.errorProneMethod();
        } catch (Exception ignored) {

        }

        try {
            proxy.otherErrorProneMethod();
        } catch (Exception ignored) {

        }

    }

    public void afterThrowing(Exception ex) throws Throwable {
        System.out.println("***");
        System.out.println("Generic Exception Capture");
        System.out.println("Caught: " + ex.getClass().getName());
        System.out.println("***\n");
    }

    public void afterThrowing(Method method, Object[] args, Object target,
            IllegalArgumentException ex) throws Throwable {
        System.out.println("***");
        System.out.println("IllegalArgumentException Capture");
        System.out.println("Caught: " + ex.getClass().getName());
        System.out.println("Method: " + method.getName());
        System.out.println("***\n");
    }
}
```

We are sure that you understand the code in the `main()` method, so now we will just focus on the two `afterThrowing()` methods. The first thing Spring looks for in a throws advice is one or more public methods called `afterThrowing()`. The return type of the methods is unimportant, although we find it best to stick with `void` because this method can't return any meaningful value. The first `afterThrowing()` method in the `SimpleThrowsAdvice` class has a single argument of type `Exception`. You can specify any type of `Exception` as the argument, and this method is ideal when you are not concerned about the method that threw the exception or the arguments that were passed to it. Note that this method catches `Exception` and any subtypes of `Exception` unless the type in question has its own `afterThrowing()` method.

In the second `afterThrowing()` method, we declared four arguments to catch the `Method` that threw the exception, the arguments that were passed to the method, and the target of the method invocation. The order of the arguments in this method is important, and you must specify all four. Notice that the second `afterThrowing()` method catches exceptions of type `IllegalArgumentException` (or its subtype). Running this example produces the following output:

```
***
Generic Exception Capture
Caught: java.lang.Exception
***

***
IllegalArgumentException Capture
Caught: java.lang.IllegalArgumentException
Method: otherErrorProneMethod
***
```

As you can see, when a plain old `Exception` is thrown, the first `afterThrowing()` method is invoked, but when an `IllegalArgumentException` is thrown, the second `afterThrowing()` method is invoked. Spring only invokes a single `afterThrowing()` method for each `Exception`, and as you saw from the example in Listing 5-18, Spring uses the method whose signature contains the best match for the `Exception` type. In the situation where your after throwing advice has two `afterThrowing()` methods, both declared with the same `Exception` type but one with a single argument and the other with four arguments, Spring invokes the four-argument `afterThrowing()` method.

As we mentioned earlier, after throwing advice is useful in a variety of situations; it allows you to reclassify entire `Exception` hierarchies as well as build centralized `Exception` logging for your application. We have found that after throwing advice is particularly useful when we are debugging a live application, because it allows us to add extra logging code without needing to modify the application's code.

Choosing an Advice Type

In general, the choice of which advice type you want to use is driven by the requirements of your application, but you should choose the most specific advice type for your needs. That is to say, don't use around advice when a before advice will do. In most cases, around advice can accomplish everything that the other three advice types can, but it may be overkill for what you are trying to achieve. By using the type of advice most appropriate for your specific circumstances, you are making the intention of your code clearer and reducing the possibility of errors. Consider an advice that counts method calls. When you are using before advice, all you need to code is the counter, but with around advice, you need to remember to invoke the method and return the value to the caller. These small things can allow spurious errors to creep into your application. By keeping the advice type as focused as possible, you reduce the scope for errors.

Advisors and Pointcuts in Spring

Thus far, all the examples you have seen have used the `ProxyFactory.addAdvice()` method to configure advice for a proxy. As we mentioned earlier, this method delegates to `addAdvisor()` behind the scenes, creating an instance of `DefaultPointcutAdvisor` and configuring it with a pointcut that points to all methods. In this way, the advice is deemed to apply to all methods on the target. In some cases, such as when you are using AOP for logging purposes, this may be desirable, but in other cases, you may want to limit the methods to which an advice applies.

Of course, you could simply check, in the advice itself, that the method that is being advised is the correct one, but this approach has several drawbacks. First, hard coding the list of acceptable methods into the advice reduces the advice's reusability. By using pointcuts, you can configure the methods to which an advice applies, without needing to put this code inside the advice; this clearly increases the reuse value of the advice. The second and third drawbacks with hard-coding the list of methods into the advice are performance related. To check the method being advised in the advice, you need to perform the check each time any method on the target is invoked. This clearly reduces the performance of your application. When you use pointcuts, the check is performed once for each method, and the results are cached for later use. The other performance-related drawback of not using pointcuts to restrict the list-advised methods is that Spring can make optimizations for nonadvised methods when creating a proxy, which results in faster invocations on nonadvised methods. These optimizations are covered in greater detail when we discuss proxies later in the chapter.

We strongly recommend that you avoid the temptation to hard-code method checks into your advice and instead use pointcuts wherever possible to govern the applicability of advice to methods on the target. That said, in some cases, you need to hard-code the checks into your advice. Consider the earlier example of the after returning advice designed to catch weak keys generated by the `KeyGenerator` class. This kind of advice is closely coupled to the class it is advising, and checking inside the advice is wise, to ensure that the advice is applied to the correct type. We refer to this coupling between advice and target as target affinity. In general, you should use pointcuts when your advice has little or no target affinity—that is, it can apply to any type or a wide range of types. When your advice has strong target affinity, try to check that the advice is being used correctly in the advice itself; this helps reduce head-scratching errors when advice is misused. We also recommend that you avoid advising methods needlessly. As you will see, needless advice results in a noticeable drop in invocation speed that can have a large impact on the overall performance of your application.

The Pointcut Interface

Pointcuts in Spring are created by implementing the `Pointcut` interface, shown in Listing 5-19.

Listing 5-19. *The Pointcut Interface*

```
public interface Pointcut {

    ClassFilter getClassFilter ();

    MethodMatcher getMethodMatcher();
}
```

As you can see from this code, the `Pointcut` interface defines two methods, `getClassFilter()` and `getMethodMatcher()`, which return instances of `ClassFilter` and `MethodMatcher`, respectively. When creating your own pointcuts from scratch, you must implement both the `ClassFilter` and `MethodMatcher` interfaces as well. Thankfully, as you will see in the next section, this is usually unnecessary because Spring provides a selection of `Pointcut` implementations that cover most, if not all, of your use cases.

When determining whether a `Pointcut` applies to a particular method, Spring first checks to see if the `Pointcut` applies to the method's class using the `ClassFilter` instance returned by `Pointcut.getClassFilter()`. Listing 5-20 shows the `ClassFilter` interface.

Listing 5-20. *The ClassFilter Interface*

```
public interface ClassFilter {

    boolean matches(Class clazz);
}
```

As you can see, the ClassFilter interface defines a single method, matches(), that is passed an instance of Class that represents the class to be checked. As you have no doubt determined, the matches() method returns true if the pointcut applies to the class and false otherwise.

The MethodMatcher interface is more complex than the ClassFilter interface, as shown in Listing 5-21.

Listing 5-21. *The MethodMatcher Interface*

```
public interface MethodMatcher {

    boolean matches(Method m, Class targetClass);

    boolean isRuntime();

    boolean matches(Method m, Class targetClass, Object[] args);

}
```

Spring supports two different types of MethodMatcher, static and dynamic, determined by the return value of isRuntime(). Before using a MethodMatcher, Spring calls isRuntime() to determine whether the MethodMatcher is static, indicated by a return value of false, or dynamic, indicated by a return value of true.

For a static pointcut, Spring calls the matches(Method, Class) method of the MethodMatcher once for every method on the target, caching the return value for subsequent invocations of those methods. In this way, the check for method applicability is performed only once for each method and subsequent invocations of a method do not result in an invocation of matches().

With dynamic pointcuts, Spring still performs a static check using matches(Method, Class) the first time a method is invoked to determine the overall applicability of a method. However, in addition to this and provided that the static check returned true, Spring performs a further check for each invocation of a method using the matches(Method, Class, Object[]) method. In this way, a dynamic MethodMatcher can determine whether a pointcut should apply based on a particular invocation of a method, not just on the method itself.

Clearly, static pointcuts—that is, pointcuts whose MethodMatcher is static—perform much better than dynamic pointcuts, because they avoid the need for an additional check per invocation. That said, dynamic pointcuts provide a greater level of flexibility for deciding whether to apply advice. In general, we recommend that you use static pointcuts wherever you can. However, in cases where your advice adds substantial overhead, it may be wise to avoid any unnecessary invocations of your advice by using a dynamic pointcut.

In general, you rarely create your own Pointcut implementations from scratch, because Spring provides abstract base classes for both static and dynamic pointcuts. We look at these base classes, along with other Pointcut implementations, over the next few sections.

Available Pointcut Implementations

Spring provides ten implementations of the Pointcut interface: two abstract classes intended as convenience classes for creating static and dynamic pointcuts and eight concrete classes. These implementations are summarized in Table 5-2.

Table 5-2. *Summary of Spring Pointcut Implementations*

Implementation Class	Description
org.springframework.aop.support.ComposablePointcut	The ComposablePointcut class is used to compose two or more pointcuts together with operations such as union() and intersection(). This class is covered in more detail in the next chapter.
org.springframework.aop.support.ControlFlowPointcut	The ControlFlowPointcut is a special case pointcut that matches all methods within the control flow of another method, that is, any method that is invoked either directly or indirectly as the result of another method being invoked. We cover ControlFlowPointcut in more detail in the next chapter.
org.springframework.aop.support.JdkRegexpMethodPointcut	The JdkRexepMethodPointcut allows you to define pointcuts using JDK 1.4 regular expression support. This class requires JDK 1.4 or higher.
org.springframework.aop.support.NameMatchMethodPointcut	Using the NameMatchMethodPointcut, you can create a pointcut that performs simple matching against a list of method names.
org.springframework.aop.StaticMethodMatcherPointcut	The StaticMethodMatcherPointcut class is intended as a base for building static pointcuts.
org.springframework.aop.DynamicMethodMatcherPointcut	The DynamicMethodMatcherPointcut class is a convenient superclass for building dynamic pointcuts that are aware of method arguments at runtime.
org.springframework.aop.AnnotationMatchingPointcut	The AnnotationMatchingPointcut class is used for creating Java 5 annotated pointcuts.
org.springframework.aop.AspectJExpressionPointcut	The AspectJExpressionPointcut convenient class is used for defining pointcuts using AspectJ expression language. Note that only method execution pointcuts can be defined, as Spring AOP does not support other AspectJ pointcuts in the current version.

We cover the basic implementations in detail in the following sections.

Using DefaultPointcutAdvisor

Before you can use any Pointcut implementation, you must first create an Advisor, more specifically a PointcutAdvisor. Remember from our earlier discussions that an Advisor is Spring's representation of an aspect, a coupling of advice and pointcuts that governs which methods should be advised and how they should be advised. Spring provides four implementations of PointcutAdvisor, but for now, we concern ourselves we just one—DefaultPointcutAdvisor. DefaultPointcutAdvisor is a simple PointcutAdvisor for associating a single Pointcut with a single Advice.

Creating a Static Pointcut Using StaticMethodMatcherPointcut

In this section, we will create a simple static pointcut using the StaticMethodMatcherPointcut class as a base. StaticMethodMatcherPointcut requires you to implement only a single method, matches (Method, Class); the rest of the Pointcut implementation is handled automatically. Although this is the only method you are required to implement, you may also want to override the getClassFilter() method as we do in this example to ensure that only methods of the correct type get advised.

For this example, we have two classes, BeanOne and BeanTwo, with identical methods defined in both. Listing 5-22 shows the BeanOne class.

Listing 5-22. *The BeanOne Class*

```
package com.apress.prospring2.ch05.staticpc;

public class BeanOne {

    public void foo() {
        System.out.println("foo");
    }

    public void bar() {
        System.out.println("bar");
    }
}
```

The BeanTwo class has identical methods to BeanOne. With this example, we want to be able to create a proxy of both classes using the same DefaultPointcutAdvisor but have the advice apply to only the foo() method of the BeanOne class. To do this, we created the SimpleStaticPointcut class shown in Listing 5-23.

Listing 5-23. *The SimpleStaticPointcut Class*

```
package com.apress.prospring2.ch05.staticpc;

import java.lang.reflect.Method;

import org.springframework.aop.ClassFilter;
import org.springframework.aop.support.StaticMethodMatcherPointcut;

public class SimpleStaticPointcut extends StaticMethodMatcherPointcut {

    public boolean matches(Method method, Class cls) {
        return ("foo".equals(method.getName()));
    }

    public ClassFilter getClassFilter() {
        return new ClassFilter() {
            public boolean matches(Class cls) {
                return (cls == BeanOne.class);
            }
        };

    }
}
```

Here, you can see that we implemented the matches(Method, Class) method as required by the StaticMethodMatcher base class. The implementation simply returns true if the name of the method is foo; otherwise, it returns false. Notice that we have also overridden the getClassFilter() method to return a ClassFilter instance whose matches() method only returns true for the BeanOne class. With this static pointcut, we are saying that only methods of the BeanOne class will be matched, and furthermore, only the foo() method of that class will be matched.

Listing 5-24 shows the SimpleAdvice class that simply writes out a message on either side of the method invocation.

Listing 5-24. *The SimpleAdvice Class*

```
package com.apress.prospring2.ch05.staticpc;

import org.aopalliance.intercept.MethodInterceptor;
import org.aopalliance.intercept.MethodInvocation;

public class SimpleAdvice implements MethodInterceptor {

    public Object invoke(MethodInvocation invocation) throws Throwable {
        System.out.println(">> Invoking " + invocation.getMethod().getName());
        Object retVal = invocation.proceed();
        System.out.println(">> Done");
        return retVal;
    }
}
```

In Listing 5-25, you can see a simple driver application for this example that creates an instance of `DefaultPointcutAdvisor` using the `SimpleAdvice` and `SimpleStaticPointcut` classes.

Listing 5-25. *The StaticPointcutExample Class*

```
package com.apress.prospring2.ch05.staticpc;

import org.aopalliance.aop.Advice;
import org.springframework.aop.Advisor;
import org.springframework.aop.Pointcut;
import org.springframework.aop.framework.ProxyFactory;
import org.springframework.aop.support.DefaultPointcutAdvisor;

public class StaticPointcutExample {

    public static void main(String[] args) {
        BeanOne one = new BeanOne();
        BeanTwo two = new BeanTwo();

        BeanOne proxyOne;
        BeanTwo proxyTwo;

        // create pointcut, advice, and advisor
        Pointcut pc = new SimpleStaticPointcut();
        Advice advice = new SimpleAdvice();
        Advisor advisor = new DefaultPointcutAdvisor(pc, advice);

        // create BeanOne proxy
        ProxyFactory pf = new ProxyFactory();
        pf.addAdvisor(advisor);
        pf.setTarget(one);
        proxyOne = (BeanOne)pf.getProxy();

        // create BeanTwo proxy
        pf = new ProxyFactory();
        pf.addAdvisor(advisor);
        pf.setTarget(two);
        proxyTwo = (BeanTwo)pf.getProxy();

        proxyOne.foo();
        proxyTwo.foo();
```

```
        proxyOne.bar();
        proxyTwo.bar();

    }
}
```

Notice that the `DefaultPointcutAdvisor` instance is then used to create two proxies: one for an instance of `BeanOne` and one for an instance of `BeanTwo`. Finally, both the `foo()` and `bar()` methods are invoked on the two proxies.

Running this example results in the following output:

```
>> Invoking foo
foo
>> Done
foo
bar
bar
```

As you can see, the only method for which the `SimpleAdvice` was actually invoked was the `foo()` method for the `BeanOne` class, exactly as expected. Restricting the methods that an advice applies is quite simple and, as you will see when we discuss the different proxy options, is key to getting the best performance out of your application.

Creating a Dynamic Pointcut Using DynamicMethodMatcherPointcut

As we will demonstrate in this section, creating a dynamic pointcut is not much different from creating a static one. For this example, we create a dynamic pointcut for the class shown in Listing 5-26.

Listing 5-26. *The SampleBean Class*

```
package com.apress.prospring2.ch05.dynamicpc;

public class SampleBean {

    public void foo(int x) {
        System.out.println("Invoked foo() with: "  +x);
    }

    public void bar() {
        System.out.println("Invoked bar()");
    }
}
```

For this example, we want to advise only the `foo()` method, but unlike the previous example, we want to advise this method only if the `int` argument passed to it is greater or less than 100.

As with static pointcuts, Spring provides a convenience base class for creating dynamic pointcuts—`DynamicMethodMatcherPointcut`. The `DynamicMethodMatcherPointcut` class has a single abstract method, `matches(Method, Class, Object[])`, that you must implement, but as you will see, implementing the `matches(Method, Class)` method to control the behavior of the static checks is also prudent. Listing 5-27 shows the `SimpleDynamicPointcut` class.

Listing 5-27. *The SimpleDynamicPointcut Class*

```
package com.apress.prospring2.ch05.dynamicpc;

import java.lang.reflect.Method;

import org.springframework.aop.ClassFilter;
import org.springframework.aop.support.DynamicMethodMatcherPointcut;

public class SimpleDynamicPointcut extends DynamicMethodMatcherPointcut {

    public boolean matches(Method method, Class cls) {
        System.out.println("Static check for " + method.getName());
        return ("foo".equals(method.getName()));
    }

    public boolean matches(Method method, Class cls, Object[] args) {
        System.out.println("Dynamic check for " + method.getName());
        int x = (Integer) args[0];
        return (x != 100);
    }

    public ClassFilter getClassFilter() {
        return new ClassFilter() {

            public boolean matches(Class cls) {
                return (cls == SampleBean.class);
            }
        };
    }
}
```

As Listing 5-27 shows, we override the `getClassFilter()` method in a similar manner to the previous example shown in Listing 5-23. This removes the need to check the class in the method-matching methods—something that is especially important for the dynamic check. Although we are only required to implement the dynamic check, we implement the static check as well, because we know the `bar()` method will never be advised. By indicating this using the static check, Spring ensures it never has to perform a dynamic check for this method. If we neglect the static check, Spring performs a dynamic check each time the `bar()` method is invoked even though it always returns `false`. In the `matches(Method, Class, Object[])` method, you can see that we return `false` if the value of the `int` argument passed to the `foo()` method is `false`; otherwise, we return `true`. Note that in the dynamic check, we know that we are dealing with the `foo()` method, because no other method makes it past the static check.

In Listing 5-28, you can see an example of this pointcut in action.

Listing 5-28. *The DynamicPointcutExample Class*

```
package com.apress.prospring2.ch02.dynamicpc;

import org.springframework.aop.Advisor;
import org.springframework.aop.framework.ProxyFactory;
import org.springframework.aop.support.DefaultPointcutAdvisor;

import com.apress.prospring.ch6.staticpc.SimpleAdvice;

public class DynamicPointcutExample {
```

```
    public static void main(String[] args) {
        SampleBean target = new SampleBean();

        // create advisor
        Advisor advisor = new DefaultPointcutAdvisor(
                new SimpleDynamicPointcut(), new SimpleAdvice());

        // create proxy
        ProxyFactory pf = new ProxyFactory();
        pf.setTarget(target);
        pf.addAdvisor(advisor);
        SampleBean proxy = (SampleBean)pf.getProxy();

        proxy.foo(1);
        proxy.foo(10);
        proxy.foo(100);

        proxy.bar();
        proxy.bar();
        proxy.bar();
    }
}
```

Notice that we have used the same advice class as in the static pointcut example. However, in this example, only the first two calls to `foo()` should be advised. The dynamic check prevents the third call to `foo()` from being advised, and the static check prevents the `bar()` method from being advised. Running this example yields the following output:

```
Static check for foo
Static check for bar
Static check for toString
Static check for clone
Static check for foo
Dynamic check for foo
>> Invoking foo
Invoked foo() with: 1
>> Done
Dynamic check for foo
>> Invoking foo
Invoked foo() with: 10
>> Done
Dynamic check for foo
Invoked foo() with: 100
Static check for bar
Invoked bar()
Invoked bar()
Invoked bar()
```

As we expected, only the first two invocations of the `foo()` method were advised. Notice that none of the `bar()` invocations is subject to a dynamic check, thanks to the static check on `bar()`. An interesting point to note here is that the `foo()` method is actually subject to *two* static checks: one during the initial phase when all methods are checked and another when it is first invoked.

As you can see, dynamic pointcuts offer a greater degree of flexibility than static pointcuts, but due to the additional runtime overhead they require, you should only use a dynamic pointcut when absolutely necessary.

Using Simple Name Matching

Often when creating a pointcut, you want to match based on just the name of the method, ignoring the method signature and return type. In this case, you can avoid needing to create a subclass of `StaticMethodMatcherPointcut` and use the `NameMatchMethodPointcut` to match against a list of method names instead. When you are using `NameMatchMethodPointcut`, no consideration is given to the signature of the method, so if you have methods `foo()` and `foo(int)`, they are both matched for the name `foo`.

Now for a demonstration, look at Listing 5-29, which shows a simple class with four methods.

Listing 5-29. *The NameBean Class*

```
package com.apress.prospring2.ch05.namepc;

public class NameBean {

    public void foo() {
        System.out.println("foo");
    }

    public void foo(int x) {
        System.out.println("foo " + x);
    }

    public void bar() {
        System.out.println("bar");
    }

    public void yup() {
        System.out.println("yup");
    }
}
```

For this example, we want to match the `foo()`, `foo(int)`, and `bar()` methods using the `NameMatchMethodPointcut`; this translates to matching the names `foo` and `bar`. This is shown in Listing 5-30.

Listing 5-30. *Using the NameMatchMethodPointcut*

```
package com.apress.prospring2.ch05.namepc;

import org.springframework.aop.Advisor;
import org.springframework.aop.framework.ProxyFactory;
import org.springframework.aop.support.DefaultPointcutAdvisor;
import org.springframework.aop.support.NameMatchMethodPointcut;

import com.apress.prospring2.ch05.staticpc.SimpleAdvice;

public class NamePointcutExample {

    public static void main(String[] args) {
        NameBean target = new NameBean();

        // create the advisor
        NameMatchMethodPointcut pc = new NameMatchMethodPointcut();
        pc.addMethodName("foo");
```

```
        pc.addMethodName("bar");
        Advisor advisor = new DefaultPointcutAdvisor(pc, new SimpleAdvice());

        // create the proxy
        ProxyFactory pf = new ProxyFactory();
        pf.setTarget(target);
        pf.addAdvisor(advisor);
        NameBean proxy = (NameBean)pf.getProxy();

        proxy.foo();
        proxy.foo(999);
        proxy.bar();
        proxy.yup();
    }
}
```

There is no need to create a class for the pointcut; you can simply create an instance of `NameMatchMethodPointcut`, and you are on your way. Notice that we have added two names to the pointcut, `foo` and `bar`, using the `addMethodName()` method. Running this example results in the following output:

```
>> Invoking foo
foo
>> Done
>> Invoking foo
foo 999
>> Done
>> Invoking bar
bar
>> Done
yup
```

As expected, the `foo()`, `foo(int)`, and `bar()` methods are advised, thanks to the pointcut, but the `yup()` method is left unadvised.

Creating Pointcuts with Regular Expressions

In the previous section, we discussed how to perform simple matching against a predefined list of methods. But what if you don't know all of the methods' names in advance, and instead, you know the pattern that the names follow? For instance, what if you want to match all methods whose names start with `get`? In this case, you can use one of the regular expression pointcuts, either `JdkRegexpMethodPointcut` or `Perl5RegexpMethodPointcut`, to match a method name based on a regular expression.

The code in Listing 5-31 shows a simple class with three methods.

Listing 5-31. *The RegexpBean Class*

```
package com.apress.prospring2.ch05.regexppc;

public class RegexpBean {

    public void foo1() {
        System.out.println("foo1");
    }
```

```
    public void foo2() {
        System.out.println("foo2");
    }

    public void bar() {
        System.out.println("bar");
    }
}
```

Using a regular-expression–based pointcut, we can match all methods in this class whose name starts with `foo`. This is shown in Listing 5-32.

Listing 5-32. *Using Regular Expressions for Pointcuts*

```
package com.apress.prospring2.ch05.regexppc;

import org.springframework.aop.Advisor;
import org.springframework.aop.framework.ProxyFactory;
import org.springframework.aop.support.DefaultPointcutAdvisor;
import org.springframework.aop.support.JdkRegexpMethodPointcut;

import com.apress.prospring2.ch05.staticpc.SimpleAdvice;

public class RegexpPointcutExample {

    public static void main(String[] args) {
        RegexpBean target = new RegexpBean();

        // create the advisor
        JdkRegexpMethodPointcut pc = new JdkRegexpMethodPointcut();
        pc.setPattern(".*foo.*");
        Advisor advisor = new DefaultPointcutAdvisor(pc, new SimpleAdvice());

        // create the proxy
        ProxyFactory pf = new ProxyFactory();
        pf.setTarget(target);
        pf.addAdvisor(advisor);
        RegexpBean proxy = (RegexpBean)pf.getProxy();

        proxy.foo1();
        proxy.foo2();
        proxy.bar();
    }
}
```

Notice we do not need to create a class for the pointcut; instead, we just create an instance of `JdkRegexpMethodPointcut` (which could just as easily be `Perl5RegexpMethodPointcut`) and specify the pattern to match—and we are done. The interesting thing to note is the pattern. When matching method names, Spring matches the fully qualified name of the method, so for `foo1()`, Spring is matching against `com.apress.prospring.ch6.regexppc.RegexpBean.foo1`, hence the leading `.*` in the pattern. This is a powerful concept, because it allows you to match all methods within a given package, without needing to know exactly which classes are in that package and what the names of the methods are. Running this example yields the following output:

```
>> Invoking foo1
foo1
>> Done
>> Invoking foo2
foo2
>> Done
bar
```

As you would expect, only the `foo1()` and `foo2()` methods have been advised, because the `bar()` method does not match the regular expression pattern.

Convenience Advisor Implementations

For many of the `Pointcut` implementations, Spring also provides a convenience `Advisor` implementation that acts as the `Pointcut` as well. For instance, instead of using the `NameMatchMethodPointcut` coupled with a `DefaultPointcutAdvisor` in the previous example, we could simply have used a `NameMatchMethodPointcutAdvisor`, as shown in Listing 5-33.

Listing 5-33. *Using NameMatchMethodPointcutAdvisor*

```
package com.apress.prospring.ch6.namepc;

import org.springframework.aop.framework.ProxyFactory;
import org.springframework.aop.support.NameMatchMethodPointcutAdvisor;

import com.apress.prospring2.ch6.staticpc.SimpleAdvice;

public class NamePointcutUsingAdvisor {

    public static void main(String[] args) {
        NameBean target = new NameBean();

        // create the advisor
        NameMatchMethodPointcutAdvisor advisor = new
            NameMatchMethodPointcutAdvisor(new SimpleAdvice());
        advisor.addMethodName("foo");
        advisor.addMethodName("bar");

        // create the proxy
        ProxyFactory pf = new ProxyFactory();
        pf.setTarget(target);
        pf.addAdvisor(advisor);
        NameBean proxy = (NameBean) pf.getProxy();

        proxy.foo();
        proxy.foo(999);
        proxy.bar();
        proxy.yup();
    }
}
```

Notice in Listing 6-33 that, rather than create an instance of `NameMatchMethodPointcut`, we configure the pointcut details on the instance of `NameMatchMethodPointcutAdvisor` itself. In this way, the `NameMatchMethodPointcutAdvisor` is acting as both the `Advisor` and the `Pointcut`.

You can find full details of the different convenience `Advisor` implementations by exploring the Javadoc for the `org.springframework.aop.support` package. There is no noticeable performance difference between the two approaches, and aside from slightly less code in the second approach, there are very few differences in the actual coding approaches. We prefer to stick with the first approach, because we feel that the intent is slightly clearer in the code. At the end of the day, the style you choose comes down to personal preference.

Using AspectJExpressionPointcut

The `AspectJExpressionPointcut` class enables you to write AspectJ expressions to define a pointcut. Let's see how this class is used. Listing 5-34 shows `SimpleAfterAdvice` that writes a message after returning from a method call.

Listing 5-34. *SimpleAfterAdvice Implementations*

```
public class SimpleAfterAdvice implements AfterReturningAdvice{
    public void afterReturning(Object returnValue, Method method, Object[] args, ➥
                Object target) throws Throwable {
        System.out.print("After method: " + method);
    }
}
```

Now, let's create the simple bean `SampleBean` in Listing 5-35 shows. We will advise methods on this bean using `SimpleAfterAdvice` from Listing 5-34.

Listing 5-35. *SampleBean Implementation*

```
public class SampleBean {

    public String getName() {
        return "Aleksa V";
    }

    public void setName(String name) {
        this.name=name;
    }

    public int getHeight() {
        return 201;
    }
}
```

Now, let's say that we need to log all calls to getter methods on the `SampleBean` class. For our `SampleBean` implementation, that means that we want to log calls to the `getName()` and `getHeight()` methods but not calls to the `setName()` method. We can use an AspectJ expression to define methods we want to pointcut, using `AspectJExpressionPointcut`. Listing 5-36 shows the simple demonstration class that will apply `SimpleAfterAdvice` to our `SampleBean` class.

Listing 5-36. *AspectJExpressionPoincutDemo Class*

```
public class AspectJExpressionPointcutDemo {

    public static void main(String[] args) {
        SampleBean target = new SampleBean();
```

```
        AspectJExpressionPointcut pc = new AspectJExpressionPointcut();
        pc.setExpression("execution(* com.apress.prospring2.➥
                ch05.aspectj..SampleBean.get*(..))");

        SampleBean proxy = getProxy(pc, target);
        proxy.getName();
        proxy.setName("New Name");
        proxy.getHeight();

    }

    private static SampleBean getProxy(AspectJExpressionPointcut pc, ➥
              SampleBean target) {
        // create the advisor

        Advisor advisor = new DefaultPointcutAdvisor(pc,
                new SimpleAfterAdvice());

        // create the proxy
        ProxyFactory pf = new ProxyFactory();
        pf.setTarget(target);
        pf.addAdvisor(advisor);

        return (SampleBean) pf.getProxy();
    }

}
```

In the bold code lines, we simply instantiate the AspectJExpressionPointcut and set the expression value. The expression execution(* com.apress.prospring2.ch05.aspectj..*.get*(..)) says we should pointcut all method executions in the class com.apress.prospring2.ch05.aspectj.SampleBean that start with get. After that, we simply instantiate the proxy, like in previous examples, with our AspectJExpressionPointcut and SimpleAfterAdvice.

We make calls to all three methods of the proxied SampleBean class, and we get the following console output:

```
After method: public java.lang.String com.apress.prospring2.➥
ch05.aspectj.SampleBean.getName()
After method: public int com.apress.prospring2.➥
ch05.aspectj.SampleBean.getHeight()
```

As expected, advice has been called on methods getName() and getHeight() but not on method setName().

The AspectJ expression language is a very powerful language, allowing a lot of different joinpoints in a pointcut expression. However, since AspectJExpressionPointcut is used with Spring AOP, which supports only method execution joinpoints, execution is the only joinpoint from AspectJ expression language that can be used.

You can still write very powerful AspectJ pointcut expressions. In this section, you have seen only basic syntax and usage; more in-depth examples will follow in the next chapter.

Using AnnotationMatchingPointcut

Think about the following situation: we have several methods we want to advise for performance-monitoring purposes while testing. However, these methods come from different packages and classes. More, we want to be able to change the methods or classes that are monitored with as little configuration as possible. One solution is to implement annotation, and annotate all classes or methods we want to advise with this annotation. That is where AnnotationMatchingPointcut comes into play. We can define a pointcut for methods and classes annotated with specific annotation using this convenient class.

We will use our custom SimpleAnnotation, which Listing 5-37 shows.

Listing 5-37. *SimpleAnnotation Example*

```
@Target({ElementType.METHOD, ElementType.TYPE})
@Retention(RetentionPolicy.RUNTIME)
public @interface SimpleAnnotation {

}
```

This simple annotation can be applied to either methods or classes. Let's now modify the SampleBean class from Listing 5-35 by adding an annotation to the getName() method, as shown in Listing 5-38.

Listing 5-38. *Annotated SampleBean Class*

```
public class SampleBean {

    @SimpleAnnotation
    public String getName() {
        return "Aleksa V";
    }

    public void setName(String name) {

    }

    public int getHeight() {
        return 201;
    }
}
```

We will reuse SimpleAfterAdvice from the previous section (see Listing 5-34) and apply it to all methods and/or classes annotated with @SimpleAnnotation. Listing 5-39 shows a demonstration for AnnotationMatchingPointcut.

Listing 5-39. *AnnotationMatchingPointcutDemo Example*

```
public class AnnotationMatchingPointcutDemo {

    public static void main(String[] args) {
        SampleBean target = new SampleBean();

        AnnotationMatchingPointcut pc = ➥
new AnnotationMatchingPointcut(null, SimpleAnnotation.class);

        SampleBean proxy = getProxy(pc, target);

        proxy.getName();

        proxy.getHeight();
    }
```

```
    private static SampleBean getProxy(AnnotationMatchingPointcut pc, ➥
SampleBean target) {
        // create the advisor

        Advisor advisor = new DefaultPointcutAdvisor(pc,
                new SimpleAfterAdvice());

        // create the proxy
        ProxyFactory pf = new ProxyFactory();
        pf.setTarget(target);
        pf.addAdvisor(advisor);

        return (SampleBean) pf.getProxy();
    }
}
```

As you can see in the bold code in Listing 5-39, we have simply instantiated `AnnotationMatchingPointcut` and used it in proxy instantiation. The `AnnotationMatchingPointcut` constructor accepts two parameters, a class-level annotation class, and a method-level annotation class. In our example, the class-level annotation is `null`, so we are advising all methods annotated with method-level annotation (in our case, `SimpleAnnotation.class`). We then invoke two methods, `getName()` and `getHeight()`, on the proxied `SampleBean` instance.

When we run the example, we get the following console output:

```
After method: public java.lang.String ➥
com.apress.prospring2.ch05.annotation.SampleBean.getName()
```

As expected, only the `getName()` method is advised, as it is the only method that is annotated with the method-level annotation, `@SimpleAnnotation`.

If the `AnnotationMatchingPointcut` constructor is instantiated with a class-level annotation (for example, `new AnnotationMatchingPointcut(SimpleAnnotation.class, null)`), all methods in annotated classes would be advised.

If you supply both class- and method-level annotations (`new AnnotationMatchingPointcut (SimpleAnnotation.class, SimpleAnnotation.class)` for example), both will need to be applied for the method to be advised. See Listing 5-40 for this example.

Listing 5-40. *Modified SampleBean with Class-Level Annotation*

```
@SimpleAnnotation
public class SampleBean {

    @SimpleAnnotation
    public String getName() {
        return "Aleksa V";
    }

    public void setName(String name) {

    }

    public int getHeight() {
        return 201;
    }
}
```

Using both method- and class-level annotations, the getName() method will be advised but the getHeight() method won't, as it isn't annotated on the method level.

Using Control Flow Pointcuts

Spring control flow pointcuts, implemented by the ControlFlowPointcut class, are similar to the cflow construct available in many other AOP implementations, although they are not quite as powerful. Essentially, a control flow pointcut in Spring pointcuts all method calls below a given method or below all methods in a class. This is quite hard to visualize and is better explained using an example.

Listing 5-41 shows a SimpleBeforeAdvice that writes a message out describing the method it is advising.

Listing 5-41. *The SimpleBeforeAdvice Class*

```
public class SimpleBeforeAdvice implements MethodBeforeAdvice {

    public void before(Method method, Object[] args, Object target) ➥
throws Throwable {
        System.out.println("Before method " + method);
    }
}
```

This advice class allows us to see which methods are being pointcut by the ControlFlowPointcut. In Listing 5-42, you can see a simple class with one method—the method that we want to advise.

Listing 5-42. *The TestBean Class*

```
public class TestBean {

    public void foo() {
        System.out.println("foo");
    }

}
```

In Listing 5-42, you can see the simple foo() method that we want to advise. We have, however, a special requirement—we only want to advise this method when it is called from another specific method. Listing 5-43 shows a simple driver program for this example.

Listing 5-43. *Using the ControlFlowPointcut Class*

```
public class ControlFlowDemo {

    public static void main(String[] args) {
        new ControlFlowDemo().run();
    }

    private void run() {
        TestBean target = new TestBean();

        // create advisor
        Pointcut pc = new ControlFlowPointcut(ControlFlowDemo.class, "test");
        Advisor advisor = new DefaultPointcutAdvisor(pc,
                new SimpleBeforeAdvice());

        // create proxy
        ProxyFactory pf = new ProxyFactory();
```

```
        pf.setTarget(target);
        pf.addAdvisor(advisor);

        TestBean proxy = (TestBean) pf.getProxy();

        System.out.println("Trying normal invoke");
        proxy.foo();
        System.out.println("Trying under ControlFlowDemo.test()");
        test(proxy);
    }

    private void test(TestBean bean) {
        bean.foo();
    }

}
```

In Listing 5-43, the advised proxy is assembled with `ControlFlowPointcut` and the `foo()` method is invoked twice: once directly from the `run()` method and once from the `test()` method. Here is the line of particular interest:

```
Pointcut pc = new ControlFlowPointcut(ControlFlowDemo.class, "test");
```

In this line, we are creating a `ControlFlowPointcut` instance for the `test()` method of the `ControlFlowDemo` class. Essentially, this says, "pointcut all methods that are called from the `ControlFlowDemo.test()` method." Note that although we said "pointcut all methods," in fact, this really means "pointcut all methods on the proxy object that is advised using the `Advisor` corresponding to this instance of `ControlFlowPointcut`." Running this example yields the following output:

```
Trying normal invoke
foo
Trying under ControlFlowExample.test()
Before method public void com.apress.prospring2.ch05.cflow.TestBean.foo()
foo
```

As you can see, when the `foo()` method is first invoked outside of the control flow of the `test()` method, it is unadvised. When it executes for a second time, this time inside the control flow of the `test()` method, the `ControlFlowPointcut` indicates that its associated advice applies to the method, and thus the method is advised. Note that if we had called another method from within the `test()` method, one that was not on the advised proxy, it would not have been advised.

Control flow pointcuts can be extremely useful, allowing you to advise an object selectively only when it is executed in the context of another. However, be aware that you take a substantial performance hit for using control flow pointcut over other pointcuts. Figures from the Spring documentation indicate that a control flow pointcut is typically five times slower than other pointcuts on a version 1.4 JVM.

Using ComposablePointcut

In previous pointcutting examples, we used just a single pointcut for each `Advisor`. In most cases, this is enough, but in some cases, you may need to compose two or more pointcuts together to achieve the desired goal. Consider the situation where you want to pointcut all getter and setter methods on a bean. You have a pointcut for getters and a pointcut for setters, but you don't have one for both. Of course, you could just create another pointcut with the new logic, but a better approach is to combine the two pointcuts into a single pointcut using `ComposablePointcut`.

ComposablePointcut supports two methods: union() and intersection(). By default, ComposablePointcut is created with a ClassFilter that matches all classes and a MethodMatcher that matches all methods, although you can supply your own initial ClassFilter and MethodMatcher during construction. The union() and intersection() methods are both overloaded to accept ClassFilter and MethodMatcher arguments.

Invoking the union() method for a MethodMatcher replaces the MethodMatcher of the ComposablePointcut with an instance of UnionMethodMatcher using the current MethodMatcher of the ComposablePointcut and the MethodMatcher passed to the union() method as arguments. The UnionMethodMatcher then returns true for a match if either of its wrapped MethodMatchers match. You can invoke the union() method as many times as you want, with each call creating a new UnionMethodMatcher that wraps the current MethodMatcher with the MethodMatcher passed to the union() method. A similar structure is followed when you are using ClassFilter with the union() method.

Internally, the intersection() method works in a similar way to union(). However, the IntersectionMethodMatcher class only returns true for a match if both of the embedded MethodMatcher instances match. Essentially, you can think of the union() method as an *any* match, in that it returns true if any of the matchers it is wrapping return true. And you can think of the intersection() method as an *all* match, in that it only returns true if all its wrapped matchers return true.

As with control flow pointcuts, it is quite difficult to visualize the ComposablePointcut, and it is much easier to understand with an example. Listing 5-44 shows a simple bean with three methods.

Listing 5-44. *The SampleBean Class*

```
public class SampleBean {

    public String getName() {
        return "Springfield Springy";
    }

    public void setName(String name) {

    }

    public int getAge() {
        return 100;
    }
}
```

With this example, we are going to generate three different proxies using the same ComposablePointcut instance, but each time, we are going to modify the ComposablePointcut using either the union() or intersection() method. Following this, we will invoke all three methods on the SampleBean proxy and look at which ones have been advised. Listing 5-45 shows the code for this.

Listing 5-45. *Investigating ComposablePointcut*

```
public class ComposablePointcutDemo {

    public static void main(String[] args) {
        // create target
        SampleBean target = new SampleBean();

        ComposablePointcut pc = new ComposablePointcut(ClassFilter.TRUE,
                new GetterMethodMatcher());

        System.out.println("Test 1");
        SampleBean proxy = getProxy(pc, target);
        testInvoke(proxy);
```

```
        System.out.println("Test 2");
        pc.union(new SetterMethodMatcher());
        proxy = getProxy(pc, target);
        testInvoke(proxy);

        System.out.println("Test 3");
        pc.intersection(new GetAgeMethodMatcher());
        proxy = getProxy(pc, target);
        testInvoke(proxy);

    }

    private static SampleBean getProxy(ComposablePointcut pc, SampleBean target) {
        // create the advisor

        Advisor advisor = new DefaultPointcutAdvisor(pc,
                new SimpleBeforeAdvice());

        // create the proxy
        ProxyFactory pf = new ProxyFactory();
        pf.setTarget(target);
        pf.addAdvisor(advisor);

        return (SampleBean) pf.getProxy();
    }

    private static void testInvoke(SampleBean proxy) {
        proxy.getAge();
        proxy.getName();
        proxy.setName("John Doe");
    }

    private static class GetterMethodMatcher extends StaticMethodMatcher {

        public boolean matches(Method method, Class cls) {
            return (method.getName().startsWith("get"));
        }

    }

    private static class GetAgeMethodMatcher extends StaticMethodMatcher {
        public boolean matches(Method method, Class cls) {
            return "getAge".equals(method.getName());
        }
    }

    private static class SetterMethodMatcher extends StaticMethodMatcher {

        public boolean matches(Method method, Class cls) {
            return (method.getName().startsWith("set"));
        }

    }
}
```

The first thing to notice in this example is the set of three private MethodMatcher implementations. The GetterMethodMatcher matches all methods that start with get. This is the default MethodMatcher that we use to assemble the ComposablePointcut. Because of this, we expect that the first round of invocations on the SampleBean methods will result in only the getAge() and getName() methods being advised.

The SetterMethodMatcher matches all methods that start with set, and it is combined with the ComposablePointcut using union() for the second round of invocations. At this point, we have a union of two MethodMatcher instances: one that matches all methods starting with get and one that matches all methods starting with set. To this end, we expect that all invocations during the second round will be advised.

The GetAgeMethodMatcher is very specific and only matches the getAge() method. This MethodMatcher is combined with the ComposablePointcut using intersection() for the third round for invocations. Because the GetAgeMethodMatcher is being composed using intersection(), the only method that we expect to be advised in the third round of invocations is getAge(), because this is the only method that matches all the composed MethodMatchers.

Running this example results in the following output:

```
Test 1
Before method public int com.apress.prospring2.ch06.cflow.SampleBean.getAge()
Before method public java.lang.String ➥
com.apress.prospring2.ch06.cflow.SampleBean.getName()
Test 2
Before method public int com.apress.prospring2.ch06.cflow.SampleBean.getAge()
Before method public java.lang.String ➥
com.apress.prospring2.ch06.cflow.SampleBean.getName()
Before method public void com.apress.prospring2.ch06.cflow.SampleBean.➥
setName(java.lang.String)
Test 3
Before method public int com.apress.prospring2.ch06.cflow.SampleBean.getAge()
```

As expected, the first round of invocations on the proxy saw only the getAge() and getName() methods being advised. For the second round, when the SetterMethodMatcher had been composed with the union() method, all methods were advised. In the final round, as a result of the intersection of the GetAgeMethodMatcher, only the getAge() method was advised.

Although this example only demonstrated the use of MethodMatchers in the composition process, you can see that Spring offers a powerful set of Pointcut implementations that should meet most, if not all, of your application's requirements. Remember that if you can't find a pointcut to suit your needs, you can create your own implementation from scratch by implementing Pointcut, MethodMatcher, and ClassFilter. Use ClassFilter when you are building the pointcut. Indeed, you can use a combination of MethodMatcher and ClassFilter implementations when building your composite pointcut.

Composition and the Pointcut Interface

In the last section, you saw how to create a composite pointcut using multiple MethodMatcher and ClassFilter instances. You can also create composite pointcuts using other objects that implement the Pointcut interface. You can perform an intersection of pointcuts using the ComposablePointcut.intersection() method, but for a union, you need to use the org.springframework.aop.support.Pointcuts class that has both intersection() and union() methods.

You can compose pointcuts in the same way you can for method matchers, so we do not go into any detail here. You can find more information about composition by reading the Javadoc for the Pointcuts class.

Pointcutting Summary

From the discussions in this and the previous chapter, you can see that Spring offers a powerful set of Pointcut implementations that should meet most, if not all, of your application's requirements. Remember that if you can't find a pointcut to suit your needs, you can create your own implementation from scratch by implementing Pointcut, MethodMatcher, and ClassFilter.

There are two patterns you use to combine pointcuts and advisors together. The first pattern, the one that we have used so far, involves having the pointcut implementation decoupled from the advisor. In the code you have seen up to this point, we have created instances of Pointcut implementations and used the DefaultPointcutAdvisor to add advice along with the Pointcut to the proxy.

The second option, one that is adopted by many of the examples in the Spring documentation, is to encapsulate the Pointcut inside your own Advisor implementation. That way, you have a class that implements both Pointcut and PointcutAdvisor, with the PointcutAdvisor.getPointcut() method simply returning this. This is an approach many classes, such as StaticMethodMatcherPointcutAdvisor, use in Spring.

We find that the first approach is the more flexible, allowing you to use different Pointcut implementations with different Advisor implementations. However, the second approach is useful in situations where you are going to be using the same combination of Pointcut and Advisor in different parts of your application or across many different applications. The second approach is useful when each Advisor must have a separate instance of a Pointcut; by making the Advisor responsible for creating the Pointcut, you can ensure that this is the case.

If you recall the discussion on proxy performance from the previous chapter, you will remember that unadvised methods perform much better than methods that are advised. For this reason, you should ensure that, by using a Pointcut, you only advise those methods that are absolutely necessary. This way, you reduce the amount of unnecessary overhead added to your application by using AOP.

All About Proxies

So far, we have taken only a cursory look at the proxies generated by ProxyFactory. We mentioned that there are two types of proxy available in Spring: JDK proxies created using the JDK Proxy class and CGLIB-based proxies created using the CGLIB Enhancer class. Understanding the differences between these proxies is key to making the AOP code in your application perform as well as it can. In this section, we take a detailed look at the differences between the proxies and how these differences affect the performance of your application.

You may be wondering exactly what the difference is between the two proxies and why Spring needs two different types of proxy. Prior to version 1.1 of Spring, the two types of proxy shared much in common in the way they were implemented, and the performance of both types of proxy was very similar. There are two types of proxy because of the poor performance of Proxy under JDK 1.3. Spring overcame this by providing CGLIB proxies, which performed better than the JDK 1.4 proxies when running on a version 1.3 JVM.

The initial intention of the CGLIB proxy was to overcome the performance issues of the Proxy class in JDK 1.3, so the implementation was as similar to the JDK proxy as possible. The only drawback with this was that Spring was not taking full advantage of the feature set available with CGLIB. In version 1.1, things have changed dramatically. The CGLIB proxy is now heavily optimized and outperforms the JDK proxy quite dramatically in many cases. Before we take a look at the differences in proxy implementations, we must make sure you understand exactly what the generated proxies have to do.

Caution Before version 1.1 of Spring, a bug in the CGLIB proxy code resulted in an inordinate amount of dynamically generated classes being created unnecessarily. In the long run, this resulted in excess memory being used and eventually `OutOfMemoryError` errors occurring. This bug is fixed in Spring 1.1.

Understanding Proxies

The core goal of a proxy is to intercept method invocations, and where necessary, execute chains of advice that apply to a particular method. The management and invocation of advice is largely proxy independent and is managed by the Spring AOP Framework. However, the proxy is responsible for intercepting calls to all methods and passing them as necessary to the AOP framework for the advice to be applied.

In addition to this core functionality, the proxy must also support a set of additional features. You can configure the proxy to expose itself via the `AopContext` class so that you can retrieve the proxy and invoke advised methods on the proxy from the target object. The proxy is responsible for ensuring that, when this option is enabled via `ProxyFactory.setExposeProxy()`, the proxy class is appropriately exposed. In addition to this, all proxy classes implement the `Advised` interface by default, which (among other things) allows the advice chain to be changed after the proxy has been created. A proxy must also ensure that any methods that return `this`—that is, return the proxied target—do in fact return the proxy and not the target.

As you can see, a typical proxy has quite a lot of work to perform, and all of this logic is implemented in both the JDK and CGLIB proxies. As of version 1.1 of Spring, the way in which this logic is implemented differs quite drastically depending on which of the proxy types you are using.

Using JDK Dynamic Proxies

JDK proxies are the most basic type of proxy available in Spring. Unlike the CGLIB proxy, the JDK proxy can only generate proxies of interfaces, not classes. In this way, any object you wish to proxy must implement at least one interface. In general, it is good design to use interfaces for your classes, but doing so is not always possible, especially when you are working with third-party or legacy code. In this case, you *must* use the CGLIB proxy.

When you are using the JDK proxy, all method calls are intercepted by the JVM and routed to the `invoke()` method of the proxy. This method then determines whether or not the method in question is advised, and if so, it invokes the advice chain and then the method itself using reflection. In addition to this, the `invoke()` method performs all the logic discussed in the previous section.

The JDK proxy makes no determination between methods that are advised and unadvised until it is in the `invoke()` method. This means that for unadvised methods on the proxy, the `invoke()` method is still called, all the checks are still performed, and the method is still invoked using reflection. Obviously, invoking the method on the proxy incurs a runtime overhead each time the method is invoked, even though the proxy often performs no additional processing other than to invoke the unadvised method via reflection.

You can instruct the `ProxyFactory` to use a JDK proxy by specifying the list of interfaces to proxy using `setProxyInterfaces()`.

Using CGLIB Proxies

With the JDK proxy, all decisions about how to handle a particular method invocation are taken at runtime each time the method is invoked. When you use CGLIB, you avoid this approach in favor of one that performs much better. A full discussion of the inner workings of CGLIB is well beyond the scope of this chapter, but essentially, CGLIB dynamically generates the bytecode for a new class on the fly for each proxy, reusing already generated classes wherever possible. This approach allows you to make extensive optimizations.

When a CGLIB proxy is first created, CGLIB asks Spring how it wants to handle each method. This means that many of the decisions that are performed in each call to `invoke()` on the JDK proxy are performed just once for the CGLIB proxy. Because CGLIB generates actual bytecode, there is also a lot more flexibility in the way you can handle methods. For instance, the CGLIB proxy generates the appropriate bytecode to invoke any unadvised methods directly, dramatically reducing the overhead introduced by the proxy. In addition to this, the CGLIB proxy determines whether it is possible for a method to return `this`; if not, it allows the method call to be invoked directly, again reducing the overhead substantially.

The CGLIB proxy also handles fixed advice chains differently than the JDK proxy. A fixed advice chain is one that you guarantee will not change after the proxy has been generated. By default, you are able to change the advisors and advice on a proxy even after it is created, although this is rarely a requirement. The CGLIB proxy handles fixed advice chains in a particular way, reducing the runtime overhead for executing an advice chain.

In addition to all these optimizations, the CGLIB proxy utilizes the bytecode generation capabilities to gain a slight increase in performance when invoking advised methods; this results in advised methods that perform slightly better than those on JDK proxies.

Comparing Proxy Performance

So far, all we have done is discuss in loose terms the differences in implementation between the different proxy types. In this section, we are going to run a simple performance test to compare the performance of the CGLIB proxy with the JDK proxy.

Listing 5-46 shows the code for the performance test.

Listing 5-46. *Testing Proxy Performance*

```
package com.apress.prospring2.ch05.proxies;

import org.springframework.aop.Advisor;
import org.springframework.aop.framework.Advised;
import org.springframework.aop.framework.ProxyFactory;
import org.springframework.aop.support.DefaultPointcutAdvisor;

public class ProxyPerfTest {

    public static void main(String[] args) {
        ISimpleBean target = new SimpleBean();

        Advisor advisor = new DefaultPointcutAdvisor(new TestPointcut(),
                new NoOpBeforeAdvice());

        runCglibTests(advisor, target);
        runCglibFrozenTests(advisor, target);
        runJdkTests(advisor, target);
    }

    private static void runCglibTests(Advisor advisor, ISimpleBean target) {
        ProxyFactory pf = new ProxyFactory();
        pf.setTarget(target);
        pf.addAdvisor(advisor);

        ISimpleBean proxy = (ISimpleBean)pf.getProxy();
        System.out.println("Running CGLIB (Standard) Tests");
        test(proxy);
    }
```

```
    private static void runCglibFrozenTests(Advisor advisor, ISimpleBean target) {
        ProxyFactory pf = new ProxyFactory();
        pf.setTarget(target);
        pf.addAdvisor(advisor);
        pf.setFrozen(true);

        ISimpleBean proxy = (ISimpleBean)pf.getProxy();
        System.out.println("Running CGLIB (Frozen) Tests");
        test(proxy);
    }

    private static void runJdkTests(Advisor advisor, ISimpleBean target) {
        ProxyFactory pf = new ProxyFactory();
        pf.setTarget(target);
        pf.addAdvisor(advisor);
        pf.setInterfaces(new Class[]{ISimpleBean.class});

        ISimpleBean proxy = (ISimpleBean)pf.getProxy();
        System.out.println("Running JDK Tests");
        test(proxy);
    }

    private static void test(ISimpleBean bean) {
        long before = 0;
        long after = 0;

        // test advised method
        System.out.println("Testing Advised Method");
        before = System.currentTimeMillis();
        for(int x = 0; x < 500000; x++) {
            bean.advised();
        }
        after = System.currentTimeMillis();;

        System.out.println("Took " + (after - before) + " ms");

        // testing unadvised method
        System.out.println("Testing Unadvised Method");
        before = System.currentTimeMillis();
        for(int x = 0; x < 500000; x++) {
            bean.unadvised();
        }
        after = System.currentTimeMillis();;

        System.out.println("Took " + (after - before) + " ms");

        // testing equals() method
        System.out.println("Testing equals() Method");
        before = System.currentTimeMillis();
        for(int x = 0; x < 500000; x++) {
            bean.equals(bean);
        }
        after = System.currentTimeMillis();;

        System.out.println("Took " + (after - before) + " ms");

        // testing hashCode() method
```

```
        System.out.println("Testing hashCode() Method");
        before = System.currentTimeMillis();
        for(int x = 0; x < 500000; x++) {
            bean.hashCode();
        }
        after = System.currentTimeMillis();;

        System.out.println("Took " + (after - before) + " ms");

        // testing method on Advised
        Advised advised = (Advised)bean;

        System.out.println("Testing Advised.getProxyTargetClass() Method");
        before = System.currentTimeMillis();
        for(int x = 0; x < 500000; x++) {
            advised.getProxyTargetClass();
        }
        after = System.currentTimeMillis();;

        System.out.println("Took " + (after - before) + " ms");

        System.out.println(">>>\n");
    }
}
```

In this code, you can see that we are testing three kinds of proxy: a standard CGLIB proxy, a CGLIB proxy with a frozen advice chain, and a JDK proxy. For each proxy type, we run the following five test cases:

- *Advised method*: A method is advised. The advice type used in the test is a before advice that performs no processing, so it reduces the effects of the advice itself on the performance tests.
- *Unadvised method*: A method on the proxy is unadvised. Often, your proxy has many methods that are not advised. This test looks at how well unadvised methods perform for the different proxies.
- *The* `equals()` *method*: This test looks at the overhead of invoking the `equals()` method. This method is especially important when you use proxies as keys in a `HashMap` or similar collection.
- *The* `hashCode()` *method*: As with the `equals()` method, the `hashCode()` method is important when you are using `HashMaps` or similar collections.
- *Executing methods on the* `Advised` *interface*: As we mentioned earlier, a proxy implements the `Advised` interface by default, allowing you to modify the proxy after creation and to query information about the proxy. This test looks at how quickly methods on the `Advised` interface can be accessed using the different proxy types.

We ran the test on two processors: a dual-core Xeon at 2.65 GHz with 2GB of RAM and a 32-bit Sun 1.5 JVM on Ubuntu Linux 7.10 i386. When running the test, we set the initial heap size of the JVM to 1024MB to reduce the effects of heap resizing on test results. The results are shown in Table 5-3.

Table 5-3. *Proxy Performance Test Results (in milliseconds)*

Test	Standard CGLIB	Frozen CGLIB	JDK
Advised method	239	155	442
Unadvised method	126	24	322
`equals()`	36	35	504
`hashCode()`	53	40	180
`Advised.getProxyTargetClass()`	24	28	212

The results in this table clearly show that the CGLIB proxy performs much better than the JDK proxies. A standard CGLIB proxy only performs marginally better than the JDK proxy when executing an advised method, but the difference is noticable when you are using a proxy with a frozen advice chain. For unadvised methods, the CGLIB proxy is over eight times faster than the JDK proxy. Similar figures apply to the `equals()` and `hashCode()` methods, which are noticeably faster when you are using the CGLIB proxy. Notice that `hashCode()` is faster than `equals()`. The reason for this is that `equals()` is handled in a specific way to ensure that the `equals()` contract is preserved for the proxies. For methods on the `Advised` interface, you will notice that they are also faster on the CGLIB proxy, although not to the same degree. The reason why they are faster is that `Advised` methods are handled early on in the `intercept()` method, and they avoid much of the logic that is required for other methods.

In the test results, notice that, for the standard CGLIB proxy, the invocation on `Advised.getProxyTargetClass()` took 0 milliseconds. This indicates that this call was optimized out by the just-in-time (JIT) compiler. On subsequent runs of the test, we noticed that sometimes calls to `hashCode()` were also optimized out when either CGLIB proxy was used. Interestingly, none of the method calls was ever optimized out for the JDK proxy.

Which Proxy to Use?

Deciding which proxy to use is typically easy. The CGLIB proxy can proxy both classes and interfaces, whereas the JDK proxy can only proxy interfaces. Add to this the fact that the CGLIB proxy clearly performs better than the JDK proxy, and it becomes apparent that the CGLIB proxy is the correct choice. The only thing to be aware of when using the CGLIB proxy is that a new class is generated for each distinct proxy, although with version 1.1, the reuse of proxy classes is now functioning correctly, reducing the runtime overhead of frequent class generation and reducing the amount of memory used by the CGLIB proxy classes. When proxying a class, the CGLIB proxy is the default choice, because it is the only proxy capable of generating a proxy of a class. In order to use the CGLIB proxy when proxying an interface, you must set the value of the `optimize` flag in the `ProxyFactory` to `true` using the `setOptimize()` method.

Summary

In this chapter, we introduced the core concepts of AOP and looked at how these concepts translate into the Spring AOP implementation. We discussed the features that are and are not implemented in Spring AOP, and we pointed to AspectJ as an AOP solution for those features Spring does not implement. We spent some time explaining the details of the advice types available in Spring, and you have seen examples of all types in action. We also looked at how you limit the methods to which advice applies using pointcuts. In particular, we looked at the pointcut implementations available with Spring. Finally, we covered the details of how the AOP proxies are constructed, the various options, and what makes the proxies different. We wrapped up the discussion of proxies with a comparison of the performance among three different proxy types, and we concluded that the CGLIB proxy performs the best and is suitable for most, if not all, the proxies you will use.

In Chapter 6, we will look at Spring's `@AspectJ` annotation support for easy configuration of your advices and pointcuts. We will also look at how AOP is supported by Spring Framework services, which means you can define and configure advice declaratively rather than programmatically. Chapter 6 finishes with a look at how to integrate AspectJ with Spring to extend the AOP feature set available to your application.

CHAPTER 6

Advanced AOP

In this chapter, we go into more detail about the AOP features available in Spring. In particular, we look at the topic in a much more real-world light: we explore the framework services in Spring that allow for transparent application of AOP; we cover real-world usage of AOP in the context of the sample application; and we discuss overcoming the limitations of Spring AOP using Spring/AspectJ integration.

First, we'll cover @AspectJ. Spring 2.5 brings a new way of writing aspects; it automatically turns classes with specific annotations into Spring AOP aspects. The @AspectJ support allows you to very easily and cleanly define aspects. Because the @AspectJ aspects are Spring beans, you have full access to Spring's DI features.

Introductions, mentioned briefly in the previous chapter, allow you to add interface implementations dynamically to any object on the fly using the familiar interceptor concept. In this chapter, we'll cover these in more detail.

After introductions, we'll look at how the `ProxyFactoryBean`, the class at the heart of Spring AOP, can affect the behavior of your application. We explain the difference between direct and proxied calls.

Next, we'll cover integrating AspectJ, which is a full featured, statically compiled AOP implementation. The feature set of AspectJ is much greater than that of Spring AOP, but AspectJ is much more complicated to use. As mentioned in the previous chapter, AspectJ is a good solution when you find that Spring AOP lacks a feature you need (particularly when it comes to the various pointcut types).

Finally, we will take a look at how you can use aspect-oriented programming in your applications. We will ignore the usual choices (e.g., logging and security) and offer a more realistic example.

In order to run some of the examples in this chapter, you need to obtain AspectJ. You can download it from `http://eclipse.org/aspectj`. We used version 1.5.4 of AspectJ for the examples in this chapter.

@AspectJ

@AspectJ has nothing to do with AspectJ; it is a set of Java 5 annotations that Spring uses to parse the pointcuts and advice. This also means that @AspectJ aspects have no dependency on AspectJ; they use pure Spring AOP. The @AspectJ support offers a very easy and convenient way to create aspects; some IDEs come with @AspectJ support, simplifying the process of creating aspects.

Let's begin by writing the infamous logging aspect in Listing 6-1. We will write a single piece of around advice for every method call on the `TestBean` class.

Listing 6-1. *Simple @AspectJ Aspect*

```
@Aspect
public class LoggingAspect {

    @Around("execution(* com.apress.prospring2.ch06.simple.TestBean.*(..))")
    public Object log(ProceedingJoinPoint pjp) throws Throwable {
        System.out.println("Before");
        Object ret = pjp.proceed();
        System.out.println("After");
        return ret;
    }

}
```

The first annotation, `@Aspect` simply tells Spring to treat this bean as an aspect, that is, to extract the pointcuts and advice from it. Next, we have the `@Around` annotation with an AspectJ pointcut expression. The advice is very simple: it "logs" the start of the call to the method, proceeds to invoke the advised method, and finally "logs" the end of the method call. Next, let's create a sample application and the `TestBean` class (see Listing 6-2).

Listing 6-2. *The TestBean and Sample Application for the Aspect*

```
// TestBean.java
public class TestBean {

    public void work() {
        System.out.println("work");
    }

    public void stop() {
        System.out.println("stop");
    }

}

// LoggingAspectDemo.java
public class LoggingAspectDemo {

    public static void main(String[] args) {
        ApplicationContext ac = new ClassPathXmlApplicationContext(
                "/META-INF/spring/ataspectjdemo1-context.xml"
        );
        TestBean testBean = (TestBean) ac.getBean("test");
        testBean.work();
        testBean.stop();
    }

}
```

Finally, we put in the last piece of the puzzle: the `ataspectjdemo1-context.xml` file in Listing 6-3.

Listing 6-3. *ApplicationContext Configuration File*

```
<?xml version="1.0" encoding="UTF-8"?>
<beans xmlns="http://www.springframework.org/schema/beans"
       xmlns:xsi="http://www.w3.org/2001/XMLSchema-instance"
       xmlns:aop="http://www.springframework.org/schema/aop"
```

```
        xsi:schemaLocation="http://www.springframework.org/schema/beans
                http://www.springframework.org/schema/beans/spring-beans.xsd
                http://www.springframework.org/schema/aop
                http://www.springframework.org/schema/aop/spring-aop.xsd">

    <bean id="test" class="com.apress.prospring2.ch06.simple.TestBean"/>

</beans>
```

When we run the application, it gets the test bean and calls its `work()` and `stop()` methods, but the aspect doesn't seem to work. We have forgotten to enable the @AspectJ support, and we haven't declared the `LoggingAspect` as a Spring bean in Listing 6-3. Luckily, both these things are easy to do; in fact, all we have to do is update the `ataspectjdemo1-context.xml` file (see Listing 6-4).

Listing 6-4. *Modified ataspectjdemo1-context.xml*

```
<?xml version="1.0" encoding="UTF-8"?>
<beans xmlns="http://www.springframework.org/schema/beans"
       xmlns:xsi="http://www.w3.org/2001/XMLSchema-instance"
       xmlns:aop="http://www.springframework.org/schema/aop"
       xsi:schemaLocation="
            http://www.springframework.org/schema/beans
            http://www.springframework.org/schema/beans/spring-beans.xsd
            http://www.springframework.org/schema/aop
            http://www.springframework.org/schema/aop/spring-aop.xsd">

    <bean id="test" class="com.apress.prospring2.ch06.simple.TestBean"/>
    <bean class="com.apress.prospring2.ch06.simple.LoggingAspect"/>
    <aop:aspectj-autoproxy />

</beans>
```

The bold lines show the critical points of the configuration. First, we define the `aop` namespace. Next, we declare the `LoggingAspect` as a regular Spring bean, and finally, we use the `<aop:aspectj-autoproxy />` tag. The code behind the `<aop:aspectj-autoproxy />` tag is responsible for post-processing all beans that have at least one piece of advice. Spring will create a proxy for all advised beans. When we run the application now, we will see that our logging advice gets called, and the application prints out the following:

```
Before
work
After
Before
stop
After
```

Notice that the aspect is a regular Spring bean, which means we can use Spring to set its dependencies. As an example, let's improve the `LoggingAspect` to include a custom message for the before and after log entries (see Listing 6-5).

Listing 6-5. *ImprovedLoggingAspect*

```
@Aspect
public class ImprovedLoggingAspect {
    private String beforeMessage;
    private String afterMessage;
```

```
    @Around("execution(* com.apress.prospring2.ch06.simple.TestBean.*(..))")
    public Object log(ProceedingJoinPoint pjp) throws Throwable {
        System.out.println(String.format(this.beforeMessage,
                pjp.getSignature().getName(), Arrays.toString(pjp.getArgs())));
        Object ret = pjp.proceed();
        System.out.println(String.format(this.afterMessage,
                pjp.getSignature().getName(), Arrays.toString(pjp.getArgs())));
        return ret;
    }

    @PostConstruct
    public void initialize() {
        Assert.notNull(this.beforeMessage,
           "The [beforeMessage] property of [" + getClass().getName() +
           "] must be set.");
        Assert.notNull(this.afterMessage,
           "The [afterMessage] property of [" + getClass().getName() +
           "] must be set.");
    }

    public void setBeforeMessage(String beforeMessage) {
        this.beforeMessage = beforeMessage;
    }

    public void setAfterMessage(String afterMessage) {
        this.afterMessage = afterMessage;
    }
}
```

Here, you can see that we are treating the aspect as a plain Spring bean: we have defined two properties and a @PostConstruct-annotated method. Listing 6-6 shows the modifications to the ataspectjdemo1-context.xml to use the ImprovedLoggingAspect.

Listing 6-6. *Modified ApplicationContext Configuration File*

```
<?xml version="1.0" encoding="UTF-8"?>
<beans xmlns="http://www.springframework.org/schema/beans"
       xmlns:xsi="http://www.w3.org/2001/XMLSchema-instance"
       xmlns:aop="http://www.springframework.org/schema/aop"
       xsi:schemaLocation="
            http://www.springframework.org/schema/beans
            http://www.springframework.org/schema/beans/spring-beans.xsd
            http://www.springframework.org/schema/aop
            http://www.springframework.org/schema/aop/spring-aop.xsd">

    <bean id="test" class="com.apress.prospring2.ch06.simple.TestBean"/>
    <bean class="com.apress.prospring2.ch06.simple.ImprovedLoggingAspect">
        <property name="beforeMessage" value="Before %s %s"/>
        <property name="afterMessage" value="After %s %s"/>
    </bean>
    <aop:aspectj-autoproxy />

</beans>
```

When we run the application, we see that the new aspect is working; its properties are set to the values in the configuration file. The application now prints this:

```
Before work []
work
After work []
Before stop []
stop
After stop []
```

You can see that creating aspects is no more difficult than writing standard Java code. Most IDEs will also offer some assistance with the @AspectJ work (Figure 6-1 shows IDE support in IntelliJ IDEA 7).

```
@Aspect
public class ImprovedLoggingAspect {
    private String beforeMessage;
    private String afterMessage;

    @Around("execution(* com.apress.prospring2.ch06.simple.|.*(..))")
    public Object log(ProceedingJoinPoint pjp) throws   ImprovedLoggingAspect
        System.out.println(String.format(this.beforeMe:  LoggingAspect
                pjp.getSignature().getName(), Arrays.t(   LoggingAspectDemo
        Object ret = pjp.proceed();                       TestBean
        System.out.println(String.format(this.afterMessage,
                pjp.getSignature().getName(), Arrays.toString(pjp.getArgs())));
        return ret;
    }
```

Figure 6-1. *IntelliJ IDEA 7 @AspectJ support*

In the next section, we will take a more detailed look at the @AspectJ support in Spring.

@AspectJ Aspects in Detail

Now that we have written our first @AspectJ aspect, we need to take a more detailed look at its features. We need to take a look at how to create pointcuts (including best and recommended practices) and how we can write advice. Let's begin by looking at pointcuts; we will use @pointcut whenever we are going to reference an `@Pointcut`-annotated method. We will say @pointcut expression when we refer to the code used in the `@Pointcut` annotation. To illustrate this, take a look at the following code snippet:

```
@Pointcut("execution(* com.apress.prospring2.ch06.simple.TestBean.*(..))")
private void testBeanExecution() { }
```

In this snippet, the `testBeanExecution` method is an @pointcut, and `"execution(* com.apress.prospring2.ch06.simple.TestBean.*(..))"` is a pointcut expression.

Pointcuts

In our first aspect, we have used a pointcut in the around advice. We have specified the pointcut expression as constant. If we wanted to create another advice using the same pointcut, we'd have to duplicate the pointcut expression constant. To prevent this duplication, we can use the `@Pointcut` annotation to create a pointcut. Let's modify our logging aspect to use the @pointcut (see Listing 6-7).

Listing 6-7. *Using the @Pointcut Annotation*

```
@Aspect
public class LoggingAspectPC {
    private String beforeMessage;
    private String afterMessage;

    @Pointcut("execution(* com.apress.prospring2.ch06.simple.TestBean.*(..))")
    private void testBeanExecution() { }

    @Around("testBeanExecution()")
    public Object log(ProceedingJoinPoint pjp) throws Throwable {
        System.out.println(String.format(this.beforeMessage,
                pjp.getSignature().getName(), Arrays.toString(pjp.getArgs())));
        Object ret = pjp.proceed();
        System.out.println(String.format(this.afterMessage,
                pjp.getSignature().getName(), Arrays.toString(pjp.getArgs())));
        return ret;
    }

    @PostConstruct
    public void initialize() {
        Assert.notNull(this.beforeMessage,
           "The [beforeMessage] property of [" + getClass().getName() +
           "] must be set.");
        Assert.notNull(this.afterMessage,
            "The [afterMessage] property of [" + getClass().getName() +
           "] must be set.");
    }

    public void setBeforeMessage(String beforeMessage) {
        this.beforeMessage = beforeMessage;
    }

    public void setAfterMessage(String afterMessage) {
        this.afterMessage = afterMessage;
    }
}
```

The code in bold shows that we have created the `testBeanExecution` @pointcut with the expression `execution(* com.apress.prospring2.ch06.simple.TestBean.*(..))`. The `log` advice uses the @pointcut, but we can now add another advice using the same @pointcut. Listing 6-8 shows a fragment of the `LoggingAspectPC` that uses the same `testBeanExecution` @pointcut.

Listing 6-8. *Using the Same Pointcut*

```
@Aspect
public class LoggingAspectPC {
    @Pointcut("execution(* com.apress.prospring2.ch06.simple.TestBean.*(..))")
    private void testBeanExecution() { }

    @Around("testBeanExecution()")
    public Object log(ProceedingJoinPoint pjp) throws Throwable {
        ...
    }

    @After("testBeanExecution()")
    public void afterCall(JoinPoint jp) {
```

```
        System.out.println("After");
    }

    ....
}
```

The code in bold shows that we have used the same @pointcut in two pieces of advice. Also note that the @pointcut is private, which means that we can only use it within this class. Let's expand this example a bit further: we will create a common set of @pointcuts and then use those in our aspects. Because an @pointcut is simply a method with the `@Pointcut` annotation, we can create the `SystemPointcuts` class in Listing 6-9.

Listing 6-9. *The SystemPointcuts Class*

```
public final class SystemPointcuts {

    private SystemPointcuts() {

    }

    @Pointcut("execution(* com.apress.prospring2.ch06.simple.TestBean2.*(..))")
    public void testBeanExecution() { }

    @Pointcut("within(com.apress.prospring2.ch06.simple.TestBean2)")
    public void fromTestBeanExecution() { }
}
```

Notice that we have made the class final and created a private constructor: because we intend this class only as a holder for the @pointcut methods, we want to prevent anyone from creating instances of this class. Next, Listing 6-10 shows that we can now use the `SystemPointcuts` in any number of advices.

Listing 6-10. *Usage of the Pointcuts from the SystemPointcuts Class*

```
@Aspect
public class PointcutDemoAspect {

    @Around("SystemPointcuts.testBeanExecution()")
    public Object log(ProceedingJoinPoint pjp) throws Throwable {
        System.out.println("Before");
        Object ret = pjp.proceed();
        System.out.println("After");
        return ret;
    }

    @Around("SystemPointcuts.fromTestBeanExecution()")
    public Object inTestBean(ProceedingJoinPoint pjp) throws Throwable {
        System.out.println("In Test Bean>");
        Object ret = pjp.proceed();
        System.out.println("<");
        return ret;
    }

}
```

The code in bold shows that we use the @pointcut methods declared in the `SystemPointcuts` class. We will complete the example with the `TestBean2` and `SimpleBean` classes, diagramed in Figure 6-2.

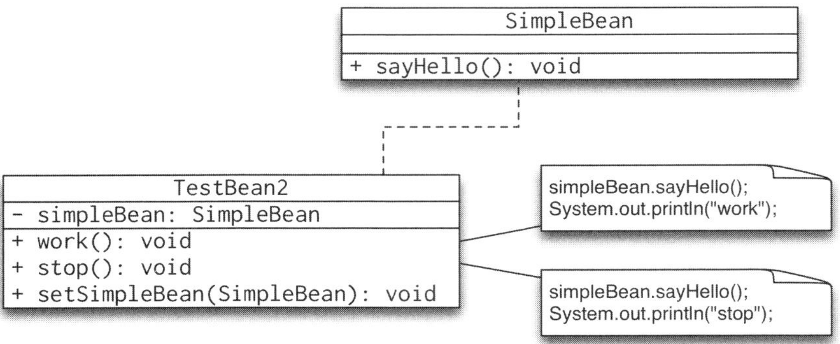

Figure 6-2. *UML class diagram of TestBean2 and SimpleBean*

We create the `ApplicationContext` configuration file that defines the `test` and `simple` beans, and we inject the `simple` bean into the `test` bean (see Listing 6-11).

Listing 6-11. *ApplicationContext Confiuration File*

```
<?xml version="1.0" encoding="UTF-8"?>
<beans xmlns="http://www.springframework.org/schema/beans"
       xmlns:xsi="http://www.w3.org/2001/XMLSchema-instance"
       xmlns:aop="http://www.springframework.org/schema/aop"
       xsi:schemaLocation="
            http://www.springframework.org/schema/beans
            http://www.springframework.org/schema/beans/spring-beans.xsd
            http://www.springframework.org/schema/aop
            http://www.springframework.org/schema/aop/spring-aop.xsd">

    <bean id="test" class="com.apress.prospring2.ch06.simple.TestBean2">
        <property name="simpleBean" ref="simple"/>
    </bean>
    <bean id="simple" class="com.apress.prospring2.ch06.simple.SimpleBean"/>
    <bean class="com.apress.prospring2.ch06.simple.PointcutDemoAspect"/>
    <aop:aspectj-autoproxy/>

</beans>
```

The example application uses the configuration file from Listing 6-11 and demonstrates that Spring applies the advices correctly according to the @pointcut methods. Because we wanted to demonstrate the `within` @pointcut, we have called the `SimpleBean.sayHello()` from outside `TestBean2` (see Listing 6-12).

Listing 6-12. *Example Application for the SystemPointcuts Class*

```
public class PointcutDemo {

    public static void main(String[] args) {
        ApplicationContext ac = new ClassPathXmlApplicationContext(
                "/META-INF/spring/ataspectjdemo2-context.xml"
        );
        TestBean2 testBean = (TestBean2) ac.getBean("test");
        SimpleBean simpleBean = (SimpleBean) ac.getBean("simple");
        testBean.work();
```

```
        testBean.stop();
        simpleBean.sayHello();
    }

}
```

When we run the example application, its output shows that Spring created the advised beans correctly. We have also used the `execution` and `within` @pointcut expressions. Let's now complete our discussion of @pointcut expressions by looking at available @AspectJ pointcut expressions.

Pointcut Expressions

Even though @AspectJ supports use of AspectJ syntax for pointcut expressions, Spring AOP does not support the entire range of AspectJ pointcuts. Table 6-1 summarizes the AspectJ pointcut expressions you can use in Spring AOP.

Table 6-1. *@AspectJ Pointcut Expressions Supported in Spring AOP*

Expression	Description
`execution`	Matches method execution join points; you can specify the package, class and method name, its visibility, return type, and type of arguments. This is the most widely used pointcut expression. For example, `execution(* com.apress..TestBean.*(..)` means to execute any method in `TestBean` in the `com.apress` subpackage with any return type and any arguments.
`within`	Matches join points when executed from the declared type. For example, `within(com.apress..TestBean)` matches calls made from methods of `TestBean`.
`this`	Matches join points by comparing the type of bean reference (the AOP proxy) with the specified type. For example, `this(SimpleBean)` will match only calls from a bean of type `SimpleBean`.
`target`	Matches join points by comparing the type of bean being invoked with the specified type. `target(SimpleBean)` will match only calls made to a bean of type `SimpleBean`, for example.
`args`	Matches join points by comparing the method argument types with the specified argument types. As an example, `args(String, String)` will match only methods with two arguments of type `String`.
`@target`	Matches join points by checking that the target class of the invocation has the specified annotation. `@target(Magic)`, for example, will match calls to methods from classes with the `@Magic` annotation.
`@args`	Similar to `args`, `@args` checks the annotations on the method arguments instead of their types. An example of `@args` is `@args(NotNull)`, which would match all methods with a single argument with the `@NotNull` annotation.
`@within`	Similar to `within`, this expression matches join points when executed from a type with the specified annotation. An example of the `@within` expression might be `@within(Magic)`, which will match calls from within bean of type with the `@Magic` annotation.
`@annotation`	Matches join points by checking the annotation on the method to be called with the specified annotation. For example, `@annotation(Magic)` will match calls to all methods with the `@Magic` annotation.
`bean`	Matches join points by comparing the bean's ID (or names); you can also use wildcards in the bean name pattern. An example might be `bean("simple")`, which will match join points in the bean with ID or name `simple`.

You can combine pointcut expressions using the || (disjunction) and && (conjunction) operators and negate the expression using the ! (not) operator. You can apply these operators on both the @pointcut methods as well as the pointcut expressions. You can write pointcut expression directly (using code similar to Listing 6-13).

Listing 6-13. *Combining AspectJ Pointcut Expressions*

```
execution(* com.apress.prospring2.ch06.simple.TestBean2.*(..))
&& within(com.apress.prospring2..*)
```

Alternatively, you can combine the @Pointcut-annotated methods with other @Pointcut-annotated method or a pointcut expression. The code in Listing 6-14 shows public @pointcuts same1, same2, and same3: the only difference among them is the code in the @Pointcut annotation.

Listing 6-14. *Combining the @Pointcut-Annotated Methods*

```
public final class SystemPointcuts {

    private SystemPointcuts() {

    }

    @Pointcut("execution(* com.apress.prospring2.ch06.simple.TestBean2.*(..))")
    private void testBeanExec() { }

    @Pointcut("within(com.apress.prospring2..*)")
    private void withinProSpringPackage() { }

    @Pointcut("execution(* com.apress.prospring2.ch06.simple.TestBean2.*(..)) &&" +
            "within(com.apress.prospring2..*)")
    public void same1() { }

    @Pointcut("execution(* com.apress.prospring2.ch06.simple.TestBean2.*(..)) &&" +
            "withinProSpringPackage()")
    public void same2() { }

    @Pointcut("testBeanExec() && withinProSpringPackage()")
    public void same3() { }

}
```

Here, you can see that we have two private @pointcuts—testBeanExec and withinProSpringPackage—and that we use the private @pointcuts in the public @pointcuts same2 and same3. Before we take a look at how we can use the @pointcuts outside the @AspectJ infrastructure, we need to explore the pointcut expressions in more detail.

Exploring the Pointcut Expressions

There are ten types of pointcut expressions; each type has its specific syntax. Even the execution expression, which seems fairly straightforward, can become quite complex when you make full use of its full syntax range.

The execution Expression

The syntax of the execution pointcut expression Spring uses is the same as the AspectJ execution syntax. Listing 6-15 defines the syntax formally.

Listing 6-15. *Formal Definition of the Execution Pointcut Expression Syntax*

```
execution(modifiers-pattern?
    ret-type-pattern
    declaring-type-pattern? name-pattern(param-pattern)
    throws-pattern?)
```

The question mark (?) suffix marks the expression element as optional; in other words, we can leave it out. Let's analyze the `* com.apress.prospring2.ch06.simple.TestBean2.*(..)` expression we have already used: the * indicates any return type (`ret-type-pattern`) followed by a full class name (`declaring-type-pattern`). We follow the class name with another `*(..)`, which means a method with any name and any number (including zero) and type of arguments. Because we did not specify the `modifiers-pattern` or the `throws-pattern`, Spring AOP will match methods with any modifiers and throwing any exceptions.

To declare a pointcut that matches any method (with any return type and any arguments, throwing any exception) in any class in a subpackage of `com.apress.prospring2.ch06`, we would need to write `* com.apress.prospring2.ch06..*.*(..)`. Analyzing the expression tells us to match a method with any name and any arguments (the last `*()`), returning any type (the first *) in any class (the middle *) in the package whose name starts with `com.apres.prospring2.ch06` (notice the `..` between the package name and class name). As a more realistic example, consider the pointcut expression in Listing 6-16.

Listing 6-16. *A More Realistic Pointcut Expression*

```
public final class SystemPointcuts {

    private SystemPointcuts() {

    }

    @Pointcut("execution(* com.apress.prospring2.ch06..*.*(..)) &&" +
            "!execution(* com.apress.prospring2.ch06..*.set*(..)) &&" +
            "!execution(* com.apress.prospring2.ch06..*.get*(..))")
    public void serviceExecution() { }
    ...
}
```

You can probably guess what we will use the `serviceExecution` @pointcut for: we can use it in the `tx:advice` and make every method in all classes in the `com.apress.prospring2.ch06.services` package transactional, as long it is not a simple getter or setter. For simplicity, we say that a getter is a method whose name starts with get and takes no arguments, and a setter is simply any method whose name begins with `set`.

Tip We prefer to use the @Transactional annotation to mark a method to be transactional; it is even simpler than using @pointcuts.

The within Expression

The `within` expression's formal syntax is far simpler than the syntax of the execution expression (see Listing 6-17).

Listing 6-17. *Syntax of the within Pointcut Expression*

```
within(declaring-type-pattern)
```

You can use the usual `..` and * wildcards; for example, to declare a pointcut that would match execution of any method invoked from within any class in the `com` package and its subpackages, you'd need to write `within(com..*)`.

The this Expression

The syntax of the `this` pointcut expression is similar to the syntax of the `within` expression. The only difference is that we cannot use the `..` and * wildcards: the semantics of the `this` pointcut are such that it would match any method execution on an object whose class matches the specified expression, but how could we match any class in the `com` package and its subpackages? Therefore, the only allowed syntax is `this(`*`class-name`*`)`, for example, `this(com.apress.prospring2.ch06.simple.TestBean2)`.

The target Expression

The syntax of the `target` expression is exactly the same as the syntax of the `this` expression. Because the `target` expression defines a pointcut that would match execution of any method on an object whose class matches the specified expression, we cannot use the wildcards. Therefore, the only valid syntax is `target(`*`class-name`*`)`, for example, `target(com.apress.prospring2.ch06.simple.SimpleBean)`.

The args Expression

The syntax of the `args` expression is `args(type-pattern? (, type-pattern)*)`; in other words, we can specify zero, one, or more `type-pattern` expressions. It is important to note that while you can use the `argument-pattern` in the `execution` expression, the `execution` matching evaluates the formal argument types. The `args` expression matching evaluates the actual types of arguments passed to the method. As an example, take the class in Listing 6-18.

Listing 6-18. *The SimpleBean Class*

```
public class SimpleBean {

    public void sayHello() {
        System.out.println("Hello");
    }

    public void x(CharSequence a, String b) {

    }

}
```

The pointcut `execution(* SimpleBean.*(CharSequence, String))` would match calls to the method `x("A", "B")`, because the name and formal argument types match. However, the pointcut `execution(* SimpleBean.*(String, String))` would not match, even if the call to the method uses two `String` arguments (and not a `StringBuilder` and `String`, for example). If we wanted to create a pointcut that matches calls to the `x(CharSequence, String)` method if and only if the actual argument types are `String, String`, we'll need to write `args(String, String)`.

You can also use the `..` wildcard in the `type-pattern`; to match calls to the method with the first argument of type `Integer`, followed by any number of arguments of any type and ending with a `String` argument, we'd write `args(Integer, .., String)`.

The most common use of the `args` expression is in argument binding, which we will explore in the next section.

The @target Expression

The `@target` expression is another example of a simple expression that requires a full type name. Moreover, the type name should represent an @interface. Example uses of this expression are, therefore, `@target(Magic)` or `@target(org.springframework.transaction.annotation.Transactional)`, where both `Magic` and `Transactional` are @interfaces with the `@Retention(RetentionPolicy.RUNTIME)` annotation and whose `@Target` annotations include `ElementType.TYPE`. The pointcut will match the call to all methods in the type with the annotation; to match methods with a particular annotation, use the `@annotation` expression.

The @within Expression

The `@within` expression requires a full @interface type name, and it will match calls to any methods originating from objects (or methods) with the specified annotation. As an example, we can write `@within(StartsTransaction)`, where `StartsTransaction` is an @interface.

The @annotation Expression

Like the `@target` expression, the `@annotation` expression will match execution of any method with the specified annotation. A good example is `@annotation(Transactional)`, which will match execution of any method with the `Transactional` annotation.

The @args Expression

The `@args` expression is similar to the `args` expression; the only difference is that it compares argument annotations rather than argument types. We can use this expression to match calls to methods with the specified annotated arguments. You can use the same wildcards as in the `args` expression.

The bean Expression

This last expression is truly Spring specific; it will match calls to all methods in a bean with an `id` or a `name` that matches the specified name. You can use the * wildcard in the bean name. To match calls to all methods in the `simple` bean, we'd write `bean(simple)`; to match calls to all methods in beans whose `id` (or one of its `names`) ends with `Service`, we'd write `bean(*Service)`.

Using the @Pointcuts in XML

Because the pointcuts defined using the `@Pointcut` annotation are Spring AOP–specific, we can use them even in the XML configuration. If we wanted to make all method executions in the `TestBean2` participate in a transaction, we could use the `SystemPointcuts.testBeanExecution()` in the `<aop:advisor . . ./>` element. The XML configuration file in Listing 6-19 shows an example of this approach.

Listing 6-19. *Using the @Pointcuts in the XML Configuration File*

```
<?xml version="1.0" encoding="UTF-8"?>
<beans xmlns="http://www.springframework.org/schema/beans"
       xmlns:xsi="http://www.w3.org/2001/XMLSchema-instance"
       xmlns:tx="http://www.springframework.org/schema/tx"
       xmlns:aop="http://www.springframework.org/schema/aop"
       xsi:schemaLocation="
            http://www.springframework.org/schema/beans
            http://www.springframework.org/schema/beans/spring-beans.xsd
            http://www.springframework.org/schema/aop
```

```
        http://www.springframework.org/schema/aop/spring-aop.xsd
        http://www.springframework.org/schema/tx
        http://www.springframework.org/schema/tx/spring-tx.xsd">

    <bean id="test" class="com.apress.prospring2.ch06.simple.TestBean2">
        <property name="simpleBean" ref="simple"/>
    </bean>
    <bean id="simple" class="com.apress.prospring2.ch06.simple.SimpleBean"/>
    <aop:config>
        <aop:advisor advice-ref="tx-advice"
                     pointcut="com.apress.prospring2.ch06.simple.➥
                         SystemPointcuts.testBeanExecution()"/>
    </aop:config>

    <bean id="transactionManager"
        class="com.apress.prospring2.ch06.simple.NoopTransactionManager"/>

    <tx:advice id="tx-advice" transaction-manager="transactionManager">
        <tx:attributes>
            <tx:method name="*" propagation="REQUIRED"/>
        </tx:attributes>
    </tx:advice>
</beans>
```

Do not worry about the `transactionManager` bean and the `tx:advice`; the important portions of code are in bold. We define an advice (using the `<aop:advisor . . ./>` element); the advice is referencing the `@Pointcut`-annotated method from the `SystemPointcuts` class; the body of the advice is `tx:advice`. We give more detail about declarative transaction support in Spring in Chapter 16; for now, it is enough to say that the method execution will take part in a transaction, and the advice will commit the transaction if the method execution does not throw any exceptions; it will roll back the transaction if the target method throws any exception.

Types of Advice

Now that we know how to write pointcut expressions (whether we use the `@Pointcut`-annotated methods or write the pointcut expressions directly in XML), we need to take a look at the types of advices we can use. We have already used an around advice (in the `@Aspect` example in Listing 6-1 and in the `tx:advice` in the XML configuration in Listing 6-19). We will cover the basic advices (before, after, after throwing, and around); we will then take a look at how we can access the arguments in the join point.

Before Advice

Let's begin with the before advice. As the name suggests, it runs before execution proceeds to the method's body, but unless we throw an exception, we cannot avoid the execution of the target method. This makes the before advices suitable for access control: we check whether the caller is allowed to call the target; if not, we throw an exception. Take a look at the UML class diagram in Figure 6-3, which shows the classes we are going to be using in the discussion of the before advice.

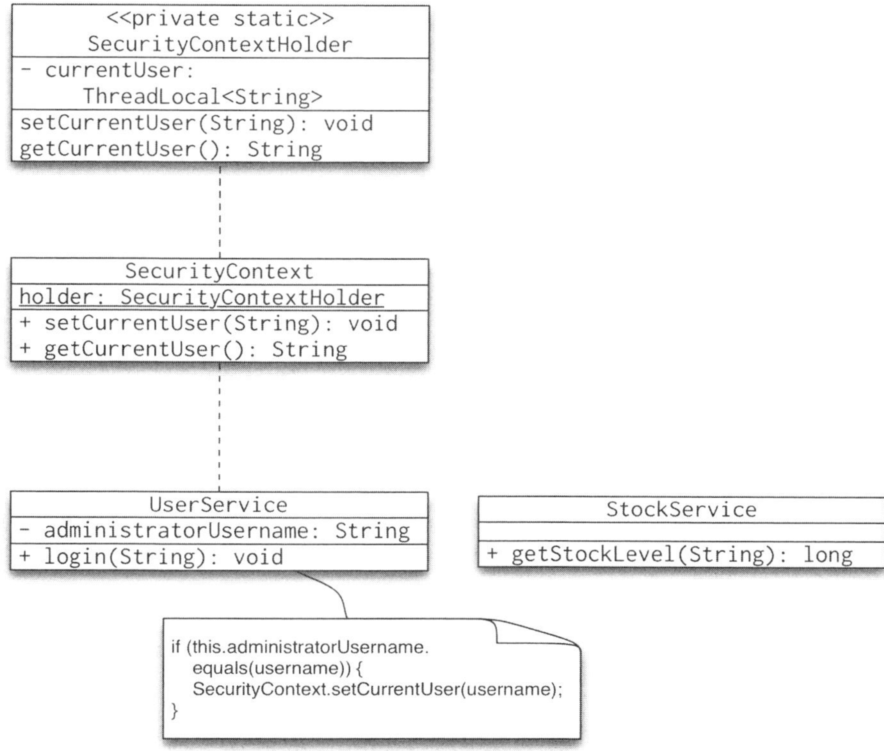

Figure 6-3. *UML class diagram for the before advice classes*

We now want to secure the StockService so that we can only call its methods after we have logged in. In fact, we'll say that we want to secure all classes in the com.apress.prospring2.ch06.services package so that we don't have to worry about security in the future. A naïve attempt at implementation of the before advice is in Listing 6-20.

Listing 6-20. *Naïve Implementation of the Before Advice*

```
@Aspect
public class BeforeAspect {

    @Before("execution(* com.apress.prospring2.ch06.services.*.*(..))")
    public void beforeLogin() throws Throwable {
        if (SecurityContext.getCurrentUser() == null)
            throw new RuntimeException("Must login to call this method.");
    }

}
```

At first glance, this looks absolutely fine. To test the advice, we will combine the BeforeAspect with the XML configuration in Listing 6-21.

Listing 6-21. *The XML Configuration File for the Before Advice*

```
<?xml version="1.0" encoding="UTF-8"?>
<beans xmlns="http://www.springframework.org/schema/beans"
       xmlns:xsi="http://www.w3.org/2001/XMLSchema-instance"
       xmlns:aop="http://www.springframework.org/schema/aop"
       xsi:schemaLocation="
            http://www.springframework.org/schema/beans
            http://www.springframework.org/schema/beans/spring-beans.xsd
            http://www.springframework.org/schema/aop
            http://www.springframework.org/schema/aop/spring-aop.xsd">

    <bean id="userService" class="com.apress.prospring2.ch06.services.UserService"/>
    <bean id="stockService"
        class="com.apress.prospring2.ch06.services.StockService"/>
    <bean class="com.apress.prospring2.ch06.before.BeforeAspect"/>

    <aop:aspectj-autoproxy />

</beans>
```

We have the BeforeAspect as a Spring bean, and we use the aspectj-autoproxy: we can therefore use the code from Listing 6-22 to access the advised services.

Listing 6-22. *Sample Application for the Before Advice*

```
public class BeforeDemo {

    public static void main(String[] args) {
        ApplicationContext ac = new ClassPathXmlApplicationContext(
                "/META-INF/spring/beforedemo1-context.xml"
        );
        StockService stockService = (StockService) ac.getBean("stockService");
        System.out.println(stockService.getStockLevel("ABC"));
    }
}
```

When we run the application, it fails with a RuntimeException with the message "Must login to call this method." Great, it works! To test that we can call the service methods after logging in, we will add a call to get the UserService bean and call its login method. Listing 6-23 shows a code fragment that does just that.

Listing 6-23. *Code Fragment to Get the UserService and login*

```
UserService userService = (UserService) ac.getBean("userService");
userService.login("janm");
```

The trouble is that the login method is also in a class in the services package; therefore, it is advised by the beforeLogin advice. Thus, we cannot log in, because we're not logged in. We'll need to modify our pointcut expression to exclude the login method. We can write the pointcut expression directly, but we're going to create two private @pointcut expressions and use them in the before advice's pointcut expression. Listing 6-24 shows how we've implemented the change.

Listing 6-24. *Change to the BeforeAspect*

```
@Aspect
public class BeforeAspect {
```

```
    @Pointcut("execution(* com.apress.prospring2.ch06.services.*.*(..))")
    private void serviceExecution() { }

    @Pointcut(
        "execution(* com.apress.prospring2.ch06.services.UserService.login(..))")
    private void loginExecution() { }

    @Before("serviceExecution() && !loginExecution()")
    public void beforeLogin() throws Throwable {
        if (SecurityContext.getCurrentUser() == null)
            throw new RuntimeException("Must login to call this method.");
    }

}
```

When we run the sample application now, it succeeds: we are allowed to call the `UserService.login` method even without being logged in, but we must be logged in to call all other methods.

After Returning Advice

As its name suggests, after returning advice runs after the target method finishes normally. To "finish normally" means that the method has not thrown any exceptions. The usual application for after returning advice is to perform auditing. Let's take the code in Listing 6-25, which shows after returning advice.

Listing 6-25. *After Returning Advice*

```
@Aspect
public class AfterAspect {

    @AfterReturning("execution(* com.apress.prospring2.ch06.services.*.*(..))")
    public void auditCall() {
        System.out.println("After method call");
    }

}
```

This aspect defines one piece after returning advice for execution of all methods in all classes in the `com.apress.prospring2.ch06.services` package. To implement the sample application, let's begin the configuration file from Listing 6-26.

Listing 6-26. *XML Configuration File for the Sample Application*

```
<?xml version="1.0" encoding="UTF-8"?>
<beans xmlns="http://www.springframework.org/schema/beans"
       xmlns:xsi="http://www.w3.org/2001/XMLSchema-instance"
       xmlns:aop="http://www.springframework.org/schema/aop"
       xsi:schemaLocation="
            http://www.springframework.org/schema/beans
            http://www.springframework.org/schema/beans/spring-beans.xsd
            http://www.springframework.org/schema/aop
            http://www.springframework.org/schema/aop/spring-aop.xsd">

    <bean id="userService" class="com.apress.prospring2.ch06.services.UserService"/>
    <bean id="stockService"
        class="com.apress.prospring2.ch06.services.StockService"/>
```

```
    <bean class="com.apress.prospring2.ch06.afterreturning.AfterAspect"/>

    <aop:aspectj-autoproxy />

</beans>
```

Here, we define two service beans (the `userService` and `stockService`) and the `AfterAspect` bean. The anonymous `AfterAspect` bean contains our `auditCall()` after returning advice. We use this configuration file in the sample application that simply obtains the `userService` and `stockService` beans and uses their methods. The sample application's source code is in Listing 6-27.

Listing 6-27. *Sample Application for After Returning Advice*

```
public class AfterDemo {

    public static void main(String[] args) {
        ApplicationContext ac = new ClassPathXmlApplicationContext(
                "/META-INF/spring/afterreturningdemo1-context.xml"
        );
        UserService userService = (UserService) ac.getBean("userService");
        userService.login("janm");

        StockService stockService = (StockService) ac.getBean("stockService");
        System.out.println(stockService.getStockLevel("ABC"));
    }

}
```

When we run this application, the output verifies that the `auditCall` after returning advice works; the application prints `After method call, After method call, 193734`. The problem is that the audit messages cannot access any details of the call: the advice, as we have written it, only knows that a method that matched the pointcut finished normally. We don't know which method it is, nor do we know the returned value. We can improve the advice by using the `JoinPoint` argument or by using the returning field of the `@AfterReturning` annotation. Listing 6-28 shows the first option—adding the `JoinPoint` argument to the advice method.

Listing 6-28. *Using the JoinPoint Argument*

```
@Aspect
public class AfterAspect {

    @AfterReturning("execution(* com.apress.prospring2.ch06.services.*.*(..))")
    public void auditCall(JoinPoint jp) {
        System.out.println("After method call of " + jp);
    }

}
```

We can use the `JoinPoint` argument interface to find out details about the method that has just returned: perhaps the most interesting information we can obtain from the `JoinPoint` is the `Method` being executed and its arguments. The only trouble is that we can't use the `JoinPoint` to find the return value. To do this, we must stop using the `JoinPoint` argument and explicitly set the `returning()` and `argNames()` properties of the `@AfterReturning` annotation. Listing 6-29 shows the advice that can examine (and modify) the return value.

Listing 6-29. *Using the returning() and argNames() Properties*

```
@Aspect
public class AfterAspect {

    @AfterReturning(
        pointcut = "execution(* com.apress.prospring2.ch06.services.*.*(..))",
        returning = "ret", argNames = "ret")
    public void auditCall(Object ret) {
        System.out.println("After method call of " + ret);
        if (ret instanceof User) {
            ((User)ret).setPassword("****");
        }
    }

}
```

Notice that we have defined the `pointcut()`, `returning()`, and `argNames()` properties of the `@AfterReturning` annotation to create much more powerful after returning advice. We can see the return value from the method call. We cannot change the returned value directly, but if the return type allows it, we can change the returned value's properties. This is similar to attempting to modify the value of a method argument and passing the modified value to the calling code.

After Throwing Advice

The next type of advice is after throwing, which executes when its target method throws an exception. As with the after returning advice, we can create advice that can have access to the thrown exception. Furthermore, the type of the exception in the advice's argument filters the exception type. Listing 6-30 shows an aspect that filters all `IOExceptions` thrown in the service calls.

Listing 6-30. *IOException After Throwing Advice*

```
@Aspect
public class AfterThowingAspect {

    @AfterThrowing(
        pointcut = "execution(* com.apress.prospring2.ch06.services.*.*(..))",
        throwing = "ex", argNames = "ex")
    public void logException(IOException ex) {
        System.out.println("After method call of " + ex);
    }

}
```

The code in bold shows the most important areas of the advice: the `throwing()` property of the `@AfterThrowing` advice specifies the argument that will receive the exception, and the `argNames()` specifies the names of the arguments in the order in which they are declared. Now, when we run the sample application from Listing 6-31, it will fail, because the `StockService.getStockLevel(String)` method will throw a `NullPointerException` if the `sku` argument is `null`.

Listing 6-31. *Sample Application for the After Throwing Advice*

```
public class AfterThrowingDemo {

    public static void main(String[] args) {
        ApplicationContext ac = new ClassPathXmlApplicationContext(
                "/META-INF/spring/afterthrowingdemo1-context.xml"
        );
        UserService userService = (UserService) ac.getBean("userService");
        userService.login("janm");

        StockService stockService = (StockService) ac.getBean("stockService");
        System.out.println(stockService.getStockLevel(null));
    }

}
```

Even though we have written after throwing advice (and configured the beans correctly in `afterthrowingdemo1-context.xml`), the advice does not get executed, because the type of the exception in its argument is `IOException`, not `NullPointerException`. If we change the advice's argument to `Exception`, it will work, printing the following.

```
...
Exception in thread "main" java.lang.NullPointerException
After method call of java.lang.NullPointerException
   at com.apress.prospring2.ch06.services.StockService.➥
    getStockLevel(StockService.java:9)
    ...
```

After Advice

The final type of after advice is the after or, more formally, finally advice. This executes regardless of whether the target method completes normally or throws an exception. However, we cannot access the method's return value or any exceptions it may have thrown. In most cases, you will use the finally advice to release resources, very much as you would in a `try` / `catch` / `finally` construct in Java.

Around Advice

The most powerful and most complicated advice is the around advice. It executes around the target method invocation. Therefore, the advice needs at least one argument, and it must return a value. The argument specifies the target being invoked, and the return value specifies the return value, regardless of where the return value comes from. You would typically find around advice in transaction management: the advice will begin a transaction before proceeding to call the target. If the target returns normally, the advice will commit the transaction; in case of any exceptions, it will perform a rollback. Another example is caching: the code in Listing 6-32 shows simple caching around advice.

Listing 6-32. *Around Advice for Caching*

```
@Aspect
public class CachingAspect {
    private Map<MethodAndArguments, Object> cache =
            Collections.synchronizedMap(
                    new HashMap<MethodAndArguments, Object>());
    private Object nullValue = new Object();
```

```
    private static class MethodAndArguments {
        private Object target;
        private Object[] arguments;

        private MethodAndArguments(Object target, Object[] arguments) {
            this.target = target;
            this.arguments = arguments;
        }

        public boolean equals(Object o) {
            if (this == o) return true;
            if (o == null || getClass() != o.getClass()) return false;

            MethodAndArguments that = (MethodAndArguments) o;

            return Arrays.equals(arguments, that.arguments) &&
                target.equals(that.target);
        }

        public int hashCode() {
            int result;
            result = target.hashCode();
            result = 31 * result + Arrays.hashCode(arguments);
            return result;
        }
    }

    @Around("execution(* com.apress.prospring2.ch06.services.*.*(..))")
    public Object cacheCalls(ProceedingJoinPoint pjp) throws Throwable {
        Object cacheRet;
        final MethodAndArguments methodAndArguments =
            new MethodAndArguments(pjp.getTarget(), pjp.getArgs());
        cacheRet = this.cache.get(methodAndArguments);
        if (cacheRet == this.nullValue) return null;
        if (cacheRet == null) {
            Object ret = pjp.proceed();
            cacheRet = ret;
            if (cacheRet == null) cacheRet = this.nullValue;
            this.cache.put(methodAndArguments, cacheRet);
            return ret;
        }
        return cacheRet;
    }

}
```

The cache implemented in this aspect is definitely not an enterprise-grade cache, but it will demonstrate the around advice quite nicely. It takes the `ProceedingJoinPoint` argument and returns an `Object`; the argument gives everything we need to know about the execution of the target method, and the calling code will receive the value returned from the advice.

You may be wondering whether we must invoke the target method at all or whether we can invoke it more than once; the answer is yes. We can do anything we wish in the advice: we can implement advice that can handle retries, attempting to call the target three times before giving up. Or, as you have seen in Listing 6-32, we can skip the call to the target completely!

Argument Binding

You may have noticed that we sometimes need to access the values of the arguments passed to the target from the advice. So far, you have only seen explicit access to the return value; you can also use the `JoinPoint.getArgs()` to access the arguments. While this is possible, it feels like too much work, because the arguments are passed in as an `Object[]`, and we would have to perform bounds checking and casting ourselves. Luckily, `@AspectJ` supports binding, where we can bind a value from the target to an argument in the advice. As an example, let's take a look at the code in Listing 6-33.

Listing 6-33. *An Aspect with Bound Arguments*

```
@Aspect
public class BindingAspect {

    @Around(value =
            "execution(* com.apress.prospring2.ch06.services.StockService.*(..)) " +
            "&& args(cutoffDate, minimumDiscount)",
            argNames = "pjp, cutoffDate, minimumDiscount")
    public Object discountEnforcement(ProceedingJoinPoint pjp, Date cutoffDate,
                                      BigDecimal minimumDiscount)
            throws Throwable {
        return pjp.proceed();
    }
}
```

Here, we can see that the `discountEnforcement` advice will execute on execution of any method in the `StockService` class (the `execution` clause), as long as it has two arguments (the `args` clause) and as long as the type of the `cutoffDate` argument's type is `Date` and the `minimumDiscount` argument's type is `BigDecimal` (inferred from the advice method arguments). In addition to the two arguments passed in from the target, the advice method will receive the `ProceedingJoinPoint` instance. Also note the `argNames()` property of the `@Around` annotation: it explicitly specifies that the advice method's arguments are named `pjp`, `cutoffDate`, and `minimumDiscount`. The Spring AOP infrastructure will use the `argNames()` to decide which argument gets the bound value from the pointcut expression.

■Note The reason for the `argNames()` method's existence is that, once Java source code is compiled into bytecode, determining the argument names is impossible; we can obtain only their indexes and types. However, we refer to the argument names in pointcut and bind expressions; the `argNames()` method, therefore, represents a mechanism that can resolve an argument name to its index.

Even though you can leave out the `JoinPoint` (and its subinterfaces) from the `argNames()` property if it appears as the first argument of the advice method, we do not recommend doing so. Forgetting that the `JoinPoint` needs to be the first argument is far too easy; in addition, some IDEs will report errors if the names in `argNames` do not match the advice method's arguments (see Figure 6-4).

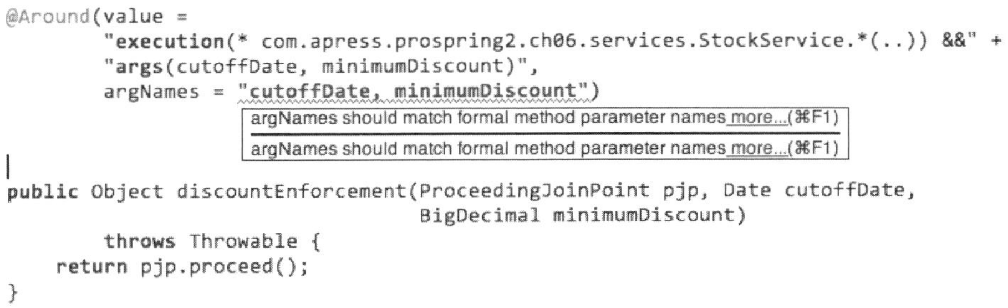

```
@Around(value =
        "execution(* com.apress.prospring2.ch06.services.StockService.*(..)) &&" +
        "args(cutoffDate, minimumDiscount)",
        argNames = "cutoffDate, minimumDiscount")
                    argNames should match formal method parameter names more...(⌘F1)
                    argNames should match formal method parameter names more...(⌘F1)

public Object discountEnforcement(ProceedingJoinPoint pjp, Date cutoffDate,
                                  BigDecimal minimumDiscount)
        throws Throwable {
    return pjp.proceed();
}
```

Figure 6-4. *IntelliJ IDEA reporting a problem with argNames()*

If you find that argNames is a bit clumsy, you do not have to specify it, and Spring AOP will use the debug information in the class files to determine the argument names. This is usually not enabled by default, but you can turn on argument names debug information using the -g:vars javac directive. Apart from allowing Spring AOP to determine the argument names, it will slightly increase the size of the compiled *.class files, which is usually not a problem at all.

More significant problems may be that the *.class files compiled with the -g:vars directive will be more readable when decompiled and that the compiler will not be able to apply an optimization to remove unused arguments. If you are working on an open source application, the first problem should not trouble you at all; the second problem is also moot if you write your code carefully and do not leave in unused arguments. If your class files do not have the necessary debugging information, Spring will attempt to match the arguments using their types. In our example in Listing 6-33, Spring can easily do this matching: ProceedingJoinPoint does not share a class hierarchy with either Date or BigDecimal. Similarly, Date and BigDecimal are different classes. If Spring cannot safely match the arguments using their types (for example, the advised method takes the ProceedingJoinPoint as its argument), it will throw an AmbiguousBindingException.

Introductions

Introductions are an important part of the AOP feature set available in Spring. By using introductions, you can add new functionality to an existing object dynamically. In Spring, you can introduce an implementation of any interface to an existing object. You may well be wondering exactly why this is useful—why would you want to add functionality dynamically at runtime when you can simply add that functionality at development time? The answer to this question is easy. You add functionality dynamically when the functionality is crosscutting and thus not easily implementable using traditional object-oriented programming.

The Spring documentation gives two typical examples of introduction use: object locking and modification detection. In the case of object locking, which is implemented in the Spring documentation, we have an interface, Lockable, that defines the method for locking and unlocking an object. The intended application for this interface involves enabling the application to lock an object so that its internal state cannot be modified. Now, you could simply implement this interface manually for every class you wish to make lockable. However, this would result in a lot of duplicated code across many classes. Sure, you can refactor the implementation into an abstract base class, but you lose your one shot at concrete inheritance, and you still have to check the lock status in every method that modifies the state of the object. Clearly, this is not an ideal situation and has the potential to lead to many bugs and no doubt some maintenance nightmares.

By using introductions, you can overcome all of these issues. Using an introduction, you can centralize the implementation of the `Lockable` interface into a single class and, at runtime, have any object you wish adopt this implementation of `Lockable`. Not only does the object adopt the implementation of `Lockable` but it becomes an instance of `Lockable` in that it passes the `instanceof` test for the `Lockable` interface, even though its class does not implement this interface.

Using introductions obviously overcomes the problem of centralizing the implementation logic without affecting the concrete inheritance hierarchy of your classes, but what about all the code you need to write to check the lock status? Well, an introduction is simply an extension of a method interceptor, and as such, it can intercept any method on the object on which the introduction was made. Using this feature, you could check the lock status before any calls are made to setter methods and throw an `Exception` if the object is locked. All of this code is encapsulated in a single place, and none of the `Lockable` objects need to be aware of this.

Introductions are key to providing declarative services in applications. For instance, if you build an application that is fully aware of the `Lockable` interface, by using introductions, you declaratively define exactly which objects should be made `Lockable`.

We won't be spending any more time looking at the `Lockable` interface and how to implement it using introductions, because this is fully discussed in the Spring documentation. Instead, we focus on the other, unimplemented, example from the documentation—object modification detection. However, before we start, we will take a look at the basics behind building an introduction.

Call Tracking with Introductions

Object modification detection is a useful technique for many reasons. Typically, you apply modification detection to prevent unnecessary database access when you are persisting object data. If an object is passed to a method for modification but comes back unmodified, there is little point in issuing an update statement to the database. Using a modification check in this way can increase application throughput, especially when the database is already under a substantial load or is located on some remote network making communication an expensive operation.

Unfortunately, this kind of functionality is difficult to implement by hand, because it requires you to add to every method that can modify object state to check if the object state is actually being modified. When you consider all the null checks that have to be made and the checks to see if the value is actually changing, you are looking at around eight lines of code per method. You could refactor this into a single method, but you still have to call this method every time you need to perform the check. Spread this across a typical application with many different classes that require modification checks, and the maintenance of such an application will become much more difficult.

This is clearly a place where introductions will help. We do not want to have to make it so each class that requires modification checks inherits from some base implementation, losing its only chance for inheritance as a result, nor do we really want to be adding checking code to each and every state-changing method. Using introductions, we can provide a flexible solution to the modification detection problem without having to write a bunch of repetitive, error-prone code.

In this example, we are going to build a statistics collection framework using introductions. The modification check logic is encapsulated by the `CallTracker` interface, an implementation of which will be introduced into the appropriate objects, along with interception logic to perform modification checks automatically.

The CallTracker Interface

Central to the statistics solution is the `CallTracker` interface, which our fictional application uses to track its health. We do not look at how the application would use `CallTracker`; instead, we focus on the implementation of the introduction. Listing 6-34 shows the `CallTracker` interface.

Listing 6-34. *The CallTracker Interface*

```
public interface CallTracker {

    void markNormal();

    void markFailing();

    int countNormalCalls();

    int countFailingCalls();

    String describe();

}
```

Nothing special here—the `mark*` methods simply increase a counter of normal or failing calls, and the `count*` methods return the appropriate counter value.

Creating a Mix In

The next step is to create the code that implements `CallTracker` and is introduced to the objects; this is referred to as a mix in. Listing 6-35 shows the implementation of the `CallTracker` interface; again, the implementation does nothing difficult.

Listing 6-35. *The DefaultCallTracker Class*

```
public class DefaultCallTracker implements CallTracker {
    private int normalCalls;
    private int failingCalls;

    public void markNormal() {
        this.normalCalls++;
    }

    public void markFailing() {
        this.failingCalls++;
    }

    public int countNormalCalls() {
        return this.normalCalls;
    }

    public int countFailingCalls() {
        return this.failingCalls;
    }

    public String describe() {
        return toString();
    }

    @Override
    public String toString() {
        final StringBuilder sb = new StringBuilder();
        sb.append("DefaultCallTracker");
        sb.append("{normalCalls=").append(normalCalls);
        sb.append(", failingCalls=").append(failingCalls);
```

```
        sb.append('}');
        return sb.toString();
    }
}
```

The first thing to notice here is the implementation of CallTracker, which is made up of the private normalCalls and failingCalls fields. This example highlights why you must have one mix in instance per advised object: the mix in introduces not only methods to the object but also a state. If you share a single instance of this mix in across many different objects, you are also sharing the state, which means all objects show as modified the first time a single object becomes modified.

Creating the Mix-In Aspect

The next step is to create an aspect that will include the after returning and after throwing advice as well as the mix-in declaration. Listing 6-36 shows the code we have written.

Listing 6-36. *Creating Advice for the Mix In*

```
@Aspect
public class CallTrackerAspect {

    @Pointcut("execution(* com.apress.prospring2.ch06.services.*.*(..))")
    private void serviceCall() { }

    @DeclareParents(
        value = "com.apress.prospring2.ch06.services.*",
        defaultImpl = DefaultCallTracker.class)
    public static CallTracker mixin;

    @AfterReturning(
        value = "serviceCall() && this(tracker)",
        argNames = "tracker")
    public void normalCall(CallTracker tracker) {
        tracker.markNormal();
    }

    @AfterThrowing(
        value = "serviceCall() && this(tracker)",
        throwing = "t",
        argNames = "tracker, t")
    public void failingCall(CallTracker tracker, Throwable t) {
        tracker.markFailing();
    }

}
```

The new code in this aspect is the @DeclareParents annotation for the mixin field; it declares that for all classes in com.apress.prospring2.ch06.services we will introduce the CallTracker interface (the type of the field) using the DefaultCallTracker implementation.

Next, we define an @pointcut serviceCall() (because we will use it in the two separate pieces of advice).

Then, we create the after returning advice using the pointcut serviceCall() && this(tracker). The serviceCall() references to the @pointcut, and this(tracker) will match execution of all methods on an object that implements the CallTracker interface (because the type of the tracker expression is CallTracker in the advice method argument). Spring AOP will bind the tracker argument to the advised object; therefore, we can use the tracker argument in the advice body.

Finally, we write the after throwing advice using the same pointcut expression (serviceCall() && this(tracker)); Spring AOP will bind the tracker argument to the argument of the failingCall advice method. In addition to the CallTracker argument, we define in the @AfterThrowing annotation that we want to receive the exception thrown as the second argument of the failingCall method. Spring AOP infers the type of the exception from the type of the argument (Throwable, in this case).

Putting It All Together

Now that we have the aspect that introduces the mix in and the appropriate advice, we can write a sample application that uses the UserService and StockService beans we have already implemented. Listing 6-37 shows the source code of the sample application.

Listing 6-37. *The Introductions Sample Application*

```
public class IntroductionDemo {

    public static void main(String[] args) {
        ApplicationContext ac = new ClassPathXmlApplicationContext(
                "/META-INF/spring/introductionsdemo1-context.xml"
        );
        UserService userService = (UserService) ac.getBean("userService");
        describeTracker(userService);
        userService.login("janm");
        userService.setAdministratorUsername("x");
        describeTracker(userService);

        StockService stockService = (StockService) ac.getBean("stockService");
        describeTracker(stockService);
        try {
            stockService.getStockLevel(null);
        } catch (Exception ignored) {

        }
        System.out.println(stockService.getStockLevel("ABC"));
        stockService.applyDiscounts(new Date(), new BigDecimal("10.0"));
        describeTracker(stockService);
    }

    private static void describeTracker(Object o) {
        CallTracker t = (CallTracker)o;
        System.out.println(t.describe());
    }

}
```

Notice that we are using the userService and stockService beans as usual: we call userService.login("janm"), followed by userService.setAdministratorUsername("x"); calls to the stockService bean are similar. However, we can now cast the userService and stockService beans to CallTracker; they now implement the newly introduced interface. We are sure you won't be too surprised to learn that we did not need to write any additional configuration apart from the standard XML configuration file in Listing 6-38.

Listing 6-38. *XML Configuration File for the Introductions Demonstration*

```
<?xml version="1.0" encoding="UTF-8"?>
<beans xmlns="http://www.springframework.org/schema/beans"
       xmlns:xsi="http://www.w3.org/2001/XMLSchema-instance"
       xmlns:aop="http://www.springframework.org/schema/aop"
       xsi:schemaLocation="
            http://www.springframework.org/schema/beans
            http://www.springframework.org/schema/beans/spring-beans.xsd
            http://www.springframework.org/schema/aop
            http://www.springframework.org/schema/aop/spring-aop.xsd">

    <bean id="userService"
        class="com.apress.prospring2.ch06.services.DefaultUserService"/>
    <bean id="stockService"
        class="com.apress.prospring2.ch06.services.DefaultStockService"/>
    <bean class="com.apress.prospring2.ch06.introductions.CallTrackerAspect"/>

    <aop:aspectj-autoproxy />

</beans>
```

That is really all we needed to do. Spring AOP will proxy the `DefaultUserService` and `DefaultStockService`. Let's examine the `DefaultUserService` in more detail: it implements only the `UserService`, but the type of the `userService` bean after applying the `CallTrackerAspect` is `JdkDynamicAopProxy`—it is not an instance of the `DefaultUserService`. The proxy implements both the `UserService` interface and `CallTracker` mix-in interface. It intercepts calls to all methods and delegates the calls on the `UserService` interface to the `DefaultUserService`. The proxy also creates an instance of the `DefaultCallTracker` (defined in the `@DeclareParents` annotation) and delegates all calls on the `CallTracker` interface to the `DefaultCallTracker` instance.

The output from running the sample application should therefore come as no surprise:

```
before userService.login("janm"):
    DefaultCallTracker{normalCalls=0, failingCalls=0}

after userService.setAdministratorUsername("x"):
    DefaultCallTracker{normalCalls=2, failingCalls=0}

before stockService.getStockLevel(null):
    DefaultCallTracker{normalCalls=0, failingCalls=0}
193734

after stockService.applyDiscounts(...):
    DefaultCallTracker{normalCalls=2, failingCalls=1}
```

This output verifies that the `CallTracker` interface introduced to all classes in the `com.apress.prospring2.ch06.services` package worked and that we got one instance of the `DefaultCallTracker` for every advised class.

Introductions Summary

Introductions are one of the most powerful features of Spring AOP; they allow you not only to extend the functionality of existing methods but also to extend the set of interfaces an object implements dynamically. Using introductions is the perfect way to implement crosscutting logic that your application interacts with through well-defined interfaces. In general, this is the kind of logic that you want to apply declaratively rather than programmatically.

Obviously, because introductions work via proxies, they add a certain amount of overhead, and all methods on the proxy are considered to be advised, because the proxy needs to route every call to the appropriate target at runtime. However, in the case of many of the services you can implement using introductions, this performance overhead is a small price to pay for the reduction in code required to implement the service, as well the increase in stability and maintainability that comes from fully centralizing the service logic and adding management interface to your application.

The Aspect Life Cycle

So far, the aspects we have written are singletons—more accurately, Spring takes the singleton @Aspect-annotated beans and advices the targets using a singleton instance of the aspect. Let's take the aspect from Listing 6-39 and use it in our sample application.

Listing 6-39. *Simple Singleton Aspect*

```
@Aspect
public class CountingAspect {
    private int count;

    @Before("execution(* com.apress.prospring2.ch06.services.*.*(..))")
    public void count() {
        this.count++;
        System.out.println(this.count);
    }

}
```

Let's complete the example with code from Listing 6-40, which shows the demonstration application. It obtains the familiar `userService` and `stockService` beans and makes two calls to the `userService.login()` method, followed by one call to the `stockService.getStockLevel()` method.

Listing 6-40. *Sample Application for the Singleton Aspect*

```
public class LifecycleDemo {

    public static void main(String[] args) {
        ApplicationContext ac = new ClassPathXmlApplicationContext(
                "/META-INF/spring/lifecycledemo1-context.xml"
        );
        UserService userService = (UserService) ac.getBean("userService");
        StockService stockService = (StockService) ac.getBean("stockService");

        for (int i = 0; i < 2; i++) {
            userService.login("janm");
        }
        stockService.getStockLevel("A");
    }

}
```

The last piece of the puzzle is the XML configuration file, which simply declares the `userService`, `stockService`, and `CountingAspect` beans.

Listing 6-41. *XML Configuration for the LifecycleDemo Application*

```
<?xml version="1.0" encoding="UTF-8"?>
<beans xmlns="http://www.springframework.org/schema/beans"
       xmlns:xsi="http://www.w3.org/2001/XMLSchema-instance"
       xmlns:aop="http://www.springframework.org/schema/aop"
       xsi:schemaLocation="
            http://www.springframework.org/schema/beans
            http://www.springframework.org/schema/beans/spring-beans.xsd
            http://www.springframework.org/schema/aop
            http://www.springframework.org/schema/aop/spring-aop.xsd">

    <bean id="userService"
        class="com.apress.prospring2.ch06.services.DefaultUserService"/>
    <bean id="stockService"
        class="com.apress.prospring2.ch06.services.DefaultStockService"/>
    <bean class="com.apress.prospring2.ch06.lifecycle.CountingAspect"/>

    <aop:aspectj-autoproxy />

</beans>
```

Now, when we run the application, it will print `1, 2, 3`, thus proving that the aspect exists in a single instance. If we want to keep state for different targets, we'll need to change the scope of the aspect bean to `prototype`. If we modify the `CountingAspect` bean definition in the XML configuration file from Listing 6-41 to the following

```
<bean class="com.apress.prospring2.ch06.lifecycle.CountingAspect"
    scope="prototype"/>
```

and run the sample application again with the new aspect bean scope, it will print `1, 2, 1`: the application now maintains one instance of the aspect for every target. In effect, we have implemented a per this aspect; we can make this explicit by using a `perthis` expression in the @Aspect annotation:

```
@Aspect("perthis(execution(" +
        "* com.apress.prospring2.ch06.services.UserService.*(..)))")
public class PertargetCountingAspect {
...
}
```

The result of the modification is that Spring AOP will create a new instance of the aspect for each unique object executing the advised object.

Another life cycle strategy Spring AOP supports is `pertarget`. This works just like `perthis`, except it will create a new instance of the aspect for every unique target object at the matched join points.

Framework Services for AOP

Up to now, we have used the @AspectJ support in Spring to write aspects. We have relied on the underlying Spring AOP framework services to process the annotated beans and instrument the beans. If you cannot use annotations (perhaps you are running on a pre-1.5 JDK or you just don't like them), you can use XML configuration using the `aop` namespace. In this section, we will discuss the XML configuration and look under the hood of Spring AOP to find out how the @AspectJ support turns the annotated beans into a format usable for Spring AOP support.

Creating Our First Aspect Using the aop Namespace

To get us started, let's write an aspect that works just like the aspect in Listing 6-1, but this time we will use only XML configuration. We will start with Listing 6-42, which shows the XML configuration for the aspect.

Listing 6-42. *XML Configuration File*

```
<?xml version="1.0" encoding="UTF-8"?>
<beans xmlns="http://www.springframework.org/schema/beans"
       xmlns:xsi="http://www.w3.org/2001/XMLSchema-instance"
       xmlns:aop="http://www.springframework.org/schema/aop"
       xsi:schemaLocation="
            http://www.springframework.org/schema/beans
            http://www.springframework.org/schema/beans/spring-beans.xsd
            http://www.springframework.org/schema/aop
            http://www.springframework.org/schema/aop/spring-aop.xsd">

    <bean id="userService"
        class="com.apress.prospring2.ch06.services.DefaultUserService"/>
    <bean id="stockService"
        class="com.apress.prospring2.ch06.services.DefaultStockService"/>

    <bean id="aspectBean" class="com.apress.prospring2.ch06.xml.AspectBean"/>

    <aop:config>
        <aop:pointcut id="serviceCall"
            expression="execution(* com.apress.prospring2.ch06.services.*.*(..))"/>

        <aop:aspect id="firstAspect" ref="aspectBean">
            <aop:before method="logCall" pointcut-ref="serviceCall"/>
        </aop:aspect>
    </aop:config>

</beans>
```

The code in bold declares a pointcut that matches execution of any method with any arguments in any class in the `com.apress.prospring2.ch06.services` package. The code we have written is similar to the @AspectJ code; the only code we need to show is the `AspectBean` in Listing 6-43.

Listing 6-43. *AspectBean Code*

```
public class AspectBean {

    public void logCall(JoinPoint jp) {
        System.out.println(jp);
    }

}
```

The code is similar to the @AspectJ code; the difference is that there are no annotations at all. The sample application in Listing 6-44 uses the XML configuration and calls the now well-known methods of the `userService` and `stockService` beans.

Listing 6-44. *Sample Application for the XML aop Support*

```
public class XmlDemo1 {

    public static void main(String[] args) {
        ApplicationContext ac = new ClassPathXmlApplicationContext(
                "/META-INF/spring/xmldemo1-context.xml"
        );
        UserService userService = (UserService) ac.getBean("userService");
        StockService stockService = (StockService) ac.getBean("stockService");

        userService.login("janm");
        stockService.getStockLevel("A");
    }

}
```

The code in the sample application remains the same as the code with @AspectJ aspects; in other words, the XML configuration is completely transparent, and the calling code is not aware that it is calling methods on advised beans. When we run the sample application, it prints the following:

```
> userService.login("janm"):
    org.springframework.aop.aspectj.MethodInvocationProceedingJoinPoint: ➥
        execution(login)

> stockService.getStockLevel("A)":
    org.springframework.aop.aspectj.MethodInvocationProceedingJoinPoint: ➥
        execution(getStockLevel)
```

We can see that both `userService` and `stockService` are correctly advised and that the `AspectBean.logCall()` method executes.

Pointcuts in the aop Namespace

Just like in the @AspectJ support section, we will take a look at configuration elements for pointcut definitions. To define a pointcut, you need to write an `<aop:pointcut . . ./>` element as a child of the `<aop:config>` element. Let's take a look at the code from Listing 6-43 in more detail: Listing 6-45 shows a section of the XML configuration file.

Listing 6-45. *AOP Section of the XML Configuration File*

```
...
    <aop:config>
        <aop:pointcut id="serviceCall"
            expression="execution(* com.apress.prospring2.ch06.services.*.*(..))"/>

        <aop:aspect id="firstAspect" ref="aspectBean">
            <aop:before method="logCall" pointcut-ref="serviceCall"/>
        </aop:aspect>
    </aop:config>
...
```

The code in bold shows that we have a pointcut with `id="serviceCall"`, which we then use in the definition of the before advice in the `firstAspect`. Just as with @AspectJ support, we can refer to an @pointcut in the expression of the pointcut. Listing 6-46 shows a familiar definition of an @pointcut.

Listing 6-46. *@pointcut Definition*

```
public final class Pointcuts {
    private Pointcuts() {

    }

    @Pointcut("execution(* com.apress.prospring2.ch06.services.*.*(..))")
    public void serviceExecution() { }

}
```

We can now use the `Pointcuts.serviceExecution()` @pointcut in the XML configuration by making a simple change to the `<aop:pointcut . . ./>` element.

```
<aop:pointcut id="serviceCall"
        expression="com.apress.prospring2.ch06.xml.Pointcuts.➥
        serviceExecution()"/>
```

The only drawback is that we are using annotations again. We believe that it is better to choose one configuration style in your application and stick with it; a mixture of @AspectJ and XML configuration can quickly get too complex to manage.

Going back to pure XML configuration, you can use all Spring AOP–supported pointcut expressions, and some IDEs come with code completion even for the XML-based Spring AOP (see Figure 6-5).

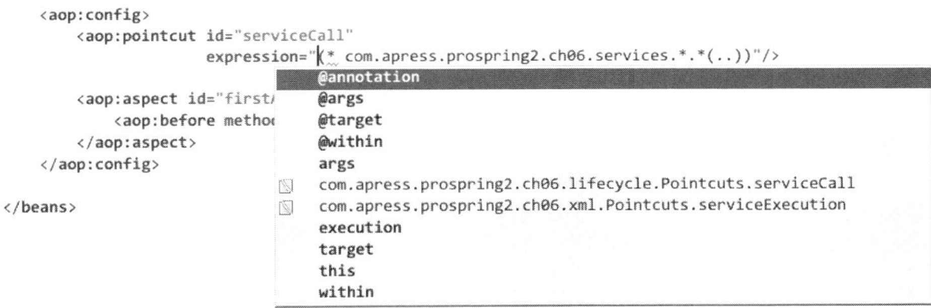

Figure 6-5. *Code completion for XML AOP confiruation in IntelliJ IDEA*

Creating Advice Using the aop Namespace

Advice in the XML configuration is similar to advice in @AspectJ; the only differences are that the beans representing the aspects are simple Spring beans and the configuration is split between the XML files and Java code in the aspect beans. The `aop` namespace is as powerful as the @AspectJ support. We have already seen an example of a simple before advice in Listing 6-42; let's explore the XML advice in more detail. Just like @AspectJ advice, XML advice needs a pointcut. You can refer to an existing pointcut (using the `pointcut-ref` attribute in the advice definition), or you can specify a pointcut expression directly (using the `pointcut` attribute in the advice definition). Listing 6-47 shows equivalent definitions of the before advice.

Listing 6-47. *Using pointcut-ref and pointcut Attributes*

```
...
<aop:aspect id="firstAspect" ref="aspectBean">
    <aop:before method="logCall" pointcut-ref="serviceCall"/>
</aop:aspect>

<aop:aspect id="firstAspect" ref="aspectBean">
    <aop:before method="logCall"
        pointcut="execution(* com.apress.prospring2.ch06.services.*.*(..))"/>
</aop:aspect>
...
```

The difference is obvious: in the first snippet, we reference an existing pointcut declared using the <pointcut . . ./> element; in the second snippet, we specify the pointcut expression.

Next, we will look into the advices in the aop namespace in more detail.

Before Advice

To declare before advice, we need to create the <before> element as a child of the <aspect> element. The attributes of the <before> element are method, pointcut or pointcut-ref, and arg-names. You must always set the method and pointcut or pointcut-ref attributes. The method attribute is the name of a public method in a bean you reference in the <aspect> element; its arguments can vary, ranging from no arguments at all, through JoinPoint, to all arguments you are binding in the pointcut expression. If you are using binding, you should consider using the arg-names attribute to help the Spring AOP Framework correctly identify the bound arguments.

After Returning Advice

To create after returning advice, create an <after-returning> element as a child of the <advice> element. Just like in the before advice, you need to set the method and pointcut or pointcut-ref attributes. In most cases, you would also want to know the return value; to obtain this, set the returning attribute to the name of an Object argument of the method. Finally, you can also use arg-names to specify the argument names of the method in the method attribute. Let's take a look at the code in Listing 6-48, which shows how we can create an aspect that will audit calls to every method and censor some return values.

Listing 6-48. *Using the After Returning Advice*

```
<?xml version="1.0" encoding="UTF-8"?>
<beans xmlns="http://www.springframework.org/schema/beans"
       xmlns:xsi="http://www.w3.org/2001/XMLSchema-instance"
       xmlns:aop="http://www.springframework.org/schema/aop"
       xsi:schemaLocation="
            http://www.springframework.org/schema/beans
            http://www.springframework.org/schema/beans/spring-beans.xsd
            http://www.springframework.org/schema/aop
            http://www.springframework.org/schema/aop/spring-aop.xsd">

    <bean id="userService"
         class="com.apress.prospring2.ch06.services.DefaultUserService"/>
    <bean id="stockService"
         class="com.apress.prospring2.ch06.services.DefaultStockService"/>

    <bean id="aspectBean" class="com.apress.prospring2.ch06.xml.AspectBean"/>
```

```
    <aop:config>
        <aop:aspect id="firstAspect" ref="aspectBean">
            <aop:after-returning method="auditCall"
                                 pointcut="execution(* com.apress.prospring2.➥
                                                ch06.services.*.*(..)) ➥
                                                &amp;&amp; target(target)"
                                 arg-names="target, ret"
                                 returning="ret"/>
        </aop:aspect>
    </aop:config>

</beans>
```

Notice that our pointcut expression specifies execution of any method in any class in the `services` package and that we are binding the invocation target to an argument called `target`. We are also going to receive the return value the target returned in the `AspectBean.auditCall()` method. Looking at the `arg-names` attribute, you can clearly see that the `auditCall` method needs two arguments, and because we want to receive a target of any type and process any type of return value, the type of the arguments needs to be `Object`. We can now write the code for the `AspectBean.auditCall` method (see Listing 6-49).

Listing 6-49. *The AspectBean auditCall Method*

```
public class AspectBean {

    public void auditCall(Object target, Object ret) {
        System.out.println("After method call of " + ret);
        if (ret instanceof User) {
            ((User)ret).setPassword("****");
        }
 }

}
```

We now have the `auditCall` method with two arguments: `target` and `ret`. Notice that the XML configuration in Listing 6-48 file specified the argument names in the correct order. This is quite easy to get wrong. Luckily, some IDEs will detect this and suggest a correction; Figure 6-6 shows this error correction in IntelliJ IDEA when we swapped the order of arguments from the correct `target, ret` to `ret, target`.

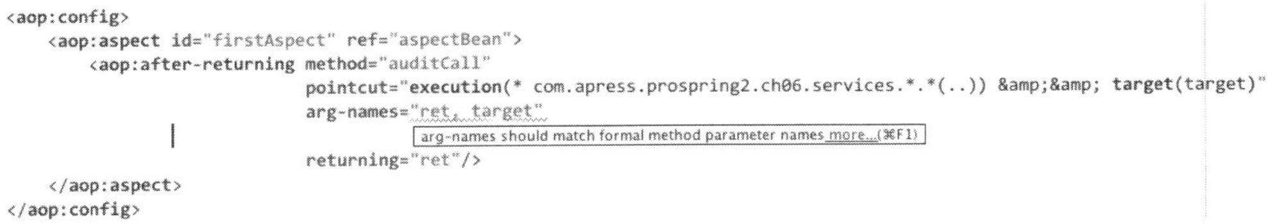

```
<aop:config>
    <aop:aspect id="firstAspect" ref="aspectBean">
        <aop:after-returning method="auditCall"
                             pointcut="execution(* com.apress.prospring2.ch06.services.*.*(..)) &amp;&amp; target(target)"
                             arg-names="ret, target"
                                       arg-names should match formal method parameter names more...(⌘F1)
                             returning="ret"/>
    </aop:aspect>
</aop:config>
```

Figure 6-6. *Arg-names error detection in IntelliJ IDEA*

You can see that the `<after-returning>` element gives you the same configuration options as the `@AfterReturning` annotation in @AspectJ.

After Throwing Advice

As you already know, after throwing advice executes only when the matching method throws an exception. To create after throwing advice declaratively, we'll use the `%(after-throwing%)` element in the `<aspect>` element. We need to set at least the `method`, `pointcut` or `pointcut-ref`, and `throwing` attributes; in most cases, we will also set the `arg-names` attribute. Without any delay, let's take a look at the XML configuration in Listing 6-50.

Listing 6-50. *After Throwing Advice in XML*

```
<?xml version="1.0" encoding="UTF-8"?>
<beans xmlns="http://www.springframework.org/schema/beans"
       xmlns:xsi="http://www.w3.org/2001/XMLSchema-instance"
       xmlns:aop="http://www.springframework.org/schema/aop"
       xsi:schemaLocation="
            http://www.springframework.org/schema/beans
            http://www.springframework.org/schema/beans/spring-beans.xsd
            http://www.springframework.org/schema/aop
            http://www.springframework.org/schema/aop/spring-aop.xsd">

    <bean id="userService"
        class="com.apress.prospring2.ch06.services.DefaultUserService"/>
    <bean id="stockService"
        class="com.apress.prospring2.ch06.services.DefaultStockService"/>

    <bean id="aspectBean" class="com.apress.prospring2.ch06.xml.AspectBean"/>

    <aop:config>
        <aop:aspect id="afterThrowingAspect" ref="aspectBean">
            <aop:after-throwing method="healthMonitoring"
                                pointcut="execution(* com.apress.prospring2.➥
                                          ch06.services.*.*(..)) &amp;&amp; ➥
                                          target(target)"
                                arg-names="target,ex"
                                throwing="ex"/>
        </aop:aspect>
    </aop:config>

</beans>
```

This after throwing advice binds the target of the invocation and the exception thrown to the arguments of method `healthMonitoring`. This means that the `healthMonitoring` method needs to have two arguments; to catch any exception on any target, the arguments' types would have to be `Object` and `Throwable`. However, to show filtering based on argument types, we will take the code from Listing 6-51.

Listing 6-51. *After Throwing Method and Argument Filtering*

```
public class AspectBean {

    public void healthMonitoring(Object target, NullPointerException ex) {
        System.out.println("Target " + target + " has thrown " + ex);
    }

}
```

Notice that the second argument's type is `NullPointerException`, so the advice will only run if the exception thrown by the target method is `NullPointerException`. To demonstrate after throwing advice, we will take the code from Listing 6-44, but call this:

```
stockService.getStockLevel(null);
```

After Advice

The after, or finally, advice executes after the target method completes, regardless of whether the target method finished normally or threw any exceptions. We declare the after advice using the `<after>` element in the `<aspect>` element; because it is after advice, we only need to set the `method` and `pointcut` or `pointcut-ref` attributes. We can use the `arg-names` attribute if we are using argument binding. Because of the nature of the advice, we cannot use the `returning` and `throwing` attributes. As an example, Listing 6-52 shows a simple after advice.

Listing 6-52. *After Advice Configuration*

```
<?xml version="1.0" encoding="UTF-8"?>
<beans xmlns="http://www.springframework.org/schema/beans"
       xmlns:xsi="http://www.w3.org/2001/XMLSchema-instance"
       xmlns:aop="http://www.springframework.org/schema/aop"
       xsi:schemaLocation="
            http://www.springframework.org/schema/beans
            http://www.springframework.org/schema/beans/spring-beans.xsd
            http://www.springframework.org/schema/aop
            http://www.springframework.org/schema/aop/spring-aop.xsd">

    <bean id="userService"
         class="com.apress.prospring2.ch06.services.DefaultUserService"/>
    <bean id="stockService"
         class="com.apress.prospring2.ch06.services.DefaultStockService"/>

    <bean id="aspectBean" class="com.apress.prospring2.ch06.xml.AspectBean"/>

    <aop:config>
        <aop:aspect id="afterAspect" ref="aspectBean">
            <aop:after-throwing method="after"
                                pointcut="execution(* com.apress.prospring2.➥
                                                 ch06.services.*.*(..)) ➥
                                                 &amp;&amp; target(target)"
                                arg-names="target"/>
        </aop:aspect>
    </aop:config>

</beans>
```

The advice method (AspectBean.after) needs only one argument, and because we only want to advise the UserService bean, we declare it as public void after(UserService target).

Around Advice

We've left the most general advice til last. As the name suggests, it runs around the matched method's execution, so you can write code that will execute before the matched method (you can manipulate the arguments or even skip the matched method execution completely). You can also execute any code after the matched method completes; you are free to catch any exceptions using a standard try / catch block. You can also manipulate the return value, as long as you return a type that is assignable to the return value of the matched method (e.g., you can return Long from advice that advises a method that returns Number, but you can't return String). To declare around advice, use the <around> element in the <aspect> element; you must set the method and pointcut or pointcut-ref attributes, and you may want to set the arg-names attribute. The code in Listing 6-53 shows our around advice.

Listing 6-53. *XML Configuration of Around Advice*

```
<?xml version="1.0" encoding="UTF-8"?>
<beans xmlns="http://www.springframework.org/schema/beans"
       xmlns:xsi="http://www.w3.org/2001/XMLSchema-instance"
       xmlns:aop="http://www.springframework.org/schema/aop"
       xsi:schemaLocation="
            http://www.springframework.org/schema/beans
            http://www.springframework.org/schema/beans/spring-beans.xsd
            http://www.springframework.org/schema/aop
            http://www.springframework.org/schema/aop/spring-aop.xsd">

    <bean id="userService"
        class="com.apress.prospring2.ch06.services.DefaultUserService"/>
    <bean id="stockService"
        class="com.apress.prospring2.ch06.services.DefaultStockService"/>

    <bean id="aspectBean" class="com.apress.prospring2.ch06.xml.AspectBean"/>

    <aop:config>
        <aop:aspect id="aroundAspect" ref="aspectBean">
            <aop:around method="censorStringArguments"
                        pointcut="execution(* com.apress.prospring2.ch06.➥
                                  services.*.*(..)) and ➥
                                  args(argument)"
                        arg-names="pjp, argument"/>
        </aop:aspect>
    </aop:config>

</beans>
```

Notice that we have defined two arguments, but we don't use the `pjp` argument in the pointcut expression at all. Your around advice method must have at least the `ProceedingJoinPoint` argument (otherwise, you would not be able to invoke the matched method!) and must return `Object`. In addition to the `ProceedingJoinPoint` argument, you are free to use as many bound arguments as you need. In our example, we have implemented a censoring advice method (its source code is in Listing 6-54).

Listing 6-54. *Around Advice Method*

```
public class AspectBean {

    public Object censorStringArguments(ProceedingJoinPoint pjp, String argument)
        throws Throwable {
        Object[] arguments;
        if (argument != null) {
            System.out.println("censored " + argument + "!");
            arguments = new Object[] { "****" };
        } else {
            arguments = new Object[] { null };
        }
        return pjp.proceed(arguments);
    }
...
}
```

Here, you can see that the method's arguments match the value in the `arg-names` attribute and that the type of the second argument is `String`, which means that we'll only match methods that have one argument of type `String`; in our small application, those are `UserService.setAdministratorUsername`, `UserService.login`, and `StockService.getStockLevel`.

Now that we have covered all types of advice using XML configuration, we will take a look at the last area, introductions.

Introductions in the aop Namespace

The last area we will cover in this section is introductions; if you recall, introductions offer a way to add additional methods to existing objects by proxying the advised objects, making the proxy implement the interfaces that the original implements plus any interfaces we declare. To use XML introductions, you need to use the `<declare-parents>` element under the `<aspect>` element; to actually make use of the newly declared parents (e.g., a newly implemented interface), you will need to create at least one piece of advice that uses the introduced interface. We are going to rework the example from Listing 6-36: we will introduce the `CallTracker` interface to the `DefaultUserService` and `DefaultStockService`. Listing 6-55 shows the configuration of the introduction of the `CallTracker` interface in XML.

Listing 6-55. *Introduction Declared in XML*

```
<?xml version="1.0" encoding="UTF-8"?>
<beans xmlns="http://www.springframework.org/schema/beans"
       xmlns:xsi="http://www.w3.org/2001/XMLSchema-instance"
       xmlns:aop="http://www.springframework.org/schema/aop"
       xsi:schemaLocation="
            http://www.springframework.org/schema/beans
            http://www.springframework.org/schema/beans/spring-beans.xsd
            http://www.springframework.org/schema/aop
            http://www.springframework.org/schema/aop/spring-aop.xsd">

    <bean id="userService"
        class="com.apress.prospring2.ch06.services.DefaultUserService"/>
    <bean id="stockService"
        class="com.apress.prospring2.ch06.services.DefaultStockService"/>

    <bean id="aspectBean" class="com.apress.prospring2.ch06.xml.AspectBean"/>

    <aop:config>
        <aop:aspect id="aroundAspect" ref="aspectBean">
            <aop:declare-parents
                                     types-matching="com.apress.prospring2.➥
                                         ch06.services.*"
                                     implement-interface="com.apress.prospring2.➥
                                         ch06.introductions.CallTracker"
                                     default-impl="com.apress.prospring2.ch06.➥
                                         introductions.DefaultCallTracker"/>

            <aop:after-returning method="normalCall"
                                     arg-names="tracker"
                                     pointcut="execution(* com.apress.prospring2.➥
                                         ch06.services.*.*(..)) and this(tracker)"/>
            <aop:after-throwing method="failingCall"
                                    arg-names="tracker"
                                    pointcut="execution(* com.apress.prospring2.➥
                                        ch06.services.*.*(..)) and this(tracker)"/>
        </aop:aspect>
    </aop:config>

</beans>
```

In the `<declare-parents>` element, the `types-matching` attribute specifies the classes to which we want to introduce the interface defined in the `implement-interface`. To complete the `<declare-parents>` element, we need to specify the `default-impl`—the name of the class that implements the interface in `implement-interface`. If we stopped there, we could write

```
CallTracker usct = (CallTracker)ac.getBean("userService");
```

Assuming that `ac` is the `ApplicationContext` instance configured using the XML configuration file from Listing 6-55, this would verify that the `userService` bean now implements the `CallTracker` interface, even though the `DefaultUserService`, the actual class of the bean, only implements the `UserService`. The only problem is that the application would not track calls; the values in the `normalCalls` and `failingCalls` fields in the `DefaultCallTracker` would never change. To complete this example, we need to create two pieces of advice: after returning and after throwing. Listing 6-56 shows the configuration of these two.

Listing 6-56. *After Returning and After Throwing Advices*

```
...
    <aop:config>
        <aop:aspect id="aroundAspect" ref="aspectBean">
            <aop:declare-parents ... />

            <aop:after-returning method="normalCall"
                                 arg-names="tracker"
                                 pointcut="execution(* com.apress.prospring2.➥
                                     ch06.services.*.*(..)) and this(tracker)"/>
            <aop:after-throwing method="failingCall"
                                arg-names="tracker"
                                pointcut="execution(* com.apress.prospring2.➥
                                    ch06.services.*.*(..)) and this(tracker)"/>
        </aop:aspect>
    </aop:config>
...
```

To complete the advice, we need to implement the `normalCall` and `failingCall` methods in the `AspectBean`. Both pieces of after advice have the `arg-names` attribute set to `tracker`, so the methods will need one argument with the name `tracker`. Its type should be `CallTracker`; we will use its methods to count the calls. Listing 6-57 shows the implementation of the two advice methods.

Listing 6-57. *Implementation of the After Advice Methods*

```
public class AspectBean {
...
    public void normalCall(CallTracker tracker) {
        tracker.markNormal();
    }

    public void failingCall(CallTracker tracker) {
        tracker.markFailing();
    }
...
}
```

The methods are very simple: they use the tracker argument to increment the appropriate call counter. We will complete the example with Listing 6-58, which shows the demonstration application. The application makes calls to the `userService` and `stockService` beans and displays the call statistics using the introduced `CallTracker` interface.

Listing 6-58. *Example Application for the Introductions*

```
public class XmlDemo6 {

    public static void main(String[] args) {
        ApplicationContext ac = new ClassPathXmlApplicationContext(
                "/META-INF/spring/xmldemo6-context.xml"
        );
        UserService userService = (UserService) ac.getBean("userService");
        StockService stockService = (StockService) ac.getBean("stockService");

        userService.login("janm");
        stockService.getStockLevel("A");
        stockService.applyDiscounts(new Date(), BigDecimal.ONE);
```

```
        describeTracker(userService);
        describeTracker(stockService);
    }

    private static void describeTracker(Object o) {
        CallTracker t = (CallTracker)o;
        System.out.println(t.describe());
    }

}
```

The application works and proves that we have successfully introduced the `CallTracker` interface on both beans.

Which Style Should You Use?

You may be wondering which Spring AOP style to choose? @AspectJ is easy to use but requires that you use 1.5 JDK; XML-based configuration works with a pre-1.5 JDK. Our recommendation is to use @AspectJ wherever you can. The XML-based configuration may feel more familiar to seasoned Spring developers, but the issue is that, in XML-based configuration, the developers may not be aware that they are working on an aspect, and the XML configuration splits the functionality of a single unit into two files. Moreover, you cannot combine pointcuts with as much flexibility as you can with @AspectJ. If you recall, you can use a pointcut to specify the pointcut expression or `pointcut-ref` attribute to specify a reference to an existing pointcut expression in the XML configuration. However, you cannot combine a reference to an existing pointcut and a pointcut expression. For example, you cannot write code similar to the code in Listing 6-59.

Listing 6-59. *Illegal Combination of pointcut and pointcut-ref*

```
<aop:config>
    <aop:pointcut id="x" expression="..."/>
    <aop:aspect ...>
        <aop:before pointcut="x() and target(y)" />
    </aop:aspect>
</aop:config>
```

The line in bold is not valid, because the pointcut expression `x() and target(y)` is not valid. The same value in the `pointcut-ref` attribute is also invalid, because no (pointcut) bean with ID `x() and target(y)` exists.

Possibly the worst approach is to combine the two approaches and use both @AspectJ and XML-based configuration: this can only lead to confusion and possibly duplicate advice.

Working with Spring AOP Proxies

Spring AOP support uses proxies; Figure 6-7 shows a UML class diagram of a proxy pattern.

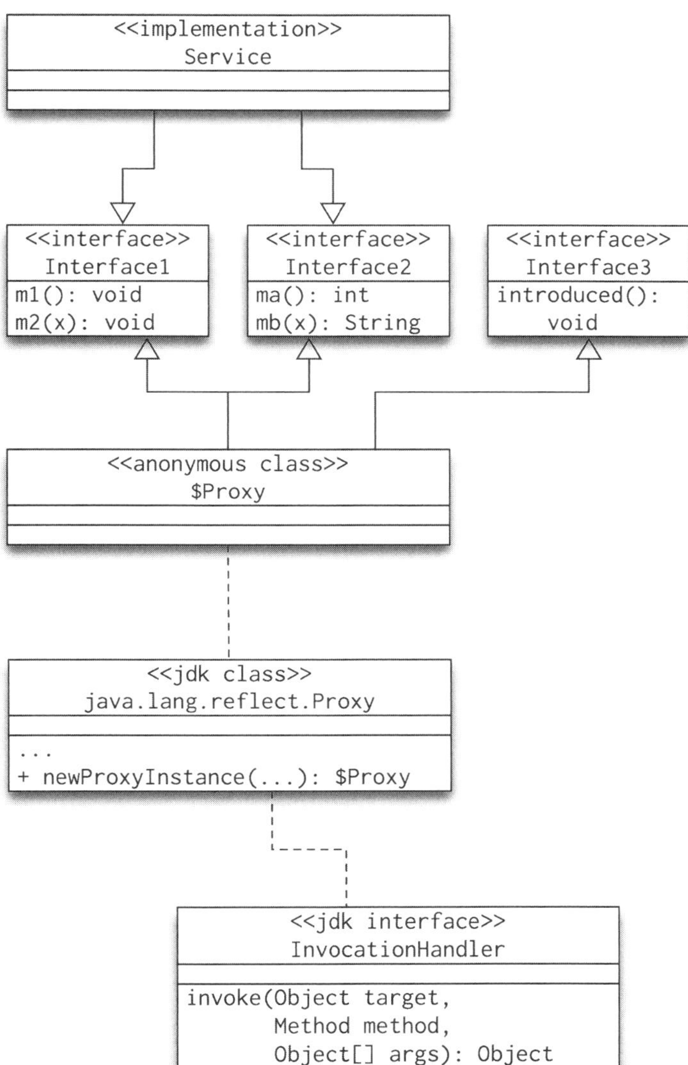

Figure 6-7. *UML class diagram of a proxy pattern*

The figure shows a JDK dynamic proxy; the proxy implements `Interface1`, `Interface2`, and `Interface3`. The implementation of the `InvocationHandler.invoke()` method handles all calls to all methods of the interfaces implemented by the proxy. In the case of Spring AOP, the `InvocationHandler` holds a reference to the advised object; it handles all before, after returning, after throwing, or around advice pertaining to the target method. If the target objects do not implement any interfaces or if you do not wish to use JDK dynamic proxies, you can use CGLIB proxies. CGLIB is a bytecode manipulation library, which you can use to proxy a class that does not implement any interface. Figure 6-8 shows the class diagram of a CGLIB proxy.

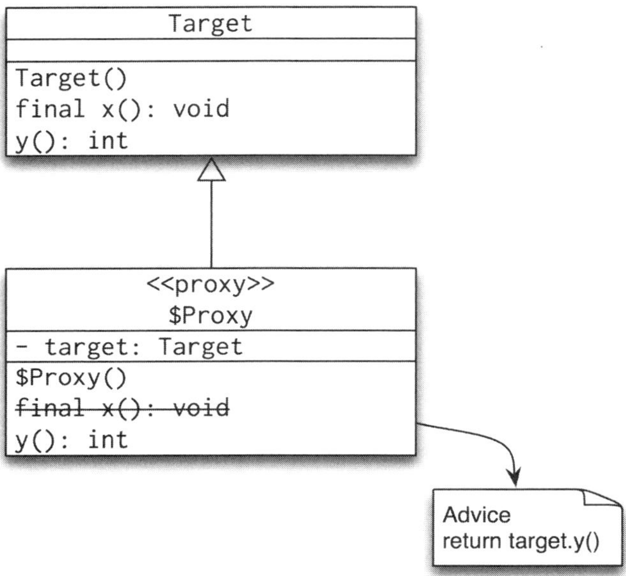

Figure 6-8. *CGLIB proxy class diagram*

Essentially, CGLIB proxies are subclasses of the target class; because you cannot override `final` methods, advice on `final` methods will not work. Also, the constructor of the target (the advised class) will be called twice: once to create the advised class and the second time to create the proxy. Usually, two constructor calls do not cause any problems; if all you do in a constructor is check the arguments and set the instance fields, then you can run the constructor as many times as you want. However, if there is some kind of business logic in the constructor, it may cause problems. You can control which type of proxy Spring creates by setting the `proxy-target-class="true"` in the `<aop:config . . ./>` or the `<aop:aspectj-autoproxy . . ./>` elements. If you have more than one `<aop:config . . ./>` or `<aop:aspectj-autoproxy . . ./>` element in your configuration files and if at least one of them specifies `proxy-target-class="true"`, then all proxies will use CGLIB as if we set `proxy-target-class="true"` in every configuration element.

Impact of Proxies

Let's now take a look at the impact the proxying may have on your code. As an example, we will take the `StockService` interface and its implementation, the `DefaultStockService`. To demonstrate some of the concepts we will discuss in this section, we will make a subtle modification to the `DefaultStockService`. Listing 6-60 shows the modifications.

Listing 6-60. *Modified DefaultStockService*

```
public class DefaultStockService implements StockService {

    public long getStockLevel(String sku) {
        try {
            Thread.sleep(2000L);
        } catch (InterruptedException ignored) {
        }
        return getPredictedStockLevel (sku) / 2L;
    }

    public long getPredictedStockLevel(String sku) {
        return 6L * sku.hashCode();
    }

    public void applyDiscounts(Date cutoffDate, BigDecimal maximumDiscount) {
        // do some work
    }

}
```

If we create an unproxied instance of the `DefaultStockService` and then call the `getStockLevel("X")` method, the call to `getPredictedStockLevel` operates on the same instance. Listing 6-61 demonstrates this concept more clearly.

Listing 6-61. *Calling Unproxied Methods*

```
public class ProxyDemo {

    public static void main(String[] args) {
        StockService dss = new DefaultStockService();
        dss.getStockLevel("X");
    }

}
```

When we call `dss.getStockLevel("X")`, the `dss` references the `DefaultStockService` directly and therefore when the `DefaultStockService.getStockLevel()` calls the `DefaultStockService.getPredictedStockLevel()` method, it is the same as if we called `((DefaultStockService)dss).getPredictedStockLevel()` from the `main()` method.

Next, consider a similar scenario, but this time, the `StockService` interface will be a proxy to the `DefaultStockService`. We will begin with JDK dynamic proxies. Listing 6-62 shows a JDK dynamic proxy for the `StockService`.

Listing 6-62. *JDK Dynamic Proxy for the StockService*

```
public class ProxyDemo2 {

    private static class DelegatingInvocationHandler
        implements InvocationHandler {
        private Object target;

        private DelegatingInvocationHandler(Object target) {
            this.target = target;
        }
```

```
        public Object invoke(Object target,
                             Method method,
                             Object[] args) throws Throwable {
            return method.invoke(this.target, args);
        }
    }

    public static void main(String[] args) {
        DefaultStockService targetReference = new DefaultStockService();
        StockService proxyReference =
                (StockService) Proxy.newProxyInstance(
                        ProxyDemo2.class.getClassLoader(),
                        new Class<?>[] {StockService.class},
                        new DelegatingInvocationHandler(
                                targetReference
                        ));
        proxyReference.getStockLevel("X");
    }

}
```

When we call `proxyReference.getStockLevel("X")`, we are in fact calling the proxy. The proxy's `InvocationHandler` uses the `DefaultStockService` instance to delegate the method calls. Therefore, the `proxyReference.getStockLevel()` method operates on a different instance than the call to `getPredictedStockLevel()` in the `DefaultStockService`.

Before we can discuss the practical impact of proxying, we need to take a look at how Spring creates proxies. As you saw in Listing 6-62, creating even the simplest proxy is a lot of work. Spring simplifies this by providing the `ProxyFactory` class, which can not only create a proxy to the target object but also add any advice. Listing 6-63 shows a simple use of the `ProxyFactory`.

Listing 6-63. *Using the ProxyFactory*

```
public class ProxyDemo3 {

    public static void main(String[] args) {
        DefaultStockService target = new DefaultStockService();
        ProxyFactory pf = new ProxyFactory(target);
        pf.addInterface(StockService.class);

        StockService stockService = (StockService) pf.getProxy();
        stockService.getStockLevel("A");
    }

}
```

We have created the target object (the `DefaultStockService`) and then used the `ProxyFactory` to create a proxy that implements the `StockService`. Next, we need to take a look at how we can use a subclass of the `ProxyFactory` to create advised proxies. To do this, we will look at the simple before advice in Listing 6-64.

Listing 6-64. *Simple Aspect with Before Advice*

```
public class BeforeAspect {

    @Before("execution(* com.apress.prospring2.ch06.services.*.*(..))")
    public void simpleLog(JoinPoint jp) {
```

```
        System.out.println("Before " + jp);
    }

}
```

There is nothing extraordinary about the aspect; it simply prints a message before the call to the advised method. Now that we have the aspect, we will use the `AspectJProxyFactory` to create an advised proxy. Listing 6-65 shows the code needed to create the advised proxy.

Listing 6-65. *Using AspectJProxyFactory*

```
public class ProxyDemo4 {

    public static void main(String[] args) {
        DefaultStockService target = new DefaultStockService();
        AspectJProxyFactory pf = new AspectJProxyFactory(target);
        pf.addInterface(StockService.class);
        pf.addAspect(BeforeAspect.class);

        StockService stockService = (StockService) pf.getProxy();
        stockService.getStockLevel("A");
    }

}
```

When we now run this example, it will show the same output as if we used Spring's `ApplicationContext` configured with `<aop:aspectj-autoproxy . . ./>` and the aspect bean.

Now that we know how to use Spring to create advised proxies, we need to look at the implication of the proxy calls, which can become significant: imagine an advised object with an around advice that begins and commits every transaction for every method call. If you get the advised object (the proxy) and call its methods, the advice will work. However, when you call an advised method from within an advised object, the call will not go through the proxy, and the advice will not run. Therefore, when we use the `StockService` proxy in the sample application, we'll see that only the `getStockLevel` call is advised; the internal call to the `getPredictedStockLevel` method is not.

The best way to avoid this situation is not to chain method calls in your advised classes. In some situations, this chaining can in fact lead to problems (we explore some of the problems you can face in Chapter 11). However, there is another way that will allow you to make calls in the advised objects but direct them through the appropriate proxy. We strongly discourage you from doing so, but if you must, you can use the `AopContext.currentProxy()` method to obtain the proxy representing `this`. Listing 6-66 shows a modification to the `DefaultStockService` that demonstrates how to use this call.

Listing 6-66. *Modified DefaultStockService*

```
public class DefaultStockService implements StockService {

    public long getStockLevel(String sku) {
        try {
            Thread.sleep(2000L);
        } catch (InterruptedException ignored) {
        }
        return ((StockService)AopContext.currentProxy()).
            getPredictedStockLevel(sku) / 2L;
    }
```

```
    public long getPredictedStockLevel(String sku) {
        return 6L * sku.hashCode();
    }

    public void applyDiscounts(Date cutoffDate, BigDecimal maximumDiscount) {
        // do some work
    }

}
```

Instead of calling `this.getPredictedStockLevel(sku)`, we obtain the proxy from `AopContext.currentProxy()` and call the `getPredictedStockLevel` on the proxy. If we attempt to run the sample application now, it will fail. We have to expose the current proxy in the configuration of the `ProxyFactory` (see Listing 6-67).

Listing 6-67. *Modified ProxyFactory Configuration*

```
public class ProxyDemo4 {

    public static void main(String[] args) {
        DefaultStockService target = new DefaultStockService();
        AspectJProxyFactory pf = new AspectJProxyFactory(target);
        pf.addInterface(StockService.class);
        pf.setExposeProxy(true);
        pf.addAspect(BeforeAspect.class);

        StockService stockService = (StockService) pf.getProxy();
        stockService.getStockLevel("A");
    }

}
```

This is the final change needed to make the application work—when we run it, it shows that the before advice from Listing 6-64 ran for `getStockLevel` and `getPredictedStockLevel`:

```
Before org.springframework.aop.aspectj.➥
MethodInvocationProceedingJoinPoint: ➥
execution(getStockLevel)
Before org.springframework.aop.aspectj.➥
MethodInvocationProceedingJoinPoint: ➥
execution(getPredictedStockLevel)
```

Even though this is the solution to the problem caused by proxying when chaining advised methods, we strongly urge you to rethink your design to prevent such chained calls. Only if there is no other option should you consider using the `AopContext` and changing the configuration of the `ProxyFactory`. Doing so will tie your beans very closely to Spring AOP; making your code dependent on the framework you use is the very thing Spring tries to avoid!

AspectJ Integration

AOP provides a powerful solution to many of the common problems that arise with OOP applications. When using Spring AOP, you can take advantage of a select subset of AOP functionality that, in most cases, allows you to solve problems you encounter in your application. However, in some cases, you may wish to use some AOP features that are outside the scope of Spring AOP. In this case, you need to look at an AOP implementation with a fuller feature set. Our preference, in this case, is to use AspectJ, and because you can now configure AspectJ aspects using Spring, AspectJ forms the perfect complement to Spring AOP.

AspectJ is a fully featured AOP implementation that uses compile-time weaving to introduce aspects into your code. In AspectJ, aspects and pointcuts are built using a Java-like syntax, which reduces the learning curve for Java developers. We are not going to spend too much time looking at AspectJ and how it works, because that is beyond the scope of this book. Instead, we present some simple AspectJ examples and show you how to configure them using Spring. For more information on AspectJ, you should definitely read *AspectJ in Action* by Raminvas Laddad (Manning, 2003).

Creating Your First AspectJ Aspect

Let's get started with a simple example: we'll create an aspect and use the AspectJ compiler to weave it in. Next, we will configure the aspect as a standard Spring bean. We can do this because each AspectJ aspect exposes a method, `aspectOf()`, which can be used to access the aspect instance. Using the `aspectOf()` method and a special feature of Spring configuration, you can have Spring configure the aspect for you. The benefits of this cannot be overstated. You can take full advantage of AspectJ's powerful AOP feature set without losing out on Spring's excellent DI and configuration abilities. This also means that you do not need two separate configuration methods for your application; you can use the same Spring `ApplicationContext` approach for all your Spring-managed beans and for your AspectJ aspects.

As an example, we are going to use AspectJ to advise all methods of all classes in the `com.apress.prospring2.ch06.services` package and write out a message before and after the method invocation. These messages will be configurable using Spring. Listing 6-68 shows the `StockServiceAspect` aspect (the file name is `StockServiceAspect.aj` in `com/apress/prospring2/ch06/aspectj`).

Listing 6-68. *StockServiceAspect Aspect*

```
package com.apress.prospring2.ch06.aspectj;

public aspect StockServiceAspect {
    private String suffix;
    private String prefix;

    public void setPrefix(String prefix) {
        this.prefix = prefix;
    }

    public void setSuffix(String suffix) {
        this.suffix = suffix;
    }

    pointcut doServiceCall() :
        execution(* com.apress.prospring2.ch06.services.*.*(..));

    before() : doServiceCall() {
        System.out.println(this.prefix);
    }

    after() : doServiceCall() {
        System.out.println(this.suffix);
    }
}
```

Much of this code should look familiar. Essentially, we create an aspect called StockServiceAspect, and just like for a normal Java class, we give the aspect two properties, suffix and prefix, which we will use when advising all methods in all classes in the com.apress.prospring2.ch06.services package. Next, we define a named pointcut, doServiceCall(), for a single joinpoint, in this case, the execution of the service methods (AspectJ has a huge number of joinpoints, but coverage of those is outside the scope of this example). Finally, we define two pieces of advices: one that executes before the doServiceCall() pointcut and one that executes after it. The before advice writes a line containing the prefix, and the after advice writes a line containing the suffix. Listing 6-69 shows how this aspect is configured in Spring.

Listing 6-69. *Configuring an AspectJ Aspect*

```
<?xml version="1.0" encoding="UTF-8"?>
<beans xmlns="http://www.springframework.org/schema/beans"
       xmlns:xsi="http://www.w3.org/2001/XMLSchema-instance"
       xsi:schemaLocation="
            http://www.springframework.org/schema/beans
            http://www.springframework.org/schema/beans/spring-beans.xsd">

    <bean id="userService"
        class="com.apress.prospring2.ch06.services.DefaultUserService"/>
    <bean id="stockService"
        class="com.apress.prospring2.ch06.services.DefaultStockService"/>
    <bean class="com.apress.prospring2.ch06.aspectj.StockServiceAspect"
        factory-method="aspectOf">
        <property name="prefix" value="Before call"/>
        <property name="suffix" value="After call"/>
    </bean>

</beans>
```

As you can see, much of the configuration of the aspect bean is very similar to standard bean configuration. The only difference is the use of the factory-method attribute of the <bean> tag. The factory-method attribute is intended to allow classes that follow a traditional Factory pattern to be integrated seamlessly into Spring. For instance, if you have a class Foo with a private constructor and a static factory method, getInstance(), using factory-method allows a bean of this class to be managed by Spring. The aspectOf() method exposed by every singleton AspectJ aspect allows you to access the instance of the aspect and thus allows Spring to set the properties of the aspect. However, notice that we have not used the aop namespace at all; on top of that, the StockServiceAspect is not a valid Java source. To complete the example, Listing 6-70 shows a familiar code that uses the stockService and userService beans.

Listing 6-70. *AspectJ Sample Application*

```
public class AspectJDemo1 {
    public static void main(String[] args) {
        ApplicationContext ac = new ClassPathXmlApplicationContext(
                "/META-INF/spring/aspectjdemo1-context.xml"
        );
        UserService userService = (UserService) ac.getBean("userService");
        userService.login("janm");

        StockService stockService = (StockService) ac.getBean("stockService");
        System.out.println(stockService.getStockLevel("ABC"));
    }

}
```

If we try to run the application directly from our IDE, it will fail. The output will indicate that there is no StockServiceAspect class; we expected this problem, because the StockServiceAspect is an aspect, not a Java class.

```
...
Exception in thread "main" ➥
org.springframework.beans.factory.CannotLoadBeanClassException: ➥
Cannot find class [com.apress.prospring2.ch06.aspectj.StockServiceAspect] ➥
for bean with name 'com.apress.prospring2.ch06.aspectj.StockServiceAspect#0'➥
defined in class path resource [META-INF/spring/aspectjdemo1-context.xml]; ➥
nested exception is java.lang.ClassNotFoundException: ➥
    com.apress.prospring2.ch06.aspectj.StockServiceAspect
...
```

To make the sample application run, we must use the AspectJ compiler. The AspectJ compiler is going to turn the StockServiceAspect into a Java class file, and it will weave in the aspect's code into the advised classes. In other words, the AspectJ compiler is going to produce different bytecode for the DefaultStockService than a standard Java compiler would, because it will weave in the StockServiceAspect. In addition to compile-time weaving, the AspectJ compiler will produce a valid Java bytecode file from the StockServiceAspect.aj source file. Perhaps the most important method in the compiled StockServiceAspect class is the public static Aspect aspectOf() method that we use in the Spring bean definition.

Compiling the Sample Application

If you are familiar with AspectJ, you can skip this section; otherwise, read on to find out how to set up your computer to work with the AspectJ compiler. The first step is to get the AspectJ distribution from http://www.eclipse.org/aspectj. Download the installation package (.jar file) and install AspectJ to $ASPECTJ_HOME—typically /usr/share/aspectj-1.5 or C:\Program Files\aspectj1-5. Once you have the AspectJ compiler installed, modifying the PATH environment variable to include $ASPECTJ_HOME/bin is convenient. When you now type ajc -version at the command prompt, you should see this:

```
AspectJ Compiler 1.5.4 built on Thursday Dec 20, 2007 at 13:44:10 GMT
```

Because using the AspectJ compiler directly is rather complex, we are going to use Apache Ant to simplify the work (for more information about Ant, go to http://ant.apache.org). The AspectJ distribution includes custom Ant tasks; to get these custom tasks installed, copy aspectjtools.jar from $ASPECTJ_HOME/lib to $ANTHOME/lib.

Now that we have installed the AspectJ compiler and configured Ant to include the AspectJ custom tasks, we can take a look at the build file (see Listing 6-71).

Listing 6-71. *The Ant Build File*

```
<?xml version="1.0"?>
<project name="ch06" default="all" basedir="."
        xmlns:aspectj="antlib:org.aspectj">

    <property name="dir.src.main.java" value="./src/main/java"/>
    <property name="dir.src.main.resources" value="./src/main/resources"/>
    <property name="dir.module.main.build" value="./target/build-main"/>
    <property name="dir.lib" value="../../lib"/>
```

```
    <property name="module.jar" value="ch06.jar"/>
    <path id="module.classpath">
        <fileset dir="${dir.lib}" includes="**/*.jar"/>
        <fileset dir="${dir.lib}" includes="**/*/*.jar"/>
    </path>

    <target name="all">
        <aspectj:iajc
            outjar="${module.jar}"
            sourceRootCopyFilter="**/*.java"
            source="1.5"
            target="1.5">
            <classpath refid="module.classpath"/>
            <sourceroots>
                <path location="${dir.src.main.java}➥
                    /com/apress/prospring2/ch06/services"/>
                <path location="${dir.src.main.java}➥
                    /com/apress/prospring2/ch06/aspectj"/>
                <path location="${dir.src.main.java}➥
                    /com/apress/prospring2/ch06/common"/>
                <path location="${dir.src.main.resources}"/>
            </sourceroots>
        </aspectj:iajc>

        <java classname="com.apress.prospring2.ch06.aspectj.AspectJDemo1"
            fork="yes">
            <classpath>
                <path refid="module.classpath"/>
                <pathelement location="${module.jar}"/>
            </classpath>
        </java>

    </target>
</project>
```

When we build the sample application using this Ant script, the AspectJ compiler will weave in the aspect and create the `StockServiceAspect`. When we run the sample application (using `ant`) from Listing 6-70, it will print the following:

```
...
[java] DEBUG [main] CachedIntrospectionResults.<init>(265) | ➥
    Found bean property 'suffix' of type [java.lang.String]
...
[java] DEBUG [main] AbstractBeanFactory.getBean(197) | ➥
    Returning cached instance of singleton bean 'userService'

userService.login("janm")
[java] Before call
[java] After call
[java] DEBUG [main] AbstractBeanFactory.getBean(197) | ➥
    Returning cached instance of singleton bean 'stockService'

stockService.getStockLevel("ABC")
[java] Before call
    stockService.getPredictedStockLevel("ABC")
    [java] Before call
```

```
    [java] After call
[java] After call
[java] 193734
```

This output clearly shows that the aspect worked! We have successfully advised the `DefaultStockService` and `DefaultUserService` methods and set the aspect's `prefix` and `suffix` properties. Because the AspectJ compiler performs compile-time weaving, we do not need to worry about any proxying issues: the `getPredictedStockLevel` call from `DefaultStockService.getStockLevel` was advised without applying any `AopContext` wizardry.

AspectJ's Aspect Scope

By default, AspectJ aspects are singletons—you get a single instance per classloader. If you need to use different instances of the aspect depending on a pointcut, you'll have to write and configure the aspects differently. Listing 6-72 shows a per this aspect; "per this" means that AspectJ will create a different instance of the aspect for every match of the pointcut.

Listing 6-72. *Stateful (Per This) Aspect*

```
package com.apress.prospring2.ch06.aspectj;

public aspect ThisCountingAspect perthis(doServiceCall()) {
    private int count;

    pointcut doServiceCall() :
        execution(* com.apress.prospring2.ch06.services.*.*(..));

    before() : doServiceCall() {
        this.count++;
        System.out.println("Before call");
    }

    after(Object target) : doServiceCall() && this(target) {
        System.out.println(target + " executed " + this.count + " times");
    }
}
```

The only problem is that we cannot configure this aspect in Spring: if we configure it with the usual prototype code, it will set the property only in one instance of the aspect, but that instance won't be the one that gets used in the join points. If we need a scoped AspectJ aspect, we cannot use Spring to configure its properties.

Load-Time Weaving

Load-time weaving is a process during which the weaver applies the aspects when the `ClassLoader` loads the advised class. AspectJ supports load-time weaving using a Java agent; you need to specify the agent's JAR file (see JVM's `-javaagent` command-line argument for details). However, agents bring some limitations: the obvious one is that agents only work with 1.5 and later JVMs, and a second limitation is that the JVM loads and uses the agent for the entire JVM. This may not be a significant problem in smaller applications, but when you get to a point where you need to deploy more than one application in a virtual machine, you may need more fine-grained control over the load-time weaving process.

Spring's load-time weaving support does just that: it allows you to control the load-time weaving for each ClassLoader. This is a great help when you are deploying a web application in a servlet container or an application server. You can configure a different load-time weaver for each web application and leave the container's class loading intact. Further, if you use Spring load-time weaving support, you may not need to change the configuration of some application servers and servlet containers.

Your First Load-Time Weaving Example

We'll get started with a simple aspect that just tracks calls to all service methods. The aspect is trivial; its source code is in Listing 6-73.

Listing 6-73. *A Load-Time Weaving Demonstration Aspect*

```
@Aspect
public class AuditAspect {

    @After(value =
            "execution(* com.apress.prospring2.ch06.services.*.*(..)) && " +
            "this(t)",
         argNames = "jp,t")
    public void audit(JoinPoint jp, Object t) {
        System.out.println("After call to " + t + " (" + jp + ")");
    }

}
```

Now that we have the aspect, we'll use it to advise our userService and stockService beans. Instead of using the <aop:aspectj-autoproxy />, we will use spring-agent.jar as the JVM agent and use the context namespace to initiate the load-time weaving. In addition to the ApplicationContext XML configuration file, we need to create the META-INF/aop.xml file. The aop.xml file is a standard component of AspectJ; it tells the AspectJ weaver which classes to weave at load time. Listing 6-74 shows the contents of the aop.xml file.

Listing 6-74. *The META-INF/aop.xml File*

```
<!DOCTYPE aspectj PUBLIC
        "-//AspectJ//DTD//EN"
        "http://www.eclipse.org/aspectj/dtd/aspectj.dtd">
<aspectj>
    <weaver>
        <include within="com.apress.prospring2.ch06.services.*"/>
    </weaver>
    <aspects>
        <aspect name="com.apress.prospring2.ch06.ltw.AuditAspect"/>
    </aspects>
</aspectj>
```

The code in bold tells the AspectJ weaver to weave in the AuditAspect into all classes in the com.apress.prospring2.ch06.services package. To complete the example, Listing 6-75 shows the ApplicationContext XML configuration file with the <context:load-time-weaver> tag. The <context:load-time-weaver> tag has a single attribute, aspectj-weaving. You can set it to "on" to turn on load-time weaving, "off" to turn the load-time weaving, well, off, and "autodetect" to turn on load-time weaving if there is at least one META-INF/aop.xml file. If you omit the aspectj-weaving attribute, Spring assumes the value is "autodetect".

Listing 6-75. *The ApplicationContext XML Configuration File*

```
<?xml version="1.0" encoding="UTF-8"?>
<beans xmlns="http://www.springframework.org/schema/beans"
       xmlns:xsi="http://www.w3.org/2001/XMLSchema-instance"
       xmlns:context="http://www.springframework.org/schema/context"
       xsi:schemaLocation="
            http://www.springframework.org/schema/beans
            http://www.springframework.org/schema/beans/spring-beans.xsd
            http://www.springframework.org/schema/context
            http://www.springframework.org/schema/context/spring-context.xsd">

    <bean id="userService"
        class="com.apress.prospring2.ch06.services.DefaultUserService"/>
    <bean id="stockService"
        class="com.apress.prospring2.ch06.services.DefaultStockService"/>

    <context:load-time-weaver />

</beans>
```

Before we can run this application to find out whether the load-time weaving worked, we need to add the -javaagent JVM argument. In our particular setup, the argument's value is -javaagent:../lib/org/springframework/spring/spring-agent.jar. Without the agent, the application would fail with an IllegalStateException:

```
...
Caused by: java.lang.IllegalStateException: ➥
ClassLoader [sun.misc.Launcher$AppClassLoader] ➥
does NOT provide an 'addTransformer(ClassFileTransformer)' method. ➥
Specify a custom LoadTimeWeaver or start your Java virtual machine with ➥
Spring's agent: -javaagent:spring-agent.jar
```

The error message tells us what we already know: we need to specify the spring-agent.jar library as a JVM agent. When we do this, the application runs and prints this:

```
userService.login("janm")
After call to com.apress.prospring2.ch06.services.➥
    DefaultUserService@4cb44131 ➥
    (execution(void com.apress.prospring2.ch06.services.➥
        DefaultUserService.login(String)))

stockService.getStockLevel("ABC")
After call to com.apress.prospring2.ch06.services.➥
    DefaultStockService@197a64f2 ➥
    (execution(long com.apress.prospring2.ch06.services.➥
        DefaultStockService.getPredictedStockLevel(String)))
    DefaultStockService.getPredictedStockLevel("ABC")
    After call to com.apress.prospring2.ch06.services.➥
        DefaultStockService@197a64f2 ➥
        (execution(long com.apress.prospring2.ch06.services.➥
            DefaultStockService.getStockLevel(String)))
193734
```

Not only does the application work with load-time weaving but the call from `DefaultStockService.getStockLevel` to `DefaultStockService.getPredictedStockLevel` is advised, demonstrating that there are no problems with proxying—the bytecode of the `DefaultStockService` class is not the same as the bytecode on disk, and the AspectJ weaver completed its work before the application's `ClassLoader` loaded the class. Not only does load-time weaving solve the proxying problems, it also removes any performance decrease introduced by the proxies. Because there is no proxy, the code runs as if it were compiled with the advice's code coded into every matching join point.

LoadTimeWeaver Lookup Strategies

Spring uses the `InstrumentationSavingAgent` in the JVM agent library `spring-agent.jar` to save the current instance of the `Instrumentation` interface the JVM exposes. The `DefaultContextLoadTimeWeaver` will attempt to automatically detect the `LoadTimeWeaver` instance that best matches the application's environment. Table 6-2 shows the `LoadTimeWeaver` implementations for different environments.

Table 6-2. *LoadTimeWeaver Implementations*

LoadTimeWeaver	Environment
`InstrumentationLoadTimeWeaver`	JVM started with Spring `InstrumentationSavingAgent` (using `-javaagent:$LIB/spring-agent.jar`)
`WebLogicLoadTimeWeaver`	`LoadTimeWeaver` implementation in a running BEA WebLogic 10 or later application server
`GlassFishLoadTimeWeaver`	Works in the GlassFish application server V2.
`OC4JLoadTimeWeaver`	The implementation of the `LoadTimeWeaver` that works with Oracle Application Server version 10.1.3.1 or later
`ReflectiveLoadTimeWeaver`	Intended to be used with the `TomcatInstrumentableClassLoader` to provide load-time weaving in the Tomcat servlet container and the default fallback `LoadTimeWeaver` implementation
`SimpleLoadTimeWeaver`	A test-only implementation of the `LoadTimeWeaver` (By "test-only," we mean that it performs the necessary weaving transformations on a newly created `ClassLoader`.)

Whichever strategy you use, it is important to realize that load-time weaving uses AspectJ, not @AspectJ, as you might think after looking at the code in Listing 6-74. This means that we cannot use the `bean()` pointcut @AspectJ supports.

Practical Uses of AOP

The first thing that comes to mind when someone mentions AOP is logging, followed by transaction management. However, these are just special applications of AOP. In our application development experience, we have used AOP for health and performance monitoring, call auditing, caching, and error recovery. More advanced uses of AOP include compile-time checks of architecture standards. For example, you can write an aspect that will enforce that you only call certain methods from certain classes. However, the more advanced cases have little to do with Spring AOP, so we will demonstrate performance and health monitoring. You can also refer to Chapter 22 for an example of the Cache SpringModule, which uses AOP to implement declarative caching support.

Performance and Health Monitoring

Being able to monitor applications is critical when they are deployed in the production environment. While you can use logging, finding a particular problem in the log is often difficult. It would be much better if we could track the performance of the application and quickly find any significant drops in performance. Also, it would be useful to record the exceptions that occurred during the application's runtime. Apart from recording the exception type (and message), recording the values of all arguments that could have caused the exception is important. To help us focus on the problems causing the most trouble in the application most of the time, we will also group the exception reports by exception type and argument values.

Before we can proceed with the implementation of the aspects, we will take a look at the other components of the application. Figure 6-9 shows the UML class diagram of the application's components.

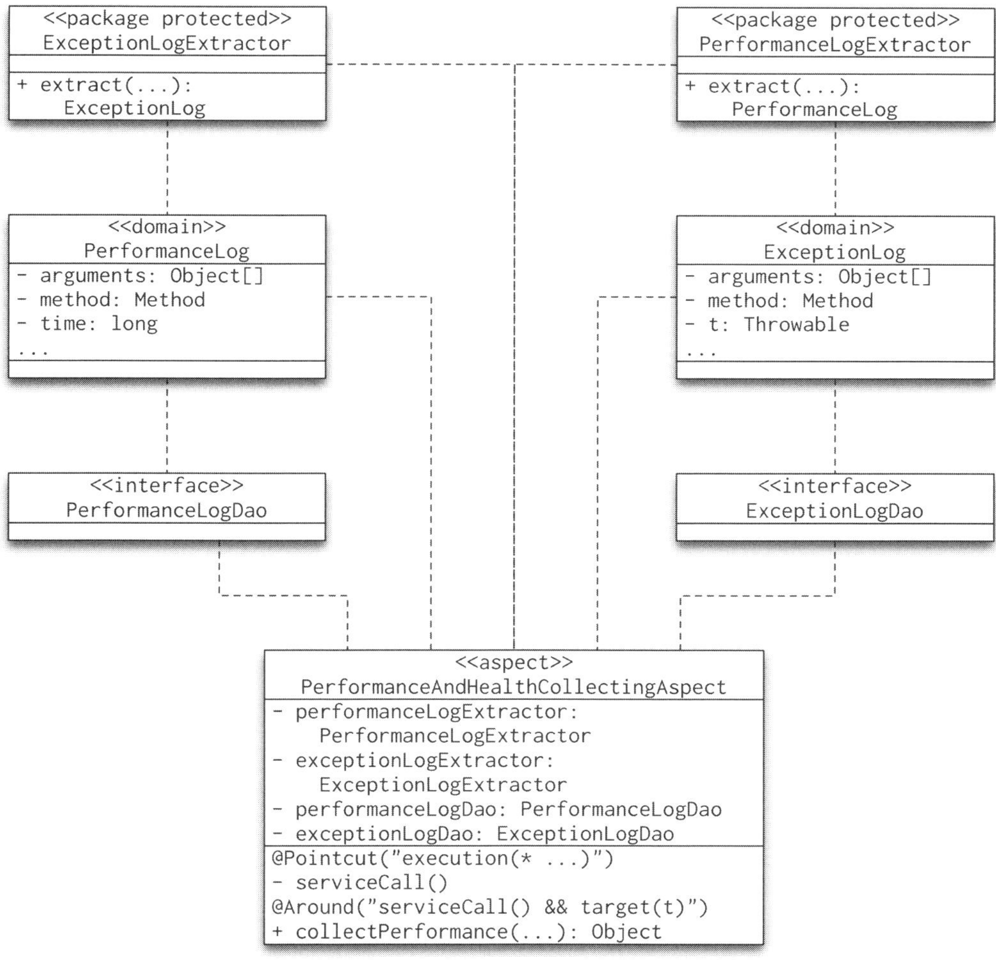

Figure 6-9. *UML class diagram of the main components*

Now, we can take a look at the implementation of the PeformanceAndHealthCollectingAspect. The aspect only has one piece of around advice; this advice collects statistics about method execution times and possible exceptions. Listing 6-76 shows the PerformanceAndHealthCollectingAspect.

Listing 6-76. *PerformanceAndHealthCollectingAspect*

```
@Aspect
public class PerformanceAndHealthCollectingAspect {

    private PerformanceLogDao performanceLogDao;
    private ExceptionLogDao exceptionLogDao;
    private PerformanceLogExtractor performanceLogExtractor =
            new PerformanceLogExtractor();
    private ExceptionLogExtractor exceptionLogExtractor =
            new ExceptionLogExtractor();

    @Pointcut("execution(* com.apress.prospring2.ch06.services.*.*(..))")
    private void serviceCall() { }

    @Around(value = "serviceCall() && target(target)",
            argNames = "pjp, target")
    public Object collectPerformance(ProceedingJoinPoint pjp, Object target)
            throws Throwable {
        Throwable exception = null;
        Object ret = null;

        StopWatch stopWatch = new StopWatch();
        stopWatch.start();
        try {
            ret = pjp.proceed();
        } catch (Throwable t) {
            exception = t;
        }
        stopWatch.stop();

        if (exception == null) {
            this.performanceLogDao.insert(
                    this.performanceLogExtractor.extract(pjp, target),
                    stopWatch.getLastTaskTimeMillis()
        } else {
            this.exceptionLogDao.insert(
                    this.exceptionLogExtractor.extract(pjp, target),
                    exception
            );
        }

        if (exception != null) throw exception;
        return ret;
    }

    public void setPerformanceLogDao(PerformanceLogDao performanceLogDao) {
        this.performanceLogDao = performanceLogDao;
    }
```

```
    public void setExceptionLogDao(ExceptionLogDao exceptionLogDao) {
        this.exceptionLogDao = exceptionLogDao;
    }
}
```

You can see that we record method performance and possible exceptions. We will use this information in the PerformanceMonitoringAspect. As its name suggests, this aspect is going to monitor the performance of the application. The aspect needs before and after advice; the before advice will record a start of the method call; the after advice will match and remove the start record. You may ask why we cannot use an around advice, as doing so would simplify tracking. The reason is that we need to be able to find out that a particular method is taking much longer than usual *while it is still running*. If we had implemented the health monitoring using around advice, our code would only find out that the method took much longer after it completed. Listing 6-77 outlines the implementation of the aspect.

Listing 6-77. *Outline Implementation of the PerformanceMonitoringAspect*

```
@Aspect
public class PerformanceMonitoringAspect {

    @Pointcut("execution(* com.apress.prospring2.ch06.services.*.*(..))")
    private void serviceCall() { }

    @Before(value = "serviceCall() && target(target)",
            argNames = "jp, target")
    public void logStartCall(JoinPoint jp, Object target) {
        // log start call
    }

    @After(value = "serviceCall() && target(target)",
            argNames = "jp, target")
    public void logEndCall(JoinPoint jp, Object target) {
        // log end call
    }

}
```

The logging infrastructure must insert a record for each start call and remove it after the method finishes. The last component is the PerformanceMonitor class, which periodically scans the call log and for all entries found in the call log, checks the statistics collected in the PerformanceAndHealthMonitoringAspect. If the PerformanceMonitor finds a call that is taking much longer than usual, it can alert the application's administrators.

Summary

In this chapter, we concluded our discussion on AOP. We looked at the advanced options for pointcutting, as well as how to extend the set of interfaces implemented by an object using introductions. A large part of this chapter focused on using Spring Framework services to configure AOP declaratively, thus avoiding the need to hard-code AOP proxy construction logic into your code. We spent some time looking at how Spring and AspectJ are integrated to allow you to use the added power of AspectJ without losing any of the flexibility of Spring. Next, we looked at how you can use AspectJ with load-time weaving to minimize the overhead Spring AOP's proxies add to the application. Finally, we looked at how we can use AOP to solve an application-specific problems in real-life applications.

Even though we have discussed *how* to use AOP in Spring applications, we have barely scratched the surface of all the features AspectJ provides. If you are interested in more details about AspectJ, we recommend two excellent books. The first one is *Eclipse AspectJ* by Adrian Colyer, Andy Clement, George Harley, and Matthew Webster (Addison-Wesley, 2005), which provides a comprehensive introduction and reference for the AspectJ language; the second book, *AspectJ in Action* by Ramnivas Laddad (Manning, 2003), focuses on the syntax of AspectJ as well as covering a lot of general AOP topics.

CHAPTER 7

Spring Schemas and Namespaces

In this chapter, we are going to look at Spring namespaces. You are going to learn about the new and simplified way to write Spring bean XML files, and we will discuss all the schemas provided out of the box by the Spring Framework. In addition, you will see how easy it is to write a custom Spring schema and its handler.

The main attraction of the new schema- and namespace-style configurations is their simplicity and expressiveness. They allow you to be very precise about the values allowed in each element and attribute. Because you can create your own schemas and namespaces, you can make the configuration much easier to write. It is not unusual to have a shared component—say in your company's Maven 2 repository—with its own custom Spring configuration schema and parser. Developers who then use the shared component do not have to spend so much time reading the documentation. You can also dramatically reduce the chance of misconfiguration.

Why the New Configuration?

In Spring 1.x, we used quite complex XML files to describe the configuration and dependencies of our beans. We can certainly continue to do so in Spring 2.5, but we can now take advantage of several standard XSD schemas and schema handlers.

Consider the old-style configuration file (see Listing 7-1): it is perfectly readable for a seasoned Spring 1.x developer but still very verbose.

Listing 7-1. *Very Verbose Spring 1.x–Style Context File*

```
<?xml version="1.0" encoding="UTF-8"?>
<!DOCTYPE beans PUBLIC "-//SPRING//DTD BEAN//EN" ➥
"http://www.springframework.org/dtd/spring-beans.dtd">

<beans>

    <bean id="transactionManager"
          class="com.apress.prospring2.namespaces.➥
NoopPlatformTransactionManager"/>
```

```
    <bean id="greetingsList"
          class="org.springframework.beans.factory.config.ListFactoryBean">
        <property name="sourceList">
            <list>
                <value>Hello, World</value>
                <value>What do you want to do tomorrow?</value>
                <value>Nazdar, prdi</value>
            </list>
        </property>
    </bean>

    <bean id="greeterService"
          class="org.springframework.transaction.interceptor.➥
TransactionProxyFactoryBean">
        <property name="transactionManager" ref="transactionManager"/>
        <property name="target">
            <bean class="com.apress.prospring2.namespaces.ComplexGreeterService">
                <property name="greetings" ref="greetingsList"/>
            </bean>
        </property>
        <property name="transactionAttributes">
            <props>
                <prop key="greet*">PROPAGATION_REQUIRED</prop>
            </props>
        </property>
    </bean>

</beans>
```

A Spring 2.5–style configuration file is not necessarily less verbose, but it is a lot cleaner and much easier to understand at a glance. Listing 7-2 shows the new style configuration file.

Listing 7-2. *The Configuration File from Listing 7-1 in Spring 2.5*

```
<?xml version="1.0" encoding="UTF-8"?>
<beans xmlns="http://www.springframework.org/schema/beans"
       xmlns:xsi="http://www.w3.org/2001/XMLschema-instance"
       xmlns:util="http://www.springframework.org/schema/util"
       xmlns:tx="http://www.springframework.org/schema/tx"
       xmlns:aop="http://www.springframework.org/schema/aop"
       xsi:schemaLocation="http://www.springframework.org/schema/beans
                http://www.springframework.org/schema/beans/spring-beans-2.5.xsd
                    http://www.springframework.org/schema/util
                http://www.springframework.org/schema/util/spring-util-2.5.xsd
                    http://www.springframework.org/schema/tx
                http://www.springframework.org/schema/tx/spring-tx-2.5.xsd
                    http://www.springframework.org/schema/aop
                http://www.springframework.org/schema/aop/spring-aop-2.5.xsd">

    <bean id="transactionManager"
          class="com.apress.prospring2.namespaces.NoopPlatformTransactionManager"/>
```

```
    <util:list id="greetingsList">
        <value>Hello, world</value>
        <value>What do you want to do tomorrow?</value>
        <value>Nazdar, prdi</value>
    </util:list>

    <bean id="greeterService"
          class="com.apress.prospring2.namespaces.ComplexGreeterService">
        <property name="greetings" ref="greetingsList"/>
    </bean>

    <tx:advice id="greeterServiceAdvice" transaction-manager="transactionManager">
        <tx:attributes>
            <tx:method name="greet*" propagation="REQUIRED"/>
        </tx:attributes>
    </tx:advice>

    <aop:config>
        <aop:pointcut id="greeterServiceOperation"
                expression="execution(* com.apress.*.*.GreeterService.*(..))"/>
        <aop:advisor advice-ref="greeterServiceAdvice"
                pointcut-ref="greeterServiceOperation"/>
    </aop:config>

</beans>
```

As you can see, the new configuration file is not necessarily shorter, even though a lot of it consists of XML schema definitions. The main advantage is that the new code is much easier to understand: the `greeterService` is no longer hidden as the target bean of the `TransactionProxyFactoryBean`. Apart from the advantages of cleaner code, consider that your favorite IDE probably comes with code completion; with the specific XSD definition files, you can now invoke code completion for the propagation values and many others (see Figure 7-1).

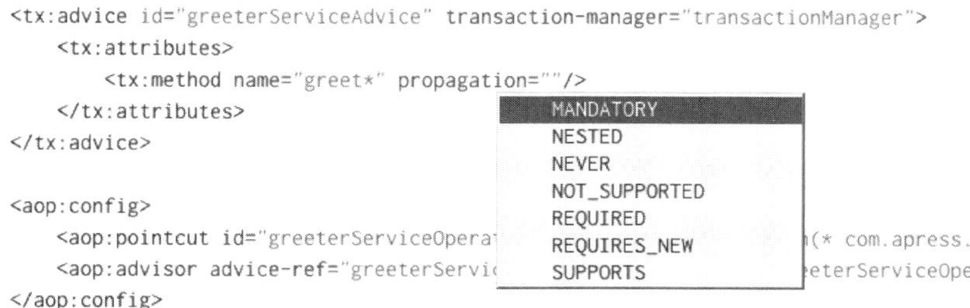

Figure 7-1. *Code completion in IntelliJ IDEA*

Schemas Included in Spring 2.5

Let's now take a look at the various schemas supplied in the Spring Framework. Table 7-1 summarizes the available schemas and their intended usage.

Table 7-1. *Schemas Included in the Spring 2.5 Distribution*

Schema	Usage
`util`	Utility functions for declaration of constants, lists, maps, properties, and property paths.
`j2ee`	J2EE functions for working with the JNDI and EJBs.
`jms`	Adds support for simple configuration of JMS beans.
`lang`	Allows objects exposed by languages such as JRuby to be used as Spring beans.
`tx`	Allows you to declare transactional properties of your Spring beans.
`aop`	Deals with aspect-oriented programming elements, such as pointcuts and advice.
`tool`	This schema is intended to be used by developers of additional components; the developers use the `tool` schema to add metadata that the third-party components use.
`context`	Allows you to control the wiring up process and bean post-processing.
`beans`	Use this schema to declare beans, aliases, and imports; this is usually the default schema in the XML file.

Apart from these, there are lots of other products in the Spring Portfolio, like Spring Security, and many third-party products, such as Oracle Coherence, supply their own custom namespaces. Now that you know the schemas that come standard with Spring 2.5, we can go ahead and discuss each schema in more detail.

The beans Schema

Let's start with the most important schema of all, the `beans` schema. These are the same tags that have been present in Spring since the early days of the framework. To make a schema the default schema for a particular XML file, simply declare it as the default in that XML file. Listing 7-3 shows how to do this.

Listing 7-3. *beans Schema Example*

```
<?xml version="1.0" encoding="UTF-8"?>
<beans xmlns="http://www.springframework.org/schema/beans"
       xsi:schemaLocation="http://www.springframework.org/schema/beans
                 http://www.springframework.org/schema/beans/spring-beans-2.5.xsd">

    <!-- bean declarations here -->

</beans>
```

Put simply, the elements without a schema reference the `beans` schema. The `beans` schema contains four elements: `bean`, `alias`, `import`, and `description`. The `bean` element matches the definition of the bean element from the Spring DTD. Refer to Chapters 3 and 4 for a detailed overview of the elements in the `beans` schema.

The context Schema

Spring 2.5 introduces the `context` schema. This is the second most fundamental schema, even though you will not have to use it in most applications. It modifies the core behavior of Spring's bean creation process. Listing 7-4 shows how to configure the property placeholders in the Spring context files.

Listing 7-4. *Beans for the Property Placeholder Configuration*

```
<?xml version="1.0" encoding="UTF-8"?>
<beans xmlns="http://www.springframework.org/schema/beans"
       xmlns:xsi="http://www.w3.org/2001/XMLSchema-instance"
       xmlns:context="http://www.springframework.org/schema/context"
       xsi:schemaLocation="http://www.springframework.org/schema/beans ➥
http://www.springframework.org/schema/beans/spring-beans-2.5.xsd
            http://www.springframework.org/schema/context ➥
http://www.springframework.org/schema/context/spring-context-2.5.xsd">

    <bean id="test" class="com.apress.prospring2.ch07.context.TestBean">
        <property name="name" value="${name}"/>
    </bean>

    <context:property-placeholder location= ➥
"classpath:/com/apress/prospring2/ch07/context/test.properties" />

</beans>
```

The code in Listing 7-4 shows how to configure a property placeholder using the `context` schema. It is possible to configure a property placeholder with one location (as shown in Listing 7-4), or with multiple locations by providing a comma-separated list. The property placeholder will also check against the Java system properties if it can't find a property you are trying to use.

The util Schema

The next schema to look at is the `util` schema. It contains definitions that are shorthand for the old factory beans. Consider the code in Listing 7-5.

Listing 7-5. *Usage of the util Schema*

```
<beans xmlns="http://www.springframework.org/schema/beans"
       xmlns:xsi="http://www.w3.org/2001/XMLschema-instance"
       xmlns:util="http://www.springframework.org/schema/util"
       xsi:schemaLocation="http://www.springframework.org/schema/beans
                 http://www.springframework.org/schema/beans/spring-beans-2.5.xsd
                           http://www.springframework.org/schema/util
                 http://www.springframework.org/schema/util/spring-util-2.5.xsd">

    <!-- bean declarations here -->

</beans>
```

Let's take a look at the various elements of the `util` schema, starting from the simplest one, `util:constant`. Listing 7-6 shows its usage.

Listing 7-6. *Constant Declaration*

```
<util:constant id="X" static-field="java.lang.Integer.MAX_VALUE"/>
```

This code declares a bean with ID X with the value set to Integer.MAX_VALUE.

The next element, util:list, declares a bean that implements java.util.List—more specifically java.util.List<Object>. You can specify the class of the List implementation and, naturally, add the values of the list. Listing 7-7 shows how to do this.

Listing 7-7. *Declaration of the list Bean*

```
<util:constant id="Y" static-field="java.lang.Integer.MAX_VALUE"/>

<util:list id="X" list-class="java.util.ArrayList">
    <value>value1</value>
    <ref bean="Y"/>
</util:list>
```

This code declares bean ID X of type java.util.ArrayList<Object> with values String("value1") and Integer.MAX_VALUE. We can verify the contents of this bean in Java code as shown in Listing 7-8.

Listing 7-8. *Usage of the util:list Declaration*

```
List y = (List)context.getBean("X");
for (Object o : y) {
    System.out.println(o.getClass() + " " + o);
}
```

Running this code snippet prints the following:

```
class java.lang.String value1
class java.lang.Integer 2147483647
```

Now, let's move to the next element in the util schema, the util:map element. You can specify the class that implements the java.util.Map interface and the elements of the map. Listing 7-9 shows typical usage of the util:map element.

Listing 7-9. *Usage of the map Declaration*

```
<util:constant id="Y" static-field="java.lang.Integer.MAX_VALUE"/>

<util:map id="Z" map-class="java.util.HashMap">
    <entry key="x" value="y"/>
    <entry key="y"><ref bean="X"/></entry>
</util:map>
```

This bean declares bean ID Z as an implementation of the java.lang.Map<Object, Object> map with values of "x" => String("y") and "y" => Integer.MAX_VALUE. Printing the contents of the map using code similar to Listing 7-8 gives us the following:

```
y => class java.lang.Integer 2147483647
x => class java.lang.String y"
```

The next element in the util schema is the util:properties element (see Listing 7-10).

Listing 7-10. *Declaration of the properties Element*

```
<util:properties id="BeanId"
    location="classpath:com/apress/prospring2/ch07/util/Main.properties"/>
```

The bean identified by `BeanId` declares a `java.util.Properties` bean with values loaded from a properties file in the classpath location `com/apress/prospring2/ch07/util/Main.properties`. As you can see, the `location` attribute can be a Spring resource, which means that you can use any pattern recognized by the Spring resource editor in the value of the attribute.

The next element from the `util` schema is the `util:property-path` element. It allows us to extract a property from an existing bean. Consider the code in Listing 7-11, where we have the bean ID `simple` as an instance of the `SimpleBean` class. We then create a `util:property-path` bean with ID `Q` with a value obtained from calling `simple.getName()`.

Listing 7-11. *Declaration of the simple and property-path Beans*

```
// SimpleBean.java
public class SimpleBean {
    private String name;
    private String value;

    public SimpleBean() {
        this.name = "Name";
        this.value = "Anirvan Chakraborty";
    }

    public String getName() {
        return name;
    }

    public String getValue() {
        return value;
    }
}

// greeter-context-2.0.xml
<bean id="simple" class="com.apress.prospring2.namespaces.util.SimpleBean"/>
<util:property-path id="Q" path="simple.name"/>
```

Here, the `util:property-path` bean with ID `Q` will be set to "Name".

Finally, the `util:set` element declares a bean implementing the `java.util.Set<Object>` interface. See Listing 7-12 for an example definition of such a bean.

Listing 7-12. *Showing a util:set Configuration*

```
<util:constant id="X" static-field="java.lang.Integer.MAX_VALUE"/>

<util:set id="S" set-class="java.util.HashSet">
    <value>foo</value>
    <ref bean="X"/>
</util:set>
```

The elements of the set must conform to the contract specified by the `Set` implementation class; if we were to change the `set-class` to `java.util.TreeSet`, the bean construction would fail, because a `TreeSet` can't contain objects of different types.

The tx Schema

Spring provides comprehensive support for transactions and the <tx> tags deal with configuring transactional beans. Listing 7-13 shows a code snippet to reference the correct schema that will enable you to use the tags in the tx namespace.

Listing 7-13. *Code Snippet for Transactional Bean Declaration Using the tx Namespace*

```
<beans xmlns="http://www.springframework.org/schema/beans"
       xmlns:xsi="http://www.w3.org/2001/XMLschema-instance"
       xmlns:util="http://www.springframework.org/schema/util"
       xmlns:tx="http://www.springframework.org/schema/tx"
       xmlns:aop="http://www.springframework.org/schema/aop"
       xsi:schemaLocation="http://www.springframework.org/schema/beans
                http://www.springframework.org/schema/beans/spring-beans-2.0.xsd
                         http://www.springframework.org/schema/util
                http://www.springframework.org/schema/util/spring-util-2.0.xsd
                         http://www.springframework.org/schema/tx
                http://www.springframework.org/schema/tx/spring-tx-2.0.xsd
                         http://www.springframework.org/schema/aop
                http://www.springframework.org/schema/aop/spring-aop-2.0.xsd">

    <!–transactional bean declarations here -->

</beans>
```

You can find a comprehensive discussion of Spring's support for transactions in Chapter 16, which also demonstrates the different attributes of the <tx> tag.

The aop Schema

AOP-related Spring beans configuration is dealt with by the <aop> tags, including Spring's own proxy-based AOP framework and Spring's integration with the AspectJ AOP framework. These tags are comprehensively covered in Chapters 5 and 6, so we have not repeated the same information here. For completeness, Listing 7-14 shows the correct usage of the aop schema.

Listing 7-14. *Correct Usage of the aop Schema*

```
<?xml version="1.0" encoding="UTF-8"?>
<beans xmlns="http://www.springframework.org/schema/beans"
   xmlns:xsi="http://www.w3.org/2001/XMLSchema-instance"
   xmlns:aop="http://www.springframework.org/schema/aop"
   xmlns:tx="http://www.springframework.org/schema/tx"
   xsi:schemaLocation="
http://www.springframework.org/schema/beans ➥
http://www.springframework.org/schema/beans/spring-beans-2.5.xsd
http://www.springframework.org/schema/tx ➥
http://www.springframework.org/schema/tx/spring-tx-2.5.xsd
http://www.springframework.org/schema/aop ➥
http://www.springframework.org/schema/aop/spring-aop-2.5.xsd">

<!-- <bean/> definitions here -->

</beans>
```

The jee Schema

Spring provides support for Java Enterprise Edition (Java EE or JEE) configuration using the jee schema. It is now possible to configure JNDI object lookup in a much simpler way. Listing 7-15 shows the correct usage of the jee namespace.

Listing 7-15. *Configuration for Correct Usage of the jee Namespace*

```
<?xml version="1.0" encoding="UTF-8"?>
<beans xmlns="http://www.springframework.org/schema/beans"
       xmlns:xsi="http://www.w3.org/2001/XMLSchema-instance"
       xmlns:jee="http://www.springframework.org/schema/jee"
       xsi:schemaLocation="
http://www.springframework.org/schema/beans ➥
http://www.springframework.org/schema/beans/spring-beans-2.5.xsd
http://www.springframework.org/schema/jee ➥
http://www.springframework.org/schema/jee/spring-jee-2.5.xsd">

<!-- <bean/> definitions here -->

</beans>
```

Just for comparison, let's take a look at a simple JNDI object lookup configuration in Spring 1.x (see Listing 7-16).

Listing 7-16. *Spring 1.x–Specific Configuration of JNDI Object Lookup*

```
<bean id="dataSource" class="org.springframework.jndi.JndiObjectFactoryBean">
    <property name="jndiName" value="jdbc/dataSource"/>
</bean>

<bean id="someDao" class="com.apress.chapter7.JdbcSomeDao">
    <property name="dataSource" ref="dataSource"/>
</bean>
```

Here, you can see that we have configured a JndiObjectFactoryBean as a simple Spring bean and passed the reference of this bean to a Spring data access object bean.

Now, let's take a quick look at the much simpler configuration using Spring 2.5's jee namespace support. Listing 7-17 shows a code snippet to configure a JNDI object lookup using the <jee> tag.

Listing 7-17. *JNDI Object Lookup Using the <jee> Tag*

```
<jee:jndi-lookup id="dataSource" jndi-name="jdbc/MyDataSource"/>

<bean id="userDao" class="com.foo.JdbcUserDao">
    <property name="dataSource" ref="dataSource"/>
</bean>
```

The lang Schema

The lang schema deals with exposing objects written in a dynamic language such as JRuby or Groovy as beans in the Spring container. These tags (and the dynamic language support) are comprehensively covered in Chapter 14. Please consult that chapter for full details of this support and the <lang> tags themselves.

Listing 7-18 shows the correct use of the lang schema.

Listing 7-18. *Correct Usage of the lang Schema*

```
<?xml version="1.0" encoding="UTF-8"?>
<beans xmlns="http://www.springframework.org/schema/beans"
       xmlns:xsi="http://www.w3.org/2001/XMLSchema-instance"
       xmlns:lang="http://www.springframework.org/schema/lang"
       xsi:schemaLocation="
http://www.springframework.org/schema/beans ➥
http://www.springframework.org/schema/beans/spring-beans-2.5.xsd
http://www.springframework.org/schema/lang ➥
http://www.springframework.org/schema/lang/spring-lang-2.5.xsd">

<!-- <bean/> definitions here -->

</beans>
```

■ **Note** We have ignored Spring 2.5's `tool` schema, as it is currently undergoing review. To learn about the `tool` schema, please take a look at the `spring-tool-2.5.xsd` file.

Behind the Schema Scenes

Knowing how to use the standard schemas is good, but learning how Spring handles the new configuration files is also interesting. Let's take a look at what happens when Spring encounters a schema reference.

Figure 7-2 is a UML sequence diagram showing the most important parts of Spring's configuration loading and processing steps.

A good starting point is a call to create an `ApplicationContext` implementation, for example, by calling `new ClasspathXmlApplicationContext()`. If we leave the default settings, Spring will use (in `AbstractXmlApplicationContext`) the `XmlBeanDefinitionReader` class to read the bean definitions, using the `DefaultBeanDefinitionDocumentReader` in the process.

The `DefaultBeanDefinitionDocumentReader` creates the `BeanDefinitionParserDelegate`, which is used to handle the XML events as the `DefaultBeanDefinitionDocumentReader` encounters them. The `BeanDefinitionParserDelegate` uses the `DefaultNamespaceHandlerResolver` to obtain the appropriate `NamespaceHandlerResolver` for the given `namespaceUri`.

The `DefaultNamespaceHandlerResolver` uses the `META-INF/spring.handlers` file to determine the class that implements the `NamespaceHandler` interface for the given namespace URI. As the `XmlBeanDefinitionReader` reads the XML configuration file, it calls the `NamespaceHandler` implementation for every element encountered in its namespace. As the elements are read, the `NamespaceHandler` is called to provide a `BeanDefinition` or to update a `BeanDefinitionHolder` instance. The `BeanDefinitions` are then used to instantiate the configured beans; for more information on bean factories, see Chapter 3.

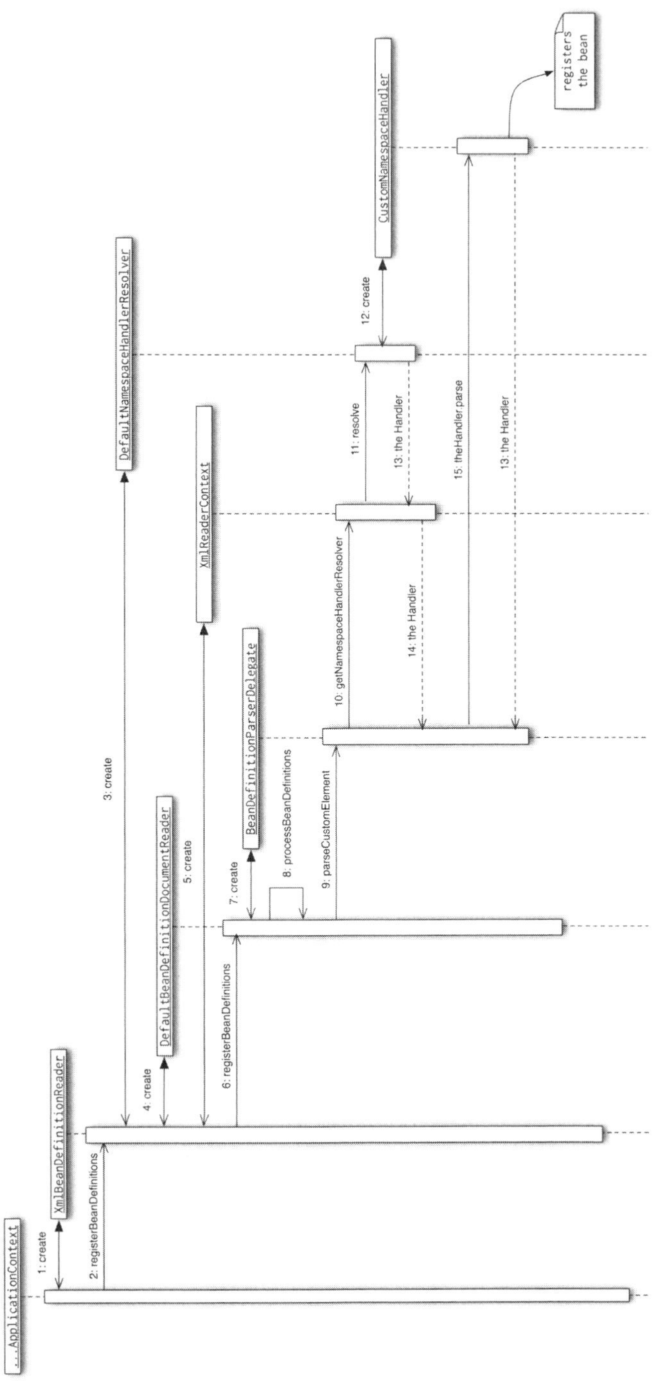

Figure 7-2. *Loading Spring configuration*

Let's take a look at Listing 7-19, which shows the default `META-INF/spring.handlers` file.

Listing 7-19. *Default META-INF/spring.handlers File*

```
http\://www.springframework.org/schema/util=
    org.springframework.beans.factory.xml.UtilNamespaceHandler
http\://www.springframework.org/schema/aop=
    org.springframework.aop.config.AopNamespaceHandler
http\://www.springframework.org/schema/lang=
    org.springframework.scripting.config.LangNamespaceHandler
http\://www.springframework.org/schema/tx=
    org.springframework.transaction.config.TxNamespaceHandler
http\://www.springframework.org/schema/jee=
    org.springframework.ejb.config.JeeNamespaceHandler
http\://www.springframework.org/schema/p=
    org.springframework.beans.factory.xml.SimplePropertyNamespaceHandler
```

As you can see, it is a simple properties-style file, where the key is the namespace URI and the value is the class that implements the `NamespaceHandler` for the namespace URI. In reality, most implementations do not implement the interface directly but extend the `NamespaceHandlerSupport` convenience superclass.

The `NamespaceHandlerSupport` class allows your `NamespaceHandler` implementation to be really simple and allows you to register a `BeanDefinitionParser` to process different elements of the custom schema. In a typical scenario, you register the `BeanDefinitionParser` (usually implemented as a static inner class) in the `init()` method (see Listing 7-20).

Listing 7-20. *Typical Implementation of a Class that Extends NamespaceHandlerSupport*

```
public class CustomNamespaceHandler extends NamespaceHandlerSupport {

    private static class GreeterBeanDefinitionParser
        extends AbstractSingleBeanDefinitionParser {

        protected Class getBeanClass(Element element) {
            return GreeterFactoryBean.class;
        }

        protected void doParse(Element element,
            ParserContext parserContext, BeanDefinitionBuilder builder) {
            // implementation of the doParse method.
    }

    public void init() {
        registerBeanDefinitionParser("greeter", new GreeterBeanDefinitionParser());
    }
}
```

Custom Schemas

Now that you know how Spring handles configuration file loading, you can easily create your custom schema and an appropriate `NamespaceHandler`. Let's begin by looking at Figure 7-3, which shows the structure of the source files we are going to create.

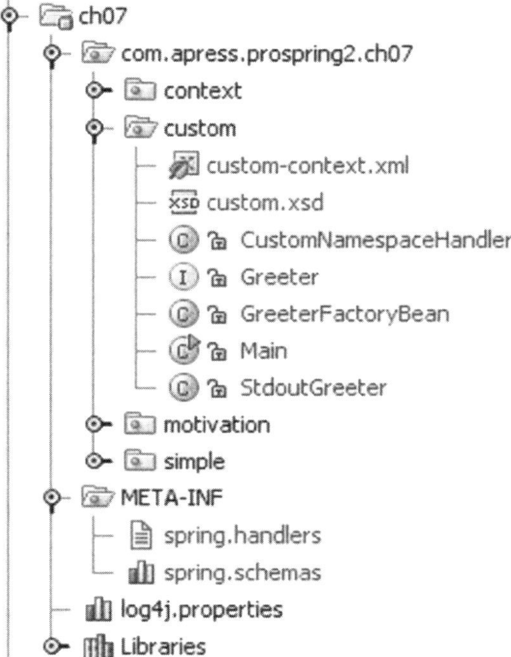

Figure 7-3. *Files for the custom namespace handler*

As you can see, we have nine files; the simplest ones to explain are the `Greeter` interface and `StdoutGreeter`, which is a very simple implementation of the interface. Then we have the `Main` class, which is the test runner, which uses the `ClasspathXmlApplicationContext` to load the `custom-context.xml` file. From the namespace-handling point of view, the most important files are `spring.handlers`, `spring.schemas`, `custom.xsd`, `GreeterFactoryBean`, and `CustomNamespaceHandler`. Let's begin analyzing the sample application by looking at Listing 7-21, which shows the contents of the `custom.xsd` schema file.

Listing 7-21. *The custom.xsd Schema File*

```
<?xml version="1.0" encoding="UTF-8" standalone="no"?>

<xsd:schema xmlns="http://prospring2.apress.com/namespaces/custom"
            xmlns:xsd="http://www.w3.org/2001/XMLschema"
            targetNamespace="http://com.apress.prospring2/ch07/custom"
            elementFormDefault="qualified">

    <xsd:import namespace="http://www.w3.org/XML/1998/namespace"/>

    <xsd:element name="greeter">
        <xsd:annotation>
            <xsd:documentation>...</xsd:documentation>
        </xsd:annotation>
        <xsd:complexType>
            <xsd:attribute name="id" type="xsd:ID"/>
            <xsd:attribute name="count" type="xsd:integer" use="required">
```

```
                <xsd:annotation>
                    <xsd:documentation>...</xsd:documentation>
                </xsd:annotation>
            </xsd:attribute>
            <xsd:attribute name="message" type="xsd:string" use="required">
                <xsd:annotation>
                    <xsd:documentation>...</xsd:documentation>
                </xsd:annotation>
            </xsd:attribute>
        </xsd:complexType>
    </xsd:element>

</xsd:schema>
```

Here, we define one element, `greeter`, which has three required attributes. They are the `id` of type `xsd:ID`, `count` of type `xsd:integer`, and `message` of type `xsd:string`. By strictly specifying the allowed data types for each attribute, we force any developer who uses our component to supply the correct data types. To help our developer, we have also added documentation for the main element and for each attribute.

Notice that the schema location is `http://com.apress.prospring2/ch07/custom`; this is a URI that may not be accessible when the application is running. That is why we must go ahead and create the `META-INF/spring.schemas` file, which specifies a classpath location for the URI. Listing 7-22 shows the contents of this file.

Listing 7-22. *The spring.schemas File*

```
http\://com.apress.prospring2/ch07/custom =\
/com/apress/prospring2/ch07/custom/custom.xsd
```

Note that the key in this properties-style file matches the URI of the schema and the value is the classpath location of the `custom.xsd` file. Next, we will register a `NamespaceHandler` implementation that can process elements in the `http://com.apress.prospring2/ch07/custom` schema. We do this in the `META-INF/spring.handlers` file, which is shown in Listing 7-23.

Listing 7-23. *The spring.handlers File*

```
http\://com.apress.prospring2/ch07/custom =\
com.apress.prospring2.namespaces.custom.CustomNamespaceHandler
```

This file tells Spring to load the `CustomNamespaceHandler` class and use it to handle elements in the custom schema.

Before we can write the implementation of the `NamespaceHandler`, we must create a `GreeterFactoryBean`. This is a standard Spring `FactoryBean` whose responsibility is to create appropriately configured instances of the `Greeter` interface implementations. Listing 7-24 shows how we have implemented the factory bean.

Listing 7-24. *Implementation of the GreeterFactoryBean*

```
public class GreeterFactoryBean extends AbstractFactoryBean {

    private String message;
    private int count;

    public void setMessage(String message) {
        this.message = message;
    }
```

```
    public void setCount(int count) {
        this.count = count;
    }

    protected Object createInstance() {
        if (this.message == null) {
            throw new IllegalArgumentException("'message' is required");
        }
        return new StdoutGreeter(this.count, this.message);
    }

    public Class getObjectType() {
        return Greeter.class;
    }
}
```

The implementation is not difficult to understand: the method `createInstance()` uses the `message` and `count` properties to create instances of the `StdoutGreeter`, which is a simple implementation of the `Greeter` interface. We use this bean factory in the `CustomNamespaceHandler`, shown in Listing 7-25.

Listing 7-25. *CustomNamespaceHandler Implementation*

```
public class CustomNamespaceHandler extends NamespaceHandlerSupport {

    private static class GreeterBeanDefinitionParser extends
        AbstractSingleBeanDefinitionParser {

        protected Class getBeanClass(Element element) {
            return GreeterFactoryBean.class;
        }

        protected void doParse(Element element, ParserContext parserContext,
            BeanDefinitionBuilder builder) {
            builder.addPropertyValue("message", element.getAttribute("message"));
            String countString = element.getAttribute("count");
            try {
                int count = Integer.parseInt(countString);
                builder.addPropertyValue("count", count);
            } catch (NumberFormatException ex) {
                throw new RuntimeException(ex);
            }
        }
    }

    public void init() {
        registerBeanDefinitionParser("greeter", new GreeterBeanDefinitionParser());
    }
}
```

There are several key points in this file. The first point is that it extends the convenience superclass `NamespaceHandlerSupport`. So we only have to implement the `init()` method, where we register the parser for all `custom:greeter` elements. The parser is a static inner class that extends `AbstractSingleBeanDefinitionParser`; all we have to do is implement the `getBeanClass()` method and the `doParse()` method. Spring will create an instance of the class returned by the `getBeanClass()` method and invoke its setters for all properties added by the `builder.addPropertyValue()` calls in the `doParse()` method. In our case, the methods that will be called are `GreeterFactoryBean.setMessage()`

and `GreeterFactoryBean.setCount()`. This is also all we have to do in the `doParse()` method. We know that the attributes exist, because their existence is enforced by the schema validation process. We also know that the count value is really an integer, but we have no choice but to parse it from `String`, because `element.getAttribute()` returns `String`. Therefore, the `catch` block should never get executed.

The final piece of the puzzle is the `custom-context.xml` file and its testing application, the `Main` class. The context file shown in Listing 7-26 is very simple indeed: it only references the `custom` schema and declares one `greeter`.

Listing 7-26. *The custom-context.xml File*

```
<?xml version="1.0" encoding="UTF-8"?>
<beans xmlns="http://www.springframework.org/schema/beans"
       xmlns:xsi="http://www.w3.org/2001/XMLschema-instance"
       xmlns:custom="http://prospring2.apress.com/namespaces/custom"
       xsi:schemaLocation="http://www.springframework.org/schema/beans ➥
 http://www.springframework.org/schema/beans/spring-beans-2.5.xsd
                       http://prospring2.apress.com/namespaces/custom ➥
 http://prospring2.apress.com/namespaces/custom.xsd">

    <custom:greeter id="greeter" count="10" message="goo"/>

</beans>
```

Here, you can see that we have nice clear definitions of the properties; the usage of the `greeter` bean is shown in Listing 7-27.

Listing 7-27. *Code Fragment Showing Usage of the Custom Namespace Handler*

```
// code fragment of Main.java
ApplicationContext context =
    new ClassPathXmlApplicationContext("classpath*:**/custom-context.xml");
Greeter greeter = (Greeter)context.getBean("greeter");
greeter.greet();
```

IDE Configuration

Depending on your IDE, you can now configure it to use the `custom.xsd` file to perform XML validation on the fly. First, let's take a look at how to set up IntelliJ IDEA. We begin with a situation similar to the one shown in Figure 7-4: IntelliJ IDEA doesn't know where the XSD file is located, so it is showing it in red and offers a quick fix.

```
<?xml version="1.0" encoding="UTF-8"?>
<beans xmlns="http://www.springframework.org/schema/beans"
       xmlns:xsi="http://www.w3.org/2001/XMLSchema-instance"
       xmlns:custom="http://prospring2.apress.com/namespaces/custom"
       xsi:schemaLocation="http://www.springframework.org/schema/beans http://www.springframework.org/schema/beans/spring-beans-2.0.xsd
                           http://prospring2.apress.com/namespaces/custom http://prospring2.apress.com/namespaces/custom.xsd">
                                                  Fetch External Resource
    <custom:greeter id="greeter" count="10" message="goo"/>              Manually Setup External Resource
                                                  Ignore External Resource
</beans>
```

Figure 7-4. *Missing external resource*

Select Manually Setup External Resource, and in the next window, click Edit and select the location of the `custom.xsd` file. Figure 7-5 shows how to do this.

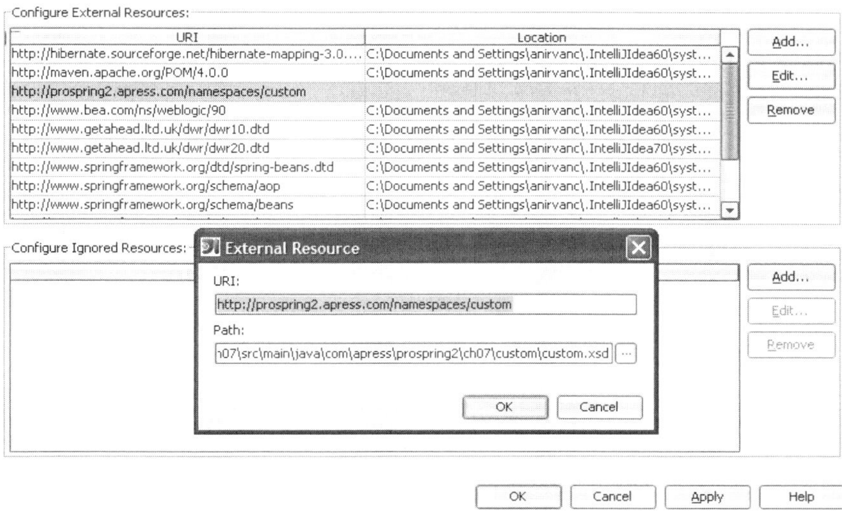

Figure 7-5. *Edit the path to the external resource.*

After confirming the location, IntelliJ IDEA will use the `custom.xsd` file to validate the schema of the `custom-context.xml` file. It will show errors when attributes are missing or when an attribute's value does not match the required data type. Figure 7-6 shows this kind of validation error.

```
<?xml version="1.0" encoding="UTF-8"?>
<beans xmlns="http://www.springframework.org/schema/beans"
       xmlns:xsi="http://www.w3.org/2001/XMLSchema-instance"
       xmlns:custom="http://prospring2.apress.com/namespaces/custom"
       xsi:schemaLocation="http://www.springframework.org/schema/beans
       http://www.springframework.org/schema/beans/spring-beans-2.5.xsd
       http://prospring2.apress.com/namespaces/custom
       http://prospring2.apress.com/namespaces/custom.xsd">

    <custom:greeter id="greeter" count="f10" message="goo"/>
                    The value 'f10' of attribute 'count' on element 'custom:greeter' is not valid with respect to its type, 'integer'.
</beans>
```

Figure 7-6. *Validation errors in IntelliJ IDEA*

Eclipse, too, supports XML schema validation. Unfortunately, XML support does not come with the standard Eclipse installation. Unless you want to rely on Eclipse plug-ins, download the WTP project from `http://www.eclipse.org/webtools/`.

As with IntelliJ IDEA, you have to register a custom location for the XSD file to allow the Eclipse validator to use it. Figure 7-7 shows how to do this.

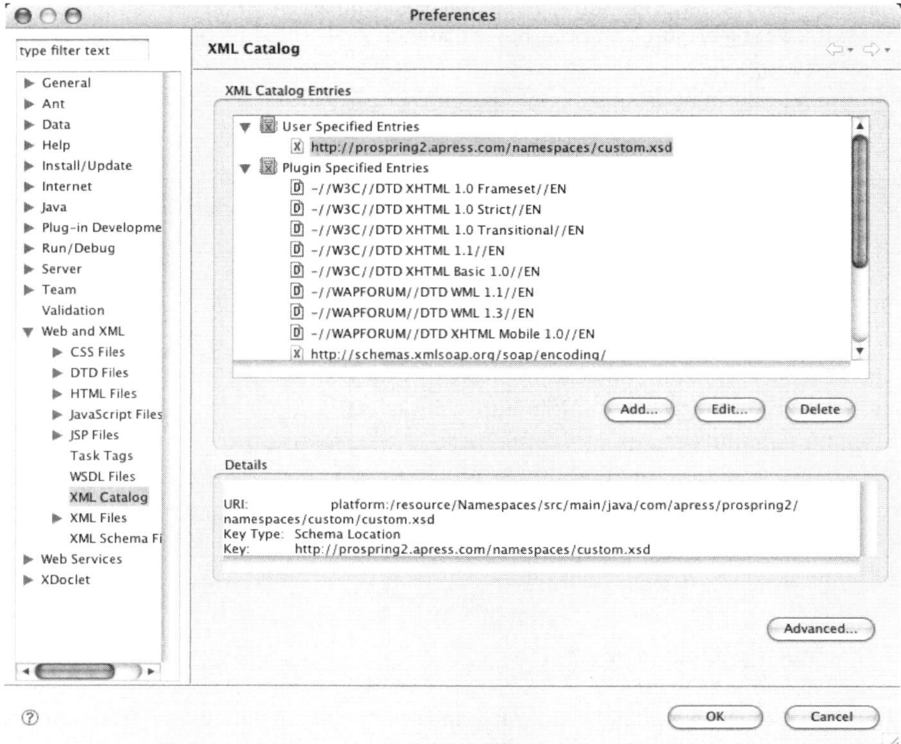

Figure 7-7. *Eclipse schema file registration*

When setting up the XML catalog entry, make sure that you select Schema Location as the key type. Once you've added the `custom.xsd` reference, you can use the XML schema validation, shown in Figure 7-8.

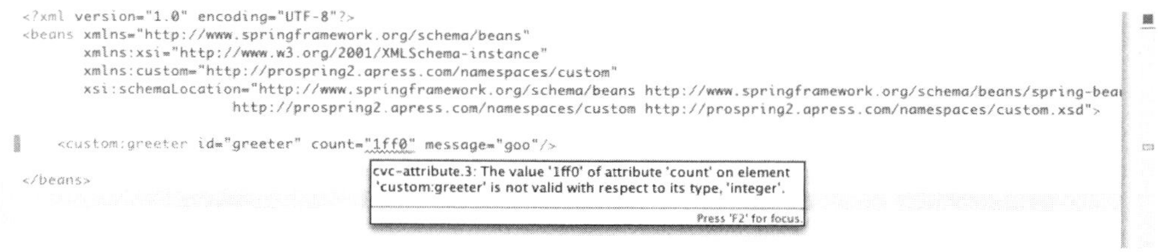

```
<?xml version="1.0" encoding="UTF-8"?>
<beans xmlns="http://www.springframework.org/schema/beans"
       xmlns:xsi="http://www.w3.org/2001/XMLSchema-instance"
       xmlns:custom="http://prospring2.apress.com/namespaces/custom"
       xsi:schemaLocation="http://www.springframework.org/schema/beans http://www.springframework.org/schema/beans/spring-bea
                           http://prospring2.apress.com/namespaces/custom http://prospring2.apress.com/namespaces/custom.xsd">

    <custom:greeter id="greeter" count="1ff0" message="goo"/>

</beans>
```

cvc-attribute.3: The value '1ff0' of attribute 'count' on element 'custom:greeter' is not valid with respect to its type, 'integer'.

Press 'F2' for focus.

Figure 7-8. *XML schema validation in Eclipse*

As you can see from these figures, the combination of custom namespace and schema with a modern IDE gives you a powerful set of tools to hide the sometimes complex configuration of your beans.

Summary

In this chapter, you have seen how Spring 2.5 handles the new XML context files. Like previous releases of the Spring Framework, Spring 2.5 is fully backward compatible, so all your existing Spring 1.x document-type-definition–based (DTD-based) configuration will still work. But even though you can still use Spring 1.x DTD context files, you will get much more flexibility from using the new schema-based context files. In fact, some Spring 2.5 features are quite verbose to configure using the standard DTD-based approach. Good examples of this are the configuration of AspectJ beans and dynamic languages (for more information about AspectJ and Spring, see Chapter 6; for dynamic languages, see Chapter 14).

As well as understanding the standard namespaces provided by Spring, you now know how to create your own custom namespace. This is particularly helpful if you are developing a component of an application that many developers of your organization are going to use. If you write a custom namespace for its configuration, you can ensure that the beans will not be misconfigured.

CHAPTER 8

Spring Patterns

In this chapter, we are going to discuss typical design patterns of Spring applications. We will start with simple console applications and conclude with complex Java EE applications. We are not going to limit ourselves to a pure academic discussion of object-oriented programming and will include recommendations for directory structure, build procedures, testing, and deployment.

We will begin with a description of the directory structure of a typical Spring project, followed by Java design patterns, and a section on Spring application patterns. We will describe some of the typical situations we have solved in Spring applications. We believe that this section will help you tackle some of the more complex requirements in your own applications.

After reading this chapter, you should be able to create and manage even very complex Spring applications; moreover, you will have a good overview of how you can combine the technologies in the Spring Framework to create elegant and well maintainable applications.

Directory Structure

Before we begin discussing programming patterns, we need to have a look at the directory structure. An elegant directory structure will simplify the build process and make it easy to find any part of the application's source (be it Java code, script, or JSP file) and to exclude the output of the compilers or code generators from source control.

The project's directory structure should also make it easy to split the project in to modules. Large Java EE applications mostly need to be split across several modules, which are usually packaged in separate JAR files.

Simple Applications

Let's begin by looking at relatively simple applications. Take a look at Listing 8-1, which shows the directory structure of a simple Spring application. Such an application could be a command-line database manipulation utility, with only a handful of classes and one Spring context file.

Listing 8-1. *Simple Application Directory Structure*

```
./src
./src/main
./src/main/java
./src/main/resources
./src/main/sql
./src/test/java
./src/test/resources
./target/test/classes
./target/production/classes
```

The src directory contains all source files needed to build and test the application; the target directory contains compiled classes and copied resources. Following the Maven 2 directory structure recommendations, the src directory is split into main and test. These correspond to the main source code and test code; code in the test directory can depend on the code in the main directory, but code in the main directory cannot depend on code in the test directory. The resources subdirectories contain non-Java files that are part of the source code, such as Spring context files; the sql directory contains SQL scripts needed to create the database, for example. The target directory contains all compiled code; this directory should not be versioned in your source control system.

The directory structure in Listing 8-1 works fine for a simple Spring application or a shared module, but it does not fit a web application very well. The web application directory structure looks like Listing 8-2.

Listing 8-2. *Web Application Directory Structure*

```
./web
./web/WEB-INF/webapp-servlet.xml
./web/WEB-INF/web.xml
./web/WEB-INF/views
./web/WEB-INF/views/**/*.jsp
```

You can see that we have not included any Java code in our web application. There is a good reason for this: we usually package the Java code for the web application in a separate JAR file, so the web application's code is split into two directories: one containing only the Java code and one containing only the web code.

The overall structure of a web application's directory structure looks very similar to the one in Listing 8-3.

Listing 8-3. *Overall Structure of the Web Application*

```
core
  src
    main
      java
      sql
    test
      java

web
  src
    main
      java
    test
      java

webapp
  src
    resources
      images
      styles
    war
      WEB-INF
        views
        tags
        web.xml
      META-INF
```

We consider this to be the least intrusive approach for applications where you do not need to use Java EE features that require more complex packaging and deployment strategies. The core directory contains the application's domain, data, and service layers; the web directory contains only the web code. It must be said that this structure does not enforce strict layer separation (for that, you'd need to split the core module into domain, data access, and service modules), but for homogeneous and not overly complex applications, we've found that it is the best match.

The intramodule dependencies are very simple: `core` depends only on external libraries; `web` depends on `core`; and `webapp` depends on `web` (and transitively on `core`).

Complex Applications

Complex applications will, in most cases, require a more detailed directory structure. The main reason for this is the need to logically separate the application into several reusable modules. Even though the reusable modules are not easy to identify, they are easy to set up in the standard directory structure: simply create a top-level directory for each independent module.

Packaging and Naming

This can be a highly controversial topic; each developer has a preferred way of naming classes, interfaces, and packages. However, it is very important that the entire team share the same naming conventions. We recommend following standard Sun Java programming naming conventions. Packaging is a far more complex issue, and in most cases, it determines how flexible your application is going to be. Figure 8-1 shows a large application split into several packages and deployed across two JVMs.

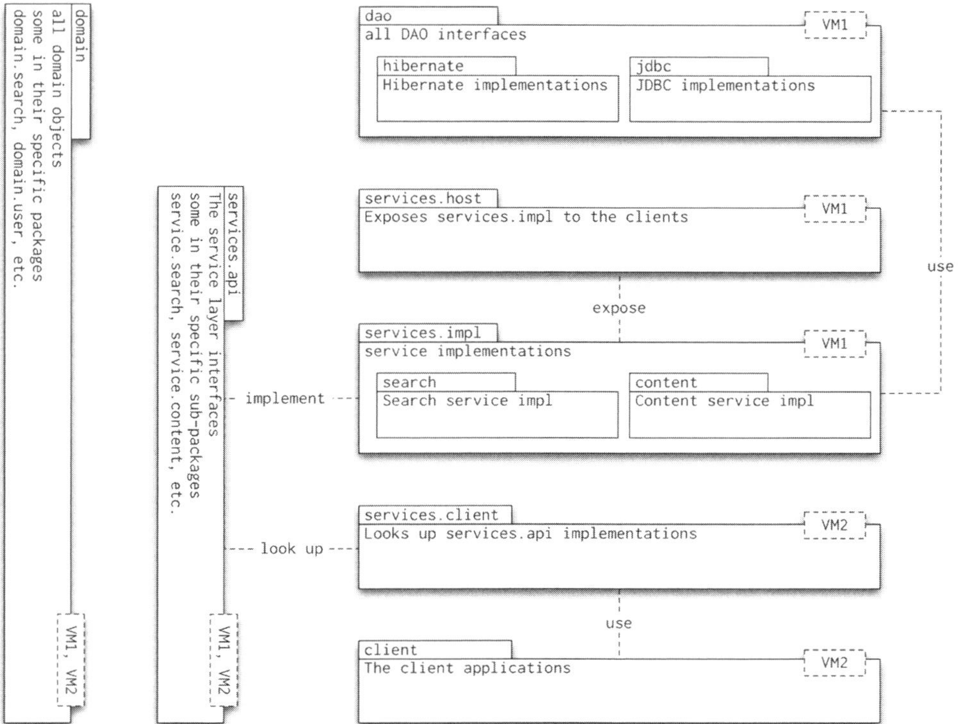

Figure 8-1. *Packaging of a large application*

We found that splitting the service layer into service APIs, service API implementation, and service host and client packages allows us to use the service host in integration tests even outside an application server. This is certainly an advantage that outweighs the more complex packaging.

In the next section, we will take a look at the logical building blocks of a Spring application.

Design Patterns Introduction

Now that you know how to structure the source code of your application, it is time to look at Java design patterns in Spring applications. We shall reiterate Spring's "programming against interfaces" mantra by showing the practical impact of the two injection strategies (constructor and dependency injection). Next, we will focus on the creational design patterns: Singleton, Factory, and Factory Method. Then we will look at the Template Method pattern, which is extensively used in Spring's data access libraries.

Programming Against Interfaces

This is not a design pattern as such, but it is a very important part of all Spring applications. As you know, interfaces separate the purpose of a component from the internal details of any implementation.

When creating interfaces that will be used in a Spring application, keep the interfaces focused on a very specific task and never mix concerns. Listing 8-4 shows an example of an interface that has more than one concern.

Listing 8-4. *Mixed-Concern Interface*

```
public interface InvoiceManagementService {
    void file(Invoice invoice);
    void dispute(Long id, String reason);
    BigDecimal getDiscount(Long customerId, Long productId);
}
```

The first two methods are perfectly valid in the `InvoiceManagementService` interface. The actions they are likely to perform match the name of the interface. The third method does not really belong to the `InvoiceManagementService` interface. The `getDiscount(Long, Long)` method is the most obviously misplaced one.

The situation becomes much more apparent if we attempt to implement this interface. The implementation is forced to deal with discount calculation, even though it may be more appropriate to deal with just the invoice manipulation. The solution to this is to create two interfaces, `InvoiceManagementService` and `DiscountCalculationService` (see Listing 8-5).

Listing 8-5. *Specialized Interfaces*

```
public interface InvoiceManagementService {
    void file(Invoice invoice);
    void dispute(Long id, String reason);
}

public interface DiscountCalculationService {
    BigDecimal getDiscount(Long customerId, Long productId);
}

}
```

Creational Patterns

This group of patterns deals with object creation. In most cases, the objects you create can be fully initialized by passing appropriate arguments to the constructor or by calling a few setter methods. There are, however, situations where object creation is either very complex or very resource intensive. In those situations, it can be more efficient to use one of the creational patterns. The first of these is the Singleton pattern, closely followed by the Factory pattern. The Prototype pattern is also widely used in Spring; the same is true for the Object Pool and Lazy Initialization pattern. Finally, the Builder pattern is used in the configuration handlers. Let's now take a closer look at all of these patterns, see where we can find them in Spring and how we can use them in our application code.

Singleton

The first pattern we will take a look at is the Singleton pattern. This restricts the existence of objects in the JVM to one and only one instance of the particular class. The objects created are called singletons.

Note Spring has a slightly different concept of singletons: Spring will manage one and only one instance of a class *for any bean definition.* In other words, using Spring, you can have multiple instances of the same class in the same JVM, as long as they are defined as separate beans in your Spring configuration files.

To prevent calling code from accidentally creating multiple instances of a singleton class, we provide only a private constructor and one static method that returns the sole instance of the class. Figure 8-2 shows the UML diagram for the Singleton pattern.

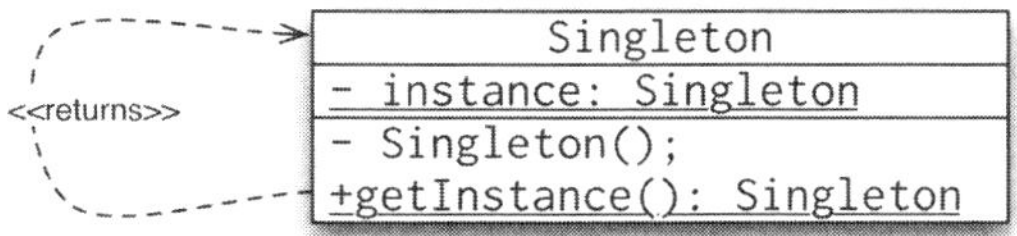

Figure 8-2. *UML diagram for the Singleton pattern*

It is very likely that most, if not all, of the beans in your applications can be singletons. In the stateless architecture that Spring applications usually follow, the implementations of the data access interfaces should not keep state between calls; the same applies to the service objects and holds true for the controllers in the web tier. Unless you specifically request your beans to be prototypes, Spring's `BeanFactory` implementations will treat your beans as singletons (in the Spring sense, the one and only one instance per bean definition). That means that when you call the `getBean()` methods with the same arguments for nonprototype beans, you will get the same instance of the bean. This brings us nicely to the next design pattern, Factory.

Factory

The Factory pattern is responsible for creating objects, but it is different from the Singleton pattern in that the factory class is usually a different class from the class being created and the construction process is generally more complex. Figure 8-3 shows the UML diagram for the Factory pattern.

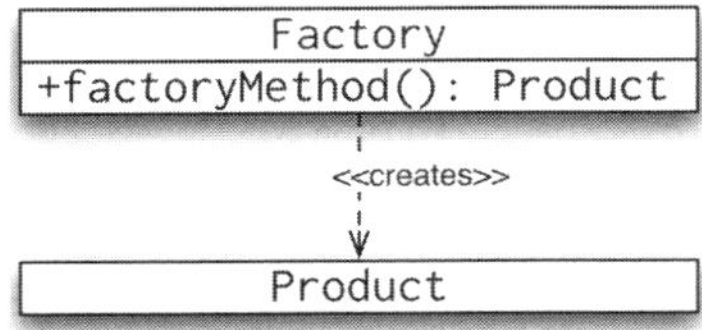

Figure 8-3. *UML diagram for the Factory pattern*

Builder

Another object creational pattern is the Builder pattern. In conjunction with a director, the builder is responsible for creating instances of objects. The director calls methods of the builder so that it can return the finished object at the end. The builder itself is usually an abstract class or an interface; the director can therefore use different implementations of the builder. Figure 8-4 shows a UML diagram of the Builder pattern.

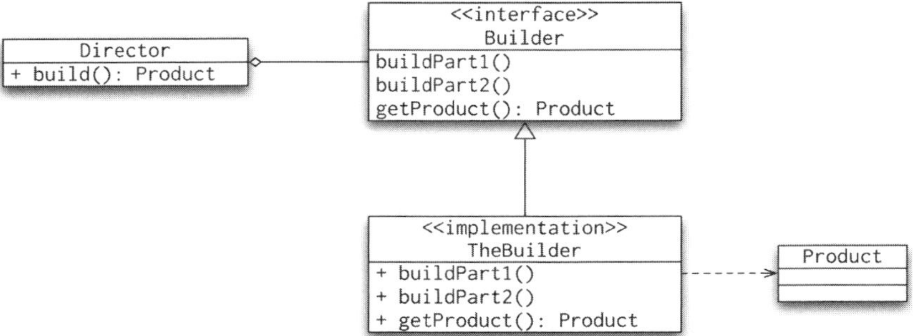

Figure 8-4. *UML diagram of the Builder pattern*

It is not unusual to see the Builder pattern use the Singleton or Factory patterns. This approach is used in Spring in its use of the Builder pattern. The `BeanDefinitionBuilder` (which combines the factory pattern) is used by the namespace handlers to create instances of the `BeanDefinitions` that are then used to construct the Spring-managed beans.

Prototype

Prototype is another creational pattern; the prototype uses a template object that can be used to create and initialize multiple individual instances of a class as well as instances of any subclasses. It is usual to initialize the prototype with some default values and then obtain its copies (or its subclasses). Figure 8-5 shows the UML diagram for the Prototype pattern.

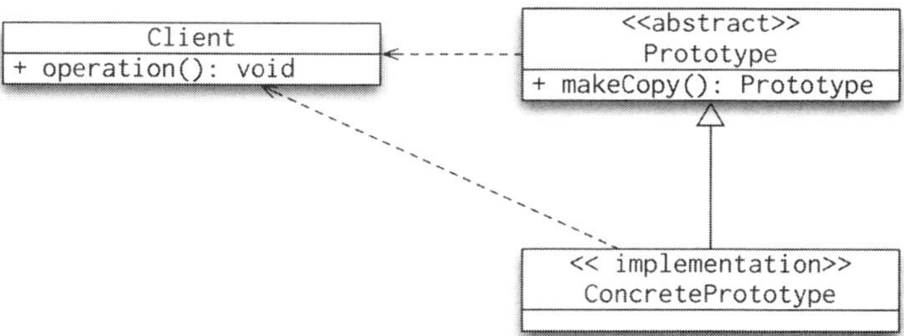

Figure 8-5. *UML diagram of the Prototype pattern*

The usage of the prototype in pure Java code (without Spring) involves the implementation of the abstract `Prototype` class and its `makeCopy()` method. The only difficulty is that the `makeCopy()` method should return any possible subclasses. The code in Listing 8-6 shows the implementation of the Prototype pattern in plain Java.

Listing 8-6. *Prototype Implementation Example*

```
public abstract class Message {
    private String sender;
    public Message makeCopy() {
        try {
            Message copy =  this.getClass().newInstance();
            copy.setSender(this.sender);
            return copy;
        } catch (InstantiationException e) {
            return null;
        } catch (IllegalAccessException e) {
            return null;
        }
    }
}

public class EmailMessage extends Message {
    @Override
    public String toString() {
        return "EmailMessage";
    }
}

public class PrototypeDemo {
     private Message message;
     PrototypeDemo(Message message) {
        this.message = message;
    }
    Message makeMessage() {
        return this.message.makeCopy();
    }
    public static void main(String[] args) {
        Message prototype = new EmailMessage();
        PrototypeDemo demo = new PrototypeDemo(prototype);
        System.out.println("Message "  + demo.makeMessage());
    }
}
```

In the code example, the Message class is the prototype, the EmailMessage is the concrete prototype, and the PrototypeDemo is the client that uses the prototype to obtain additional instances. Listing 8-7 shows the Spring context file for the prototype object declaration.

Listing 8-7. *Spring Context File for the Prototype Example*

```
<!DOCTYPE beans PUBLIC "-//SPRING//DTD BEAN//EN"
    "http://www.springframework.org/dtd/spring-beans.dtd">
<beans>
    <bean id="prototypeClient"
          class="com.apress.prospring2.ch08.➥
creational.prototype.SpringPrototypeClient">
        <property name="message1" ref="message"/>
        <property name="message2" ref="message"/>
    </bean>

    <bean id="message"
        class="com.apress.prospring2.ch08.creational.prototype.EmailMessage"
       scope="prototype"/>
</beans>
```

The context file looks like any other Spring context file; the only notable line is the scope="prototype" attribute. The BeanFactory will create a new instance of the message bean every time it is referenced. The message1 and message2 properties of the prototypeClient bean will therefore receive copies of the original message bean. Listing 8-8 shows code we can use to prove that the messages are indeed new instances.

Listing 8-8. *Sample Application Using the Spring Prototype Pattern*

```
public class SpringPrototypeClient {
    private Message message1;
    private Message message2;

    public void run() {
        System.out.println("Message1 " + this.message1.toString());
        System.out.println("Message2 " + this.message2.toString());
        System.out.println("Messages == " + (this.message1 == this.message2));
    }

    public void setMessage1(Message message1) {
        this.message1 = message1;
    }

    public void setMessage2(Message message2) {
        this.message2 = message2;
    }
}

public class SpringPrototypeDemo {

    public static void main(String[] args) {
        ApplicationContext context =
            new ClassPathXmlApplicationContext("prototype-context.xml", ➥
SpringPrototypeDemo.class);
        SpringPrototypeClient client = ➥
(SpringPrototypeClient) context.getBean("prototypeClient");
```

```
        client.run();
    }
}
```

The `run()` method in the `SpringPrototypeClient` prints out the values of `message1` and `message2` and finally indicates whether the two messages are the same objects. The output of running the `SpringPrototypeDemo` follows:

```
Message1 EmailMessage
Message2 EmailMessage
Messages == false
```

Structural Patterns

The patterns in this group are used in the implementation of interactions between elements of the application. They are used to alter behavior of existing classes, make existing classes appear as other classes, and add functionality to existing classes.

Proxy

Proxy is a widely-used pattern in Spring applications; its use is often hidden behind standard Spring beans. A proxy is an object that stands in place of the original object, and thus intercepts (and thus sees first) all method calls to the target object. Because of this, the proxy can modify the behavior of the target object; the range of the modifications spans from simple tracing, before and after processing, to invoking completely different methods. A complete proxy UML diagram is shown in Figure 8-6.

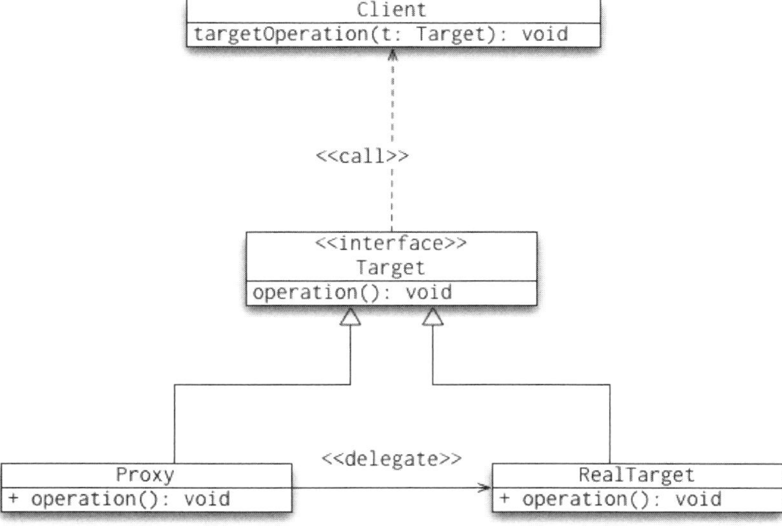

Figure 8-6. *UML diagram for the Proxy pattern*

You have seen proxy examples in the AOP chapters of this book. If you like, you can revisit Chapter 5 and Chapter 6 for more details.

Adapter

The next pattern to discuss is Adapter. As the name suggests, it is used to make an alien interface or class usable for a client. Figure 8-7 shows the UML diagram of the classical representation of the Adapter pattern.

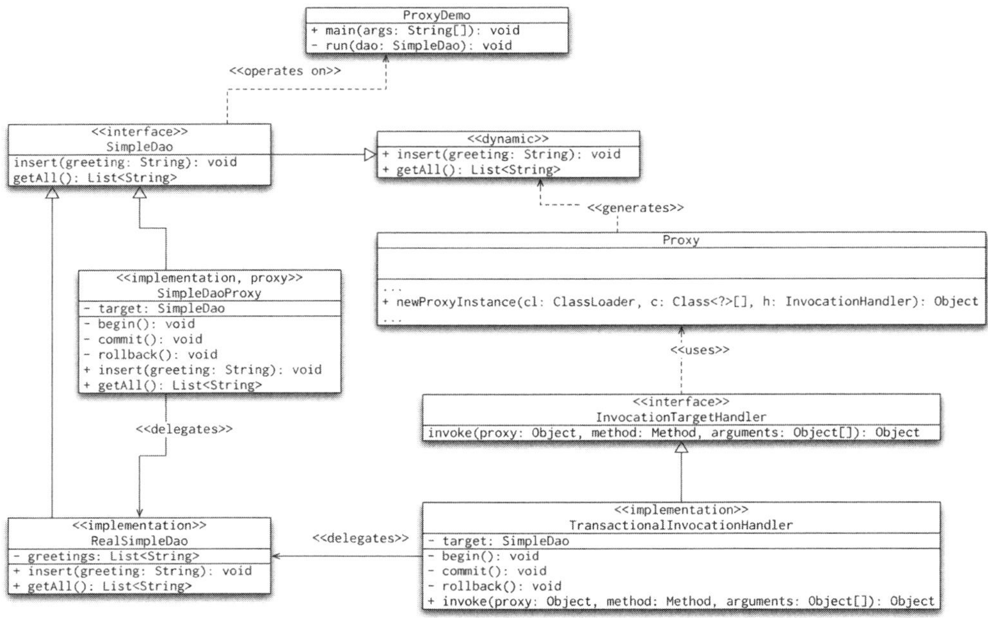

Figure 8-7. *UML diagram of the Adapter pattern*

The uses of the Adapter pattern are mainly in the domain of application code, not Spring itself. Nevertheless, Spring makes use of the Adapter pattern in the JMS and AOP packages. A good example can be found in `MessageListenerAdapter` and `MessageListenerAdapter102`. Both these classes implement the `MessageListener` interface but then adapt the `onMessage(Message, Session)` call to the adaptee. The adaptee does not have to implement the `MessageListener` (or the `SessionAwareMessageListener`) interface. The adapters can delegate to any other method of the adaptee.

Wrapper and Decorator

The Wrapper and Decorator patterns are very similar to one another; in fact, you can say that a wrapper is a special type of decorator. Let's therefore focus on decorator, which, as the name suggests, adds additional functionality to the decorated object. A good example of the Decorator pattern in action is in web programming, when we might want a decorator to display results. If, for example, the result received from a service layer call is a collection of domain objects, but the presentation needs additional information about each element, you do not want to complicate your domain objects with fields and methods needed only for the presentation. That's why you should consider implementing a decorator. This decorator will take the domain object as its argument and add the necessary functionality. The presentation tier will receive the decorated domain objects. Figure 8-8 shows the UML diagram of the Decorator pattern.

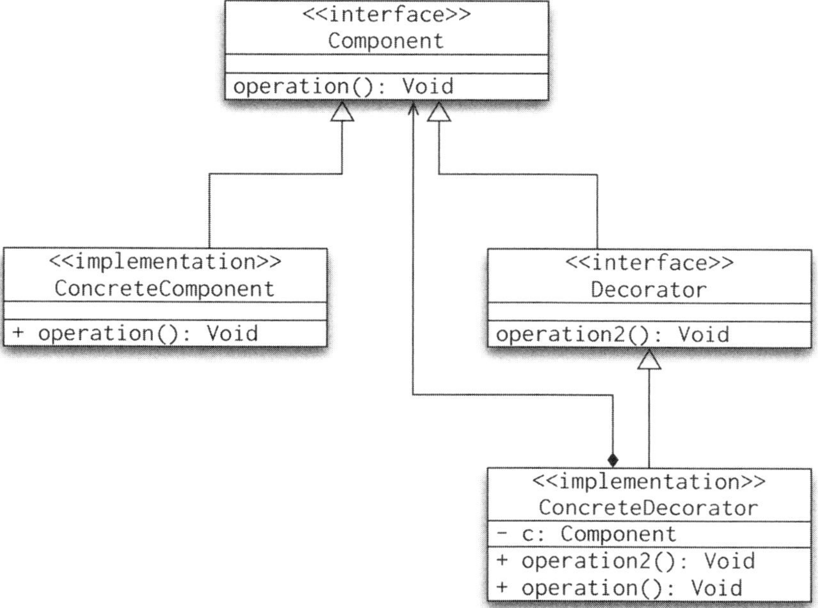

Figure 8-8. *UML diagram of the Decorator pattern*

As already mentioned, the most frequent use of Decorator is in the presentation tier. Our favorite JSP tag library for displaying tabular data is DisplayTag (`http://displaytag.sourceforge.net/11/`), and it makes extensive use of the Decorator pattern.

Facade

The purpose of the Facade pattern is to hide a complex structure of calls behind a simple interface that clients can use. Typically, a call to a facade method involves various calls to the methods behind the facade. That is why this pattern is sometimes referred to as the business or service facade. The UML diagram in Figure 8-9 shows the potentially complex interactions in a facade.

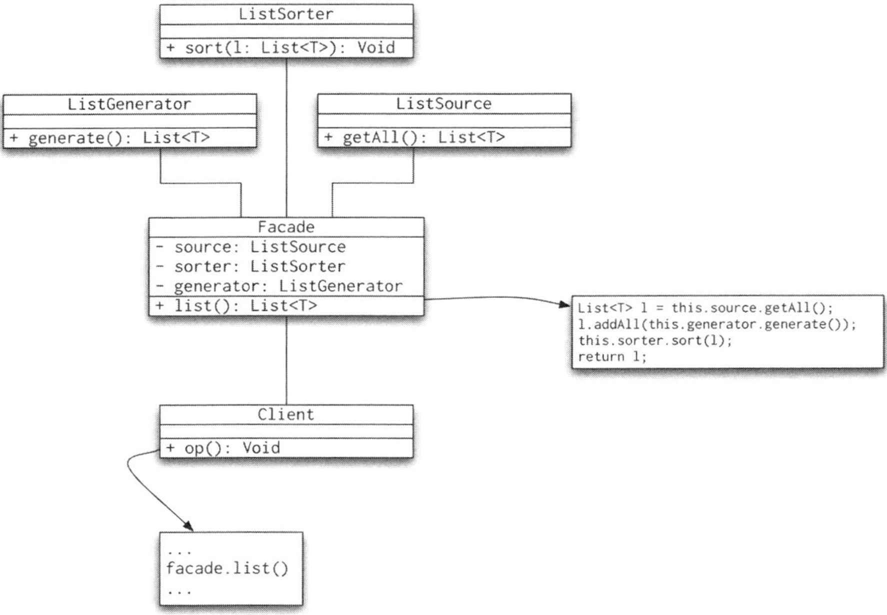

Figure 8-9. *Facade UML diagram*

Behavioral Patterns

Of all the many patterns in this group, the patterns that we will focus on are Observer, Strategy, and Template Method. You will probably be familiar with some of these patterns already, because the Observer pattern is rather widely used. Let's take a look at these patterns in more detail.

Observer

Observer is used in situations where any number of other objects (observers) need to be notified when the observed object changes its state. Its use in Spring may represent a situation where you implement the `ApplicationListener` to receive notifications from Spring. Following our convention of illustrating patterns with UML diagrams, Figure 8-10 shows the Observer pattern diagram.

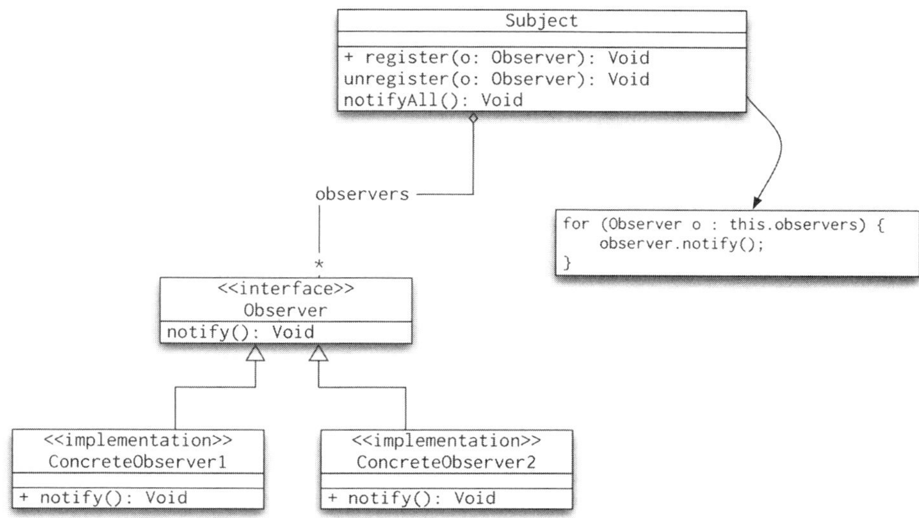

Figure 8-10. *The Observer pattern in UML*

Strategy

Strategy is a specific programming pattern where the algorithm for obtaining a result can be selected at runtime. The UML diagram for this pattern is shown in Figure 8-11.

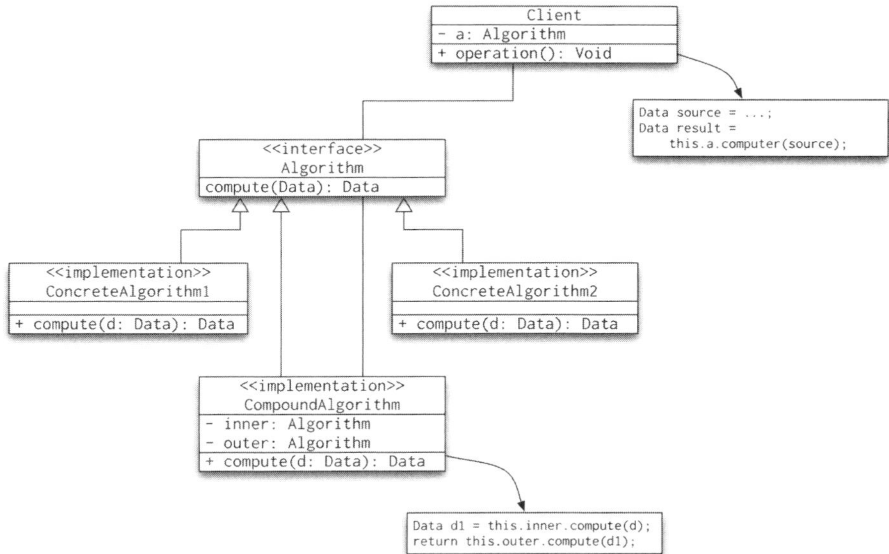

Figure 8-11. *Strategy UML diagram*

Template Method

The Template Method pattern is used to implement a skeleton of an algorithm. In other words, it implements the common parts of a computation and delegates the details to the implementation subclasses. This way, the subclasses cannot disrupt the overall computation but are free to perform their subtasks in any way necessary. The UML diagram for this pattern is shown in Figure 8-12.

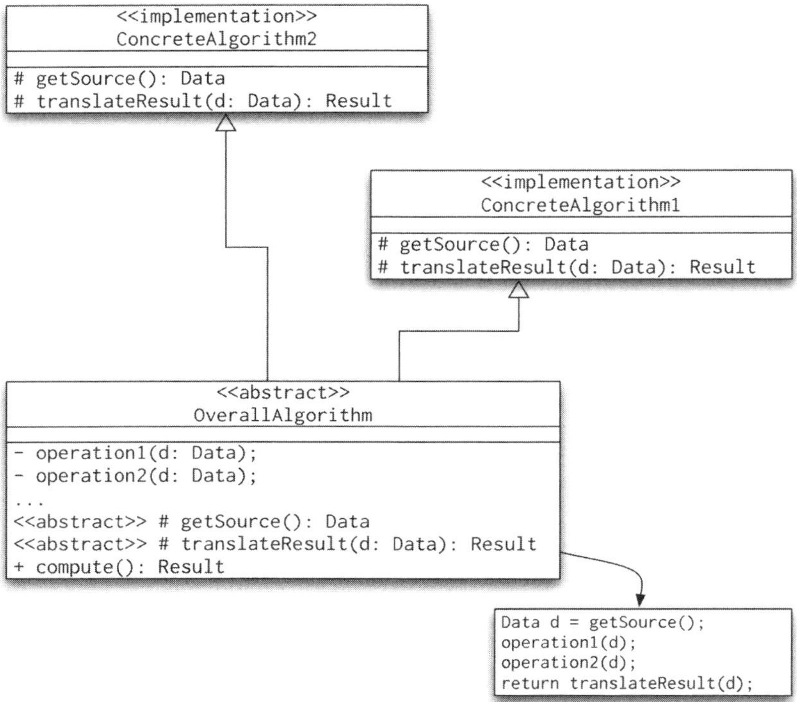

Figure 8-12. *The Template Method pattern*

This is perhaps the most widely used pattern in Spring applications—or at least in the ones that use Spring's data access classes. In short, the Template Method pattern represents a fragment of an algorithm or some other process. This process is completely enclosed and guarded by the framework.

You may have noticed that this pattern is widely used in Spring's data access template classes, namely in `JdbcTemplate`, `HibernateTemplate`, `SqlMapClientTemplate`, `JdoTemplate`, and `ToplinkTemplate`. Let's focus our discussion on the `HibernateTemplate` class: consider its `Object execute (HibernateCallback action)` method. Its argument is an implementation of the `HibernateCallback`, which represents the code fragment that needs to be executed in a guarded section provided in the `HibernateTemplate.execute()` method. As programmers, we do not need to worry about error management in the body of the `HibernateCallback.doInHibernate()` method; this exactly represents the Template Method pattern.

Another example of the template method is in the DAO support convenience superclasses that Spring provides. Take, for example, the `HibernateDaoSupport class`: it implements the `InitializingBean` interface, and the attendant `afterPropertiesSet` method is declared as `final`. That means that any subclasses cannot change the initialization, but Spring offers them a chance to provide additional initialization by overriding the `initDao` method. The code in Listing 8-9 shows a similar situation in a web application.

Listing 8-9. *Template Method Pattern in a Web Tier*

```
public abstract class ProductServiceSupport implements InitializingBean {
    protected ProductDao productDao;

    /**
     * Subclasses may override this method to perform additional initialization
     * that will be performed as the last action of the afterPropertiesSet method.
     * This implementation does nothing.
     */
    protected void initService() throws Exception { /* do nothing */ }

    public final void afterPropertiesSet() throws Exception {
        Assert.notNull(this.productDao, "The productDao must be set");
        initController();
    }

    public final void setProductDao(ProductDao productDao) {
        this.productDao =productDao;
    }
}

public class IndexController extends ProductControllerSupport {
```

Another example is a failover block, where you attempt to acquire a resource and if the acquire call fails, you try another resource. Whichever resource you manage to acquire, you want to execute the same code.

Spring Application Patterns

Now that we have covered some of the design patterns and their usage in isolation, it is time to look at the patterns we have identified in the context of various enterprise applications we have implemented using Spring. In this section, we will present typical features of large applications and the solution we believe will give the best results. Along with the solution, we will explain why we have chosen it and what its potential shortcomings are. Remember that the solutions we will discuss in this section are not the only ones available.

Also keep in mind that this section is not an exhaustive list of enterprise application patterns; it is a selection of problems we encounter most often when implementing Java EE applications with Spring.

Layered Design

The first concept we will mention here is the logical layered design of applications, which is the fundamental concept of maintainable applications. All the layers of your application may run in the same virtual machine and use local calls; you don't necessarily have to write a complex distributed application. The layers are illustrated in Figure 8-13.

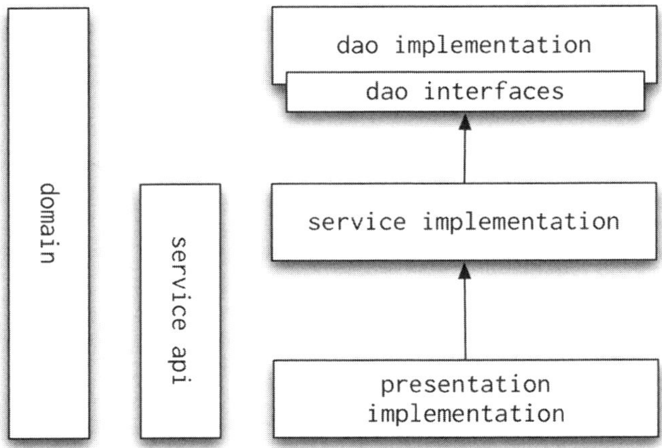

Figure 8-13. *A layered Spring application*

As you can see from the diagram, the domain layer spans the entire application; the domain objects are accessible to every layer of the application. Next, the service API defines the interfaces of the application services. The services are accessible to the presentation tier. The presentation layer accesses the service APIs using the service lookup code, which connects to the service API implementation exposed by the service host.

Next, the service implementations use the data access interfaces, which are ultimately implemented in the DAO implementation. The important point to observe here is that the presentation implementation cannot access the DAO interfaces, not to mention the DAO implementation. You can see in Figure 8-13 that the presentation layer can only access the service layer, which in turn, has access to the DAO interfaces. The presentation implementation is limited to using the service API interfaces.

Distributed applications can be set up using the same logical layering as Figure 8-13 shows, because the Spring setup can be left unchanged as the dependencies between layers are on interfaces. If you need to create a distributed application, you can set up the application in a more complex way, as illustrated in Figure 8-14.

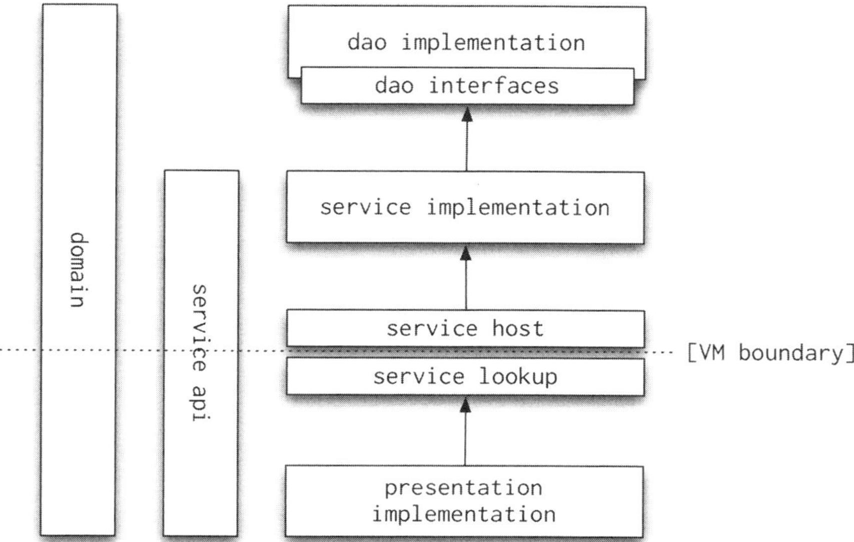

Figure 8-14. *Distributed layered application*

As you can see, the difficulty with a distributed application is the virtual machine boundary between the service host and service lookup. These two layers are responsible for exposing the service implementation so that it is accessible to the service lookup code. The service lookup code finds the service APIs and returns them to the presentation implementation.

All of the patterns we will show in this chapter work with both distributed and local applications.

High-Performance Paging

In most applications, you need to deal with potentially large result sets. For performance and usability reasons, displaying the entire result set at once is often unacceptable. You need to implement some kind of paging mechanism, and you have two fundamental choices: either leave the presentation layer to deal entirely with the paging or add support for paging to all layers. While the first option is the easier to implement (indeed, with projects like DisplayTag, you add one attribute to a JSP tag, and all your paging is done), such approaches could suffer from severe performance and memory usage limitations. Imagine calling a service method that returns thousands of objects—each time you want to display one page of the result all these objects are collected from the database and then the presentation layer pages them. Or if the presentation layer has to keep thousands of large objects in memory so it can perform the paging correctly, a memory usage problem would be expected. So, while using presentation layer paging as a short-term fix is possible, the long-term solution should use an approach similar to the one we will show now.

Let's begin by looking at Figure 8-15; it shows a typical data flow without paging support.

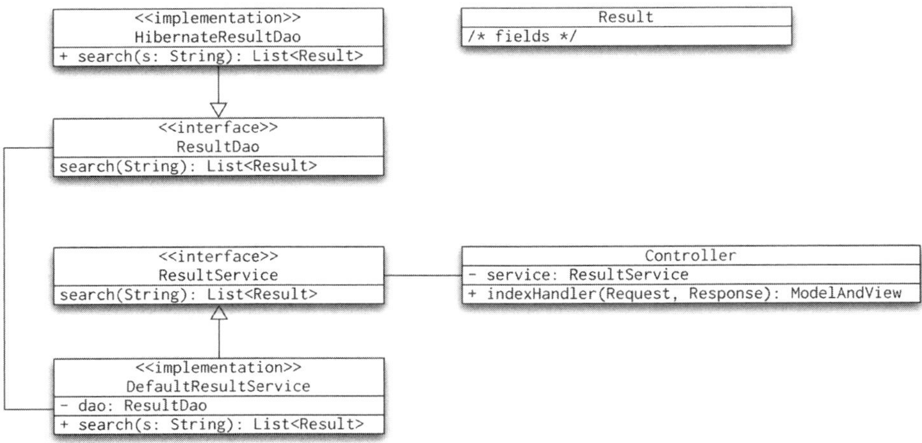

Figure 8-15. *Typical design with no support for paging*

Now, you can see that the Controller uses the ResultService (and indirectly its implementation, the DefaultResultService) to perform some kind of search and gets a List of Result object back. The data access layer (defined by the ResultDao and implemented in HibernateResultDao) acts on the requests of the DefaultResultService, goes to the database, and fetches all Result objects that matched the search strings. Unfortunately, this means that any paging must be left to the presentation tier (the Controller or a JSP page).

The widely accepted solution to this problem is to pass a search argument object to the service and DAO layers and receive a search result back. The argument will include the first record and a maximum number of records to fetch; the result will include up to a maximum number of Result objects and a number of total Result objects. Because the search argument and result objects are likely to be very similar for various types of searches, expressing them as abstract classes can be useful, as illustrated in Figure 8-16.

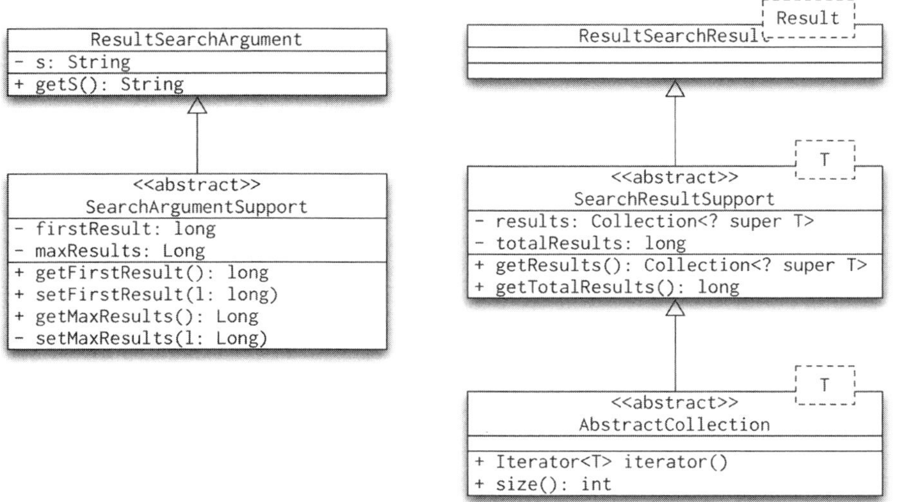

Figure 8-16. *Search argument and result classes*

As you can see, the `ResultSearchArgument` only adds the search strings, and the `ResultSearchResult` does not add any fields to their superclasses. The service and DAO layers need to be modified so that they take the argument object and return the result object. Listing 8-10 shows how this might look in code.

Listing 8-10. *Paging Implementation in Hibernate*

```
public interface ResultDao {
    ResultSearchResult search(ResultSearchArgument a);
}

public class HibernateResultDao ➥
extends HibernateResultSupport implements ResultDao {
    public ResultSearchResult search(final ResultSearchArgument a) {
        return (ResultSearchResult) getHibernateTemplate().execute(➥
new HibernateCallback() {
            public Object doInHibernate(Session session)
                                    throws HibernateException, SQLException {
                Query query;
                ResultSearchResult result = new ResultSearchResult();
                query = session.createQuery("from Result where name = :s");
                query.setString("s", a.getS());
                query.setFirstResult(a.getFirstResult());
                query.setMaxResults(a.getMaxResults());
                result.setResult(query.list());

                query = session.createQuery(➥
"select count(*) from Result where name = :s");
                query.setString("s", a.getS());
                result.setTotalResults((Long)query.uniqueResult());

                return result;
            }
        });
    }}

public interface ResultService {
    ResultSearchResult search(ResultSearchArgument a);
}

public class DefaultResultService implements ResultService {
    private ResultDao resultDao;

    public ResultSearchResult search(ResultSearchArgument a) {
        return this.resultDao.search(a);
    }
}

   public void setResultDao(ResultDao resultDao) {
        this.resultDao = resultDao;
    }
}
```

Even though the implementation uses Hibernate, the general principle would remain the same for any other DAO implementation. You select the specific page and a total number of results that would match the search argument. It means two trips to the database, but the performance benefit over fetching all records, passing them up the call stack, and leaving the presentation tier to discard most of the results, can be substantial. For more information about Hibernate, see Chapter 11.

The specifics of processing the paging requests on the client side depend on the final presentation layer; we give an example of a JSP page using a simple `Controller` and the DisplayTag library in Chapter 17.

Multiple Error Reporting

Some applications need to process the user input, and if the user input contains errors, the application has to return a number of possible problems. An example you should be familiar with is the Java compiler. It processes input (compiles code) and returns compilation errors (if any). If you were to write an application that compiles and runs Java sources received from the user, indicating all discoverable errors at once would be best, rather than stopping at the first erroneous line.

Making error messages localizable and maximizing code reuse for the result reports are also desirable. Thus we can create the `ResultSupport` class as shown in Figure 8-17.

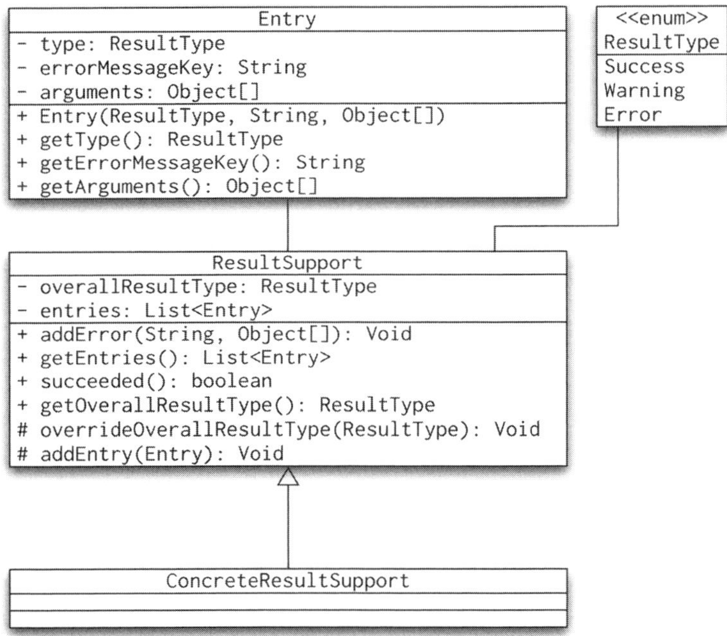

Figure 8-17. *UML diagram of the ResultSupport class*

The service calls in our application now return the `ResultSupport` subclasses, which can report multiple errors from one call. In addition to reporting multiple errors, the callers (usually in the presentation layer) can easily check whether the call succeeded or not. Finally, you can very easily write a custom JSP tag that can be used in a JSP page in code similar to the one shown in Listing 8-11.

Listing 8-11. *JSP Page Displaying a Result*

```
<%@ page contentType="text/html;charset=UTF-8" language="java" %>
<%@ taglib prefix="c" uri="http://java.sun.com/jsp/jstl/core" %>
<%@ taglib prefix="ps" uri="http://www.apress.com/prospring2/tags" %>
```

```
<html xmlns="http://www.w3.org/1999/xhtml"
     xmlns:xsi="http://www.w3.org/2001/XMLSchema-instance"
     xsi:schemaLocation="http://www.w3.org/MarkUp/SCHEMA/xhtml11.xsd"
     xml:lang="en" >
<head>
    <title>Result</title>
</head>
<body>
<h2>We have processed the data</h2>
<ps:result result="${result}">
    <c:if test="${succeeded}">
        <b>The update was successful</b><br/><br/>
    </c:if>
    <c:if test="${!succeeded}">
        <b>The update has failed</b><br/><br/>
     </c:if>
</ps:result>
</body>
</html>
```

The `ps:result` tag's implementation is shown in Listing 8-12. We found this to be a very efficient way of passing complex results back to the user interface.

Listing 8-12. *ResultSupportTag Implementation*

```
public class ResultSupportTag extends RequestContextAwareTag implements BodyTag {
    private ResultSupport result;
    private boolean showDetail = true;
    private boolean showHeader = true;
    private boolean hideSuccess = true;
    private static final Pattern LOCALISED_PATTERN = Pattern.compile("@L(.*)");
    private static Map<ResultSupport.ResultType, String> resultTypeClasses =
        new HashMap<ResultSupport.ResultType, String>();

    static {
        for (ResultSupport.ResultType resultType : ➥
               ResultSupport.ResultType.values()) {
            resultTypeClasses.put(resultType, resultType.name().toLowerCase());
        }
    }

    public void setResult(ResultSupport result) {
        this.result = result;
    }

    public void setShowDetail(boolean showDetail) {
        this.showDetail = showDetail;
    }

    public void setShowHeader(boolean showHeader) {
        this.showHeader = showHeader;
    }

    public void setHideSuccess(boolean hideSuccess) {
        this.hideSuccess = hideSuccess;
    }
```

```
    protected int doStartTagInternal() throws Exception {
        if (this.result == null) return Tag.SKIP_BODY;

        ResultSupport.ResultType overallResultType = ➥
this.result.getOverallResultType();
        //noinspection UnnecessaryBoxing
        pageContext.setAttribute("succeeded", Boolean.valueOf(result.succeeded()));

        if (overallResultType == ResultSupport.ResultType.Success ➥
&& this.hideSuccess) {
            // the result is a success and the user doesn't want to see ➥
the success message
            return Tag.EVAL_BODY_INCLUDE;
        }

        String resultTypeText =
                    HtmlUtils.htmlEscape(getResultTypeMessage(overallResultType));[HL1]
        JspWriter out = pageContext.getOut();

        out.write("<div class=\"result\">\n");
        if (this.showHeader) {
            // write out the overall result (if requested)
            out.write("<span class=\"");
            out.write(resultTypeClasses.get(overallResultType)); out.write("\">");
            out.write(resultTypeText);
            out.write("</span>\n");
        }

        // write out the details, if requested
        if (this.showDetail) {
            out.write("<ul>");
            for (ResultSupport.Entry entry : this.result.getEntries()) {
                out.write("<li class=\"");
                out.write(resultTypeClasses.get(entry.getType())); out.write("\">");
                writeMessage(out, entry);
                out.write("</li>\n");
            }
            out.write("</ul>\n");
        }

        // close the main element
        out.write("</div>\n");

        return Tag.EVAL_BODY_INCLUDE;
    }

    private void writeMessage(JspWriter out, ResultSupport.Entry entry) ➥
throws IOException {
        String key = entry.getErrorMessageKey();
        Matcher matcher = LOCALISED_PATTERN.matcher(key);
        if (matcher.matches()) {
            key = matcher.group(1);
        }
        String message = getRequestContext().getMessage(key, ➥
entry.getArguments(), key);
        out.write(HtmlUtils.htmlEscape(message));
    }
```

```
    private String getResultTypeMessage(ResultSupport.ResultType resultType) {
        switch (resultType) {
            case Error:
                 return getRequestContext().getMessage("error", "Error");
            case Success:
                return getRequestContext().getMessage("success", "Success");
            case Warning:
                return getRequestContext().getMessage("warning", "Warning");
        }
        // not really possible if we're careful not to forget to add to ➥
the switch above
        throw new IllegalArgumentException("Result type not supported");
    }

    public void setBodyContent(BodyContent bodyContent) {
        // noop
    }

    public void doInitBody() throws JspException {
        // noop
    }
}
```

User Interface Transactions

Some applications require what are best described as user interface transactions. The Java EE pattern name for this is Unit of Work. The user sequentially adds more information about the work that is to be performed in a transaction. Starting a transaction in the traditional sense (to treat the whole process of user interaction as one unit that has to be completed before we commit any work) and keeping it open across many user interface interactions is not a good idea. Doing so will cause performance bottlenecks when the user makes modifications to data that other transactions might use. Even worse, the user may simply close the browser, leaving our transaction stranded until the session expires.

Clearly, using transactions is not an option. Instead, we must collect all information about the work the user wants to run transactionally and perform the actual work only when the user clicks the final submit button. Following the pattern we will show here, giving feedback to the user at each step is easy, and you can just as easily store the unit of work data so that the user can come back to an unfinished unit of work and complete it later. Finally, this pattern can also be used to submit the unit of work for asynchronous processing with minimal impact on the code.

Let's begin with a definition of the domain object that represents the unit of work. We will show a document upload with additional metadata. Listing 8-13 shows the domain object for our unit of work.

Listing 8-13. *DocumentUploadTransaction Domain Object*

```
public class DocumentUploadTransaction {
    private Long id;
    private byte[] content;
    private String headline;
    private List<Category> categories;

    public Long getId() {
        return id;
    }
```

```
    public void setId(Long id) {
        this.id = id;
    }

    public byte[] getContent() {
        return content;
    }

    public void setContent(byte[] content) {
        this.content = content;
    }

    public String getHeadline() {
        return headline;
    }

    public void setHeadline(String headline) {
        this.headline = headline;
    }

    public List<Category> getCategories() {
        return categories;
    }

    public void setCategories(List<Category> categories) {
        this.categories = categories;
    }
}
```

The actual meaning of headline and categories properties is not our main concern at this point. The main concern is how the presentation layer will use this object. We will create the `DocumentService` with the methods shown in Listing 8-14.

Listing 8-14. *DocumentService Interface*

```
public interface DocumentService {

    Long begin();
    DocumentUploadResult upload(long id, byte[] content);
    DocumentUploadResult setCategories(long id, List<Category> categories);
    DocumentUploadResult setHeadline(long id, String headline);
    DocumentUploadResult commit(long id, boolean synchronous);
    void abandon(long id);

}
```

The interface itself is very simple; its use is slightly more complex. The presentation tier code will call the `begin()` method to obtain an identifier for the unit of work. It will then repeatedly call the `upload`, `setCategories`, and `setHeadline` methods until the user is satisfied or until the returned `DocumentUploadResults` indicate failures. Notice that the `DocumentUploadResult` here extends the `ResultSupport` class from the multiple errors reporting pattern. Once the user is satisfied with the result and clicks the final submit button, the presentation tier code calls the `commit()` method. Notice that the commit method includes the `synchronous` argument. The outline of the implementation is shown in Figure 8-18.

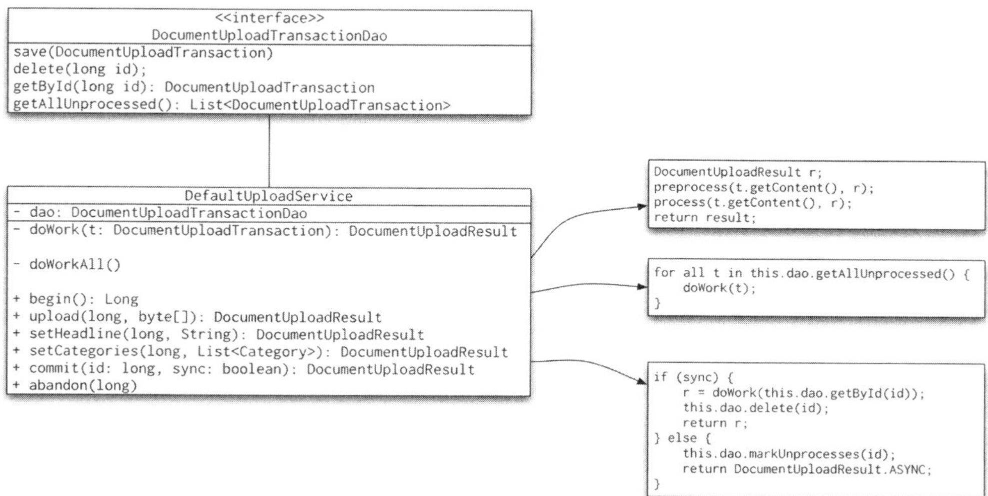

Figure 8-18. *The DefaultUploadService implementation*

The implementation of the `upload`, `setHeadline`, and `setCategories` methods simply updates the `DocumentUploadTransaction` object and then performs processing similar to that done in the `doWork(DocumentUploadTransaction)` method, except it does not perform any data updates. This means that the returned result is not absolutely guaranteed to be correct. It is possible, though unlikely, that the methods will indicate success though the call to the `commit` method ultimately fails. This is why even the commit method returns a `DocumentUploadResult` object.

The interesting part of this pattern is the implementation of the commit code for asynchronous requests. We simply mark the `DocumentUploadTransaction` object as unprocessed, which means that it will be picked up by the `doWorkAll()` method. You may notice that no code explicitly calls the `doWorkAll` method; it is up to a scheduler (see Chapter 12 for more details) to invoke this method periodically to perform the processing. This method then calls the `doWork(DocumentUploadTransaction)` method that performs the processing.

The final, and perhaps most important, point is that the `doWorkAll()` and `doWork (DocumentUploadTransaction)` methods must be marked as transactional in the Spring transaction configuration (see Chapter 16 for more details). This way, we ensure that the user sees the upload process as a transaction (unit of work in our application). The transaction semantics are enforced by processing the definition of the unit of work in an actual transaction.

Notice that you do not have to implement the `DocumentUploadTransactionDao` to actually go to the database, because for some applications, it may be quite enough to implement with code similar to that shown in Listing 8-15.

Listing 8-15. *Simple Implementation of DocumentUploadTransactionDao*

```
public class HeapDocumentUploadTransactionDao ➥
implements DocumentUploadTransactionDao {
    private Map<Long, DocumentUploadTransaction> data =
            Collections.synchronizedMap(➥
new HashMap<Long, DocumentUploadTransaction>());

    public void save(DocumentUploadTransaction transaction) {
        long id = this.data.size() + 1;
        transaction.setId(id);
        this.data.put(id, transaction);
    }

    public void delete(long id) {
        this.data.remove(id);
    }

    public DocumentUploadTransaction getById(long id) {
        return this.data.get(id);
    }

    public synchronized List<DocumentUploadTransaction> getAllUnprocessed() {
        List<DocumentUploadTransaction> result = ➥
new LinkedList<DocumentUploadTransaction>();
        for (DocumentUploadTransaction t : this.data.values()) {
            if (t.isUnprocessed()) result.add(t);
        }
        return result;
    }
}
```

This approach will work quite well when the expected number of active units of work is fairly low. If you expect a high volume of units of work, you will be better off using a real database. Using a database will give you the additional benefit of being able to save a unit of work, thus allowing the users to stop their work and return to it at some later point. Automatically saving the unit of work before the session expires is also possible, thus sparing the users the inconvenience of preparing the unit of work again, is also possible.

The database approach will also allow you to add permission control to the upload process; it is quite possible to have a group of users who can prepare the units of work but cannot actually commit them. This task can be reserved to a power user who will check the unit of work and decide to commit or abandon it.

Background Processes

Most enterprise applications need some kind of background processing. Background processes are those that are not triggered by the user interface. To put it more precisely, the user cannot see the result of the processing immediately. Using scheduling in Spring (see Chapter 12) is not difficult, but managing the jobs is harder. Though we found that the JMX console provides adequate support for management of scheduled jobs, we do not want to restrict our options to JMX alone. Figure 8-19 shows the solution we found to be most flexible.

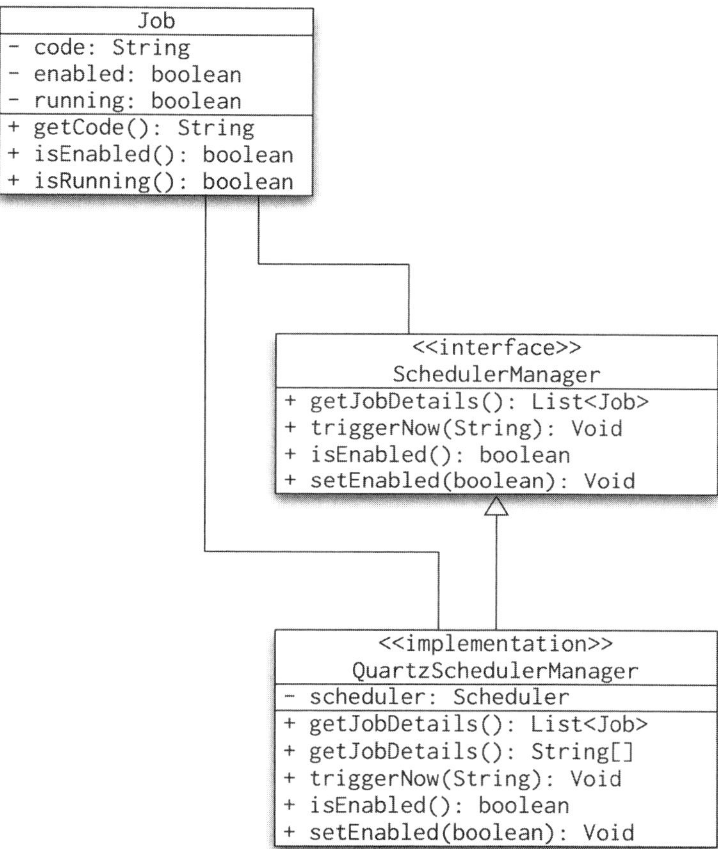

Figure 8-19. *UML diagram of the scheduler managers*

The diagram shows quite clearly that the `Job` class is an object that records information about the `Job` objects in a scheduler-agnostic way. The Quartz scheduler, for example, uses a concept of job groups and job names. What the UML diagram doesn't show is that the implementation of the `SchedulerManager` interface prepares the name returned in the `Job` class and parses it back in the `triggerNow(String)` method. In addition to the code building and parsing, we have also marked the `QuartzSchedulerManager` as a JMX resource. Listing 8-16 shows the full source of the `QuartzSchedulerManager`.

Listing 8-16. *JMX-Annotated Scheduler Manager*

```
@ManagedResource(objectName = "com.apress.prospring.ch08.scheduler:name=manager", ➥
description = "The scheduler manager")
public class QuartzSchedulerManager implements SchedulerManager {
    private Scheduler scheduler;
    private static final Pattern JOB_NAME_PATTERN = ➥
Pattern.compile("([^:]*)::(.*)");
```

```
public List<Job> getJobsDetails() {
    try {
        List<Job> result = new LinkedList<Job>();
        String[] groups = this.scheduler.getJobGroupNames();
        for (String group : groups) {
            String[] names = this.scheduler.getJobNames(group);
            for (String name : names) {
                Job job = new Job(String.format("%s::%s", group, name));
                job.setEnabled(true);
                result.add(job);
            }
        }
        return result;
    } catch (SchedulerException ex) {
        throw new RuntimeException(ex);
    }
}

@ManagedAttribute(description = "The scheduled jobs")
public String[] getJobs() {
    try {
        List<String> result = new LinkedList<String>();
        String[] groups = this.scheduler.getJobGroupNames();
        for (String group : groups) {
            String[] names = this.scheduler.getJobNames(group);
            for (String name : names) {
                result.add(String.format("%s::%s", group, name));
            }
        }
        return result.toArray(new String[result.size()]);
    } catch (SchedulerException ex) {
        throw new RuntimeException(ex);
    }
}

@ManagedOperation(description = "Trigger a job identified by the argument now")
@ManagedOperationParameters({
    @ManagedOperationParameter(name = "job", description = "The job name")
})
public void triggerNow(String job) {
    Matcher matcher = JOB_NAME_PATTERN.matcher(job);
    if (matcher.matches()) {
        try {
            this.scheduler.triggerJob(matcher.group(2), matcher.group(1));
        } catch (SchedulerException ex) {
            throw new RuntimeException(ex);
        }
    }
}

@ManagedAttribute(description = "Indicates whether the scheduler is enabled")
public boolean isEnabled() {
    return true;
}

@ManagedOperation(description = "Enables or disables the scheduler")
@ManagedOperationParameters({
```

```
        @ManagedOperationParameter(name = "enabled", ➥
description = "Enable or disable")
    })
    public void setEnabled(boolean enabled) {
        // noop
    }

    public void setScheduler(Scheduler scheduler) {
        this.scheduler = scheduler;
    }
}
```

Now, we can define as many Quartz triggers in our application's Spring context files as we need. But we also need to declare them in the reference of the `SchedulerFactoryBean`; this is not a problem in a smaller application, but it becomes an issue with a large enterprise application. Therefore, we have created a new implementation of the `SchedulerFactoryBean`, the `AutodiscoveringSchedulerFactoryBean`. Figure 8-20 shows a high-level overview of our implementation: we have added the `autodiscoverJobsAndTriggers()` method, which we call from the `afterPropertiesSet()` method; the remainder of the code is taken from the original `SchedulerFactoryBean`.

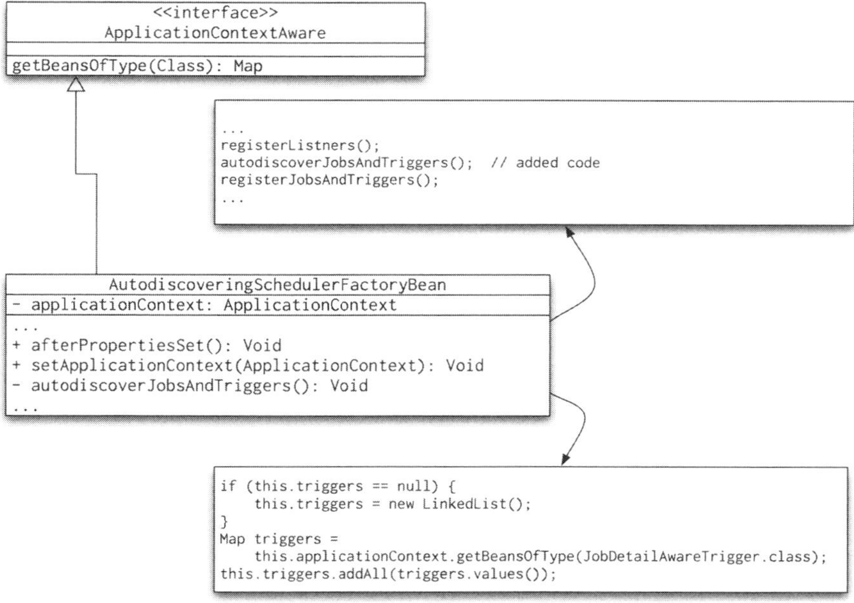

Figure 8-20. *UML diagram of the new SchedulerFactoryBean*

To complete the picture, look at the code shown in Listing 8-17. We define the `AutodiscoveringSchedulerFactoryBean` and all necessary JMX beans. After we have completed this configuration, all we need to do is to create a Quartz `JobDetail` bean. It will automatically be discovered when the application starts up. It will be exposed in the JMX `SchedulerManager` MBean, and it will be made available to scheduling management that uses the `SchedulerManager` bean.

Listing 8-17. *Spring Context File for the Scheduler Manager*

```
<?xml version="1.0" encoding="UTF-8"?>
<beans xmlns="http://www.springframework.org/schema/beans"
                         ...>

    <bean id="mbeanServer" ➥
class="org.springframework.jmx.support.MBeanServerFactoryBean">
        <property name="locateExistingServerIfPossible" value="true"/>
    </bean>
    <bean id="mainScheduler" class="uk.gov.ukti.bpb.services.➥
host.scheduler.AutodiscoveringSchedulerFactoryBean">
        <property name="autoStartup" value="true"/>
    </bean>
    <bean id="schedulerManager"
        class="uk.gov.ukti.bpb.services.host.scheduler.QuartzSchedulerManager">
        <property name="scheduler" ref="mainScheduler"/>
    </bean>

    <bean id="jmxAttributeSource"
          class="org.springframework.jmx.export.➥
annotation.AnnotationJmxAttributeSource"/>

    <bean id="assembler"
          class="org.springframework.jmx.export.➥
assembler.MetadataMBeanInfoAssembler">
        <property name="attributeSource" ref="jmxAttributeSource"/>
    </bean>

    <bean id="namingStrategy"
          class="org.springframework.jmx.export.naming.MetadataNamingStrategy">
        <property name="attributeSource" ref="jmxAttributeSource"/>
    </bean>

    <bean class="org.springframework.jmx.export.MBeanExporter">
        <property name="autodetect" value="true"/>
        <property name="server" ref="mbeanServer"/>
        <property name="assembler" ref="assembler"/>
        <property name="namingStrategy" ref="namingStrategy"/>
    </bean>

</beans>
```

Here, we can see all the important elements of the scheduling management code: the `MBeanServer` (see Chapter 21) and the Quartz scheduler (see Chapter 12). The demonstration application consists of a simple Java class whose code is shown in Listing 8-18.

Listing 8-18. *Sample Application for the Scheduler Manager*

```
public class Main {

    public static void main(String[] args) throws Exception {
        new ClassPathXmlApplicationContext(new String[] {
                "scheduler-context.xml",
                "main-context.xml"
        }, Main.class);
```

```
        new BufferedReader(new InputStreamReader(System.in)).readLine();
    }

}
```

When we run this application with the -Dcom.sun.management.jmxremote JVM argument (this is required in JVMs before version 1.6; if you're using Java 1.6, you don't have to add this parameter), we can then see the JConsole window shown in Figure 8-21.

■ **Note** JConsole is a graphical tool that connects to the running JVM, usually for application monitoring purposes. You can find more about JMX and JConsole in Chapter 16 or on the Sun web site at http://java.sun.com/developer/technicalArticles/J2SE/jconsole.html.

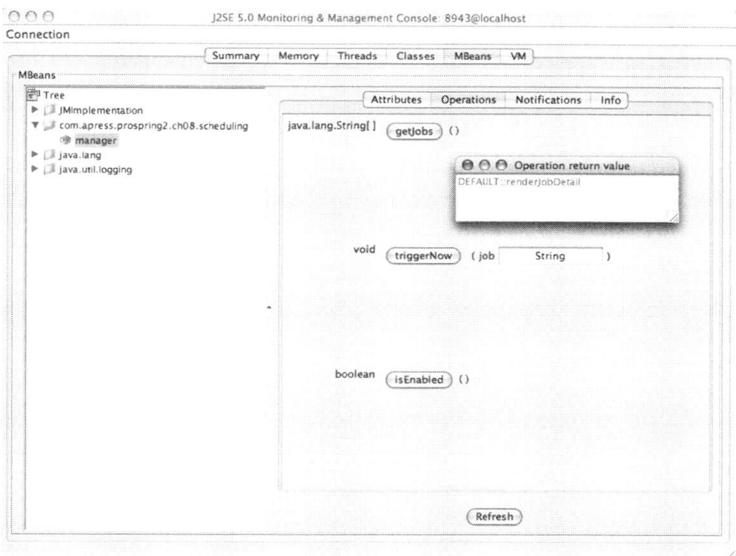

Figure 8-21. *Image of JConsole showing the MBean view*

Now that you know how to deal with scheduled jobs, we can move ahead and see how we can use this knowledge to send e-mail.

E-mail Notifications

Most applications need to notify their users by e-mail. Simpler applications can get away with using Spring's e-mail integration and synchronously sending the e-mails using an SMTP mail transport. However, more advanced applications usually cannot tolerate the delay of connecting to the SMTP server and may require scheduling of the delivery of the e-mails and infrastructure for retries and reports on e-mails sent.

To do this, we usually create a message queue with a scheduled process that processes the queue and sends the messages asynchronously. Together with the scheduling infrastructure we introduced earlier, you can build efficient e-mail–sending applications. In addition to the sending process, adding some kind of templating engine is useful so that you can customize the e-mail being sent out. We will show how we can separate template generation from storage.

The main components of the solution are illustrated in Figure 8-22.

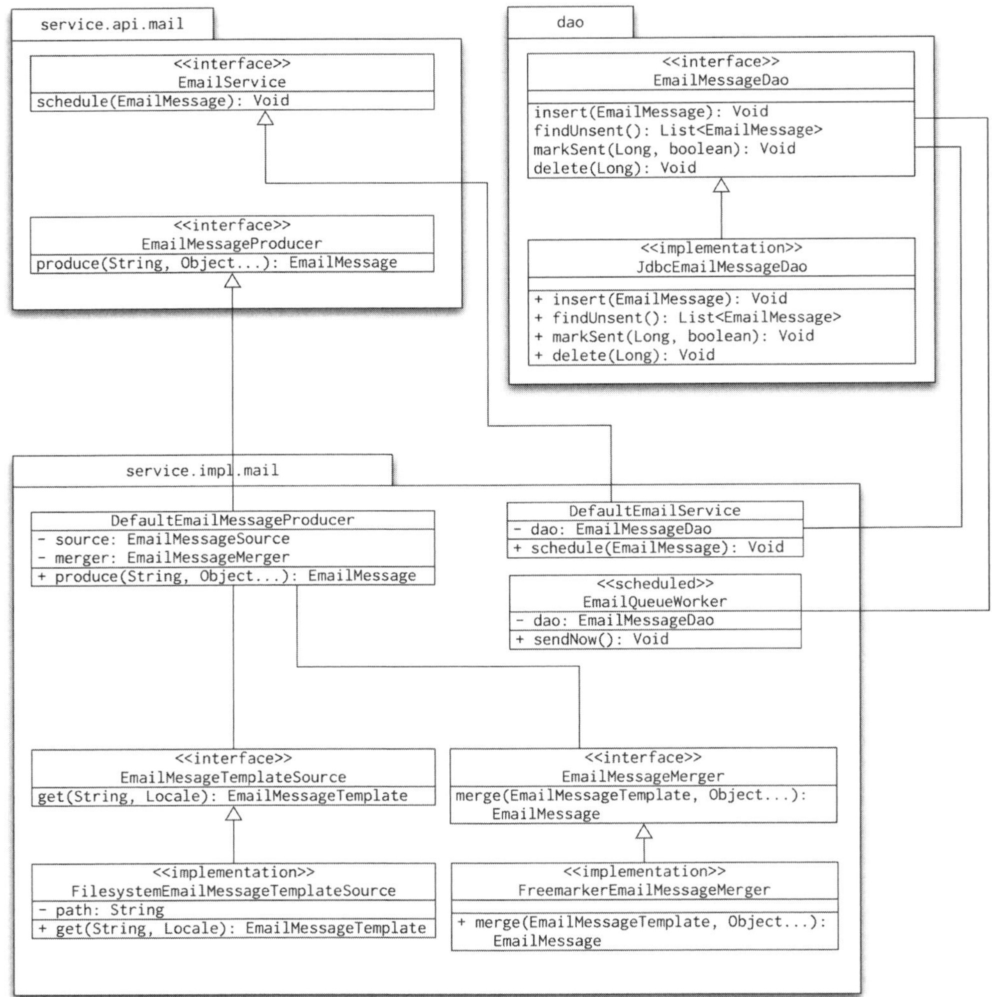

Figure 8-22. *UML diagram of the e-mail infrastructure*

The diagram shows the main components of the system. The data access tier implements storage of the `EmailMessage` objects. The service APIs are represented by the `EmailService` and `EmailMessageProducer`. The implementation of the `EmailService` (the `DefaultEmailService`) simply validates the passed `EmailMessage` class and stores it in the database. It then gets picked up by the `EmailQueueWorker`, which operates on the message queue in the database. The clients (that is the code that uses the service APIs) use the `EmailMessageProducer` to obtain an `EmailMessage`. The `EmailMessage` is identified by its code; it usually includes placeholders for arguments, which are passed to the producer in the `Object . . . argument` parameter. The implementation of the

EmailMessageProducer (the DefaultEmailMessageProducer) uses implementations of the EmailMessageTemplateSource and EmailMessageMerger. The task of the EmailMessageTemplateSource is to look up the e-mail template identified by its code; the merger will take the content of the template and merge it with the arguments to produce the final EmailMessage, which is almost ready to be queued using the EmailService. By "almost ready," we mean that the message body and subject are set; all that remains to be done is to specify the recipient and add any potential attachments.

As you can see, there are important things to consider in a real implementation. The e-mail templates should be stored externally, perhaps on the filesystem or in the database. Also, including the locale is important when looking up the e-mail templates. You may argue that your application does not need to support different languages, but adding this feature is easy, and you can always produce templates in your default language.

When implementing the scheduler, you should add some management information: you may find it useful to track the numbers of retry e-mails sent, the size of the queue, and many other values.

Error Collecting and Logging

The final section of this chapter deals with error reporting. This is an extremely important aspect of good application design. With enough information about the errors that occur, debugging becomes a lot easier. However, recording just enough information about application failures is very tricky. I am sure you would never write code similar to that shown in Listing 8-19.

Listing 8-19. *Bad Example of Error Handling*

```
public class SimpleClient {
    private FileUploadService fileUploadService;
    private static final Log logger = LogFactory.getLog(SimpleClient.class);

    public void uploadTerrible() {
        try {
            this.fileUploadService.upload("me", "text/plain",
                System.currentTimeMillis(), new byte[] { 1, 2, 3 });
        } catch (Exception e) {
            // Go away!
        }
    }

    public void setFileUploadService(FileUploadService fileUploadService) {
        this.fileUploadService = fileUploadService;
    }
}
```

Silently ignoring exceptions is not good practice in Java (or any other type of) programming. The code in Listing 8-19 gives no feedback to the user in case of an error. When the users complain that the application did not work as it should, the programmers may find it hard to reproduce the problem. A solution that addresses some of these issues is shown in Listing 8-20.

Listing 8-20. *Slightly Improved Error Logging*

```
public class SimpleClient {
    private FileUploadService fileUploadService;
    private static final Log logger = LogFactory.getLog(SimpleClient.class);

    public void uploadBetter() {
        try {
            this.fileUploadService.upload("me", "text/plain",
```

```
                System.currentTimeMillis(), new byte[] { 1, 2, 3 });
        } catch (Exception e) {
            logger.error(e);
        }
    }

    public void setFileUploadService(FileUploadService fileUploadService) {
        this.fileUploadService = fileUploadService;
    }
}
```

The code here addresses the issue of silently swallowing the exception. However, it simply writes it out to a log. Now, even if we turned the logging down to the `ERROR` level, if we had 1,000 requests, the log would still contain 26 lines; at the `DEBUG` level, we would have to go through 2,865 lines to locate the errors!

However, we are still missing more information about the errors. We get the message, but that is usually not enough information. Ideally, we would have the method arguments that contain additional information, so that we can create a test to expose the failure. In addition to this, it would be better if we didn't have to scan through the log files to find problems. Consider this solution: for every service-layer method call, we create an around advice that logs the arguments supplied and proceeds with the invocation. If the invocation fails with an exception, we write the details of the exception to a database, together with the method arguments and stack trace. We then transparently rethrow the exception so that the clients do not notice that there was advice. The database could very quickly become clogged with exception reports. Chances are, however, that most of the exceptions will be the same or very similar. Therefore, we can record a count of each exception. Ultimately, we would like to see a report that looks like Table 8-1.

Table 8-1. *Sample Exception Report*

Count	Last Date	Exception	Stack Trace	Method
1312	03/10/2007	NullPointerException	...	DefaultUploadService.fileUpload (null, "Foo", 10, null);
10	03/10/2007	FileNotFoundException	...	DefaultFileAccessService.load ("/vaar/content/file.txt");
1	02/10/2007	NumberFormatException	...	DefaultUserService.updateCount ("janm", "one hundred");

This report shows clearly that the exception we need to look at (because it happened 1,312 times!) is the `NullPointerException` thrown from the call to the `DefaultUploadSercvice.fileUpload` method with `null`, `"Foo"`, `10`, and `null` arguments. We can now write a test to verify what the correct functionality should be. Generally, we should not throw low-level exceptions such as `NullPointerException` from methods that should have verified their arguments and thrown more specific exceptions, hence `NullPointerException` may indicate that we have forgotten such a check.

To achieve all this, we will make use of the Spring AspectJ support (for more information, see Chapter 6). The most important component is the aspect, which is shown in Listing 8-21.

Listing 8-21. *The Around Error Collecting Aspect*

```
@Aspect
public class ErrorLoggingAroundAspect {
    private ErrorLogDao errorLogDao;
```

```
    @Around("execution(* com.apress.prospring2.ch08.errorreporting.*Service.*(..))")
    public Object doBasicProfiling(ProceedingJoinPoint pjp) throws Throwable {
        try {
            return pjp.proceed();
        } catch (Throwable t) {
            insertThrowable(t, pjp);
            throw t;
        }
    }

    private void insertThrowable(Throwable t, ProceedingJoinPoint pjp) ➥
throws IOException {
        StringWriter writer = new StringWriter();
        t.printStackTrace(new PrintWriter(writer));
        writer.close();
        this.errorLogDao.insert(writer.toString(), pjp.getSignature().getName());
    }

    public void setErrorLogDao(ErrorLogDao errorLogDao) {
        this.errorLogDao = errorLogDao;
    }
}
```

This around advice applies to all invocations in classes with names matching the `*Service` pattern in the `com.apress.prospring2.ch08.errorreporting` package. The aspect simply proceeds with the invocation, and if invocation fails, will log the failed method using the `ErrorLogDao` and then rethrow the exception. The `ErrorLogDao` implementation is very straightforward, and it does not differ from any other DAO implementation—it simply collects the `ErrorLog` domain objects. The implementation is shown in Listing 8-22.

Listing 8-22. *The ErrorLogDao Interface and Domain Object*

```
public interface ErrorLogDao {

    void insert(String stackTrace, String method);

    List<ErrorLog> getAll();
}

public class HeapErrorLogDao implements ErrorLogDao {

    private List<ErrorLog> errors = new LinkedList<ErrorLog>();

    public void insert(String stackTrace, String method) {
        for (ErrorLog log : this.errors) {
            if (log.getMethod().equals(method) &&
                    log.getStackTrace().equals(stackTrace)) {
                log.setCount(log.getCount() + 1);
                return;
            }
        }
        this.errors.add(new ErrorLog(stackTrace, method));
    }
```

```
    public List<ErrorLog> getAll() {
        return this.errors;
    }
}

public class ErrorLog {
    private String stackTrace;
    private String method;
    private int count = 1;

    // getters and setters
}
```

The only important bit to consider is that the `insert()` method does not just blindly add a new record; it checks whether there is another identical exception report, in which case it simply increases its count. The final piece of the puzzle is the Spring context file, which is shown in Listing 8-23.

Listing 8-23. *The Spring Context File for the Error Reporting Demonstration*

```
<?xml version="1.0" encoding="UTF-8"?>
<beans xmlns="http://www.springframework.org/schema/beans"
                              ...>

    <bean id="fileUploadService"
        class="com.apress.prospring2.ch08.errorreporting.DefaultFileUploadService"/>

    <bean id="client" ➥
class="com.apress.prospring2.ch08.errorreporting.SimpleClient">
        <property name="fileUploadService" ref="fileUploadService"/>
    </bean>

    <bean id="errorLogDao" ➥
class="com.apress.prospring2.ch08.errorreporting.HeapErrorLogDao"/>

    <bean class="com.apress.prospring2.ch08.➥
errorreporting.ErrorLoggingAroundAspect">
        <property name="errorLogDao" ref="errorLogDao"/>
    </bean>
    <aop:aspectj-autoproxy/>

</beans>
```

The lines in bold define the aspect and wire it into the Spring beans so that when we run the application, we get output like this:

```
[2 * upload(me,text/plain,11,[B@578426, Stack trace
com.apress.prospring2.ch08.errorreporting.InvalidLevelException: ➥
Level must not be divisible by 11.
    at com.apress.prospring2.ch08.errorreporting.DefaultFileUploadService.➥
    upload(DefaultFileUploadService.java:19)
    SNIP
, 1 * upload(me,text/plain,22,[B@578426, Stack trace
com.apress.prospring2.ch08.errorreporting.InvalidLevelException: ➥
Level must not be divisible by 11.
    at com.apress.prospring2.ch08.errorreporting.DefaultFileUploadService➥
    upload(DefaultFileUploadService.java:19)
    SNIP
, 1 * upload(me,text/plain,33,[B@578426, Stack trace ➥
com.apress.prospring2.ch08.errorreporting.InvalidLevelException: ➥
Level must not be divisible by 11.
    at com.apress.prospring2.ch08.errorreporting.DefaultFileUploadService➥
    upload(DefaultFileUploadService.java:19)
    SNIP
```

This is exactly what we were looking for: we get a list of the exceptions encountered, and we can see how many times each exception occurred, what the method arguments were, and the stack trace of the exception. All you have to do now is to provide a more production-ready implementation of the DAO, and you'll be ready to keep a close eye on your application.

Summary

In this chapter, we discussed some high-level designs we use in large Spring applications. The standard design patterns allow you to communicate a particular object-oriented programming concept easily to other members of your team. If everyone understands the design patterns, you can use them as building blocks when describing your solution.

We also had a look at some of the patterns we ourselves have encountered and implemented in building Spring applications. We have tried to find as many practical examples as possible. With a complex framework such as Spring, you can easily overlook useful ways of combining the different features of the framework to get the most out of it. Use the patterns we have described as ideas for your own applications.

After reading this chapter, you should try out some of the concepts we talked about and see how they can be applied to your current or future projects.

PART 2

Data Access

CHAPTER 9

JDBC Support

In this chapter, we begin the discussion of the data access support in Spring. Almost every application needs to store and retrieve the data it works with. Storage options range from simple text files to complex proprietary data storage systems. However, in most cases, the best option is to use a relational database.

Virtually all of today's databases can be used from Java. Java code accesses the database using a JDBC driver (see `http://java.sun.com/javase/technologies/database/`). The driver translates JDBC operations to commands that the database can understand. The driver needs to be able to handle core JDBC concepts; for Spring's JDBC support to be considered complete, it too must support all JDBC operations.

Note You will notice that we use the term *database* quite freely and, in many cases, incorrectly! Strictly speaking, a database is the information that we store in a database management system. The database management system manipulates and retrieves the data it stores. In virtually all situations, you will be working with a relational database management system, which is sometimes called just a "database" for short.

We will continue to mix these two terms, as we are sure you will understand from the context which meaning is intended.

Key JDBC Concepts

The JDBC framework is very complex, but at the highest level, you should understand that it contains the driver, the `DriverManager`, the connection, various types of statements, and finally the `ResultSet`. Figure 9-1 shows these concepts in a UML class diagram.

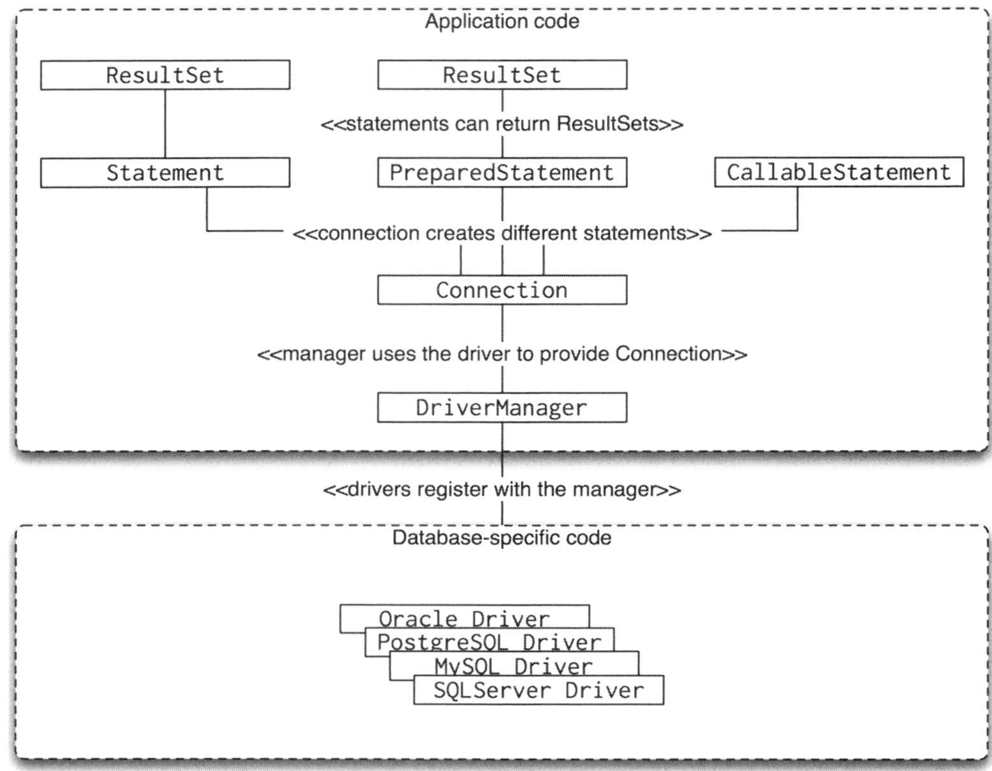

Figure 9-1. *Class diagram of the JDBC core*

You can see that the drivers are not part of the JDBC core; instead, each database vendor supplies its own implementation of the driver. However, the drivers have a common behavior: once loaded by the class loader, they register themselves with the `DriverManager`. The application code then uses the `DriverManager` to obtain a `Connection` to the database. The `Connection` object represents a session as well as a logical connection to the database. Once it has the `Connection` object, it can use it to create different types of `Statement` objects depending on the nature of the statement to be executed. The two core types of statements are

- `PreparedStatement`: This statement can be used to perform operations that change or select rows from the database. As the name implies, most databases prepare the statement; usually, this means that the database parses the SQL code of the statement, creates its execution plan, and caches this plan. Therefore, it does not have to perform the sometimes quite complex analysis of the SQL code and can immediately begin its execution. It returns a `ResultSet` or a number (`int`) of affected rows.
- `CallableStatement`: This statement can be used to execute stored procedures and functions. Unlike the `PreparedStatement`, most databases do not perform any preparation for the call, because it is such a simple command. The `CallableStatement` instances can be used to return the object that the stored procedure—or function, to be more exact—returned.

Another powerful feature of the JDBC framework is batching. JDBC batches allow us to perform a large number of JDBC operations (operations with the `Statement` instances) as one logical block. If your application performs many inserts or updates, batching these operations performs them an order of magnitude faster than using the individual, non-batched operations.

Let's take a more detailed look at some of the important concepts of the JDBC framework. Before we get into the details of the various JDBC concepts, glance at Figure 9-2, which shows the table diagram for our examples.

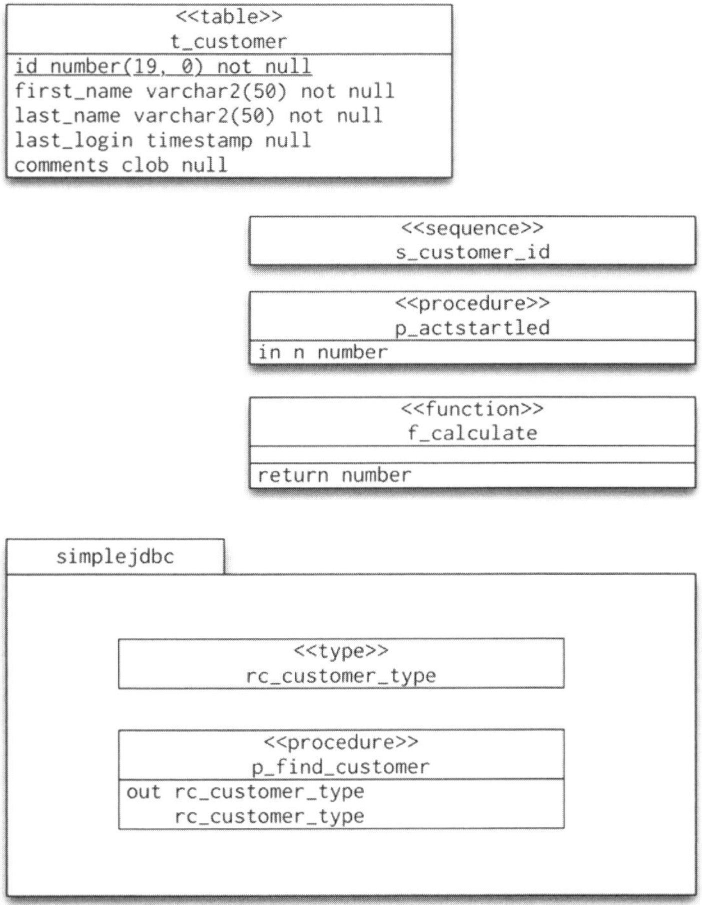

Figure 9-2. *Table diagram of the example database*

Listing 9-1 shows the SQL code needed to create the tables and stored procedures.

Listing 9-1. *SQL Code to Create the Tables and Procedures*

```
create table t_customer (
    id number(19, 0) not null,
    first_name varchar2(50) not null,
    last_name varchar2(50) not null,
    last_login timestamp null,
```

```
    comments clob null,
    constraint pk_customer primary key(id)
)
/
create sequence s_customer_id start with 1000
/

create or replace procedure p_actstartled(n number)
is
begin
    dbms_output.put_line(n || '?! Really?');
end;
/

create or replace function f_calculate
return number
as
begin
    return 42;
end;
/

create or replace package simplejdbc as
    type rc_customer_type is ref cursor return t_customer%rowtype;
    procedure p_find_customer(rc_customer_type out rc_customer_type);
end;
/

create or replace package body simplejdbc as
    procedure p_find_customer (rc_customer_type out rc_customer_type) is
    begin
        open rc_customer_type for select * from t_customer;
    end;
end;
/
```

You do not have to retype this SQL code; it is available in the source code for the book. We used Oracle 10g for our tests, but kept the SQL code as close to ANSI SQL as possible. It should not be difficult for you to adapt the SQL code to match your database.

Using the DriverManager and Connections

Before you begin using any of the JDBC objects, you need to learn how to register a driver and how to use the `DriverManager` to obtain a `Connection` to your database. The code in Listing 9-2 illustrates how to do this.

Listing 9-2. *Registering a Driver and Obtaining a Connection*

```
public class ConnectionDemo {
    private static final String CONNECTION_STRING =
        "jdbc:oracle:thin:@oracle.devcake.co.uk:1521:INTL";

    public static void main(String[] args) {
        try {
            Class.forName("oracle.jdbc.OracleDriver");
        } catch (ClassNotFoundException e) {
```

```
            return;
        }
        Connection connection;
        try {
            connection = DriverManager.getConnection(CONNECTION_STRING,
                "PROSPRING", "x******6");
        } catch (SQLException e) {
            return;
        }
        // work with the  connection
        try {
            connection.commit();
        } catch (SQLException e) {
            return;
        }
        try {
            connection.close();
        } catch (SQLException e) {
            // noop
        }
    }

}
```

As you can see, the code is not very difficult; the only complexity comes from handling the various checked exceptions. We have left all the exception handling code in place just to demonstrate how cumbersome the code can become. Spring hides these details of the JDBC framework and provides a translation layer between JDBC exceptions and Spring unchecked exceptions. Jump ahead to the "Concepts in Spring Data Access Support" section if you are impatient.

Apart from the clumsiness that the exception handling code has brought in, we can see that the Connection is a bottleneck. Imagine a web application that handles hundreds of concurrent requests. If, for each request, we get a new connection and then close it, we put a significant strain on the database. We can improve the situation using two techniques: smart connection management and connection pooling. However, using these without the help of a framework is very difficult. Spring provides all the necessary tools for smart connection management, and it can use connection pools as well. Now that you know how to get a Connection, we can consider how to use it to work with the data in the database.

Using PreparedStatements

We begin by looking at how we can use the PreparedStatement instances to insert, select, update, and delete data. (These four operations are sometimes referred to as CRUD (create, read, update, and delete).

We will begin by performing an insert into the t_customer table. If you were to write the SQL command directly, you would write code similar to Listing 9-3.

Listing 9-3. *Insert Code in Plain SQL*

```
insert  into t_customer (id,  first_name, last_name, last_login, comments)
values (1, 'Jan', 'Machacek', null, null);
```

You could construct the same SQL in Java using the code in Listing 9-4.

Listing 9-4. *Insert Statement Constructed in Java*

```
StringBuilder sb = new StringBuilder(100);
sb.append("insert into " +
    "t_customer (id, first_name, last_name, last_login, comments) values (");
sb.append(customerId).append(", ");
sb.append("'").append(firstName).append("', ");
sb.append("'").append(lastName).append("', ");
sb.append("null, ");
sb.append("null)");
```

We hope you would never even consider writing code like this. It is ugly (while that is a subjective opinion, we hope you agree with us), but more importantly, it is susceptible to SQL injection attacks. Listing 9-5 shows how to use the `PreparedStatement` to perform the insert operation.

Listing 9-5. *Using the PreparedStatement to Insert Data*

```
class InsertDemo {
    private static final String CONNECTION_STRING =
        "jdbc:oracle:thin:@oracle.devcake.co.uk:1521:INTL";

    public static void main(String[] args) {
        try {
            Class.forName("oracle.jdbc.OracleDriver");
        } catch (ClassNotFoundException e) {
            return;
        }
        Connection connection;
        try {
            connection = DriverManager.getConnection(CONNECTION_STRING,
                "PROSPRING", "x******6");
        } catch (SQLException e) {
            return;
        }
        PreparedStatement preparedStatement;
        try {
            preparedStatement = connection.prepareStatement(
                 "insert into t_customer (id, first_name, last_name, last_login, " +
                    "comments) "values (?, ?, ?, ?, ?)");
        } catch (SQLException e) {
            return;
        }
        try {
            preparedStatement.setLong(1, 1L);
            preparedStatement.setString(2, "Jan");
            preparedStatement.setString(3, "Machacek");
            preparedStatement.setNull(4, Types.TIMESTAMP);
            preparedStatement.setNull(5, Types.CLOB);
            preparedStatement.executeUpdate();
        } catch (SQLException e) {
            return; // 1
        }
        try {
            connection.commit();
        } catch (SQLException e) {
            return;
        }
```

```
        try {
            connection.close();
        } catch (SQLException e) {
            // noop
        }
    }

}
```

The code in bold shows how we have used the `Connection` object to create a `PreparedStatement` for the insert operation. It also shows that we have not included the values to be inserted in the SQL statement itself; instead, we have used the ? parameter placeholder. We set the values of the parameters using the `setLong`, `setString`, and `setNull` methods. Finally, we call the `executeUpdate` method, which performs the insert operation in the database.

The problem with the code we have written is that it will only work once. The second time we run it, it will fail with a primary key constraint violation (we will not see any evidence of this, because we silently ignore the exception on line `// 1` in Listing 9-4). We need to be able to select the next value of the `s_customer_id` sequence. The code in Listing 9-6 shows how to use a `PreparedStatement` to select data.

Listing 9-6. *Selecting Data Using a PreparedStatement*

```
class SelectDemo {
    private static final String CONNECTION_STRING =
        "jdbc:oracle:thin:@oracle.devcake.co.uk:1521:INTL";

    public static void main(String[] args) {
        // same code to obtain the Connection
        PreparedStatement preparedStatement;
        try {
            preparedStatement = connection.prepareStatement(
                    "select s_customer_id.nextval from dual");
        } catch (SQLException e) {
            return;
        }
        long id;
        try {
            ResultSet resultSet = preparedStatement.executeQuery();
            if (resultSet.next()) {
                id = resultSet.getLong(1);
                System.out.println("The id was " + id);
            }
        } catch (SQLException e) {
            return;
        }

        // use the id

       // same code to close the connection
    }

}
```

The code in bold shows the use of the `PreparedStatement` to get data from the result of running a SQL statement; in this particular case, we have selected the next value of a sequence.

You have now seen two different uses of the PreparedStatement: we can use it to insert, update, and delete data as well as to select data. The main difference between the uses is that data selection returns a ResultSet, while data modification returns the number of affected rows.

However, we cannot use the PreparedStatement to call stored procedures and functions; for that, we must use the CallableStatement.

Using CallableStatements

To call a stored procedure or a function, we must use the CallableStatement. To get a CallableStatement instance, we need to call the prepareCall method on the Connection object. Listing 9-7 shows the procedure and function we need to demonstrate the use of the CallableStatement.

Listing 9-7. *The Stored Procedure and Function*

```
create or replace procedure p_actstartled(n number)
is
begin
    dbms_output.put_line(n || '?! Really?');
end;
/

create or replace function f_calculate
return number
as
begin
    return 42;
end;
/
```

Neither p_actstartled nor f_calculate does anything profound, but we can show how to call them from our Java code. Listing 9-8 shows the Java code that demonstrates how to execute the procedure and call the function.

Listing 9-8. *Java Code That Calls the Procedure and Function*

```
class CallableDemo {

    public static void main(String[] args) throws SQLException {
        CallableStatement cs;
        Connection connection = ConnectionFactory.createConnection(); // 1

        cs = connection.prepareCall("{? = call f_calculate}");        // 2
        cs.registerOutParameter(1, Types.INTEGER);                     // 3
        cs.execute();                                                  // 4
        long meaningOfLife = cs.getLong(1);                            // 5
        System.out.println(meaningOfLife);

        cs = connection.prepareCall("{call p_actstartled(?)}");       // 6
        cs.setLong(1, meaningOfLife);                                  // 7
        cs.execute();                                                  // 8

        connection.close();
    }

}
```

The code we have written obtains the connection and calls the stored function `f_calculate` to get the meaning of life, and then passes the calculated value to the `p_actstartled` stored procedure.

We have moved the complex code to get the `Connection` to a utility class; we get a valid `Connection` on line `// 1`. Next, on line `// 2`, we prepare the call to the `f_calculate` stored function. The statement argument for the `prepareCall` method must be formatted in this way: `{? = call name(`***A***`)}`, where the first question mark (`?`) is the return value, `name` is the name of the function to call, and the ***A*** is the list of arguments. Line `// 3` registers the type of the value returned from the function call—in our case, the `number` type in Oracle maps to the `Types.INTEGER`. Line `// 4` executes the function, and line `// 5` gets the value returned from the function. To call a stored procedure, use the `prepareCall` method with slightly different syntax of the statement SQL code than the SQL code we used to call a stored function. The only difference is that a stored procedure does not return a value, so the statement syntax is just `{call name(`***A***`)}`, where the `name` is the name of the stored procedure, and ***A*** represents the arguments (see line `// 6`). On line `// 7`, we set the value of the argument to the procedure call, and finally, on line `// 8` we execute the call.

Other JDBC Concepts

There are many other JDBC concepts to discuss, but we will do so in the context of Spring's JDBC support. The other concepts that you are likely to use include handling binary large objects (BLOBs) and character large objects (CLOBs), and using cursors returned from stored procedures and functions.

Another important feature of the JDBC framework is batch updates. This feature allows you to execute a large number of JDBC operations in a set, thus dramatically improving performance.

Spring supports all the basic JDBC operations you have seen in this short introduction and adds elegant exception handling and connection management. Spring JDBC support simplifies all of the JDBC operations. Simplification does not mean that Spring hides the details, just that it contains all the boilerplate code so you can focus on the actual database code you need to implement.

Concepts in Spring Data Access Support

Before we start discussing the specifics of Spring JDBC support, we need to take a look at Spring's general approach to data access. The examples in the previous section should have made very apparent the difficulties with verbose code and the use of checked exceptions. Another consideration is the management of open connections. Obviously, connections to the database are a scarce resource: if we open too many, the performance of the database will degrade rapidly; if we maintain only one active connection for the entire application, we are not using the database's full potential. However, reliably managing a pool of connections is difficult.

Spring addresses all these concerns. Take a look at the exception hierarchy in Figure 9-3.

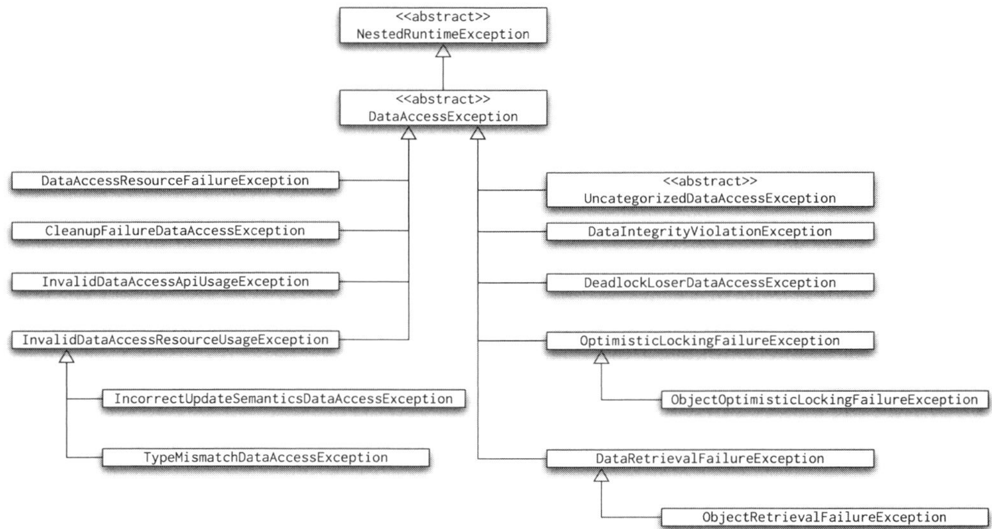

Figure 9-3. *Exception hierarchy in Spring data support*

Notice that all these exceptions are runtime exceptions, which make much more sense than the checked exceptions used in JDBC. Checked exceptions should be used to indicate an error that the application can recover from. But how can you recover from an exception caused by a malformed SQL statement?

Alongside the rich exception hierarchy, all Spring data access code follows the same pattern as `HibernateTemplate`, `JdoTemplate`, and `JpaTemplate`. All of these classes maintain the safety of the underlying scarce resources (e.g., database connections or Hibernate sessions). Spring also provides convenience superclasses for your data access implementations; their names are `JdbcDaoSupport`, `HibernateDaoSupport`, `JdoDaoSupport`, and `JpaDaoSupport`.

Let's look at how Spring simplifies the JDBC programming.

JDBC Data Access Support

At the core of Spring JDBC support is the `JdbcTemplate` class. The `JdbcTemplate` allows you to work directly with instances of the `Statement`, `PreparedStatement`, and `CallableStatement` classes. The `JdbcTemplate` helps manage the connection and translates any `SQLException` to a Spring data access exception.

Before we begin looking at the JDBC support, we need a `DataSource`. A `DataSource` is a JDBC interface that represents an alternative to `DriverManager`. Because it is an interface, many different implementations exist, from simple ones that just use the JDBC driver to get a connection to advanced pooling implementations. For our experiments in this chapter, we will use the Apache Commons `BasicDataSource`. Listing 9-9 shows how we have configured the `dataSource` bean.

Listing 9-9. *Definition of the DataSource Bean*

```
<?xml version="1.0" encoding="UTF-8"?>
<beans xmlns="...">

    <bean id="dataSource"
        class="org.apache.commons.dbcp.BasicDataSource" destroy-method="close">
        <property name="driverClassName" value="oracle.jdbc.driver.OracleDriver"/>
        <property name="url"
                 value="jdbc:oracle:thin:@oracle.devcake.co.uk:1521:INTL"/>
        <property name="username" value="PROSPRING"/>
        <property name="password" value="x******6"/>
    </bean>

</beans>
```

You can see that the `dataSource` bean is similar to the `DriverManager` we used before in that we must specify the JDBC driver to use, the connection string, and (optionally) the username and password. Once configured, we can call its `getConnection(String, String)` method to obtain a connection to the database.

You can choose between two main approaches to writing JDBC data access code in Spring: you can either use the `JdbcTemplate` class, or you can use subclasses of the `RdbmsOperation` class. The `JdbcTemplate` offers features that allow you to do everything from just running a hard-coded SQL statement to complexly creating the statement, setting its parameters, and extracting results. Use the `RdbmsOperation` subclasses to create fine-grained implementations, each of which performs a specialized task (e.g., to insert a row into a particular table).

Using the JdbcTemplate

The `JdbcTemplate` class is at the core of Spring JDBC support. Using the `JdbcTemplate`, you can perform call, execute, query, and update operations on the database. Each of these operations has a number of variations, which differ in the number of arguments and the return types of the `JdbcTemplate` methods. The `JdbcTemplate` makes heavy use of callback interfaces. The implementations perform the required functions. The `JdbcTemplate` performs the common steps and delegates to the callbacks at appropriate points.

Consider the code we'd need to select rows from a table:

1. Open the connection to the database.
2. Specify the statement to be executed on the connection.
3. Set any required parameters and execute the statement.
4. If required, obtain the `ResultSet`, iterate through the results, and close the `ResultSet` regardless of any exception.
5. Run the code for each iteration, or return a single value if no iteration is required.
6. Process the `SQLException` instances.
7. Process any active transaction (decide whether to commit, roll back, or continue).
8. Close the connection (depending on the `DataSource` used, this may actually close the connection or simply return it to the pool).

That is quite a lot of work to do for every statement we execute, especially if you consider that only steps 2 and 4 are different for every statement. Let's see if using Spring JDBC support can save us some steps.

Figure 9-4 illustrates how the JdbcTemplate operates.

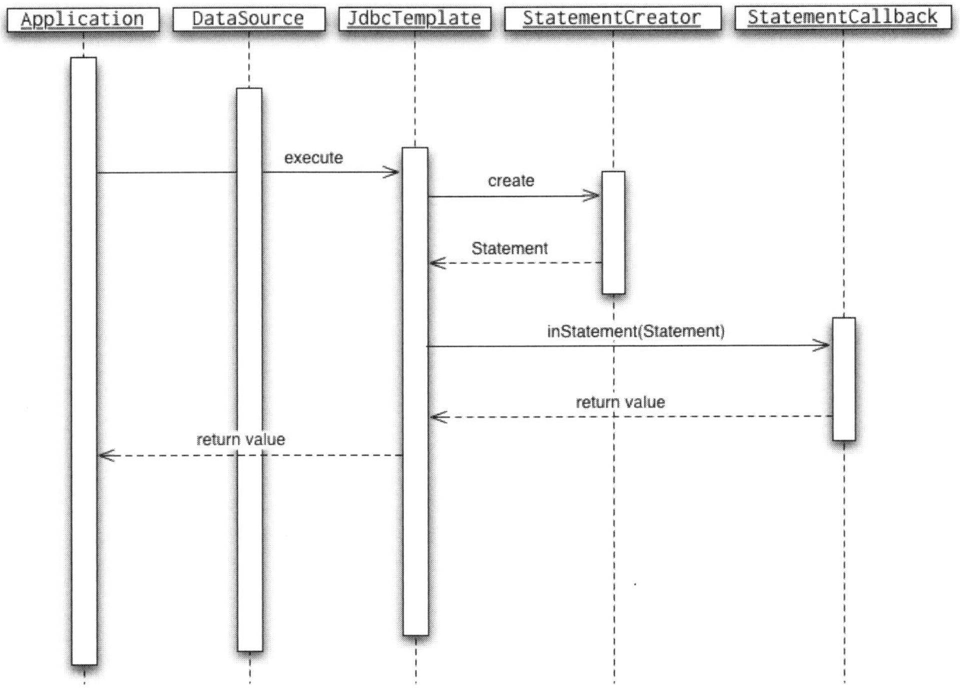

Application DataSource JdbcTemplate StatementCreator StatementCallback
execute
create
Statement
inStatement(Statement)
return value
return value

Figure 9-4. *Sequence diagram of the JdbcTemplate operations*

The JdbcTemplate uses the DataSource to obtain a connection (step 1). Then, it calls the StatementCreator instance to create the statement to be executed (steps 2 and 3). Next, it calls the StatementCallback to perform step 4. Once the StatementCallback returns the result, the JdbcTemplate performs all necessary housekeeping to close the connection (steps 4 through 8). If StatementCreator or the StatementCallback throw exceptions, the JdbcTemplate class catches them and translates them to Spring data access exceptions.

Now that you know how the JdbcTemplate works, we can take a look at the JDBC operations it can perform.

JdbcTemplate.execute

Even though the call method is the easiest one to use, we will begin with the execute method. There are seven overloaded execute methods:

Object execute(ConnectionCallback): This performs the code in ConnectionCallback.doInConnection and returns the value returned from the callback. Use this execute overload to perform data structure modifications using more than one statement. It is a bit too low-level to use for simple queries.

`Object execute(StatementCallback)`: This method performs the callback in `StatementCallback.doInStatement` and returns the value returned from the callback. Use this overload to perform operations on a single statement obtained from the connection. Use this operation in situations similar to `execute(ConnectionCallback)`, but where you need only one statement.

`void execute(String)`: This `execute` overload is the simplest one: it performs a single statement using the `String` argument supplied. You can use this overload whenever you need to execute a single statement and are not interested in the result.

`Object execute(PreparedStatementCreator, PreparedStatementCallback)`: Performs the code in `PreparedStatementCallback.doInPreparedStatement`. The argument in this callback is the `PreparedStatement` returned from the `PreparedStatementCreator.createPreparedStatement(Connection)` method. This overload is best used when you have an implementation of `PreparedStatementCreator` and `PreparedStatementCallback` not as an anonymous implementation but as a reusable class.

`Object execute(String, PreparedStatementCallback)`: This overload is similar to the previous one, except it creates the `PreparedStatement` from the `String` argument. It executes the `PreparedStatementCallback.doInPreparedStatement` when the `PreparedStatement` is created.

`Object execute(CallableStatementCreator, CallableStatementCallback)`: This overload behaves exactly like the `execute(PreparedStatementCreator, PreparedStatementCallback)`; the only difference is that it operates on callable statements. It can therefore execute stored procedures and functions. Again, this overload is commonly used when you have implementations of the `CallableStatementCreator` and `CallableStatementCallback` as reusable classes rather than anonymous implementations.

`Object execute(String, CallableStatementCallback3)`: The final overload of the `execute` method creates the `CallableStatement` from the first `String` argument, and once created, it invokes the `CallableStatementCallback` to process the result.

Now that you know all the overloaded variants of the `execute` method, it is time to look at how you can use it in practice. Before showing you the code, we must make a slight modification to the Spring context file: we must add the definition for the `jdbcTemplate` and `jdbcTemplateDemo` beans. Listing 9-10 shows the new context file.

Listing 9-10. *New Beans in the Spring Context File*

```
<?xml version="1.0" encoding="UTF-8"?>
<beans xmlns="...">

    <bean id="dataSource"
        class="org.apache.commons.dbcp.BasicDataSource" destroy-method="close">
        <property name="driverClassName" value="oracle.jdbc.driver.OracleDriver"/>
        <property name="url"
              value="jdbc:oracle:thin:@oracle.devcake.co.uk:1521:INTL"/>
        <property name="username" value="PROSPRING"/>
        <property name="password" value="x******6"/>
    </bean>

    <bean id="jdbcTemplate" class="org.springframework.jdbc.core.JdbcTemplate">
        <property name="dataSource" ref="dataSource"/>
    </bean>
```

```
    <bean id="jdbcTemplateDemo"
         class="com.apress.prospring2.ch09.spring.JdbcTemplateDemo">
        <property name="jdbcTemplate" ref="jdbcTemplate"/>
    </bean>

</beans>
```

The `jdbcTemplate` is the most important bean; we inject it into our `JdbcTemplateDemo`. We could just as easily have created an instance of `JdbcTemplate` in `JdbcTemplateDemo`; all we would need to do so is the `DataSource` object (in fact, this is the approach used in the `JdbcDaoSupport`). Nevertheless, our code takes the injected `JdbcTemplate` instance and demonstrates the usage of all `execute` overloads (see Listing 9-11).

Listing 9-11. *Usage of the JdbcTemplate.execute Method*

```
class JdbcTemplateDemo {
    private JdbcTemplate jdbcTemplate;

    private static class MyPreparedStatementCreator
        implements PreparedStatementCreator {

        public PreparedStatement createPreparedStatement(Connection connection)
            throws SQLException {
            PreparedStatement ps = connection.prepareStatement(
                    "select * from t_x where id=?");
            ps.setLong(1, 1L);
            return ps;
        }
    }

    private static class MyPreparedStatementCallback
        implements PreparedStatementCallback {

        public Object doInPreparedStatement(PreparedStatement preparedStatement)
            throws SQLException, DataAccessException {
            ResultSet rs = preparedStatement.executeQuery();
            List<Long> ids = new LinkedList<Long>();
            while (rs.next()) {
                ids.add(rs.getLong(1));
            }
            rs.close();
            return ids;
        }
    }

    private static class MyCallableStatementCreator
        implements CallableStatementCreator {

        public CallableStatement createCallableStatement(Connection connection)
            throws SQLException {
            CallableStatement cs = connection.prepareCall("{? = call f_calculate}");
            cs.registerOutParameter(1, Types.INTEGER);
            return cs;
        }
    }
```

```
private static class MyCallableStatementCallback
    implements CallableStatementCallback {

    public Object doInCallableStatement(CallableStatement callableStatement)
        throws SQLException, DataAccessException {
        callableStatement.execute();
        return callableStatement.getLong(1);
    }
}

private void run() {
    this.jdbcTemplate.execute(new ConnectionCallback() {
        public Object doInConnection(Connection connection) throws SQLException,
            DataAccessException {
            PreparedStatement createTable = connection.prepareStatement(
                  "create table t_x (id number(19,0) not null, " +
                  "constraint pk_x primary key(id))");
            createTable.execute();
            return null;
        }
    });

    this.jdbcTemplate.execute(new StatementCallback() {
        public Object doInStatement(Statement statement)
             throws SQLException, DataAccessException {
            return statement.execute("insert into t_x (id) values (1)");
        }
    });

    this.jdbcTemplate.execute("insert into t_x (id) values (2)");

    List<Long> ids;
    ids = (List<Long>) this.jdbcTemplate.execute(
        new MyPreparedStatementCreator(),
        new MyPreparedStatementCallback());
    System.out.println(ids);

    ids = (List<Long>) this.jdbcTemplate.execute("select id from t_x",
        new MyPreparedStatementCallback());
    System.out.println(ids);

    System.out.println(this.jdbcTemplate.execute(
       new MyCallableStatementCreator(),
       new MyCallableStatementCallback()));

    this.jdbcTemplate.execute("{call p_actstartled(42)}",
        new CallableStatementCallback() {
             public Object doInCallableStatement(
                  CallableStatement callableStatement)
                  throws SQLException, DataAccessException {
                 callableStatement.execute();
                 return null;
             }
        });

    this.jdbcTemplate.execute("drop table t_x");
}
```

```
    public static void main(String[] args) {
        ApplicationContext ac = new ClassPathXmlApplicationContext(
            "jdbcdao-context.xml",
            JdbcTemplateDemo.class);
        JdbcTemplateDemo demo = (JdbcTemplateDemo) ac.getBean("jdbcTemplateDemo");
        demo.run();
    }

    public void setJdbcTemplate(JdbcTemplate jdbcTemplate) {
        this.jdbcTemplate = jdbcTemplate;
    }

}
```

The run method demonstrates the use of all variants of the execute method. We begin with execute(ConnectionCallback) and continue with execute(StatementCallback), execute (String), execute(PreparedStatementCreator, PreparedStatementCallback), execute(String, PreparedStatementCallback), execute(CallableStatementCreator, CallableStatementCallback), and finally execute(String, CallableStatementCallback). We have also demonstrated how to use the callbacks and creators as classes rather than anonymous implementations of the interfaces. Running this example produces the expected output:

```
/System/Library/Frameworks/JavaVM.framework/Home/bin/java -Dfile.encoding=UTF-8
[1]
[1, 2]
42

Process finished with exit code 0
```

You can use the various JdbcTemplate.execute methods to perform all data access operations. You can execute both data definition (create and drop tables and views, etc.) and data modification (insert, update, delete, and select) statements. Because the execute methods are so general, you may end up writing code that is unnecessarily difficult. We will now take a look at how you can use other methods of the JdbcTemplate to simplify some of the JDBC code.

JdbcTemplate.query and Friends

Perhaps the most often used method in the JdbcTemplate is query. As you can probably guess from its name, it is used to query for existing data. Just like the execute method, it has a number of overloads, each with different argument types and each returning a different value back to the caller. Three overload groups differ by the returned type. The first group returns void, the second returns Object, and the third returns List. The type of the return value is determined by the actions that the JdbcTemplate performs on the ResultSet. In the case of the first group, which returns void, the callback is of type RowCallbackHandler. The query overloads in the Object-returning group use the ResultSetExtractor. The value returned from the ResultSetExtractor.extractData is the value returned from the query method. Finally, the group of overloads that returns List uses the RowMapper, and the Object instances returned from the RowMapper.mapRow method are added to the List that the query method overloads return to the caller.

The following list shows all the different versions of the query method and their arguments, results, and typical usage:

`Object query(String, ResultSetExtractor)`: Use this method to execute the query from the first argument and extract the results using the `ResultSetExtractor` instance. The `Object` returned from `ResultSetExtractor.extractData(ResultSet)` will be returned from the call. Because the method returns only one object and the SQL statement cannot use parameters, this method is quite suitable for simple queries that return only one value—for example, `select count(*) from table`. Note that you have to call `ResultSet.next()` to get to the first row of the result.

`void query(String, RowCallbackHandler)`: This method executes the statement in the first argument, and once executed, it calls the `RowCallbackHandler.processRow(ResultSet)` method. This method does not return any value, and is therefore suitable for processing that does not return any result. For example, we can use it to process all customers who have not logged in yet and send them e-mail reminders. All the sending code is performed in the callback, and there is no need to return any value to the caller.

`List query(String, RowMapper)`: This is an interesting method for executing simple `select` statements. The `JdbcTemplate` executes the statement from the first argument and then, for each row in the `ResultSet`, calls the `RowMapper.mapRow(ResultSet, int)`. The first argument of the `mapRow` method is the `ResultSet`; the second argument is the row number. The objects you return from the `mapRow` method will be added to the returned `List`. Typically, you would use this method to select all rows from a table and map them to useful objects (`Strings` or full-blown domain objects).

`Object query(PreparedStatementCreator, PreparedStatementSetter, ResultSetExtractor)`: This method performs a similar function to `execute(String, ResultSetExtractor)`; the difference is that this overload of the `query` method gives you full control over the `PreparedStatement`. The `PreparedStatement` is returned from the `PreparedStatementCreator.createPreparedStatement (Connection)` call. You can use as many parameters as necessary, and you can use the `PreparedStatementSetter` implementation to set their values. Finally, the `ResultSetExtractor` extracts the value from the returned `ResultSet` and returns the value to the caller. This is perhaps the most baroque overload of the `query` method; if you end up using it in your code, you should consider creating classes that implement the callback arguments rather than using anonymous implementations.

`Object query(PreparedStatementCreator, ResultSetExtractor)`: This is a slightly simplified version of the previous overload. It does not use the `PreparedStatementSetter`, which means that you either cannot use parameters at all or you have to set them directly in the `PreparedStatementCreator`. Once the statement executes, the `JdbcTemplate` calls the `ResultSetExtractor.extractData` method to process the `ResultSet` and return the value to the caller. Again, we recommend that you do not use anonymous implementations of the interfaces and that the value you return is a single value (`count`, `avg`, etc.).

`Object query(String, PreparedStatementSetter, ResultSetExtractor)`: This prepares the statement and discovers any parameters. The implementation of the `PreparedStatementSetter` sets the values of the parameters. The `JdbcTemplate` then executes the `PreparedStatement` and calls the `ResultSetExtractor` to process the returned `ResultSet` and return the extracted value to the caller.

`Object query(String, Object[], int[], ResultSetExtractor)`: The overload prepares the statement using the first argument, discovers all parameters, and then uses the `Object[]` array to set the values of the parameters. It uses the `int[]` array to determine the SQL data type of the argument. Therefore, the number of elements in the `Object[]` and `int[]` arrays must be the same, and the elements in the `int[]` array must be the constants in the `java.sql.Types` class. The `JdbcTemplate` prepares the statement and sets all parameters before executing the statements and calling the `ResultSetExtractor.extractData(ResultSet)`. Finally, the extracted value is returned to the caller. The only time you would favor this overload over the `Object query(String, Object[], ResultSetExtractor)` is when at least one parameter is null and you need to specify its type.

`Object query(String, Object[], ResultSetExtractor)`: This performs exactly the same code as the previous overload, except it tries to guess the type of the parameter from the class of the element in the `Object[]` array. The only limitation is that no element in the `Object[]` array can be `null`. If that is the case, the `JdbcTemplate` cannot guess the SQL type for it, and you must use the previous overload.

`void query(PreparedStatementCreator, RowCallback)`: This one executes the `PreparedStatement` returned from the `PreparedStatementCreator.createPreparedStatement(Connection)` method and executes the `RowCallback.processRow(ResultSet)`. Just like the previous overload with the `RowCallback` argument, this overload cannot return any value.

`void query(String, PreparedStatementSetter, RowCallback)`: This creates the `PreparedStatement` from the first argument. After the `JdbcTemplate` class creates the statement, it calls the `PreparedStatementSetter.setValues(PreparedStatement)` method to set the values of the parameters. Finally, it executes the statement and calls the `RowCallbackHandler.processRow (ResultSet)`. Just like the other overloads with the `RowCallbackHandler` argument, it doesn't return any value to the caller.

`void query(String, Object[], int[], RowCallback)`: This overload prepares the statement using the first argument and, for each element in the `Object[]` array, sets the parameter to the value of the element. The type of the parameter must be specified in the `int[]` array. Therefore, the lengths of the two arrays must be equal. Once the statement is ready, the `JdbcTemplate` executes it and calls the `RowCallback.processRow`. Again, no result is returned to the caller.

`void query(String, Object[], RowCallback)`: Just like the previous overload, the `JdbcTemplate` creates the `PreparedStatement` and sets the parameters to the values of elements in the `Object[]` array. Because the `JdbcTemplate` will try to determine the type of the element by looking at its class, none of the elements can be null. The `JdbcTemplate` then executes the statement and calls `RowCallback.processRow`.

`List query(PreparedStatementCreator, RowMapper)`: This overload allows the `JdbcTemplate` to take the `PreparedStatement` returned from the `PreparedStatementCreator`, execute it, and iterate over every row in the `ResultSet`. For each row, it calls the `RowMapper.mapRow(ResultSet, int)` method. The first argument is the `ResultSet` and its position points to the `i` row. The `Objects` returned from `RowMapper.mapRow` will be added to the `List` that the method returns to the caller.

`List query(String, PreparedStatementSetter, RowMapper)`: This overload of the `query` method creates the `PreparedStatement` using the SQL statement in the first argument. The `JdbcTemplate` class then calls the `PreparedStatementSetter.setValues(PreparedStatement)` to set the parameter values in the statement. Finally, it executes the `PreparedStatement`, and for each row in the `ResultSet`, it increments the counter and calls the `RowMapper.mapRow(ResultSet, int)`. The values returned from the `RowMapper.mapRow` method are added to the `List`.

`List query(String, Object[], int[], RowMapper)`: This version of the `query` method creates the `PreparedStatement` using the SQL statement in the first argument and then sets the parameter values to the values in the `Object[]` array. It uses the SQL types specified in the `int[]` array. As expected, it calls the `RowMapper.mapRow` method for every row in the `ResultSet`.

`List query(String, Object, RowMapper)`: The last overload of the `query` method works just like the previous overload, except that it determines the types of the parameters from the class of the elements in the `Object[]` array. It then executes the `PreparedStatement` and calls the `RowMapper.mapRow` method for every row in the `ResultSet`.

By now you may have noticed that the overloads of the `query` method fall into two main categories. The first category represents simple `String` values and query arguments as `Object` instances and their types as `int` values (values in the `javax.sql.Types` class). The second category represents callback interfaces; each specific interface creates the `PreparedStatement` instances (using the SQL statement); another callback sets the arguments in the `PreparedStatement` instances; and finally, another callback runs after the `PreparedStatement` has been executed. Because these callback interfaces are used in other methods of the `JdbcTemplate` class, we will cover them in more detail. Table 9-1 lists callback interfaces you can implement to handle the returned rows.

Table 9-1. *JdbcTemplate Row-Handling Callback Interfaces*

Interface	Usage
`ResultSetExtractor`	This interface extracts a single `Object` from the open `ResultSet` passed to its `extractData` method. To get the first result, call the passed `ResultSet`'s `next` method.
`RowCallbackHandler`	The `JdbcTemplate` calls this interface's `processRow(ResultSet)` method for every row in the `ResultSet`; therefore, the code in `processRow` should not call the `ResultSet.next` method to advance to the next row.
`RowMapper`	This callback interface is used to map every row in the `ResultSet` to an `Object`. Again, the `JdbcTemplate` takes care of iterating through the `ResultSet`; the implementation should not call `ResultSet.next`. Typically, the `Object` instances returned from this method will be returned as members of a `List` from the `JdbcTemplate` method that takes the `RowMapper` as its argument.

If you need fine control over the statements that the `JdbcTemplate` executes, you can implement and use one of the statement callback interfaces listed in Table 9-2.

Table 9-2. *JdbcTemplate Statement Callback Interfaces*

Interface	Usage
`PreparedStatementCreator`	The implementations of this interface return a `PreparedStatement` from its `createPreparedStatement(Connection)` method.
`PreparedStatementSetter`	This interface's `setValues(PreparedStatement)` method is used to set the parameters in a `PreparedStatement` (either created from a `String` or returned from `PreparedStatementCreator.createPreparedStatement`).

We believe there is no need to show code for every overload of the `query` method, but we will show you a very complicated example with `PreparedStatementCreator`, `PreparedStatementSetter`, and `ResultSetExtractor`. In this example, a query processes all rows from the `t_customer` table using a SQL `String` and a `RowCallbackHandler` (see Listing 9-12).

Listing 9-12. *Examples of the JdbcTemplate.query Method*

```
class JdbcTemplateDemo {
    private JdbcTemplate jdbcTemplate;

    public void runQuery() {
        this.jdbcTemplate.query(
           "select first_name, last_name, last_login from t_customer " +
           "where last_login is null",
                new RowCallbackHandler() {
                    public void processRow(ResultSet resultSet)
                        throws SQLException {
                        while (resultSet.next()) {
                            // send email to resultSet.getString(1)
                        }
                    }
                });

        String machaceksName = (String) this.jdbcTemplate.query(
            new PreparedStatementCreator() {
                public PreparedStatement createPreparedStatement(
                    Connection connection)
                    throws SQLException {
                    return connection.prepareStatement(
                         "select first_name from t_customer where " +
                        "last_name like ?");
                }
            },
            new PreparedStatementSetter() {
                public void setValues(PreparedStatement preparedStatement)
                    throws SQLException {
                    preparedStatement.setString(1, "Mach%");
                }
            },
           new ResultSetExtractor() {
                public Object extractData(ResultSet resultSet)
                    throws SQLException, DataAccessException {
                    if (resultSet.next()) {
                        return resultSet.getLong(1);
                    }
                    return null;
                }
            });
    }
}
```

Alongside the generic query method, the JdbcTemplate class contains convenience versions of the query method that return specific data types. Each of these methods takes arguments that range from a simple String to the callback interfaces we have described. Table 9-3 shows these convenience methods.

Table 9-3. *Convenience query Methods in the JdbcTemplate Class*

Method	Usage
queryForInt	This method executes the statement (created from String, PreparedStatementCreator, or a PreparedStatementCreator/ PreparedStatementSetter pair). The result is expected to contain only one row and one column, whose value is converted to int and returned.
queryForList	This executes the statement; the execution of the statement can return more than one row, but must return only one column. The elementType argument specifies the type of the elements in the returned List. The values of the elements in the returned List come from the first column in each returned row.
queryForLong	Just like queryForInt, this executes the statement and returns the value in the first row and first column converted to long.
queryForMap	This method executes the statement, which must not return more than one row; it returns a Map containing the column name as the key and the column value as the value.
queryForObject	This one executes a single-row–returning statement and then uses the RowMapper to convert the ResultSet to an Object, which is then returned. If you do not want to use a RowMapper implementation, you can use the Class requiredType argument, as long as the column's requiredType is one that the ResultSet can return (Integer, Long, String, etc.).
queryForRowSet	This method executes the statement that can return any number of rows and returns the result as a RowSet. You are responsible for closing the returned RowSet.

JdbcTemplate.update

Now that we can execute any statement, and insert and query data, we must take a look at how we can modify existing data. To do this, we can use the JdbcTemplate.update(..) method. We use the word update in its broadest meaning—modification or removal. Take a closer look at the overloads of the update method and their arguments:

int update(String): This overload method executes the statement in the String and returns the number of affected rows. This is the simplest version of the update method and should be only used for updates that do not need any parameters.

int update(PreparedStatementCreator): This executes the statement returned from the PreparedStatementCreator and returns the number of rows affected.

int update(PreparedStatementCreator, KeyHolder): This method executes the statement returned from the PreparedStatementCreator and stores the generated keys in the KeyHolder. It assumes that the PreparedStatement returned from the PreparedStatementCreator will be an insert statement and that the insert execution will generate at least one primary key. In fact, most simple inserts will insert only one row with one key. However, the KeyHolder (and its implementation GeneratedKeyHolder) lets you access multiple keys for every inserted row. The method returns the number of rows affected.

int update(String, PreparedStatementSetter): This one executes the statement in the String parameter and uses the PreparedStatementSetter to set the parameters in the SQL statement in the first argument. Again, it returns the number of rows affected.

int update(String, Object[], int[]): This overload executes the statement in the String argument and uses the elements in the Object[] argument to set the parameters in the PreparedStatement. The parameter types are taken from the int[] array, which must contain constants from the java.sql.Types class. This overload is useful if some of the values are null—the PreparedStatement cannot infer the database type from the Java null reference. The return value is the number of affected rows.

int update(String, Object[]): If all parameters in the PreparedStatement constructed from the String argument are not null, we can allow the JDBC code to infer the database types from the Java objects. The return value is the number of affected rows.

Again, as an example, we will show a simple update using just the SQL code as the argument and further example of the update(String, Object[], int[]) method; the usage of the remaining two overloads of the update method should be clear from their descriptions (see Listing 9-13).

Listing 9-13. *JdbcTemplate.update Example*

```
class JdbcTemplateDemo {
    private JdbcTemplate jdbcTemplate;

    private void runUpdate() {
        this.jdbcTemplate.update(
            "update t_customer set first_name = first_name||'x'");

        this.jdbcTemplate.update("update t_customer set first_name=? where id=?",
            new Object[] { "Jenda", 1L },
            new int[] { Types.VARCHAR, Types.INTEGER });
    }
```

You now know how to perform any single operation using the JdbcTemplate. Next, we need to explore how to perform a large number of JDBC operations in the most efficient way. Imagine that we are inserting 10,000 rows into a table. If we were to issue 10,000 separate insert statements, the performance would be atrocious. We need to take advantage of JDBC batching to speed things up!

JdbcTemplate.batchUpdate

Batch updates offer a significant performance improvement over a large number of individual statement executions. A typical scenario for batch update is when you need to insert a large number of rows (to import them from an external source, for example). The JdbcTemplate offers two batchUpdate methods. One takes a simple array of strings as its argument and executes the SQL statements in the array in a batch. This is useful when performing a large number of SQL statements that do not have any parameters. The second overload of the batchUpdate method takes a single String representing the SQL statement and a BatchPreparedStatementSetter. The JdbcTemplate class calls the implementation of BatchPreparedStatementSetter.setValues(PreparedStatement, int) for every statement in the batch. Listing 9-14 shows examples of both batchUpdate calls.

Listing 9-14. *JdbcTemplate.batchUpdate Example*

```
class JdbcTemplateDemo {
    private static Log logger = LogFactory.getLog(JdbcTemplateDemo.class);
    private JdbcTemplate jdbcTemplate;

    private void runBatch() {
        final int count = 2000;
        final List<String> firstNames = new ArrayList<String>(count);
        final List<String> lastNames = new ArrayList<String>(count);
        for (int i = 0; i < count; i++) {
            firstNames.add("First Name " + i);
            lastNames.add("Last Name " + i);
        }
        this.jdbcTemplate.batchUpdate(
            "insert into t_customer (" +
            "id, first_name, last_name, last_login, comments) " +
            "values (?, ?, ?, ?, ?)",
            new BatchPreparedStatementSetter() {
                public void setValues(PreparedStatement ps, int i)
                    throws SQLException {
                    ps.setLong(1, i + 10);
                    ps.setString(2, firstNames.get(i));
                    ps.setString(3, lastNames.get(i));
                    ps.setNull(4, Types.TIMESTAMP);
                    ps.setNull(5, Types.CLOB);
                }

                public int getBatchSize() {
                    return count;
                }
            });

        this.jdbcTemplate.batchUpdate(new String[] {
                "update t_customer set first_name = 'FN#'||id",
                "delete from t_customer where id > 2"
        });
    }
}
```

The example shows how to insert 2,000 rows into the `t_customer` table in a batch (using a single SQL statement with many different values) and how to perform two different SQL statements in a batch. It is important to remember that running statements in a batch is not the same as running them in a transaction; there is no transactional behavior.

RdbmsOperation Subclasses

The RdbmsOperation abstract class is the root of a hierarchy of classes that let you write specialized subclasses to perform specific operations (update, insert, delete, and select). Take a look at Figure 9-5, which shows the class diagram of the RdbmsOperation subclasses.

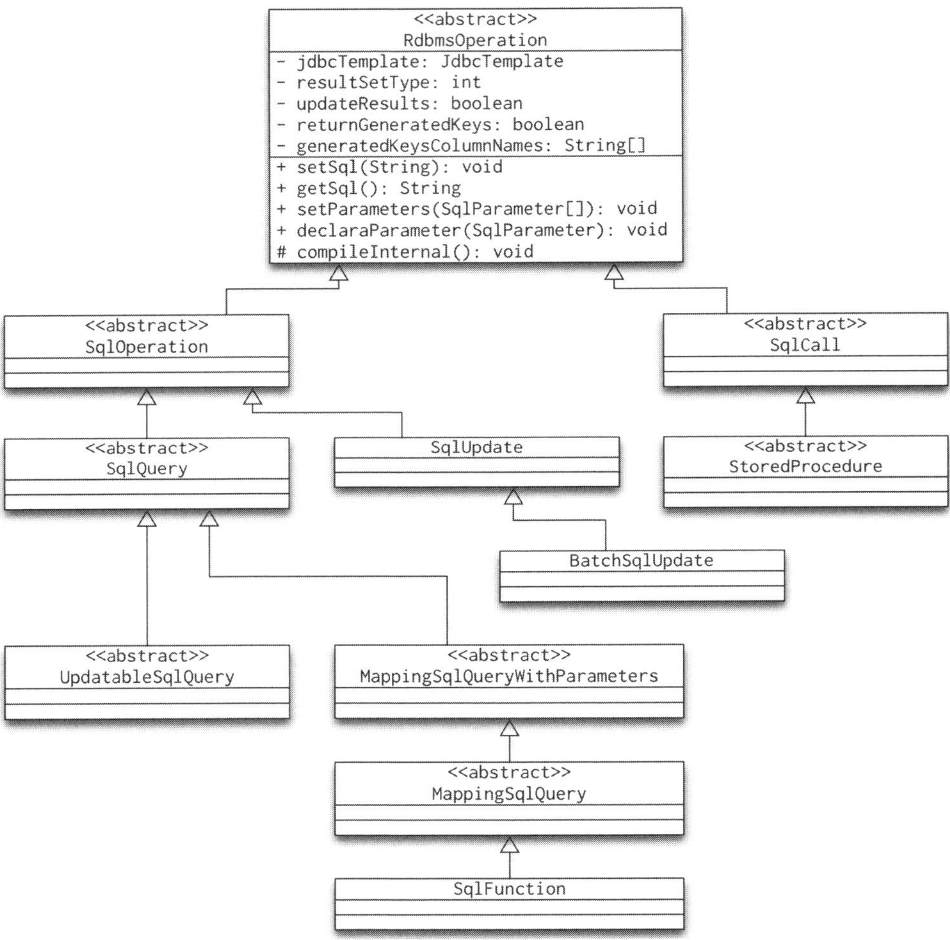

Figure 9-5. *RdbmsOperation class diagram*

Notice that the hierarchy is split into two main paths: the SqlCall hierarchy, which represents statements that do not return results (other than output parameters in a stored procedure) and the SqlOperation hierarchy, which deals with statements that return results. It is also noteworthy that the RdbmsOperation class uses the JdbcTemplate internally.

We will begin our discussion with the simplest RdbmsOperation subclass, SqlUpdate, follow it by discussing subclasses of SqlQuery, and wrapping up with StoredProcedure.

SqlUpdate

As you can probably guess, this class is used to run SQL updates; again, by "update" we mean insert, update, or delete. We will begin by implementing an insert operation using the SqlUpdate. Listing 9-15 shows the Insert class and auxiliary code around it to get the sample application running.

Listing 9-15. *SqlUpdate Subclass*

```
class SqlUpdateDemo {
    private Insert insert;

    private static class Insert extends SqlUpdate {
        private static final String SQL =
                "insert into t_customer (id, first_name, last_name, last_login, " +
                "comments) values (?, ?, ?, ?, ?)";

        Insert(DataSource dataSource) {
            super(dataSource, SQL);    // 2
            declareParameter(new SqlParameter(Types.INTEGER));    // 3.1
            declareParameter(new SqlParameter(Types.VARCHAR));    // 3.2
            declareParameter(new SqlParameter(Types.VARCHAR));    // 3.3
            declareParameter(new SqlParameter(Types.TIMESTAMP)); // 3.4
            declareParameter(new SqlParameter(Types.CLOB));       // 3.5
        }
    }

    SqlUpdateDemo(DataSource dataSource) {
        this.insert = new Insert(this.dataSource);    // 1
    }

    private void runInsert() {
        this.insert.update(new Object[] { 3L, "J", "Machacek", null, null });   // 4
        this.insert.update(new Object[] { 4L, "J", "Doe", null, null });        // 5
    }

    public static void main(String[] args) {
        ApplicationContext ac = new ClassPathXmlApplicationContext(
            "jdbcdao-context.xml",
            SqlUpdateDemo.class);
        SqlUpdateDemo me = new SqlUpdateDemo((DataSource)ac.getBean("dataSource"));
        me.runInsert();
    }

}
```

The code in bold is the most important. The line marked `// 1` constructs a new instance of the Insert class, supplying the DataSource we got from Spring in the main method. In the constructor of the Insert class, we invoke the super constructor and supply the DataSource and SQL statement to be executed. Next, we declare the parameters in the SQL statement on lines `// 3.1` to `// 3.5`. Once we have the Insert instance constructed, we can use its update(Object[]) method on lines `// 4` and `// 5`. Notice that we insert two rows: if we were using two calls using the JdbcTemplate, we would need to create two PreparedStatement instances (either explicitly in PreparedStatementCreator or implicitly by supplying the statement to the JdbcTemplate as a String). In this case, we reuse the same statement, which can be seen in the log output when we run the application:

```
DEBUG [main] RdbmsOperation.checkCompiled(365) | ➥
SQL operation not compiled before execution - invoking compile
DEBUG [main] RdbmsOperation.compile(342) |
RdbmsOperation with SQL [insert into t_customer (id, first_name,➥
last_name, last_login, comments) values (?, ?, ?, ?, ?)] compiled
DEBUG [main] JdbcTemplate.update(765) | Executing prepared SQL update
DEBUG [main] JdbcTemplate.execute(549) | Executing prepared SQL statement➥
[insert into t_customer (id, first_name, last_name, last_login, comments) ➥
values (?, ?, ?, ?, ?)]
DEBUG [main] DataSourceUtils.doGetConnection(112) | ➥
Fetching JDBC Connection from DataSource
DEBUG [main] StatementCreatorUtils.setParameterValueInternal(150) | ➥
Setting SQL statement parameter value: column index 1, parameter value [3],➥
value class [java.lang.Long], SQL type 4
DEBUG [main] StatementCreatorUtils.setParameterValueInternal(150) | ➥
Setting SQL statement parameter value: column index 2, parameter value [J], ➥
value class [java.lang.String], SQL type 12
DEBUG [main] StatementCreatorUtils.setParameterValueInternal(150) | ➥
Setting SQL statement parameter value: column index 3, parameter value [Machacek],➥
value class [java.lang.String], SQL type 12
DEBUG [main] StatementCreatorUtils.setParameterValueInternal(150) | ➥
Setting SQL statement parameter value: column index 4, parameter value [null], ➥
value class [null], SQL type 93
DEBUG [main] StatementCreatorUtils.setParameterValueInternal(150) | ➥
Setting SQL statement parameter value: column index 5, parameter value [null], ➥
value class [null], SQL type 2005
DEBUG [main] JdbcTemplate$2.doInPreparedStatement(775) | SQL update affected 1 rows
DEBUG [main] DataSourceUtils.doReleaseConnection(312) | ➥
Returning JDBC Connection to DataSource
DEBUG [main] JdbcTemplate.update(765) | Executing prepared SQL update
DEBUG [main] JdbcTemplate.execute(549) | Executing prepared SQL statement ➥
[insert into t_customer (id, first_name, last_name, last_login, comments) ➥
values (?, ?, ?, ?, ?)]
DEBUG [main] DataSourceUtils.doGetConnection(112) |➥
Fetching JDBC Connection from DataSource
DEBUG [main] StatementCreatorUtils.setParameterValueInternal(150) |➥
Setting SQL statement parameter value: column index 1, parameter value [4],➥
value class [java.lang.Long], SQL type 4
DEBUG [main] StatementCreatorUtils.setParameterValueInternal(150) |➥
Setting SQL statement parameter value: column index 2, parameter value [J], ➥
value class [java.lang.String], SQL type 12
DEBUG [main] StatementCreatorUtils.setParameterValueInternal(150) |➥
Setting SQL statement parameter value: column index 3, parameter value [Doe], ➥
value class [java.lang.String], SQL type 12
DEBUG [main] StatementCreatorUtils.setParameterValueInternal(150) |➥
Setting SQL statement parameter value: column index 4, parameter value [null], ➥
value class [null], SQL type 93
DEBUG [main] StatementCreatorUtils.setParameterValueInternal(150) |➥
Setting SQL statement parameter value: column index 5, parameter value [null],➥
value class [null], SQL type 2005
DEBUG [main] JdbcTemplate$2.doInPreparedStatement(775) | SQL update affected 1 rows
DEBUG [main] DataSourceUtils.doReleaseConnection(312) |➥
Returning JDBC Connection to DataSource
```

Notice that the statement is compiled (or prepared in the database) only once; the second `update` call reuses the prepared statement. Another detail to notice is that we supplied the values for the `last_login` and `comments` columns as `null`. We could do this because we declared the type of the parameter in the `Insert` constructor.

However, the array of objects supplied to the `update` method is clumsy. The order of elements in the array must match the order of parameters in the statement. Even though you can say that the `Insert` statement is a private inner class that we expect to use only in our data access layer, because the SQL statement is inside the inner class, it would be better to implement another method in the `Insert` class that ensures type safety of the arguments. Listing 9-16 shows how we could do this.

Listing 9-16. *Type-Safe update Method*

```
class SqlUpdateDemo {
...
    private static class Insert extends SqlUpdate {
        private static final String SQL =
              "insert into t_customer (id, first_name, last_name, last_login, " +
              "comments) values (?, ?, ?, ?, ?)";

        Insert(DataSource dataSource) {
            super(dataSource, SQL);
            declareParameter(new SqlParameter(Types.INTEGER));
            declareParameter(new SqlParameter(Types.VARCHAR));
            declareParameter(new SqlParameter(Types.VARCHAR));
            declareParameter(new SqlParameter(Types.TIMESTAMP));
            declareParameter(new SqlParameter(Types.CLOB));
        }

        void insert(long id, String firstName, String lastName, Date lastLogin,
            String comments) {
            update(new Object[] { id, firstName, lastName, lastLogin, comments });
        }
    }
...
    private void runInsert() {
        this.insert.update(new Object[] { 3L, "Jan", "Machacek", null, null });
        this.insert.update(new Object[] { 4L, "Joe", "Doe", null, null });

        this.insert.insert(5L, "Anirvan", "Chakraborty", null, null);
    }
...
}
```

The difference is now obvious: the calling code does not need to worry about the position of the parameters in the SQL statement, and the compiler checks them for types. This compile-time type checking is especially important if you ever need to change the SQL statement and add a parameter. It is far too easy to forget to modify all calls to `update(Object[])`.

In some databases, you can specify that the database should generate the key values on insert. In most applications, you need to know the generated value. To discuss this, we will create our `t_customer` table in MySQL and declare the `id` column as serial. Listing 9-17 shows the SQL code we used in MySQL.

Listing 9-17. *The t_customer Table in MySQL*

```
create table t_customer (
    id int auto_increment not null,
    first_name varchar(50) not null,
    last_name varchar(50) not null,
    last_login timestamp null,
    comments text null,
    constraint pk_customer primary key(id)
);
```

Even though the RdbmsOperation class has two methods with encouraging names—setGeneratedKeyColumnNames and setReturnGeneratedKeys—at the time of writing, the SqlUpdate class does not use them to return the value of the generated keys (we plan to submit a patch to the SqlUpdate class that adds this support). Instead, you must explicitly call the update method that takes the KeyHolder instance as its argument. Listing 9-18 illustrates this.

Listing 9-18. *Using Automatically Generated Keys in the SqlUpdate Subclass*

```
class SqlUpdateDemo {
...
    private static class MySqlInsert extends SqlUpdate {
        private static final String SQL =
              "insert into t_customer (first_name, last_name, last_login, " +
              "comments) values (?, ?, ?, ?)";

        MySqlInsert(DataSource dataSource) {
            super(dataSource, SQL);
            declareParameter(new SqlParameter(Types.VARCHAR));
            declareParameter(new SqlParameter(Types.VARCHAR));
            declareParameter(new SqlParameter(Types.TIMESTAMP));
            declareParameter(new SqlParameter(Types.CLOB));
            setGeneratedKeysColumnNames(new String[] { "id" });
            setReturnGeneratedKeys(true);
        }

        long insert(String firstName, String lastName, Date lastLogin,
            String comments) {
            List<String> generatedKeys = new ArrayList<String>(1);    // 1
            generatedKeys.add("id");
            KeyHolder kh = new GeneratedKeyHolder(generatedKeys);    // 2
            update(new Object[] { firstName, lastName, lastLogin, comments },
                  kh);    // 3
            return (Long) kh.getKey();    // 4
        }
    }
...
}
```

Notice the name of the class: MySqlInsert. This name implies that we have switched from Oracle to MySQL—and we have, because Oracle does not support automatically generated keys. We could have used PostgreSQL, which supports automatically generated keys at the database level (using the serial data type and implicit sequences), but, at the time of this writing, its JDBC driver does not return the keys; instead, it fails with a "not implemented yet" exception.

Leaving the various database quirks aside, let's look at the code. On line // 1, we create a List that will hold the column names of the generated keys; we use this List on line // 2 where we create an instance of the GeneratedKeyHolder class. Line // 3 calls the update method with the values of the columns to be inserted and passes in the `KeyHolder` implementation. Finally, on line `// 4`, we use the convenience method `getKey` of the `GeneratedKeyHolder` class. Remember that the database can theoretically generate multiple keys for multiple insert operations, in which case the call to `getKey` would throw an exception. If, however, we have inserted only one row with only one generated key, we can get it using the `getKey` method.

Note The `KeyHolder`'s keys are modified during the call to `update`. Therefore, the `List` that you supply to the `GeneratedKeyHolder` constructor must be modifiable. This is why you cannot use the convenient `GeneratedKeyHolder(Arrays.asList("id"))`.

Apart from the anonymous position-based parameters, we can use named JDBC parameters. When you use named parameters in the SQL statement, you can then use the `update` method that takes a `Map` as its first argument and supply the values as `"parameter name" => parameter value`. Listing 9-19 shows code that demonstrates this.

Listing 9-19. *Using Named Parameters in SqlUpdate*

```
class SqlUpdateDemo {
...
    private static class NamedInsert extends SqlUpdate {
        private static final String SQL =
            "insert into t_customer (id, first_name, last_name, last_login, " +
           "comments) values (:id, :firstName, :lastName, :lastLogin, :comments)";

        NamedInsert(DataSource dataSource) {
            super(dataSource, SQL);
            declareParameter(new SqlParameter(Types.INTEGER));
            declareParameter(new SqlParameter(Types.VARCHAR));
            declareParameter(new SqlParameter(Types.VARCHAR));
            declareParameter(new SqlParameter(Types.TIMESTAMP));
            declareParameter(new SqlParameter(Types.CLOB));
        }
    }
...
    private void runInsert() {
        Map<String, Object> parameterMap = new HashMap<String, Object>();
        parameterMap.put("id", 6L);
        parameterMap.put("firstName", "John");
        parameterMap.put("lastName", "Appleseed");
        parameterMap.put("lastLogin", null);
        parameterMap.put("comments", null);
        this.namedInsert.updateByNamedParam(parameterMap);
    }
...
}
```

This approach is safer than using an array of objects and relying on the position of elements in the array, even though the calling code is more complicated. If you do not want to write your own method to handle the updates in your subclasses of `SqlUpdate`, we recommend that you use named parameters instead of position parameters.

Finally, the `SqlUpdate` class provides convenience overloads of the `update` method that take only a few `int`, `long`, or `String` parameters. These methods are particularly elegant for deletes (see Listing 9-20).

Listing 9-20. *A Deletion Operation Demonstration*

```
class SqlUpdateDemo {
...
    private static class DeleteWhereIdGreater extends SqlUpdate {
        private static final String SQL = "delete from t_customer where id > ?";

        DeleteWhereIdGreater(DataSource dataSource) {
            super(dataSource, SQL);
            declareParameter(new SqlParameter(Types.INTEGER));
        }
    }
...
    private void runInsert() {
        this.deleteWhereIdGreater.update(1L);
    }
...
}
```

The DeleteWhereIdGreater performs a simple delete statement and is self-explanatory. The new bit of code is in bold and shows that we can use one of the convenience update methods, in this case one that takes one argument of type long.

It is good safe coding practice to include a check for the maximum number of affected rows. As an example, imagine an update statement that should modify only one row. However, you have made a mistake in the SQL and ended up modifying the entire table. It would be useful to catch this situation, and thus be able to take recovery steps immediately, rather than waiting until someone notices that all the rows have been modified. To perform this check, call the setMaxRowsAffected(int) method, supplying the maximum number of rows that should be affected by the statement execution. If the number of affected rows is greater than the maximum, the SqlUpdate call will throw JdbcUpdateAffectedIncorrectNumberOfRowsException. If you are running the JDBC code in a transaction, this check may just save your neck!

BatchSqlUpdate

As the name implies, this subclass of SqlUpdate is used to perform batch queries. This class takes care of automatically splitting the batch into chunks that the database (and its JDBC driver) can handle. Using batch operation implies that there will be many updates, and this means that you cannot use LOB columns. Using the BatchSqlUpdate is incredibly simple: call the update method for every row you want to update, supplying the necessary parameters. The BatchSqlUpdate will use the batchSize property (you can set it using setBatchSize(int)) and implicitly call the flush method once the number of updates have reached batchSize. You *can* call flush explicitly to immediately execute the batched up statements during the updates, but you *must* call it after the last call to update. Listing 9-21 demonstrates the use of the BatchSqlUpdate.

Listing 9-21. *Using BatchSqlUpdate*

```
class BatchSqlUpdateDemo {
...
    private static class BatchInsert extends BatchSqlUpdate {
        private static final String SQL =
           "insert into t_customer (id, first_name, last_name, last_login, " +
           "comments) values (?, ?, ?, ?, null)";

        BatchInsert(DataSource dataSource) {
            super(dataSource, SQL);
```

```
            declareParameter(new SqlParameter(Types.INTEGER));
            declareParameter(new SqlParameter(Types.VARCHAR));
            declareParameter(new SqlParameter(Types.VARCHAR));
            declareParameter(new SqlParameter(Types.TIMESTAMP));

            setBatchSize(101);
        }

    }

    private void run() {
        int count = 5000;
        for (int i = 0; i < count; i++) {
            this.batchInsert.update(
                new Object[] { i + 100L, "a" + i, "b" + i, null });
        }
        this.batchInsert.flush();
    }
...
}
```

This example inserts all 5,000 rows in batches of 101 rows each; using this code is an order of magnitude faster than performing 5,000 individual inserts (using either the `JdbcTemplate` or the `SqlUpdate` subclass for the inserts).

Everything we have written about the usage of the `SqlUpdate` holds true for the `BatchSqlUpdate`—the only difference is that the update call does not execute the statement immediately and instead places it in a batch.

SqlCall and StoredProcedure

The next two classes we will look at are used to call database functions and procedures. The limiting factor is that the stored function or procedure must not return a row set. Naturally, a stored procedure can have as many in/out or out parameters as necessary and a stored function can return a scalar value. Under the hood, the `SqlCall` and `StoredProcedure` classes construct `CallableStatement` instances rather than the `PreparedStatement` instances we used in the `SqlUpdate`. Even though the statement in use is different, the semantics and behavior are similar to those of the `SqlUpdate`.

We discuss using stored functions and procedures that return row sets in the section about `SqlFunction`.

Listing 9-22 shows code that calls our `f_calculate` stored function and uses the value in the in parameter in a call to the `p_actstartled` stored procedure.

Listing 9-22. *Calling the Stored Function and Procedure*

```
class SqlCallDemo {
    private static final Log logger = LogFactory.getLog(SqlCallDemo.class);

    private MeaningOfLife meaningOfLife;
    private ActStartled actStartled;

    private static class MeaningOfLife extends StoredProcedure {
        private static final String SQL = "f_calculate";

        MeaningOfLife(DataSource dataSource) {
            super(dataSource, SQL);
            setFunction(true);
```

```
            declareParameter(new SqlOutParameter("n", Types.INTEGER));
        }
    }

    private static class ActStartled extends StoredProcedure {
        private static final String SQL = "p_actstartled";

        ActStartled(DataSource dataSource) {
            super(dataSource, SQL);
            declareParameter(new SqlParameter("n", Types.INTEGER));
        }
    }

    private void run() {
        Map result = this.meaningOfLife.execute(Collections.emptyMap());
        logger.debug(result.values().iterator().next());

        this.actStartled.execute(result);
    }
...
}
```

Notice that we did not have to worry about the CallableStatement syntax for functions ([?=]call function-name). All we had to do was to supply the function name and call setFunction (true). Because of this and because we declared one output parameter, the StoredProcedure code did all the hard work for us and produced statement ? = call f_calculate(). Because the stored functions or procedures can return multiple output parameters, the result of the execute method is a Map, whose keys are the parameter names and whose values are their values.

Also notice that we explicitly named the parameter "n". Without names, we could not obtain the keys for the returned map. Because the f_calculate stored function returns one number that the p_actstartled stored procedure uses, we can name it "n" in both cases. This allows us to take the value returned from this.meaningOfLife.execute(Collections.emptyMap()) and use it in the call to this.actStartled.execute.

Recall from our discussion of the SqlUpdate subclasses that you should not directly call the execute method; doing so ties the calling code too closely to the SQL statement. If the parameter names change, you have to remember to change them whenever you call the execute method. It is better to provide methods with meaningful names that convert any passed arguments to the Map and extract the result (see Listing 9-23).

Listing 9-23. *Removing the Calls to the execute Method*

```
class SqlCallDemo {
    private MeaningOfLife meaningOfLife;
    private ActStartled actStartled;

    private static class MeaningOfLife extends StoredProcedure {
        private static final String SQL = "f_calculate";

        MeaningOfLife(DataSource dataSource) {
            super(dataSource, SQL);
            setFunction(true);
            declareParameter(new SqlOutParameter("n", Types.INTEGER));
        }
```

```
        int executeAndGet() {
            return (Integer)execute(Collections.emptyMap()).
                values().iterator().next();
        }
    }

    private static class ActStartled extends StoredProcedure {
        private static final String SQL = "p_actstartled";

        ActStartled(DataSource dataSource) {
            super(dataSource, SQL);
            declareParameter(new SqlParameter("n", Types.INTEGER));
        }

        void execute(int value) {
            Map<String, Object> parameters = new HashMap<String, Object>(1);
            parameters.put("n", value);
            execute(parameters);
        }
    }

    private void run() {
        ...
        int m = this.meaningOfLife.executeAndGet();
        this.actStartled.execute(m);
    }

}
```

The code in bold shows the improvements we have made, and if you look at the run method, the improvements are clearly visible. We get a single value from a simple call to the MeaningOfLife.executeAndGet method and use it in the ActStartled.execute call.

SqlQuery and Its Subclasses

As you can guess, SqlQuery and its subclasses work with rows returned by running SQL statements. The subclasses differ in the way they handle the rows selected from the database.

The SqlQuery contains a number of overloads of the execute method. Just like with the SqlCall and SqlUpdate classes, we can use the overloads to pass values to the parameters of the SQL statements. We can use position-based parameters and the execute(Object[])–style overloads or use named parameters and the execute(Map)–style overloads. In addition to these generic overloads, the SqlUpdate class defines several convenience overloads of the execute method that take one or two int, long, or String values. Some subclasses further widen the range of available overloads of the execute method.

In addition to the execute methods, which return List objects, the SqlQuery class contains findObject method overloads. These methods return the first element of the List returned from the equivalent call to the execute method. If the returned List contains more than one element, the findObject overloads throw IncorrectResultSizeDataAccessException. If the List returned from the execute method is empty, the findObject overloads return null.

We will begin by discussing the SqlQuery class; Listing 9-24 shows code that selects all rows from the t_customer table.

Listing 9-24. *Using SqlQuery*

```
class SqlQueryDemo {
    private static final Log logger = LogFactory.getLog(SqlQueryDemo.class);

    private static class SelectCustomer extends SqlQuery {
        private static final String SQL = "select * from t_customer";

        SelectCustomer(DataSource ds) {
            super(ds, SQL);
        }

        protected RowMapper newRowMapper(Object[] parameters, Map context) {
           return new ColumnMapRowMapper();
        }
    }

    private SelectCustomer selectCustomer;

    SqlQueryDemo(DataSource dataSource) {
        this.selectCustomer = new SelectCustomer(dataSource);
    }

    public void run() {
        List customers = this.selectCustomer.execute();
        logger.debug(customers);
    }

    public static void main(String[] args) {
        ApplicationContext ac = new ClassPathXmlApplicationContext(
            "jdbcdao-context.xml",
            SqlUpdateDemo.class);
        SqlQueryDemo me = new SqlQueryDemo((DataSource)ac.getBean("dataSource"));
        me.run();
    }

}
```

When we run this application, we will see the following output:

```
DEBUG [main] RdbmsOperation.checkCompiled(365) |➥
SQL operation not compiled before execution - invoking compile
DEBUG [main] RdbmsOperation.compile(342) |➥
RdbmsOperation with SQL [select * from t_customer] compiled
DEBUG [main] JdbcTemplate.query(614) | Executing prepared SQL query
DEBUG [main] JdbcTemplate.execute(549) |➥
Executing prepared SQL statement [select * from t_customer]
DEBUG [main] DataSourceUtils.doGetConnection(112) |➥
Fetching JDBC Connection from DataSource
DEBUG [main] DataSourceUtils.doReleaseConnection(312) |➥
Returning JDBC Connection to DataSource
DEBUG [main] SqlQueryDemo.run(41) |~CC
[{ID=1, FIRST_NAME=FN#1, LAST_NAME=Machacek, LAST_LOGIN=null, COMMENTS=null}]

Process finished with exit code 0
```

You can see that the result is a List of Map objects; the elements in the List are the selected rows, each row being a Map whose key is the column name and whose value is the column value. The strategy that decides which objects will appear as the elements of the returned List is the RowMapper returned from the newRowMapper(Object[], Map) method. In this example, we have used the ColumnMapRowMapper, which returns a Map of columns and their values. Figure 9-6 shows the hierarchy of RowMapper elements.

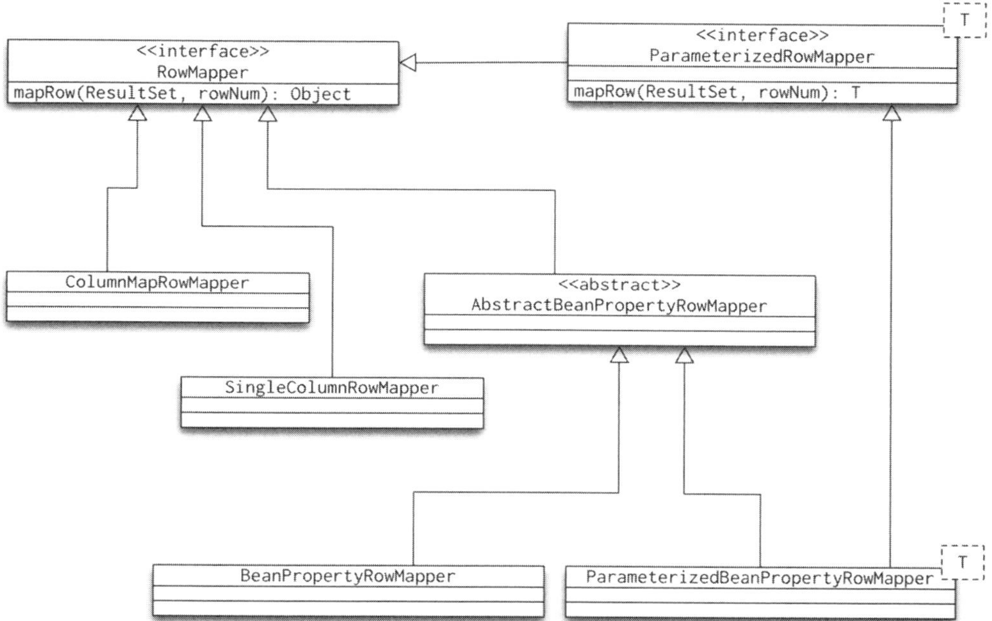

Figure 9-6. *RowMapper class diagram*

The implementations follow three main paths: one that returns a Map and therefore does not need to know anything about the structure of the table, one that returns a value in a single column, and finally one that maps returned rows to objects. The usage of the Map and single-column RowMapper implementations are obvious; the BeanPropertyRowMapper and ParameterizedBeanPropertyRowMapper are more interesting.

Before we can look at the BeanPropertyRowMapper, we need to create the object that we will be selecting from the database. Because the t_customer table is very simple, our domain object will define only the getters and setters for each column. In addition to the getters and setters, we will implement the toString method (see Listing 9-25).

Listing 9-25. *Customer Domain Object*

```
public class Customer {
    private Long id;
    private String firstName;
    private String lastName;
    private Date lastLogin;
    private String comments;
```

```
    public Long getId() {
        return id;
    }

    public void setId(Long id) {
        this.id = id;
    }

    // and other getters and setters

    @Override
    public String toString() {
        final StringBuilder sb = new StringBuilder();
        sb.append("Customer");
        sb.append("{id=").append(id);
        sb.append(", firstName='").append(firstName).append('\'');
        sb.append(", lastName='").append(lastName).append('\'');
        sb.append(", lastLogin=").append(lastLogin);
        sb.append(", comments='").append(comments).append('\'');
        sb.append('}');
        return sb.toString();
    }
}
```

Using this domain object and the BeanPropertyRowMapper, we can use the BeanPropertyRowMapper implementation of the RowMapper interface (see Listing 9-26).

Listing 9-26. *Modified SelectCustomer Class*

```
class SqlQueryDemo {
...
    private static class SelectCustomer extends SqlQuery {
        private static final String SQL = "select * from t_customer";

        SelectCustomer(DataSource ds) {
            super(ds, SQL);
        }

        protected RowMapper newRowMapper(Object[] parameters, Map context) {
            return new BeanPropertyRowMapper(Customer.class);
        }
    }
...
}
```

The output includes a line that clearly shows that the List returned from the execute method contains the Customer objects rather than Maps:

```
DEBUG [main] SqlQueryDemo.run(64) | [Customer{id=1, firstName='FN#1',➥
lastName='Machacek', lastLogin=null, comments='null'}]
```

Notice that we have successfully set the value of the firstName, lastName, and lastLogin properties, even though the column names are first_name, last_name, and last_login. The AbstractBeanPropertyRowMapper uses the BeanWrapperImpl implementation to handle conversions between common naming conventions. If you are using JDK 1.5 or later, you can use the generic ParameterizedRowMapper and its only implementation, ParameterizedBeanPropertyRowMapper, in place of BeanPropertyRowMapper. However, in order to take full advantage of the type inference, you should call ParameterizedBeanPropertyRowMapper.newInstance(<T>) instead of the new ParameterizedBeanPropertyRowMapper<T>().

If the column names cannot be converted to property names using the BeanWrapper strategies, you will have to use MappingSqlQueryWithParameters or its subclasses. Take a look at the code in Listing 9-27, where we implement the MappingSqlQueryWithParameters class and swap the values in the first_name and last_name columns.

Listing 9-27. *MappingSqlQueryWithParameters Usage*

```
class SqlQueryDemo {
...
    private static class MappingSelectCustomer
        extends MappingSqlQueryWithParameters {
        private static final String SQL = "select * from t_customer";

        MappingSelectCustomer(DataSource ds) {
            super(ds, SQL);
        }

        protected Object mapRow(ResultSet rs, int rowNum, Object[] parameters,
            Map context)
            throws SQLException {
            Customer customer = new Customer();
            customer.setId(rs.getLong("id"));
            customer.setFirstName(rs.getString("last_name"));
            customer.setLastName(rs.getString("first_name"));
            customer.setLastLogin(rs.getDate("last_login"));
            if (rs.wasNull()) customer.setLastLogin(null);

            return customer;
        }
    }
...
    public void run() {
        List result;
        ...
        result = this.mappingSelectCustomer.execute();
        logger.debug(result);
    }
...
}
```

When we run the application, the output will show that we have one Customer object, but the value in its firstName property matches the value in the last_name column, and the lastName property matches the value in the first_name column.

```
DEBUG [main] SqlQueryDemo.run(70) | [Customer{id=1, firstName='Machacek',➥
lastName='FN#1', lastLogin=null, comments='null'}]
```

As the name suggests, MappingSqlQueryWithParameters allows you to see the parameters passed to the execute method as well as an arbitrary Map. The implementation of mapRow(ResultSet rs, int n, Object[] parameters, Map context) can examine the parameters or context to change its behavior. As an example, Listing 9-28 shows an implementation that favors the "lastLogin" key in the context map for the value of the lastLogin property.

Listing 9-28. *Use of the Context Map*

```
class SqlMapDemo {
...
    private static class
         MappingSelectCustomer extends MappingSqlQueryWithParameters {
        private static final String SQL = "select * from t_customer";

        MappingSelectCustomer(DataSource ds) {
            super(ds, SQL);
        }

        protected Object mapRow(ResultSet rs, int rowNum, Object[] parameters,
            Map context)
            throws SQLException {
            Customer customer = new Customer();
            customer.setId(rs.getLong("id"));
            customer.setFirstName(rs.getString("last_name"));
            customer.setLastName(rs.getString("first_name"));
            customer.setLastLogin(rs.getDate("last_login"));
            if (rs.wasNull()) customer.setLastLogin(null);
            if (context != null) {
                if (context.containsKey("lastLogin"))
                    customer.setLastLogin((Date)context.get("lastLogin"));
            }
            return customer;
        }
    }
...
    public void run() {
        List result;
        Map context = new HashMap();
        context.put("lastLogin", new Date());
        result = this.mappingSelectCustomer.execute(context);
        logger.debug(result);
    }
...
}
```

This code is clumsy and difficult to maintain. If you find that you need to specify a context parameter to be passed to the `mapRow` method, consider using a custom overload of the `execute` method. Listing 9-29 greatly improves the code in Listing 9-28.

Listing 9-29. *Improved Use of the Context Map*

```
class SqlDemo {
...
    private static class
        MappingSelectCustomer extends MappingSqlQueryWithParameters {
        private static final String SQL = "select * from t_customer";
        private static final String LAST_LOGIN_DATE = "last_login";

        MappingSelectCustomer(DataSource ds) {
            super(ds, SQL);
        }

        protected Object mapRow(ResultSet rs, int rowNum, Object[] parameters,
```

```
            Map context) throws SQLException {
            Customer customer = new Customer();
            customer.setId(rs.getLong("id"));
            customer.setFirstName(rs.getString("last_name"));
            customer.setLastName(rs.getString("first_name"));
            customer.setLastLogin(rs.getDate("last_login"));
            if (rs.wasNull()) customer.setLastLogin(null);
            if (context != null) {
                if (context.containsKey(LAST_LOGIN_DATE))
                   customer.setLastLogin((Date)context.get("lastLogin"));
            }
            return customer;
        }

        public List execute(Date defaultLastLoginDate) {
            Map<String, Object> context = new HashMap<String, Object>();
            context.put(LAST_LOGIN_DATE, defaultLastLoginDate);
            return execute(context);
        }
    }
...
    public void run() {
        List result;
        result = this.mappingSelectCustomer.execute(new Date());
        logger.debug(result);
    }
...
}
```

This code is far better, as there are no maintenance issues, and the type of the `defaultLoginDate` is actually checked at compile time. In most cases, you do not need to examine the values of the parameters passed to the `execute` method, nor do you need to pass any contextual information. If so, it is more convenient to use `MappingSqlQuery`, whose `mapRow` method only includes the `ResultSet` and row number; its signature is only `Object mapRow(ResultSet rs, int rowNum)`.

Finally, we sometimes need to call functions that return a single value—for example, `select sysdate from dual`. The `SqlFunction` class is an ideal candidate to use in this situation; in fact, in most cases, you do not even need to subclass it to call the function. Notice that we use the `select` keyword, indicating that we will receive a standard result set. You cannot use this class to call complex stored functions or procedures. As an example, Listing 9-30 shows how to use the Oracle database to calculate `1 + 1` (which is obscenely ridiculous but very enterprise-like!).

Listing 9-30. *Selecting sysdate*

```
class SqlFunctionDemo {
    private SqlFunction two;
    private static final Log logger = LogFactory.getLog(SqlFunctionDemo.class);

    SqlFunctionDemo(DataSource dataSource) {
        this.two = new SqlFunction(dataSource, "select 1+1 from dual");
    }

    private void run() {
        logger.debug(this.two.runGeneric());
    }
```

```
    public static void main(String[] args) {
        ApplicationContext ac = new ClassPathXmlApplicationContext(
            "jdbcdao-context.xml",
            SqlFunctionDemo.class);
        SqlFunctionDemo me = new SqlFunctionDemo(
            (DataSource)ac.getBean("dataSource"));
        me.run();
    }

}
```

JdbcTemplate or RdbmsOperation?

Implementing the RdbmsOperation subclasses requires a bit more work than using the JdbcTemplate, so what is the benefit of doing this work? Remember the work the database has to do in order to execute a SQL statement: it must parse the statement to verify that it is syntactically correct, create an execution plan, and finally run the plan. The process of creating the execution plan can be difficult, especially if the SQL statement contains a large number of joins and the tables have a lot of indexes. The database examines statistics for each table and index to decide the best strategy to execute the statement. All this can be a lot of work, so most databases cache statements' execution plans.

If you use the JdbcTemplate class, you create a new statement every time you call any of its methods, and only some databases would recognize that the repeated SQL code should be treated as the same statement. The RdbmsOperation subclasses keep their statements between executions, thus allowing the database to reuse the execution plan. Therefore, for high-performance operations, writing the specialized RdbmsOperation subclass is best. Another benefit is that the subclasses are usually very specific, allowing you to pass in parameters in a more elegant way than using an array of Object instances.

Large Binary Objects

LOBs are large blocks of text or binary data; their size can range from just a few kilobytes of text all the way to megabytes of binary data. Each database has its own strategy for storing this data and, unfortunately, its own way of accessing it. Take, for example, the setClob(int, Clob) method in PreparedStatement. If all databases followed the JDBC specification, we could use this without any problems. Unfortunately, Oracle does not work very well with the standard JDBC code. Even if all databases worked smoothly with the standard JDBC implementation, using this method causes some issues with resource management.

Luckily, Spring comes to the rescue with its LobHandler interface and its implementations DefaultLobHandler and OracleLobHandler. Most LOB support code in the JDBC driver is closely tied to the underlying database. This can cause problems when you are using, for example, a connection pool instead of the implementation of the JDBC. The connection pool implements Connection, but not the native Connection the LOB code expects. Therefore, the LobHandler can use a NativeJdbcExtractor interface that can return the native Connection from a number of Connection adapters. Table 9-4 shows the available NativeJdbcExtractor implementations in Spring.

Table 9-4. *NativeJdbcExtractor Implementations*

Extractor	Description
C3P0NativeJdbcExtractor	This is the NativeJdbcExtractor for the C3P0 connection pool. This works with C3P0 version 0.8.5 or later; if you are using an earlier version of C3P0, use SimpleNativeJdbcExtractor.
CommonsDbcpNativeJdbcExtractor	This extracts a native Connection from the Commons DBCP connection pool.
JBossNativeJdbcExtractor	This is the extractor for the JBoss connection pool.
Jdbc4NativeJdbcExtractor	If you are using JDK 1.6 and JDBC 4, you can use this extractor to get the unwrapped connection. The driver must be a JDBC 4 driver; an attempt to run a JDBC 3 driver in JDK 1.6 will fail.
SimpleNativeJdbcExtractor	This extractor attempts to extract the native Connection from the wrapped Connection's metadata. The wrapper wraps only the Connection instances, not the DatabaseMetaData.
WebLogicNativeJdbcExtractor	This extractor handles connection pools in WebLogic 8.1 and above.
WebSphereNativeJdbcExtractor	This is an implementation of the NativeJdbcExtractor that works with connection pools in WebLogic 5.1 and higher.
XAPoolNativeJdbcExtractor	This is the extractor for XAPool connections.

Before we can show the code that actually inserts a LOB, we should show you the configuration of the lobHandler and nativeJdbcExtractor beans. Listing 9-31 shows the necessary details.

Listing 9-31. *LobHandler and NativeJdbcExtractor Implementation Beans*

```
<?xml version="1.0" encoding="UTF-8"?>
<beans xmlns="http://www.springframework.org/schema/beans"
   ...>
...
    <bean id="dataSource" class="org.apache.commons.dbcp.BasicDataSource"
        destroy-method="close">
        <property name="driverClassName" value="oracle.jdbc.driver.OracleDriver"/>
        <property name="url"
             value="jdbc:oracle:thin:@oracle.devcake.co.uk:1521:INTL"/>
        <property name="username" value="PROSPRING"/>
        <property name="password" value="x******6"/>
    </bean>

    <bean id="nativeJdbcExtractor"
        class="org.springframework.jdbc.support.nativejdbc.➥
                    CommonsDbcpNativeJdbcExtractor"/>

    <bean id="lobHandler"
        class="org.springframework.jdbc.support.lob.OracleLobHandler">
        <property name="nativeJdbcExtractor" ref="nativeJdbcExtractor"/>
    </bean>
...
</beans>
```

Here, we have configured the nativeJdbcExtractor bean to be CommonsDbcpNativeJdbcExtractor, because our dataSource bean is the Commons DBCP BasicDataSource. Next, we have defined the lobHandler bean—in our case, the OracleLobHandler—because we are connecting to an Oracle 10g database. Finally, Listing 9-32 shows how we can use the lobHandler inside a JdbcTemplate call to set a CLOB column.

Listing 9-32. *Using the LobHandler to Set the Value of a CLOB Column*

```
class LobDemo {
    private JdbcTemplate jdbcTemplate;
    private LobHandler lobHandler;

    LobDemo(DataSource dataSource, LobHandler lobHandler) {
        this.jdbcTemplate = new JdbcTemplate(dataSource);
        this.lobHandler = lobHandler;
    }

    private void runInTemplate() {
        this.jdbcTemplate.update(
                "insert into t_customer " +
                "(id, first_name, last_name, last_login, comments) " +
                "values (?, ?, ?, ?, ?)",
                new PreparedStatementSetter() {
                    public void setValues(PreparedStatement ps)
                       throws SQLException {
                       ps.setLong(1, 2L);
                       ps.setString(2, "Jan");
                       ps.setString(3, "Machacek");
                       ps.setTimestamp(4,
                           new Timestamp(System.currentTimeMillis()));
                      lobHandler.getLobCreator().setClobAsString(ps, 5,
                         "This is a loooong String!");
                    }
        });
    }

    public static void main(String[] args) {
        ApplicationContext ac = new ClassPathXmlApplicationContext(
             "jdbcdao-context.xml",
            LobDemo.class);
        LobDemo me = new LobDemo((DataSource)ac.getBean("dataSource"),
                                            (LobHandler)ac.getBean("lobHandler"));
        me.runInTemplate();
    }
}
```

The code in bold is all we needed to write! We used the LobCreator returned by the LobHandler.getLobCreator method, and we created a CLOB from a simple String. To select LOB data, we just have to use the LobHandler directly. Listing 9-33 shows you how.

Listing 9-33. *Using the LobHandler to Extract the Value of a CLOB Column*

```
class LobDemo {
...
    private void runInTemplate() {
        this.jdbcTemplate.update(
                "insert into t_customer " +
                "(id, first_name, last_name, last_login, comments) " +
                "values (?, ?, ?, ?, ?)", new PreparedStatementSetter() {
            public void setValues(PreparedStatement ps) throws SQLException {
                ps.setLong(1, 2L);
                ps.setString(2, "Jan");
                ps.setString(3, "Machacek");
                ps.setTimestamp(4, new Timestamp(System.currentTimeMillis()));
                lobHandler.getLobCreator().setClobAsString(ps, 5,
                    "This is a loooong String!");
            }
        });

        logger.debug(this.jdbcTemplate.query(
            "select comments from t_customer where id=?",
            new Object[] { 2L }, new RowMapper() {
            public Object mapRow(ResultSet rs, int rowNum) throws SQLException {
                return lobHandler.getClobAsString(rs, 1);
            }
        }));

    }
...
}
```

Again, not at all difficult, and the result is as expected:

```
DEBUG [main] LobDemo.runInTemplate(44) | [This is a loooong String!]
```

The `LobHandler` interface has many more methods than just `getClobAsString`; their names are intuitive enough to suggest their purposes immediately. You just have to remember to close the stream when using the `InputStream`-returning methods. In the case of our Oracle 10g example, the `InputStream` we got back is `oracle.jdbc.driver.OracleClobInputStream`, and Oracle Technology Network (`www.oracle.com/technology/index.html`) explicitly warns developers to close the stream, particularly if reading large LOBs. In Oracle, such LOBs use up space in the temporary table space, and failing to close the streams could tie up the temporary space longer than necessary.

JdbcDaoSupport

You could use all the JDBC support classes we have introduced in any class in your application. However, it is very likely that you will only use them in your data access tier. That is why Spring comes with the convenience class `JdbcDaoSupport`. If you use this class as the superclass of your data access tier classes, you will be able to access the `JdbcTemplate` and the `DataSource` by calling the `getJdbcTemplate` and `getDataSource` methods. In addition, the `JdbcDaoSupport` implements `InitializingBean`, and even though it implements the `afterPropertiesSet` method as `final`, it provides an `initDao` method that you can override to perform any additional initialization code. Look over the class diagram in Figure 9-7, which shows the code we are going to demonstrate.

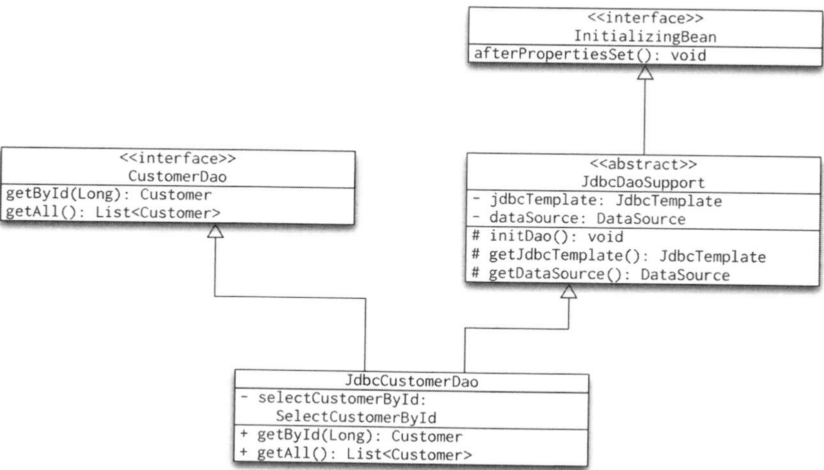

Figure 9-7. *Class diagram of the JdbcDaoSupport example*

The diagram in Figure 9-7 shows that the `CustomerDao` is a simple interface, and we have provided a single implementation, `JdbcCustomerDao`, with `JdbcDaoSupport` as its superclass. Now, we can take advantage of this in the Spring context file (see Listing 9-34).

Listing 9-34. *Spring Context File for the JdbcDaoSupport Example*

```
<?xml version="1.0" encoding="UTF-8"?>
<beans xmlns="http://www.springframework.org/schema/beans"
    ...>

    <bean id="dataSource" class="org.apache.commons.dbcp.BasicDataSource"
        destroy-method="close">
        <property name="driverClassName" value="oracle.jdbc.driver.OracleDriver"/>
        <property name="url"
             value="jdbc:oracle:thin:@oracle.devcake.co.uk:1521:INTL"/>
        <property name="username" value="PROSPRING"/>
        <property name="password" value="x******6"/>
    </bean>

    <bean id="abstractJdbcDao" abstract="true"
        class="org.springframework.jdbc.core.support.JdbcDaoSupport">
        <property name="dataSource" ref="dataSource"/>
    </bean>
    <bean id="customerDao"
        class="com.apress.prospring2.ch09.dataaccess.jdbc.JdbcCustomerDao"
        parent="abstractJdbcDao"/>

</beans>
```

Notice, in particular, the declaration of the `abstractJdbcDao` bean. If all our JDBC DAO classes extend `JdbcDaoSupport`, we can add a new DAO implementation by writing just one line, saving us two lines of XML. While that may not seem like much, if you have a lot of DAO implementations, you will be grateful for any such savings. Listing 9-35 shows the implementation of `JdbcCustomerDao`.

Listing 9-35. *JdbcCustomerDao Implementation*

```
public class JdbcCustomerDao extends JdbcDaoSupport implements CustomerDao {
    private SelectCustomerById selectCustomerById;

    private static class SelectCustomerById extends SqlQuery {

        SelectCustomerById(DataSource ds) {
            super(ds, "select * from t_customer where id=?");
            declareParameter(new SqlParameter(Types.INTEGER));
        }

        protected RowMapper newRowMapper(Object[] parameters, Map context) {
            return ParameterizedBeanPropertyRowMapper.newInstance(Customer.class);
        }
    }

    @Override
    protected void initDao() throws Exception {
        this.selectCustomerById = new SelectCustomerById(getDataSource());
    }

    @SuppressWarnings({"unchecked"})
    public List<Customer> getAll() {
        return getJdbcTemplate().query("select * from t_customer",
            ParameterizedBeanPropertyRowMapper.newInstance(Customer.class));
    }

    public Customer getById(long id) {
        return (Customer)this.selectCustomerById.findObject(id);
    }
}
```

The code here should come as no surprise to you now. The only important point is the `initDao` method. We need it because we must create the instance of the `SelectCustomerById` class after the `JdbcDaoSupport` has initialized itself, but before we use it in the `getById` method. Finally, we can implement the demonstration application in Listing 9-36.

Listing 9-36. *JdbcDaoSupport Demonstration Application*

```
class DataAccessTierDemo {
    private static final Log logger = LogFactory.getLog(DataAccessTierDemo.class);
    private CustomerDao customerDao;

    DataAccessTierDemo(CustomerDao customerDao) {
        this.customerDao = customerDao;
    }

    private void run() {
        logger.debug(this.customerDao.getAll());
        logger.debug(this.customerDao.getById(1L));
    }

    public static void main(String[] args) {
        ApplicationContext ac = new ClassPathXmlApplicationContext(
           "dataaccess-tier-context.xml",
            DataAccessTierDemo.class);
```

```
        DataAccessTierDemo me = new DataAccessTierDemo(
            (CustomerDao)ac.getBean("customerDao"));
        me.run();
    }

}
```

The use of `CustomerDao` is trivial, and indeed, this is the recommended way to design and implement data access code: the data access methods are in an interface, which we later implement; you will see in the next chapter how to use Hibernate object-relational mapping to make data access coding even simpler.

Simple Spring JDBC

You may have noticed that throughout the JDBC support code, the Spring code uses no JDK 1.5 features. This is necessary to make the Spring core run in older JVMs, but if you are using a modern JVM, it would be nice to take away all the type casts that older JDKs require when using nongeneric `List` and `Map` elements.

Spring 2.5 comes with several simplified core classes of the classic JDBC support. The simplification is twofold: through the use of generics, the calling code is simpler and safer, and the simplified classes contain only the most commonly used methods. Figure 9-8 shows the structure of the simplified classes and their relationships with the classic classes.

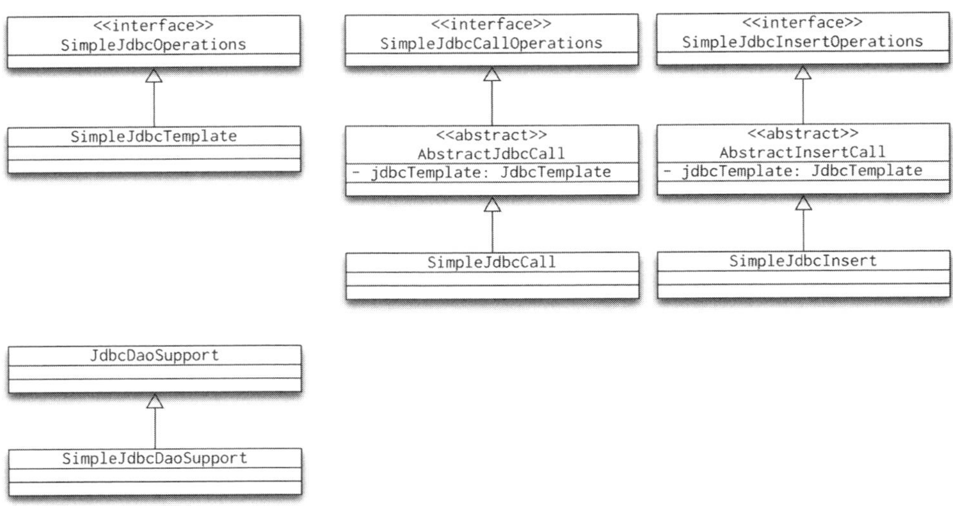

Figure 9-8. *Simple JDBC support class diagram*

We are going to begin our discussion with the `SimpleJdbcTemplate` class, followed by `SimpleJdbcCall` and `SimpleJdbcInsert`. Finally, we will wrap up this section with the `SimpleJdbcDaoSupport` class.

SimpleJdbcTemplate

The SimpleJdbcTemplate class offers the same functionality as the classic JdbcTemplate class, but it gives you support for generics and has a few other simplifications, most notably in the batch update area. You will recognize its methods from the JdbcTemplate:

<T> List<T> query(String sql, ParameterizedRowMapper<T> rm, Map args): This method returns the Object instances (T instances) returned from the ParameterizedRowMapper<T> implementation and sets the named parameters of the SQL statement from the values in the map.

<T> List<T> query(String sql, ParameterizedRowMapper<T> rm, SqlParameterSource args): This returns Object instances (T instances) returned from the ParameterizedRowMapper<T> implementation. It takes the parameters that will be passed to the SQL statement from the SqlParameterSource value.

<T> List<T> query(String sql, ParameterizedRowMapper<T> rm, Object . . . args): The last overload of the query method executes the statement, maps the returned objects, and gives you the chance to set position-based SQL parameters using the values in the args vararg.

In addition, there are the usual queryForObject, queryForInt, queryForLong, and queryForMap methods. All of these use arguments similar to the query arguments to execute the SQL statement and return the selected value.

These methods are undoubtedly similar to the query overloads in the classic JdbcTemplate, but SqlParameterSource is a new class. As you can guess, this class is used to pass parameters to the statement to be executed. There are several implementations of this interface in the default Spring distribution. Figure 9-9 shows the hierarchy of the SqlParameterSource.

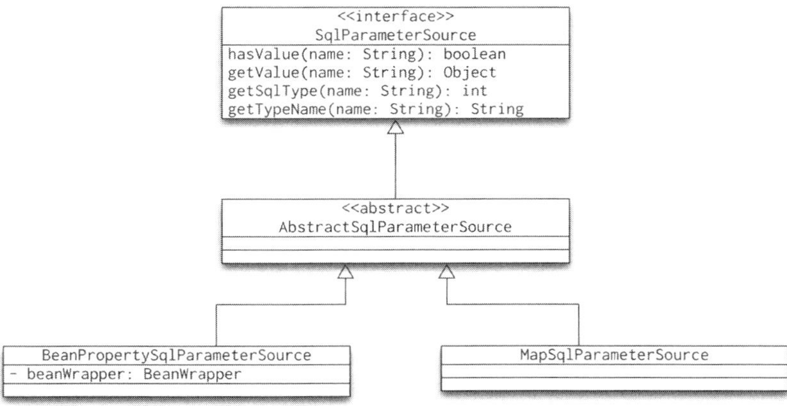

Figure 9-9. *SqlParameterSource class diagram*

The two SqlParameterSource implementations we can use are BeanPropertySqlParameterSource and MapSqlParameterSource. Both allow the calling code to get the named SQL parameters and their values. Take a look at Listing 9-37, which shows how to use BeanPropertySqlParameterSource to insert a new row.

Listing 9-37. *Using BeanPropertySqlParameterSource to Insert Data*

```
class SimpleJdbcTemplateDemo {
    private static final Log logger =
        LogFactory.getLog(SimpleJdbcTemplateDemo.class);
    private SimpleJdbcTemplate jdbcTemplate;

    SimpleJdbcTemplateDemo(DataSource dataSource) {
        this.jdbcTemplate = new SimpleJdbcTemplate(dataSource);
    }

    private void run() {
        Customer customer = new Customer();
        customer.setId(3L);
        customer.setFirstName("FN");
        customer.setLastName("LN");
        customer.setLastLogin(new Date());
        SqlParameterSource parameterSource =
           new BeanPropertySqlParameterSource(customer);
        this.jdbcTemplate.update(
                "insert into t_customer " +
                "(id, first_name, last_name, last_login, comments) " +
               "values (:id, :firstName, :lastName, :lastLogin, :comments)",
                parameterSource);
    }

    public static void main(String[] args) {
        ApplicationContext ac = new ClassPathXmlApplicationContext(
           "jdbcdao-context.xml",
           SimpleJdbcTemplateDemo.class);
        SimpleJdbcTemplateDemo me = new SimpleJdbcTemplateDemo(
            (DataSource)ac.getBean("dataSource"));
        me.run();
    }

}
```

Here, you can see that we have used the `:id`, `:firstName`, `:lastName`, `:lastLogin`, and `:comments` named parameters, and these names match the properties of the `Customer` object we are inserting. Using named parameters is particularly useful in batch updates. The code needed to insert a large number of objects becomes a lot easier, as you can see in Listing 9-38.

Listing 9-38. *Batch Inserts Using SimpleJdbcTemplate*

```
class SimpleJdbcTemplateDemo {
...
    private void run() {
        ...
        int count = 1000;
        SqlParameterSource[] source = new SqlParameterSource[count];
        for (int i = 0 ; i < count; i++) {
            Customer c = new Customer();
            c.setId(i + 100L);
            c.setFirstName("FN #" + i);
            c.setLastName("LN #" + i);
            c.setLastLogin(new Date());
            source[i] = new BeanPropertySqlParameterSource(c);
```

```
        }
        this.jdbcTemplate.batchUpdate(
                "insert into t_customer " +
               "(id, first_name, last_name, last_login, comments) " +
               "values (:id, :firstName, :lastName, :lastLogin, :comments)",
               source);
    }
...
}
```

The call to batchUpdate is a simple affair, where we only supply the SqlParameterSource array. This array contains elements that contain the values to be set in the SQL statement we will execute in the batch. As with the insert operation, we use parameter names that match the property names of the Customer objects.

Finally, we will discuss the querying methods in SimpleJdbcTemplate. Unlike the classic overloads of the query method, there are only three, which focus on the most common scenarios of querying data. Listing 9-39 shows how to select all rows from the t_customer table and return List of Customer objects. We will use the ParameterizedBeanPropertyRowMapper<T> to map the rows to Customer objects.

Listing 9-39. *Using SimpleJdbcTemplate to Query Data*

```
class SimpleJdbcTemplateDemo {
...
    private void run() {
        List<Customer> customers = this.jdbcTemplate.query(
                "select * from t_customer",
                ParameterizedBeanPropertyRowMapper.newInstance(Customer.class));
        logger.debug(customers);
        ...
    }
...
}
```

Here, you can see a very simple way of selecting data from a database and dealing with the mapping between the columns and returned Object instances.

SimpleJdbcCall

The SimpleJdbcCall class is an impressive simplification. When using it, you chain the calls to the original instance, further specifying the SQL call details with every method call (this approach is very similar to JMocks's). Take a look at Listing 9-40 for an example of this class.

Listing 9-40. *Using SimpleJdbcCall*

```
class SimpleJdbcTemplateDemo {
...
    private void runCall() {
        BigDecimal meaningOfLife = new SimpleJdbcCall(this.dataSource).
                withFunctionName("f_calculate").
                withReturnValue().
                executeObject(BigDecimal.class, Collections.emptyMap());
        logger.debug(meaningOfLife);
    }
...
}
```

The code in bold reads almost like a story: we take the original SimpleJdbcCall instance, call withFunctionName(String) to set the name of the function to call, and then call withReturnValue() to indicate that it is a stored function, not a stored procedure. Finally, we call executeObject(Class<T>, Map) to indicate that we will receive a single result of type T. Therefore, there is no need to even cast the returned value. Table 9-5 summarizes the methods available in the SimpleJdbcCall.

Table 9-5. *SimpleJdbcCall Methods*

Method	Description
withProcedureName(String procedureName)	Sets the function name (internally, sets function = true).
withFunctionName(String functionName)	Sets the function name (internally, sets function = false).
withSchemaName(String schemaName)	Sets the name of the schema where the callable objects are.
withCatalogName(String catalogName)	Sets the name of the catalog where the callable objects are.
withReturnValue()	Indicates that the callable object will return a value.
declareParameters (SqlParameter... sqlParameters)	Declares all of the parameters in the object to be called.
useInParameterNames (String... inParameterNames)	Sets the names of the in parameters.
returningResultSet (String parameterName, ParameterizedRowMapper rowMapper)	Indicates that the callable object will return a result set. The SimpleJdbcCall class will use the rowMapper to map the rows in the result set.
withoutProcedureColumnMetaDataAccess()	Turns off automatic discovery of parameters (this is particularly useful for out parameters).

Notice in particular the last method, withoutProcedureColumnMetaDataAccess(). We begin the discussion by looking at the source code for the stored procedure that returns refcursor for all rows in the t_customer table (see Listing 9-41).

Listing 9-41. *Stored Procedure That Returns All Rows in t_customer*

```
create or replace package simplejdbc as
    type rc_customer_type is ref cursor return t_customer%rowtype;
    procedure p_find_customer(rc_customer_type out rc_customer_type);
end;
/

create or replace package body simplejdbc as
    procedure p_find_customer (rc_customer_type out rc_customer_type) is
    begin
        open rc_customer_type for select * from t_customer;
    end;
end;
/
```

Next, we use this stored procedure in Listing 9-42, which shows how to deal with a procedure that returns a refcursor as one of its out parameters.

Listing 9-42. *Using the Stored Procedure in SimpleJdbcCall*

```
class SimpleJdbcTemplateDemo {
...
    private void runCall() {
        ...
        Map<String,Object> result = new SimpleJdbcCall(this.dataSource).
                withProcedureName("simplejdbc.p_find_customer").
                withoutProcedureColumnMetaDataAccess().
                returningResultSet("rc_customer_type",
                    ParameterizedBeanPropertyRowMapper.newInstance(Customer.class)).
                execute(new MapSqlParameterSource("rc_customer_type", null));
        logger.debug(result);

    }
...
}
```

We had to use the `withoutProcedureColumnMetaDataAccess()` call because we declared the `rc_customer_type` parameter of the stored procedure as `out`. Therefore, Spring cannot discover that the parameter exists at all. When we call this method, Spring will take our word for the existence of the call parameters. The result of running this code is exactly what we expect: a `Map`, which contains an instance of the mapped `Customer` object under the `rc_customer_type` key:

```
DEBUG [main] SimpleJdbcTemplateDemo.runCall(80) | {rc_customer_type=➥
[Customer{id=1, firstName='FN#1', lastName='Machacek', ➥
lastLogin=null, comments='null'}]}
```

SimpleJdbcInsert

Finally, let's look at a simple way of inserting data. This class offers similar functionality to the `SimpleJdbcCall`. Some of its methods modify the instance they are invoked on and return `this`, allowing you to chain the calls. To get us started, look at Listing 9-43, which shows how to insert a row into the `t_customer` table.

Listing 9-43. *Using SimpleJdbcInsert to Insert a Row*

```
class SimpleJdbcDemo {
...
    private void runInsert() {
        Customer customer = new Customer();
        customer.setId(3L);
        customer.setFirstName("FN");
        customer.setLastName("LN");
        customer.setLastLogin(new Date());
        customer.setComments("This is a long CLOB string. Mu-har-har!");

        SimpleJdbcInsert insert = new SimpleJdbcInsert(this.dataSource);
        insert.
                withTableName("t_customer").
                usingColumns(
                    "id", "first_name", "last_name", "last_login", "comments").
                execute(new BeanPropertySqlParameterSource(customer));
    }
...
}
```

The code in bold shows the critical calls: `withTableName(String)` sets the table name we will be inserting into; `usingColumns(String . . .)` sets the columns we will insert; and finally, the call to `execute` performs the insert using the values obtained from properties of the customer object. Notice that the `SimpleJdbcInsert` also inserted values into the CLOB column `comments`!

The `SimpleJdbcInsert` also offers an elegant way to retrieve the values of the generated keys. To demonstrate this, we must use our MySQL database and the code in Listing 9-44.

Listing 9-44. *Inserting and Retrieving the Value of a Generated Key*

```
class SimpleJdbcDemo {
...
    private void runInsert() {
        Customer customer = new Customer();
        customer.setId(3L);
        customer.setFirstName("FN");
        customer.setLastName("LN");
        customer.setLastLogin(new Date());
        customer.setComments("This is a long CLOB string. Mu-har-har!");

        long id = new SimpleJdbcInsert(this.mysqlDataSource).
                withTableName("t_customer").
                usingColumns("first_name", "last_name", "last_login", "comments").
                usingGeneratedKeyColumns("id").
                executeAndReturnKey(new BeanPropertySqlParameterSource(customer)).
                    longValue();
        logger.debug(id);
    }
...
}
```

The lines in bold show that we declare the column `id` as automatically generated, and we call the `executeAndReturnKey` method to perform the update. This method returns a `Number` that indicates the value of the generated key. We can use this method because the statement generates only one key. If your insert operation generates more than one key, you must use the `executeAndReturnKeyHolder` method and use the returned `KeyHolder` instance to query the value of all generated keys.

SimpleJdbcDaoSupport

The final class to discuss in this section (and chapter) is `SimpleJdbcDaoSupport`. Just like `JdbcDaoSupport`, you can use it as a convenience superclass of your JDBC DAO implementations. In addition to `JdbcDaoSupport`, it offers a single method, `getSimpleJdbcTemplate`. However, because `SimpleJdbcTemplate` is easy to use, your DAO implementations will rarely need to use the classic `JdbcTemplate` returned from `getJdbcTemplate`. Listing 9-45 shows the `SimpleJdbcCustomerDao` implementation of the `CustomerDao` interface using `SimpleJdbcDaoSupport`.

Listing 9-45. *SimpleJdbcDaoSupport Implementation of the CustomerDao Interface*

```
public class SimpleJdbcCustomerDao extends SimpleJdbcDaoSupport
    implements CustomerDao {

    public List<Customer> getAll() {
        return getSimpleJdbcTemplate().query("select * from t_customer",
                ParameterizedBeanPropertyRowMapper.newInstance(Customer.class));
    }
```

```
    public Customer getById(long id) {
        return getSimpleJdbcTemplate().queryForObject(
                "select * from t_customer where id=?",
                Customer.class,
                id);
    }
}
```

The implementation is trivial and lets the power of Spring JDBC and the new Simple JDBC classes really stand out, especially if you consider just how much code you would have to write if you wanted to implement the same functionality using plain JDBC.

Summary

In this chapter, we have discussed Spring's JDBC support. Spring 2.5 builds on the strong foundation of Spring 1.x and brings further simplification while keeping the complexity of the calling code minimal.

The new Simple JDBC classes offer an excellent way to implement very low-level data access code without having to spend too much time writing tedious JDBC code. This allows you to use the most efficient data access method for critical parts of your application.

In our experience, the best combination for the data access tier code in large applications is to use object-relational mapping code for most of the data access and Spring JDBC for specialized or performance-critical sections. Indeed, the batching capabilities of Spring JDBC allow you to run a large number of operations in a very short time. Hibernate and other ORM tools cannot always batch operations correctly when you interleave data reads and writes. Using Spring JDBC is also useful when you are dealing with exotic data types (such as extremely large LOBs) or SQL syntax (such as Oracle hierarchical queries). Again, in all these cases, most ORM tools fail to use the database-specific features.

Even if database vendor independence is a requirement for your application, you can still use vendor-specific SQL and data types as long as you "hide" the vendor-specific DAO implementations behind an interface, as you saw in Figure 9-7.

In the next chapter, we will leave the complex area of manual JDBC code and look at Hibernate, an object-relational mapping framework.

CHAPTER 10

iBATIS Integration

In the previous chapter, you saw how to use JDBC in Spring applications. Even though Spring goes a long way toward simplifying JDBC development, you will find that you still have a lot of code to write to use JDBC.

One elegant solution to avoiding all this code is to use an object-relational mapping (ORM) tool, which maps the data rows and creates appropriate Java objects. In order for such mapping tools to access Java objects in a standardized fashion, they have to follow Java bean naming conventions. For example, the mapping tools can also set referenced objects that result from a join operation.

There are two basic types of ORM frameworks: those in which you can rely on the framework to generate all the SQL statements for you and those in which you have to write the SQL statements yourself. The first case speeds up development, but sometimes the generated SQL code is not efficient enough. With the second approach, you write the SQL code yourself, making sure to select the correct columns that the ORM framework uses to create instances of the Java beans.

In this chapter, we are going to focus on implementing the data access layer of a Spring application using the iBATIS ORM framework. Specifically, we will cover configuration, including the various configuration files you need to use iBATIS successfully in the data layer of your application. We'll also discuss mapping files; you'll learn how to create these files and how iBATIS uses them to map selected rows to the properties of the domain objects. And finally, we'll cover basic database operations: you'll learn how to implement the select, delete, and update operations using iBATIS, and you'll see how to implement select operations that represent all types of data relationships and how you can make sure that insert operations are using correct primary key values.

What Is iBATIS?

iBATIS (`http://www.ibatis.com`) is an ORM tools that allows the developer to write the custom SQL code needed to populate bean properties. iBATIS uses the same approach for data inserts and updates, which is very good news indeed, because sometimes, you do not want to update an entire row (especially when a row is quite large). In a lot of cases, you have just one value to update, and with iBATIS, you can write custom code to update only a particular column in the table.

iBATIS also allows you to fully use your database's extensions to the standard SQL syntax. You may object on the grounds that portability is an important feature of a Java EE application, but remember that, in most cases, full database portability is often a phantom requirement (for further discussion of application design in Spring, check out Chapter 4). Besides, because iBATIS uses XML mapping files, you can easily have different mapping files for different databases. This is similar to the level of abstraction you gain from using stored procedures.

Note Some databases do not even support stored procedures.

---

iBATIS Versions

iBATIS has two distinct versions, 1.x and 2.x, which have similar high-level functions, but the syntax of their configuration files is very different. Spring does actually support both versions. However, only version 2.x support is an integral part of core Spring 2.0. The iBATIS 1.x support has been moved to the Spring Modules project as of Spring 2.0. As iBATIS 2.x is supported only by core Spring 2.0, this chapter will cover only iBATIS SQL maps for version 2.x. For version 1.x information, please see the Spring Modules project documentation.

Infrastructure and Configuration

Let's take a look at iBATIS configuration and mapping files. One central XML file contains references to mapping files that define the Java beans and all database operations. You can specify the location of this reference configuration file when you create an instance of the iBATIS beans in Spring.

The mapping files usually represent a single domain object and contain the appropriate SQL code for persisting that object's data to the database. It is important that you realize that all mapping files are loaded at start-up, and the mappings specified are validated against the actual objects. If a property is not present in the domain object, bean creation fails.

Unlike stand-alone iBATIS applications, the only things you need to configure in a Spring iBATIS application are the reference file and the mapping files. The Spring iBATIS factory bean (`org.springframework.orm.ibatis.SqlMapClientFactoryBean`) takes care of loading the configuration files. Just as with JDBC, you should not create and manage database transactions manually in the iBATIS mapping files; always delegate the transaction management to Spring.

Figure 10-1 gives you a basic overview of the structure of the configuration files. We take a more detailed look at the recommended file locations and the exact content of the files in the next section.

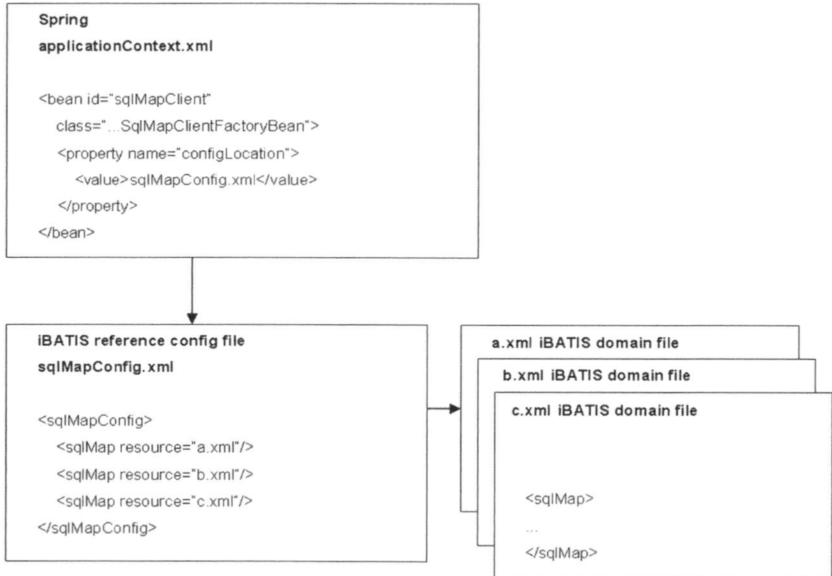

Figure 10-1. *Configuration files structure*

Mapping Files

Let's begin with a description of the reference configuration file. Unlike stand-alone iBATIS applications, you normally include references to only the concrete `sqlMap` files.

Listing 10-1 shows a sample reference configuration file.

Listing 10-1. *SqlMapConfig.xml Reference Configuration File*

```
<?xml version="1.0" encoding="UTF-8" ?>
<!DOCTYPE sqlMapConfig
    PUBLIC "-//iBATIS.com//DTD SQL Map Config 2.0//EN"
    "http://www.ibatis.com/dtd/sql-map-config-2.dtd">

<sqlMapConfig>
    <sqlMap resource="Customer.xml" />
</sqlMapConfig>
```

As Listing 10-2 shows, the configuration file references a single `sqlMap` file, `Customer.xml`, which in turn declares the domain object type.

Listing 10-2. *sqlMap File for Customer Class*

```
<?xml version="1.0" encoding="UTF-8" standalone="no"?>
<!DOCTYPE sqlMap PUBLIC "-//iBATIS.com//DTD SQL Map 2.0//EN" ➥
"http://www.ibatis.com/dtd/sql-map-2.dtd">

<sqlMap>

</sqlMap>
```

At this point, we have the basic infrastructure of the application ready. The missing piece of the puzzle is the Spring context file that links all the configuration files together (see Listing 10-3).

Listing 10-3. *Spring applicationContext.xml File*

```
<?xml version="1.0" encoding="UTF-8"?>
<!DOCTYPE beans PUBLIC "-//SPRING//DTD BEAN//EN" ➥
"http://www.springframework.org/dtd/spring-beans.dtd">

<beans>

    <!-- SqlMap setup for iBATIS Database Layer -->
    <bean id="sqlMapClient"
        class="org.springframework.orm.ibatis.SqlMapClientFactoryBean">
        <property name="configLocation"
            value="sqlMapConfig.xml"/ >
     </bean>

</beans>
```

Listing 10-3 shows you how to instruct Spring to create an instance of the `sqlMapClient` bean, which loads the `sqlMapConfig.xml` file. We now have a configured `sqlMapClient` bean that can be used in the DAO implementations. All we need to do is define the DAO interfaces, create the implementation, and create the `dataSource` bean; but before we can do that, we should take a more detailed look at the map files.

Table 10-1 lists the files we have and how we are going to structure them.

Table 10-1. *Locations of the Configuration Files*

File	Source Location	Build/Run Location
sqlMapClient.xml	src/ibatis	build
Customer.xml	src/ibatis	build
applicationContext	src/conf	build

The build scripts should take care of building the application and make sure that the configuration files are copied from their source locations to the appropriate destinations to run the application. Before we move ahead to complete the configuration files and make the application work, let's take a closer look at the `sqlMap` files.

The location of the files is specific to the application type you are developing. You need to realize that the configuration files are resources, and as such, they are handled by `ResourceLoaders`, usually, the default `ResourceLoader`. Refer to Chapter 4 for more information on resources.

sqlMap Files

`sqlMap` files define types, result maps, and database statements. Even though you can use a single file to define these, creating a separate `sqlMap` file for each domain object is a good idea. If you follow this simple rule, you will keep the `sqlMap` files easy to read, and as the number of domain objects grows, the project will remain easy to manage.

We will use Oracle as our database for examples in this chapter. In Listing 10-4, we create a simple database with a single table to demonstrate the iBATIS functionality.

Listing 10-4. *SQL Create Script*

```
create table T_Customer (
    Id number(19, 0) not null,
    First_Name varchar(50) not null,
    Last_Name varchar(50) not null,
    Last_Login timestamp not null,
     constraint PK_CustomerId primary key (Id),
};
create sequence s_customer_id start with 1000;
```

Next, we create a domain object to map in the `sqlMap` file. The domain object (see Listing 10-5) has the same class name as the `sqlMap` file, `Customer`, and will have the same properties as the `T_CUSTOMER` table columns.

Listing 10-5. *Customer Domain Object*

```
import java.util.Date;

public class Customer {

    private Long id;
    private String firstName;
    private String lastName;
    private Date lastLogin;

    public String getFirstName() {
        return firstName;
    }
```

```
    public void setFirstName(String firstName) {
        this.firstName = firstName;
    }

    public String getLastName() {
        return lastName;
    }

    public void setLastName(String lastName) {
        this.lastName = lastName;
    }

    public Date getLastLogin() {
        return lastLogin;
    }

    public void setLastLogin(Date lastLogin) {
        this.lastLogin = lastLogin;
    }
    public Long getId() {
        return id;
    }

    public void setId(Long id) {
        this.id = id;
    }
```

The domain object has four properties: `id`, `firstName`, `lastName`, and `lastLogin`. We need to tell iBATIS how to interpret the data that will be selected from the database. To do this, we create a `resultMap` element that tells iBATIS what object to instantiate and what properties to set (see Listing 10-6).

Listing 10-6. *sqlMap File for the Customer Domain Object*

```
<?xml version="1.0" encoding="UTF-8" standalone="no"?>
<!DOCTYPE sqlMap PUBLIC "-//iBATIS.com//DTD SQL Map 2.0//EN" ➥
"http://www.ibatis.com/dtd/sql-map-2.dtd">

<sqlMap>

    <typeAlias type="com.apress.prospring2.ch10.domain.Customer" alias="customer"/>

    <resultMap class="customer" id="result">
        <result property="id" column="Id"/>
        <result property="firstName" column="First_Name"/>
        <result property="lastName" column="Last_Name"/>
        <result property="lastLogin" column="Last_Login"/>
    </resultMap>

</sqlMap>
```

Listing 10-6 actually shows how to create a `typeAlias` that tells iBATIS that `customer` actually means `com.apress.prospring2.ch10.domain.Customer`; this is a merely a convenience feature to save you typing. Table 10-2 lists all predefined aliases and their corresponding Java types.

Table 10-2. *Predefined iBATIS Type Aliases*

Alias	Java Type	Details
boolean	java.lang.Boolean	Use #value# to access the object's primitive boolean property.
byte	java.lang.Byte	Use #value# to access the object's primitive byte property.
short	java.lang.Short	Use #value# to access the object's primitive short property.
int	java.lang.Integer	Use #value# to access the object's primitive int property.
long	java.lang.Long	Use #value# to access the object's primitive long property.
float	java.lang.Float	Use #value# to access the object's primitive float property.
double	java.lang.Double	Use #value# to access the object's primitive double property.
string	java.lang.String	Use #value# to access the object's value.
date	java.util.Date	Use #value# to access the object's value.
decimal	java.math.BigDecimal	Use #value# to access the object's value.
map	java.util.Map	Use #key# to get or set the item in the Map.

Next, we define a resultMap with an ID of result. When a resultMap with name result is used, iBATIS instantiates the Customer object and sets its properties with the values in the appropriate columns (see Listing 10-7).

Listing 10-7. *sqlMap File for the Select Statement of the Customer Domain Object*

```
<?xml version="1.0" encoding="UTF-8" standalone="no"?>
<!DOCTYPE sqlMap PUBLIC "-//iBATIS.com//DTD SQL Map 2.0//EN" ➥
"http://www.ibatis.com/dtd/sql-map-2.dtd">

<sqlMap>

    <typeAlias type="com.apress.prospring2.ch10.domain.Customer" alias="customer"/>

    <resultMap class="customer" id="result">
        <result property="id" column="Id"/>
        <result property="firstName" column="First_Name"/>
        <result property="lastName" column="Last_Name"/>
        <result property="lastLogin" column="Last_Login"/>
    </resultMap>

    <select id="getAllCustomers" resultMap="result">
        select * from T_Customer
    </select>
</sqlMap>
```

Don't worry if you don't understand what a select node does or what to use it for, we will discuss this further in the "Selecting Data" section later in this chapter.

Configuring iBATIS and Spring

Finally, we can define the CustomerDao interface and its iBATIS implementation and add the familiar dataSource bean.

■ **Note** If you cannot remember how to configure `dataSource` beans, go back to Chapter 9, where we discussed different `DataSource` objects you can use in a Spring application.

In Listing 10-8, we begin with `CustomerDao`, a DAO interface, and the `SqlMapClientCustomerDao` implementation.

Listing 10-8. *CustomerDao Interface*

```
public interface CustomerDao {
    public List<Customer> getAll();
    public List<Customer> getByNameAndRunDate(String name, Date runDate);
    public void save(Customer customer);
    public void delete(Long id);
    public Customer getById(Long id);
    public List<Customer> getByLastNameAndLastLogin(String lastName, ➥
            Date lastLogin);
    public void updateLastName(long id, String lastName);
}
```

We now proceed to implement this interface (see Listing 10-9). We use a convenience Spring superclass, `SqlMapClientDaoSupport`. Just like `JdbcDaoSupport`, this class already has a property for a `dataSource` and provides `getSqlMapClientTemplate()`, which allow us to call iBATIS methods.

Listing 10-9. *CustomerDao iBATIS Implementation*

```
public class SqlMapClientCustomerDao
    extends SqlMapClientDaoSupport
    implements CustomerDao {

    // CustomerDao methods are implemented as stubs
}
```

In Listing 10-10, we finish the `applicationContext.xml` file to link the beans together.

Listing 10-10. *Spring applicationContext.xml File*

```
<?xml version="1.0" encoding="UTF-8"?>
<beans xmlns="http://www.springframework.org/schema/beans"
....>
    <!-- Data source bean -->
    <bean id="dataSource" class="org.apache.commons.dbcp.BasicDataSource"
        destroy-method="close">
        <property name="driverClassName" value="oracle.jdbc.driver.OracleDriver"/>
        <property name="url" value="jdbc:oracle:thin:@localhost:1521:INTL"/>
        <property name="username" value="PROSPRING"/>
        <property name="password" value="x******6"/>
    </bean>

    <!-- SqlMap setup for iBATIS Database Layer -->
    <bean id="sqlMapClient"
        class="org.springframework.orm.ibatis.SqlMapClientFactoryBean">
        <property name="configLocation" value="sqlMapConfig.xml"/>
        <property name="dataSource" ref local="dataSource"/>
    </bean>
```

```
    <bean id="customerDao"
        class="com.apress.prospring2.ch10.data.SqlMapClientCustomerDao">
        <property name="sqlMapClient" ref="sqlMapClient"/>
    </bean>

</beans>
```

We're almost there now. We have a full Spring application context file with the `dataSource`, `sqlMapClient`, and `customerDao` beans. Note that the `dataSource` property is injected into the `sqlMapClient` bean directly; there is no need to inject it to every DAO bean separately. Now, we can create a `Main` class (see Listing 10-11) that creates the application context from the context file on the classpath and selects and prints the data.

Listing 10-11. *The Sample Application's Main Class*

```
public class Main {

    private ApplicationContext context;

    private void run() {
        System.out.println("Initializing application");
        context = new ClassPathXmlApplicationContext("dataaccess-context.xml");

        System.out.println("Getting customerDao");
        CustomerDao customerDao = (CustomerDao)context.getBean("customerDao");

        System.out.println("Done");
    }

    public static void main(String[] args) {
        new Main().run();
    }
}
```

The framework for the application is now ready. Once executed, the Spring application context is loaded, and all beans are successfully configured. However, we cannot see any data just yet, so let's move on to the next section.

Selecting Data

In this section, we discuss how to select rows from the database and how to pass parameters from DAO implementations to the select statements. We start by discussing select operations from a single table that uses a single domain object, and we move on to discuss selecting data from one-to-one (1:1), one-to-many (1:*n*), and finally many-to-many (*m*:*n*) database relationships.

Simple Selects

We start with a select-all statement that does not need any parameters and selects the data from only one table into one domain object (see Listing 10-12); the only addition to the `Customer.xml` `sqlMap` file is the select node.

Listing 10-12. *sqlMap File for the Customer Domain Object*

```
<typeAlias type="com.apress.prospring2.ch10.domain.Customer" alias="customer"/>

    <resultMap class="customer" id="result">
        <result property="id" column="Id"/>
        <result property="firstName" column="First_Name"/>
        <result property="lastName" column="Last_Name"/>
        <result property="lastLogin" column="Last_Login"/>
    </resultMap>

    <select id="getAllCustomers" resultMap="result">
        select * from T_Customer
    </select>
```

This simple `<select>` node actually tells iBATIS that there is a SQL statement named `getAllCustomers` and that this statement is a select statement. The SQL code for the statement is `select * from T_Customer`. The `resultMap` is `result`, which in turn represents `customer`—that is, the `Customer` domain object. In Listing 10-13, we implement `CustomerDao`'s `getAll()` method to see all this in action.

Listing 10-13. *CustomerDao getAll() iBATIS Implementation*

```
public class SqlMapClientCustomerDao
    extends SqlMapClientDaoSupport
    implements CustomerDao {

public List getAll() {
        return getSqlMapClientTemplate().queryForList("getAllCustomers");
    }

    // other CustomerDao methods are implemented as stubs
}
```

That is all the code you need to write! The `getAll()` method delegates the database call and domain object instantiation to iBATIS. All we need to provide is the name of the statement, which must be defined in one of the `sqlMap` files referenced from the `SqlMapConfig` file. iBATIS locates the statement, checks that it is a select statement, performs the database operation, and processes the `resultSet`. After that, for each row, iBATIS instantiates the domain object, sets its properties, and adds it to the resulting `List`.

In Listing 10-14, we make a final change to the `Main` class to utilize the new implementation.

Listing 10-14. *Main Class Modified to Call the Select Method*

```
public class Main {

    private ApplicationContext context;

    private void run() {
        System.out.println("Initializing application");
        context = new ClassPathXmlApplicationContext("dataaccess-context.xml");

        System.out.println("Getting customerDao");
        CustomerDao customerDao = (CustomerDao)context.getBean("customerDao");
        List<Customer> customers = customerDao.getAll();
        for (Customer customer : customers) {
```

```
            System.out.println(customer);
        }
        System.out.println("Done");
    }

    public static void main(String[] args) {
        new Main().run();
    }
}
```

When we run the application, it creates the Spring `ApplicationContext`, which is used to get a `CustomerDao` bean. After the bean is created, we call its `getAll()` method to get a `List` of `Customer` domain objects. The output is exactly what we expect:

```
Getting customerDao
Customer { id: 1, firstName: John, lastName: Smith, ➥
lastLogin: Wed Aug 08 00:00:00 GMT 2007}
Done
```

The application runs, connects to the database, selects the data, and returns a `List` of our domain objects. In most cases, however, you need to filter out the rows that are selected. In other words, you need to pass parameters to the select statements. As an example, in Listing 10-15, we begin with a select by primary key operation, implemented in the `getById(int)` method.

Listing 10-15. *sqlMap File for the Customer Domain Object*

```
<?xml version="1.0" encoding="UTF-8" standalone="no"?>
<!DOCTYPE sqlMap PUBLIC "-//iBATIS.com//DTD SQL Map 2.0//EN" ➥
"http://www.ibatis.com/dtd/sql-map-2.dtd">

<sqlMap>
    <!-- as previous -->
    <select id="getCustomerById" resultMap="result" parameterClass="long">
        select * from T_Customer where Id=#value#
    </select>
</sqlMap>
```

Here, we added the `getCustomerById` select statement with a parameter class of `long`, which is a type alias for `java.lang.Long`. The implementation of the `getById(Long)` method (shown in Listing 10-16) is quite simple as well. All we need to do is pass the primary key value to iBATIS.

Listing 10-16. *CustomerDao getById(int) iBATIS Implementation*

```
public class SqlMapClientCustomerDao  extends SqlMapClientDaoSupport ➥
                      implements CustomerDao {
    public Customer getById(Long id) {
          return (Customer)getSqlMapClientTemplate().queryForObject(➥
              "getCustomerById", id);
    }
    // other CustomerDao methods are implemented as stubs
}
```

The implementation calls the `queryForObject()` method that returns a single `java.lang.Object` or a `null` value that results from executing the select statement. If more than one row is selected, a `DataAccessException` is thrown. Even though the result of `queryForObject()` is `java.lang.Object`, we can safely cast it to `Customer`, because our `resultMap` states that the object type is `Customer`. We are also passing a Long object with its value set to the primary key value as a parameter instance to the iBATIS call. Again, the code is very straightforward and easy to follow.

There are some cases where you will want to pass more than one value to the database operation. You are free to use any type, but in most cases, you will find yourself using either a domain object or a java.util.Map implementation. There is no difference between using a Map and a concrete domain object in sqlMap files. However, in the Java code, you gain type safety if you use the domain objects. The rule of thumb is that if you find yourself updating only a few fields in a table with a large number of columns, you are better off using a Map. If you are updating all or most of the columns in a table, using the domain object is better. In Listing 10-17, we show you both implementations.

Listing 10-17. *sqlMap File for the Customer Domain Object*

```
<?xml version="1.0" encoding="UTF-8" standalone="no"?>
<!DOCTYPE sqlMap PUBLIC "-//iBATIS.com//DTD SQL Map 2.0//EN" ➥
"http://www.ibatis.com/dtd/sql-map-2.dtd">

<sqlMap>
    <select id="getCustomersByLastNameAndLastLoginMap"
        resultMap="result" parameterClass="map">
        select * from T_Customer where Last_Name like #lastName# and ➥
              Last_Login=#lastLogin#
    </select>
    <select id="getCustomersByLastNameAndLastLoginDO"
        resultMap="result" parameterClass="customer">
        select * from T_Customer where Last_Name like #lastName# and ➥
                Last_Login=#lastLogin#
    </select>

</sqlMap>
```

Here, we added two select statements: one uses the parameterClass of the map and the other uses the customer domain object. Apart from this, the body of the select statements is exactly the same. In Listing 10-18 you can see that the Java implementation of CustomerDao is also very similar.

Listing 10-18. *CustomerDao getByLastNameAndLastLogin*() iBATIS Implementation*

```
public class SqlMapClientCustomerDao  extends SqlMapClientDaoSupport ➥
                         implements CustomerDao {

public List<Customer> getByLastNameAndLastLoginMap(String lastName, ➥
            Date lastLogin) {
        Map<String, Object> parms = new HashMap<String, Object>();
        parms.put("lastName", lastName);
        parms.put("lastLogin", lastLogin);
        return getSqlMapClientTemplate().queryForList(➥
                 "getCustomersByLastNameAndLastLoginMap", parms);
    }

public List<Customer> getByLastNameAndLastLoginDO(String lastName, Date lastLogin) {
        Customer customer = new Customer();
        customer.setLastName(lastName);
        customer.setLastLogin(lastLogin);
        return getSqlMapClientTemplate().queryForList(➥
                  "getCustomersByLastNameAndLastLoginDO", lastLogin);
    }
```

```
    // other CustomerDao methods are implemented as stubs
}
```

The two methods demonstrate different ways in which we can pass data to the select statements. In the `getByLastNameAndLastLoginMap` method, we create a `Map` instance and put the values required in the select statement, while the code in the `getByLastNameAndLastLoginDO` method instantiates the `Customer` domain object, sets the property values, and passes the instance of the domain object to the iBATIS call. You'll experience a slight performance hit when you use the `java.util.HashMap` implementation of `Map` to update the same number of fields. We have tested 25,000 select calls using a `java.util.HashMap` and a domain object as parameters to the iBATIS calls. The `HashMap` implementation took 13,594 milliseconds, whereas the domain object implementation took 12,328 milliseconds.

One-to-One Selects

To demonstrate how to select data in one-to-one mapping, we'll add another table and another domain object. Let's create a few tables and domain objects. In Listing 10-19, we edit the `T_Customer` table and create `T_Customer_Detail` table.

Listing 10-19. *One-to-One Relationship SQL Script*

```
create table T_Customer_Detail (
    Id number(19, 0) not null,
    Data varchar2(512) not null,
    constraint PK_CustomerDetailId primary key (Id)
);
create table T_Customer (
    Id number(19, 0) not null,
    First_Name varchar(50) not null,
    Last_Name varchar(50) not null,
    Last_Login timestamp not null,
    Customer_Detail int not null,
    Customer_Gossip int null,
    constraint PK_CustomerId primary key (Id),
           constraint FK_CustomerDetail foreign key (Customer_Detail)
        references T_Customer_Detail(Id) on delete cascade,
    constraint FK_CustomerGossip foreign key (Customer_Gossip)
        references T_Customer_Detail(Id) on delete cascade
);
create sequence s_customer_id start with 1000;
insert into T_Customer_Detail (Id, Data) values (100, 'Detail 1');
insert into T_Customer_Detail (Id, Data) values (101, 'Foo');
insert into T_Customer_Detail (Id, Data) values (102, 'Bar');
insert into T_Customer (Id, First_Name, Last_Name, Last_Login, ➥
Customer_Detail, Customer_Gossip) values (1, 'John', 'Smith',➥
TO_DATE('08-08-2007', 'dd-MM-YYYY'), 100, null);
insert into T_Customer (Id, First_Name, Last_Name, ➥
                                Last_Login, Customer_Detail, Customer_Gossip)
    values (2, 'Jane', 'Doe', TO_DATE('08-08-2007', 'dd-MM-YYYY'), 101, 102);
```

As the SQL script shows, a record in the `T_Customer` table must have one record in the `T_Customer_Detail` table referenced by `Customer_Detail` and may have one record in the `T_Customer_Detail` table referenced by `Customer_Gossip`.

On the Java front, we create the two domain objects: `CustomerDetail` and `Customer` (as shown in Listing 10-20).

Listing 10-20. *Customer and CustomerDetail Domain Objects*

```
// Customer.java:
public class Customer {

    private int id;
    private String firstName;
    private String lastName;
    private CustomerDetail customerDetail;
    private CustomerDetail customerGossip;
    // getters and setters as usual
}

// CustomerDetail.java:
package com.apress.prospring2.ch10.domain;
public class CustomerDetail {

    private int customerDetailId;
    private String data;

    //getters and setters as usual
}
```

Next, in Listing 10-21, we create a sqlMap for the domain objects.

Listing 10-21. *Customer.xml sqlMap File*

```
<?xml version="1.0" encoding="UTF-8" standalone="no"?>
<!DOCTYPE sqlMap PUBLIC "-//iBATIS.com//DTD SQL Map 2.0//EN" ➥
"http://www.ibatis.com/dtd/sql-map-2.dtd">

<sqlMap>

    <typeAlias type="com.apress.prospring2.ch10.domain.Customer" ➥
               alias="customer"/>

    <typeAlias type="com.apress.prospring2.ch10.domain.CustomerDetail"
               alias="customerDetail"/>

    <resultMap class="customer" id="result">
        <result property="id" column="Id"/>
        <result property="firstName" column="First_Name"/>
        <result property="lastName" column="Last_Name"/>
        <result property="lastLogin" column="Last_Login"/>
    </resultMap>

    <resultMap class="customerDetail" id="gossipResult">
        <result property="id" column="Id"/>
        <result property="data" column="Data"/>
    </resultMap>

    <resultMap class="customer" id="resultDetail" extends="result">
        <result property="customerDetail.id"
                column="Customer_Detail_Id"/>
        <result property="customerDetail.data" column="Customer_Detail_Data"/>
        <result property="customerGossip" select="getCustomerGossipById"
                column="Customer_Gossip"/>
    </resultMap>
```

```
    <select id="getCustomerById" resultMap="resultDetail" parameterClass="long">
        select
        c.Id as Id,
        c.First_Name as First_Name,
        c.Last_Name as Last_Name,
        c.Customer_Detail as Customer_Detail,
        c.Customer_Gossip as Customer_Gossip,
        c.Last_Login as Last_Login,
        cd.Id as Customer_Detail_Id,
        cd.Data as Customer_Detail_Data
        from
        T_Customer c inner join T_Customer_Detail cd on
        c.Customer_Detail = cd.Id
        where
        c.Id=#value#
    </select>

    <select id="getCustomerGossipById" resultMap="gossipResult"
            parameterClass="int">
        select * from T_Customer_Detail where Id=#value#
    </select>

</sqlMap>
```

This sqlMap file has a lot of new features, so let's take a closer look at them. First of all, we are using resultMap inheritance. This is useful for situations where you want to create a resultMap that adds more fields to the super resultMap. Let's say you're implementing a search method that returns a list of customers based on the lastName field. You are not interested in customerDetail or customerGossip properties, so you can leave them set to their default values, null in both cases. However, if you are getting a customer by Customer.id, you want to get all available information about the customer. This is why we created both a simple result resultMap and the resultDetail resultMap that extends result and adds definitions for customerDetail and customerGossip.

In Listing 10-22, you can take a closer look at the resultDetail, which also reveals that we are telling iBATIS that there will always be data for a customerDetail object, while there may not be data for customerGossip.

Listing 10-22. *Detail of the resultDetail resultMap*

```
<sqlMap>
    <resultMap class="customer" id="resultDetail" extends="result">
        <result property="customerDetail.id"
                column="Customer_Detail_Id"/>
        <result property="customerDetail.data"
                 column="Customer_Detail_Data"/>
        <result property="customerGossip" select="getCustomerGossipById"
            column="CustomerGossip"/>
    </resultMap>
</sqlMap>
```

The code in bold in Listing 10-22 states that the Customer_Detail_Id and Customer_Detail_Data columns will always be present in the resultSet, and that they should be set on the customerDetail object's id and data properties. The customerGossip object, however, should be set to the result of the getCustomerrGossipById select statement. This statement takes a single long parameter. The value of this parameter should be taken from Customer_Gossip column of the T_Customer table. In other words, the customerDetail property is never null, whereas customerGossip can be null. After some hard work to create a configuration file from Listing 10-22, the CustomerDao interface and its implementation are very simple, as you can see in Listing 10-23.

Listing 10-23. *The CustomerDao Interface and Its Implementation*

```
// CustomerDao.java

public interface CustomerDao {
    Customer getById(int customerId);
}

// SqlMapClientCustomerDao.java

public class SqlMapClientCustomerDao
    extends SqlMapClientDaoSupport implements CustomerDao {
    public Customer getById(Long id) {
        return (Customer)getSqlMapClientTemplate().
            queryForObject("getCustomerById", id);
    }
}
```

We must not forget to include the new Customer.xml sqlMap in the SqlMapConfig.xml file and to add the customerDao bean to the applicationContext.xml file. Once all the changes to the configuration files are complete, we can add the code in Listing 10-24 to the Main class.

Listing 10-24. *New Code to Test the One-to-One Relationship*

```
CustomerDao customerDao = (CustomerDao)context.getBean("customerDao");

Customer c1 = customerDao.getById(1L);
Customer c2 = customerDao.getById(2L);

System.out.println(c1);
System.out.println(c2);
```

Running the Main class using the test data from the SQL script produces the following output:

```
Customer { id: 1, firstName: John, lastName: Smith, ➥
lastLogin: Wed Aug 08 00:00:00 GMT 2007, ➥
detail: CustomerDetail { id: 100, date: Detail 1}, gossip: null}
Customer { id: 2, firstName: Jane, lastName: Doe, ➥
lastLogin: Wed Aug 08 00:00:00 GMT 2007, ➥
detail: CustomerDetail { id: 101, date: Foo}, ➥
gossip: CustomerDetail { id: 102, date: Bar}}
```

Performance of One-to-One Selects

There is one performance issue you need to consider: using a select statement to set a property on a domain object results in *n* plus one select operations being performed. Consider a situation where you load a single Customer object: an extra query is run to select the Customer_Detail row to set the customerGossip property. This extra step may become a major issue. Imagine a situation where we issue a select statement that returns 100 Customer domain objects. iBATIS now needs to run 100 separate selects to set the customerGossip property, making the total number of queries 101.

We have seen a way around this, though—we can return the customerDetail object as a part of the result set, so no more queries need to be executed. Unfortunately, we cannot use this workaround if the one-to-one relationship is optional.

The best way to resolve this situation is to set only the properties you really need. Use a simplified resultMap that sets only the basic properties for selects that return a large number of rows, and use this basic resultMap as a supermap for a detailed map that sets all properties.

Since one-to-one relationships are not very common, you will find the discussion of one-to-many relationships in the next sections more applicable.

One-to-Many Selects

Let's move away from the CustomerGossip objects we have used in the previous section and implement standard order tables. Each order can have zero or more lines. As you can see in Listing 10-25, adding to SQL script is simple enough.

Listing 10-25. *Adding to the Create SQL Script*

```
create table T_Order (
    Id number(19, 0) not null,
    Customer number(19, 0) not null,

    constraint PK_OrderId primary key (Id),
    constraint FK_Customer foreign key (Customer) references T_Customer(Id)
);
create sequence s_order_id start with 1000;

create table T_Order_Line (
    Id number(19, 0) not null,
    "Order" number(19, 0) not null,
    Product varchar(200) not null,
    Price decimal(10, 2) not null,

    constraint PK_OrderLineId primary key (Id),
    constraint FK_Order foreign key ("Order") references T_Order(Id)
);
create sequence s_order_line_id start with 1000;
insert into T_Order (Id, Customer) values (100, 1);
insert into T_Order_Line (Id, "Order", Product, Price)
    values (200, 100, 'Punch people over the internet client application', 19.95);
insert into T_Order_Line (Id, "Order", Product, Price)
    values (201, 100, 'The Mangelfreuzer Switch', 12.95);
```

The Java domain objects are also going to be pretty standard. The Order object is going to contain all the properties for columns in the T_Order table plus a List for holding instances of the OrderLine domain object. The list, in turn, is going to have properties for all columns in the T_Order_Line table.

In Listing 10-26, we begin the implementation of the iBATIS mapping files by creating the sqlMap file, Order.xml.

Listing 10-26. *The Order.xml sqlMap File*

```
<?xml version="1.0" encoding="UTF-8" standalone="no"?>
<!DOCTYPE sqlMap PUBLIC "-//iBATIS.com//DTD SQL Map 2.0//EN" ➥
"http://www.ibatis.com/dtd/sql-map-2.dtd">

<sqlMap>
     <typeAlias type="com.apress.prospring2.ch10.domain.Order" alias="order"/>
    <typeAlias type="com.apress.prospring2.ch10.domain.OrderLine"
        alias="orderLine"/>
```

```
<resultMap class="order" id="result">
    <result property="id" column="Id"/>
    <result property="customer" column="Customer"/>
    <result property="orderLines" select="getOrderLinesByOrder"
        column="Id"/>
</resultMap>

<resultMap class="orderLine" id="resultLine">
    <result property="id" column="Id"/>
    <result property="order" column="Order"/>
    <result property="product" column="Product"/>
    <result property="price" column="Price"/>
</resultMap>

<select id="getOrderById" resultMap="result" parameterClass="long">
    select * from T_Order where Id=#value#
</select>

<select id="getOrderLinesByOrder" resultMap="resultLine" parameterClass="long">
    select * from T_Order_Line where "Order"=#value#
</select>
```

The elements in the `sqlMap` file from Listing 10-26 should come as no surprise. We have two types, `order` and `orderLine`. We have also declared that to set the `orderLines` property, iBATIS must execute the `getOrderLinesByOrder` select statement and add the results of that query to the `orderLines List` property of the `Order` object. The domain objects follow the properties we declared in the `sqlMap` file, as shown in Listing 10-27.

Listing 10-27. *Order and OrderLine Domain Objects*

```
// Order.java
public class Order {

    private Long id;
    private Long customer;
    private List<OrderLine> orderLines;

    // Getters and Setters
}

// OrderLine.java
public class OrderLine {

    private Long id;
    private Long order;
    private String product;
    private BigDecimal price;

    // Getters and Setters
}
```

The `OrderDao` interface and its implementation are also very simple (see Listing 10-28); it merely passes the required parameters to the iBATIS calls.

Listing 10-28. *OrderDao Interface and Its Implementation*

```
// OrderDao.java
public interface OrderDao {
    public Order getById(Long orderId);
}

// SqlMapClientOrderDao.java

public class SqlMapClientOrderDao
    extends SqlMapClientDaoSupport implements OrderDao {

    public Order getById(Long id) {
        return (Order)getSqlMapClientTemplate().queryForObject(
            "getOrderById", id);
    }

}
```

If we add a reference to the new `sqlMap` file to `SqlMapConfig.xml` and add a bean definition for `orderDao` to the `applicationContext.xml` file, we can use the code in the `Main` class to test the application (see Listing 10-29).

Listing 10-29. *Testing Code for the OderDao Implementation*

```
OrderDao orderDao = (OrderDao)context.getBean("orderDao");
Order order = orderDao.getById(1);
System.out.println(order);
```

The result of running this code is the following nice output that shows that `Order` with `OrderId: 1` has two order lines:

```
Order { id: 1, customer: 1, orderlines:
[  OrderLine { id: 2, order: 1, product: The Mangelfreuzer Switch},
   OrderLine { id: 1, order: 1, product: Punch people over the ➥
internet client application},]}
```

Performance

In one-to-many relationships, you have no way to avoid n-plus-one selects. However, you can still use the basic `resultMap` to set the basic properties and extend this simple `resultMap` in a detailed `resultMap` that sets all properties. For example, if you are displaying a list of orders, you do not really need to know the `orderLines`. You only need this extra information when you want to display a detailed summary of the order. This usually means selecting an order domain object by its primary key, which results in another query being executed to return all order lines.

Excellent! We now have two relationships: one-to-one and one-to-many. The last one remaining is many-to-many.

Many-to-Many Selects

Finally, a many-to-many select is a simple question of creating two one-to-many selects. For example, consider `User` and `Role` objects. A `User` can appear in more than one `Role` and one `Role` can be assigned to more than one `User`. We need a linking table `T_User_Role`, that creates a one-to-many relationship between `User` and `UserRole` and a one-to-many relationship between `UserRole` and `Role`; making the whole relationship many-to-many.

Updating Data

Now that you have learned how to select data from the database, you must be keen to learn how to update existing data. Updating data is very similar to selecting it; we use parameter maps and domain objects extensively. Let's start with the simple example: updating name columns in the `T_Customer` table. In Listing 10-30, we modify the `sqlMap` file for `Customer` domain objects and add an update statement.

Listing 10-30. *sqlMap File for the Customer Domain Object*

```
<?xml version="1.0" encoding="UTF-8" standalone="no"?>
<!DOCTYPE sqlMap PUBLIC "-//iBATIS.com//DTD SQL Map 2.0//EN" ➥
"http://www.ibatis.com/dtd/sql-map-2.dtd">

<sqlMap>
    <!-- as previous -->

    <update id="updateCustomer" parameterClass="customer">
        update T_Customer
                set First_Name=#firstName#, ➥
                      Last_Name=#lastName#, ➥
                      Last_Login=#lastLogin#
                where Id=#id#
    </update>

</sqlMap>
```

Unsurprisingly, the update SQL statement is in the body of an update element in the `sqlMap` file, and it does exactly what is expected of it—it updates the `First_Name`, `Last_Name`, and `Last_Login` columns in a row identified by `customer id` and passed in through the `int parameterClass`. The `long parameterClass` is an alias for `java.lang.Long`, and we can access its `long` property in `#value#`.

The implementation in the Java code is slightly more complex; because our `CustomerDao` interface contains only one method to update or insert the domain object, we need to decide whether the object is to be updated or inserted (see Listing 10-31).

Listing 10-31. *CustomerDao save() iBATIS Implementation*

```
public class SqlMapClientCustomerDao
    extends SqlMapClientDaoSupport
    implements CustomerDao {
    private void insert(Customer customer) {

    }

    private void update(Customer customer) {
        getSqlMapClientTemplate().update("updateCustomer", customer);
    }

    public void save(Customer customer) {
        if (customer.getId() == null) {
            insert(customer);
        } else {
            update(customer);
        }
    }

    // other CustomerDao methods are implemented as stubs
}
```

Having only a single method for insert and update saves coding, and because our DAO implementation knows how the domain object is stored, it can decide whether to perform an insert or update. Now, we are going to ignore the `insert(Customer)` method for the moment and focus on the `update(Customer)` method.

Rules similar to type usage apply to the update statements: you are free to use any Java type or iBATIS alias. To demonstrate this, we create a method that updates the name of a `Customer` record identified by its primary key. Again, we have two options: we can either use a `Map` instance or the domain object. Tests show that using a `Map` is slightly slower. When using a `Map`, we are creating another instance of `java.lang.Long`, whereas when we are using the `Customer` domain object, we can use the `setId(long)` method and pass the primitive rather than an instance of `java.lang.Long`.

■ **Note** Keep in mind that `Map` is slower in *this case*. If you find yourself updating only two fields out of 20, using a `Map` implementation is definitely more efficient.

Listing 10-32 shows two update elements: the first one takes the `Customer` domain object and the second one a `Map`.

Listing 10-32. *sqlMap File for the Customer Domain Object*

```
<?xml version="1.0" encoding="UTF-8" standalone="no"?>
<!DOCTYPE sqlMap PUBLIC "-//iBATIS.com//DTD SQL Map 2.0//EN" ➥
"http://www.ibatis.com/dtd/sql-map-2.dtd">

<sqlMap>
    <!-- as previous -->

    <update id="updateCustomerLastNameDO" parameterClass="customer">
        update T_Customer set Last_Name=#lastName# where Id=#id#
    </update>

    <update id="updateCustomerLastNameMap" parameterClass="map">
        update T_Customer set Last_Name=#lastName# where Id=#id#
    </update>
</sqlMap>
```

The implementation of the DAO interface is very straightforward (see Listing 10-33). We are not going to discuss the `Map` implementation; we leave this to you in case you wish to do your own performance testing.

Listing 10-33. *CustomerDao updateName() iBATIS Implementation*

```
public class SqlMapClientCustomerDao
    extends SqlMapClientDaoSupport
    implements CustomerDao {

    public void updateLastName(Long id, String lastName) {
        Customer customer = new Customer();
        customer.setId(id);
        customer.setLastName(lastName);
        getSqlMapClientTemplate().update("updateCustomerNameDO", customer);
    }

    // other CustomerDao methods are implemented as stubs
}
```

The performance tests reveal that the Map implementation took 19,063 milliseconds to perform 5,000 updates, whereas the domain object implementation took 15,937 milliseconds in a table of less than 1,000 rows. Do not be too concerned about using Map implementations; if your application is performing very complicated updates, the overhead of object creation and lookup is absolutely minimal compared to the actual database work.

There is one final point to make about data updates. Each DAO interface-implementation pair should be responsible for updating its own domain objects. Consider this situation: you have two domain objects, Order and OrderLine. Order has a List that contains instances of OrderLine objects. You may be tempted to code the SQL statement for the save () operation in the OrderDao implementation so that it saves all its orderLine objects, but this is not a very good idea. If you do so, OrderDao and OrderLineDao no longer have clear responsibilities. You have to document that once OrderDao.save(Order) is called, you do not need to call OrderLineDao.save(OrderLine) for each OrderLine in Order. Also, you might be tempted to include the entire operation in a transaction, which is not the best idea because you should try not to control transactions manually in the code. Delegate transaction management to Spring; if you can't wait to read about transaction management, go to Chapter 12.

Deleting Data

Now that we have covered data selects and updates, we can take a look at deletes. A delete is very similar to an update; just like an update, it takes a number of parameters and does not return any results. Let's start by implementing a delete(int) method in CustomerDao that deletes a row in the T_Customer table identified by the primary key. In Listing 10-34, we modify the sqlMap Customer.xml file and CustomerDao implementation.

Listing 10-34. *sqlMap File for the Customer Domain Object*

```
<?xml version="1.0" encoding="UTF-8" standalone="no"?>
<!DOCTYPE sqlMap PUBLIC "-//iBATIS.com//DTD SQL Map 2.0//EN" ➥
"http://www.ibatis.com/dtd/sql-map-2.dtd">

<sqlMap>
    <!-- as previous -->

    <delete id="deleteCustomer" parameterClass="long">
        delete from T_Customer where Id=#value#
    </delete>
</sqlMap>
```

The <delete> node declares a delete operation named deleteCustomer, which takes one parameter of type long that represents the primary key.

The addition to the DAO implementation class simply calls the delete method, passing it the name of the delete statement and the primary key value wrapped in a java.lang.Long (as shown in Listing 10-35).

Listing 10-35. *CustomerDao delete(int) iBATIS Implementation*

```
public class SqlMapClientCustomerDao
    extends SqlMapClientDaoSupport
    implements CustomerDao {

    public void delete(Long id) {
        getSqlMapClientTemplate().delete("deleteCustomer", id);
    }
```

```
    // other CustomerDao methods are implemented as stubs
}
```

The Java code is very simple and does exactly what we expect it to do: it removes a row from the table identified by its primary key.

You should consider concern slush when coding delete operations.

■**Note** Concern slush is a practice in application development when the application code doesn't have strictly defined tiers of responsibility (for example data access tier, business logic tier, presentation tier), making the application an almost unreadable mixture of code.

The considerations about concern slush apply to the delete operations: a DAO implementation class should delete only rows that belong to its domain object. It is absolutely valid to use `on delete cascade` in your foreign key definitions, which effectively means that a delete of a master record propagates to the child rows, but do not delete the referenced records yourself.

■**Note** Technically, this is *just* a same-layer concern slush. The real and nasty concern slush happens when a web layer contains parts of business logic, for example.

Inserting Data

It is time to tackle the last data operation—insert. An insert is very similar to an update operation, with one exception: you must concern yourself with the primary key value. You need to generate the primary key value before you perform the insert, or you need to get the generated primary key value after the insert.

■**Note** Most databases let you create a table without a primary key, but you should *always* have a primary key in a table.

For the insert example, we are again going to use Oracle, which allows us to demonstrate how to select a primary key value before, as well as after, an insert operation. If you are using automatically generated values and your database system offers no way to know what the next primary key value is going to be, it certainly will offer a way to retrieve a value that was generated by the *previous* insert operation. The catch is in the word "previous." In a high-contention system, another insert operation may complete and change the previously generated value before you can select it. The result is that even though the rows have been inserted with unique primary keys, your application has two different domain objects with the same value for their primary key. This problem is discussed more extensively in Chapter 9.

Let's take a look at an ideal scenario: we select the next value from a sequence and attempt an insert operation. It is impossible for two processes to get the same value from a sequence as each `select s_customer_id.nextval from dual` statement increases the sequence counter. Our insert operation consists of two separate steps: selecting the next value from the sequence and performing the actual insert operation. We also want to modify the property of the domain object that stores the primary key value. This process sounds complicated, but with iBATIS, it is not at all difficult. Listing 10-36 shows how to select a value from the sequence and perform the insert operation.

Listing 10-36. *sqlMap File Showing How to Select the Primary Key Values*

```
<?xml version="1.0" encoding="UTF-8" standalone="no"?>
<!DOCTYPE sqlMap PUBLIC "-//iBATIS.com//DTD SQL Map 2.0//EN"➥
"http://www.ibatis.com/dtd/sql-map-2.dtd">

<sqlMap>
    <!-- as previous -->

    <insert id="insertCustomer" parameterClass="customer">
        <selectKey keyProperty="id" resultClass="int">
            select s_customer_id.nextval from dual
        </selectKey>
        insert into T_Customer (Id, First_Name, Last_Name, Last_Login) ➥
                    values (#id#, #firstName#, #lastName#, #lastLogin#)
    </insert>
</sqlMap>
```

If you look at the `<insert>` element, you can see that the first step is to select a key from the sequence. After that, you simply use the selected key in the insert operation. The `<selectKey>` element also sets the domain object's `id` property to the value of the selected value from the sequence. The Java implementation of the `insert(Customer)` method is incredibly simple, as you can see in Listing 10-37.

Listing 10-37. *CustomerDao insert(Customer) iBATIS Implementation*

```
public class SqlMapClientCustomerDao
    extends SqlMapClientDaoSupport
    implements CustomerDao {

    private void insert(Customer customer) {
        getSqlMapClientTemplate().insert("insertCustomer", customer);
    }

    // other CustomerDao methods are implemented as stubs
}
```

That is all the code you have to write, honest. In Listing 10-38, we modify the source code for the `Main` class to test that our new object does indeed get inserted.

Listing 10-38. *Main Class Calling the save(Customer) Method*

```
public class Main {

    private ApplicationContext context;

    private void run() {
        // get the context and customerDao
        Date today = Calendar.getInstance().getTime();

        System.out.println("Inserting new Customer record");
        Customer customer = new Customer();
        customer.setFirstName("Jack");
        customer.setLastName("Bower");
        customer.setLastLogin(today);
        CustomerDetail detail = new CustomerDetail();
        detail.setId(101L);
```

```
        customer.setCustomerDetail(detail);
        customerDao.save(customer);

        System.out.println("Customer inserted " + customer);

    }

    public static void main(String[] args) {
        new Main().run();
    }

}
```

Running the application, as the following output shows, proves that we are selecting the next value from the sequence, setting the customer `id` property to the `sequence` value, and inserting a row with the selected `id` primary key:

```
Inserting new Customer record
Customer inserted Customer { id: 8, firstName: Jack, lastName: Bower, ➥
lastLogin: Wed Oct 17 10:36:31 GMT 2007, ➥
detail: CustomerDetail { id: 101, date: null}, gossip: null}
```

Unfortunately, some databases do not support sequences, or do not allow us to obtain the value that *is* generated for the primary key in an insert operation. The only thing we can do is to get the value generated by the previous insert operation. One such database is MySQL. If we use MySQL, we have to modify the SQL script (as shown in Listing 10-39) as well as the `<insert>` element in the `sqlMap` file.

Listing 10-39. *MySQL Create Script*

```
create table Customers (
    Id int auto_increment not null,
    FirstNameName varchar(50) not null,
    LastNameName varchar(50) not null,
    LastLogin timestamp not null,

    constraint PK_CustomerId primary key (Id)
);
```

The only difference is the `Id` column definition; instead of using sequence data type, we are using `int` with the `auto_increment` modifier. This tells MySQL that it should generate a unique value for the primary key if no value is supplied for the column in the insert statement.

The `sqlMap` also needs to be modified to select the generated key after the insert operation (see Listing 10-40).

Listing 10-40. *sqlMap File for the Customer Domain Object for MySQL*

```
<?xml version="1.0" encoding="UTF-8" standalone="no"?>
<!DOCTYPE sqlMap PUBLIC "-//iBATIS.com//DTD SQL Map 2.0//EN"➥
"http://www.ibatis.com/dtd/sql-map-2.dtd">

<sqlMap>
    <!-- as previous -->

    <insert id="insertCustomer" parameterClass="test">
        insert into Customers (Id, FirstName, LastName, LastLogin) ➥
```

```
            values (#id#, #firstName#, #lastName#, #lastLogin#)
        <selectKey keyProperty="id" resultClass="int">
            select select last_insert_id()
        </selectKey>
    </insert>
</sqlMap>
```

The implementation of CustomerDao remains the same. If we create a MySQL database, create the T_Customer table in it, modify the dataSource bean connection properties, and run the application, we get the same output and in almost all cases. We also get the correct value for the generated primary key.

■ **Note** The chances of selecting a primary key value generated by another insert operation are remote. An insert operation takes thousands of CPU instructions to finish; the chance that the scheduler of the operating system will switch threads so that this situation would arise are as likely as another Big Bang happening in your coffee mug—but remember, even the Big Bang happened at least once!

What's Missing from iBATIS?

Even though iBATIS offers a very good performance-to-code complexity ratio, several features are missing. Perhaps the most annoying absence is lack of support for persistent enumerations and object canonization.

Take a User domain object for example. Usually, a limited number of roles are used in a system. If a User object has a userRole property, a select statement that returns 1,000 User objects also creates 1,000 UserRole objects, even though most of the UserRole objects actually represent the same Role. This very inefficient practice results in a lot of memory being used up. This situation is similar to the java.lang.Boolean problem, where you can create 1,000 Boolean objects that represent Boolean.TRUE—even though these 1,000 objects represent the *same information*, you have 1,000 distinct objects. Another side effect of missing object canonization is that you have to use the equals (Object) method to compare the values, whereas if you had 1,000 references to the same object, you could use the equals (==) operator.

Also, a persistent enumeration would be a nice addition to iBATIS. Hibernate allows you to use persistent enumeration. This actually refers to an object that has public static <T> fromInt() and public int toInt() methods, which return an int value that represents value in the enumeration. Hibernate, however, creates an instance of the object.

The issues just discussed are the only problems in iBATIS we can think of, which makes it an exceptional DAO framework.

Overall Performance

Overall, the performance of iBATIS is very good. Because iBATIS allows you to write your own SQL statements in the sqlMap files, you are free to use native features of the database server you are using. You also have full control over the data that is selected into the columns. For instance, you can select custom data in your select statement, without selecting any column from the table you're referencing. There is no reason why you cannot use the code in Listing 10-41.

Listing 10-41. *sqlMap file for the Customer Domain Object*

```
<?xml version="1.0" encoding="UTF-8" standalone="no"?>
<!DOCTYPE sqlMap PUBLIC "-//iBATIS.com//DTD SQL Map 2.0//EN" ➥
"http://www.ibatis.com/dtd/sql-map-2.dtd">
```

```
<sqlMap>

    <typeAlias type="com.apress.prospring2.ch10.domain.Customer" alias="customer"/>

    <resultMap class="customer" id="result">
        <result property="id" column="Id"/>
        <result property="firstName" column="First_Name"/>
        <result property="lastName" column="Last_Name"/>
        <result property="lastLogin" column="Last_Login"/>
    </resultMap>

    <select id="getAllCustomers" resultMap="result">
        select (1+1) as Id, 'foo' as FirstName, 'bar' as LastName, ➥
                to_date('2004-01-01', 'yyyy-MM-dd') as LastLogin
    </select>
</sqlMap>
```

Even though the code in bold is not a typical select statement, it demonstrates your full control over the selected data and the way the data is selected.

You need to consider the possible performance implications of *n* plus one selects when selecting object properties of domain objects. In most cases, however, you can absorb the performance hit by splitting the `resultMap` implementations into a basic one that is used for selects that return large numbers of rows and another one that extends the basic `resultMap` to set more complex properties when the number of rows won't be very large. As always, do not guess; measure the performance!

As we said in the chapter introduction, the most important advantage of iBATIS is that it does not generate any code. Therefore, you have no data selection language to learn, and you do not have to translate to the database's SQL code. This allows you to use any nonstandard SQL extensions that your database may provide.

Bean configuration in separate XML files also helps you to keep the code relatively easy to manage.

The actual data operations are incredibly simple; the built-in types allow you to pass almost any parameters to the database operations without having to create specific Java beans for them.

We have highlighted several limitations in the code. The one that bothers us most is that there is no support for persistent enumerations and object canonicalization. This is an unfortunate side effect of almost every ORM framework we have worked with so far. You have to sacrifice a bit of the ideal design to accommodate the features or the lack of features of the framework you are using. These limitations notwithstanding, iBATIS is the least obtrusive framework we have seen so far. However, we do encourage you to read about Hibernate—the SQL code it generates is very good.

Summary

In this chapter, you have learned how to use iBATIS in your Spring applications. We believe that iBATIS offers the best trade-off between ease of development and code control. In fact, iBATIS does not generate SQL code, which means that your code is not interpreted in any way by the ORM framework. Caching is there to speed up data access in time-critical applications, and if you are aware of the few limitations of the framework, we believe you will be able to write very efficient, elegant, and high-performing applications.

For more information about iBATIS, including its latest source code, binaries, and documentation, go to `http://www.ibatis.com`.

CHAPTER 11

Hibernate Support

In this chapter, we will take a look at the Hibernate support code in Spring. We will begin with a short description of the Hibernate versions and their support in Spring. Next, you will read about configuration of the Hibernate session factory and transaction manager. After that, we will take a look at how to write efficient data manipulation code, focusing especially on using Hibernate with other data access methods. Next, we will take a look at lazy loading and session management—these areas are not very difficult conceptually but can become very complex in their implementation. Finally, we will you show some integration testing approaches.

Hibernate Primer

Before we start the discussion of Spring Hibernate support, we should take a quick look at how Hibernate works. Hibernate is an object-relational mapping (ORM) tool; it finds, saves, and deletes plain Java objects in a database with minimal impact on the Java code. Let's take a look at a simple `LogEntry` object defined in Listing 11-1.

Listing 11-1. *LogEntry Domain Object*

```
public class LogEntry {
    private Long id;
    private String name;
    private Date date;

    public Date getDate() {
        return date;
    }

    public void setDate(Date date) {
        this.date = date;
    }

    public Long getId() {
        return id;
    }

    public void setId(Long id) {
        this.id = id;
    }
```

```
    public String getName() {
        return name;
    }

    public void setName(String name) {
        this.name = name;
    }
}
```

We need to tell Hibernate how we want to store the LogEntry objects. Next, we define the table name and the column names for the properties we want to persist. We must pay special attention to the primary key. Listing 11-2 shows the final Hibernate mapping file.

Listing 11-2. *Hibernate Mapping for the LogEntry Object*

```
<?xml version="1.0"?>
<!DOCTYPE hibernate-mapping PUBLIC "-//Hibernate/Hibernate Mapping DTD 3.0//EN"
    "http://hibernate.sourceforge.net/hibernate-mapping-3.0.dtd">

<hibernate-mapping default-lazy="false">

    <class name="com.apress.prospring2.ch11.domain.LogEntry" table="t_log_entry">
        <id name="id" type="long" unsaved-value="null">
            <generator class="sequence">
                <param name="sequence">s_log_entry_id</param>
            </generator>
        </id>
        <property name="name" column="name_" not-null="true"/>
        <property name="date" column="date_" not-null="true"/>
    </class>

</hibernate-mapping>
```

Here, you see that the primary key (the id column and property) is generated from a sequence named s_log_entry_id. Hibernate can tell (again through the information from the configuration file) when to perform a SQL insert and when to do an update. In this particular case, if the value returned from the getId() method is null, Hibernate will issue an insert; otherwise, it will issue an update. The name property is stored in a not null column called name_ and the date property is stored in a not null column called date_.

Now, to insert a new LogEntry object, we simply create its instance and call session.saveOrUpdate(Object). To find a mapped object identified by its primary key, we use session.load(Class, Serializable) or session.get(Class, Serializable). We will explore the differences between these two calls later on in the chapter. To select more than one log entry, we use many of the Query methods (we create the Query instances by calling one of the session.createQuery() methods). Finally, to delete objects, we use the session.delete() methods.

Before we get to the details of the Spring Hibernate support, we must take a look at how Spring organizes the support classes in its distribution.

Packaging

There are currently two major versions of Hibernate: Hibernate 2.x and Hibernate 3.x. Since the packaging of the two Hibernate versions in Spring is very similar, the Spring distribution, by default, includes Hibernate 3 support. If you want to use Hibernate 2.x, you must include the spring-hibernate2.jar package and be careful not to accidentally use one of the org.springframework.orm.hibernate3 classes. Alternatively, you may choose the Spring modular distribution and include only the specific Spring packages your application needs. However, for new applications, we recommend that you use Hibernate 3, which means that you can carry on using the default spring.jar package.

The Spring Hibernate support works with versions 2.1.8 for Hibernate 2 support and version 3.2.5ga for Hibernate 3 support.

Introduction to Hibernate Support

The main Hibernate class is Session, which provides methods to find, save, and delete mapped objects. To create a Hibernate Session, you must first create the SessionFactory; creating and configuring SessionFactory to create the Sessions can be quite complex and cumbersome. Luckily, Spring comes to your aid with its implementation of the AbstractSessionFactoryBean subclasses: LocalSessionFactoryBean and AnnotationSessionFactoryBean. The LocalSessionFactoryBean needs to be configured with the mapping file locations, and these file locations need to be local from the application's point of view. In most cases, this means that the mapping resources are on the classpath. The second subclass, the AnnotationSessionFactoryBean, picks up Hibernate mappings from annotations on the classes we wish to use in Hibernate.

■ **Note** We do not encourage the use of annotations on the objects you will persist using Hibernate. In most cases, the persistent objects will be your application's domain objects. Using Hibernate-specific annotations exposes too much information to the tiers above the data access tier. We prefer the old-fashioned way of creating mapping files—leaving the domain objects completely independent of the DAO implementation you choose.

If you annotate your domain objects with Hibernate-specific annotations, you are implying that you have implemented the data access in Hibernate.

Regardless of the mapping information source, we need to supply some common dependencies to construct a SessionFactory using the appropriate factory bean. Listing 11-3 shows the minimalist LocalSessionFactoryBean configuration.

Listing 11-3. *Minimal Configuration of the LocalSessionFactoryBean*

```
<?xml version="1.0" encoding="UTF-8"?>
<beans xmlns="http://www.springframework.org/schema/beans"
       xmlns:xsi="http://www.w3.org/2001/XMLSchema-instance"
       xmlns:jee="http://www.springframework.org/schema/jee"
       xsi:schemaLocation="http://www.springframework.org/schema/beans
          http://www.springframework.org/schema/beans/spring-beans-2.5.xsd
          http://www.springframework.org/schema/jee
         http://www.springframework.org/schema/j2ee/spring-jee-2.5.xsd">

    <jee:jndi-lookup id="dataSource" jndi-name="java:comp/env/jdbc/prospring2/ch11"
        expected-type="javax.sql.DataSource"/>

    <bean id="hibernateSessionFactory"
       class="org.springframework.orm.hibernate3.LocalSessionFactoryBean">
        <property name="dataSource" ref="dataSource"/>
        <property name="mappingLocations">
            <list>
```

```
                <value>classpath*:/com/apress/prospring2/ch11/dataaccess/➥
                    hibernate/*.hbm.xml</value>
            </list>
        </property>
        <property name="hibernateProperties">
            <value>hibernate.dialect=org.hibernate.dialect.Oracle9Dialect</value>
        </property>
    </bean>
</beans>
```

First, we declare the `dataSource` bean of type `JndiObjectFactoryBean` (for a detailed explanation of why we use JNDI, see Chapter 22). Next, we declare the `hibernateSessionFactory` bean and set its `dataSource`, `mappingLocations`, and `hibernateProperties` properties. The `dataSoruce` property is necessary but not really very interesting. The `mappingLocations` property is much more intriguing. It is a list of values that can be converted into a Spring `Resource`; in this particular case, we include all `*.hbm.xml` files in the `com.apress.prospring2.ch11.dataaccess.hibernte` package. Finally, we need to tell Hibernate what SQL dialect to use. To do that, we set the `hibernate.dialect` property in the properties list of the `hibernateProperties` property (we honestly have to use the word property four times!). In this particular case, the database can be Oracle 9 or later (we use Oracle 10*g*). To verify that everything works, we will run the code from Listing 11-4.

Listing 11-4. *Sample Application to Verify That the Hibernate Configuration Works*

```
public class DaoDemo {

    public static void buildJndi() {
        try {
            TestUtils.NamingContextBuilder builder;
            builder = TestUtils.NamingContextBuilder.emptyActivatedContextBuilder();

            String connectionString = "jdbc:oracle:thin:@oracle.devcake.co.uk" +
                ":1521:INTL";
            builder.bind("java:comp/env/jdbc/prospring2/ch11",
                     new DriverManagerDataSource(
                    "oracle.jdbc.driver.OracleDriver", connectionString,
                    "PROSPRING", "x******6"));
        } catch (NamingException ignored) {
        }
    }

    public static void main(String[] args) throws NamingException {
        buildJndi();
        ApplicationContext ac =
            new ClassPathXmlApplicationContext("datasource-context-minimal.xml",
                DaoDemo.class);
    }

}
```

The sample application only creates and destroys the Hibernate beans. It is important to take note of the dependencies of this code. We need to set the following packages on the classpath; otherwise, we will get dreaded `ClassNotFound` exceptions:

- antlr-2.7.6.jar
- cglib-2.1_3.jar
- commons-logging-1.1.jar
- spring-2.0.6.jar
- hibernate-3.2.5ga.jar
- log4j-1.2.14.jar

When we run the application with the correct classpath, we should see the following log entries as the application starts up:

```
INFO [main] SessionFactoryImpl.<init>(161) | building session factory
DEBUG [main] SessionFactoryImpl.<init>(173) | ➥
Session factory constructed with filter configurations : {}
DEBUG [main] SessionFactoryImpl.<init>(177) | instantiating session factory with ➥
properties: {java.runtime.name=Java(TM) 2 Runtime Environment, Standard Edition,
...
hibernate.bytecode.use_reflection_optimizer=false,
...
hibernate.dialect=org.hibernate.dialect.Oracle9Dialect,
...
hibernate.connection.provider_class=➥
org.springframework.orm.hibernate3.LocalDataSourceConnectionProvider,
... }
...
DEBUG [main] SessionFactoryObjectFactory.<clinit>(39) | ➥
initializing class SessionFactoryObjectFactory
DEBUG [main] SessionFactoryObjectFactory.addInstance(76) | ➥
registered: 40284884158164670115816467d30000 (unnamed)
...
```

Notice that Spring builds the Hibernate SessionFactory by providing the properties in the Hibernate Spring context file and the hibernate.connection.provider_class property, which allows Spring to provide an implementation of Hibernate's ConnectionProvider so that Hibernate can access Spring-managed DataSource beans.

Using Hibernate Sessions

If, for some reason, you need to access the low-level Hibernate SessionFactory and Session instances created by calls to the factory, you can easily reference the Spring-managed bean that extends the AbstractSessionFactoryBean. Listing 11-5 shows you how to do that.

Listing 11-5. *Direct Access to Hibernate SessionFactory and Session*

```
public class DaoDemo {

    public static void buildJndi() { /* same code */ }

    public static void main(String[] args) throws NamingException {
        buildJndi();
        ApplicationContext ac =
            new ClassPathXmlApplicationContext("datasource-context-minimal.xml",
            DaoDemo.class);
```

```
        SessionFactory sessionFactory =
            (SessionFactory)ac.getBean("hibernateSessionFactory");
        Session session = sessionFactory.openSession();
        // use the Session
        session.close();
    }
}
```

Notice that you have to manually request a new session and that you have to explicitly close the session. The call to `session.close()` should really happen even if the operations we perform on the session fail with an exception. In addition to this, Hibernate sessions should typically begin with a call to the `beginTransaction()` method and end with a call to the `Transaction.commit()` method. We would also like to roll back the transaction if there are exceptions. The refactored code of the `main` method is shown in Listing 11-6.

Listing 11-6. *Refactrored Code of the main Method*

```
public class DaoDemo {

    public static void main(String[] args) throws Exception {
        buildJndi();
        ApplicationContext ac =
            new ClassPathXmlApplicationContext("datasource-context-minimal.xml",
            DaoDemo.class);
        SessionFactory sessionFactory =
            (SessionFactory)ac.getBean("hibernateSessionFactory");

        Session session = null;
        Transaction transaction = null;
        try {
            session = sessionFactory.openSession();
            transaction = session.beginTransaction();
            // do work
            transaction.commit();
        } catch (Exception e) {
            if (transaction != null) transaction.rollback();
            throw e;
        } finally {
            if (session != null) session.close();
        }
    }

}
```

The code in bold shows the important refactorings: first of all the `// do work` line performs whatever database work we wish to do. If the work succeeds (i.e., there are no exceptions), we commit the transaction; otherwise, we perform a rollback. Finally, we close the session. This code is acceptable if it only appears in the main method. If we find that we're writing the same code (except for the actual database work represented by the `// do work` marker here), we should look at using the template method pattern. This is exactly what we have done in Spring. The `HibernateTemplate` has operations that take instances of the `HibernateCallback` interface. This interface performs the actual work in the database, but the calling code takes care of session management. Figure 11-1 shows the concept behind the implementation of the `HibernateTemplate` callback.

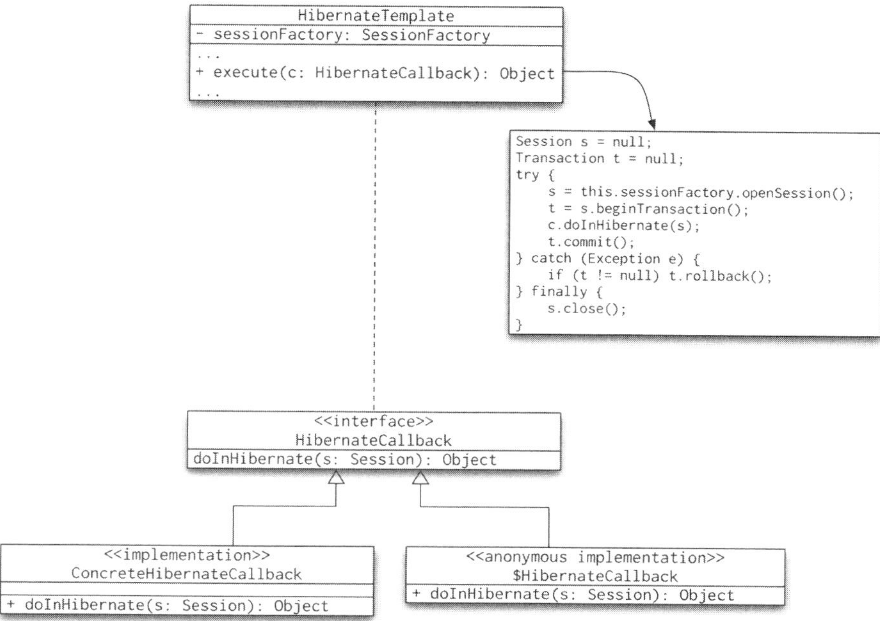

Figure 11-1. *UML diagram of the HibernateTemplate concept*

As you can see, all the hard work gets done in the `HibernateTemplate` class. All you have to do is supply the `HibernateCallback` implementation that performs the work you want to do in the session. Usually, the `HibernateCallback` implementation is an anonymous class; Listing 11-7 shows an example of its use.

Listing 11-7. *Use of the HibernateTemplate Class*

```
public class HibernateTemplateDemo {

    public static void main(String[] args) throws Exception {
        DaoDemoUtils.buildJndi();
        ApplicationContext ac =
            new ClassPathXmlApplicationContext("datasource-context-minimal.xml",
            DaoDemo.class);
        SessionFactory sessionFactory =
            (SessionFactory)ac.getBean("hibernateSessionFactory");
        HibernateTemplate template = new HibernateTemplate(sessionFactory);
        template.execute(new HibernateCallback() {
            public Object doInHibernate(Session session)
                throws HibernateException, SQLException {
                // do the work
                return null;
            }
        });
    }

}
```

The preceding listing illustrates most of the points we discussed. We create the HibernateTemplate class and give it the SessionFactory instance. Next, we call its execute method and supply an anonymous implementation of the HibernateCallback that does all the database work. We get the Session as the argument of the doInHibernate method in the callback. The session argument is never null, and we do not have to worry about closing it or about managing exceptions in the implementation. In addition to this, the code in the callback supplied to the doInHibernate method can participate in Spring transactions (we discuss transactions in much more detail in Chapter 16). The value we return from the doInHibernate method simply gets propagated to the caller as the result of the execute method.

In most applications, we will set the HibernateTemplate as a dependency; you can do this because all methods of the HibernateTemplate are thread safe, and you can, therefore, share a single instance of HibernateTemplate among many DAO beans. Listing 11-8 shows how to declare the hibernateTemplate bean; it can then be used in the same manner as the manually created HibernateTemplate instance.

Listing 11-8. *hibernateTemplate Bean and Its Use*

```
<?xml version="1.0" encoding="UTF-8"?>
<beans xmlns="http://www.springframework.org/schema/beans"
       xmlns:xsi="http://www.w3.org/2001/XMLSchema-instance"
       xmlns:jee="http://www.springframework.org/schema/jee"
       xsi:schemaLocation="http://www.springframework.org/schema/beans
           http://www.springframework.org/schema/beans/spring-beans-2.5.xsd
           http://www.springframework.org/schema/jee
           http://www.springframework.org/schema/j2ee/spring-jee-2.5.xsd">

    <jee:jndi-lookup id="dataSource" jndi-name="java:comp/env/jdbc/prospring2/ch11"
        expected-type="javax.sql.DataSource"/>

    <bean id="hibernateSessionFactory"
       class="org.springframework.orm.hibernate3.LocalSessionFactoryBean">
        <property name="dataSource" ref="dataSource"/>
        <property name="mappingLocations">
            <list>
                <value>classpath*:/com/apress/prospring2/ch11/dataaccess/➥
                    hibernate/*.hbm.xml</value>
            </list>
        </property>
        <property name="hibernateProperties">
            <props>
                <prop key="hibernate.dialect">
                    org.hibernate.dialect.Oracle9Dialect
                </prop>
            </props>
        </property>
    </bean>

    <bean id="hibernateTemplate"
        class="org.springframework.orm.hibernate3.HibernateTemplate">
        <property name="sessionFactory" ref="hibernateSessionFactory"/>
    </bean>

</beans>

public class HibernateTemplateBeanDemo {
```

```
    public static void main(String[] args) throws Exception {
        DaoDemoUtils.buildJndi();
        ApplicationContext ac =
            new ClassPathXmlApplicationContext("datasource-context-ht.xml",
            DaoDemo.class);
        HibernateTemplate template =
            (HibernateTemplate) ac.getBean("hibernateTemplate");
        template.execute(new HibernateCallback() {
            public Object doInHibernate(Session session)
                throws HibernateException, SQLException {
                // do the work
                return null;
            }
        });
    }

}
```

This change makes the implementation of any potential DAO interfaces quite straightforward; the `HibernateTemplate` instance is a Spring-managed bean, which means that we do not have to worry about creating new instances in our DAO implementations. The only reservation we may have is that setting up the implementation simply requires too much typing: we need to declare a property of type `HibernateTemplate` and its setter in every DAO. This is why Spring contains the `HibernateDaoSuppot` convenience superclass. This class gives us access to the `HibernateTemplate` and the Hibernate `Session` and `SessionFactory`.

Using HibernateDaoSupport

The convenient, abstract `HibernateDaoSupport` superclass allows us to implement our DAO interfaces in Hibernate with as little code as possible. Let's take a look at the code in Listing 11-9, which shows the `LogEntryDao` interface and its Hibernate implementation.

Listing 11-9. *LogEntryDao and Its Implementation*

```
public interface LogEntryDao {

    void save(LogEntry logEntry);

    List<LogEntry> getAll();

}

public class HibernateLogEntryDao extends
    HibernateDaoSupport implements
    LogEntryDao {

    public void save(LogEntry logEntry) {
        getHibernateTemplate().saveOrUpdate(logEntry);
    }

    @SuppressWarnings({"unchecked"})
    public List<LogEntry> getAll() {
        return getHibernateTemplate().find("from LogEntry");
    }
}
```

You can see that the implementation is incredibly simple—all the code we really need to insert or update a `LogEntry` object to the database is really `getHibernateTemplate().saveOrUpdate(logEntry)`. Selecting all `LogEntry` objects from the database is equally simple.

■ **Note** The `@SuppressWarnings({"unchecked"})` annotation tells the `javac` compiler not to report the unchecked operations warning. Hibernate does not support generics (and how could it know what classes to return without first parsing the query?) and neither does `HibernateTemplate`. You need to unit and integration test your DAO code to make sure you are getting the correct objects back.

Listing 11-10 shows the only configuration needed to create the `HibernateLogEntryDao`.

Listing 11-10. *Spring Context File for the HibernateLogEntryDao*

```
<?xml version="1.0" encoding="UTF-8"?>
<beans xmlns="http://www.springframework.org/schema/beans"
       xmlns:xsi="http://www.w3.org/2001/XMLSchema-instance"
       xmlns:jee="http://www.springframework.org/schema/jee"
       xsi:schemaLocation="http://www.springframework.org/schema/beans
           http://www.springframework.org/schema/beans/spring-beans-2.5.xsd
           http://www.springframework.org/schema/jee
           http://www.springframework.org/schema/j2ee/spring-jee-2.5.xsd">

    <jee:jndi-lookup id="dataSource" jndi-name="java:comp/env/jdbc/prospring2/ch11"
        expected-type="javax.sql.DataSource"/>

    <bean id="hibernateSessionFactory"
       class="org.springframework.orm.hibernate3.LocalSessionFactoryBean">
        <property name="dataSource" ref="dataSource"/>
        <property name="mappingLocations">
            <list>
                <value>classpath*:/com/apress/prospring2/ch11/dataaccess/➥
                    hibernate/*.hbm.xml</value>
            </list>
        </property>
        <property name="hibernateProperties">
            <props>
                <prop key="hibernate.dialect">
                    org.hibernate.dialect.Oracle9Dialect
                 </prop>
            </props>
        </property>
    </bean>

    <bean id="logEntryDao"
        class="com.apress.prospring2.ch11.dataaccess.hibernate.➥
            HibernateLogEntryDao">
        <property name="sessionFactory" ref="hibernateSessionFactory"/>
    </bean>

</beans>
```

We can now use the `logEntryDao` as a standard Spring-managed bean. This configuration shows only one `HibernateSupportDao` subclass; in real-world applications, having tens of such DAO implementations is not unusual. We could repeat the `<property name="sessionFactory"> . . .`

line in every DAO bean definition, but we could save even this bit of additional typing by declaring an abstract `hibernateDaoSupport` bean and creating the real DAO subbeans (see Listing 11-11).

Listing 11-11. *Abstract hibernateDaoSupport Bean and Its Use*

```
<?xml version="1.0" encoding="UTF-8"?>
<beans xmlns="http://www.springframework.org/schema/beans"
    ....>
    <bean id="hibernateDaoSupport" abstract="true"
        class="org.springframework.orm.hibernate3.support.HibernateDaoSupport">
        <property name="sessionFactory" ref="hibernateSessionFactory"/>
    </bean>

    <bean id="logEntryDao"
        class="com.apress.prospring2.ch11.dataaccess.hibernate.HibernateLogEntryDao"
       parent="hibernateDaoSupport"/>

</beans>
```

This is exactly what we need: we can now add a new `HibernateDaoSupport` subclass with as little Spring configuration as possible.

Deciding Between HibernateTemplate and Session

Recall that the `JdbcTemplate`'s work is twofold: it provides common resource management and translates the JDBC checked exceptions to the Spring data access exceptions. Hibernate 3 uses runtime exceptions, and Spring 2.5's `@Repository` annotation gives you resource management similar to what you get in `HibernateTemplate`. Therefore, we can say that, in most cases, using the `HibernateTemplate` is not necessary at all. Consider the code in Listing 11-12.

Listing 11-12. *Using Hibernate SessionFactory Instead of HibernateTemplate*

```
@Repository
public class TemplatelessHibernateInvoiceLogEntryDao implements LogEntryDao {
    private SessionFactory sessionFactory;

    public TemplatelessHibernateInvoiceLogEntryDao(SessionFactory sessionFactory) {
        this.sessionFactory = sessionFactory;
    }

    public LogEntry getById(Long id) {
        return (LogEntry) this.sessionFactory.getCurrentSession().
            get(LogEntry.class, id);
    }

    public void save(LogEntry logEntry) {
        this.sessionFactory.getCurrentSession().saveOrUpdate(logEntry);
    }

    public List<LogEntry> getAll() {
        return this.sessionFactory.getCurrentSession().
            createQuery("from LogEntry").list();
    }
}
```

This clearly shows that we are using the SessionFactory interface from Hibernate, and we are using its getCurrentSession method. This method, according to the Hibernate documentation, returns a Session bound to the current thread. Listing 11-13 shows how we use the TemplatelessHibernateInvoiceLogEntryDao bean in a sample application.

Listing 11-13. *Using the templatelessLogEntryDao Bean*

```
public class TemplatelessHibernateLogEntryDaoDemo {

    public static void main(String[] args) throws Exception {
        DaoDemoUtils.buildJndi();
        ApplicationContext ac = new ClassPathXmlApplicationContext(
            "datasource-context-dao.xml", DaoDemo.class);
        LogEntryDao logEntryDao =
            (LogEntryDao) ac.getBean("templatelessLogEntryDao");
        logEntryDao.getAll();
    }

}
```

When we run the example in Listing 11-13, it fails:

```
Exception in thread "main" org.hibernate.HibernateException:
No Hibernate Session bound to thread, and configuration does not allow
creation of non-transactional one here.
```

The exception makes sense: the SessionFactory.getCurrentSession method tries to return the Session bound to the current thread, but there is no such Session, and the SessionFactory configuration does not include information about how to create one. We can tell Hibernate how to create a new thread-bound Session (and which transaction manager to use) by modifying the hibernateSessionFactory bean definition. Listing 11-14 shows the modified datasource-context-dao.xml file.

Listing 11-14. *The Modified hibernateSessionFactory Bean*

```
<?xml version="1.0" encoding="UTF-8"?>
<beans xmlns="http://www.springframework.org/schema/beans"
    ...>

...

     <bean id="hibernateSessionFactory"
          class="org.springframework.orm.hibernate3.LocalSessionFactoryBean">
          <property name="dataSource" ref="dataSource"/>
          <property name="mappingLocations">
               <list>
                    <value>classpath*:/com/apress/prospring2/ch11/dataaccess/➥
                       hibernate/*.hbm.xml</value>
               </list>
          </property>
          <property name="hibernateProperties">
               <props>
                    <prop key="hibernate.dialect">
                        org.hibernate.dialect.Oracle9Dialect
                     </prop>
```

```
                <prop key="hibernate.current_session_context_class">
                    thread
                </prop>
                <prop key="hibernate.transaction.factory_class">
                       org.hibernate.transaction.JDBCTransactionFactory</prop>
            </props>
        </property>
    </bean>
...
</beans>
```

This change allows Hibernate to create a new thread-bound `Session` in the call to `getCurrentSession`. However, the application still fails when we call the `createQuery` method; the exception is

```
org.hibernate.HibernateException: createQuery is not valid ➥
without active transaction
```

We will need to make one last modification to our code and include an explicit call to create a `Hibernate` transaction. Listing 11-15 shows the new `TemplatelessHibernateLogEntryDao` class.

Listing 11-15. *Modified Templateless DAO*

```
@Repository
public class TemplatelessHibernateInvoiceLogEntryDao implements LogEntryDao {
    ...
    public List<LogEntry> getAll() {
        Transaction transaction = this.sessionFactory.getCurrentSession().
            beginTransaction();
        try {
            return this.sessionFactory.getCurrentSession().
                createQuery("from LogEntry").list();
        } finally {
            transaction.commit();
        }
    }
}
```

The text in bold shows the code we needed to add to make the sample work. But let's not stop here. We need to take a look at the exception handling and translation. To do this, we will add the `getByName(String)` method to the `LogEntryDao` interface but make a deliberate mistake in its implementation. Both implementations of the `LogEntryDao` interface (`HibernateLogEntryDao` and `TemplatelessLogEntryDao`) are going to run the same Hibernate code (see Listing 11-16).

Listing 11-16. *Incorrect Hibernate Code in the LogEntryDao Implementations*

```
public class HibernateLogEntryDao extends HibernateDaoSupport
    implements LogEntryDao {
...
    public LogEntry getByName(final String name) {
        return (LogEntry) getHibernateTemplate().execute(new HibernateCallback() {
            public Object doInHibernate(Session session)
                throws HibernateException, SQLException {
                return session.
                       createQuery("from LogEntry where name = :name").
                       setParameter("name", name).
```

```
                        uniqueResult();
            }
        });
    }
...
}

@Repository
public class TemplatelessHibernateInvoiceLogEntryDao implements LogEntryDao {
    private SessionFactory sessionFactory;

...
    public LogEntry getByName(String name) {
        Transaction transaction = this.sessionFactory.getCurrentSession().
            beginTransaction();
        try {
            return (LogEntry) this.sessionFactory.getCurrentSession().
                    createQuery("from LogEntry where name = :name").
                    setParameter("name", name).
                    uniqueResult();
        } finally {
            transaction.commit();
        }
    }
...
}
```

You can see that the code in bold is the same in both classes. However, when we run it, with more than one row with the same value in the name_ column, we get the following exception when we use the HibernateTemplate:

```
org.springframework.dao.IncorrectResultSizeDataAccessException:
query did not return a unique result: 2
```

However, we get the following one when we use the Session directly:

```
org.hibernate.NonUniqueResultException: query did not return a unique result: 2
```

Obviously, there was no exception translation. However, we can add a bean post processor that will instruct the framework to intercept all calls to the beans annotated with @Repository and perform the standard exception translation. Listing 11-17 shows the one-line post processor definition.

Listing 11-17. *The Exception Translator Bean Post Processor*

```
<bean class="org.springframework.dao.annotation.➥
    PersistenceExceptionTranslationPostProcessor"/>
```

With this bean in place, we can run TemplatelessHibernateLogEntryDaoDemo, and even though we are not using the HibernateTemplate at all, we still get the Spring data access exception when we call the getByName method.

You can see that your DAO implementation does not need to use hardly any Spring code at all, and when you use the Spring declarative transaction management and your DAO templateless bean implementation in a transactional context, you do not even need to worry about the explicit Hibernate transaction management code. Even though this approach makes your Hibernate DAO classes almost completely independent of Spring (save for the `@Repository` annotation), we still favor the `HibernateTemplate` approach. Using `HibernateTemplate` makes your code framework dependent, but chances are that you will not need to change the framework in the life cycle of the application.

Using Hibernate in Enterprise Applications

The code in the examples in the previous section is perfectly functional Hibernate code. In fact, you can take the code we have written and use it in almost any enterprise application. But it will not work as efficiently as we would like.

The first problem is that we have done nothing to prevent updates of stale data. The code we have will simply update the rows in the database without any checks.

Next, we do not consider transactional behavior. Without any additional code, the code in the callback supplied to the `doInHibernate` method does not automatically run in a transaction. Enterprise applications certainly need to support transactions in the traditional sense of the word, conforming to the ACID (atomicity, consistency, independence, and durability) rules. Moreover, enterprise applications often include other resources (a JMS queue, for example) in a transaction.

Next, the examples we have given work with `LogEntry` objects. The `LogEntry` class does not have any associations; it can be fully constructed using data from a single database row. Enterprise applications usually manipulate complex objects with many associations. Handling these associations efficiently is important; otherwise, you may end up with extremely complex SQL statements.

Finally, if the `t_log_entry` table contained hundreds of thousands of rows, the examples we gave would simply crash with a `java.lang.OutOfMemoryException`. Real applications need to be able to deal efficiently and elegantly with very large data sets.

In this section, we will take a look at how we can solve each of these problems in a way that is as close to real-world application code as possible.

Preventing Stale Data Updates

Table 11-1 shows a scenario in which our application can overwrite data updated by another user.

Table 11-1. *Stale Data Updates Scenario*

Time	Thread A	Thread B	Database
0	`LogEntry e = load(1L)`		`1, "Test", 12/10/2007`
1		`LogEntry e = load(1L)`	`1, "Test", 12/10/2007`
2	`e.setName("X")`		`1, "Test", 12/10/2007`
3	`save(e)`		`1, "X", 12/10/2007`
4		`e.setName("Z")`	`1, "X", 12/10/2007`
5		`save(e)`	`1, "Z", 12/10/2007`

The critical operation happens in Thread B at time 5. Thread B is allowed to overwrite an update performed by Thread A at time 3. This is most likely a problem, because Thread B thinks it is changing `Name` to `Z`, while in fact it is changing `X` to `Z`. In this particular case, it is not a major problem, but if you replace the `name` column for `account_balance`, the problem becomes much more serious.

There are several ways to prevent this situation: Thread A can lock the entire row so that Thread B cannot read it until Thread A has finished updating it. This approach is called pessimistic locking—we believe that problems will happen so we lock the row to guarantee exclusive access to it. This approach will prevent the problem described in Table 11-1, but it will also introduce a significant performance bottleneck. If the application is performing a lot of updates, we may end up with the majority of the table locked, and the system will be forever waiting for rows to become unlocked.

If you perform more reads than writes, it is better to leave the rows unlocked and use optimistic locking. With optimistic locking, we do not explicitly lock the row for updates, because we believe that conflicts will not happen. To identify stale data, we add a `version` column to the table and to our domain object. When we save, we check that the version in the database matches the version in our object. If it does, no other thread has modified the row we are about to update, and we can proceed. If the version in our object differs from the version of the row in the database, we throw an exception indicating that we attempted to save stale data. Hibernate makes optimistic locking very easy; Listing 11-18 shows the optimistic-locking-enabled `LogEntry` object.

Listing 11-18. *Optimistic Locking LogEntry Object*

```
public class LogEntry {
    private Long id;
    private String name;
    private Date date;
    private Long version;

    // getters and setters

    public Long getVersion() {
        return version;
    }

    public void setVersion(Long version) {
        this.version = version;
    }
}
```

Next, take a look at Listing 11-19, where we tell Hibernate to perform optimistic locking checks on the `LogEntry` object.

Listing 11-19. *Hibernate Mapping Configuration for the LogEntry Class*

```
<?xml version="1.0"?>
<!DOCTYPE hibernate-mapping PUBLIC
        "-//Hibernate/Hibernate Mapping DTD 3.0//EN"
        "http://hibernate.sourceforge.net/hibernate-mapping-3.0.dtd">

<hibernate-mapping default-lazy="false">

    <class name="com.apress.prospring2.ch11.domain.LogEntry" table="t_log_entry">
        <id name="id" type="long" unsaved-value="null">
            <generator class="sequence">
                <param name="sequence">s_log_entry_id</param>
            </generator>
        </id>
        <version name="version" column="version" unsaved-value="null" type="long" />
        <property name="name" column="name_" not-null="true"/>
        <property name="date" column="date_" not-null="true"/>
    </class>

</hibernate-mapping>
```

The code in bold shows the only modification we needed to instruct Hibernate to perform optimistic-locking checks whenever we attempt to save the `LogEntry` object. To test that Hibernate will do what we expect, we issue the SQL command `alter table t_log_entry add version number(19, 0) null` and run the code in Listing 11-20.

Listing 11-20. *Testing the Optimistic Locking*

```
public class VersioningDemo {

    public static void main(String[] args) throws Exception {
        DaoDemoUtils.buildJndi();
        ApplicationContext ac =
            new ClassPathXmlApplicationContext("datasource-context-dao.xml",
          DaoDemo.class);
        LogEntryDao logEntryDao = (LogEntryDao) ac.getBean("logEntryDao");
        // save the original entry
        LogEntry le = new LogEntry();
        le.setName("Name");
        le.setDate(Calendar.getInstance().getTime());
        logEntryDao.save(le);

        // load two instances of the same LogEntry object
        LogEntry le1 = logEntryDao.getById(le.getId());
        LogEntry le2 = logEntryDao.getById(le.getId());
        // modify and save le1
        le1.setName("X");
        logEntryDao.save(le1);
        // now, let's try to modify and save le2.
        // remember, le2 represents the same row as le1
        le2.setName("Z");
        logEntryDao.save(le2);
    }
}
```

The code simulates the behavior of the application from Table 11-1. It loads two `LogEntry` objects that refer to the same row, makes a modification to one, and tries to modify the second one. However, once `le1` is saved, `le2` contains stale data, and the line in bold should not allow it to be persisted. When we run the application, we can see that that is exactly what happens:

```
* 1 logEntryDao.save(le1);
DEBUG [main] AbstractBatcher.log(401) | update t_log_entry set version=?, name_=?,
 date_=? where id=? and version=?
DEBUG [main] NullableType.nullSafeSet(133) | binding '1' to parameter: 1
DEBUG [main] NullableType.nullSafeSet(133) | binding 'X' to parameter: 2
DEBUG [main] NullableType.nullSafeSet(133) | binding '2007-10-12 10:35:06' to ➥
parameter: 3
DEBUG [main] NullableType.nullSafeSet(133) | binding '1160' to parameter: 4
DEBUG [main] NullableType.nullSafeSet(133) | binding '0' to parameter: 5
...

* 2 logEntryDao.save(le2);
DEBUG [main] AbstractBatcher.log(401) | update t_log_entry set version=?, name_=?,
date_=? where id=? and version=?
DEBUG [main] NullableType.nullSafeSet(133) | binding '1' to parameter: 1
DEBUG [main] NullableType.nullSafeSet(133) | binding 'Z' to parameter: 2
DEBUG [main] NullableType.nullSafeSet(133) | binding '2007-10-12 10:35:06' to ➥
```

```
parameter: 3
DEBUG [main] NullableType.nullSafeSet(133) | binding '1160' to parameter: 4
DEBUG [main] NullableType.nullSafeSet(133) | binding '0' to parameter: 5
...
ERROR [main] AbstractFlushingEventListener.performExecutions(301) |
    Could not synchronize database state with session
org.hibernate.StaleObjectStateException: Row was updated or deleted by another➥
transaction (or unsaved-value mapping was incorrect): ➥
[com.apress.prospring2.ch11.domain.LogEntry#1160]
    at org.hibernate.persister.entity.AbstractEntityPersister.➥
        check(AbstractEntityPersister.java:1765)
    ...
    at com.apress.prospring2.ch11.dataaccess.VersioningDemo.➥
       main(VersioningDemo.java:34)
```

The line marked `* 1` in the output shows the point where we call `logEntryDao.save(le1)`. The update operation includes both the primary key (`id`) and the version. The version gets increased on update, and Hibernate checks that exactly one row has been modified. We try to run `logEntryDao.save(le2)` at the line marked `* 2`. We see a similar update statement, but the version in the database is now set to `1`. Therefore, the update affects zero rows, and at that point, Hibernate throws the `StaleObjectStateException`.

Object Equality

Now that we can safely prevent stale data updates, we need to consider another important limitation. When we persist collections in Hibernate, we are likely to use some kind of `Collection`. When we are modeling a 1-to-*n* relationship, we are most likely to use a `Set`. A `Set` is a collection that does not guarantee order of elements and does not allow duplicate elements; this is precisely what a 1-to-*n* relationship in a database represents. We will be adding our domain objects to the `Sets`, so we need to consider their equality. We can implement natural equality or database equality. Natural equality means that two objects are equal if they contain the same data from the application logic point of view. Consider the domain object in Listing 11-21.

Listing 11-21. *The Customer Domain Object*

```
public class Customer {
    private Long id;
    private String title;
    private String firstName;
    private String lastName;
    private String address;

    // getters and setters
}
```

When should we consider two `Customer` objects equal? Is it when their IDs are equal or when their `title`, `firstName`, `lastName`, and `address` fields are equal, regardless of the value of `id`? When it comes to data persistence, we favor the first approach. The database does not care if it contains two rows with all other columns set to the same value as long as the rows' primary keys are unique and the rows do not violate any other constraints. If you need to enforce natural equality, consider using a unique index. With this in mind, we can take a look at the implementation of the `equals` and `hashCode` methods in our `LogEntry` class; see Listing 11-22.

Listing 11-22. *LogEntry equals and hashCode Implementation*

```
public class LogEntry {
    // same as before

    public boolean equals(Object o) {
        if (this == o) return true;
        if (o == null || getClass() != o.getClass()) return false;

        //noinspection CastToConcreteClass
        final LogEntry that = (LogEntry) o;

        if (this.id != null ? !this.id.equals(that.id) : that.id != null)
            return false;
        //noinspection RedundantIfStatement
        if (this.version != null ?
            !this.version.equals(that.version) : that.version != null) return false;

        return true;
    }

    public int hashCode() {
        int result = super.hashCode();
        result = 31 * result + (this.version != null ? this.version.hashCode() : 0);
        result = 31 * result + (this.id != null ? this.id.hashCode() : 0);
        return result;
    }

}
```

We have implemented database equality with a twist: two objects are equal if they have the same id and the same version. There is one slight problem with this: it is likely that our domain will contain many other classes, not just LogEntry. We will therefore refactor the code, move the common implementation of equals and hashCode to a new class, and have LogEntry extend the new class. Listing 11-23 shows this refactoring.

Listing 11-23. *Refactored LogEntry Class*

```
public abstract class AbstractIdentityVersionedObject<T> implements Serializable {
    protected Long version;
    protected T id;

    public AbstractIdentityVersionedObject() {

    }

    public AbstractIdentityVersionedObject(T id) {
        this.id = id;
    }

    protected final boolean idEquals(Object o) {
        if (this == o) return true;
        if (o == null || getClass() != o.getClass()) return false;

        //noinspection CastToConcreteClass
        final AbstractIdentityVersionedObject that =
           (AbstractIdentityVersionedObject) o;
```

```
        if (this.id != null ? !this.id.equals(that.id) : that.id != null)
            return false;
        //noinspection RedundantIfStatement
        if (this.version != null ?
            !this.version.equals(that.version) : that.version != null) return false;

        return true;
    }

    protected final int idHashCode() {
        int result = super.hashCode();
        result = 31 * result + (this.version != null ? this.version.hashCode() : 0);
        result = 31 * result + (this.id != null ? this.id.hashCode() : 0);
        return result;
    }

    @Override
    public boolean equals(final Object o) {
        return idEquals(o);
    }

    @Override
    public int hashCode() {
        return idHashCode();
    }

    public T getId() {
        return id;
    }

    public void setId(final T id) {
        this.id = id;
    }

    public Long getVersion() {
        return version;
    }

    public void setVersion(final Long version) {
        this.version = version;
    }
}

public class LogEntry extends AbstractIdentityVersionedObject<Long> {
    private String name;
    private Date date;

    public Date getDate() {
        return date;
    }

    public void setDate(Date date) {
        this.date = date;
    }

    public String getName() {
        return name;
```

```
    }

    public void setName(String name) {
        this.name = name;
    }

}
```

The AbstractIdentityVersionedObject class contains the id and version properties (and the id is a generic type, which allows us to use any type for the primary key value, even a compound value!). It also implements database equality. The LogEntry object simply extends AbstractIdentityVersionedObject<Long> and adds only the columns it declares. This makes our domain code much more readable, and we do not have to worry about forgetting to implement the equals and hashCode methods in a new domain class. However, even though this code breaks the usual contract for the equals and hashCode methods, it is useful for objects that you expect to persist in a database. It assumes that an id with the value null represents an object that you have not yet inserted. Additionally, it assumes that you will not explicitly modify the values of the id and version properties.

This forms a good starting point for our discussion of lazy loading, but before we get to that, we need to take a look at one other crucial enterprise requirement.

Transactional Behavior

The next area we need to look at is the transactional behavior of Hibernate support. Spring uses the PlatformTransactionManager interface in its transactional support; for use with Hibernate, we have the HibernateTransactionManager implementation. This bean needs the SessionFactory reference; Listing 11-24 shows its configuration.

Listing 11-24. *Transactional Support in Hibernate*

```
<?xml version="1.0" encoding="UTF-8"?>
<beans xmlns="http://www.springframework.org/schema/beans"
    ....>
    <bean id="hibernateDaoSupport" abstract="true"
        class="org.springframework.orm.hibernate3.support.HibernateDaoSupport">
        <property name="sessionFactory" ref="hibernateSessionFactory"/>
    </bean>

    <bean id="logEntryDao"
        class="com.apress.prospring2.ch11.dataaccess.hibernate.HibernateLogEntryDao"
       parent="hibernateDaoSupport"/>

    <bean id="transactionManager"
        class="org.springframework.orm.hibernate3.HibernateTransactionManager">
        <property name="sessionFactory" ref="hibernateSessionFactory"/>
    </bean>

</beans>
```

We now have the `transactionManager` bean, which allows us to control Hibernate transactions using the common Spring transaction framework. However, declaring only the `transactionManager` bean does not mean we get transactional behavior, as code in Listing 11-25 shows.

Listing 11-25. *Still Nontransactional Behavior*

```
public class HibernateLogEntryDaoTx1Demo {

    private static LogEntry save(LogEntryDao dao, String name) {
        LogEntry le = new LogEntry();
        le.setName(name);
        le.setDate(Calendar.getInstance().getTime());
        dao.save(le);
        return le;
    }

    public static void main(String[] args) throws Exception {
        DaoDemoUtils.buildJndi();
        ApplicationContext ac =
            new ClassPathXmlApplicationContext("datasource-context-dao.xml",
            DaoDemo.class);
        LogEntryDao logEntryDao = (LogEntryDao) ac.getBean("logEntryDao");

        try {
            save(logEntryDao, "Hello, this works");
            save(logEntryDao, null);
        } catch (Exception e) {
            // we don't want anything here, but Alas!
            System.out.println(logEntryDao.getAll());
        }
    }

}
```

The first Hibernate operation in the `save` method succeeds, but the second one fails. Because we have not defined the boundary of the transaction, we will find one row in the catch block. We need to rethink our transaction strategy at this point: we could make the `HibernateLogEntryDao.save(LogEntry)` method transactional, but that would not give us any benefit. In fact, making a single DAO method transactional is not a good practice—it is up to the service layer to define transactional boundaries. The DAO layer should be a relatively simple translator between domain objects and some data store.

Let's create a simple service interface and its implementation. The service implementation will use the log, and we will ensure that the service method is transactional. Figure 11-2 shows a diagram of the service we will create.

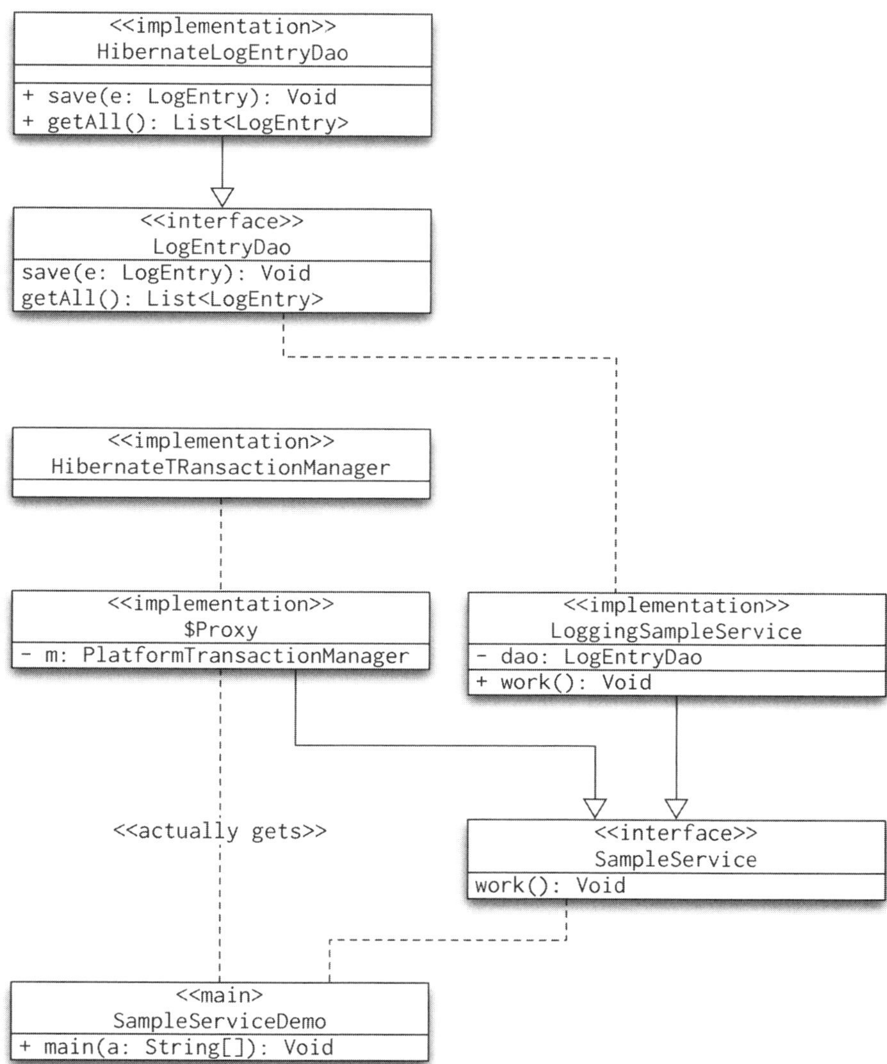

Figure 11-2. *UML diagram of the service*

Figure 11-2 shows that the code in the `SampleServiceDemo` example does not use the `LoggingSampleService` implementation of the `SampleService`; instead, it uses a dynamically generated proxy. This proxy, in turn, uses the `HibernateTransactionManager` to maintain the transactional behavior of the `work()` method. The `LogEntryDao` and its `HibernateLogEntryDao` implementation are shown for completeness. For further discussion on AOP and transactions, see Chapters 5, 6, and 16.

Listing 11-26 shows the service interface, the implementation, and the Spring context file.

Listing 11-26. *The Service Layer and Its Configuration*

```
public interface SampleService {

    void work();

}

public class LoggingSampleService implements SampleService {
    private LogEntryDao logEntryDao;

    private void log(String message) {
        LogEntry entry = new LogEntry();
        entry.setDate(Calendar.getInstance().getTime());
        entry.setName(message);
        this.logEntryDao.save(entry);
    }

    public void work() {
        log("Begin.");
        log("Processing...");

        if (System.currentTimeMillis() % 2 == 0) log(null);
        log("Done.");
    }

    public void setLogEntryDao(LogEntryDao logEntryDao) {
        this.logEntryDao = logEntryDao;
    }
}

<?xml version="1.0" encoding="UTF-8"?>
<beans xmlns="http://www.springframework.org/schema/beans"
        ...>

    <tx:advice id="txAdvice" transaction-manager="transactionManager">
        <tx:attributes>
            <tx:method name="work"/>
        </tx:attributes>
    </tx:advice>

    <aop:config>
        <aop:pointcut id="sampleServiceOperation"
            expression="execution(* com.apress.prospring2.ch11.service.➥
                SampleService.*(..))"/>
        <aop:advisor advice-ref="txAdvice" pointcut-ref="sampleServiceOperation"/>
    </aop:config>

    <bean id="sampleService"
        class="com.apress.prospring2.ch11.service.LoggingSampleService">
        <property name="logEntryDao" ref="logEntryDao"/>
    </bean>
</beans>
```

Looking at the code of the LoggingSampleService, we can see that we deliberately try to save the LogEntry object with a null name, which causes an exception. The advice catches the exception and rolls back the transaction and, therefore, the first two log entries. If the timing is favorable, we do not insert the LogEntry object with null name and insert only the final LogEntry object. So, for a successful call, we should get three rows in the t_log_entry table, and we should get no rows for a failed call. Let's verify this in code (see Listing 11-27) as well as in SQL*Plus client.

Listing 11-27. *Using the SampleService*

```
public class SampleServiceDemo {

    public static void main(String[] args) throws Exception {
        DaoDemoUtils.buildJndi();
        ApplicationContext ac = new ClassPathXmlApplicationContext(new String[] {
            "classpath*:/com/apress/prospring2/ch11/dataaccess/➥
                datasource-context-tx.xml",
            "classpath*:/com/apress/prospring2/ch11/service/*-context.xml"
        });
        SampleService sampleService = (SampleService)ac.getBean("sampleService");
        LogEntryDao logEntryDao = (LogEntryDao) ac.getBean("logEntryDao");
        int successCount = 0;
        int failureCount = 0;
        int before = logEntryDao.getAll().size();
        for (int i = 0; i < 10; i++) {
            if (tryWork(sampleService)) {
                successCount++;
            } else {
                failureCount++;
            }
        }
        System.out.println("Inserted " + (logEntryDao.getAll().size() - before) +
            ", for " + successCount + " successes and " +
           failureCount + " failures");
    }

    private static boolean tryWork(SampleService sampleService) {
        try {
            sampleService.work();
            return true;
        } catch (Exception e) {
            // do nothing (BAD in production)
        }
        return false;
    }

}
```

The result of running this class varies every time, but the numbers of inserted objects match the expected results:

```
Inserted 15, for 5 successes and 5 failures
```

We can also verify this in SQL*Plus using the code shown in Listing 11-28.

Listing 11-28. *Further Verification of the Transaction Code*

```
$ sqlplus PROSPRING/x*****6@//oracle.devcake.co.uk/INTL
SQL> truncate table t_log_entry
  2  /

Table truncated.

SQL> exit

$ java -cp $CLASSPATH com.apress.prospring2.ch11.service.SampleServiceDemo
... output truncated ...
Inserted 15, for 5 successes and 5 failures

$ sqlplus PROSPRING/x*****6@//oracle.devcake.co.uk/INTL
SQL> select count(0) from t_log_entry
  2  /

  COUNT(0)
----------
        15
```

It worked! We have run the sample application and verified that for five successful service calls we have 15 rows in the t_log_entry table, exactly as we expected.

Lazy Loading

This section is just as important as the transactional behavior one; in fact, these two areas are closely connected. The principle of lazy loading is simple: fetch data only when it is needed. It means more trips to the database, but the throughput is better because Hibernate only fetches data the application needs. Lazy loading generally applies to associated collections; imagine an Invoice object with a Set of InvoiceLine objects; each InvoiceLine will have a Set of Discount objects.

Let's consider an application that loads all invoices in a particular date range, for example. Imagine that the number of matching records is 10,000; that means that we will get 10,000 Invoice objects. On average, we can expect an Invoice to have five lines; that means 50,000 InvoiceLine objects. In addition to that, let's say that every other line has a discount applied to it. That means 25,000 Discount objects. In total, a single Hibernate operation will create 85,000 objects! By using lazy loading, we can reduce the number of objects created to just 10,000; we instruct Hibernate to fetch the InvoiceLine objects only when we need them. Hibernate does this by instrumenting the fetched objects' code and using its own implementations of the Collection interfaces.

In theory, it should work quite nicely; let's write code that implements the model from Figure 11-3.

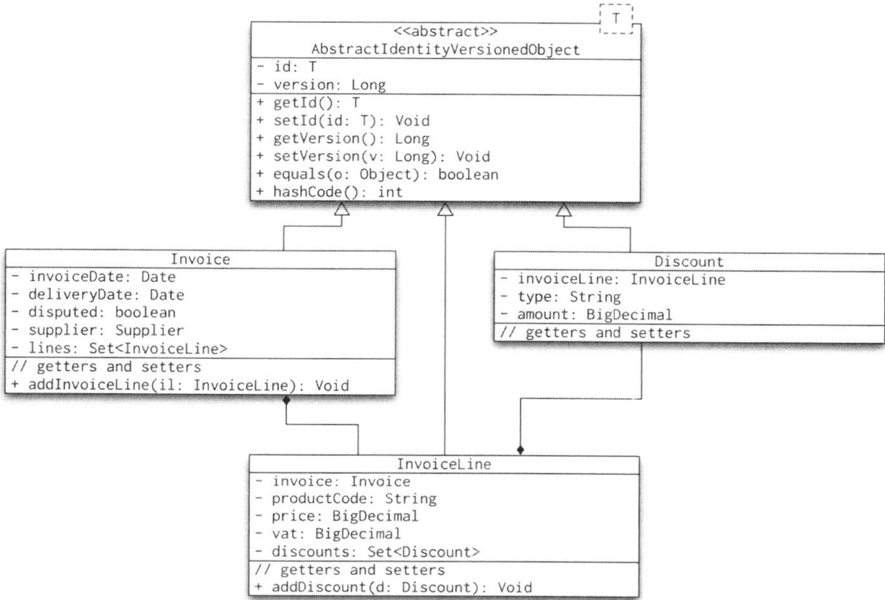

Figure 11-3. *Invoice domain model*

The domain objects are not difficult to implement; the only thing we want to show in Listing 11-29 are the `Invoice.addInvoiceLine` and `InvoiceLine.addDiscount` methods.

Listing 11-29. *The addInvoiceLine and addDiscount Methods*

```
public class Invoice extends AbstractIdentityVersionedObject<Long> {
    public void addInvoiceLine(InvoiceLine invoiceLine) {
        invoiceLine.setInvoice(this);
        this.invoiceLines.add(invoiceLine);
    }
}

public class InvoiceLine extends AbstractIdentityVersionedObject<Long> {
    public void addDiscount(Discount discount) {
        discount.setInvoiceLine(this);
        this.discounts.add(discount);
    }
}
```

This code clearly shows that the addInvoiceLine and addDiscount methods establish a bidirectional relationship between the object being added and its container. This is important for Hibernate, and it makes our code clearer; it is better and much less error-prone than the code in Listing 11-30.

Listing 11-30. *Avoiding the Error-Prone addInvoiceLine and addDiscount Methods*

```
Invoice invoice = new Invoice();
InvoiceLine il = new InvoiceLine();
invoice.getInvoiceLines().add(il);    // 1

Discount discount = new Discount();
discount.setInvoiceLine(invoiceLine);    //2
invoiceLine.getDiscounts().add(discount);    //3
```

The line marked //1 represents a bug: the il instance we've added to the invoice object does not contain a reference to the invoice object. Lines //2 and //3 are simply clumsy code. Even though the tables for the Invoice domain model are straightforward, Listing 11-31 shows the SQL code to create them.

Listing 11-31. *SQL Code to Create the Invoice Domain Model Tables*

```
create table t_supplier (
    id number(19, 0) not null,
    version number(19, 0) null,
    name varchar2(200) not null,
    constraint pk_supplier primary key (id)
)
/
create sequence s_supplier_id start with 10000
/

create table t_invoice (
    id number(19, 0) not null,
    version number(19, 0) null,
    invoice_date date not null,
    delivery_date date not null,
    supplier number(19, 0) not null,
    constraint pk_invoice primary key (id),
    constraint fk_i_supplier foreign key (supplier) references t_supplier(id)
)
/
create sequence s_invoice_id start with 10000
/

create table t_invoice_line (
    id number(19, 0) not null,
    version number(19, 0) null,
    invoice number(19, 0) not null,
    price number(20, 4) not null,
    vat number(20, 4) not null,
    product_code varchar2(50) not null,
    constraint pk_invoice_line primary key (id),
    constraint fk_il_invoice foreign key (invoice) references t_invoice(id)
)
/
```

```
create sequence s_invoice_line_id start with 10000
/

create table t_discount (
    id number(19, 0) not null,
    version number(19, 0) null,
    invoice_line number(19, 0) not null,
    type_ varchar2(50) not null,
    amount number(20, 4) not null,
    constraint pk_discount primary key (id),
    constraint fk_d_invoice_line foreign key (invoice_line)
       references t_invoice_line(id)
)
/
create sequence s_discount_id start with 10000
/
```

Because we will implement the DAOs in Hibernate, we have to create the Hibernate mapping files for our new domain objects. It is usual practice to keep one mapping file for each domain object; Listing 11-32, therefore, shows four mapping files (for the `Supplier`, `Invoice`, `InvoiceLine`, and `Discount` objects).

Listing 11-32. *Mapping Files for the Newly Created Domain Objects*

```
<!—Supplier.hbm.xml -->
<?xml version="1.0"?>
<!DOCTYPE hibernate-mapping PUBLIC
        "-//Hibernate/Hibernate Mapping DTD 3.0//EN"
        "http://hibernate.sourceforge.net/hibernate-mapping-3.0.dtd">

<hibernate-mapping default-lazy="true">

    <class name="com.apress.prospring2.ch11.domain.Supplier" table="t_supplier">
        <id name="id" type="long" unsaved-value="null">
            <generator class="sequence">
                <param name="sequence">s_supplier_id</param>
            </generator>
        </id>
        <version name="version" column="version" unsaved-value="null" type="long" />
        <property name="name" column="name" not-null="true" />
    </class>

</hibernate-mapping>

<!—Invoice.hbm.xml -->
<?xml version="1.0"?>
<!DOCTYPE hibernate-mapping PUBLIC
        "-//Hibernate/Hibernate Mapping DTD 3.0//EN"
        "http://hibernate.sourceforge.net/hibernate-mapping-3.0.dtd">

<hibernate-mapping default-lazy="true">

    <class name="com.apress.prospring2.ch11.domain.Invoice" table="t_invoice">
        <id name="id" type="long" unsaved-value="null">
            <generator class="sequence">
                <param name="sequence">s_invoice_id</param>
            </generator>
```

```
        </id>
        <version name="version" column="version" unsaved-value="null" type="long" />
        <property name="deliveryDate" column="delivery_date" not-null="true" />
        <property name="invoiceDate" column="invoice_date" not-null="true" />
        <many-to-one name="supplier" not-null="true"
             class="com.apress.prospring2.ch11.domain.Supplier"/>
        <set name="lines" cascade="all" inverse="true">
            <key column="invoice" not-null="true"/>
            <one-to-many class="com.apress.prospring2.ch11.domain.InvoiceLine"/>
        </set>
    </class>

</hibernate-mapping>

<!—InvoiceLine.hbm.xml -->
<?xml version="1.0"?>
<!DOCTYPE hibernate-mapping PUBLIC
        "-//Hibernate/Hibernate Mapping DTD 3.0//EN"
        "http://hibernate.sourceforge.net/hibernate-mapping-3.0.dtd">

<hibernate-mapping default-lazy="true">

    <class name="com.apress.prospring2.ch11.domain.InvoiceLine"
        table="t_invoice_line">
        <id name="id" type="long" unsaved-value="null">
            <generator class="sequence">
                <param name="sequence">s_invoice_line_id</param>
            </generator>
        </id>
        <version name="version" column="version" unsaved-value="null" type="long" />
        <property name="price" column="price" not-null="true" />
        <property name="productCode" column="product_code" not-null="true" />
        <property name="vat" column="vat" not-null="true" />
        <many-to-one name="invoice"
            class="com.apress.prospring2.ch11.domain.Invoice"
            not-null="true"/>
        <set name="discounts" inverse="true" cascade="all">
            <key column="invoice_line" not-null="true"/>
            <one-to-many class="com.apress.prospring2.ch11.domain.Discount"/>
        </set>
    </class>

</hibernate-mapping>

<!—Discount.hbm.xml -->
<?xml version="1.0"?>
<!DOCTYPE hibernate-mapping PUBLIC
        "-//Hibernate/Hibernate Mapping DTD 3.0//EN"
        "http://hibernate.sourceforge.net/hibernate-mapping-3.0.dtd">

<hibernate-mapping default-lazy="true">

    <class name="com.apress.prospring2.ch11.domain.Discount" table="t_discount">
        <id name="id" type="long" unsaved-value="null">
            <generator class="sequence">
                <param name="sequence">s_discount_id</param>
            </generator>
```

```
        </id>
        <version name="version" column="version" unsaved-value="null" type="long" />
        <property name="amount" column="amount" not-null="true" />
        <property name="type" column="type_" not-null="true" />
        <many-to-one name="invoiceLine" column="invoice_line"
            class="com.apress.prospring2.ch11.domain.InvoiceLine" not-null="true" />
    </class>

</hibernate-mapping>
```

The listing shows the simplest mapping first: `Supplier` has no references to any other objects. The mapping for the `Invoice` object is quite complex: it shows a many-to-one mapping to the `Supplier` object and the lines set, which represents one-to-many mapping to the `InvoiceLine` objects. The `InvoiceLine` and `Discount` mappings follow the same pattern we have in the mapping for the `Invoice` object. Also notice that the `default-lazy` attribute of the `hibernate-mapping` element is set to `true`.

Now that we have the domain objects with convenience methods to set the dependencies and their Hibernate mappings, we need to create the appropriate DAOs and services. Figure 11-4 shows the UML diagram of the code we will write.

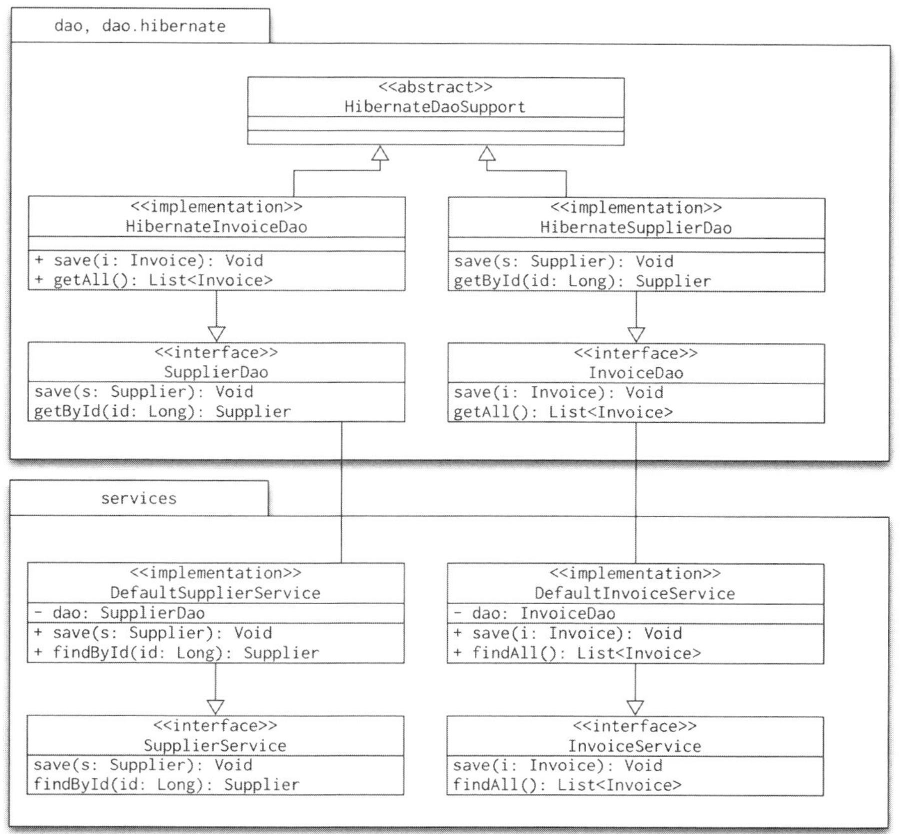

Figure 11-4. *UML diagram of the DAOs and services*

Finally, let's modify the `dataaccess-context-tx.xml` and create the `services-context.xml` Spring configuration files to wire up the new DAOs and services. We will use the code in Listing 11-33 in a sample application.

Listing 11-33. *The Changed dataaccess-context-tx.xml and New services-context.xml Files*

```
<?xml version="1.0" encoding="UTF-8"?>
<beans xmlns="http://www.springframework.org/schema/beans"
    ...>

    <bean id="invoiceDao"
        class="com.apress.prospring2.ch11.dataaccess.hibernate.HibernateInvoiceDao"
       parent="hibernateDaoSupport"/>
    <bean id="supplierDao"
       class="com.apress.prospring2.ch11.dataaccess.hibernate.HibernateSupplierDao"
       parent="hibernateDaoSupport"/>

</beans>

<?xml version="1.0" encoding="UTF-8"?>
<beans xmlns="http://www.springframework.org/schema/beans"
    ....>

    <bean id="invoiceService"
        class="com.apress.prospring2.ch11.service.DefaultInvoiceService">
        <property name="invoiceDao" ref="invoiceDao"/>
    </bean>
    <bean id="supplierService"
        class="com.apress.prospring2.ch11.service.DefaultSupplierService">
        <property name="supplierDao" ref="supplierDao"/>
    </bean>
</beans>
```

We have the Spring context files, and we are now ready to try to run the sample application shown in Listing 11-34. The sample application will only verify that the Spring configuration is correct; it does not actually do any database work yet.

Listing 11-34. *Sample Application*

```
public class InvoiceServiceDemo {
    private SupplierService supplierService;
    private InvoiceService invoiceService;

    private void run() throws Exception {
        DaoDemoUtils.buildJndi();
        ApplicationContext ac = new ClassPathXmlApplicationContext(new String[] {
            "classpath*:/com/apress/prospring2/ch11/dataaccess/➥
                datasource-context-tx.xml",
            "classpath*:/com/apress/prospring2/ch11/service/*-context.xml"
        });
        this.invoiceService = (InvoiceService)ac.getBean("invoiceService");
        this.supplierService = (SupplierService)ac.getBean("supplierService");

        findAllInvoices();
    }
```

```
    private void findAllInvoices() {
    }

    public static void main(String[] args) throws Exception {
        new InvoiceServiceDemo().run();
    }

}
```

We will work on the findAllInvoices() method to find out what Hibernate does behind the scenes. We will begin by creating some sample data by running the code in Listing 11-35.

Listing 11-35. *Stored Procedure to Create the Sample Data*

```
CREATE OR REPLACE PROCEDURE "PROSPRING"."CREATE_SAMPLE_DATA"
is
    i number;
    j number;
    l number;
begin
    dbms_output.put_line('begin');
    for i in 1 .. 50 loop
        insert into t_supplier (id, version, name) values (
           s_supplier_id.nextval, 1, 'Supplier '||i);
        for j in 1 .. 100 loop
            insert into t_invoice (id, version, invoice_date,
               delivery_date, supplier)
            values (s_invoice_id.nextval, 1, sysdate,
               sysdate, s_supplier_id.currval);
            for l in 1 .. 5 loop
                insert into t_invoice_line (id, version, invoice, price,
                    vat, product_code)
                values (s_invoice_line_id.nextval, 1, s_invoice_id.currval,
                   dbms_random.value(1, 1000),
                   dbms_random.value(1, 100), 'Product '||l);
            end loop;
        end loop;
    end loop;
end;
```

This code simply inserts 50 suppliers; each invoice has 100 invoices; and each invoice, five lines. This should give us a representative data set for our experiments. Let's modify the findAllInvoices() method to actually go to the database and return all Invoice objects (see Listing 11-36).

Listing 11-36. *Finding All Invoices*

```
    private void findAllInvoices() {
        List<Invoice> invoices = this.invoiceService.findAll();
        System.out.println(invoices.size());
    }
```

We expect this code to print 5,000 lines, and running it indeed prints out 5,000. This is perhaps the most inefficient way to count the rows in the t_invoice table. The benefit, however, is that we have not loaded 25,000 InvoiceLine objects! Hibernate runs the SQL statement only on the t_invoice table:

```
select invoice0_.id as id1_, invoice0_.version as version1_,
invoice0_.delivery_date as delivery3_1_,
invoice0_.invoice_date as invoice4_1_,
invoice0_.supplier as supplier1_ from t_invoice invoice0_
```

Let's write a method that gets an invoice by its id, the `InvoiceService.findById(Long)` method, and examine the structure of the `Invoice` object we get back. Figure 11-5 shows the debugger view of the returned `Invoice` object.

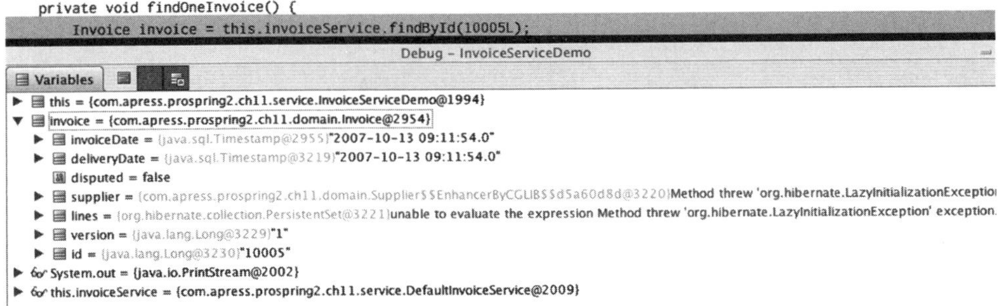

Figure 11-5. *The debugger view of the Invoice object*

The debugger shows that we have successfully loaded the `Invoice` object, but it also shows that when we try to access the `supplier` and `lines` properties, we get the `LazyInitializationException`. The reason is that the `Session` that has loaded the `Invoice` object has ended. Remember that the `HibernateTemplate` ensures that the session closes correctly at the end of the work performed by the callback. This is where the Hibernate transactional support comes into play. Whenever application code requests Spring Hibernate support to get a session, Spring registers the `Session` as a transaction synchronization object. Therefore, code that executes in a single transaction always operates under the same `Session`, even if it uses more than one `HibernateTemplate` call. You must, however, be careful with how you deal with the transactional nature of your beans. Take a look at Table 11-2, which shows an application that declared its service layer and DAO layer to be transactional and, to make matters even worse, it has declared that operations on both the DAO and the service beans require a new transaction.

Table 11-2. *Nested Transactions*

Service Call	DAO Call	Hibernate Session
`Invoice i = findById(1L)`		Session 1
	`Invoice i = getById(1L)`	Session 2
	`i.getSupplier()`	Session 2
`i.getSupplier()`		Session 1

Because we have configured the service bean with the `REQUIRES_NEW` transaction propagation, the service call starts a new transaction and gets Hibernate session one. It then proceeds to call the DAO's `getId` method. Because we have configured the DAO bean with the `REQUIRES_NEW` transaction propagation for every call, it gets Hibernate session two. Using session two, the DAO bean loads the `Invoice` object: `i.getSupplier()` will work, because `i` was loaded in session two. However, when the DAO bean returns back to the service layer, the call to `i.getSupplier()` in the service call will fail. Even though we still have a Hibernate `Session` open, it is not the same `Session` that loaded the original `Invoice` object. Do not worry if you do not fully understand the transaction propagation, we cover this in more detail in Chapter 16.

You can argue that you would not make such a mistake, but imagine that the service call is actually a web tier call and that the DAO call is the service call. Suddenly, you are dealing with the same situation. The problem becomes even worse, because all your integration and DAO tests will work. The solution we take is to perform an explicit eager fetch when we need it in the DAO or to access the objects we need in an active transaction in the service layer. An eager fetch is the opposite of lazy fetch: we instruct Hibernate to select the associations in a single `select` statement. The service call should always return all data that the nontransactional presentation tier needs.

Explicit Eager Fetching

Let's take a look at the first way to prevent lazy loading exceptions. If we expect that the subsequent layers will require the entire object graph, we can instruct Hibernate to eagerly fetch all objects. This is frequently useful when implementing DAO calls—typically, the `getById` calls—that return a single result, or a very small number of results. Listing 11-37 shows the modification to the `HibernateInvoiceDao`'s `getById()` method.

Listing 11-37. *Eager getById Method*

```
public class HibernateInvoiceDao extends HibernateDaoSupport implements InvoiceDao {

    // other methods omitted

    public Invoice getById(Long id) {
        return (Invoice) DataAccessUtils.uniqueResult(
                getHibernateTemplate().find("from Invoice i inner join fetch" +
                        "i.supplier inner join fetch i.lines il " +
                        "left outer join fetch il.discounts where i.id = ?", id)
        );
    }
}
```

The eager fetch looks just like a SQL statement with explicit inner and left-outer joins. Figure 11-6 shows the `Invoice` object we get back in the debugger view.

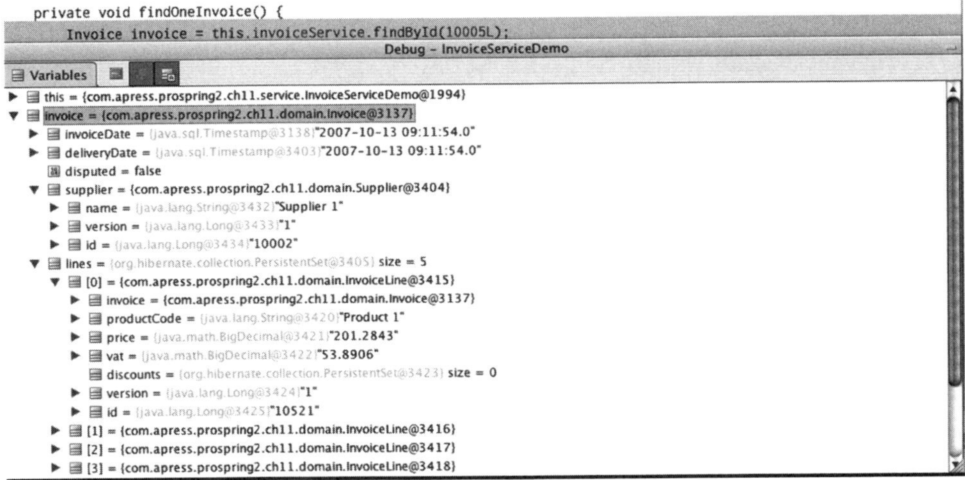

Figure 11-6. *Debugger view of the eagerly loaded Invoice object*

This is exactly what we need: we have a DAO that returns an eagerly fetched object only when we need it.

Other Lazy Loading Considerations

Even if your code is running in a clean service layer transaction, you should consider the performance hit caused by using lazy loading. Consider the code in Listing 11-38, where the `InvoiceDao.getByIdLazy(Long)` method returns the `Invoice` object without eager fetching.

Listing 11-38. *Very Slow Performance of Lazy Loading*

```
public class Invoice extends AbstractIdentityVersionedObject<Long> {
...
    public BigDecimal getLinesTotalPrice() {
        BigDecimal total = new BigDecimal(0);
        for (InvoiceLine line : this.lines) {
            total = total.add(line.getPrice());
        }
        return total;
    }
...
}

public class DefaultInvoiceService implements InvoiceService {

    // rest of the code omitted
    public void recalculateDiscounts(Long id) {
        Invoice invoice = this.invoiceDao.getByIdLazy(id);
        BigDecimal total = invoice.getLinesTotalPrice();
        if (total.compareTo(BigDecimal.TEN) > 0) {
            // do something special
        }
    }
}
```

The seemingly innocent call to `invoice.getLinesTotalPrice()` forces Hibernate to fetch all `InvoiceLines` for this invoice.

Some applications use the Open Session in View (anti)pattern. The reasoning behind this pattern is that the application keeps the `Session` open while it displays a view (a JSP page, for example). This simplifies the decision between lazy and eager fetches: the session is open in the view, and it can fetch any lazy association. We sometimes call this an antipattern because it may lead to inconsistent data views. Imagine you display the `Invoice` object and show only a count of its invoice lines. You then rely on lazy loading to get the invoice lines. In the meantime, the system (or other users) might have updated the invoice lines of the displayed invoice, thus making the actually lazily loaded `InvoiceLine` objects inconsistent with the count.

Dealing with Large Data Sets

Most applications need to be able to handle very large data sets; the code you have seen so far works quite nicely with hundreds of records in the database, but when we start to approach larger record set sizes, our application may crash with a `java.lang.OutOfMemoryException`—we may simply select too much data. Worse, a web application would most likely discard the vast majority of the result set to display only one page of results to the users. We need to make the DAO layer aware of paging. Hibernate supports paging in its `Query` object; it provides the `setFirstResult(int)` and `setMaxResults(int)` methods. Our first attempt at implementing paging might look like the code in Listing 11-39.

Listing 11-39. *The First Attempt at Implementing Paging*

```
public interface InvoiceService {
    List<Invoice> search(int firstResult, int pageSize);
    ...
}

public class DefaultInvoiceService implements InvoiceService {
    private InvoiceDao invoiceDao;

    public List<Invoice> search(int firstResult, int pageSize) {
        return this.invoiceDao.search(firstResult, pageSize);
    }
    ....
}

public interface InvoiceDao {
    ...
    List<Invoice> search(int firstResult, int pageSize);

}

public class HibernateInvoiceDao extends HibernateDaoSupport implements InvoiceDao {
    ...
    @SuppressWarnings({"unchecked"})
    public List<Invoice> search(final int firstResult, final int pageSize) {
        return (List<Invoice>) getHibernateTemplate().execute(
            new HibernateCallback() {
                public Object doInHibernate(Session session)
                    throws HibernateException, SQLException {
                    Query query = session.createQuery("from Invoice");
                    query.setFirstResult(firstResult);
                    query.setMaxResults(pageSize);
```

```
                    return query.list();
                }
            });
    }
}
```

We can now use the search method and give it the first result and the maximum number of results to be returned. This certainly works, but the downside is that we can't return the maximum number of results. We can, therefore, show a link to only the next page; we can't show the total number of pages (or results). One solution would be to implement a method that would return the total number of rows in the `Invoices` table. What if we made our search more complicated, perhaps by introducing conditions that can result in selecting only a subset of all rows? We would have to implement a matching counting method for every search method. In addition to this, the code that uses our service would have to explicitly call two methods. There is a better solution; we illustrate it with the UML diagram in Figure 11-7.

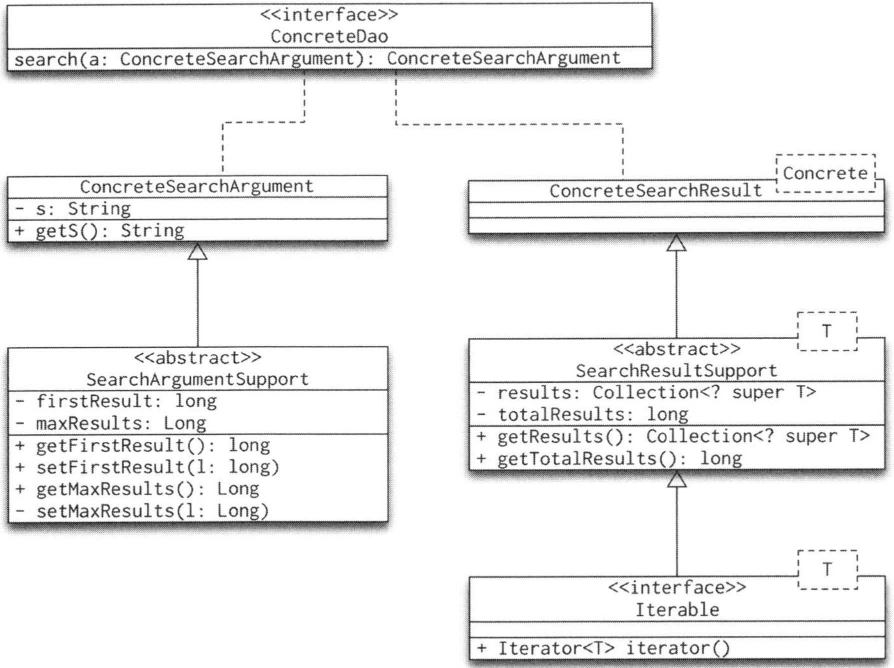

Figure 11-7. *UML diagram of paging support*

The search method performs all necessary search operations, taking the `SearchArgumentSupport` subclass as its argument and returning `SearchResultSupport` subclass. The returned `SearchResultSupport` contains the page of fetched objects as well as the total number of results. In addition to containing the results, it implements `Iterable<T>`. That means that we can use the `ResultSupport` subclass in a JSP's `c:forEach` loop (see Listing 11-40).

Listing 11-40. *JSP Page That Lists the Invoice Objects*

```
<%@ page contentType="text/html;charset=UTF-8" language="java" %>
<%@ taglib prefix="c" uri="http://java.sun.com/jsp/jstl/core" %>
<html xmlns="http://www.w3.org/1999/xhtml"
     xmlns:xsi="http://www.w3.org/2001/XMLSchema-instance"
     xsi:schemaLocation="http://www.w3.org/MarkUp/SCHEMA/xhtml11.xsd"
     xml:lang="en" >
<head>
    <title>Result</title>
</head>
<body>
<h2>Invoices found</h2>
<c:forEach items="${invoices}" var="invoice">
    ${invoice.invoiceDate} <!-- etc -->
</c:forEach>
</body>
</html>
```

As you can see, no additional effort was needed in our JSP views; in fact, if we change the returned type from a `Collection<T>` to the `ResultSupport<T>` subclass later on in the development of a web application, we do not have to change the views in any way.

Handling Large Objects

It is possible to use Hibernate to fetch objects from tables that use large objects (LOBs). There are two types of LOBs: character large binary objects (CLOBs) and binary large objects (BLOBs). CLOBs are usually mapped to `String`, while BLOBs are usually mapped to `byte[]`. Because the standard JDBC infrastructure does not deal with large binary objects, we must use an appropriate `LobHandler` implementation for the database we are using. Take a look at Listing 11-41, which shows a table with BLOB and CLOB fields.

Listing 11-41. *Table with Large Object Columns*

```
create table t_lob_test (
    id number(19, 0) not null,
    version number(19, 0) null,
    text_content clob not null,
    binary_content blob not null,
    mime_type varchar2(200) not null,
    constraint pk_lob_test primary key (id)
)
/
create sequence s_lob_test_id start with 10000
/
```

This class is very simple, so its domain object is going to be very simple as well (see Listing 11-42).

Listing 11-42. *Domain Object for the t_lob_test Table*

```
public class LobTest extends AbstractIdentityVersionedObject<Long> {
    private String textContent;
    private byte[] binaryContent;
    private String mimeType;
```

```
    public String getTextContent() {
        return textContent;
    }

    public void setTextContent(String textContent) {
        this.textContent = textContent;
    }

    public byte[] getBinaryContent() {
        return binaryContent;
    }

    public void setBinaryContent(byte[] binaryContent) {
        this.binaryContent = binaryContent;
    }

    public String getMimeType() {
        return mimeType;
    }

    public void setMimeType(String mimeType) {
        this.mimeType = mimeType;
    }

    @Override
    public String toString() {
        StringBuilder sb = new StringBuilder();
        sb.append("LobTest { id=").append(this.id).append(", ");
        sb.append("textContent=").append(this.textContent).append(", ");
        sb.append("binaryContent=");
        for (int i = 0; i < this.binaryContent.length && i < 50; i++) {
            sb.append(String.format("%x", (int)this.binaryContent[i]));
        }
        sb.append("}");

        return sb.toString();
    }
}
```

The only addition to the usual getters and setters is the `toString()` method, but that is really only for our convenience. Next, we need to create the Hibernate mapping file for the `LobTest` domain object. Listing 11-43 shows that we use subclasses of the `AbstractLobType`: `BlobByteArrayType` and `ClobStringType`.

Listing 11-43. *Mapping File for the LobTest Domain Object*

```
<?xml version="1.0"?>
<!DOCTYPE hibernate-mapping PUBLIC
        "-//Hibernate/Hibernate Mapping DTD 3.0//EN"
        "http://hibernate.sourceforge.net/hibernate-mapping-3.0.dtd">

<hibernate-mapping default-lazy="true">

    <class name="com.apress.prospring2.ch11.domain.LobTest" table="t_lob_test">
        <id name="id" type="long" unsaved-value="null">
            <generator class="sequence">
                <param name="sequence">s_lob_test_id</param>
```

```
            </generator>
        </id>
        <version name="version" column="version" unsaved-value="null" type="long" />
        <property name="binaryContent" column="binary_content" not-null="true"
              type="org.springframework.orm.hibernate3.support.BlobByteArrayType" />
        <property name="textContent" column="text_content" not-null="true"
                type="org.springframework.orm.hibernate3.support.ClobStringType"/>
        <property name="mimeType" column="mime_type" not-null="true" />
    </class>
</hibernate-mapping>
```

The final complex part of using this domain object is setting up the Hibernate mapping and Spring configuration. We need to tell Hibernate how our database (Oracle 10*g*) handles LOBs. To do that, we create an instance of the `LobHandler` implementation and reference it in the `HibernateSessionFactoryBean`; Listing 11-44 shows how to do this.

Listing 11-44. *Hibernate Configuration for LOB Handling*

```
<?xml version="1.0" encoding="UTF-8"?>
<beans xmlns="http://www.springframework.org/schema/beans"
    ...>

    <bean id="nativeJdbcExtractor"
        class="org.springframework.jdbc.support.nativejdbc.➥
            SimpleNativeJdbcExtractor"/>
    <bean id="lobHandler"
        class="org.springframework.jdbc.support.lob.OracleLobHandler">
        <property name="nativeJdbcExtractor" ref="nativeJdbcExtractor"/>
    </bean>

    <bean id="hibernateSessionFactory"
        class="org.springframework.orm.hibernate3.LocalSessionFactoryBean">
        <property name="dataSource" ref="dataSource"/>
        <property name="lobHandler" ref="lobHandler"/>
        <property name="mappingLocations">
            <list>
                <value>classpath*:/com/apress/prospring2/ch11/dataaccess/➥
                    hibernate/*.hbm.xml</value>
            </list>
        </property>
    </bean>

...
    <bean id="lobTestDao"
        class="com.apress.prospring2.ch11.dataaccess.hibernate.HibernateLobTestDao"
        parent="hibernateDaoSupport"/>

</beans>
```

The final difficulty we need to deal with is that the LOB support requires an active Spring transaction or a JTA transaction synchronization. Therefore, we must create a service layer interface and its implementation (remember, we do not ever want to make our DAOs transactional!). Listing 11-45 shows the service interface and its implementation.

Listing 11-45. *Service Code for the LOB Demonstration*

```
public interface LobTestService {

    void save(LobTest lobTest);

    LobTest findById(Long id);

}

public class DefaultLobTestService implements LobTestService {
    private LobTestDao lobTestDao;

    public void save(LobTest lobTest) {
        this.lobTestDao.save(lobTest);
    }

    public LobTest findById(Long id) {
        return this.lobTestDao.getById(id);
    }

    public void setLobTestDao(LobTestDao lobTestDao) {
        this.lobTestDao = lobTestDao;
    }
}
```

The Spring configuration for the service layer simply defines the `LobTestService` bean with its dependencies; Listing 11-46 shows only the sample application that uses the service implementation and verifies that the LOB handling works as expected.

Listing 11-46. *LOB Sample Application*

```
public class LobTestServiceDemo {

    private void run() throws Exception {
        DaoDemoUtils.buildJndi();
        ApplicationContext ac = new ClassPathXmlApplicationContext(new String[] {
            "classpath*:/com/apress/prospring2/ch11/dataaccess/➥
                datasource-context-tx.xml",
            "classpath*:/com/apress/prospring2/ch11/service/*-context.xml"
        });
        LobTestService lobTestService =
           (LobTestService)ac.getBean("lobTestService");
        LobTest lobTest = new LobTest();
        lobTest.setTextContent("Hello, world");
        lobTest.setBinaryContent("Hello, world".getBytes());
        lobTest.setMimeType("text/plain");
        lobTestService.save(lobTest);

        LobTest lobTest2 = lobTestService.findById(lobTest.getId());
        System.out.println(lobTest2);
    }

    public static void main(String[] args) throws Exception {
        new LobTestServiceDemo().run();
        new BufferedReader(new InputStreamReader(System.in)).readLine();
    }

}
```

Running this application produces output that verifies that the LobTest object gets inserted and fetched without any problems:

```
DEBUG [main] ConnectionManager.cleanup(380) | performing cleanup
DEBUG [main] ConnectionManager.closeConnection(441) | releasing JDBC connection
[ (open PreparedStatements: 0, globally: 0) (open ResultSets: 0, globally: 0)]
DEBUG [main] JDBCContext.afterTransactionCompletion(215) |
after transa version 3.2.5ga ction completion
DEBUG [main] ConnectionManager.afterTransaction(302) | transaction completed on
session with on_close connection release mode; be sure to close the session
to release JDBC resources!
DEBUG [main] SessionImpl.afterTransactionCompletion(422) |
after transaction completion
LobTest { id=10004, textContent=Hello, world,
binaryContent=48656c6c6f2c20776f726c64}
```

The only difficulty with this approach is that the LOB columns usually contain fairly large amounts of data, and unfortunately, setting lazy="true" on the column does not work. Using the AbstractLobType subclasses, Hibernate will always fetch the entire contents of the column. This is why, in our large applications, we tend to use Spring JDBC to handle the LOBs and Hibernate to handle all other data access code.

Combining Hibernate with Other DAO Code

You can use Hibernate in almost every application; it can deal with complex object structures, and its lazy loading will decrease the performance of your application only slightly. There is one situation in which we found Hibernate more difficult to use efficiently: if you are dealing with tables with large objects and the large objects are significant in size (10kB and above). In that case, it is best to combine Hibernate with Spring-managed JDBC code. Even though Hibernate supports column-level lazy loading, support for this is not always possible for all column types and all databases.

There is nothing stopping you from implementing part of your DAO in Hibernate and part in JDBC. Because you still need to declare the DataSource bean, you can use it in your Spring JDBC DAOs. In addition to this, both the Hibernate and JDBC DAO implementations participate in the same transaction. This is very useful but can lead to a problem when you insert a row with Hibernate, then use JDBC, and expect to see the inserted row. The HibernateTransactionManager typically does not flush the Hibernate Session until the transaction commits; therefore, the row we have inserted using session.saveOrUpdate() will not appear in the database. This will cause the JDBC operation that expects to see the row to fail. The solution is to call session.flush() before performing JDBC DAO operations that depend on rows inserted as a result of the Hibernate session operations.

Summary

In this chapter, you have learned what Hibernate does and how to use it in Spring applications. We started by looking at the simplest code and quickly moved on to more complicated examples. Now, you know how to prevent stale data updates, and we paid special attention to creating efficient data access code. Lazy loading plays an important role in this, and to properly use lazy loading, you must understand how Hibernate and Spring cooperate in handling transactions.

Finally, we discussed how we can use Hibernate to store large object data in a database, even though, as you saw, it may not be the most appropriate solution. We will end the chapter by saying that the best combination is Hibernate with Spring-managed JDBC; this way, you can implement critical pieces of data access code in a very low-level way using JDBC and use Hibernate's incredible convenience and power for all other DAO code.

PART 3

■ ■ ■

Enterprise Application Components

CHAPTER 12

Job Scheduling with Spring

Most application logic happens in response to some form of user action, such as a button click or a form submission. However, in many applications certain processes must be invoked *without* user interaction, usually at a given interval. For example, you might have a process that cleans out temporary files once an hour or a process that creates a data export from a database and sends it to an external system once a day at midnight. Most nontrivial applications require some kind of scheduling support—if not directly related to business logic of the application then to support system housekeeping.

When you are building scheduled tasks for your application, creating a task that runs once an hour or once a day is fairly simple. But what about a task that runs at 3:00 p.m. every Monday, Wednesday, and Friday? This is a little more difficult to code, and it makes sense to use prebuilt scheduling solutions rather than attempt to create your own scheduling framework.

When talking about scheduling from a programming perspective, we tend to talk about three distinct concepts. A job is a unit of work that needs to be scheduled to run at a specific interval. A trigger is a condition, perhaps a fixed interval or a given piece of data, that causes a job to run. A schedule is a collection of triggers that govern the complete timeline of a job. Typically, you encapsulate a job by implementing an interface or extending a given base class. You define your triggers in whatever terms your scheduling framework supports. Some frameworks may support only basic interval-based triggers, whereas others, such as Quartz, provide much more flexible trigger schemes. In general, a job has only a single trigger in its schedule, and the terms "schedule" and "trigger" are often used interchangeably.

Scheduling support in Spring comes in two distinct forms: JDK `Timer`-based and Quartz-based. The JDK `Timer`-based approach provides scheduling capabilities on any version 1.3 or later JVM, and it does not need external dependencies beyond Spring. `Timer`-based scheduling is quite primitive and provides limited flexibility when defining job schedules. However, `Timer` support is included with Java and requires no external libraries, which might be beneficial if you are restricted by application size or corporate policy. Quartz-based scheduling is much more flexible and allows triggers to be defined in a much more real-world way, such as the earlier example of 3:00 p.m. every Monday, Wednesday, and Friday.

In this chapter, we explore both of the scheduling solutions included with Spring. In particular, this chapter discusses three core topics: scheduling with the JDK `Timer`, Quartz-based scheduling, and job scheduling considerations.

We'll start our discussion by exploring Spring's support for JDK `Timer`-based scheduling. This section introduces the different trigger types available with `Timer`-based scheduling and looks at how you can schedule any arbitrary logic without needing to create additional Java code.

After that, we'll look at the comprehensive Quartz scheduling engine and how it is integrated into Spring. In particular, we examine Quartz support for cron expressions allowing highly complex schedules to be configured using a concise format. As with the JDK `Timer`, you'll see how to schedule any logic without needing to encapsulate it.

Finally, we'll discuss the various points to consider when choosing a scheduling implementation and patterns to use when creating logic for scheduled execution.

Scheduling Jobs Using JDK Timer

The most basic scheduling support with Spring is based on the JDK `java.util.Timer` class. When scheduling using `Timer`, you are limited to simple interval-based trigger definitions, which makes `Timer`-based scheduling suitable only for jobs that you need to execute just once at some given future time or that you need to execute at some fixed frequency.

Trigger Types with Timer

`Timer`-based scheduling offers you three types of triggers:

- *One-off*: When you use a one-off trigger, job execution is scheduled for some given point in the future, defined as the number of milliseconds from a given date. After the job executes, it is not rescheduled for further execution. We have found that one-off triggers are great for scheduling jobs that need to be done once that you might forget to do yourself. For instance, if a web application has scheduled maintenance coming up in a week, we can schedule a task to switch on the In Maintenance page when the maintenance is due to begin.
- *Repeating and fixed-delay*: When you use a fixed-delay trigger, you schedule the first execution of the job just like for a one-off trigger, but after that, the job is rescheduled to execute after a given interval. When you are using fixed-delay, the interval is relative to the actual execution time of the previous job. This means that the interval between successive executions is always approximately the same, even if executions occur "late" when compared to the original schedule. With this type of trigger, the interval you specify is the actual interval between subsequent executions. Use this approach when the interval between executions must be kept as constant as possible.
- *Repeating and fixed-rate*: Fixed-rate triggers function in a similar way to fixed-delay triggers, but the next execution time is always calculated based on the initial scheduled execution time. This means that if a single execution is delayed, subsequent executions are not delayed as a result. With this type of trigger, the interval you specify is not necessarily the actual interval between subsequent executions. Use this approach when the actual execution time is important, rather than the interval between executions.

You may find it difficult to visualize the differences between fixed-delay and fixed-rate triggers, and unfortunately, creating an example that causes enough of a delay in execution to fully clarify the differences reliably is difficult. That said, here is a simple example that should help highlight the differences.

Consider a task that starts executing at 1:00 p.m. and has a specified interval of 30 minutes. The task runs fine until 4:30 p.m., when the system experiences a heavy load and a particularly nasty garbage collection; these cause the actual execution time to be a minute late—4:31 p.m. Now, with fixed-delay scheduling it is the *actual interval* that is important, that is to say, we want 30 minutes between each actual execution, so the next execution is scheduled for 5:01 p.m. rather than 5:00 p.m. With fixed-rate scheduling, the interval defines the *intended* interval—that is to say, we intend the job to execute every 30 minutes based on the start time, not on the time of the last job—so the job is scheduled for execution at 5:00 p.m.

Both of these trigger types are useful in different ways. In general, you use fixed-delay triggers for situations where you want the time between each execution to be as regular as possible or when you want to avoid the possibility of two executions happening too close together, which can happen with fixed-rate execution if a particular execution is delayed long enough. You use fixed-rate triggers for real-time–sensitive operations such as those that must execute every hour on the hour.

Creating a Simple Job

To create a job to use with the `Timer` class, you simply extend the `TimerTask` class and implement the `run()` method to execute your job's logic. Listing 12-1 shows a simple `TimerTask` implementation that writes "Hello, World" to `stdout`.

Listing 12-1. *Creating a Basic TimerTask*

```
package com.apress.prospring2.ch12.timer;

import java.util.TimerTask;

public class HelloWorldTask extends TimerTask {

    public void run() {
        System.out.println("Hello World!");
    }
}
```

Here, you can see that in the `run()` method, we simply write the "Hello, World" message to `stdout`. Each time a job is executed, `Timer` invokes the `TimerTask`'s `run()` method. The simplest possible trigger we can create for this job is a one-off trigger to start the job in 1 second; Listing 12-2 shows this.

Listing 12-2. *Using a One-Off Trigger with the HelloWorldTask*

```
package com.apress.prospring2.ch12.timer;

import java.util.Timer;

public class OneOffScheduling {

    public static void main(String[] args) {
        Timer t = new Timer();
        t.schedule(new HelloWorldTask(), 1000);
    }
}
```

To schedule a job using a given trigger when you are using the JDK `Timer` class, you must first create an instance of the `Timer` class and then create the trigger using one of the `schedule()` or `scheduleAtFixedRate()` methods. In Listing 12-2, we used the `schedule()` method to schedule an instance of `HelloWorldTask` to run after a delay of 1,000 milliseconds. If you run this example, after the initial delay of 1 second, you get the following message:

```
Hello World!
```

This kind of one-off trigger is fairly useless—how often are you going to need to schedule a one-off task to run an arbitrary period of time after application start-up? For this reason, you can also specify an absolute date when you create a one-off trigger. So if we want to create a job to remind us seven days before an important birthday, we can replace our call to `Timer.schedule()` with something like this:

```
Calendar cal = Calendar.getInstance();
cal.set(2008, Calendar.NOVEMBER, 30);
t.schedule(new HelloWorldTask(), cal.getTime());
```

In this example, you can see that we created an instance of Calendar for the date November 30, 2008. Then, using the Calendar instance, we scheduled the HelloWorldTask to run. This is clearly more useful than the first example, because no matter what time the application starts, the job is always scheduled to run at the same time. The only drawback with this approach is that we will not be reminded about the birthday in 2009 or 2010 unless we explicitly add more triggers. By using a repeating trigger, we can get around this.

Both types of repeating trigger, fixed-delay and fixed-rate, are configured in the same way: you specify a starting point, using either a number of milliseconds relative to the call to schedule() or an absolute date, and you specify an interval in milliseconds to control when subsequent executions occur. Remember that "interval" is interpreted differently depending on whether you are using a fixed-delay or fixed-rate trigger.

We can schedule the HelloWorldTask job to run every 3 seconds with a 1-second delay using the code shown in Listing 12-3.

Listing 12-3. *Scheduling a Repeating Task*

```
package com.apress.prospring2.ch12.timer;

import java.util.Timer;

public class FixedDelayScheduling {

    public static void main(String[] args) throws Exception{
        Timer t = new Timer();
        t.schedule(new HelloWorldTask(), 1000, 3000);
    }
}
```

If you run this application, you will see the first "Hello, World" message displayed after about 1 second, followed by further "Hello, World" messages every 3 seconds. To schedule this job using a fixed-rate trigger, simply replace the call to Timer.schedule() with a call to Timer.scheduleAtFixedRate(), as shown in Listing 12-4.

Listing 12-4. *Scheduling a Job Using a Fixed-Rate Trigger*

```
package com.apress.prospring2.ch12.timer;

import java.util.Timer;

public class FixedRateScheduling {

    public static void main(String[] args) throws Exception {
        Timer t = new Timer();
        t.scheduleAtFixedRate(new HelloWorldTask(), 1000, 1000);
    }
}
```

As with the one-off trigger, you can start both fixed-delay and fixed-rate triggers using an absolute date. Using this approach, we can create a trigger for our birthday reminder example that runs on a given date and then repeats each year. This is shown in Listing 12-5.

Listing 12-5. *Scheduling Birthday Reminders*

```
package com.apress.prospring2.ch12.timer;

import java.util.Calendar;
```

```
import java.util.Timer;

public class SimpleBirthdayReminderScheduling {

    private static final long MILLIS_IN_YEAR = 1000 * 60 * 60 * 24 * 365;

    public static void main(String[] args) {
        Timer t = new Timer();

        Calendar cal = Calendar.getInstance();
        cal.set(2008, Calendar.NOVEMBER, 30);
        t.schedule(new HelloWorldTask(), cal.getTime());

        t.scheduleAtFixedRate(new HelloWorldTask(), cal.getTime(),
                MILLIS_IN_YEAR);
    }
}
```

In this example, you can see that we calculate the number of milliseconds in a year, and using a `Calendar` instance, we define a starting point of November 30 and define the interval to be one year. Now, every year on November 30, provided that this application is running and conveniently ignoring the existence of leap years, the "Hello, World" message is written to `stdout`. Clearly, this is not a fully functional example, because there is no real notification mechanism, and each time we want to add a new birthday reminder, we need to change the code. In the next section, we create a more robust birthday reminder application using Spring's JDK `Timer` support classes.

Spring Support for JDK Timer Scheduling

As you saw in the previous section, you can easily create and schedule jobs using the JDK `Timer` and `TimerTask` classes. That said, the approach we took in the previous examples has some problems. First, we created the `TimerTask` instances within the application rather than using Spring. For the `HelloWorldTask`, this is acceptable, because we did not need to configure the job at all. However, many jobs require some configuration data, so we should manage these using Spring to allow for easy configuration. Second, the trigger information is hard-coded into the application, meaning that any changes to the time a job is triggered require a change to the application code and a recompilation. Finally, scheduling new jobs or removing a job requires changes to the application code; ideally, we should be able to configure this externally. By using Spring's `Timer` support classes, we can externalize all job and trigger configuration as well as hand over control of `Timer` creation to Spring, thus allowing jobs and their triggers to be defined externally.

The core of Spring's `Timer` support comes in the form of the `ScheduledTimerTask` and `TimerFactoryBean` classes. The `ScheduledTimerTask` class acts as a wrapper around your `TimerTask` implementations and allows you to define trigger information for the job. Using the `TimerFactoryBean`, you can have Spring automatically create `Timer` instances for a given list of `ScheduledTimerTask` beans using the trigger configuration data when creating the trigger.

Using ScheduledTimerTask and TimerFactoryBean

Before we dive in and look at our new and improved birthday reminder application, we should first look at the basics of how `ScheduledTimerTask` and `TimerFactoryBean` work. For each scheduled job you want to create, you need to configure an instance of the job class and an instance of `ScheduledTimerTask` containing the trigger details. You can share the same `TimerTask` instance across many `ScheduledTimerTask` instances if you want to create many triggers for the same job. Once you have these components configured, simply configure a `TimerFactoryBean` and specify the list of ScheduledTimerTask beans. Spring then creates an instance of Timer and schedules all the jobs defined by the ScheduledTimerTask beans using that Timer class.

This might sound complex at first, but in reality, it is not. Listing 12-6 shows a simple configuration for scheduling the HelloWorldTask to run every 3 seconds with a delay of 1 second before the first execution.

Listing 12-6. *Configuring Job Scheduling Using TimerFactoryBean*

```
<?xml version="1.0" encoding="UTF-8"?>
 <beans xmlns=http://www.springframework.org/schema/beans
         xmlns:xsi=http://www.w3.org/2001/XMLSchema-instance
         xsi:schemaLocation="http://www.springframework.org/schema/beans
         http://www.springframework.org/schema/beans/spring-beans-2.0.xsd">

    <bean id="job" class="com.apress.prospring2.ch12.timer.HelloWorldTask"/>

    <bean id="timerTask"
         class="org.springframework.scheduling.timer.ScheduledTimerTask">
        <property name="delay" value="1000" />
        <property name="period" value="3000" />
        <property name="timerTask" ref="job" />
    </bean>

    <bean id="timerFactory"
         class="org.springframework.scheduling.timer.TimerFactoryBean">
        <property name="scheduledTimerTasks">
            <list>
                <ref local="timerTask"/>
            </list>
        </property>
    </bean>
</beans>
```

Here, you can see that we have configured a bean, job, of type HelloWorldTask, and using this bean, we have configured a bean of type ScheduledTimerTask, setting the delay to 1,000 milliseconds and the period to 3,000 milliseconds. The final part of the configuration is the timerFactory bean, which is passed a list of beans of type ScheduledTimerTask. In this case, we have only one task to schedule, represented by the timerTask bean. Be aware that when specifying trigger information using ScheduledTimerTask, you can supply a delay only in milliseconds, not an initial date for startup. We'll show you a way around this when we build the birthday reminder application in the next section.

With all of the scheduling and job definition information contained in the configuration, our sample application has very little to do. In fact, all we need to do is load the ApplicationContext, and Spring creates the Timer class and schedules the HelloWorldTask as per the configuration file. This code is shown in Listing 12-7.

Listing 12-7. *The TimerFactoryBeanExample Class*

```
package com.apress.prospring2.ch12.timer;

import org.springframework.context.ApplicationContext;
import org.springframework.context.support.FileSystemXmlApplicationContext;

public class TimerFactoryBeanExample {
```

```
    public static void main(String[] args) throws Exception {
        ApplicationContext ctx = new FileSystemXmlApplicationContext(
                "./ch12/src/conf/timer-context.xml");
        System.in.read();
    }
}
```

If you run this application, you will see that the message “Hello, World” is written to stdout every 3 seconds after an initial delay of 1 second. As you can see from this example, it is very simple to configure job scheduling external to your application’s code. Using this approach, it is much simpler to make changes to a job’s schedules or to add new scheduled jobs and remove existing ones.

A More Comprehensive Birthday Reminder Application

In this section, we create a more complex birthday reminder application using Spring’s Timer support. With this example, we want to be able to schedule multiple reminder jobs, each with a specific configuration, to identify whose birthday the reminder indicates. We also want to be able to add and remove reminders without having to modify the application code.

To get started, we need to create a job to perform the actual reminder. Because we are going to create these jobs using Spring, we can allow all configuration data to be provided using DI. Listing 12-8 shows the BirthdayReminderTask.

Listing 12-8. *The BirthdayReminderTask*

```
package com.apress.prospring2.ch12.timer.bday;

import java.util.TimerTask;

public class BirthdayReminderTask extends TimerTask {

    private String who;

    public void setWho(String who) {
        this.who = who;
    }

    public void run() {
        System.out.println("Don't forget it is " + who
                + "'s birthday is 7 days");
    }
}
```

Notice here that we defined a property on the task, who, that allows us to specify of whose birthday we’re being reminded. In a real birthday reminder application, the reminder would no doubt be sent to e-mail or some similar medium. For now, however, you’ll have to be content with reminder messages written to stdout!

With this task complete, we are almost ready to move on to the configuration stage. However, as we pointed out earlier, you cannot specify the start time of a scheduled job using a date when you are using ScheduledTimerTask. This is problematic for our sample application, because we do not want to have to specify reminder dates as a relative offset to the start-up time of the application. Thankfully, we can overcome this problem quite easily by extending the ScheduledTimerTask class and overriding the getDelay() method used by TimerFactoryBean to determine what delay it should assign to a trigger. At the same time, we can also override the getPeriod() method to return the number of milliseconds in a year so that you do not have to add that literal into configuration files. Listing 12-9 shows the code for our custom ScheduledTimerTask, BirthdayScheduledTask.

Listing 12-9. *Customizing ScheduledTimerTask*

```
package com.apress.prospring2.ch12.timer.bday;

import java.text.DateFormat;
import java.text.ParseException;
import java.text.SimpleDateFormat;
import java.util.Calendar;
import java.util.Date;

import org.springframework.scheduling.timer.ScheduledTimerTask;

public class BirthdayScheduledTask extends ScheduledTimerTask {

    private static final long MILLIS_IN_YEAR = 1000 * 60 * 60 * 24 * 365;

    private DateFormat dateFormat = new SimpleDateFormat("yyyy-MM-dd");

    private Date startDate;

    public void setDate(String date) throws ParseException {
        startDate = dateFormat.parse(date);
    }

    public long getDelay() {
        Calendar now = Calendar.getInstance();
        Calendar then = Calendar.getInstance();
        then.setTime(startDate);

        return (then.getTimeInMillis() - now.getTimeInMillis());
    }

    public long getPeriod() {
        return MILLIS_IN_YEAR;
    }
}
```

In this example, you can see that we define a new property for the `BirthdayScheduledTask` class, `date`, which allows us to specify the start date as a date rather than a delay period. This property is of type `String`, because we use an instance of `SimpleDateFormat` configured with the pattern `yyyy-MM-dd` to parse dates such as `2008-11-30`. We override the `getPeriod()` method, which `TimerFactoryBean` uses when it configures the interval for the trigger, to return the number of milliseconds in a year. Also notice that we override `getDelay()`, and using the `Calendar` class, we calculate the number of milliseconds between the current time and the specified start date. This value is then returned as the delay. With this complete, we can now complete the configuration for our sample application, as shown in Listing 12-10.

Listing 12-10. *Configuring the Birthday Reminder Application*

```
<?xml version="1.0" encoding="UTF-8"?>
<beans xmlns="http://www.springframework.org/schema/beans"
     xmlns:xsi="http://www.w3.org/2001/XMLSchema-instance"
     xsi:schemaLocation="http://www.springframework.org/schema/beans
        http://www.springframework.org/schema/beans/spring-beans-2.0.xsd">
```

```
    <bean id="mum"
          class="com.apress.prospring2.ch12.timer.bday.BirthdayScheduledTask">
        <property name="date" value="2008-11-30" />
        <property name="fixedRate" value="true" />

        <property name="timerTask">
          <bean class="com.apress.prospring2.ch12.timer.bday.BirthdayReminderTask">
              <property name="who" value="Mum">
          </bean>
        </property>
    </bean>

    <bean id="timerFactory"
          class="org.springframework.scheduling.timer.TimerFactoryBean">
        <property name="scheduledTimerTasks">
            <list>
                <ref local="mum"/>
            </list>
        </property>
    </bean>
</beans>
```

This code should look familiar to you by now. Notice that we used our `BirthdayScheduledTask` class in place of the `ScheduledTimerTask` class, and instead of specifying a delay and a period, we have simply specified the date. Also, we rely on the overridden `getDelay()` and `getPeriod()` methods to provide the `TimerFactoryBean` with the delay and period values. In addition, notice that we set the `fixedRate` property of the `BirthdayScheduledTask` bean to `true`. This property is inherited from `ScheduledTimerTask`; `TimerFactoryBean` uses it to decide whether or not it should create a fixed-rate or fixed-delay trigger.

Scheduling Arbitrary Jobs

When scheduling jobs, you often need to schedule the execution of logic that already exists. If this is the case, you might not want to go through the trouble of creating a `TimerTask` class just to wrap your logic. Thankfully, you don't have to. Using the `MethodInvokingTimerTaskFactoryBean`, you can schedule the execution of any method on any given bean or a static method on a specific class; you can even provide method arguments if your logic method requires them.

As an example of this, consider the `FooBean` shown in Listing 12-11.

Listing 12-11. *The FooBean Class*

```
package com.apress.prospring2.ch12.timer;

public class FooBean {

    public void someJob(String message) {
        System.out.println(message);
    }
}
```

If we want to schedule the `someJob()` method to run every 3 seconds with a given argument rather than create a `TimerTask` just to do that, we can simply use the `MethodInvokingTimerTaskFactoryBean` to create a `TimerTask` for us. The configuration for this is shown in Listing 12-12.

Listing 12-12. *Using MethodInvokingTimerTaskFactoryBean*

```
<?xml version="1.0" encoding="UTF-8"?>
<beans xmlns=http://www.springframework.org/schema/beans
       xmlns:xsi=http://www.w3.org/2001/XMLSchema-instance
       xsi:schemaLocation="http://www.springframework.org/schema/beans
       http://www.springframework.org/schema/beans/spring-beans-2.0.xsd">

    <bean id="target" class="com.apress.prospring2.ch12.timer.FooBean"/>

    <bean id="task" class="org.springframework.scheduling.timer.➥
                                        MethodInvokingTimerTaskFactoryBean">
        <property name="targetObject" ref="target" />
        <property name="targetMethod" value="someJob" />
        <property name="arguments" value="Hello World!" />
    </bean>

    <bean id="timerTask"
            class="org.springframework.scheduling.timer.ScheduledTimerTask">
        <property name="delay" value="1000" />
        <property name="period" value="3000" />
        <property name="timerTask" ref="task" />
    </bean>

    <bean id="timerFactory"
            class="org.springframework.scheduling.timer.TimerFactoryBean">
        <property name="scheduledTimerTasks">
            <list>
                <ref local="timerTask"/>
            </list>
        </property>
    </bean>

</beans>
```

We can replace the definition of our own custom `TimerTask` bean with a definition using the `MethodInvokingTimerTaskFactoryBean`. To configure `MethodInvokingTimerTaskFactoryBean`, we specify the target of the invocation as a reference to another bean, the method to execute, and the argument to use when executing. The `TimerTask` supplied by `MethodInvokingTimerTaskFactoryBean` is used in the normal way, wrapped in a `ScheduledTimerTask`, and passed to the `TimerFactoryBean`.

Listing 12-13 shows a simple driver program to test this out.

Listing 12-13. *Testing the MethodInvokingTimerTaskFactoryBean*

```
package com.apress.prospring2.ch12.timer;

import org.springframework.context.ApplicationContext;
import org.springframework.context.support.FileSystemXmlApplicationContext;

public class MethodInvokerScheduling {

    public static void main(String[] args) throws Exception {
        ApplicationContext ctx = new FileSystemXmlApplicationContext(
                "./ch12/src/conf/timerMethodInvoker.xml");
        System.in.read();
    }
}
```

Running this example gives you the now familiar timed appearance of "Hello, World" messages on your console. Clearly, using `MethodInvokingTimerTaskFactoryBean` removes the need to create custom `TimerTask` implementations that simply wrap the execution of a business method.

JDK `Timer`-based scheduling provides support for an application's basic scheduling needs using a simple and easy-to-understand architecture. Although the trigger system for JDK `Timer` is not extremely flexible, it does provide basic schemes that allow you to control simple scheduling. Using Spring's support classes for `Timer`, you externalize a task scheduling configuration and make it easier to add and remove tasks from the scheduler without having to change any application code. Using `MethodInvokingTimerTaskFactoryBean`, you avoid having to create `TimerTask` implementations that do nothing more than invoke a business method, thus reducing the amount of code you need to write and maintain.

The main drawback of JDK `Timer` scheduling comes when you need to support complex triggers such as a trigger to execute a job every Monday, Wednesday, and Friday at 3:00 p.m. In the next part of this chapter, we look at the Quartz scheduling engine, which provides much more comprehensive support for scheduling and, just like `Timer`, is fully integrated into Spring.

Scheduling Jobs Using OpenSymphony Quartz

The open source Quartz project is a dedicated job scheduling engine designed to be used in both Java EE and Java SE settings. Quartz provides a huge range of features such as persistent jobs, clustering, and distributed transactions, though we do not look at the clustering or distributed transaction features in this book—you can find out more about these online at `www.opensymphony.com/quartz`. Spring's Quartz integration is similar to its `Timer` integration in that it provides for declarative configuration of jobs, triggers, and schedules. In addition to this, Spring provides additional job persistence features that allow the scheduling of a Quartz job to take part in a Spring-managed transaction.

Introducing Quartz

Quartz is an extremely powerful job scheduling engine, and we cannot hope to explain everything about it in this chapter. However, we do cover the main aspects of Quartz that are related to Spring, and we discuss how you can use Quartz from a Spring application. As with our `Timer` discussion, we start by looking at Quartz separately from Spring, and then we look at integrating Quartz and Spring.

The core of Quartz is made up of two interfaces, `Job` and `Scheduler`, and two classes, `JobDetail` and `Trigger`. From their names, it should be apparent what `Job`, `Scheduler`, and `Trigger` do, but the role of the `JobDetail` class is not so clear. Unlike `Timer`-based scheduling, tasks are not executed using a single instance of your job class; instead, Quartz creates instances as it needs them. You can use the `JobDetail` class to encapsulate the job state and to pass information to a job between subsequent executions of a job. `Timer`-based scheduling has no notion of a `Trigger` class; `Trigger` logic is encapsulated by the `Timer` class itself. Quartz supports a pluggable architecture for triggers, which allows you to create your own implementations as you see fit. That said, you rarely create your own `Trigger` implementations because Quartz provides the superpowerful `CronTrigger` class out of the box, which allows you to use cron expressions (more on that shortly) to have fine-grained control over job execution.

Simple Job Scheduling

To create a job for use in Quartz, simply create a class that implements the `Job` interface. The `Job` interface defines a single method, `execute()`, from which you call your business logic. Quartz passes an instance of `JobExecutionContext` to the `execute()` method, allowing you to access context data about the current execution. We'll look at this in more detail in the next section.

Listing 12-14 show a simple `Job` implementation that writes "Hello, World" to `stdout`.

Listing 12-14. *Creating a Simple Job*

```
package com.apress.prospring2.ch12.quartz;

import org.quartz.Job;
import org.quartz.JobExecutionContext;
import org.quartz.JobExecutionException;

public class HelloWorldJob implements Job {

    public void execute(JobExecutionContext context)
            throws JobExecutionException {
        System.out.println("Hello World!");
    }

}
```

To schedule this job to run, we first need to obtain a Scheduler instance, then create a JobDetail bean that contains information about the job, and finally create a Trigger to govern job execution. The code for this is shown in Listing 12-15.

Listing 12-15. *Scheduling Jobs in Quartz*

```
package com.apress.prospring2.ch12.quartz;

import java.util.Date;

import org.quartz.JobDetail;
import org.quartz.Scheduler;
import org.quartz.SimpleTrigger;
import org.quartz.Trigger;
import org.quartz.impl.StdSchedulerFactory;

public class HelloWorldScheduling {

    public static void main(String[] args) throws Exception {

        Scheduler scheduler = new StdSchedulerFactory().getScheduler();
        scheduler.start();

        JobDetail jobDetail = new JobDetail("helloWorldJob",
                Scheduler.DEFAULT_GROUP, HelloWorldJob.class);

        Trigger trigger = new SimpleTrigger("simpleTrigger",
                Scheduler.DEFAULT_GROUP, new Date(), null,
                SimpleTrigger.REPEAT_INDEFINITELY, 3000);

        scheduler.scheduleJob(jobDetail, trigger);
    }
}
```

This code starts by obtaining an instance of Scheduler using the StdSchedulerFactory class. We are not going to look at this class in any detail here, but you can find out more information in the Quartz tutorial, which is available on the OpenSymphony web site. For now, it is enough to know that the StdSchedulerFactory.getScheduler() class returns a Scheduler instance that is ready to run. In Quartz, a Scheduler can be started, stopped, and paused. If a Scheduler has not been started or is paused, no triggers fire, so we start the Scheduler using the start() method.

Next, we create the JobDetail instance of the job we are scheduling, passing in three arguments to the constructor. The first argument is the job name and refers to this job when using one of the Scheduler interface's administration methods, such as pauseJob(), which allows a particular job to be paused. The second argument is the group name, for which we are using the default. Group names can be used to refer to a group of jobs together, perhaps to pause them all using Scheduler.pauseJobGroup(). You should note that job names are unique within a group. The third and final argument is the Class that implements this particular job.

With the JobDetail instance created, we now move on to create a Trigger. In this example, we use the SimpleTrigger class, which provides JDK Timer-style trigger behavior. The first and second arguments passed to the SimpleTrigger constructor are the trigger name and group name, respectively. Both of these arguments perform similar functions for a Trigger as they do for a JobDetail. Also note that trigger names must be unique within a group, as otherwise, an exception is raised. The third and fourth arguments, both of type Date, are the start and end dates for this Trigger. By specifying null for the end date, we are saying there is no end date. The ability to specify an end date for a trigger is not available when you are using Timer. The next argument is the repeat count, which allows you to specify the maximum number of times the Trigger can fire. We use the constant REPEAT_INDEFINITELY to allow the Trigger to fire without a limit. The final argument is the interval between Trigger firings and is defined in milliseconds. We have defined an interval of 3 seconds.

The final step in this example is to schedule the job with a call to Scheduler.schedule() that passes in the JobDetail instance and the Trigger. If you run this application, you will see the familiar stream of "Hello, World" messages appearing gradually in your console.

Using JobDataMaps

In the previous example, all information for the job execution was contained in the job itself. However, you can pass state into the job using the JobDetail or Trigger class. Each instance of JobDetail and Trigger has an associated JobDataMap instance, which implements Map, and allows you to pass in job data in key/value pairs. Your jobs can modify data in the JobDataMap to allow for the passing of data between subsequent executions of the job. However, there are some considerations related to job persistence when using this approach. We discuss these later in the "About Job Persistence" section.

Storing data about a Trigger is useful when you have the same job scheduled with multiple Trigger implementations and want to provide the job with different data on each independent triggering. Entries of this map are made available via the JobDataMap on the JobExecutionContext that can be retrieved via the getMergedJobDataMap() method. As the method name suggests, the JobDataMap on the JobExecutionContext is a merge of the JobDataMap found on the JobDetail and the JobDataMap found on the Trigger, whereas data stored in the Trigger overrides data stored on the JobDetail.

In Listing 12-16, you can see an example of a Job that uses data contained in the merged JobDataMap to perform its processing.

Listing 12-16. *Using the JobDataMap*

```
package com.apress.prospring2.ch12.quartz;

import java.util.Map;

import org.quartz.Job;
import org.quartz.JobExecutionContext;
import org.quartz.JobExecutionException;

public class MessageJob implements Job {

    public void execute(JobExecutionContext context) throws JobExecutionException {
```

```
        Map properties = context.getMergedJobDataMap();

        System.out.println("Previous Fire Time: "
                + context.getPreviousFireTime());
        System.out.println("Current Fire Time: " + context.getFireTime());
        System.out.println("Next Fire Time: " + context.getNextFireTime());
        System.out.println(properties.get("message"));
        System.out.println(properties.get("jobDetailMessage"));
        System.out.println(properties.get("triggerMessage"));
        System.out.println("");
    }
}
```

From the merged `JobDataMap`, we are able to extract the `Objects` that are keyed as `message`, `jobDetailMessage`, and `triggerMessage` and write them to `stdout`. Also notice that we are able to get information about the previous, current, and next execution of this job from the `JobExecutionContext`.

In Listing 12-17, you can see an example of how you populate the `JobDataMap` on `JobDetail` with data when scheduling the `Job`.

Listing 12-17. *Adding Data to the JobDetail JobDataMap*

```
package com.apress.prospring2.ch12.quartz;

import org.quartz.Scheduler;
import org.quartz.SimpleTrigger;
import org.quartz.JobDetail;
import org.quartz.Trigger;
import org.quartz.impl.StdSchedulerFactory;

import java.util.Map;
import java.util.Date;

public class JobDetailMessageScheduling {

    public static void main(String[] args) throws Exception {
        Scheduler scheduler = new StdSchedulerFactory().getScheduler();
        scheduler.start();

        JobDetail jobDetail = new JobDetail("messageJob",
                Scheduler.DEFAULT_GROUP, MessageJob.class);

        Map map = jobDetail.getJobDataMap();
        map.put("message", "This is a message from Quartz");
        map.put("jobDetailMessage", "A jobDetail message");

        Trigger trigger = new SimpleTrigger("simpleTrigger",
                Scheduler.DEFAULT_GROUP, new Date(), null,
                SimpleTrigger.REPEAT_INDEFINITELY, 3000);

        scheduler.scheduleJob(jobDetail, trigger);
    }
}
```

You will recognize much of this code from the example in Listing 12-15, but notice that once the `JobDetail` instance has been created here, we access the `JobDataMap` and add two messages to it, keyed as `message` and `jobDetailMessage`. If you run this example and leave it running for a few iterations, you end up with output similar to this:

```
Previous Fire Time: null
Current Fire Time: Tue Oct 23 11:02:19 BST 2007
Next Fire Time: Tue Oct 23 11:02:22 BST 2007
This is a message from Quartz
A jobDetail message
null

Previous Fire Time: Tue Oct 23 11:02:19 BST 2007
Current Fire Time: Tue Oct 23 11:02:22 BST 2007
Next Fire Time: Tue Oct 23 11:02:25 BST 2007
This is a message from Quartz
A jobDetail message
null

Previous Fire Time: Tue Oct 23 11:02:22 BST 2007
Current Fire Time: Tue Oct 23 11:02:25 BST 2007
Next Fire Time: Tue Oct 23 11:02:28 BST 2007
This is a message from Quartz
A jobDetail message
null
```

You can see that both messages contained in the `JobDataMap` are written to `stdout` after the information about the execution times of the previous, current, and next execution is displayed.

Listing 12-18 gives you an example of also providing data on the `Trigger` and the effect that merging the two `JobDataMap` instances has on the values.

Listing 12-18. *Using the JobDataMap on the Trigger*

```
package com.apress.prospring2.ch12.quartz;

import org.quartz.JobDetail;
import org.quartz.Scheduler;
import org.quartz.SimpleTrigger;
import org.quartz.Trigger;
import org.quartz.impl.StdSchedulerFactory;

import java.util.Date;

public class TriggerMessageScheduling {

    public static void main(String[] args) throws Exception {
        Scheduler scheduler = new StdSchedulerFactory().getScheduler();
        scheduler.start();

        JobDetail jobDetail = new JobDetail("triggerMessageJob",
                Scheduler.DEFAULT_GROUP, MessageJob.class);
        jobDetail.getJobDataMap().put("message", "This is a message from Quartz");
        jobDetail.getJobDataMap().put("jobDetailMessage", "My job details data.");

        Trigger trigger = new SimpleTrigger("simpleTrigger",
                Scheduler.DEFAULT_GROUP, new Date(), null,
                SimpleTrigger.REPEAT_INDEFINITELY, 3000);
        trigger.getJobDataMap().put("message", "Message from Trigger");
        trigger.getJobDataMap().put("triggerMessage", "Another trigger message.");
```

```
        scheduler.scheduleJob(jobDetail, trigger);
    }
}
```

As you can see, the JobDetail is configured exactly as before. We simply add two messages to the Trigger: a keyed message and a trigger message. Running this example produces output similar to the following:

```
Previous Fire Time: null
Current Fire Time: Tue Oct 23 11:14:22 BST 2007
Next Fire Time: Tue Oct 23 11:14:25 BST 2007
Message from Trigger
My job details data.
Another trigger message.

Previous Fire Time: Tue Oct 23 11:14:22 BST 2007
Current Fire Time: Tue Oct 23 11:14:25 BST 2007
Next Fire Time: Tue Oct 23 11:14:28 BST 2007
Message from Trigger
My job details data.
Another trigger message.

Previous Fire Time: Tue Oct 23 11:14:25 BST 2007
Current Fire Time: Tue Oct 23 11:14:28 BST 2007
Next Fire Time: Tue Oct 23 11:14:31 BST 2007
Message from Trigger
My job details data.
Another trigger message.
```

Note that the value of the key message is what we added to the Trigger JobDataMap, not what we defined in the JobDetail.

As you will see shortly, when using Spring to configure Quartz scheduling, you can create the JobDataMap in your Spring configuration file, allowing you to externalize all Job configuration completely.

Using the CronTrigger

In the previous examples, we used the SimpleTrigger class, which provides trigger functionality very similar to that of the JDK Timer class. However, Quartz excels in its support for complex trigger expressions using the CronTrigger. CronTrigger is based on the Unix cron daemon, a scheduling application that supports a simple, yet extremely powerful, trigger syntax. Using CronTrigger, you can quickly and accurately define trigger expressions that would be extremely difficult or impossible to do with the SimpleTrigger class. For instance, you can create a trigger that says, "Fire every 5 seconds of every minute, starting at the third second of the minute, but only between the hours of 2:00 and 5:00 p.m." Or it could say, "Fire on the last Friday of every month."

A CronTrigger syntax expression, referred to as a cron expression, contains six required components and one optional component. A cron expression is written on a single line, and each component is separated from the next by a space. Only the last, or rightmost, component is optional. Table 12-1 describes the cron components in detail.

Table 12-1. *Components of a cron Expression*

Position	Meaning	Allowed Special Characters
1	Seconds (0–59)	,, -, *, and /
2	Minutes (0–59)	,, -, *, and /
3	Hours (0–23)	,, -, *, and /
4	Day of the month (1–31)	,, -, *, /, ?, L, W, and C
5	Month (either JAN–DEC or 1–12)	,, -, *, and /
6	Day of the week (either SUN–SAT or 1–7)	,, -, *, /, ?, L, C, and #
7	Year (optional, 1970–2099), when empty, full range is assumed	,, -, *, and /

Each component accepts the typical range of values that you would expect, such as 0–59 for seconds and minutes and 1–31 for the day of the month. For the month and day of the week components, you can use numbers, such as 1–7 for day of the week, or text such as SUN–SAT.

Each field also accepts a given set of special symbols, so placing an asterisk (*) in the hours component means "every hour," and using an expression such as 6L in the day of the week component means "last Friday of the month." Table 12-2 describes cron wildcards and special characters in detail.

Table 12-2. *cron Expression Wildcards and Special Characters*

Special Character	Description
*	Any value. This special character can be used in any field to indicate that the value should not be checked. Therefore, our example cron expression will be fired on every day of the month, every month, and every day of the week between 1970 and 2099.
?	No specific value. This special character is usually used with other specific values to indicate that a value must be present but will not be checked.
-	Range. For example, 10-12 in the hours field means hours 10:00, 11:00, and 12:00 a.m.
,	List separator. Allows you to specify a list of values, such as MON, TUE, WED in the day of the week field.
/	Increments. This character specifies increments of a value. For example, 0/1 in the minute field means the job should run on every 1-minute increment of the minute field, starting from 0.
L	An abbreviation for "last." The meaning of L is a bit different in the day of the month field than for the day of the week. When used in the day of the month field, it means the last day of the month (March 31, February 28 or 29, and so on). When used in the day of the week field, it has the same value as 7—Saturday. The L special character is most useful when you use it with a specific day of the week value. For example, 6L in the day of the week field means the last Friday of each month.
W	W is only allowed for the day of the month field and specifies the nearest weekday (Monday–Friday) to the given day of the same month. Set the value to 7W, and the trigger will be fired on the sixth day if the seventh happens to be a Saturday. If the seventh day is a Sunday, the trigger fires on Monday, the eighth day. Note that a trigger due on Saturday the first will actually fire on the third.

Continued

Table 12-2. *Continued*

Special Character	Description
#	This value is allowed only for the day of the week field, and it specifies the *n*th day in a month. For example 1#2 means the first Monday of each month.
C	The calendar value. This is allowed for the day of the month and day of the week fields. The values of days are calculated against a specified calendar. Specifying 20C in the day of the month field fires the trigger on the first day included in the calendar on or after the twentieth day. Specifying 6C in the day of the week field is interpreted as the first day included in the calendar on or after Friday.

The last thing to bear in mind when writing cron expressions is daylight saving time. Changes because of daylight saving time may cause a trigger to fire twice in spring or to never fire in autumn.

There are many more permutations for cron expressions than we can discuss here; you can find a detailed description of cron syntax in the Javadoc for the CronTrigger class.

Listing 12-19 shows an example of the CronTrigger class in action.

Listing 12-19. *Using the CronTrigger Class*

```
package com.apress.prospring2.ch12.quartz;

import java.util.Map;

import org.quartz.CronTrigger;
import org.quartz.JobDetail;
import org.quartz.Scheduler;
import org.quartz.Trigger;
import org.quartz.impl.StdSchedulerFactory;

public class CronTriggerExample {

    public static void main(String[] args) throws Exception {
        Scheduler scheduler = new StdSchedulerFactory().getScheduler();
        scheduler.start();

        JobDetail jobDetail = new JobDetail("messageJob",
                Scheduler.DEFAULT_GROUP, MessageJob.class);

        Map map = jobDetail.getJobDataMap();
        map.put("message", "This is a message from Quartz");

        String cronExpression = "3/5 * 14,15,16,17 * * ?";

        Trigger trigger = new CronTrigger("cronTrigger",
                Scheduler.DEFAULT_GROUP, cronExpression);

        scheduler.scheduleJob(jobDetail, trigger);
    }
}
```

Much of this code should look familiar to you; the only major difference here is that we use the cron expression. The actual creation of the CronTrigger class is very similar to the creation of the SimpleTrigger class in that you have a name and a group name. To help you understand the cron expression in the example, we'll break it down into components.

The first component, `3/5`, means every 5 seconds starting at the third second of the minute. The second component, *, simply says every minute. The third component, `14, 15, 16, 17`, restricts this trigger to running between 2:00 and 5:59 p.m.—that is, when the time begins with 14, 15, 16, or 17. The next two components are both wildcards saying that this trigger can run in any month or any year. The final component uses the queston mark wildcard, ?, to indicate that this trigger can run on any day of the week. This expression has the net effect of firing every 5 seconds, starting on the third second of the minute, but only between 2:00 and 5:59 p.m.

If you run this example, depending on the time of day, you see either a blank screen or the ever increasing list of "Hello, World" printouts. Try modifying the first component in the expression to change the frequency of the trigger or at which second in the minute the trigger starts. You should also try modifying other components to see what effects you get.

The `CronTrigger` class is great for almost all trigger requirements. However, expressions can quickly become convoluted when you need to program exceptions to the rule. For instance, consider a process that checks a task list for a user every Monday, Wednesday, and Friday at 11:00 a.m. and 3:00 p.m. Now, consider what happens when you want to prevent this trigger from firing when the user is on vacation. Thankfully, Quartz provides support for this via the `Calendar` interface. Using the `Calendar` interface, you can accurately define a period that should either be explicitly included or explicitly excluded from a trigger's normal schedule. Quartz comes with six implementations of `Calendar`, one of which is the `HolidayCalendar` that stores a list of days to be excluded from a trigger's schedule. Listing 12-20 shows a modification of the previous example that uses a `HolidayCalendar` to exclude December 25, 2007.

Listing 12-20. *Explicitly Excluding Dates with HolidayCalendar*

```
package com.apress.prospring2.ch12.quartz;

import java.util.Calendar;
import java.util.Map;

import org.quartz.CronTrigger;
import org.quartz.JobDetail;
import org.quartz.Scheduler;
import org.quartz.Trigger;
import org.quartz.impl.StdSchedulerFactory;
import org.quartz.impl.calendar.HolidayCalendar;

public class CronWithCalendarExample {

    public static void main(String[] args) throws Exception {
        Scheduler scheduler = new StdSchedulerFactory().getScheduler();
        scheduler.start();

        // create a calendar to exclude a particular date
        Calendar cal = Calendar.getInstance();
        cal.set(2007, Calendar.DECEMBER, 25);

        HolidayCalendar calendar = new HolidayCalendar();
        calendar.addExcludedDate(cal.getTime());

        // add to scheduler
        scheduler.addCalendar("xmasCalendar", calendar, true, false);

        JobDetail jobDetail = new JobDetail("messageJob",
                Scheduler.DEFAULT_GROUP, MessageJob.class);
```

```
        Map map = jobDetail.getJobDataMap();
        map.put("message", "This is a message from Quartz");

        String cronExpression = "3/5 * 14,15,16,17 * * ?";

        Trigger trigger = new CronTrigger("cronTrigger",
                Scheduler.DEFAULT_GROUP, cronExpression);

        trigger.setCalendarName("xmasCalendar");

        scheduler.scheduleJob(jobDetail, trigger);
    }
}
```

Here, you can see that we create an instance of HolidayCalendar, and using the addExcludedDate() method, we exclude December 25. With the Calendar instance created, we add the Calendar to the Scheduler using the addCalendar() method, giving it a name of xmasCalendar. Later, before adding the CronTrigger, we associate it with xmasCalendar. Using this approach saves you from having to create complex cron expressions just to exclude a few arbitrary dates.

About Job Persistence

Quartz provides support for Job persistence, allowing you to add jobs at runtime or make changes to existing jobs and persist these changes and additions for subsequent executions of the Job. Central to this concept is the JobStore interface, implementations of which are used by Quartz when it is performing persistence. By default, Quartz uses the RAMJobStore implementation, which simply stores Job instances in memory. Other available implementations are JobStoreCMT and JobStoreTX. Both of these classes persist job details using a configured DataSource and support the creation and modification of jobs as part of a transaction. The JobStoreCMT implementation is intended to be used in an application server environment and takes part in container-managed transactions. For stand-alone applications, you should use the JobStoreTX implementation. Spring provides its own LocalDataSourceJobStore implementation of JobStore, which can take part in Spring-managed transactions. We will take a look at this implementation when we discuss Spring support for Quartz.

Earlier on, you saw how you can modify the contents of the JobDataMap to pass information between different executions of the same Job. However, if you try to run that example using a JobStore implementation other than RAMJobStore, you will be surprised to see that it doesn't work. The reason for this is that Quartz supports the notion of stateless and stateful jobs. When using the RAMJobStore and modifying the JobDataMap, you are actually modifying the store directly, so the type of Job is unimportant, but this is not the case when you are using implementations other than RAMJobStore. A stateless Job only has the data in the JobDataMap persisted when it is added to the Scheduler, whereas stateful Jobs have their JobDataMap persisted after every execution. To mark a Job as stateful, implement the StatefulJob interface instead of the Job interface. StatefulJob is a subinterface of Job, so you do not need to implement Job as well. You should also be aware that any data you place in the JobDataMap when using Job persistence must be serializable, because Quartz writes the JobDataMap as a serialized blob to the database.

Quartz Support in Spring

Spring's Quartz integration follows a similar pattern to the integration with Timer in that it allows you to configure your job scheduling fully within the Spring configuration file. In addition to this, Spring provides further classes to integrate with the Quartz JobStore, thus allowing you to configure Job persistence in your configuration and for Job modification to take part in Spring-managed transactions.

Scheduling a Job with Spring

As you would expect, much of the code you need to schedule a Quartz Job using Spring goes into the Spring configuration file. Indeed, you only need to load the ApplicationContext in your application for the configuration to take effect and for Spring to start the Scheduler automatically.

In Listing 12-21, you can see the configuration code required to configure the MessageJob class you saw in Listing 12-16 to run once every 3 seconds.

Listing 12-21. *Configuring Scheduling Declaratively*

```
<?xml version="1.0" encoding="UTF-8"?>
<beans xmlns="http://www.springframework.org/schema/beans"
     xmlns:xsi="http://www.w3.org/2001/XMLSchema-instance"
     xsi:schemaLocation="http://www.springframework.org/schema/beans
        http://www.springframework.org/schema/beans/spring-beans-2.0.xsd">

        <bean id="job" class="org.springframework.scheduling.quartz.JobDetailBean">
            <property name="jobClass"
                value="com.apress.prospring2.ch12.quartz.MessageJob"/>
            <property name="jobDataAsMap">
                <map>
                    <entry key="message"
                        value="This is a message from the Spring config file!"/>
                </map>
            </property>
        </bean>

        <bean id="trigger"
                class="org.springframework.scheduling.quartz.SimpleTriggerBean">
            <property name="jobDetail" ref="job"/>
            <property name="startDelay" value="1000"/>
            <property name="repeatInterval" value="3000"/>
            <property name="jobDataAsMap">
                <map>
                    <entry key="triggerMessage"
                            value="Trigger message from the Spring config file!"/>
                </map>
            </property>
        </bean>

    <bean id="schedulerFactory"
            class="org.springframework.scheduling.quartz.SchedulerFactoryBean">
        <property name="triggers">
            <list>
                <ref local="trigger"/>
            </list>
        </property>
    </bean>
</beans>
```

Here, you can see that we use the JobDetailBean class, which extends the JobDetail class, to configure the job data in a declarative manner. The JobDetailBean provides more JavaBean-style properties that are accessible by Spring, and it also provides sensible defaults for properties that you usually have to specify yourself. For instance, notice that we did not specify a job name or a group name. By default, the JobDetailBean uses the ID of the <bean> tag as the job name and the default group of the Scheduler as the group name. Notice that we are able to add data to the JobDataMap property using the jobDataAsMap property. The name of this property is not a typographical error—

you can't add directly to the jobDataMap property. It is of type JobDataMap, and this type is not supported in Spring configuration files.

With the JobDetailBean configured, the next step is to create a trigger. Spring offers two classes, SimpleTriggerBean and CronTriggerBean, that wrap the SimpleTrigger and CronTrigger classes, allowing you to configure them declaratively and to associate them with a JobDetailBean—all within your configuration file. Notice that in Listing 12-21, we defined a starting delay of 1 second and a repeat interval of 3 seconds. By default, the SimpleTriggerBean sets the repeat count to infinity.

The final piece of configuration you need is the SchedulerFactoryBean. By default, the SchedulerFactoryBean creates an instance of StdSchedulerFactory, which, in turn, creates the Scheduler implementation. You can override this behavior by setting the schedulerFactoryClass property to the name of a class that implements SchedulerFactory, which you wish to use in place of StdSchedulerFactory. The only property that you need to configure scheduling is the triggers property, which accepts a List of TriggerBean elements.

Because all of the job scheduling configuration is contained in the configuration, you need very little code to actually start the Scheduler and execute the Job instances. In fact, all you need to do is create the ApplicationContext, as shown in Listing 12-22.

Listing 12-22. *Testing Declarative Quartz Configuration*

```
package com.apress.prospring2.ch12.quartz.spring;

import org.springframework.context.ApplicationContext;
import org.springframework.context.support.FileSystemXmlApplicationContext;

public class SimpleSpringQuartzIntegrationExample {

    public static void main(String[] args) {
        ApplicationContext ctx = new FileSystemXmlApplicationContext(
                "./ch12/src/conf/quartz-simple.xml ");
    }
}
```

As you can see, this class does nothing more than create an instance of ApplicationContext using the configuration shown in Listing 12-21. If you run this application and leave it running for a few iterations, you end up with something like this:

```
Previous Fire Time: null
Current Fire Time: Tue Oct 23 11:24:31 BST 2007
Next Fire Time: Tue Oct 23 11:24:34 BST 2007
This is a message from the Spring configuration file!
null
Trigger message from the Spring configuration file!

Previous Fire Time: Tue Oct 23 11:24:31 BST 2007
Current Fire Time: Tue Oct 23 11:24:34 BST 2007
Next Fire Time: Tue Oct 23 11:24:37 BST 2007
This is a message from the Spring configuration file!
null
Trigger message from the Spring configuration file!

Previous Fire Time: Tue Oct 23 11:24:34 BST 2007
Current Fire Time: Tue Oct 23 11:24:37 BST 2007
Next Fire Time: Tue Oct 23 11:24:40 BST 2007
This is a message from the Spring configuration file!
null
Trigger message from the Spring configuration file!
```

Notice that it is running just like it was for the previous MessageJob example, but the messages displayed are the messages configured in the Spring configuration file.

Using Persistent Jobs

One of the great features of Quartz is its ability to create stateful, persistent jobs. This opens up some great functionality that is not available when you are using Timer-based scheduling. With persistent jobs, when you can add jobs to Quartz at runtime, they will still be in your application after a restart. Plus, you can modify the JobDataMap passed between executions of a Job, and the changes will still be in effect after a restart.

In this example, we are going to schedule two jobs, one using Spring configuration mechanisms and one at runtime. We'll see how the Quartz persistence mechanism copes with changes to the JobDataMap for these jobs and what happens in subsequent executions of the application.

To start with, you need to create a database in which Quartz can store the Job information. In the Quartz distribution—we used version 1.6.0—you will find a selection of database scripts for a variety of different RDBMS flavors. For the example here, we use Oracle, but you should not encounter problems using a different database as long as Quartz has a database script for it. For version 1.6.0, try the docs/dbTables subfolder of the Quartz distribution. Once you have located the script for your database, execute it against your database and verify that 12 tables, each with the prefix qrtz, have been created.

Next, create your test Job. Because we want to make changes to JobDataMap during Job execution, we need to flag to Quartz that it should treat this as a stateful Job. We do this by implementing the StatefulJob interface rather than the Job interface. This is shown in Listing 12-23.

Listing 12-23. *Creating a Stateful Job*

```
package com.apress.prospring2.ch12.quartz.spring;

import java.util.Map;

import org.quartz.JobExecutionContext;
import org.quartz.JobExecutionException;
import org.quartz.StatefulJob;

public class PersistentJob implements StatefulJob {

    public void execute(JobExecutionContext context)
            throws JobExecutionException {
        Map map = context.getJobDetail().getJobDataMap();
        System.out.println("[" + context.getJobDetail().getName() + "]"
                + map.get("message"));
        map.put("message", "Updated Message");
    }
}
```

The StatefulJob interface does not declare additional methods for your class to implement; it is simply a marker telling Quartz that it should persist the JobDetail after every execution. Here, you can see that we display the message that is stored in the JobDataMap along with the name of the Job.

The next steps are to configure the Job in Spring and configure the Scheduler with a DataSource it can use for persistence, as shown in Listing 12-24.

Listing 12-24. *Configuring Quartz Persistence in Spring*

```
<?xml version="1.0" encoding="UTF-8"?>
<beans xmlns="http://www.springframework.org/schema/beans"
     xmlns:xsi="http://www.w3.org/2001/XMLSchema-instance"
     xsi:schemaLocation="http://www.springframework.org/schema/beans
        http://www.springframework.org/schema/beans/spring-beans-2.0.xsd">

    <bean id="job" class="org.springframework.scheduling.quartz.JobDetailBean">
        <property name="jobClass"
            value="com.apress.prospring2.ch12.quartz.spring.PersistentJob"/>
        <property name="jobDataAsMap">
            <map>
                <entry key="message" value="Original Message"/>
            </map>
        </property>
    </bean>

    <bean id="dataSource"
            class="org.springframework.jdbc.datasource.SingleConnectionDataSource">
        <property name="driverClassName" value="oracle.jdbc.driver.OracleDriver"/>
        <property name="url"
                        value="jdbc:oracle:thin:@oracle.devcake.co.uk:1521:INTL"/>
        <property name="username" value="PROSPRING"/>
        <property name="password" value="x******6"/>
    </bean>

    <bean id="trigger"
                class="org.springframework.scheduling.quartz.SimpleTriggerBean">
        <property name="jobDetail" ref="job"/>
        <property name="startDelay" value="1000"/>
        <property name="repeatInterval" value="3000"/>
    </bean>

    <bean id="schedulerFactory"
              class="org.springframework.scheduling.quartz.SchedulerFactoryBean">
        <property name="triggers">
            <list>
                <ref local="trigger"/>
            </list>
        </property>
        <property name="dataSource" ref="dataSource"/>
    </bean>
</beans>
```

You will recognize much of this configuration code from Listing 12-21; the important part here is the dataSource bean. In this code, we use the Spring class SingleConnectionDataSource; this DataSource implementation is handy for testing, but never use it in production (check the Javadoc for this class if you are unsure why). Also, remember, you need to modify the connection details in the configuration as appropriate for your environment. For more details on configuring other DataSources with Spring, see Chapter 8.

Using the configured dataSource bean, we set the dataSource property of the SchedulerFactoryBean. By doing this, we instruct Spring to create a Scheduler that is configured to persist Job data using the given DataSource. Internally, this is achieved using Spring's own JobStore implementation, LocalDataSourceJobStore.

With the configuration complete, all that remains is to load it in an application and add another `Job` to the `Scheduler` at runtime. Listing 12-25 shows the code for this.

Listing 12-25. *Testing Job Persistence*

```
package com.apress.prospring2.ch12.quartz.spring;

import java.util.Date;

import org.quartz.JobDetail;
import org.quartz.Scheduler;
import org.quartz.SimpleTrigger;
import org.quartz.Trigger;
import org.springframework.context.ApplicationContext;
import org.springframework.context.support.FileSystemXmlApplicationContext;

public class SpringWithJobPersistence {

    public static void main(String[] args) throws Exception {
        ApplicationContext ctx = new FileSystemXmlApplicationContext(
                "./ch12/src/conf/quartzPersistent.xml");

        // get the scheduler
        Scheduler scheduler = (Scheduler) ctx.getBean("schedulerFactory");

        JobDetail job = scheduler.getJobDetail("otherJob",
                Scheduler.DEFAULT_GROUP);

        if (job == null) {
            // the job has not yet been created
            job = (JobDetail) ctx.getBean("job");
            job.setName("otherJob");
            job.getJobDataMap().put("message", "This is another message");

            Trigger trigger = new SimpleTrigger("simpleTrigger",
                    Scheduler.DEFAULT_GROUP, new Date(), null,
                    SimpleTrigger.REPEAT_INDEFINITELY, 3000);

            scheduler.scheduleJob(job, trigger);
        }
    }
}
```

This code requires little explanation. However, note that before we schedule the second job, we check to see if it already exists using the `Scheduler.getJobDetail()` method. This prevents us from overwriting the `Job` on subsequent runs of the application.

The first time you run this example, you get output something like this:

```
[otherJob]This is another message
[job]Original Message
[otherJob]Updated Message
[job]Updated Message
[otherJob]Updated Message
[job]Updated Message
```

As you can see, the first time each Job executes, the message displayed is the original message configured in the JobDataMap when the Job was scheduled. On subsequent executions, each Job displays the updated message that was set during the previous execution. If you stop the application and restart it, you see something slightly different:

```
[otherJob]Updated Message
[job]Updated Message
[otherJob]Updated Message
[job]Updated Message
[otherJob]Updated Message
[job]Updated Message
```

This time, you can see that, because the Job data was persisted, you do not need to re-create the second Job, and the JobDataMap accurately reflects changes that were made during the last run of the application.

Scheduling Arbitrary Jobs with Quartz

Like the Timer-based scheduling classes, Spring provides the ability to schedule the execution of arbitrary methods using Quartz. We won't go into detail on this, because it works in an almost identical manner to the Timer approach. Instead of using MethodInvokingTimerTaskFactoryBean, you use MethodInvokingJobDetailFactoryBean, and instead of automatically creating TimerTask implementations, you automatically create JobDetail ones.

Job Scheduling Considerations

If you are going to be adding job scheduling to your application, you should bear in mind a few considerations when you choose a scheduler and a scheduling approach.

Choosing a Scheduler

The first decision you have to make when adding scheduling to your application is which scheduler to use. This choice is actually quite easy. If you have only very simple scheduling requirements or are restricted in the external libraries that you can package with your application, you should use Timer-based scheduling. Otherwise, use Quartz.

Even if you find that your requirements are simple, you might want to go with Quartz, especially if you have to create an explicit Job implementation. If you use Quartz from the outset, if your requirements become more advanced, you can easily add persistence, transactions, or more complex triggers without having to change a TimerTask to a Job. In general, we have found that using Quartz for all of our scheduling allows us to become familiar with a single scheduling approach and saves our developers from having to worry about two different approaches when one provides everything they need.

Packaging Job Logic Separately from the Job Class

A common approach that we see many developers take when adding scheduling to an application is to place business logic inside a Job or TimerTask. Generally, this is a bad idea. In many cases, you need to have scheduled tasks available for execution on demand, which requires the logic to be separate from the scheduling framework.

Also, you should not unnecessarily couple your business logic to a particular scheduler. We have found that a better approach is to keep business logic in separate classes and either create a simple wrapper around those classes that is specific to your scheduler or, preferably, use the appropriate MethodInvoker*FactoryBean to create the wrapper for you.

Task Execution and Thread Pooling

So far in this chapter, we have discussed various ways of scheduling jobs to be executed at a specific point in time, at defined intervals, or using a combination of both times and intervals. Now, we are going to look at another way to schedule jobs in Spring that depend less on a specific time or interval than on immediate or event-triggered execution.

For example, think of a web server handling incoming requests. A simple approach for building such a server application would be to process each job in a new thread. Depending on the server you are building and its environment, this might work absolutely fine. But as the creation of a thread needs time and system resources, you might end up spending more time creating and destroying threads than executing jobs, not to mention that you might run out of system resources. To run stably, a server needs some way of managing how much can be done at the same time. The concept of thread pools and work queue offers just this.

The java.util.concurrent Package

One welcome addition to Java 5 was the java.util.concurrent package based on Doug Lea's util.concurrent package, a library offering efficient and well-tested tools to simplify the development of multithreaded applications. This package provides the Executor interface, which defines only one method execute(Runnable command) to execute Runnable tasks. It abstracts the submission of tasks away from the details of how they are run. Implementations of this interface offer all sorts of execution policy: thread-per-task, thread pooling, or even synchronous execution just to name a few (you can find some implementations of these in the Javadoc for the Executor interface).

To give you a little example of how this interface and its subinterface ExecutorService can be used, we will first create a task to execute using a slightly amended version of our former HelloWorldTask from Listing 12-1. We could just as well use the HelloWorldTask straight away, as it extends TimerTask that implements Runnable, but we wouldn't be able to see the task scheduling differences between various Executor implementations.

Listing 12-26. *HelloWorldCountDownTask*

```
package com.apress.prospring2.ch12;

public class HelloWorldCountDownTask implements Runnable {

    private String name;
    private int count = 4;

    public HelloWorldCountDownTask(String name) {
        this.name = name;
    }

    public void run() {
        while (count > 0) {
            count--;
            if (count == 0) {
                System.out.println(name + " says 'Hello World!");
            } else {
                System.out.println(name + ": " + count);
                Thread.yield();
            }
```

```
        }
    }
}
```

All this task does is print out a countdown from 3, calling the Thread.yield() method afterward to pause this thread's executions and allow other threads to be executed. As a last statement, the task will say hello to the world and finish execution.

Next, as shown in Listing 12-27, we are going to use an ExecutorService implementation to schedule and execute this task.

Listing 12-27. *Use ExecutorService to Schedule and Execute a Task*

```
package com.apress.prospring2.ch12.executor;
import com.apress.prospring2.ch12.HelloWorldCountDownTask;
import java.util.concurrent.ExecutorService;
import java.util.concurrent.Executors;

public class ExecutorServiceExample {

    public static void main(String[] args) {
        ExecutorService service = Executors.newFixedThreadPool(2);

        service.execute(new HelloWorldCountDownTask("Anna"));
        service.execute(new HelloWorldCountDownTask("Beth"));
        service.execute(new HelloWorldCountDownTask("Charlie"));
        service.execute(new HelloWorldCountDownTask("Daniel"));

        service.shutdown();
    }
}
```

The java.util.concurrent.Executors class provides convenient factory and utility methods for Executor and ExecutorService classes. We are using its newFixedThreadPool() method to retrieve a ThreadPoolExecutor with a fixed number of two threads in the pool. We then submit four tasks to execution and call the ExecutorService's shutdown() method to shut down the ExecutorService after all tasks have been executed. After calling this method, no further tasks can be added to the service. Running this example will print out the following:

```
Anna: 3
Anna: 2
Beth: 3
Anna: 1
Anna says 'Hello World!
Charlie: 3
Beth: 2
Charlie: 2
Beth: 1
Charlie: 1
Beth says 'Hello World!
Daniel: 3
Charlie says 'Hello World!
Daniel: 2
Daniel: 1
Daniel says 'Hello World!
```

Note that there are only two tasks being executed at the same time, and task Charlie is only getting executed after task Anna has finished. Try a different number of threads in the pool or a different Executor implementation, and you will find the printout to be different.

Spring's TaskExecutor Abstraction

Since version 2.0, Spring has offered an abstraction to the previously discussed Java 5 Executor framework. Identical to the java.util.concurrent.Executor interface, the TaskExecutor interface defines only the single method execute(Runnable command). Intended to be used internally in other Spring components such as asynchronous JMS and JCA environment support, it now lets you add thread pooling behavior to your own application without creating the need for Java 5.

Spring comes with a variety of TaskExecutor implementations, which are described in Table 12-3.

Table 12-3. *Springs TaskExecutor Implementations*

Implementation	Description
SimpleAsyncTaskExecutor	This implementation provides asynchronous threading with a new thread per invocation policy. It also allows setting a concurrency limit that will block further invocations.
SyncTaskExecutor	When you choose this implementation task, execution happens synchronously in the calling thread.
ConcurrentTaskExecutor	This class implements Spring's SchedulingTaskExecutor interface as well Java 5's java.util.concurrent.Executor interface and acts as a wrapper for the latter.
SimpleThreadPoolTaskExecutor	This is a subclass of Quartz's SimpleThreadPool and useful if a thread pool needs to be shared by Quartz and non-Quartz components.
ThreadPoolTaskExecutor	Behaving similarly to the ConcurrentTaskExecutor, it exposes the java.util.concurrent.ThreadPoolExecutor parameters as bean properties (it needs Java 5).
TimerTaskExecutor	This implementation uses a TimerTask behind the scenes. Invocations are executed in a separate thread but synchronously within that thread.
WorkManagerTaskExecutor	This uses the CommonJ WorkManager implementation and implements the WorkManager interface.

The differences in how the various implementations work is easiest to see in a small example. Listing 12-28 shows the configuration of three TaskExecutor implementations in Spring: ThreadPoolTaskExecutor, SyncTaskExecutor, and TimerTaskExecutor.

Listing 12-28. *task-executor-context.xml*

```
<?xml version="1.0" encoding="UTF-8"?>
<beans xmlns="http://www.springframework.org/schema/beans"
   xmlns:xsi="http://www.w3.org/2001/XMLSchema-instance"
   xsi:schemaLocation="http://www.springframework.org/schema/beans
        http://www.springframework.org/schema/beans/spring-beans-2.5.xsd">

    <bean id="threadPoolTaskExecutor"
          class="org.springframework.scheduling.concurrent.ThreadPoolTaskExecutor">
        <property name="corePoolSize" value="5"/>
```

```
        <property name="maxPoolSize" value="10"/>
        <property name="queueCapacity" value="25"/>
    </bean>

    <bean id="synchTaskExecutor"
            class="org.springframework.core.task.SyncTaskExecutor"/>

    <bean id="timerTaskExecutor"
            class="org.springframework.scheduling.timer.TimerTaskExecutor">
        <property name="delay" value="3000"/>
        <property name="timer" ref="timer"/>
    </bean>

    <bean id="timer" class="java.util.Timer"/>
</beans>
```

We can then use the defined beans to load them from the `ApplicationContext` and use them in a `TaskExecutorExample`, as shown in Listing 12-29.

Listing 12-29. *TaskExecutorExample*

```
package com.apress.prospring2.ch12.taskexecutor;

import org.springframework.core.task.TaskExecutor;
import com.apress.prospring2.ch12.HelloWorldCountDownTask;

public class TaskExecutorExample {

    private TaskExecutor taskExecutor;

    public TaskExecutorExample(TaskExecutor taskExecutor) {
        this.taskExecutor = taskExecutor;
    }

    public void executeTasks() {
        this.taskExecutor.execute(new HelloWorldCountDownTask("Anna"));
        this.taskExecutor.execute(new HelloWorldCountDownTask("Beth"));
        this.taskExecutor.execute(new HelloWorldCountDownTask("Charlie"));
        this.taskExecutor.execute(new HelloWorldCountDownTask("Daniel"));
    }
}
```

As you see, we use the same four `HelloWorldCountDownTask` instances as before. The generated output will highlight the different execution strategies. As expected, the `SyncTaskExecutorExample`, shown in Listing 12-30, executes the tasks synchronously:

Listing 12-30. *SyncTaskExecutorExample*

```
package com.apress.prospring2.ch12.taskexecutor;

import org.springframework.context.ApplicationContext;
import org.springframework.context.support.ClassPathXmlApplicationContext;
import org.springframework.core.task.TaskExecutor;

import java.io.IOException;

public class SynchTaskExecutorExample {
```

```
    public static void main(String[] args) throws IOException {
        ApplicationContext ctx = new ClassPathXmlApplicationContext(
              "com/apress/prospring2/ch12/taskexecutor/task-executor-context.xml");

        TaskExecutor taskExecutor =
              (TaskExecutor)ctx.getBean("synchTaskExecutor", TaskExecutor.class);
        TaskExecutorExample example = new TaskExecutorExample(taskExecutor);
        example.executeTasks();
    }
}
```

Running this code will create output like what's shown here:

```
Anna: 3
Anna: 2
Anna: 1
Anna says 'Hello World!
Beth: 3
Beth: 2
Beth: 1
Beth says 'Hello World!
Charlie: 3
Charlie: 2
Charlie: 1
Charlie says 'Hello World!
Daniel: 3
Daniel: 2
Daniel: 1
Daniel says 'Hello World!
```

If your application is running on Java 5 or higher, you can configure this abstraction to delegate to any of Java 5's implementations. Spring's `ThreadPoolTaskExecutor` enables you to configure a JDK 1.5 `ThreadPoolExecutor` through bean properties and exposes it as a Spring `TaskExecutor`. Additionally, Spring provides the `ConcurrentTaskExecutor` as an adapter class for other Java 5 `Executor` implementations, making upgrading from Java 1.4 even easier.

The adapter class implements both the `TaskExecutor` and `Executor` interfaces. Because the primary interface is the `TaskExecutor`, exception handling follows its contract. For example, when a task cannot be accepted for execution, a Spring `TaskRejectedException` is thrown rather than a `java.util.concurrent.RejectedExecutionException`.

A further convenient feature of the `TaskExecutor` interface is its wrapping of exceptions in runtime exceptions. When a task fails with an exception, the situation is usually considered fatal. Without the need or possibility to recover, the exception can go unchecked—your code stays more portable, and you can quite easily switch between `TaskExecutor` implementations.

Summary

In this chapter, we showed you various mechanisms for scheduling jobs with Spring. We looked at the basic support offered when you use JDK `Timer` and the more sophisticated support offered through Quartz. You saw how the different trigger types are used, and in particular, we explored the `CronTrigger` in Quartz as a means of creating complex schedules that match real-world scenarios.

Job scheduling is an important part of enterprise applications, and Spring provides excellent support for adding scheduling to your own applications. In the next chapter, we are going to examine Spring's support for sending e-mail messages.

CHAPTER 13

Mail Support in Spring

Many applications make use of electronic mail (e-mail). E-mail is a perfect medium for a wide variety of different tasks, such as sending notification, marketing materials, and periodic reports about application usage and in some cases, facilitating application integration. The Java world boasts a large selection of e-mail solutions, the most well known being JavaMail from Sun. While JavaMail is exceptionally powerful, it is quite a complex API and even sending simple e-mail with it is not a trivial task. The JavaMail API is hard to mock or stub, mainly because of its use of static methods and final classes. On top of that, its heavy dependency on system properties makes testing application code that directly uses the JavaMail API difficult. Spring makes your life much easier by providing an abstraction layer that allows easy mocking and testing.

Fortunately, Spring provides full support for e-mail through a much simplified API. The Spring Mail API is fully pluggable, and you get two out-of-the-box implementations: one based on JavaMail and another using Jason Hunter's `MailMessage` class (included in the com.oreilly.servlet package available at `http://www.servlets.com`).

Spring's e-mail abstraction layer is split into two parts: one for basic mail support and one for more complex mail support. The JavaMail implementation supports both parts, whereas the COS (com.oreilly.servlet) implementation only supports the simple message-sending feature. For this reason, this chapter will focus on the JavaMail implementation. To get the most out of the examples in this chapter, you should familiarize yourself with the JavaMail and MailMessage APIs, since we won't be going into great detail about either of these.

This chapter will explain the Spring Mail API structure, show you how to send simple e-mails and complex messages, and offer insight into enterprise-level e-mail handling.

First, we will introduce the various interfaces and classes that make up the Spring Mail API and the two out-of-the-box implementations. We will also look at how the Mail API is structured for use in a DI-based environment and how this benefits the application.

Next, we'll tackle sending e-mail messages. We will start with basic examples of sending plain text e-mail with both JavaMail and COS using a completely programmatic approach. The final example in this chapter will demonstrate how to use the Spring Mail API in a more declarative fashion.

After that, we will show you how to assemble nontrivial mail messages using the JavaMail implementation of the Spring API. In particular, we will look at how to construct complex multipart messages with embedded image content, alternative formats, and attachments.

Finally, we will take a quick peek into real-life uses of Spring mail in a large enterprise-level web application. Specifically, we will look at how to send e-mails asynchronously.

To run the examples in this chapter, you will need to download both JavaMail and COS MailMessage. If you have downloaded the full Spring distribution with all the dependencies included, you will find all the necessary JAR files there. Otherwise, you can obtain JavaMail along with the JavaBeans Activation Framework, which is required by JavaMail, at `http://java.sun.com`. COS MailMessage can be obtained at `http://servlets.com/cos`.

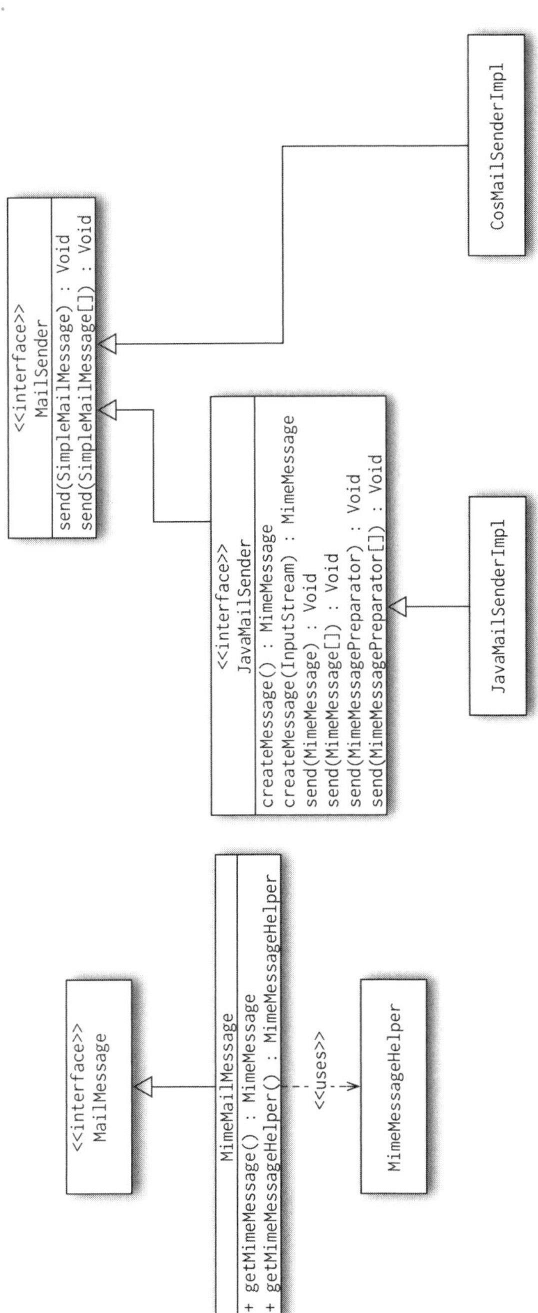

Figure 13-1. *Spring Mail API*

The Spring Mail API Structure

The Spring mail abstraction layer is centered around the `MailSender` and `JavaMailSender` interfaces shown in Figure 13-1.

The `MailSender` interface is the central interface and is intended for implementations that support only simple, plain text e-mails. As you can see, `JavaMailSender` extends the `MailSender` interface with methods for constructing and sending MIME (multipurpose Internet mail extensions) messages.

COS `MailMessage` interface does not support complex MIME messages and can only be used for sending plain text e-mails; it also includes an implementation of `MailSender`. When you require something more complex, you should use the JavaMail-based solution, which provides an implementation of the `JavaMailSender` interface allowing you to send complex MIME messages.

In general, if you are just sending plain text e-mails, code your application to the `MailSender` interface, which provides an extremely simple API for sending messages. If you need to send more complex messages, perhaps with attachments or inline images, you will need to code to the `JavaMailSender` interface and use the `JavaMail` implementation of the mail abstraction layer.

Configuring Mail Settings Using Spring

To be able to use Spring's e-mail library, you need to add the following JARs to the classpath of your application.

- The JavaMail `mail.jar` library
- The JavaBeans Activation Framework (JAF) `activation.jar` library

Both of these libraries are available in the `spring-with-dependencies` distribution of the Spring Framework as well as being freely available on the Web.

Both the JavaMail and COS MailMessage mail layer implementations provide JavaBean-style properties to let you adjust mail settings in your Spring configuration file. For the COS implementation, the only parameter you can set is the host name of the SMTP server to use for sending mail. But the JavaMail implementation provides a much wider set of parameters to control the protocol, including mail host, host port, and server authentication details. In addition to the JavaBean properties for basic configuration, the JavaMail implementation allows you to provide any of the recognized JavaMail configuration parameters using an instance of `Properties` and the `<properties>` tag in your configuration file.

Sending Simple E-mails

The simplest case of sending e-mail is a plain text message. Both the COS and JavaMail implementations support this basic functionality using programmatic as well as declarative mechanisms. In the first part of this section, you will see how to create and send messages programmatically. In the second part, we will look at an alternative implementation that uses the declarative approach to configure both the `MailSender` implementation and the `SimpleMailMessage` that is to be sent.

Constructing and Sending E-mail Programmatically

To send mail programmatically, the first task is to create an instance of `SimpleMailMessage` and configure it with the appropriate details, such as subject, body text, and recipient address. The next step is to create an instance of `MailSender` and set the appropriate configuration details; in particular, you need to set the host address of the mail server.

In Listing 13-1, you can see the SimpleMailSender class, which acts as a base class for the examples in this section.

Listing 13-1. *The SimpleMailSender Class*

```
package com.apress.prospring2.ch13.simple;

import org.springframework.mail.MailSender;
import org.springframework.mail.SimpleMailMessage;
import org.springframework.mail.MailException;

public abstract class SimpleMailSender {
    protected abstract MailSender getMailSender();

    public void sendMessage(String to, String text) {
        SimpleMailMessage msg = new SimpleMailMessage();
        msg.setTo(to);
        msg.setSubject("Test Message");
        msg.setFrom("test@apress.com");
        msg.setText(text);

        MailSender sender = getMailSender();
        try {
            sender.send(msg);
        } catch (MailException e) {
            e.printStackTrace();
        }
    }
}
```

The first thing to notice here is that this class is declared abstract and has an abstract method, getMailSender(). We create two different base classes, one that returns an instance of CosMailSenderImpl and one that returns JavaMailSenderImpl, so we can reuse the logic in sendMessage(). In the sendMessage() method, we assemble an instance of SimpleMailMessage with addresses for the sender and recipient, a subject line, and body content. Once this instance is assembled, we use the instance of MailSender returned by the getMailSender() method to send the message. The MailSender interface includes two send() methods, one that accepts a single instance of SimpleMailMessage and another that accepts an array of SimpleMailMessage objects for sending messages in bulk.

Listing 13-2 shows the JavaMailSimpleMailSender class that extends SimpleMailSender to return an instance of JavaMailSenderImpl from the getMailSender() method.

Listing 13-2. *The JavaMailSimpleMailSender Class*

```
package com.apress.prospring2.ch13.simple;

import org.springframework.mail.MailSender;
import org.springframework.mail.javamail.JavaMailSenderImpl;

public class JavaMailSimpleMailSender extends SimpleMailSender {

    protected MailSender getMailSender() {
        JavaMailSenderImpl sender = new JavaMailSenderImpl();
        sender.setHost("localhost");
        return sender;
    }
}
```

Notice that, in the getMailSender() method, we create an instance of JavaMailSenderImpl and configure the mail host using the setHost() method. You will most likely need to change the mail host address for your environment. Be aware that the setHost() method is not defined on either the MailSender or JavaMailSender interfaces, so you can't configure the mail host in an implementation-agnostic manner when using this approach. Listing 13-3 shows the CosSimpleMailSender class, which is a simple implementation for the CosMailSenderImpl class like the one shown in Listing 13-2.

Listing 13-3. *The CosSimpleMailSender Class*

```
package com.apress.prospring2.ch13.simple;

import org.springframework.mail.MailSender;
import org.springframework.mail.cos.CosMailSenderImpl;

public class CosSimpleMailSender extends SimpleMailSender {

    protected MailSender getMailSender() {
        CosMailSenderImpl sender = new CosMailSenderImpl();
        sender.setHost("localhost");
        return sender;
    }
}
```

Aside from the class instance that is created, this implementation is identical to that of the JavaMailSimpleMailSender class. At this point, we have two classes that, using different MailSender implementations, can send a message containing some arbitrary text to a single recipient. Listing 13-4 shows the SimpleMailTest class that tests out the CosSimpleMailSender and JavaMailSimpleMailSender classes.

Listing 13-4. *Sending the E-mail*

```
package com.apress.prospring2.ch13.simple;

public class SimpleMailTest {
    private static final String TO = "anirvanc@cakesolutions.net";
    private static final String JAVAMAIL_TEXT = "Hello World! Email generated using ➥
JavaMail.";
    private static final String COS_TEXT = "Hello World! Email generated ➥
using COS MailMessage.";

    public static void main(String[] args) {

        SimpleMailSender sender1 = new JavaMailSimpleMailSender();
        SimpleMailSender sender2 = new CosSimpleMailSender();

        sender1.sendMessage(TO, JAVAMAIL_TEXT);
        sender2.sendMessage(TO, COS_TEXT);
    }
}
```

Here, we are using an instance of JavaMailSimpleMailSender and an instance of CosSimpleMailSender to send two copies of the same message to the same recipient. When you run this example, it will take a few seconds to execute depending on your mail server and the connection speed; once it finishes, it will then terminate. In Figure 13-2, you can see the results of this code rendered in one of our mail clients.

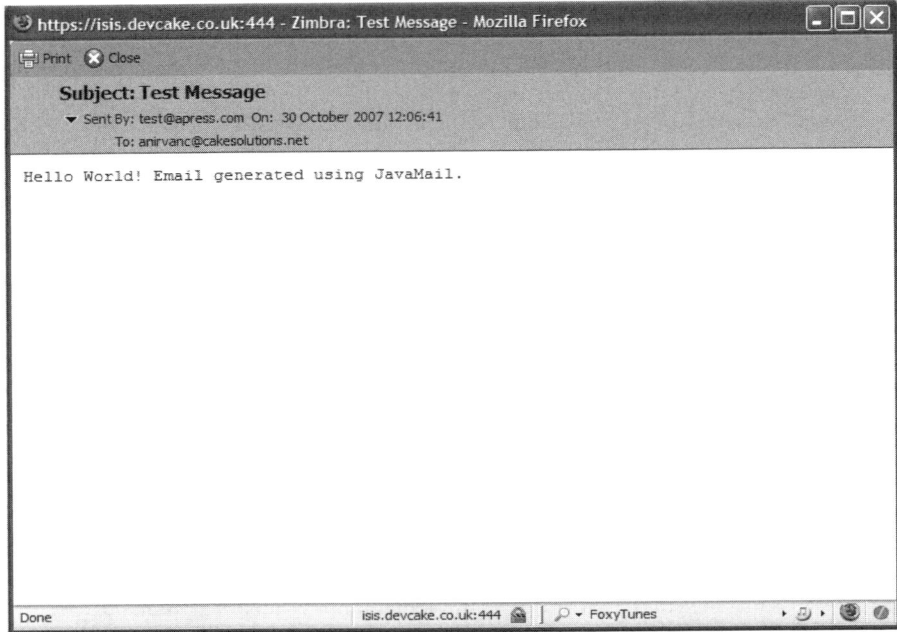

Figure 13-2. *The mail message using JavaMail*

As you can see from this example, sending plain text e-mails is extremely simple. However, this approach has a big drawback: all configuration data for the `MailSender` implementations and the `SimpleMailMessage` objects is contained in the code. In the next example, we will see how to configure the `MailSender` and `SimpleMailMessage` in the Spring configuration file.

Constructing E-mail Declaratively

In the previous section, we mentioned that you can also configure a `MailSender` in your Spring configuration file and create a template `SimpleMailMessage` containing the basic details of your mail. In this section, we are going to revisit the birthday reminder example from the previous chapter to add e-mail–based reminders.

The first step in this example is to create a `TimerTask` implementation that will send e-mail reminders. This is shown in Listing 13-5.

Listing 13-5. *The ReminderTask Class*

```
package com.apress.prospring2.ch13.birthday;

import java.util.TimerTask;

import org.springframework.mail.MailSender;
import org.springframework.mail.SimpleMailMessage;

public class ReminderTask extends TimerTask {

    private SimpleMailMessage defaultMessage;
    private MailSender sender;
```

```
    private String who;

    public void setMailMessage(SimpleMailMessage defaultMessage) {
        this.defaultMessage = defaultMessage;
    }

    public void setMailSender(MailSender sender) {
        this.sender = sender;
    }

    public void setWho(String who) {
        this.who = who;
    }

    public void run() {
        SimpleMailMessage msg = new SimpleMailMessage(defaultMessage);
        msg.setText("Remember! It is " + who + "'s birthday in 7 days.");
        sender.send(msg);
        System.out.println("Sent reminder for: " + who);
    }
}
```

The first thing to notice in this code is that we have defined two JavaBean properties: `mailSender` and `mailMessage`. These will allow instances of `MailSender` and `SimpleMailMessage` to be set using dependency injection (DI). In the `run()` method, we create an instance of `SimpleMailMessage` using the externally provided instance as a template. Then, we set the message text to be the reminder and send it using the externally provided `MailSender` instance. Notice that we have specified neither any configuration properties for the `MailSender` nor a subject, sender address, or recipient address for the `SimpleMailMessage`. These parameters are all set in the configuration file shown in Listing 13-6.

Listing 13-6. *Configuring Mail Settings Externally*

```
<?xml version="1.0" encoding="UTF-8"?>
<beans xmlns="http://www.springframework.org/schema/beans"
       xmlns:xsi="http://www.w3.org/2001/XMLSchema-instance"
       xmlns:util="http://www.springframework.org/schema/util"
       xmlns:tx="http://www.springframework.org/schema/tx"
       xsi:schemaLocation="http://www.springframework.org/schema/beans
http://www.springframework.org/schema/beans/spring-beansxsd
                           http://www.springframework.org/schema/util
http://www.springframework.org/schema/util/spring-util.xsd
                           http://www.springframework.org/schema/tx
 http://www.springframework.org/schema/tx/spring-tx-.xsd

    <bean id="scheduledTask" class=
"com.apress.prospring2.ch12.timer.bday.BirthdayScheduledTask">
        <property name="date" value="2007-10-30"/>
        <property name="fixedRate" value=true/>
        <property name="timerTask">
            <bean class="com.apress.prospring2.ch13.birthday.ReminderTask">
                <property name="who" value="Ria"/>
                <property name="mailSender ref="sender"/>
                <property name="mailMessage" ref="mailMessage"/>
            </bean>
        </property>
    </bean>
```

```
    <bean id="sender" class="org.springframework.mail.javamail.JavaMailSenderImpl">
        <property name="host">
            <value>localhost</value>
        </property>
    </bean>

    <bean id="mailMessage" class="org.springframework.mail.SimpleMailMessage">
        <property name="from">
            <value>reminders@apress.com</value>
        </property>
        <property name="to">
            <value>anirvanc@cakesolutions.net</value>
        </property>
        <property name="subject">
            <value>Birthday Reminder!!</value>
        </property>
    </bean>

    <bean id="timerFactory" class=
"org.springframework.scheduling.timer.TimerFactoryBean">
        <property name="scheduledTimerTasks">
            <list>
                <ref local=" scheduledTask "/>
            </list>
        </property>
    </bean>
</beans>
```

You should recognize much of this configuration code from the previous chapter; the important parts are the `mailMessage` and sender bean declarations. For the sender bean, we are using the `JavaMailSenderImpl` class, and we have configured the `host` property to be localhost as we did when using the programmatic approach. For the `mailMessage` bean we have set the `to`, `from`, and `subject` properties. Each of these properties will be inherited by the instance of `SimpleMailMessage` created in the `run()` method, since we use this instance of `SimpleMailMessage` as a template.

Listing 13-7 shows a simple driver class that simply loads the configuration shown in Listing 13-6 and waits.

Listing 13-7. *Loading the Mail Configuration*

```
package com.apress.prospring2.ch13.birthday;

import org.springframework.context.support.ClassPathXmlApplicationContext;

import java.io.BufferedReader;
import java.io.InputStreamReader;

public class Runner {
    public static void main(String[] args) throws Exception {
        new ClassPathXmlApplicationContext(
"/com/apress/prospring2/ch13/birthday/birthdayReminder.xml");

        BufferedReader reader =
new BufferedReader(new InputStreamReader(System.in));
        reader.readLine();
    }
}
```

Until the date in the configuration file is reached, no e-mail will be sent, so you might want to change the date to one that is more relevant or change the configuration for the scheduled task to use a different schedule altogether. Figure 13-3 shows a sample message generated by this example.

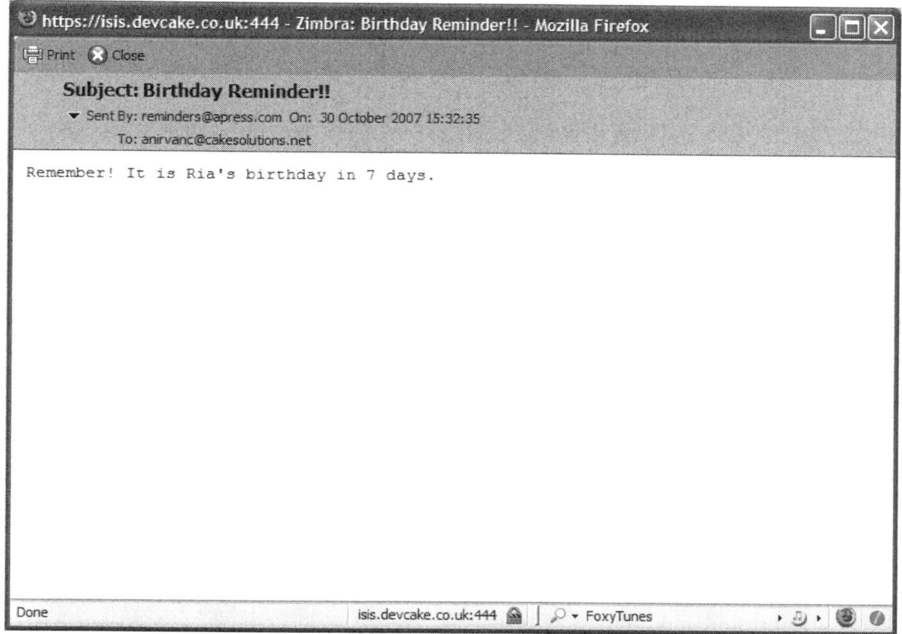

Figure 13-3. *The birthday reminder e-mail*

Using the declarative approach for configuration is generally preferred to the wholly programmatic approach, as it allows you to fully externalize all configuration, including basic message configuration. You can also take advantage of Spring's DI when providing your application components with instances of `MailSender` and `SimpleMailMessage`. This allows you to easily swap one `MailSender` implementation for another, but you can also pass in a custom implementation of the `SimpleMailMessage` if you need some custom processing.

Constructing and Sending MIME Messages

In the previous section, all the e-mails we created were plain text messages with no fancy extras like HTML formatting, embedded images, or attachments. That might be OK for applications where e-mail is just for sending simple messages across or is used only within an organization, but often, applications require the ability to send much more complex messages. The JavaMail implementation of `MailSender`, or more accurately of `JavaMailSender`, provides the ability to send MIME messages. `JavaMailSender` also supports messages in HTML format, messages with embedded images, and messages with attachments.

In this section, we are going to take a look at sending complex MIME messages in five separate scenarios:

- A basic HTML message
- An HTML message with embedded images
- An HTML message with attachments
- An HTML message with a plain text alternative
- A MIME message with a complex structure

All of these examples rely on features in the `JavaMailSenderImpl` class, so they will not work with `CosMailSenderImpl`. A major drawback of sending MIME messages is that you cannot use the `SimpleMailMessage` class for external configuration, since the MIME-aware methods of `JavaMailSenderImpl` do not work with this class. For this reason, it is often better to create a class that can be configured externally by Spring to encapsulate your MIME message. For the examples in this section, we have defined a common base class that allows for external configuration of the messages; the class is shown in Listing 13-8.

Listing 13-8. *The AbstractMessageSender Class*

```
package com.apress.prospring2.ch13.mime;

import org.springframework.mail.javamail.JavaMailSender;

public abstract class AbstractMessageSender {
    protected String to;
    protected String from;
    protected String subject;
    protected JavaMailSender sender;

    public void setTo(String to) {
        this.to = to;
    }

    public void setFrom(String from) {
        this.from = from;
    }

    public void setSubject(String subject) {
        this.subject = subject;
    }

    public void setJavaMailSender(JavaMailSender sender) {
        this.sender = sender;
    }
}
```

The idea behind this class is that each of our examples will inherit from it and can then be configured in the Spring configuration file. Also, all examples in this section require an instance of `JavaMailSender`, which will be set via the `javaMailSender` property exposed by the `AbstractMessageSender`. To configure this `JavaMailSender` instance, we will use the shared configuration file shown in Listing 13-9 across all of the examples.

Listing 13-9. *The Shared Configuration File*

```
<?xml version="1.0" encoding="UTF-8"?>
<beans xmlns="http://www.springframework.org/schema/beans"
       xmlns:xsi="http://www.w3.org/2001/XMLSchema-instance"
       xmlns:util="http://www.springframework.org/schema/util"
       xmlns:tx="http://www.springframework.org/schema/tx"
       xmlns:aop="http://www.springframework.org/schema/aop"
       xsi:schemaLocation="http://www.springframework.org/schema/beans
http://www.springframework.org/schema/beans/spring-beans-2.5.xsd
                           http://www.springframework.org/schema/util
http://www.springframework.org/schema/util/spring-util-2.5.xsd
                           http://www.springframework.org/schema/tx
http://www.springframework.org/schema/tx/spring-tx-2.5.xsd
                           http://www.springframework.org/schema/aop
http://www.springframework.org/schema/aop/spring-aop-2.5.xsd">

    <bean id="sender" class="org.springframework.mail.javamail.JavaMailSenderImpl">
        <property name="host">
            <value>localhost</value>
        </property>
    </bean>
</beans>
```

Here, you can see that we have configured a `sender` bean, of type `JavaMailSenderImpl`, and we have configured the `host` property for our environment. You may need to modify the host for these examples to work in your environment.

In addition to the shared configuration file, each example uses a custom configuration like the one shown in Listing 13-10.

Listing 13-10. *The Example Specific Configuration File*

```
<?xml version="1.0" encoding="UTF-8"?>
<beans xmlns="http://www.springframework.org/schema/beans"
       xmlns:xsi="http://www.w3.org/2001/XMLSchema-instance"
       xmlns:util="http://www.springframework.org/schema/util"
       xmlns:tx="http://www.springframework.org/schema/tx"
       xmlns:aop="http://www.springframework.org/schema/aop"
       xsi:schemaLocation="http://www.springframework.org/schema/beans
http://www.springframework.org/schema/beans/spring-beans.xsd
                           http://www.springframework.org/schema/util
http://www.springframework.org/schema/util/spring-util.xsd
                           http://www.springframework.org/schema/tx
http://www.springframework.org/schema/tx/spring-tx.xsd
                           http://www.springframework.org/schema/aop
http://www.springframework.org/schema/aop/spring-aop.xsd">

    <bean id="messageSender" class=
"com.apress.prospring2.ch13.mime.AlternativeFormatMessageSender">
        <property name="javaMailSender">
            <ref bean="sender"/>
        </property>
        <property name="to">
            <value>anirvanc@cakesolutions.net</value>
        </property>
        <property name="from">
            <value>mail@apress.com</value>
```

```
        </property>
        <property name="subject">
            <value>Alternative Formats</value>
        </property>
    </bean>
</beans>
```

The only thing that changes in each of these configuration files is the `class` attribute of the `messageSender` bean. For this reason, we won't show you each of these configurations, but you can find them in the code download.

Sending a Basic HTML Message

An HTML message is created in a similar manner to plain text e-mail, but you must be sure to specify the MIME type of the message that you are creating, in this case `text/html`. Although you can't use the `SimpleMailMessage` class when working with MIME messages, Spring provides the `MimeMessageHelper` class that allows you to work with MIME messages in a similar manner to the `SimpleMailMessage` class and to avoid some of the complexities of working with the JavaMail API directly. Listing 13-11 shows the `SimpleHtmlMessageSender` class that builds and sends a simple HTML message.

Listing 13-11. *The SimpleHtmlMessageSender Class*

```
package com.apress.prospring2.ch13.mime;

import javax.mail.MessagingException;
import javax.mail.internet.MimeMessage;

import org.springframework.context.ApplicationContext;
import org.springframework.context.support.ClassPathXmlApplicationContext;
import org.springframework.mail.javamail.MimeMessageHelper;

public class SimpleHtmlMessageSender extends AbstractMessageSender {

    public void sendMessage() throws MessagingException {
        MimeMessage msg = sender.createMimeMessage();
        MimeMessageHelper helper = new MimeMessageHelper(msg);

        helper.setTo(to);
        helper.setFrom(from);
        helper.setSubject(subject);
        helper.setText("<html><head></head><body><h1>Hello World!"
                + "</h1></body></html>", true);

        sender.send(msg);
    }

    public static void main(String[] args) throws Exception {
        ApplicationContext ctx = new ClassPathXmlApplicationContext(
                new String[] {
"/com/apress/prospring2/ch13/mime/simpleHtmlMessageSender.xml",
"/com/apress/prospring2/ch13/mime/javaMailSender.xml" });

        SimpleHtmlMessageSender sender =
(SimpleHtmlMessageSender) ctx.getBean("messageSender");
        sender.sendMessage();
    }
}
```

Much of this code is fairly self-explanatory, but there are a few points to note. First, notice that an instance of `MimeMessage` is retrieved by calling the `createMimeMessage()` method of the `JavaMailSender` interface. Second, this instance is wrapped in an instance of `MimeMessageHelper`, and we use this to set the various parameters. The third and final point of interest in this example is that, in the call to `MimeMessageHelper.setText()`, we pass in `true` as the second argument to flag this message as an HTML formatted one. Once the message is assembled, it is sent with a call to `JavaMailSender.send()`. Figure 13-4 shows an HTML formatted message.

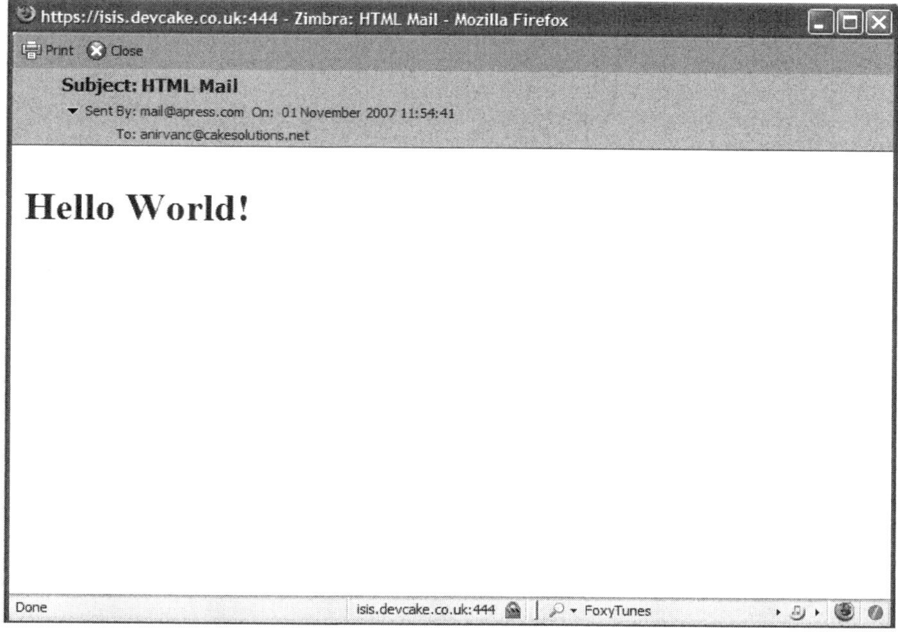

Figure 13-4. *The results of this code rendered in an e-mail client*

Sending an HTML Message with Embedded Images

In the previous example, you saw how to assemble and send an HTML formatted e-mail. In this section, you will see how to add embedded images to your message and display these in the HTML message body content.

■ **Note** In general, we have found that avoiding embedded images is best; instead, use images that are accessed via a standard URL in your e-mails. Many e-mail clients have trouble dealing with embedded images, especially when they form part of complex MIME structures like the one shown in the "Sending Complex MIME Messages" section.

To send an HTML e-mail that uses embedded images, you first have to assemble the HTML message; then, you can add the images as additional *parts* of the MIME message. When adding a MIME part, you can associate a `Content-ID` with it that is used when referring to the image from the HTML. When using `MimeMessageHelper`, Spring takes care of much of the logic behind this process for you.

Listing 13-12 shows the `InlineImageMessageSender` class that demonstrates how to build a message with inline images.

Listing 13-12. *The InlineImageMessageSender Class*

```
package com.apress.prospring2.ch13.mime;

import java.io.File;

import javax.mail.MessagingException;
import javax.mail.internet.MimeMessage;

import org.springframework.context.ApplicationContext;
import org.springframework.context.support.ClassPathXmlApplicationContext;
import org.springframework.core.io.FileSystemResource;
import org.springframework.mail.javamail.MimeMessageHelper;

public class InlineImageMessageSender extends AbstractMessageSender {

    public void sendMessage() throws MessagingException {
        MimeMessage msg = sender.createMimeMessage();
        MimeMessageHelper helper = new MimeMessageHelper(msg, true);

        helper.setTo(to);
        helper.setFrom(from);
        helper.setSubject(subject);

        helper.setText("<html><head></head><body><h1>Hello World!</h1>"
                + "<img src=\"cid:abc\"></body></html>", true);

        // add the image
        FileSystemResource img =
new FileSystemResource(
new File("./ch13/src/main/resources/images/apress.gif"));
        helper.addInline("abc", img);

        sender.send(msg);
    }

    public static void main(String[] args) throws Exception {
        ApplicationContext ctx = new ClassPathXmlApplicationContext(
                new String[] {
"/com/apress/prospring2/ch13/mime/inlineImageMessageSender.xml",
"/com/apress/prospring2/ch13/mime/javaMailSender.xml" });

        InlineImageMessageSender sender =
(InlineImageMessageSender) ctx.getBean("messageSender");
        sender.sendMessage();
    }
}
```

This example is very similar to the previous one, but the `sendMessage()` method has two important differences. First, the HTML that is added to the message body contains an `<img>` tag whose `src` attribute is set to `cid:abc`. This tells the mail client to use the embedded resource with the `Content-ID` of `abc` when rendering this image. Second, the image resource itself is embedded in the message using the `MimeMessageHelper.addInline()` method. When adding inline resources, it is important that you add the message body first and the resources second; otherwise, the message will not render correctly in the mail client.

Figure 13-5 shows the result of running this example, rendered in a mail client.

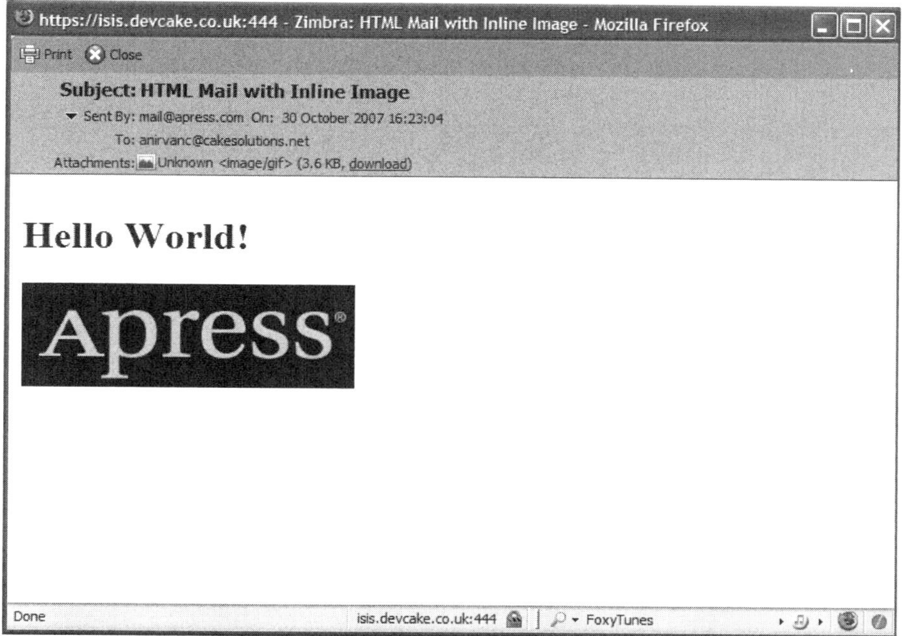

Figure 13-5. *Displaying a message with an embedded image*

As Figure 13-5 shows, the embedded image is rendered as part of the message body. Using this approach to include images in your messages means that you avoid the need to store images on a server that is accessible by the recipients. However, many mail clients do not handle embedded images well when they are combined with other MIME features, such as alternative message formats.

Sending a Message with Attachments

Sending attachments with a message is very much like including embedded resources; in fact, both features create additional MIME parts in your message behind the scenes. The main difference is that embedded resources have their content disposition set to `inline`, indicating that they should not be considered attachments.

Listing 13-13 shows a slight modification to the previous example; instead of embedding the image, it now attaches it to the message instead.

Listing 13-13. *Sending Attachments*

```
package com.apress.prospring2.ch13.mime;

import org.springframework.context.ApplicationContext;
import org.springframework.context.support.ClassPathXmlApplicationContext;
import org.springframework.core.io.FileSystemResource;
import org.springframework.mail.javamail.MimeMessageHelper;

import javax.mail.MessagingException;
import javax.mail.internet.MimeMessage;
import java.io.File;

public class AttachmentMessageSender extends AbstractMessageSender {

    public void sendMessage() throws MessagingException {
        MimeMessage msg = sender.createMimeMessage();
        MimeMessageHelper helper = new MimeMessageHelper(msg, true);

        helper.setTo(to);
        helper.setFrom(from);
        helper.setSubject(subject);

        helper.setText(
                "<html><head></head><body><h1>Hello World!</h1></body></html>",
                true);

        // add the image
        FileSystemResource img = new FileSystemResource(
new File("./ch13/src/main/resources/images/apress.gif"));
        helper.addAttachment("apress.gif", img);

        sender.send(msg);
    }

    public static void main(String[] args) throws Exception {
        ApplicationContext ctx = new ClassPathXmlApplicationContext(
                new String[] {
"/com/apress/prospring2/ch13/mime/attachmentMessageSender.xml",
"/com/apress/prospring2/ch13/mime/javaMailSender.xml" });

        AttachmentMessageSender sender =
(AttachmentMessageSender) ctx.getBean("messageSender");
        sender.sendMessage();
    }
}
```

As we mentioned, this example is very similar to the last. The only important difference here is that we have swapped the call to `addInline()` with a call to `addAttachment()`. Since attachments are included in the mail in the same way as embedded resources, they are also given a `Content-ID`, which most mail clients recognize as the file name. Figure 13-6 shows this message in the mail client; notice the file name that is displayed for the attachment.

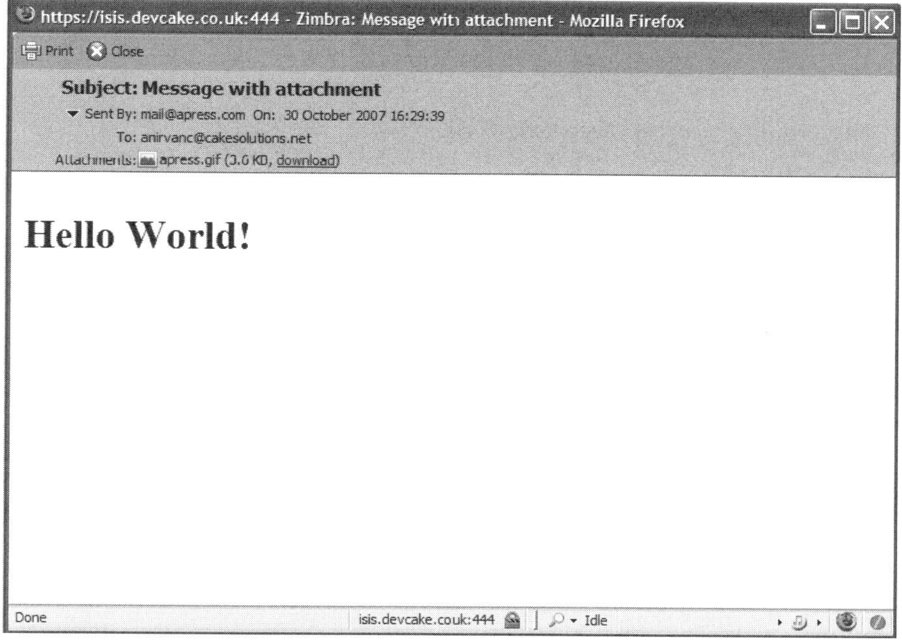

Figure 13-6. *A message with an attachment*

Sending an HTML Message with a Plain Text Alternative

The examples so far have required very little direct interaction with the JavaMail APIs, and we have been able to rely on Spring helper classes when assembling MIME messages. However, in some cases, the complexity of the MIME message structure requires you to interact directly with the JavaMail API, as this example and the following one illustrate.

When you need more control over how a MIME message is assembled, you can create an implementation of the `MimeMessagePreparator` interface and pass this to the `JavaMailSender.send()` method in place of the `MimeMessage`. The main reason for doing this, rather than attempting to assemble the `MimeMessage` directly, is that Spring will take care of wrapping the checked exceptions thrown by JavaMail—many of which cannot be recovered from—in runtime exceptions, reducing the complexity of your code. You should note that you can still use the `MimeMessageHelper` class when assembling your own `MimeMessages`, but we avoid doing so here in order to illustrate how to interact directly with JavaMail.

In this example, you will see how to assemble an HTML message with a plain text alternative. When rendered in a mail client that either doesn't support HTML or has had HTML disabled, the plain text alternative contained in the message is used in place of the HTML. This is like sending two copies of the same letter, each in a different language, in the same envelope: both the HTML and plain text message parts contain the same message albeit in different formats. In this example, though, we are going to make the plain text message differ from the HTML one, just to illustrate how this works.

The code for this example is quite complex, so we will explain it one piece at a time. Listing 13-14 shows the basic class that obtains the required beans from Spring and sends the message with a call to JavaMailSender.sender().

Listing 13-14. *The AlternativeFormatMessageSender Class*

```
package com.apress.prospring2.ch13.mime;

import org.springframework.context.ApplicationContext;
import org.springframework.context.support.ClassPathXmlApplicationContext;
import org.springframework.mail.javamail.MimeMessagePreparator;

import javax.mail.BodyPart;
import javax.mail.Message;
import javax.mail.internet.InternetAddress;
import javax.mail.internet.MimeBodyPart;
import javax.mail.internet.MimeMessage;
import javax.mail.internet.MimeMultipart;

public class AlternativeFormatMessageSender extends AbstractMessageSender {

    public void sendMessage() {
        sender.send(new MessagePreparator());
    }

    public static void main(String[] args) throws Exception {
        ApplicationContext ctx = new ClassPathXmlApplicationContext(
                new String[] {
"/com/apress/prospring2/ch13/mime/alternativeFormatMessageSender.xml",
"/com/apress/prospring2/ch13/mime/javaMailSender.xml" });

        AlternativeFormatMessageSender sender =
(AlternativeFormatMessageSender) ctx.getBean("messageSender");
        sender.sendMessage();
    }
```

Much of this code will be familiar to you by now, but notice that the call to send() passes in an instance of the MessagePreparator class instead of an instance of MimeMessage. The MessagePreparator class is an inner class that implements the MimeMessagePreparator interface and is responsible for actually constructing the MimeMessage object. Note that Spring will create the MimeMessage instance and pass it to the MimeMessagePreparator.prepare() method—MessagePreparator is only responsible for configuring this object; it does not need to create the MimeMessage itself.

Listing 13-15 shows the MimeMessagePreparator class.

Listing 13-15. *The MimeMessagePreparator Class*

```
private class MessagePreparator implements MimeMessagePreparator {

        public void prepare(MimeMessage msg) throws Exception {

            // set header details
            msg.addFrom(InternetAddress.parse(from));
            msg.addRecipients(Message.RecipientType.TO, InternetAddress.parse(to));
            msg.setSubject(subject);
```

```
            // create wrapper multipart/alternative part
            MimeMultipart ma = new MimeMultipart("alternative");
            msg.setContent(ma);

            // create the plain text
            BodyPart plainText = new MimeBodyPart();
            plainText.setText("This is the plain text version of the mail.");
            ma.addBodyPart(plainText);

            //  create the html part
            BodyPart html = new MimeBodyPart();
            html.setContent(
                    "<html><head></head><body>
<h1>This is the HTML version of the mail."
                            + "</h1></body></html>", "text/html");
            ma.addBodyPart(html);
        }
    }
}
```

Here, the prepare() method starts by setting the sender and recipient addresses along with the subject. Notice that, when setting the addresses of the sender and recipient, we have to use the InternetAddress.parse() method to create an instance of InternetAddress from a String. This is one of the details that are hidden by the MimeMessageHelper class, and often, using MimeMessageHelper is preferable for configuring message properties even when assembling the message directly.

Next, we create an instance of MimeMultipart, a wrapper class to hold multiple message parts, and we specify the MIME type as multipart?FORSLASH?alternative, signifying that the parts contained in this multipart message are alternative formats of the same data. This MimeMultipart instance is specified as the content of the MimeMessage instance using the MimeMessage.setContent() method.

Then, we create two instances of MimeBodyPart, one for the plain text body and one for the HTML body. When assembling the plain text BodyPart, simply calling the setText() method and passing in the part content is sufficient. This will set the MIME type of the BodyPart to text/plain. For the HTML BodyPart, we use the setContent() method in place of setText(), and we explicitly pass in the MIME type of text/html as the second argument. Both of these BodyPart instances are then added to the MimeMultipart instance, and as a result, they are added to the MimeMessage. The order in which you add BodyPart instances to the MimeMultipart is important, and you should add the BodyPart with the most preferable message format last.

The result of this code is to populate a MimeMessage instance in such a way that the top-level MIME type is multipart/alternative, and within the message, there are two parts: one with the MIME type text/plain and the other with the MIME type text/html.

Figure 13-7 shows this message rendered as HTML in the mail client, and Figure 13-8 shows it rendered as plain text.

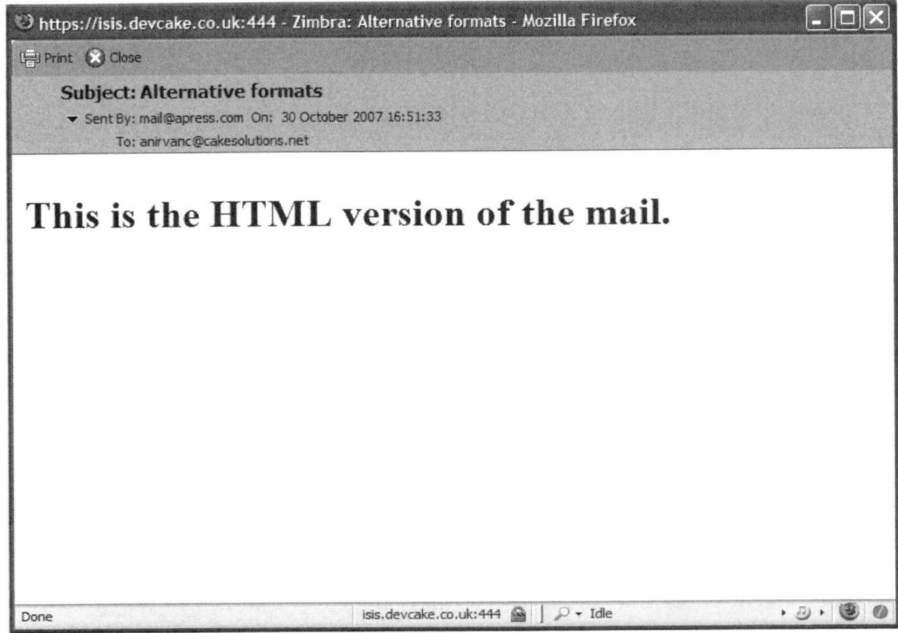

Figure 13-7. *The HTML message*

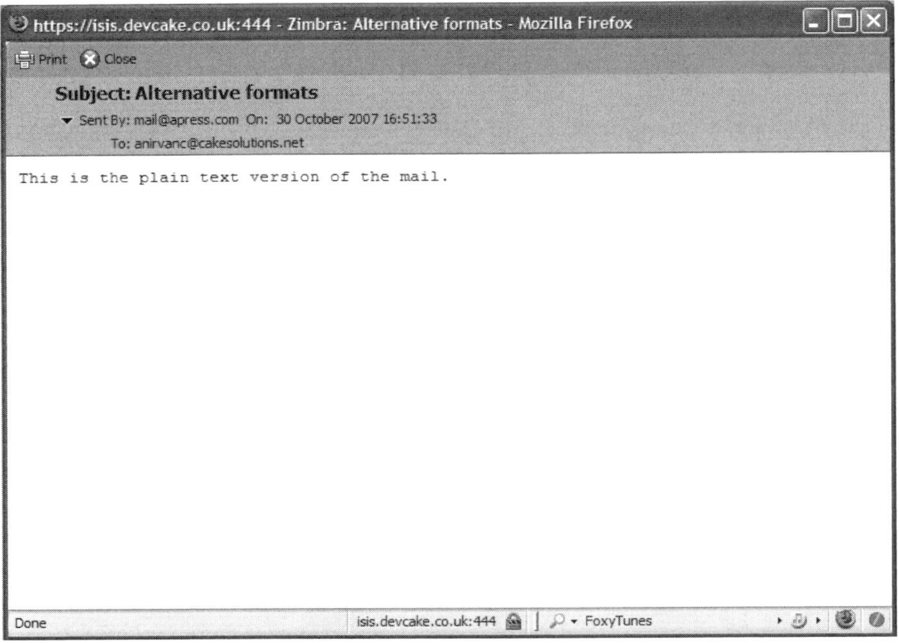

Figure 13-8. *The plain text message*

Sending Complex MIME Messages

So far, you have seen how to send a variety of different MIME messages, including HTML messages with embedded images and messages with both HTML and plain text content. But how can you send a message that has HTML content with embedded images and a plain text alternative? In this section, we show you how.

The code required to send an HTML message with both embedded images and a plain text alternative is not that different from the code required to send the HTML message with the plain text alternative. The main change is that we need to wrap the HTML content, along with the embedded images, inside an additional multipart wrapper. This wrapper will group the HTML together with the embedded images and instruct the mail client that the second message format consists of the HTML plus the images, not just the HTML on its own. Listing 13-16 shows the code required to assemble the message.

Listing 13-16. *Assembling Complex MIME Messages*

```
package com.apress.prospring2.ch13.mime;

import org.springframework.context.ApplicationContext;
import org.springframework.context.support.ClassPathXmlApplicationContext;
import org.springframework.mail.javamail.MimeMessagePreparator;

import javax.activation.DataHandler;
import javax.activation.FileDataSource;
import javax.mail.BodyPart;
import javax.mail.Message;
import javax.mail.MessagingException;
import javax.mail.internet.InternetAddress;
import javax.mail.internet.MimeBodyPart;
import javax.mail.internet.MimeMessage;
import javax.mail.internet.MimeMultipart;

public class ComplexMessageSender extends AbstractMessageSender {

    public void sendMessage() throws MessagingException {
        sender.send(new MessagePreparator());
    }

    public static void main(String[] args) throws Exception {
        ApplicationContext ctx = new ClassPathXmlApplicationContext(
                new String[] {
                        "/com/apress/prospring2/ch13/mime/complexMessageSender.xml",
                        "/com/apress/prospring2/ch13/mime/javaMailSender.xml" });

        ComplexMessageSender sender =
(ComplexMessageSender) ctx.getBean("messageSender");
        sender.sendMessage();
    }

    private class MessagePreparator implements MimeMessagePreparator {

        public void prepare(MimeMessage msg) throws Exception {

            // set header details
            msg.addFrom(InternetAddress.parse(from));
            msg.addRecipients(Message.RecipientType.TO, InternetAddress.parse(to));
            msg.setSubject(subject);
```

```
            // create wrapper multipart/alternative part
            MimeMultipart ma = new MimeMultipart("alternative");
            msg.setContent(ma);

            // create the plain text
            BodyPart plainText = new MimeBodyPart();
            plainText.setText("This is the plain text version of the mail.");
            ma.addBodyPart(plainText);

            //  create the html and image multipart wrapper
            BodyPart related = new MimeBodyPart();
            MimeMultipart mr = new MimeMultipart("related");
            related.setContent(mr);
            ma.addBodyPart(related);

            BodyPart html = new MimeBodyPart();
            html.setContent(
                    "<html><head></head>
<body><h1>This is the HTML version of the mail."
                   + "</h1><img src=\"cid:0001\"></body></html>", "text/html");
            mr.addBodyPart(html);

            BodyPart img = new MimeBodyPart();
            img.setHeader("Content-ID", "0001");
            img.setDisposition("inline");
            img.setDataHandler(
new DataHandler(
new FileDataSource("./ch13/src/main/resources/images/apress.gif")));
            mr.addBodyPart(img);
        }
    }
}
```

The important piece of this code is the `prepare()` method of the `MessagePreparator` class. Up to and including the code that adds the plain text `BodyPart`, the `prepare()` method is identical to the one in the last example. When it comes to the HTML format message, we start by creating a `BodyPart` and a second `MimeMultipart` instance. This `MimeMultipart` instance is given the MIME type `multipart/related`, indicating that the `BodyPart` instances it contains are related and that these parts, for the purposes of the enclosing `MimeMultipart` message, should be treated as one part. The `MimeMultipart` of type `multipart/related` is then set as the content type for a `BodyPart`, and this `BodyPart` is added to the top-level `multipart/alternative` `MimeMultipart` instance. We create an additional `BodyPart` in this case because we cannot add one `MimeMultipart` instance to another without first wrapping it in a `BodyPart`—essentially, we need to say that a part of the top-level multipart instance is made up of another one.

Next, we add the HTML `BodyPart` to the `multipart/related MimeMultipart` instance, and then we add the embedded image. In general, using the `MimeMessageHelper` class to add embedded resources to a `MimeMultipart` is much easier than this section's manual approach, but we wanted to show how to do it. The first two steps required when adding an embedded, inline resource are to set the `Content-ID` header of the multipart and to set the content disposition to `inline`. Once this is done, you can supply the content of the actual `BodyPart` using the `setDataHandler()` method. The `setDataHandler()` method requires an instance of `javax.activation.DataHandler`, which in turn requires an instance of a class that implements `javax.activation.DataSource`; we use the `javax.activation.FileDataSource` class. JavaMail and the JavaBeans Activation Framework take care of encoding the resource data for inclusion in the message, as well identifying the correct MIME type for the data and including this in the `BodyPart`.

Figure 13-9 shows the plain text version of this message, and Figure 13-10 shows the HTML version with the embedded image.

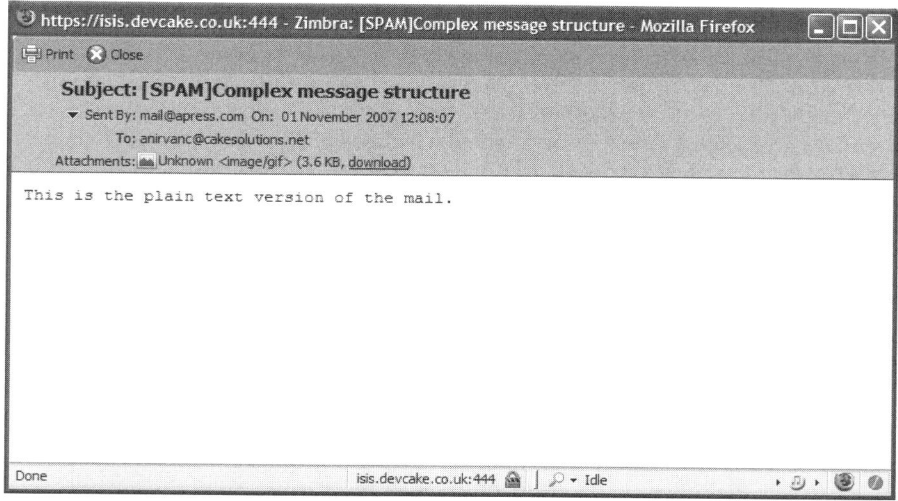

Figure 13-9. *The plain text message*

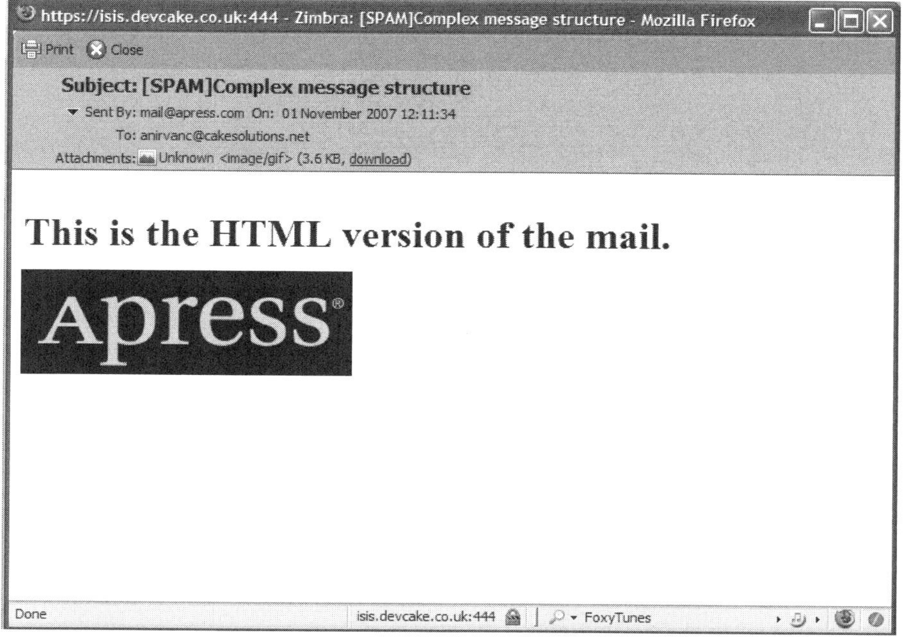

Figure 13-10. *The HTML message*

Notice that in the plain text view, the inline image is treated as an attachment even though we set the content disposition to inline. This is just one example of how different mail clients treat the mail structure in different ways.

Insight into Enterprise-Level E-mail Handling

Until now, we have seen different ways of integrating Spring e-mail with an application and sending e-mails from that application using an SMTP mail transport *synchronously*. Simple applications can get away with sending e-mail synchronously. However, more advanced and complex applications cannot tolerate the delay imposed by connecting to the SMTP server, and they may need to schedule delivery of e-mail and set up an infrastructure for retries and reports on e-mail sent.

To achieve this, we will model our solutions on the background processes design described in Chapter 8. Essentially, we create a message queue with a scheduled process that goes through the queue and sends out the messages *asynchronously*. In this section, we are mainly concerned with implementing the chosen design pattern (refer to Chapter 8 for the details of the design pattern).

Our previous examples may incline you to think that using a wholly programmatic approach to message construction puts too much of the message content inside your application, making it hard to modify. We have found adding some kind of templating engine useful; that way, we can customize the e-mail messages that are sent out. We will show you how to separate template generation from storage in this section.

By combining the scheduling infrastructure and the templating engine, you can add an efficient e-mail–sending feature to your application.

Let's get into some more detail and have a look at the main components of the solution, illustrated in Figure 13-11.

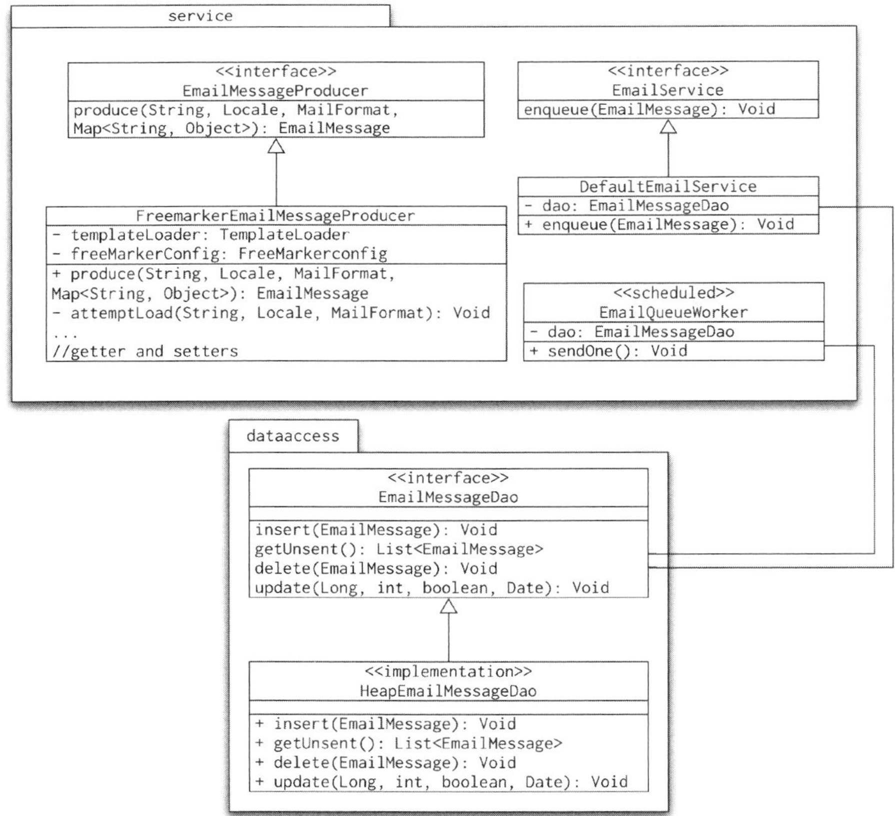

Figure 13-11. *UML class diagram of the e-mail–sending solution*

Figure 13-11 shows the central components that make up our solution.

The data access tier implements storage of the EmailMessage. For the sake of simplicity, we are storing the queue in memory and have provided a HeapEmailMessageDao as the implementation of EmailMessageDao. You can easily substitute HeapEmailMessageDao with a database-specific implementation, as you have seen in Chapter 9.

The service layer is composed of the EmailService and EmailMessageProducer interfaces. The implementation of the EmailService (the DefaultEmailService) simply validates the supplied EmailMessage class and saves it. It then gets picked up by the EmailQueueWorker, which operates on the existing message queue. The clients (pieces of code that rely on the e-mail service) use the EmailMessageProducer to obtain an EmailMessage, which is identified by its code. The implementation of the EmailMessageProducer (i.e., the FreemarkerEmailMessageProducer) uses instances of the TemplateLoader and FreeMarkerConfig. We will take a better look at them later in this section. The main task achieved here is to generate the EmailMessage, using the e-mail template and the arguments. Now, the EmailMessage is almost ready to be queued using the EmailService; all that remains to be done is to specify the recipient and add any potential attachments. The EmailQueueWorker takes this EmailMessage, completes it, and produces a MimeMessage, which is then sent out as a complete e-mail.

Now, look at Figure 13-12, which shows the structure and suggested fields of the EmailMessage object.

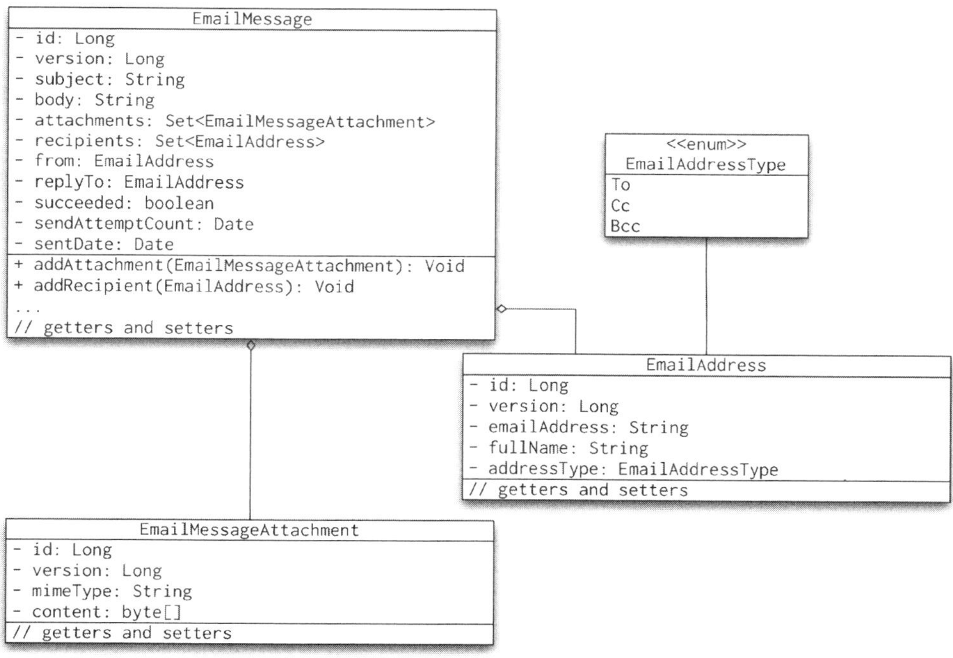

Figure 13-12. *UML diagram showing the structure of the EmailMessage*

As you can see, there are important things to consider when you are developing a solution for an enterprise-level application. The e-mail templates should be stored externally, perhaps on the filesystem or in a database. Also, including the locale is important when looking up the e-mail templates. You may argue that your application does not need to support different languages, but adding this feature is easy, and you can always produce templates in your default language.

When implementing the scheduler, you need to add some management information. You may find it useful to track the numbers of retry e-mails sent, the size of the queue, and many other values. We leave these details to you to configure according to your needs. See Chapter 21 for a detailed discussion on how to gather management information for a Java application.

Now, let's take a quick look at the implementation of the data access tier in Listing 13-17.

Listing 13-17. *The EmailMessageDao Interface and Its Implementation*

```
package com.apress.prospring2.ch13.dataaccess;

import com.apress.prospring2.ch13.domain.EmailMessage;
import java.util.List;
import java.util.Date;

public interface EmailMessageDao {

    void insert(EmailMessage emailMessage);

    List<EmailMessage> getUnsent();

    void delete(EmailMessage emailMessage);

    void update(Long id, int sendAttemptCount, boolean success, Date date);
}

package com.apress.prospring2.ch13.dataaccess;

import com.apress.prospring2.ch13.domain.EmailMessage;
import java.util.*;

public class HeapEmailMessageDao implements EmailMessageDao {
    private long lastId = 0L;
    private Map<Long, EmailMessage> mailQueue = new HashMap<Long, EmailMessage>();

    public void insert(EmailMessage emailMessage) {
        if (emailMessage.getId() == null) {
            this.lastId ++;
            emailMessage.setId(this.lastId);
        }
        this.mailQueue.put(emailMessage.getId(), emailMessage);
    }

    public List<EmailMessage> getUnsent() {
        List<EmailMessage> messages = new ArrayList<EmailMessage>();
        for(Long id : this.mailQueue.keySet()) {
            if(! mailQueue.get(id).isSucceeded()) {
                messages.add(mailQueue.get(id));
            }
        }
        if (!messages.isEmpty()) return messages;
        return null;
    }

    public void delete(EmailMessage emailMessage) {
        this.mailQueue.remove(emailMessage.getId());
    }
```

```
    public void update(Long id, int sendAttemptCount, boolean success, Date date) {
        EmailMessage message = this.mailQueue.get(id);
        message.setSentDate(date);
        message.setSendAttemptCount(sendAttemptCount);
        if (success) message.setSucceeded(true);
        this.mailQueue.put(id, message);
    }
}
```

The important method here is the `unsent()` method, which returns all the `EmailMessages` that are still to be sent out. The `EmailQueueWorker` makes use of this method to send e-mails.

Moving on to the central part of the solution, now we will look deeper into the `DefaultEmailService`. Although this is the central part of the system, it is trivial compared to the other parts. Listing 13-18 shows the `DefaultEmailService` class.

Listing 13-18. *Showing the DefaultEmailService Class*

```
package com.apress.prospring2.ch13.service;

import com.apress.prospring2.ch13.domain.EmailMessage;
import com.apress.prospring2.ch13.dataaccess.EmailMessageDao;

public class DefaultEmailService implements EmailService {
    private EmailMessageDao emailMessageDao;

    public void enqueue(final EmailMessage message) {
        try {
            message.validate();
        } catch (IllegalArgumentException e) {
            // Invalid message, handle it
            return;
        }

        // the message is valid; insert it to the queue
        this.emailMessageDao.insert(message);
    }

    public void setEmailMessageDao(final EmailMessageDao emailMessageDao) {
        this.emailMessageDao = emailMessageDao;
    }
}
```

The `DefaultEmailService` uses the `EmailMassageDao` to insert new `EmailMessages` into the mail queue, which is dependency injected into the service. The `enqueue()` method takes an `EmailMessage` and validates it. If the validation succeeds, it inserts the `EmailMessage` into the mail queue using the `EmailMessageDao`.

This brings us to the `EmailMessageProducer` interface and its FreeMarker-based implementation. `EmailMessageProducer` creates a message in a common structure and obtains the message content from FreeMarker templates.

FreeMarker is a templating engine that allows you to create any kind of textual output by merging text-based templates with Java objects. FreeMarker is most widely used as a replacement or complement to JSP in the web tier, as discussed in Chapter 17, but it has many other uses. If you are unfamiliar with FreeMarker, you can visit the web site at `http://www.freemarker.org` to find out more.

From our experience of building large-scale enterprise applications, we have found that a message structure that works well in most mail clients is simply to provide both plain text and HTML content in a single multipart message. We have also found that it is better to avoid embedded images, hosting them on a web server instead and linking to them in the standard way from within the HTML content.

For the solution shown in this section, we have created a class, `FreemarkerEmailMessageProducer`, which implements `EmailMessageProducer` and Spring's `InitializingBean`. Listing 13-19 shows the `FreemarkerEmailMessageProducer` class.

Listing 13-19. *The FreemarkerEmailMessageProducer Class*

```
package com.apress.prospring2.ch13.service;

import com.apress.prospring2.ch13.domain.EmailMessage;
import com.apress.prospring2.ch13.domain.MailFormat;
import freemarker.template.Configuration;
import freemarker.template.Template;
import freemarker.template.TemplateException;
import org.springframework.beans.FatalBeanException;
import org.springframework.beans.factory.InitializingBean;
import org.springframework.web.servlet.view.freemarker.FreeMarkerConfig;

import java.io.IOException;
import java.io.StringWriter;
import java.util.Locale;
import java.util.Map;

public class FreemarkerEmailMessageProducer
implements EmailMessageProducer, InitializingBean {

    private TemplateLoader templateLoader;
    private FreeMarkerConfig freeMarkerConfig;

    public void afterPropertiesSet() throws Exception {
        if (this.freeMarkerConfig == null)
            throw new
FatalBeanException("Property
[freeMarkerConfig] of [" + getClass().getName() + "] is required.");
        this.templateLoader = new DefaultTemplateLoader ➥
("", ".ftl", freeMarkerConfig);
    }
```

The interesting thing to notice here is that the `FreemarkerEmailMessageProducer` also implements the `InitializingBean` interface from Spring's factory package. This gives us the ability to do initialization work after properties are set up for a bean in the `BeanFactory`. The `afterPropertiesSet()` method allows you to check if all the properties are set properly, or if some operation has to be completed after the properties have been set. Here, we check whether the `FreeMarkerConfig` property is properly set or not; if it is properly set, we create the `TemplateLoader`. The `FreeMarkerConfig` class will be provided using DI and we will be using Spring's `FreeMarkerConfigurer`, an out-of-the-box implementation for using FreeMarker as a templating engine.

Note FreeMarkerConfigurer is typically used in a web-app (web-based application). For non-web-apps, add a `FreeMarkerConfigurationFactoryBean` to your application context definition file.

Listing 13-20. *The FreemarkerEmailMessageProducer Class*

```
    static interface TemplateLoader {
        Template load(final String name, final Locale locale, ➥
final MailFormat format) throws IOException;
    }

    static class DefaultTemplateLoader implements TemplateLoader {
        private FreeMarkerConfig config;
        private String prefix;
        private String suffix;

        public DefaultTemplateLoader(final String prefix, final String suffix,
final FreeMarkerConfig config) {
            this.config = config;
            this.prefix = prefix;
            this.suffix = suffix;
        }

        private String resolveTemplateName(final String name,
final Locale locale, final MailFormat format) {
            StringBuilder result = new StringBuilder(50);
            result.append(prefix);
            result.append(locale.getLanguage());
            result.append("_");
            result.append(locale.getCountry());
            result.append("/");
            result.append(name);
            result.append("_");
            result.append(format.toString());
            result.append(suffix);
            return result.toString();
        }

        public Template load(final String name, final Locale locale,
final MailFormat format) throws IOException {
            Configuration configuration = config.getConfiguration();
            return configuration.getTemplate(
resolveTemplateName(name, locale, format));
        }
    }

    private Template attemptLoad(final String templateName, final Locale locale,
final MailFormat format) {
        try {
            return this.templateLoader.load(templateName, locale, format);
        } catch (IOException e) {
            // log error here
            return null;
        }
    }
```

The `TemplateLoader` interface and its implementation (the `DefaultTemplateLoader`) loads the appropriate FreeMarker template file (`.ftl`) based on the supplied template code, mail format, and locale. As you can see from the code, the main objective is to programmatically load a template based on some parameters. The `resolveTemplateName()` method returns the fully qualified path of the required template file based on the passed-in values of name, locale, and format. Here, `name` is the template code (e.g., registrationSuccessful); locale is the country and language combination of the required template (e.g., en_GB); and format is the desired format of the mail message (e.g., plain text or HTML). The returned value of the resolveTemplateName() method would look something like this: en_GB/registrationSuccessful_plain.ftl.

The load() method returns a FreeMarker Template object. This method uses the FreeMarker Configuration class. The Configuration.getTemplate() method retrieves a template specified by the name passed into this method.

Listing 13-21. *The FreemarkerEmailMessageProducer Class*

```
    public EmailMessage produce(String emailTemplateCode, Locale locale,
MailFormat format, Map<String, Object> arguments) {
        EmailMessage message = new EmailMessage();
        Template template = attemptLoad(emailTemplateCode, locale, format);
        if (template == null) throw new ➥
RuntimeException("Cannot load email template.");
        try {
            StringWriter body = new StringWriter();
            template.process(arguments, body);
            message.setBody(body.toString());
        } catch (TemplateException e) {
            //handle it
            return null;
        } catch (IOException impossible) {
        }

        return message;
    }

    public void setFreeMarkerConfig(FreeMarkerConfig freeMarkerConfig) {
        this.freeMarkerConfig = freeMarkerConfig;
    }
}
```

The only special thing to notice in Listing 13-21 is the Template.process() method, which takes in the StringWriter and the Map of arguments. This method processes the template, using the data from the Map, outputs the resulting text to the supplied StringWriter, and produces the merged result. This merged result will form the body of the e-mail message.

The only part of the system that still has to be written is the EmailQueueWorker class. Listing 13-22 shows the full source of the EmailQueueWorker class.

Listing 13-22. *The EmailQueueWorker Class*

```
package com.apress.prospring2.ch13.service;

import com.apress.prospring2.ch13.dataaccess.EmailMessageDao;
import com.apress.prospring2.ch13.domain.EmailAddress;
import com.apress.prospring2.ch13.domain.EmailMessage;
import com.apress.prospring2.ch13.domain.EmailMessageAttachment;
import com.apress.prospring2.ch13.domain.EmailAddressType;
import org.springframework.jmx.export.annotation.ManagedOperation;
import org.springframework.jmx.export.annotation.ManagedResource;
import org.springframework.mail.javamail.JavaMailSender;

import javax.activation.DataHandler;
import javax.activation.DataSource;
```

```
import javax.mail.BodyPart;
import javax.mail.MessagingException;
import javax.mail.Multipart;
import javax.mail.Message;
import javax.mail.internet.*;
import java.io.ByteArrayInputStream;
import java.io.ByteArrayOutputStream;
import java.io.InputStream;
import java.io.OutputStream;
import java.util.Date;
import java.util.List;

@ManagedResource(objectName = "com.apress.prospring2.ch13:name=EmailQueueWorker")
public class EmailQueueWorker {

    private EmailMessageDao emailMessageDao;
    private JavaMailSender javaMailSender;

    @ManagedOperation(description = "Runs the queue now")
    public void run() {
        List<EmailMessage> messages = this.emailMessageDao.getUnsent();
        for (EmailMessage message : messages) {
            sendOne(message);
        }
    }

    private void sendOne(EmailMessage message) {
        MimeMessage mimeMessage = javaMailSender.createMimeMessage();

        prepareMimeMessage(mimeMessage, message);
        javaMailSender.send(mimeMessage);

        // update the queue
        this.emailMessageDao.update(message.getId(),
message.getSendAttemptCount() + 1, true, new Date());
    }

    private void prepareMimeMessage(MimeMessage mimeMessage,
EmailMessage emailMessage) {
        try {
            mimeMessage.setFrom(getAddress(emailMessage.getFrom()));
            setRecipients(mimeMessage, emailMessage);
            mimeMessage.setSubject(emailMessage.getSubject());
            if (emailMessage.getReplyTo() != null)
                mimeMessage.setReplyTo(
new InternetAddress[]{getAddress(emailMessage.getReplyTo())});
            Multipart multipart = new MimeMultipart("related");

            //plain text
            BodyPart plainTextPart = new MimeBodyPart();
            plainTextPart.setContent(emailMessage.getBody(), "text/plain");
            multipart.addBodyPart(plainTextPart);

            //html part
            BodyPart htmlPart = new MimeBodyPart();
            htmlPart.setContent(emailMessage.getBody(), "text/html");
            multipart.addBodyPart(htmlPart);
```

```
            //attachments
            for (EmailMessageAttachment attachment : ➥
emailMessage.getAttachments())
{
                BodyPart attachmentPart = new MimeBodyPart();
                DataSource dataSource = new DataSource() {
                    public String getContentType() {
                        return attachment.getMimeType();
                    }

                    public InputStream getInputStream() {
                        return new ByteArrayInputStream(attachment.getContent());
                    }

                    public String getName() {
                        return attachment.getFileName();
                    }

                    public OutputStream getOutputStream() {
                        return new ByteArrayOutputStream();
                    }
                };
                attachmentPart.setDataHandler(new DataHandler(dataSource));
                attachmentPart.setFileName(attachment.getFileName());
                multipart.addBodyPart(attachmentPart);
            }
            mimeMessage.setContent(multipart);
        } catch (MessagingException me) {
            // handle the exception
            throw new RuntimeException(me);
        }

    }

    private void setRecipients(MimeMessage mimeMessage, EmailMessage emailMessage) {
        try {
            for (EmailAddress emailAddress : emailMessage.getRecipients()) {
                mimeMessage.addRecipient(
resolveType(emailAddress.getAddressType()), getAddress(emailAddress));
            }

        } catch (AddressException ae) {
            // handle exception
            throw new RuntimeException(ae);
        } catch (MessagingException me) {
            // handle exception
            throw new RuntimeException(me);
        }
    }

    private Message.RecipientType resolveType(EmailAddressType addressType) {
        switch (addressType) {
            case To:
                return Message.RecipientType.TO;
            case Cc:
                return Message.RecipientType.CC;
```

```
            case Bcc:
                return Message.RecipientType.BCC;
        }
        throw new RuntimeException("Unknown recipient type");
    }

    private InternetAddress getAddress(EmailAddress emailAddress) {
        try {
            return new InternetAddress(emailAddress.getEmailAddress());
        } catch (AddressException ae) {
            // handle exception
            throw new RuntimeException(ae);
        }
    }

    public void setJavaMailSender(JavaMailSender javaMailSender) {
        this.javaMailSender = javaMailSender;
    }

    public void setEmailMessageDao(EmailMessageDao emailMessageDao) {
        this.emailMessageDao = emailMessageDao;
    }
}
```

The `EmailQueueWorker` is a background process, which, when run, starts sending out e-mail messages in the mail queue. The solution discussed here is based on the Spring application pattern for background processes as described in Chapter 8. To manage the scheduled `EmailQueueWorker`, we have exposed it as a JMX bean (see Chapter 21 for details about JMX).

Here, we are only going to focus on the part relating to Spring e-mail. The `prepareMimeMessage()` method is what we are interested in at this point. Most of the code should be familiar to you by now from the previous examples shown in this chapter. The `prepareMimeMessage()` takes in an `EmailMessage` and turns it into a `MimeMessage` by filling in all the relevant details. The `JavaMailSender` then takes the prepared `MimeMessage` and sends it using its `send()` method.

Summary

In this chapter, you have seen how to use Spring to simplify the creation of e-mail messaging functionality for your applications. You saw how to use both JavaMail and COS MailMessage to create and send plain text messages, and you also saw how these messages can be configured externally using Spring DI features.

In the second half of the chapter, you saw how JavaMail can be used to construct complex MIME messages to support advanced features such as HTML message content, embedded images, and message attachment. You also learned how to build an enterprise-level e-mail infrastructure with built-in scheduling and templating.

Sending e-mail is an important part of many enterprise applications, and Spring provides excellent support for adding this feature to your own applications. In the next chapter, we examine how to use dynamic languages in a Spring application.

CHAPTER 14

Dynamic Languages

Spring 2.0 brought support for dynamic languages and Spring 2.5 continues the support. By "dynamic language," we mean code that is not compiled and has an interpreter written in Java. In other words, a dynamic language can be anything you wish as long as there is a Java library that can execute it. Spring comes with support for JRuby, Groovy, and BeanShell.

Dynamic language support means that you can now have Spring-managed beans that are not written in Java! Imagine having an external script that handles validation, for example. The traditional approach would be to implement the `Validator` interface in Java and then set the validator implementation bean as a dependency of a form controller. If the validation rules change, we change the validator and redeploy the application. It would be better to be able to use a different approach, where the validator is still a Spring-managed bean but can be changed without having to redeploy the application. In fact, Spring can detect any change to the script source code and rebuild the bean definition while the application is running!

In this chapter, you will learn how to use Spring's dynamic language support; we will begin with a simple example and use it to take a look at how the dynamic language support works behind the scenes. Once we understand how the dynamic language framework works, we will take a look at more complicated examples. We will show how to externalize some aspect of the application's business logic using a dynamic language.

Supported Languages Primer

Before we begin discussing Spring's support for the three dynamic languages, we need to take a quick look at the basic features of each language. We will not discuss detailed aspects of each language's syntax, but we will try to show the main differences so that you can choose the most appropriate dynamic language in your application.

Notice that the languages we are going to show here are not exactly domain-specific languages. They are a bit too complex for even the power users of your application. For more details about domain-specific languages, go to Chapter 8. However, the administrators of your application can use the scripting languages to make more complex changes to your application without having to modify the application's Java code.

BeanShell

BeanShell is a simple Java-like scripting language. The BeanShell source code can mix typed and untyped statements. To try it out, download it from `http://www.beanshell.org`. Copy the `bsh-2.0b4.jar` file to `$BSH_HOME` (`/usr/local/bsh-2.0b4` in our example). Next, we create the `bsh` shell script that invokes the `bsh.Interpreter` and passes it the arguments we specify. Listing 14-1 shows the `bsh` script (on Windows, you will need to create an equivalent `.bat` file).

Listing 14-1. *The bsh Script*

```
#!/bin/sh
BSH_HOME=/usr/local/bsh-2.0b4
java -cp $BSH_HOME/bsh-2.0b4.jar bsh.Interpreter $@
```

This shell script allows us to run any BeanShell script using just the `bsh <script-name>` command. To get a feel for the BeanShell code, take a look at Listing 14-2, which shows the ultimate beginner's program.

Listing 14-2. *"Hello, World" in BeanShell*

```
greeting = "Hello";
print(greeting + ", world");
```

When we run this program, we get "Hello, world" printed in the standard output. The BeanShell language looks and behaves just like Java; the only interesting feature that BeanShell adds to its Java-like syntax is closure. Closure is effectively a function assigned to a variable; using closure means we can pass the function as an argument of other functions.

Let's now leave the details of the BeanShell language itself and take a quick look at how we can use it in our Java applications. Listing 14-3 shows a simple example of BeanShell code running in a Java application.

Listing 14-3. *BeanShell in a Java Application*

```
public class BeanShellDemo {

    public static class Bean {
        private String name;
        private int value;

        public String getName() {
            return name;
        }

        public void setName(String name) {
            this.name = name;
        }

        public int getValue() {
            return value;
        }

        public void setValue(int value) {
            this.value = value;
        }
    }

    private void run() throws Exception {
        Interpreter i = new Interpreter(new StringReader(
                "print(bean.name); bean.value = 20;"),
                System.out, System.err, false);
        Bean bean = new Bean();
        bean.setName("My bean");
        i.set("bean", bean);
        i.run();
        bean = (Bean)i.get("bean");
```

```
        System.out.println(bean.getName());
        System.out.println(bean.getValue());
    }

    public static void main(String[] args) throws Exception {
        new BeanShellDemo().run();
    }

}
```

This code does not do anything too exciting, but it shows that we can pass objects from our Java code into the BeanShell code. The BeanShell code can access or modify the passed objects, and we can then retrieve them.

Groovy

Another scripting language Spring 2.5 supports out of the box is Groovy. To download Groovy, go to http://groovy.codehaus.org/Download, and download the distribution package for your operating system. The package comes with the necessary shell scripts; to execute the code in Listing 14-4 in Groovy, we just need to add the Groovy installation directory to the $PATH.

Listing 14-4. *"Hello, world" in Groovy*

```
world = "World";
println("Hello, " + world);
```

Groovy is a far more complex language than BeanShell. It even allows you to interact with databases, JMX servers, and many other resources. In addition to the functionality offered by the Groovy runtime environment, the language itself contains many advanced concepts. The notable ones are closures (again), functional programming, and constraint programming. Constraint programming is particularly interesting; constraint programs describe the set of legal operations and the solution, rather than the steps needed to reach the solution. This is very similar to backward chaining rule languages such as Prolog. You could use this to implement a simple rule engine in Java, though if you want to use a rule engine you will be better off using a "real" one, such as JESS or Drools.

Let's now take a look at how we can use Groovy directly from Java code; Listing 14-5 shows code very similar to the code in Listing 14-3.

Listing 14-5. *Groovy in a Java Application*

```
public class GroovyDemo {

    public static class Bean {
        private String name;
        private int value;

        public String getName() {
            return name;
        }

        public void setName(String name) {
            this.name = name;
        }

        public int getValue() {
            return value;
        }
```

```
        public void setValue(int value) {
            this.value = value;
        }
    }

    public static void main(String[] args) {
        GroovyShell gs = new GroovyShell();
        Bean bean = new Bean();
        bean.setName("Jan Machacek");
        gs.setVariable("bean", bean);
        Script script = gs.parse("println(bean.name);bean.value = 100;");
        script.run();
        System.out.println(bean.getValue());
    }
}
```

You can see the Groovy code using and modifying a bean passed in from the calling Java code.

JRuby

The last language we will take a quick look at is JRuby; following the pattern of the previous two languages, download JRuby from `http://jruby.codehaus.org/`. Follow the download link to obtain the latest distribution archive and uncompress it to complete the installation. The default distribution includes all necessary shell scripts; we can immediately run the code from Listing 14-6, a "Hello, world" program in JRuby.

Listing 14-6. *"Hello, World" Program in JRuby*

```
world = "World"
puts "Hello, " + world
```

As expected, running this program prints "Hello, World" on the standard output. Let's take a look at the code in Listing 14-7, which shows how we can interact with JRuby from our Java applications.

Listing 14-7. *Using JRuby from Java*

```
public class JRubyDemo {

    public static class Bean {
        private String name;
        private int value;

        public String getName() {
            return name;
        }

        public void setName(String name) {
            this.name = name;
        }

        public int getValue() {
            return value;
        }

        public void setValue(int value) {
            this.value = value;
```

```
        }
    }

    public static void main(String[] args) {
        GroovyShell gs = new GroovyShell();
        Bean bean = new Bean();
        bean.setName("Jan Machacek");
        gs.setVariable("bean", bean);
        Script script = gs.parse("println(bean.name);bean.value = 100;");
        script.run();
        System.out.println(bean.getValue());
    }

}
```

This completes our quick primer on the three dynamic languages supported in Spring. You should now have enough information to start using one of these dynamic languages in your Spring applications. However, the code we have shown is not very Spring-like. In fact, it does not use any code from the Spring Framework at all. Let's see how we could use the dynamic languages in a Spring application; to be more specific, let's explore how we can define Spring beans in the dynamic languages and use those beans in the rest of our application.

Using Dynamic Languages As Spring Beans

Let's begin our discussion of the dynamic languages as Spring beans with a simple example. We will create the `textSource` Spring bean, but we will define it in Groovy. Listing 14-8 shows how we can do this using the Spring 2.5–style schema configuration.

Listing 14-8. *The textSource Bean Definition*

```
<?xml version="1.0" encoding="UTF-8"?>
<beans xmlns="http://www.springframework.org/schema/beans"
       xmlns:xsi="http://www.w3.org/2001/XMLSchema-instance"
       xmlns:util="http://www.springframework.org/schema/util"
       xmlns:tx="http://www.springframework.org/schema/tx"
       xmlns:aop="http://www.springframework.org/schema/aop"
       xmlns:lang="http://www.springframework.org/schema/lang"
       xsi:schemaLocation="http://www.springframework.org/schema/beans
        ...
       http://www.springframework.org/schema/lang
       http://www.springframework.org/schema/lang/spring-lang.xsd">

    <lang:groovy id="textSource">
        <lang:inline-script>
            class Messenger {
                public String getMessage() { return "Hello "}
            }
        </lang:inline-script>
    </lang:groovy>


</beans>
```

Here, we can see that the `textSource` bean defined in Groovy and its source code is embedded in the Spring configuration file. However, calling the methods declared in the Groovy `Messenger` bean would be difficult. Listing 14-9 shows that we can obtain the bean in Java code, but we are unable to use it.

Listing 14-9. *Accessing the textSource Bean*

```
public class BeansDemo {

    public static void main(String[] args) {
        ApplicationContext ac =
            new ClassPathXmlApplicationContext("beans-context.xml",
                BeansDemo.class);
        Object textSouce = ac.getBean("textSource");
        System.out.println(textSouce);
    }

}
```

When we run the application, it loads the bean and indeed prints out a Java-style object reference (`Messenger@da52a1`), but we cannot use it. Figure 14-1 shows the debugger view of the `textSource` object.

```
public static void main(String[] args) {
    ApplicationContext ac = new ClassPathXmlApplicationContext("beans-context.xml", BeansDemo.class)
    Object textSouce = ac.getBean("textSource");
    System.out.println(textSouce);
```

```
Debug - BeansDemo
Vari...
static = com.apress.prospring2.ch14.beans.BeansDemo
args = {java.lang.String[0]@1471}
ac = {org.springframework.context.support.ClassPathXmlApplicationContext@1472}"org.springframework.context.support.ClassP
textSouce = {Messenger@1473}
    metaClass = {groovy.lang.MetaClassImpl@1738}"groovy.lang.MetaClassImpl@90690e[class Messenger]"
        registry = {groovy.lang.MetaClassRegistry@1742}
        classNode = null
        classMethodIndex = {java.util.HashMap@1743} size = 3
        classMethodIndexForSuper = {java.util.HashMap@1744} size = 2
        classStaticMethodIndex = {java.util.HashMap@1745} size = 2
        classPropertyIndex = {java.util.HashMap@1746} size = 3
        classPropertyIndexForSuper = {java.util.HashMap@1747} size = 3
```

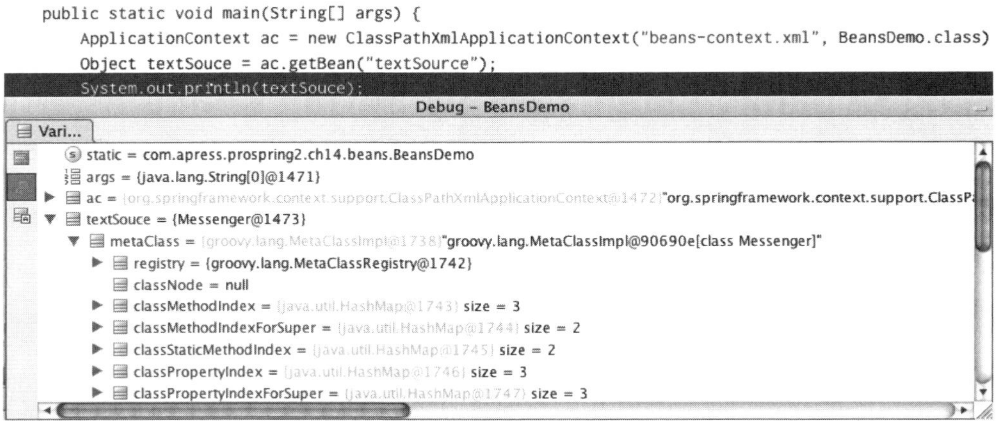

Figure 14-1. *Debugger view of the textSource object*

Figure 14-1 shows that we cannot actually invoke the `getMessage()` method without resorting to using reflection. To bind Groovy (or any other dynamic language) to Java and Spring, we need to define an interface that the dynamic language bean will implement.

Listing 14-10 shows our `TextSource` interface; we then modify the `textSource` bean in the `beans-context.xml` Spring file.

Listing 14-10. *The TextSource Interface and Its Groovy Implementation*

```
TextSource.java:
public interface TextSource {

    String getMessage();

}
```

```
dynamic-beans-context.xml:
<?xml version="1.0" encoding="UTF-8"?>
<beans xmlns="http://www.springframework.org/schema/beans"
       xmlns:xsi="http://www.w3.org/2001/XMLSchema-instance"
       xmlns:util="http://www.springframework.org/schema/util"
       xmlns:tx="http://www.springframework.org/schema/tx"
       xmlns:aop="http://www.springframework.org/schema/aop"
       xmlns:lang="http://www.springframework.org/schema/lang"
       xsi:schemaLocation="http://www.springframework.org/schema/beans
       ...>

    <lang:groovy id="textSource">
        <lang:inline-script>
            class Messenger implements com.apress.prospring2.ch14.beans.TextSource {
                public String getMessage() { return "Hello "}
            }
        </lang:inline-script>
    </lang:groovy>


</beans>
```

Now, we can modify the code of the demo application and cast the bean identified by `"textSource"` to `TextSource` and call its `getMessage()` method. Listing 14-11 shows how we have done this.

Listing 14-11. *Using the textSource Bean*

```
public class BeansDemo {

    public static void main(String[] args) {
        ApplicationContext ac =
            new ClassPathXmlApplicationContext("beans-context.xml",
                 BeansDemo.class);
        TextSource textSouce = (TextSource) ac.getBean("textSource");
        System.out.println(textSouce);
        System.out.println(textSouce.getMessage());
    }

}
```

The output from this program includes the result of the default `toString()` method (`Messenger@aea8cf`), followed by the value returned from the `Messenger.getMessage()` defined in Groovy (`Hello`).

Behind the Scenes of Dynamic Language Support

We have successfully created the `textSource` bean implemented in Groovy, but we have not really explored what Spring does to bring Groovy and Java together. We can shed some light on the steps Spring takes by using an old-style DTD context file, like the one shown in Listing 14-12.

Listing 14-12. *DTD Configuration for the Groovy Bean*

```
<?xml version="1.0" encoding="UTF-8"?>
<!DOCTYPE beans PUBLIC "-//SPRING//DTD BEAN 2.0//EN"
      "http://www.springframework.org/dtd/spring-beans-2.0.dtd">
<beans>

     <bean class=
         "org.springframework.scripting.support.ScriptFactoryPostProcessor"/>

    <bean id="textSource"
        class="org.springframework.scripting.groovy.GroovyScriptFactory">
        <constructor-arg>
            <value>inline:
                class Messenger implements com.apress.prospring2.ch14.beans.TextSource {
                    public String getMessage() { return &quot;Hello&quot; }
                }
            </value>
        </constructor-arg>
    </bean>

</beans>
```

This code brings some clarity to the creation of beans implemented in Groovy (similar approaches apply for other dynamic languages). We register the `ScriptFactoryPostProcessor` bean and then declare the scripted bean in an appropriate `ScriptFactory` bean (`GroovyScriptFactory` in this case). The `GroovyScriptFactory` bean takes a `String` as its constructor argument; this `String` either identifies a `Resource` or contains the script itself. Next, we declare the `ScriptFactoryPostProcessor`; it is a `BeanPostProcessor` that takes the `scriptSource` argument of the `ScriptFactory` subclasses and replaces the instances of `ScriptFactory` by the code the script implements. You can try it out by commenting out the `<bean class="org.springframework.scripting.support.ScriptFactoryPostProcessor"/>` definition and running the example again. You will see an exception message rather than the `Hello` message.

```
Exception in thread "main" java.lang.ClassCastException:
    org.springframework.scripting.groovy.GroovyScriptFactory
        at com.apress.prospring2.ch14.beans.BeansDemo.main(BeansDemo.java:13)
```

Proxying Dynamic Language Beans

We mentioned that Spring creates a proxy to the dynamic language object. Let's explore this in more detail. When the application requests the `Messenger` bean in Groovy, Spring calls Groovy to create an object that represents the script. It then creates a proxy to the Groovy script object and returns the proxy. The proxy implements the interfaces we specified in the XML configuration file. The `InvocationHandler` directs all calls to the methods defined in the interface to the Groovy script object. Figure 14-2 illustrates the proxies Spring creates.

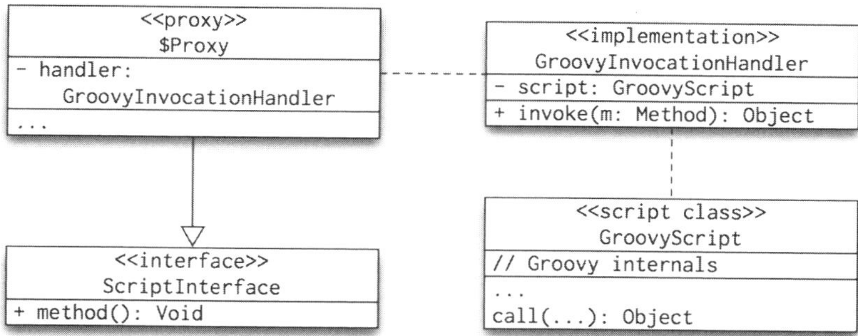

Figure 14-2. *UML class diagram of the Messenger proxy*

Performance

It is important to realize that dynamic languages are inherently slower than compiled Java code, mainly because the appropriate interpreter needs to do a lot of work for dynamic languages: it needs to check the syntax of the script, build its internal representation, and then execute the internal model of the script. Most interpreters do not optimize the execution; for example, they always use late binding (they always resolve the target method at runtime, rather than compile time—there is no compile time!).

Let's write a few tests that measure how the dynamic languages compare to standard Java beans. We will measure the performance of each of the dynamic languages and the efficiency of the supporting code necessary to invoke it. We will implement and measure the performance of the Messenger bean example in Groovy, BeanShell, and JRuby. Listing 14-13 shows the Spring context file for the performance-measuring application.

Listing 14-13. *Spring Context File for the Performance-Measuring Application*

```
<?xml version="1.0" encoding="UTF-8"?>
<beans xmlns="http://www.springframework.org/schema/beans"
   ...>

    <lang:groovy id="textSource">
        <lang:inline-script>
            class Messenger implements com.apress.prospring2.ch14.beans.TextSource {
                public String getMessage() { return "Hello "}
            }
        </lang:inline-script>
    </lang:groovy>

    <lang:bsh id="bshTextSource"
         script-interfaces="com.apress.prospring2.ch14.beans.TextSource">
        <lang:inline-script>
            String getMessage() {
                return "Hello";
            }
        </lang:inline-script>
    </lang:bsh>

    <lang:jruby id="jrubyTextSource"
```

```
        script-interfaces="com.apress.prospring2.ch14.beans.TextSource">
        <lang:inline-script>
        <![CDATA[
            require 'java'

            class Messenger

              def getMessage
                "Hello"
              end

            end
        ]]>
        </lang:inline-script>
    </lang:jruby>

    <bean id="javaTextSource"
       class="com.apress.prospring2.ch14.beans.JavaTextSource"/>

</beans>
```

The testing application will get instances of all four beans, call the getMessage() method 10,000 times, and print how long it took (see Listing 14-14).

Listing 14-14. *Performance-Measuring Application*

```
public class PerformanceDemo {
    private ApplicationContext applicationContext;

    private void run() {
        this.applicationContext =
                new ClassPathXmlApplicationContext("beans-context.xml",
                    BeansDemo.class);
        measure("bshTextSource");
        measure("textSource");
        measure("jrubyTextSource");
        measure("javaTextSource");
    }

    private void measure(String beanName) {
        TextSource ts = (TextSource) this.applicationContext.getBean(beanName);
        long start = System.currentTimeMillis();
        for (int i = 0; i < 10000; i++) {
            ts.getMessage();
        }
        System.out.println("Bean " + beanName + " took " +
            (System.currentTimeMillis() - start) + " ms.");
    }

    public static void main(String[] args) {
        new PerformanceDemo().run();
    }
}
```

The output of the application shows that the Java implementation is the fastest, followed by Groovy, BeanShell, and JRuby.

```
DEBUG [main] AbstractBeanFactory.getBean(203) | Returning cached instance of ➥
singleton bean 'bshTextSource'
Bean bshTextSource took 52 ms.
DEBUG [main] AbstractBeanFactory.getBean(203) | Returning cached instance of ➥
singleton bean 'textSource'
Bean textSource took 5 ms.
DEBUG [main] AbstractBeanFactory.getBean(203) | Returning cached instance of ➥
singleton bean 'jrubyTextSource'
Bean jrubyTextSource took 212 ms.
DEBUG [main] AbstractBeanFactory.getBean(203) | Returning cached instance of ➥
singleton bean 'javaTextSource'
Bean javaTextSource took 1 ms.
```

Do not take this performance test as a definitive measure of the various dynamic languages' performance; we merely wanted to show that any dynamic language is slower than compiled Java code.

Refreshable Beans

The code in the previous examples was interesting, but it didn't give us any additional benefits over standard Java code. On the contrary, the code needed to build the application context was more complicated and the performance of the scripted bean was slower than that of a standard Java bean. However, there is one very compelling reason for using dynamic languages in your Spring beans: Spring can automatically reload the bean if the script changes, without even having to restart the application. Note that you can only make use of this feature if you move your script code outside the Spring context file.

Let's write an application that uses this feature. Continuing with the implementation of the `textSource` bean, we will move the Groovy implementation of the `TextSource` interface to the `TextSource.groovy` file. Listing 14-15 shows the Spring context file for the refreshable dynamic language bean.

Listing 14-15. *Refreshable textSource Context File*

```
<?xml version="1.0" encoding="UTF-8"?>
<beans xmlns="http://www.springframework.org/schema/beans"
    ...>

    <lang:groovy id="textSource"
        script-source="file:ch14/src/main/java/com/apress/➥
            prospring2/ch14/dynamic/TextSource.groovy"
        refresh-check-delay="1000" />

</beans>
```

As you can see, we removed the `inline-script` definition but added the `script-source` and `refresh-check-delay` attributes to the `lang:groovy` element. The `script-source` attribute represents a Spring `Resource`, so the path can be any value that Spring's built-in `PropertyEditor` for the `Resouce` type can parse, for example, `classpath:/com/apress/prospring2/ch14/dynamic/TextSource.groovy`.

Next, in Listing 14-16, you can see a simple testing application. It gets the `textSource` bean, invokes its `getMessage()` method, and waits for input from the standard input. If we type **exit**, the application stops; otherwise, it gets the `textSource` bean again and prints the message.

Listing 14-16. *The Sample Application*

```
public class DynamicDemo {

    public static void main(String[] args) throws IOException {
        ApplicationContext ac =
                new ClassPathXmlApplicationContext("dynamic-beans-context.xml",
                   DynamicDemo.class);
        BufferedReader reader = new BufferedReader(
                new InputStreamReader(System.in));
        while (true) {
            TextSource textSouce = (TextSource) ac.getBean("textSource");
            System.out.println(textSouce.getMessage());
            System.out.println("Press Enter to continue, exit to stop.");
            if ("exit".equals(reader.readLine())) break;
        }
    }

}
```

Finally, let's add the Groovy script (see Listing 14-17).

Listing 14-17. *TextSource Groovy Script*

```
class GroovyTextSource implements com.apress.prospring2.ch14.beans.TextSource {
    public String getMessage() { return "Hello"}
}
```

When we run the application from Listing 14-16, we get the following output:

```
DEBUG [main] AbstractBeanFactory.getBean(203) | Returning cached instance of ➥
singleton bean 'textSource'
DEBUG [main] AbstractRefreshableTargetSource.refreshCheckDelayElapsed(123) | ➥
Refresh check delay elapsed - checking whether refresh is required
Hello
Press Enter to continue, exit to stop.

<< enter

DEBUG [main] AbstractBeanFactory.getBean(203) | Returning cached instance of ➥
singleton bean 'textSource'
DEBUG [main] AbstractRefreshableTargetSource.refreshCheckDelayElapsed(123) | ➥
Refresh check delay elapsed - checking whether refresh is required
Hello
Press Enter to continue, exit to stop.

* edit the TextSource.groovy; make the getMessage return "Hello, world"
<< enter

DEBUG [main] AbstractBeanFactory.getBean(203) | Returning cached instance of ➥
singleton bean 'textSource'
DEBUG [main] AbstractRefreshableTargetSource.refreshCheckDelayElapsed(123) | ➥
Refresh check delay elapsed - checking whether refresh is required
DEBUG [main] AbstractRefreshableTargetSource.refresh(95) |➥
Attempting to refresh target
DEBUG [main] AbstractAutowireCapableBeanFactory.createBean(342) | ➥
Creating instance of bean 'scriptedObject.textSource' with merged definition
...
```

```
DEBUG [main] AbstractRefreshableTargetSource.refresh(101) |➥
Target refreshed successfully
Hello, world
Press Enter to continue, exit to stop.

<< enter

DEBUG [main] AbstractBeanFactory.getBean(203) | Returning cached instance of ➥
singleton bean 'textSource'
DEBUG [main] AbstractRefreshableTargetSource.refreshCheckDelayElapsed(123) | ➥
Refresh check delay elapsed - checking whether refresh is required
Hello, world
Press Enter to continue, exit to stop.

<< exit
```

The bean indeed got reloaded when we changed the code in the TextSource.groovy file. However, if there is no change to the file, Spring returns the cached instance of the textSource bean. If you do not want to use the automatic refresh checking, set the value of the refresh-check-delay attribute to -1 or leave it out completely.

You now know how to declare Spring beans in the three dynamic languages, but you can only write very simple dynamic language beans. In the next section, we will look at the specifics of bean creation using the various dynamic languages.

BeanShell Beans

If you closely examine the BeanShell syntax, you will notice that there is no top-level class or method. The script begins simply by executing the first command it finds in the source code, continues to the second one, and so on. However, BeanShell's functions come with a twist: because a function can be assigned to a variable, the functions define the this symbol. If a function returns this, the calling code can save the value and access any elements defined in the function. As an example, take a look at the code in Listing 14-18.

Listing 14-18. *Function References*

```
demo() {
    int value = 100;
    main() {
        super.value = 200;
    }
    return this;
}

demoInstance = demo();
demoInstance.main();
print(demoInstance.value);
```

This construct looks like object-oriented programming, where demo is a class and main is its method. However, in BeanShell, both demo and main are functions; the demoInstance variable is a reference to a function, not an object. This is why Spring's <lang:bsh /> bean definition needs the script-interfaces attribute. This attribute defines the interfaces that the script implements. Take a look at the code in Listing 14-19, which shows two new interfaces that we wish to implement in the dynamic languages.

Listing 14-19. *Interfaces to be Implemented in Dynamic Languages*

```
public interface Checker {

    boolean check(String value);

}

public interface Corrector {

    String correct(String value);

}
```

We will use these interfaces in our sample applications. Now look at Listing 14-20, which shows the bean dynamic language bean that implements these two interfaces.

Listing 14-20. *Implementation of the Two Interfaces in BeanShell*

```
<?xml version="1.0" encoding="UTF-8"?>
<beans xmlns="http://www.springframework.org/schema/beans"
    ...>


    <lang:bsh id="bean"
              script-interfaces="com.apress.prospring2.ch14.Checker,➥
                 com.apress.prospring2.ch14.Corrector">
        <lang:inline-script>
            foo() { }
        </lang:inline-script>
    </lang:bsh>

</beans>
```

Notice that the code in the implementation of the bean does not actually implement any of the methods found in the interfaces. We can still get its instance in the sample application shown in Listing 14-21.

Listing 14-21. *Using the Dynamic Bean*

```
public class ImplementationDemo {

    public static void main(String[] args) {
        ApplicationContext ac =
                new ClassPathXmlApplicationContext("beans-context.xml",
                     ImplementationDemo.class);
        Object bean = ac.getBean("bean");
        Corrector corrector = (Corrector)bean;
        Checker checker = (Checker)bean;
        String corrected = corrector.correct("foo");
        System.out.println(checker.check(corrected));
    }
}
```

The line in bold, however, fails with a message that indicates that the desired method (`correct (String)`) has not been found. We fix this by writing the two methods in the `<inline-script>` element (see Listing 14-22).

Listing 14-22. *Implementing the Interfaces in BeanShell*

```
<?xml version="1.0" encoding="UTF-8"?>
<beans xmlns="http://www.springframework.org/schema/beans"
    ...>


    <lang:bsh id="bean"
            script-interfaces="com.apress.prospring2.ch14.Checker,➥
               com.apress.prospring2.ch14.Corrector">
        <lang:inline-script>
            correct(s) { return s; }
            check(s) { return true; }
        </lang:inline-script>
    </lang:bsh>

</beans>
```

As you can see, BeanShell is not a strictly object-oriented language; we therefore need to specify which Java interfaces the script implements. Moreover, even if we specify the interfaces, we must still make sure that the dynamic language script actually declares the methods found in the interface. The bean class will implement the interfaces, but we may not notice a problem until we call a method on the interface.

JRuby Beans

JRuby's syntax allows for first-class object definitions, but the `<lang:jruby />` element still needs the `script-interfaces` attribute. Spring needs to know which Java interfaces the script implements, because it is not possible to find this from the JRuby code. The Spring-generated proxy for the JRuby dynamic language bean will implement all specified `script-interfaces`. Let's run the demonstration code from Listing 14-21 using the Spring context file shown in Listing 14-23.

Listing 14-23. *Spring Context File for the JRuby Bean*

```
<?xml version="1.0" encoding="UTF-8"?>
<beans xmlns="http://www.springframework.org/schema/beans"
    ...>

    <lang:jruby id="bean"
            script-interfaces="com.apress.prospring2.ch14.Checker,➥
                com.apress.prospring2.ch14.Corrector">
        <lang:inline-script>
            <![CDATA[
                require 'java'

                class Impl

                    def correct(s)
                        return s
                    end

                    def check(s)
                        return true
                    end

                end
```

```
                Impl.new
            ]]>
        </lang:inline-script>
    </lang:jruby>

</beans>
```

Notice the line in bold, `Impl.new`. This makes JRuby create an instance of the `Impl` class, which is then used when the Spring-generated proxy delegates the method calls to the JRuby code. If we leave the `Impl.new` line out, the code will still run, but the Spring proxy will use reflection to find the method to execute, which will affect the performance. Also notice that we have not specified the interfaces to be implemented in the `Impl` class definition in JRuby.

Groovy Beans

The final language we will take a look at is Groovy. It is a full object-oriented language, so Groovy classes can directly implement the Java interfaces, and the `<lang:groovy />` element does not need the `script-interfaces` attribute. Again, we create a demonstration application using the code in Listing 14-21. The only change is the `beans-context.xml` Spring context file, which is shown in Listing 14-24.

Listing 14-24. *Spring Context File for Groovy*

```
<?xml version="1.0" encoding="UTF-8"?>
<beans xmlns="http://www.springframework.org/schema/beans"
    ...>

    <lang:groovy id="bean">
        <lang:inline-script>
            class Messenger implements
                com.apress.prospring2.ch14.Checker,
                com.apress.prospring2.ch14.Corrector {
                public boolean check(String s) { return true; }
                public String correct(String s) { return s; }
            }

        </lang:inline-script>
    </lang:groovy>

</beans>
```

You can see that the Groovy implementation is the most straightforward of the languages we've looked at; as well as being easily and clearly implemented, Groovy is also the fastest option for simple scripts.

Typical Usage for Dynamic Languages in Spring Applications

In this section, we will take a look at how we can use the dynamic languages in a realistic Spring application. The first area of usage is auxiliary code in the application, for example web form validators. These validators can now be implemented in a dynamic language. If we use an external file for the script source codes, we will be able to change the validation rules while the application is running. This is indeed a very compelling reason to use a dynamic language.

Another, though not very typical example, is domain-specific language (DSL) creation. If you choose to use one of the dynamic languages (BeanShell, JRuby, or Groovy) for your DSL, you must keep in mind that none of the dynamic languages are particularly user friendly for nondevelopers. This makes these dynamic languages suitable only for portions of your applications that are intended for power users and administrators.

■ Tip While the dynamic languages in their raw forms may be unfriendly, you can implement code that transforms a user-friendly script into one of the dynamic languages. This way, you will be able to offer a user-friendly language and still have all the power of the dynamic languages in your application.

Of the three languages, we believe JRuby is the most object oriented. "Object oriented" in this context means closest to the definition of pure OO language: it is not strongly typed; everything in JRuby is an object; and objects react to messages. However, the Spring abstraction of the dynamic languages means that you can choose the dynamic language you feel most comfortable with for your DSL implementation.

Take a look at Listing 14-25, which shows the JRuby script of a discount calculator.

Listing 14-25. *DiscountCalculator Engine*

```
require 'java'

include_class 'java.math.BigDecimal'

class DiscountCalculator

    def calculate(i)
        d = BigDecimal.valueOf(0)
        i.lines.each {|l|
            if (l.sku == 'a') then
                d = d.add(BigDecimal.valueOf(1))
            end
        }
        d
    end

end

DiscountCalculator.new
```

Even if we do not tell you any details of the implementation, we are confident you can guess what the returned discount will be for an `Invoice` object like the one created in Listing 14-26.

Listing 14-26. *Discount Calculator Demonstration*

```
public class DslDemo {

    public static void main(String[] args) throws IOException {
        ApplicationContext ac =
                new ClassPathXmlApplicationContext("dsl-context.xml",
               DslDemo.class);
        DiscountCalculator dc =
              (DiscountCalculator)ac.getBean("discountCalculator");
        Invoice invoice = new Invoice();
```

```
        invoice.addLine(new InvoiceLine("a"));
        invoice.addLine(new InvoiceLine("b"));
        invoice.addLine(new InvoiceLine("c"));
        System.out.println(dc.calculate(invoice));
    }
}
```

The only difficulty this code presents is that the `DiscountCalculator` in JRuby can only deal with the instance of the `Invoice` class passed to it. It is not difficult to imagine that the script will sometimes need to access other Spring beans. Figure 14-3 best illustrates the class model we are going to use; the implementation of the `DiscountCalculator` is in JRuby.

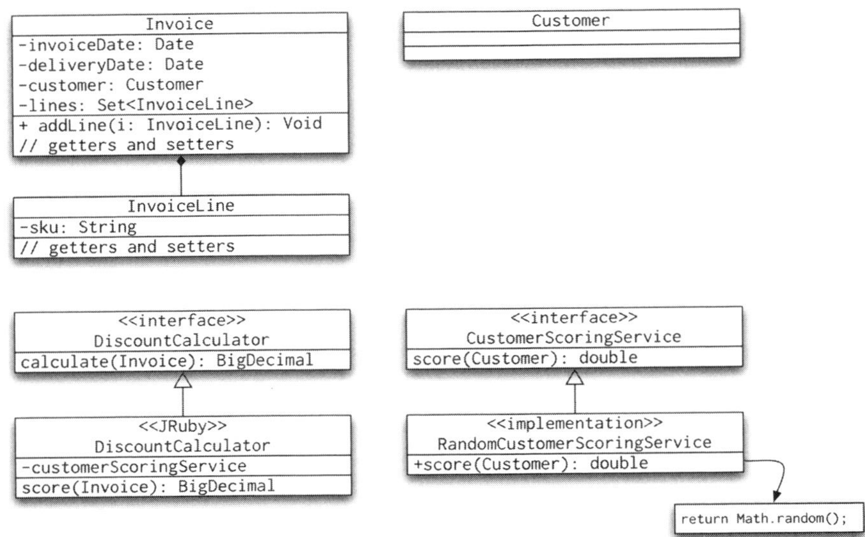

Figure 14-3. *UML class diagram of the sample application*

As Figure 14-3 shows, the `DiscountCalculator`'s JRuby implementation references the `RandomCustomerScoringService` bean. We update the JRuby script and Spring context file with the code from Listing 14-27.

Listing 14-27. *Updated JRuby Script and Spring Context File*

```
// Dsl.rb
require 'java'

include_class 'java.math.BigDecimal'

class DiscountCalculator

    def calculate(i)
        d = BigDecimal.valueOf(0)
        i.lines.each {|l|
            if (l.sku == 'a') then
                d = d.add(BigDecimal.valueOf(1))
            end
        }
```

```
        if @@customerScoringService.score(i.customer) < 0.5 then
            d = BigDecimal.valueOf(0)
        end
        d
    end

    def setCustomerScoringService(css)
        @@customerScoringService = css
    end
end

DiscountCalculator.new

// Spring context file
<?xml version="1.0" encoding="UTF-8"?>
<beans xmlns="http://www.springframework.org/schema/beans"
    ...>

    <bean id="customerScoringService"
        class="com.apress.prospring2.ch14.dsl.RandomCustomerScoringService"/>

    <lang:jruby id="discountCalculator"
            script-interfaces="com.apress.prospring2.ch14.dsl.DiscountCalculator"
            script-source="/com/apress/prospring2/ch14/dsl/Dsl.rb">
        <lang:property name="customerScoringService" ref="customerScoringService"/>
    </lang:jruby>

</beans>
```

Here, we see that the JRuby script—just like any other dynamic language script—can easily access other (Java) Spring beans; other applications can follow this pattern. Examples include the implementation of `Validator` interfaces, or—as the Spring documentation suggests—the implementation of `Controllers`. Before wrapping up this chapter, we will examine how well aware Spring is that scripted beans are not implemented in Java. As you have seen, the proxies to the scripted beans implement the interfaces specified either in the script itself (JRuby) or defined in the `script-interfaces` attribute of the appropriate `<lang: />` element. This has one major implication for Spring's AOP support: we can only advise the interface methods, not the actual implementations, because by the time the script beans are created, we have only proxies. If we modify the Spring context file as show in Listing 14-28, our JRuby bean will be advised correctly.

Listing 14-28. *Transactional Advice for the JRuby Bean*

```
<?xml version="1.0" encoding="UTF-8"?>
<beans xmlns="http://www.springframework.org/schema/beans"
    ...>

    <bean id="customerScoringService"
        class="com.apress.prospring2.ch14.dsl.RandomCustomerScoringService"/>

    <bean id="transactionManager"
        class="com.apress.prospring2.ch14.dsl.NoopTransactionManager"/>

    <tx:advice id="allTransactionalAdvice" transaction-manager="transactionManager">
        <tx:attributes>
            <tx:method name="*"/>
        </tx:attributes>
    </tx:advice>
```

```
    <aop:config>
        <aop:pointcut id="discountCalculationOperation"
            expression="execution(* com.apress.prospring2.ch14.dsl.➥
                                    DiscountCalculator.*(..))"/>
        <aop:advisor advice-ref="allTransactionalAdvice"
             pointcut-ref="discountCalculationOperation"/>
    </aop:config>

    <lang:jruby id="discountCalculator"
            script-interfaces="com.apress.prospring2.ch14.dsl.DiscountCalculator"
            script-source="/com/apress/prospring2/ch14/dsl/Dsl.rb">
        <lang:property name="customerScoringService" ref="customerScoringService"/>
    </lang:jruby>

</beans>
```

Notice, though, that we had to advise the interface operation; we can't advise the scripted bean operations (say, if we added `def foo . . . end` to the JRuby bean).

Summary

In this chapter, you learned how to create Spring-managed beans in three dynamic languages: BeanShell, JRuby, and Groovy. You can now externalize parts of your application's code and allow this code to be changed dynamically even while the application is running. This way, you can change the behavior of the dynamic language beans and thus your entire application without needing to restart.

We also looked into what happens behind the scenes and how Spring actually manages to create beans in dynamic languages. Finally, we showed you how you can use the dynamic language beans to implement a domain-specific language in your application.

PART 4

Java EE 5

CHAPTER 15

Using Spring Remoting

So far, all of the examples we have looked at have assumed that all the components in your application will be running on the same machine, and indeed, in the same JVM. All other things being equal, this architecture is preferable to one where components are distributed across many different machines. In some cases, however, running an application on a single machine is not sufficient to meet the requirements of the application, and component distribution is needed in order to meet these requirements. In general, we see these distributed Java applications fall into two general categories: Java EE and non–Java EE.

For Java EE applications (and by that we mean applications that make use of EJB or have EJB available to use), component distribution is best achieved by using built-in features of the EJB specification. In recent times, EJB has come under a lot of scrutiny in the industry, but the fact remains that it does simplify the creation of distributed applications, making it a useful tool when developing distributed Java EE applications.

For non–Java EE applications (that is, applications without EJB access), the common choice for building distributed applications is Java Remote Method Invocation (RMI), which allows for Java objects running in one JVM to be accessed from another JVM. RMI is quite complex to work with, and part of the allure of EJB is that it hides the underlying details of RMI from the developer.

For both Java EE and non–Java EE applications, the most common kind of distribution is to have one Java component talking to another Java component, but in many cases, the components that make up a distributed system are not written in the same language. Using RMI, Java components cannot interoperate with components written in other languages using Common Object Request Broker Architecture (CORBA). More recently, Java has gained support for web services, allowing you to build applications in Java that interoperate with arbitrary services using XML as a means of communication.

The two main problems faced when creating distributed applications in Java are the complexity and sheer amount of code required to create distributed components. EJB goes some way toward solving these problems by hiding some of the details of RMI and, as of Java EE 1.4, web services from your applications. However, for non–Java EE applications, in which EJB is not available, the EJB fix doesn't help, and in Java EE applications, we are seeing a shift away from EJB toward lightweight frameworks such as Spring, which also limits the effectiveness of the EJB solution.

Thankfully, Spring provides a comprehensive set of features known as Spring Remoting that ease the creation of distributed applications. For non–Java EE applications, you can use Spring Remoting to radically simplify the creation of remote services and to reduce the amount of code needed to access these services. For Java EE applications, Spring Remoting provides a viable alternative to EJB for building many distributed applications which, when coupled with other features in Spring, may remove the need for EJB altogether, allowing much more flexibility in how you choose to deploy your Java EE application.

Note Although Spring's RMI support provides a viable alternative to EJB in many cases, there is no out-of-the-box support for standard role-based authentication or for the propagation of remote transactions. You can add this support yourself, although explaining how is outside the scope of this chapter. If you require either of these two features, we recommend that you use EJB for creating your remote components.

Spring provides support for five distinct types of remoting architectures covering both homogeneous (Java-to-Java) and heterogeneous (Java-to-other) communication. These architectures are detailed in Table 15-1.

Table 15-1. *Remoting Support in Spring*

Architecture	Description
RMI	RMI is a standard part of J2SE, allowing for the creation of distributed applications. Using Spring's RMI support, you can reduce the amount of code needed to expose and access RMI services and have Spring handle most of the plumbing associated with RMI, such as the handling of `RemoteException` instances. Spring also provides integration support for RMI and JNDI, which is most useful when exposing and accessing CORBA services.
JAX-RPC	The Java API for XML-based Remote Procedure Calls (JAX-RPC) provides a standard Java API for accessing and exposing RPC-style SOAP web services. Spring provides support classes to ease the creation of JAX-RPC client applications and the creation of servlet-based service endpoints. Like many of the Java XML APIs, JAX-RPC comes in many different flavors, the most popular of which is Apache Axis, a fully JAX-RPC–compliant SOAP stack available from `http://ws.apache.org/axis`. We use Axis for the JAX-RPC examples in this chapter.
JAX-WS	JAX-WS 2.0 is the successor of the JAX-RPC 1.1. It provides an API for exposing and accessing SOAP 1.2 web services. Like JAX-RPC, Spring provides convenient classes for easily exposing JAX-WS services, as well as creating client applications. We will use XFire for JAX-WS examples in this chapter. XFire is Java framework for exposing JAX-WS web services, and it is available from `http://xfire.codehaus.org`.
HTTP Invoker	HTTP Invoker architecture is a Spring-native remoting architecture that uses standard Java serialization and HTTP to provide a simple solution for building remote components. The HTTP Invoker relies on a servlet container at the server side to host remote services. A benefit of this is that you can secure your remote services using HTTP authentication methods.
Hessian	Hessian is a binary protocol created by Caucho (`www.caucho.com`) to simplify the creation of web services. Hessian is not linked to any particular transport, although in general it is used with HTTP. Spring provides support classes to ease the creation of Hessian services, using HTTP as the transport, and provides proxy support, allowing for Hessian services to be accessed transparently.
Burlap	Burlap is an XML-based protocol also created by Caucho and is a complement to the Hessian protocol. Aside from the details of the protocol, Burlap is used in an identical manner to Hessian. Burlap support in Spring is a mirror of the support offered for Hessian; indeed, the Burlap classes are designed to be drop-in replacements for Hessian's, should you need to swap protocols.

In this chapter, we are going to discuss four of these remoting architectures in turn, looking at how you can use Spring's support classes to create, expose, and access remote services using each different architecture. Although Spring provides full support for Hessian and Burlap remoting architectures, we won't cover these two protocols in the book, mainly because they are not commonly used in Java Enterprise applications. HTTP Invoker provides the same functionality as Hessian and Burlap, with much better support for Java object serialization, making it a better choice.

In this chapter, we assume that you have a basic understanding of both RMI options: JAX-RPC and JAX-WS. If you are not familiar with the basics of either of these, we suggest that you read the RMI tutorial at `http://java.sun.com/docs/books/tutorial/rmi/` and the Java web services tutorials at `http://java.sun.com/webservices/docs/1.6/tutorial/doc/index.html` and `https://java.sun.com/webservices/docs/2.0/tutorial/doc/JAXWS.html`.

Spring Remoting Architecture

Central to the Spring Remoting architecture are the concepts of a service exporter and a proxy generator. One of the first tasks that you need to perform when building a distributed application is to expose your remote services so that clients can access them. Spring simplifies this by providing a set of service exporters that allow you to configure and expose services declaratively, dramatically reducing the amount of code you need to write in order to expose remote services.

Once a remote service is exposed, the next step is to create a client that will access the service. This is often one of the most complex areas of building a distributed application, since you need to be intimately aware of the plumbing of your remote architecture of choice. With Spring, you can use a proxy generator to create a proxy to the remote resource, which allows you to access the remote service via a simple Java interface. Using this approach not only reduces the complexity of client code, since Spring is dealing with the plumbing, but it also decouples your application from your chosen remote architecture, since Spring hides all the implementation-level details.

Both of these components are available for four of the five remoting architectures supported by Spring. Neither JAX-RPC nor JAX-WS has a service exporter, since the method for service exposure is dependent on the JAX-RPC/JAX-WS implementation you are using. However, Spring does provide the `ServletEndpointSupport` class to simplify the creation of JAX-RPC service endpoints that are exposed via a servlet.

Remote Method Invocation

RMI has been part of Java since version 1.1 and is central to many of the platform's remoting solutions. CORBA support in Java is provided using RMI, and EJB uses RMI as the underlying mechanism for bean communication. Also, as you will see later in the "Web Services with JAX-RPC" section, JAX-RPC builds on RMI concepts to expose Java objects as web services.

■ **Note** CORBA support in Java can be provided using Interface Definition Language (IDL) instead of RMI. IDL is a declarative language that enables the creation of objects that interact with one another—although they may be written in different programming languages. However, RMI is used much more frequently with Java nowadays, mostly because of its better security and garbage collection capabilities.

In this section, we are going to look at four distinct examples. First, you will see how to expose an arbitrary Java object as an RMI service, and next, you will see how to access this service via a proxy. The third topic we will look at is how to expose an RMI service to CORBA using Spring, and last, you will see how to access this service using a Spring-created proxy.

Exposing Arbitrary Services

To build an RMI service, you would traditionally start by defining an interface for your service that extended the `java.rmi.Remote` interface. Your RMI service would then implement this interface and most likely extend the `java.rmi.server.UnicastRemoteObject` class. The main drawback with this approach is that your remote service is coupled to the RMI framework, reducing the chances for component reuse and making it difficult to change the remoting architecture used by your application.

Spring Remoting allows you to overcome this problem using the `RmiServiceExporter` class. Using `RmiServiceExporter`, you can expose any arbitrary Java object as an RMI service using any Java interface. Your interface is not required to extend `Remote`, nor is your service class required to extend `UnicastRemoteObject`. In addition to this, `RmiServiceExporter` allows your remote service to be configured and exposed declaratively, reducing the need to create executable code just to expose remote services. Another benefit of using Spring to expose RMI services is that you can avoid the need to create stubs for your service, since stub creation is handled automatically by Spring.

The main benefit of Spring's approach to RMI service exposure is that it allows you to expose existing service objects in your application as remote services with no modifications. Provided that your service classes implement an interface, which is good design anyway, you can easily expose your application services remotely with minimal effort.

In Listing 15-1, you can see the `HelloWorld` interface that will act as the interface for our remote service.

Listing 15-1. *The HelloWorld Interface*

```
package com.apress.prospring2.ch15.remoting;

public interface HelloWorld {

    public String getMessage();
}
```

Notice that this interface does not extend the `Remote` interface and the `getMessage()` method is not declared to throw `RemoteException` as required by the RMI specification—in fact, this interface provides no indication that it will be exposed remotely at all. Likewise, the implementation of the `HelloWorld` interface shown in Listing 15-2 is equally RMI-independent.

Listing 15-2. *The SimpleHelloWorld Class*

```
package com.apress.prospring2.ch15.remoting;

public class SimpleHelloWorld implements HelloWorld {

    public String getMessage() {
        return "Hello World";
    }
}
```

As with the `HelloWorld` interface, the `SimpleHelloWorld` class is free from any RMI-specific details; indeed, we could have created the `SimpleHelloWorld` class before exposing it as an RMI service was even considered. To expose the `SimpleHelloWorld` class as an RMI service via the `HelloWorld` interface, you simply configure an instance of `RmiServiceExporter` in your `ApplicationContext` with the appropriate details, as shown in Listing 15-3.

Listing 15-3. *Exposing RMI Services with RmiServiceExporter*

```
<?xml version="1.0" encoding="UTF-8"?>
<beans xmlns="http://www.springframework.org/schema/beans"
       ...>

    <bean id="helloWorldService"
                class="com.apress.prospring2.ch15.remoting.SimpleHelloWorld"/>

    <bean id="serviceExporter"
                class="org.springframework.remoting.rmi.RmiServiceExporter">
        <property name="serviceName" value="HelloWorld" />

        <property name="service" ref="helloWorldService" />

        <property name="serviceInterface"
                value="com.apress.prospring2.ch15.remoting.HelloWorld" />

        <property name="registryPort" value="9000" />

        <property name="servicePort" value="9001" />

    </bean>

</beans>
```

Here, we have declared two beans: the helloWorldService bean, which is the bean to be exposed, and the serviceExporter bean, which will expose the helloWorldService bean as an RMI service. In the serviceExporter bean, we have set the serviceName property to "HelloWorld". The RmiServiceExporter class requires this property and uses it as the service name when registering the service with the RMI registry. The service property is used to pass the RmiServiceExporter and the bean instance that should be exported, and the serviceInterface property defines the interface that should be used as the remote interface. Only methods on the service interface can be invoked remotely—if you have a method on your service object but not on the service interface, it can't be invoked remotely. The registryPort property allows you to specify the port of the RMI registry, and the servicePort property allows you to specify which port the service will use for communication. By default, servicePort is set to 0, meaning an anonymous port number will be used.

With the configuration of the RmiServiceExporter complete, all you need to do in your server application is load the ApplicationContext; Spring will invoke the RmiServiceExporter automatically and expose the service. Internally, the RmiServiceExporter class uses the InitializingBean interface to perform the actual service exposure process. This means that if you want service exposure to happen automatically, you must use an ApplicationContext, not a BeanFactory, since a BeanFactory does not automatically instantiate singletons.

Listing 15-4 shows a simple class that loads the configuration from Listing 15-3 and then simply waits for connections to the service.

Listing 15-4. *Hosting the HelloWorld Service*

```
package com.apress.prospring2.ch15.remoting.rmi;

public class HelloWorldHost {

    public static void main(String[] args) throws Exception {
        ApplicationContext ctx = new ClassPathXmlApplicationContext(
            "classpath*:/com/apress/prospring2/ch15/remoting/rmi/helloWorld.xml");
        System.out.println("Host Started...");
    }
}
```

If you run this example, you will notice that it does not exit immediately, because the remote service is running in the background waiting for connections from clients.

As you can see from the examples in this section, you can expose any of your service objects as a remote service quickly and easily using the `RmiServiceExporter` class, all without modifications to the service object or to the service interface. In the next section, you will see how to access this remote service transparently using a Spring-generated proxy.

Accessing an RMI Service Using Proxies

One of the most complex parts of building RMI-based applications is creating the client application. With the traditional approach to creating RMI clients, your client application becomes coupled to RMI, making it difficult to change to any new remoting architecture, and you are forced to deal with all the messy internals of RMI such as `RemoteExceptions` and service lookup.

Thankfully, Spring provides a much simpler mechanism for interacting with an RMI service—a proxy generator that removes the need to create plumbing code and eliminates the coupling of your application to Spring. Using the proxy generator, you can have Spring generate a proxy to the remote service that implements the service interface, allowing you to interact with the remote service via the service interface as though it were a local component. Spring hides all the RMI details, such as service lookup and exception handling, allowing you to code to the business interface rather than to a particular implementation.

The RMI proxy generator, as with all proxy generators, implements the `FactoryBean` interface, allowing the proxy to be created and configured declaratively and then injected into a component as a dependency. Listing 15-5 shows a class that defines such a dependency:

Listing 15-5. *The HelloWorldClient Class*

```
package com.apress.prospring2.ch15.remoting.rmi;

public class HelloWorldClient {

    private HelloWorld helloWorldService;

    public static void main(String[] args) throws Exception {
        ApplicationContext ctx = new ClassPathXmlApplicationContext(
                "classpath*:/com/apress/prospring2/ch15/ ➥
remoting/rmi/helloWorldClient.xml");

        HelloWorldClient helloWorldClient = (HelloWorldClient) ctx
                .getBean("helloWorldClient");
        helloWorldClient.run();

    }
```

```
    public void run() {
        System.out.println(helloWorldService.getMessage());
    }

    public void setHelloWorldService(HelloWorld helloWorldService) {
        this.helloWorldService = helloWorldService;
    }
}
```

Here, you can see that the `HelloWorldClient` class defines the `helloWorldService` property that expects an instance of `HelloWorld` to be provided. By using the RMI proxy generator, we can create a proxy to the `SimpleHelloWorld` service exposed in the previous example that implements the `HelloWorld` interface and inject it into an instance of the `HelloWorldClient` class. Listing 15-6 shows the appropriate configuration for this.

Listing 15-6. *Configuring an RMI Proxy*

```
<?xml version="1.0" encoding="UTF-8"?>
<beans xmlns="http://www.springframework.org/schema/beans"
       ...>

    <bean id="helloWorldService"
                class="org.springframework.remoting.rmi.RmiProxyFactoryBean">
        <property name="serviceUrl" value="rmi://localhost:9000/HelloWorld" />

        <property name="serviceInterface"
               value="com.apress.prospring2.ch15.remoting.HelloWorld"/>

    </bean>

    <bean id="helloWorldClient"
             class="com.apress.prospring2.ch15.remoting.rmi.HelloWorldClient">
        <property name="helloWorldService" ref="helloWorldService" />

    </bean>
</beans>
```

The important piece of code here is the `helloWorldService` declaration. Notice that two properties are required: `serviceUrl` and `serviceInterface`. The `serviceInterface` property tells the proxy generator which interface the generated proxy should implement, and the `serviceUrl` points the proxy at the correct RMI service, in this case the `HelloWorld` service running in the registry at port 9000 on the localhost.

Since the `RmiProxyFactoryBean` class implements the `FactoryBean` interface, it can be treated as though it were an instance of the service interface, since this is the type that the `FactoryBean` is defined to return. Therefore, you can use the `helloWorldService` bean to satisfy the `helloWorldService` dependency of the `helloWorldClient` bean.

To test this example, make sure the host class from Listing 15-4 is running and run the `HelloWorldClient` class. After a short delay, you will see the message "Hello World" displayed in the `HelloWorldClient` console. Note that you can run the `HelloWorldClient` class as many times as you wish, provided the `HelloWorldHost` class is still running.

As is evident from this example, using proxies is a simple yet powerful way to access remote services. By using a proxy, you free yourself from the burden of handling all the plumbing involved with your remoting architecture of choice, thereby decreasing the chance of bugs creeping into your application and increasing the speed at which you can create applications. Another key benefit of using proxies is that doing so reduces the coupling between your application and your remoting architecture, making it easier for you to replace remote components with local ones or to change the remoting architecture for another one.

Exposing CORBA Services

One excellent feature offered by RMI is that it allows you to expose services using Internet Inter-Orb Protocol (IIOP) so that they can be accessed by CORBA components written in other languages. CORBA is a popular solution for remote interoperation between components written in different languages and enjoys extensive support in many programming languages.

Exposing a Java service via RMI using the IIOP protocol rather than the default Java Remote Method Protocol (JRMP) is simply a matter of generating the correct stubs and then exposing the service via a CORBA Object Request Broker (ORB). As you saw in the earlier examples, when exposing a service using JRMP, Spring removes the need for your components to be coupled to the RMI infrastructure and also removes the need to create stubs. When exposing CORBA services, Spring is not quite as helpful, although it does take care of registering your service with the ORB.

In fact, Spring doesn't really supply classes to simplify CORBA service exposure and utilization; instead, it provides features to expose and look up remote services using JNDI. However, a feature to use JNDI for service lookup is most useful when dealing with CORBA components, since your application can interact with the ORB via JNDI.

In this section, you will see how to build an RMI service, generate the appropriate IIOP stubs, and expose the IIOP service to the ORB using Spring. In order to run the example in this section, you need to obtain a JNDI provider for the CORBA Common Object Services (COS) name server. You can obtain the Sun implementation from the JNDI home page at `http://java.sun.com/products/jndi/`. This provider allows for the COS naming service to be accessed using the JNDI API, thus allowing Spring to interact with it as well.

The first step you need to take when building an RMI service is to create the remote service interface. Your remote service interface must extend the `java.rmi.Remote` interface, and all methods in the interface must throw `RemoteException`. Listing 15-7 shows the remote service interface for this example.

Listing 15-7. *The RemoteHelloWorld Interface*

```
package com.apress.prospring2.ch15.remoting.rmi;

public interface RemoteHelloWorld extends Remote {

    String getMessage() throws RemoteException;

}
```

You will notice that this interface is very similar to the `HelloWorld` interface shown in Listing 15-1, except that it now meets the contract required by the RMI specification. Next, you need to create an implementation of your remote interface. Listing 15-8 shows a trivial implementation of the `RemoteHelloWorld` interface.

Listing 15-8. *The SimpleRemoteHelloWorld Class*

```
package com.apress.prospring2.ch15.remoting.rmi;

public class SimpleRemoteHelloWorld implements RemoteHelloWorld {

    public String getMessage() throws RemoteException {
        return "Hello World";
```

```
    }
}
```

As with the RemoteHelloWorld interface, this class is not much different from its corresponding nonremote implementation shown in Listing 15-2. At this point, you should compile both the RemoteHelloWorld interface and the SimpleRemoteHelloWorld class so that they are available to create the IIOP stub.

Note If you are unfamiliar with the concepts of stubs or ties, we recommend that you read *Java RMI* by William Grosso (O'Reilly, 2001) for a comprehensive discussion of all things RMI.

Generating IIOP Stubs and Ties

To generate a remote stub for an RMI service, you use the rmic tool that is included with your JDK. The rmic tool takes the remote service class and from this generates the appropriate stubs. By default, rmic generates stubs for JRMP, but by specifying the -iiop switch, you can tell it to generate IIOP stubs and ties instead. To generate stubs for the SimpleRemoteHelloWorld class, you must run the following command:

```
rmic -classpath bin -d bin -iiop ➥
com.apress.prospring2.ch15.remoting.rmi.SimpleRemoteHelloWorld
```

The -classpath switch specifies the location of any classes needed by rmic. The rmic tool needs to be able to access both the class and the interface for your remote service, so you should ensure that they are both on the classpath specified by the -classpath switch. The -d switch specifies the root folder where the generated classes should be written. The final argument is the fully qualified class name of the service class for which you are generating stubs. Running this command generates the _SimpleRemoteHelloWorld_Tie and _RemoteHelloWorld_stub class files in the same directory as the SimpleRemoteHelloWorld class.

Exposing the Service to CORBA Using Spring and JNDI

With the stubs generated, the next step is to configure an instance of JndiRmiServiceExporter in your ApplicationContext to export the remote service to a JNDI location. In this case, we are going to use the COS provider for JNDI to register the service with the CORBA ORB. Listing 15-9 shows the configuration file.

Listing 15-9. *Exposing an RMI Service to CORBA Using JNDI*

```
<?xml version="1.0" encoding="UTF-8"?>
<beans xmlns="http://www.springframework.org/schema/beans"
       ...>

    <bean id="helloWorldService"
                class="com.apress.prospring2.ch15. ➥
remoting.rmi.SimpleRemoteHelloWorld"/>
    <bean class="org.springframework.remoting.rmi.JndiRmiServiceExporter">
        <property name="jndiName" value="HelloWorld"/>
        <property name="serviceInterface" ➥
value="com.apress.prospring2.ch15.remoting.rmi.RemoteHelloWorld"/>

        <property name="service" ref="helloWorldService" />
```

```
        <property name="jndiEnvironment">
            <value>
                java.naming.factory.initial=com.sun.jndi.cosnaming.CNCtxFactory
                java.naming.provider.url=iiop://localhost:1050
            </value>
        </property>
    </bean>
</beans>
```

In this configuration, we have declared two beans, `helloWorldService` and `serviceExporter`. The `helloWorldService` bean is simply an instance of the `SimpleRemoteHelloWorld` class to be managed by Spring. The important part of this code is the `serviceExporter` bean. For the `serviceExporter` bean, we have specified three properties: `jndiName`, which is the name used to register the remote service with the ORB; `service`, which is the actual service object and must be of type `Remote`; and `jndiEnvironment`.

The `jndiEnvironment` property allows you to configure the `InitialContext` that is used internally to perform JNDI operations. Here, we are specifying that the `CNCtxFactory` class should be used to create the actual `InitialContext` implementation. `CNCtxFactory` is part of the COS JNDI provider and performs lookup and registration operations against the CORBA ORB specified using the `java.naming.provider.url` property. We are saying that operations should be executed against the ORB running on port 1050 of the local machine. Do not worry about this yet—we will discuss the ORB later in this section.

Creating a Host Application

With the configuration of the service exporter complete, all that remains from a code perspective is to create the host application that loads the `ApplicationContext`. Listing 15-10 shows the `HelloWorldJndiHost` class that loads the `ApplicationContext` and waits for user connections to the service:

Listing 15-10. *The HelloWorldJndiHost Class*

```
package com.apress.prospring2.ch15.remoting.rmi;

public class HelloWorldJndiHost {

    public static void main(String[] args) throws Exception {
        ApplicationContext ctx = new ClassPathXmlApplicationContext(
                "classpath*:/com/apress/prospring2/ch15/ ➥
remoting/rmi/helloWorldJndi.xml");
        System.out.println("Host Started...");
    }
}
```

Here, the `main()` method simply loads the `ApplicationContext` using the configuration shown in Listing 15-9 and prints a message to the console to notify the user that the host has started. As with the host class shown in Listing 15-4, this class will not exit automatically when run, since it is kept alive by the RMI framework that is exposing the remote service to CORBA.

Starting the Object Request Broker

If you try to run the host application at this point, it will return an error, informing you that it is unable to connect to the ORB. The JDK comes complete with an ORB that you can use when developing CORBA applications using Java. You can start the ORB using the `orbd` application found in the bin directory of your JDK. To start the ORB using port 1050 as required by the host application in Listing 15-10, run the following command:

```
orbd -port 1050 -ORBInitialPort 1050  -ORBInitialHost localhost
```

Once the ORB is started, you will be able to start up the host and host your CORBA component.

Accessing a CORBA Service

Just as Spring provides proxy support for JRMP RMI services, it can also generate a proxy for any remote service that can be accessed via JNDI. Using this feature, you can also create a proxy to a remote IIOP service that is hosted in an ORB. In this section, you will see how to use the JndiRmiProxyFactoryBean to generate a proxy to an RMI/IIOP service exposed via an ORB.

In order to create a proxy from a JNDI-accessible RMI resource, you must configure an instance of JndiRmiProxyFactoryBean with the appropriate JNDI access information and the name of the interface you want the proxy to implement. Listing 15-11 shows a configuration that generates a proxy for the SimpleRemoteHelloWorld service we created in the last section.

Listing 15-11. *Configuring a JNDI RMI Proxy*

```
<?xml version="1.0" encoding="UTF-8"?>
<beans xmlns="http://www.springframework.org/schema/beans"
       ...>

    <bean id="helloWorldService"
              class="org.springframework.remoting.rmi.JndiRmiProxyFactoryBean">
        <property name="jndiName" value="HelloWorld" />

        <property name="serviceInterface"
                  value="com.apress.prospring2.ch15.remoting.HelloWorld" />

        <property name="jndiEnvironment">
            <value>
                java.naming.factory.initial=com.sun.jndi.cosnaming.CNCtxFactory
                java.naming.provider.url=iiop://localhost:1050
            </value>
        </property>
    </bean>
</beans>
```

Here, you can see that we have configured the JndiRmiProxyFactoryBean class with the same JNDI information used to configure the JndiRmiServiceExporter in Listing 15-9, since that is the service we want to access. An interesting point of note here is that we have used the HelloWorld interface from Listing 15-1 as the service interface, not the RemoteHelloWorld interface from Listing 15-7. One of the major benefits of the Spring-generated proxies is that you can use any interface you want for the proxy, as long as the names, return types, and parameter lists of the methods match those exposed by the remote service. In this case, we use the HelloWorld interface, which exposes a getMessage() method, which is identical to the RemoteHelloWorld.getMessage() method but doesn't throw RemoteException. The Spring-generated proxy will take care of handling any RemoteException on your behalf, leaving your client code free to code to the business interface rather the remote interface.

Using the proxy is as simple as loading the ApplicationContext and obtaining the corresponding bean in your application, as shown in Listing 15-12:

Listing 15-12. *The HelloWorldJndiClient Class*

```
package com.apress.prospring2.ch15.remoting.rmi;

public class HelloWorldJndiClient {

    public static void main(String[] args) throws Exception {
        ApplicationContext ctx = new ClassPathXmlApplicationContext(
                "classpath*:/com/apress/prospring2/ch15/ ➥
remoting/rmi/helloWorldJndiClient.xml");

        HelloWorld helloWorld = (HelloWorld) ctx.getBean("helloWorldService");
        System.out.println(helloWorld.getMessage());

    }
}
```

Running this example with the `HelloWorldJndiHost` class also running will result in the following output:

```
Hello World
```

From this example and the earlier example showing the creation of a proxy to an RMI/JRMP service, you can plainly see that Spring proxies greatly reduce the amount of code you need to write to access remote RMI services. One of the biggest benefits of Spring RMI proxies is that you can hide the fact that the service is remote, allowing your application to work directly with a business interface and relying on Spring to take care of all the RMI plumbing.

Web Services with JAX-RPC

Just as RMI provides a standard API for creating remote services that are exposed using binary protocols, JAX-RPC provides a standard API for creating remote services that are exposed using RPC-style SOAP messages. JAX-RPC is used to create SOAP-based services, called endpoints in web service lingo, and clients in an implementation-agnostic way. On the server side, JAX-RPC itself is a simple API that borrows much from RMI. The complexity lies in the definition of service endpoints, which is often an implementation-specific issue, and the code on the client side, which is convoluted and problematic.

Unfortunately, Spring can't help much with service endpoint issues, as so much depends on which JAX-RPC implementation you are using. However, Spring does provide the `ServletEndpointSupport` class, which makes it simple for endpoints that sit behind a servlet to access a Spring `ApplicationContext`. On the client side, Spring provides the `JaxRpcPortProxyFactoryBean` class, which allows you to create a proxy to a SOAP web service, reducing the complexity inherent in creating a JAX-RPC client and shielding your client application from any JAX-RPC–specific details.

In this section, you are going to see how to create a simple web service that uses the `ServletEndpointSupport` class to load dependencies from a Spring `ApplicationContext`, and we will introduce a useful pattern for building service endpoints when using Spring. You will also see how to use the `JaxRpcPortProxyFactoryBean` to create a proxy for accessing your service. Finally, we give Axis-specific details for handling complex Java objects in your services.

Introducing Apache Axis

For the examples in this section, we are going to use the Apache Axis SOAP stack, which provides a fully compliant JAX-RPC implementation. Axis provides support for SOAP over a variety of different transports such as HTTP, JMS, and SMTP. In this section, we will be using the HTTP transport, which is implemented as a servlet that dispatches requests to your service automatically. HTTP is the traditional transport for SOAP, and Spring provides additional support for service endpoints that sit behind a servlet.

In this section, we assume a basic knowledge of the Axis framework and JAX-RPC. If you are unfamiliar with JAX-RPC, you should visit the tutorial mentioned at the beginning of this chapter. For a quick introduction to Axis, check out the user guide at `http://ws.apache.org/axis/java/user-guide.html`, which provides a rundown of the features of Axis and how they work.

If you downloaded the full distribution of Spring including all the dependencies, you will already have Axis and its dependencies. Otherwise, you can download Axis from `http://ws.apache.org/axis`. For the examples in this section, we used version 1.4 of Axis.

Creating a Web Service with ServletEndpointSupport

In this section, you will see how to build a basic web service that is analogous to the "Hello, World" RMI services you saw earlier. Creating JAX-RPC services is where most of the implementation-specific details come into play. From a Java code perspective, everything is standard, but on the deployment front, everything is implementation specific. If you want to build a web service using a JAX-RPC implementation other than Axis, you will need to modify the deployment details as appropriate for your implementation of choice.

A basic Axis web service has four parts: the Axis servlet, the Axis deployment descriptor, the remote interface, and the service implementation. The Axis servlet sits between your services and the SOAP clients and is responsible for creating the Web Services Description Language (WSDL) description of your service so that a SOAP client can access your service, for translating SOAP requests into Java method calls, and for translating method return values into SOAP responses. The Axis servlet hides most of the plumbing code related to building a web service; indeed, you will rarely, if ever, have to create code to handle SOAP messages manually, since that is all handled by the Axis servlet.

The Axis deployment descriptor is an XML document that provides information to the Axis servlet about the services you wish to expose and how they should be exposed. Axis uses the information contained in the deployment descriptor to determine which classes in your web application should be exposed via SOAP and to obtain additional service information that cannot be obtained from the remote interface or the service implementation.

The remote interface is identical to the remote interface used for an RMI service. It must extend the `java.rmi.Remote` interface, and we have to declare all methods to throw `RemoteException`. This similarity with RMI makes it simple to reuse remote interfaces across RMI services and web services; indeed, in this example we will reuse the `RemoteHelloWorld` interface from Listing 15-7 for our web service.

The service implementation is simply an implementation of the remote interface similar to the `SimpleRemoteHelloWorld` implementation you saw in Listing 15-8. Indeed, we could have reused this implementation to create our services; however, unlike the RMI service, your application is not responsible for creating instances of the service class; that is the job of Axis, which makes it impossible to use Spring dependency injection. As a workaround to this, Spring provides the `ServletEndpointSupport` base class that can be used to automatically obtain a Spring `ApplicationContext` that is configured as part of your web application. This functionality sits on top of the special support for `ApplicationContext` loading in web applications that is provided by Spring. `ServletEndpointSupport` is covered in more detail in Chapter 17, but for now, just know that Spring provides a mechanism for loading an ApplicationContext once in a web application and making it available through the ServletContext class.

Creating the Remote Interface

The first step when building a JAX-RPC web service is to create the remote interface. As we mentioned in the previous section, JAX-RPC remote interfaces are exactly the same as RMI remote interfaces. For this example, we are going to reuse the RemoteHelloWorld interface shown in Listing 15-7.

Implementing the Web Service

After you have created the remote interface for your web service, the next step is to create your service implementation class. As we mentioned previously, creating a basic service class is just like creating a service class for an RMI service: you simply implement the remote interface. Indeed, we could have chosen to reuse the SimpleRemoteHelloWorld class from Listing 15-8. However, this approach has a drawback—you cannot use dependency injection. A much better solution is to make your service class a simple wrapper around a POJO service object that is loaded from a Spring ApplicationContext and thus can be configured using DI. Spring makes this simple by providing the ServletEndpointSupport class, which allows you to access the ApplicationContext that is loaded for a web application. In Listing 15-13, you can see the JaxRpcHelloWorld class, which shows an example of this approach.

Listing 15-13. *Creating a JAX-RPC Service Wrapper*

```
package com.apress.prospring2.ch15.remoting.jaxrpc;

public class JaxRpcHelloWorld extends ServletEndpointSupport implements
        RemoteHelloWorld {

    private HelloWorld helloWorld;

    protected void onInit() throws ServiceException {
        helloWorld = (HelloWorld) getApplicationContext().getBean(
                "helloWorldService");
    }

    public String getMessage() throws RemoteException {
        return helloWorld.getMessage();
    }

}
```

There are two important parts to this class: the getMessage()and onInit() methods. In getMessage(), you can see that the actual processing is delegated to an instance of the HelloWorld interface shown in Listing 15-1. The HelloWorld interface and the RemoteHelloWorld interface share methods with the same signature, but HelloWorld does not extend Remote and its methods do not throw RemoteException. Implementations of the HelloWorld interface can easily be tested away from the servlet container and can easily be reused in many environments, since they are not coupled to the Java remote interfaces. We could have made the JaxRpcHelloWorld class delegate to another RemoteHelloWorld, but the reusability of implementations of RemoteHelloWorld is impaired by the fact that all methods throw the checked RemoteException. By using the HelloWorld interface, we can use implementations that can be used easily in other environments.

In the onInit() method, you can see that an actual implementation of HelloWorld is loaded from a Spring ApplicationContext. The ServletEndpointSupport class provides the getApplicationContext() method, which allows you to access the ApplicationContext that is configured for the web application containing the service class. The actual mechanism for configuring this ApplicationContext is discussed later in the "Creating the Web Application Deployment Descriptor" section, but in Listing 15-14, you can see the contents of the ApplicationContext configuration file.

Listing 15-14. *ApplicationContext Configuration for JaxRpcHelloWorld*

```
<?xml version="1.0" encoding="UTF-8"?>
<beans xmlns="http://www.springframework.org/schema/beans"
       ...>

    <bean id="helloWorldService"
              class="com.apress.prospring2.ch15.remoting.SimpleHelloWorld"/>
</beans>
```

As you can see, the helloWorldService bean is defined as an instance of the SimpleHelloWorld class shown in Listing 15-2. This class implements the HelloWorld interface but has nothing to do with the RemoteHelloWorld interface implemented by the JaxRpcHelloWorld service class.

Behind the scenes, the ServletEndpointSupport class implements the javax.xml.rpc.server.ServiceLifecycle interface, which allows the service to receive notifications from Axis at certain points throughout its life cycle. Through this interface, the ServletEndpoint class is able to access the ServletContext of the currently running web application, and from there, it can access the ApplicationContext that is configured for the web application.

Creating the Axis Deployment Descriptor

Once you have created the service implementation class, you are ready to create the Axis deployment descriptor for your web service. The Axis deployment descriptor is an XML file that should be named server-config.wsdd and should be placed in the WEB-INF directory of your web application. Listing 15-15 shows the server-config.wsdd file for the JaxRpcHelloWorld service.

Listing 15-15. *Axis Deployment Descriptor for JaxRpcHelloWorld*

```
<deployment xmlns="http://xml.apache.org/axis/wsdd/" ➥
xmlns:java="http://xml.apache.org/axis/wsdd/providers/java">
    <handler name="URLMapper" type="java:org.apache.axis.handlers.http.URLMapper"/>
    <service name="HelloWorld" provider="java:RPC">
        <parameter name="className"
              value="com.apress.prospring2.ch15.remoting.jaxrpc.JaxRpcHelloWorld"/>
        <parameter name="allowedMethods" value="*"/>
    </service>
    <transport name="http">
        <requestFlow>
            <handler type="URLMapper"/>
        </requestFlow>
    </transport>
</deployment>
```

There are three important parts to this deployment descriptor: the <handler> tag, the <service> tag, and the <transport> tag. The <handler> tag allows you to configure a Handler, which can be integrated into the control flow for a SOAP request/response sequence. The URLMapper Handler is required as part of the request flow of the HTTP transport, which is configured using the <transport> tag. The URLMapper is used by Axis to map the URIs of incoming requests to service names, which is the desirable approach when using HTTP as the transport. For instance, if the Axis servlet is mapped to handle requests on http://localhost:8080/app/services and you have a service called FooService, the URL for your service will be http://localhost:8080/app/services/FooService. Without this

Handler, your service will not be accessible, and Axis will not be able to generate the WSDL for it since it won't be able to locate the service for the given URI. You can find more details on the <handler> and <transport> tags on the Axis web site.

The most important tag is the <service> tag, which is used to configure the actual service. The <service> tag itself has two attributes: name and provider. The name attribute can take any value, but each service must have a valid name. Bear in mind that this name will form part of the URL for your web service, so it should be concise, and you should avoid special characters that would over-complicate the URL. The provider attribute specifies what kind of web service you are creating. In this case, we specify java:RPC, indicating that this is an RPC-style service. Inside of the <service> tag are two <parameter> tags: one that specifies the fully qualified name of the service implementation class and one that defines a filter for which methods of the service are exposed in the service.

Axis supports many more configuration parameters than those shown in this example, but they are outside the scope of this chapter. For more details, you should read the Axis reference guide at http://ws.apache.org/axis/java/reference.html.

Creating the Web Application Deployment Descriptor

Once you have created the Axis deployment descriptor, all that remains is to create the web application deployment descriptor, package the web application for deployment, and deploy the application in your servlet container of choice.

In the deployment descriptor for a web service built using ServletEndpointSupport, you need to configure not only the Axis servlet but also the Spring ContextLoaderServlet (or ContextLoaderListener for 2.4 servlet containers) to load the ApplicationContext for your web service. Listing 15-16 shows an example of this configuration for the JaxRpcHelloWorld service.

Listing 15-16. *Configuring the Axis Servlet and Spring ContextLoaderServlet*

```
<?xml version="1.0" encoding="UTF-8"?>
<web-app version="2.4"
         xmlns="http://java.sun.com/xml/ns/j2ee"
         xmlns:xsi="http://www.w3.org/2001/XMLSchema-instance"
         xsi:schemaLocation="http://java.sun.com/xml/ns/j2ee ➥
http://java.sun.com/xml/ns/j2ee/web-app_2_4.xsd">
    <context-param>
        <param-name>contextConfigLocation</param-name>
        <param-value>
            classpath*:/com/apress/prospring2/ch15/remoting/remoting-context.xml
        </param-value>

     <servlet>
        <servlet-name>context</servlet-name>
        <servlet-class>
              org.springframework.web.context.ContextLoaderServlet
        </servlet-class>
        <load-on-startup>1</load-on-startup>
    </servlet>

    <servlet>
        <servlet-name>axis</servlet-name>
        <servlet-class>org.apache.axis.transport.http.AxisServlet</servlet-class>
        <load-on-startup>2</load-on-startup>
    </servlet>

    <servlet-mapping>
```

```
        <servlet-name>axis</servlet-name>
        <url-pattern>/services/*</url-pattern>
    </servlet-mapping>
</web-app>
```

Here, you can see a deployment descriptor that configures two servlets: the Spring ContextLoaderServlet and the Axis AxisServlet class. The ContextLoaderServlet loads an ApplicationContext using the path provided in the context parameter contextConfigLocation and then stores it in the ServletContext. Without this servlet declaration, the ServletEndpointSupport class would not be able to locate the ApplicationContext, and thus JaxRpcHelloWorld would not be able to load the helloWorldService bean it requires. You should always ensure that the ContextLoaderServlet is loaded before all other servlets by explicitly setting the <load-on-startup> parameter for each servlet. This avoids problems arising when a servlet attempts to access an ApplicationContext that is not yet loaded.

The configuration of the Axis service is fairly basic, and you should be more than familiar with the code you see. Note that the choice of URL mapping was not arbitrary; Axis generates a web page for your services, which expects them to be mapped under /services/*. Figure 15-1 shows an example of the page generated by Axis for the HelloWorld service configured in Listing 15-16.

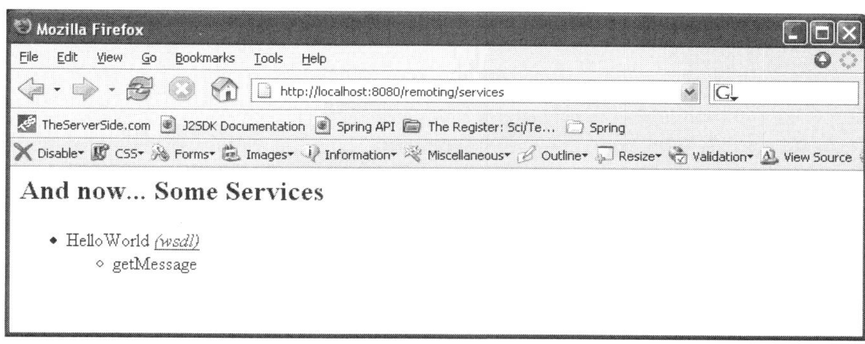

Figure 15-1. *Viewing web services in your web browser*

Clicking the wsdl link next to the listing for the HelloWorld service will bring up the WSDL definition for your service. It is evident from looking at the WSDL that Axis is saving you an awful lot of work by generating the WSDL automatically; you would not want to have to generate WSDL manually for every service created.

Accessing RPC-Style Web Services using Proxies

Traditionally, accessing a web service using JAX-RPC has been quite a complex process that bears little resemblance to working with the service interface of the web service. Although some web service toolkits, Axis included, provide the ability to generate proxies to a web service, these are generally implementation dependent and might not work exactly as you would expect.

Thankfully, Spring provides a JAX-RPC proxy generator, allowing you to access any RPC-style SOAP service using a simple Java interface. In this example, you will see how to configure an instance of JaxRpcPortProxyFactoryBean to create a proxy to the HelloWorld service that you built and deployed in the previous section.

One of the biggest benefits of using a Spring proxy for accessing JAX-RPC services is that you can have the proxy implement a business interface rather than the remote interface of the JAX-RPC service. The remote interface is still required, so that Spring can use it internally, but externally, you can interact with a proxy through the business interface. In this example, you will see how to construct a proxy to the `HelloWorld` service that uses the `HelloWorld` interface shown in Listing 15-1 rather than the `RemoteHelloWorld` interface that is implemented by the `JaxRpcHelloWorld` service class.

Configuring the JaxRpcPortProxyFactoryBean

Creating a JAX-RPC proxy is very similar to creating an RMI proxy—all you need to do is configure an instance of the `JaxRpcPortProxyFactoryBean` in your `ApplicationContext`. You can access this instance in the application using your chosen business interface. Listing 15-17 shows an example configuration that uses `JaxRpcPortProxyFactoryBean` to create a proxy to the `HelloWorld` service.

Listing 15-17. *Configuring a JAX-RPC Proxy*

```
<?xml version="1.0" encoding="UTF-8"?>
<beans xmlns="http://www.springframework.org/schema/beans"
       ...>

    <bean id="helloWorldService" class="org.springframework.remoting. ➥
jaxrpc.JaxRpcPortProxyFactoryBean" >
         <property name="serviceFactoryClass"
                value="org.apache.axis.client.ServiceFactory"/>

         <property name="wsdlDocumentUrl"
               value="http://localhost:8080/remoting/services/HelloWorld?wsdl" />

         <property name="namespaceUri"
                value="http://localhost:8080/remoting/services/HelloWorld" />

         <property name="serviceName" value="JaxRpcHelloWorldService"/>

         <property name="portName" value="HelloWorld" />

         <property name="portInterface"
               value="com.apress.prospring2.ch15.remoting.rmi.RemoteHelloWorld"/>

         <property name="serviceInterface"
                value="com.apress.prospring2.ch15.remoting.HelloWorld" />

    </bean>
</beans>
```

Here, you can see that we have configured an instance of `JaxRpcPortProxyFactoryBean` with values for seven properties. The values for four of these properties—`serviceFactoryClass`, `wsdlDocumentUrl`, `portInterface`, and `serviceInterface`—are simple to obtain. Obtaining values for the rest requires peeking inside the WSDL that is generated for your service.

The `serviceFactoryClass` is used to point Spring at the implementation of the `javax.xml.rpc.ServiceFactory` interface provided by your SOAP stack. In the case of Axis, this class is `org.apache.axis.client.ServiceFactory`.

The `wsdlDocumentUrl`, obviously, specifies the URL of the WSDL document for your service and can be obtained by browsing to your service in a web browser and clicking the wsdl link.

The `serviceInterface` property allows you to specify which interface you want the generated proxy to implement. If this is the remote interface of the JAX-RPC service, you do not need to provide a value for the `portInterface` property; otherwise, `portInterface` must be set to the fully qualified name of the remote interface. As you can see, we have specified that the proxy should implement the HelloWorld interface, which is not a remote interface, so we also specify that the portInterface is RemoteHelloWorld. In general, using a separate service interface for your proxies, rather than the remote interface, is preferable, as doing so removes the need for your application code to deal with RemoteExceptions explicitly.

To obtain values for the namespaceUri, portName, and serviceName properties, you need to look at the WSDL that is generated for your service. The root node of the WSDL document is <wsdl:definitions>, which has an attribute, targetNamespace, the value of which corresponds to the value of the namespaceUri property.

Toward the end of your WSDL document, you will see a snippet of code similar to the one shown in Listing 15-18.

Listing 15-18. *Service Definition in WSDL*

```
<wsdl:service name="JaxRpcHelloWorldService">
    <wsdl:port binding="impl:HelloWorldSoapBinding" name="HelloWorld">
      <wsdlsoap:address ➥
location="http://localhost:8080/remoting/services/HelloWorld"/>
    </wsdl:port>
  </wsdl:service>
```

Here, the value of the name attribute of the <wsdl:service> tag corresponds to the value of the serviceName property, and the value of the name attribute of the <wsdl:port> tag corresponds to the value of the portName property.

These several properties provide the JaxRpcPortProxyFactoryBean class with all the information it needs to generate a proxy that implements the HelloWorld interface but internally uses the RemoteHelloWorld interface. The proxy will be generated using the WSDL document at http://localhost:8080/remoting/services/HelloWorld?wsdl, and it expects that the target namespace of this WSDL document will be http://localhost:8080/remoting/services/HelloWorld.

Using JAX-RPC Proxies

As with the RmiProxyFactoryBean, the JaxRpcPortProxyFactoryBean class implements the FactoryBean interface so that when the class is accessed using ApplicationContext.getBean(), it will in fact return the proxy instead of a reference to itself. Listing 15-19 shows the JaxRpcHelloWorld class, which loads an ApplicationContext using the configuration shown in Listing 15-17, grabs the proxy, and uses it to execute the getMessage() method of the web service.

Listing 15-19. *Using a JAX-RPC Proxy*

```
package com.apress.prospring2.ch15.remoting.jaxrpc;

public class JaxRpcHelloWorld extends ServletEndpointSupport implements
        RemoteHelloWorld {

    private HelloWorld helloWorld;

    protected void onInit() throws ServiceException {
        helloWorld = (HelloWorld) getApplicationContext().getBean(
                "helloWorldService");
    }

    public String getMessage() throws RemoteException {
        return helloWorld.getMessage();
    }

}
```

As you can see from this example, the client is free to interact with the web service using the `HelloWorld` interface, which is much simpler than the `RemoteHelloWorld` interface, as it does not require code to deal with the checked `RemoteExceptions`.

Make sure that you deploy your web service in your servlet container and that the servlet container is running; then run this application. After a short delay, you should see the message "Hello, World" written to the console. As this example shows, building a web service client is extremely simple when using Spring, thanks to the support for proxies. By allowing proxies to implement a business interface that is separate from the remote interface of a service, Spring also makes the code required to interact with the proxy much simpler as well.

Working with JavaBeans in Axis Services

In the previous example, the value returned by the `getMessage()` method of the `HelloWorld` service was a simple `String`, which is mapped directly to the `xsd:string` type in SOAP. This mapping is handled automatically by Axis, but when you are using complex return types such as JavaBeans, Axis cannot map the type automatically, and using such a type requires additional configuration on both the server and client sides.

As an example of this, consider the remote interface shown in Listing 15-20.

Listing 15-20. *The MessageService Interface*

```
package com.apress.prospring2.ch15.remoting.jaxrpc;

public interface MessageService extends Remote {

    MessageBean getMessage() throws RemoteException;
}
```

Here, you can see that the `getMessage()` method of the `MessageService` interface doesn't return a `String` like `RemoteHelloWorld.getMessage()`; instead, it returns an instance of the `MessageBean`, the code for which is shown in Listing 15-21.

Listing 15-21. *The MessageBean Class*

```
package com.apress.prospring2.ch15.remoting;

public class MessageBean implements Serializable {

    private String message;
    private String senderName;

    public String getMessage() {
        return message;
    }

    public void setMessage(String message) {
        this.message = message;
    }

    public String getSenderName() {
        return senderName;
    }

    public void setSenderName(String senderName) {
        this.senderName = senderName;
```

```
    }

    public String toString() {
        return "Message: " + message + "\nSender: " + senderName;
    }
}
```

As you can see, MessageBean is just a simple JavaBean class with two properties, both of type String. Additional configuration is required when using this class as part of an Axis service as the return type of a method or as a method parameter.

■ **Note** Although the MessageBean class implements Serializable, doing so is *not* a requirement of JAX-RPC. We use MessageBean in a later example that does require it to implement Serializable.

Deploying a Service with Complex Types

On the server side, when configuring your service in server-config.wsdd, you need to specify additional configuration details telling Axis how it should serialize and deserialize your complex types to and from SOAP messages. Axis provides built-in support for serializing and deserializing JavaBean-style classes, meaning that apart from a small amount of additional configuration information, no effort is required on your part to use JavaBeans in your web services.

For non-JavaBean–style classes you must provide custom implementations of the SerializerFactory and DeserializerFactory interfaces. Indeed, behind the scenes Axis's JavaBean support is implemented using prebuilt implementations of these interfaces. The topic of custom serialization is outside the scope of this chapter, but you can find more details in the Axis user guide.

To configure a JavaBean for use with an Axis web service, you need to add a <beanMapping> definition to the <service> for your service. In Listing 15-22, you can see the <service> definition for the MessageService complete with <beanMapping>.

Listing 15-22. *Configuring with <beanMapping>*

```
<service name="MessageService" provider="java:RPC">
       <parameter name="className" ➥
value="com.apress.prospring2.ch15.remoting.jaxrpc.JaxRpcMessageService"/>
       <parameter name="allowedMethods" value="*"/>
       <beanMapping qname="apress:MessageBean" xmlns:apress=http://www.apress.com ➥
languageSpecificType="java:com.apress.prospring2.ch15.remoting.MessageBean"/>
</service>
```

Here, you can see that we have defined a <beanMapping> tag for the MessageBean class, specifying that the XML-qualified name of the MessageBean class in SOAP form should be apress:MessageBean, where apress is the namespace and MessageBean is the local name. Further, we map the apress namespace to the URI http://www.apress.com.

You also notice from the service configuration in Listing 15-22 that the implementation class is set to JaxRpcMessageService, the code for which is shown in Listing 15-23.

Listing 15-23. *The JaxRpcMessageService Class*

```
package com.apress.prospring2.ch15.remoting.jaxrpc;

import com.apress.prospring2.ch15.remoting.MessageBean;
```

```
import java.rmi.RemoteException;

public class JaxRpcMessageService implements MessageService {

    public MessageBean getMessage() throws RemoteException {
        MessageBean bean = new MessageBean();
        bean.setMessage("Hello World!");
        bean.setSenderName("Mr No");
        return bean;
    }

}
```

This implementation is trivial and requires no explanation. At this point, you are ready to deploy your web service. Once the web service is deployed in your servlet container, you should navigate to the WSDL for it, to ensure that the `<beanMapping>` has been correctly applied. In Listing 15-24, you can see a snippet of the WSDL from the `MessageService` that is created by the `<beanMapping>`.

Listing 15-24. *Complex Types in WSDL*

```
<wsdl:types>
    <schema targetNamespace="http://www.apress.com"
                               xmlns="http://www.w3.org/2001/XMLSchema">
        <import namespace="http://schemas.xmlsoap.org/soap/encoding/" />
        <complexType name="MessageBean">
            <sequence>
                <element name="message" nillable="true" type="xsd:string" />
                <element name="senderName" nillable="true" type="xsd:string" />
            </sequence>
        </complexType>
    </schema>
</wsdl:types>
```

In the definition of the `MessageBean` `<complexType>`, the name for which is derived from the `qname` attribute of your `<beanMapping>`, you can see that Axis has successfully defined two attributes, `message` and `senderName`, based on the JavaBean properties of the `MessageBean` class.

Accessing a Service with Complex Types

Once you have successfully deployed a service using complex types, all that remains is to create a client application to access the service. Unfortunately, Spring has no declarative way to define complex type mappings for use with JAX-RPC clients. Instead, you must subclass the `JaxRpcPortProxyFactoryBean` class in order to post-process the JAX-RPC service created by the proxy creator and add your custom type mappings.

When registering custom type mappings, you are essentially informing your JAX-RPC framework which implementations of the `SerializerFactory` and `DeserializerFactory` classes to use for a given type. Although the code to register a custom type mapping is largely provider independent, the implementations of `SerializerFactory` and `DeserializerFactory` will be supplied by either your SOAP stack or your application. In this case, we will use the `BeanSerializerFactory` and `BeanDeserializerFactory` classes provided by Axis when registering our custom type mapping, as shown in Listing 15-25.

Listing 15-25. *Registering a Custom Type Mapping*

```
package com.apress.prospring2.ch15.remoting.jaxrpc;

public class MessageServiceJaxRpcProxyFactoryBean extends
```

```
        JaxRpcPortProxyFactoryBean {

    protected void postProcessJaxRpcService(Service service) {
        TypeMappingRegistry tmr = service.getTypeMappingRegistry();
        TypeMapping tm = tmr.createTypeMapping();

        QName qname = new QName("http://www.apress.com", "MessageBean");

        tm.register(MessageBean.class, qname,
                new BeanSerializerFactory(MessageBean.class, qname),
                new BeanDeserializerFactory(MessageBean.class, qname));

        tmr.register("http://schemas.xmlsoap.org/soap/encoding/", tm);
    }
}
```

To register a custom type mapping in your custom `JaxRpcPortProxyFactoryBean` implementation, you must override the `postProcessJaxRpcService()` method, which allows you to access the `Service` instance once it is configured by the base class.

To access a service that uses complex types using a proxy, you should replace `JaxRpcPortProxyFactoryBean` with your custom implementation in the `ApplicationContext` configuration. In this case, we are replacing `JaxRpcPortProxyFactoryBean` with `MessageServiceJaxRpcProxyFactoryBean`, as shown in Listing 15-26.

Listing 15-26. *Proxy Configuration Using Custom Proxy Factory*

```
<?xml version="1.0" encoding="UTF-8"?>
<beans xmlns="http://www.springframework.org/schema/beans"
       ...>

    <bean id="messageService" class="com.apress.prospring2.ch15.remoting. ➥
jaxrpc.MessageServiceJaxRpcProxyFactoryBean">
        <property name="serviceFactoryClass"
               value="org.apache.axis.client.ServiceFactory" />

        <property name="wsdlDocumentUrl"
              value="http://localhost:8080/remoting/services/MessageService?wsdl"/>

        <property name="namespaceUri"
              value="http://localhost:8080/remoting/services/MessageService"/>

        <property name="serviceName" value="JaxRpcMessageServiceService"/>

        <property name="portName" value="MessageService"/>

        <property name="serviceInterface"
               value="com.apress.prospring2.ch15.remoting.jaxrpc.MessageService"/>

    </bean>
</beans>
```

As you can see, the proxy is configured in the same way it would be if you were using the standard `JaxRpcPortProxyFactoryBean` class; the only thing that changes is the class used in the `<bean>` declaration. You will notice that in this example we have used the remote interface as the value for the `serviceInterface` property, meaning that the proxy itself will actually implement the remote interface of the service. We have done this for illustrative purposes only; using a nonremote business interface as the interface for your proxy is certainly preferable.

Using the proxy from your application code is no different from working with any other object that implements the MessageService interface, as shown by the code in Listing 15-27.

Listing 15-27. *The MessageServiceClient Class*

```
package com.apress.prospring2.ch15.remoting.jaxrpc;

public class MessageServiceClient {

    public static void main(String[] args) throws Exception {
        ApplicationContext ctx = new FileSystemXmlApplicationContext(
                "classpath*:/com/apress/prospring2/ch15/ ➥
remoting/jaxrpc/messageServiceClient.xml");
        MessageService service = (MessageService) ctx.getBean("messageService");
        MessageBean bean = service.getMessage();
        System.out.println(bean);
    }
}
```

Provided that the MessageService is deployed in your servlet container, running this example will result in the following output to the console after a short delay:

```
Message: Hello World!
Sender: Mr No
```

Using JAX-WS Web Services

If you are using Sun JDK 1.6, you can take advantage of the built-in HTTP server, as well as the JAX-WS provider, to expose your web service easily. JAX-WS was developed as a natural successor of the JAX-RPC architecture and was designed to be easier to understand and therefore easier to use for exposing and accessing web services in Java.

Exposing Web Services Using SimpleJaxWsServiceExporter

Let's see how we can easily expose a web service using Spring's SimpleJaxWsServiceExporter. Listing 15-28 shows the web service class that we are going to expose.

Listing 15-28. *JaxWSHelloWorld Class*

```
package com.apress.prospring2.ch15.remoting.jaxws;

@WebService(serviceName=”JaxWsHelloWorld”)
public class JaxWsHelloWorld{
    @Autowired
    private HelloWorld helloWorld;

    @WebMethod
    public String getMessage() throws RemoteException {
        return helloWorld.getMessage();
    }
}
```

All we have to do is to define the SimpleJaxWsServiceExporter bean in the Spring ApplicationContext, and that will take care of all exposed web services. Listing 15-29 shows a simple Spring XML configuration:

Listing 15-29. *Web service Spring Configuration*

```
<bean class="org.springframework.remoting.jaxws.SimpleJaxWsServiceExporter">
    <property name="baseAddress" value="http://localhost:9800/"/>
</bean>

<bean id="jaxWsHelloWorld"
        class=" com.apress.prospring2.ch15.remoting.jaxws .JaxWsHelloWorld" />
```

SimpleJaxWsServiceExporter will expose all web services that have been defined as Spring beans, using its baseAddress property, and the serviceName defined in the annotation. For our example, the JaxWsHelloWorld web service will be accessible from the following URL: http://localhost:9800/JaxWsHelloWorld.

Exposing a Web Service Using XFire

XFire is a lightweight SOAP framework that provides a full JAX-WS implementation (for more information, see http://xfire.codehaus.org).

We will reuse the RemoteHelloWorld interface introduced in Listing 15-7 and expose its implementation from Listing 15-30 as our web service.

Listing 15-30. *JaxWsHelloWorld Implementation*

```
package com.apress.prospring2.ch15.remoting.jaxws;

@WebService
public class JaxWsHelloWorld extends SpringBeanAutowiringSupport ➥
implements RemoteHelloWorld {
    @Autowired
    private HelloWorld helloWorld;

    @WebMethod
    public String getMessage() throws RemoteException {
        return helloWorld.getMessage();
    }
    public void setHelloWorld(HelloWorld helloWorld) {
        this.helloWorld = helloWorld;
    }
}
```

To expose your web services using XFire, you will first have to download xfire.jar and configure the xfire servlet in your web.xml. Listing 15-31 shows basic web.xml configuration.

Listing 15-31. *web.xml for the xfire Servlet*

```
<?xml version="1.0" encoding="ISO-8859-1"?>

<web-app xmlns="http://java.sun.com/xml/ns/j2ee"
         xmlns:xsi="http://www.w3.org/2001/XMLSchema-instance"
         xsi:schemaLocation="http://java.sun.com/xml/ns/j2ee ➥
http://java.sun.com/xml/ns/j2ee/web-app_2_4.xsd"
         version="2.4">

    <context-param>
        <param-name>contextConfigLocation</param-name>
        <param-value>
```

```
            classpath*:/org/codehaus/xfire/spring/xfire.xml                1
        </param-value>

    </context-param>
    <listener>
        <listener-class>
              org.springframework.web.context.ContextLoaderListener
        </listener-class>
    </listener>
    <servlet>
        <servlet-name>context</servlet-name>
        <servlet-class>
              org.springframework.web.context.ContextLoaderServlet
        </servlet-class>
        <load-on-startup>1</load-on-startup>
    </servlet>
    <servlet>
        <servlet-name>xfire</servlet-name>
        <servlet-class>
              org.springframework.web.servlet.DispatcherServlet
        </servlet-class>
        <load-on-startup>5</load-on-startup>
    </servlet>
    <servlet-mapping>
        <servlet-name>xfire</servlet-name>
        <url-pattern>/ws/*</url-pattern>
    </servlet-mapping>
</web-app>
```

In the line marked with //1, in Listing 15-31, we include XFire configuration by adding the xfire.xml file shipped with XFire. We also configured the xfire servlet and mapped it to the /ws/* request URLs. The next step is to export the actual web service, which will be done in the xfire servlet configuration file, xfire-servlet.xml, shown in Listing 15-32.

Listing 15-32. *xfire-servlet.xml*

```
<?xml version="1.0" encoding="UTF-8"?>
<beans xmlns="http://www.springframework.org/schema/beans"
...>

    <bean name="/JaxWsHelloWorld"
                class="org.codehaus.xfire.spring.remoting.XFireExporter">
        <property name="serviceInterface"
              value="com.apress.prospring2.ch15.remoting.rmi.RemoteHelloWorld"/>
        <property name="serviceBean" ref="jaxWsHelloWorld" />
        <property name="namespace" value="http://localhost:8080/remoting/ws" />
        <property name="xfire" ref="xfire"/>
    </bean>

<bean id="jaxWsHelloWorld" ➥
class="com.apress.prospring2.ch15.remoting.jaxws.JaxWsHelloWorld" >
        <property name="helloWorld" ref="helloWorldService"/>
    </bean>
</beans>
```

A bean name will correspond to the web service name (/JaxWsHelloWorld). This bean is of the class org.codehaus.xfire.spring.remoting.XFireExporter, which is a convenient class for Spring integration provided by XFire. We set the `serviceBean` property to our `JaxWsHelloWorld` web service implementation and `serviceInterface` to `com.apress.prospring2.ch15.remoting.rmi.RemoteHelloWorld`, the remote interface that our web service implements. The XFire bean is defined in the `xfire.xml` file provided by XFire.

And that's it! XFire will take care of all other aspects of exposing web services, including generating the WSDL. You can see generated WSDL after deploying your web service using following URL: `http://localhost:8080/remoting/ws/JaxWsHelloWorld?WSDL`.

Accessing JAX-WS Web Services

Accessing JAX-WS web services from Spring is pretty straightforward. Spring provides `org.springframework.remoting.jaxws.JaxWsPortProxyFactoryBean`, which is configured to look for generated WSDL code, and accesses the web service like the JAX-RPC configuration from the previous section (JAX-RPC). Listing 15-33 shows the Spring configuration of `JaxWsPortProxyFactoryBean` for our example, which is saved in the `client.xml` file.

Listing 15-33. *JaxWsPortProxyFactoryBean Configuration—client.xml*

```
<?xml version="1.0" encoding="UTF-8"?>
<beans xmlns="http://www.springframework.org/schema/beans"
...>

    <bean id="helloWorldService" ➥
class="org.springframework.remoting.jaxws.JaxWsPortProxyFactoryBean">
        <property name="serviceInterface" ➥
value="com.apress.prospring2.ch15.remoting.rmi.RemoteHelloWorld"/>
        <property name="wsdlDocumentUrl" ➥
value="http://localhost:8080/remoting/ws/JaxWsHelloWorld?WSDL"/>
        <property name="namespaceUri" value="http://localhost:8080/remoting/ws"/>
        <property name="serviceName" value="HelloWorld"/>
        <property name="portName" value="HelloWorldHttpPort"/>

    </bean>

</beans>
```

Now, let's create a simple client class that will load our `client.xml` definition and access the exposed web service methods (see Listing 15-34).

Listing 15-34. *JAX-WS HelloWorldClient Implementation*

```
package com.apress.prospring2.ch15.remoting.jaxws;

public class HelloWorldClient {

    public static void main(String[] args) throws Exception{
        ApplicationContext ctx = new FileSystemXmlApplicationContext(
                "classpath*:/com/apress/prospring2/ch15/remoting/jaxws/client.xml");

        RemoteHelloWorld helloWorld =
                            (RemoteHelloWorld) ctx.getBean("helloWorldService");
        System.out.println(helloWorld.getMessage());
    }
}
```

Our client simply loads Spring ApplicationContext from the XML file, gets the helloWorldService bean, and calls its getMessage() method. Behind the scenes, Spring connects to the web service URL and performs calls on exposed methods. We have the output we expected:

```
Hello World!
```

The ServiceInterface property is the interface that our web service implements. wsdlDocumentUri defines a URL to the generated WSDL. ServiceName defines the name of the web service, and portName defines the web service port name.

Accessing Java Web Services from Other Clients

One of the main advantages of web services is that different platforms and technologies can communicate with each other using a language both servers and clients understand, namely XML. We will show an example of this by accessing Java web services deployed using Spring, exposed in previous sections from a .NET client.

We will expose the JaxWsHelloWorld web service from the JAX-WS section, as well as the MessageService web service from the JAX-RPC section.

The first thing to do is to generate .NET proxies for the Java web services and objects they use. For this, we will use the wsdl.exe tool, provided by Microsoft. Listing 15-35 shows console output when calling the wsdl.exe tool with arguments we provide.

Listing 15-35. *Generating Proxies Using the wsdl.exe Tool*

```
c:\Program Files\Microsoft Visual Studio .NET 2003\SDK\v1.1\Bin>wsdl ➥
/out:HelloWorldProxy.cs http://localhost:8080 /remoting/ws/JaxWsHelloWorld?wsdl
Microsoft (R) Web Services Description Language Utility
[Microsoft (R) .NET Framework, Version 1.1.4322.573]
Copyright (C) Microsoft Corporation 1998-2002. All rights reserved.
Writing file 'HelloWorldProxy.cs'.
```

This will generate C# source files that we can include in our Visual Studio project and use as proxies to our web services. Listing 15-36 shows the generated HelloWorldProxy.cs file.

Listing 15-36. *HelloWorldProxy.cs*

```
//------------------------------------------------------------------------------
// <autogenerated>
//     This code was generated by a tool
//     Runtime Version: 1.1.4322.2407
//
//     Changes to this file may cause incorrect behavior and will be lost if
//     the code is regenerated.
// </autogenerated>
//------------------------------------------------------------------------------

//
// This source code was auto-generated by wsdl, Version=1.1.4322.2407.
//
using System.Diagnostics;
using System.Xml.Serialization;
using System;
using System.Web.Services.Protocols;
using System.ComponentModel;
using System.Web.Services;
```

```
/// <remarks/>
 [System.Diagnostics.DebuggerStepThroughAttribute()]
 [System.ComponentModel.DesignerCategoryAttribute("code")]
 [System.Web.Services.WebServiceBindingAttribute(Name= ➥
"RemoteHelloWorldHttpBinding", Namespace="http://localhost:8080/remoting/ws")]
public class RemoteHelloWorld :
                  System.Web.Services.Protocols.SoapHttpClientProtocol {
    /// <remarks/>
    public RemoteHelloWorld() {
        his.Url = "http://192.168.100.101:8080/remoting/ws/JaxWsHelloWorld";
    }

    /// <remarks/>
    [System.Web.Services.Protocols.SoapDocumentMethodAttribute("",
                RequestNamespace="http://localhost:8080/remoting/ws",
                ResponseNamespace="http://localhost:8080/remoting/ws",
                Use=System.Web.Services.Description.SoapBindingUse.Literal,
                ParameterStyle=System.Web.Services.Protocols. ➥
SoapParameterStyle.Wrapped)]
    [return: System.Xml.Serialization.XmlElementAttribute("out", IsNullable=true)]
    public string getMessage() {
        object[] results = this.Invoke("getMessage", new object[0]);
        return ((string)(results[0]));
    }

    /// <remarks/>
    public System.IAsyncResult BegingetMessage(System.AsyncCallback callback, ➥
object asyncState) {
        return this.BeginInvoke("getMessage", new object[0], callback, asyncState);
    }
    /// <remarks/>
    public string EndgetMessage(System.IAsyncResult asyncResult) {
        object[] results = this.EndInvoke(asyncResult);
        return ((string)(results[0]));
    }
}
```

Now, we can use generated proxies to call the web service methods, as if they are local implementations in .NET. Listing 15-37 shows the .NET client code used to call web service methods.

Listing 15-37. *.NET Client Web Service Calling Code*

```
RemoteHelloWorld hello = new RemoteHelloWorld();
Console.WriteLine(hello.message);
```

The output we get is what we expect, the same as when we called the same service from the Java client:

```
Hello World!
```

So we have returned a simple `String` from the Java web service method. But what will happen when we want to return a Java object? Let's now try the same thing with `JaxRpcMessageService` from Listing 15-23, which we deployed in the "Web Services with JAX-RPC" section. First, let's use the `wsdl.exe` tool to generate a .NET proxy from the WSDL of the exposed Java service (see Listing 15-38).

Listing 15-38. *Using wsdl.exe to Generate a Proxy for JaxRpcMessageService*

```
c:\Program Files\Microsoft Visual Studio .NET 2003\SDK\v1.1\Bin>wsdl ➥
/out:MessageServiceProxy.cs http://localhost:8080 /remoting/ws/MessageService?wsdl
Microsoft (R) Web Services Description Language Utility
[Microsoft (R) .NET Framework, Version 1.1.4322.573]
Copyright (C) Microsoft Corporation 1998-2002. All rights reserved.
Writing file 'MessageServiceProxy.cs'.
```

Now we have generated C# source code for the proxy. Listing 15-39 shows the generated code.

Listing 15-39. *Generated Proxy Source Code*

```
//------------------------------------------------------------------------------
// <autogenerated>
//  This code was generated by a tool.
// Runtime Version: 1.1.4322.2407
//
// Changes to this file may cause incorrect behavior and will be lost if
//  the code is regenerated.
// </autogenerated>
//------------------------------------------------------------------------------

//
// This source code was auto-generated by wsdl, Version=1.1.4322.2407.
//
using System.Diagnostics;
using System.Xml.Serialization;
using System;
using System.Web.Services.Protocols;
using System.ComponentModel;
using System.Web.Services;

/// <remarks/>
[System.Diagnostics.DebuggerStepThroughAttribute()]
[System.ComponentModel.DesignerCategoryAttribute("code")]
[System.Web.Services.WebServiceBindingAttribute(Name="MessageServiceSoapBinding",
            Namespace="http://192.168.100.101:8080/remoting/services/MessageService")]
public class JaxRpcMessageServiceService :
                            System.Web.Services.Protocols.SoapHttpClientProtocol {
/// <remarks/>
public JaxRpcMessageServiceService() {
this.Url = "http://192.168.100.101:8080/remoting/services/MessageService";
}

/// <remarks/>
[System.Web.Services.Protocols.SoapRpcMethodAttribute("",
              RequestNamespace="http://jaxrpc.remoting.ch15.prospring2.apress.com",
              ResponseNamespace="http://192.168.100.101:8080/remoting/ ➥
services/MessageService")]
[return: System.Xml.Serialization.SoapElementAttribute("getMessageReturn")]
public MessageBean getMessage() {
object[] results = this.Invoke("getMessage", new object[0]);
return ((MessageBean)(results[0]));
}

/// <remarks/>
```

```
public System.IAsyncResult BegingetMessage(System.AsyncCallback callback, ➥
object asyncState) {
return this.BeginInvoke("getMessage", new object[0], callback, asyncState);
}

/// <remarks/>
public MessageBean EndgetMessage(System.IAsyncResult asyncResult) {
object[] results = this.EndInvoke(asyncResult);
return ((MessageBean)(results[0]));
}
}

/// <remarks/>
[System.Xml.Serialization.SoapTypeAttribute("MessageBean", "http://www.apress.com")]
public class MessageBean {

/// <remarks/>
public string message;

/// <remarks/>
public string senderName;
}
```

You can see that the generated code includes the `MessageBean` class, which was not available in the .NET code. This means we can get a reference to the `MessageBean` object returned from the web service method, although we haven't implemented that class in our .NET source code. Now, we can use a proxy to call the methods of our web service, as Listing 15-40 shows.

Listing 15-40. *.NET Client Web Service Calling Code*

```
MessageBean messagebean = new JaxRpcMessageServiceService().getMessage();
Console.WriteLine(messageBean.senderName + ": " +messageBean.message);
```

We can see the expected output:

```
Mr No: Hello World!
```

Creating Web Services with HTTP Invoker

As you saw in the previous section, JAX-RPC and JAX-WS are quite complex ways to expose services over HTTP. Not only that, the use of XML adds a certain amount of overhead, as incoming requests and outgoing responses have to be converted to and from SOAP. In many cases, all you require is a simple mechanism for two Java applications to communicate with each other using HTTP as the transport.

In this case, using JAX-RPC or JAX-WS may be overkill, since both the client and server sides are using Java, and the use of XML as a communication fabric adds unnecessary complexity. Likewise, RMI is unsuitable for this scenario, since it cannot be used over HTTP. Thankfully, quite a few solutions provide simple mechanisms for exposing services over HTTP. Spring provides support for three such services on top of the support offered by JAX-RPC and JAX-WS: Hessian, Burlap, and Spring HTTP Invoker. In this section, you will see how to use Spring's native HTTP Invoker remoting architecture to build distributed components in a 100 percent Spring environment.

From a user perspective, using Spring HTTP Invoker is deceptively simple and provides a powerful mechanism for remote component communication. On the server side, services are exposed on top of Spring's comprehensive web framework, using a 100 percent Spring-native configuration mechanism. Unlike JAX-RPC or JAX-WS, you are in full control of the creation semantics for your service objects, and thus you can configure them using Spring DI.

On the client side, Spring provides proxy capabilities allowing you to access HTTP Invoker–exposed services via a business interface. Internally, Spring uses the built-in capabilities of the JDK for HTTP communication, although it can be configured to use Jakarta Commons HttpClient (`http://jakarta.apache.org/commons/httpclient`), which provides a more complete HTTP implementation. By using HttpClient on the client and standard servlet security on the server, you can secure your HTTP Invoker services using HTTP basic authentication.

In this section, you will see how to build services using the HTTP Invoker architecture and how to access these services using Spring-generated proxies. You will also see how Spring handles the transmission of complex types and how to provide basic security using HTTP basic authentication.

Exposing Simple Services

Building and deploying a service using the HTTP Invoker architecture requires four distinct steps. The first step is to create the service interface. Spring does not place any special constraints on the service interface, so you are free to use one of your normal business interfaces. However, you may wish to restrict the operations that are exported in your service, in which case you can create a specific interface for your service. For the example in this section, we are going to use the standard `HelloWorld` interface from Listing 15-1.

The second step you need to take is to build the actual service implementation. Again, Spring places no special constraints on the implementation class such as those specified by RMI. Indeed, when using Spring HTTP Invoker, using one of your standard service classes is generally easier. If you need to restrict the exposure of operations on your service class, you can do this in the service interface. For the example in this section, we will use the `SimpleHelloWorld` implementation of `HelloWorld` shown in Listing 15-2.

The third step is to configure an instance of `HttpInvokerServiceExporter` in your `ApplicationContext`. Behind the scenes, `HttpInvokerServiceExporter` is implemented as a Spring `Controller` that is capable of receiving an HTTP request and returning an arbitrary response. In addition, when configuring your `HttpInvokerServiceExporter`, you must specify a mapping for the service to a URL. There are many different mechanisms for mapping beans to a URL discussed in Chapter 17, but for the examples in this section, we will use `BeanNameUrlHandlerMapping`, which uses the name of the bean as the URL mapping.

The fourth step you need to follow is to configure an instance of Spring's `DispatcherServlet` in your web application deployment descriptor. `DispatcherServlet` is responsible for routing incoming HTTP requests to the appropriate `Controllers` based on their URL mappings. If you are unclear of the basic concept behind the MVC pattern in a web application, you might want to look ahead to Chapter 17 for a rundown of MVC and the roles played by Spring's `DispatcherServlet` class and `Controller` interface.

Creating the Service Interface and Service Implementation

As we mentioned, Spring places no special constraints on your service interface or service implementation when using the HTTP Invoker stack. In most cases, you will simply use standard business interfaces along with some arbitrary implementation, although in some cases, you may choose to restrict the operations that are exposed remotely using a specific service interface.

For the example in this section, we are going to use the `HelloWorld` interface and `SimpleHelloWorld` class from Listings 15-1 and 15-2 respectively. Since we have already shown and discussed these, we will not cover them again here.

Exporting an HTTP Invoker Service

Configuring the HttpInvokerServiceExporter is much like configuring the RmiServiceExporter, although HttpInvokerServiceExporter requires only two properties: the service bean and the service interface. Listing 15-41 shows a sample configuration that configures an HttpInvokerServiceExporter for the helloWorldService bean that we configured in Listing 15-3:

Listing 15-41. *Exporting an HTTP Invoker Service*

```
<?xml version="1.0" encoding="UTF-8"?>
<beans xmlns="http://www.springframework.org/schema/beans"
       ...>

    <bean id="defaultHandlerMapping" ➥
class="org.springframework.web.servlet.handler.BeanNameUrlHandlerMapping"/>

    <bean name="/helloWorld" ➥
class="org.springframework.remoting.httpinvoker.HttpInvokerServiceExporter">
        <property name="service" ref="helloWorldService" />
        <property name="serviceInterface" ➥
                   value=com.apress.prospring2.ch15.remoting.HelloWorld />
    </bean>

</beans>
```

This configuration is fairly straightforward, although there are two points of note. First, notice that the bean name for the HttpInvokerServiceExporter is specified as /helloWorld. When processing incoming requests, Spring's DispatcherServlet will use any defined HandlerMapping beans to find a Controller that the request should be routed to. In this case, we have defined a BeanNameUrlHandlerMapping bean as our only HandlerMapping implementation. As its name implies, BeanNameUrlHandlerMapping attempts to map the URL of the incoming request to a bean based on the bean's name. So in this case, if a request comes whose URL contains /helloWorld after taking out the host name, context path, and servlet mapping, BeanNameUrlHandlerMapping will route it to the /helloWorld bean.

The second point to note here is that when we set the service property of the HttpInvokerServiceExporter, we are pointing to a bean that is contained in a separate configuration file. When you create a web application using Spring, it is traditional to separate your bean definitions into at least two ApplicationContexts. You place all non-web-specific bean definitions, such as service objects and data access objects, in one ApplicationContext and all web–specific beans such as Controllers and HandlerMappings in another. The ContextLoaderServlet loads the ApplicationContext containing your business interfaces, while the DispatcherServlet loads the ApplicationContext containing the web components. Spring ensures that beans in the web-specific ApplicationContext can access beans in the business ApplicationContext but not vice versa. The reason for this separation is simple—it increases reusability. Since the business ApplicationContext doesn't contain any web-specific bean declarations, it can be reused in other applications.

In our example, we are reusing the helloWorldBean definition that you can see in Listing 15-3. This single bean definition constitutes the business ApplicationContext, and the ContextLoaderServlet will load it. The defaultHandlerMapping and /helloWorld beans shown in Listing 15-41 make up our web ApplicationContext, which will be loaded by the DispatcherServlet. The name and location of the web ApplicationContext file is very important. The file must be placed in the WEB-INF directory of your web application, and it must be named <servlet_name>-servlet.xml, where <servlet_name> is the name given to the DispatcherServlet in your web application deployment descriptor.

Configuring Spring's DispatcherServlet

Configuring the `DispatcherServlet` is simple; it is just a standard servlet configuration. The only point to note is that you must remember to configure the `ContextLoaderServlet` as well if you have split your bean definitions across multiple files (as we have). Listing 15-42 shows the `DispatcherServlet` configuration for this example.

Listing 15-42. *HTTP Invoker Servlet Configuration*

```
<?xml version="1.0" encoding="UTF-8"?>
<web-app version="2.4"
         xmlns="http://java.sun.com/xml/ns/j2ee"
         xmlns:xsi="http://www.w3.org/2001/XMLSchema-instance"
         xsi:schemaLocation="http://java.sun.com/xml/ns/j2ee ➥
http://java.sun.com/xml/ns/j2ee/web-app_2_4.xsd">

    <context-param>
        <param-name>contextConfigLocation</param-name>
        <param-value>
            classpath*:/com/apress/prospring2/ch15/remoting/remoting-context.xml
            /WEB-INF/httpinvoker-servlet.xml
        </param-value>

    </context-param>

    <servlet>
        <servlet-name>context</servlet-name>
        <servlet-class>org.springframework.web.context.ContextLoaderServlet</servlet-class>
        <load-on-startup>1</load-on-startup>
    </servlet>

    <servlet>
        <servlet-name>httpinvoker</servlet-name>
        <servlet-class>
               org.springframework.web.servlet.DispatcherServlet
         </servlet-class>
        <load-on-startup>2</load-on-startup>
    </servlet>
<servlet-mapping>
        <servlet-name>httpinvoker</servlet-name>
        <url-pattern>/http/*</url-pattern>
    </servlet-mapping>
</web-app>
```

Unfortunately, unlike Axis, the `HttpInvokerServiceExporter` does not provide a nice interface to test whether or not the service is deployed correctly. However, you can test to see whether the servlet is configured correctly by pointing your browser at the service URL, in this case `http://localhost:8080/remoting/http/helloWorld`. If the error screen that is displayed indicates that a `java.io.EOFException` has been thrown, then the service is being invoked as desired but there is no data available. If you get another error, Spring most likely cannot find your `ApplicationContext` configuration files, because they contain errors or the URL mapping is incorrectly defined. Check all the configuration files for mistakes, and ensure that you correctly named all of them and that they sit in the correct places in your web application. Then redeploy.

Accessing an HTTP Invoker Service Using Proxies

As with both RMI and JAX-RPC, accessing an HTTP Invoker service is done using proxies that hide all the messy details from your application, allowing you to code purely to business interfaces. Just like the FactoryBeans provided for RMI and JAX-RPC proxies, Spring provides the HttpInvokerProxyFactoryBean, which will create a proxy for your HTTP Invoker service. Listing 15-43 shows a sample configuration that uses HttpInvokerProxyFactoryBean to create a proxy to the service created in the last section.

Listing 15-43. *Creating an HTTP Invoker Proxy*

```
<?xml version="1.0" encoding="UTF-8"?>
<beans xmlns="http://www.springframework.org/schema/beans"
       ...>

    <bean id="helloWorldService" ➥
class="org.springframework.remoting.httpinvoker.HttpInvokerProxyFactoryBean">
        <property name="serviceUrl"
                  value="http://localhost:8080/remoting/http/helloWorld" />

        <property name="serviceInterface"
                  value="com.apress.prospring2.ch15.remoting.HelloWorld" />

    </bean>
</beans>
```

This configuration is self-explanatory and demonstrates the ease with which you can configure a proxy for HTTP Invoker services. You can use this proxy in your application just like you would use any instance of HelloWorld, as shown in Listing 15-44.

Listing 15-44. *Using an HTTP Invoker Proxy*

```
package com.apress.prospring2.ch15.remoting.http;

public class HelloWorldClient {

    public static void main(String[] args) {
        ApplicationContext ctx = new FileSystemXmlApplicationContext(
                    "classpath*:/com/apress/prospring2/ch15/ ➥
remoting/http/helloWorld.xml");

        HelloWorld helloWorld = (HelloWorld) ctx.getBean("helloWorldService");
        System.out.println(helloWorld.getMessage());
    }
}
```

As with earlier examples of the HelloWorld service, running this class will result in a short delay before the message “Hello, World” is printed to the console.

Using Arbitrary Objects in HTTP Invoker Services

In the previous example, the return type of the getMessage() method was a java.util.String. The String class implements the Serializable interface and thus is transmittable by HTTP Invoker, which builds on top of Java serialization as a mechanism for transmitting objects across the wire. You will recall from the discussion of JAX-RPC that substantial effort was required to use a complex Java type as a return type or argument of a remote method. With HTTP Invokers, very little effort is required to make your own types transmittable—all you need to do is implement Serializable for any classes you wish to use in your service.

As an example of this, consider the MessageService interface that was shown earlier in Listing 15-20. This interface defines a single method, getMessage(), that returns an instance of MessageBean. You will recall from Listing 15-21 that the MessageBean class implements the Serializable interface and as such is perfectly acceptable for use in an HTTP Invoker service. Listing 15-45 shows an HttpInvokerServiceExporter that configures a new HTTP Invoker service at the URL /messageService.

Listing 15-45. *Configuring the /messageService HTTP Invoker Service*

```
    <bean name="/messageService" ➥
class="org.springframework.remoting.httpinvoker.HttpInvokerServiceExporter">
        <property name="service">
            <ref bean="messageService"/>
        </property>
        <property name="serviceInterface">
            <value>com.apress.prospring2.ch15.remoting.MessageService</value>
        </property>
    </bean>
```

Notice that in this example we are pointing the HttpInvokerServiceExporter to the messageService, which needs to be added to the business ApplicationContext as shown in Listing 15-46.

Listing 15-46. *Adding the messageService Bean to the ApplicationContext*

```
<?xml version="1.0" encoding="UTF-8"?>
<beans xmlns="http://www.springframework.org/schema/beans"
       ...>
    <bean id="messageService" ➥
class="com.apress.prospring2.ch15.remoting.http.SimpleMessageService"/>
</beans>
```

Since a DispatcherServlet is already configured for the ApplicationContext containing the HTTP Invoker services, no additional modifications are required by the deployment descriptor for the web application.

As with the previous HTTP Invoker service, you can test that this service has been deployed correctly by pointing your browser at the correct location, but to test it fully, you need to build a client. As you saw in the previous section, building the client is much simplified by the use of proxies. Listing 15-47 shows a proxy configuration for accessing the MessageService.

Listing 15-47. *HTTP Invoker Proxy for MessageService*

```
    <bean name="/messageService" ➥
class="org.springframework.remoting.httpinvoker.HttpInvokerServiceExporter">
        <property name="service">
            <ref bean="messageService"/>
        </property>
        <property name="serviceInterface">
            <value>com.apress.prospring2.ch15.remoting.MessageService</value>
        </property>
    </bean>
```

You should be more than familiar with code needed for this proxy, but it is included in Listing 15-48 for the sake of completeness.

Listing 15-48. *Accessing the MessageService*

```
package com.apress.prospring2.ch15.remoting.http;

        public class MessageServiceClient {

            public static void main(String[] args) {
                ApplicationContext ctx = new FileSystemXmlApplicationContext(
                        "classpath*:/com/apress/prospring2/ch15/remoting/ ➥
http/messageService.xml");

                MessageService messageService =
                            (MessageService) ctx.getBean("messageService");
            System.out.println(messageService.getMessage());
    }
}
```

Running this class results in the following output:

```
Message: Hello World!
Sender: Superman
```

Using HTTP Basic Authentication

One of the best features of the HTTP Invoker architecture is that it can use built-in servlet container security services to provide secure services. In this example, you will see how to create a secure version of the `MessageService` created in the previous section that requires users to authenticate using HTTP basic authentication.

For the purposes of this example, we are going to reuse most of the server-side configuration from the previous example. The only modifications will be to the web `ApplicationContext` file (to add a new URL mapping) and to the web application deployment descriptor (to configure the security). The bulk of the work in this example is on the client side where we create an authentication-aware proxy.

Configuring a URL Mapping for the Secure Service

The new secure service requires a new URL mapping that can be mapped as a secured resource in the web application deployment descriptor. This is shown in Listing 15-49.

Listing 15-49. *URL Mapping for Secure Service*

```
    <bean name="/messageServiceSecure" ➥
class="org.springframework.remoting.httpinvoker.HttpInvokerServiceExporter">
        <property name="service" ref ="messageService" />
        <property name="serviceInterface" ➥
                    value=com.apress.prospring2.ch15.remoting.MessageService />
    </bean>
```

Configuring Container Security

You may already be familiar with the details of container security—it is a fairly well known part of the servlet specification—so we won't go into a great amount of detail on this topic. To secure a service, you need to configure the web application to use HTTP basic authentication, map a security role into your application, and then mark the service URL as secure. Listing 15-50 shows a configuration that achieves these three tasks.

Listing 15-50. *Configuring Container Security*

```
<security-constraint>
        <web-resource-collection>
            <web-resource-name>Secure HTTP Services</web-resource-name>
            <url-pattern>/http/messageServiceSecure</url-pattern>
        </web-resource-collection>
        <auth-constraint>
            <role-name>manager</role-name>
        </auth-constraint>
    </security-constraint>

    <login-config>
        <auth-method>BASIC</auth-method>
        <realm-name>remoting</realm-name>
    </login-config>

    <security-role>
        <role-name>manager</role-name>
    </security-role>
```

In this configuration, a security role named manager is defined. The way these roles are obtained is container specific. For testing, we used Tomcat, which allows you to specify users and roles in a simple XML file called tomcat-users.xml.

The <login-config> element configures the servlet container to use HTTP basic authentication, and the <security-constraint> element restricts access to the /http/messageServiceSecure URL to users in the manager role only. If you deploy this example to your servlet container, you can check that the security is active by pointing your browser at http://localhost:8080/remoting/http/messageServiceSecure, which should prompt you for a username and password.

Adding Authentication Capabilities to a Proxy

Deploying a secure HTTP service is the easy part; accessing it is not quite so simple. You will recall from our initial discussion of the HttpInvokerProxyFactoryBean that internally it can use either built-in JDK HTTP support or the Jakarta Commons HttpClient project. The built-in support for HTTP in the JDK does not include support for HTTP basic authentication, meaning that you need to use HttpClient if you want to use HTTP basic authentication to access a secure service.

Configuring HttpInvokerProxyFactoryBean to use HttpClient is simply a matter of setting the httpInvokerRequestExecutor property to an instance of CommonsHttpInvokerRequestExecutor—this configuration gets complex. CommonsHttpInvokerRequestExecutor doesn't allow you to set username and password as properties, but it does allow you to pass in an instance of the HttpClient class, which is the core to the HttpClient project. However, it is not possible to configure HttpClient with credentials for HTTP basic authentication using Spring DI. The workaround for this is to create a FactoryBean implementation that can return an appropriately configured implementation of HttpClient, as shown in Listing 15-51.

Listing 15-51. *The HttpClientFactoryBean Class*

```
package com.apress.prospring2.ch15.remoting.http;

public class HttpClientFactoryBean implements FactoryBean, InitializingBean {

    private HttpClient httpClient = null;

    private String username = null;

    private String password = null;

    private String authenticationHost = null;

    private String authenticationRealm = null;

    public Object getObject() throws Exception {
        return httpClient;
    }

    public Class getObjectType() {
        return HttpClient.class;
    }

    public boolean isSingleton() {
        return true;
    }

    public void setPassword(String password) {
        this.password = password;
    }

    public void setUsername(String username) {
        this.username = username;
    }

    public void setAuthenticationHost(String authenticationHost) {
        this.authenticationHost = authenticationHost;
    }

    public void setAuthenticationRealm(String authenticationRealm) {
        this.authenticationRealm = authenticationRealm;
    }

    public void afterPropertiesSet() throws Exception {
        if ((username == null) || (password == null)) {
            throw new IllegalArgumentException(
                    "You must set the username, password and "
                            + "authenticationHost properties");
        }

        httpClient = new HttpClient();
        httpClient.getState().setAuthenticationPreemptive(true);
```

```
        Credentials credentials = new UsernamePasswordCredentials(username,
                password);
        httpClient.getState().setCredentials(authenticationRealm,
                authenticationHost, credentials);
    }
}
```

Most of the code in the `HttpClientFactoryBean` class is easy to understand. The important part is the `afterPropertiesSet()` method. The `afterProperties()` method ensures that values for the `username` and `password` properties have been supplied before moving on to create an instance of `HttpClient`, which is stored in the `httpClient` field. The call to `setAuthenticationPreemptive()` instructs `HttpClient` that it should send credentials to the server in advance of any requests from the server in an attempt to authenticate preemptively.

In the final part of `afterPropertiesSet()`, an instance of `UsernamePasswordCredentials` is created and assigned to the `HttpClient`, along with the values of the `authenticationRealm` and `authenticationHost` properties. Both of these properties can be left blank, but specifying them allows you to restrict the supplied credentials to a set host or authentication realm.

Using the `HttpClientFactoryBean`, you cannot configure an instance of `CommonsHttpInvokerRequestExecutor` with a correctly configured instance of `HttpClient`. In turn, this `CommonsHttpInvokerRequestExecutor` bean can be used to configure an instance of `HttpInvokerProxyFactoryBean` so that it can take advantage of HTTP basic authentication, as shown in Listing 15-52.

Listing 15-52. *Configuring HttpInvokerProxyFactoryBean for HTTP Basic Authentication*

```
<?xml version="1.0" encoding="UTF-8"?>
<beans xmlns="http://www.springframework.org/schema/beans"
       ...>

    <bean id="messageService" ➥
class="org.springframework.remoting.httpinvoker.HttpInvokerProxyFactoryBean">
        <property name="serviceUrl" ➥
value="http://localhost:8080/remoting/http/messageServiceSecure" />

        <property name="serviceInterface" ➥
value="com.apress.prospring2.ch15.remoting.MessageService" />

        <property name="httpInvokerRequestExecutor" ref="requestExecutor" />
    </bean>

    <bean id="requestExecutor" ➥
class="org.springframework.remoting.httpinvoker.CommonsHttpInvokerRequestExecutor">
        <property name="httpClient">
            <bean class="com.apress.prospring2.ch15.remoting.http.HttpClientFactoryBean">
                <property name="username" value="tomcat" />
                <property name="password" value="tomcat" />
            </bean>
        </property>
    </bean>
</beans>
```

The resulting proxy created by this configuration can be used just like any proxy, as shown in Listing 15-53.

Listing 15-53. *The MessageServiceSecureClient Class*

```
package com.apress.prospring2.ch15.remoting.http;

public class MessageServiceSecureClient {

    public static void main(String[] args) {
        ApplicationContext ctx = new FileSystemXmlApplicationContext(
                "classpath*:/com/apress/prospring2/ch15/remoting/http/ ➥
messageServiceSecure.xml");

        MessageService messageService = (MessageService) ctx
                .getBean("messageService");
        System.out.println(messageService.getMessage());
    }
}
```

If you run this example, provided you have configured validation credentials in the `ApplicationContext`, you will see output similar to the previous example's output. You should experiment with different sets of credentials to see the security in action.

Choosing a Remoting Architecture

With so many options available for remoting, you may wonder which solution to use. Thankfully, the decision is often quite clear for a given set of requirements. The Spring documentation provides quite a comprehensive discussion on how to choose a remoting implementation; you should certainly read it in conjunction with this discussion, which expands on that documentation.

As the documentation states, RMI is a good solution for Java-to-Java solutions that require transmission of complex objects. Since RMI uses built-in Java serialization capabilities, creating a distributed application that transmits complex models across the network requires very little effort on your part. Using RMI in conjunction with Spring allows you to hide RMI-specific implementation details from your application, making it easier to plug in a new remoting architecture should your requirements change.

RMI is also a good solution for use in heterogeneous environments, since it allows for communication using the CORBA IIOP protocol, which is widely supported in a variety of other languages. Indeed, you may find that if you are deploying a new component into an existing environment, the architecture in place is CORBA. In this case, RMI is the best solution for your needs.

The biggest drawback of RMI is that it is not easily usable across HTTP, so if you need communication across the Internet, one of the other architectures will better meet your needs.

The use of JAX-RPC or JAX-WS is usually mandated if you need to communicate across HTTP with systems written in other languages, since SOAP is widely supported. You should think twice about adopting JAX-RPC or JAX-WS for Java-to-Java communication, as many other solutions are more efficient. Even if you feel that you may need SOAP support in the future, you can easily create a SOAP service for non-Java clients and use some other framework for your Java clients with both services being backed by the same implementation class.

Spring-native HTTP Invoker architecture is a good candidate for Spring-to-Spring communication, and since it builds on Java serialization, it is more than capable of transmitting complex object models between components.

Summary

In this chapter, you saw how to create and access remote services using Spring and a wide variety of different remoting architectures. In the first part of the chapter, you saw how to use Spring Remoting to simplify the creation of RMI-based services and how Spring can be used to create and access CORBA services via JNDI. In the second part of the chapter, you saw how to create and access SOAP web services using Spring's support for JAX-RPC and JAX-WS. The third part of this chapter introduced Spring's native remoting solution—HTTP Invoker. Using HTTP Invoker architecture, you can easily expose and access remote services over HTTP, using Java serialization to format complex object graphs for transmission across the wire.

In the next chapter, you can read about Spring support for transactions. Transactional behavior is the main part of any business-oriented Java application. The next chapter will give you an overview of transactions in Spring, as well as in-depth examples of transaction configuration and management.

CHAPTER 16

Transaction Management

Transactions are pivotal parts of a reliable enterprise application. The simplistic view of a transaction includes the `begin transaction` command; SQL updates, deletes, and so on; and finally the `commit/rollback` command. But there's much more to transactions than this! In this chapter, we show you how to use declarative, rather than manually coded, transactions and how to span transactions across multiple transactional resources. We will also show you how to write code that can be synchronized with a transaction, in other words, how to write code that can participate in a transaction and receive `commit/rollback` notifications. Finally, we give you some advice on how to test transactional code.

Spring offers excellent support for declarative transactions, which means you do not need to clutter your code with transaction management code. You can use the traditional approach, where Spring creates proxies to the methods in a target bean, or you can use AOP and the `tx-advice` tag. In addition to these two methods, we will cover the following topics in this chapter.

First, we will take a look at the Spring transaction abstraction layer. We discuss the base components of Spring transaction abstraction classes and explain how to use these classes to control transaction properties.

Next, we will cover declarative transaction management. We show you how to use Spring to implement declarative transaction management using just plain Java objects. We offer examples for declarative transaction management using the configuration files as well as source-level metadata.

We will follow the declarative transaction management with programmatic transaction management. Even though programmatic transaction management is not used very often, we explain how to use the `PlatformTransactionManager` interface, which gives you ultimate control over the transaction management code.

Toward the end of the chapter, we will show you how to use the Java Transaction API (JTA) `TransactionManager` to manage transactions over multiple transactional resources. We also give examples of how to use the `JtaTransactionManager`, which allows you to include multiple transactional resources, such as a database and message queue, in a single transaction.

Finally, we will show you how to implement your own transaction synchronization to receive callbacks from the `TransactionSynchronizationManager` whenever the active transaction's status changes.

Exploring the Spring Transaction Abstraction Layer

Whether you use Spring or not, you have to make a fundamental choice when you use transactions—whether to use global or local transactions. Local transactions are specific to a single transactional resource (a JDBC connection, for example), whereas global transactions are managed by the container and can include multiple transactional resources.

Local transactions are easy to manage, and because most operations work with just one transactional resource (such as a JDBC transaction), using local transactions is enough. However, if you are not using Spring, you still have a lot of transaction management code to write, and if at some time in the future the scope of the transaction needs to be extended across multiple transactional resources, you will have to drop the local transaction management code and rewrite it to use global transactions.

Global transactions in non-Spring applications are, in most cases, coded using JTA, a complex API that depends on JNDI, which means that you almost invariably have to use a Java EE application server. Rather than implementing JTA transactions programmatically, you can use EJB Container Managed Transactions (CMT) functionality, which is provided by a Java EE application server. This allows you to simply declare which operations are to be enlisted in a transaction; once you do, the container takes care of transaction management. This is the preferred management strategy because the code you write does not contain any explicit transactional code and all the hard work is delegated to the container. Another great advantage of EJB CMT is that it removes the need to work with the JTA API directly, though by definition, you still have to use EJBs.

Ideally, you will have a container that supports global and local declarative and programmatic transactions without needing EJBs. Even though declarative transactions are the favored approach, there can sometimes be a place for programmatic transactions.

Analyzing Transaction Properties

We start with a summary of a standard transaction. However, keep in mind that everything we are going to write applies to more than just database operations. In most cases, it is true that a database is heavily involved, but nothing stops us from extending the concept of transactions from the database to other transactional resources.

Transactions have the four well-known ACID properties—atomicity, consistency, isolation, and durability—and the transactional resources must maintain these aspects of a transaction. You cannot control the atomicity, consistency, or durability of a transaction, but you can control the timeout, set whether the transaction should be read-only, and specify the isolation level.

■ **Note** In an ideal situation, you would not have to worry about independence, either: all transactions would be completely independent. In reality, having independent transactions means executing the transactions serially (i.e., one after another). This ensures complete isolation but severely limits the throughput of the system. You can use the isolation level value to control how independent the transactions really are.

Spring encapsulates all these settings in the `TransactionDefinition` interface. This interface is used in the core interface of the transaction support in Spring, the `PlatformTransactionManager`, whose implementations perform transaction management on a specific platform, such as JDBC or JTA. The core method, `PlatformTransactionManager.getTransaction()`, returns a `TransactionStatus` reference, which is used to control the transaction execution; more specifically, it can be used to set the transaction result and to check whether the transaction is read-only or whether it is a new transaction.

Exploring the TransactionDefinition Interface

As we mentioned earlier, the `TransactionDefinition` interface controls the properties of a transaction. Let's take a more detailed look at the `TransactionDefinition` interface (see Listing 16-1) and describe its methods.

Listing 16-1. *TransactionDefinition Interface*

```
public interface TransactionDefinition {
    int getPropagationBehavior();
    int getIsolationLevel();
    int getTimeout();
    boolean isReadOnly();
}
```

The simple and obvious methods of this interface are `getTimeout()`, which returns the time (in seconds) in which the transaction must complete, and `isReadOnly()`, which indicates whether the transaction is read-only. The transaction manager implementation can use this last value to optimize transaction execution and to make sure that the transaction is performing only reads.

The other two methods, `getPropagationBehavior()` and `getIsolationLevel()`, need to be discussed in more detail. We begin with `getIsolationLevel()`, which controls what changes to the data other transactions see. Table 16-1 lists the transaction isolation levels you can use and explains what changes made in the current transaction other transactions can access.

Table 16-1. *Transaction Isolation Levels*

Isolation Level	Description
`TransactionDefinition.ISOLATION_DEFAULT`	This is the default isolation level for an individual `PlatformTransactionManager` (`ISOLATION_READ_COMMITTED` for most databases).
`TransactionDefinition.ISOLATION_READ_UNCOMMITTED`	This is the lowest level of isolation; we cannot really call this an isolation level, because other transactions can see data modified by this transaction even before it completes. This transaction can also see all changes other transactions perform even before they are committed.
`TransactionDefinition.ISOLATION_READ_COMMITTED`	This is the default level in most databases; it specifies that other transactions cannot see the data modifications before this transaction completes. Unfortunately, you can select data *inserted* or *updated* by other transactions once they commit in this transaction. This means that at different points in this transaction, you can see different data as other transactions modify it.
`TransactionDefinition.ISOLATION_REPEATABLE_READ`	More strict than `ISOLATION_READ_COMMITTED`, this isolation level ensures that if you select a data set in this transaction, you can select at least the same set again, even if other transactions modify the selected data. However, if another transaction *inserts* new data, you can select the newly inserted data.
`TransactionDefinition.ISOLATION_SERIALIZABLE`	This is the most expensive and reliable isolation level; all transactions are treated as if they were executed one after another.

Choosing the appropriate isolation level is very important for the consistency of the data, but the choices you make can have a great impact on performance. The highest isolation level, `TransactionDefinition.ISOLATION_SERIALIZABLE`, is particularly expensive to maintain.

The `getPropagationBehavior()` method specifies what Spring does when your code requests a new transaction. The values for this method are listed in Table 16-2.

Table 16-2. *Propagation Behavior Values*

Propagation Behavior	Description
TransactionDefinition.PROPAGATION_REQUIRED	Spring will use an active transaction if it exists. If not, Spring will begin a new transaction.
TransactionDefinition.PROPAGATION_SUPPORTS	Spring will use an active transaction; if there is no active transaction, Spring will not start a new one.
TransactionDefinition.PROPAGATION_MANDATORY	Spring will use an active transaction; if there is no active transaction, Spring will throw an exception.
TransactionDefinition.PROPAGATION_REQUIRES_NEW	Spring will always start a new transaction. If an active transaction already exists, it is suspended.
TransactionDefinition.PROPAGATION_NOT_SUPPORTED	Spring will not execute the code in an active transaction. The code always executes nontransactionally and suspends any existing transaction.
TransactionDefinition.PROPAGATION_NEVER	This always executes nontransactionally even if an active transaction exists. It throws an exception if an active transaction exists.
TransactionDefinition.PROPAGATION_NESTED	This runs in a nested transaction if an active transaction exists. If there is no active transaction, the code runs as if TransactionDefinition.PROPAGATION_REQUIRED is set.

Using the TransactionStatus Interface

The TransactionStatus interface, shown in Listing 16-2, allows a transaction manager to control transaction execution. The code can check whether the transaction is a new one or whether it is a read-only transaction. You can also use the TransactionStatus reference to initiate a rollback.

Listing 16-2. *TransactionStatus Declaration*

```
public interface TransactionStatus {
    boolean isNewTransaction();
    void setRollbackOnly();
    boolean isRollbackOnly();
}
```

The methods of the TransactionStatus interface are fairly self-explanatory; the most notable one is setRollbackOnly(), which marks the transaction as uncommittable. In other words, the only operation you can perform after calling setRollbackOnly() is a rollback. In most cases, the transaction manager will detect this and end the transaction immediately after it notices that it would have to commit. The pseudo code in Listing 16-3 demonstrates this.

Listing 16-3. *Usage of setRollbackOnly()*

```
begin
SQL: select * from t_user;
Java: setRollbackOnly();
SQL: select * from t_user_address where user = ?
SQL: update t_user_address set primary = 1 where id = ?
SQL: select * from t_product
```

After the call to `setRollbackOnly()`, most databases allow the next `select` statement to execute but will fail on the `update` statement—it would be pointless to perform the `update`; because the transaction is read-only, the modification would not be committed.

Implementations of the PlatformTransactionManager

The `PlatformTransactionManager` interface uses the `TransactionDefinition` and `TransactionStatus` interfaces to create and manage transactions. The actual implementations of this interface must have detailed knowledge of the transaction manager. The `DataSourceTransactionManager` controls transactions performed on JDBC `Connection` instances obtained from a `DataSource`; `HibernateTransactionManager` controls transactions performed on a Hibernate session; `JdoTransactionManager` manages JDO transactions; and `JtaTransactionManager` delegates transaction management to JTA.

Exploring a Transaction Management Sample

The first part of this chapter gave you a quick overview of the transaction infrastructure in Spring, but we are sure you will appreciate an example that demonstrates how to use Spring transaction support.

There are three basic ways to implement an operation that uses transactions: you can use declarative transactions, where you simply declare that a method requires a transaction; you can use source-level metadata to indicate that a method requires a transaction; or you can actually write code that handles the transactions. Spring supports all three approaches; we begin with the most flexible and convenient one—declarative transaction management.

First, we will show you several implementations of transaction support. Take a look at the UML diagram in Figure 16-1 to get a sense of what is in store in the sample application.

Even though the class diagram may seem complex, we will be implementing a naïve banking application. We have the `Account` class that holds the account balance (this is a gross simplification of real bank accounts, but it is all we need for this example); we use the `AccountIdentity` to uniquely identify the bank account. The `BalanceMutator` interface has a single method, `mutate(BigDecimal)`. We implement this interface in the `BankServiceSupport`; the `CreditBalanceMutator` adds the amount to be credited to the `balance` argument. The `DebitBalanceMutator` is slightly more complicated; it checks whether there is enough money in the account to debit the specified amount. If you want to explore this concept further, you can modify the `DebitBalanceMutator` to allow for overdrafts, for example.

The `AccountDao` defines a data access interface, which we implement in the `JdbcAccountDao` class. Next, we have the `BankService` interface with the `transfer` and `getBalance` methods. The `BankServiceSupport` implements these two methods, even if only as protected methods with the `do` prefix. We will use the `BankServiceSupport` subclasses to demonstrate the various transaction management techniques.

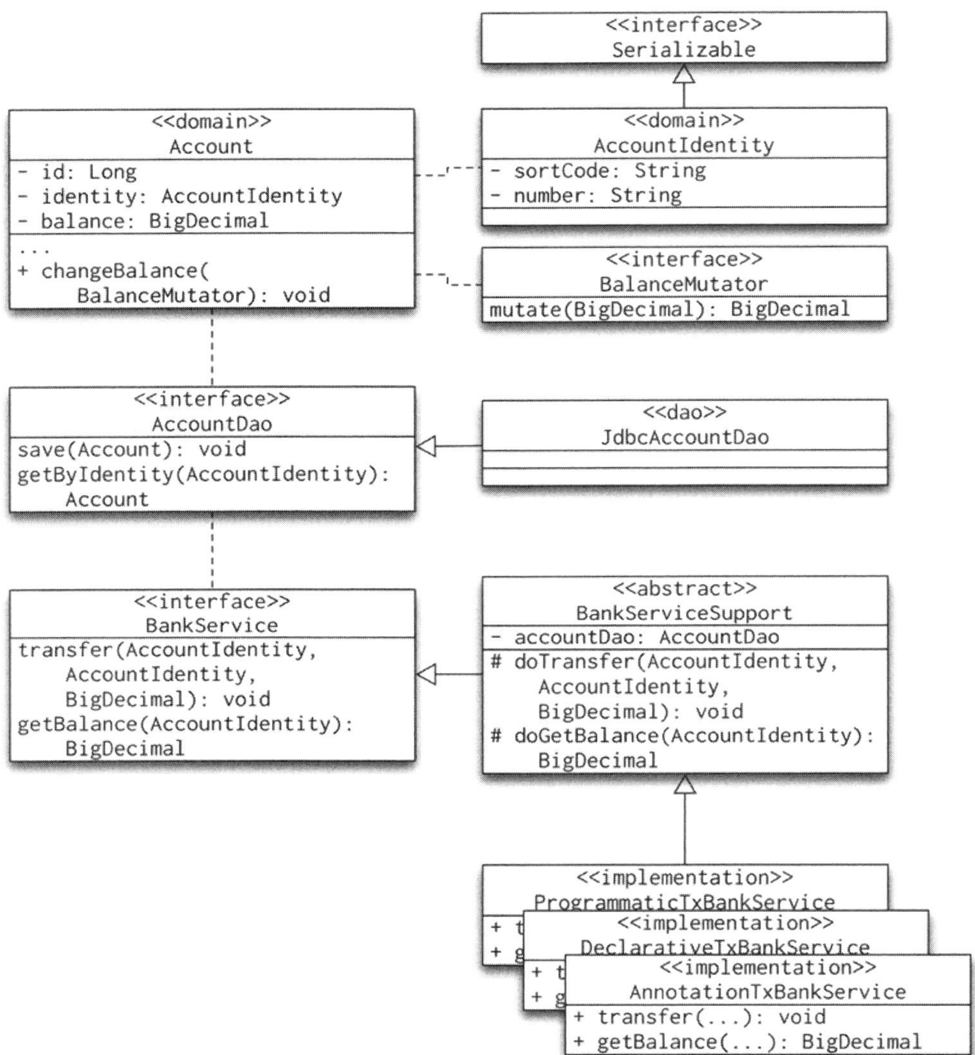

Figure 16-1. *UML class diagram for the transactional banking sample application*

Nontransactional Code

Before we can begin discussing transactional management, we need to write the necessary support code. Let's begin with the SQL code in Listing 16-4 that creates the `t_account` table and inserts several testing accounts.

Listing 16-4. *SQL Code for the Sample Banking Application*

```
create table t_account (
    id number(19, 0) not null,
    sort_code varchar2(6) not null,
```

```
    number_ varchar2(8) not null,
    balance number(19, 2) not null,
    constraint pk_account primary key (id)
)
/

insert into t_account (id, sort_code, number_, balance)
               values (1, '011001', '12345678', 1000.0)
/
insert into t_account (id, sort_code, number_, balance)
               values (2, '011001', '87654321', 100.0)
/
insert into t_account (id, sort_code, number_, balance)
               values (3, '011001', '10203040', 0.0)
/
insert into t_account (id, sort_code, number_, balance)
               values (4, '011001', '50607080', 30.0)
/
insert into t_account (id, sort_code, number_, balance)
               values (5, '011001', '10000000', 1000000.0)
/
```

There is nothing unusual about the SQL code; if you are not using an Oracle 10g database, you may need to tweak the SQL syntax to make the code run in your particular database. Next, we need to look at the `Account` and `AccountIdentity` classes and the `BalanceMutator` interface. For brevity, we show the two classes and interface in Listing 16-5.

Listing 16-5. *Account, AccountIdentity, and BalanceMutator*

```
Account.java:
public class Account {
    private Long id;
    private AccountIdentity identity;
    private BigDecimal balance;

    public void changeBalance(BalanceMutator mutator) {
        this.balance = mutator.mutate(this.balance);
    }

    // getters and setters
}

AccountIdentity.java:
public final class AccountIdentity implements Serializable {
    private static final long serialVersionUID = 3287882727785753918L;
    private String sortCode;
    private String number;

    public AccountIdentity() {
    }

    public AccountIdentity(String sortCode, String number) {
        Assert.notNull(sortCode, "The 'sortCode' argument must not be null.");
        Assert.notNull(number, "The 'number' argument must not be null.");
```

```
        this.sortCode = sortCode;
        this.number = number;
    }
    ...
    // getters and setters
}
```

BalanceMutator.java:

```
public interface BalanceMutator {

    BigDecimal mutate(BigDecimal balance);

}
```

You can see that the Account class has a synthetic identity (Long id). The synthetic identity is the implementation detail: we need the synthetic ID in our code, but it is meaningless to the users; they use the account number and sort code to identify their accounts. The Account class has only one significant method: changeBalance(BalanceMutator). This method uses the BalanceMutator instance to update the balance of the account.

■ **Note** We have chosen to use the BalanceMutator to update the balance of the accounts, because we suspect that the rules that govern balance updates may be quite complex. Using an interface that we implement in the service layer is more flexible than having simple credit(BigDecimal) and debit(BigDecimal) methods on the Account class.

Next, we take a look at the sample application's data access layer. For simplicity, we will use the SimpleJdbcTemplate (go to Chapter 9 for more details on Spring JDBC support). We take an approach typical for Spring applications: we create the AccountDao interface and a single implementation, JdbcAccountDao. Listing 16-6 shows the source code of both the interface and the implementation.

Listing 16-6. *The AccountDao Interface and the JdbcAccountDao Implementation*

AccountDao.java:

```
public interface AccountDao {

    void save(Account account);

    Account getByIdentity(AccountIdentity accountIdentity);

}
```

JdbcAccountDao.java

```
public class JdbcAccountDao extends SimpleJdbcDaoSupport implements AccountDao {
    private static final String INSERT_SQL =
            "insert into t_account (id, sort_code, number_, balance) values " +
                    "(?, ?, ?, ?)";
    private static final String UPDATE_SQL =
            "update t_account set balance=? where id=?";
    private static final String SELECT_SQL =
            "select id, sort_code, number_, balance from t_account " +
                    "where sort_code=? and number_=?";
```

```
    public void save(Account account) {
        if (account.getId() == null) {
            // insert
            getSimpleJdbcTemplate().update(INSERT_SQL,
                    account.getId(),
                    account.getIdentity().getSortCode(),
                    account.getIdentity().getNumber(),
                    account.getBalance());
        } else {
            // update
            getSimpleJdbcTemplate().update(UPDATE_SQL,
                    account.getBalance(),
                    account.getId());
        }
    }

    public Account getByIdentity(AccountIdentity accountIdentity) {
        return getSimpleJdbcTemplate().queryForObject(SELECT_SQL,
                new ParameterizedRowMapper<Account>() {
                    public Account mapRow(ResultSet rs, int rowNumber)
                            throws SQLException {

                        Account account = new Account();
                        account.setId(rs.getLong(1));
                        AccountIdentity identity = new AccountIdentity(
                                rs.getString(2),
                                rs.getString(3)
                        );
                        account.setIdentity(identity);
                        account.setBalance(rs.getBigDecimal(4));
                        return account;
                    }
                }, accountIdentity.getSortCode(), accountIdentity.getNumber());
    }
}
```

We have tried to keep the code as simple as possible; keep in mind that we are not showing Spring JDBC, just implementing the data access layer code to demonstrate Spring transaction management. Finally, we implement the `BankServiceSupport`; we will use this class as the superclass for our transactional `BankService` implementations. To that effect, the `BankServiceSupport` implements the `BankService` methods as protected methods with the `do` prefix. Listing 16-7 shows the `BankServiceSupport` implementation.

Listing 16-7. *BankServiceSupport Code*

```
public abstract class BankServiceSupport {
    private AccountDao accountDao;

    protected abstract static class BalanceMutatorSupport
            implements BalanceMutator {
        private BigDecimal amount;

        BalanceMutatorSupport(BigDecimal amount) {
            Assert.notNull(amount, "The 'amount' argument must not be null.");
            this.amount = amount;
        }
```

```
        protected final BigDecimal getAmount() {
            return this.amount;
        }

        protected abstract BigDecimal doMutate(BigDecimal balance);

        public final BigDecimal mutate(BigDecimal balance) {
            return doMutate(balance);
        }
    }

    protected static class CreditBalanceMutator
            extends BalanceMutatorSupport {

        CreditBalanceMutator(BigDecimal amount) {
            super(amount);
        }

        protected BigDecimal doMutate(BigDecimal balance) {
            return balance.add(getAmount());
        }
    }

    protected static class NoOverdraftDebitBalanceMutator
            extends BalanceMutatorSupport {

        NoOverdraftDebitBalanceMutator(BigDecimal amount) {
            super(amount);
        }

        protected BigDecimal doMutate(BigDecimal balance) {
            BigDecimal result = balance.subtract(getAmount());
            if (result.compareTo(new BigDecimal(0)) < 0)
                throw new InsufficientFundsException(getAmount().subtract(balance));
            return result;
        }
    }

    protected void doTransfer(AccountIdentity from, AccountIdentity to,
                          BigDecimal amount) {
        Account fromAccount = this.accountDao.getByIdentity(from);
        if (fromAccount == null) throw new UnknownAccount(from);
        Account toAccount = this.accountDao.getByIdentity(to);
        if (toAccount == null) throw new UnknownAccount(to);

        fromAccount.changeBalance(new NoOverdraftDebitBalanceMutator(amount));
        toAccount.changeBalance(new CreditBalanceMutator(amount));

        this.accountDao.save(fromAccount);
        this.accountDao.save(toAccount);
    }

    protected BigDecimal doGetBalance(AccountIdentity accountIdentity) {
        Account account = this.accountDao.getByIdentity(accountIdentity);
        if (account == null) throw new UnknownAccount(accountIdentity);
        return account.getBalance();
    }
```

```
    public void setAccountDao(AccountDao accountDao) {
        this.accountDao = accountDao;
    }
}
```

The doTransfer and doGetBalance methods implement the functionality of the BankService.transfer and BankService.getBalance methods; we have implemented them as protected methods because we will create different subclasses of the BankServiceSupport to demonstrate the different transaction management techniques Spring offers. Let's complete our nontransactional code with a nontransactional implementation of the BankServiceSupport class (see Listing 16-8).

Listing 16-8. *Nontransactional Implementation of the BankServiceSupport Class*

```
public class DefaultBankService extends BankServiceSupport
        implements BankService {

    public void transfer(AccountIdentity from, AccountIdentity to,
                         BigDecimal amount) {
        doTransfer(from, to, amount);
    }

    public BigDecimal getBalance(AccountIdentity accountIdentity) {
        return doGetBalance(accountIdentity);
    }
}
```

The last pieces of the sample application are the Spring XML configuration files. We will split the configuration into two files: dao-context.xml and svc-context-*.xml. The dao-context.xml file will define the dataSource and accountDao beans; the svc-context-*.xml file will define the bankService bean. Listing 16-9 shows the dao-context.xml file.

Listing 16-9. *The dao-context.xml Configuration File*

```
<?xml version="1.0" encoding="UTF-8"?>
<beans xmlns="http://www.springframework.org/schema/beans"
       xmlns:xsi="http://www.w3.org/2001/XMLSchema-instance"
       xsi:schemaLocation="
            http://www.springframework.org/schema/beans
           http://www.springframework.org/schema/beans/spring-beans.xsd">


    <bean id="dataSource"
        class="org.apache.commons.dbcp.BasicDataSource" destroy-method="close">
        <property name="driverClassName" value="oracle.jdbc.driver.OracleDriver"/>
        <property name="url"
            value="jdbc:oracle:thin:@oracle.devcake.co.uk:1521:INTL"/>
        <property name="username" value="PROSPRING"/>
        <property name="password" value="x******6"/>
    </bean>

    <bean id="transactionManager"
       class="org.springframework.jdbc.datasource.DataSourceTransactionManager">
        <property name="dataSource" ref="dataSource"/>
    </bean>

    <bean id="accountDao"
```

```
        class="com.apress.prospring2.ch16.dao.jdbc.JdbcAccountDao">
        <property name="dataSource" ref="dataSource"/>
    </bean>

</beans>
```

There are no surprises here: the dataSource bean is the Apache DBCP implementation of the DataSource, and we use the Oracle 10g database. The accountDao bean is the JdbcAccountDao implementation from Listing 16-6. To verify that the application works without Spring transaction support, we will create the svc-context-nt.xml file (see Listing 16-10).

Listing 16-10. *Nontransactional bankService Bean Configuration*

```
<?xml version="1.0" encoding="UTF-8"?>
<beans xmlns="http://www.springframework.org/schema/beans"
       xmlns:xsi="http://www.w3.org/2001/XMLSchema-instance"
       xsi:schemaLocation="
            http://www.springframework.org/schema/beans
            http://www.springframework.org/schema/beans/spring-beans.xsd">


    <bean id="bankService"
          class="com.apress.prospring2.ch16.services.DefaultBankService">
        <property name="accountDao" ref="accountDao"/>
    </bean>
</beans>
```

The final piece is the sample application that creates the ClassPathXmlApplicationContext and uses the bankService bean to transfer some virtual money between two accounts. Listing 16-11 shows a simple application that displays the account balances, transfers some money, and displays the final balances.

Listing 16-11. *Sample Application for bankService*

```
public class Main {

    public static void main(String[] args) {
        ApplicationContext ac = new ClassPathXmlApplicationContext(
                new String[] {
                        "/META-INF/spring/*-context.xml",
                        "/META-INF/spring/*-context-nt.xml"
                }
        );
        BankService bankService = (BankService) ac.getBean("bankService");
        final AccountIdentity a1 = new AccountIdentity("011001", "12345678");
        final AccountIdentity a2 = new AccountIdentity("011001", "10203040");

        System.out.println("Before");
        System.out.println(a1 + ": " + bankService.getBalance(a1));
        System.out.println(a2 + ": " + bankService.getBalance(a2));
        try {
            bankService.transfer(a1, a2, new BigDecimal("200.00"));
        } catch (Exception ignored) {

        }
        System.out.println("After");
```

```
        System.out.println(a1 + ": " + bankService.getBalance(a1));
        System.out.println(a2 + ": " + bankService.getBalance(a2));
    }

}
```

Using the data we inserted in the SQL script in Listing 16-4, the application runs and prints the following:

```
Before
AccountIdentity {01-10-01 1234-5678}: 1000
AccountIdentity {01-10-01 1020-3040}: 0
After
AccountIdentity {01-10-01 1234-5678}: 800
AccountIdentity {01-10-01 1020-3040}: 200
```

The application works: it can find an account in the database using the `AccountIdentity` object, modify the amount in each account, and persist it to the database. The only trouble is that the debit and credit operations are not tied together. If the credit operation fails, the system will not reverse the debit operation: in other words, we take money out of the payer account, fail to pay it into the payee account, and the money is lost. We need to ensure that the debit and credit operations are treated as a single command. Accountants would also like to see that the amounts transferred match—the account records need to be consistent at all times. Also, we need to make sure that while we are debiting the payer account, the account holder cannot use an ATM card to withdraw more money than there would be when the transfer completes. Finally, we also need to guarantee that once we complete the transfer, the information about the transfer will survive even if the database server goes down. In short, our `transfer` method needs to conform to the ACID requirements.

Before we begin discussing the different transaction management approaches, we need to write code that will simulate possible problems. We will modify the `JdbcAccountDao` class to fail randomly; Listing 16-12 shows the unreliable implementation of `JdbcAccountDao`.

Listing 16-12. *Randomly Failing JdbcAccountDao Class*

```
public class JdbcAccountDao extends SimpleJdbcDaoSupport implements AccountDao {
    ...

    public void save(Account account) {
        Grinch.ruin();
        if (account.getId() == null) {
            // insert
            getSimpleJdbcTemplate().update(INSERT_SQL,
                    account.getId(),
                    account.getIdentity().getSortCode(),
                    account.getIdentity().getNumber(),
                    account.getBalance());
        } else {
            // update
            getSimpleJdbcTemplate().update(UPDATE_SQL,
                    account.getBalance(),
                    account.getId());
        }
    }
    ...
}
```

The Grinch.ruin() method throws a RuntimeException randomly, which is precisely what we need in order to demonstrate transaction management fully. We complete the nontransactional code with Listing 16-13, which shows the Grinch class.

Listing 16-13. *Implementation of the Grinch Class*

```
public final class Grinch {
    private static final Random RND = new Random();
    private static final String MESSAGE = "Muhehe! It's broken now.";

    private Grinch() {

    }

    public static void ruin() {
        if (RND.nextInt() % 3 == 0) {
            System.out.println(MESSAGE);
            throw new RuntimeException(MESSAGE);
        }
    }

}
```

Programmatic Transaction Management

We begin by looking at how you can use the PlatformTransactionManager directly, that is, programmatically. We will use the nontransactional code from the previous section but implement another subclass of the BankServiceSupport. Listing 16-14 shows the ProgrammaticTxBankService.

Listing 16-14. *ProgrammaticTxBankService Implementaiton*

```
public class ProgrammaticTxBankService
        extends BankServiceSupport implements BankService{
    private PlatformTransactionManager transactionManager;

    public void transfer(AccountIdentity from, AccountIdentity to,
                         BigDecimal amount) throws Throwable {
        TransactionDefinition transactionDefinition =
                new DefaultTransactionDefinition(
                        TransactionDefinition.PROPAGATION_REQUIRED);
        TransactionStatus transactionStatus =
                this.transactionManager.getTransaction(transactionDefinition);
        try {
            doTransfer(from, to, amount);
            this.transactionManager.commit(transactionStatus);
        } catch (Throwable t) {
            this.transactionManager.rollback(transactionStatus);
            throw t;
        }
    }

    public BigDecimal getBalance(AccountIdentity accountIdentity) {
        return doGetBalance(accountIdentity);
    }
```

```
    public void setTransactionManager(
            PlatformTransactionManager transactionManager) {
        this.transactionManager = transactionManager;
    }
}
```

The ProgrammaticTxBankService demonstrates how to write transaction management code manually. If we take a closer look at the transfer method, it is not difficult code. We create a new TransactionDefinition instance (the DefaultTransactionDefinition) and, to be explicit, we set the transaction propagation to TransactionDefinition.PROPAGATION_REQUIRED. We could have used the DefaultTransactionDefinition() constructor, which assumes that the propagation level is TransactionDefinition.PROPAGATION_REQUIRED.

Next, we use PlatformTransactionManager.getTransaction to start a transaction. When the PlatformTransactionManager begins the transaction, it returns a TransactionStatus instance, which identifies the transaction. We will need TransactionStatus in calls to PlatformTransactionManager.commit or PlatformTransactionManager.rollback. The rules for commit and rollback are quite simple: if the doTransfer method completes without any exception, we commit the changes; if it throws any exception, we roll back the changes. While the code to manually manage the transaction is not difficult, it obfuscates the important code. In fact, the only line in the transfer method that actually implements the requirements is doTransfer(from, to, amount). The rest of the code just implements transaction management.

Nevertheless, we have the code now, so let's use the ProgrammaticTxBankService in a sample application similar to the one in Listing 16-11; the only difference is that instead of using *-context-nt.xml we are going to use *-context-ptx.xml in the ClassPathXmlApplicationContext constructor. Listing 16-15 shows the svc-context-ptx.xml configuration file.

Listing 16-15. *The svc-context-ptx.xml Configuration File*

```
<?xml version="1.0" encoding="UTF-8"?>
<beans xmlns="http://www.springframework.org/schema/beans"
       xmlns:xsi="http://www.w3.org/2001/XMLSchema-instance"
       xsi:schemaLocation="
            http://www.springframework.org/schema/beans
            http://www.springframework.org/schema/beans/spring-beans.xsd">

    <bean id="bankService"
          class="com.apress.prospring2.ch16.services.ProgrammaticTxBankService">
        <property name="accountDao" ref="accountDao"/>
        <property name="transactionManager" ref="transactionManager"/>
    </bean>
</beans>
```

This XML configuration file defines the bankService bean as an instance of the ProgrammaticTxBankService and sets the transactionManager reference. If we run the application a few times, the Grinch.ruin() method will do its worst and the application will print this:

```
Before
AccountIdentity {01-10-01 1234-5678}: 600
AccountIdentity {01-10-01 1020-3040}: 400
Muhehe! It's broken now.
After
AccountIdentity {01-10-01 1234-5678}: 600
AccountIdentity {01-10-01 1020-3040}: 400
```

The Grinch.ruin() method threw the RuntimeException, but we caught the exception in the ProgrammaticTxBankService.transfer method and rolled back the transaction. Therefore, the payer and payee accounts show the same balances before and after the failed transaction. No money got lost during the transfer.

Using the TransactionTemplate Class

If we wanted to use programmatic transaction control in more than one area of the system, we should refactor the way we interact with the PlatformTransactionManager. If we take a closer look at the transfer method, we can see that we have some common code that surrounds some specific code. This calls for the template method pattern, and Spring transaction support provides the TransactionTemplate class that implements the common code for the programmatic transaction management. All we have to do is supply the TransactionCallback implementation; its doInTransaction method represents the specialized section of the algorithm in the template method pattern. Listing 16-16 shows the ProgrammaticTxBankService using TransactionTemplate.

Listing 16-16. *ProgrammaticTxBankService Using TransactionTemplate*

```
public class ProgrammaticTxBankService
        extends BankServiceSupport implements BankService{
    private TransactionTemplate transactionTemplate;

    public void transfer(final AccountIdentity from,
                         final AccountIdentity to,
                         final BigDecimal amount) throws Throwable {
        this.transactionTemplate.execute(new TransactionCallbackWithoutResult() {
            protected void doInTransactionWithoutResult(TransactionStatus status) {
                doTransfer(from, to, amount);
            }
        });
    }

    public BigDecimal getBalance(AccountIdentity accountIdentity) {
        return doGetBalance(accountIdentity);
    }

    public void setTransactionManager(
            PlatformTransactionManager transactionManager) {
        this.transactionTemplate = new TransactionTemplate(transactionManager);
    }
}
```

You can see that the preceding code is much simpler: all the transaction creation and exception-handling code is in the TransactionTemplate. Also notice that we have not implemented the TransactionCallback interface directly. Instead, we have chosen to implement the abstract class TransactionCallbackWithoutResult. This was only for convenience: the TransactionCallback.doInTransaction implementation must return Object, but we do not want to return anything at all. The TransactionCallbackWithoutResult is an abstract class that implements the TransactionCallback.doInTransaction method as final and delegates the processing to protected abstract void doInTransactionWithoutResult; when this method completes, the TransactionCallbackWithouResult.doInTransaction returns null.

Programmatic Transaction Management Summary

Even though you can use programmatic transaction support (and the TransactionTemplate class greatly simplifies this), it is still a lot of work. If you cast your mind back to the AOP chapters (Chapters 5 and 6), you can see that transaction management is a good application of around advices. In the next section, we will take a look at the different options for declarative transaction management.

Declarative Transaction Management

Declarative transaction management means that you don't write transaction management code in your beans at all; instead, you configure the beans to be transactional. We can therefore take the DefaultBankService from Listing 16-8 and specify in the bean configuration that we want the transfer method to be transactional. The simplest way to achieve this is to use a proxy: the proxy will intercept all method calls, and if the method name is included in the transactional configuration, the proxy will act as around advice. It will begin the transaction before the call to the target method and execute the target method in a try / catch block. If the target method finishes normally, the proxy commits the transaction; if the target method throws a runtime exception, the proxy performs a rollback. To do all this work, the proxy will use the configured PlatformTransactionManager. This is the core concept of declarative transaction management; the differences are in the way we can create the proxy. Let's begin with the legacy way, using the TransactionProxyFactoryBean.

Using the TransactionProxyFactoryBean

The TransactionProxyFactoryBean has been with us since Spring 1.0, and Spring 2.5 still supports its functions, even though the implementation has changed substantially. In short, the factory bean creates a JDK proxy to the target bean and intercepts every method call. It decides how to handle any transactional code depending on additional configuration. Let's jump straight into an example; Listing 16-17 shows how we can create the proxy bean. We are going to use the TransactionProxyFactoryBean to declaratively specify transactional behavior of your beans.

Listing 16-17. *Using the TransactionProxyFactoryBean*

```
<?xml version="1.0" encoding="UTF-8"?>
<beans xmlns="http://www.springframework.org/schema/beans"
       xmlns:xsi="http://www.w3.org/2001/XMLSchema-instance"
       xsi:schemaLocation="
            http://www.springframework.org/schema/beans
            http://www.springframework.org/schema/beans/spring-beans.xsd">

    <bean id="bankService"
          class="org.springframework.transaction.interceptor.➥
                     TransactionProxyFactoryBean">
        <property name="target">
            <bean class="com.apress.prospring2.ch16.services.DefaultBankService">
                <property name="accountDao" ref="accountDao"/>
            </bean>
        </property>
```

```
        <property name="transactionAttributes">
            <value>
                *=PROPAGATION_REQUIRED
            </value>
        </property>
        <property name="transactionManager" ref="transactionManager"/>
    </bean>
</beans>
```

This configuration is not pretty, but it does an excellent job: the code in the `DefaultBankService` is not aware that the `transfer` method now runs in a transaction. Even though the `TransactionProxyFactoryBean` is the Spring 1.x–style of declarative transaction management, we will describe it in more detail in case you encounter it in existing Spring applications.

The `TransactionProxyFactoryBean` creates a JDK, which intercepts calls to all methods. For any method whose name appears as the key in the `transactionProperties`, it starts a transaction with the specified propagation level. In the example in Listing 16-17, all methods will be transactional, and the proxy will call code equivalent to that shown in Listing 16-18.

Listing 16-18. *Pseudo Code for the Calls to the bankService.transfer Method*

```
TransactionDefinition transactionDefinition = new TransactionDefinition() {
    public int getPropagationBehavior() {
        return TransactionDefinition.PROPAGATION_REQUIRED;
    }

    public int getIsolationLevel() {
        return TransactionDefinition.ISOLATION_DEFAULT;
    }

    public int getTimeout() {
        return TransactionDefinition.TIMEOUT_DEFAULT;
    }

    public boolean isReadOnly() {
        return false;
    }

    public String getName() {
        return "Transaction-1";
    }
};
TransactionStatus transactionStatus =
           this.transactionManager.getTransaction(transactionDefinition);
try {
    target.invoke(arguments);
} catch (Throwable t) {
    if (t ( allowedExceptions)
       this.transactionManager.commit(transactionStatus);
    else if (t ( disallowedExceptions || disallowedExceptions.isEmpty())
       this.transactionManager.rollback(transactionStatus);
    throw t;
}
```

You can see that the proxy handles the transaction in exactly the same way as in Listing 16-14. However, the code is slightly more complex because the `TransactionProxyFactoryBean` gives you finer control over the transaction-handling code than the `TransactionTemplate` or our programmatic code.

First, you may notice that the proxy sets all properties of the TransactionDefinition instance and that the proxy will commit the transaction even if the target method throws an exception, as long as that exception is in the set of allowed exceptions. You can control all aspects of transaction handling in the transactionAttributes property entry. Listing 16-19 shows the detailed syntax of the property entry.

Listing 16-19. *The Syntax of the transactionAttributes Property Expression*

```
expr ::=
   method = propagation
       isolation? read-only? timeout? allowedExceptions? disallowedExceptions?

method ::= IDENT*;
propagation ::= 'PROPAGATION_' IDENT;
isolation ::= 'ISOLATION_' IDENT;
read-only ::= 'readOnly';
timeout ::= 'TIMEOUT_' INT;
allowedExceptions ::= '+' exceptions+;
disallowedExceptions ::= '-' exceptions+;
exceptions ::= exception (, exception)*;
exception ::= IDENT;

IDENT ::= java identifier pattern;
IDENT* ::= java identifier pattern + * (wildcard);
INT ::= integer pattern;
```

At the least, the expression must specify the method name and propagation, for example transfer=PROPAGATION_REQUIRED. The most complex expression can look like this:

```
transfer=PROPAGATION_REQUIRED, ISOLATION_SERIALIZABLE, readOnly, ➥
timeout_500, +MyBenignException, +AnotherAllowedException, -BadException
```

You may notice that the TransactionProxyFactoryBean has other properties, for example exposeProxy and pointcut; their names sound like some of the terms we explored in the AOP chapters. In fact, Spring 2.5 uses AOP in the implementation of the TransactionProxyFactoryBean. Moreover, AOP transaction handling is the preferred declarative transaction management approach in Spring 2.5.

Implications of Using Proxies in Transaction Management

If you recall, in Chapter 6, we discussed the impact of proxying on the advised objects. The transactional proxies are no different from any other proxies. Let's change our DefaultBankService to perform additional balance checking before calling the doTransfer method (see Listing 16-20).

Listing 16-20. *DefaultBankService Calling the getBalance Method in the transfer Method*

```
public class DefaultBankService extends BankServiceSupport
        implements BankService {

    public void transfer(AccountIdentity from, AccountIdentity to,
                         BigDecimal amount) {
        if (getBalance(to).compareTo(new BigDecimal("1000000000")) > 0) {
            throw new RuntimeException("Billionaires do not need more money!");
        }
        doTransfer(from, to, amount);
    }
```

```
    public BigDecimal getBalance(AccountIdentity accountIdentity) {
        return doGetBalance(accountIdentity);
    }
}
```

If we run this application, the proxy will intercept the call to the transfer method and start a new transaction, but the getBalance(BigDecimal) method will not start a new transaction, because the getBalance(BigDecimal) method is being executed not on the proxy but on the proxy target.

In this simple example, the fact that the getBalance method is not being executed in its own transaction is not a problem; in fact, it is the desired behavior. There can be situations where nested transactions (or the lack of them) can cause problems. In Chapter 11, we explored the implications of nested transactions on Hibernate sessions and the problems transaction nesting may cause with lazy loading.

If you do require nested transactional behavior, you must take the approach we explored in Chapter 6: use ((BankService)AopContext.currentProxy()).getBalance(to), which binds the implementation to Spring AOP. Alternatively, you can use Spring AOP transaction management with load-time weaving.

AOP Transaction Management

AOP transaction management makes use of the Spring AOP infrastructure; in most cases, Spring AOP will create a JDK proxy to intercept the method calls. You can use load-time weaving to weave the aspect in at load time, eliminating the need for proxies (refer to Chapter 6 if you would like to refresh your memory about load-time weaving). You have two alternative ways to configure Spring AOP transaction management: annotation-based configuration or XML configuration.

Using Annotation-Based AOP Transaction Management

You can use annotations with AOP automatic proxying to introduce transactional behavior to existing beans. Let's begin with Listing 16-21, which shows the DeclarativeTxBankService class.

Listing 16-21. *The DeclarativeTxBankService Implementation*

```
public class DeclarativeTxBankService
        extends BankServiceSupport implements BankService{

    @Transactional
    public void transfer(final AccountIdentity from,
                         final AccountIdentity to,
                         final BigDecimal amount) {
        doTransfer(from, to, amount);
    }

    @Transactional
    public BigDecimal getBalance(AccountIdentity accountIdentity) {
        return doGetBalance(accountIdentity);
    }

}
```

Notice the @Transactional attribute; to allow Spring's transaction management infrastructure to use this attribute to create the appropriate pointcuts and advice, we need to use AOP's automatic proxying and transaction annotation-driven support. Listing 16-22 shows the XML configuration for annotation-based transaction management.

Listing 16-22. *Configuration for Annotation-Based Transaction Management*

```
<?xml version="1.0" encoding="UTF-8"?>
<beans xmlns="http://www.springframework.org/schema/beans"
       xmlns:aop="http://www.springframework.org/schema/aop"
       xmlns:tx="http://www.springframework.org/schema/tx"
       xmlns:xsi="http://www.w3.org/2001/XMLSchema-instance"
       xsi:schemaLocation="
            http://www.springframework.org/schema/beans
            http://www.springframework.org/schema/beans/spring-beans.xsd
            http://www.springframework.org/schema/tx
            http://www.springframework.org/schema/tx/spring-tx.xsd
            http://www.springframework.org/schema/aop
            http://www.springframework.org/schema/aop/spring-aop.xsd">

    <bean id="bankService"
          class="com.apress.prospring2.ch16.services.DefaultBankService">
        <property name="accountDao" ref="accountDao"/>
    </bean>

    <tx:annotation-driven transaction-manager="transactionManager"/>
    <aop:aspectj-autoproxy />

</beans>
```

This XML configuration file shows the standard bankService bean declaration, followed by the <tx:annotation-driven /> and <aop:aspectj-autoproxy /> tags. The <tx:annotation-driven /> tag creates the appropriate transaction management aspects using the @Transactional annotation. The <aop:aspectj-autoproxy /> tag then advises the matching beans.

Exploring the tx:annotation-driven Tag

The <tx:annotation-driven /> tag is at the core of the annotation-driven transaction management support. Table 16-3 lists all attributes of the <tx:annotation-driven /> tag.

Table 16-3. *Attributes of the <tx:annotation-driven /> Tag*

Attribute	Description
transactionManager	Specify a reference to an existing PlatformTransactionManager bean that the advices will use.
mode	Specify how the Spring transaction management framework creates the advised beans. The allowed values are proxy and aspectj. The proxy value is the default; it specifies that the advised object will be a JDK proxy. The aspectj parameter instructs Spring AOP to use AspectJ to create the proxy.
order	Specify the order in which the created aspect will be applied. This is applicable if you have more than one advice for the target object.
proxy-target-class	Set to true to specify that you wish to proxy the target class rather than all interfaces the bean implements.

Exploring the @Transactional Annotation

The `@Transactional` annotation allows you to control all aspects of the transaction definition the advice is going to create. Just as with the `transactionAttributes` property expression, you can specify the propagation, isolation level, timeout, and allowed and disallowed exceptions. Table 16-4 lists all attributes of the `@Transactional` annotation.

Table 16-4. *Attributes of the @Transactional Annotation*

Attribute	Type	Description
`propagation`	`org.springframework.annotaion.transaction.Propagation`	Specifies the propagation to be used in the transaction definition
`isolation`	`org.springframework.annotation.transaction.Isolation`	Sets the isolation level the transaction should have
`timeout`	`int`	Specifies the transaction timeout in seconds
`readOnly`	`boolean`	If `true`, the transaction will be marked as read-only
`noRollbackFor`	`Class<? extends Throwable>[]`	Array of exceptions that the target method can throw but the advice will still commit the transaction
`rollbackFor`	`Class<? extends Throwable>[]`	Array of exceptions that will make the advice roll back the transaction if the target method throws them

Annotation-Based Transaction Management Summary

Using the `@Transactional` annotation is an easy way to declare a method transactional. The advantage is that you can immediately see that the method is transactional, because it has the annotation. The disadvantage is that you have to repeat the `@Transactional` annotation for every transactional method. This is not a problem if you are happy with the default transaction attributes but quickly becomes a clumsy copy-and-paste affair when you are setting additional transaction attributes. An alternative is to annotate the class with the `@Transactional` annotation. This would make all methods in the class transactional. The problem with this approach is that all methods, even simple getters and setters, would run in a transaction, even though there is absolutely no need for that. The XML AOP transaction management handles such situations much better.

■ **Note** In saying that using `@Transactional` will make all methods execute in a transaction, we are being a bit sloppy: more accurately, we should say that all methods of a Spring bean instantiated from a class with the `@Transactional` annotation will be transactional.

Using XML AOP Transaction Management

XML AOP declarative transaction management is the preferred approach in Spring 2.5. Spring comes with the `<tx:advice />` tag, which creates a transaction-handling advice. All we need do to get us started is to create a pointcut that matches all methods we wish to make transactional and reference the transactional advice. Listing 16-23 shows an XML configuration that uses XML AOP transaction management.

Listing 16-23. *XML AOP Transaction Management Configuration*

```
<?xml version="1.0" encoding="UTF-8"?>
<beans xmlns="http://www.springframework.org/schema/beans"
       xmlns:aop="http://www.springframework.org/schema/aop"
       xmlns:tx="http://www.springframework.org/schema/tx"
       xmlns:xsi="http://www.w3.org/2001/XMLSchema-instance"
       xsi:schemaLocation="
            http://www.springframework.org/schema/beans
            http://www.springframework.org/schema/beans/spring-beans.xsd
            http://www.springframework.org/schema/tx
            http://www.springframework.org/schema/tx/spring-tx.xsd
            http://www.springframework.org/schema/aop
            http://www.springframework.org/schema/aop/spring-aop.xsd">


    <bean id="bankService"
          class="com.apress.prospring2.ch16.services.DefaultBankService">
        <property name="accountDao" ref="accountDao"/>
    </bean>

    <aop:config>
        <aop:pointcut id="allServiceMethods"
                      expression="execution(* ➥
                               com.apress.prospring2.ch16.services.*.*(..))"/>

        <aop:advisor advice-ref="defaultTransactionAdvice"
                     pointcut-ref="allServiceMethods"/>
    </aop:config>

    <tx:advice id="defaultTransactionAdvice"
           transaction-manager="transactionManager"/>

</beans>
```

This configuration file may seem much more complex than the `TransactionProxyFactoryBean` in Listing 16-17, so let's examine it in more detail. First, we used the `defaultTransactionAdvice`, which can specify the actions the proxy needs to perform when it intercepts the method call. If we leave the tag empty, it will assume that all methods should be transactional, that the propagation level is `PROPAGATION_DEFAULT`, that the isolation is `ISOLATION_DEFAULT`, that the timeout is `TIMEOUT_DEFAULT`, that the `read-only` property is `false`, and that all runtime exceptions cause rollbacks. To use the advice, we create the `allServiceMethods` pointcut for all methods in all classes in the com.apress.prospring2.ch16.services package. Finally, we create an aspect using the `defaultTransactionAdvice` for all methods matched by the `allServiceMethods` pointcut.

Before we take a more detailed look at the `<tx:advice />` tag, you may be wondering why this approach is preferred, because the `TransactionProxyFactoryBean` seems a lot easier. But the `TransactionProxyFactoryBean` is easier only if you have very few transactional beans. When you get to a point where you have several beans whose methods you want to declare transactional, you would have to create a `TransactionProxyFactoryBean` for every bean; moreover, you would have to repeat the `transactionAttributes` declaration in the proxy factory beans. The XML configuration in Listing 16-23 will apply the same transaction management to any number of new beans we create in the services package; all we have to do is to create a plain bean definition for every new bean. We won't have to configure anything else to have the transactional advice applied to all new service beans.

Exploring the tx:advice Tag

As you saw in Listing 16-23, you need to set the `id` and `transaction-manager` attributes in the `<tx:advice />` tag. The `id` is the identity of the advice bean, and the `transaction-manager` must reference a `PlatformTransactionManager` bean.

Beyond these two attributes, you can customize the behavior of the advice the `<tx:advice />` tag creates by using the `<tx:attributes />` tag. This allows you to configure everything that the `transactionAttributes` properties expression allowed you to do but in a more structured way. Let's take a look at Listing 16-24, which shows a more complicated `<tx:advice />` tag.

Listing 16-24. *A More Complex <tx:advice /> Tag*

```
<tx:advice id="defaultTransactionAdvice"
    transaction-manager="transactionManager">
    <tx:attributes>
        <tx:method
                name="*"
                isolation="READ_COMMITTED"
                propagation="REQUIRED"
                timeout="100"/>
        <tx:method
                name="get*"
                read-only="true"/>
    </tx:attributes>
</tx:advice>
```

We have transaction advice that will start a transaction using the `PROPAGATION_REQUIRED` propagation, `READ_COMMITTED` isolation level, and a 100-second timeout for all methods unless the method's name begins with `get`; in which case, the transaction definition will include `PROPAGATION_DEFAULT`, `ISOLATION_DEFAULT`, `TIMEOUT_DEFAULT`, and the `read-only` property will be set to `true`. In both cases, any runtime exception will cause a rollback.

As you can see, the `<tx:attributes />` tag allows you to create the `transactionAttributes` property expression in a more concise way; in addition, most IDEs will offer code completion (see Figure 16-2).

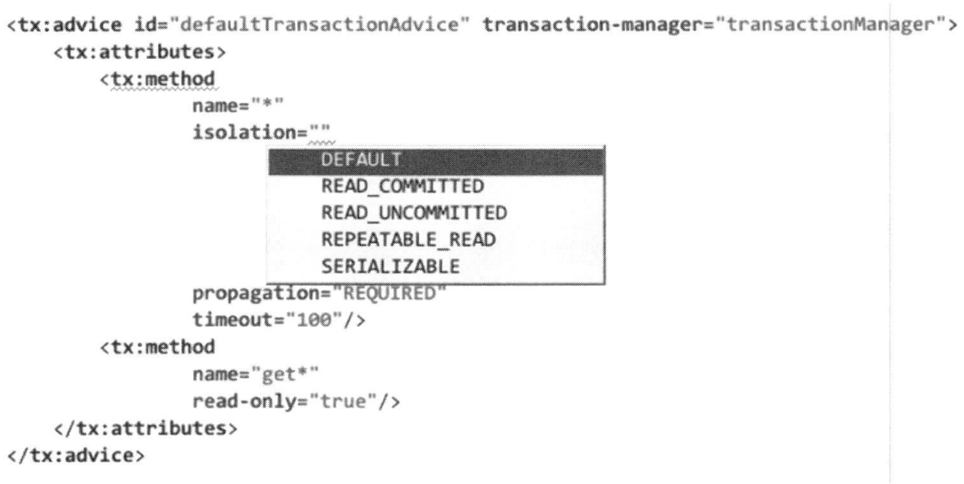

```
<tx:advice id="defaultTransactionAdvice" transaction-manager="transactionManager">
    <tx:attributes>
        <tx:method
                name="*"
                isolation=""
                          DEFAULT
                          READ_COMMITTED
                          READ_UNCOMMITTED
                          REPEATABLE_READ
                          SERIALIZABLE
                propagation="REQUIRED"
                timeout="100"/>
        <tx:method
                name="get*"
                read-only="true"/>
    </tx:attributes>
</tx:advice>
```

Figure 16-2. *<tx:attributes> code completion in IntelliJ IDEA*

The `<tx:attributes />` tag allows only `<tx:method />` tags to appear as its children. To complete the description of the `<tx:attributes />` tag, Table 16-5 details the attributes of the `<tx:method />` tag.

Table 16-5. *<tx:method /> Tag Attributes*

Attribute	Description
`name`	The pattern the method name needs to match for the advice to apply. You can use the asterisk (*) wildcard in this attribute.
`propagation`	Sets the propagation level to be used in the transaction definition.
`isolation`	Sets the isolation level to be used for the transaction.
`timeout`	Specifies the transaction timeout in seconds.
`read-only`	Set to `true` to mark the transaction as read-only (typically, you'd do this for transactions that only perform `select` statements; databases will usually fail read-only transaction on the first `update`, `insert`, or `delete` statement).
`no-rollback-for`	Comma-separated list of class names of exceptions that the target method can throw without causing the advice to perform a rollback.
`rollback-for`	Comma-separated list of class names of exceptions that will cause the advice to perform a rollback when thrown from the target method. By default, this list is empty; therefore, any runtime exception that is not in the `no-rollback-for` list will cause a rollback.

XML AOP Summary

Unlike annotation-based AOP transaction management, when you use XML AOP transaction management, the code in your beans does not reflect any transactional behavior at all. The XML configuration easily offsets this disadvantage with the fact that you do not need to repeat any details of the transaction management configuration. In addition, you can refer to pointcuts you use in your application's AOP configuration to allow the most effective code reuse.

We usually use the annotation-based approach during the implementation of the application, but in the production environment, we always try to use XML configuration only.

Working with Transactions Over Multiple Transactional Resources

So far, all our examples have used only one resource in the transactions: the JDBC connection. If you need to implement an application whose transactions include multiple resources, you will need to use the `JtaTransactionManager`.

■ **Note** You will also need to use the `JtaTransactionManager` if you are using an application-server–managed `DataSouce`.

Even though the Java EE application server specification does not require an application server to provide a `javax.transaction.TransactionManager`, all application servers we have used expose it, even though different application servers bind the `TransactionManager` to a different JNDI name. All that is required to start using the `JtaTransactionManager` in Spring applications is to define a `JtaTransactionManager` bean. Listing 16-25 shows the simplest possible configuration of a `JtaTransactionManager` bean.

Listing 16-25. *JtaTransactionManager Bean*

```
<?xml version="1.0" encoding="UTF-8"?>
<beans xmlns="http://www.springframework.org/schema/beans"
       xmlns:xsi="http://www.w3.org/2001/XMLSchema-instance"
       xsi:schemaLocation="
               http://www.springframework.org/schema/beans
               http://www.springframework.org/schema/beans/spring-beans.xsd">

...

    <bean id="jtaTransactionManager"
          class="org.springframework.transaction.jta.JtaTransactionManager"/>

...
</beans>
```

By default, the `JtaTransactionManager` will attempt to automatically detect a `UserTransaction` bound to the `java:comp/UserTransaction` JNDI name; if the `java:comp/UserTransaction` object also implements the `TransactionManager`, the `JtaTransactionManager` will use that; if the `java:comp/UserTransaction` does not implement the `TransactionManager`, the `JtaTransactionManager` will attempt to find the `TransactionManager` under these JNDI names:

- `java:comp/UserTransaction`: The default JNDI name, used by Resin 2.x, Oracle OC4J (Orion), JOnAS (JOTM), BEA WebLogic, and IBM WebSphere
- `java:pm/TransactionManager`: JNDI name for `TransactionManager` in Borland Enterprise Server and Sun Application Server (Sun ONE 7 and later)
- `java:comp/TransactionManager`: JNDI name used in Resin 3.x
- `java:/TransactionManager`: The name used in the JBoss Application Server

As you can see, the default names cover most of today's application servers. You can configure the `JtaTransactionManager` to match your application server; Table 16-6 shows the properties you may need to configure for your application server.

Table 16-6. *Properties of the JtaTransactionManager*

Property	Description
`userTransactionName`	The JNDI name that the application server uses to bind the instance of the `UserTransaction`; if the object bound to this name also implements `TransactionManager`, the `JtaTransactionManager` will not need to attempt to find the `TransactionManager` bound to JNDI name set in the `transactionManagerName`.
`transactionManagerName`	Specifies the JNDI name that contains the `TransactionManager` implementation.
`transactionSynchronizationRegistryName`	If you are using the Java EE 5 specification, and if your application server does not use the default name `java:comp/TransactionSynchronizationRegistry`, set this property to the JNDI name of a `TransactionSynchronizationRegistry` implementation your application server exposes.

These are the crucial properties to successfully create the JtaTransactionManager; the other properties specify the behavior of the transaction management—in particular, the boolean failEarlyOnGlobalRollbackOnly property specifies whether the transaction should fail as soon as possible when a global rollback is signaled, and boolean rollbackOnCommitFailure specifies whether the JtaTransactionManager should roll back when the commit command fails.

In most cases, you will not need to modify any of the properties exposed by the JtaTransactionManager. If this is the case, you can use the <tx:jta-transaction-manager /> element, which defines a JtaTransactionManager bean with its default values.

The Spring documentation outlines the latest notes about any potential issues with the JtaTransactionManager in different application servers.

Implementing Your Own Transaction Synchronization

If you are developing a large application, you may find yourself in a situation where you need to attach your code to the transaction. In this section, we will show how to implement transaction synchronization of your own object. We will create a simple Worker interface (see Listing 16-26).

Listing 16-26. *The Worker Interface*

```
public interface Worker {

    void work(int value);

    void commit();

    void rollback();
}
```

The interface is very simple indeed. Ideally, we will only use the work(int) method in code that uses the implementation of the Worker interface; we would like the commit() and rollback() methods to get called automatically whenever we use an instance of the Worker interface in a transactional method. To demonstrate this behavior, we will create a simple AccountService interface and its implementation. Listing 16-27 shows the interface.

Listing 16-27. *AccountService and Its Implementation*

```
public interface AccountService {

    AccountIdentity create();

}
```

We will use the AccountService in a small sample application. Listing 16-28 shows a pseudo code implementation of the AccountService.

Listing 16-28. *Pseudo Code Implementation of the AccountService*

```
public class DefaultAccountService implements AccountService {
    private AccountDao accountDao;

    @Transactional
    public AccountIdentity create() {
       Worker worker = getWorker();
       worker.work(10);
       AccountIdentity id = createAndSaveAccount();
       Worker.work(20);

       Grinch.ruin();

        return id;
    }

}
```

This pseudo code implementation shows the core concepts. We have a transactional method, `AccountIdentity create()`. In the method's body, we somehow obtain an instance of the `Worker` class that is synchronized with the current transaction. We then call the `worker.work(10)` method. Next, we use `createAndSaveAccount()`, which returns the `AccountIdentity` of the new account. We follow that with another call to the `worker.work` method. Finally, we use `Grinch.ruin()` to randomly simulate failure. We would like to call the `worker.commit()` method when the transaction commits and `worker.rollback()` when the transaction rolls back.

If we forget about transaction synchronization for a moment, we can implement the pseudo code from Listing 16-28 using the classes and interfaces from Figure 16-3.

You can see that we have a `WorkerFactory` interface, and we use this interface in the `DefaultAccountService`. The `WorkerFactory` implementation will be responsible for registering a `TransactionSynchronization` with the `TransactionSynchronizationManager`. The `TransactionSynchronizationManager` will then notify all registered `TransactionSynchronization` objects when the transaction completes. All we need to do is keep the instance of the worker we are synchronizing with the synchronization key. The UML diagram in Figure 16-4 shows the class diagram of the final solution.

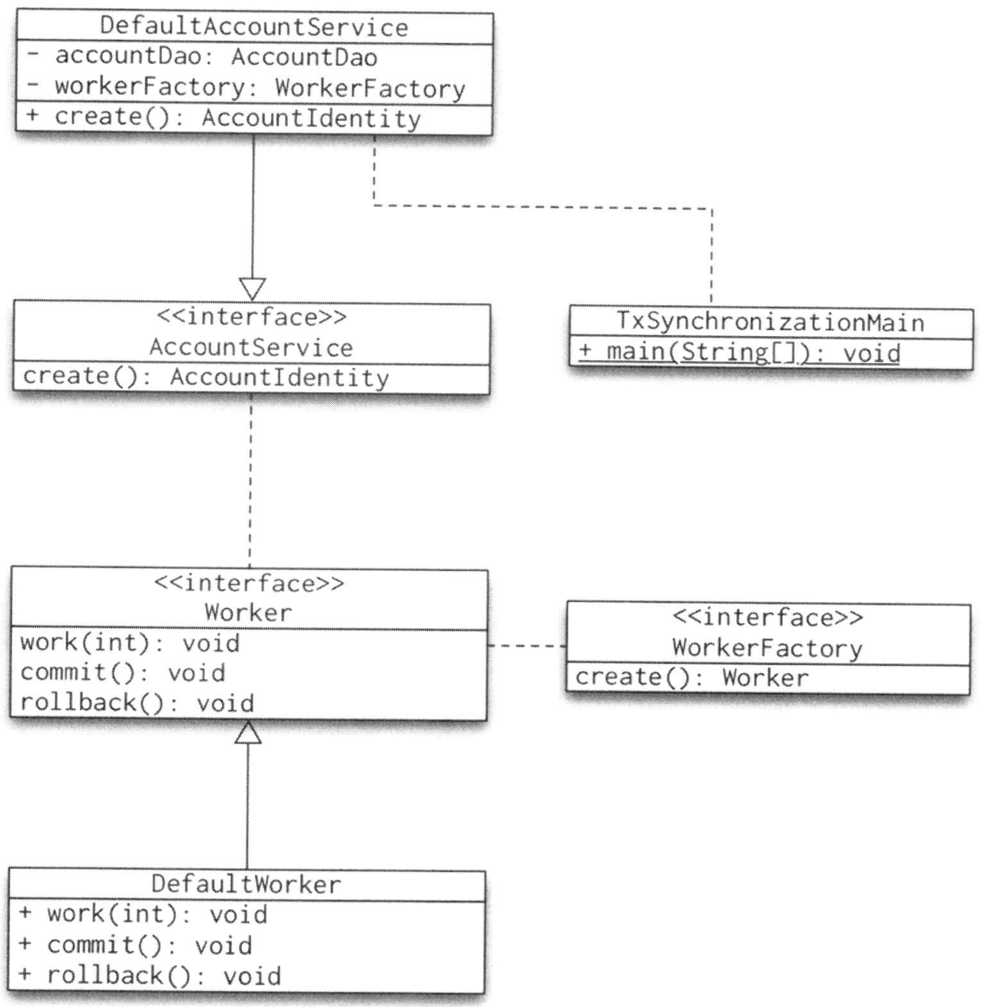

Figure 16-3. *UML class diagram of the worker example*

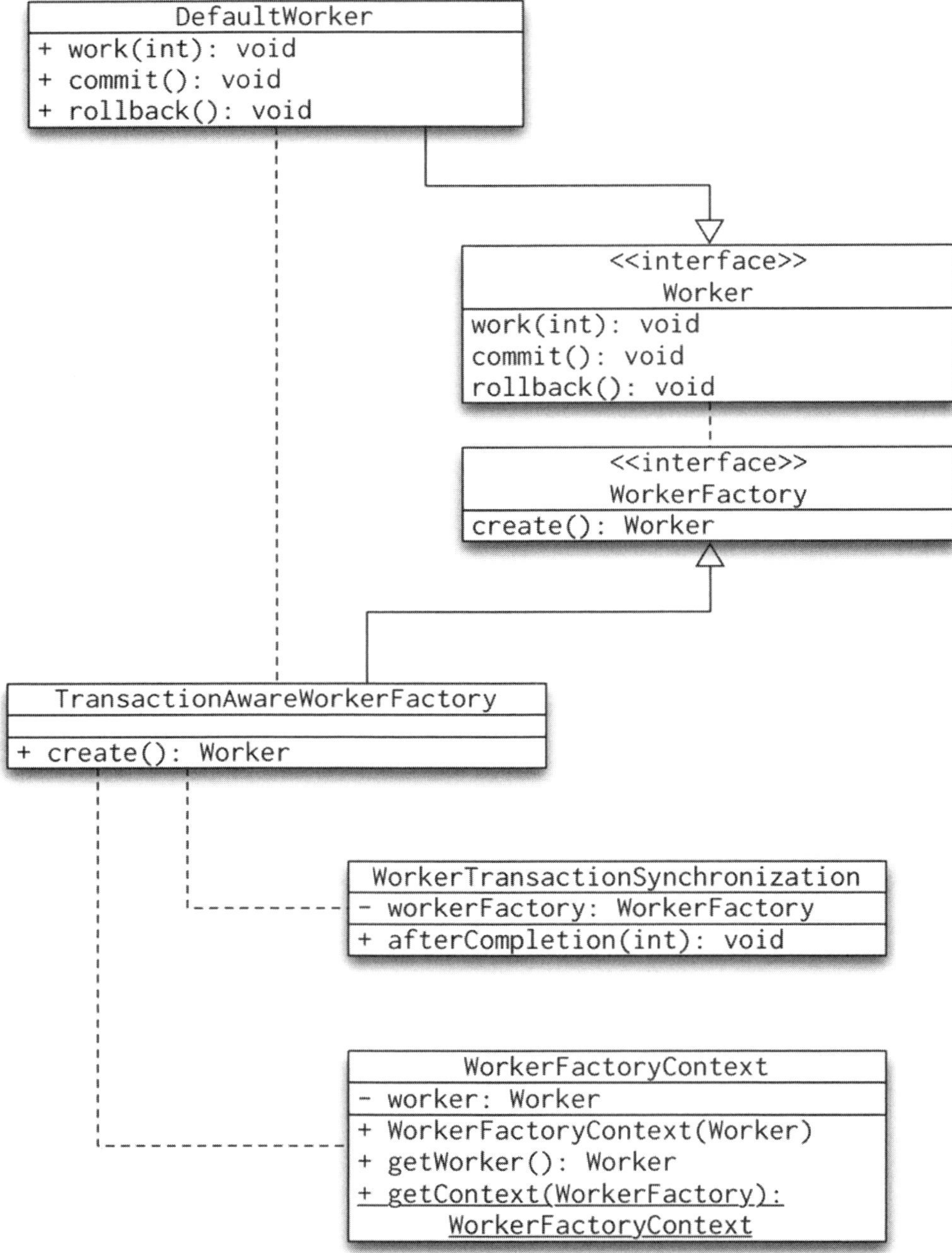

Figure 16-4. *UML class diagram of the synchronization solution*

Let's explore the classes from Figure 16-4 in more detail. We will begin with Listing 16-29, which shows the code of the WorkerFactoryContext.

Listing 16-29. *The Implementation of the WorkerFactoryContext Class*

```
public class WorkerFactoryContext {
    private Worker worker;

    public WorkerFactoryContext(Worker worker) {
        Assert.notNull(worker, "The argument 'worker' must not be null.");
        this.worker = worker;
    }

    public Worker getWorker() {
        return worker;
    }

    public static WorkerFactoryContext getContext(WorkerFactory workerFactory) {
        if (TransactionSynchronizationManager.isSynchronizationActive() &&
                TransactionSynchronizationManager.hasResource(workerFactory)) {

            WorkerFactoryContext context =
                    (WorkerFactoryContext) TransactionSynchronizationManager.
                            getResource(workerFactory);
            if (context == null) {
                throw new IllegalStateException(String.format(
                        "Null WorkerFactoryContext bound as " +
                                "transactional resource for [%s].",
                        workerFactory));
            }
            return context;
        }
        throw new IllegalStateException(String.format(
                "Cannot access WorkerFactoryContext for [%s] when " +
                        "transaction synchronozation is not active.",
                workerFactory));
    }

}
```

The constructor simply stores the worker argument in the worker field; the getWorker() method is a getter for the worker field. The getContext(WorkerFactory) method seems complex but only because of the error-handling code. If we removed all error-handling code, it would be simply this:

```
public static WorkerFactoryContext getContext(WorkerFactory workerFactory) {
    if (TransactionSynchronizationManager.isSynchronizationActive() &&
            TransactionSynchronizationManager.hasResource(workerFactory)) {
        return (WorkerFactoryContext) TransactionSynchronizationManager.
                getResource(workerFactory);
    }
    return null;
}
```

If we examine the code closely, we can see that it checks whether transaction synchronization is active (i.e., whether there is an active transaction) and whether we registered a resource (WorkerFactoryContext) with the key workerFactory. If so, the method returns the registered WorkerFactoryContext. We use the WorkerFactoryContext in the TransactionAwareWorkerFactory implementation of the WorkerFactory interface (see Listing 16-30).

Listing 16-30. *The TransactionAwareFactoryWorker Implementation*

```
public class TransactionAwareWorkerFactory implements WorkerFactory {

    public TransactionAwareWorkerFactory() {
    }

    public Worker create() {
        if (TransactionSynchronizationManager.hasResource(this)) {
            return getTransactionBoundWorker();
        } else {
            return createNewTransactionBoundWorker();
        }
    }

    private Worker createNewTransactionBoundWorker() {
        Worker worker = new DefaultWorker();
        WorkerFactoryContext context = new WorkerFactoryContext(worker);

        TransactionSynchronization synchronization =
                new WorkerTransactionSynchronization(this);
        TransactionSynchronizationManager.registerSynchronization(synchronization);
        TransactionSynchronizationManager.bindResource(this, context);

        return worker;
    }


    private Worker getTransactionBoundWorker() {
        WorkerFactoryContext context = (WorkerFactoryContext)
                TransactionSynchronizationManager.getResource(this);
        return context.getWorker();
    }


}
```

The implementation of the `create()` method checks whether we registered a resource with the key `this` in this transaction. If so, we return the worker bound to the `WorkerFactoryContext` that we registered for the active transaction. If not, we need to create the `WorkerFactoryContext` and register the `WorkerTransactionSynchronization` with the `TransactionSynchronizationManager`. The `createNewTransactionBoundWorker()` method does just that. The final piece of code we need to look at is the `WorkerTransactionSynchronization` class in Listing 16-31.

Listing 16-31. *Implementation of the WorkerTransactionSynchronization*

```
public class WorkerTransactionSynchronization
    extends TransactionSynchronizationAdapter {
    private WorkerFactory workerFactory;

    public WorkerTransactionSynchronization(WorkerFactory workerFactory) {
        this.workerFactory = workerFactory;
    }

   @Override
    public void afterCompletion(int status) {
        if (!TransactionSynchronizationManager.hasResource(this.workerFactory)) {
```

```
            throw new IllegalStateException(String.format(
                    "Required synchronization resource missing under key '%s'.",
                    this.workerFactory));
        }
        WorkerFactoryContext context = WorkerFactoryContext.
                getContext(this.workerFactory);
        Worker worker = context.getWorker();

        try {
            if (STATUS_COMMITTED == status) {
                worker.commit();
            } else {
                worker.rollback();
            }
        } finally {
            TransactionSynchronizationManager.unbindResource(this.workerFactory);
        }
    }
}
```

We have not implemented the `TransactionSynchronization` interface directly; instead, we used the convenience `TransactionSynchronizationAdapter`, which implements all methods of the `TransactionSynchronization` interface as empty and allows its subclasses to override them. This implementation allowed us to override only the `afterCompletion(int)` method; the `TransactionSynchronizationManager` calls this method after the transaction has completed, regardless of whether it was committed or rolled back. We obtain the `WorkerFactoryContext` from the `TransactionSynchronizationManager` using the `workerFactory` as the key. We call the context's `getWorker()` method, and depending on whether the transaction committed or rolled back, we call either `worker.commit()` or `worker.rollback()`. With all this code in place, we can finally show the `DefaultAccountService` implementation in Java in Listing 16-32.

Listing 16-32. *Java Implementation of the DefaultAccountService*

```
public class DefaultAccountService implements AccountService {
    private AccountDao accountDao;
    private WorkerFactory workerFactory;

    @Transactional
    public AccountIdentity create() {
        Random random = new Random();
        StringBuilder number = new StringBuilder(8);
        for (int i = 0; i < 8; i++) {
            number.append(random.nextInt(9));
        }
        AccountIdentity ai = new AccountIdentity("011001", number.toString());
        Account account = new Account();
        account.setId(System.currentTimeMillis());
        account.setIdentity(ai);
        account.setBalance(BigDecimal.ZERO);

        Worker worker = this.workerFactory.create();
        worker.work(10);
        this.accountDao.save(account);
        worker.work(20);
```

```
        Grinch.ruin();

        return ai;
    }

    public void setAccountDao(AccountDao accountDao) {
        this.accountDao = accountDao;
    }

    public void setWorkerFactory(WorkerFactory workerFactory) {
        this.workerFactory = workerFactory;
    }
}
```

You can see that, apart from the `Account` creation code, we use the `WorkerFactory` to create an instance of the `Worker`. We then call the worker's `work` method, use the `accountDao` to insert the newly set up account, and then call the `work` method again. We complete with a potentially deadly call to `Grinch.ruin()`. The final class we need to show is `TxSynchronizationMain`, the sample program that demonstrates the transaction synchronization (see Listing 16-33).

Listing 16-33. *Sample Application for the Transaction Synchronization*

```
public class TxSynchronizationMain {

    public static void main(String[] args) {
        ApplicationContext ac = new ClassPathXmlApplicationContext(
                new String[] {
                        "/META-INF/spring/*-context.xml",
                        "/META-INF/spring/*-context-worker.xml"
                }
        );
        AccountService accountService =
            (AccountService) ac.getBean("accountService");
        try {
            accountService.create();
        } catch (Exception ignored) {

        }
    }

}
```

The very last piece of code is the XML configuration file that contains definitions for the `accountService` and `workerFactory` beans in Listing 16-34.

Listing 16-34. *The XML Configuration for the Sample Banking Application*

```
<?xml version="1.0" encoding="UTF-8"?>
<beans xmlns="http://www.springframework.org/schema/beans"
       xmlns:aop="http://www.springframework.org/schema/aop"
       xmlns:tx="http://www.springframework.org/schema/tx"
       xmlns:xsi="http://www.w3.org/2001/XMLSchema-instance"
       xsi:schemaLocation="
            http://www.springframework.org/schema/beans
            http://www.springframework.org/schema/beans/spring-beans.xsd
```

```
        http://www.springframework.org/schema/tx
        http://www.springframework.org/schema/tx/spring-tx.xsd
        http://www.springframework.org/schema/aop
        http://www.springframework.org/schema/aop/spring-aop.xsd">


    <bean id="bankService"
          class="com.apress.prospring2.ch16.services.DefaultBankService">
        <property name="accountDao" ref="accountDao"/>
    </bean>

    <bean id="workerFactory"
          class="com.apress.prospring2.ch16.synchronization.➥
                      TransactionAwareWorkerFactory"/>
    <bean id="accountService"
        class="com.apress.prospring2.ch16.services.DefaultAccountService">
        <property name="accountDao" ref="accountDao"/>
        <property name="workerFactory" ref="workerFactory"/>
    </bean>

    <tx:annotation-driven transaction-manager="transactionManager"/>
    <aop:aspectj-autoproxy />

</beans>
```

Depending on whether the `Grinch` did its damage in the `JdbcAccountDao.save(Account)` or in the `DefaultAccountService.create()` or not at all, the sample application will print something like the following:

```
Failure in the JdbcAccountDao.save(Account) method:
Muhehe! It's broken now.
Rolling back 10

Failure in the DefaultAccountService.create() method:
Muhehe! It's broken now.
Rolling back 20

Successful execution:
Committed 20
```

This clearly demonstrates that we have successfully registered the `TransactionSynchronization` callback with the `TransactionSynchronizationManager` and that the `WorkerTransactionSynchronization` correctly calls the `Worker.commit()` or `Worker.rollback()` methods depending on the completed transaction's status.

In the real world, the `Worker` class would be far more complex. It might be an e-mail–sending interface: if your application sends multiple e-mails during a transactional process and the process ultimately fails, you don't want to send any e-mails at all. Another example may be indexing using the Lucene index: if your application is modifying some database structures and the index, you should ensure that the data in the index will always match the data in the database, and one way of doing so is to implement transaction synchronization for the Lucene index bean.

Summary

Transactions are a key part of ensuring data integrity in almost any type of application. In this chapter, you learned how to use Spring to manage transactions with almost no impact on your source code. You now know how to use local and global transactions and can synchronize your code with the active transaction.

We provided various examples of transaction implementation—declarative using application context files, declarative using annotations, and programmatic—and discussed the practical uses and implications of the coding style and manageability of each.

Local transactions are supported outside a Java EE application server, and almost no additional configuration is required to enable local transaction support in Spring. Unfortunately, the setup for global transactions greatly depends on your Java EE application server, and you will most likely need to refer to your application server's configuration for details.

CHAPTER 17

Web Applications with Spring MVC

Web applications have become a very important part of any enterprise system. The key requirement for a web framework is to simplify development of the web tier as much as possible. In this chapter, you will learn how to develop web applications using Spring. We will start with an explanation of Spring MVC architecture and the request cycle of Spring web applications, introducing handler mappings, interceptors, and controllers. Then we will show how we can use different technologies to render HTML in the browser.

Before we dive into a discussion of Spring MVC, we should take a look at what MVC stands for and how it can help develop more flexible web applications.

MVC Architecture

MVC is the acronym for the model view controller architectural pattern. The purpose of this pattern is to simplify the implementation of applications that need to act on user requests and manipulate and display data. There are three distinct components of this pattern:

- The model represents data that the user expects to see. In most cases, the model will consist of JavaBeans.
- The view is responsible for rendering the model. A view component in a text editor will probably display the text in appropriate formatting; in a web application, it will, in most cases, generate HTML output that the client's browser can interpret.
- The controller is a piece of logic that is responsible for processing and acting on user requests: it builds an appropriate model and passes it to the view for rendering. In the case of Java web applications, the controller is usually a servlet. Of course, the controller can be implemented in any language a web container can execute.

Currently, there are two MVC models. In the domain of web applications, model one architecture is illustrated in Figure 17-1.

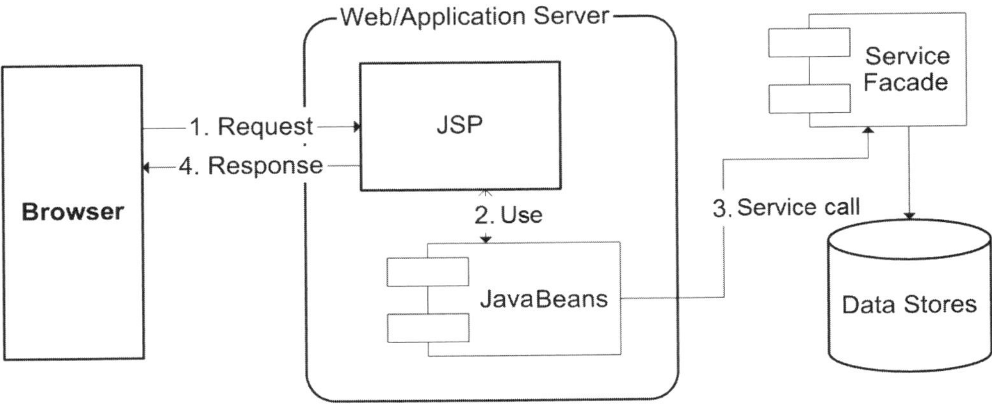

Figure 17-1. *MVC model one architecture*

As Figure 17-1 shows, the JSP pages are at the center of the application. They include both the control logic and presentation logic. The client makes a request to a JSP page, and the logic in the page builds the model (typically using POJOs) and renders the model. The separation of the presentation layer and control layer is not very clear. In fact, with the exception of "Hello, World" applications, model one quickly grows out of control, simply because of the amount of logic that different JSP pages need to perform.

Model two is far more manageable in a larger application. Whereas in model one, a JSP page acted as both view and controller, model two adds a separate controller (see Figure 17-2).

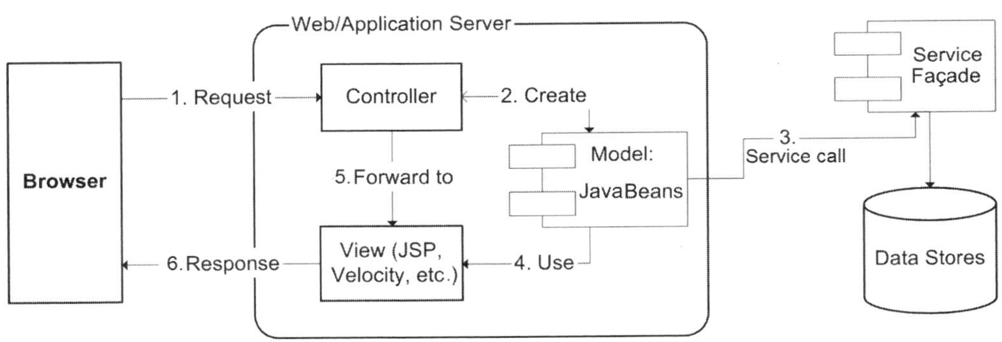

Figure 17-2. *MVC model two architecture*

Now, the controller accepts user requests, prepares the model, and passes it to the view for rendering. The JSP pages no longer contain logic for processing the requests; they simply display the model prepared by the controller.

We have used JSP pages in place of the view and controller in model one's diagram and in place of the view in model two's diagram. Using JSP pages as the view illustrates only one type of MVC implementation. However, as Spring MVC architecture is an implementation of model two MVC, the view can be created using anything that can render the model and return it to the client.

Now that we have covered the basics of the MVC pattern, we can take a more detailed look at how this pattern is implemented in Spring and how you can use it in your web applications.

Spring MVC

Spring MVC support allows us to build flexible applications using MVC model two. The implementation is truly generic. The model is a simple `Map` that holds the data; the view is an interface whose implementations render the data; and the controller is an implementation of the `Controller` interface.

■ **Note** We have addressed Spring MVC support for servlet-based web applications in this chapter. Spring goes beyond that and offers full support for JSR 168 portlet development. The major difference between servlets and portlets is that a portlet can have two distinct phases: the action phase and the render phase. The action phase is executed only once, when some business layer changes are invoked (such as a database update). The render phase is executed whenever a user requests a page. The Spring portlet MVC framework is designed to be a mirror image of Spring web MVC architecture, as much as possible. A detailed explanation of the Spring portlet framework is beyond the scope of this book, but the full reference and documentation can be found on the Spring Framework web site.

Spring's implementation of the MVC architecture for web applications is based around `DispatcherServlet`. This servlet processes requests and invokes appropriate `Controller` elements to handle them.

The `DispatcherServlet` intercepts incoming requests and determines which controller will handle the request. The Spring controllers return a `ModelAndView` class from their handling methods. The `ModelAndView` instance holds a reference to a view and a model. The model is a simple `Map` instance that holds JavaBeans that the `View` interface is going to render. The `View` interface, when implemented, defines the render method. It follows that the `View` implementation can be virtually anything that can be interpreted by the client.

MVC Implementation

If we want to create a web application with Spring, we need to start with the basic `web.xml` file, where we specify the `DispatcherServlet` and set the mapping for the specified `url-pattern`. Listing 17-1 shows a sample `web.xml` file.

Listing 17-1. *A Web.Example*

```
<?xml version="1.0" encoding="ISO-8859-1"?>
<web-app xmlns="http://java.sun.com/xml/ns/j2ee"
         xmlns:xsi="http://www.w3.org/2001/XMLSchema-instance"
         xsi:schemaLocation="http://java.sun.com/xml/ns/j2ee ➥
         http://java.sun.com/xml/ns/j2ee/web-app_2_4.xsd"
         version="2.4">
    <servlet>
        <servlet-name>ch17</servlet-name>
        <servlet-class>
            org.springframework.web.servlet.DispatcherServlet
        </servlet-class>
    </servlet>
    <servlet-mapping>
        <servlet-name>ch17</servlet-name>
        <url-pattern>*.html</url-pattern>
    </servlet-mapping>
    <servlet-mapping>
        <servlet-name> ch17</servlet-name>
        <url-pattern>*.tile</url-pattern>
    </servlet-mapping>
</web-app>
```

This `web.xml` file defines the `ch17` servlet of the class `DispatcherServlet` that maps to all requests to `*.html` or `*.tile`.

Note We usually create a mapping to `*.html` because it is a recognized extension and easily fools search engines into thinking that the page is not dynamically generated.

Using Handler Mappings

How does our web application know which servlet (controller implementation) to invoke on a specific request? This is where Spring handler mappings kick in. In a few easy steps, you can configure URL mappings to Spring controllers. All you need to do is edit the Spring application context file.

Spring uses `HandlerMapping` implementations to identify the controller to invoke and provides three implementations of `HandlerMapping`, as shown in Table 17-1.

Table 17-1. *HandlerMapping Implementations*

HandlerMapping	Description
`BeanNameUrlHandlerMapping`	The bean name is identified by the URL. If the URL were `/product/index.html`, the controller bean ID that handles this mapping would have to be set to `/product/index.html`. This mapping is useful for small applications, as it does not support wildcards in the requests.
`SimpleUrlHandlerMapping`	This handler mapping allows you to specify in the requests (using full names and wildcards) which controller is going to handle the request.
`ControllerClassNameHandlerMapping`	This handler mapping is part of the convenience over configuration approach introduced with Spring 2.5. It automatically generates URL paths from the class names of the controllers. This implementation is covered in more detail later in this chapter.

All three `HandlerMapping` implementations extend the `AbstractHandlerMapping` base class and share the following properties:

- `interceptors`: This property indicates the list of interceptors to use. `HandlerInterceptors` are discussed in the next section.
- `defaultHandler`: This property specifies the default handler to use when this handler mapping does not result in a matching handler.
- `order`: Based on the value of the `order` property (see the `org.springframework.core.Ordered` interface), Spring will sort all handler mappings available in the context and apply the first matching handler.
- `alwaysUseFullPath`: If this property is set to `true`, Spring will use the full path within the current servlet context to find an appropriate handler. If this property is set to `false` (the default), the path within the current servlet mapping will be used. For example, if a servlet is mapped using `/testing/*` and the `alwaysUseFullPath` property is set to `true`, `/testing/viewPage.html` would be used, whereas if the property is set to `false`, `/viewPage.html` would be used.
- `urlPathHelper`: Using this property, you can tweak the `UrlPathHelper` used when inspecting URLs. Normally, you shouldn't have to change the default value.

- `urlDecode`: The default value for this property is `false`. The `HttpServletRequest` returns request URLs and URIs that are *not* decoded. If you do want them to be decoded before a `HandlerMapping` uses them to find an appropriate handler, you have to set this to `true` (which requires JDK 1.4). The decoding method uses either the encoding specified by the request or the default ISO-8859-1 encoding scheme.
- `lazyInitHandlers`: This allows for lazy initialization of *singleton* handlers (prototype handlers are always lazily initialized). The default value is `false`.

■ **Note** The last four properties are only available to subclasses of `org.springframework.web.servlet.handler.AbstractUrlHandlerMapping`.

We will start with the example of `BeanNameUrlHandlerMapping`. This is the simple `HandlerMapping` implementation that maps controller bean IDs to the servlet URLs. This `HandlerMapping` implementation is used by default if no `HandlerMapping` is defined in the Spring context files. Listing 17-2 shows an example of the `BeanNameUrlHandlerMapping` configuration, without the actual `BeanNameUrlHandlerMapping` bean (`DispatcherServlet` will instantiate it by default, if no other `HandlerMapping` has been configured).

Listing 17-2. *BeanNameUrlHandlerMapping Configuration*

```
<?xml version="1.0" encoding="UTF-8"?>
<beans xmlns="http://www.springframework.org/schema/beans"
...>

<beans>
    <bean name="/index.html.form" ➥
class=" com.apress.prospring.ch17.web.IndexController "/>
</beans>
```

`SimpleUrlHandlerMapping` offers more flexibility in the request mappings. You can configure the mapping as key/value properties in the `publicUrlMapping` bean. In Listing 17-3, you can see a simple example of a Spring application context file containing the handler mapping configuration.

Listing 17-3. *SimpleUrlHandlerMapping Definitions*

```
<?xml version="1.0" encoding="UTF-8"?>
<beans xmlns="http://www.springframework.org/schema/beans"
...>

<beans>
    <bean id="publicUrlMapping"
        class="org.springframework.web.servlet.handler.SimpleUrlHandlerMapping">
                <property name="mappings">
            <value>
                /index.html=indexController
                /product/index.html=productController
                /product/view.html=productController
                /product/edit.html=productFormController
            </value>
        </property>
    </bean>
</beans>
```

Spring Controllers

Controllers do all the work to process the request, build the model based on the request, and pass the model to the view for rendering. Spring's DispatcherServlet intercepts the requests from the client and uses a HandlerAdapter implementation that is responsible for delegating the request for further processing. You can implement the HandlerAdapter yourself, allowing you to modify the chain of command the request must pass through.

The DispatcherServlet has a List handlerAdapters property that allows you to specify the HandlerAdapter implementations you wish to use. To make sure the HandlerAdapter implementations are called in the right order, you can choose to implement the Ordered interface in your HandlerAdapter to indicate the position among other HandlerAdapter implementations.

If the handlerAdapters property of DispatcherServlet is null, the DispatcherServlet will use SimpleControllerHandlerAdapter. Because we are not going to provide any additional HandlerAdapter implementations, our application will use the SimpleControllerHandlerAdapter.

SimpleControllerHandlerAdapter delegates the request to the implementation of the Controller interface, hence, the beans—handlers that are to act as controllers must implement the Controller interface. This approach provides you the flexibility to write your own implementation from scratch or to use one of the convenient implementations already provided. The Controller interface depends on HttpServletRequest and HttpServletResponse, which means that you can use it only in web applications.

Let's take a look at the most basic implementation of the Controller interface. We are going to create an IndexController that simply writes "Hello, World" to the response stream, as shown in Listing 17-4.

Listing 17-4. *IndexController Implementation*

```
public class IndexController implements Controller {

    public ModelAndView handleRequest(HttpServletRequest request,
        HttpServletResponse response) throws Exception {

        response.getWriter().println("Hello, world");

        return null;
    }

}
```

The only method we need to implement is ModelAndView handleRequest(HttpServletRequest, HttpServletResponse). We are returning null as the return value of ModelAndView, which means that no view will be rendered and the result will be written directly to the output of the response, which will be committed and returned to the client.

Implementing the Controller interface is, in most cases, too much work, so Spring provides a number of useful superclasses.

AbstractController

At first glance, it might seem that AbstractController is simply a wrapper around the interface that will force you to implement the handleRequestInternal method to process the request. This is only partially true, as AbstractController extends the WebContentGenerator class that allows you to set additional properties to control the request and response. Additionally, WebContentGenerator extends WebApplicationObjectSupport, which, in turn, extends the ApplicationObjectSupport class that implements ApplicationContextAware. In other words, extending your controller from AbstractController rather than implementing the Controller interface directly gives you access to ServletContext, WebApplicationContext, ApplicationContext, Log, and MessageSourceAccessor.

Table 17-2 provides a closer look at properties you can set that are related to the web application environment.

Table 17-2. *WebContentGenerator and AbstractController Properties*

Property	Description	Default Value
supportedMethods	Supported and allowed HTTP methods	GET, POST
requiresSession	Specifies whether an HttpSession instance is required to process the request	false
useExpiresHeader	Specifies whether to use the HTTP 1.0 expires header	true
useCacheControlHeader	Specifies whether to use the HTTP 1.1 cache-control header	true
cacheSeconds	Instructs the client to cache the generated content for the specified number of seconds	-1
synchronizeOnSession	Specifies whether the controller should synchronize an instance of HttpSession before invoking handleRequestInternal. Useful for serializing reentrant request handling from a single client	false

As an example, we can set the cacheSeconds property to 10 and refresh the page in the client (making sure we are not instructing the client to bypass the cache), and we should receive new content from the server only every 10 seconds (see Listing 17-5).

Listing 17-5. *IndexController Implementation Using AbstractController*

```
public class IndexController extends AbstractController {

    protected ModelAndView handleRequestInternal(HttpServletRequest request,
        HttpServletResponse response) throws Exception {
        setCacheSeconds(10);
        response.getWriter().println("Hello, world at " + ➥
System.currentTimeMillis());
        return null;
    }

}
```

If you compare the implementation of IndexController from Listings 17-4 and 17-5, you will see that there is very little difference, except for the fact that code in Listing 17-5 now has full access to the context (both Servlet and Application) and can manipulate the HTTP headers more easily.

ParameterizableViewController

The ParameterizableViewController is a very simple subclass of AbstractController; it implements the handleRequestInternal method to return a new model with a name set in its viewName property. No data is inserted into the model, and the only reason you would choose to use this controller is simply to display a view using its name.

Listing 17-6 shows the ParameterizableIndexController we have created to demonstrate the functionality of the ParameterizableViewController.

Listing 17-6. *ParametrizableIndexController Implementation*

```
public class ParametrizableIndexController extends ParameterizableViewController {

}
```

We will add a `parameterizableIndexController` bean to the application context file, set its `viewName` property to `product-index`, and add a reference to it to the `publicUrlMapping` bean as shown in Listing 17-7.

Listing 17-7. *parametrizableIndexController Bean Declarations*

```
<beans xmlns="http://www.springframework.org/schema/beans"
       ...>

<beans>
    <bean id="publicUrlMapping"
        class="org.springframework.web.servlet.handler.SimpleUrlHandlerMapping">
        <property name="mappings">
            <value>
                /index.html=indexController
                /pindex.html=parametrizableIndexController
                /product/index.html=productController
                /product/view.html=productController
                /product/edit.html=productFormController
                /product/image.html=productImageFormController
            </value>
        </property>
    </bean>

    <bean id="parametrizableIndexController"
        class="com.apress.prospring.ch17.web.ParametrizableIndexController">
        <property name="viewName" value=products-index/ >
    </bean>
</beans>
```

MultiActionController

This `Controller` implementation is far more interesting than the `ParameterizableViewController`. It is also a subclass of `AbstractController`, giving it access to all its properties and methods. Most importantly, it lets you provide as many implementations of `public ModelAndView(HttpServletRequest, HttpServletResponse)` as you need. You can choose to implement the methods in your subclass of `MultiActionController`, or you can specify a delegate object that implements these methods and the `MultiActionController` will invoke the methods on the delegate object. Using this `Controller` implementation, you can map multiple URLs to the same controller and use different methods to process the various URLs.

The two additional properties of `AbstractController`—`delegate` and `methodNameResolver`—are used to tell the `MultiActionController` which method on which object to invoke for each request. If the delegate property is left to its default value of `null`, the controller will look up and invoke the method on the `MultiActionController` subclass itself; if the delegate is not `null`, the method will be invoked on the delegate.

The `methodNameResolver` must be set to an implementation of `MethodNameResolver`. The three implementations of `MethodNameResolver` are shown in Table 17-3.

Table 17-3. *MethodNameResolver Implementations*

Implementation	Description
`InternalPathMethodNameResolver`	The method name will be taken from the last part (the file part) of the path, excluding the extension. When using this resolver the path, `/servlet/foo.html`, will map to the method `public ModelAndView foo(HttpServletRequest, HttpServletResponse)`. This is also the default implementation used in `MultiActionController`.
`ParameterMethodNameResolver`	The method name will be taken from the specified request parameter. The default parameter name is `action`; you can change the parameter name in the context file.
`PropertiesMethodNameResolver`	The method name will be resolved from an external properties file. You can specify exact mapping, such as `/test.html=handleTest`, or you can use wildcards, such as `/*=handleAll`.

■ **Note** You won't be able to map URLs like `/view-product.html` using `InternalPathMethodNameResolver`. You cannot define method `public ModelAndView view-product()` in Java, because the hyphen is an illegal character in Java definitions. If you need to use URLs like this, you'll have to implement your own `MethodNameResolver`. However, for most cases, the resolvers that Spring provides are sufficient.

Let's take a look at the simplest implementation of the `MultiActionController` subclass.

Listing 17-8. *MultiActionController Subclass*

```
public class ProductController extends MultiActionController {

    public ModelAndView view(HttpServletRequest request,
        HttpServletResponse response) throws Exception{

        response.getOutputStream().print("Viewing product " +
            request.getParameter("productId"));

        return null;
    }

}
```

The `ProductController` from Listing 17-8 adds only one method, `view()`. If the path `/product/*` is mapped to this controller and if the request is `/product/view.html?productId=10`, the output displayed in the browser is going to be "Viewing product 10".

The fact that the URL from the previous section invoked the method `public ModelAndView view(HttpServletRequest request, HttpServletResponse response)` of `ProductController` proves that the `MultiActionController` defaults to using `InternalPathMethodNameResolver` as a method name resolver and that the delegate property is `null`.

If you want to use `InternalPathMethodNameResolver` with custom properties, you can always define it as a Spring-managed bean and add any properties you like. In the example shown in Listing 17-9, we add the suffix property, with the value "Handler". Using this configuration, Spring will look for a method whose name matches the last part of the URL without the extension with the string "Handler" appended to it.

Listing 17-9. *MultiActionController Subclass*

```
<bean id="internalPathMethodNameResolverclass="org.springframework.web.➥
            servlet.mvc.multiaction.InternalPathMethodNameResolver">
        <property name="suffix" value="Handler"/>
    </bean>

    <bean id="productController"
        class="com.apress.prospring2.ch17.web.product.ProductController">
        <property name="methodNameResolver" ref="internalPathMethodNameResolver"/>
    </bean>
```

Now, the `view.html` URL will be mapped to the `public ModelAndView viewHandler()` method of `MultiActionController`. Let's take a look at how we can configure other `methodNameResolvers`, starting with the `ParameterMethodNameResolver`.

By default, `ParameterMethodNameResolver` uses the `action` parameter name to derive the method name; we can change that by setting the `paramName` property. We can also specify a method name that will be invoked when the `paramName` parameter is not present in the request by setting the `defaultMethodName` property to the name of the method to be invoked (see Listing 17-10).

Listing 17-10. *The ch17-servlet.xml Definition with ParameterMethodNameResolver*

```
<?xml version="1.0" encoding="UTF-8"?>
<beans xmlns="http://www.springframework.org/schema/beans"
   ...>
    <!-- other beans -->
    <bean id="productController"
        class="com.apress.prospring2.ch17.web.product.ProductController">
        <property name="methodNameResolver" ref="productMethodNameResolver"/>
    </bean>

    <bean id="productMethodNameResolver"
        class="org.springframework.web.servlet.mvc.multiaction.➥
            ParameterMethodNameResolver">
            <property name="paramName" value="method"/>
            <property name="defaultMethodName" value="view"/>
    </bean>
</beans>
```

If we now make a request to `/product/a.html` and do not specify the method parameter, `ProductController.view` will be invoked, and we will get the same behavior if we make a request to `/product/a.html?method=view`. However, if we make a request to `/product/a.html?method=foo`, we will get an error message, because the method `public ModelAndView foo(HttpServletRequest, HttpServletResponse)` is not implemented in `ProductController`.

The last method name resolver we will discuss is the `PropertiesMethodNameResolver`. This method resolver relies on the request URI, but unlike `InternalPathMethodNameResolver`, we can specify the method names in the Spring context file.

Listing 17-11. *The ch17-servlet.xml Definition with PropertiesMethodNameResolver*

```
<?xml version="1.0" encoding="UTF-8"?>
<beans xmlns="http://www.springframework.org/schema/beans"
        ...>
    <!-- other beans -->
    <bean id="productController"
        class="com.apress.prospring2.ch17.web.product.ProductController">
        <property name="methodNameResolver" ref="productMethodNameResolver"/>
```

```
....
    <bean id="productMethodNameResolver"
        class="org.springframework.web.servlet.mvc.multiaction.➥
            PropertiesMethodNameResolver">
        <property name="mappings">
            <value>
                /product/view.html=view
                /product/v*.html=view
            </value>
        </property>
    </bean>
</beans>
```

This code listing demonstrates how to use `PropertiesMethodNameResolver`: we need to configure its mappings property and add a list of mappings and their handler methods. The example from Listing 17-11 declares that `/product/view.html` as well as `/product/v*.html` will map to the `public ModelAndView view(HttpServletRequest, HttpServletResponse)` method in `ProductController`. The benefit of this `MethodNameResolver` is that we can use wildcards in the mapping strings.

All these controllers are very useful, but if we had to process input submitted by a user, we would have to write a lot of code to get the submitted values and process error messages. Spring simplifies this process by providing several command `Controllers`. Before we can move ahead to the command controllers, however, we must discuss views and interceptors. These, with handlers (explained previously), will enable us to create pages in which the command controllers process the data that users enter.

Interceptors

Interceptors are closely related to mappings, as you can specify a list of interceptors that will be called for each mapping. `HandlerInterceptor` implementations can process each request before or after it has been processed by the appropriate controller. You can choose to implement the `HandlerInterceptor` interface or extend `HandlerInterceptorAdapter`, which provides default do-nothing implementations for all `HandlerInterceptor` methods. As an example, we are going to implement a `BigBrotherHandlerInterceptor` that will process each request.

Listing 17-12. *BigBrotherHandlerInterceptor Implementation*

```
public class BigBrotherHandlerInterceptor extends HandlerInterceptorAdapter {

    public void postHandle(HttpServletRequest request,
        HttpServletResponse response, Object handler,
        ModelAndView modelAndView) throws Exception {
        // process the request
    }
}
```

The actual implementation of such an interceptor would probably process the request parameters and store them in an audit log. To use the interceptor, we will create a URL mapping and interceptor bean definitions in the Spring application context file as shown in Listing 17-13.

Listing 17-13. *HandlerMapping and HandlerInterceptor Definitions*

```
<?xml version="1.0" encoding="UTF-8"?>
<beans xmlns="http://www.springframework.org/schema/beans"
       ...>
```

```
    <bean id="bigBrotherHandlerInterceptor"
        class="com.apress.prospring2.ch17.web.BigBrotherHandlerInterceptor"/>

    <bean id="publicUrlMapping"
        class="org.springframework.web.servlet.handler.SimpleUrlHandlerMapping">
        <property name="interceptors">
            <list>
                <ref local="bigBrotherHandlerInterceptor"/>
            </list>
        </property>
        <property name="mappings">
            <value>
                /index.html=indexController
                /product/index.html=productController
                /product/view.html=productController
                /product/edit.html=productFormController
            </value>
        </property>
    </bean>
</beans>
```

You can specify as many `HandlerMapping` and `HandlerInterceptor` beans as you like, provided that the actual mappings do not collide with each other (one URL mapping can have one corresponding handler).

Now, we have mapped URL requests to invoking controllers. But how can we display the actual web page in the browser? We will now take a look at Spring views.

Views, Locales, and Themes

When we touched on the `View` interface, we merely stated its uses. Now, let's take a look at it in more detail. We'll start with a custom implementation of the `View` interface that will demonstrate how simple it is to create a custom view and what Spring does to look up (and instantiate) an appropriate instance of `View` when we refer to the `View` by its name.

Using Views Programmatically

In this example, we are going to manually implement a view and return the implementation in the `ModelAndView` class, which is the return value of a call to the `AbstractController.handleRequestInternal` method.

A custom view must implement the single method from the `View` interface: `render(Map, HttpServletRequest, HttpServletResponse)`. The `View` implementation we are going to create will output all data from the model to a text file and set the response headers to indicate to the client that the returned content is a text file and should be treated as an attachment (see Listing 17-14).

Listing 17-14. *PlainTextView Implementation*

```
public class PlainTextView implements View {

    public void render(Map model, HttpServletRequest request,
        HttpServletResponse response) throws Exception {

        response.setContentType("text/plain");
        response.addHeader("Content-disposition", ➥
                                "attachment; filename=output.txt");
```

```
        PrintWriter writer = response.getWriter();
        for (Iterator k = model.keySet().iterator(); k.hasNext();) {
            Object key = k.next();
            writer.print(key);
            writer.println(" contains:");
            writer.println(model.get(key));
        }
    }

}
```

We will modify the IndexController class from the "Spring Controllers" section to return our custom view (see Listing 17-15).

Listing 17-15. *Modified IndexController Class*

```
public class IndexController extends AbstractController {

    protected ModelAndView handleRequestInternal(
        HttpServletRequest request, HttpServletResponse response) throws Exception {

        setCacheSeconds(10);
        Map model = new HashMap();
        model.put("Greeting", "Hello World");
        model.put("Server time", new Date());

        return new ModelAndView(new PlainTextView(), model);
    }
    public String getContentType() {
        return "text/plain";
    }
}
```

Let's now send a request to the /index.html path. The IndexController.handleRequestInternal method will be called and will return an instance of ModelAndView with View set to an instance of PlainTextView and a model Map containing the keys Greeting and Server time. The render method of PlainTextView will set the header information that will prompt the client to display an Opening window (see Figure 17-3).

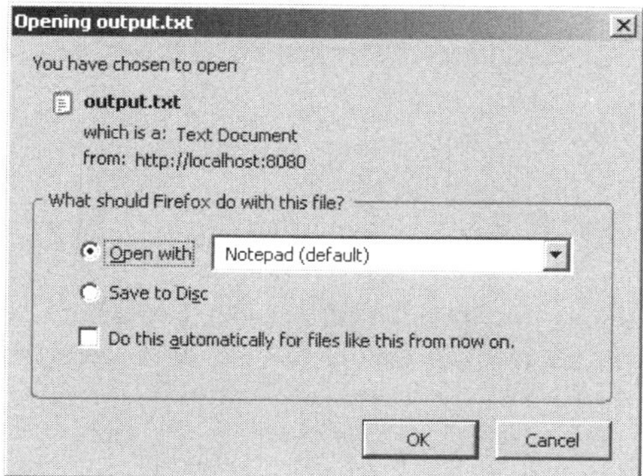

Figure 17-3. *PlainTextView prompts the client to display the Opening window to allow you to save the file.*

The content of the `output.txt` file is simply the model displayed as plain text, as shown in Figure 17-4.

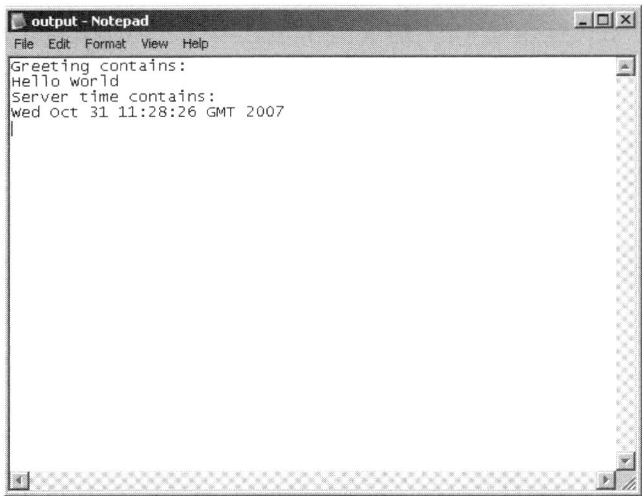

Figure 17-4. *The downloaded output.txt file*

The result is exactly what we expected: there were two entries in the model map, "Greeting" and "Server time" with "Hello World" and current date value.

This example has one disadvantage: the code in `IndexController` will create an instance of `PlainTextView` for each request. This is not necessary as the `PlainTextView` is a stateless object. Let's improve the application and make `PlainTextView` a Spring singleton bean. You can simply insert this bean into the `IndexController` via dependency injection, as Listing 17-16 shows.

Listing 17-16. *PlainTextView As a Spring Bean*

```
<?xml version="1.0" encoding="UTF-8"?>
<beans xmlns="http://www.springframework.org/schema/beans"
       ...>
    <bean id="plainTextView"
        class="com.apress.prospring2.ch17.web.views.PlainTextView"/>
    <bean id="indexController"
        class="com.apress.prospring2.ch17.web.IndexController">
        <property name="view" ref="plainTextView" />
   </bean>
    <!-- other beans as usual -->
</beans>
```

The `IndexController` will need to be modified to use the `plainTextView` bean instead of instantiating `PlainTextView` for each request. We will add a view property to `IndexController`, and implement a public setter method to inject the `PlainTextView` bean (see Listing 17-17).

Listing 17-17. *Modified IndexController Class*

```
public class IndexController extends AbstractController {
    private View view;
```

```
    protected ModelAndView handleRequestInternal(
        HttpServletRequest request, HttpServletResponse response) throws Exception {

        setCacheSeconds(10);
        Map model = new HashMap();
        model.put("Greeting", "Hello World");
        model.put("Server time", new Date());

        return new ModelAndView(this.view, model);
    }

    public setView(View view){
         this.view = view;
    }

}
```

This approach is better than the one used in Listing 17-15, because each request gets the same instance of the `PlainTextView` bean. However, it is still far from ideal. A typical web application consists of a rather large number of views, and configuring all views this way would be inconvenient. Moreover, certain views require further configuration. Take a JSP view, for example: it needs a path to the JSP page. If we were to configure all views as Spring beans manually, we would have to configure each JSP page as a separate bean. An easier way to define the views and delegate all the work to Spring would be nice to have. This is where view resolvers come into the picture.

Using View Resolvers

A `ViewResolver` is a strategy interface that Spring MVC uses to look up and instantiate an appropriate view based on its name and locale. There are various view resolvers that all implement the `ViewResolver` interface's single method: `View resolveViewName(String viewName, Locale locale) throws Exception`. This allows your applications to be much easier to maintain. The locale parameter suggests that the `ViewResolver` can return views for different client locales, which is indeed the case.

Table 17-4 shows the implementations of the `ViewResolver` interface that are supplied with the Spring Framework.

Table 17-4. *ViewResolver Implementations*

Implementation	Description
`BeanNameViewResolver`	This simple `ViewResolver` implementation will try to get the `View` as a bean configured in the application context. This resolver may be useful for small applications, where you do not want to create another file that holds the view definitions. However, this resolver has several limitations; the most annoying one is that you have to configure the views as Spring beans in the application context. Also, it does not support internationalization.
`ResourceBundleViewResolver`	This resolver is far more complex. The view definitions are kept in a separate configuration file, so you do not have to configure the `View` beans in the application context file. This resolver supports internationalization.

Continued

Table 17-4. *Continued*

Implementation	Description
UrlBasedViewResolver	This resolver instantiates the appropriate view based on the URL, which can configure the URL with prefixes and suffixes. This resolver gives you more control over views than BeanNameViewResolver but can become difficult to manage in a large application and does not support internationalization.
XmlViewResolver	This view resolver is similar to ResourceBundleViewResolver, as the view definitions are kept in a separate file. Unfortunately, this resolver does not support internationalization.

Now that you know the advantages and disadvantages of your ViewResolver options in Spring, we can improve the sample application. We are going to discuss the ResourceBundleViewResolver, because it offers the most complete functionality.

We will start off by updating the application context file to include the viewResolver bean definition, as shown in Listing 17-18.

Listing 17-18. *ResourceBundleViewResolver Definition*

```
<?xml version="1.0" encoding="UTF-8"?>
<beans xmlns="http://www.springframework.org/schema/beans"
...>
    <bean id="viewResolver"
        class="org.springframework.web.servlet.view.ResourceBundleViewResolver">
        <property name="basename" value="views"/>
    </bean>
    <!-- etc -->
</beans>
```

This introduces the viewResolver bean that Spring will use to resolve all view names. The class is ResourceBundleViewResolver, and its basename property value is views, which means that the ViewResolver is going to look for a views_<LID>.properties file on the classpath, where LID is the locale identifier (EN, FR, ES, CS, etc.). If the resolver cannot locate a views_<LID>.properties file, it will try to open views.properties. To demonstrate the internationalization support in this resolver, we are going to create views_ES.properties, which is the Spanish language file, and views.properties, which will be used for any other language. In general, the syntax of the properties file looks like this: viewname.class=class-name and viewname.url=view-url. Our example's syntax is shown in Listing 17-19.

Listing 17-19. *views.properties File Syntax*

```
#index
products-index.class=org.springframework.web.servlet.view.JstlView
products-index.url=/WEB-INF/views/en_GB/product/index.jsp
```

Probably the best way to keep this file reasonably easy to maintain is to follow the logical structure of the application, using a dash as a directory separator. To create a user edit view definition, we can use the code in Listing 17-20.

Listing 17-20. *Additions to views.properties*

```
#index
user-edit.class=org.springframework.web.servlet.view.JstlView
user-edit.url=/WEB-INF/views/en_GB/user/edit.jsp
```

In Listing 17-21, you can see that the Spanish versions of the views definition files (views_es.properties) look very similar.

Listing 17-21. *views_es.properties File*

```
#index
products-index.class=org.springframework.web.servlet.view.JstlView
products-index.url=/WEB-INF/views/es_ES/product/index.jsp
```

Note that we kept the same view name (products-index) and changed only the path to the translated JSP file.

Similarly, we are going to create index.jsp in English in the /WEB-INF/views/en_GB/product directory and index.jsp in Spanish in /WEB-INF/views/es_ES/product. Finally, we are going to modify the ProductController to return a dummy list of Product objects and display this list in the view (see Listing 17-22).

Listing 17-22. *Modified ProductController*

```
public class ProductController extends MultiActionController {
    private List products;

    private Product createProduct(Long productId, String name, ➥
                               Date expirationDate) {
        Product product = new Product();
        product.setId(productId);
        product.setName(name);
        product.setExpirationDate(expirationDate);

        return product;
    }

    public ProductController() {
        products = new ArrayList();
        Date today = new Date();
        products.add(createProduct(1L, "test", today));
        products.add(createProduct(2L, "Pro Spring Appes", today));
        products.add(createProduct(3L, "Pro Velocity", today));
        products.add(createProduct(4L, "Pro VS.NET", today));
    }

    public ModelAndView index(HttpServletRequest request,
        HttpServletResponse response) {

        return new ModelAndView("products-index", "products", products);
    }
    // other methods omitted for clarity
}
```

As you can see, we have not modified the ProductController in any unexpected way. However, the ModelAndView constructor we are calling in the index() method is ModelAndView (String, String, Object) rather than ModelAndView (View, Map).

To test the application, make sure the preferred language in your browser is set to anything other than Spanish. Spring will create a product-index view of type JstlView with the URL set to /WEB-INF/views/en_GB/product/index.jsp and render the output shown in Figure 17-5.

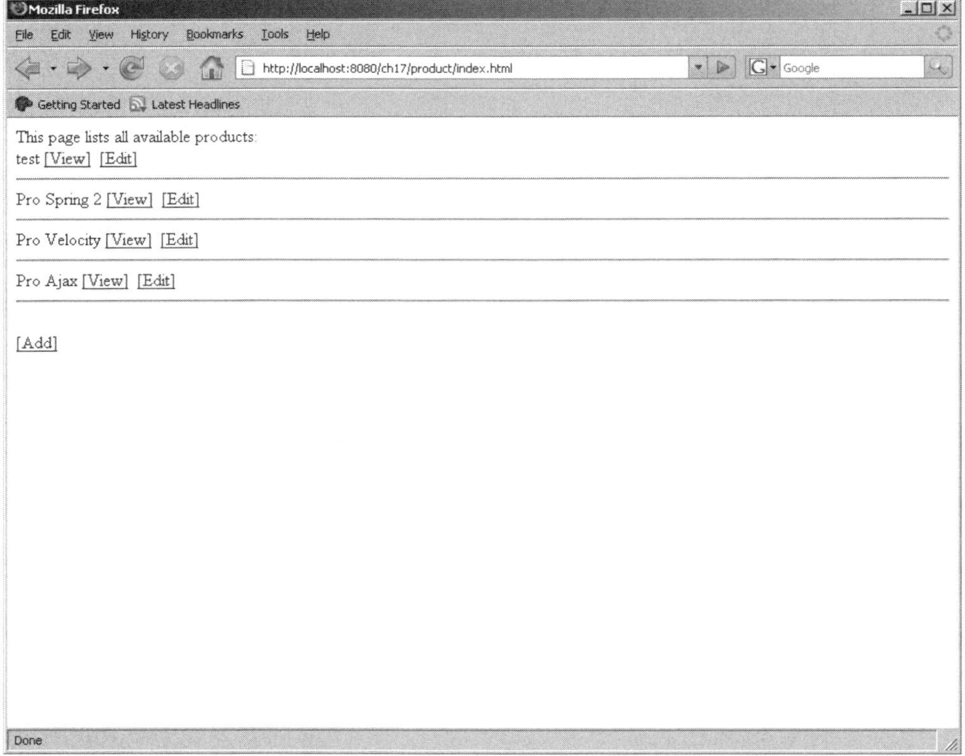

Figure 17-5. *The English version of the site*

If we now change the preferred language to Spanish, the view resolver is going to create an instance of `index_ES`, which is a `JstlView`, and its URL property points to `/WEB-INF/views/en_ES/products/index.jsp`. This renders the page shown in Figure 17-6.

Using view resolvers rather than manually instantiating the views has the obvious benefit of simpler configuration files, but it also reduces the application's memory footprint. If we defined each view as a Spring bean, it would be instantiated on application start; if we use view resolvers, however, the view will be instantiated and cached on first request.

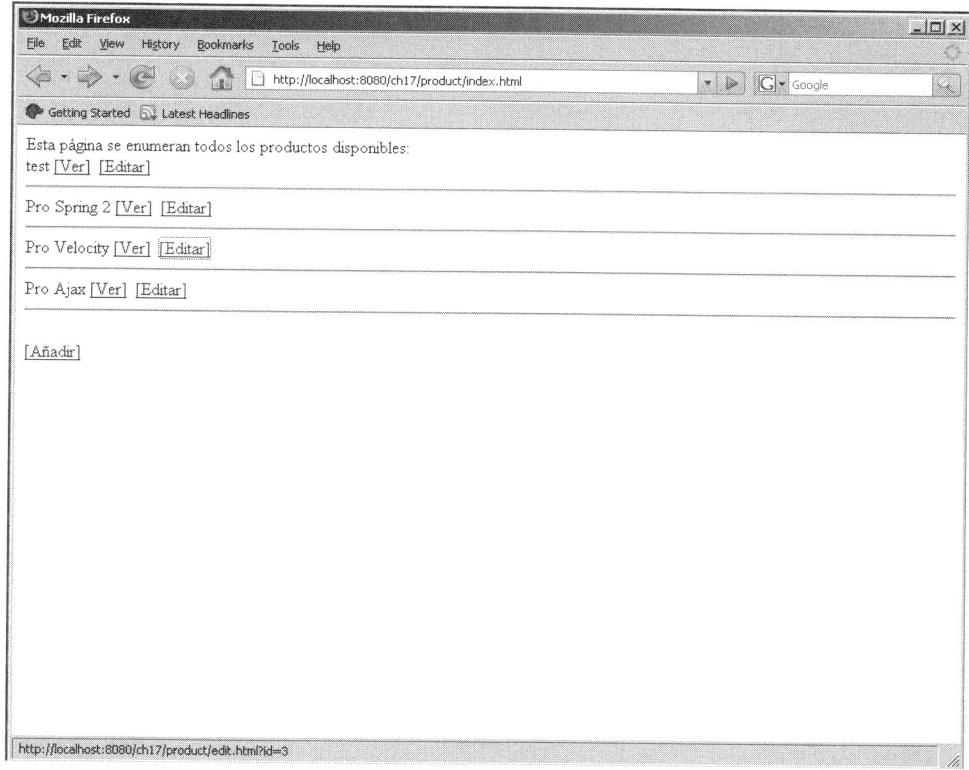

Figure 17-6. *The Spanish version of the site*

Using Localized Messages

Before we can discuss using locales in Spring web applications, we must take a look at how Spring resolves the actual text for messages to be displayed either in the `spring:message` tag (covered in more depth in the "Using Locales" section of this chapter) or as part of the validation process. The core interface, `MessageSource`, uses the `MessageSourceResolvable` interface to find the message key to be displayed. Spring comes with two implementations of the `MessageSource` interface: `ResourceBundleMessageSource` and `ReloadableResourceBundleMessageSource`. Both implementations use a standard properties file to load the messages, but `ReloadableResourceBundleMessageSource` can reload the contents of the properties file if it detects a change, eliminating the need to restart the application when the contents of the properties file are updated.

The default bean name Spring looks up is `messageSource`; our definition of this bean is shown in Listing 17-23.

Listing 17-23. *messageSource Bean Definition*

```
<?xml version="1.0" encoding="UTF-8"?>
<beans xmlns="http://www.springframework.org/schema/beans"
...
    <bean id="messageSource"
        class="org.springframework.context.support.ResourceBundleMessageSource">
        <property name="basename"><value>messages</value></property>
    </bean>
</beans>
```

Using Locales

We have already discussed the internationalization support in ResourceBundleViewResolver; let's now take a look at how things work under the hood. Spring uses the LocaleResolver interface to intercept the request and calls its methods to get or set the Locale. The implementations of LocaleResolver, each with its particular uses and properties, are shown in Table 17-5.

Table 17-5. *LocaleResolver Implementations*

Implementation	Description
AcceptHeaderLocaleResolver	This locale resolver returns the locale based on the accept-language header sent by the user agent to the application. If this resolver is used, the application will automatically appear in the user's preferred language (if we took the time to implement that language). If users wish to switch to another language, they have to change their browser settings.
CookieLocaleResolver	This locale resolver uses a cookie on the client's machine to identify the locale. This allows users to specify the language they want the application to appear in without changing their browser settings. It is not hard to imagine that users in Prague could have an English web browser, yet expect to see the application in Czech. Using this locale resolver, we can store the locale settings using users' browser cookie stores.
FixedLocaleResolver	The fixed locale resolver is a very simple implementation of LocaleResolver that always returns one configured locale.
SessionLocaleResolver	This resolver works very much like CookieLocaleResolver, but the locale settings are not persisted in a cookie and are lost when the session expires.

Using Themes

In addition to providing the application's views in users' languages, themes can be used to further improve the user experience. A theme is usually a collection of style sheets and images that are embedded into the rendered output. Spring also provides a tag library that you can use to enable theme support in your JSP pages. Listing 17-17 shows a typical directory structure of a Spring web application, with specific directory for themes.

As you can see from Figure 17-7, we have added a themes directory and created two new properties files: cool.properties and default.properties. Each line in these properties files specifies the location of a static theme resource. The key is the name of the resource, and the value is the path to the resource file, as shown in Listing 17-24. The path is relative to the context root of the web application.

Figure 17-7. *Directory and file structure for themes*

Listing 17-24. *The cool.properties File*

```
css=/themes/cool/main.css
```

We can use this definition in a JSP page using the Spring tag library, as shown in Listing 17-25.

Listing 17-25. *index.jsp*

```
<%@ taglib prefix="c" uri="http://java.sun.com/jstl/core_rt" %>
<%@taglib prefix="spring" uri="http://www.springframework.org/tags"%>

<html>
    <head>
        <c:set var="css"><spring:theme code="css"/></c:set>
        <c:if test="${not empty css}">
            <link rel="stylesheet" href="<c:url value="${css}"/>" type="text/css" />
        </c:if>
    </head>
<body>
```

```
This page lists all available products:<br>
<c:forEach items="${products}" var="product">
    <c:out value="${product.name}"/>
    <a href="view.html?productId=
        <c:out value="${product.productId}"/>">[View]</a> 
    <a href="edit.html?productId=
        <c:out value="${product.productId}"/>">[Edit]</a> <br>
    <hr>
</c:forEach><br>
<a href="edit.html">[Add]</a>
</body>
</html>
```

Finally, we need to modify the Spring application context and add a `themeResolver` bean, as shown in Listing 17-26.

Listing 17-26. *The themeResolver Bean Definition*

```
<?xml version="1.0" encoding="UTF-8"?>
<beans xmlns="http://www.springframework.org/schema/beans"
...>
    <bean id="themeResolver"
         class="org.springframework.web.servlet.theme.FixedThemeResolver">
        <property name="defaultThemeName"><value>cool</value></property>
    </bean>
    <!-- other beans as usual -->
</beans>
```

This application context file specifies that the application is going to be using `FixedThemeResolver` with `defaultThemeName` set to `cool`, which is going to be loaded from the `cool.properties` file in the root of the classpath because we have set the `defaultThemeName` to `cool`.

Themes can contain not only style sheets but references to any kind of static content, such as images and movies. Therefore, themes must support internationalization, as images may contain text that needs to be translated into other languages. The internationalization support in theme resolvers works exactly the same way as internationalization support in `ResourceBundleViewResolver`. The theme resolver will try to load `theme_<LID>.properties`, where LID is the locale identifier (`EN`, `ES`, `CS`, etc.). If the properties file with the LID does not exist, the resolver will try to load properties file without it.

Just like the `ViewResolvers` and the `LocaleResolvers`, there are several implementations of `ThemeResolvers`; they are shown in Table 17-6.

Table 17-6. *ThemeResolver Implementations*

ThemeResolver	Description
`CookieThemeResolver`	Allows the theme to be set per user and stores the theme preferences by storing a cookie on the client's computer
`FixedThemeResolver`	Returns one fixed theme, which is set in the bean's `defaultThemeName` property
`SessionThemeResolver`	Allows the theme to be set per user's session, so the theme is not persisted between sessions

Adding support for themes can give your application an extra visual kick with very little programming effort.

Command Controllers

Until now, we have been talking about ways to get the data to the user based on the request parameters and how to render the data passed from the controllers. A typical application also gathers data from the user and processes it. Spring supports this scenario by providing command controllers that process the data posted to the controllers. Before we can start discussing the various command controllers, we must take a more detailed look at the concept of command controllers.

The command controller allows a command object's properties to be populated from the <FORM> submission. Because the command controllers work closely with the Spring tag libraries to simplify data validation, they are an ideal location to perform all business validation. As validation occurs on the server, it is impossible for the users to bypass it. However, you should not rely on the web tier to perform all validation, and you should revalidate in the business tier.

On the technical side, the command controller implementations expose a command object, which is (in general) a domain object. These are the possible implementations:

- `AbstractCommandController`: Just like `AbstractController`, `AbstractCommandController` implements the `Controller` interface. This class is not designed to actually handle HTML `FORM` submissions, but it provides basic support for validation and data binding. You can use this class to implement your own command controller, in case the Spring controllers are insufficient to your needs.
- `AbstractFormController`: The `AbstractFormController` class extends `AbstractCommandController` and can actually handle HTML `FORM` submissions. In other words, this command controller will process the values in `HttpServletRequest` and populate the controller's command object. The `AbstractFormController` also has the ability to detect duplicate form submission, and it allows you to specify the views that are to be displayed in the code rather than in the Spring context file. This class has the useful method `Map referenceData()`, which returns the model (`java.util.Map`) for the form view. In this method, you can easily pass any parameter that you would use on the form page (a typical example is a `List` of values for an HTML `SELECT` field).
- `SimpleFormController`: This is the most commonly used command controller to process HTML `FORM` submissions. It is also designed to be very easy to use; you can specify the views to be displayed for the initial view and a success view; and you can set the command object you need to populate with the submitted data.
- `AbstractWizardFormController`: As the name suggests, this command controller is useful for implementing wizard-style sets of pages. This also implies that the command object must be kept in the current `HttpSession`, and you need to implement the `validatePage()` method to check whether the data on the current page is valid and whether the wizard can continue to the next page. In the end, the `AbstractWizardFormController` will execute the `processFinish()` method to indicate that it has processed the last page of the wizard process and that the data is valid and can be passed to the business tier. Instead of this command controller, Spring encourages the use of Spring Web Flow, which offers the same functionality with greater flexibility.

Using Form Controllers

Now that you know which form controller to choose, let's create an example that will demonstrate how a form controller is used. We will start with the simplest form controller implementation and move on to add validation and custom formatters.

The most basic controller implementation will extend `SimpleFormController`, override its `onSubmit()` method, and provide a default constructor.

Listing 17-27. *ProductFormController Implementation*

```
public class ProductFormController extends SimpleFormController {

    public ProductFormController() {
        setCommandClass(Product.class);
 setCommandName("product");
        setFormView("products-edit");
    }

    protected ModelAndView onSubmit(HttpServletRequest request,
        HttpServletResponse response, Object command,
        BindException errors) throws Exception {
        System.out.println(command);

        return new ModelAndView("products-index-r");
    }

}
```

The ProductFormController's constructor defines that the command class is Product.class; this means that the object this controller creates will be an instance of Product.

Next, we override the onSubmit() method, which is going to get called when the user submits the form. The command object will have already passed validation so passing it to the business layer is safe, if doing so is appropriate. The onSubmit() method will return a products-index-r view, which is a RedirectView that will redirect to the products/index.html page. We need the products-index-r view because we want the ProductController.handleIndex() method to take care of the request.

Finally, the call to setFormView() specifies the view that will be used to display the form. In our case, it will be a JSP page, as shown in Listing 17-28.

Listing 17-28. *The edit.jsp Page*

```
<%@ taglib prefix="c" uri="http://java.sun.com/jstl/core_rt" %>
%@ taglib prefix="form" uri="http://www.springframework.org/tags/form" %>

<html>
<head>
    <c:set var="css"><spring:theme code="css"/></c:set>
        <c:if test="${not empty css}">
            <link rel="stylesheet" href="<c:url value="${css}"/>" type="text/css" />
        </c:if>
</head>
<body>
<form:form commandName="product" action="edit.html" method="post">
<input type="hidden" name="productId"
    value="<c:out value="${product.productId}"/>">
<table>
    <tr>
        <td>Name</td>
        <td><form:input path="name" />

        </td>
    </tr>
    <tr>
        <td>Expiration Date</td>
        <td><form:input path="expirationDate" />
```

```
        </td>
    </tr>
    <tr>
        <td></td>
        <td><input type="submit"></td>
    </tr>
</table>
</form:form>
</body>
</html>
```

The form tag library is provided in Spring version 2.0 or higher. It allows us to pass the values from the form in a very simple way. The form tag renders HTML's `<form>` tag and exposes its path for inner tags binding. The method and action attributes are the same as the HTML `<form>` tag's, and the `commandName` attribute sets the command name as it is set in the form controller (`setCommandName(String name)` method). If omitted, the `commandName` value defaults to `command`. The input tags render the HTML `<input>` tag of type text, with value as the bound property of the form object.

The form tag library is explained in more depth later in this chapter.

The last things we need to do are modify the application context file and the `productFormController` bean and add mapping for `/product/edit.html` to the form controller.

Listing 17-29. *The ProductFormController Definition and URL Mapping*

```
<?xml version="1.0" encoding="UTF-8"?>
<beans xmlns="http://www.springframework.org/schema/beans"
...>
    <bean id="publicUrlMapping"
         class="org.springframework.web.servlet.handler.SimpleUrlHandlerMapping">
        <property name="mappings">
            <value>
                /index.html=indexController
                /product/index.html=productController
                /product/view.html=productController
                /product/edit.html=productFormController
            </value>
        </property>
    </bean>

    <!-- Product -->
    <bean id="productFormController"
        class="com.apress.prospring2.ch17.web.product.ProductFormController">
    </bean>
    <!-- other beans as usual -->
</beans>
```

As you can see, there is nothing unusual about the new definitions in the Spring application context file. If we now navigate to `http://localhost:8080/ch17/product/edit.html`, we will find a typical web page with a form to enter the data, as shown in Figure 17-8.

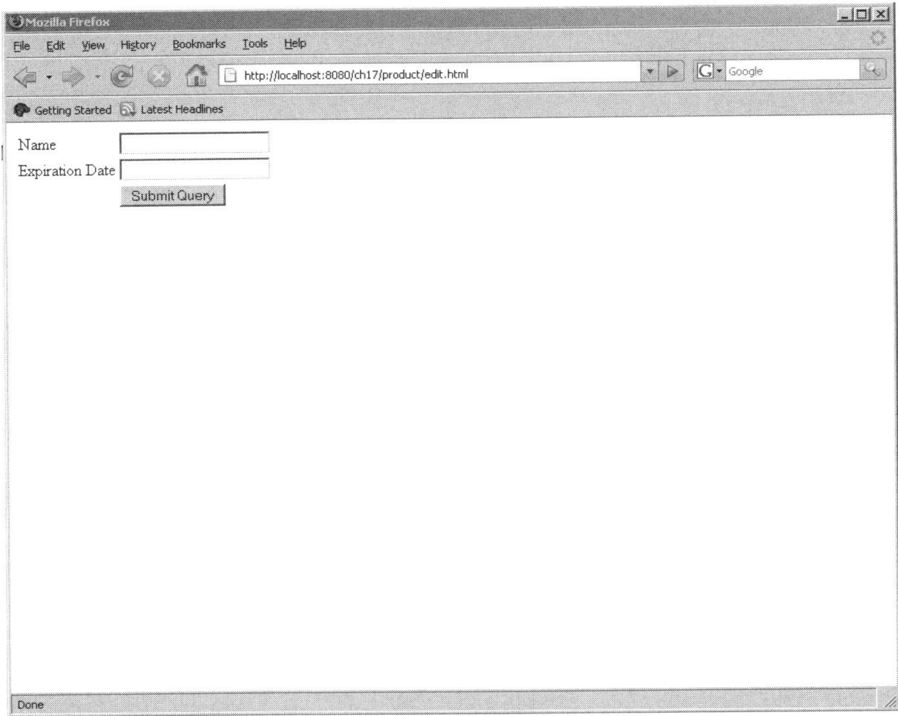

Figure 17-8. *The product editing form*

Unfortunately, the `expirationDate` property is of type `Date`, and Java date formats are a bit difficult to use. You cannot expect users to type **Sun Oct 24 19:20:00 BST 2004** for a date value. To make things a bit easier for the users, we will make our controller accept the date as a user-friendly string, for example, "24/10/2004". To do this, we must use an implementation of the `PropertyEditor` interface, which gives users support to edit bean property values of specific types. In this example, we will use `CustomDateEditor`, which is the `PropertyEditor` for `java.util.Date`. Now, we have to let our controller know to use our date editor (`CustomDateEditor`) to set properties of type `java.util.Date` on the command object. We will do this by registering `CustomDateEditor` for the `java.util.Date` class to the `ServletRequestDataBinder`. `ServletRequestDataBinder` extends the `org.springframework.validation.DataBinder` class to bind the request parameters to the JavaBean properties. To register our date editor, we are going to override the `initBinder()` method (see Listing 17-30).

Listing 17-30. *CustomEditor Registration in ProductFormController*

```
public class ProductFormController extends SimpleFormController {

    // other methods omitted for clarity

    protected void initBinder(HttpServletRequest request,
        ServletRequestDataBinder binder) throws Exception {
        SimpleDateFormat dateFormat = new SimpleDateFormat("dd/MM/yyyy");
        dateFormat.setLenient(false);
        binder.registerCustomEditor(Date.class, null,
```

```
            new CustomDateEditor(dateFormat, false));
    }
}
```

The newly registered custom editor will be applied to all `Date.class` values in the requests processed by `ProductFormController`, and the values will be parsed as `dd/MM/yyyy` values, thus accepting "24/10/2004" instead of "Sun Oct 24 19:20:00 BST 2004" as a valid date value.

There is one other important thing missing from our `Controller`—validation. We do not want to allow users to add a product with no name. To implement validation, Spring provides `Validator` interface, which we have implemented in Listing 17-31. Next, we need to register the `ProductValidator` bean as a Spring-managed bean and set the `ProductFormController`'s validator property to the `productValidator` bean (Listing 17-32 shows the bean definition).

Listing 17-31. *ProductValidator Bean Implementation*

```
public class ProductValidator implements Validator {

    public boolean supports(Class clazz) {
        return clazz.isAssignableFrom(Product.class);
    }

    public void validate(Object obj, Errors errors) {
        Product product = (Product)obj;
        if (product.getName() == null || product.getName().length() == 0) {
            errors.rejectValue("name", "required", "");
        }
    }

}
```

This `Validator` implementation will add a validation error with `errorCode` set to `required`. This code identifies a message resource, which needs to be resolved using a `messageSource` bean. The `messageSource` bean allows externalization of message strings and supports internationalization as well. The rules for creating internationalized messages are exactly the same as rules for creating internationalized views and themes, so we will show only the final application context file in Listing 17-32, without going into the details of the `messages.properties` and `messages_CS.properties` files.

Listing 17-32. *The ProductFormController Definition and URL Mapping*

```
<?xml version="1.0" encoding="UTF-8"?>
<beans xmlns="http://www.springframework.org/schema/beans"
...>
    <bean id="messageSource"
        class="org.springframework.context.support.ResourceBundleMessageSource">
        <property name="basename" value="messages/>
    </bean>

    <bean id="productValidator"
        class="com.apress.prospring2.ch17.business.validators.ProductValidator"/>

    <!-- Product -->
    <bean id="productFormController"
        class="com.apress.prospring2.ch17.web.product.ProductFormController">
        <property name="validator" ref="productValidator"/>
    </bean>
```

```
    <!-- other beans as usual -->
</beans>
```

Spring provides the convenience utility class `ValidationUtils` for easier, more intuitive validation. Using `ValidationUtils`, we can improve our `ProductValidator` as shown in Listing 17-33.

Listing 17-33. *ProductValidator Bean Implementation*

```
public class ProductValidator implements Validator {

    public boolean supports(Class clazz) {
        return clazz.isAssignableFrom(Product.class);
    }

    public void validate(Object obj, Errors errors) {
        Product product = (Product)obj;
       ValidationUtils.rejectIfEmptyOrWhitespace(errors, ➥
                    "name", "required", "Field is required.");
    }

}
```

If we want validation errors to be displayed on the form page to the user, we must edit the `edit.jsp` page as shown in Listing 17-34.

Listing 17-34. *The edit.jsp Page with Errors*

```
<%@ taglib prefix="c" uri="http://java.sun.com/jstl/core_rt" %>
%@ taglib prefix="form" uri="http://www.springframework.org/tags/form" %>

<html>
<head>
    <c:set var="css"><spring:theme code="css"/></c:set>
        <c:if test="${not empty css}">
            <link rel="stylesheet" href="<c:url value="${css}"/>" type="text/css" />
        </c:if>
</head>
<body>
<form:form commandName="product" action="edit.html" method="post">
<input type="hidden" name="productId"
    value="<c:out value="${product.productId}"/>">
<table>
    <tr>
        <td>Name</td>
        <td><form:input path="name" />
                  <form:errors path="name" />
        </td>
    </tr>
    <tr>
        <td>Expiration Date</td>
        <td><form:input path="expirationDate" />
                <form:errors path="expirationDate" />
        </td>
    </tr>
    <tr>
        <td></td>
        <td><input type="submit"></td>
```

```
    </tr>
</table>
</form:form>
</body>
</html>
```

If we rebuild and redeploy the application, go to the `product/edit.html` page, and try to submit the form with a valid expiration date but no product name, we will see an error message in the appropriate language, as shown in Figure 17-9.

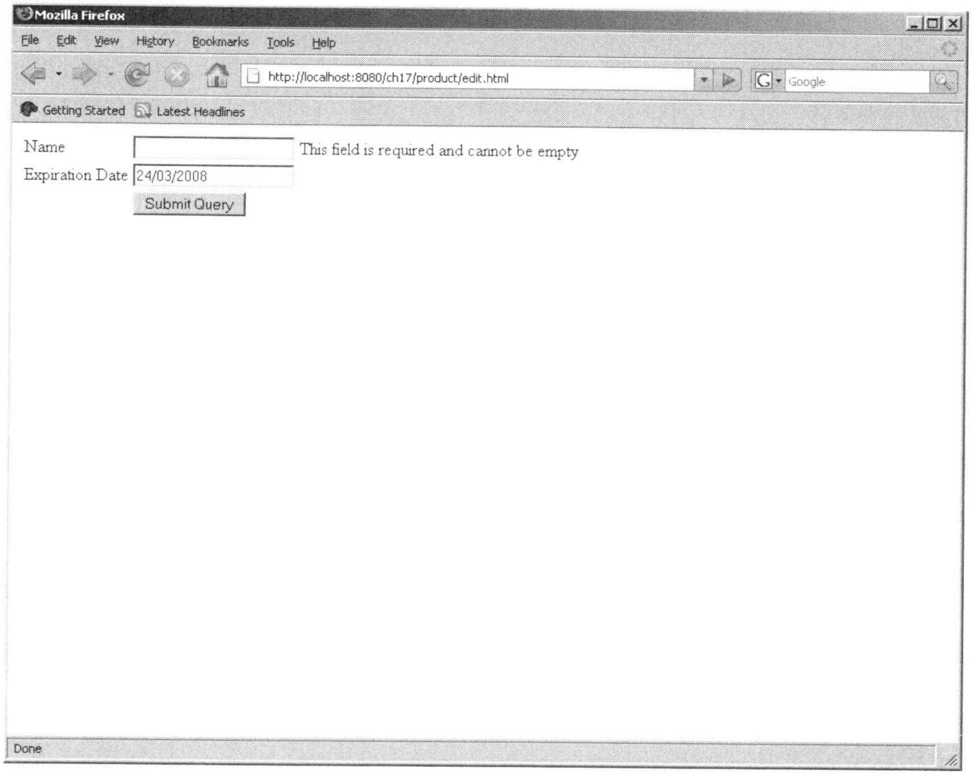

Figure 17-9. *The edit page with validation errors*

You now know how to get new data from users, but in a typical application, you have to deal with edits as well. There must be a way to prepare the command object so it contains data retrieved from the business layer. Typically, this means that the request to the edit page will contain a request parameter that specifies the object identity. The object will then be loaded in a call to the business layer and presented to the user. To do this, override the `formBackingObject()` method.

Listing 17-35. *Overriding the formBackingObject() Method*

```
public class ProductFormController extends SimpleFormController {

    // other methods omitted for clarity
```

```
        protected Object formBackingObject(HttpServletRequest request) ➥
                        throws Exception {
        Product command = new Product();
        long productId = ServletRequestUtils.getLongParameter(request, "id", 0);
        if (id != 0) {
            // load the product
            command.setId(id);
            command.setName("loaded");
        }

        return command;
}
```

And behold: when we make a request to `edit.html` with the request parameter product ID set to 2, the command object's `name` property will be set to `loaded`. Of course, instead of creating an instance of the `Product` object in the controller, we would use a business layer to pass the object identified by the ID.

The other controllers follow the same rules for processing form submission and validation, and the Spring sample applications explain the uses of other controllers, so there is no need to describe them in further detail.

Exploring the AbstractWizardFormController

As we stated in the previous section, Spring advocates using Spring Web Flow for implementing wizard-style forms. However, since `AbstractWizardFormController` is the predecessor of Spring Web Flow, we believe familiarity with this `Controller` implementation would be useful. To demonstrate how to use `AbstractWizardFormController`, we are going to begin with a simple set of JSP pages: `step1.jsp`, `step2.jsp`, and `finish.jsp`. The code of these JSP pages (see Listing 17-36) is not too different from the code used in the `edit.jsp` page from the previous section (see Listing 17-34).

Listing 17-36. *Code for the step1.jsp, step2.jsp, and finish.jsp Pages*

```
// step1.jsp
<%@ taglib prefix="c" uri="http://java.sun.com/jstl/core_rt" %>
<%@taglib prefix="spring" uri="http://www.springframework.org/tags"%>

<html>
<head>
    <c:set var="css"><spring:theme code="css"/></c:set>
       <c:if test="${not empty css}">
            <link rel="stylesheet" href="<c:url value="${css}"/>" ➥
                  type="text/css" />
       </c:if>
</head>
<body>
<form action="wizard.html?_target1" method="post">
<input type="hidden" name="_page" value="0">
<table>
    <tr>
        <td>Name</td>
        <td><spring:bind path="command.name">
                <input name="name" value="<c:out value="${status.value}"/>">
                <span class="error"><c:out value="${status.errorMessage}"/></span>
            </spring:bind>
        </td>
```

```
    </tr>
    <tr>
        <td></td>
        <td><input type="submit" value="Next"></td>
    </tr>
</table>
</form>
</body>
</html>

// step2.jsp
<%@ taglib prefix="c" uri="http://java.sun.com/jstl/core_rt" %>
<%@taglib prefix="spring" uri="http://www.springframework.org/tags"%>

<html>
<head>
    <c:set var="css"><spring:theme code="css"/></c:set>
       <c:if test="${not empty css}">
          <link rel="stylesheet" href="<c:url value="${css}"/>➥
                " type="text/css" />
       </c:if>
</head>
<body>
<form action="wizard.html?_target2" method="post">
<input type="hidden" name="_page" value="1">
<table>
    <tr>
        <td>Expiration Date</td>
        <td><spring:bind path="command.expirationDate">
                <input name="expirationDate" ➥
                       value="<c:out value="${status.value}"/>">
                <span class="error"><c:out value="${status.errorMessage}"/></span>
            </spring:bind>
        </td>
    </tr>
    <tr>
        <td></td>
        <td><input type="submit" value="Next"></td>
    </tr>
</table>
</form>
</body>
</html>

// finish.jsp
<%@ taglib prefix="c" uri="http://java.sun.com/jstl/core_rt" %>
<%@taglib prefix="spring" uri="http://www.springframework.org/tags"%>

<html>
<head>
    <c:set var="css"><spring:theme code="css"/></c:set>
       <c:if test="${not empty css}">
            <link rel="stylesheet" href="<c:url value="${css}"/>" ➥
                        type="text/css" />
       </c:if>
</head>
<body>
```

```
<form action="wizard.html?_finish" method="post">
<input type="hidden" name="_page" value="2">
<table>
    <tr>
        <td>Register now?</td>
        <td><c:out value="${command}"/></td>
    </tr>
    <tr>
        <td></td>
        <td><input type="submit" value="Next"></td>
    </tr>
</table>
</form>
</body>
</html>
```

As you can see, the step1.jsp and step2.jsp pages simply populate the name and expirationDate properties of the command object, which is an instance of the Product domain object.

The AbstractWizardFormController uses several request parameters to control the page flow of the wizard. All possible parameters are summarized in Table 17-7.

Table 17-7. *Page Flow Request Parameters*

Parameter	Description
_target<value>	The value is a number that specifies the pages[] property's index that the controller should go to when the current page is submitted. The current page must be valid, or the allowDirtyForward or allowDirtyBack properties must be set to true.
_finish	If this parameter is specified, the AbstractWizardFormController will invoke the processFinish() method and remove the command object from the session.
_cancel	If this parameter is specified, the AbstractWizardFormController will invoke the processCancel() method, which, if not overridden, will just remove the command object from the session. If you choose to override this method, do not forget to call the super() method or remove the command object from the session yourself.
_page	This parameter (usually specified as <input type="hidden" name="_page" value="">) specifies the index of the page in the pages property.

Now that we have the JSP pages that form the wizard steps, we need to implement the RegistrationController as a subclass of the AbstractWizardFormController, as shown in Listing 17-37.

Listing 17-37. *RegistrationController Implementation*

```
package com.apress.prospring2.ch17.web.registration;

public class RegistrationController extends AbstractWizardFormController {

    public RegistrationController() {
        setPages(new String[] {"registration-step1", "registration-step2",
            "registration-finish"});
        setSessionForm(true);
        setCommandClass(Product.class);
    }
```

```
    protected ModelAndView processFinish(HttpServletRequest request,
        HttpServletResponse response, Object command,
        BindException errors) throws Exception {
        Product product = (Product)command;

        System.out.println("Register " + product);
        return null;
    }

    protected void initBinder(HttpServletRequest request,
        ServletRequestDataBinder binder) throws Exception {
        SimpleDateFormat dateFormat = new SimpleDateFormat("dd/MM/yyyy");
        dateFormat.setLenient(false);
        binder.registerCustomEditor(Date.class, null,
            new CustomDateEditor(dateFormat, false));
    }

    protected void validatePage(Object command, Errors errors, int page,
        boolean finish) {
        getValidator().validate(command, errors);
    }
}
```

The code shown represents almost the simplest implementation of the AbstractWizardFormController subclass. Technically, all we have to implement is the processFinish() method, but in our case, we also needed to register a custom editor for the Date class. Finally, we wanted set the commandClass property to Product.class. We could have set the pages and sessionForm properties in the bean definition, which is shown in Listing 17-38, but we have decided to set the properties in the constructor.

Listing 17-38. *The RegistrationController Bean and URL Mappings*

```
<beans xmlns="http://www.springframework.org/schema/beans"
       ...>
    <bean id="publicUrlMapping"
        class="org.springframework.web.servlet.handler.SimpleUrlHandlerMapping">
        <property name="interceptors">
            <list>
                <ref local="bigBrotherHandlerInterceptor"/>
            </list>
        </property>
        <property name="mappings">
            <value>
                <!-- other  omitted -->
                /registration/wizard.html=registrationController
            </value>
        </property>
    </bean>
    <bean id="registrationController"
        class="com.apress.prospring.ch17.web.registration.RegistrationController">
        <property name="validator"><ref bean="productValidator"/></property>
    </bean>
</beans>
```

Notice that we have not created mappings for the step1.jsp, step2.jsp, and finish.jsp pages; instead, we have only created a single mapping for /registration/wizard.html, which is handled by the registrationController bean. We also set the validator property of the registrationController to the productValidator bean. We use the validator property in the validatePage() method to show that we can validate each page. The implementation we have chosen is exactly the same as the default implementation in AbstractWizardFormController, but if we wanted to, we could allow the user to move to the next page. The AbstractWizardFormController performs the validation before calling the processFinish() method, so there is no way to avoid validation and skipping validation on certain pages is safe—the command object in the processFinish() method is guaranteed to be valid.

Note The command object will be valid only if we have supplied an appropriate Validator implementation.

The explanation of the AbstractWizardFormController we have offered here is quite simple, but it should give you a good starting point if you decide to use AbstractWizardFormController subclasses in your application.

File Upload

Spring handles file upload through implementations of the MultipartResolver interface. Out of the box, Spring comes with support for Commons FileUpload (http://commons.apache.org/fileupload/). By default, there is no default multipartResolver bean declared, so if you want to use the Commons implementation or provide your own implementation, you have to declare the multipartResolver bean in the Spring application context, as shown in Listing 17-39.

Listing 17-39. *MultipartResolver Declaration for Commons FileUpload*

```
<?xml version="1.0" encoding="UTF-8"?>
<beans xmlns="http://www.springframework.org/schema/beans"
...>
    <bean id="multipartResolver"
        class="org.springframework.web.multipart.➥
            commons.CommonsMultipartResolver">
        <property name="maxUploadSize"> <value>100000</value> </property>
    </bean>

    <!-- other beans as usual -->
</beans>
```

Do not forget that you can only have one multipartResolver bean, so you have to choose which one to use when you declare the beans. Once the multipartResolver bean is configured, Spring will know how to handle multipart form-data-encoded requests; that means it will transform the form data into a byte[] array. To demonstrate that our newly configured multipartResolver works, we are going to create ProductImageFormController and ProductImageForm classes. The first one will extend SimpleFormController and handle image upload, while the second one is going to contain properties for the image name and contents. The ProductImageForm implementation is shown in Listing 17-40.

Listing 17-40. *ProductImageForm Implementation*

```
public class ProductImageForm {

    private String name;
    private byte[] contents;

    public byte[] getContents() {
        return contents;
    }

    public void setContents(byte[] contents) {
        this.contents = contents;
    }

    public String getName() {
        return name;
    }

    public void setName(String name) {
        this.name = name;
    }
}
```

There is nothing spectacular about this class; it is a simple Java bean that exposes the `name` and `contents` properties. The `ProductImageFormController` class's `initBinder()` method makes it much more interesting; Listing 17-41 shows this class.

Listing 17-41. *ProductImageFormController Implementation*

```
public class ProductImageFormController extends SimpleFormController {

    public ProductImageFormController() {
        super();
        setCommandClass(ProductImageForm.class);
        setFormView("products-image");
        setCommandName("product");
    }

    protected ModelAndView onSubmit(HttpServletRequest request,
        HttpServletResponse response, Object command,
        BindException errors) throws Exception {
        ProductImageForm form = (ProductImageForm)command;

        System.out.println(form.getName());
        byte[] contents = form.getContents();
        for (int i = 0; i < contents.length; i++) {
            System.out.print(contents[i]);
        }

        return new ModelAndView("products-index-r");
    }
```

```
    protected void initBinder(HttpServletRequest request,
        ServletRequestDataBinder binder) throws Exception {
        binder.registerCustomEditor(byte[].class,
            new ByteArrayMultipartFileEditor());
    }

}
```

The ByteArrayMultipartResolver class uses the multipartResolver bean from the application context to parse the contents of the multipart stream and return it as byte[] array, which is then processed in the onSubmit() method.

Be careful when coding the JSP page for the file upload: the most usual error is to forget the enctype attribute of the form element (as shown in Listing 17-42).

Listing 17-42. *The image.jsp Form*

```
<%@ taglib prefix="c" uri="http://java.sun.com/jstl/core_rt" %>
<%@ taglib prefix="form" uri="http://www.springframework.org/tags/form" %>

<html>
<head>
    <c:set var="css"><spring:theme code="css"/></c:set>
        <c:if test="${not empty css}">
            <link rel="stylesheet" href="<c:url value="${css}"/>" type="text/css" />
        </c:if>
</head>
<body>
<form:form commandName="product" action="image.html" ➥
              method="post" enctype="multipart/form-data">
<input type="hidden" name="productId"
    value="<c:out value="${product.productId}"/>">
<table>
    <tr>
        <td>Name</td>
        <td><form:input path="name" />
                <form:errors path="name" />
        </td>
    </tr>
    <tr>
        <td>Expiration Date</td>
        <td><input name="contents" type="file" />
                <form:errors path="contents" />
        </td>
    </tr>
    <tr>
        <td></td>
        <td><input type="submit"></td>
    </tr>
</table>
</form:form>
</body>
</html>
```

As you can see, the JSP page is a plain HTML page, except for the enctype attribute. You must not forget to define this JSP page as a view in the views.properties file. Once you have defined the view and recompiled and redeployed the application, you should be able to use the file upload page at products/image.html, which is shown in Figure 17-10.

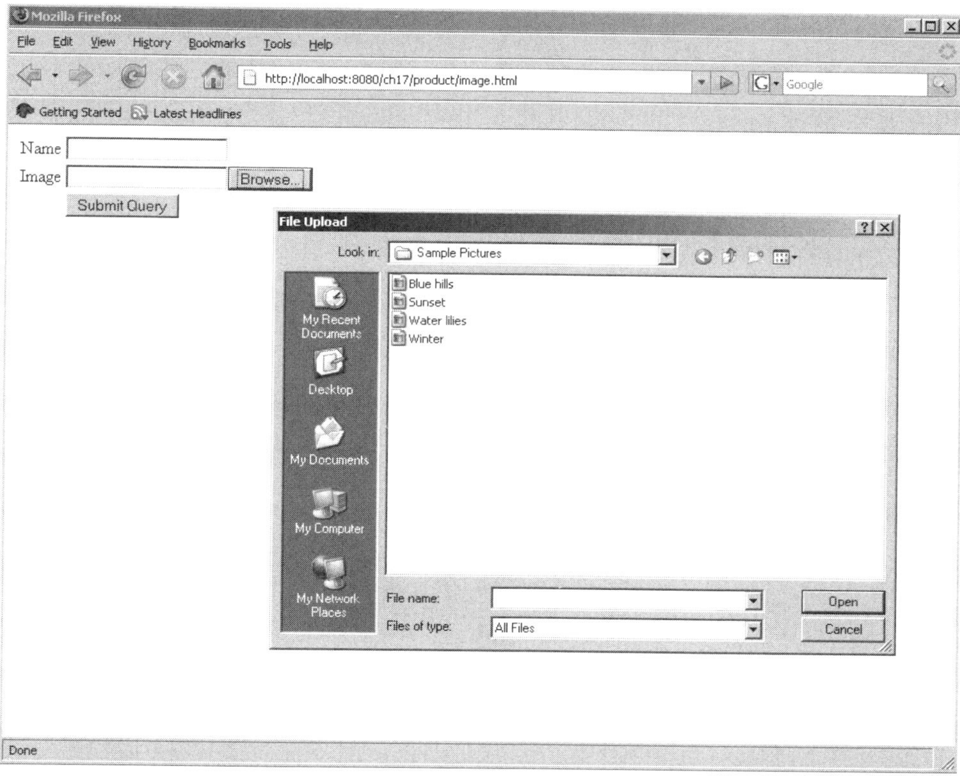

Figure 17-10. *File uploading*

Handling Exceptions

What will you do when something unexpected happens in your web application and an exception gets thrown? Showing the web user an ugly nested exception message isn't very nice. Fortunately, Spring provides `HandlerExceptionResolver` to make life easy when handling exceptions in your controllers. `HandlerExceptionResolver` provides information about what handler was executing when the exception was thrown, as well as many options to handle the exception before the request is forwarded to a user-friendly URL. This is the same end result as when using the exception mappings defined in `web.xml`.

Spring MVC provides one convenient, out-of-the-box implementation of `HandlerExceptionResolver`: `org.springframework.web.servlet.handler.SimpleMappingExceptionResolver`. This resolver enables you to take the class name of any exception that might be thrown and map it to a view name. It is easily configured in your Spring configuration files, as shown in Listing 17-43.

Listing 17-43. *ExceptionResolver Spring Configuration*

```
<bean id="exceptionResolver"
    class="org.springframework.web.servlet.handler.SimpleMappingExceptionResolver">
        <property name="defaultErrorView" value=""/>
        <property name="exceptionMappings">
                  <value>
```

```
                java.lang.NullPointerException=nullPointerErrorView
                javax.servlet.ServletException=servletErrorView
            </value>
        </property>
</bean>
```

The ExceptionMappings property in our example maps java.lang.NullPointerException to a view named nullPointerErrorView and javax.servlet.ServletException to servletErrorView. The defaultErrorView property maps a view to which the request will be forwarded if the exception thrown is not mapped in the exceptionMappings property.

These views have to be defined in views.properties, urlMapping, and Controller, just like any other views (see Listing 17-44).

Listing 17-44. *Exception Views Definitions*

```
defaultErrorView.class=org.springframework.web.servlet.view.JstlView
defaultErrorView.url=/WEB-INF/views/en_GB/exception/default.jsp

nullPointerErrorView.class=org.springframework.web.servlet.view.JstlView
nullPointerErrorView.url=/WEB-INF/views/en_GB/exception/nullpointer.jsp

servletErrorView.class=org.springframework.web.servlet.view.JstlView
servletErrorView.url=/WEB-INF/views/en_GB/exception/servlet.jsp

<bean id="urlMapping" class="org.springframework.web.➥
            servlet.handler.SimpleUrlHandlerMapping">
        <property name="mappings">
            <value>

              /exception/*.html=exceptionController
              ...
            </value>
        </property>
</bean>
```

Listing 17-45 shows Controller implementation:

Listing 17-45. *ExceptionController Implementation*

```
public class ExceptionController extends MultiActionController{

          public ModelAndView defaultErrorHandler(HttpServletRequest request,
            HttpServletResponse response){
                    return new ModelAndView("defaultErrorView");
        }

        public ModelAndView nullPointerErrorHandler(HttpServletRequest request,
             HttpServletResponse response){
               return new ModelAndView("nullPointerErrorView");
      }

       public ModelAndView servletErrorHandler(HttpServletRequest request,
             HttpServletResponse response){
               return new ModelAndView("servletErrorView");
     }
}
```

Let's now look at a simple controller example. In Listing 17-46, you can see the IndexController implementation, which has only one method, handleRequestInternal(). Inside the method, we have only one line of code, throw new NullPointerException(). Every time this controller is invoked, NullPointerException will be thrown. You won't see an implementation like this in the real world; it's just a simplified example.

Listing 17-46. *IndexController Implementation*

```
public class IndexController extends AbstractController {

        protected ModelAndView handleRequestInternal(HttpServletRequest request, ➥
                    HttpServletResponse response) throws Exception {

                throw new NullPointerException();

        }
```

As we would expect, after pointing the browser to /index.html, we will see the NullPointerException view message shown in Figure 17-11.

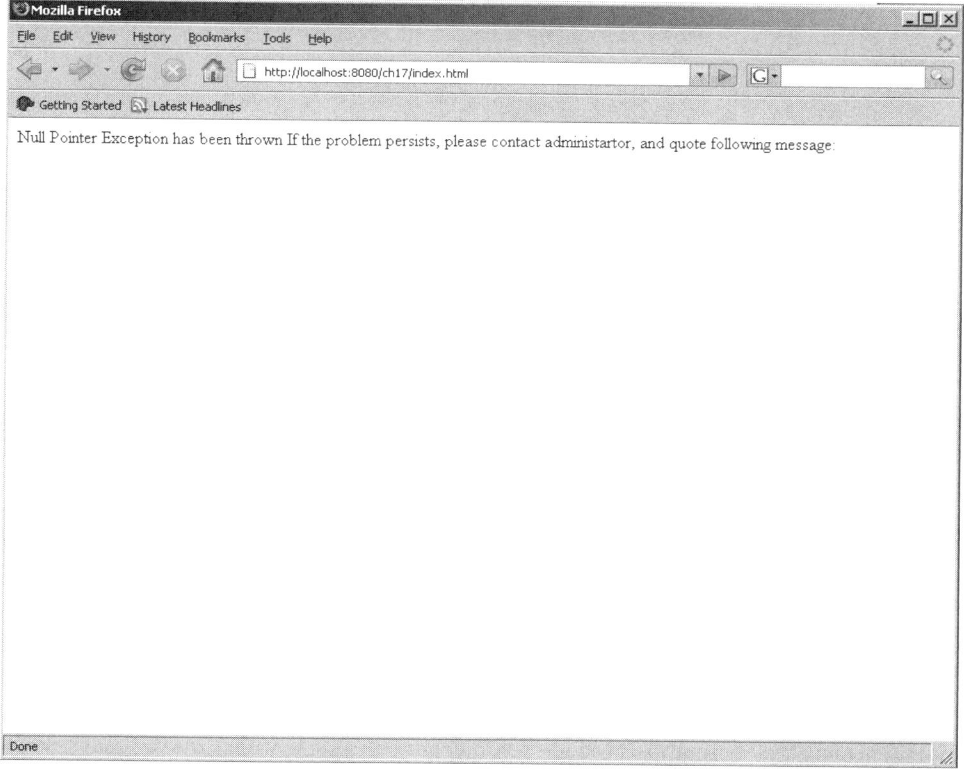

Figure 17-11. *Exception message in the browser*

This is functionally the same as the exception mapping feature from the Servlet API, but you could also implement finer grained mappings of exceptions from different handlers. Also, you can always implement your own `HandlerExceptionResolver`; all you have to do is implement its `public ModelAndView resolveException(HttpServletRequest request, HttpServletResponse response, Object handler, Exception ex)` method. In example in the Listing 17-47, we create a custom exception resolver, that simply display an `Exception` message in the browser.

Listing 17-47. *Custom Implementation and Configuration of ExceptionResolver*

```
<bean id="exceptionResolver" class="com.apress.prospring2. ➥
       ch17.web.exception.ApressExceptionResolver"/>
...
public class ApressExceptionResolver implements HandlerExceptionResolver {

            public ModelAndView resolveException(HttpServletRequest request, ➥
                      HttpServletResponse response, Object handler, Exception ex) {

                  Map<String, Object> model = new HashMap<String, Object>();

                   model.put("message", ex.getMessage());

                  return new ModelAndView("exception", model);
        }
}
```

Note that only exceptions that occur before rendering the view are resolved by the `ExceptionResolver`. If your application throws an exception while rendering the view to the browser (for example if you have used a variable in your JSP pages without passing it to the model), you will still get a long ugly generic exception message. However, these situations are not supposed to happen in a web application, so this isn't a big complication after all.

Spring and Other Web Technologies

In the previous sections, we used JSP pages to generate output that is sent to the client's browser for rendering. We could naturally build the entire application using just JSP pages, but the application and JSP pages would probably become too complex to manage.

Even though JSP pages are very powerful, they can present a considerable processing overhead. Because Spring MVC fully decouples the view from the logic, the JSP pages should not contain any Java scriptlets. Even if this is the case, the JSP pages still need to be compiled, which is a lengthy operation, and their runtime performance is sometimes not as good as we would like. The Velocity templating engine from Apache (described in more detail in the "Using Velocity" section later in this chapter) is a viable alternative, offering much faster rendering times while not restricting the developer too much.

In addition to Velocity, we are going to explore the Tiles framework, which allows you to organize the output generated by the controllers into separate components that can be assembled together using a master template. This greatly simplifies the visual design of the application, and any changes to the overall layout of the output can be made very quickly with fewer coding mistakes and easier code management.

Further, we will explain how to use a PDF or an Excel spreadsheet as output instead of HTML. In some cases, HTML output is simply not suitable, and we have to use PDF or Excel output to present data to the user.

Using JSP

JSP is a tested technology that many developers are familiar with. Because JSP pages are compiled into Java classes and can contain Java code, the developers may be too tempted to move parts of the business logic into the JSP pages (in JSP technology, a code fragment that performs some business logic and is run at request-time processing is called scriptlet). Needless to say, that is a very bad thing that not only violates the MVC model two architecture but makes the application very difficult to maintain.

There is no way to stop developers from using Java scriptlets in JSP pages, but there should be no need to use them. If you ever find yourself in need of a scriptlet or creating a lot of logic using the standard JSTL (Java Standard Tag Library) tags, you should consider writing a custom tag.

Spring offers a list of specific tags that simplify access to Spring features in your JSP pages, as shown in Table 17-8.

Table 17-8. *Spring Tags*

Custom Tag	Description
`htmlEscape`	Sets a value indicating whether the output of other Spring tags should be escaped. If `true`, the HTML formatting strings (such as `<`, `/>`, and `&`) will be replaced by their HTML visual codes.
`message`	Displays a message, identified by its code, that is retrieved from the Spring `messageSource` beans.
`theme`	Retrieves a value for the element defined in the current theme.
`hasBindErrors`	Binds to the errors object, enabling you to inspect any binding errors and display them in the HTML page.
`nestedPath`	Sets a nested path that is then used by the `bind` tag.
`bind`	Binds to an object and provides the object that allows you to access the bound value and any error messages.
`transform`	Transforms a variable to a string using the currently registered `PropertyEditor`. It can be used only with the bind tag.

Using the message Tag

Let's take a closer look at Spring custom tags, beginning with the `message` tag. First, let's create a `messageSource` bean definition in the application context file and create an appropriate `message.properties` file. Listing 17-48 shows the definition of the `messageSource` bean.

Listing 17-48. *messageSource Bean Definition*

```
<?xml version="1.0" encoding="UTF-8" ?>
<beans xmlns="http://www.springframework.org/schema/beans"
...>
    <bean id="messageSource"
        class="org.springframework.context.support.ResourceBundleMessageSource">
        <property name="basename"><value>messages</value></property>
    </bean>
    <!-- other beans omitted -->
</beans>
```

Next, we will create our trivial `message.properties` file, though if you want, you can create `message.properties` files for multiple languages. Listing 17-49 shows the `message.properties` file in English.

Listing 17-49. *message.properties File*

```
greeting=Hello <b>Spring</b> Framework
required=This field is required and cannot be empty
```

Next, we are going to create a `default.jsp` page that will use the Spring JSTL library to display the greeting message inside an `H1` element. Listing 17-50 shows the code for this page.

Listing 17-50. *Code for the default.jsp Page*

```
<%@taglib prefix="spring" uri="http://www.springframework.org/tags"%>
<%@ taglib prefix="c" uri="http://java.sun.com/jstl/core_rt" %>

<html>
<head>
<title>Pro Spring</title>
</head>
<body>
<h1><spring:message code="greeting"/></h1>
</body>
</html>
```

The usage of the `message` tag is quite simple: it simply outputs the text that is looked up in the `messageSource` bean. This is obviously the simplest use of this tag, which can be modified by setting its attributes, shown in Table 17-9.

Table 17-9. *message Tag Attributes*

Attribute	Description
`code`	The code used to look up the message text in the `messageSource` bean.
`arguments`	Comma-separated list of arguments that will be passed to the `getMessage()` method of the `messageSource` bean.
`text`	Text that will be displayed if the entry code is not found in the `messageSource`. Internally, this is used as an argument in the `MessageSource.getMessage()` call.
`var`	Specifies the object that will be set to the value of the message.
`scope`	Specifies the scope to which the object specified in the `var` attribute is going to be inserted.
`htmlEscape`	Indicates whether the message tag should escape the HTML text. If not specified, the global value defined by the `htmlEscape` tag is used.

Using the theme Tag

The `theme` tag allows you to create themed pages. It uses the `themeResolver` bean to load all theme element definitions. To see the tag work, we need to make sure that the application context file contains a `themeResolver` bean definition, as shown in Listing 17-51.

Listing 17-51. *themeResolver Bean Definition*

```
<?xml version="1.0" encoding="UTF-8"?>
<beans xmlns=http://www.springframework.org/schema/beans...>
    <bean id="themeResolver"
        class="org.springframework.web.servlet.theme.FixedThemeResolver">
        <property name="defaultThemeName"><value>cool</value></property>
```

```
    </bean>
    <!-- other beans omitted -->
</beans>
```

Typical usage of the theme bean is shown in the code fragment of the default.jsp page in Listing 17-52.

Listing 17-52. *theme Tag Usage*

```
<link rel="stylesheet" href="<spring:theme code="css"/>">
```

The theme tag has similar attributes to the message tag, allowing you to further control the values it generates. The attributes you can use are summarized in Table 17-10.

Table 17-10. *theme Tag Attributes*

Attribute	Description
code	The code used to look up the theme element text in the themeResolver bean.
arguments	Comma-separated list of arguments that will be passed to the getMessage() method of the messageSource bean.
text	Text that will be displayed if the entry code is not found in the messageSource. Internally, this is used as an argument in the MessageSource.getMessage() call.
var	Specifies the object that will be set to the value of the theme resource.
scope	Specifies the scope to which the object specified in the var attribute is going to be inserted.
htmlEscape	Indicates whether the message tag should escape the HTML text. If not specified, the global value defined by the htmlEscape tag is used.

In fact, the theme tag is a subclass of the message tag; the only difference is that the codes are looked up in a themeResolver rather than messageSource bean.

Using the hasBindErrors Tag

The hasBindErrors tag evaluates its body if the bean specified in its name attribute has validation errors. If there are no errors, the body of the tag is skipped. The usage of this tag in a JSP page is best demonstrated by the code fragment in Listing 17-53.

Listing 17-53. *The hasBindErrors Tag*

```
<spring:hasBindErrors name="command">
    There were validation errors: <c:out value="${errors}"/>
</spring:hasBindErrors>
```

Table 17-11 lists the attributes you can use to fine-tune the behavior of this tag.

Table 17-11. *hasBindErrors Attributes*

Attribute	Description
`name`	Name of the bean for which errors will be looked up.
`htmlEscape`	Indicates whether the message tag should escape the HTML text. If not specified, the global value defined by the `htmlEscape` tag is used.

Using the nestedPath Tag

The `nestedPath` tag is useful to include another object in the path resolution performed by the `bind` tag. The `nestedPath` tag will also copy objects in an existing `nestedPath` to the `nestedPath` it creates.

The only attribute of this tag is `path`, which specifies the path to the object that is to be included in the nested path. The code in Listing 17-54 shows the use of the `nestedPath` tag to add a user attribute to the nested path, giving the `bind` tag access to properties exposed by the `user` bean.

Listing 17-54. *nestedPath Tag Usage*

```
<spring:nestedPath name="user"/>
```

Using the bind Tag

The `bind` tag is the Spring tag used to simplify data entry and validation. In its simplest form, it looks up an object's property identified by the `path` attribute and exposes a new variable named status that holds the object's value and validation errors. This is the most common usage scenario and is shown in the code fragment in Listing 17-55.

Listing 17-55. *The bind Tag*

```
<spring:bind path="command.name">
    <input name="name" value="<c:out value="${status.value}"/>">
    <span class="error"><c:out value="${status.errorMessage}"/></span>
</spring:bind>
```

This code assumes there is a `command` object in the current scope, and that it exposes the `name` property. The `bind` tag will then create a status object and set its `status` property to an instance of the `BindStatus` object for the property identified by the `path` attribute. If there are any validation errors, the `errors` property will contain an instance of `Errors`; the `PropertyEditor` used to parse the value is in the `propertyEditor` property.

This tag can be further controlled through the attributes listed in Table 17-12.

Table 17-12. *bind Tag Attributes*

Attribute	Description
`path`	This attribute identifies the object and its property that will be used to create the `status`, `errors`, and `propertyEditor` properties.
`ignoreNestedPath`	If this is set to `true`, the `bind` tag will ignore any available nested paths as set by the `nestedPath` tag.
`htmlEscape`	This indicates whether the message tag should escape the HTML text. If not specified, the global value defined by the `htmlEscape` tag is used.

Using the transform Tag

The `transform` tag tag looks up the appropriate `PropertyEditor` for the object specified in the value attribute and uses it to output the `String` representation. You can use this attribute instead of the format JSTL tags to keep the formatting rules in Spring. The usage is shown in Listing 17-56.

Listing 17-56. *transform Tag Usage*

```
<spring:transform value="command.expirationDate"/>
```

If the `expirationDate` property of the command object is of `Date` class and if there is a `PropertyEditor` registered for `Date.class` with specified formatting rules, the `transform` tag will output the appropriately formatted date string. All attributes of the transform tag are listed in Table 17-13.

Table 17-13. *transform Tag Attributes*

Attribute	Description
`value`	Identified the value to be formatted
`var`	If set, the tag will set the formatted output to an object with the name set to the specified value.
`scope`	Specifies the scope into which the object specified in the `var` attribute is going to be inserted.
`htmlEscape`	Indicates whether the `message` tag should escape the HTML text. If not specified, the global value defined by the `htmlEscape` tag is used.

The Spring Form Tag Library

Spring 2.0 introduces a new tag library used to bind HTML form elements when working with JSP and Spring controllers. Each tag provides support for an HTML tag counterpart, which makes use easy and intuitive. All tags in the Form Tag library generate HTML 4.01–compliant and XHTML 1.0–compliant code.

Spring form tag library support is included in Spring MVC, so you'll be able to easily integrate it with your controllers.

To take advantage of this library, each of your JSP pages include the library declaration in the beginning of its file (see Listing 17-57).

Listing 17-57. *Form Tag Library Declaration*

```
<%@ taglib prefix="form" uri="http://www.springframework.org/tags/form" %>
```

You can choose the value of the `prefix` attribute as you like and use the tag library on your page with that prefix (in our example `"form"`).

The form Tag

The `form` tag is the main one in the library and is used to generate the HTML `form` tag, and all other tags in the Spring form tag library are nested tags of the `form` tag. The `form` tag will put the command object in the `PageContext` and make the command object available to inner tags.

Let's assume we have a domain object called `Customer`. It is a Java Bean with properties such as `username` and `fullName`. We will use it as the form-backing object of our form controller, which returns `form.jsp`. Listing 17-58 shows an example `form.jsp` file. This example just uses the provided binding of the `form` tag, and actual input fields are built using regular HTML input tags.

Listing 17-58. *The form Tag Example*

```
<form:form action="edit.html" commandName="customer">
    <table>
        <tr>
            <td>Username:</td>
            <td><input name="username" type="text" ➥
                                   value="${customer.username}"/></td>
        </tr>
        <tr>
            <td>Full Name:</td>
            <td><input name="fullName" type="text" ➥
                                 value="${customer.fullName}"/></td>
        </tr>
        <tr>
            <td>
                <input type="submit" value="Save" />
            </td>
        </tr>
    </table>
</form:form>
```

The `firstName` and `lastName` values are retrieved from the command object placed in the `PageContext` by the page controller.

The generated HTML looks like a standard form; see Listing 17-59.

Listing 17-59. *The HTML Generated by Listing 17-58*

```
<form method="POST" action="edit.html">
    <table>
      <tr>
          <td>Username:</td>
          <td><input name="firstName" type="text" value="janed"/></td>
          <td></td>
      </tr>
      <tr>
          <td>Full Name:</td>
          <td><input name="fullName" type="text" value="Jane Doe"/></td>
          <td></td>
      </tr>
      <tr>
          <td>
            <input type="submit" value="Save Changes" />
          </td>
      </tr>
    </table>
</form>
```

The `commandName` attribute of the form tag can be omitted; in that case, the command name will default to `"command"`.

This tag can be further controlled through the attributes. Main attributes are listed in Table 17-14.

Table 17-14. *form Tag Attributes*

Attribute	Description
`modelAttribute`	Identifies the name of the command object, same as `commandName`.
`acceptCharset`	A list of character encodings that are valid for the server. The list has to be a space- or comma-delimited set of values.
`htmlEscape`	Controls the HTML escaping of the rendered values.

Note The `form` tag can use certain regular HTML attributes, such as `encoding`, `action`, and `method`. At the same time, all standard HTML attributes and HTML event attributes can be used, such as `title`, `name`, `onclick`, and `onmouseover`. All HTML standard attributes and events can also be used on all nested attributes. For style purposes, all tags in the Spring form tag library have `cssStyle`, `cssClass`, and `cssErrorClass` attributes. The `cssStyle` tag is equivalent to standard HTML `style` attribute, and `cssClass` is equivalent to the standard HTML `class` attribute. The `cssErrorClass` attribute is used as a `class` attribute when the `errors` object is provided for given filed, for example, when a field has validation errors.

The example in Listings 17-58 and 17-59 uses just the `form` tag, but it uses normal HTML input tags in the form. We will now use the Spring form tag library input tag instead of HTML input tag.

The input Tag

The most common type of a field in forms is the `input` field. In Listing 17-59, we used a standard HTML `input` tag for `input` fields. Listing 17-60 shows how we can improve that example, using the `form:input` tag.

Listing 17-60. *An input Form Tag Example*

```
<form:form action="edit.html" commandName="customer">
    <table>
        <tr>
            <td>Username:</td>
            <td><form:input path="username" /></td>
        </tr>
        <tr>
            <td>Full Name:</td>
            <td><form:input path="fullName" /></td>
        </tr>
        <tr>
            <td colspan="3">
                <input type="submit" value="Save Changes" />
            </td>
        </tr>
    </table>
</form:form>
```

The `input` fields will bind to paths: `customer.username` and `customer.fullName` respectively (as supplied via the `path` attribute). Table 17-15 shows some useful attributes for further controlling the `input` tag.

Table 17-15. *input Tag Attributes*

Attribute	Description
path	Identifies the object and its property that will be used to create the status and/or errors
htmlEscape	Controls the HTML escaping of the rendered values

Standard CSS style attributes, mentioned earlier, are also available for this tag.

The checkbox Tag

The checkbox tag renders an HTML input tag with type checkbox. There are three common scenarios for using the checkbox tag; these should meet all your check box needs. The scenarios are based on the type of the object that is bound to the field, depending weather the object is of the Boolean, Collection, or any other type.

When the bound value is of type java.lang.Boolean, the check box is marked as checked if the value of the property is true. Listing 17-61 shows Customer object with new property subscribed.

Listing 17-61. *Customer Bean Properties*

```
public class Customer{
    //other fields omitted for clarity
    private Boolean subscribed;
    public isSubscribed(){
        return subscribed;
}
    public setSubscribed(Boolean subscribed){
        this.subscribed=subscribed;

    }
}
```

In Listing 17-62, we have created appropriate form, with the subscribed property bound to the checkbox field.

Listing 17-62. *The checkbox Form Tag*

```
<form:form action="edit.html" commandName="customer">
    <table>
        <!-- Other properties, omitted for clarity-- >
        <tr>
            <td>Subscribe to newsletter?:</td>
            <td><form:checkbox path="customer.subscribed"/></td>
            <td> </td>
        </tr>

    </table>
</form:form>
```

If the customer command's subscribed property is set to true, the check box will be checked. Otherwise, it will remain unchecked.

The second usual scenario is that the bound property is of type java.util.Collection (or an array of any type). The check box is marked as checked if the property (Collection or array) contains the value.

To see an example of this property, we will add property `Set<String> categories` to the `Customer` object, referencing the product categories that the `Customer` is interested in (see Listing 17-63).

Listing 17-63. *Changed Customer Object with categories Property*

```
...
private Set<String> categories;
public getCategories(){
      return categories;
}
...
public setCategories(Set<String> categories){
      this.categories=categories;
}...
```

Listing 17-64 shows the form, with the check box bound to the `customer.categories` property.

Listing 17-64. *The Check Box Mapped to the Collection*

```
<form:form action="edit.html" commandName="customer">
    <table>
        <!-- Other properties, omitted for clarity-- >
        <tr>
            <td>Books:</td>
            <td><form:checkbox path="customer.categories" value="Books"/></td>
            <td> </td>
        </tr>
    </table>
</form:form>
```

This form will generate a check box that will be checked if the bound property `customer.categories` contains the value `Books`. If the `Books` value is not contained in the `categories` property of the `Customer`, the check box will not be checked.

The third scenario includes all other types of bound properties.

For this example, add the property `favouriteProduct` to the `Customer` bean, and add this property to the customer editing form (see Listings 17-65 and 17-66).

Listing 17-65. *Changed Customer Java Bean with favouriteProduct property*

```
private String favouriteProduct;
public getFavouriteProduct(){
      return favouriteProduct;
}
public setFavouriteProduct(String favouriteProduct){
      this.favouriteProduct=favouriteProduct;
}
```

Listing 17-66. *A Form with the checkbox Tag*

```
<form:form action="edit.html" commandName="customer">
    <table>
        <!-- Other properties, omitted for clarity-- >
        <tr>
            <td>Pro Spring 2 favourite artist:</td>
            <td><form:checkbox path="customer.favouriteProduct" ➥
                                  value="Amy Winehouse CD"/></td>
            <td> </td>
```

```
        </tr>
    </table>
</form:form>
```

The customer.favouriteProduct property value is compared to the value attribute of the checkbox tag, and if they are the equal, the check box status will be checked; otherwise, the box will be unchecked.

The generated HTML will look exactly the same, no matter which approach we choose. In Listing 17-67, you can see an example of generated HTML for the categories property.

Listing 17-67. *Generated HTML for the categories Property*

```
<tr>
    <td>Categories:</td>
    <td>
        Books: <input name="customer.categories" type="checkbox" value="Books"/>
        <input type="hidden" value="1" name="_customer.categories "/>
        MP3 Players: <input name="customer.categories" type="checkbox" ➥
                            value="MP3 Players"/>
        <input type="hidden" value="1" name="_customer.categories"/>
        CDs: <input name="customer.categories" type="checkbox"
            value="CDs"/>
        <input type="hidden" value="1" name="_customer.categories"/>
    </td>
    <td> </td>
</tr>
```

The only uncommon things in this example are the hidden fields after every check box, which are there to overcome HTML restrictions within Spring. When a check box in an HTML page is not checked, its value will not be sent to the server as part of the HTTP request parameters when the form is submitted. But we need that information in the request, as otherwise, Spring form binding will not work (Spring would complain if a bound field were not found). We need a workaround to keep Spring's form data binding working. The checkbox tag follows the existing Spring convention of including a hidden parameter prefixed by an underscore (_) for each check box. This way, you will be telling Spring what check boxes were visible in the form and to bind data to properties of check box fields even if they are not part of the request (i.e., if they are not checked).

Table 17-16 lists some specific attributes for the checkbox tag.

Table 17-16. *checkbox Tag Attributes*

Attribute	Description
path	Identifies the object and its property that will be used to create the status and/or errors
label	Label to be displayed with the tag path property value
htmlEscape	Controls the HTML escaping of the rendered values

Standard CSS style attributes, mentioned earlier, are also available for this tag.

The checkboxes Tag

Spring provides the convenient checkboxes tag for rendering multiple check box fields.

This tag works in a similar way to the checkbox tag. The main addition is the items attribute, which accepts the java.util.Collection of values on which to build check boxes. Using the items attribute, you would render a check box for each value in the items' Collection in your HTML.

Let's use the example from Listing 17-61, the `Set<String> categories` property of the `Customer` object. We will create form page, using the `checkboxes` tag for binding categories (see Listing 17-68).

Listing 17-68. *checkbox Tag Mapped to Collection*

```
<form:form action="edit.html" commandName="customer">
    <table>
        <!-- Other properties, omitted for clarity-- >
        <tr>
            <td>Books:</td>
            <td><form:checkbox path="customer.categories" ➥
                           items="availableCategories"/></td>
            <td> </td>
        </tr>
    </table>
</form:form>
```

We will have to make the `availableCategories Collection` available as a model attribute by passing it to the model in our controller. Listing 17-69 shows how to achieve this.

Listing 17-69. *Controller Passing Available Check Boxes' Values*

```
Public class EditCustomerController extends SimpleFormController{
       //other methods omitted for clarity
    Map referenceData(HttpServletRequest request){
        Map<String, Object> model = new HashMap<String, Object>();
        List<String> availableCategories = new LinkedList<String>();
        availableCategories.add("Books");
        availableCategories.add("CDs");
        availableCategories.add("MP3Players");
        model.put("availableCategories", availableCategories);.
        return model;
    }
}
```

The generated HTML will have three check boxes rendered, with values passed via `availableCategories` list in the model (see Listing 17-70).

Listing 17-70. *Generated HTML for Check Boxes from Listing 17-68*

```
<tr>
    <td>Categories:</td>
    <td>
        Books: <input name="customer.categories" type="checkbox" value="Books"/>
        <input type="hidden" value="1" name="_customer.categories "/>
        MP3 Players: <input name="customer.categories" type="checkbox" ➥
                                 value="MP3 Players"/>
        <input type="hidden" value="1" name="_customer.categories"/>
        CDs: <input name="customer.categories" type="checkbox"
            value="CDs"/>
        <input type="hidden" value="1" name="_customer.categories"/>
    </td>
    <td> </td>
</tr>
```

The value of the `items` attribute can be the `Map` as well. In this case, the `Map` keys will be the values of rendered check boxes, and the `Map` value for the specific key will be the label for that check box.

Table 17-17 shows main attributes that can be used with the `checkboxes` tag.

Table 17-17. *checkboxes Tag Attributes*

Attribute	Description
`path`	Identifies the object and its property that will be used to create the status and/or errors.
`items`	The `Collection`, `Map`, or array that holds values for the rendered multiple check boxes.
`itemLabel`	The label to be displayed.
`itemValue`	The name of the property to be used as value for the check boxes.
`delimiter`	The HTML tag or any `String` to be used as delimiter between the check boxes. The default is `none`.
`element`	The HTML tag used to enclose every rendered check box. By default, all `<input type="checkbox">` tags will be enclosed with `<span>` HTML tags.
`htmlEscape`	Controls the HTML escaping of the rendered values.

Standard CSS style attributes, mentioned earlier, are also available for this tag.

The radiobutton Tag

The `radiobutton` tag renders an HTML `input` tag with type `radio`.

Listing 17-71 shows a typical radio button example. The `String` property `"answer"` is bound to multiple radio button tags. Only one of the radio buttons bound to the same property can be selected at any time.

Listing 17-71. *Radio Button Example*

```
private String answer;
//getters and setters
<tr>
    <td>Answer:</td>
    <td>A: <form:radiobutton path="answer" value="A"/> <br/>
        B: <form:radiobutton path="answer " value="B"/> </td>
    <td> </td>
</tr>
```

Table 17-18 shows some attributes that can be used with the `radiobutton` tag.

Table 17-18. *radiobutton Tag Attributes*

Attribute	Description
`path`	Identifies the object and its property that will be used to create the status and/or errors
`label`	Label to be displayed with the tag path property value
`htmlEscape`	Controls the HTML escaping of the rendered values

Standard CSS style attributes, mentioned earlier, are also available for this tag.

The radiobuttons Tag

The `radiobuttons` tag is convenient for rendering multiple radio buttons based on the values of the `Collection`, `Map`, or array of objects passed to this tag using the `items` attribute.

Listing 17-72 shows the form example using `radiobuttons` tag.

Listing 17-72. *A radiobuttons Tag Mapped to a Collection*

```
<form:form action="edit.html" >
    <table>
        <!-- Other properties, omitted for clarity-- >
        <tr>
            <td>Who is the murderer?</td>
            <td><form:radiobuttons path="command.answer" ➥
                        items="availableAnswers" delimiter="<br/>"/></td>m
            <td> </td>
        </tr>
    </table>
</form:form>
```

We will have to make `availableAnswers` available as a model attribute. Listing 17-73 gives example of how to do it using `Map`.

Listing 17-73. *Controller Passing Available radiobuttons Values*

```
Public class AnswerController extends SimpleFormController{
       //other methods omitted for clarity
    Map referenceData(HttpServletRequest request){
        Map<String, Object> model = new HashMap<String, Object>();
        Map<String, String> availableAnswers = new HashMap<String, String>();
        availableAnswers.put("A", "Butler");
        availableAnswers.put("B", "Gardener");
        availableAnswers.put("C", "Lawyer");
        availableAnswers.put("D", "Inspector");
        model.put("availableCategories", availableCategories);.
        return model;
    }
}
```

The map keys will be used for radio button values, and the `Map` entry for the specific key will be used for the radio button label. Listing 17-74 shows generated HTML.

Listing 17-74. *Generated HTML for the radiobuttons Tag from Listing 17-72*

```
<tr>
    <td>Who is the murderer:</td>
    <td>
        Butler: <input name="answer" type="radio" value="A"/><br/>
        Gardener: <input name="answer" type="radio" value="B"/><br/>
        Lawyer: <input name="answer" type="radio" value="C"/><br/>
        Inspector: <input name="answer" type="radio" value="D"/><br/>
</tr>
```

The `<br/>` HTML tag is used as delimiter as specified in the `tag` attribute. Similar to the `checkboxes` tag, items can be either `Map`, `Collection`, or array of objects. Table 17-19 shows attributes that can be used with the `radiobuttons` tag.

Table 17-19. *radiobuttons Tag Attributes*

Attribute	Description
`path`	Identifies the object and its property that will be used to create the status and/or errors.
`items`	The `Collection`, `Map`, or array that holds values for the rendered multiple radio buttons.
`itemLabel`	Label to be displayed.
`itemValue`	Name of the property to be used as value for the radio buttons.
`delimiter`	The HTML tag or any `String` to be used as delimiter between the radio buttons. The default is `none`.
`element`	The HTML tag used to enclose every rendered radio button. By default, all `<input type="radio">` tags will be enclosed with `<span>` HTML tags.
`htmlEscape`	Controls the HTML escaping of the rendered values.

Standard CSS style attributes, mentioned earlier, are also available for this tag.

The password Tag

The `password` tag renders an HTML `input` tag with type `password`. By default, the value of the field will not be shown in the browser. However, you can overcome this by setting the attribute `showPassword` to `true`. Listing 17-75 shows simple example.

Listing 17-75. *Password tag Example*

```
<tr>
    <td>Password:</td>
    <td>
        <form:password path="password" />
    </td>
</tr>
```

This tag can be further controlled using the attributes listed in Table 17-20.

Table 17-20. *password Tag Attributes*

Attribute	Description
`path`	Identifies the object and its property that will be used to create the status and/or errors.
`showPassword`	Determines if the password should be shown in the browser. The default is `false`.
`htmlEscape`	Controls the HTML escaping of the rendered values.

Standard CSS style attributes, mentioned earlier, are also available for this tag.

The select tag

The `select` tag renders an HTML `select` element and works in similar fashion to the `checkboxes` tag. The only difference is that it will be rendered as a `select` HTML element, not as multiple check boxes.

You can see example of the `select` tag in the Listing 17-76.

Listing 17-76. *The select Form Tag*

```
<form:form action="edit.html" commandName="customer">
    <table>
        <!-- Other properties, omitted for clarity-- >
        <tr>
            <td>Category:</td>
            <td><form:select path="customer.categories" ➥
                                 items="availableCategories"multiple="true"/></td>
            <td> </td>
        </tr>
    </table>
</form:form>
```

We will need to pass the available categories as a model attribute using the controller, in the same way as in Listing 17-69.

The value of the `items` attribute can be the `Map` as well. In this case, the `Map` keys will be the values of rendered check boxes, and the `Map` value for the specific key will be the label for that check box.

Table 17-21 shows main attributes that can be used with the `select` tag.

Table 17-21. *select Tag Attributes*

Attribute	Description
`path`	Identifies the object and its property that will be used to create the status and/or errors
`items`	The `Collection`, `Map`, or array that hold values for the `select` field
`itemLabel`	Name of the property to be displayed as visible text for the option
`itemValue`	Name of the property to be used as the value for the options
`htmlEscape`	Controls the HTML escaping of the rendered values

Standard CSS style attributes, mentioned earlier, are also available for this tag.

The option Tag

The `option` tag renders an HTML `option`. When using this tag, we don't have to supply an `items` attribute to the `select` tag, but we do need to add all options inside the `select` tag.

Listing 17-77. *The option Form Tag*

```
<form:form action="edit.html" commandName="customer">
    <table>
        <!-- Other properties, omitted for clarity-- >
        <tr>
            <td>Category:</td>
            <td><form:select path="customer.categories" multiple="true">
                            <form:option value="Books"/>
                            <form:option value="CDs"/>
                            <form:option value="MP3"/>
                    </form:select></td>
            <td> </td>
        </tr>
    </table>
</form:form>
```

Table 17-22 shows the attribute that can be used with the option tag.

Table 17-22. *option Tag Attribute*

Attribute	Description
htmlEscape	Controls the HTML escaping of the rendered values

Standard CSS style attributes, mentioned earlier, are also available for this tag.

The options Tag

The options tag renders a list of HTML option tags and is typically used with the singular option tag when we want to add an option for a select field that is not one of the values provided in the items attribute for that select field. See Listing 17-78 for an example.

Listing 17-78. *The options Form Tag*

```
<form:form action="edit.html" commandName="customer">
    <table>
        <!-- Other properties, omitted for clarity-- >
        <tr>
            <td>Category:</td>
            <td><form:select path="customer.categories">
                           <form:option value="-" label="--Please Select--"/>
                           <form:options items="${availableCategories}" />
                   </form:select></td>
            <td> </td>
        </tr>
    </table>
</form:form>
```

Table 17-23 shows the main attributes that can be used with the options tag.

Table 17-23. *options Tag Attributes*

Attribute	Description
items	The Collection, Map, or array that hold values for the select field
itemLabel	Name of the property to be displayed as visible text for the option
itemValue	Name of the property to be used as value for the options
htmlEscape	Controls the HTML escaping of the rendered values

Standard CSS style attributes, mentioned earlier, are also available for this tag.

The textarea tag

The textarea tag simply renders a textarea HTML field. See Listing 17-79 for a simple example.

Listing 17-79. *The textarea Form Tag*

```
<tr>
    <td>Comments:</td>
    <td><form:textarea path="comments" rows="3" cols="20" /></td>
```

```
    <td><form:errors path="comments " /></td>
</tr>
```

This tag can be further controlled using the attributes listed in Table 17-24.

Table 17-24. *textarea Tag Attributes*

Attribute	Description
path	Identifies the object and its property that will be used to create the status and/or errors
htmlEscape	Controls the HTML escaping of the rendered values

Standard CSS style attributes, mentioned earlier, are also available for this tag.

The hidden tag

The hidden tag is used for rendering hidden fields in HTML forms; see Listing 17-80.

Listing 17-80. *The hidden Form Tag*

```
<form:hidden path="id" />
```

The hidden tag can be further controlled using the attributes listed in Table 17-25.

Table 17-25. *hidden Tag Attributes*

Attribute	Description
path	Identifies the object and its property that will be used to create the status and/or errors
htmlEscape	Controls the HTML escaping of the rendered values

Standard CSS style attributes, mentioned earlier, are also available for this tag.

The errors tag

The errors tag provides easy and convenient access to the errors created either in your controller or by any validators associated with the controller.

Listing 17-81 shows an example using EditProductController, which edits product properties using ProductValidator.

Listing 17-81. *ProductValidator Implementation*

```
public class ProductValidator implements Validator {

    public boolean supports(Class product) {
        return Product.class.isAssignableFrom(product);
    }

    public void validate(Object obj, Errors errors) {
        ValidationUtils.rejectIfEmptyOrWhitespace(errors, "name", ➥
                                        "required", "Field is required.");
        ValidationUtils.rejectIfEmptyOrWhitespace(errors, "expirationDate", ➥
                                        "required", "Field is required.");
```

```
    }
}
```

In Listing 17-82, we create the form that will be validated with our `ProductValidator`.

Listing 17-82. *The Form with the errors Tag*

```
<form:form>
    <table>
        <tr>
            <td>Name:</td>
            <td><form:input path="name" /></td>
            <td><form:errors path="name" /></td>
        </tr>
        <tr>
            <td>Expiration Date:</td>
            <td><form:input path="expirationDate " /></td>
            <td><form:errors path="expirationDate "  /></td>
        </tr>
        <tr>
            <td colspan="3">
                <input type="submit" value="Save Changes" />
            </td>
        </tr>
    </table>
</form:form>
```

Now, let's see what happens if we submit the form with errors in it. If we submit a form with empty values in the name and `expirationDate` fields, the validator will pick up those errors, and the `form:errors` tag will display them in the HTML. In Listing 17-83, you can see how the generated HTML looks after validation.

Listing 17-83. *Generated HTML for the errors Tag Example from Listing 17-82*

```
<form method="POST">
    <table>
        <tr>
            <td>Name:</td>
            <td><input name="name" type="text" value=""/></td>
            <td><span name="name.errors">Field is required.</span></td>
        </tr>

        <tr>
            <td>Expiration Date:</td>
            <td><input name="expirationDate" type="text" value=""/></td>
            <td><span name="expiration.errors">Field is required.</span></td>
        </tr>
        <tr>
            <td colspan="3">
                <input type="submit" value="Save Changes" />
            </td>
        </tr>
    </table>
</form>
```

You can use the wildcard character (*) in the `path` attribute of the `errors` tag. If you, for example, want to display all errors associated with the form on the top of the page, you can just add this line to your code: `<form:errors path="*" cssClass="errors" />`.

If you want to display all errors for one field, use standard wildcard character syntax:

```
<form:errors path="name*" cssClass=" errors " />
```

Table 17-26 shows attributes that can be used with this tag.

Table 17-26. *errors Tag Attributes*

Attribute	Description
path	Identifies the object and its property that will be used to create the status and/or errors.
delimiter	The HTML tag or any String to be used as delimiter between the errors. The default is the tag.
element	The HTML tag used to enclose every rendered error.
htmlEscape	Controls the HTML escaping of the rendered values.

Standard CSS style attributes, mentioned earlier, are also available for this tag.

JSP Best Practices

As we have stated before, JSP pages offer the largest set of features you can use to generate HTML output. Because JSP pages are compiled into Java classes, applications using JSP pages (as opposed to, for example, Velocity) can suffer from low performance, especially when the pages are still being compiled. Another consideration is that if the content of the page is too big, the JSP will not compile into a Java class, as Java methods cannot be more than 64kB long.

From an architectural point of view, there is danger that developers will use Java code in the pages to perform business operations, which clearly violates the MVC architecture and will cause problems in the future development of the application.

If you keep all these potential limitations in mind, you will find that JSP pages are an excellent technology to use, especially when combined with tag libraries. However, there are other view technologies that may not be as feature-rich as JSP but offer other benefits—the first in line is Velocity.

Using Velocity

Velocity (http://velocity.apache.org) is another view templating engine that can be used in Spring. Unlike JSP pages, Velocity templates are not compiled into Java classes. They are interpreted by the Velocity engine every time they are used—even though the pages are interpreted, the time needed to generate the output is very short. In fact, in most cases, Velocity templates will outperform JSP pages. However, using Velocity has some drawbacks: JSP custom tags cannot be used in Velocity, and developers have to familiarize themselves with the syntax of the Velocity Template Language.

Velocity is a stand-alone project of the Apache Software Foundation that is used in many applications that produce text output. You can download the latest version of the Velocity libraries from http://velocity.apache.org.

Integrating Velocity and Spring

The Velocity engine requires initialization before it can be used. This initialization is performed by the VelocityConfigurer class. We need this bean to set up resource paths to the Velocity template files.

Once an instance of VelocityConfigurer class is created in the application context, we can use Velocity templates just like any other view in our application. Listing 17-84 shows how to declare a velocityConfigurer bean.

Listing 17-84. *velocityConfigurer Bean Declaration*

```
<?xml version="1.0" encoding="UTF-8"?>
<beans xmlns="http://www.springframework.org/schema/beans"
...>
    <bean id="velocityConfigurer"
        class="org.springframework.web.servlet.view.velocity.VelocityConfigurer">
        <property name="resourceLoaderPath">
            <value>WEB-INF/views/</value></property>
    </bean>
</beans>
```

Next, we need to add a view definition in the views.properties file, as shown in Listing 17-85.

Listing 17-85. *A Velocity View Definition*

```
#product/index
product-index.class=org.springframework.web.servlet.view.velocity.VelocityView
product-index.url=product/index.vm
```

The product-index view is going to be created as an instance of VelocityView, and the template file will be loaded from WEB-INF/views/product/index.vm. The first part of the path to the template file is defined in the velocityConfigurer bean, and the second part is declared in the views.properties file. Next, we create a simple Velocity template, as shown in Listing 17-86.

Listing 17-86. *product/.vm Velocity Template*

```
<html>
<head>
</head>
<body>

All products:<br>
#foreach($product in $products)
    ${product.name}<br>
#end

</body>
</html>
```

Finally, we are going to modify the ProductController used in this chapter to make sure it returns an instance of the ModelAndView ("product-index", . . .).

Listing 17-87. *Modified ProductController That Returns the Velocity View*

```
public class ProductController extends MultiActionController {
    private List<Product> products;

    public ModelAndView index(HttpServletRequest request,
        HttpServletResponse response) {
        return new ModelAndView("product-index", "products", products);
    }

}
```

When the application is rebuilt and deployed, we should see a list of products at `/ch17/product/index.html`, as shown in Figure 17-12.

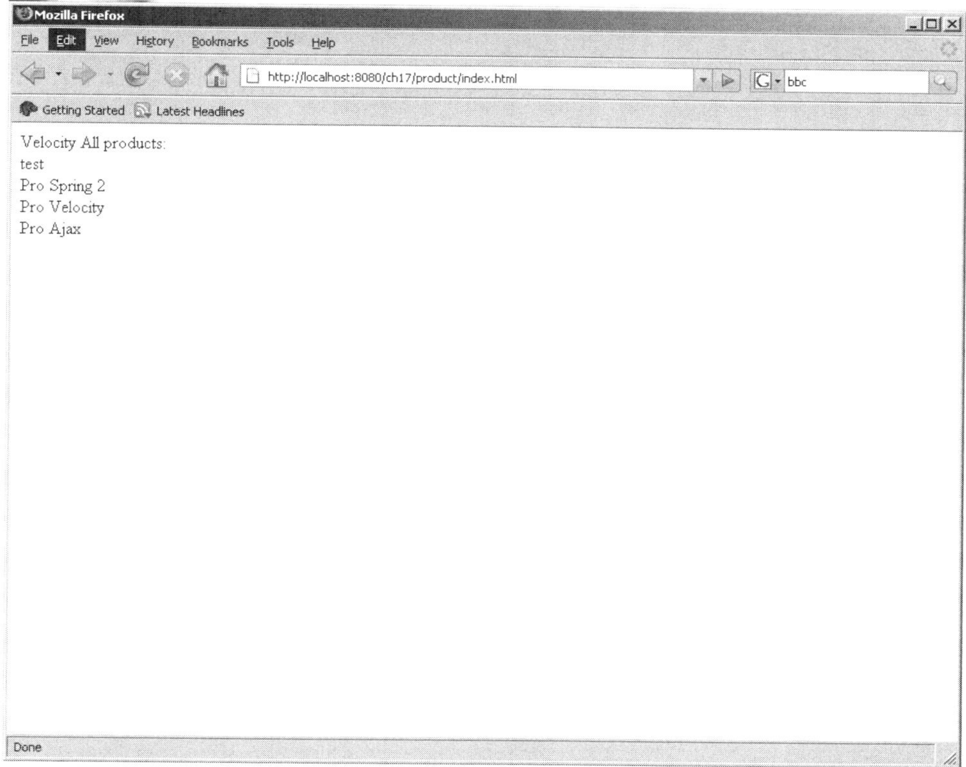

Figure 17-12. *The Velocity example output*

Advanced Velocity Concepts

So far, you have seen simple examples of what Velocity can do used on its own. Using Velocity together with Spring allows you to go much further: you can customize the properties of the Velocity Engine by setting its properties through the `velocityConfigurer` bean and provide macros with functionality similar to the Spring JSTL tags introduced in the "Using JSP Pages" section earlier in this chapter.

There are two ways to set properties of the Velocity Engine: provide a standard properties file or set the properties directly in the `velocityConfigurer` bean definition, as shown in Listing 17-88.

Listing 17-88. *Setting Velocity Engine Properties*

```
<?xml version="1.0" encoding="UTF-8"?>
<beans xmlns="http://www.springframework.org/schema/beans"
...>
    <bean id="velocityConfigurer"
        class="org.springframework.web.servlet.view.velocity.VelocityConfigurer">
        <property name="resourceLoaderPath" value="WEB-INF/views/"/>
        <property name="velocityProperties">
```

```
            <value>
                file.resource.loader.cache=false
            </value>
        </property>
        <property name="configLocation"
value="/WEB-INF/classes/velocity.properties"/>
    </bean>
</beans>
```

Naturally, you have to decide whether you want to set the Velocity Engine properties in a properties file or keep them in the bean definition.

Perhaps the most important Velocity support comes from the Velocity macros Spring exposes in the Velocity templates. These macros work just like the Spring JSTL tags; the most important macro is the `#springBind` macro. It gives you access to the Spring Validator framework from your Velocity templates. To use the Spring macros in a particular view, the `exposeSpringMacroHelpers` property must be set to `true` (the value of this property is `true` by default).

To demonstrate the usage of the Velocity macros, we are going to create a Velocity template that will allow the users to enter product details, with full validation and error control. We will use the `ProductFormController` introduced earlier in this chapter, but with a modified `views.properties` file and a new `edit.vm` template. We'll start with the modified `views.properties` file, which is shown in Listing 17-89.

Listing 17-89. *The Velocity views.properties File*

```
#products
product-index.class=org.springframework.web.servlet.view.velocity.VelocityView
product-index.url=product/index.vm
product-index-r.class=org.springframework.web.servlet.view.RedirectView
product-index-r.url=/ch17/product/index.html
product-edit.class=org.springframework.web.servlet.view.velocity.VelocityView
product-edit.url=product/edit.vm

#other views omitted
```

The code in bold shows the lines we have added to support the `product-edit` view as a Velocity template. There was no need to set the `exposeSpringMacroHelpers` property to `true`, as it is `true` by default. This configuration allows us to create the `edit.vm` template, shown in Listing 17-90.

Listing 17-90. *The edit.vm Template Contents*

```
<form action="edit.html" method="post">
<input type="hidden" name="productId" value="${command.productId}">
<table>
    <tr>
        <td>Name</td>
        <td>#springBind("command.name")
                <input name="name" value="$!status.value">
                <span class="error">$status.errorMessage</span>
        </td>
    </tr>
    <tr>
        <td>Expiration Date</td>
        <td>#springBind("command.expirationDate")
                <input name="expirationDate" value="$!status.value">
                <span class="error">$status.errorMessage</span>
        </td>
```

```
    </tr>
    <tr>
        <td></td>
        <td><input type="submit"></td>
    </tr>
</table>
</form>
```

Notice that we can use the #springBind macro in the template. This macro does precisely the same work its JSTL counterpart: it allows us to access the Spring Validator framework from the template. The result is exactly what you would expect: Figure 17-13 shows a standard HTML form with a working validator in the browser.

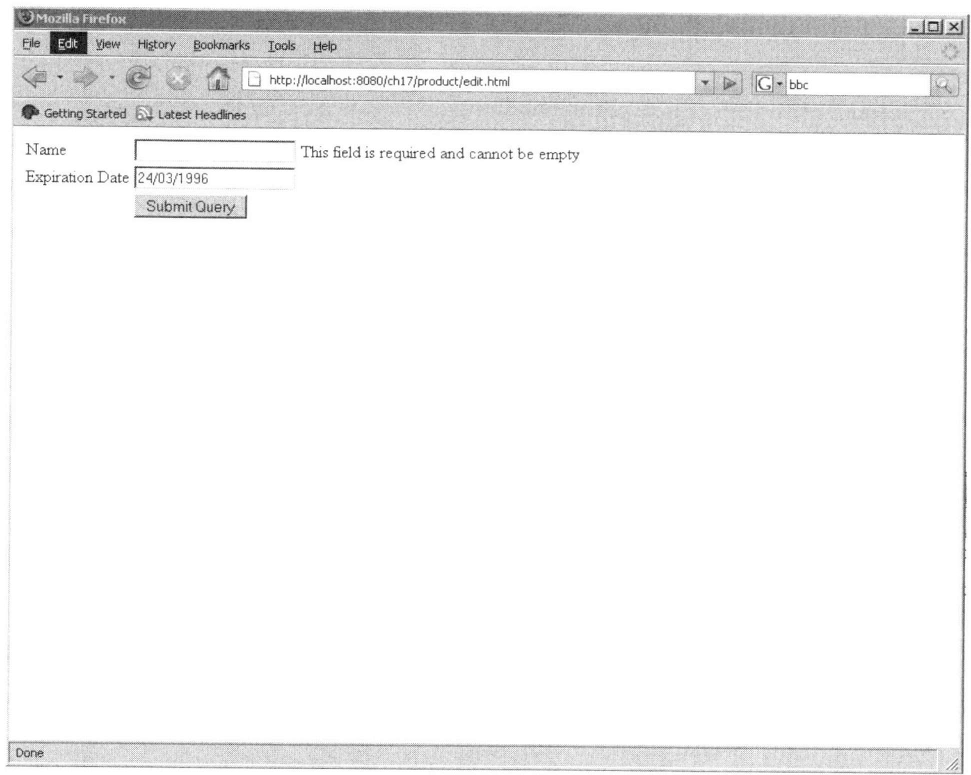

Figure 17-13. *The edit form with a validator message*

There is no difference in the ProductFormController code from previous examples; the only difference is the view definition in the views.properties file and the presence of the velocityConfigurer bean in the application context.

The code in the edit.vm file in Listing 17-90 still doesn't take full advantage of the available Spring macros. You could further simplify the code by using the #springFormInput, #springFormTextarea, #springFormSingleSelect, #springFormMultiSelect, #springFormRadioButtons, #springCheckboxes, and #showErrors macros.

Velocity provides a good alternative to JSP pages; the lack of features is well justified by its speed.

FreeMarker

FreeMarker is another templating engine that can be used as view technology in Spring. It is a stand-alone project and can be found at `http://freemarker.org/`. Although FreeMarker has some programming capabilities, it is *not* a full-blown programming language. It is designed to be a view-only templating engine, and Java programs are responsible for preparing all the data for the template.

You will have to include `freemarker-2-x.jar` in your application classpath to be able to use FreeMarker as templating language.

Spring Configuration with FreeMarker

As with the Velocity, all you have to do is to add the configurer bean to your `application-servlet.xml` file, as shown in Listing 17-91.

Listing 17-91. *freemarkerConfig Declaration*

```
<bean id="freemarkerConfig" class="org.springframework.web.➥
                servlet.view.freemarker.FreeMarkerConfigurer">
    <property name="templateLoaderPath" value="/WEB-INF/views/"/>
</bean>
```

`TemlateLoaderPath` specifies the path where Spring will look for your FreeMarker templates.

If you want to use FreeMarker as view technology for your web application, you will have to define the `viewResolver` bean in your servlet context file, as shown in Listing 17-92.

Listing 17-92. *Freemarker viewResolver Bean Declaration*

```
<bean id="viewResolver" class="org.springframework.web.➥
              servlet.view.freemarker.FreeMarkerViewResolver">
  <property name="cache" value="true"/>
  <property name="prefix" value=""/>
  <property name="suffix" value=".ftl"/>
</bean>
```

This example configuration has the default prefix and `.ftl` suffix, which indicates a FreeMarker template. Let's create simple FreeMarker template and save it as `/WEB-INF/views/en_GB/product/index.ftl`. Listing 17-93 shows the template code.

Listing 17-93. *FreeMarker Template index.ftl File*

```
<html>
<head>
</head>
<body>

Freemarker All products:<br>
<#list products as product>
    {product.name}<br>
</#list>

</body>
</html>
```

All we have to do now is add a handler method to our `Controller`. Let's add the `indexHandler()` method to previously introduced `ProductController`, as shown in Listing 17-94.

Listing 17-94. *ProductController's Handler Method*

```
    //other methods omitted for clarity
public ModelAndView indexHandler(request, response){
    return new ModelAndView("product/index");
}
```

View with name `product/index` will automatically be mapped to template `index.ftl`, located in directory set in FreeMarker configurer bean (`/WEB-INF/views/en_GB/`). Spring will load the template, populate the variables, and display rendered result in the browser (see Figure 17-14).

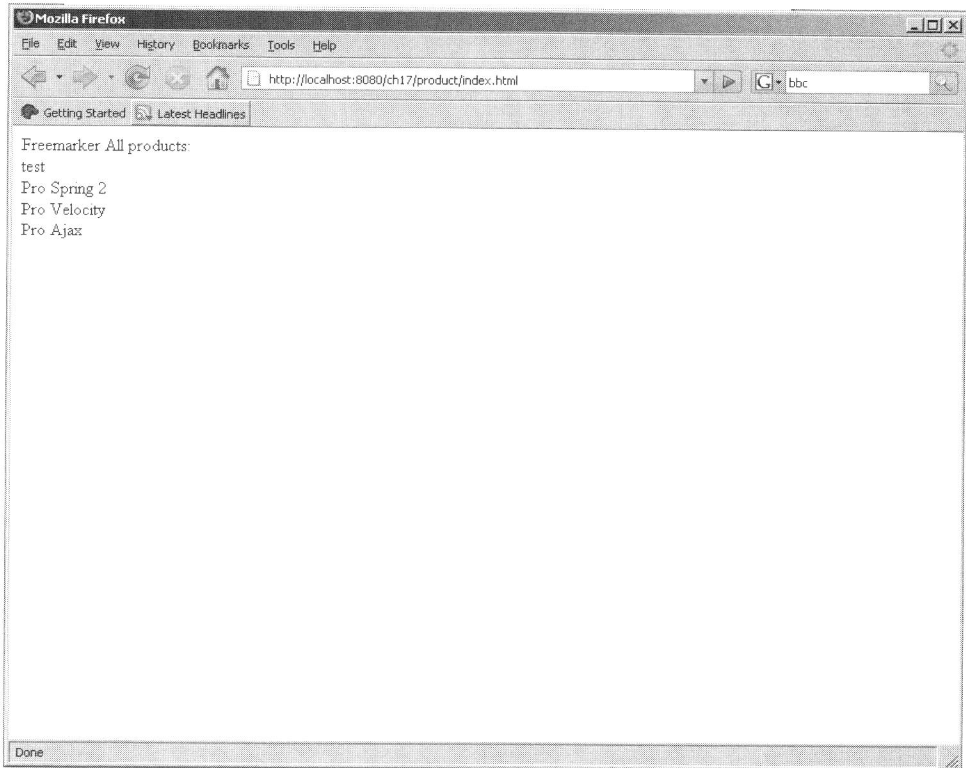

Figure 17-14. *The FreeMarker page in the browser*

As of version 1.1, Spring provides macros for form binding as well as additional convenient macros for easily building form elements in FreeMarker templates. To use Spring FreeMarker macros, you will have to include a macros definition file at the beginning of your template file. The macro definition file is called `spring.ftl` and can be found in the package `org.springframework.web.servlet.view.freemarker` of the `spring.jar` distribution file. Listing 17-95 shows how to import and use the Spring macro library in your FreeMarker templates.

Listing 17-95. *FreeMarker Binding Tags Example*

```
<#import "/spring.ftl" as spring />

<!-- freemarker macros have to be imported into a namespace.  We strongly
recommend sticking to 'spring' -->
```

```
<#import "spring.ftl" as spring />
<html>

<form action="" method="POST">
  Name:
  <@spring.bind "product.name" />
  <input type="text"
    name="${spring.status.expression}"
    value="${spring.status.value?default("")}" /><br>
  <#list spring.status.errorMessages as error> <b>${error}</b> <br> </#list>
  <br>
  Name:
  <@spring.bind "product.expirationDate" />
  <input type="text"
    name="${spring.status.expression}"
    value="${spring.status.value?default("")}" /><br>
  <#list spring.status.errorMessages as error> <b>${error}</b> <br> </#list>
  <br>

  <input type="submit" value="submit"/>
</form>

</html>
```

Figure 17-15 shows how will this template look when rendered in the browser.

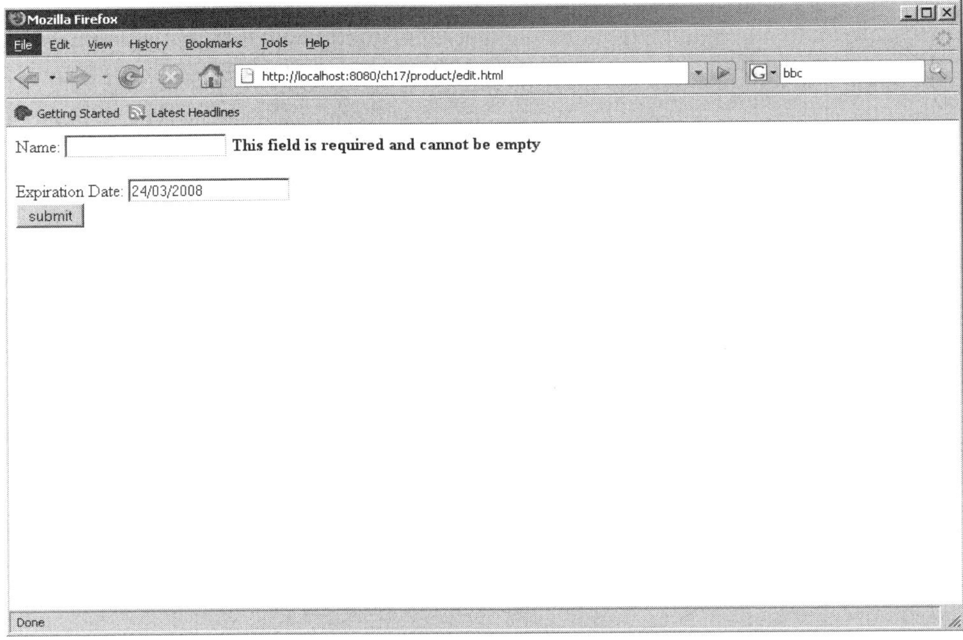

Figure 17-15. *A FreeMarker form*

The Spring.ftl FreeMarker macro library has additional convenience macros for HTML input field generation. These macros also include easy binding and validation errors display.

Let's write the example in Listing 17-96 by extending the form in Listing 17-95.

Listing 17-96. *A Spring FreeMarker Macro Library Example*

```
<#import "spring.ftl" as spring />

<!-- freemarker macros have to be imported into a namespace.  We strongly
recommend sticking to 'spring' -->
<#import "spring.ftl" as spring />
<html>

<form action="" method="POST">
  Name:
  <@spring.formInput "product.name" value="${product.name}"/>

  <br>
  Name:
    <@spring.formInput "product.expirationDate" value="${product.expirationDate}"/>

  <input type="submit" value="submit"/>
</form>

</html>
```

The formInput macro takes the path parameter (product.name) and an additional attributes parameter (empty in our example). The macro binds the field to provided path. The attributes parameter is usually used for style information or additional attributes required by HTML input field (like rows and columns of a text area).

The showErrors macro takes a separator parameter (the characters that will be used to separate multiple errors on the field) and accepts, as a second parameter, a class name or style attribute.

In FreeMarker, macros can have default parameters, so we can often call macro with fewer parameters than are defined for it (like in the preceding example, where we haven't passed a second parameter for the formInput macro).

Table 17-27 lists all of the macros available in the Spring FreeMarker macros library, with brief descriptions.

Table 17-27. *Spring FreeMarker Available Macros*

Macro	Description
<@spring.message code/>	Output a string from a resource bundle based on the code parameter.
<@spring.messageText code, text/>	Output a string from a resource bundle based on the code parameter, falling back to the value of the default parameter.
<@spring.url relativeUrl/>	Prefix a relative URL with the application's context root.
<@spring.formInput path, attributes, fieldType/>	This is the standard input field for gathering user input.
<@spring.formHiddenInput path, attributes/>	This hidden input field is for submitting nonuser input.

Continued

Table 17-27. *Continued*

Macro	Description
`<@spring.formPasswordInput path, attributes/>`	This standard input field gathers passwords. Note that no value will ever be populated in fields of this type.
`<@spring.formTextarea path, attributes/>`	This large text field gathers long, free-form text input.
`<@spring.formSingleSelect path, options, attributes/>`	This is a drop-down box of options allowing a single required value to be selected.
`<@spring.formMultiSelect path, options, attributes/>`	This list box of options allows the user to select zero or more values.
`<@spring.formRadioButtons path, options separator, attributes/>`	Create a set of radio buttons allowing a single selection to be made from the available choices.
`<@spring.formCheckboxes path, options, separator, attributes/>`	Create a set of check boxes allowing zero or more values to be selected.
`<@spring.showErrors separator, classOrStyle/>`	Simplify the display of validation errors for the bound field.

Selection field macros accept a `java.util.Map` attribute, containing the options of the select field. Map keys represent option values, and map values are displayed as the labels for those values. Let's see an example of the multiple `select` HTML fields:

```
<@spring.formMultiSelect "customer.categories", |categoriesMap />
```

If the web application expects category IDs as passed values, you can provide `categoriesMap` in the `referenceData()` method of your controller, as shown in Listing 17-97.

Listing 17-97. *referenceData() Method*

```
protected Map referenceData(HttpServletRequest request) throws Exception {
  Map categoriesMap = new LinkedHashMap();
  categoriesMap.put("1", "Books");
  categoriesMap.put("2", "CDs");
  categoriesMap.put("3", "MP3 Playes");

  Map m = new HashMap();
  m.put("categoriesMap", categoriesMap);
  return m;
}
```

FreeMarker offers good speed and some programming capabilities, but its main strength is great macro support that can improve reusability and customization of your web application.

Using XSLT Views

XSLT offers an elegant way to transform XML data into any other plain text format. If you already have an XML document, it may be worth using XSLT views to transform it to HTML output.

Let's create a `ProductsXsltView` that takes the `List` of `Product` objects, builds an XML document, and uses XSLT to transform the list to HTML. Listing 17-98 shows the implementation of the `ProductsXsltView` class.

Listing 17-98. *ProductsXsltView Implementation*

```
public class ProductsXsltView extends AbstractXsltView {

    protected Node createDomNode(Map model, String root,
        HttpServletRequest request, HttpServletResponse response)
        throws Exception {

        List products = (List)model.get("products");
        if (products == null) throw new IllegalArgumentException➥
("Products not in model");
        Document document = new Document();
        Element rootElement = new Element(root);
        document.setRootElement(rootElement);

        for (Product product : products) {
            Element pe = new Element("product");
            pe.setAttribute("productId", Integer.toString(product.getProductId()));
            pe.setAttribute("expirationDate", ➥
product.getExpirationDate().toString());
            pe.setText(product.getName());

            rootElement.addContent(pe);
        }

        return new DOMOutputter().output(document);
    }

}
```

Remember that it is not important how you create the Node object that the createDomNode() method returns; in this case, we have used JDOM (Java Document Object Model), because it is a bit easier to use than the W3C XML API.

The AbstractXsltView class allows you to add additional name/value pairs that you can pass as style sheet parameters. For each <xsl:param name="param-name">param-value</xsl:param>, you must add an entry to a Map returned from the getParameters() method.

To test our view, we are going to create an XSLT template that will transform the XML document to a very simple HTML page, as shown in Listing 17-99.

Listing 17-99. *An XSLT Template*

```
<?xml version="1.0"?>
<xsl:stylesheet version="1.0" xmlns:xsl="http://www.w3.org/1999/XSL/Transform">
    <xsl:template match="/">
        <html>
            <head>
                <title>Pro Spring 2</title>
            </head>
            <body>
                <h1>Available Products</h1>
                <xsl:for-each select="products/product">
                    <xsl:value-of select="."/>
                    <br />
                </xsl:for-each>
            </body>
        </html>
    </xsl:template>
</xsl:stylesheet>
```

Just like with any other view, we need to declare it in the views.properties file.

Listing 17-100. *views.properties Declaration of ProductsXsltView*

```
product-index.class=com.apress.prospring2.ch17.web.views.ProductsXsltView
product-index.root=root
product-index.stylesheetLocation=/WEB-INF/views/product/index.xslt
```

When we deploy the application, we can see the product listing as a regular HTML page.

You should use XSLT views with caution as the processing involved is very complex, and in most cases, an XSLT view is the slowest to render view available. In our example, we have actually built the XML document and used XSLT to transform it to HTML—this is without any doubt the worst way to use XSLT views. However, if you already have XML document and all you need is to transform it to HTML, you can certainly benefit from implementing an XSLT view.

Using PDF Views

Even though the previous view technologies are powerful, they still depend on the browser to interpret the generated HTML code. Though basic HTML is rendered without any problems on all browsers, you cannot guarantee that a page with complex formatting is going to look the same on all browsers. Even more, there are situations where HTML is just not enough, if you need to print the output, for example. If this is the case, the best solution is to use a document format that will be rendered consistently on all clients.

You will see in this section how to use PDF files as the view technology. To use a PDF as a Spring View, you will need to include the iText (http://www.lowagie.com/iText/) and PDFBox (http://www.pdfbox.org/) JAR files; both are included in the Spring distribution.

Unfortunately, there is no PDF template language, so we have to implement the views ourselves. As you saw in this chapter's XSLT view example, implementing a custom view is not a difficult task, and Spring provides a convenience superclass, AbstractPdfView, which you can use in your PDF view implementation.

Implementing a PDF View

Generating a PDF from your Spring web application is not too difficult, even though there can be a lot of coding involved. The PDF view we are going to implement will display product details. We are not going to make any change to the ProductController whose view() method processes requests to view a product. We will need to make a change to the views.properties file and implement the ProductPdfView class to create the PDF output. Let's begin by looking at Listing 17-101, which shows the implementation of ProductPdfView class.

Listing 17-101. *ProductPdfView Implementation*

```
public class ProductPdfView extends AbstractPdfView {

    protected void buildPdfDocument(Map model, Document document,
        PdfWriter writer, HttpServletRequest request,
        HttpServletResponse response) throws Exception {
        Product product = (Product) model.get("product");
        if (product == null) throw new
            IllegalArgumentException("Product not present in the model");
```

```
        Paragraph header = new Paragraph("Product details");
        header.font().setSize(20);
        document.add(header);

        Paragraph content = new Paragraph(product.getName());
        document.add(content);

        Paragraph footer = new Paragraph("Pro Spring Chapter 17");
        footer.setAlignment(Paragraph.ALIGN_BOTTOM);
        document.add(footer);
    }

}
```

This view simply extracts the Product domain object from the model and uses its data to add paragraphs to the document instance. Because ProductPdfView is a subclass of AbstractPdfView, we do not have to worry about setting the appropriate HTTP headers or performing any I/O—the superclass takes care of all that.

Before we can verify that the newly created ProductPdfView class works, we need to modify the views.properties file and make sure that the product-view's class is set to ProductPdfView and that the ProductController.view() adds a Product instance to the model. Listing 17-102 shows the changes we need to make to views.properties file.

Listing 17-102. *views.properties File for the product-view*

```
product-view.class=com.apress.prospring2.ch17.web.views.ProductPdfView
```

You may notice that we do not need to set any additional properties on the product-view. Next, we need to make sure that the ProductController.view() method returns the correct instance of ModelAndView, as shown in Listing 17-103.

Listing 17-103. *ProductController.view Implementation*

```
public class ProductController extends MultiActionController {
    private Product createProduct(int productId, String name, Date expirationDate) {
        Product product = new Product();
        product.setProductId(productId);
        product.setName(name);
        product.setExpirationDate(expirationDate);

        return product;
    }

    public ModelAndView view(HttpServletRequest request,
        HttpServletResponse response) throws Exception {
        Product product = createProduct(1, "Pro Spring", new Date());
        return new ModelAndView("product-view", "product", product);
    }
}
```

When the application is rebuilt and deployed, the PDF document in Figure 17-16 should be returned for `/product/view.html`.

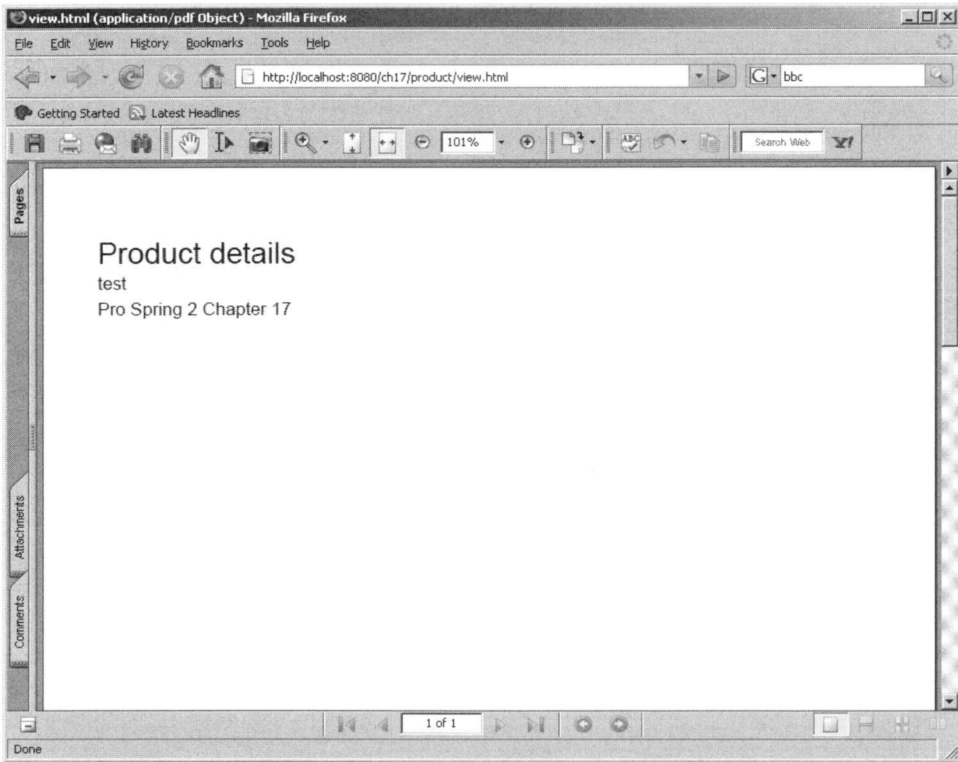

Figure 17-16. *ProductPdfView output*

Using Excel Views

If your application requires Excel output, you can use Spring to create an Excel view rather than directly writing the contents of an Excel file to the output stream. Just like `AbstractPdfView`, Spring provides `AbstractExcelView`, which you can subclass to further simplify development of new Excel views. You will need the Jakarta POI library (`http://jakarta.apache.org/poi/`) to perform the actual Excel I/O; the POI JAR file comes with the Spring distribution.

We are going to show a simple `ProductsExcelView` that renders the list of products into an Excel spreadsheet. We will implement `ProductsExcelView` and modify `views.properties`. The implementation of `ProductsExcelView` is going to extend `AbstractExcelView`, as shown in Listing 17-104.

Listing 17-104. *ProductsExcelView Implementation*

```
public class ProductsExcelView extends AbstractExcelView {

    private static final int COL_PRODUCT_ID = 0;
    private static final int COL_NAME = 1;
    private static final int COL_EXPIRATION_DATE = 2;

    protected void buildExcelDocument(Map model, HSSFWorkbook wb,
        HttpServletRequest request, HttpServletResponse response) throws Exception {
        List<Product> products = (List<Product>)model.get("products");
        HSSFSheet sheet = wb.createSheet("Products");
        int row = 0;
        getCell(sheet, row, COL_PRODUCT_ID).setCellValue("Id");
        getCell(sheet, row, COL_NAME).setCellValue("Name");
        getCell(sheet, row, COL_EXPIRATION_DATE).setCellValue("ExpirationDate");
        row++;
        for (Product product : products) {
            getCell(sheet, row, COL_PRODUCT_ID).setCellValue(
                product.getProductId());
            getCell(sheet, row, COL_NAME).setCellValue(
                product.getName());
            getCell(sheet, row, COL_EXPIRATION_DATE).setCellValue(
                product.getExpirationDate());
            row++;
        }
    }

}
```

The code for the `ProductsExcelView` class is quite simple: we get a `List` of `Product` objects and iterate over the list, adding a row to the Excel workbook in each iteration.

Next, we need to make sure that the `product-index` view declared in `views.properties` is referencing the newly created `ProductsExcelView` class, as shown in Listing 17-105.

Listing 17-105. *views.properties with the ProductsExcelView Definition*

```
product-index.class=com.apress.prospring.ch17.web.views.ProductsExcelView
```

Again, we do not need to set any additional properties for this view. The `ProductController.index()` method does not need any modification, as it already returns `ModelAndView ("product-index", . . .)`. When we make a request to `/product/index.html`, we will get an Excel spreadsheet, as shown in Figure 17-17.

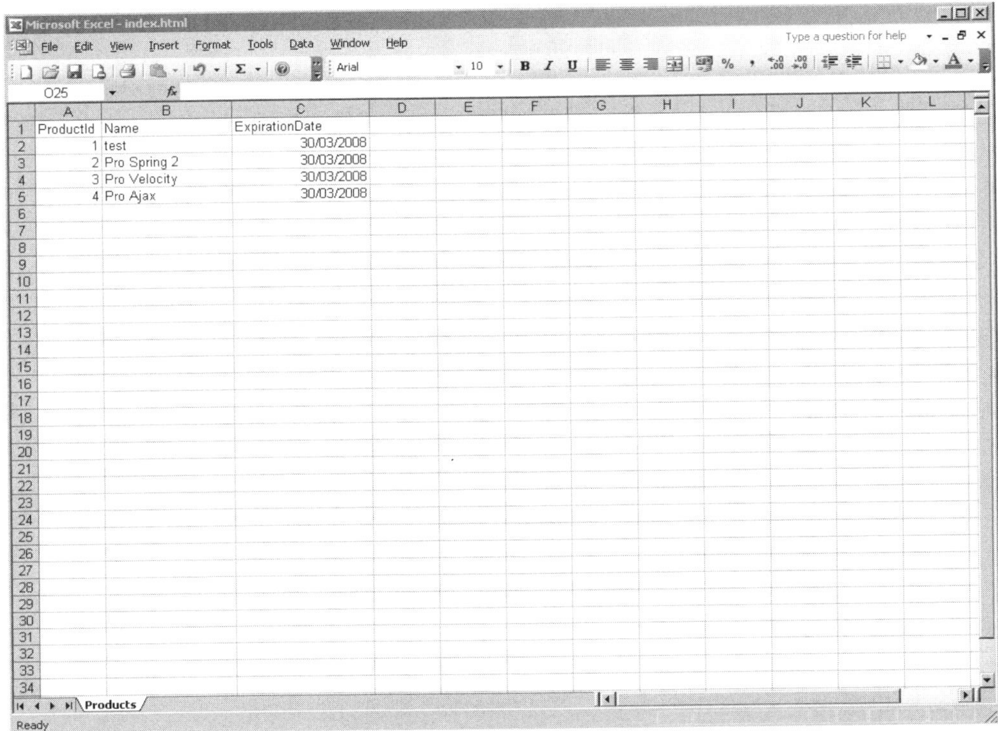

Figure 17-17. *Output of the ProductsExcelView*

As you can see, using `AbstractExcelView` is very similar to using `AbstractPdfView`: in both cases, we have to implement code that will create the content of the document, and we do not need to handle the I/O.

Using Tiles

Unlike all the previous view technologies, Tiles (`http://tiles.apache.org/`) is not actually used to generate output. Instead, it can combine the output from various views into a master view. Each individual tile can consist of a collection of tiles, a JSP page, or output directly written to the `HttpResponse` object in the `handle()` method of a Spring controller.

Tiles was a part of the Jakarta Struts project (`http://struts.apache.org/`). However, due to its growing popularity, it was split off into an independent project with a new version, known as Tiles 2. You will have to include the following dependencies in your project to be able to use Tiles: Tiles version 2.0.4 or higher, Commons BeanUtils, Commons Digester, and Commons Logging.

Integrating Tiles and Spring

Tiles requires some initialization before you can use it. In a Struts application, Tiles is initialized when loaded as a plug-in. In Spring, we need to create a `TilesConfigurer` bean that will load the tile definition XML files and configure the Tiles framework, as shown in Listing 17-106.

Listing 17-106. *TilesConfigurer Definition in the Application Context*

```
<?xml version="1.0" encoding="UTF-8"?>
<beans xmlns="http://www.springframework.org/schema/beans"
...>
    <bean id="tilesConfigurer"
        class="org.springframework.web.servlet.view.tiles2.TilesConfigurer">
        <property name="definitions">
            <list>
                <value>/WEB-INF/tiles-layout.xml</value>
            </list>
        </property>
    </bean>
</beans>
```

This bean creates the `TilesDefinitionsFactory` instance using the definition files listed in the `definitions` property of the `TilesConfigurer` bean.

Before we can use Tiles in our application, we must create the `tiles-layout.xml` file; we will start with a very simple one. You can build and deploy your web application to check that the Tiles support is properly configured (if there is a problem in the configuration, the deployment will fail).

Listing 17-107. *Simple Tiles Definition File*

```
<!DOCTYPE tiles-definitions PUBLIC
      "-//Apache Software Foundation//DTD Tiles Configuration 2.0//EN"
      "http://tiles.apache.org/dtds/tiles-config_2_0.dtd">

<tiles-definitions>
    <definition name=".dummy"/>
</tiles-definitions>
```

When we build and deploy the application, the application server's console will print debug messages from the `TilesConfigurer` class indicating that the Tiles support has been correctly configured; see Listing 17-108.

Listing 17-108. *TilesConfigurer Debug Messages*

```
21:07:58,001 INFO  [TilesConfigurer] TilesConfigurer: initializion started
21:07:58,011 INFO  [TilesConfigurer] TilesConfigurer: adding definitions ➥
[/WEB-INF/tiles-layout.xml]
21:07:58,211 INFO  [TilesConfigurer] TilesConfigurer: initialization completed
```

Now that we have verified that the Tiles support is working, we need to think about the tiles we want to use in our application. A typical web page layout might look like the one shown in Figure 17-18. We are going to call this page a root page; it is a JSP page that uses the Tiles tag library to insert the appropriate tiles according to their definitions in the tiles configuration files.

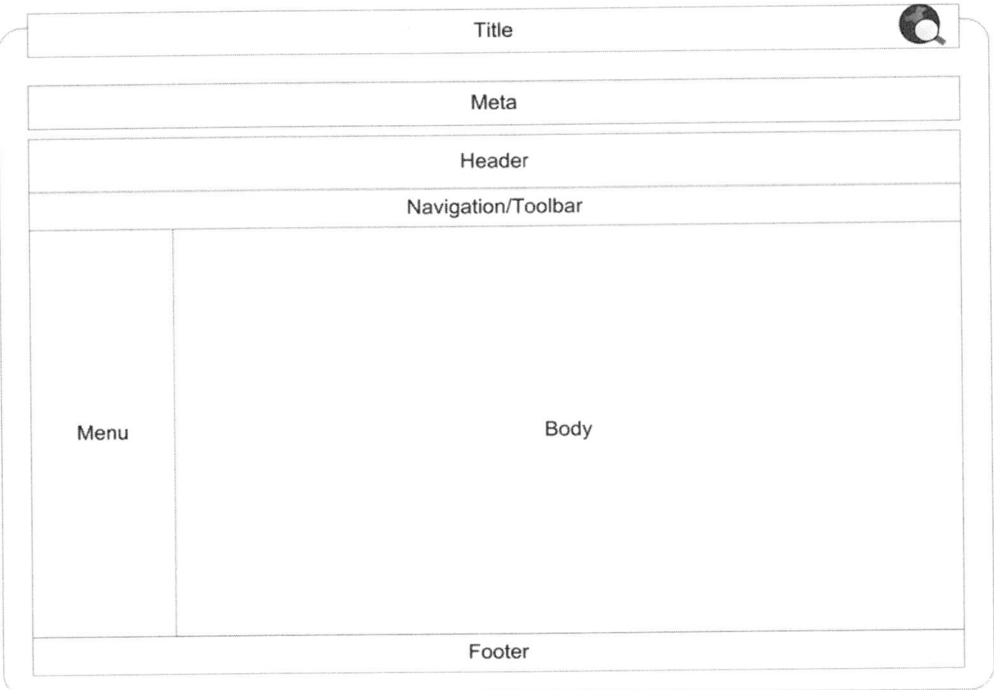

Figure 17-18. *Tiles layout*

Looking at this layout, you might think that we are going to create five tiles: one for each section of the final page layout. But we are going to add sixth tile, which is going to output the content of the `<meta>` tag in the root layout.

Let's begin by creating the `root.jsp` page that will place all the tiles into a HTML table, as shown in Listing 17-109.

Listing 17-109. *The root.jsp Page*

```
<%@taglib prefix="spring" uri="http://www.springframework.org/tags"%>
<%@ taglib uri="http://tiles.apache.org/tags-tiles" prefix="tiles" %>

<%@ taglib prefix="c" uri="http://java.sun.com/jstl/core_rt" %>

<html>
<head>
    <c:set var="css"><spring:theme code="css"/></c:set>
       <c:if test="${not empty css}">
            <link rel="stylesheet" href="<c:url value="${css}"/>" type="text/css" />
        </c:if>
    <tiles:insertAttribute name="meta"/>
    <title><tiles:getAsString name="title"/></title>
</head>

<table cellspacing="0" cellpadding="0" width="700px" align="center"
    bgcolor="#ffffff">
    <tr>
```

```
        <td colspan="2"><tiles:insertAttribute name="header"/></td>
    </tr>
    <tr>
        <td colspan="2"><tiles:insertAttribute name="toolbar"/></td>
    </tr>
    <tr height="400px">
        <td width="150px" valign="top"><tiles:insertAttribute name="menu"/></td>
        <td width="550px" valign="top"><tiles:insertAttribute name="body"/></td>
    </tr>
    <tr>
        <td colspan="2"><tiles:insertAttribute name="footer"/></td>
    </tr>
</table>

</body>
</html>
```

The root layout page is straightforward: we define the layout of the page, and we use Tiles tags to specify where Tiles should insert the appropriate pages. However, the Tiles framework still doesn't know what content to insert for all `<tiles:insertAttribute>` and `<tiles:getAsString>` tags. We need to create the Tiles definition file shown in Listing 17-110.

Listing 17-110. *Tiles Definition File*

```
<!DOCTYPE tiles-definitions PUBLIC
       "-//Apache Software Foundation//DTD Tiles Configuration 2.0//EN"
       "http://tiles.apache.org/dtds/tiles-config_2_0.dtd">
<tiles-definitions>
    <!-- Abstract root definition -->
    <definition name=".root" template="/WEB-INF/views/en_GB/tiles/root.jsp">
        <put-attribute name="title" value="CHANGE-ME"/>
        <put-attribute name="meta" value="/WEB-INF/views/en_GB/tiles/meta.jsp"/>
        <put-attribute name="header" value="/WEB-INF/views/en_GB/tiles/header.jsp"/>
        <put-attribute name="menu" value="/WEB-INF/views/en_GB/tiles/menu.jsp"/>
        <put-attribute name="toolbar" value="/WEB-INF/views/➥
                  en_GB/tiles/toolbar.jsp"/>
        <put-attribute name="footer" value="/WEB-INF/views/en_GB/tiles/footer.jsp"/>
    </definition>

    <!-- Index -->

    <definition name=".index" extends=".root">
                <put-attribute name="title" value="Main Page"/>
                <put-attribute name="body" value="/WEB-INF/views/en_GB/index.jsp"/>
            </definition>

    <definition name=".status" extends=".root">
        <put-attribute name="title" value="Status"/>
        <put-attribute name="body" value="/tile/status.tile"/>
    </definition>
</tiles-definitions>
```

This definition file introduces a number of Tiles concepts, so let's go through the features used line by line. The first definition element's attribute name is set to `.root`, and the element also includes the `path` attribute, which instructs Tiles to use the JSP page specified in the path attribute and instructs the values specified in the `put` elements to display their content.

However, the .root definition is missing the body attribute we are using in the root.jsp page. The definition we have created is an abstract definition, as it does not define all the attributes used. We must extend this abstract definition to ensure that all the necessary attributes are defined, as shown in the second definition element. Its name attribute is set to .index, and its extends attribute specifies that it should inherit all values in the put elements from the definition element whose name is .root. The name attribute overrides the title value and adds the body value—just as you would expect in Java code.

Before we can move ahead and configure the Spring views to use Tiles, we need to stress that the individual pages that are used as tiles must not include the standard HTML headers, but if you are using JSP pages, they must include all tag library references. The prohibition against using document HTML tags is obvious, as the document tags are already included in the root page. The taglibs must be included in the JSP pages, because Tiles will request each tile individually; the tiles are not actually aware of the fact that the output they are rendering is being collected by another layer and formatted using the root layout.

Now that you know the requirements for individual tiles, we must configure the Spring views to use the Tiles framework. To do this, we are going to modify the views.properties file as shown in Listing 17-111.

Listing 17-111. *views.properties Definition*

```
#index
index.class=org.springframework.web.servlet.view.tiles2.TilesView
index.url=.index
```

This file defines that the view name index is going to be created as an instance of TilesView and its URL is going to be .index.

Note You may be wondering why we are using dots (.) in the Tiles definition names and no dots in the view names. This is simply a practice we find useful when managing applications with a large number of views and Tiles definitions. By looking at the names, you can immediately identify Tiles and Spring views.

The last step we need to take before we can test our application is to make sure that the IndexController's handleRequestInternal() method is returning the correct view; see Listing 17-112.

Listing 17-112. *The IndexController Class*

```
public class IndexController extends AbstractController {

    protected ModelAndView handleRequestInternal(HttpServletRequest request,
            HttpServletResponse response) throws Exception {

        return new ModelAndView("index", model);
    }

}
```

When we now deploy the application and make a request to the /index.html page, the TilesConfigurer bean will parse the Tiles configuration, load the .root and .index definitions, call each JSP page and render its output, and finally take the JSP output and output it into the appropriate places in the root.jsp page, whose output will be returned to the client as shown in Figure 17-19.

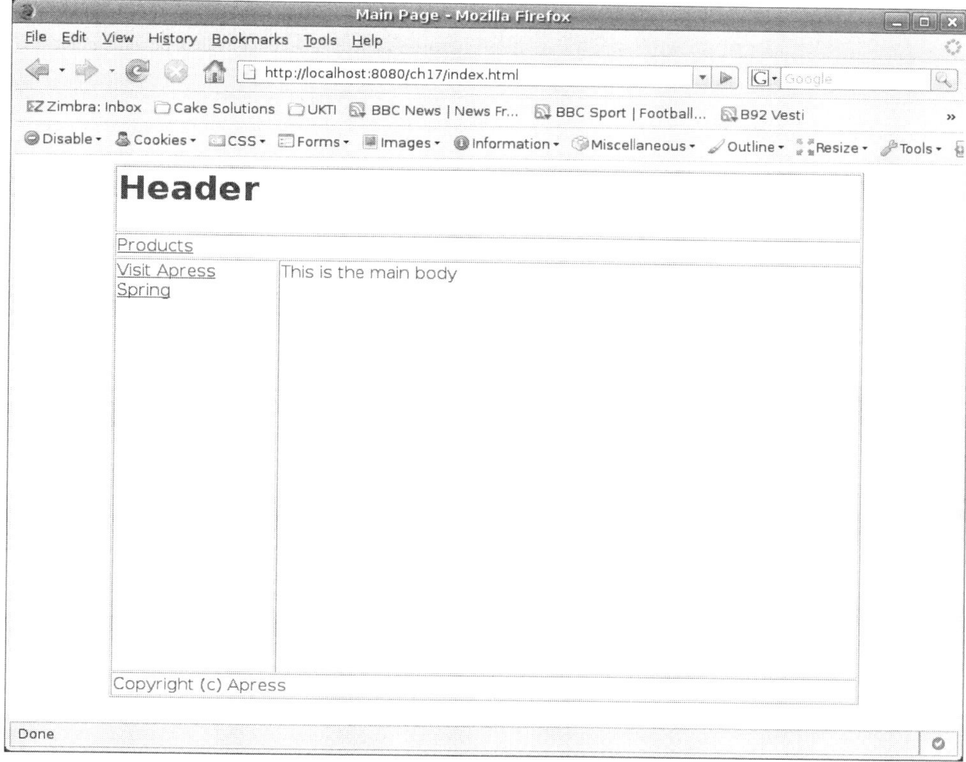

Figure 17-19. *The .root Tiles view*

Advanced Tiles Concepts

In the previous section, we showed you how to use Tiles in your Spring application in a way that is not too different from the `@include` JSP directive. The true power of Tiles comes from the fact that Tiles can take any output and paste it into the appropriate place. A tile can consist of other tiles, JSP pages, or even simple output from a `Controller`. We are going to start with a tile whose content is the output written to the response stream by a simple controller.

We are going to create a tile that prints out the memory usage information. It will print this information directly to the `HttpServletResponse`'s `Writer` object. We are going to create another servlet mapping in `web.xml` to map all `*.tile` requests to the `ch17` servlet. The only reason for this is to keep the request namespace clean of any ambiguous request URLs. The modified `web.xml` file is shown in Listing 17-113.

Listing 17-113. *web.xml Descriptor*

```
<?xml version="1.0" encoding="ISO-8859-1"?>
<web-app xmlns="http://java.sun.com/xml/ns/j2ee"
         xmlns:xsi="http://www.w3.org/2001/XMLSchema-instance"
         xsi:schemaLocation="http://java.sun.com/xml/ns/j2ee ➥
http://java.sun.com/xml/ns/j2ee/web-app_2_4.xsd"
         version="2.4">    <!-- omitted for clarity -->
    <servlet-mapping>
```

```
        <servlet-name>ch17</servlet-name>
        <url-pattern>*.tile</url-pattern>
    </servlet-mapping>
</web-app>
```

Next, we are going to create a TileController, which is going to be a subclass of MultiActionController. We are going to implement only one method in the TileController, the handleStatus(); it will print out the memory information. Listing 17-114 shows that the implementation is quite trivial.

Listing 17-114. *TileController.handleStatus Implementation*

```
public class TileController extends MultiActionController {

    private void writeMemoryPoolMXBean(MemoryPoolMXBean bean,
        PrintWriter writer) {
        writer.append("<pre><tt>");

        writer.append("Name: "); writer.append(bean.getName());
        writer.append("\n");
        writer.append("Type: "); writer.append(bean.getType().name ());
        writer.append("\n");
        writer.append("Usage: "); writer.append(bean.getUsage().toString());
        writer.append("\n");

        writer.append("</pre></tt>");
    }

    public ModelAndView handleStatus(HttpServletRequest request,
        HttpServletResponse response) throws Exception {
        List<MemoryPoolMXBean> beans =
                ManagementFactory.getMemoryPoolMXBeans();
        PrintWriter writer = response.getWriter();
        for (MemoryPoolMXBean bean : beans) {
            writeMemoryPoolMXBean(bean, writer);
        }
        return null;
    }

}
```

Notice that the handleStatus() method returns null, which means that Spring will not attempt to perform any view processing.

Next, we are going to declare the tileController bean in the application context file together with a tileMethodNameResolver bean and an entry in the publicUrlMapping bean, as shown in Listing 17-115.

Listing 17-115. *The tileController and tileMethodNameResolver Beans*

```
<?xml version="1.0" encoding="UTF-8"?>
<beans xmlns="http://www.springframework.org/schema/beans"
...>
    <bean id="publicUrlMapping"
        class="org.springframework.web.servlet.handler.SimpleUrlHandlerMapping">
        <property name="mappings">
            <value>
                /index.html=indexController
                /product/index.html=productController
                /product/view.html=productController
                /product/edit.html=productFormController
                /product/image.html=productImageFormController

               /tile/*.tile=tileController
            </value>
        </property>
    </bean>

    <!-- Tile -->
    <bean id="tileController"
        class="com.apress.prospring2.ch17.web.tiles.TileController">
        <property name="methodNameResolver"
             ref="tileMethodNameResolver"/>
    </bean>
    <bean id="tileMethodNameResolver"
        class="org.springframework.web.servlet.mvc.multiaction.➥
PropertiesMethodNameResolver">
        <property name="mappings">
            <value>
                /tile/status.tile=handleStatus
            </value>
        </property>
    </bean>
</beans>
```

We can test that our tileController works by making a request to /ch17/tile/status.tile. This should print the JVM memory status information. Finally, we are going to create StatusController as a subclass of AbstractController, add it to the application context file, and add an entry to the publicUrlMapping bean to map /status.html URL to the StatusController, as shown in Listing 17-116.

Listing 17-116. *The statusController Bean Definition and the New Entry in the publicUrlMapping Bean*

```
<?xml version="1.0" encoding="UTF-8"?>
<beans xmlns="http://www.springframework.org/schema/beans"
...>
    <bean id="publicUrlMapping"
        class="org.springframework.web.servlet.handler.SimpleUrlHandlerMapping">
        <property name="mappings">
```

```
            <value>
                /index.html=indexController
                /status.html=statusController
                /product/index.html=productController
                /product/view.html=productController
                /product/edit.html=productFormController
                /product/image.html=productImageFormController

                /tile/*.tile=tileController</prop>
            </value>
        </property>
    </bean>
    <bean id="statusController"
        class="com.apress.prospring2.ch17.web.StatusController"/>
</beans>
```

The code in the `StatusController.handleRequestInternal` method simply returns an instance of `ModelAndView ("status")`. This means that we need to add an entry to the `tiles-layout.xml` file and an entry to `views.properties`, as shown in Listing 17-117.

Listing 17-117. *Additions to tiles-layout.xml and views.properties*

```
//tiles-layout.xml:
 <!DOCTYPE tiles-definitions PUBLIC
       "-//Apache Software Foundation//DTD Tiles Configuration 2.0//EN"
       "http://tiles.apache.org/dtds/tiles-config_2_0.dtd">

<tiles-definitions>
    <!-- other definitions omitted -->

   <definition name=".status" extends=".root">
        <put-attribute name="title" value="Status"/>
        <put-attribute name="body" value="/tile/status.tile"/>
    </definition>
</tiles-definitions>

//views.properties:
status.class=org.springframework.web.servlet.view.tiles2.TilesView

status.url=.status
```

When we make a request to `/ch17/status.html`, Spring will instantiate the `status` view defined in `views.properties`. This view points to the `.status` tile definition, which specifies that the value for the body element should be taken from the output generated by `/ch17/tile/status.tile`. The final result should look something like the page shown in Figure 17-20.

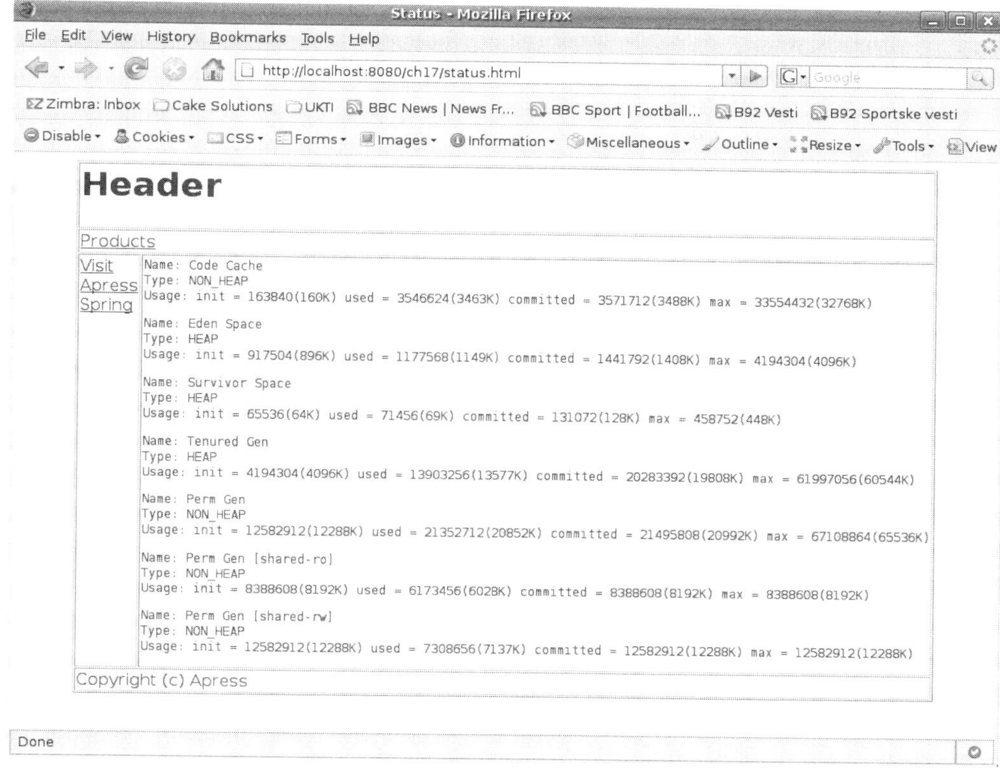

Figure 17-20. *Rendered /ch17/status.html page*

You would rarely use a controller that prints output directly to the output stream as our previous example does; in most cases, a controller returns a `ModelAndView` object that identifies a view and data to be rendered by that view. You can use this approach in a Tiles application as well. To demonstrate, we are going to add `handleMenu()` method to the `TileController`; this method reads the links from the configuration file and renders them using a JSP page.

First, we are going to modify the `TileController` as shown in Listing 17-118.

Listing 17-118. *Modified TileController*

```
public class TileController extends MultiActionController {
    private Map menu;
    public ModelAndView handleMenu(HttpServletRequest request,
        HttpServletResponse response) throws Exception {
        return new ModelAndView("tile-menu", "menu", menu);
    }

    public void setMenu(Map menu) {
        this.menu = menu;
    }
}
```

The handleMenu() method takes the menu property set in the application context file and forwards to the tile-menu view, which is defined as JstlView in views.properties, as shown in Listing 17-119.

Listing 17-119. *JstlView Definition in views.properties File*

```
#index
index.class=org.springframework.web.servlet.view.tiles2.TilesView

index.url=.index

#status
status.class=org.springframework.web.servlet.view.tiles2.TilesView

status.url=.status

#menu tile
tile-menu.class=org.springframework.web.servlet.view.JstlView

tile-menu.url=/WEB-INF/views/tiles/menu2.jsp
```

Listing 17-120 shows that the JSP page that displays the menu is quite trivial; it uses the core JSTL tags to iterate over all items in a map.

Listing 17-120. *The tile/menu2.jsp Page*

```
<%@ taglib prefix="c" uri="http://java.sun.com/jstl/core_rt" %>

<c:forEach items="${menu}" var="item">
    <a href="<c:out value="${item.value}"/>"><c:out value="${item.key}"/></a><br>
</c:forEach>
```

Finally, we will modify the tiles-layout.xml and ch17-servlet.xml files to use the newly created menu; see Listing 17-121.

Listing 17-121. *Updated tiles-layout.xml and ch17-servlet.xml Files*

```
tiles-layout.xml:
<tiles-definitions>
    <!-- Abstract root definition -->
     <definition name=".root" template="/WEB-INF/views/en_GB/tiles/root.jsp">
        <put-attribute name="title" value="CHANGE-ME"/>
        <put-attribute name="meta" value="/WEB-INF/views/en_GB/tiles/meta.jsp"/>
        <put-attribute name="header" value="/WEB-INF/views/en_GB/tiles/header.jsp"/>
        <put-attribute name="menu" value="/tile/menu.tile"/>
        <put-attribute name="toolbar" ➥
                value="/WEB-INF/views/en_GB/tiles/toolbar.jsp"/>
        <put-attribute name="footer" value="/WEB-INF/views/en_GB/tiles/footer.jsp"/>
    </definition>

ch17-servlet.xml:
.......
    <bean id="tileController" class="com.apress.prospring2➥
            .ch17.web.tiles.TileController">
        <property name="methodNameResolver" ref ="tileMethodNameResolver"/>
        <property name="menu">
            <map>
                <entry key="Apress" value="http://www.apress.com"/>
```

```
                <entry key="Spring" value="http://www.springframework.org"/>
                <entry key="Cake Solutions" ➥
                    value="http://www.cakesolutions.net"/>
            </map>
        </property>
    </bean>
    <bean id="tileMethodNameResolver"
        class="org.springframework.web.servlet.mvc.multiaction.➥
PropertiesMethodNameResolver">
        <property name="mappings">
            <value>
                /tile/status.tile=handleStatus
                /tile/menu.tile=handleMenu
            <value/>
        </property>
    </bean>
</beans>
```

Because we have modified the `.root` tile definition, our new menu is going to be used in all definitions that extend the `.root` definition, and the newly displayed menu is shown in Figure 17-21.

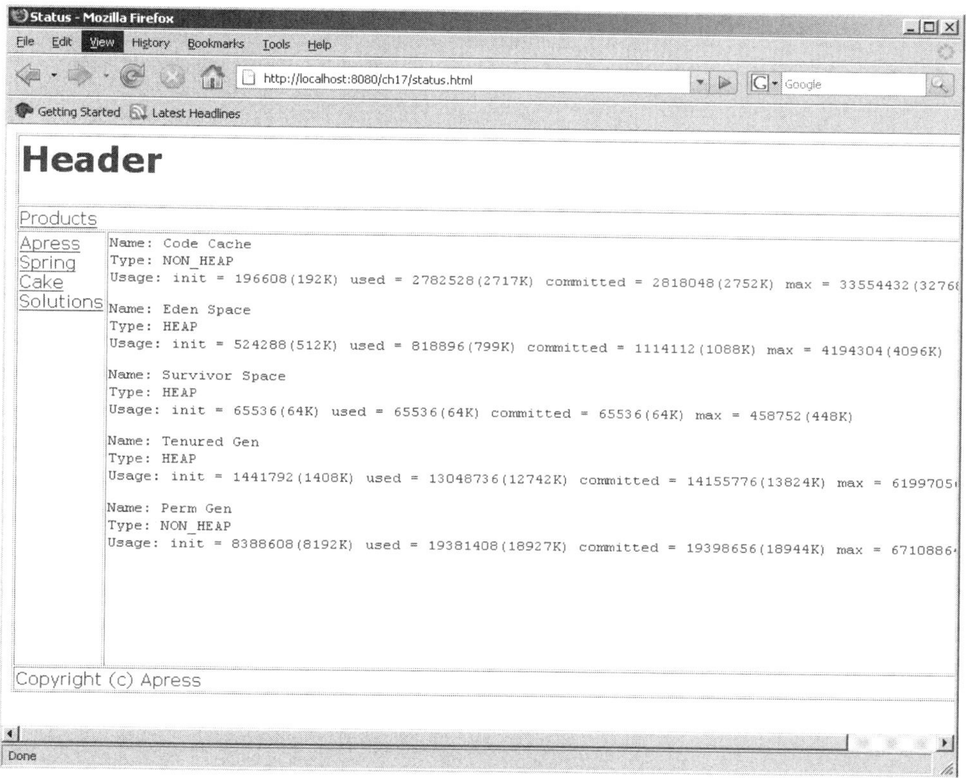

Figure 17-21. *Our new menu tile*

Tiles Best Practices

Tiles is a very powerful framework that can greatly simplify the development of web applications. With its power comes the complexity of configuration files and different request paths. Therefore, using a logical naming convention and enforcing this naming convention throughout the whole project is important. We feel that the best way to organize the URLs to be rendered as tiles is to use `*.html` for the final pages returned to the client, and `*.tile` for requests whose output is to be rendered as a tile. The view naming conventions follow the directory structure of the source files, so a Spring `JstlView` definition for a JSP page located in `tile/menu.jsp` will be named `tile-menu`. Finally, a tile definition that will be used to render the output of the `/product/index.html` page is best named `.product.index`.

Note You should take a look at the SiteMesh layout framework as well, which is based on the Decorator pattern. SiteMesh uses servlet filters instead of JSP includes, which means it intercepts request at lower level. So there is no other special or Spring-specific configuration; you just configure the SiteMesh filter in your `web.xml` file. This makes SiteMesh extremely easy to configure and maintain. It uses template files called detectors, which describe how the page will be rendered. Decorators can be written using different technologies, like JSP, FreeMarker, or Velocity.

SiteMesh is written in Java but can be used with all web technologies, whether they're Java based or not. The pages don't even know they are being decorated, unlike in Tiles, where each individual page has to be associated with a layout. However, SiteMesh doesn't allow inheritance of page definitions or overriding attributes. It also lacks debugging support, so you could have problem identifying the errors, especially if you use nested decorators. SiteMesh is available at `http://www.opensymphony.com/sitemesh/`.

JasperReports

JasperReports (`http://jasperreports.sourceforge.net`) is an open source reporting engine written entirely in Java. Its main goal is to deliver print-ready documents in any of the supported formats: CSV, Microsoft Excel, HTML, or PDF.

JasperReports uses one XML-based format for report design files. You can create the design files by yourself in any text editor, and you can change any report details at a low level. Thankfully, however, you do not need to hand-code all of your report files, because a wide range of graphical tools is available for working with JasperReports design files. You can find the complete list of these tools on the JasperReports web site.

Again, the design files are actually XML files, with the extension `.jrmxl`. Before you can use a report design file, it has to be compiled into a report file with the `.jasper` extension. JasperReports reports are distributed with Ant task for this compilation. However, when using JasperReports with Spring, you can let Spring compile your reports on the fly. You can supply either a `.jrxml` or `.jasper` file to Spring when generating your reports: if you supply a `.jrxml` design file, Spring compiles the report to `.jasper` format and caches the compiled file to serve future requests. You can supply already compiled `.jasper` file as well, which will Spring use directly, without compiling.

Let's design a simple report that will display the list of `Product` objects. Listing 17-122 shows our `Product` class.

Listing 17-122. *Product Java Object*

```
public class Product {
    private String name;
    private Date expirationDate;
```

```
    public String getName() {
        return name;
    }

    public void setName(String name) {
        this.name = name;
    }

    public Date getExpirationDate() {
        return expirationDate;
    }

    public void setExpirationDate(Date expirationDate) {
        this.expirationDate = expirationDate;
    }
}
```

The next thing to do is to design the report.jrxml file. You can do so manually in any text editor or using a design tool. Listing 17-123 shows the XML content of the report file.

Listing 17-123. *The report.jrxml File*

```
<?xml version="1.0" encoding="UTF-8"  ?>
<!-- Created with iReport - A designer for JasperReports -->
<!DOCTYPE jasperReport PUBLIC "//JasperReports//DTD Report Design//EN" ➥
"http://jasperreports.sourceforge.net/dtds/jasperreport.dtd">
<jasperReport
        name="catalogue"
         columnCount="1"
         printOrder="Vertical"
         orientation="Portrait"
         pageWidth="595"
         pageHeight="842"
         columnWidth="555"
         columnSpacing="0"
         leftMargin="20"
         rightMargin="20"
         topMargin="30"
         bottomMargin="30"
         whenNoDataType="NoPages"
         isTitleNewPage="false"
         isSummaryNewPage="false">
    <property name="ireport.scriptlethandling" value="0" />
    <property name="ireport.encoding" value="UTF-8" />
    <import value="java.util.*" />
    <import value="net.sf.jasperreports.engine.*" />
    <import value="net.sf.jasperreports.engine.data.*" />

    <field name="name" class="java.lang.String"/>
    <field name="expirationDate" class="java.util.Date"/>

        <detail>
    <band height="20">
     <textField>
        <reportElement x="170" y="0" width="200" height="20"/>
      <textFieldExpression   class="java.lang.String">➥
          <![CDATA[$F{name}]]></textFieldExpression>
```

```
    </textField>
<textField>
        <reportElement x="170" y="0" width="200" height="20"/>
       <textFieldExpression   class="java.lang.String">➥
            <![CDATA[$F{expirationDate}]]></textFieldExpression>
    </textField>

   </band>
  </detail>

</jasperReport>
```

Configuring JasperReports

To be able to use JasperReports in your Spring application, you will have to download latest versions of JasperReports and the following dependencies: BeanShell, Commons BeanUtils, Commons Collections, Commons Digester, Commons Logging, iText, and POI.

Next, we need to configure the view resolver; see Listing 17-124. For JasperReports, you should use ResourceBundleViewResolver and map view names to View classes in the properties file.

Listing 17-124. *The viewResolver Definition*

```
<bean id="viewResolver" class="org.springframework.web.➥
servlet.view.ResourceBundleViewResolver">
    <property name="basename" value="views"/>
</bean>
```

JasperReports Views

An overview of Spring's View implementation for JasperReports is given in Table 17-28.

Table 17-28. *Spring's JasperReportsView Implementations*

Class Name	Description
JasperReportsCsvView	Generates reports as comma-separated values files.
JasperReportsHtmlView	Generates reports in HTML format.
JasperReportsPdfView	Generates reports in PDF format.
JasperReportsXlsView	Generates reports in Microsoft Excel format.
JasperReportsMultiFormatView	Wrapper class that allows the report format to be specified at runtime. Actual rendering of the report is delegated to one of the other JasperReports view classes.

Mapping these View implementations is simply the case of adding them to the views.properties file (see Listing 17-125).

Listing 17-125. *view.properties for a JasperReport View*

```
simpleReport.class=org.springframework.web.➥
servlet.view.jasperreports.JasperReportsPdfView
simpleReport.url=/WEB-INF/reports/report.jasper
```

SimpleReport view is now mapped to PDF format report of the report.jasper file.

Using JasperReportsMultiFormatView

`JasperReportMultiFromatView` allows us to determine the format of the report at runtime. If you specify this as your view class, you have to provide mode parameter with the name `format` and a value that determines the report format. Spring has default values for standard JasperReports views. Table 17-29 shows these values.

Table 17-29. *Default Key Values for JasperReportViews in JasperReportMultiFormatView*

View Class	Format
JasperReportsCsvView	csv
JasperReportsHtmlView	html
JasperReportsPdfView	pdf
JasperReportsXlsView	xls

Let's now edit the `views.properties` file to add a multiformat view for the report (see Listing 17-126).

Listing 17-126. *view.properties for JasperReport View Using JasperReportsMultiFormatView*

```
Products-report.class=org.springframework.web.➥
servlet.view.jasperreports.JasperReportsMultiFormatView
products-report.url=/WEB-INF/views/en_GB/jasper/report.jrxml
```

And finally, let's add a handler method to our `ProductController`, as shown in Listing 17-127.

Listing 17-127. *Controller Code for JasperReports*

```
public ModelAndView pdfReportHandler(HttpServletRequest request,
        HttpServletResponse response) {
            Map model = new HashMap();
            String format = request.getParameter("format");
            JRBeanCollectionDataSource source = ➥
                    new JRBeanCollectionDataSource(products);
            model.put("products", source);
            model.put("format", format"pdf");
            return new ModelAndView("products-report", model);
    }
...
```

In our controller code, we use `JRBeanCollectionDataSource` to pass the data source to the JasperReports engine. This simple implementation maps `java.util.Collection` to the JasperReports data source (you can find more about JasperReports on the project's web site).

Note that we are using request `"format"` parameter to specify the report's format.

After mapping `pdfReport.html` to `pdfReportHandler()` and `xlsReport.html` to `xlsReportHandler()` using any of the `MethodNameReolvers`, if we point the browser to `http://localhost:8080/ch17/product/report.html?fomat=pdf`, we can access the PDF report. Figure 17-22 displays the browser output.

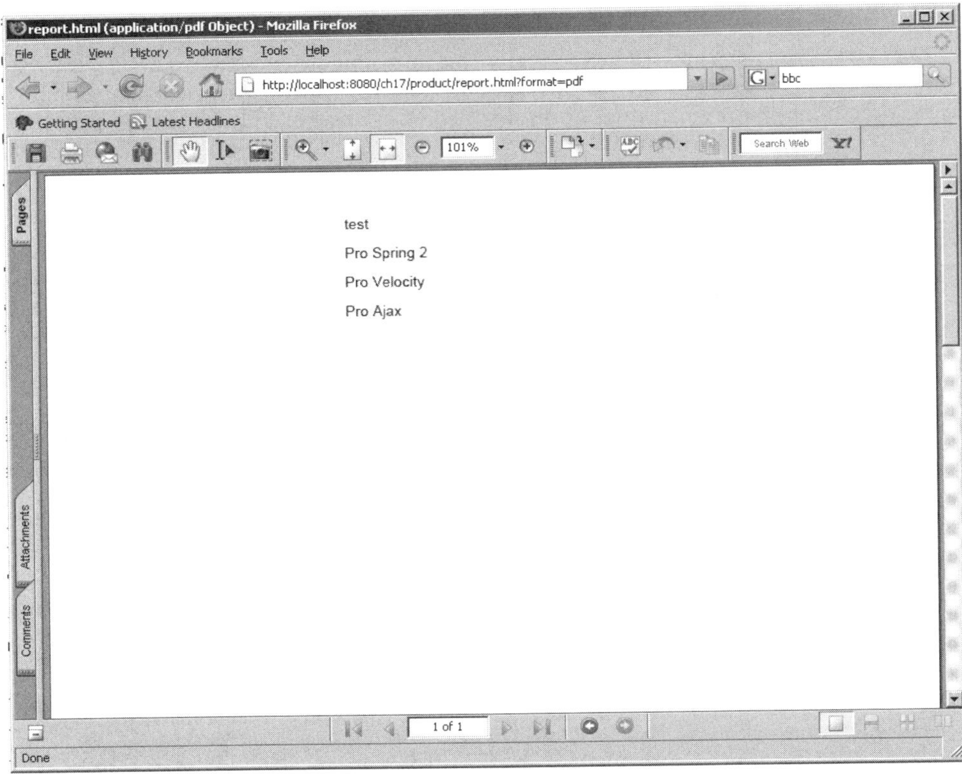

Figure 17-22. *JasperReportsPdfView browser output*

If we change format parameter to `xls`, we'll have `http://localhost:8080/ch17/product/report.html?format=xls`, as Figure 17-23 shows.

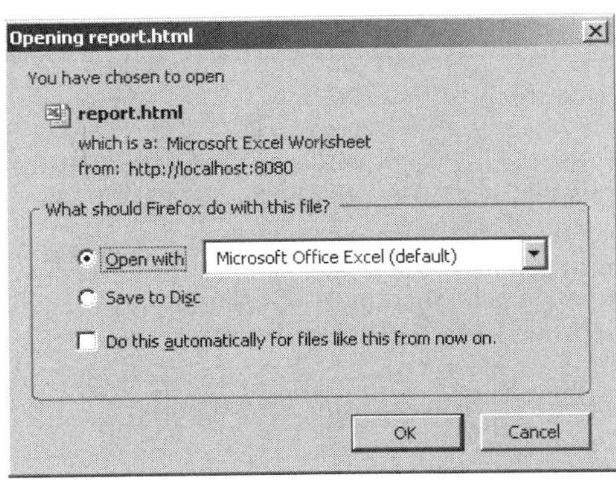

Figure 17-23. *JasperReportsExcelView browser output*

Configuring Export Parameters

Additional parameters are available in JasperReports to specify export options such as page size, headers, or footers. Using Spring, we can easily manage these parameters.

You can export additional parameters to your `JasperReportsView` using a simple declaration in the Spring configuration file. All you have to do is set the `exporterParameters` property of the view class. This property is actually a `Map`: the key is the fully qualified name of the static field from the `JasperReports` class, and the value should be the value you want to assign to the parameter (see Listing 17-128).

Listing 17-128. *ExporterParameters Declaration*

```
<bean id="report" class="org.springframework.web.➥
               servlet.view.jasperreports.JasperReportsHtmlView">
  <property name="url" value="/WEB-INF/reports/simpleReport.jrxml"/>
  <property name="exporterParameters">
    <map>
      <entry key="net.sf.jasperreports.engine.➥
               export.JRHtmlExporterParameter.HTML_FOOTER">
        <value>This is footer! </value>
      </entry>
    </map>
  </property>
</bean>
```

Here, you can see that the `JasperReportsHtmlView` is being configured with an export parameter for `net.sf.jasperreports.engine.export.JRHtmlExporterParameter.HTML_FOOTER`, which will output a footer in the resulting HTML.

Spring Conventions Over Configuration

For many smaller projects, configuring a Spring MVC model can be time consuming, even for fairly simple projects. Sometimes, we need to quickly develop a prototype, without worrying about all aspects of Spring MVC configuration. Imagine how much time you would save if you didn't have to configure all the handler mappings, view resolvers, model instances, views, and so on.

To that end, Spring developers came up with a convention-over-configuration setup to make programmers' lives easier. The convention separately supports core parts of MVC architecture, that is, the models, views, and controllers.

Controller Conventions

Spring 2.0 provides `ControllerClassHandlerMapping` class, which is basically an implementation of the `HandlerMapping` interface. This class uses the convention of mapping the requests' URL to controller classes based on names of controller classes in the Spring configuration file. Let's look at an example in Listing 17-129.

Listing 17-129. *ViewProductController Implementation*

```
public class ViewProductController implements Controller {

    public ModelAndView handleRequest(HttpServletRequest request, ➥
             HttpServletResponse response) {
       return new ModelAndView("/WEB-INF/views/product/viewProduct.jsp");
    }
}
```

Listing 17-130 shows the usual Spring context configuration for this controller.

Listing 17-130. *ViewProductController Spring Configuration*

```
<bean class="org.springframework.web.➥
            servlet.mvc.support.ControllerClassNameHandlerMapping"/>

<bean class="com.apress.ch17.web.ViewProductController" />
```

And that's it! If you point your browser to `/viewProduct.html`, you will get the content of the `/WEB-INF/views/product/viewProduct.jsp` file as implemented in `ViewProductController`. With this simple configuration, you have mapped the `viewProduct.html` URL to your `ViewProductController`—in fact, this convention maps all `/viewProduct*` URLs to the `ViewProductController`.

Behind the scenes, `ControllerClassNameHandlerMapping` looks for all `Controller` beans in the application context and defines its handler mappings by stripping the `"Controller"` string off its class name.

So, if we define another controller, lets say `IndexController`, it will automatically be mapped to the `/index*` request URL.

Note that `ViewProductController` (in camel case) is mapped to `/viewproduct*` (lowercase) request URLs.

MultiActionController Conventions

If we have a `MultiActionController` implementation, the convention is slightly different. Let's look at the examples in Listing 17-131 and Listing 17-132.

Listing 17-131. *AdminController Implementation*

```
public class AdminController extends MultiActionController {

    public ModelAndView usersHandler(HttpServletRequest request, ➥
            HttpServletResponse response) {
        //implementation not relevant
    }
public ModelAndView productsHandler(HttpServletRequest request, ➥
            HttpServletResponse response) {
        //implementation not relevant
    }
}
```

Listing 17-132. *AdminController Spring Configuration*

```
<bean class="org.springframework.web.➥
         servlet.mvc.support.ControllerClassNameHandlerMapping"/>

<bean id="internalPathMethodNameResolver"class="org.springframework.web.➥
            servlet.mvc.multiaction.InternalPathMethodNameResolver">
        <property name="suffix" value="Handler"/>
    </bean>
<bean id="adminController" class="com.apress.ch17.web.AdminController">
<property name="methodNameResolver" ref="internalPathMethodNameResolver"/>
</bean>
```

This configuration will map all request URLs like `/admin/*` to `AdminController`. The different methods inside `AdminController` will be mapped based on the `methodNameResolver` of the controller (in our example, `InternalPathMethodResolver`).

If you follow naming conventions for your Controller implementation (***Controller), which is the best practice in Spring, you can use this convention and have your web application up and running without having to maintain something like a SimpleHandlerMapping bean definition.

Model Conventions

Spring introduces the ModelMap class, which is actually a Map implementation that automatically generates the key for any object that is added to it. ModelAndVew implementation uses this ModelMap, allowing us to use it in Spring controllers. For scalar objects, the object key is generated from the short class name of the object added, with the first character in lowercase. Based on this, we have following rules:

- A User instance will have a user key generated for it.
- A Product instance will have a product key generated for it.
- A java.util.HashMap will have a hashMap key generated for it.
- Adding null will result in an IllegalArgumentException being thrown. If the object (or objects) that you are adding could potentially be null, you will also want to be explicit about the name.

If you're adding the object that is a Set, List, or array object, the map key is generated from the short class name of the first object contained in the Set, List, or array, followed by List. The general rules for key generation follow:

- A User[] array with one or more User elements added will have a userList key generated for it.
- An x.y.User[] array with one or more x.y.Customer elements added will have a userList key generated for it.
- A java.util.ArrayList with one or more x.y.User elements added will have a userList key generated for it.
- A java.util.HashSet with one or more x.y.Customer elements added will have a customerList key generated for it.
- An empty java.util.ArrayList will not be added at all (basically, it will be the no-op).

The ModelMap and the fact that it is part of ModelAndView class allow us to add objects to the model without the hassle of instantiating the Map and adding objects to it using invented keys. In Listing 17-133, you can see how easy it is to add objects to the model.

Listing 17-133. *Adding Objects to ModelMap in the Controller*

```
public class ViewOrderController implements Controller {

    public ModelAndView handleRequest(HttpServletRequest request, ➥
            HttpServletResponse response) {

        List orderItems = // get a List of OrderItem objects
        User user = // get the User making the order

        ModelAndView mav = new ModelAndView("viewOrder"); <-- the logical view name

        mav.addObject(orderItems);
        mav.addObject(user);

        return mav;
    }
}
```

This example will expose model that contains two objects, orderItems with the key orderItemList and User with key user.

View Conventions

In this section, we will show some conventions over configuration applied to the view. Let's take a look at the example in the Listing 17-134, which shows a Controller that returns ModelAndView without a view name being set.

Listing 17-134. *Controller Code Without a View Name*

```
public class RegistrationController implements Controller {

    public ModelAndView handleRequest(HttpServletRequest request, ➥
            HttpServletResponse response) {

        ModelAndView mav = new ModelAndView();

        return mav;
        // notice that no View or logical view name has been set
    }
}
```

At first glance, this code seems incorrect, because no View or view name has been set for the ModelAndView instance. But this code works!

The trick is in the RequestToViewNameTranslator interface introduced in Spring 2.0, which has one implementation, DefaultRequestToViewNameTraslator. To understand what's happening in Listing 17-134, we need to take a look at that example's Spring web application context in Listing 17-135.

Listing 17-135. *viewNameTranslator Configuration*

```
<?xml version="1.0" encoding="UTF-8"?>
<beans xmlns="http://www.springframework.org/schema/beans"
...">
    <bean id="viewNameTranslator" class="org.springframework.web.➥
            servlet.view.DefaultRequestToViewNameTranslator"/>

    <bean class="com.apress.prospring2.ch17.web.ProductController">
    </bean>

    <bean class="org.springframework.web.➥
          servlet.mvc.support.ControllerClassNameHandlerMapping"/>

    <bean id="viewResolver" class="org.springframework.web.➥
            servlet.view.InternalResourceViewResolver">
        <property name="prefix" value="/WEB-INF/views/"/>
        <property name="suffix" value=".jsp"/>
    </bean>

</beans>
```

If the View has not been set and no logical view name is passed to the ModelAndView instance, the DefaultRequestToViewNameTraslator will kick in. The RegistrationController in our example is used with ControllerClassNameHandlerMapping, which maps it to the /registration* request

URLs. The /registration.html URL will be mapped to the RegistrationController, which will in turn set default logical view to registration (generated by DefaultRequestToViewNameTraslator). This logical view will be resolved into /WEB-INF/views/registration.jsp, by the defined view resolver.

The DefaultRequestToViewNameTraslator strips the leading slash and file extension of the URL and returns the result as the logical view name.

Another example is /admin/users.html, which resolves to the logical view admin/index.

You can even skip the definition of the viewNameTranslator bean in the configuration. If no viewNameTranslator bean is explicitly defined, Spring DispatchedServlet will instantiate the DefaultRequestToViewNameTraslator itself. However, if you want to customize default settings of the DefaultRequestToViewNameTraslator or to implement your own RequestToViewNameTraslator, you will have to explicitly define the bean.

Using Annotations for Controller Configuration

Using annotations instead of XML-style configurations has become a trend in Java programming. Spring 2.5 introduces an annotation-based programming model for MVC controllers. This annotation support is available for both Servlet MVC and Portlet MVC. Controllers implemented in this style do not have to extend specific base classes or implement specific interfaces. We will discuss Servlet MVC in this section.

@Controller

The @Controller annotation simplifies controller class declaration. There is no need to implement a Controller interface, extend any Spring controller class, or even reference the Servlet API. All you have to do is to add the annotation to your Controller class as shown in Listing 17-136.

Listing 17-136. *@Controller Annotation in IndexController*

```
@Controller
public class IndexController{

    public ModelAndView displayIndex(
  //omitted for clarity
    }

}
```

To be able to use this annotation, you have to add component scanning to your configuration files, as shown in Listing 17-137.

Listing 17-137. *@Controller Annotation Configuration*

```
<?xml version="1.0" encoding="UTF-8"?>
<beans xmlns="http://www.springframework.org/schema/beans"
    xmlns:xsi="http://www.w3.org/2001/XMLSchema-instance"
    xmlns:p="http://www.springframework.org/schema/p"
    xmlns:context="http://www.springframework.org/schema/context"
    xsi:schemaLocation="
        http://www.springframework.org/schema/beans
        http://www.springframework.org/schema/beans/spring-beans-2.5.xsd
        http://www.springframework.org/schema/context
        http://www.springframework.org/schema/context/spring-context-2.5.xsd">
```

```
    <context:component-scan base-package="com.apress.prospring2.ch17.web" />

    ...

</beans>
```

@RequestMapping

The @RequestMapping annotation is used to map URLs to the Controller class or a particular method (in MultiActionControllers, for example). Listing 17-138 provides an example.

Listing 17-138. *@RequestMapping Annotation in IndexController*

```
@Controller
@RequestMapping("/index.html")
public class IndexController{

    public ModelAndView displayIndex(
  //omitted for clarity
    }

}
@Controller

public class IndexController{

 @RequestMapping("/product/list.html")
    protected ModelAndView listProductsHandler(
  //omitted for clarity
    }
@RequestMapping("/product/view.html")
    protected ModelAndView viewProductHandler(
  //omitted for clarity
    }

}
```

If you want to use this mapping as a class-level annotation, you will have to configure AnnotationMethodHandlerAdapter for your servlet. If you want to use the @RequestMapping annotation at the method level, you need to configure DefaultAnnotationHandlerMapping. This is done by default for DispatcherServlet, but if you are implementing your own handler adapter, you will have to define AnnotationMethodHandlerAdapter—just as if you use custom handler mapping, DefaultAnnotationHandlerMapping must be defined in the Spring configuration files. Listing 17-139 shows an example of this configuration.

Listing 17-139. *@RequestMapping Configuration*

```
<?xml version="1.0" encoding="UTF-8"?>
<beans xmlns="http://www.springframework.org/schema/beans"
    xmlns:xsi="http://www.w3.org/2001/XMLSchema-instance"
    xmlns:p="http://www.springframework.org/schema/p"
    xmlns:context="http://www.springframework.org/schema/context"
    xsi:schemaLocation="
        http://www.springframework.org/schema/beans
        http://www.springframework.org/schema/beans/spring-beans-2.5.xsd
        http://www.springframework.org/schema/context
```

```
        http://www.springframework.org/schema/context/spring-context-2.5.xsd">
    <context:component-scan base-package="com.apress.prospring2.ch17.web" />
    <bean class="org.springframework.web.➥
        servlet.mvc.annotation.AnnotationMethodHandlerAdapter"/>
   <bean class="org.springframework.web.➥
        servlet.mvc.annotation.DefaultAnnotationHandlerMapping"/>

    ...

</beans>
```

@RequestParam

The @RequestParam annotation is used to bind request parameters to a method parameter in the controller; Listing 17-140 shows an example.

Listing 17-140. *@RequestParam Annotation*

```
@Controller
@RequestMapping("/product/edit.html")
public class EditProductController {

        @RequestMapping(type = "GET")
        public String setupForm(@RequestParam("productId") int productId, ➥
                        ModelMap model) {
                Product product = this.productManager.findProductById(productId);
                model.addAttribute("product", product);
                return "productForm";
        }
```

All parameters used with this annotation are mandatory by default. If you want to add an optional parameter, set the @RequestParam annotation's required attribute to false: @RequestParam ("productId", required="false")

@ModelAttribute

If your method returns the Object that is going to be used in your model, you can annotate it with the @ModelAttribute annotation. This annotation will populate the model attribute with the return value of the method, using its parameter, the model name, as shown in Listing 17-141.

Listing 17-141. *@ModelAttribute Annotation Example*

```
        @ModelAttribute("products")
        public Collection<Product> populateProducts() {
                return this.productManager.findAllProducts();
        }
```

This annotation can also be placed as a method parameter. In that case, the model attribute with a specified name is mapped to method parameter. This can be used to get the command object after filling in the HTML form (see Listing 17-142).

Listing 17-142. *Using @ModelAttribute to Get the Command Object in the Form Controller*

```
        public String processSubmit(@ModelAttribute("product") Product product, ➥
                        BindingResult result,SessionStatus status) {
                this.productManager.saveProduct(product);
```

```
            return getSuccessView();
        }
```

Using Annotations with the Command Controller

Let's now look at how can we use an annotation-based controller for functionality that was usually implemented using a command controller (like the simple form submission).

Listing 17-143 shows the annotation-based implementation of `ProductFormController`:

Listing 17-143. *Annotation-Based ProductFormController Implementation*

```
@Controller
@RequestMapping("/products/edit.html")
@SessionAttributes("product")
public class ProductFormController {

    @Autowired
    private ProductService productService;

    @ModelAttribute("types")
    public Collection<String> populateProductTypes() {
                List<String> types = new ArrayList<String>();
                types.add("Books");
                types.add("CDs");
                types.add("MP3 Players");

                return types;
    }

    @RequestMapping(method = RequestMethod.GET)
    public String showForm(@RequestParam("productId") int productId, ➥
ModelMap model) {
        Product product;
        if(productId == 0)
            product = new Product();
        else
            product = this.productService.findById(productId);
        model.addAttribute("product", product);
        return "products-edit";
        }

    @RequestMapping(method = RequestMethod.POST)
    public String submit(@ModelAttribute("product")Product product, ➥
BindingResult result,SessionStatus status) {

        this.productService.save(product);
        return "products-index";
    }

}
```

To the controller in the preceding listing, we have added three class-level annotations: `@Controller` to mark the class as `Controller`, `@RequestMapping` to set the URL that maps to this controller, and `@SessionAttribute` to set the name of our command object to be used in the view.

The method public String showForm() shows the actual form view. This method is annotated with @RequestMapping(method = RequestMethod.GET), which tells Spring to call it only when the request method is GET. It takes the productId request parameter (as defined with @RequestParam annotation), which we use to create the command object named product. Since we have annotated the controller with @SessionAttribute("product"), the value of this attribute will be saved in the session. Listing 17-144 shows the actual form.

Listing 17-144. *The Product Editing Form*

```
<%@ taglib prefix="form" uri="http://www.springframework.org/tags/form" %>

<form:form commandName="product" action="editProduct.html">
    <table>
        <tr>
            <td>Product name:</td>
            <td><form:input path="name" /></td>
        </tr>
         <tr>
            <td>Product type:</td>
            <td><form:select path="type">
            <form:option value="-" label="--Please Select"/>
            <form:options items="${types}"/>
        </form:select></td>
        </tr>
        <tr>
            <td colspan="2">
                <input type="submit" value="Save Changes" />
            </td>
        </tr>
    </table>
</form:form>
```

The method public Collection<String> populateProductTypes() populates the productTypes List with values that are later used as options in the form's select input field. The @ModelAttribute (?QUOT?types?QUOT?) method-level annotation tells Spring to include the return value of this method (that is, a java.util.Collection of product types) in the ModelMap for this model.

The public String submit() method is called whenever POST is the request method. It takes as a parameter a Product that is directly loaded from the model (annotated with @ModelAttribute ("product")). Now, we can save the product we got from the attribute and return the success view (in our case, the products-index view defined in the views.properties file introduced in Tiles section of this chapter).

Summary

In this chapter, you have learned how to use Spring MVC architecture to build flexible and powerful web applications. You know how to use Spring to configure your controllers; you know which controller to use for different usage scenarios. You also know how to validate the data the users enter on the forms, build applications that display the output in the user's language, and make the user's experience even better by providing themes. File upload is now quite a trivial task to implement.

In this chapter, you have also learned about the view technologies available for use in a Spring application and saw that there's a lot more to generating web output than using JSP pages. You can use Velocity if you need top performance or FreeMarker for macro support; you can control PDF or Excel file output if you need to ensure that the formatting is the same on all browsers or to generate output that users will print out. You also know how to set up Tiles to integrate all the different views together. We have also introduced Spring 2.5 features like the Spring form tag library, convention-over-configuration methodology, and annotation-based controllers.

If you are interested in mastering Velocity, check out Rob Harrop's book *Pro Jakarta Velocity* (Apress, 2004), which covers the Velocity Template Language and its uses as well as all the internals of Velocity.

CHAPTER 18

Spring Web Flow

When we go back a couple of decades and think about the beginnings of the World Wide Web, we realize how much—and at the same time how little—has changed. Some things have changed a great deal: the number of people using the Web; its availability, accessibility, and speed; and of course the range of services on offer. If you never enjoyed the dissonant sounds of a modem, you can't fully appreciate the ease with which we now watch high-quality videos via mobile broadband, fiber optic cable, and the like.

The vast increases in the number of users, performance, and services have also had a great influence on the development of the Web as we know it today. Changes to a system introduce new requirements that usually lead to the invention of new solutions (and new buzzwords) to meet those new requirements. These new technologies often come with their own sets of requirements, what brings us back to the beginning of this chapter and how little has changed since the birth of the Internet. Never mind the actual content of a web site; when browsing the Net, we are still mainly downloading HTML code via the same old protocols: mainly HTTP over TCP/IP.

The eight methods that HTTP defines (`GET`, `POST`, `DELETE`, `PUT`, `HEAD`, `TRACE`, `OPTION`, and `CONNECT`) were all that was needed when the Web merely consisted of linked text pages, all users were nice to each other, and it was bad manners to exploit security holes. Times have changed with a vengeance, and web developers these days have to cope with entirely different conditions.

While "free browsing" was trendy in the 1990s, almost every web application developer nowadays must have been confronted with the requirement to limit the user's navigational freedom and guide the user through a series of consecutive pages in a specific way for a business process to be completed. If you haven't had to implement such a process yourself yet, you have certainly participated in one the last time you placed an order with your favorite online retailer or booked a flight online.

Figure 18-1 shows a basic flowchart of a simplified version of such an airline ticket booking process. At the beginning, the user can search for flights until she has picked a suitable one. So far, the process is pretty straightforward. However, by confirming her flight selection, she enters a more complex booking process involving a set of steps that all need to be completed successfully before the selected flight can be booked. In our simple example, the user will have to enter her personal details correctly before she is asked to provide the airline with payment details. Once those details have been accepted, a final confirmation is requested before the tickets are booked, and the user can finally start looking forward to visiting her travel destination.

Figure 18-1. *Ticket booking process*

This is a very simple example, but we're sure you get the idea. Page sequences like this and more complex conversations usually require some sort of state management. HTTP is a stateless protocol, meaning that each request is completely independent of previous or later requests. Information is passed on through request parameters or session attributes. Achieving stateful navigational control spanning a sequence of pages in a stateless environment can be quite cumbersome.

There are other situations that can also cause problems in a web application. What if a user in the example flow entered the postal code of his old address in the personal details form, but only realized it after submitting his entries? Even if a link to the previous page is provided, many users will just click the Back button to go back. Theoretically, this should prompt the browser to display the last page purely retrieved from its own cache, but in practice, all browsers implement their own strategies. Some browsers even reload data from the server. Surely a web application should behave the same with all browsers; and especially in a way that the web developer can predict.

Another situation of concern is related to a user moving through the pages in the other direction. By knowing the correct URLs and the parameters that these URLs expect, a user can theoretically hop from one stage of a process to another while leaving out other stages in between. In our ticket booking example, we would want to make sure the user can't take an illegal shortcut and just skip, say, the page for entering payment details.

To mention a last common problem in web applications, think of a situation where a page seems to hang after you click a link or submit a form. Instead of just waiting in front of the screen, most of us would probably press the refresh button. The undesirable state this can lead to, especially if your last request was a `POST` request, is known as the *double-submit* problem. When you were just posting a comment for a blog, the worst thing that could happen was to post the same comment twice. People might think you're an impatient user; but now imagine if your last post had nothing to do with a blog but was a confirmation to take money out of your account. How painful could that be?

You may be wondering why we list all these problems. As you might have guessed by now, we're about to introduce you to a Spring module that offers solutions to all of them.

Introducing Spring Web Flow

Spring Web Flow is a controller framework for implementing page flows in web applications that are based on MVC frameworks like Spring MVC, Struts, or JSF. In the MVC model two architecture shown in last chapter's Figure 17-2, Spring Web Flow takes its place in the box labeled "Controller," which is responsible for handling incoming requests, preparing the model, and passing the model to the view for rendering. However, unlike other web controller frameworks that operate on a request-to-request basis, Spring Web Flow allows you to capture full navigational paths—even very complex ones—involving a series of pages in a clear and concise way. It does this by representing them as flows.

A flow in Spring Web Flow is a self-contained module fulfilling the role of a template for a user–web-site session. The conversational scope was introduced by Spring Web Flow to fill the gap between the very granular request scope and the full-blown session scope. Conversations can make up the whole of a user session but usually only span a series of requests.

These templates, or flow definitions, describe the order and dependencies of all possible steps and tasks involved in fulfilling a business process or user conversation. They define which pages should be displayed, what business logic needs to be executed, and how these pages and the business logic are related to each other. Due to their modular character, flow definitions can easily be reused throughout an application.

Core Concepts

Usually, before development work on a web site project begins, a concept of what is about to be developed is created. This can involve clients getting together with business analysts and interface architects creating loads of documentation. Or it can just as well be only you sitting down with pen and paper, making notes on what you want your web site to be like.

In either case, a common way to sketch out functional and behavioral requirements is to draw up a flowchart. Figure 18-2 shows the flowchart for a charity shop that wants to make its collection of second-hand books available online. Its users will be allowed to browse what's available and purchase the books they're interested in.

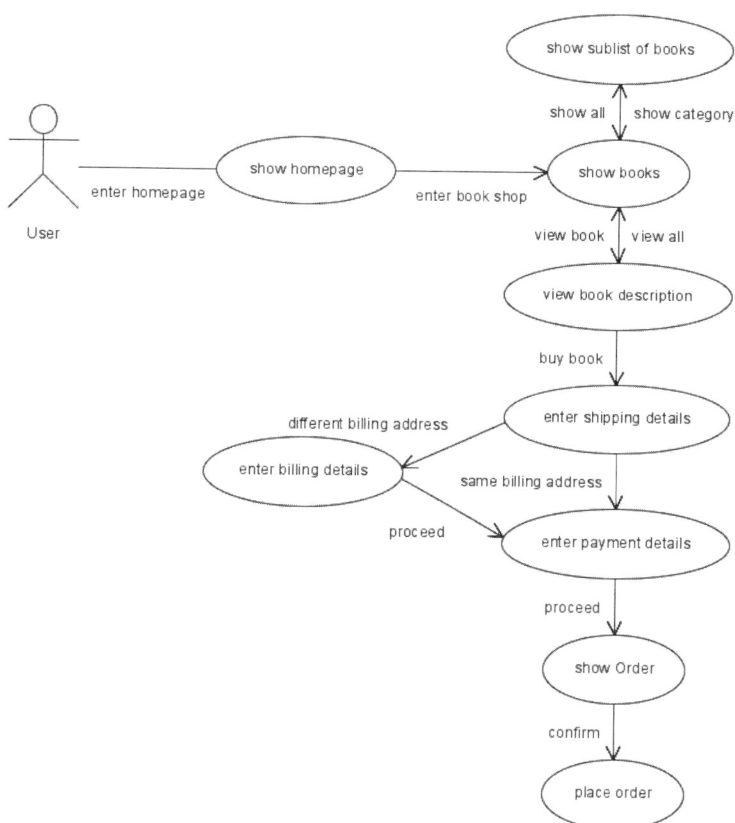

Figure 18-2. *Imaginary charity online bookstore flowchart*

Flowcharts make it easier to visualize processes; in this respect, their role is similar to that of UML state diagrams. In general terms, state diagrams are used to describe the behavior of a system. They describe the possible states the system can be in, the internal and external events that can occur at these states, and the possible transitions between states triggered by the events.

State diagrams have a limited number of elements. All state diagrams begin with an initial state that describes the system when it is created. Beginning with this initial state, the system starts changing state. In diagrams, the initial state is represented by a filled circle. All other states are symbolized by rounded boxes. States can have activities associated with them that are depicted in the activity section of the state symbol using a do/action syntax. In addition to their main activities, states can also define entry and exit actions that are executed when a state is entered or left (see Figure 18-3).

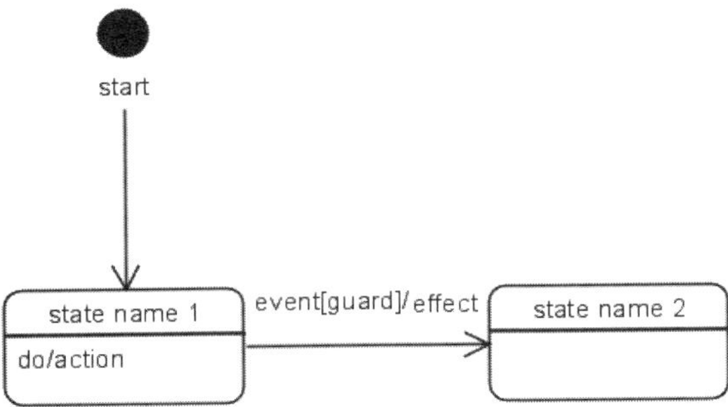

Figure 18-3. *State diagram example*

Arrows between two states indicate possible transitions from one state to another in the direction of the arrow. Transitions are labeled with the event they are triggered by and can optionally also be tagged with an `event [guard]/effect` label. A guard is an expression that evaluates to a Boolean value and offers further control over the execution of a transition. A transition matching an event won't fire if the guard expression doesn't evaluate to `true`. If the transition does fire, the optionally defined actions get executed.

UML state diagrams also include the concept of superstates. Superstates are used when multiple states define the same transition(s) to another state. Instead of noting each transition for every state individually, the superstate declares the transition for all states that are members of the superstate.

Unless the system models an infinite loop, all systems come to an endpoint that declares the process completed. These end states are displayed by bordered, filled circles and don't declare any transitions, as that would defeat the purpose of an end state.

Coming back to our charity shop example, Figure 18-4 shows the previously described use case in UML state diagram notation.

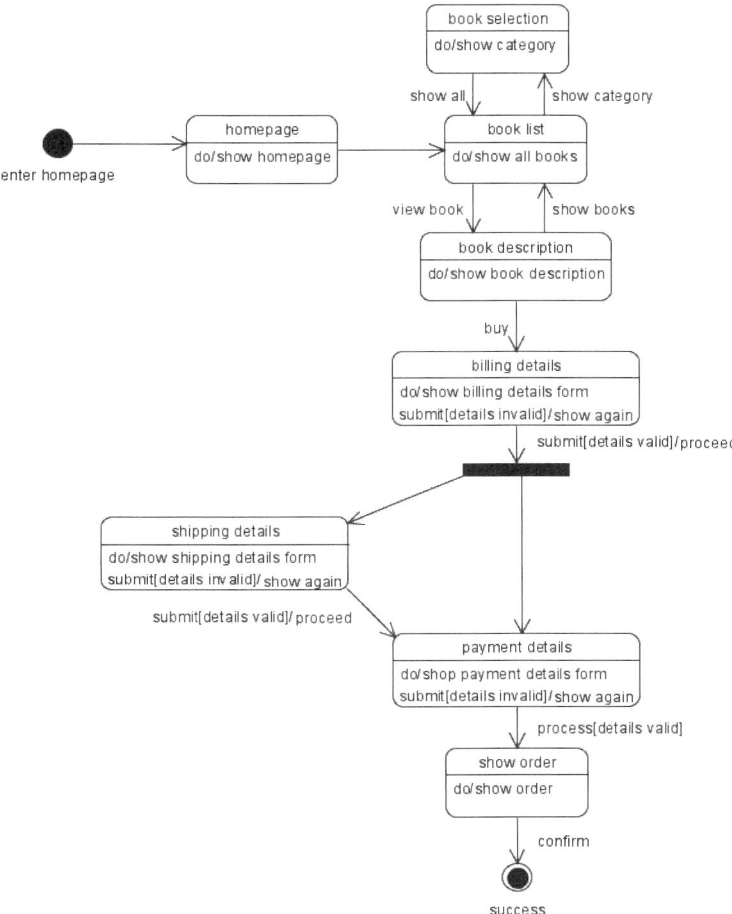

Figure 18-4. *Imaginary charity shop UML state diagram*

You may be wondering why we're explaining UML state diagrams in a chapter on Spring Web Flow. The point is that state diagrams are used to visualize the type of model known as a finite state machine (FSM). Spring Web Flow is an implementation of an FSM. When you compare the flowchart in Figure 18-2 with the state diagram in Figure 18-4, you will see that the views map nicely onto states. Spring Web Flow does pretty much the same thing by treating all steps and tasks of a web application as states. So flow definitions show a high level of resemblance to state diagrams, which is why we found it important to explain them.

In the course of this chapter, you will see how closely Spring Web Flow follows the concept of FSMs and how the various elements are implemented. Better than just talking about Spring Web Flow is actually using it and seeing it in action. On the following pages, we'll guide you through getting hold of Spring Web Flow and show you step by step how to use it.

Obtaining Spring Web Flow

Before we can start building web applications with Spring Web Flow, we need to obtain the necessary libraries. Hence, our first step will be to download the Spring Web Flow distribution from the Spring Framework home page, at `www.springframework.org/download`. Like the Spring Framework libraries, the Spring Web Flow libraries are also available on a SourceForge download page where you can choose among all releases (`http://sourceforge.net/project/showfiles.php?group_id=73357&package_id=148517`). At the time of this writing, Spring Web Flow 2.0 is the latest release, and all the following examples in this chapter will be based on this version.

When the final version of Spring Web Flow 1.0 was released, it contained quite a few drastic changes compared to previous release candidates, causing quite a stir among users and prompting the developers to publish an upgrade guide. Initially, assuming that a lesson had been learned from this, we hoped fewer changes would arise while this chapter was being written. But since nothing is really final until the final release (and even then development still goes on), please be aware that depending on your version of Spring Web Flow, you might have to amend our samples to make them run. In case you experience any problems, the Spring Framework home page and the Spring Web Flow forum (`http://forum.springframework.org/index.php`) are good resources.

Spring Web Flow Nightly Builds

Like the Spring Framework itself, Spring Web Flow is under constant development with new features being added frequently. If you want to try out the latest features that haven't made their way into a full release yet, you can download nightly builds from `http://static.springframework.org/downloads/nightly/snapshot-download.php?project=SWF`.

Building Spring Web Flow from Source

It is also possible to build your own version of Spring Web Flow from scratch. To check out the latest version of the code, you first need a Subversion client installed. You can find the Subversion source code or precompiled binaries for a variety of operating systems at `http://subversion.tigris.org/`.

Windows users who prefer a graphical user interface might find the free tool TortoiseSVN helpful. It can be found at `http://tortoisesvn.tigris.org/`. With this tool installed, all SVN commands are just a right-click away. In addition, little icons directly indicate the status of a file (if it is up-to-date, modified, or deleted, just to name a few of the available options).

Either way, the repository URL you will have to connect to is `https://springframework.svn.sourceforge.net/svnroot/springframework/spring-webflow/`. You won't need a username or password.

You will find the latest development efforts in the `trunk` folder and all previous releases named accordingly in the `tags` folder. Figure 18-5 shows a screenshot of Spring Web Flow's Subversion repository as seen through TortoiseSVN. As already mentioned in the equivalent "Building Spring from Source Code" section in Chapter 2, it is possible to compile the trunk version, but we recommend compiling one of the tagged releases or milestones.

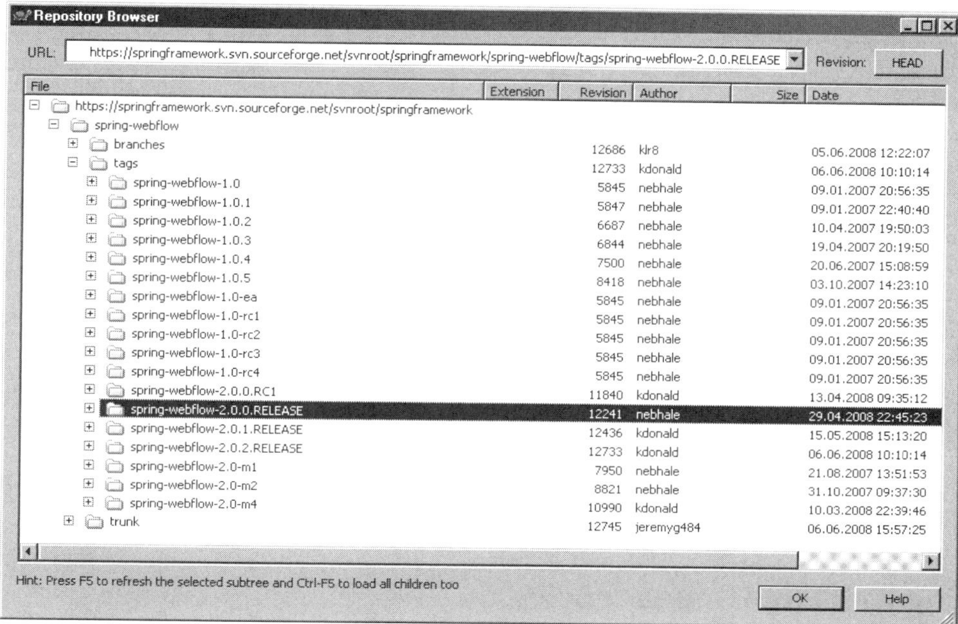

Figure 18-5. *TortoiseSVN repository browser screenshot*

Checking out Spring Web Flow through a graphical user interface is straightforward. Now let's see how to achieve the same goal through the command line (see Listing 18-1).

Listing 18-1. *SVN Command to Check Out the 2.0 Release*

```
svn checkout https://springframework.svn.sourceforge.net/svnroot/springframework/➥
spring-webflow/tags/spring-webflow-2.0.0.RELEASE
```

Running this command will check out the aforementioned release into the directory the command has been issued from. For more details on how to use Subversion, see the online book *Version Control with Subversion*, freely available at `http://svnbook.red-bean.com/`. With the same command, you can check out any other tag (or branch, or even the trunk) of the repository. All you need to do is adjust the preceding URL to reflect your choice.

To build Spring Web Flow, you will need Java 1.5 or higher and Apache Ant 1.7 or higher. Spring Web Flow uses Apache Ivy as its dependency manager. If you haven't already installed Apache Ivy, there is a version bundled with Apache Ant that will be used automatically. If all these requirements are met, you should navigate to the `build-spring-webflow` subdirectory of your checkout directory. Then you can start the build by typing **ant**. This will compile all source code, produce the Spring Web Flow JAR files, and build the sample applications included in the source code distribution. If you want to build a different tag than the one in our example, it's worth checking the `readme.txt` file in your checkout directory for the correct `ant` target information.

Table 18-1 gives a list of the created JAR files that can be found in multiple subdirectory locations (e.g., in the `target/artifacts` subdirectory of each module and under the `integration-repo` directory). These JARs are the same ones you can download from the aforementioned SourceForge page. We will discuss the sample applications that are provided at the end of this chapter.

Table 18-1. *Spring Web Flow Distribution JARs*

JAR File	Description
`org.springframework.webflow-2.0.0.RELEASE.jar`	This library contains all elements of the Spring Web Flow system.
`org.springframework.binding-2.0.0.RELEASE.jar`	This JAR contains the Spring Data Binding framework used internally by Spring Web Flow.
`org.springframework.faces-2.0.0.RELEASE.jar`	`spring-faces.jar` contains Spring Web Flow's integration with JavaServer Faces (JSF) and additional JSF functionality.
`org.springframework.js-2.0.0.RELEASE.jar`	The spring-js library is one of the latest additions. It packages a JavaScript abstraction framework facilitating AJAX calls and other client-side behaviors. The `ResourceServlet` allows for serving static resources such as CSS and JavaScript files from JAR files.

Now that we have the necessary Spring Web Flow libraries, let us see what else we need to start building our first application.

Spring Web Flow Dependencies

In order to use Spring Web Flow in your application, you will need to include a few additional libraries to fulfill Spring Web Flow's dependency requirements. Table 18-2 provides a list of the additional libraries that are absolutely mandatory, as Spring Web Flow references them internally. Depending on which additional functionality you want to make use of (e.g., persistence with JPA), you will have to extend this list further. For a brief description of the mentioned libraries, refer to Chapter 2.

Table 18-2. *Spring Web Flow Runtime Requirements*

Dependency Group	JAR Files	Description
Logging	`commons-logging.jar`	Additionally add `log4j.jar` to configure Spring Web Flow to use log4j logging.
Spring	`spring-beans.jar`, `spring-context.jar`, `spring-core.jar`, `spring-web.jar`, `spring-mvc.jar`	Spring Web Flow 2.0.0.RELEASE requires the Spring Framework 2.5.4 or higher and at least Java 1.4.
Spring Web Flow	`org.springframework.webflow-2.0.0.RELEASE.jar`, `org.springframework.binding-2.0.0.RELEASE.jar`, `org.springframework.js-2.0.0.RELEASE.jar`	Depending on whether you want to integrate Spring Web Flow with JSF, you also need to add `org.springframework.faces-2.0.0.RELEASE.jar`.
Expression Language	An Expression Language (EL) implementation (e.g., `ognl.jar` or `jboss-el.jar`).	JUnit is not required at runtime; it is only used for building and running the test suite.
Testing	`junit.jar`	

Hello, Web Flow!

Now then! It's time to get our hands dirty—not literally—and what could be more suitable to start with than building a Spring Web Flow version of the so well-known "Hello, World"? It will be a pretty simple version to get you started, but we're going to introduce new features with examples as we go along, slowly but surely enabling you to build complex web applications with Spring Web Flow.

First, we need a web application directory structure. It doesn't matter how you create it—whether you do it manually or with the help of your favorite IDE—as long as you have a directory for source code and libraries and a WEB-INF directory for the deployment descriptor and further configuration and application files.

To run this example, you will only need the minimum set of JAR files, as discussed previously—namely commons-logging.jar, spring-beans.jar, spring-context.jar, spring-core.jar, spring-web.jar, spring-webmvc.jar, an expression language implementation (we use ognl.jar), and of course spring-webflow.jar, spring-binding.jar, and spring-js.jar.

Underneath the WEB-INF directory, you should now create a new folder named flows. Within this directory, create two simple JSP files named hello.jsp and helloWorld.jsp, as shown in Listing 18-2 and Listing 18-3, respectively. These are the two files we are going to use to communicate with the world.

Listing 18-2. *hello.jsp*

```
<%@ taglib prefix="form" uri="http://www.springframework.org/tags/form"%>
<!DOCTYPE html PUBLIC "-//W3C//DTD XHTML 1.0 Transitional//EN"
          "http://www.w3.org/TR/xhtml1/DTD/xhtml1-transitional.dtd">
<html>
<head>
  <title>Welcome to Spring Web Flow</title>
</head>
<body>
  <h1>Welcome to Spring Web Flow</h1>
  <form:form id="start">
    <input type="submit" name="_eventId" value="Click to say hello!" />
  </form:form>
</body>
</html>
```

Listing 18-3. *helloWorld.jsp*

```
<!DOCTYPE html PUBLIC "-//W3C//DTD XHTML 1.0 Transitional//EN"
"http://www.w3.org/TR/xhtml1/DTD/xhtml1-transitional.dtd">
<html>
<head>
    <title>Welcome to Spring Web Flow</title>
</head>
<body>
    <h1>Hello, Web Flow!</h1>
</body>
</html>
```

Your directory structure should now look similar to Figure 18-6.

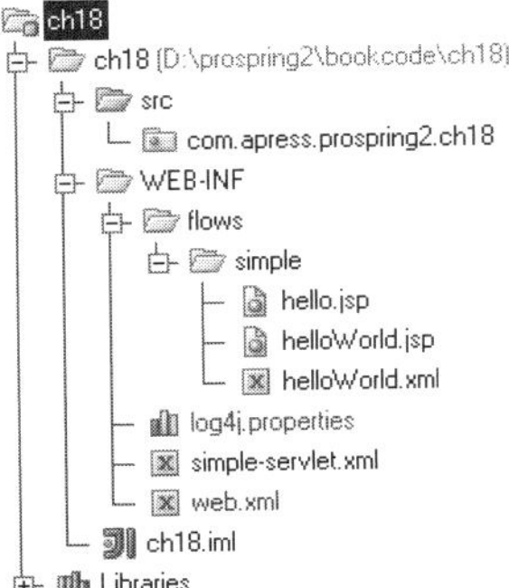

Figure 18-6. *"Hello, World" sample application*

Next, we need a flow definition. Spring Web Flow offers you a convenient way to build flows using a simple XML-based definition language. Let us now add the `helloWorld.xml` file shown in Listing 18-4 to the `flows` directory.

Listing 18-4. *Basic XML Flow Template*

```
<?xml version="1.0" encoding="UTF-8"?>
<flow xmlns="http://www.springframework.org/schema/webflow"
        xmlns:xsi="http://www.w3.org/2001/XMLSchema-instance"
        xsi:schemaLocation="http://www.springframework.org/schema/webflow
        http://www.springframework.org/schema/webflow/spring-webflow-2.0.xsd">

    <view-state id="hello">
        <transition on="*" to="helloWorld" />
    </view-state>

    <end-state id="helloWorld" view="helloWorld.jsp" />

</flow>
```

All Spring Web Flow flow definitions begin with this namespace declaration. All other elements that should become part of the flow definition are defined between the `<flow>` root element tags. For our example, we have added a single `view-state` with a `transition` child element and an `end-state`.

Now we have the sample views and the sample flow definition, but we're still missing the system configuration. In the last chapter, we covered Spring's `DispatcherServlet`, which we will also use in our Spring Web Flow application. We configure it in the `web.xml` file, as displayed in Listing 18-5. Our servlet is called `simple`, and we map all requests ending in `*.html` to it.

Listing 18-5. *Web Application Deployment Descriptor*

```
<?xml version="1.0" encoding="ISO-8859-1"?>
<web-app xmlns="http://java.sun.com/xml/ns/j2ee"
    xmlns:xsi="http://www.w3.org/2001/XMLSchema-instance"
    xsi:schemaLocation="http://java.sun.com/xml/ns/j2ee
        http://java.sun.com/xml/ns/j2ee/web-app_2_4.xsd" version="2.4">

    <display-name>Pro Spring Chapter 18 Simple Hello World</display-name>
    <description>Introduction to Spring Web Flow</description>
```

```
    <context-param>
      <param-name>contextConfigLocation</param-name>
      <param-value>/WEB-INF/simple-servlet.xml</param-value>
    </context-param>

    <servlet>
      <servlet-name>simple</servlet-name>
      <servlet-class>
          org.springframework.web.servlet.DispatcherServlet
      </servlet-class>
      <load-on-startup>1</load-on-startup>
    </servlet>

    <servlet-mapping>
      <servlet-name>simple</servlet-name>
      <url-pattern>*.html</url-pattern>
    </servlet-mapping>
</web-app>
```

The final step to finish the setup of Spring Web Flow is done in the `simple-servlet.xml` application context file you can see in Listing 18-6.

Listing 18-6. *simple-servlet.xml*

```
<beans xmlns="http://www.springframework.org/schema/beans"
       xmlns:xsi="http://www.w3.org/2001/XMLSchema-instance"
       xmlns:webflow="http://www.springframework.org/schema/webflow-config"
       xsi:schemaLocation="
           http://www.springframework.org/schema/beans
           http://www.springframework.org/schema/beans/spring-beans.xsd
           http://www.springframework.org/schema/webflow-config
           http://www.springframework.org/schema/webflow-config/➥
           spring-webflow-config.xsd">

    <bean id="publicUrlMappings"
          class="org.springframework.web.servlet.handler.SimpleUrlHandlerMapping">
        <property name="mappings">
            <value>
                /helloWorld.html=helloWorldHandler
            </value>
        </property>
    </bean>

    <bean id="helloWorldHandler"
          class="org.springframework.webflow.mvc.servlet.AbstractFlowHandler" />

    <bean class="org.springframework.webflow.mvc.servlet.FlowHandlerAdapter">
        <constructor-arg ref="flowExecutor" />
    </bean>

    <!-- Spring Web Flow Configuration -->
    <webflow:flow-executor id="flowExecutor" flow-registry="flowRegistry" />

    <webflow:flow-registry id="flowRegistry">
        <webflow:flow-location path="/WEB-INF/flows/helloWorld.xml" />
    </webflow:flow-registry>

</beans>
```

The SimpleUrlHandlerMapping should be an old friend by now. In its mapping property, we specify the URL we want to make our little application available under and map it to a handler. In the last chapter, you saw that the DispatcherServlet can delegate requests to any implementation of the HandlerAdapter interface. For Spring MVC controllers, there is the SimpleControllerHandlerAdapter, which is also used automatically if no HandlerAdapter is configured specifically. Since we're not using Spring MVC controllers in our example application, this class is not suitable for us. Fortunately, Spring Web Flow comes with its own HandlerAdapter implementation, FlowHandlerAdapter. Just as the SimpleControllerHandlerAdapter delegates requests to implementations of the Controller interface, the FlowHandlerAdapter handles requests with the help of implementations of the FlowHandler interface. (Actually, it's not as simple as that as you can imagine, but that's enough for you to know for the time being. You'll see exactly how it works in the "Flow Execution Architecture" section later in this chapter.)

Spring Web Flow ships with a default implementation of this interface, namely the AbstractFlowHandler. In spite of its name, it is not an abstract class, and we can instantiate it and use it for our example. We'll cover the interface and the class in more detail later. To enable the DispatcherServlet to use the FlowHandlerAdapter, we just need to add it to a context file and it will be picked up automatically when the context is initialized.

If you've asked yourself already how the flow definitions and flow handling find their way into the application, the FlowHandlerAdapter holds the answer. It has a FlowExecutor property that handles the execution of flows and needs to be set on construction.

To perform flow handling, the flowExecutor needs to have access to the flow definition(s). These are added to a flowRegistry that we define at the bottom of the simple-servlet.xml file. The flowExecutor holds a reference to the created flowRegistry and can hence access the flow definitions. (If all this explanation has been too quick for your liking, we will cover all the relevant components in more depth later in this chapter.)

Now that we have created all necessary files and configurations, it's time to build the application and deploy it. When we then direct the browser to http://localhost:8080/simple/helloWorld.html, we should see something like Figure 18-7.

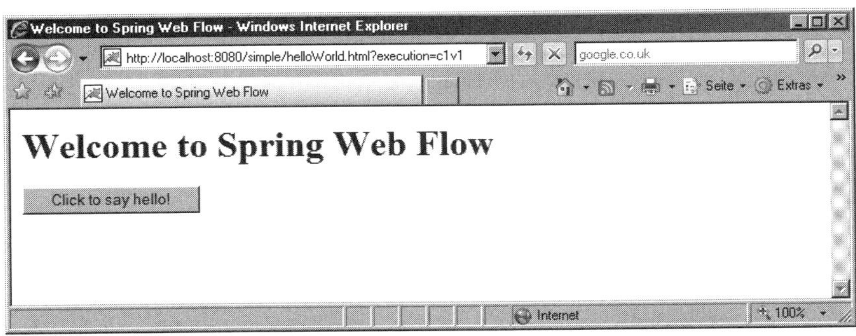

Figure 18-7. *The sample application welcome page*

Clicking the "Click to say hello!" button will then take us to the next page, which should look like Figure 18-8. Hooray!

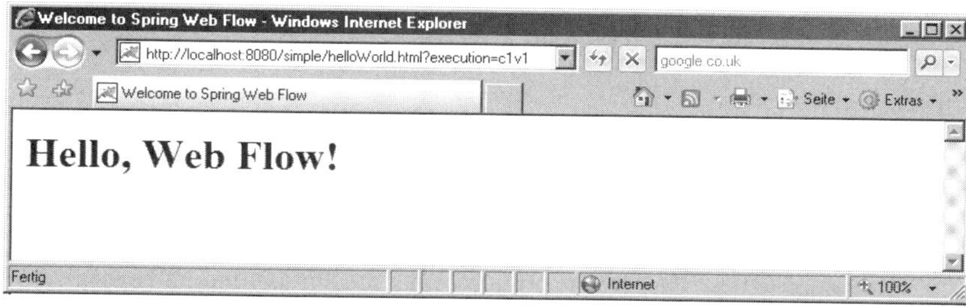

Figure 18-8. *The "Hello, Web Flow!" page*

This use case is so simple that you normally wouldn't choose Spring Web Flow to implement it. We'll now introduce some more of the elements you can use to build a flow to highlight the areas where Spring Web Flow's advantages lie.

Exploring States

Going back to the concept of states in a state diagram, you'll remember that states are executing behaviors. In the state diagram examples, you've seen that the executed behaviors can be quite different from each other. Our example diagram in Listing 18-4 had states like "show" and "validate." To cater for these different behaviors, Spring Web Flow comes with a set of five different state types. You already used two of them in the "Hello, Web Flow!" sample application: `<view-state>` and `<end-state>`. Table 18-3 provides a list of the existing states and a description of the behaviors they execute.

Table 18-3. *Spring Web Flow States*

State Type	XML Element	Behavior
View state	`<view-state>`	The behavior of a view state is generally to issue a response to the user; this is usually done by rendering a view. Once the user signals an event, the flow execution is resumed.
Decision state	`<decision-state>`	The responsibility of decision states is to make flow-routing decisions. A series of expressions can be configured, and the first expression that evaluates to `true` determines which transition out of this state is to be executed.
Subflow state	`<subflow-state>`	When a subflow state is executed, a new flow is spawned as a subflow. The higher-level flow is put on hold while the new flow is executed. When the subflow terminates, execution of the higher-level flow is resumed. Potential end results returned by the subflow can determine the higher-level flow's next transition.
Action state	`<action-state>`	An action state effects the execution of some logic—typically, this will be underlying business layer code. The result of this execution decides which transition to execute next. We mention the action state here for completeness. Spring Web Flow 2.0 favors the usage of the `<evaluate>` element, which we'll introduce in the section "Implementing Actions."
End state	`<end-state>`	If an end state is entered, the currently active flow session is terminated and the flow outcome is returned. If the active flow session is a subflow, only the subflow is terminated, and control is handed back to the parent flow. Terminating the top-level flow removes all information about the previous flow execution; the flow can't be resumed.

We're now going to have a closer look at three of these states and how we can make use of them. Subflow states and action states will be covered in the "Advanced Concepts" section.

View State

View states form the main way to communicate with the user. They display web application output and react to user input, enabling the user to actively take part in the flow. This section is going to explain how to use the `<view-state>` element to render views. The minimum configuration you need to define a view state is its ID. All states need to have IDs that are unique within the flow definition. There is no reason why you can't have two view states with the ID `index` within a web application, as long as those two IDs are elements of two different flows. Following is an example of a view state definition:

```
<view-state id="showPage" />
```

By convention, this view state will resolve to the view template `showPage.jsp`, which is located in the same directory as the flow definition. We took advantage of this convention in our "Hello, Web Flow!" application earlier. This convention is fine for small applications, but it can quickly grow out of hand as you get more view templates. With the `view` attribute, you can make more specific declarations as to exactly which view template to use. You have three options for the view identifiers.

The first option is to specify your view templates as relative to the flow-containing directory:

```
<view-state id="showPage" view="myPage.jsp" />
```

The path to your view template can also be relative to the web application root context. Generally, all view identifiers starting with a / will be treated as root-context–relative paths.

```
<view-state id="showPage" view="/WEB-INF/views/myPage.jsp" />
```

Some frameworks such as Spring MVC also allow you to use logical view names that are resolved by the framework. Spring MVC, for example, uses the `ViewResolver` infrastructure. In the "Integration with Spring MVC" section, we're going to show you how this is done.

```
<view-state id="showPage" view="myPage" />
```

You can then define view states as shown, without tying your flow definition to a specific view template technology.

Decision State

Decision states are useful if the continuation of a flow depends on circumstances that need to be evaluated at runtime. They allow expressions to be set that are then evaluated in order to determine which transition to execute. Decision states are defined with the `<decision-state>` element.

```
<decision-state id="requiresShippingAddress">
    <if test="requestParameters.billingAddressIsAlsoShippingAddress"
        then="enterPaymentDetails" else="enterShippingAddress" />
</decision-state>
```

The `else` attribute of the `<if>` element is not mandatory. It is also perfectly OK to define multiple `<if test=". . ." then=". . .">` child elements. If you have more than one expression to test, be aware that they are evaluated in order of their definition, and the first one to result in `true` will trigger its transition. If you define an `<if>` element with an `else` attribute and it's not the last expression defined in the decision state, you might end up wondering why certain transitions are not executed even though they should be.

The expression to evaluate can be anything the EL parser can evaluate—hence there is nothing to stop you from executing business logic here. However, the responsibility of the decision state is to execute controller logic, not business logic. Don't misuse the decision state for something that should rather be handled by an action.

End State

End states mark the endpoints of a flow, declaring that the process is finished. If a flow reaches an end state, the flow session is terminated. If the terminated flow is a top-level flow, the entire flow execution ends and can't be resumed again. If instead a subflow session is terminated, the parent flow resumes and uses the outcome of the terminated subflow as the base for further transitions.

```
<end-state id="finished" />
```

Without any further configuration, end states return events that match their IDs. The previously defined end state would therefore return a finished event. As you will see in the "Advanced Concepts" section, you can also explicitly map any flow scope attributes as output attributes that will then be returned as data alongside the logical flow outcome.

By default, end states don't render any views. This is fine for subflows, since the parent flow will take over control. If the end state terminates a top-level flow, you can set the view attribute to specify which view to return. The same rules as for the view state also apply here, giving you full control over the view selection strategy.

```
<end-state id="helloWorld" view="helloWorld.jsp"/>
```

Now that we've covered a few basic state types, it is time to find out how we can navigate between them.

Working with Transitions

Transitions are used to progress the flow from one state to another. They are defined as child elements of any of the state elements except the end state, using the <transition> element, as shown following:

```
<transition on="event" to="otherState" />
```

You've seen a transition declared in the view state of our sample application in Listing 18-4. Since a state can react on multiple events with different transitions, you can define a list of <transition> child elements per state. When an event occurs, it is matched against the event specified in the on attribute, one transition after the other. The transitions are matched in order of their definition, and the first match will be executed.

```
<view-state id="chooseColor">
    <transition on="red" to="showRed" />
    <transition on="green" to ="showGreen" />
    <transition on="blue" to="showBlue" />
    <transition on="yellow" to="showYellow" />
    <transition on="red" to ="showOrange" /> <!-- never executes! -->
</view-state>
```

If you have a collection of states in a flow that all have one or more transitions in common, the <global-transitions> element allows you to declare those transitions once for all states. A good example is a cancel transition that should be available for every page in the flow (see Figure 18-9).

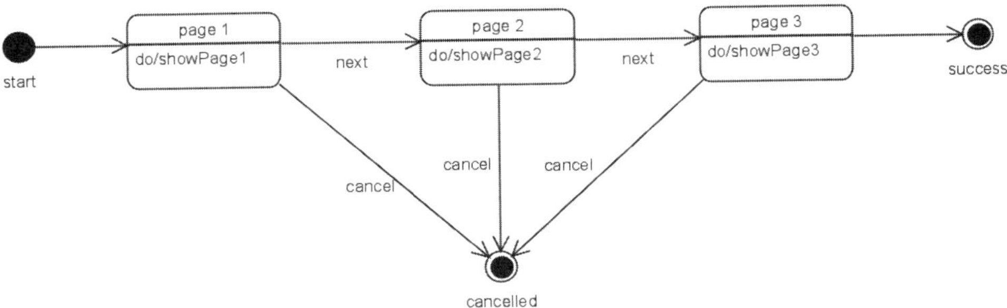

Figure 18-9. *A state diagram for cancel on every page*

The definition of this global transition could look like Listing 18-7.

Listing 18-7. *Global Transitions*

```
<global-transitions>
    <transition on="cancel" to="cancelled" />
</global-transitions>
```

Now that we've discussed the various states and how to transition from one to another, it's time to have a look at the events that trigger transitions. An event is basically the flow execution outcome of a state. When a decision state is executed, the flow evaluates the defined expression and chooses a transition based on this result. A view state, however, is executed by a view being rendered and returned. Even though the web application doesn't do anything after the response is generated, the state itself is theoretically still being executed. The flow execution result of a view state is generated when the user interacts with the view by clicking links or submitting forms back to the server.

Allowing the user to create events is simpler than you might think. All you need to do is include an `_eventId` parameter in the request. We assume you're already familiar with adding request parameters to URLs, but just for completeness, here's a simple example of a parameterized `GET` request:

```
Click <a href="${flowExecutionUrl}&_eventId=red">here</a> for RED
```

To transmit the event ID in a `POST` request, you have a few other options in conjunction with the `<input>` element in `<form>` elements. You can either use a `hidden` input field or `submit` buttons, as shown in forms `one` and `two` in Listing 18-8.

Listing 18-8. *Input Type Events*

```
<html>
<head>
    <title>Colors</title>
</head>
<body>
    <form id="one" action="${flowExecutionUrl}" method="post">
        [...]
        <p>Lorem ipsum dolor sit amet...</p>
        <<input type="hidden" name="_eventId" value="yellow" />
        [...]
    </form>

    <form id="two" action="${flowExecutionUrl}" method="post">
        [...]
```

```
        <p>Lorem ipsum dolor sit amet...</p>
        <p><input type="submit" name="_eventId" value="blue" /></p>

        <p><input type="submit" name="_eventId_green" value="Go green!" /></p>
    </form>
</body>
</html>
```

In form two, you can see two options to transmit the value of the _eventId parameter. The first option is to use the value from the value attribute of the input element. The second option is to append the value to the request parameter name following the pattern _eventId_${value}.

Don't worry too much about the ${flowExecutionUrl} expression. It is part of the context and scope variables that get automatically generated and added to the model by Spring Web Flow. We will cover those in the "Expression Languages and Scopes" section.

In the "Advanced Concepts" section, we will explain further features and elements you can use in your flow definition.

Advanced Concepts

So far, we have introduced the essential elements of Spring Web Flow and how to configure them in a flow definition. You are now able to quickly draft a web site by simply concatenating views. In this section, we will explore some of the more complicated concepts in Spring Web Flow. We will begin by looking at how we can use an expression language to access the model, followed by how to invoke business logic. We will further discuss other ways to interact with the model scope and how to partially rerender views.

Expression Languages and Scopes

To access the data model, invoke bean methods, and defer evaluation of variables to runtime, Spring Web Flow uses EL. It supports two implementations of it: the Unified EL and OGNL (Object Graph Navigation Language). The current default EL implementation is jboss-el. If this library and the el-api library are already set on the classpath, they will be used automatically. Spring Web Flow versions 1.0.x use OGNL as the default implementation. Switching between the two implementations is as easy as copying a couple of JAR files or updating your project's dependency management configuration.

With the help of EL, Spring Web Flow can

- Resolve and evaluate expressions, such as view names and transition criteria
- Access client-side data in terms of request parameters and flow attributes
- Access server-side held data structures such as applicationContext and flowScope
- Invoke methods on Spring beans

Spring Web Flow distinguishes between expressions that should simply be resolved and expressions that need to be evaluated. Evaluate expressions can only be defined as single string expressions and don't require (or rather allow) EL delimiters like ${ } and #{ }. An IllegalArgumentException will let you know if you did use them nevertheless. Evaluate expressions are defined as follows:

```
<evaluate expression="order.recalculateCosts()" />
```

Evaluate expressions that return a result can expose this through setting another expression in the result attribute. The following line of code would on execution call the findAllBooks method on the bookShopService bean and add the result list as attribute books to the flowScope:

```
<evaluate expression="bookShopService.findAllBooks()" result="flowScope.books" />
```

If your method returns a value that needs type conversion, you can specify the desired type in the `result-type` attribute as shown following. Spring Web Flow's `DefaultConversionService` adds four `Converter` implementations by default: `TextToClass`, `TextToBoolean`, `TextToLabeledEnum`, and `TextToNumber`. We think their names are self-explanatory.

```
<evaluate expression="bookShopService.findBookById(bookId)" result="flowScope.book"
      result-type="com.apress.prospring2.ch18.sample.Book
```

On the other hand, you will need the EL delimiters to specify expressions that are only to be resolved, like the `locale` attribute of the `requestContext` in this view:

```
<view-state id="index" view="index_${requestContext.locale}.jsp" />
```

There are also several variables that are managed by Spring Web Flow that you can access from within a flow. First, let's have a look at the different scopes and contexts Spring Web Flow provides.

requestParameters

With the help of `requestParameters`, you can access all parameters transmitted in the incoming request:

```
<set name="flowScope.bookId" value="requestParameters.bookId" type="long" />
```

requestScope

The `requestScope` variable allows for setting attributes in the request scope. The request scope exists for as long as the flow handles the request. It gets created when the flow is called and is destroyed when the flow has responded.

```
<set name="requestScope.bookId" value="requestParameters.bookId" type="long" />
```

viewScope

To assign variables for a view, you can use the `viewScope` variable. Since the view scope's life span lasts from when a view state enters until the view state exits, it can't be referenced outside of that view state.

```
<view-state id="list" view="shop/list">
    <on-render>
      <evaluate expression="bookShopService.findAllBooks()"
            result="viewScope.books" />
    </on-render>
    [...]
</view-state>
```

Usage of the following EL variables is the same as shown in the earlier examples. Hence, we won't give any further examples unless there is a good reason.

flashScope

Spring Web Flow supports the concept of a flash scope. While the request scope only exists for the duration of a request, the flash scope is defined to store its values for a request and the subsequent request. After the second request has been handled, the flash scope is automatically cleared.

This scope was introduced to solve a common problem in web applications (which we'll describe further in the "Problem Solver" section later in this chapter). Generally, when an application processes a request and returns with a redirect response, the client will issue a new request to retrieve the resource (see Figure 18-10). Sometimes, however, some of the parameters in the initial request are needed by the handler of the redirect request. This is the gap between request scope and session scope that flash scope fills.

Spring Web Flow stores flash variables in `flashScope`. The flash scope exists for as long as the flow is alive but gets cleared after each view rendering. This is due to Spring Web Flow's `alwaysRedirectOnPause` property, which defaults to `true`. This property configures Spring Web Flow to always issue a redirect to render a view. Every user request is ultimately served by two requests.

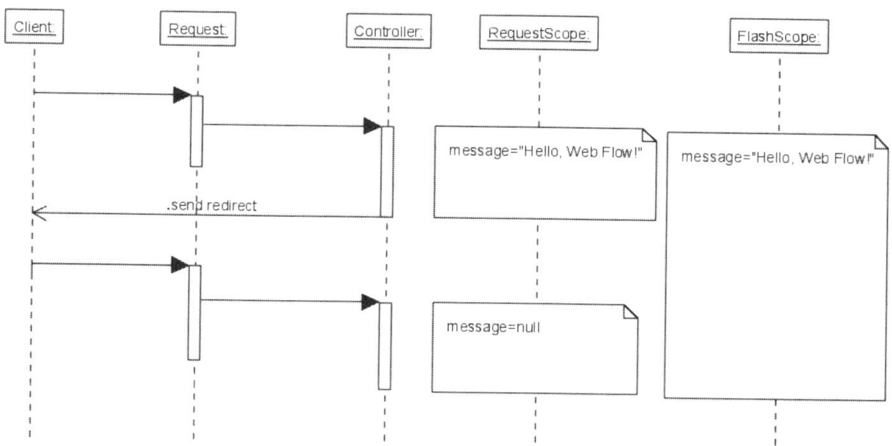

Figure 18-10. *Flash scope life cycle*

flowScope

For variables that are needed throughout the execution of a flow, you can use the flow scope. You gain access to it via the `flowScope` variable. Flow scope exists from when a flow is started until it ends.

conversationScope

The conversation scope exists for the length of a user–web-site conversation. It is allocated when a top-level flow is started and destroyed when it ends. All subflows spawned by a top-level flow also have access to variables in this scope via the `conversationScope` variable.

Figure 18-11 should help visualize the lifetimes of the different scopes. When you set a variable into one of the scopes, you should address it with this scope when you retrieve it. If no scope is specified, Spring Web Flow will try each scope individually to resolve it. The scopes are searched in order of their lifetimes, starting with the most short-lived one: `requestScope`, `flashScope`, `flowScope`, and then `conversationScope`.

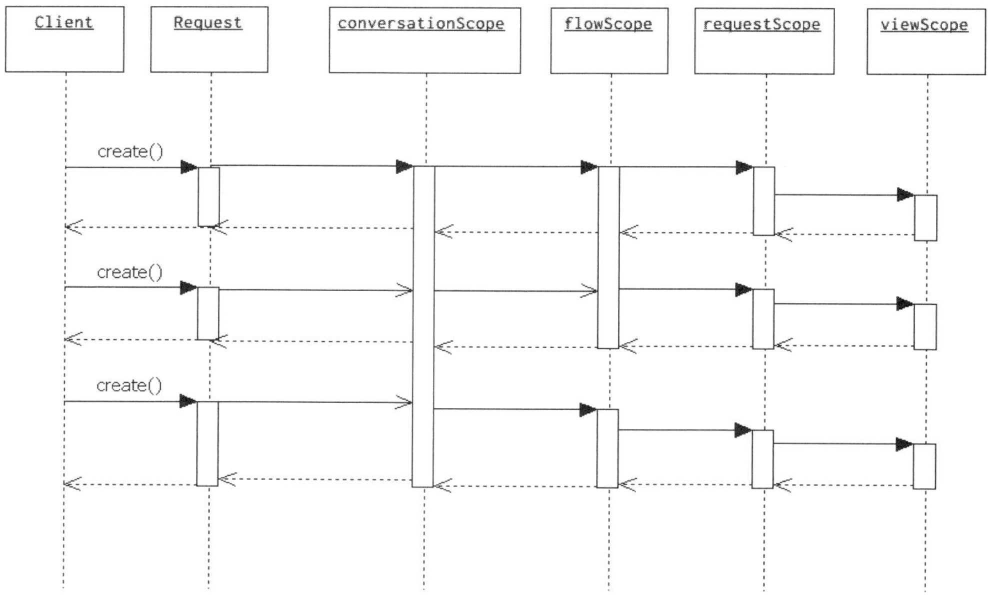

Figure 18-11. *Scopes in Spring Web Flow*

Table 18-4 gives a summary of the rest of Spring Web Flow's special EL variables.

Table 18-4. *Spring Web Flow EL Variables*

Variable	Description
`flowRequestContext`	This context variable gives you access to the current flow request represented by an instance of `RequestContext`. This includes the request locale and theme, as well as error and message resources, through a reference to the `WebApplicationContext`.
`flowExecutionContext`	An instance of `FlowExecutionContext` holds a representation of the current flow execution state. Retrievable details are, for example, the underlying flow definition or an indication of whether a flow has started, is active, or has ended.
`externalContext`	The external context represents a client call into the flow. The `ExternalContext` interface defines methods giving you, among other things, access to several request and session attribute maps.
`currentEvent`	This variable lets you access data on the current `Event`.
`currentUser`	For authentication purposes, a `Principal` object can be held in this EL variable.
`messageContext`	This variable is used to store and retrieve messages that should be displayed, such as flow execution messages or error messages. The supported methods are defined in the `MessageContext` interface.
`resourceBundle`	With the `resourceBundle` variable, you can easily do things like look up localized messages.

Variable	Description
flowExecutionUrl	This variable contains the context-relative URL to the current flow execution's view state. You need it, for example, to let the user post back data to the application.
flowExecutionKey	This variable contains the identifier of the current flow execution snapshot. You can use it to address certain flow execution snapshots directly.

Implementing Actions

So far, we've mainly covered how to get the user-facing page flow up and running, more or less ignoring that web applications mainly display dynamically generated content and process and store transmitted data. Being a controller framework, Spring Web Flow is also able to call underlying service layer code using evaluate expressions and actions.

Following the concept of an FSM, Spring Web Flow provides for calling actions at various points in the flow life cycle. Regardless of when an action is invoked, the definition syntax is always the same: all actions are declared with the `<evaluate>` element. The most basic form to declare it is just to define it with an expression to evaluate. This expression can be a method on a variable the flow has access to and includes Spring beans in the application context.

```
<evaluate expression="bookStoreService.saveOrder()" />
```

In case the invoked method returns a result that you want to make available to the whole flow, you can assign it to a flow scope variable by using the `result` attribute:

```
<evaluate expression=" bookStoreService.findAllBooks" result="flowScope.books" />
```

A last attribute of the `<evaluate>` element makes it possible to specify the type of the result in case it's not a simple list as in our example:

```
<evaluate expression=" bookStoreService.findBookById" result="flowScope.book"
       result-type="com.apress.prospring2.ch18.sample.Book" />
```

Actions can be invoked at various points in a flow. For one, they can be invoked when the flow starts or ends, as shown in Listing 18-9.

Listing 18-9. *Invoking an Action on Flow Start or End*

```
<?xml version="1.0" encoding="UTF-8"?>
<flow xmlns="http://www.springframework.org/schema/webflow"
    xmlns:xsi="http://www.w3.org/2001/XMLSchema-instance"
    xsi:schemaLocation="http://www.springframework.org/schema/webflow
        http://www.springframework.org/schema/webflow/spring-webflow-2.0.xsd">

  <on-start>
    <evaluate expression="exampleService.onStart()" />
  </on-start>

  [...]

  <on-end>
    <evaluate expression="exampleService.onEnd()" />
  </on-end>

</flow>
```

They can also be invoked when a state is entered or left, as in Listing 18-10.

Listing 18-10. *Invoking an Action on State Entry or Exit*

```
<view-state id="showPage">
  <on-entry>
    <evaluate expression="exampleService.onEntry()" />
  </on-entry>
  <on-exit>
    <evaluate expression="exampleService.onExit()" />
  </on-exit>
</view-state>
```

They can be invoked when a view is rendered, as in Listing 18-11.

Listing 18-11. *Invoking an Action When a View is Rendered*

```
<view-state id="list" view="shop/list">
  <on-render>
    <evaluate expression="service.findAllBooks()" result="requestScope.books" />
  </on-render>
</view-state>
```

And they can be invoked when a transition is executed, as in Listing 18-12.

Listing 18-12. *Invoking an Action on a Transition*

```
<view-state id="list" view="shop/list">
  <on-render>
    <evaluate expression="service.findAllBooks()" result="requestScope.books" />
  </on-render>
  <transition on="view" to="viewBook">
    <set name="requestScope.id" value="requestParameters.bookId" type="long" />
    <evaluate expression="service.findBookById(requestScope.id)"
            result="flowScope.book" />
  </transition>
</view-state>
```

Model Data Binding

In the previous chapter, we talked you through a series of Spring MVC controller implementations. One of them was the `AbstractFormController`, which can automatically bind request parameters to a POJO command object. The same functionality is also available in Spring Web Flow.

A model object for a view to bind request parameters to is declared with the `model` attribute of the `<view-state>` element. If you have a page in the flow where a user should, for example, enter address details, you could have an `Address` POJO as in Listing 18-13 with address detail attributes and define this class to be used as the data binding model.

Listing 18-13. *Address POJO*

```
package com.apress.prospring2.ch18.sample;

import java.io.Serializable;

public class Address implements Serializable {
```

```
    private static final long serialVersionUID = 100L;

    private String address1;
    private String address2;
    private String postcode;
    private String town;

    /** getters and setters left out for brevity **/
}
```

Listing 18-14 gives the flow definition of the very basic `address` flow. This flow consists of two pages. The first page will show four input fields to enter address details. After the Next button is clicked, a second page will simply print these entries out.

Listing 18-14. *address.xml Flow State Definition*

```
<?xml version="1.0" encoding="UTF-8"?>
<flow xmlns="http://www.springframework.org/schema/webflow"
    xmlns:xsi="http://www.w3.org/2001/XMLSchema-instance"
    xsi:schemaLocation="http://www.springframework.org/schema/webflow
        http://www.springframework.org/schema/webflow/spring-webflow-2.0.xsd">

    <var name="address" class="com.apress.prospring2.ch18.sample.Address" />

    <view-state id="start" view="address/shippingAddress" model="address">
      <transition on="next" to="confirm" />
    </view-state>

    <view-state id="confirm" view="address/showAddress" />

</flow>
```

At the beginning, we create the flow variable `address`, which is an instance of `Address`. By setting this variable as a model attribute in the start view, we tell Spring Web Flow to use this object for data binding. This allows us to implement a simple submit form by using the convenient `spring-form` tags (Listing 18-15).

Listing 18-15. *Simple Address Details Input Form*

```
<%@ taglib prefix="form" uri="http://www.springframework.org/tags/form" %>
<!DOCTYPE html PUBLIC "-//W3C//DTD HTML 4.01 Transitional//EN"
"http://www.w3.org/TR/html4/loose.dtd">
<html>
<head>
<title>Web Flow Book Shop</title>
</head>
<body>
  <h1>Shipping Address Details</h1>
  <p>Please enter your shipping address details:</p>
    <form:form id="shippingDetails" modelAttribute="address">
      <table>
      <tr>
       <td>Address 1: </td>
       <td><form:input path="address1"/></td>
      </tr>
```

```
      <tr>
        <td>Address 2: </td>
        <td><form:input path="address2"/></td>
      </tr>
      <tr>
        <td>Post code: </td>
        <td><form:input path="postcode"/></td>
      </tr>
      <tr>
        <td>Town/City: </td>
        <td><form:input path="town"/></td>
      </tr>
      <tr>
        <td><input type="submit" name="_eventId" value="next"></td>
      </tr>
    </table>
  </form:form>
</body>
</html>
```

The `confirm` event submitted by clicking the button triggers the transition to the second view state, which is called `confirm`. In this transition, the posted parameters are automatically bound to the `address` object in flow scope. When, afterward, the `confirm` state is rendered, the EL expressions are resolved against the objects in the scopes. That allows us to print them out, as shown in Listing 18-16.

Listing 18-16. *Display Details Page Fragment*

```
[...]
<table>
  <tr>
    <td>Address 1: </td>
    <td>${address.address1}</td>
  </tr>
  <tr>
    <td>Address 2: </td>
    <td>${address.address2}</td>
  </tr>
  <tr>
    <td>Post code: </td>
    <td>${address.postcode}</td>
  </tr>
  <tr>
    <td>Town/City: </td>
    <td>${address.town}</td>
  </tr>
</table>
[...]
```

If for any reason you don't want to bind the input parameters on a certain event, you can declare this on the transition. You just have to add `bind="false"`.

```
<view-state id="start" view="address/shippingAddress" model="order">
    <transition on="next" to="confirm" />
    <transition on="cancel" to="end" bind="false" />
</view-state>
```

Usually, all forms on web sites have one or more mandatory input fields. If a submitted form is lacking parameters that are essential for further request processing, it makes sense to check for these parameters as soon as possible. As you've seen in the last chapter, you can make use of `Validator` implementations to validate the submitted command object. The same is also possible in Spring Web Flow.

You can validate your model programmatically in two ways. The first is to define `validate` methods on the model. The method signatures have to follow this convention:

```
public void validate${viewStateId}(MessageContext context)
```

To enable postcode validation on our address in the example, we can add the `validateStart` method to the `Address` class:

```
public void validateStart(MessageContext context) {
    if(!StringUtils.hasLength(postcode)) {
        context.addMessage(new MessageBuilder().error().source("postcode").
        defaultText("Postcode is missing.").build());
    }
}
```

If the postcode is `null` or empty, an error message is added to the message context marking that the validation has failed. Referring back to the concept of FSMs, a validation method basically acts as the guard for a transition. If the guard expression doesn't evaluate to `true`, the transition isn't executed, and the source state is rerendered. In our example, this means that if the address isn't validated successfully, the transition to the second page isn't executed, but the `start` state is reentered.

The other way to validate a model is by using validator classes. Method signatures in such a validator need to follow this convention:

```
public void validate${viewStateId}(<<Model object>>, MessageContext context)
```

To perform the same validation of the `Address` object with this approach, all we need to do is create an `AddressValidator` class, as shown in Listing 18-17, and comment out the `validate` method in the `Address` class.

Listing 18-17. *AddressValidator Class*

```
@Component
public class AddressValidator {

    public void validateStart(Address address, MessageContext context) {
        if(!StringUtils.hasLength(address.getPostcode())) {
            context.addMessage(new MessageBuilder().error().source("postcode")
                    .defaultText("Enter Postcode").build());
        }
    }
}
```

We add this bean to the application context by marking it with the `@Component` annotation. If in your project you haven't already done so, you'd have to add the `<context:component-scan />` element to your application context to let the bean be picked up on context initialization, as shown in Listing 18-18.

Listing 18-18. *Enabling Annotations*

```
<?xml version="1.0" encoding="UTF-8"?>
<beans xmlns="http://www.springframework.org/schema/beans"
    xmlns:xsi="http://www.w3.org/2001/XMLSchema-instance"
    xmlns:context="http://www.springframework.org/schema/context"
    [...]
```

```
    xsi:schemaLocation="
           http://www.springframework.org/schema/beans
           http://www.springframework.org/schema/beans/spring-beans-2.5.xsd
           http://www.springframework.org/schema/context
           http://www.springframework.org/schema/context/spring-context-2.5.xsd
           [...]">

    <context:component-scan base-package="com.apress.prospring2"/>

    [...]

</beans>
```

Partial Rendering of Views

Spring Web Flow also allows you to react to user events by rerendering only certain parts of a web site. All you need to do is to specify a transition matching the user event and the needed actions. In the following example, we have a transition for a `children` event. If this event occurs, the `findAllByCategory` of the `bookShopService` bean is invoked and the returned result is added as the attribute `books` to `viewScope`.

With the `<render>` element, you specify the IDs of the HTML elements you wish to rerender (see Listing 18-19). Multiple IDs need to be comma separated.

Listing 18-19. *Partial Rerendering of Views*

```
<view-state id="list" view="shop/list">
  <on-render>
    <evaluate expression="bookShopService.findAllBooks()"
        result="flowScope.books" />
  </on-render>

  <transition on="all" to="list" />
    <transition on="children">
        <evaluate expression="bookShopService.findAllByCategory(currentEvent)"
                result="viewScope.books" />
        <render fragments="bookTable" />
    </transition>
     <transition on="computer">
        <evaluate expression="bookShopService.findAllByCategory(currentEvent)"
                result="viewScope.books" />
        <render fragments="bookList" />
    </transition>
</view-state>
```

Mapping Flow Input and Output Parameters

All flows, whether top-level flows or subflows, can be passed input parameters and can pass back output parameters. This is particularly useful if a flow needs to operate on request-specific data or a subflow is used to create an object that has to be passed back to the initiating flow.

To define input parameters, use the `<input>` element at the beginning of the flow definition. In the basic version, you only need to specify the name and value of the argument. If the expression language parser can evaluate the value, the name is used as the key when the argument is put into the flow scope.

```
<input name="book" value="flowScope.book" />
```

If you add the attribute `required="true"`, a `FlowInputMapperException` will be raised if the value couldn't be found when the subflow state was entered.

```
<input name="book" value="flowScope.book" required="true" />
```

An extract of a flow definition could look like the code fragment in Listing 18-20. From a `viewBook` state, the `buy` event will trigger a transition to the `checkout` subflow. We pass the `book` object of the higher-level flow into the subflow.

Listing 18-20. *Parent Flow Passing Input to Subflow*

```
<view-state id="viewBook" view="shop/view">
    <transition on="buy" to="startCheckout" />
</view-state>

<subflow-state id="startCheckout" subflow="checkout">
    <input name="book" />
    <transition on="success" to="orderConfirmed" />
</subflow-state>

<end-state id="orderConfirmed" />
```

Flow output parameters are defined with the `<output>` element of the end state. The example checkout flow might want to return a Boolean value or another object as a checkout result to report back to the higher-level flow.

```
<end-state id="orderCheckedOut">
    <output name="checkoutResult" />
</end-state>
```

The output result can also be retrieved through an expression:

```
<output name="checkoutResult" value="order.id" />
```

Using Subflows

As we've just discussed, a flow can call another flow and start it as a subflow. Execution of the parent flow is put on hold until the subflow returns. The subflow returns a specific outcome as an event to the parent flow. This event triggers the next transition in the resumed parent flow.

Subflows are called with the `<subflow-state>` element shown following:

```
<subflow-state id="enterShop" subflow="shop">
    <transition on="orderConfirmed" to="thankYou">
        <evaluate expression="bookShopService.saveOrder(currentEvent.order)" />
    </transition>
      <transition on="orderCancelled" to="start" />
</subflow-state>
```

In this case, the parent flow will call the `shop` flow as a subflow. If the `shop` flow returns with an `orderConfirmed` event, the order is saved and the parent flow transitions to a `thankYou` state. If the subflow returns with an `orderCancelled` event, the parent flow will move to the `start` state.

As with regular flows, you can pass input parameters into the subflow. To do so, declare the parameters with the `<input>` element, in the subflow state (Listing 18-21) as well as in the subflow definition (Listing 18-22).

Listing 18-21. *Subflow State in Higher-Level Flow Definition*

```
<?xml version="1.0" encoding="UTF-8"?>
<flow xmlns="http://www.springframework.org/schema/webflow"
    xmlns:xsi="http://www.w3.org/2001/XMLSchema-instance"
    xsi:schemaLocation="http://www.springframework.org/schema/webflow
        http://www.springframework.org/schema/webflow/spring-webflow-2.0.xsd">

    [...]

    <subflow-state id="enterShop" subflow="shop">
        <input name="bookId" />
        <transition on="orderConfirmed" to="thankYou" />
        <transition on="orderCancelled" to="start" />
    </subflow-state>

    [...]

</flow>
```

Listing 18-22. *Subflow Flow Definition*

```
<?xml version="1.0" encoding="UTF-8"?>
<flow xmlns="http://www.springframework.org/schema/webflow"
    xmlns:xsi="http://www.w3.org/2001/XMLSchema-instance"
    xsi:schemaLocation="http://www.springframework.org/schema/webflow
        http://www.springframework.org/schema/webflow/spring-webflow-2.0.xsd">

    [...]
    <input name="bookId" value="flowScope.bookId" required="true"/>
    [...]

</flow>
```

Flow definitions encapsulate business processes in little modules. If you have two or more business processes that have a sequence of steps in common, you can define the common steps as a separate flow that can then be reused as subflows in the higher-level business process flows.

Spring Web Flow Behind the Scenes

Architecturally, Spring Web Flow is separated into three main components that each have their own responsibilities, and two convenience components for configuration and testing, as Figure 18-12 illustrates.

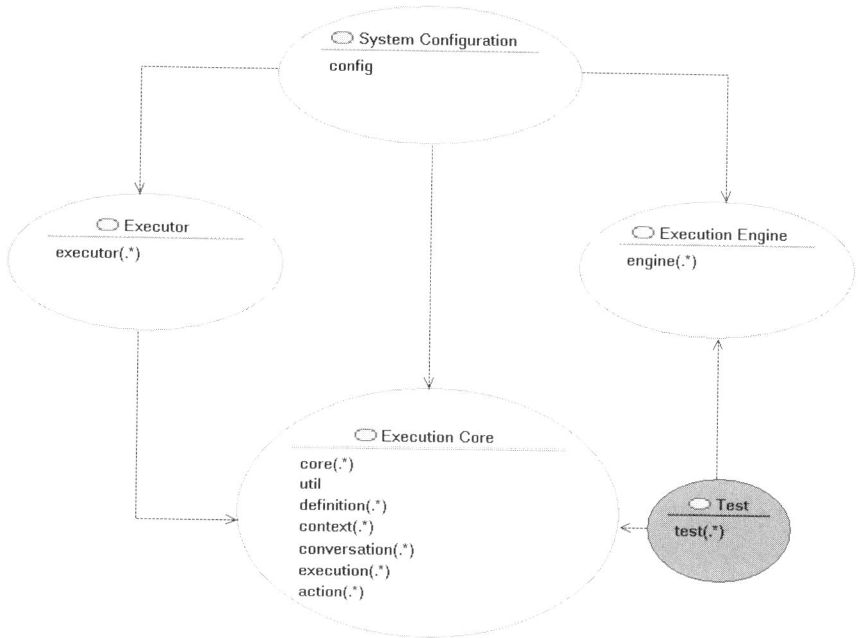

Figure 18-12. *Spring Web Flow architectural components*

So far in this chapter, we've looked at the elements of the execution core component: the definition of flows, states, transitions, and so forth, and how to configure them. We'll now take a look at the other two components, namely the executor and the execution engine component.

If the execution core gives you the templates for elements to construct a flow, the execution engine gives you the building materials, tools, and construction plan to instantiate and execute a flow definition. The responsibility of the executor is to drive and coordinate these flow executions.

Flow Execution Architecture

We just explained the three core flow execution components and what their responsibilities are. This section will further explain how these components interact with each other.

Figure 18-13 shows a simple activity diagram that should help you visualize the steps, especially the functions that the flow executor performs.

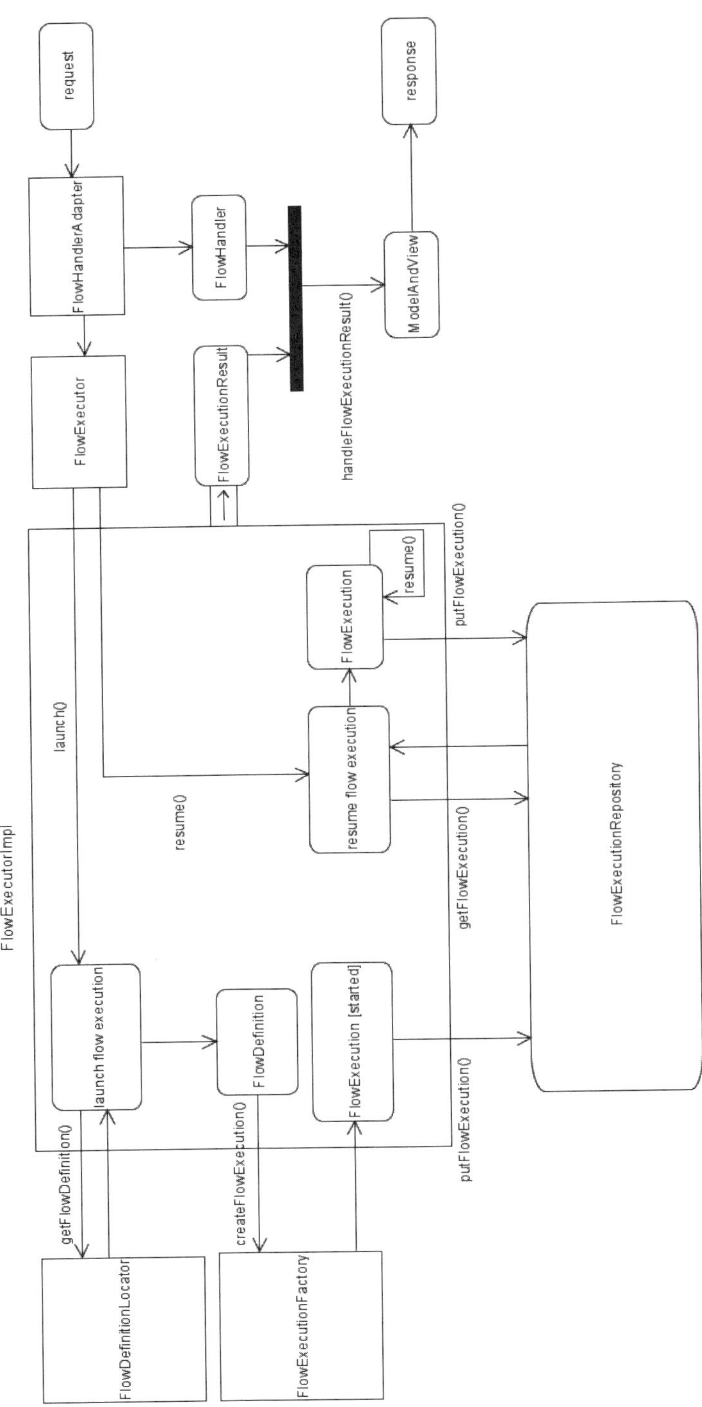

Figure 18-13. *Flow execution*

When a request comes in, the `DispatcherServlet` will map it to a `FlowHandler` via the `FlowHandlerAdapter`. The `FlowHandlerAdapter` checks for flow execution parameters in the request. If no flow execution details are found, the `FlowExecutor` is called to launch a new `FlowExecution`. For this process, the `FlowExecutor` retrieves the `FlowDefinition` from the `FlowDefinitionLocator` (flow repository). The `FlowDefinition` is then passed to the `FlowExecutionFactory` as a template for a `FlowExecution`. Before the `FlowExecutionResult` is calculated, the newly created `FlowExecution` is stored in the `FlowExecutionRepository`.

In the case where flow execution parameters are found in the incoming request, the parameters are used to retrieve the `FlowExecution` from the repository. Execution of this `FlowExecution` is then resumed and executed. The `FlowExecution`'s new state is then stored as a new entry in the flow execution repository before the `FlowExecutionResult` is calculated.

The `FlowExecutionResult` object that the `FlowExecutor` passed back to the `FlowHandlerAdapter` is then used together with a `FlowHandler` in the `handleFlowExecutionResult` method. This method eventually returns a `ModelAndView` object, and the response can then be rendered.

Flow Executor

As illustrated in Figure 18-13, the flow executor is the central component of Spring Web Flow responsible for handling all aspects related to the execution of flow definitions. The `FlowExecutor` interface exposes only two methods: `launchExecution` and `resumeExecution`. This abstraction successfully hides the internal complexity of the flow execution life cycle: creating and launching new flow executions and resuming already existing flow executions. Behind the scenes, the default implementation `FlowExecutorImpl` has three helpers in the form of properties to be set (see Table 18-5).

Table 18-5. *FlowExecutorImpl Properties*

Property Type	Description	Default
`definitionLocator`	`FlowDefinitionLocator`	The responsibility of the `definitionLocator` is to retrieve flow definitions by ID. The `FlowDefinitionLocator` interface is extended by the `FlowDefinitionRegistry` interface, and the default `FlowDefinitionRegistryImpl` implementation holds all flow definitions we register in the application context.
`executionFactory`	`FlowExecutionFactory`	The `executionFactory` constructs and assembles `FlowExecution` instances from given `FlowDefinition` instances. It is also responsible for registering listeners with the constructed flow execution.
`executionRepository`	`FlowExecutionRepository`	The `executionRepository` manages the persistence of flow executions. It is responsible for storing, restoring, and removing flow executions in or from the repository. Each `FlowExecution` object in the repository represents the state of a flow at a single point in time, and is indexed under its unique `flowExecutionKey`, allowing the `executionRepository` to retrieve it easily, hence restoring the state of a flow from a different point in time.

On the following pages, we'll have a closer look at these interfaces and their default implementations, starting with the flow definition registry.

Flow Definition Registry

To make your flow definitions eligible for execution, you need to register them with a flow definition registry. As you've seen in the "Hello, Web Flow!" application, this is done via the `<webflow:flow-registry>` element in the application context. You can specify individual flow definitions using the child element `<webflow:flow-location path=". . ." />`. By setting the `id` attribute on this element, you can override the filename-equals-flow-ID convention. For example, the flow defined in `myFlow.xml` can have the ID `myId` instead of the default ID of `myFlow`. Multiple flow definitions can be added at the same time by specifying a directory or file name pattern within `<webflow:flow-location-pattern value=". . ." />`. The two `<flow-location/>` child elements are not mutually exclusive and can be used together.

```
<webflow:flow-registry id="flowRegistry">
    <webflow:flow-location path="/WEB-INF/myFlowDirectory/singleFlow.xml" />
    <webflow:flow-location path="/WEB-INF/otherDirectory/myFlow.xml" id="myId" />
    <webflow:flow-location-pattern value="/WEB-INF/otherFlows/**/*.xml" />
</webflow:flow-registry>
```

A declaration in this form uses the default flow builder service implementations. These flow builder services are hooks into Spring Web Flow's flow builder, allowing you to customize services like `conversionService`, `formatterRegistry`, `expressionParser`, and `viewFactoryCreator`. The following is a sample configuration of custom flow builder services:

```
<webflow:flow-registry id="flowRegistry"
        flow-builder-services=" flowBuilderServices ">

<webflow:flow-builder-services id="flowBuilderServices"
        conversion-service="conversionService"
        formatter-registry="formatterRegistry"
        expression-parser="expressionParser"
        view-factory-creator="viewFactoryCreator" />

<bean id="conversionService" class="..." />

<bean id="formatterRegistry" class="..." />

<bean id="expressionParser" class="..." />

<bean id="viewFactoryCreator" class="..." />
```

conversionService

You came across the `ConversionService` before in the "Expression Languages and Scopes" section. During flow execution, the `Converters` defined on the `ConversionService` are used to convert one object type into another. As mentioned previously, the default implementation `DefaultConversionService` is configured with four default `Converter` implementations: `TextToClass`, `TextToBoolean`, `TextToLabeledEnum`, and `TextToNumber`. In case you need your own custom object conversion behavior instead of or in addition to these four standard converters, Spring Web Flow allows for easy extension. We'll quickly show how to add a converter for our custom class `FlightNumber`. We'll start with the `FlightNumber` class shown in Listing 18-23.

Listing 18-23. *FlightNumber Class*

```
public class FlightNumber {

    private String carrier;
    private Integer number;
```

```
    /** getters and setters ommitted for brevity **/
}.
```

The next step is to create our TextToFlightNumber converter by implementing the three methods the Converter interface defines (see Listing 18-24).

Listing 18-24. *TextToFlightNumber Converter*

```
public class TextToFlightNumber implements Converter {

    public Object convert(Object source, Class targetClass, Object context)
            throws ConversionException {
        /** conversion code **/
    }

    public Class[] getSourceClasses() {
        return new Class[] { String.class };
    }

    public Class[] getTargetClasses() {
        return new Class[] { FlightNumber.class };
    }
}
```

The next step will be to implement our own ConversionService. One possibility is to simply extend the DefaultConversionService and override its protected addDefaultConverters method, as shown in Listing 18-25.

Listing 18-25. *Extending DefaultConversionService*

```
public class MyConversionService extends DefaultConversionService {
    @Override
    protected void addDefaultConverters() {
        super.addDefaultConverters();
        addConverter(new TextToFlightNumber());
    }
}.
```

The last step is to register the MyConversionService with the flow builder services (see Listing 18-26).

Listing 18-26. *Register MyConversionService*

```
<webflow:flow-builder-services id="builderService"
        conversion-service="myService" />

<bean id="myService" class="com.apress.prospring2.ch18.MyConversionService"/>
```

Using the FormatterRegistry

The FormatterRegistry controls a list of Formatter implementations that are registered with it. Unlike Converters, which can perform conversion from any defined source class to any defined target class, Formatters only convert from String to Object and vice versa. Formatter implementations are used by views to control the string representations of object types. The default FormatterRegistry implementation DefaultFormatterRegistry registers Formatter instances for the number, Boolean, and date object types on initialization.

Listing 18-27 shows a Formatter implementation for our FlightNumber class.

Listing 18-27. *FlightNumberFormatter Class*

```
public class FlightNumberFormatter implements Formatter {
    public String format(Object object) throws IllegalArgumentException {
        FlightNumber fn = (FlightNumber)object;
        return fn.getCarrier() + fn.getNumber();
}

    public Object parse(String formattedString) throws InvalidFormatException {
        FlightNumber fn = new FlightNumber();
        /** omitted for brevity **/
        return fn;
    }
}
```

Again, we simply extend the default implementation DefaultFormatterRegistry and override the registerDefaultFormatters method (see Listing 18-28).

Listing 18-28. *MyFormatterRegistry Class*

```
public class MyFormatterRegistry extends DefaultFormatterRegistry {
    @Override
    protected void registerDefaultFormatters() {
        super.registerDefaultFormatters();
        registerFormatter(FlightNumber.class, new FlightNumberFormatter());
    }
}
```

To configure the flow builder services to use this implementation, we'll have to change our context file (Listing 18-29).

Listing 18-29. *Registering MyFormatterRegistry*

```
<webflow:flow-builder-services id="builderService"
        formatter-registry="myRegistry" />

<bean id="myRegistry" class="com.apress.prospring2.ch18.MyFormatterRegistry"/>
```

expressionParser

The expressionParser allows you to customize expression parsing in your Spring Web Flow applications. Spring Web Flow currently supports two EL libraries: JBoss (the default) and OGNL.

viewFactoryCreator

You can use the viewFactoryCreator attribute to enable a custom ViewFactoryCreator. There are currently two implementations of this interface shipped with Spring Web Flow: the JsfViewFactoryCreator, which creates JsfViewFactory instances for integration with JSF; and the MvcViewFactoryCreator, which creates MvcViewFactories for integration with Spring MVC.

By default, the MvcViewFactoryCreator creates view factories that resolve their views as resources relative to the flow's working directory. We're going to show you how you can customize the MvcViewFactoryCreator to resolve views via Spring MVC's ViewResolver infrastructure in the section on Integration with Spring MVC.

Flow Execution Repository

The FlowExecutionRepository interface is the subsystem interface responsible for saving and restoring flow executions. Each flow execution represents a state of an active flow definition. This interface completely hides the way the execution state is actually stored.

Spring Web Flow's default implementation is the DefaultFlowExecutionRepository, which extends the AbstractSnapshottingFlowExecutionRepository class. This repository stores snapshots of flow executions. A *snapshot* is a copy of a flow execution at a specific moment. Each snapshot is assigned a unique execution key under which it is indexed in the repository. With their unique IDs, snapshots can be restored and continued. This is particularly useful if you need to provide full support of the browser navigation buttons. When the Back button is clicked, you can just retrieve the previous snapshot from the repository.

The DefaultFlowExecutionRepository holds references to helper properties, as summarized in Table 18-6.

Table 18-6. *DefaultFlowExecutionRepository Properties*

Property Type	Description
ConversationManager	This is a service for managing conversations. This interface defines three methods, which handle the creation of a conversation (beginConversation), the retrieval of a conversation by ID (getConversation), and the parsing of the string representation of an encoded conversation ID into its object form of ConversationId (parseConversationId).
SessionBindingConversationManager	This interface uses the session as a conversation container.
FlowExecutionStateRestorer	This interface defines one method, restore, to restore the transient flow execution state.
FlowExecutionImplStateRestorer	This interface restores flow executions as instances of FlowExecutionImpl.
FlowExecutionSnapshotFactory	This interface specifies the contract for FlowExecutionSnaphot implementations. It defines two methods that both return a FlowExecutionSnapshot: createSnaphot(FlowExecution) and restoreSnapshot(byte[]).
SerializedFlowExecutionSnapshotFactory	This interface creates and restores snapshots from flow executions by serializing or deserializing them to or from byte arrays.

The ConversationManager handles the persistence of conversations. The default implementation SessionBindingConversationManager stores conversations in the HttpSession. By creating your own implementation, you can hook in a different approach to persist conversations.

The DefaultFlowExecutionRepository defines two parameters for performance tuning, as shown following:

```
<webflow:flow-executor id="flowExecutor" flow-registry="flowRegistry">
    <webflow:flow-execution-repository max-executions="5"
        max-execution-snapshots="9"/>
</webflow:flow-executor>
```

Use the max-executions attribute to put an upper limit on the number of flow executions stored per user session. The max-execution-snapshots attribute lets you further limit the number of snapshots per flow execution to be kept as history in storage.

Integration with Spring MVC

This section is going to show you how to integrate Spring Web Flow into a Spring MVC environment. To fully demonstrate the integration between Web Flow and Spring MVC, we will extend the "Hello, Web Flow!" application.

Flow Handling

When we went through the configuration of the "Hello, Web Flow!" example, we explained that Spring Web Flow integrates with the Spring MVC `DispatcherServlet` by registering the `FlowHandlerAdapter`. All you need do is add the following bean declaration to the application context:

```
<bean class="org.springframework.webflow.mvc.servlet.FlowHandlerAdapter">
    <constructor-arg ref="flowExecutor" />
</bean>
```

Back then, we also promised to cover this class and its responsibilities in more detail later—so here we go. The `FlowHandlerAdapter` encapsulates the chain of command associated with executing flows; that is launching and resuming flows, as well as handling the outcomes of these two commands. Launching and resuming flows are activities that get delegated to the `launchExecution` and `resumeExecution` methods of the `flowExecutor` property set on construction of the `FlowHandlerAdapter`. These two methods return a `FlowExecutionResult` object. Together with the original request and response objects, the application context, and the correct `FlowHandler` implementation, this result object is then passed on to the `handleFlowExecutionResult` method, which completes handling of the request and eventually returns a `ModelAndView` object for rendering.

A `FlowHandler` implementation is a helper utility to access a single flow definition in your application. If you do not want to fully implement the `FlowHandler` interface yourself, you can use the convenience `AbstractFlowHandler` superclass. It simply returns `null` for all defined operations, and since (despite its name) it is not abstract, your subclasses are not forced to override methods other than the ones they need.

Using the `FlowHandlerAdapter`-based integration approach, you will need to create one `FlowHandler` per flow. If many of your flows don't require specific handling, but follow the default rules, creating a class for each can quickly feel a bit excessive.

A different approach to integrating Spring Web Flow with Spring MVC is to use a `FlowController`. A `FlowController` is an adapter between a Spring MVC `Controller` and the Spring Web Flow engine. It extends Spring MVC's `AbstractController` and has the same attributes for interacting with Spring Web Flow as the `FlowHandlerAdapter`: a reference to a `FlowExecutor`, a reference to a `FlowUrlHandler`, and a reference to an `AjaxHandler`.

It performs the same chain of command, implementing `AbtractController`'s `protected ModelAndView handleRequestInternal(HttpServletRequest request, HttpServletResponse response)` as the `FlowHandlerAdapter` in its `public ModelAndView handle(HttpServletRequest request, HttpServletResponse response, Object handler)` method. For simple cases, consider therefore mapping a typical `FlowController` as in Listing 18-30 as a handler for multiple flows.

Listing 18-30. *FlowController and URL Mapping*

```
<bean id="flowController"
        class="org.springframework.webflow.mvc.servlet.FlowController">
    <property name="flowExecutor" ref="flowExecutor" />
</bean>
```

```
<bean id="publicUrlMappings"
        class="org.springframework.web.servlet.handler.SimpleUrlHandlerMapping">
    <property name="mappings">
      <value>
          /sampleApp.html=helloWorldFlowHandler
          /colours.html=flowController
          /address.html=flowController
      </value>
    </property>
</bean>
```

As you can also see from this example, Spring MVC controllers and Spring Web Flow flow handlers can be used together nicely.

View Resolving

Spring Web Flow 2.0 introduced a new convention for resolving views relative to the flow's working directory. An existing Spring MVC application, however, will probably already be using the Spring MVC ViewResolver infrastructure to resolve views. Spring Web Flow allows you to make use of the existing infrastructure by registering the existing viewResolver instances with an MvcViewFactoryCreator:

```
<webflow:flow-registry id="flowRegistry" flow-builder-services="builderService">
    <webflow:flow-location-pattern value="/WEB-INF/flows/**/*.xml" />
</webflow:flow-registry>

<webflow:flow-builder-services id="builderService"
        view-factory-creator="myViewFactoryCreator" />

<bean id="myViewFactoryCreator"
        class="org.springframework.webflow.mvc.view.MvcViewFactoryCreator">
    <property name="viewResolvers" ref="internalJspViewResolver" />
</bean>

<bean id="internalJspViewResolver"
        class="org.springframework.web.servlet.view.InternalResourceViewResolver">
    <property name="prefix" value="/WEB-INF/views/" />
    <property name="suffix" value=".jsp" />
</bean>
```

This MvcViewFactoryCreator is used to customize the flow builder services that are registered with the flow registry by referencing it in the flow-builder-services attribute.

Securing Flows with Spring Security

Whatever the technology used in a web application, security is a concern that must be addressed. Security in web applications is about authenticating and authorizing users. Authentication is the process in which the user is prompted to prove that they are who they claim to be. Authorization is the subsequent process that decides if a user, once identified, should be allowed to do what she requests. Many web applications have to handle users who are granted different sets of permissions. A forum application, for example, usually categorizes users as administrators, moderators, registered users, or anonymous users. This is a typical role-based approach, since access to the web site and its functionality depends on the user's role. A web application needs to ensure that only duly authorized users can access sensitive parts of the application.

If you have been writing web applications with Spring MVC for a while, you have probably come across Spring Security (or Acegi Security System for Spring, as it was formerly known). It is a comprehensive solution to the requirement for integrating security features into Java EE–based applications. Spring Security supports a number of authentication mechanisms ranging from simple form-based authentication, through automatic "remember-me" authentication, to LDAP or CAS authentication. It also supports further security features such as channel security (to ensure requests only arrive via HTTPS) and JCaptcha to ensure the web site is interacting with a human being rather than a script.

This feature set not only extends what is offered in the servlet specification, but it also helps your application stay container-independent and hence more portable. In addition to the support you get out of the box, you can extend the feature set with custom implementations of the core interfaces.

You can use this Spring module to secure the paths in your Spring Web Flow application. On the following pages, we're going to briefly talk you through a simple integration example that shows the three steps to setting up Spring Security and configuring it once you have the necessary binaries.

It is beyond the scope of this book to explain all the Spring Security mechanisms and configurations in full. For further details and examples, please have a look at the Spring Security reference documentation available on the module's home page, at `http://static.springframework.org/spring-security/site/index.html`.

Step 1: Adding the SecurityFlowExecutionListener

Setting up Spring Security involves configuration in three places: the `web.xml` file, the application context, and the flow definition. The first step is to enable Spring Security within your web application. This is done by adding the following filter to the `web.xml` configuration:

```
<filter>
  <filter-name>springSecurityFilterChain</filter-name>
  <filter-class>org.springframework.web.filter.DelegatingFilterProxy</filter-class>
</filter>

<filter-mapping>
  <filter-name>springSecurityFilterChain</filter-name>
  <url-pattern>/*</url-pattern>
</filter-mapping>
```

This filter provides us with a hook for the Spring Security infrastructure. The next two steps handle the setup and configuration of this infrastructure.

Step 2: Basic Authentication and Authorization Handling

This step is going to show how authentication and authorization are set up.

The authentication process usually follows much the same pattern in any web application. You make a request to the web server, which decides that you've asked for a protected resource. The server then checks if you are already authorized. In the case you are not authorized, a response is sent indicating that you have to authenticate. Depending on the authentication mechanism defined, you are either redirected to a login form page or the browser tries to retrieve your identity in another way (Basic, cookie, etc.). After you provide your credentials, the server will check if they are valid and retry your initial request if validation was successful. If you have the right authorities to access the requested resource, it will be returned; otherwise, an HTTP 403 error will occur.

The decision to authenticate a user is made by Spring Security's `AuthenticationManager` with the help of `AuthenticationProvider` objects. The minimum configuration you need to define and configure an `AuthenticationManager` is to declare one or more `AuthenticationProvider` objects with the `<security:authentication-provider>` element, as shown in Listing 18-31.

Listing 18-31. *Spring Security AuthenticationProvider*

```
<security:authentication-provider user-service-ref="myUserDetailsService" />

<security:authentication-provider>
    <security:user-service>
        <security:user name="admin" password="admin" authorities="ROLE_ADMIN" />
        <security:user name="user" password="user" authorities="ROLE_USER" />
    </security:user-service>
</security:authentication-provider>
```

The AuthenticationProvider uses a UserDetailsService to access your user details in the data storage. This service can be a reference to your own implementation accessing a database, or an in-memory data storage with the <security:user-service> element. Listing 18-31 defined a user service providing the details for two users. This is a useful technique when you need to set up authentication quickly (e.g., when you're prototyping an application).

Also very useful during testing of an application is the TestingAuthenticationProvider, as it accepts any credentials. You can simply mark it with the <security:custom-authentication-provider/> element, and it will be automatically registered with the AuthenticationManager. Don't forget to take it out before going into production, though.

```
<bean id="authenticationProvider"
      class="org.springframework.security.providers.TestingAuthenticationProvider">
    <security:custom-authentication-provider/>
</bean>
```

By specifying an authentication mechanism like HTTP form login or Basic, we define how the user details should be retrieved. The following short line will fully configure simple HTTP form authentication:

```
<security:http auto-config="true" />
```

Behind the scenes, this is equivalent to the following configuration:

```
<security:http>
    <security:intercept-url pattern="/**" access="ROLE_USER" />
    <security:form-login />
    <security:anonymous />
    <security:http-basic />
    <security:logout />
    <security:remember-me />
<security:/http>
```

For our example, we're only interested in the first two child elements. For a description of other elements and their attributes, please refer to the Spring Security reference documentation.

The <security:intercept-url> element defines which URLs of the application require which access authorities. In this configuration, URLs can only be accessed from ROLE_USER authority holders. The second child element, <security:form-login />, specifies that we want to enable form-based authentication. In this basic form, Spring security will do all the login form setup work for us, including rendering a simple login page.

When authentication is requested, a default login screen will be rendered. If login is successful, the user's initial request is retried. To make use of a self-designed login screen, you will need to make a few changes to the configuration.

First add the login-page attribute to the <security:form-login> element:

```
<security:form-login login-page="/login.html" />
```

This attribute specifies the URL that handles rendering the login screen. It's the page a user gets redirected to if authentication is required. Since this is a URL that needs to be accessible by all users, including unauthenticated users, we'll need to add another `<security-intercept-url>` element. By setting `filters="none"`, we define that we don't want any security filters to be applied. Our final configuration will look like this:

```
<security:http auto-config="true">
    <security:intercept-url pattern="/login.html" filters="none" />
    <security:form-login login-page="/login.html" />
</security:http>
```

Patterns of URL interceptors are matched in order of declaration. Make sure you don't "hide" an interceptor behind another that has a more general pattern.

Step 3: Defining Security Rules in Flow Definitions

The final step is to mark a flow definition or flow definition element as requiring authentication. For this purpose, Spring Web Flow provides you with the `<secured>` element. When you add this element to a flow, state, or transition definition, only users with the correct access rights will be allowed to enter the flow or state or execute the transition. Which access requirements are needed is defined in the `attributes` attribute:

```
<secured attributes="..." />
```

A common way to separate access rights is through the use of a role-based approach, as mentioned earlier. Users are granted roles as authorities—for example, ROLE_USER and ROLE_ADMIN. Roles are created by defining strings that start with ROLE_. To secure a flow or flow element to only be accessed by registered users with the ROLE_USER authority, you define this as an attribute that needs to match:

```
<secured attributes"ROLE_USER" />
```

You can define multiple roles that should be allowed access by adding them as a comma-separated list. With the `match` attribute, you can further specify whether the user should have any or all of the roles defined. The following code sample defined on a flow would require the user to have both the ROLE_USER and ROLE_ADMIN authorities to get access to the flow. The `match` attribute defaults to any:

```
<secured attributes="ROLE_USER,ROLE_ADMIN" match="all" />
```

The role-based approach is Spring Security's default way to make access decisions. If you want to use a different approach, we suggest considering the Spring Security reference documentation for help.

After all the changes we made to the address example, we can now see Spring Security in action. When the new version is deployed, redirect your browser to `http://localhost:8080/ch18/address.html`. Instead of being shown the input form, you'll be forwarded to a login screen (see Figure 18-14).

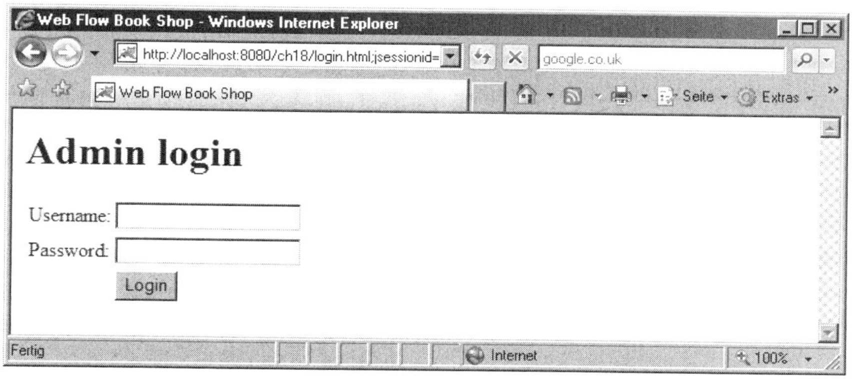

Figure 18-14. *Spring Security–invoked login screen*

Remember that we defined users `user` and `admin` in the user details service. When we now submit username `user` with password `user`, we'll be forwarded to the requested address details page (see Figure 18-15).

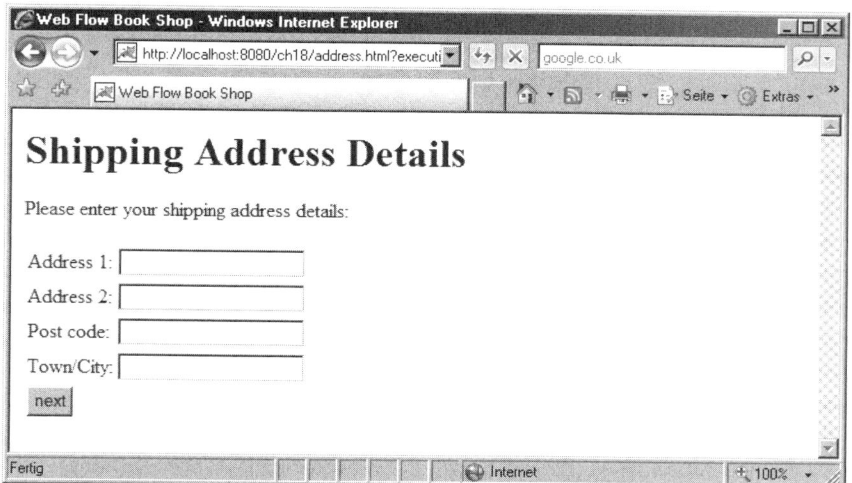

Figure 18-15. *Screen on successful authentication*

By adding a security constraint to a transition as shown in Listing 18-32, we can further ensure that only users with this authority are allowed to transition.

Listing 18-32. *Securing a Transition*

```
<?xml version="1.0" encoding="UTF-8"?>
<flow xmlns="http://www.springframework.org/schema/webflow"
    xmlns:xsi="http://www.w3.org/2001/XMLSchema-instance"
    xsi:schemaLocation="http://www.springframework.org/schema/webflow
        http://www.springframework.org/schema/webflow/spring-webflow-2.0.xsd">

    <secured attributes="ROLE_USER" />
```

```
    <var name="address" class="com.apress.prospring2.ch18.sample.Address" />

    <view-state id="start" view="address/shippingAddress" model="address">
      <transition on="admin" to="admin" bind="false">
        <secured attributes="ROLE_ADMIN"/>
      </transition>
      <transition on="next" to="confirm" />
    </view-state>

    <view-state id="confirm" view="address/showAddress" />

    <view-state id="admin" view="address/admin" />

</flow>
```

In the application, you will find that user `admin` can proceed to the admin page, while user `user` is denied access with an HTTP 403 response code, as shown in Figure 18-16.

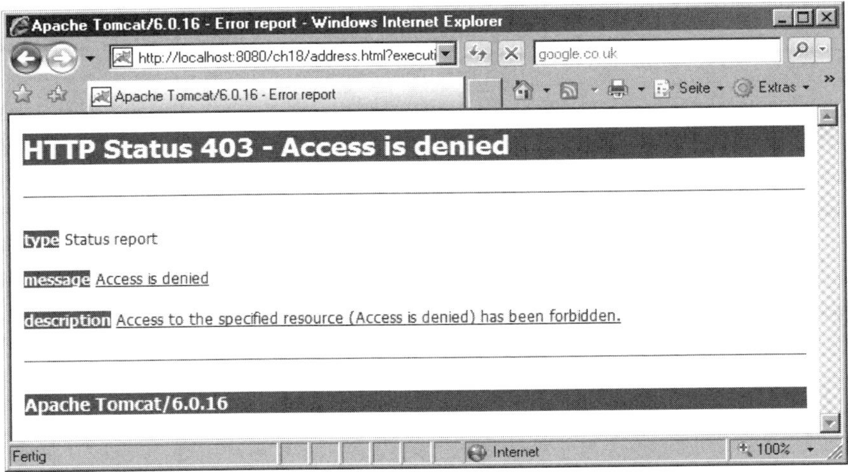

Figure 18-16. *Tomcat 6 default HTTP 403 error page*

In this section, we briefly introduced Spring Security and its features. We then explained the configuration steps to enable Spring Security in a Spring Web Flow web application and demonstrated them using a simple address details entry use case.

Problem Solver

Remember that at the very beginning of this chapter we named a few common problems and concerns in a web application and promised that Spring Web Flow would offer a solution. Let's have a look back and see how we did.

Stateful Navigational Control

Navigational control is achieved by treating a web site as a state machine. All allowed paths through the states are defined in a flow definition. Access to certain areas can also be restricted by adding security constraints.

The different scopes and automatic model binding allow the application to manage its state, adding the stateful aspect. A well-defined set of possible transitions out of a state ensures that the web site user can't just jump to a certain page, possibly trying to shortcut a process they should step through.

Browser Navigation Bar Support and Double Submit

To fully understand how Spring Web Flow goes about this issue, we need to have a look at a different concept first: the POST-REDIRECT-GET pattern. The HTTP specification calls for the GET request to "retrieve whatever information (in the form of an entity) is identified by the Request-URI." A GET request is not meant to submit data in a form that changes the state of the server. This is essentially what distinguishes it from a POST request. GET requests should allow the browser to be safe to automatically rerequest, while POST requests will prompt for user interaction.

The POST-REDIRECT-GET pattern describes the transformation of serving a POST request by serving a GET request. This is achieved by the server responding to a POST request with an HTTP redirect response, supplying a new URL for the requested resource. The browser will then automatically request the new URL with a GET request.

As you have seen, every view state rendered is stored as a snapshot in the flow execution repository. The key required to retrieve them from the repository is transmitted in the request URL. When a user clicks the Back button of his browser and the browser doesn't find the data in its cache, the URL that the browser rerequests will contain the flow execution key. With this key, Spring Web Flow can easily retrieve the state of the flow at that point in time from its repository and return it. The alwaysRedirectOnPause attribute (which tells Web Flow to always issue a redirect to render a view) is set to true by default. You can manually switch it off as shown following:

```
<webflow:flow-executor id="flowExecutor" flow-registry="flowRegistry">
      <webflow:flow-execution-attributes>
         <webflow:always-redirect-on-pause value="false"/>
     </webflow:flow-execution-attributes>
 </webflow:flow-executor>
```

Testing Flow Definitions

Spring Web Flow wouldn't be a good member of the Spring module family if testability wasn't one of its major features. While writing test code for other controller frameworks can be tiring and error prone, testing an entire flow definition is actually very simple.

Spring Web Flow comes with a test package of useful test and mock classes. To give you an example, we'll write a test case for the "Hello, Web Flow!" flow definition from the beginning of this chapter. Please be aware that you'll have to add junit.jar 3.8 or greater to your build path to make the tests run.

We start by creating a HelloWorldIntegrationTest class that extends org.springframework.webflow.test.execution.AbstractXmlFlowExecutionTests. We are forced to implement the FlowDefinitionResource getResource(FlowDefinitionResourceFactory resourceFactory) method declared in an abtract superclass of the AbstractXmlFlowExecutionTests class. This method is a hook to provide the test with the flow definition we want to test, which in our case is the helloWorld.xml file (see Listing 18-33).

Listing 18-33. *Providing an XML Flow Definition As a Resource for the Test*

```
@Override
protected FlowDefinitionResource getResource(
            FlowDefinitionResourceFactory resourceFactory) {
    String path = "webapp/WEB-INF/flows/helloWorld.xml";
    return resourceFactory.createFileResource(path);
}
```

The `flowDefinitionResourceFactory` also provides other helpful methods to create a `FlowDefinitionResource`. The `createClassPathResource` enables you to locate flow definitions on the classpath, and several overloaded `createResource` methods allow you to pass in a self-configured `AttributeMap` for further configuration possibilities.

But let's go back to our example. We're now ready to start adding the real tests. A simple test to make sure our configuration is correct is shown in Listing 18-34.

Listing 18-34. *Testing the Test Configuration*

```
public void testStartExecution() {
    MockExternalContext context = new MockExternalContext();
    startFlow(context);
    assertCurrentStateEquals("hello");
}
```

The bar is green, hooray! Let's see how we can test the transition to the `helloWorld` end state (see Listing 18-35).

Listing 18-35. *Testing Transition to End State*

```
public void testTransitionToHelloWorldState() {
    MockExternalContext context = new MockExternalContext();
    setCurrentState("hello");
    context.setEventId("submit");
    resumeFlow(context);
    assertTrue(getFlowExecution().hasEnded());
}
```

Theoretically, we could start the flow execution again as we did in `testStartExecution`. If you want to test more complex flows that have a greater number of states, you'll find the `setCurrentState` method very useful, allowing you to "cheat" and jump directly to a certain state of the flow instead of having to programmatically transition to it first.

We then specify the ID of the event we would like to occur. That way, we can fine-tune exactly which transition and hence which path we would like to test. In our example, the transition is triggered on any event that occurs, so we could specify anything we like. By calling `resumeFlow`, the flow gets executed with the information given in the context. All being well, the `helloWorld` flow will have transitioned to the `helloWorld` end state, and we can test this by checking if the flow execution has really ended.

Summary

In this chapter, we introduced the controller framework Spring Web Flow. We showed you how to get started, including getting the binaries. We covered the elements and concepts of Spring Web Flow: what a flow is and how to define one, and what its elements are and how to use them. We explained how to use automatic form binding, how to call subflows, and how to pass input and output parameters. We also gave a brief insight in securing flow definitions with Spring Security.

By exploring how Spring Web Flow works internally, we gave you an understanding of how and where you can customize the flow execution to fit your needs. We discussed which problems Spring Web Flow is trying to solve and how it goes about doing so.

If you want to have a look at more examples of certain features or see integration with another framework in action, Spring Web Flow comes with a variety of helpful sample applications. It also provides an extensive test suite that you can use as a template for your own test cases. Have a look into your Spring Web Flow distribution for the sources and visit the project home page for links to see the applications working.

CHAPTER 19

Spring and AJAX

AJAX (Asynchronous JavaScript and XML) is a new approach to web application development that uses client-side scripting to exchange data with the web server. As a result, web pages are dynamically updated without interrupting the user interaction flow by a full page refresh. With AJAX, developers can create rich browser-based web applications that look and behave more like native desktop applications.

AJAX is not one technology but a combination of several:

- XHTML and Cascading Style Sheets (CSS)
- Document Object Model (DOM)
- XML (and XSLT)
- XMLHttpRequest (XHR)
- JavaScript

Unlike many of the approaches used in the past, AJAX works in most modern browsers and doesn't require any proprietary software or hardware. In fact, one of the real strengths of AJAX is that developers who use it don't need to learn a new language or scrap their investments in server-side technology.

Several of the AJAX frameworks do not rely on Java. Most of these are implemented completely in JavaScript and designed to execute within the confines of a web browser. These frameworks leave the server-side implementation of AJAX to developers, allowing them to code in their preferred server-side languages. In this chapter, we will aim to simplify the task of adding AJAX interactions to your Spring web applications.

We will be using Direct Web Remoting (DWR). DWR is an AJAX framework that relies exclusively on Java and JavaScript. While it is not the only AJAX Remote Procedure Call (AJAX-RPC) framework available for the Java platform, it is one of the most mature and frequently used. Moreover, DWR integrates very nicely with Spring!

DWR

DWR is an open source initiative that makes calling Java functions from JavaScript easy. It is distributed under the Apache License, version 2. DWR lets JavaScript call Java methods as if they were running locally in the browser, when in fact the Java methods are running on the server. DWR has a number of features, including the ability to marshal virtually any data structure between Java and JavaScript. The two main components of DWR follow:

- A Java servlet running on the server that processes requests and sends responses back to the browser
- A set of JavaScript libraries running in the browser to send requests and dynamically update the web page

DWR dynamically generates JavaScript based on Java classes that use some AJAX calls, which gives the impression that the execution is happening on the browser, whereas in reality, the server is executing the code and DWR is marshalling the data back and forth. This method of using remote functions from Java in JavaScript gives DWR users a feel much like conventional RPC mechanisms, such as Remote Method Invocation (RMI), with the added benefit that it runs over the Web without requiring any browser plug-ins.

Installing DWR

Before we begin our examples, let's quickly install DWR. You can get started with DWR in two different ways. The easiest way is to download the WAR (web archive) file and have a look around, but this doesn't allow you to see how easily DWR integrates with your existing Spring-based web application. To start using DWR with an existing application, you will need to download the latest `dwr.jar` file from `www.getahead.org/dwr`. Starting with version 2.0, DWR also requires `commons-logging.jar`. Place the JAR files in the `WEB-INF/lib` folder of an existing Java EE web application of your choice to complete the installation.

As we mentioned, we choose DWR because of its easy integration with Spring. Now, let's go through some examples to see exactly how to expose Spring-managed beans using DWR.

Spring Configuration for DWR

Integrating DWR into your existing Spring application is also simple. From version 2.0 of DWR, a new configuration mechanism is available when using DWR with Spring 2.5. The new mechanism uses the namespace support provided by Spring 2.5 and allows you to configure DWR entirely in Spring. This eliminates the need for an extra configuration file and provides tight integration between the bean or beans that you want to use remotely and the DWR configuration. Let's look at the simple Spring configuration file shown in Listing 19-1.

Listing 19-1. *Simple Spring Configuration File*

```
<beans
xmlns="http://www.springframework.org/schema/beans"
xmlns:xsi="http://www.w3.org/2001/XMLSchema-instance"
xsi:schemaLocation="http://www.springframework.org/schema/beans
http://www.springframework.org/schema/beans/spring-beans-2.5.xsd">
```

```
    <bean id="someBean" class="BeanClass">
        <property name="someProperty" ref="someOhterBean"/>
    </bean>

    <bean id="someOtherBean" class="OtherBeanClass"/>
</beans>
```

Here, someBean is an ordinary Spring bean that has a reference to someOtherBean, which is a normal Spring bean defined in the same configuration file.

The code in Listing 19-2 shows you how to remote someOtherBean to JavaScript using DWR.

Listing 19-2. *DWR-Related Configuration*

```
<beans
        xmlns="http://www.springframework.org/schema/beans"
        xmlns:xsi="http://www.w3.org/2001/XMLSchema-instance"
        xmlns:dwr="http://www.directwebremoting.org/schema/spring-dwr"
        xsi:schemaLocation="http://www.springframework.org/schema/beans
            http://www.springframework.org/schema/beans/spring-beans-2.0.xsd
            http://www.directwebremoting.org/schema/spring-dwr
            http://www.directwebremoting.org/schema/spring-dwr-2.0.xsd">

    <bean id="someBean" class="BeanClass">
        <property name="somePropter" ref="someOtherBean"/>
        <dwr:remote javascript="Ajaxified">
            <dwr:include method="someMethod"/>
        </dwr:remote>
    </bean>

    <bean id="someOtherBean" class="OtherBeanClass"/>

    <dwr:configuration />

    <dwr:controller name="dwrController" debug="true"/>
</beans>
```

First of all, you need to define the XML namespace (xmlns) by providing an alias, in this case dwr, and link it to the URI of the schema. Note that the dwr alias can be replaced with anything you want as long as you use your alias instead of the dwr one in the following examples. Changing xmlns:dwr to xmlns:otheralias is all you need to do to change the alias.

If you have an IDE with XML schema support (e.g., IntelliJ or Eclipse), you should navigate inside the dwrService bean and use the automatic completion functionality to view all available tags provided by the DWR namespace.

Choose the dwr:remote tag, and you will see that the IDE will prompt you for the javascript name to use for exposing the bean. Note that the dwr:remote tag should be a nested tag of the someBean bean. That is all there is to it to configure DWR to remote the someBean bean under the JavaScript script named Ajaxified. However, we do need to somehow expose DWR to the outside world. Here, you have two options, and which is better depends mostly on whether you are using Spring MVC for your web application. If you are, you should use DwrServlet. If you are using any other web framework, use DwrSpringServlet.

About the Complete Example

Before explaining DWR in any detail, we will introduce a simple example scenario that we will build on throughout this chapter. We will use a minimal model based on user registration, consisting of a user representation and a data access object (DAO) to look up basic user details from a data store. The User class has id, username, and password strings. Listing 19-3 shows the User class.

Listing 19-3. *The User Class*

```
public class User {

    public String id;
    public final String username;
    public final String password;

    public User(String username, String password) {
        this.username = username;
        this.password = password;
    }

    public String getId() {
        return id;
    }

    public void setId(String id) {
        this.id = id;
    }

    public String getUsername() {
        return username;
    }

    public String getPassword() {
        return password;
    }
}
```

Next, we will demonstrate the simple UserDao interface, which provides a capability to check the availability of a new username among other general features. Listing 19-4 shows the UserDao interface.

Listing 19-4. *The UserDao Interface*

```
public interface UserDao {
    /**
     * Retrieves all the users
     * @return Collection of users
     */
    Collection<User> getAllUsers();

    /**
     * Saves a User to the datastore
     * @param user The User object to persist
     */
    void saveUser(User user);
```

```
    /**
     * Retrieves a user based on the User's identity
     * @param id The identity of the User
     * @return The retrieved User
     */
    User getUser(String id);

    /**
     * Retrieves a user based on the User's username
     * @param username The username
     * @return The retrieved User
     */
    User getUserByUsername(String username);

    /**
     * Deletes a User from the datastore
     * @param user The User to delete
     */
    void deleteUser(User user);

    /**
     * Checks whether a username is already taken or not
     * @param username The username to check
     * @return True or False based on whether the username is available or not
     */
    boolean usernameExists(String username);
}
```

For this example, we have used a static `Map<String, Value>` to hold all the existing users in the following implementation of the `UserDao` interface. Adding or deleting users will add or remove a `User` object from the `Map<String, Value>`. Listing 19-5 shows the `UserDaoImpl` class.

Listing 19-5. *The UserDaoImpl Class*

```
public class UserDaoImpl implements UserDao {

    /**
     * Static datasource
     */
    private static Map<String, User> allUsers = new HashMap<String, User>();

    public Collection<User> getAllUsers() {
        return allUsers.values();
    }

    public void saveUser(final User user) {
        String id = String.valueOf(allUsers.size() + 1);
        user.setId(id);
        if (!usernameExists(user.getUsername())) {
            allUsers.put(user.getUsername(), user);
        } else {
            throw new
IllegalArgumentException("Username " + user.getUsername() + " already exists.");
        }
    }
```

```
    public User getUser(final String id) {
        return allUsers.get(id);
    }

    public User getUserByUsername(final String username) {
        return allUsers.get(username);
    }

    public void deleteUser(final User user) {
        allUsers.remove(user);
    }

    public boolean usernameExists(final String username) {
        return allUsers.containsKey(username);
    }

    static {
        allUsers.put("janm", new User("janm", "password", "address"));
        allUsers.put("aleksav", new User("aleksav", "password", "address"));
        allUsers.put("anirvanc", new User("anirvanc", "password", "address"));
    }
}
```

By its very nature, DWR creates a tight coupling between client-side and server-side code, with a number of implications. First, changes to the API of remoted methods need to be reflected in the JavaScript that calls the DWR stubs. Second (and more significantly), this coupling causes client-side concerns to affect server-side code. To get around this, we have introduced a `DwrService` interface and its implementation, which will provide the remoted methods required for the current example. Listing 19-6 shows the `DwrService` interface.

Listing 19-6. *The DwrService Interface*

```
public interface DwrService {
    boolean usernameAvailability(String username);
}
```

Now, let's have a look at the implementation of the `DwrService` interface. Listing 19-7 shows the `DefaultDwrService` class, which implements the `DwrService` interface.

Listing 19-7. *The DefaultDwrService Class*

```
public final class DefaultDwrService implements DwrService {

    private UserDao userDao;

    public boolean usernameAvailability(final String username) {
        return !this.userDao.usernameExists(username);
    }

    public void setUserDao(final UserDao userDao) {
        this.userDao = userDao;
    }
}
```

Here, you can see that the `DefaultDwrService` only uses the `UserDao` to check the username availability for a new user. Now, if at a later stage, we need to introduce a new method for some client-side–specific concern, we can easily do that in the `DwrService` interface and in its implementation.

Next, we will have a look at the DWR configuration, which will enable AJAX clients to construct DwrService and call its methods. This is very similar to the DWR configuration you saw earlier in the chapter. Listing 19-8 shows the DWR configuration to make the DwrService implementation remote.

Listing 19-8. *The DWR Configuration for DwrService*

```
<beans
        xmlns="http://www.springframework.org/schema/beans"
        xmlns:xsi="http://www.w3.org/2001/XMLSchema-instance"
        xmlns:dwr="http://www.directwebremoting.org/schema/spring-dwr"
        xsi:schemaLocation="http://www.springframework.org/schema/beans
            http://www.springframework.org/schema/beans/spring-beans-2.5.xsd
            http://www.directwebremoting.org/schema/spring-dwr
            http://www.directwebremoting.org/schema/spring-dwr-2.0.xsd">

    <bean id="dwrService" class="com.apress.prospring2.ajax.service.DefaultDwrService">
        <property name="userDao" ref="userDao"/>
        <dwr:remote javascript="DwrService">
            <dwr:include method="usernameAvailability"/>
        </dwr:remote>
    </bean>

    <bean id="userDao" class="com.apress.prospring2.ajax.dataaccess.UserDaoImpl"/>

</beans>
```

In the preceding configuration, only the highlighted code relates to DWR. The <dwr:remote> tag has a javascript attribute, which specifies the name by which the object will be accessible from JavaScript code. In the nested <dwr:include> tag, the method parameter defines the name of the method that will be exposed. Alternately, the <dwr:remote> tag has a nested <dwr:exclude> tag, which defines the name of the method that will not be exposed. This tag can be helpful in situations where you don't want to expose one or two methods out of the many methods in the exposed object. Explicitly stating the methods to expose is good practice to avoid accidentally allowing access to potentially harmful functionality. If this element is omitted, all of the class's public methods will be exposed to remote calls.

Now to complete the configuration of our example, we need to configure DwrServlet in our web.xml file. Listing 19-9 shows the DwrServlet configuration.

Listing 19-9. *The web.xml File for DwrService*

```
<?xml version="1.0" encoding="UTF-8"?>
<web-app version="2.5"
        xmlns="http://java.sun.com/xml/ns/javaee"
        xmlns:xsi="http://www.w3.org/2001/XMLSchema-instance"
        xsi:schemaLocation="http://java.sun.com/xml/ns/javaee
            http://java.sun.com/xml/ns/javaee/web-app_2_5.xsd">

        <!-- Location of the Spring bean definition files, for initialization of
             root Spring application context -->
    <context-param>
        <param-name>contextConfigLocation</param-name>
        <param-value>
            classpath*:/com/apress/prospring2/ajax/**/*-context.xml
        </param-value>
    </context-param>
```

```
    <listener>
        <listener-class>org.springframework.web.context.ContextLoaderListener ➥
</listener-class>
    </listener>

    <servlet>
    <servlet-name>ajaxdemo</servlet-name>
    <servlet-class>org.springframework.web.servlet.DispatcherServlet</servlet-class>
    </servlet>

    <servlet-mapping>
        <servlet-name>ajaxdemo</servlet-name>
        <url-pattern>*.html</url-pattern>
    </servlet-mapping>

    <!-- DWR servlet setup -->
    <servlet>
        <servlet-name>dwr</servlet-name>
        <servlet-class>org.directwebremoting.spring.DwrSpringServlet</servlet-class>
        <init-param>
            <param-name>debug</param-name>
            <param-value>true</param-value>
        </init-param>
    </servlet>

    <servlet-mapping>
        <servlet-name>dwr</servlet-name>
        <url-pattern>/dwr/*</url-pattern>
    </servlet-mapping>

</web-app>
```

The code marked in bold shows the DwrServlet configuration. Here, we have used DwrSpringServlet and have mapped it to the path /dwr/*. The servlet will automatically retrieve its configuration from the Spring bean container loaded by the ContextLoaderListener.

If you are already using Spring MVC, using DwrController is the most obvious choice, because you will benefit from a number of services provided to you by Spring MVC, like localization support. DwrController is a normal Spring controller that has a property that takes the DWR configuration as a property. The easiest way to use this controller is again to use a tag provided by the DWR namespace, as shown in Listing 19-10.

Listing 19-10. *Code Snippet Showing DwrController Configuration*

```
<dwr:controller id="dwrController" debug="true"/>
```

Note that the debug property is optional and defaults to false. Make sure to map this controller to the path where you want to expose DWR, normally /dwr.

Testing the DWR Configuration

If DWRServlet's web.xml definition sets the init-param debug function to true, then DWR's extremely helpful test mode is enabled. Navigating to /{your-web-app}/dwr/ brings up a list of your classes that DWR has been configured to remote. Clicking through takes you to the status screen for a given class. The DWR test page for DwrService is shown in Figure 19-1. As well as providing a script tag that points to DWR's generated JavaScript for the class to paste into your web pages, this screen also provides a list of the class's methods. The list includes methods inherited from the class's supertypes.

Methods For: DwrService (com.apress.prospring2.ajax.service.DefaultDwrService)

To use this class in your javascript you will need the following script includes:

```
<script type='text/javascript' src='/dwr/interface/DwrService.js'></script>
<script type='text/javascript' src='/dwr/engine.js'></script>
```

In addition there is an optional utility script:

```
<script type='text/javascript' src='/dwr/util.js'></script>
```

Replies from DWR are shown with a yellow background if they are simple or in an alert box otherwise.
The inputs are evaluated as Javascript so strings must be quoted before execution.

There are 12 declared methods:

- usernameAvailability(""); Execute
- confirmPassword("" , ""); Execute
  (Warning: confirmPassword() is excluded: Method access is denied by rules in dwr.xml. See below)

Figure 19-1. *DWR test page showing DwrService*

You can enter parameter values into the text boxes next to the accessible methods and click the Execute button to invoke them. The server's response will be displayed using JavaScript Object Notation (JSON) in an alert box, unless it is a simple value, in which case it will be displayed inline alongside the method. These test pages are very useful. Not only do they allow you to easily check which classes and methods are exposed for remoting but they also let you test that each method is behaving as expected.

Once you're satisfied that your remoted methods are working correctly, you can use DWR's generated JavaScript stubs to call on your server-side objects from client-side code.

Running the Complete Example

We have deployed the application on the root of a locally running Tomcat server (Tomcat 5.5). Once deployed, navigating to `http://localhost:8080/index.html` will bring up the simple user registration form. Figure 19-2 shows the empty form.

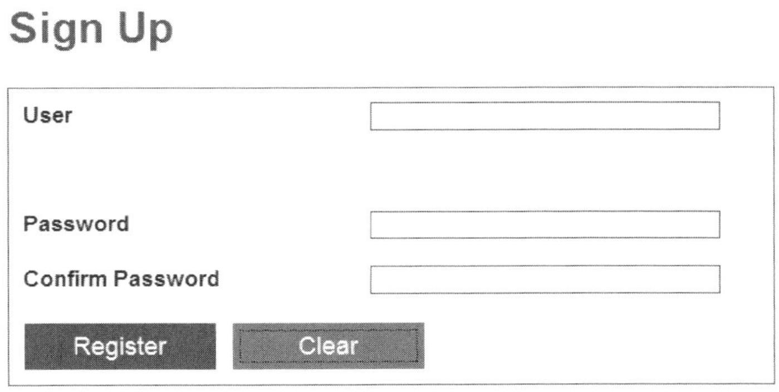

Sign Up

User

Password

Confirm Password

Register Clear

Figure 19-2. *The simple registration form*

As we explained before, the UserDao interface maintains a static list of three users: janm, aleksav, and anirvanc. If we try to register as any of these existing users, a validation error will occur, as shown in Figure 19-3.

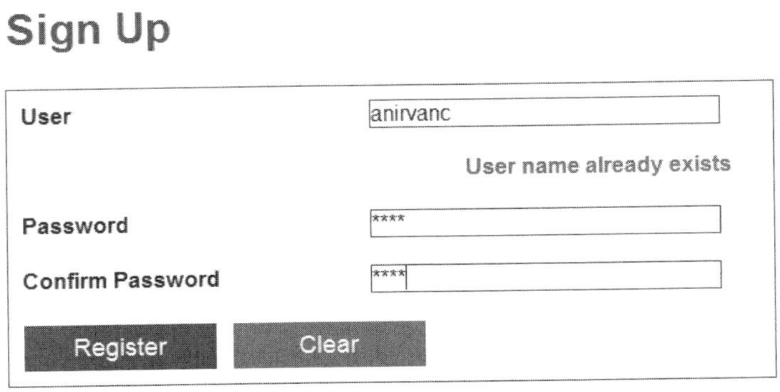

Sign Up

User anirvanc

User name already exists

Password ****

Confirm Password ****

Register Clear

Figure 19-3. *The registration form in action*

DWR Scripting Basics

Earlier in the chapter, while working through our simple example, we mentioned that once DWR is properly configured and the web application is deployed, DWR will dynamically generate a JavaScript representation of remoted Java objects. Here, the biggest challenge in creating a remote interface that matches some Java code across AJAX is the usually asynchronous nature of AJAX, compared to the synchronous nature of a normal Java call. DWR addresses this problem by introducing a callback function that is called when the data is returned from the server. There are two recommended ways to make a call using DWR: by appending the callback function to the parameter list of a JavaScript function or by appending a call metadata object to a JavaScript function.

Using Simple Callback Functions

In our example, we had a Java method that looks like the one shown in Listing 19-11.

Listing 19-11. *A Java Method Exposed Using DWR*

```
public boolean usernameAvailability(final String username) {
    return !this.userDao.usernameExists(username);
}
```

From JavaScript, we can use this method as shown in Listing 19-12.

Listing 19-12. *JavaScript Code to Call the Remote Method*

```
<script type='text/javascript' src='/dwr/interface/DwrService.js'></script>
<script type='text/javascript' src='/dwr/engine.js'></script>
...
...
```

```
function checkUsernameAvailability(username) {
    DwrService.usernameAvailability(username, displayStatus);
    return false;
}

function displayStatus(nameStatus){
    if (!nameStatus) {
        alert("Username already exists");
    } else {
        Alert("Username is available");
    }
}
```

We have passed a simple callback JavaScript function `displayStatus` to the remoted method `DwrService.usernameAvailability()`.

Calling Metadata Objects

Alternatively, we could have used a different syntax to call a metadata object. This syntax uses a call metadata object that specifies the callback function and (optionally) other options. In this syntax, the code in Listing 19-12 would have changed into the snippet shown in Listing 19-13.

Listing 19-13. *Calling a Metadata Object*

```
DwrService.usernameAvailability(username, {
  callback:function(status) { if (!status)➥
{ alert("Username not available.} else { alert("Username available");}}
});
```

Depending on your style, this approach may be easier to read than the simple callback, but more importantly, it allows you to specify extra call options.

engine.js

The `engine.js` script is vital to DWR; since it is used to marshal calls from the dynamically generated interface JavaScript function, it is needed wherever DWR is used. With DWR versions 1.0 and 1.1, all functions had the prefix `DWREngine`, but as of version 2.0, the preferred prefix is `dwr.engine`. The `engine.js` script provides some important configurable options while working with DWR. In the following sections, we will have a closer look at some of the important features provided by `engine.js`.

Call Batching

In DWR, several remote calls can be sent to the server with a single HTTP request, which saves on round-trip times to the server and reduces latency. Calling `dwr.engine.beginBatch()` tells DWR not to dispatch subsequent remoted calls straight away and instead to combine them into a single batched request. A call to `dwr.engine.endBatch()` sends the batched request to the server. The remote calls are executed in order on the server side, and each JavaScript callback is invoked.

Batching can help to reduce latency in two ways: first, you avoid the overhead of creating an `XMLHttpRequest` object and establishing the associated HTTP connection for each call. Second, in a production environment, the web server won't have to deal with so many concurrent HTTP requests, improving response times.

Call Ordering

Since AJAX is normally an asynchronous model, remote calls may not return in the order in which they were sent. `dwr.engine.setOrdered(boolean)` allows you to request that all replies are made in the strict order that they were sent. DWR achieves this by sending new requests only after older ones have been completed. By default, the Boolean parameter is set as `false`. You should always bear in mind that setting it to `true` will slow down your application and could leave users with an unresponsive browser if a message ever gets lost. Sometimes, better solutions, in which you make your application use the asynchronous model properly, are possible. Please think carefully before you decide to use this method.

Handling Errors and Warnings

Whenever DWR detects a failure, it calls an error or warning handler (depending on the severity of the error) and passes it the message. This error or warning handler could be used to display error messages in an alert box or to the status bar. To change the error handler, use `dwr.engine.setErrorHandler(function)`, and to change the warning handler, use `dwr.engine.setWarningHandler(function)`.

util.js

The `util.js` script contains a number of utility functions to help you update your web pages with JavaScript data (which might be returned from the server). You can use `util.js` outside of DWR, because (with the exception of `useLoadingMessage()`) it does not depend on the rest of DWR to function. With DWR version 1.0 and 1.1, all functions had the prefix `DWRUtil`; from version 2.0, the preferred prefix is `dwr.util`. The old prefix will still work, though it is deprecated. The documentation generally uses the new version.

The four basic page manipulation functions, `getValue[s]()`, and `setValue[s]()` work on most HTML elements except tables, lists, and images. `getText()` works with select lists. A more comprehensive list of utility functions can be found at `http://getahead.org/dwr/browser/util`.

Security in DWR

DWR has been designed with security in mind. You can use the `<dwr:include>` and `<dwr:exclude>` tags to white list only those classes and methods you wish to remote. This avoids accidental exposure of functionality that could be maliciously exploited. Moreover, using the debug test mode, you can easily audit all the classes and methods that are exposed to the Web.

DWR also supports role-based security. You can specify the Java EE role that a user must have to access a particular bean, via the bean's `<dwr:creator>` configuration. By deploying multiple URL-secured instances of the `DWRServlet`, each with its own `dwr.xml` configuration file, you can also provide different sets of users with access to different remote functionality. An example configuration to use Java EE servlet security is shown in Listing 19-14.

Listing 19-14. *Java EE Servlet-Based Security Configuration*

```
<servlet>
  <servlet-name>dwr-user-invoker</servlet-name>
  <servlet-class>uk.ltd.getahead.dwr.DWRServlet</servlet-class>
  <init-param>
    <param-name>config-user</param-name>
    <param-value>WEB-INF/dwr-user.xml</param-value>
```

```
  </init-param>
</servlet>
<servlet>
  <servlet-name>dwr-admin-invoker</servlet-name>
  <servlet-class>uk.ltd.getahead.dwr.DWRServlet</servlet-class>
  <init-param>
    <param-name>config-admin</param-name>
    <param-value>WEB-INF/dwr-admin.xml</param-value>
  </init-param>
</servlet>
<servlet-mapping>
  <servlet-name>dwr-admin-invoker</servlet-name>
  <url-pattern>/dwradmin/*</url-pattern>
</servlet-mapping>
<servlet-mapping>
  <servlet-name>dwr-user-invoker</servlet-name>
  <url-pattern>/dwruser/*</url-pattern>
</servlet-mapping>

<security-constraint>
  <display-name>dwr-admin</display-name>
  <web-resource-collection>
    <web-resource-name>dwr-admin-collection</web-resource-name>
    <url-pattern>/dwradmin/*</url-pattern>
  </web-resource-collection>
  <auth-constraint>
    <role-name>admin</role-name>
  </auth-constraint>
</security-constraint>
<security-constraint>
  <display-name>dwr-user</display-name>
  <web-resource-collection>
    <web-resource-name>dwr-user-collection</web-resource-name>
    <url-pattern>/dwruser/*</url-pattern>
  </web-resource-collection>
  <auth-constraint>
    <role-name>user</role-name>
  </auth-constraint>
</security-constraint>
```

Using DWR, an attacker can cause the server to create an instance of any Java object that you specify in your DWR configuration, and (if you are using the `BeanConverter` interface) any Java object that is in any of the parameters to the methods of those classes. Any of the properties in those classes can then be set with whatever data the attacker wishes. This is all fairly obvious if you think about what DWR is doing, but it could cause problems for the unwary. If you create a `FileBean` with an `appendStringToFile()` method and export it using DWR, you are giving an attacker a simple way of filling up your filesystem—think about the options you give attackers by using DWR. This type of scenario may make DWR sound risky, but similar issues exist with traditional web architectures; it's just that they are less obvious (and thus less likely to get fixed).

You can guard against failures in DWR access mechanisms by separating the classes accessed by DWR into a separate package and having them proxy the real code. You can double-check role-based security yourself if you wish. These options just add to the checks already made by DWR. A better idea than double-checking might be to audit the DWR source to ensure that the checks it is already doing are correct. The code has been checked over by several people already, but more eyes will always help.

Advantages and Disadvantages of DWR

You've seen how easy it is to implement a Java-backed AJAX application using DWR. Although the example scenario is a simple one, and we have taken a fairly minimal approach to implementing the use cases, you shouldn't underestimate the amount of work the DWR engine can save you over a homegrown AJAX approach. We have also shown how DWR has done all of the work for you. We wrote very few lines of JavaScript to implement the client, and on the server side, all we had to do was augment our regular `SpringBean` interface with some additional DWR-related configuration.

Of course, every technology has its drawbacks. As with any RPC mechanism, in DWR, you can easily forget that each call you make on a remoted object will take much longer than a local function call. DWR does a great job of hiding the AJAX machinery, but it's important to remember that the network is not transparent; making DWR calls involves latency, and your application should be architected so that remote methods are coarse grained.

DWR has its own solution to the latency issue in call batching (as you saw earlier in this chapter). If you can't provide a suitably coarse-grained AJAX interface for your application, use call batching wherever possible to combine multiple remote calls into a single HTTP request.

Summary

DWR has a lot to offer. It allows you to create an AJAX interface to your server-side domain objects quickly and simply, without needing to write any servlet code, object serialization code, or client-side `XMLHttpRequest` code. Deploying to your web application using DWR is extremely simple, and DWR's security features can be integrated with a Java EE role-based authentication system. DWR isn't ideal for every application's architecture, however, and it does require you to give some thought to the design of your domain objects' APIs.

If you want to learn more about the pros and cons of AJAX with DWR, the best thing would be to download it and start experimenting. While DWR has many features that we haven't covered in this chapter, `http:// getahead.org/dwr` is a good starting point for further information when you're taking DWR for a spin.

One of the most important points to take away from this chapter is that for AJAX applications, there is no one-size-fits-all solution. AJAX is a rapidly developing framework with new technologies and techniques emerging all the time. DWR itself is a very active project and is going through rapid development. Pretty soon, the next major release, DWR 3.0, will provide even more interesting features for integrating with Spring-based applications.

CHAPTER 20

JMX with Spring

Java Management Extensions (JMX) is a technology that enables the instrumentation of Java applications for management, monitoring, and configuration; it's available at `http://java.sun.com/javase/technologies/core/mntr-mgmt/javamanagement/`. Initially, JMX was available as a separate extension, but it has been a standard part of Java since the Java 5 distribution. If you want to learn more about the technology, the JMX documentation at `http://java.sun.com/products/JavaManagement` is the best initial resource. In this chapter, we will focus on explaining how JMX is supported in Spring.

The central value proposition in Spring's JMX integration is the ability to expose your Spring beans as JMX resources—MBeans—without having to couple your beans to the JMX API. This is straightforward to do and, for the most part, happens transparently.

JMX Refresher

Before going any further, let's take a quick look at some of the basic JMX concepts we will be using throughout this chapter.

JMX provides a standard way of managing resources including applications, devices, and services. Because JMX technology is dynamic in nature, you can use it to monitor and manage resources as they are created, installed, and implemented. You can also use JMX to monitor and manage the Java Virtual Machine (JVM). JMX technology was developed through the Java Community Process (JCP) as two closely related Java Specification Requests (JSR):

- *JSR 3*: Java Management Extensions Instrumentation and Agent Specification
- *JSR 160*: Java Management Extensions Remote API

JSR 3 provided the original specification for JMX. Over time, there have been many more JSRs that either reference or implement JMX or the JMX Remote API.

Managed beans (MBeans), which are the key components of an application that is instrumented using JMX, define the management interface for components within your application. According to the JMX specification, there are four different types of MBeans:

Standard MBeans: These are simple JavaBeans whose management interface is determined by using reflection on a fixed Java interface that is implemented by the bean class.

Dynamic MBeans: These are MBeans whose management interface is determined at runtime by invoking methods of the `DynamicMBean` interface. As the management interface is not defined by a static interface, it can vary at runtime.

Open MBeans: These are a variant of dynamic MBeans whose attributes and operations are limited to primitive types, primitive type class wrappers, and any type that can be decomposed into primitives or primitive wrappers.

Model MBeans: A model MBean is a special kind of dynamic MBean that connects a management interface to the managed resource. Model MBeans are not so much written as declared, and they are typically produced by a factory that uses some metainformation to assemble the management interface.

The registration of an MBean in the MBeanServer interface (i.e., the agent) requires a unique identifier called ObjectName, which represents the object name of an MBean or a pattern that can match the names of several MBeans. An object name consists of two parts: the domain, which is a string of characters not including the colon character (:), and the key properties, which are an unordered set of keys and their associated values. An example of this would be demo.service:type=message, description=Hello world. Spring provides several out-of-the-box implementations for obtaining ObjectName identifiers for each of the beans it is registering; we will take a detailed look at them later in this chapter.

Spring's JMX integration enables us to expose regular Spring beans as model MBeans so that we can see and tweak the inside of an application even when that application is running.

We will be using the Java Monitoring and Management Console (jconsole) tool in all our examples in this chapter. It uses the extensive instrumentation of the Java Virtual Machine to provide information on performance and resource consumption of applications running on the Java platform using JMX technology.

Now, let's take a detailed look at some of the basic functionality provided by Spring JMX.

Exposing Your Beans

In the following sections of this chapter, you will see different ways of exposing Java beans as Spring-managed MBeans. Spring's excellent support for JMX makes exposing your beans to JMX really easy.

MBeanExporter

The MBeanExporter is the key class in providing JMX support in Spring. This class is a bean that exports one or more of your Spring beans as MBeans and registers them with a JMX MBeanServer. An MBean server is an object registry where MBeans are managed and through which MBeans are accessed. Exporting Spring beans as JMX MBeans makes it possible for JMX-based management tools such as jconsole to peek inside a running application at the beans' properties and to invoke their methods. For an example, look at the code in Listing 20-1.

Listing 20-1. *A Simple Spring Bean*

```
package com.apress.prospring2.ch20.simple;

public class SpringManagedBean {
    private String property;
    private String anotherProperty;

    public String getProperty() {
        return property;
    }

    public void setProperty(String property) {
        this.property = property;
    }

    public String getAnotherProperty() {
        return anotherProperty;
    }
```

```
    public void setAnotherProperty(String anotherProperty) {
        this.anotherProperty = anotherProperty;
    }

    public String exposedMethod() {
        return "This method is exposed.";
    }

}
```

To expose the properties and methods of this bean as attributes and operations of an MBean, you would simply need to configure an MBeanExporter interface in your configuration file and pass in the bean as shown in Listing 20-2.

Listing 20-2. *Configuration of a Simple Bean As an MBean*

```
<?xml version="1.0" encoding="UTF-8"?>
<beans xmlns="http://www.springframework.org/schema/beans"
       xmlns:xsi="http://www.w3.org/2001/XMLSchema-instance"
       xsi:schemaLocation="http://www.springframework.org/schema/beans ➥
http://www.springframework.org/schema/beans/spring-beans-2.5.xsd">

    <bean id="exporter" ➥
class="org.springframework.jmx.export.MBeanExporter">
        <property name="beans">
            <map>
                <entry key="bean:name=springManagedMBean" ➥
value-ref="springManagedBean" />
            </map>
        </property>
    </bean>

    <bean id="springManagedBean" ➥
class="com.apress.prospring2.ch20.simple.SpringManagedBean">
        <property name="property" value="TEST"/>
    </bean>

</beans>
```

In its simplest form, an MBeanExporter can be configured through its beans property with a <map> of one or more beans that you would like to expose as model MBeans through JMX. In the preceding configuration, the springManagedBean is exposed as an MBean under the object name bean:name=springManagedMBean. An important point to note here is that, by default, Spring will expose all of the public properties and methods of the springManagedBean as MBean attributes and operations. In this case, Spring will try to locate a running MBeanServer instance, and if it finds one, it will register an MBean that defines the management interface for your bean with that MBean server.

Now, for this example, you need to run your application with the command-line arguments shown in Listing 20-3.

Listing 20-3. *Command-Line Arguments for the JMX Server*

```
-Dcom.sun.management.jmxremote
```

We now need to introduce the SimpleMain class shown in Listing 20-4.

Listing 20-4. *The Main Class to Run the Example*

```
public class SimpleMain {

    public static void main(String[] args) throws Exception {
        new ClassPathXmlApplicationContext(new String[] {
                "simple-jmx-context.xml"
        }, SimpleMain.class);
        new BufferedReader(new InputStreamReader(System.in)).readLine();
    }
}
```

Once the `SimpleMain` class is running, you can use `jconsole` to connect to the JMX server and view your `springManagedMBean` bean (see Figure 20-1).

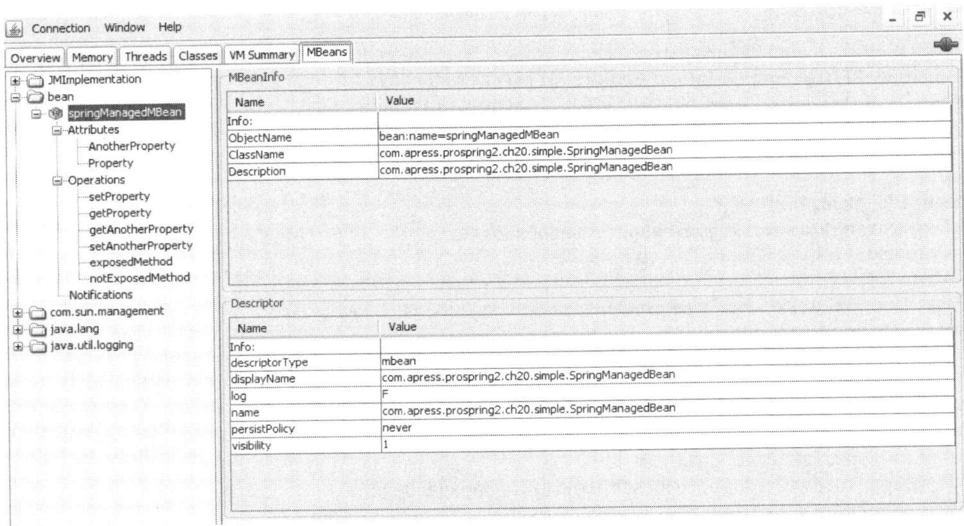

Figure 20-1. *jconsole view of the MBean*

MBeanServerFactoryBean

In the previous example, `MBeanExporter` assumes that it is running in an environment where there is a local MBean server, for example, in an application server such as JBoss or WebSphere. In such cases, Spring will attempt to locate the existing `MBeanServer` instance and register your beans with the server. This behavior is useful when your application is running inside a container.

However, if your Spring application will be running alone or in a container that doesn't provide an MBean server, this default approach is of no use. In that case, you will want to create an `MBeanServer` instance declaratively by adding an `MBeanServerFactoryBean` class in your configuration. You can also ensure that a specific MBean server is used by setting the value of `MBeanExporter`'s `server` property to the `MBeanServer` value returned by an `MBeanServerFactoryBean`, as shown in Listing 20-5.

Listing 20-5. *MBeanServerFactoryBean Example*

```
<beans xmlns="http://www.springframework.org/schema/beans"
       xmlns:xsi="http://www.w3.org/2001/XMLSchema-instance"
       xsi:schemaLocation="http://www.springframework.org/schema/beans ➥
 http://www.springframework.org/schema/beans/spring-beans-2.5.xsd">
```

```
    <bean id="mbeanServer" ➥
         class="org.springframework.jmx.support.MBeanServerFactoryBean"/>

    <bean id="exporter" class="org.springframework.jmx.export.MBeanExporter">
        <property name="beans">
            <map>
                <entry key="bean:name=springManagedMBean" ➥
                           value-ref="springManagedBean" />
            </map>
        </property>
        <property name="server" ref="mbeanServer" />
    </bean>

    <bean id="springManagedBean" ➥
            class="com.apress.prospring2.ch20.simple.SpringManagedBean">
        <property name="property" value="ANOTHER TEST"/>
    </bean>

</beans>
```

In this case, the MBean server is created by `MBeanServerFactoryBean`, and `MBeanExporter` will not try to locate a running server and will use the configured `MBeanServer` instance.

Exposing Your Beans in an Existing MBean Server

The default behavior for an `MBeanServerFactoryBean` is to create a new MBean server locally even if there is an existing MBean server running. But, `MBeanExporter` can also be configured to detect a running `MBeanServer` instance automatically if there is no server specified. This configuration will work in most cases, where there is only one `MBeanServer` running. On the other hand, if multiple `MBeanServer` instances are running, Spring cannot be sure which `MBeanServer` will be used by `MBeanExporter`, and you might need to use a specific existing `MBeanServer` to expose your MBeans. In that case, you can supply an agent ID to the `MBeanServer` to indicate which specific instance, among many running `MBeanServer` instances, you want to use. This type of MBean server agent is shown in Listing 20-6.

Listing 20-6. *An MBeanServer with an Agent*

```
<beans xmlns="http://www.springframework.org/schema/beans"
       xmlns:xsi="http://www.w3.org/2001/XMLSchema-instance"
       xsi:schemaLocation="http://www.springframework.org/schema/beans ➥
 http://www.springframework.org/schema/beans/spring-beans-2.0.xsd">

    <bean id="mbeanServer" ➥
            class="org.springframework.jmx.support.MBeanServerFactoryBean">
        <property name="locateExistingServerIfPossible" value="true" />
        <property name="agentId" value="MBeanServer instance agentId" />
    </bean>

    <bean id="exporter" class="org.springframework.jmx.export.MBeanExporter">
        <property name="beans">
            <map>
                <entry key="bean:name=springManagedMBean" ➥
                           value-ref="springManagedBean" />
            </map>
        </property>
        <property name="server" ref="mbeanServer" />
    </bean>
```

```
    <bean id="springManagedBean" ➥
            class="com.apress.prospring2.ch20.simple.SpringManagedBean">
        <property name="property" value="ANOTHER TEST"/>
    </bean>

</beans>
```

Bean Registration Behavior

So far, you have seen different ways of configuring Spring's `MBeanExporter` to expose your Spring beans as JMX beans. In each case, we have given the MBean an object name by which it will be registered with an `MBeanServer`. You shouldn't have any trouble exposing such beans to a new MBean server and, in most cases, to an existing `MBeanServer`, assuming that the existing `MBeanServer` doesn't already have an MBean with the same object name as one of our MBeans. But what happens if there *is* a name collision between our MBean and an existing MBean at registration time?

As always, Spring comes to the rescue by providing for flexible registration of MBeans with an `MBeanServer` instance. By default, `MBeanExporter` will throw an `InstanceAlreadyExistsException` when you try to expose an MBean with the object name of an MBean that's already registered in the `MBeanServer`. You can change this behavior by setting the `registrationBehaviorName` property on the `MBeanExporter`. The `registrationBehaviorName` property takes in a constant integer value defined in the `MBeanRegistrationSupport` class. These constants are also available in the `MBeanExporter` class, as `MBeanExporter` extends the `MBeanRegistrationSupport` class. Spring's JMX support allows the registration behaviors listed in Table 20-1.

Table 20-1. *Registration Behaviors Supported by Spring*

Registration Behavior	Explanation
`REGISTRATION_FAIL_ON_EXISTING`	This throws an `InstanceAlreadyExistsException` in case of a name collision between a new MBean and an existing MBean. This is the default behavior.
`REGISTRATION_IGNORE_EXISTING`	This will cause the registration of a new MBean to fail silently if an MBean with the same name already exists. No exception will be thrown.
`REGISTRATION_REPLACE_EXISTING`	In case of a name collision between a new MBean and an existing MBean, this will remove the existing MBean and register the new one.

`REGISTRATION_REPLACE_EXISTING` is particularly useful during development, when you might redeploy an application many times in a single day. If your application is exporting MBeans, specifying this registration behavior means that your JMX infrastructure doesn't have to be stopped and started with each redeploy, and you don't have to mess about with housekeeping such as unregistering MBeans.

Controlling Object Names

Spring controls the object names of MBeans using implementations of the `ObjectNamingStrategy` interface. You can make use of the following three implementations of the `ObjectNamingStrategy` provided by Spring, or you can write your own implementations as needed:

- `KeyNamingStrategy`: This is the default implementation. This implementation builds `ObjectName` instances from the key used in the `beans` map passed to `MBeanExporter`. You can configure this to look in a properties file to find the object name mappings. If no mapping is found for a given key, the key itself is used to build an `ObjectName` instance.
- `IdentityNamingStrategy`: Here, object names are generated dynamically based on the JVM identity of a bean. An `ObjectName` would be of the form `package:class=class name, hashCode=identity hash (in hex)`.
- `MetadataNamingStrategy`: This implementation of `ObjectNamingStrategy` reads the `ObjectName` from source-level metadata. It falls back to the bean name key if no source-level metadata can be found. We will take a detailed look at this strategy later in the chapter when JMX metadata is covered.

Controlling the Management Interface

You may have noticed that, so far, we don't have any control over which properties and methods of our Spring beans will be exposed when we register those Spring beans as MBeans. For very basic cases, this might be adequate, but in more complicated cases, you often want to exercise finer grained control over exactly which properties and methods of your Spring beans you want to expose as JMX attributes and operations. We can control exactly which methods and properties of a class become operations and attributes of a model MBean by using the `MBeanInfoAssembler` interface.

MBeanInfoAssembler Interface

The `MBeanInfoAssembler` interface defines the management interface of each bean that is being exposed by Spring. It builds on the standard `ModelMBean` infrastructure and allows the full feature set of JMX to be exposed. The default implementation, `SimpleReflectiveMBeanInfoAssembler`, simply defines a management interface that exposes all the public properties and methods (as you have already seen in the previous examples). Spring also provides some additional implementations of the `MBeanInfoAssembler` interface, which allow you to control the generated management interface.

MethodNameBasedMBeanInfoAssembler Interface

This implementation of the `MBeanInfoAssembler` allows you to specify method names to be exposed as MBean operations and attributes. The code in Listing 20-7 shows a sample configuration.

Listing 20-7. *MethodNameBasedMBeanInfoAssembler*

```
<?xml version="1.0" encoding="UTF-8"?>
<beans xmlns="http://www.springframework.org/schema/beans"
       xmlns:xsi="http://www.w3.org/2001/XMLSchema-instance"
       xsi:schemaLocation="http://www.springframework.org/schema/beans ➥
 http://www.springframework.org/schema/beans/spring-beans-2.0.xsd">

    <bean id="exporter" class="org.springframework.jmx.export.MBeanExporter">
        <property name="beans">
            <map>
                <entry key="bean:name=methodNameBasedMBean" ➥
                           value-ref="springManagedBean" />
            </map>
        </property>
        <property name="assembler" ref="assembler" />
    </bean>
```

```
    <bean id="assembler" ➥
class="org.springframework.jmx.export.assembler.MethodNameBasedMBeanInfoAssembler">
        <property name="managedMethods" ➥
value="anotherExposedMethod,exposedMethod,getProperty,setProperty"/>
    </bean>

    <bean id="springManagedBean" ➥
            class="com.apress.prospring2.ch20.methodnamebased.SpringBean">
        <property name="property" value="TEST"/>
    </bean>

</beans>
```

Here, we are exposing exposedMethod and anotherExposedMethod as JMX operations. The getProperty() and setProperty() methods will be exposed as JMX attributes.

Then too, MethodExclusionMBeanInfoAssembler can be used to explicitly exclude methods as MBean operations and attributes. With this implementation, you need to supply an array of method names that will be *excluded* from being exposed. Listing 20-8 shows the Spring bean being exposed using MethodNameBasedMBeanInfoAssembler.

Listing 20-8. *MethodNameBasedMBeanInfoAssembler*

```
public class SpringBean {
    private String property;
    private String anotherProperty;

    public String getProperty() {
        return property;
    }

    public void setProperty(String property) {
        this.property = property;
    }

    public String getAnotherProperty() {
        return anotherProperty;
    }

    public void setAnotherProperty(String anotherProperty) {
        this.anotherProperty = anotherProperty;
    }

    public String exposedMethod() {
        return "This method is exposed.";
    }

    public String anotherExposedMethod() {
        return "This is another method that is exposed.";
    }

    public void notExposedMethod() {
        throw new RuntimeException();
    }
}
```

Now let's take a quick look at the Spring configuration for this example, which is shown in Listing 20-9.

Listing 20-9. *Spring Configuration for MethodNameBasedMBeanInfoAssembler*

```
<?xml version="1.0" encoding="UTF-8"?>
<beans xmlns="http://www.springframework.org/schema/beans"
       xmlns:xsi="http://www.w3.org/2001/XMLSchema-instance"
       xsi:schemaLocation="http://www.springframework.org/schema/beans
http://www.springframework.org/schema/beans/spring-beans-2.5.xsd">

    <bean id="exporter" class="org.springframework.jmx.export.MBeanExporter">
        <property name="beans">
            <map>
                <entry key="bean:name=methodNameBasedMBean" ➥
value-ref="springManagedBean" />
            </map>
        </property>
        <property name="assembler" ref="assembler" />
    </bean>

    <bean id="assembler" ➥
class="org.springframework.jmx.export.assembler.MethodNameBasedMBeanInfoAssembler">
        <property name="managedMethods" ➥
value="anotherExposedMethod,exposedMethod,getProperty,setProperty"/>
    </bean>

    <bean id="springManagedBean" ➥
class="com.apress.prospring2.ch20.methodnamebased.SpringBean">
        <property name="property" value="TEST"/>
    </bean>

</beans>
```

After running this example, if you connect to the JMX server using `jconsole`, you will be able to view the bean with only two exposed methods and one exposed attribute (see Figure 20-2).

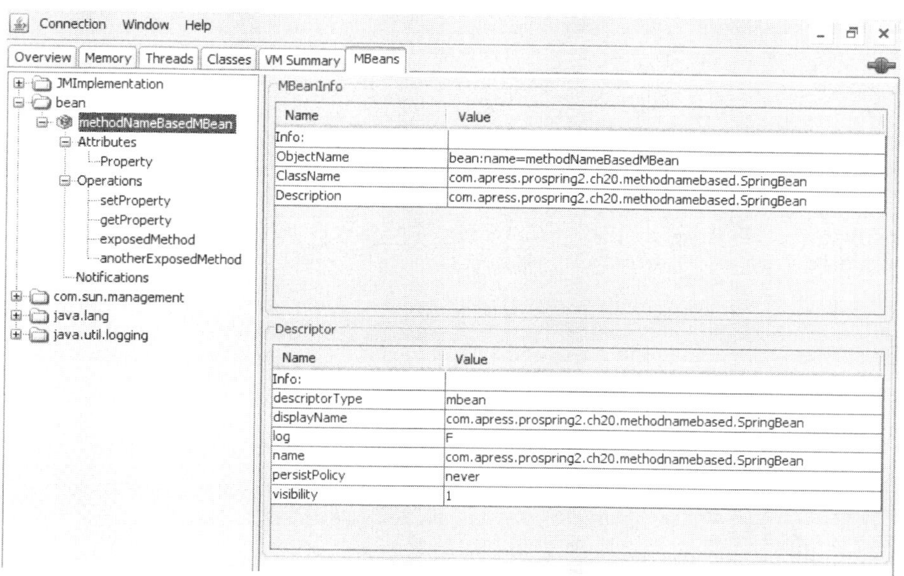

Figure 20-2. *MethodNameBasedMBeanInfoAssembler viewed in jconsole*

Using Java Interfaces to Control the Management Interface

`InterfaceBasedMBeanInfoAssembler` is another implementation of the `MBeanInfoAssembler` interface. This particular implementation allows the use of one or more Java interfaces to define the management methods.

Although the standard mechanism for exposing MBeans is to use interfaces and a simple naming scheme, the `InterfaceBasedMBeanInfoAssembler` extends this functionality by removing the need for naming conventions, allowing you to use more than one interface, and removes any need for your beans to implement the JMX specific management interfaces. Listing 20-10 shows our simple Spring bean.

Listing 20-10. *Sample Spring Bean*

```
public class SimpleSpringBean {
    private String property;
    private String anotherProperty;

    public String exposedMethod() {
        return "This method is exposed.";
    }

    public String anotherExposedMethod() {
        return "This is another method that is exposed.";
    }

    public void notExposedMethod() {
        throw new RuntimeException();
    }

    public String getProperty() {
        return property;
    }

    public void setProperty(String property) {
        this.property = property;
    }

    public String getAnotherProperty() {
        return anotherProperty;
    }

    public void setAnotherProperty(String anotherProperty) {
        this.anotherProperty = anotherProperty;
    }
}
```

Take a look at the management interface in Listing 20-11.

Listing 20-11. *ManagedInterface*

```
public interface ManagedInterface {

    void setProperty(String property);
    String getProperty();
    String exposedMethod();
    String anotherExposedMethod();
}
```

The ManagedInterface interface contains declarations of the methods to be exposed as JMX operations and attributes. Now, let's take a look at the XML configuration in Listing 20-12.

Listing 20-12. *Configuration for ManagedInterface*

```
<?xml version="1.0" encoding="UTF-8"?>
<beans xmlns="http://www.springframework.org/schema/beans"
       xmlns:xsi="http://www.w3.org/2001/XMLSchema-instance"
       xsi:schemaLocation="http://www.springframework.org/schema/beans➥
 http://www.springframework.org/schema/beans/spring-beans-2.5.xsd">

    <bean id="exporter" class="org.springframework.jmx.export.MBeanExporter">
        <property name="beans">
            <map>
                <entry key="bean:name=springManagedMBean" ➥
value-ref="springManagedBean" />
            </map>
        </property>
        <property name="assembler" ref="assembler" />
    </bean>

    <bean id="assembler" ➥
class="org.springframework.jmx.export.assembler.InterfaceBasedMBeanInfoAssembler">
        <property name="managedInterfaces">
           <list>
               <value>com.apress.prospring2.ch20.interfacebased.ManagedInterface➥
</value>
           </list>
        </property>
    </bean>

    <bean id="springManagedBean" ➥
class="com.apress.prospring2.ch20.interfacebased.SimpleSpringBean">
        <property name="property" value="TEST"/>
        <property name="anotherProperty" value="ANOTHER TEST" />
    </bean>

</beans>
```

Here, we have exposed only those methods defined on ManagedInterface on the MBean. The only difference from the method-name–based assembler you saw earlier is that we are now able to use Java interfaces to define our MBean management interfaces. Notice that our SimpleSpringBean has not implemented any interface. It is important to understand that beans processed by InterfaceBasedMBeanInfoAssembler are not required to implement the interface that is used to generate the JMX management interface.

In this particular case, ManagedInterface is used to construct all management interfaces for all beans. In many cases, this behavior is not desired, and you will often want to specify different interfaces for different beans. In those cases, you can pass a properties instance via the interfaceMapping property of the InterfaceBasedMBeanInfoAssembler, where the key of each entry is the bean name and the value of each entry is a comma-separated list of interface names to use for that bean.

If neither the managedInterfaces property nor the interfaceMapping property is set, then InterfaceBasedMBeanInfoAssembler will reflect on the beans and use all of the interfaces implemented by that bean to create the management interface.

Both InterfaceBasedMBeanInfoAssembler and MethodNameBasedMBeanInfoAssembler are suitable for assembling an MBean's managed interface, especially when you do not have access to the source code of the beans that are to be exported. Figure 20-3 shows the `jconsole` view when connected to our previous example of `ManagedInterface`.

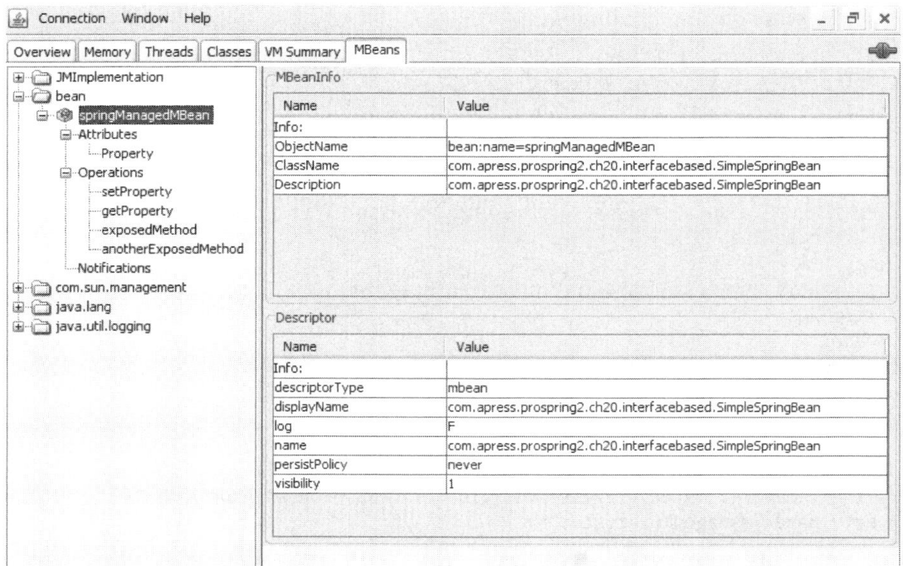

Figure 20-3. *Example of ManagedInterface usage*

Using Source-Level Metadata

At times, you might want some way to easily associate JMX metadata with a bean class in order to provide greater detail to the JMX client, such as `jconsole`.

Using `MetadataBeanInfoAssembler`, you can define the management interfaces of your beans using source-level metadata. The reading of the metadata is controlled by the `JmxAttributeSource` interface. Spring provides two implementations of this interface: `AttributesJmxAttributeSource` for using Commons Attributes and `AnnotationJmxAttributeSource` for JDK 5.0 annotations. You must configure `MetadataBeanInfoAssembler` with an implementation instance of `JmxAttributeSource` for it to function properly, as there is no default configuration.

One disadvantage of the source-level metadata approach is that the beans that can be simple Java classes when using the interface-based approach must now have Spring-specific annotations applied to their source code. In return, you can tell Spring to set much more of the generated model MBean's metadata. In the following example, we will look at using JDK annotations in the metadata. Listing 20-13 shows the annotated Java source code.

Listing 20-13. *Annotated Spring Bean*

```
package com.apress.prospring2.ch20.metadatabased;

import org.springframework.jmx.export.annotation.ManagedResource;
import org.springframework.jmx.export.annotation.ManagedAttribute;
import org.springframework.jmx.export.annotation.ManagedOperation;

@ManagedResource(objectName = "bean:name=metadataBasedMBean", ➥
description = "Metadata based MBean.")
public class SpringBean {
```

```
    private String property;
    private String anotherProperty;

    @ManagedOperation(description = "This is a managed operation.")
    public String exposedMethod() {
        return "This method is exposed.";
    }

    @ManagedOperation(description = "This is another managed operation.")
    public String anotherExposedMethod() {
        return "This is another method that is exposed.";
    }

    public void notExposedMethod() {
        throw new RuntimeException();
    }

    @ManagedAttribute(description = "An attribute.")
    public String getProperty() {
        return property;
    }

    public void setProperty(String property) {
        this.property = property;
    }

    public String getAnotherProperty() {
        return anotherProperty;
    }

    @ManagedAttribute(description = "Another attribute.")
    public void setAnotherProperty(String anotherProperty) {
        this.anotherProperty = anotherProperty;
    }
}
```

Here, the `SpringBean` class exposes multiple operations and attributes with the help of the `@ManagedOperation` and `@ManagedAttribute` annotations. Now, let's have a look at the XML configuration file shown in Listing 20-14.

Listing 20-14. *Configuration of the Annotated Spring Bean*

```
<?xml version="1.0" encoding="UTF-8"?>
<beans xmlns="http://www.springframework.org/schema/beans"
       xmlns:xsi="http://www.w3.org/2001/XMLSchema-instance"
       xsi:schemaLocation="http://www.springframework.org/schema/beans ➥
http://www.springframework.org/schema/beans/spring-beans-2.0.xsd">

    <bean id="exporter" class="org.springframework.jmx.export.MBeanExporter">
        <property name="assembler" ref="assembler" />
        <property name="namingStrategy" ref="namingStrategy" />
        <property name="autodetect" value="true" />
    </bean>
```

```
    <bean id="assembler" ➥
class="org.springframework.jmx.export.assembler.MetadataMBeanInfoAssembler">
        <property name="attributeSource" ref="jmxAttributeSource" />
    </bean>

    <bean id="namingStrategy" ➥
class="org.springframework.jmx.export.naming.MetadataNamingStrategy">
        <property name="attributeSource" ref="jmxAttributeSource" />
    </bean>

    <bean id="jmxAttributeSource" ➥
class="org.springframework.jmx.export.annotation.AnnotationJmxAttributeSource" />
    <bean id="springManagedBean" ➥
class="com.apress.prospring2.ch20.metadatabased.SpringBean">
        <property name="property" value="TEST"/>
    </bean>

</beans>
```

The most interesting aspect of the XML configuration is `MBeanExporter`'s use of `MetadataMBeanInfoAssembler` and its use of `AnnotationJmxAttributeSource`. Notice that, in this case, no beans are passed to `MBeanExporter`, but the `SpringBean` instance will still be registered since it is marked with the `@ManagedResource` annotation.

Figure 20-4 shows the `jconsole` view of the running example.

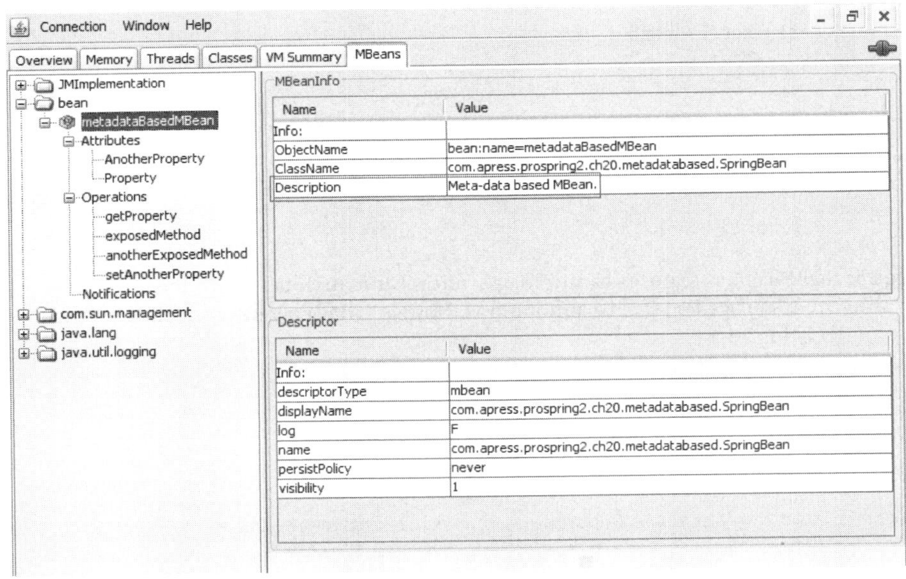

Figure 20-4. *Metadata-based MBean*

As you can see, the description of the MBean shows the value that we used to annotate our `SpringBean`.

Remoting with Spring JMX

The Java Community Process's JSR 160, the Java Management Extensions Remote API Specification, defines a standard for JMX remoting, which at minimum requires an RMI binding and optionally the JMX Messaging Protocol (JMXMP).

Spring JMX provides excellent support for remote access by offering two `FactoryBean` implementations in the `org.springframework.jmx.support` package. Using these classes, we can create both server-side and client-side connectors.

Exposing Remote MBeans

To expose Spring Beans as remote objects, we need to configure Spring's `ConnectorServerFactoryBean`. This will create and start a JSR-160–style `JMXConnectorServer`. By default the server will listen to JMXMP on port 9875 and will be bound to the URL `service:jmx:jmxmp://localhost:9875`. However, most JMX implementations do not support JMXMP, so for our examples, we will need to choose some other protocol for accessing the MBeans.

Depending on the JMX provider in use, you may have several remoting protocol options to choose from, such as RMI, SOAP, Hessian/Burlap, and IIOP. RMI is sufficient for our needs, so we will be building our examples to expose beans remotely with it. Listing 20-15 shows the configuration of `SimpleServerBean`.

Listing 20-15. *Configuration of SimpleServerBean*

```
<?xml version="1.0" encoding="UTF-8"?>
<beans xmlns="http://www.springframework.org/schema/beans"
       xmlns:xsi="http://www.w3.org/2001/XMLSchema-instance"
       xsi:schemaLocation="http://www.springframework.org/schema/beans ➥
 http://www.springframework.org/schema/beans/spring-beans-2.0.xsd">

    <bean id="springManagedBean" ➥
class="com.apress.prospring2.ch20.remote.server.SimpleServerBean">
        <property name="property" value="TEST"/>
        <property name="anotherProperty" value="ANOTHER TEST" />
    </bean>

    <bean id="exporter" class="org.springframework.jmx.export.MBeanExporter">
        <property name="beans">
            <map>
                <entry key="bean:name=springManagedMBean" ➥
                          value-ref="springManagedBean" />
            </map>
        </property>
        <property name="assembler" ref="assembler" />
    </bean>

    <bean id="assembler" ➥
class="org.springframework.jmx.export.assembler.InterfaceBasedMBeanInfoAssembler">
        <property name="managedInterfaces">
            <list>
                <value>com.apress.prospring2.ch20.remote.server. ➥
ManagedInterface</value>
            </list>
        </property>

    </bean>
```

```
    <bean id="registry" ➥
class="org.springframework.remoting.rmi.RmiRegistryFactoryBean">
        <property name="port" value="1099"/>
    </bean>

    <bean id="serverConnector" ➥
class="org.springframework.jmx.support.ConnectorServerFactoryBean" ➥
depends-on="registry">
        <property name="objectName" value="connector:name=rmi"/>
        <property name="serviceUrl" ➥
value="service:jmx:rmi://localhost/jndi/rmi://localhost:1099/jmxrmi"/>
    </bean>

</beans>
```

Here, the `serviceUrl` property is used to specify the remote binding for the `JMXConnectorService`; we are binding it to an RMI registry listening on port `1099` of the `localhost`. The registry bean creates and starts an RMI registry through Spring. The `serverConnector` references the RMI registry using the `depends-on` attribute.

Now, the MBeans are available through RMI. But there's little point in doing this if nobody ever accesses the MBeans over RMI, so now we will look at how to access the remote MBeans.

Accessing Remote MBeans

Spring provides `MBeanServerConnectionFactoryBean` for accessing a remote MBean. Let's look at the XML configuration snippet in Listing 20-16.

Listing 20-16. *Remote Bean XML Configuration Code Snippet*

```
<bean id="clientConnector" ➥
class="org.springframework.jmx.support.MBeanServerConnectionFactoryBean">
        <property name="serviceUrl" value="service:jmx:rmi://localhost:1099/jmxrmi"/>
    </bean>

<bean id="clientBean" ➥
class="com.apress.prospring2.ch20.remote.client.SimpleClient">
        <property name="mbeanServerConnection" ref="clientConnector"/>
    </bean>
```

Here, `MBeanServerConnectionFactoryBean` is a Spring `FactoryBean` that creates an `MBeanServerConnection` instance, which then acts as a local proxy to the remote MBean server. As you can see in the configuration, `clientBean`'s `mbeanServerConnection` property is wired using the `clientConnector` bean.

Proxying MBeans

Spring's `MBeanProxyFactoryBean` allows you to create proxies of MBeans that are registered in a local or remote `MBeanServer`. Instead of providing proxy-based access to remote beans via RMI or Hessian/Burlap, `MBeanProxyFactoryBean` lets you access remote MBeans directly, like any other locally configured bean. These proxies provide you with a standard Java interface through which you can interact with your MBean. The configuration code snippet in Listing 20-17 shows you how to configure a proxy for an MBean running in a local `MBeanServer`.

Listing 20-17. *Configuration for a Proxy to an MBean*

```
<bean id="clientConnector" ➥
class="org.springframework.jmx.support.MBeanServerConnectionFactoryBean">
     <property name="serviceUrl" value="service:jmx:rmi://localhost:1099/jmxrmi"/>
</bean>

<bean id="proxyBean" ➥
class="org.springframework.jmx.access.MBeanProxyFactoryBean">
     <property name="objectName" value="bean:name=springManagedBean"/>
     <property name="proxyInterface" ➥
value="com.apress.prospring2.ch20.remote.proxy.ManagedInterface"/>
</bean>
```

In the preceding configuration, a proxy is being created for the MBean registered under the `ObjectName` `bean:name=springManagedBean`. The set of interfaces that the proxy will implement is controlled by the `proxyInterface` property, and the rules for mapping methods and properties on those interfaces to operations and attributes on the MBean are the same rules used by `InterfaceBasedMBeanInfoAssembler`. The `MBeanProxyFactoryBean` can create a proxy to any MBean that is accessible via an MBean server connection (`MBeanServerConnection`). By default, the local MBean server is located and used, but you can override this and provide an `MBeanServerConnection` pointing to a remote `MBeanServer` to cater for proxies pointing to remote MBeans. In Listing 20-17, we create an `MBeanServerConnection` instance pointing to a remote machine using `MBeanServerProxyFactoryBean`. This `MBeanServerConnection` is then passed on to `MBeanProxyFactoryBean` via the `server` property. The proxy that is created will forward all invocations to `MBeanServer` via `MBeanServerConnection`.

You have now seen several ways of communicating with MBeans, and you can view and tweak your Spring bean configuration while the application is running. In the next section, we are going to take a look at listening to JMX notifications.

Notifications in Spring JMX

Notifications allow MBeans to send asynchronous messages when something interesting happens. For example, JMX notifications can be used to inform users if there's an application fault, if the application has reached or exceeded a resource usage limit, or if the state of the application has changed. Using notifications reduces, or completely eliminates, the need to constantly poll or otherwise review the state of MBeans.

Spring 2.5 provides excellent and comprehensive support for publishing JMX notifications.

Notification Listeners

Listing 20-18 shows an example of a custom notification listener that responds to changes in the state of attributes in MBeans. This simplified example doesn't do anything fancy—it just prints out the fact that a notification was published to the system console. But production implementations could, for instance, send e-mails to the support team in response to the notification.

Listing 20-18. *CustomNotificationListener*

```
public class CustomNotificationListener
             implements NotificationListener, NotificationFilter {

   public void handleNotification(Notification notification, Object handback) {
       System.out.format("Received '%s'n", notification );
   }
```

```
    public boolean isNotificationEnabled(Notification notification) {
        // since we are only interested in attribute changes, we filter out ➥
all other notification types
        return AttributeChangeNotification.class.isAssignableFrom( ➥
notification.getClass());
    }
}
```

Let's take a look at the configuration of the custom notification listener shown in Listing 20-19.

Listing 20-19. *Configuration for the CustomNotificationListener*

```
<beans>

  <bean id="exporter" class="org.springframework.jmx.export.MBeanExporter">
    <property name="beans">
      <map>
        <entry key="bean:name=notificationSpringBean" value-ref="springBean"/>
      </map>
    </property>
    <property name="notificationListenerMappings">
      <map>
        <entry key="bean:name=notificationSpringBean">
          <bean class= ➥
"com.apress.prospring2.ch20.listener.CustomNotificaitonListener"/>
        </entry>
      </map>
    </property>
  </bean>

  <bean id="springBean" ➥
class=" com.apress.prospring2.ch20.listener.SimpleSpringBean">
    <property name="someProperty" value="TEST"/>
    <property name="anotherProperty" value="1000"/>
  </bean>

</beans>
```

Now, whenever a JMX `Notification` is broadcast from the MBean with the `ObjectName` `bean:name=notificationSpringBean`, the `CustomNotificationListener` bean will be notified, and the `handleNotification(..)` method that prints a message to the system console will be invoked.

Note that your custom `NotificationListener` implementations will need to return quickly from their `handleNotification(..)` method so that they do not block the broadcasting thread. If you need to do any work in the `handleNotification(..)` method that might take a significant amount of time, consider delegating that work to another thread or placing it on a queue for execution later.

Publishing Notifications

In the previous example, you saw how to register a notification listener to listen for notifications generated by a target MBean. Spring also provides extensive support for publishing notifications. In the next example, we will demonstrate how to publish a JMX `Notification` via Spring for remote listeners. The first code, in Listing 20-20, is the Spring XML configuration.

Listing 20-20. *Configuration for Notification Publisher*

```
<?xml version="1.0" encoding="UTF-8"?>
<beans xmlns="http://www.springframework.org/schema/beans"
       xmlns:xsi="http://www.w3.org/2001/XMLSchema-instance"
       xsi:schemaLocation="http://www.springframework.org/schema/beans ➥
http://www.springframework.org/schema/beans/spring-beans-2.0.xsd">

    <bean id="simpleObject"
          class="com.apress.prospring2.ch20.notification.SimpleSpringBean" />

    <bean class="org.springframework.jmx.export.MBeanExporter">
       <property name="beans">
          <map>
             <entry key="notification.example:name=jmx,type=simpleSpringBean"
                    value-ref="simpleObject" />
          </map>
       </property>
    </bean>

    <bean id="registry" ➥
class="org.springframework.remoting.rmi.RmiRegistryFactoryBean">
       <property name="port" value="1099"/>
    </bean>

    <bean id="serverConnector"
          class="org.springframework.jmx.support.ConnectorServerFactoryBean"
          depends-on="registry">
       <property name="objectName" value="connector:name=rmi"/>
       <property name="serviceUrl"
                 value="service:jmx:rmi://localhost/jndi/ ➥
rmi://localhost:1099/jmxrmi"/>
    </bean>

</beans>
```

Interestingly, this XML configuration includes nothing specific to publishing JMX notifications, although it does contain entries to handle remote JMX. The next source code, in Listing 20-21, shows a pretty normal Java class, but it does feature the Spring-specific interface NotificationPublisherAware.

Listing 20-21. *SimpleSpringBean*

```
public class SimpleSpringBean implements NotificationPublisherAware {

   private int notificationIndex;
   private NotificationPublisher notificationPublisher;
   private String someValue = "Nada";

   public String getSomeValue() {
      return this.someValue;
   }

   public void setSomeValue(String aSomeValue) {
      notificationPublisher.sendNotification(➥
buildNotification(this.someValue, aSomeValue) );
      this.someValue = aSomeValue;
   }
```

```
   /**
    * Generate a Notification that will ultimately be published to interested
    * listeners.
    *
    * @param aOldValue Value prior to setting of new value.
    * @param aNewValue Value after setting of new value.
    * @return Generated JMX Notification.
    */
   private Notification buildNotification(String aOldValue, String aNewValue ) {
      String notificationType = "com.apress.prospring2.ch20.notification";
      String message = "Converting " + aOldValue + " to " + aNewValue;
      Notification notification =
         new Notification( notificationType,
                           this,
                           notificationIndex++,
                           System.currentTimeMillis(),
                           message );
      notification.setUserData("Example #" + notificationIndex );
      return notification;
   }

   /**
    * This is the only method required to fully implement the
    * NotificationPublisherAware interface.  This method allows Spring to
    * inject a NotificationPublisher into an instance of this class.
    *
    * @param aPublisher The NotificationPublisher that Spring injects..
    */
   public void setNotificationPublisher(NotificationPublisher aPublisher) {
      this.notificationPublisher = aPublisher;
   }
}
```

The class in Listing 20-21 is not an MBean by itself. Rather, Spring exposes it as an MBean because of our use of MBeanExporter in the XML configuration. However, some JMX-specific classes in this class enable notifications. Also, as mentioned previously, the Spring-specific NotificationPublisherAware interface is also explicitly implemented by this class so that a NotificationPublisher can be injected.

To complete our example, we need a main executable Java class to bootstrap the Spring container and to allow us the opportunity to interact and set someValue so that the JMX notifications will be broadcast by the JMX infrastructure. The source code for the main class is shown in Listing 20-22.

Listing 20-22. *The SimpleMain Class for Notifications*

```
public class SimpleMain {

public static void main(String[] args) throws Exception {
    ConfigurableApplicationContext context = ➥
new ClassPathXmlApplicationContext(new String[] {
        "notification-jmx-context.xml"
    }, SimpleMain.class);

    SimpleSpringBean simpleSpringBean = ➥
(SimpleSpringBean) context.getBean("simpleObject");
    final Console systemConsole = System.console();
    if ( systemConsole != null )
    {
```

```
        final String terminateLoop = "exit";
        String choice = null;
        do
        {
            systemConsole.printf("Enter a choice: ");
            choice = systemConsole.readLine();
            if ( choice != null && !choice.isEmpty() )
            {
                simpleSpringBean.setSomeValue(choice);
            }
        }
        while (   choice != null
            && !choice.isEmpty()
            && !choice.equals(terminateLoop) );
        }
    Else
    {
        System.err.println( ➥
"Please run this in an environment with a system console.");
    }
    context.close();
}
}
```

The class in Listing 20-22 can be run to use the Spring container to expose `SimpleSpringBean` as an MBean capable of sending JMX notifications to local or remote clients. Note that at least Java Standard Edition 6 is required to run this example, because it uses features specific to Java SE 6 (specifically the `Console` class). When this main Java class is executed, the output will look something like the screen snapshot shown in Figure 20-5.

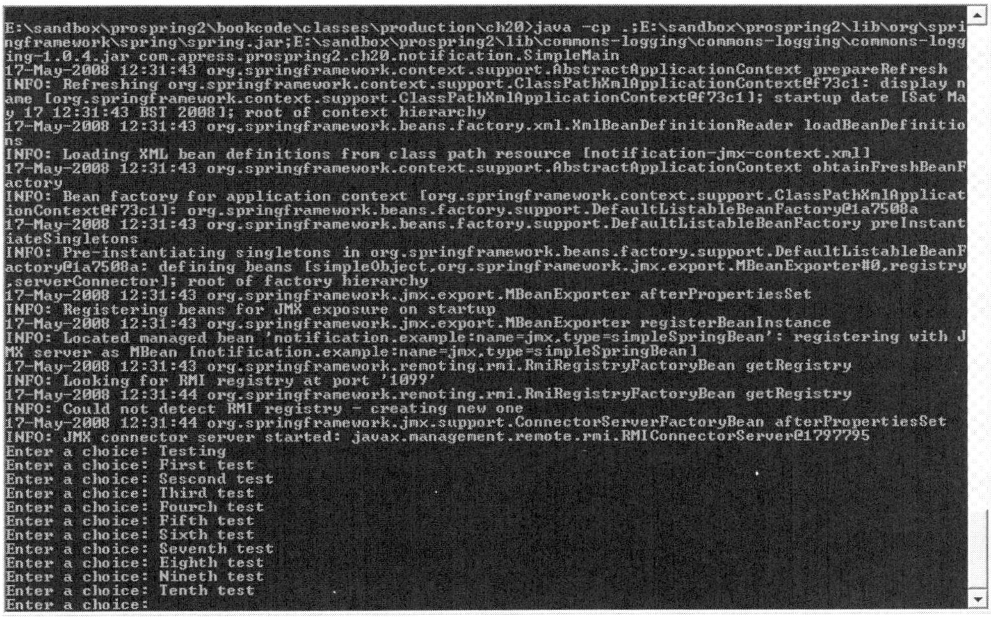

```
E:\sandbox\prospring2\bookcode\classes\production\ch20>java -cp .;E:\sandbox\prospring2\lib\org\spri
ngframework\spring\spring.jar;E:\sandbox\prospring2\lib\commons-logging\commons-logging\commons-logg
ing-1.0.4.jar com.apress.prospring2.ch20.notification.SimpleMain
17-May-2008 12:31:43 org.springframework.context.support.AbstractApplicationContext prepareRefresh
INFO: Refreshing org.springframework.context.support.ClassPathXmlApplicationContext@f73c1: display n
ame [org.springframework.context.support.ClassPathXmlApplicationContext@f73c1]; startup date [Sat Ma
y 17 12:31:43 BST 2008]; root of context hierarchy
17-May-2008 12:31:43 org.springframework.beans.factory.xml.XmlBeanDefinitionReader loadBeanDefinitio
ns
INFO: Loading XML bean definitions from class path resource [notification-jmx-context.xml]
17-May-2008 12:31:43 org.springframework.context.support.AbstractApplicationContext obtainFreshBeanF
actory
INFO: Bean factory for application context [org.springframework.context.support.ClassPathXmlApplicat
ionContext@f73c1]: org.springframework.beans.factory.support.DefaultListableBeanFactory@1a7508a
17-May-2008 12:31:43 org.springframework.beans.factory.support.DefaultListableBeanFactory preInstant
iateSingletons
INFO: Pre-instantiating singletons in org.springframework.beans.factory.support.DefaultListableBeanF
actory@1a7508a: defining beans [simpleObject,org.springframework.jmx.export.MBeanExporter#0,registry
,serverConnector]; root of factory hierarchy
17-May-2008 12:31:43 org.springframework.jmx.export.MBeanExporter afterPropertiesSet
INFO: Registering beans for JMX exposure on startup
17-May-2008 12:31:43 org.springframework.jmx.export.MBeanExporter registerBeanInstance
INFO: Located managed bean 'notification.example:name=jmx,type=simpleSpringBean': registering with J
MX server as MBean [notification.example:name=jmx,type=simpleSpringBean]
17-May-2008 12:31:43 org.springframework.remoting.rmi.RmiRegistryFactoryBean getRegistry
INFO: Looking for RMI registry at port '1099'
17-May-2008 12:31:44 org.springframework.remoting.rmi.RmiRegistryFactoryBean getRegistry
INFO: Could not detect RMI registry - creating new one
17-May-2008 12:31:44 org.springframework.jmx.support.ConnectorServerFactoryBean afterPropertiesSet
INFO: JMX connector server started: javax.management.remote.rmi.RMIConnectorServer@1797795
Enter a choice: Testing
Enter a choice: First test
Enter a choice: Sescond test
Enter a choice: Third test
Enter a choice: Fourch test
Enter a choice: Fifth test
Enter a choice: Sixth test
Enter a choice: Seventh test
Enter a choice: Eighth test
Enter a choice: Nineth test
Enter a choice: Tenth test
Enter a choice:
```

Figure 20-5. *Screen shot of the console*

We can also run `jconsole` to confirm that the JMX notifications are being broadcast and received. Figure 20-6 shows a screen snapshot of how `jconsole` appears when run alongside the application executed in Listing 20-22. Note that we had `jconsole` already running when executing the main Java application and that we had clicked its Subscribe button in the MBean's Notifications tab.

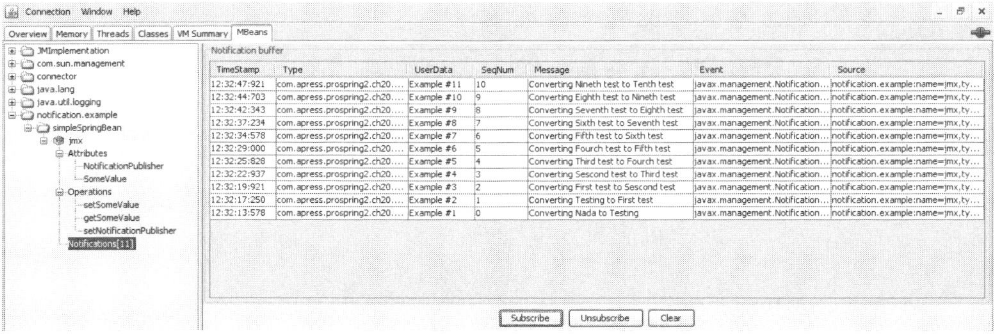

Figure 20-6. *Screen shot of jconsole running alongside Listing 20-22*

There are several interesting observations from this `jconsole` output. For one, `jconsole` nicely displays the timestamps we provided in the notification as a `long` timestamp. Another interesting observation is that the `UserData` column displays exactly the `String` we passed into the `Notification.setUserData()` method in the code. Passing the `String` value only worked because we have passed a `String` to this method that expects an `Object`. If we need to pass a class, then the class needs to have a `toString()` method overridden appropriately. Using a `String` was the easy way for the purposes of this example.

■ **Note** Any natural JMX MBeans (objects that are MBeans before Spring exposes them as such) should *not* use Spring's JMX publication support and should instead use JMX Notification APIs directly.

Summary

JMX is an important part of enterprise applications, and Spring provides excellent support for adding JMX-specific features to your own applications.

In this chapter, you have seen how to use Spring to simplify the integration of JMX functionality for your applications. You saw how to expose plain Spring beans as MBeans, and you saw some advanced features of Spring-based JMX integration like specifying the `ObjectName` attribute of exported MBeans and how to control the management interface that is exposed. In the last part of the chapter, you saw how easy it is to include notification listening and publishing in your application.

CHAPTER 21

Testing with Spring

Testing is a crucial part of software development; we believe you should not even think about releasing a piece of software that has not been tested in some way. The easiest testing technique is unit testing. It allows you to test each component of the application separately, in a controlled environment. Once you know that all components work on their own, it may be appropriate to run integration tests. However, these are difficult to implement, especially when you are dealing with large applications using EJBs and JTA transactions. In these cases, integration tests may be impossible to write. Once your application is tested and found to be fully functional, it is time to do some performance testing. This type of testing may bring up threading and JVM heap usage issues you would not otherwise notice.

Some testing methods are far too complex for the scope of this chapter, leaving us with just unit testing, integration testing, and the TestContext Framework to discuss.

First, we will take a look at how unit tests work, focusing in particular on the JUnit framework. We will discuss the importance of mock objects and of writing tests that can be repeated at any time and always get the same results. We will show you methods that will allow you to test local transactions and business logic components.

Even though integration testing is difficult to simulate because of environment setup requirements, we will show you some techniques that can be used to test component integration as thoroughly as possible.

Finally, we will cover the new TestContext testing platform introduced in Spring 2.5, including configuration, annotations, and some testing techniques.

Unit Testing

As its name suggests, unit testing individually tests the components of your applications; it allows you to prove that a single class works in terms of contract checking and functionality.

Contract checking means that the class should check that it is called within specifications—with correct arguments, correct exception handling, and so on. Let's assume there is a class with a method that returns a square root of a real (`double`) number. If the argument passed to the function is negative or `NaN` (Not a Number), the method will throw an `IllegalArgumentException`. The unit test for this class should test the contract by calling the method with a negative argument and then with a `NaN` function. In both cases, an `IllegalArgumentException` must be thrown. Once we have tested the contract, we must also test the functionality. Using our square root method, we will call it with `9` and then check that the returned value is `3`.

Note A *double* cannot represent certain numbers precisely, hence the test should allow for some tolerance. This tolerance is determined by the expected usage of the method we are testing.

Unfortunately, we will rarely be testing such simple methods. In most cases, the tests will be far more complex, making it very easy to miss a situation that might cause the tested class to fail. This is not a problem of unit testing as such; it is a problem for the programmer who writes incomplete unit tests. We will discuss ways of making sure the unit tests cover all the code later in the chapter.

To simplify the task of writing unit tests, we can use existing unit test frameworks, such as JUnit. You can download the latest version of JUnit at `http://www.junit.org/`, but if you are using a Java IDE such as IntelliJ IDEA, Eclipse, or JBuilder, chances are that JUnit is already bundled with the IDE.

Let's write our first, very simple JUnit test; Listing 21-1 shows that the code of the unit test will always succeed, as it is not actually testing anything.

Listing 21-1. *A JUnit Test*

```
public class TestAll extends TestCase {
    public void testFoo() {

    }
}
```

The individual JUnit tests are subclasses of `TestCase`, which offers basic assertion and failure methods. The failure methods are often used in contract testing, while the assertion methods are used in functionality testing. The individual tests are simple `public void` methods whose names begin with "test." Each test method is allowed to throw `Exception`.

To test our imaginary square root method, the code for the test method might look like Listing 21-2.

Listing 21-2. *A Test for the Square Root Method*

```
public void testSqrtWithNegativeNumber() {
    try {
        sqrt(-1);
        fail("This function returns only real results");
    } catch (IllegalArgumentException expected) {
        // OK
    }
}
public void testSqrtWithNaN() {
    try {
        sqrt(Double.NaN);
        fail("This function cannot take +/-NaN as argument");
    } catch (IllegalArgumentException expected) {
        // OK
    }
}
public void testSqrtCorrect() {

    assertEquals(3.0, sqrt(9), 0);
}
```

As you can see, the test for the simple `sqrt()` method is far longer than the actual implementation, but once it has been run successfully, we can be sure that the `sqrt()` method will function correctly and that any errors will be handled correctly. Listing 21-2 also demonstrates how to use the `fail()` and `assert*()` methods to perform the testing.

In most cases, the classes being tested (the targets) require other objects in order to function. Imagine a unit test for a piece of business logic; it will probably require data access classes to retrieve and store the data it processes. Let's imagine you are testing a discount calculation that applies a discount to an order based on the value of the order and those of previous orders. You *could* use the data access layer that takes the data from the database, but this is rarely a good solution. The unit test does not test the business component in isolation; instead it tests the data access components as well as the database. Furthermore, the tables in the database must contain suitable data to test all nuances of the discount calculation algorithm. This makes the test very fragile: a change in the data may influence the result of the test.

It is better to create stub or mock classes for the target's dependencies. In the case of the discount calculation business component, you will probably have to create a mock order data access component. Because you are programming a Spring application, this component will most likely be an `OrderDao` interface. It is easy to provide an implementation of `OrderDao` so that it *always* returns the correct data for the test, without accessing the database. This way, the unit test will be completely isolated and will allow you to run repeated tests without influencing any other components of your application.

However, implementing stub and mock classes for all of your classes can lead to a lot of repetitive work and is very time consuming. That's why you should use some of the available open source libraries for quick and easy ways to define mock objects. We will use jMock (`www.jmock.org`) for the examples in this chapter.

■ **Note** The terms "stub" and "mock" are often used as synonyms in programming literature. However, they are not the same: stubs are usually very simple implementations of the target interface, usually designed to respond only to calls from the test they are designed for, and they are used to create required input for the class under test. Mocks are actual implementation objects, *used* by a class under test. For more information about stubs and mocks, please see Martin Fowler's blog at `http://martinfowler.com/articles/mocksArentStubs.html#TheDifferenceBetweenMocksAndStubs`.

Unit Tests

Now that you know about unit tests and the basics of the JUnit framework, we can look at how to implement tests so that you can be sure they accurately yet unobtrusively test all aspects of your code.

It is important to realize that even though we are developing the application using Spring and taking advantage of all its dependency injection and proxy features, we still need to make sure the classes that implement our application's interfaces work correctly on their own. This is why we are not going to create the Spring application context; instead, we will manually create instances of the tested classes and set their dependencies. The dependencies are going to be mock implementations of the dependency interfaces.

For the unit test example, we will test the `DefaultInvoiceService.findById(Long id)` method, which uses the `invoiceDao` interface for database access (introduced in Chapter 11). But we will mock the `invoiceDao` for our tests, to test `DefaultInvoiceService` separately from its dependent classes.

Figure 21-1 shows the UML diagram of the `DefaultInvoiceService` class we're going to unit test (in the interests of clarity, only required methods are shown in the UML diagram).

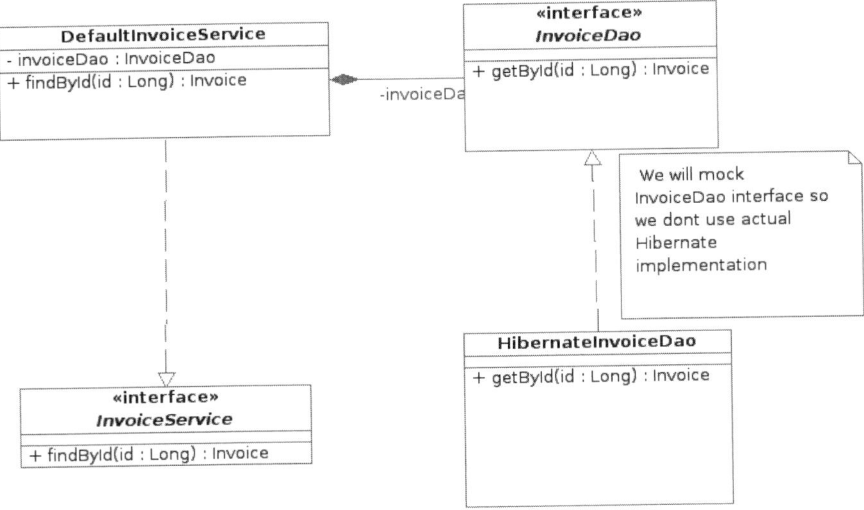

Figure 21-1. *UML diagram for the DefaultInvoiceService*

Listing 21-3 shows the InvoiceService interface declaration in Java.

Listing 21-3. *InvoiceService Interface*

```
public interface InvoiceService {

    List<Invoice> search(int firstResult, int pageSize);

    Invoice findById(Long id);

    void recalculateDiscounts(Long id);

    void save(Invoice invoice);

    List<Invoice> findAll();

}
```

Now, let's look at the implementation of this interface, DefaultInvoiceService (see Listing 21-4). This class uses invoiceDao to perform basic database operations on the invoices.

Listing 21-4. *The DefaultInvoiceService Class*

```
public class DefaultInvoiceService implements InvoiceService {
    private InvoiceDao invoiceDao;

    public List<Invoice> search(int firstResult, int pageSize) {
        return this.invoiceDao.search(firstResult, pageSize);
    }

    public Invoice findById(Long id) {
        return this.invoiceDao.getById(id);
    }
```

```
    public void recalculateDiscounts(Long id) {
        Invoice invoice = this.invoiceDao.getByIdLazy(id);
        BigDecimal total = invoice.getLinesTotalPrice();
        if (total.compareTo(BigDecimal.TEN) > 0) {
            // do something special
        }
    }

    public void save(Invoice invoice) {
        this.invoiceDao.save(invoice);
    }

    public List<Invoice> findAll() {
        return this.invoiceDao.getAll();
    }

    public void setInvoiceDao(InvoiceDao invoiceDao) {
        this.invoiceDao = invoiceDao;
    }
}
```

Let's take a look at Listing 21-5, which shows how we have implemented the tests for the `DefaultInvoiceService`. We want to test `DefaultInvoiceService` in isolation, so we will mock the `invoiceDao` implementation it uses. By creating mocks of the dependencies of the `DefaultInvoiceService`, we can be certain that any test failures indicate the problem in the `DefaultInvoiceService`.

Listing 21-5. *DefaultInvoiceServiceTest Unit Test*

```
public class DefaultInvoiceServiceTests extends MockObjectTestCase {
    private Mock invoiceDao;
    private DefaultInvoiceService invoiceService;

    protected void setUp() throws Exception {
        this.invoiceDao = new Mock(InvoiceDao.class);
        invoiceService = new DefaultInvoiceService();
        invoiceService.setInvoiceDao((InvoiceDao)this.invoiceDao.proxy());
    }

    public void testFindById(){
        Invoice expectedResult = new Invoice();
        expectedResult.setId(1L);
        expectedResult.setDisputed(true);
        Long id = 1L;
        this.invoiceDao.expects(once()).method("getById").➥
with(eq(id)).will(returnValue(expectedResult));

        Invoice invoice = this.invoiceService.findById(1L);

        assertNotNull("Invoice must not be null", invoice);
        assertEquals("Invoice id does no match!", 1L, invoice.getId().longValue());
    }
...
}
```

Notice the line in bold: it says that we expect the DefaultInvoiceService to call the InvoiceDao.getById method with a value equal to id and that the method should return the expectedResult. If this test case succeeds, we have proof that the DefaultInvoiceService calls the InvoiceDao.getById(..) method each time it tries to execute the DefaultInvoiceService .findById(..) method. The DefaultInvoiceService requires one dependency, invoiceDao; we have provided a mock implementation for this interface using the jMock library. This test does not require any other external resources. We can run it as many times as we want and still the test will succeed or fail consistently. The result of running this unit test from IntelliJ IDEA is shown in Figure 21-2.

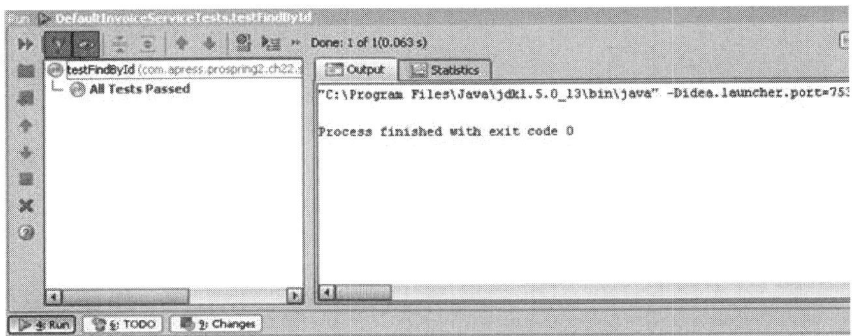

Figure 21-2. *Unit tests in IntelliJ IDEA*

Please see www.jmock.org for documentation on using mock objects for testing in your application.

Unit Testing the Web Layer

Spring provides convenient stub implementations of the interfaces used in web applications in the package org.springframework.mock.web. This package contains the collection of Servlet API stub objects, making it easy to use for testing the web layer of any Spring web application.

Recall the ProductImageFormController introduced in Chapter 17. It expects the name of the product and the image file in the request. We will show the code again in Listing 21-6.

Listing 21-6. *ProductImageFormController*

```
public class ProductImageFormController extends SimpleFormController {

    public ProductImageFormController() {
        super();
        setCommandClass(ProductImageForm.class);
        setFormView("products-image");
        setCommandName("product");
    }

    protected ModelAndView onSubmit(HttpServletRequest request,
                                    HttpServletResponse response, Object command,
                                    BindException errors) throws Exception {
        ProductImageForm form = (ProductImageForm) command;

        System.out.println(form.getName());
        byte[] contents = form.getContents();
```

```
        for (int i = 0; i < contents.length; i++) {
            System.out.print(contents[i]);
        }

        return new ModelAndView("products-index-r");
    }

    protected void initBinder(HttpServletRequest request,
                              ServletRequestDataBinder binder) throws Exception {
        binder.registerCustomEditor(byte[].class,
                new ByteArrayMultipartFileEditor());
    }

}
```

We now want to write a unit test for this Controller. However, the controller needs HttpServletRequest and HttpServletResponse interfaces to run the onSubmit method. In addition, ProductImageFormController needs MultipartHttpServletRequest to be able to accept the content of the file as part of the request. We will mock all the HttpServletRequest and HttpServletResponse interfaces by using convenience classes from the org.springframework.mock.web package. Listing 21-7 shows our test class.

Listing 21-7. *ProductImageFormControllerTests Class*

```
public class ProductImageFormControllerTests extends TestCase {
    private ProductImageFormController controller;

    public void testOnSubmit()throws Exception{
        controller = new ProductImageFormController();
        MockMultipartHttpServletRequest mockRequest = ➥
new MockMultipartHttpServletRequest();
        mockRequest.setMethod("POST");

        MockMultipartFile file = new MockMultipartFile("contents", ➥
new byte[] {1,2,1,2,23,});
        mockRequest.addFile(file);
        mockRequest.addParameter("name", "test");

        MockHttpServletResponse mockResponse = new MockHttpServletResponse();
        ModelAndView mav = controller.handleRequest(mockRequest, mockResponse);
        assertNotNull("ModelAndView returned must not ne null!", mav);
        assertEquals("Wrong view returned", "products-index-r", mav.getViewName());

    }
}
```

We have used MockMultipartHttpServletRequest (which extends MockHttpServletRequest) to mock the MultipartHttpServletRequest interface, and MockHttpServletResponse to mock HttpServletResponse. We have set the mockRequest method to "POST", as this is the method we're expecting in the controller. In addition, we have added the file to our MockMultipartHttpServletRequest. The file is actually another mock object, the MockMultipartFile. Its constructor accepts two parameters: a String object and a byte array. The String parameter is the parameter name from the mocked multipart form our tested controller expects, and the byte array contains the byte content of the file. Our test simply checks if the controller returns the correct view name.

If we do not have to deal with multipart requests, the `MockHttpServletRequest` implementation is sufficient for testing. The org.springframework.mock.web package provides a few more classes that are useful for unit testing web frameworks and web application controllers. Table 21-1 shows an overview of the main classes in this package.

Table 21-1. *The org.springframework.mock.web Package's Main Classes*

Class	Description
`MockHttpServletRequest`	This is a mock implementation of the `HttpServletRequest` interface (see previous examples in Listings 21-6 and 21-7).
`MockHttpServletResponse`	This is a mock implementation of the `HttpServletResponse` interface (see previous examples).
`MockHttpSession`	This mocks the `HttpSession` interface of the Servlet API and is used if your application controllers access the session.
`MockMultipartHttpServletRequest`	This mock implementation of the `MultipartHttpServletRequest` interface is used in your controller test to access multipart files for testing file upload from an HTML form. It's usually used with `MockMultipartFile`, as shown in the previous example.
`MockMultipartFile`	This is a mock implementation of the `MultipartFile` interface. As the example in this section shows, this class is used to populate `MockMultipartHttpServletRequest`.
`MockServletContext`	If your controllers access `ServletContext` directly, use this class to mock `ServletContext`. Point your working directory to the root of the web application directory to be able to keep the original paths.
`MockFilterConfig`	With this mock implementation of the `FilterConfig` interface, you can pass the `ServletContext` to the constructor or default to `MockServletContext`.
`MockFilterChain`	This is a mock implementation of the `FilterChain` interface.
`PassThroughFilterChain`	This is another convenient simple mock implementation of the `FilterChain` interface. You specify the servlet it should delegate the request to or specify another `Filter` and `FilterChain` if you want to delegate to the `Filter` using a given `FilterChain`.

Integration Tests

Integration tests may sound complex, but even a data-access-layer-implementation test that actually connects to the database and accesses the data in the appropriate tables is an integration test. Such a test requires interaction with the database, the Spring Framework, and the code being tested. If any part of this chain fails, the entire test fails.

Note Real integration tests used in the development process actually use much more than database interaction; they may use JMS, queues, Lucene indexing, Open Office, and more. All these tools and applications need to be configured, started, or connected when performing integration tests. For the clarity of the examples in this chapter, we use only the database for integration tests. But you should note that there are a lot more complicated cases in the development process to be considered when writing integration tests.

First, let's look at the UML diagram of the class structure we are going to use. Then we will explain every class separately before we actually start testing. Figure 21-3 shows the UML diagram of the class structure.

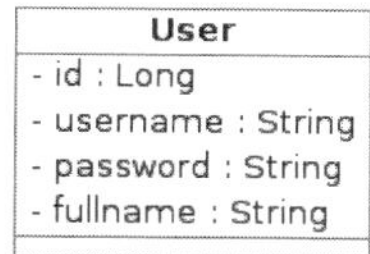

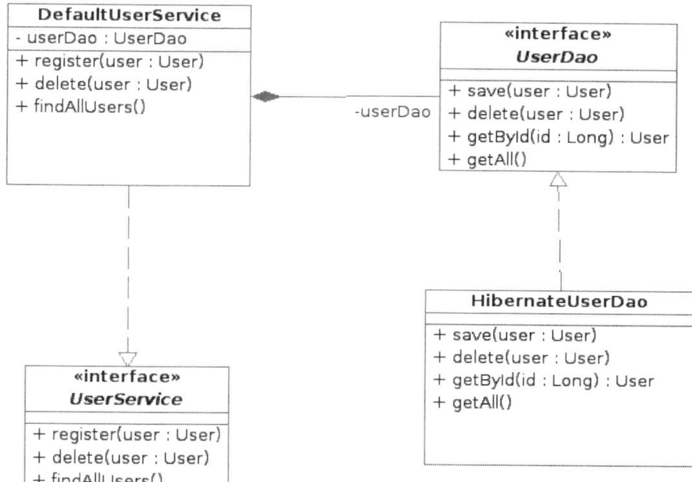

Figure 21-3. *UML diagram for the UserService class structure for testing*

Let's test the `DefaultUserService` class, which implements the `UserService` interface. Listing 21-8 shows the code for the `UserService` interface that we are going to use.

Listing 21-8. *UserService Interface*

```
public interface UserService {

    void register(User user);

    List<User> findAllUsers();

    void delete(User user);
}
```

Let's now look at how we could implement the `UserService`. We are not going to show anything complicated, in fact, except verifying the complexity of the password. The service simply delegates to the DAO (see Listing 21-9).

Listing 21-9. *DefaultUserService Implementation of UserService*

```
public class DefaultUserService implements UserService{

    private UserDao userDao;

    public void register(User user) {
        if(this.userDao.getByUsername(user.getUsername())!=null)
            throw new IllegalArgumentException("Same username already exists!");
        if(user.getPassword().length()<6)
            throw new IllegalArgumentException➥
                  ("Password must be at least 6 characters long");
        this.userDao.save(user);
    }

    public List<User> findAllUsers() {
        return this.userDao.getAll();
    }

    public void delete(User user){
        this.userDao.delete(user);
    }

    public void setUserDao(UserDao userDao) {
        this.userDao = userDao;
    }
}
```

The main method that we are going to test is `void register(User user)`; it simply saves the `User` to the database after checking the constraints for the username and password. The constraints are that the username must be unique (no other users can be already registered with the same username), and that the password must be at least six characters long. Listing 21-10 shows the `User` domain object we are using.

Listing 21-10. *The User Domain Object*

```
public class User{
    private Long id;
    private String username;
    private String fullname;
    private String password;

    public String getUsername() {
        return username;
    }

    public void setUsername(String username) {
        this.username = username;
    }

    public String getFullname() {
        return fullname;
    }

    public void setFullname(String fullname) {
        this.fullname = fullname;
    }
```

```
    public String getPassword() {
        return password;
    }

    public void setPassword(String password) {
        this.password = password;
    }
    public Long getId() {
        return id;
    }

    public void setId(Long id) {
        this.id = id;
    }
}
```

Actual database manipulation is implemented using Hibernate. Listing 21-11 shows the `UserDao` interface, which the `DefaultUserService` uses.

Listing 21-11. *The UserDao Interface*

```
public interface UserDao {

    void save(User user);

    void delete(User user);

    User getById(Long id);

    List<User> getAll();

    User getByUsername(String username);
}
```

The implementation of this class will use `hibernateTemplate` to communicate with the database. You can see the `HibernateUserDao` implementation in Listing 21-12. For more information on Hibernate and data access, please see Chapter 11.

Listing 21-12. *HibernateUserDao Implementation*

```
public class HibernateUserDao extends HibernateDaoSupport implements UserDao {

    public void save(User user) {
       getHibernateTemplate().save(user);
    }

    public void delete(User user) {
       getHibernateTemplate().delete(user);
    }

    public User getById(Long id) {
        return (User)getHibernateTemplate().get(User.class, id);
    }

    public List<User> getAll() {
        return getHibernateTemplate().find("from User");
    }
```

```
    public User getByUsername(String username) {
        List objects = getHibernateTemplate().➥
find("from User where username = ?", username);
// you can use DataAccessUtils.uniqueResult(collection).
        if (objects.size() == 1) return (User)objects.get(0);
        if (objects.size() > 1) {
            throw new InvalidResultException("Found more than one results");
        }
        return null;
    }
}
```

Next, we will need to write Spring context files for the data access layer, Hibernate, and the service layer. In Listing 21-13, you can see the `applicationContext-dataaccess.xml` file, which contains definitions for the `dataSource` bean, as well as all `userDao` beans.

Listing 21-13. *Spring Context XML File for Data Access Configuration*

```
<?xml version="1.0" encoding="UTF-8"?>
<beans xmlns="http://www.springframework.org/schema/beans"
....>

   <bean id="dataSource"➥
 class="org.springframework.jdbc.datasource.DriverManagerDataSource">
        <property name="driverClassName">
            <value>oracle.jdbc.OracleDriver</value>
        </property>
        <property name="url" value="jdbc:oracle:thin:@localhost:1521:INTL"/>
        <property name="username" value="PROSPRING"</property>
        <property name="password" value="x******6" </property>
    </bean>
    <bean id="hibernateSessionFactory" ➥
 class="org.springframework.orm.hibernate3.LocalSessionFactoryBean">
         <property name="dataSource" ref="dataSource"/>
         <property name="mappingLocations">
            <list>
               <value>classpath*:/com/apress/➥
prospring2/ch21/dataaccess/hibernate/*.hbm.xml</value>
           </list>
          </property>
         <property name="hibernateProperties">
             <props>
               <prop key="hibernate.dialect">➥
org.hibernate.dialect.Oracle9Dialect</prop>
            </props>
        </property>
    </bean>
     <bean id="hibernateDaoSupport" abstract="true" ➥
class="org.springframework.orm.hibernate3.support.HibernateDaoSupport">
        <property name="sessionFactory" ref="hibernateSessionFactory"/>
    </bean>
    <bean id="transactionManager"➥
 class="org.springframework.orm.hibernate3.HibernateTransactionManager">
        <property name="sessionFactory" ref="hibernateSessionFactory"/>
        <property name="nestedTransactionAllowed" value="false"/>
        <property name="dataSource" ref="dataSource"/>
    </bean>
```

```
    <bean id="userDao" ➥
class="com.apress.prospring2.ch21.dataaccess.hibernate.HibernateUserDao" ➥
parent="hibernateDaoSupport"/>

</beans>
```

Now that we have the data source and Hibernate beans configured, we need to write the mapping details. Hibernate uses the mapping files (`*.hbm.xml` files) to find out how to map the objects to the tables and columns in the tables. For more information about Hibernate, see Chapter 11.

Listing 21-14. *The Hibernate Configuration File*

```
<?xml version="1.0"?>
<!DOCTYPE hibernate-mapping PUBLIC
        "-//Hibernate/Hibernate Mapping DTD 3.0//EN"
        "http://hibernate.sourceforge.net/hibernate-mapping-3.0.dtd">

<hibernate-mapping default-lazy="true">

    <class name="com.apress.prospring2.ch21.domain.User" table="t_user">
        <id name="id" type="long" unsaved-value="null">
            <generator class="sequence">
                <param name="sequence">s_user_id</param>
            </generator>
        </id>
        <property name="username" column="username" not-null="true" />
        <property name="fullname" column="fullname" not-null="false" />
        <property name="password" column="password" not-null="true" />
    </class>

</hibernate-mapping>
```

Finally, we will need a Spring context file where we will define our services, which in our example means only the `userService` bean (the `DefaultUserService` implementation); see Listing 21-15.

Listing 21-15. *The applicationContext-services.xml Spring Context File for Configuring Services Beans*

```
<?xml version="1.0" encoding="UTF-8"?>
<beans xmlns="http://www.springframework.org/schema/beans"
...>
    <bean id="userService" ➥
class="com.apress.prospring2.ch21.services.DefaultUserService">
            <property name="userDao" ref="userDao"/>
    </bean>

</beans>
```

Manually creating beans for an integration test may be too difficult and unnecessary. Instead, we can create the Spring application context and let the framework instantiate the beans for us. In most cases, you will be using `XmlApplicationContext`, thus we will need to instantiate one of the `XmlApplicationContext` implementations. Let's take a look at the code in Listing 21-16 to see how we can go about this.

Listing 21-16. *Creating the Application Context*

```
public class DefaultUserServiceIntegrationTests extends TestCase {

    pprivate ApplicationContext getApplicationContext(){
        String [] paths = new String[] {
                "classpath*:/com/apress/prospring2/ch21/dataaccess/➥
applicationContext-dataaccess.xml",
                "classpath*:/com/apress/prospring2/ch21/services/➥
applicationContext-services.xml"
        };
        return new ClassPathXmlApplicationContext(paths);
    }

}
```

The paths[] array specifies the files that will be read to build the application context, and the actual implementation we are going to use is ClassPathXmlApplicationContext. We can then use the application context to programmatically get instances of the beans we need to test. Let's take a look at how we implemented the test for the DefaultUserService class in the sample application in Listing 21-17.

Listing 21-17. *DefaultUserServiceIntegrationTests Test Case*

```
public class DefaultUserServiceIntegrationTests extends TestCase {

    private ApplicationContext getApplicationContext(){
        String [] paths = new String[] {
                "classpath*:/com/apress/prospring2/ch21/dataaccess/➥
applicationContext-dataaccess.xml",
                "classpath*:/com/apress/prospring2/ch21/services/➥
applicationContext-services.xml"
        };
        return new ClassPathXmlApplicationContext(paths);
    }

    public void testRegisterSuccess(){
        ApplicationContext context = getApplicationContext();
        UserService userService = (UserService)context.getBean("userService");

        User user = new User();
        user.setUsername("jonhs");
        user.setPassword("hTy86dj");

        userService.register(user);

        assertNotNull("User not saved!", user.getId());
}
    public void testRegisterExistingUsername(){
        User user2= new User();
        user2.setUsername("jonhs");
        user2.setPassword("fGC467");
        try{
            userService.register(user2);
            fail("Cannot save user with existing username!");
        }catch(IllegalArgumentException ex){
            //OK
```

```
        }
        userService.delete(user);
    }

    public void testRegisterIncorrectPassword(){
        ApplicationContext context = getApplicationContext();
        UserService userService = (UserService)context.getBean("userService");

        User user3= new User();
        user3.setUsername("jandD");
        user3.setPassword("fgh85");
        try{
            userService.register(user3);
            fail("Password must be at least 6 characters long!");
        }catch(IllegalArgumentException ex){
            //OK
        }
    }
}
```

In this test, we used Spring to get an instance of UserService. Its property, userDao, will be loaded by the framework from the Spring configuration files. In each test method, we first call the getApplicationContext() method to load beans for XML context files. Then we look up the bean we need and get the class we use in the test.

In the first test method, void testRegister(), we first try to register a user with valid details. If registration succeeds, the id property of User will be set. In the same method, we try to register another user with the same username. We expect that the userService will throw an IllegalArgumentException, not allowing two users with the same username. If the exception is not thrown in the userService.register(..) method, we explicitly call the fail() method to signal incorrect behavior.

In the next test method, void testRegisterIncorrectPassword(), we test registering a user with a password less than six characters long, using the same technique, expecting IllegalArgumentException from userService.register() method.

And there it is—our first integration test! We have tested part of the business logic, but at the same time, we have also tested whether the Spring configuration files load beans correctly and whether database access works as it should.

Note that the user we successfully saved in this test will be permanently saved in the database. So if you try to repeat this test, it will fail unless you delete the entry from the database. That's why we have added the delete statement at the end of the successful test method, to put the database back in its original state (see the bold code in Listing 21-17). Ideally, every test should run within a transaction that rolls back when the test finishes.

But there is a lot of room for improvement in this testing code. Do we have to recreate ApplicationContext for every test method we implement? Do we really have to perform an ApplicationContext lookup in each test method whenever we want to access the bean? And do we have to write database cleanup code after every test that changes the database code?

The answer is "no" for every one of these questions; all these things can be done using one of the convenient test superclasses provided by Spring, as shown in the following sections.

Using AbstractSpringContextTests

Let's start refactoring DefaultUserServiceIntegrationTests by maintaining the Spring context throughout all our tests and caching context information so we don't need to rebuild the context for every test method. This can be done simply by making our test classes override the AbstractSpringContextTests from the org.springframework.test package that comes with the Spring distribution.

We will implement the abstract `loadContext(Objext o)` method in our test class, which loads context files and returns a built `ApplicationContext`. The `getContext(Object key)` method will return and cache the context loaded by the `loadContext(Object key)` method for the given key. If we want to access the Spring context in another test, the `getContext(Object key)` method will return cached context if the context for the specified key is already loaded, which will improve performance of the tests. If you specify the new key as a method parameter, the new context will be loaded and cached with that key. Listing 21-18 shows the refactored `DefaultUserServiceIntegrationTests` class.

Listing 21-18. *DefaultUserServiceIntegrationTests Refactored Using AbstractSpringContextTests*

```
public class DefaultUserServiceIntegrationTests extends AbstractSpringContextTests{

    protected ConfigurableApplicationContext loadContext(Object o) ➥
throws Exception {
        String [] paths = new String[] {
                "classpath*:/com/apress/prospring2/ch21/dataaccess/➥
applicationContext-dataaccess.xml",
                "classpath*:/com/apress/prospring2/ch21/services/➥
applicationContext-services.xml"
        };
        return new ClassPathXmlApplicationContext(paths);
    }

    public void testRegister() throws Exception{
        ApplicationContext context = getContext("mytestcontext");
        UserService userService = (UserService)context.getBean("userService");

        User user = new User();
        user.setUsername("jonhs");
        user.setPassword("hTy86dj");

        userService.register(user);

        assertNotNull("User not saved!", user.getId());

        User user2= new User();
        user2.setUsername("jonhs");
        user2.setPassword("fGC467");
        try{
            userService.register(user2);
            fail("Cannot save user with existing username!");
        }catch(IllegalArgumentException ex){
            //OK
        }
        userService.delete(user);
    }

    public void testRegisterIncorrectPassword() throws Exception{
        ApplicationContext context = getContext("mytestcontext");
        UserService userService = (UserService)context.getBean("userService");

        User user3= new User();
        user3.setUsername("jandD");
        user3.setPassword("fgh85");
        try{
```

```
            userService.register(user3);
            fail("Password must be at least 6 characters long!");
        }catch(IllegalArgumentException ex){
            //OK
        }
    }
}
```

You won't usually want to extend this class directly; you'll usually extend one of its subclasses, as explained later in this chapter.

Using AbstractDependencyInjectionSpringContextTests

The next step is to improve our test so we don't have to perform bean lookup in every test method for every bean we want to use. We can easily achieve this by using `AbstractDependencyInjectionSpringContextTests`, which extends `AbstractSpringContextTests` from the previous section (so we can use the context caching as shown before).

If you use the `AbstractDependencyInjectionSpringContextTests` as a superclass for your tests, it allows Spring beans to be set using either setters (the default strategy) or protected fields. You no longer have to manually get the bean you wish to test from `ApplicationContext`.

Let's see first how to populate beans using setters. We will add the private field `userService` to our test class and implement the usual setter for it (see Listing 21-19). And that's it! We can now remove the `UserService` bean lookup from the beginning of every test method in the previous examples.

Listing 21-19. *DefaultUserServiceIntegrationTests Refactored Using AbstractSpringContextTests with Setters*

```
public class DefaultUserServiceIntegrationTests ➥
         extends AbstractDependencyInjectionSpringContextTests {
    private UserService userService;

    protected String[] getConfigLocations() throws Exception {
        String [] paths = new String[] {
                "classpath*:/com/apress/prospring2/ch21/dataaccess/➥
applicationContext-dataaccess.xml",
                "classpath*:/com/apress/prospring2/ch21/services/➥
applicationContext-services.xml"
        };
        return paths;
    }

    public void testRegister() throws Exception{
        User user = new User();
        user.setUsername("jonhs");
        user.setPassword("hTy86dj");

        userService.register(user);

        assertNotNull("User not saved!", user.getId());

        User user2= new User();
        user2.setUsername("jonhs");
        user2.setPassword("fGC467");
        try{
            userService.register(user2);
```

```
            fail("Cannot save user with existing username!");
        }catch(IllegalArgumentException ex){
            //OK
        }
        userService.delete(user);
    }

    public void testRegisterIncorrectPassword() throws Exception{

        User user3= new User();
        user3.setUsername("jandD");
        user3.setPassword("fgh85");
        try{
            userService.register(user3);
            fail("Password must be at least 6 characters long!");
        }catch(IllegalArgumentException ex){
            //OK
        }
    }

    public void setUserService(UserService userService) {
        this.userService = userService;
    }
}
```

This method uses automatic wiring by type. It will look up the bean in `ApplicationContext` based on the type of the setter method of the field. If you have two or more beans of the same type declared in your configuration files, you cannot rely on `AbstractDependencyInjectionSpringContextTests` to load beans correctly using public setters.

If you don't like having setters in your test classes, or for any reason you want the Spring context to directly populate protected fields in your test class, all you have to do is to set the `populateProtectedVariables` property to `true` in the constructor and declare your fields as protected. In this case, beans are found based on the name of the protected field, and there is no automatic wiring by type, so you can load multiple beans of the same type using this method. Listing 21-20 shows an example of injecting test dependencies using protected fields.

Note that we have used the method `String[] getConfigLocations()` in this example, instead of `ConfigurableApplicationContext loadContext(Object o)` from the previous example. The `String getConfigLocations()` method is available from `AbstractDependencyInjectionSpringContextTests` and all its subclasses (see Listings 21-19 and 21-20). You should override this method to return locations of Spring configuration files in a `String` array, unless `loadContext(Object o)` is already overridden. Generally, overriding this method instead of `loadContext()` is the best practice, as doing so makes your code cleaner and more readable. We will override `getConfigLocations()` for further examples in this chapter.

Listing 21-20. *DefaultUserServiceIntegrationTests Refactored Using Protected Fields for Injecting Dependencies*

```
public class DefaultUserServiceIntegrationTests ➥
        extends AbstractDependencyInjectionSpringContextTests {
    protected UserService userService;

    public DefaultUserServiceIntegrationTests3() {
        setPopulateProtectedVariables(true);
    }
```

```
    protected String[] getConfigLocations() throws Exception {
        String [] paths = new String[] {
                "classpath*:/com/apress/prospring2/ch21/dataaccess/➥
applicationContext-dataaccess.xml",
                "classpath*:/com/apress/prospring2/ch21/services/➥
applicationContext-services.xml"
        };
        return paths;
    }

    public void testRegister() throws Exception{

        User user = new User();
        user.setUsername("jonhs");
        user.setPassword("hTy86dj");

        userService.register(user);

        assertNotNull("User not saved!", user.getId());

        User user2= new User();
        user2.setUsername("jonhs");
        user2.setPassword("fGC467");
        try{
            userService.register(user2);
            fail("Cannot save user with existing username!");
        }catch(IllegalArgumentException ex){
            //OK
        }
        userService.delete(user);
    }

    public void testRegisterIncorrectPassword() throws Exception{

        User user3= new User();
        user3.setUsername("jandD");
        user3.setPassword("fgh85");
        try{
            userService.register(user3);
            fail("Password must be at least 6 characters long!");
        }catch(IllegalArgumentException ex){
            //OK
        }
    }

}
```

If any of your tests changes the Spring context, or for any reason you want to reload the context in a test method and not use a cached one, you can call the `setDirty()` method in any of your test methods. This will tell Spring that the context should be reloaded from the context files.

Using AbstractTransactionalSpringContextTests

As you have seen in the previous examples, we have called delete statements at the end of every test method to keep the database consistent and leave its state unaffected by tests. If your test classes extend `AbstractTransactionalSpringContextTests`, Spring will take care of rolling back all transactions after the test has been executed. Every `test*()` method runs in its own transaction. In addition, this class allows you to commit some of the transactions and actually change the state of the database from the test, if you want to. Now, we will refactor `DefaultUserServiceIntegrationTests` and remove the delete statement in the `testRegister()` method (see Listing 21-21).

Listing 21-21. *DefaultUserServiceIntegrationTests Refactored Using AbstractTransactionalSpringContextTests*

```
public class DefaultUserServiceIntegrationTests4 ➥
        extends AbstractTransactionalSpringContextTests{
    protected UserService userService;
    protected String[] getConfigLocations() throws Exception {
        String [] paths = new String[] {
                "classpath*:/com/apress/prospring2/ch21/dataaccess/➥
                 applicationContext-dataaccess.xml",
                "classpath*:/com/apress/prospring2/ch21/services/➥
                 applicationContext-services.xml"
        };
        return paths;
    }

    public void testRegister() throws Exception{

        User user = new User();
        user.setUsername("jonhs");
        user.setPassword("hTy86dj");

        userService.register(user);

        assertNotNull("User not saved!", user.getId());

        User user2= new User();
        user2.setUsername("jonhs");
        user2.setPassword("fGC467");
        try{
            userService.register(user2);
            fail("Cannot save user with existing username!");
        }catch(IllegalArgumentException ex){
            //OK
        }

    }

    public void testRegisterIncorrectPassword() throws Exception{

        User user3= new User();
        user3.setUsername("jandD");
        user3.setPassword("fgh85");
        try{
            userService.register(user3);
            fail("Password must be at least 6 characters long!");
        }catch(IllegalArgumentException ex){
            //OK
        }
    }
    public void setUserService(UserService userService) {
```

```
        this.userService = userService;
    }
}
```

If, however, you want to commit a transaction programmatically from any of your tests, you can do it by calling the `setComplete()` method of the `AbstractTransactionalSpringContextTests` class.

You can also end the transaction before the end of the test case by calling the `endTransaction()` method of the `AbstractTransactionalSpringContextTests` class. The transaction will be stopped and rolled back (the default strategy) or committed (if `setComplete()` has been called). Ending transactions early can be used to test the behavior of your application if it gets disconnected from the database in the middle of the transaction or the behavior of lazily loading objects in such situations.

If you want to populate, query, or delete rows from the database directly in your tests, you should extend the `AbstractTransactionalDataSourceSpringContextTests` class, which in turn extends `AbstractTransactionalSpringContextTests`. By extending this class, you will get access to a `JdbcTemplate` instance (using the `getJdbcTemplate()` method of `AbstractTransactionalDataSourceSpringContextTests`), which is useful if you want to populate the database with some test data or delete database content for specific tests. The transaction will roll back at the end of the test method, so there is no danger of making your database inconsistent.

■ **Note** To be able to run transactional tests, the `PlatformTransactionManager` bean must be defined in the Spring configuration files. If it's not present, this class will throw an exception, and the test won't run. However, you can still use this class without the transaction manager if you turn dependency checking off, using `AbstractDependencyInjectionSpringContextTests.setDependencyCheck(false)`. Note, however, that you will be able permanently modify data from your tests in this case. Please see the transaction chapter (Chapter 16) for more information.

Using AbstractAnnotationAwareTransactionalTests

The `AbstractAnnotationAwareTransactionalTests` class extends `AbstractTransactionalDataSourceSpringContextTests`, which was covered in the previous section. It introduces Java 5 common annotations in addition to exposing `SimpleJdbcTemplate`, a Java 5 convenience class for JDBC operations (see Chapter 9 for more information on Spring JDBC support).

Let's take a look at an overview of annotations supported by `AbstractAnnotationAwareTransactionalTests`.

@Repeat

A test method annotated with `@Repeat` will be repeated as many times as indicated in the parameter. Listing 21-22 shows an example that will repeat the `testAll()` method five times.

Listing 21-22. *@Repeat Example*

```
@Repeat(5)
public void testAll(){
//test code to be repeated 5 times
}
```

@Timed

This annotation is used if you want to test functionality that needs to execute in a specific amount of time. It accepts the parameter `millis`, with the expected time for execution in milliseconds. The time measured includes all the time needed from the setup of the test until test teardown. Listing 21-23 shows a syntax example; it expects the `testSpeed()` method to execute in 500 milliseconds.

Listing 21-23. *@Timed Example*

```
@Timed(millis=500ms)
public void testSpeed(){
//test code that needs to finish in half a second
}
```

@Rollback

`@Rolledback(true)` will make a transaction roll back after the execution of a test method. If the argument is `false`, the transaction will be committed. This annotation overrides the class default rollback strategy. You can now mark some test methods to be rolled back and some to commit, without having to call the `setComplete()` method, making the code easier to read (see Listing 21-24).

Listing 21-24. *@Rollback Example*

```
@Rollback(false)
public void testPopulateDatabase(){
//test code that populates the database, and needs to be committed
}
```

@NotTransactional

The `@NotTransactional` annotation has no arguments and, when present, marks the test method as not transactional. The method will not run in a transactional context. See Listing 21-25 for a simple usage example.

Listing 21-25. *@NotTransactional Example*

```
@NotTransactional
public void testSomeNonTransactionaTest(){
//this test code will not run in the transactional context
}
```

@ExpectedException

The `@ExpectedException` annotation indicates that the test method is expected to throw an exception; the expected exception class is passed as a parameter. Using this annotation, you can write much more elegant tests to determine if an exception was thrown correctly from your code. Listing 21-26 shows the usual way to test the exception behavior, which we used in previous examples (the `testRegisterIncorrectPassword()` method from `DefaultUserServiceIntegrationTest`).

Listing 21-26. *Traditional Exception Expected Test*

```
    public void testRegisterIncorrectPassword() throws Exception{
        User user3= new User();
        user3.setUsername("jandD");
        user3.setPassword("fgh85");
```

```
        try{
            userService.register(user3);
            fail("Password must be at least 6 characters long!");
        }catch(IllegalArgumentException ex){
            //OK
        }
    }
```

If the userService.save() method throws an exception, everything is OK. If not, the test should fail (by explicitly calling the fail() method). Now, take a look at Listing 21-27, the refactored testRegisterIncorrectPassword() method using the @ExceptionExpected annotation.

Listing 21-27. *@ExceptionExpected Example*

```
@ExpectedException(IllegalArgumentException.class)
    public void testRegisterIncorrectPassword() throws Exception{
        User user3= new User();
        user3.setUsername("jandD");
        user3.setPassword("fgh85");
        userService.register(user3);
    }
```

@DirtiesContext

This annotation indicates that the test method changes the Spring context during execution. After such a method has finished, the Spring context is rebuilt from configuration files. See Listing 21-28 for a simple example.

Listing 21-28. *@DirtiesContext Example*

```
@DirtiesContext
    public void testSomething() throws Exception{
//this test changes the underlying Spring context
    }
```

The same effect can be achieved by calling the setDirty() method of AbstractDependencyInjectionSpringContextTests, but using the annotation will make the method easier to read and understand.

@IfProfileValue and @ProfileValueSourceConfiguration

The @IfProfileValue annotation checks the returned value of the supplied name (from configured ProfileValueSource), and if it matches the supplied value, the test is executed; otherwise, it is skipped. This way, you can enable selected test methods for specific test environments. Listing 21-29 shows the example of the usage.

Listing 21-29. *@ IfProfileValue Example*

```
@ IfProfileValue(name="file.encoding", value="UTF-8")
    public void testUTF8() throws Exception{
//test to be run only if file.encoding is UTF-8
    }
```

The default ProfileValueSource is SystemProfileValueSource, which uses system properties as the source. In the previous example, we use the file.encoding system property. If its value matches UTF-8, that example test method will be executed.

You can configure your own ProfileValueSource using the @ProfileValueSourceConfiguration annotation (see Listing 21-30).

Listing 21-30. *@ProfileValueSourceConfiguration Example*

```
@ProfileValueSourceConfiguration(MyProfileValueSource.class)
@IfProfileValue(name="file.encoding", value="UTF-8")
    public void testUTF8() throws Exception{
//test to be run only if file.encoding is UTF-8
    }
```

If no ProfileValueSourceConfiguration is defined, Spring will use SystemProfileValueSource by default.

Let's now see how we can refactor our DefaultUserServiceIntegrationTests class to take advantage of AbstractAnnotationAwareTransactionalTests. Listing 21-31 shows the code of the refactored DefaultUserServiceIntegrationTests.

Listing 21-31. *The DefaultUserServiceIntegrationTests Class Refactored Using AbstractAnnotationAwareTransactionalTests*

```
public class DefaultUserServiceIntegrationTests ➥
extends AbstractAnnotationAwareTransactionalTests {
    protected UserService userService;

    protected String[] getConfigLocations() {
        String[] paths = new String[]{
                "classpath*:/com/apress/prospring2/ch21/➥
dataaccess/applicationContext-dataaccess.xml",
                "classpath*:/com/apress/prospring2/ch21/➥
services/applicationContext-services.xml"
        };
        return paths;
    }

    @Repeat(10)
    @Timed(millis = 5000)
    @ExpectedException(IllegalArgumentException.class)
    public void testRegister() throws Exception {
        System.out.println("done");
        User user = new User();
        user.setUsername("jonhs");
        user.setPassword("hTy86dj");

        userService.register(user);

        assertNotNull("User not saved!", user.getId());

        User user2 = new User();
        user2.setUsername("jonhs");
        user2.setPassword("fGC467");

        userService.register(user2);

    }
```

```
    @ExpectedException(IllegalArgumentException.class)
    public void testRegisterIncorrectPassword() throws Exception {

        User user3 = new User();
        user3.setUsername("jandD");
        user3.setPassword("fgh85");
        userService.register(user3);
    }

    public void setUserService(UserService userService) {
        this.userService = userService;
    }
}
```

JNDI

In your real-world applications, you will often take advantage of JNDI for various purposes. The most common usage is probably with an application server to get access to the database connection pool. Listing 21-32 shows how your data access context (`dataSource` bean definition) would most likely look.

Listing 21-32. *JNDI dataSource Bean*

```
...
     <bean id="dataSource" class="org.springframework.jndi.JndiObjectFactoryBean">
        <property name="jndiName" value="iigDataSource"/>
    </bean>
```

However, this is usually difficult to implement in your test classes, so if you want to write an integration test that connects to the databases, you would need an additional application context for data access for the test environment, with a differently defined `dataSource` bean (using `BasicDataSource` or `DriverManagerDataSource`). You would end up with separate configuration files for you real application and for testing.

To make mocking `DataSources` easier for testing, Spring provides the org.springframework.mock.jndi package, with a JNDI implementation you can use in your test classes or even in stand-alone applications. Table 21-2 shows an overview of the three classes in org.springframework.mock.jndi.

Table 21-2. *Overview of org.springframework.mock.jndi Package*

Class	Description
`ExpectedLookupTemplate`	This basic `JndiTemplate` implementation always returns the given object.
`SimpleNamingContext`	This is a basic implementation of the JNDI naming context. You can only bind plain Java objects to `String` names using this class. You'll rarely use this class directly in an application; use the `SimpleNamingContextBuilder` instead.
`SimpleNamingContextBuilder`	This JNDI naming context builder implementation can be used in a test environment.

The class that we are most interested in is SimpleNamingContextBuilder. Take a look at Listing 21-33. It shows how we could implement a JNDI naming context to use it in our tests. In Listing 21-33, we create empty context in the line marked with //1. Note that we are not creating a context by calling the constructor, new SimpleNamingContextBuilder(), although this is allowed. Due to JNDI restrictions, only one builder can be activated in the JVM. So if we instantiated SimpleNamingContextBuilder by calling its constructor, and then wanted to do the same again (in another test class), the JVM would complain that the JNDI context builder is already activated. That is why we use the static method SimpleNamingContextBuilder.emptyActivatedContextBuilder(). This method will return an already activated builder if it exists or activate and return new one.

In the second bold code line (marked with //2 in Listing 21-33), we simply bind the DriverManagerDataSource object to the expected JNDI name. And that's it.

Listing 21-33. *SimpleNamingContextBuilder JNDI Naming Context Example*

```
public static void buildJndi() {
        try {
            SimpleNamingContextBuilder builder;
            builder = SimpleNamingContextBuilder.➥
emptyActivatedContextBuilder();//1

            String connectionString = ➥
"jdbc:oracle:thin:@oracle.devcake.co.uk:1521:INTL";
            builder.bind("java:comp/env/jdbc/prospring2/ch21", ➥
new DriverManagerDataSource(
                    "oracle.jdbc.driver.OracleDriver", connectionString, ➥
"PROSPRING", "x******6"));//2
        } catch (NamingException e) {
            // no-op
        }
    }
```

Now, your test can load the application context with the dataSource bean defined as JndiObjectFactoryBean (like in Listing 21-32). More importantly, you can use the same Spring context files in your actual application and for testing.

In order to incorporate the mocked JNDI DataSource in the testing classes introduced earlier, all you have to do is to call the buildJndi() method introduced in Listing 21-33 before you load the Spring context files (usually, you'll call it within the constructor). Listing 21-34 shows the refactored DefaultUserServiceIntegrationTests using AbstractDependencyInjectionSpringContextTests.

Listing 21-34. *Refactored DefaultUserServiceIntegrationTests Using JNDI Data Source*

```
public class DefaultUserServiceIntegrationTests3 ➥
extends AbstractDependencyInjectionSpringContextTests {
    protected UserService userService;
    public static void buildJndi() {
           try {
               SimpleNamingContextBuilder builder;
               builder = SimpleNamingContextBuilder.emptyActivatedContextBuilder();

               String connectionString = ➥
"jdbc:oracle:thin:@oracle.devcake.co.uk:1521:INTL";
               builder.bind("java:comp/env/jdbc/prospring2/ch21", ➥
new DriverManagerDataSource(
                       "oracle.jdbc.driver.OracleDriver", connectionString, ➥
"PROSPRING", "x******6"));
```

```
            } catch (NamingException e) {
                // no-op
            }
        }

    public DefaultUserServiceIntegrationTests3() {
        buildJndi();
    }

    protected String[] getConfigLocations() {
        String[] paths = new String[]{
                "classpath*:/com/apress/prospring2/ch21/➥
dataaccess/applicationContext-dataaccess.xml",
                "classpath*:/com/apress/prospring2/ch21/➥
services/applicationContext-services.xml"
        };
        return paths;
    }
...rest omitted for clarity
}
```

JNDI and Transactional Tests

Using JNDI for testing as described in the preceding section is not always possible. The transactional Spring tests (classes that extend `AbstractTransactionalSpringContextTests`) rely on `java.sql.DatSource` and `PlatformTransactionManager` being defined in the Spring context, so they do not allow the `dataSource` bean to be of any other type (like `JndiObjectFactoryBean` used in this section). In that case, you have no other option than to maintain separate data access to the Spring context for your application and the test environment.

Spring TestContext Framework

In version 2.5, Spring introduced a new approach to testing: the TestContext Framework, located in the org.springframework.test.context package. The aim of TestContext is to provide a testing environment that will not be dependent on the testing framework in use (JUnit 3.8+, JUnit 4.4+, TestNG, and so on). It is also annotation driven, making it easy to configure and maintain.

The main parts of TestContext Framework are the `TestContext` and `TestContextManager` classes and the `TestExecutionListener` interface. The `TestContext` class holds the context of the test; the text context it holds is generic, because it does not know what testing framework is being used. Every single `TestContext` is managed by `TestContextManager`. `TestContextManager` signals events to `TestExecutionListeners` registered with it. It also prepares test instances and performs final actions before the test is torn down. The `TestExecutionListener` interface defines an API for the way the framework should react to a test execution event. Spring provides three `TestExecutionListener` implementations out of the box (see Table 21-3).

Table 21-3. *Spring TestExecutionListener Implementations*

Class	Description
DependencyInjectionTestExecutionListener	Provides support for dependency injection of beans loaded from configuration files
DirtiesContextTestExecutionListener	Provides support for the @DirtiesContext annotation and processes test methods with this annotation configured
TransactionalTestExecutionListener	Provides support for tests that run in a transaction

All these TestExecutionListener implementations are configured by default, so for regular use, you don't have to think about them. However, if you require custom TestExecutionListener implementation, you can write your own class or extend one of the Spring default implementations.

Application Context and DI with the TestContext Framework

Using standard Spring test features, described in previous sections, when we wanted to load the Spring context from configuration files, we had to implement the method that would load configuration files from supplied locations (such as protected String[] getConfigLocations()).

The TestContext Framework provides annotation-driven context configuration using @ContextConfiguration annotation. The configuration files will be loaded from location paths provided as parameters (see Listing 21-35).

Listing 21-35. *@ContextConfiguration Example*

```
@ContextConfiguration(locations={"/test-context.xml", ➥
    "classpath:/com/apress/prospring2/ch21/application-context.xml"})
public class ExampleTest{
      //test methods
}
```

The first configuration file (/test-conext.xml) will be loaded from the root of the classpath. The second file shows that the same syntax can be used with this annotation as with regular Spring configuration paths (using classpath:).

If the location parameter is missing from the annotation, Spring's convention-over-configuration functionality comes into play: Spring will try to load the application context from a location generated from the full class name by default. For example, if the full class name is com.apress.prospring2.ch21.test.ExampleTest, the location generated by default will be classpath:/com/apress/prospring2/ch21/test/ExampleTest-context.xml. Listing 21-36 shows the convention-over-configuration example.

Listing 21-36. *@ContextConfiguration Without the Locations Parameter*

```
package com.apress.prospring2.ch21.test
@ContextConfiguration
public class ExampleTest{
       //the application context will be loaded from
       //"classpath:/com/apress/prospring2/ch21/test/ExampleTest-
      //context.xml"
}
```

If you define the @ContextConfiguration annotation in a test class and use that class as a superclass for your other test classes, the Spring context will be inherited from the superclass. However, if your subclass defines its own @ContextConfiguration, it will extend the one of the superclass. New beans defined will be added to the application context. If beans in configuration files of the subclass have the same names as beans in the superclass's configuration locations, the subclass's configuration files' beans will override those defined in the superclass.

If you want your class not to use the superclass application context, and use its own context instead, you can set the inheritLocations attribute to false in the @ContextConfiguration annotation. If the attribute is omitted, it will default to true, and the superclass's context will be used. Listing 21-37 shows an example of these configurations.

Listing 21-37. *Other @ContextConfiguration Examples*

```
@ContextConfiguration(locations={"classpath:/com/apress/prospring2/ch21/➥
test/superclass-context.xml"})
public class ExampleSuperClassTest{
        //test methods
}
@ContextConfiguration(locations={"classpath:/com/apress/prospring2/ch21/➥
test/subclass1-context.xml"})   // 1
//it will load all beans from superclass-context, as well as subclass1-context
public class ExampleSubClass1Test extends ExampleSuperClass {
        //test methods
}
@ContextConfiguration(locations={"classpath:/com/apress/prospring2/ch21/➥
test/subclass2-context.xml", inheritLocations=false})    //2
//This class will use subclass1-context.xml only for loading
public class ExampleSubClass2Test extends ExampleSuperClass{
        //test methods
}
```

The ExampleSubClass1 class adds additional context location, so all beans from ExampleSuperClass will be available, along with the beans loaded from the subclass1-context.xml file, as specified in ExampleSubClass1 @ContextConfiguration (see the bold line marked with //1 in Listing 21-37).

The ExampleSubClass2 class, however, specifies the inheritLocations=false parameter in the @ContextConfiguration annotation. The context from the ExampleSuperClass superclass will be discarded, and test methods of ExampleSubClass1 will only have access to beans defined in the subclass2-context.xmls file, specified in ExampleSubClass2 @ContextConfiguration (see the bold line marked with //2 in Listing 21-37).

TestContext caches the loaded application context and reuses it throughout the test, so it won't be reloaded for every test method you invoke. However, if the test method changes the application context, or if for any reason you want to reload the bean definition for the next test method, you can annotate the method with the @DirtiestContext annotation. This will cause the application context to be reloaded once the test has been executed.

Dependency Injection with TestContext Framework

Once loaded from Spring configuration files, beans can be injected into the fields of the test class. All you have to do is add specific annotations to your test class. If you add an annotation to the field, field injection will be used. If, on the other hand, you add an annotation to the setter method, setter injection will be used. If you don't add bean-loading annotations to your class, beans won't be injected.

The @Autowired annotation is used for bean loading by type. Listing 21-38 shows examples of @Autowired loading.

Listing 21-38. *DI by Type*

```
@ContextConfiguration
public class DefaultUserServiceTests{
          //userService will be loaded using field injection, autowiring by type
          @Autowired
          private UserService userService;
           //test methods...
}
public class DefaultUserServiceTests{
          private UserService userService;
            //userService will be loaded using setter injection, autowiring by type
            @Autowired
            public setUserService(UserService userService){
                      this.userService = userService
            }
            //test methods...
}
```

If you have multiple beans of the same type defined in your configuration type, automatic wiring by type cannot be used, as Spring won't know which bean to load. In that case, you can use DI by name, which will look up a bean name before loading. For this strategy, you can use the `@Resource` annotation from JSR 250. Alternately, you can use `@Autowired(required = false)`. Listing 21-39 gives examples of this strategy.

Listing 21-39. *DI by Name*

```
@ContextConfiguration
public class DefaultUserServiceTests{
            //userService will be loaded using field injection, autowiring by name
            @Resource
            private UserService userService;
            //test methods...
}
public class DefaultUserServiceTests{
            private UserService userService;
            //userService will be loaded using setter injection, autowiring by name
            @Autowired(required = false)
            public setUserService(UserService userService){
                        this.userService = userService
            }
            //test methods...
}

public class DefaultUserServiceTests{
            //userService will be loaded using field injection, autowiring by name.
            @Resource(name="myUserService")
            private UserService userService;
            //test methods...
}
```

Transactions in the TestContext Framework

The `TransactionalTestExecutionListener` manages transactions in the TestContext Framework. This listener does not have to be declared in a test class, as it is declared by default by the TestContext Framework. However, it can be configured or customized using the `@TestExecutionListener` annotation.

In order to be able to run transactional tests in your test classes, you must have the `org.springframework.transaction.PlatformTransactionManager` interface implementation in your Spring context.

@TransactionConfiguration

This class-level annotation allows you to configure transactions in a test class. It configures the `PlatformTrasactionManager` bean to be used for transactional methods. The `PlatformTransactionManager` must be defined in the Spring context files. See Listing 21-40 for a simple syntax example.

Listing 21-40. *@TransactionConfiguration Annotation Example*

```
@ContextConfiguration
@TransactionConfiguration(trasactionManager="testTransactionManager")
public class DefaultUserServiceTests{
            //test methods...
}
```

The `transactionManager` attribute value is the name of the `PlatformTransactionManager` implementation bean in your Spring context files.

The `defaultRollback` flag for the test class can be also set using `@TransactionConfiguration`, as an optional attribute (see Listing 21-41). If omitted, `defaultRollback` defaults to `true`.

Listing 21-41. *@TransactionConfiguration Annotation Example with the defaultRollback Parameter*

```
@ContextConfiguration
@TransactionConfiguration(transactionManager = ➥
"testTransactionManager". defaultRollback=true)
public class DefaultUserServiceTests{
            //test methods...
}
```

The Spring convention-over-configuration functionality is implemented for this annotation as well: if you omit the `transactionManager` attribute for the `@TransactionConfiguration` annotation, Spring will look for the default bean name `transactionManager`. You can always rely on that behavior, so you can configure your transaction test class as shown in Listing 21-42.

Listing 21-42. *@TransactionConfiguration, Convention Over Configuration*

```
@ContextConfiguration
@TransactionConfiguration
public class DefaultUserServiceTests{
            //test methods...
}
```

As you can see, we used `@TransactionConfiguration` without attributes, which will now look up the bean named `transactionManager` in the Spring context (and set `defaultRollback` to `true` by default).

@BeforeTransaction and @AfterTransaction

The Spring TestContext Framework provides these two annotations for a method you need to run right before or after the transaction but out of the transactional context: `@BeforeTransaction` and `@AfterTransaction`.

@BeforeTransaction can be used to check the database state prior to a transaction or to populate the database with transaction-specific data before execution. All you have to do to make the method run before the transaction is to add the @BeforeTransaction annotation to your method; the TestContext Framework will make sure that the method is run right before transaction starts. Listing 21-43 shows an example.

Listing 21-43. *@BeforeTransaction Example*

```
@ContextConfiguration
@TransactionConfiguration
public class DefaultUserServiceTests{
            @BeforeTransaction
            void checkDatabaseState(){
                        //method to run before transaction
            }
            void testRegister(){
                        //transactional test method
            }
}
```

The checkDatabaseState() method from the previous example will run right before the transaction for the testRegister() method starts, and it will run out of the transaction. The same scenario applies to any other transactional method implemented in the test class.

@AfterTransaction can be used for methods that, for example, check if the committed transaction has populated the data as expected or if specific statements are rolled back. Again, all you have to do is annotate the method you want to run after the transaction with the @AfterTransaction annotation. As Listing 21-44 shows, the checkCommit() will run out of the transaction, straight after the transactional test method is executed.

Listing 21-44. *@AfterTransaction Example*

```
@ContextConfiguration
@TransactionConfiguration
public class DefaultUserServiceTests{
            void testRegister(){
                        //transactional test method
            }
            @AfterTransaction
            void checkCommit(){
            //method to run after transaction
            }
}
```

Of course, you can use transaction annotation defined in AbstractAnnotationAwareTransactionalTests, such as @Trasactional to explicitly define transactional test methods and @NotTransactional to mark specific test methods to run out of the transaction. You can also use the @Rollback annotation to override the defaultRollback flag defined for the class.

Support Classes

The TestContext Framework is implemented so it does not have any knowledge of the testing framework used for testing—you can use the JUnit 3.8, JUnit 4.4, or TestNG testing environment and still use the same TestContext testing code.

However, Spring provides convenient abstract classes for each of the supported testing frameworks, and your test classes can extend these out of the box.

If you are using JUnit 3.8, Spring provides two convenient classes: `AbstractJUnit38SpringContextTests` and `AbstractTransactionalJUnit38SpringContextTests`.

`AbstractJUnit38SpringContextTests` provides application context support in the JUnit 3.8 environment. Classes extending this abstract class will have access to protected field `applicationContext`, which can be used for bean lookup and DI.

`AbstractTransactionalJUnit38SpringContextTests` extends `AbstractJUnit38SpringContextTests` and therefore provides the same `applicationContext` functionality. In addition, it provides access to the `simpleJdbcTemplate` protected field that can be used for direct database access from your test classes.

`AbstractTransactionalJUnit38SpringContextTests` also configures transactional behavior by default, so all classes extending it will have methods run in a transaction, as explained earlier in this chapter. You will need to have the `java.sql.DataSource` bean, as well as `org.springframework.transaction.PlatformTransactionManager`, defined in your Spring context files to make use of this class.

If you're using JUnit 4.4, you have a corresponding pair of classes to choose from: `AbstractJUnit4SpringContextTests` and `AbstractTransactionalJUnit4SpringContextTests`.

`AbstractJUnit4SpringContextTests`, like its JUnit 3.8 counterpart, provides access to `applicationContext` as well as DI for Spring beans.

`AbstractTransactionalJUnit4SpringContextTests`, which extends `AbstractJUnit4SpringContextTests`, provides a transactional environment as well as the `simpleJdbcTemplate` field, which is protected from direct database access.

A similar pair of classes is available for the TestNG testing framework: `AbstractTestNGSpringContextTests` and `AbstractTransactionsTestNGSpringContextTests`.

`AbstractTestNGSpringContextTests` provides access to `applicationContext`'s protected field for bean lookup and DI.

`AbstractTestNGSpringContextTests` provides a transactional environment with access to the `simpleJdbcTemplate` field.

`AbstractTransactionalJUnit4SpringContextTests` and `AbstractTransactionsTestNGSpringContextTests` also depend on the `java.sql.Datasource` and `org.springframework.transaction.PlatformTransactionManager` beans, which must be defined in the Spring context used by the test classes.

Let's now refactor our `DefaultUserServiceTests` class from previous examples so it uses the TestContext Framework. We will be extending the `AbstractTransactionalJUnit38SpringContextTests` class. Listing 21-45 shows the refactored code.

Listing 21-45. *Refactored DefaultUserServiceTests Using the TestContext Framework*

```
@ContextConfiguration(locations = ➥
{"/com/apress/prospring2/ch21/dataaccess/applicationContext-dataaccess.xml", ➥
"/com/apress/prospring2/ch21/services/applicationContext-services.xml"})
@TransactionConfiguration(transactionManager="transactionManager")
public class DefaultUserServiceIntegrationTests ➥
extends AbstractTransactionalJUnit38SpringContextTests {

    protected UserService userService;

    public DefaultUserServiceIntegrationTests() {

    }
    @AfterTransaction
    public void checkDatabaseState(){
        assertEquals("No users should be saved in this test", 0, ➥
this.userService.findAllUsers().size());
    }
```

```
    @Repeat(10)
    @Timed(millis = 5000)
    @ExpectedException(IllegalArgumentException.class)
    public void testRegister() throws Exception {
        System.out.println("done");
        User user = new User();
        user.setUsername("jonhs");
        user.setPassword("hTy86dj");

        userService.register(user);

        assertNotNull("User not saved!", user.getId());

        User user2 = new User();
        user2.setUsername("jonhs");
        user2.setPassword("fGC467");

        userService.register(user2);

    }

    @ExpectedException(IllegalArgumentException.class)
    public void testRegisterIncorrectPassword() throws Exception {

        User user3 = new User();
        user3.setUsername("jandD");
        user3.setPassword("fgh85");
        userService.register(user3);
    }

    @Autowired(required = false)
    public void setUserService(UserService userService) {
        this.userService = userService;
    }

    @Autowired(required = false)
    public void setDataSource(DataSource dataSource) {
        super.setDataSource(dataSource);
    }
}
```

Test Coverage

Your tests must be as thorough as possible, and an elegant way to make sure you are testing enough is to use a test coverage tool. There are several test coverage tools available. One example is the commercial product Clover (`http://www.cenqua.com/clover/`), which offers great analysis of your code and tests. If you want to use open source alternatives, you can use jcoverage (`http://www.jcoverage.com/downloads.html`) or EMMA (`http://emma.sourceforge.net/`).

Test coverage tools in general work by adding another layer of code to your application and generally require that you modify the build procedure to include the test coverage tool instrumentation layer in the final binary. The test coverage tools are well outside the scope of this chapter, but we do encourage you to try at least one of them.

Summary

This chapter showed you how to test the components of your application either on their own using unit tests or in cooperation with other components in integration tests. We also told you that you can gain assurance that most of your code is being tested by using test coverage tools.

Integration testing was the main part of this chapter, and you saw best practices for testing using existing testing frameworks such as JUnit. You also saw how to use the Spring TestContext Framework for integration testing. We also took a look at annotation-driven testing, with both third-party and Spring's testing frameworks.

CHAPTER 22

Spring Performance Tuning

Performance is an important aspect of all applications; improving the performance of your application is therefore an important task. We have found that many programmers follow their gut feelings in tuning the RDBMS and optimizing Java code without the facts to support their decisions. You can easily add an index here and use a different implementation of a collection there, but the results rarely justify the time spent doing these improvements.

In this chapter, we will show you how to write fast and responsive applications from the start. We cannot cover specifics of the algorithms your application will use, but we will show you how to avoid most of the performance and responsiveness pitfalls in Java EE application design. Next, we will show how to use the Spring Framework to its full potential to get the best performance from your application and other components.

We will also show you how to effectively control applications running in production mode, including automatic performance management, efficient logging, and the management interface.

Performance vs. Responsiveness

It is easy to think that good performance automatically means good responsiveness, but that isn't always the case. Imagine an application that performs some complex processing for each web request. The application takes 20 seconds to do the processing, which, because of its complexity, is excellent. However, it can only process one such request at a time. You have an application with excellent performance but poor responsiveness. The first user to make the request will wait for 20 seconds; if another user makes the same request only 1 second later, the application will take 39 seconds to produce a response. While 20 seconds may be acceptable, 40 seconds is far too long. If you then get 20 requests within the first 10 seconds, the last user will have to wait 400 seconds. There is a good chance that the users will not wait so long; they will stop the request in their browsers. Unfortunately, the application server will not be aware of this and will begin working on the users' requests even though the users will never see the results.

Whenever possible, write your applications to deliver both good performance and adequate responsiveness. If you have a long-running process, change it from an interactive process to a batch process. If it is impossible to make this change, at least consider using AJAX to report on the progress of the processing task. If users know that the application is working (especially if they can see how long they still have to wait), they may be prepared to accept some delays.

Exploring Enterprise Application Performance Issues

In our experience, many performance issues in Java EE applications come down to inefficient use of the persistence layer. If you are using some kind of ORM tool, make sure you fully understand the implications of its lazy loading capabilities. Apart from ineffective implementation of the data access tier, the most problematic area in enterprise applications is inefficient use of transactions, which is usually closely related to lazy loading issues in the data access tier. The next area of performance problems is an inefficient remoting infrastructure, where the overhead of the remote call can sometimes be greater than the time it takes for the invoked call to complete. A Spring-specific problem area is Spring AOP: if you find that dynamic advices are the root cause of performance problems and you are not using Spring-specific `bean` pointcuts, you should consider using load-time weaving or reimplementing the aspects in AspectJ and using compile-time weaving. Finally, web view rendering can take a considerable amount of time to complete, especially when you are using XSLT transformations to produce the HTML views.

Measuring Java EE Application Performance

Before we can begin tuning our application, we must know what to tune. This is the most important aspect of performance tuning: if you do not find out which specific areas of your application's code need improvement, you may spend a lot of time improving code that does not contribute significantly to the performance problem.

Finding Out What to Measure

To tune a complex application, we first need to identify the areas of code that need tuning. To do this, you can use existing Java EE performance measurement tools. We have successfully used YourKit Java Profiler (`http://yourkit.com/overview/index.jsp`) and Quest JProbe (`http://www.quest.com/jprobe/`) to collect statistics about our applications. We will use YourKit Java Profiler to measure the performance of the code in this chapter.

We will start with the application whose data model is shown in Figure 22-1 to demonstrate some of the techniques we can use to measure and then improve the application's performance.

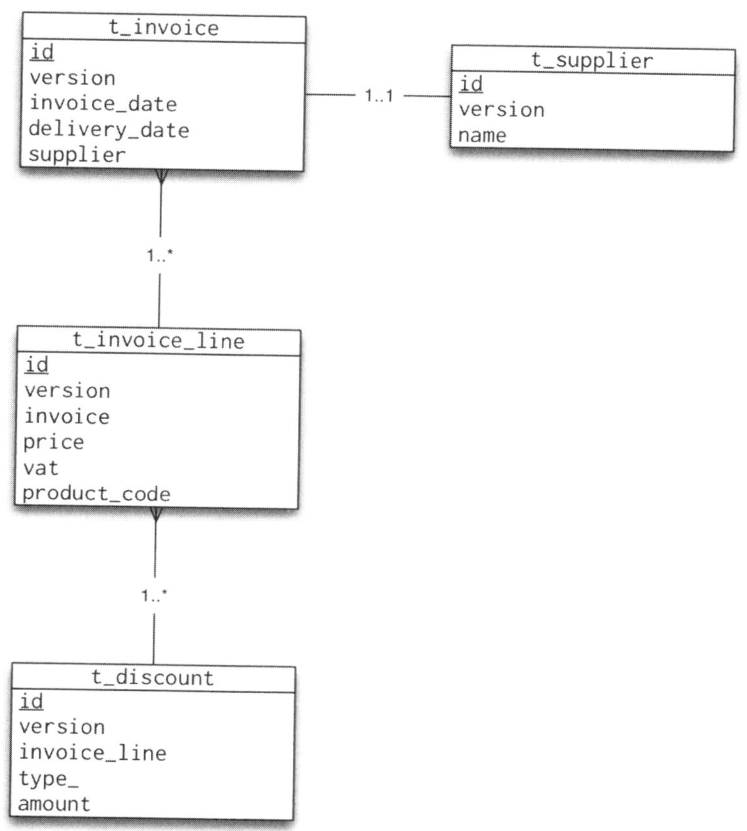

Figure 22-1. *Data model of the sample application*

The application is using Hibernate in its data tier; the data tier maps the rows from the tables to the appropriate domain objects. The services tier simply uses the data access tier and is responsible for managing transactions. Finally, we have a small stand-alone application that uses the services tier and displays the results. Figure 22-2 shows the main classes in the sample application.

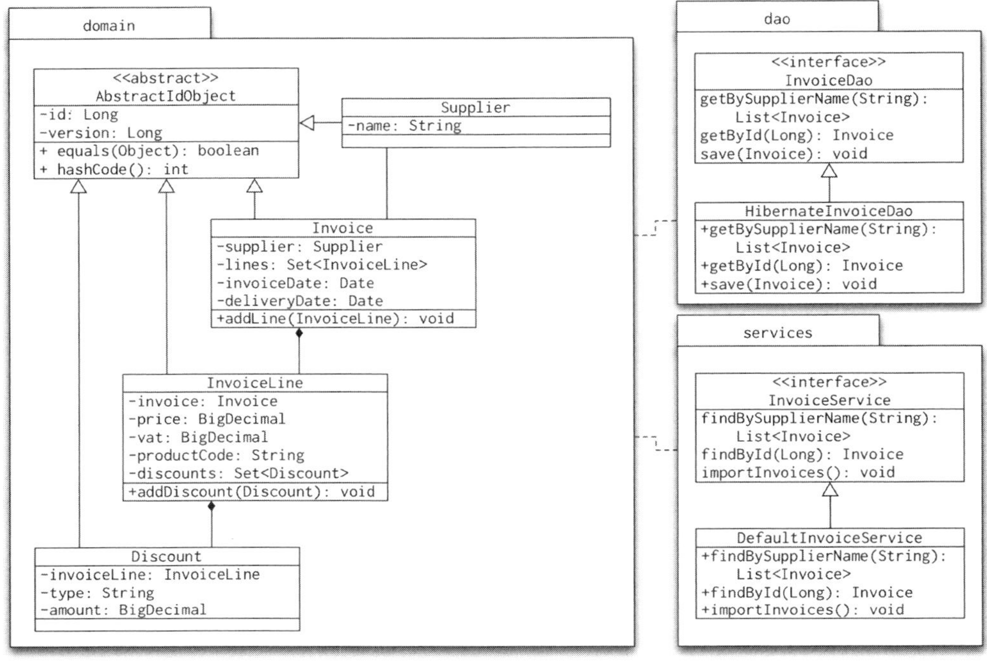

Figure 22-2. *Class diagram of the sample application*

Our task is to improve the application's performance. We will identify which areas are causing the most significant performance problems and refactor the code to improve the application's speed and responsiveness.

Listing 22-1 shows the source code of a small command line interface (CLI) application that can select one invoice or search for invoices by supplier name.

Listing 22-1. *Command Line Interface Sample Application*

```
public class CliDemo {
    private static final Pattern I_PATTERN =
        Pattern.compile("i\\W+(\\d+)");
    private static final Pattern S_PATTERN =
        Pattern.compile("s\\W+(\\d+-\\d+\\W+)?(.+)");
    private InvoiceService invoiceService;

    private void findById(String line) {
        Matcher matcher;
        matcher = I_PATTERN.matcher(line);
        if (!matcher.matches()) return;
        System.out.println(
                this.invoiceService.findById(Long.valueOf(matcher.group(1))));
    }

    private void findBySupplierName(String line) {
        Matcher matcher = S_PATTERN.matcher(line);
        if (!matcher.matches()) return;
```

```
        int firstResult = 0;
        int maxResults = Integer.MAX_VALUE;
        if (matcher.group(2) != null) {
            firstResult = Integer.valueOf(matcher.group(2));
        }
        if (matcher.group(3) != null) {
            maxResults = Integer.valueOf(matcher.group(3));
        }

        List<Invoice> invoices =
                this.invoiceService.findBySupplierName(matcher.group(4));
        List<Invoice> finalInvoices = new LinkedList<Invoice>();
        for (int i = 0; i < invoices.size(); i++) {
            if (i < firstResult) continue;
            if (i > maxResults) break;
            finalInvoices.add(invoices.get(i));
        }
        System.out.println(finalInvoices);
    }

    public static void main(String[] args) throws IOException {
        CliDemo me = new CliDemo();
        me.run();
    }

    private void run() throws IOException {
        ApplicationContext ac = new ClassPathXmlApplicationContext(
                "/META-INF/spring/*-context.xml"
        );
        this.invoiceService = (InvoiceService) ac.getBean("invoiceService");
        BufferedReader reader = new BufferedReader(
                new InputStreamReader(System.in));
        while (true) {
            String line = reader.readLine();
            findById(line);
            findBySupplierName(line);
            if ("q".equals(line)) break;
        }

    }

}
```

The application is working, but the users complain that it is too slow; in particular, selecting items by supplier name takes far too long. Our first task is to measure what is happening; we need to find out exactly how much time the application is taking to process the requests using YourKit Java Profiler. We are also going to turn on the `show_sql` Hibernate configuration option in the `dataaccess-context.xml` configuration file in Listing 22-2.

Listing 22-2. *The dataaccess-context.xml Configuration File*

```
<?xml version="1.0" encoding="UTF-8"?>
<beans xmlns="http://www.springframework.org/schema/beans"
       xmlns:xsi="http://www.w3.org/2001/XMLSchema-instance"
       xmlns:util="http://www.springframework.org/schema/util"
       xmlns:tx="http://www.springframework.org/schema/tx"
       xmlns:aop="http://www.springframework.org/schema/aop"
```

```
    xsi:schemaLocation="
        http://www.springframework.org/schema/beans
        http://www.springframework.org/schema/beans/spring-beans.xsd
        http://www.springframework.org/schema/util
        http://www.springframework.org/schema/util/spring-util.xsd
        http://www.springframework.org/schema/tx
        http://www.springframework.org/schema/tx/spring-tx.xsd
        http://www.springframework.org/schema/aop
        http://www.springframework.org/schema/aop/spring-aop.xsd">

  <bean id="dataSource" class="org.apache.commons.dbcp.BasicDataSource"
        destroy-method="close">
      ...
  </bean>

  <bean id="hibernateSessionFactory"
        class="org.springframework.orm.hibernate3.LocalSessionFactoryBean">
      <property name="dataSource" ref="dataSource"/>
      <property name="mappingLocations">
          <list>
              <value>classpath*:/META-INF/hibernate/*.hbm.xml</value>
          </list>
      </property>
      <property name="hibernateProperties">
          <props>
              <prop key="hibernate.dialect">
                  org.hibernate.dialect.Oracle9Dialect
              </prop>
              <prop key="hibernate.current_session_context_class">thread
              </prop>
              <prop key="hibernate.show_sql">true</prop>
              <prop key="generate_statistics">true</prop>
          </props>
      </property>
  </bean>

  <bean id="transactionManager"
        class="org.springframework.orm.hibernate3.HibernateTransactionManager">
      <property name="sessionFactory" ref="hibernateSessionFactory"/>
      <property name="dataSource" ref="dataSource"/>
  </bean>

  <bean id="hibernateDaoSupport" abstract="true"
        class="org.springframework.orm.hibernate3.support.HibernateDaoSupport">
      <property name="sessionFactory" ref="hibernateSessionFactory"/>
  </bean>
  <bean id="invoiceDao"
        class="com.apress.prospring2.ch23.dao.hibernate.HibernateInvoiceDao"
        parent="hibernateDaoSupport"/>

</beans>
```

Before we can start the application, we need to integrate the profiler into our IDE. YourKit's profiler installer will automatically configure your IDE; to profile the application, all we have to do is click the Profile button.

Tip If you are using NetBeans 6.1, you can take advantage of the integrated profiler.

We are now ready to profile the sample application to collect statistical information about its performance:

```
[YourKit Java Profiler 7.0.12] CPU profiling is started
[YourKit Java Profiler 7.0.12] Profiler agent is listening on port 10001...
[YourKit Java Profiler 7.0.12] Launching profiler UI (...)
[YourKit Java Profiler 7.0.12] [UI] [JavaAppLauncher] A 64-bit JVM is
    available for 1.5.0
[YourKit Java Profiler 7.0.12] [UI] [JavaAppLauncher] JVMArchs not found in
    Java dictionary
[YourKit Java Profiler 7.0.12] CPU profiling is stopped
[YourKit Java Profiler 7.0.12] CPU profiling is started

s Supplier 12
Hibernate: select invoice0_.id as id1_, ...
    where invoice0_.supplier=supplier1_.id and (supplier1_.name like ?)
Hibernate: select supplier0_.id as id3_0_, ... where supplier0_.id=?
Hibernate: select lines0_.invoice as invoice1_, ...
    where invoice0_.supplier=supplier1_.id and (supplier1_.name like ?))
Hibernate: select discounts0_.invoice_line as invoice5_1_, ...
    where invoice0_.supplier=supplier1_.id and (supplier1_.name like ?)))
[Result]

s Supplier 4%
Hibernate: select invoice0_.id as id1_, ...
    where invoice0_.supplier=supplier1_.id and (supplier1_.name like ?)
Hibernate: select ...
Hibernate: select ...
Hibernate: select ...
Hibernate: select ...
...
Hibernate: select lines0_.invoice as invoice1_, ...
    where invoice0_.supplier=supplier1_.id and (supplier1_.name like ?))
Hibernate: select discounts0_.invoice_line as invoice5_1_, ...
    where invoice0_.supplier=supplier1_.id and (supplier1_.name like ?)))
[Result]
```

```
i 12400
Hibernate: select invoice0_.id as id1_, ... where invoice0_.id=?
Hibernate: select supplier0_.id as id3_0_, ... where supplier0_.id=?
Hibernate: select lines0_.invoice as invoice1_, ... where lines0_.invoice=?
Hibernate: select discounts0_.invoice_line as invoice5_1_, ...
    where lines0_.invoice=?)
com.apress.prospring2.ch23.domain.Invoice@b8286101

i 13400
Hibernate: select invoice0_.id as id1_, ... where invoice0_.id=?
Hibernate: select supplier0_.id as id3_0_, ... where supplier0_.id=?
Hibernate: select lines0_.invoice as invoice1_, ... where lines0_.invoice=?
Hibernate: select discounts0_.invoice_line as invoice5_1_, ...
    where lines0_.invoice=?)
com.apress.prospring2.ch23.domain.Invoice@b9034a31

s Supplier 22
Hibernate: select invoice0_.id as id1_, ...
    where invoice0_.supplier=supplier1_.id and (supplier1_.name like ?)
Hibernate: select supplier0_.id as id3_0_, ... where supplier0_.id=?
Hibernate: select lines0_.invoice as invoice1_, ...
    where invoice0_.supplier=supplier1_.id and (supplier1_.name like ?))
Hibernate: select discounts0_.invoice_line as invoice5_1_, ...
    where invoice0_.supplier=supplier1_.id and (supplier1_.name like ?)))
[Result]

i 13456
Hibernate: select invoice0_.id as id1_, ... where invoice0_.id=?
Hibernate: select supplier0_.id as id3_0_, ... where supplier0_.id=?
Hibernate: select lines0_.invoice as invoice1_, ... where lines0_.invoice=?
Hibernate: select discounts0_.invoice_line as invoice5_1_, ...
    where lines0_.invoice=?)
com.apress.prospring2.ch23.domain.Invoice@b9078a34

q
[YourKit Java Profiler 7.0.12] Snapshot is saved to
    /Users/janm/Snapshots/CliDemo-2008-05-06-shutdown(1).snapshot
```

We have collected a performance snapshot with the YourKit profiler. We will analyze the performance snapshot to find out which method took the longest. To do this, we will use the method list in YourKit's CPU view (see Figure 22-3).

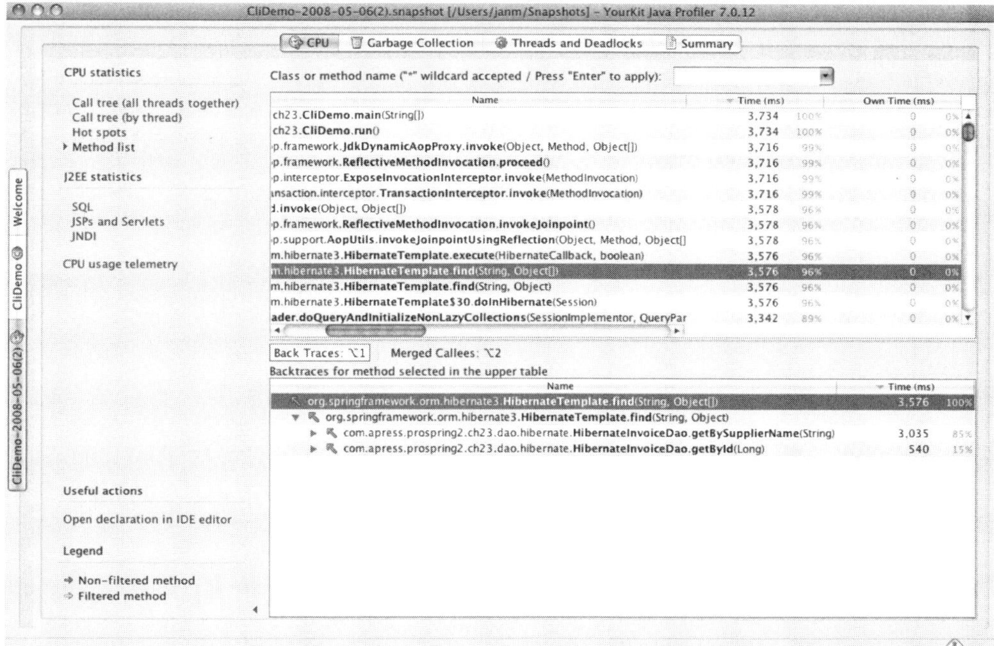

Figure 22-3. *YourKit profiler method list*

We can see that the application spends all of its time in the `CliDemo.main(String[])` method, followed by `CliDemo.run()`, `JdkDynamicAopProxy.invoke(. . .)`, and so on. There is nothing we can do about the `main` method (in fact, this is correct: the program spends all its time running the `main` method!), the first method that we can focus on tuning is `HibernateTemplate.find(String, Object)`. Further, we can see that this method is called from the `HibernateInvoiceDao.getSupplierByName` and `HibernateInvoiceDao.getById` methods. Having found which methods are causing the most delay, we can now focus our attention on improving the performance of those methods.

Determining the Necessary Data Sets

Before we proceed, we should find out whether we really need the selected suppliers, invoice lines, and discounts. Chances are that the users will only want to see a result page showing the invoice details. They can quickly page to the invoice and request its details. So we need to show the supplier, lines, and discounts only if users view the invoices.

Improving the Data Access Tier

We will begin by improving the performance of the data access tier. In our experience, there are two classes of problems in this tier: those concerning data selection, where your application unnecessarily selects more data than it needs or uses too many SQL statements to select the data, and those concerning inefficient data modification, where the applications are performing thousands of insert or update statements one by one rather than taking advantage of batching.

Improving Data Selection Performance

We will start with poor performance of the data selection code, particularly `DefaultInvoiceService`. It is not handling paging; in fact, if we used the command `s 1-1 Supplier%` to display one invoice, our code will select all rows from the `t_invoice` table. But that's not all—it will also select the appropriate rows from tables `t_supplier`, `t_invoice_line`, and `t_discount`. In total, using our test data set, our application will create 50 `Supplier`, 5,000 `Invoice`, 25,000 `InvoiceLine`, and 50,000 `Discount` objects only to throw away virtually all of them. The memory profile in Figure 22-4 clearly shows the steep increase in heap usage.

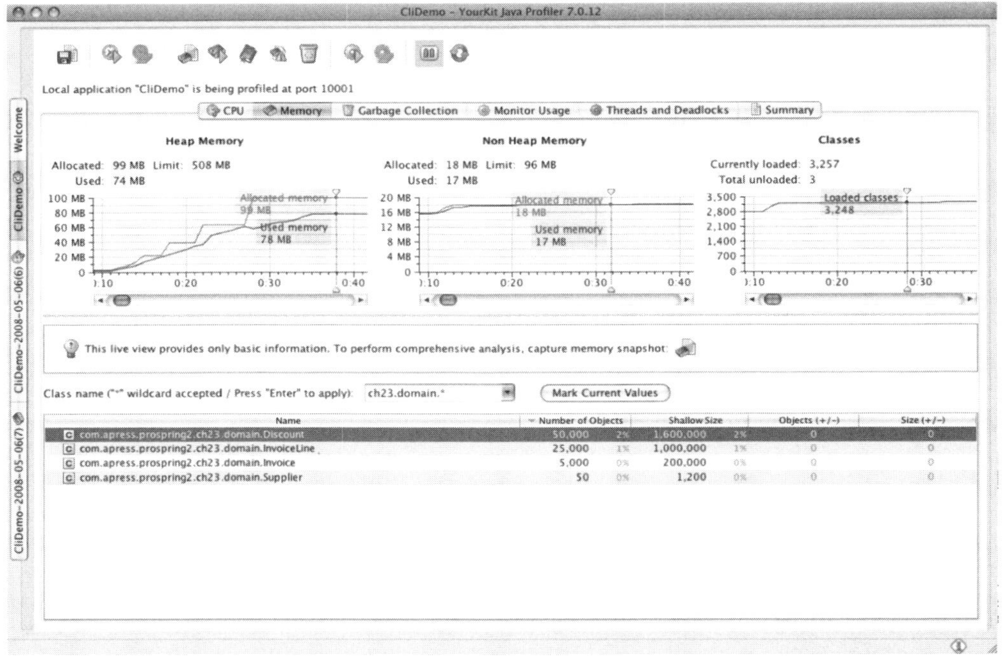

Figure 22-4. *Inefficient memory usage*

You can see that the heap usage has shot up from under 20MB to almost 100MB during the call to `DefaultInvoiceService.findBySupplierName`. We need to move paging to the services and data access tiers. Let's refactor the `InvoiceService.findBySupplierName` method to support paging; Listing 22-3 shows the `InvoiceService` and `InvoiceDao` interfaces with support for paging.

Listing 22-3. *Support for Paging in InvoiceService and InvoiceDao*

```
InvoiceService.java:
public interface InvoiceService {

    List<Invoice> findBySupplierName(String name,
        int firstResult, int maxResults);

    void save(Invoice invoice);

    Invoice findById(Long id);
```

```
}
```

InvoiceDao.java:

```
public interface InvoiceDao {

    void save(Invoice invoice);

    Invoice getById(Long id);

    List<Invoice> getBySupplierName(String name,
        int firstResult, int maxResults);
}
```

We needed to modify both the `InvoiceService` and `InvoiceDao` interfaces and their appropriate implementations. If we had only modified the `InvoiceService`, the code would not be too different from paging on the client side. The `DefaultInvoiceService` implementation of the `InvoiceService` is simply going to pass the paging information to the `HibernateInvoiceDao` (see Listing 22-4).

Listing 22-4. *Paging in HibernateInvoiceDao*

```
public class HibernateInvoiceDao extends HibernateDaoSupport implements InvoiceDao {

    public void save(Invoice invoice) {
        getHibernateTemplate().saveOrUpdate(invoice);
    }

    public Invoice getById(Long id) {
        return (Invoice) DataAccessUtils.uniqueResult(getHibernateTemplate().
            find("from Invoice where id=?", id));
    }

    @SuppressWarnings({"unchecked"})
    public List<Invoice> getBySupplierName(
            final String name, final int firstResult, final int maxResults) {
        return (List<Invoice>)
                getHibernateTemplate().execute(new HibernateCallback() {
            public Object doInHibernate(Session session)
                    throws HibernateException, SQLException {
                Query query = session.createQuery(
                        "from Invoice where supplier.name like :name");
                query.setString("name", name);
                query.setFirstResult(firstResult);
                query.setMaxResults(maxResults);

                return query.list();
            }
        });
    }

}
```

With this modification, running `s 1-1 Supplier%` in the CLI application completes in 182 milliseconds, which is a significant improvement over the previous 10,900 milliseconds! However, it still performs three select statements, even though we only need the data from the `Invoice` objects. We have configured Hibernate to eagerly load all associations. We need to modify the Hibernate mapping files and enable lazy loading for all classes. Listing 22-5 shows the required modification in the `Invoice.hbm.xml` mapping file.

Listing 22-5. *Hibernate Mapping Files*

```
<?xml version="1.0"?>
<!DOCTYPE hibernate-mapping PUBLIC
        "-//Hibernate/Hibernate Mapping DTD 3.0//EN"
        "http://hibernate.sourceforge.net/hibernate-mapping-3.0.dtd">

<hibernate-mapping default-lazy="true">
    <class name="com.apress.prospring2.ch23.domain.Invoice" table="t_invoice">
        ...
    </class>
</hibernate-mapping>
```

To enable lazy loading for all mapped classes, we need to change the value of the `default-lazy` to `true` in all mapping files. Alternatively, we can simply remove the `default-lazy` attribute, because Hibernate by default considers all associations to be lazily loaded.

We then run the profiler again to find out how it improved the performance of our application. And indeed, the profiler shows another significant decrease in the required time: from 182 milliseconds down to 6 milliseconds (see Figure 22-5).

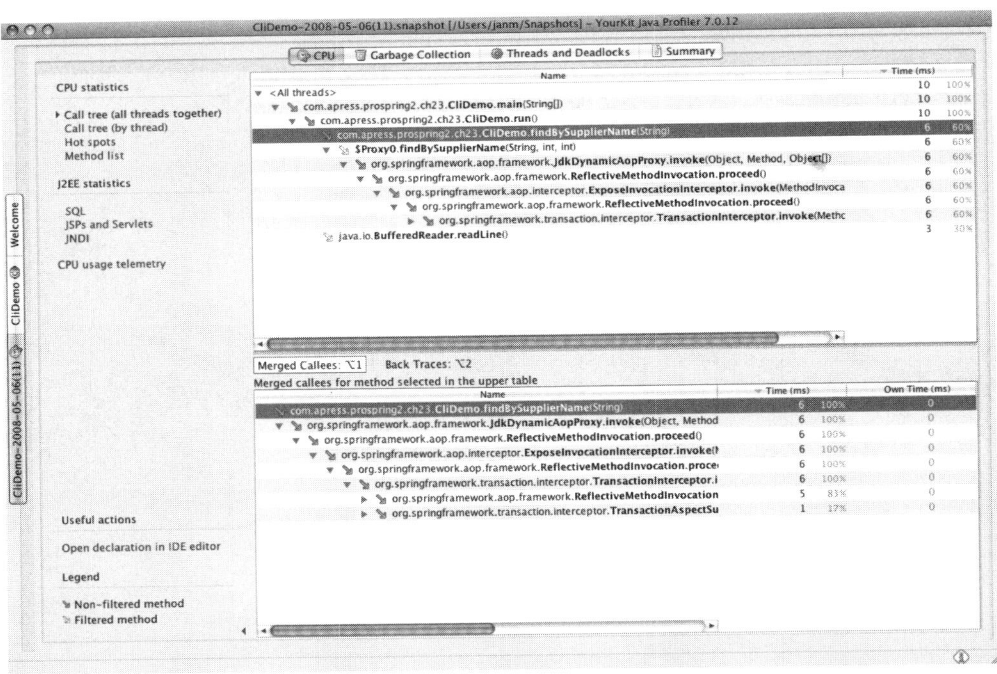

Figure 22-5. *CPU profile of the findSupplierByName call*

We have tuned the Java code as much as possible: we select only the data we are interested in, which leaves any further tuning in the database. Let's examine the SQL statement Hibernate will use for the `s 1-1 Supplier%` command from the CLI application:

```
Hibernate: select * from ( select row_.*, rownum rownum_ from
    ( select invoice0_.id as id1_, invoice0_.version as version1_,
      invoice0_.delivery_date as delivery3_1_, invoice0_.invoice_date as
      invoice4_1_, invoice0_.supplier as supplier1_ from t_invoice invoice0_,
```

```
t_supplier supplier1_ where invoice0_.supplier=supplier1_.id and
(supplier1_.name like ?) ) row_ where rownum <= ?) where rownum_ > ?
```

We can now run this statement directly against the database and view the execution plan. Figure 22-6 shows the execution plan for the preceding query.

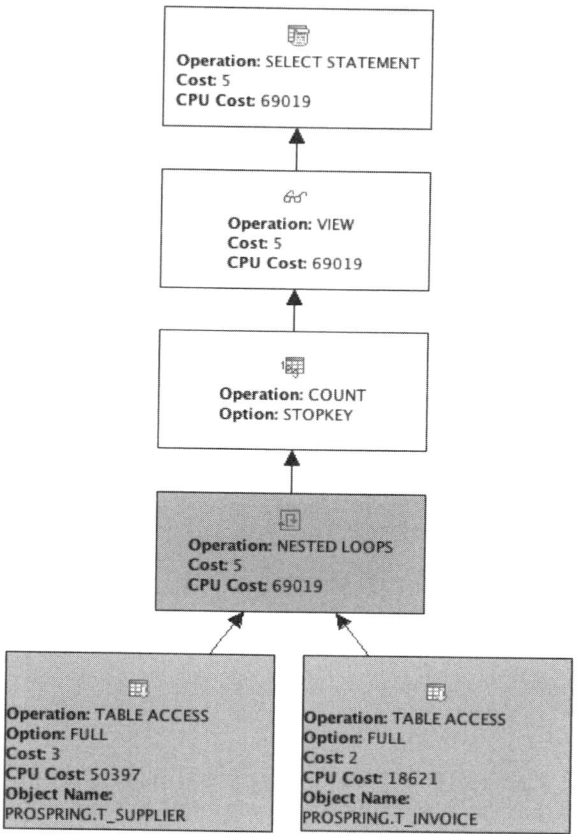

Figure 22-6. *Execution plan for the query*

Notice in particular the full table access operations on the `t_supplier` and `t_invoice` tables: even though our tables have less than 100,000 rows, the full table access will take a significant amount of time. To improve the performance of the query, we need to create an index on the name column in the `t_supplier` table. We'll create index `ix_supplier_name` using the code in Listing 22-6.

Listing 22-6. *Creating an Index*

```
create index ix_supplier_name on t_supplier (name)
```

This will reduce the full table scan of the `t_supplier` table to table access by `rowid` using a unique scan of the `ix_supplier_name` index. For further information about SQL tuning and database design, we recommend the excellent book by Tomas Kyte *Effective Oracle by Design* (McGraw-Hill Osborne Media, 2003).

The implementation of InvoiceService.findBySupplierName is as good as it can be; we will now see if we can improve InvoiceService.findById as well. First, let's modify the CliDemo.findById method to display all details about the selected invoice. Listing 22-7 shows the new code of the findById method.

Listing 22-7. *New Implementation of the CliDemo.findById Method*

```
public class CliDemo {
    private static final Pattern I_PATTERN =
        Pattern.compile("i\\W+(\\d+)");
    private static final Pattern S_PATTERN =
        Pattern.compile("s\\W+((\\d+)-(\\d+)\\W+)?(.+)");
    private InvoiceService invoiceService;

    private void findById(String line) {
        Matcher matcher;
        matcher = I_PATTERN.matcher(line);
        if (!matcher.matches()) return;
        Invoice invoice =
                this.invoiceService.findById(Long.valueOf(matcher.group(1)));

        System.out.println("Supplier: " + invoice.getSupplier());
        System.out.println("Delivery Date: " + invoice.getDeliveryDate());
        System.out.println("Invoice Date: " + invoice.getInvoiceDate());
        for (InvoiceLine invoiceLine : invoice.getLines()) {
            System.out.println("* " + invoiceLine.getProductCode() + " @ " +
                    invoiceLine.getPrice() + " + " +
                    invoiceLine.getVat());
            for (Discount discount : invoiceLine.getDiscounts()) {
                System.out.println("    * - " + discount.getAmount());
            }
        }
    }
    ...
}
```

The new implementation calls the IndexService.findById and displays all properties of the returned Invoice object. Let's measure its performance again to see if we can improve it any further. But if we run the i 10400 command in the CLI application, it fails:

```
i 10200
Hibernate: select invoice0_.id as id1_, invoice0_.version as version1_,
    invoice0_.delivery_date as delivery3_1_, invoice0_.invoice_date as invoice4_1_,
    invoice0_.supplier as supplier1_ from t_invoice invoice0_ where invoice0_.id=?
ERROR [main] LazyInitializationException.<init>(19) | could not initialize proxy
     - the owning Session was closed
org.hibernate.LazyInitializationException: could not initialize proxy
     - the owning Session was closed
    at org.hibernate.proxy.AbstractLazyInitializer.initialize(
       AbstractLazyInitializer.java:60)
    at org.hibernate.proxy.AbstractLazyInitializer.getImplementation(
       AbstractLazyInitializer.java:111)
    at org.hibernate.proxy.pojo.cglib.CGLIBLazyInitializer.invoke(
       CGLIBLazyInitializer.java:150)
    at com.apress.prospring2.ch23.domain.
       Supplier$$EnhancerByCGLIB$$73f90b98.toString(<generated>)
```

```
    at java.lang.String.valueOf(String.java:2615)
    at java.lang.StringBuilder.append(StringBuilder.java:116)
    at com.apress.prospring2.ch23.CliDemo.findById(CliDemo.java:32)
    ...
```

The exception is thrown from the line in bold: it is `invoice.getSupplier()`. We now have lazy loading enabled for all classes: Hibernate will load associations only when we request them as long as we do so while the Hibernate `Session` is open. The Hibernate transaction manager closes the Hibernate `Session` when the transaction completes, and all methods of the `DefaultIndexService` are transactional, so by the time the `DefaultIndexService.findById` method returns the `Invoice` object, the `Session` is closed. Therefore, any attempts to access the lazily loaded objects will fail. We can implement a naïve fix in the `DefaultInvoiceService` (see Listing 22-8).

Listing 22-8. *Naïve Fix of the Lazy Initialization Failure*

```
public class DefaultInvoiceService implements InvoiceService {
    ...
    public Invoice findById(Long id) {
        Invoice invoice = this.invoiceDao.getById(id);
        invoice.getSupplier().getName();
        for (InvoiceLine line : invoice.getLines()) {
            line.getDiscounts().size();
        }
        return invoice;
    }
    ...
}
```

When we run the CLI application using the new implementation of the `DefaultInvoiceService`, it works, but it performs four select statements: one when we call `invoiceDao.getById(id)`, one when we call `invoice.getSupplier().getName()`, one when we iterate over `invoice.getLines()`, and one when we call `line.getDiscounts().size()`. Because we know that we will need the `Invoice` object with all its associations, we will change the HQL statement in `HibernateInvoiceDao` so that it eagerly loads all associations. Listing 22-9 shows the new code for `HibernateInvoiceDao.getById`.

Listing 22-9. *New Implementation of the HibernateInvoiceDao.getById*

```
public class HibernateInvoiceDao extends HibernateDaoSupport implements InvoiceDao {

    public Invoice getById(Long id) {
        return (Invoice) DataAccessUtils.uniqueResult(
                getHibernateTemplate().find(
                        "from Invoice i inner join fetch i.supplier " +
                                "inner join fetch i.lines il " +
                                "inner join fetch il.discounts " +
                                "where i.id=?", id));
    }

    ...

}
```

The HQL statements tell Hibernate to fetch all associations of the `Invoice` objects eagerly. Hibernate will issue the following SQL statement to the database:

```
Hibernate: select invoice0_.id as id1_0_, supplier1_.id as id3_1_,
    lines2_.id as id2_2_, discounts3_.id as id0_3_, invoice0_.version as
    version1_0_, invoice0_.delivery_date as delivery3_1_0_,
    invoice0_.invoice_date as invoice4_1_0_, invoice0_.supplier as
    supplier1_0_, supplier1_.version as version3_1_, supplier1_.name as
    name3_1_, lines2_.version as version2_2_, lines2_.price as price2_2_,
    lines2_.product_code as product4_2_2_, lines2_.vat as vat2_2_,
    lines2_.invoice as invoice2_2_, lines2_.invoice as invoice0__, lines2_.id as
    id0__, discounts3_.version as version0_3_, discounts3_.amount as
    amount0_3_, discounts3_.type_ as type4_0_3_, discounts3_.invoice_line as
    invoice5_0_3_, discounts3_.invoice_line as invoice5_1__, discounts3_.id as
    id1__ from t_invoice invoice0_ inner join t_supplier supplier1_ on
    invoice0_.supplier=supplier1_.id inner join t_invoice_line lines2_ on
    invoice0_.id=lines2_.invoice inner join t_discount discounts3_ on
    lines2_.id=discounts3_.invoice_line
    where invoice0_.id=?
```

This statement will select all the data that Hibernate needs to create the `Invoice` object and all its associations. We can therefore remove the naïve initialization code in the `DefaultInvoiceService.findById`; Listing 22-10 shows the new implementation of this method.

Listing 22-10. *Implementation of the DefaultInvoiceService.findById*

```
public class DefaultInvoiceService implements InvoiceService {
    private InvoiceDao invoiceDao;
    ...
    public Invoice findById(Long id) {
        return this.invoiceDao.getById(id);
    }
    ...
}
```

Because `HibernateInvoiceDao` returns a fully initialized `Invoice` object, there is no need to perform any lazy loading initialization in `DefaultInvoiceService`. Because we are selecting all the data we need in as few SQL statements as possible, we can say that the `findById` method in the `DefaultInvoiceService` is now optimal.

Improving Data Update and Insert Operations

The next thing to optimize is data inserts and updates. The `DefaultInvoiceService.importInvoices()` method reads invoices from an external source and inserts all the imported invoices. The code in Listing 22-11 shows a naïve implementation of the `DefaultInvoiceService.importInvoices()` method.

Listing 22-11. *Naïve Implementation of the DefaultInvoiceService.importInvoices()*

```
public class DefaultInvoiceService implements InvoiceService {
    ...
    public void importInvoices() {
        for (int i = 0; i < 100; i++) {
            importForSupplier("Supplier 1");
            importForSupplier("Supplier 2");
            importForSupplier("Supplier 13");
        }
    }
```

```
    private void importForSupplier(String supplierName) {
        Random random = new Random();
        Invoice invoice = new Invoice();
        invoice.setDeliveryDate(new Date());
        invoice.setInvoiceDate(new Date());
        invoice.setSupplier(this.supplierDao.getByName(supplierName));
        for (int i = 0; i < random.nextInt(10); i++) {
            InvoiceLine il = new InvoiceLine();
            il.setPrice(new BigDecimal("10.00"));
            il.setVat(new BigDecimal("1.175"));
            il.setProductCode("Code");
            invoice.addInvoiceLine(il);
        }
        this.invoiceDao.save(invoice);
    }
    ...
}
```

We can see that when we call this method, it will insert 300 invoices; on average, each invoice will have five lines. The method will also perform 300 `select * from t_supplier` SQL operations to load the supplier identified by its name. When we measure the performance of this method, we find that it takes 5,500 milliseconds and runs 2,360 SQL statements! We can clearly reduce the 300 calls to find the supplier, but that will not have a significant impact. We need to use JDBC batch operations to insert the data. To improve the performance of the `importInvoices` method, we will create a `BatchInvoiceDao` interface with two methods: `addToBatch(Invoice)` and `insertAll()`. We will also modify the `importInvoices` and `importForSupplier` to eliminate the unnecessary calls to `SupplierDao.findByName`. The new code is in Listing 22-12.

Listing 22-12. *Using JDBC Batches to Improve Data Modification Performance*

```
public class DefaultInvoiceService implements InvoiceService {
    private BatchInvoiceDao batchInvoiceDao;

    ...

    public void importInvoices() {
        Supplier supplier1 = this.supplierDao.getByName("Supplier 1");
        Supplier supplier2 = this.supplierDao.getByName("Supplier 2");
        Supplier supplier3 = this.supplierDao.getByName("Supplier 13");
        List<Invoice> invoices = new LinkedList<Invoice>();
        for (int i = 0; i < 100; i++) {
            importForSupplier(supplier1, invoices);
            importForSupplier(supplier2, invoices);
            importForSupplier(supplier3, invoices);
        }
        this.batchInvoiceDao.insertAll(invoices);
    }

    private void importForSupplier(Supplier supplier, List<Invoice> invoices) {
        Random random = new Random();
        Invoice invoice = new Invoice();
        invoice.setDeliveryDate(new Date());
        invoice.setInvoiceDate(new Date());
        invoice.setSupplier(supplier);
        for (int i = 0; i < random.nextInt(10); i++) {
            InvoiceLine il = new InvoiceLine();
            il.setPrice(new BigDecimal("10.00"));
```

```
            il.setVat(new BigDecimal("1.175"));
            il.setProductCode("Code");
            invoice.addInvoiceLine(il);
        }
        invoices.add(invoice);
    }
    ...
}
```

The implementation of the BatchInvoiceDao, JdbcBatchInvoiceDao, is quite complex (see Listing 22-13), but using this approach, we have improved performance five times, reducing execution time from 5,500 milliseconds down to 1,100 milliseconds.

Listing 22-13. *JdbcBatchInvoiceDao Implementation*

```
public class JdbcBatchInvoiceDao extends JdbcDaoSupport
        implements BatchInvoiceDao {

    private static class SequenceNextvalSelect extends MappingSqlQuery {
        // omitted for brevity
    }

    private static class InsertInvoicePreparedStatementCreator
            implements PreparedStatementCreator {
        // omitted for brevity
    }

    private static class InsertInvoiceLinePreparedStatementCreator
            implements PreparedStatementCreator {
        // omitted for brevity
    }

    private static class InsertInvoicePreparedStatementSetter
            implements PreparedStatementSetter {
        // omitted for brevity
    }

    private static class InsertInvoiceLinePreparedStatementSetter
            implements PreparedStatementSetter {
        // omitted for brevity
    }

    private InsertInvoicePreparedStatementCreator
            insertInvoicePreparedStatementCreator;
    private InsertInvoiceLinePreparedStatementCreator
            insertInvoiceLinePreparedStatementCreator;

    public JdbcBatchInvoiceDao() {
        this.insertInvoicePreparedStatementCreator =
                new InsertInvoicePreparedStatementCreator();
        this.insertInvoiceLinePreparedStatementCreator =
                new InsertInvoiceLinePreparedStatementCreator();
    }
```

```
    public void insertAll(final List<Invoice> invoices) {
        getJdbcTemplate().execute(new ConnectionCallback() {
            public Object doInConnection(Connection con)
                throws SQLException, DataAccessException {
                PreparedStatement insInv =
                        insertInvoicePreparedStatementCreator.
                                createPreparedStatement(con);
                PreparedStatement insInvLine =
                        insertInvoiceLinePreparedStatementCreator.
                                createPreparedStatement(con);
                SequenceNextvalSelect snvs =
                        new SequenceNextvalSelect(getDataSource());

                for (Invoice invoice : invoices) {
                    invoice.setId((Long)snvs.findObject(new Object[]{}));
                    new InsertInvoicePreparedStatementSetter(invoice).
                            setValues(insInv);
                    insInv.addBatch();
                }

                insInv.executeBatch();

                for (Invoice invoice : invoices) {
                    for (InvoiceLine line : invoice.getLines()) {
                        new InsertInvoiceLinePreparedStatementSetter(line).
                                setValues(insInvLine);
                        insInvLine.addBatch();
                    }
                }
                insInvLine.executeBatch();
                return null;
            }
        });
    }
}
```

We admit that the JDBC batch code is not pretty, but it clearly demonstrates the point that batching the data modification operations will make a significant difference, especially as the batch size grows.

As well as JDBC batching, we recommend that you make full use of the features available in your database. For example, if your database supports CSV or Excel imports, use that functionality! The performance of the database's data import tools will, in most cases, be an order of magnitude better than the best code using JDBC batching in Java.

Improving Transaction Management

Transaction management is closely related to the data access tier: the transactional methods in the service tier usually involve more than one call to the data access tier. We have already covered the inappropriate use of transactions to fetch lazily loaded associations, but there are further optimizations we can make.

First, you should mark the transaction as read-only whenever your code will not modify any data. The databases can adopt different strategies when dealing with read-only transactions. Therefore, the `DefaultInvoiceService`'s transactional configuration should be read-only for the `find*` methods and read-write for all other methods. Further, we can consider explicitly setting the isolation level: the `find*` methods can use the `READ_COMMITTED` isolation level. You should carefully consider higher isolation levels, particularly SERIALIZABLE. Having multiple transactions in the SERIALIZABLE isolation level greatly increases the chance of reaching a deadlock. Listing 22-14 shows the service-context.xml configuration file that addresses all these considerations.

Listing 22-14. *Tuned services-context.xml*

```
<?xml version="1.0" encoding="UTF-8"?>
<beans xmlns="http://www.springframework.org/schema/beans"
       xmlns:xsi="http://www.w3.org/2001/XMLSchema-instance"
       xmlns:tx="http://www.springframework.org/schema/tx"
       xmlns:aop="http://www.springframework.org/schema/aop"
       xsi:schemaLocation="
           http://www.springframework.org/schema/beans
           http://www.springframework.org/schema/beans/spring-beans.xsd
           http://www.springframework.org/schema/tx
           http://www.springframework.org/schema/tx/spring-tx.xsd
           http://www.springframework.org/schema/aop
           http://www.springframework.org/schema/aop/spring-aop.xsd">

    <tx:advice id="txAdvice" transaction-manager="transactionManager">
        <tx:attributes>
            <tx:method name="find*"
                       read-only="true"
                       isolation="READ_COMMITTED"
                       timeout="5"/>
            <tx:method name="*" propagation="REQUIRES_NEW"/>
        </tx:attributes>
    </tx:advice>

    <aop:config>
        <aop:pointcut id="serviceOperation"
            expression="execution(* com.apress.prospring2.ch23.service.*.*(..))"/>
        <aop:advisor advice-ref="txAdvice" pointcut-ref="serviceOperation"/>
    </aop:config>

    <bean id="invoiceService"
        class="com.apress.prospring2.ch23.service.DefaultInvoiceService">
        <property name="invoiceDao" ref="invoiceDao"/>
    </bean>
</beans>
```

Here, we see that the find* methods are read-only: they execute under the READ_COMMITTED isolation level and have a very low (5 seconds) timeout. All other methods use the default isolation and default timeout. Further, we say that all other methods will start a new transaction, even if an existing transaction exists.

If your code needs to synchronize more than one transactional resource, you will need to use XA (sometimes called global) transactions. The overhead of XA transactions is far greater than the overhead of local transactions. This increased overhead comes mostly from the use of a two-phase commit. Whenever we commit a global transaction, the transaction manager contacts each resource in the transaction and sends it the query to commit request. Each resource prepares for the commit (in the case of databases, this usually means writing data to the undo log). The resource then notifies the manager whether it can commit or not. When the manager receives responses from all resources and if all responses indicate that the resources can commit, it sends the commit message to all resources. The manager must then wait for all resources to indicate that they have successfully committed. If any of the resources indicate that they cannot commit or if the commit fails, the manager sends the rollback message to all resources.

Apart from the two-phase protocol overhead, the transaction manager that deals with global transactions is far more complicated than a local transaction manager. The two-phase commit protocol we have described above skims over the details of network connections and possible failures. For example, what should the transaction manager do if all resources indicate that they will be able to commit in response to the query commit message, the manager sends the commit message, but one of the resources then fails to report that the commit was successful? Does that mean that the resource has failed to commit or that the network link between the manager and resource failed? All this potential complexity dictates that you should use XA transactions only if your application really needs them. In any case, tuning of the transaction manager, and XA data sources are beyond the scope of this chapter.

Controlling the Performance of Remote Calls

Unfortunately, we cannot improve the performance of remote calls using configuration, as we did for data access tuning. The optimization strategy for remote calls is to make them as coarse-grained as possible. This is almost opposite to the advice we gave for data access tier tuning: in the data access tier, you should select as little data as possible, but in the remoting tier, you should favor getting all the data you could possibly need in one call. Of course, the size of the data has a limitation; you should not try to load all `Invoice` objects identified by a supplier name and keep them in the session to allow for fast paging. Doing so would be fast, but it might require so much heap space that your application would very quickly run out of memory or would spend most of its time doing garbage collection.

Our advice is to use the most lightweight protocol you can. If your application does not have to interact with any other service, you can consider using Spring's `httpinvoker` instead of SOAP. You may also consider using Java RMI, which is even faster.

Understanding View Performance

It is important to make the most of the high-performance services (and transitively the data access tiers) in your web tier. You can use one of the following three fundamental approaches when writing the web tier for standard browsers:

- Use a templating engine such as Velocity or FreeMarker.
- Use standard JSP pages.
- Use XSL to transform XML into XHTML.

Templating engines are faster than JSP pages but do not offer as many features. On the other hand, if you follow the tenets of the MVC architecture, the views should not contain any logic. Therefore, the only compelling reason to use JSP pages is if you have (or plan to write) complex tag libraries. In our tests, Velocity and FreeMarker were about two to two and a half times faster than JSP pages. XSL transformations are the most complex way to prepare your views, and you should only use them if your model is in XML.

The worst-case scenario is to take a POJO model, transform it into XML, and then use XSL to transform the XML into XHTML.

Using Caching

If you have used every performance-improving approach you can think of but the application is still not as fast as required, you should think about caching. You can implement caching at different levels of abstraction: you can cache the entire HTTP responses at the web server level; you can cache global data in your singleton beans; and you can even cache the results of method invocations. Web server caching depends on the type of web server you use and is out of scope for this chapter. But storing global data in singleton beans is as easy as defining it as properties of the beans. We are going to take a look at how you can cache the results of method invocations. We will not reinvent the wheel by implementing our own caching solution, but we will briefly show you how to use the Cache SpringModule.

The concept behind method-level caching is to intercept all invocations of cacheable methods. We will check for a value in the cache that matches the method's name and arguments. If we find one, we'll return the value without calling the target method. If the cache entry for the method's name and arguments is missing, we'll invoke the target method and remember the returned value.

The concept is very simple, and you will be glad to hear that practical usage of the Cache SpringModule is just as easy. In fact, all we have to do to enable caching is to add the `service-cache-context.xml` configuration file and annotate the methods we wish to cache. Listing 22-15 shows the annotated `findById` method in the `DefaultInvoiceService`.

Listing 22-15. *Annotated DefaultInvoiceService.findById*

```
public class DefaultInvoiceService implements InvoiceService {
    ...
    @Cacheable(modelId = "Invoice")
    public Invoice findById(Long id) {
        return this.invoiceDao.getById(id);
    }
    ...
}
```

Listing 22-16 completes the caching example with the XML configuration file `service-cache-context.xml`.

Listing 22-16. *The service-cache-context.xml Configuration File*

```
<?xml version="1.0" encoding="UTF-8"?>
<beans xmlns="http://www.springframework.org/schema/beans"
       xmlns:xsi="http://www.w3.org/2001/XMLSchema-instance"
       xmlns:oscache="http://www.springmodules.org/schema/oscache"
       xsi:schemaLocation="
          http://www.springframework.org/schema/beans
          http://www.springframework.org/schema/beans/spring-beans.xsd
          http://www.springmodules.org/schema/oscache
          http://www.springmodules.org/schema/cache/springmodules-oscache.xsd">

    <bean id="cacheKeyGenerator"
          class="org.springmodules.cache.key.HashCodeCacheKeyGenerator"/>
    <bean id="cacheManager"
          class="org.springmodules.cache.provider.oscache.~CCC
                 OsCacheManagerFactoryBean">
    </bean>

    <bean id="cacheProviderFacade"
          class="org.springmodules.cache.provider.oscache.OsCacheFacade">
        <property name="cacheManager" ref="cacheManager"/>
    </bean>
```

```
    <oscache:annotations providerId="cacheProviderFacade">
        <oscache:cacheKeyGenerator refId="cacheKeyGenerator"/>
        <oscache:caching id="Invoice" refreshPeriod="3600"/>
        <oscache:flushing id="Invoice"/>
    </oscache:annotations>

</beans>
```

This is all we needed to write to enable method-level caching in our application. When we run it and use the i command, we will see the following results:

```
i 14000
Hibernate: select invoice0_.id as id1_0_, supplier1_.id ... where invoice0_.id=?
Supplier: Supplier{name='Supplier 40'}
Delivery Date: 2007-10-13 09:11:57.0
Invoice Date: 2007-10-13 09:11:57.0
* Product 5 @ 130.5423 + 43.6124
    * - 653552471
    * - 1488898877
    ...
    * - 1988962599

i 14000
Supplier: Supplier{name='Supplier 40'}
Delivery Date: 2007-10-13 09:11:57.0
Invoice Date: 2007-10-13 09:11:57.0
* Product 5 @ 130.5423 + 43.6124
    * - 653552471
    * - 1488898877
    ...
    * - 1988962599
```

You can see that there was no cache entry for `DefaultInvoiceService.findById(14000L)` for the first `i 14000` command. The second time we ran the same command (and so executed the same method), there was already an entry in the cache; therefore `DefaultInvoiceService.findById(14000L)` was never called. Notice that the code in `DefaultInvoiceService` does not implicitly handle the caching. The only addition to its code is the `@Cacheable` annotation. You should annotate the methods that invalidate the cache with the `@CacheFlush` annotation; in our case, we are going to mark the `DefaultInvoiceService.save(Invoice)` method with the `@CacheFlush` annotation. This caching approach is applicable to whatever method you choose, even methods in the web tier that return `ModelAndView` instances.

Because a lot of development effort is going into the Cache SpringModule at the time of this writing and the module is changing rapidly, rather than go into any more detail here, we will refer you to `https://springmodules.dev.java.net/`.

Performance Testing

If you are working on an application, be sure to include performance tests as part of your test suite. Listing 22-17 shows the simplest form of performance test that verifies that the `DefaultInvoiceService` works within a time limit.

Listing 22-17. *Simple Performance Test*

```
@ContextConfiguration(locations = {
        "classpath*:/META-INF/spring/*-context.xml",
        "classpath*:/META-INF/spring/*-context-t.xml"})
public class DefaultInvoiceServiceIntegrationTest
        extends AbstractTransactionalJUnit4SpringContextTests {
    @Autowired
    InvoiceService invoiceService;

    @Test
    public void testFindById() {
        long start = System.currentTimeMillis();

        Invoice invoice = this.invoiceService.findById(13000L);
        assertThat(invoice, notNullValue());
        assertThat(invoice.getSupplier().getName(), equalTo("Supplier 30"));
        assertThat(invoice.getId(), equalTo(13000L));
        assertThat(invoice.getLines().size(), equalTo(5));

        assertThat(System.currentTimeMillis() - start < 2000, is(true));
    }
}
```

However, tests of this type are tedious to write and will not show any performance benefit from using a cache. To evaluate the effect of a cache in the test, we need to run the body of the test at least twice: the first run will show the performance with cache miss, and the second run will show the performance with cache hit. However, if you are using caching on a method, you expect that the method will be called more than twice. To test accurately for this, you should repeat your test method at least 50 times.

JUnit's `@Test` annotation allows you to specify a timeout, but there is a deadly catch. If your test suite class extends the `AbstractTransactionalJUnit4SpringContextTests`, you normally expect the test method to run in a transaction that is rolled back once the test finishes. However, if you specify the `timeout` value in the `@Test` annotation, the transaction for the test method will be committed. As a workaround, Spring offers its own `@Timed` annotation. Let's refactor our `testFindById` method to make full use of Spring's performance testing annotations (see Listing 22-18).

Listing 22-18. *DefaultInvoiceServiceIntegrationTest with Spring Performance Testing Annotations*

```
@ContextConfiguration(locations = {
        "classpath*:/META-INF/spring/*-context.xml",
        "classpath*:/META-INF/spring/*-context-t.xml"})
public class DefaultInvoiceServiceIntegrationTest
        extends AbstractTransactionalJUnit4SpringContextTests {
    @Autowired
    InvoiceService invoiceService;

    @Test
    @Repeat(50)
    @Timed(millis = 20000)
    public void testFindById() {
        Invoice invoice = this.invoiceService.findById(13000L);
        assertThat(invoice, notNullValue());
        assertThat(invoice.getSupplier().getName(), equalTo("Supplier 30"));
        assertThat(invoice.getId(), equalTo(13000L));
        assertThat(invoice.getLines().size(), equalTo(5));
    }
}
```

This test proves that 50 executions of the `DefaultInvoiceService.findById` method will not take more than 20 seconds, and it passes even on a slow connection to the database.

Monitoring Application Health and Performance

Acceptable performance in unit and integration tests, and on the test platform, is no guarantee of equally good performance in the production environment. Even if your application performs well under test, you should include some performance and health monitoring infrastructure in your code. Without this, you will find it hard to pinpoint the cause of any performance problems that crop up later. If you are using Hibernate, the simplest thing to do is to expose Hibernate's statistics MBean. To do that, you need to add just a few lines to the Spring XML configuration file (see Listing 22-19).

Listing 22-19. *Exposing the Hibernate Statistics MBean*

```
<?xml version="1.0" encoding="UTF-8"?>
<beans xmlns="http://www.springframework.org/schema/beans"
       xmlns:xsi="http://www.w3.org/2001/XMLSchema-instance"
       xmlns:util="http://www.springframework.org/schema/util"
       xmlns:tx="http://www.springframework.org/schema/tx"
       xmlns:aop="http://www.springframework.org/schema/aop"
       xsi:schemaLocation="
            http://www.springframework.org/schema/beans
            http://www.springframework.org/schema/beans/spring-beans.xsd
            http://www.springframework.org/schema/util
            http://www.springframework.org/schema/util/spring-util.xsd
            http://www.springframework.org/schema/tx
            http://www.springframework.org/schema/tx/spring-tx.xsd
            http://www.springframework.org/schema/aop
            http://www.springframework.org/schema/aop/spring-aop.xsd">

    <bean id="dataSource" class="org.apache.commons.dbcp.BasicDataSource"
        ...
    </bean>

    <bean id="hibernateSessionFactory"
          class="org.springframework.orm.hibernate3.LocalSessionFactoryBean">
        <property name="dataSource" ref="dataSource"/>
        <property name="mappingLocations">
            <list>
                <value>classpath*:/META-INF/hibernate/*.hbm.xml</value>
            </list>
        </property>
        <property name="hibernateProperties">
            <props>
                <prop key="hibernate.dialect">
                    org.hibernate.dialect.Oracle9Dialect
                </prop>
                <prop key="hibernate.current_session_context_class">thread
                </prop>
                <prop key="hibernate.show_sql">true</prop>
                <prop key="generate_statistics">true</prop>
            </props>
        </property>
    </bean>
```

```
    <bean id="statisticsBean" class="org.hibernate.jmx.StatisticsService">
        <property name="statisticsEnabled" value="true"/>
        <property name="sessionFactory">
            <ref local="hibernateSessionFactory"/>
        </property>
    </bean>

    <bean id="exporter" class="org.springframework.jmx.export.MBeanExporter">
        <property name="beans">
            <map>
                <entry key="bean:name=statistics" value-ref="statisticsBean"/>
            </map>
        </property>
    </bean>

...
</beans>
```

We have configured the Hibernate `StatisticsService` bean and the `MBeanExporter` in the `dataaccess-context.xml` file; in large applications, you will probably place the `MBeanExporter` in a separate XML configuration file. Let's take a look at Figure 22-7 to see what we can find out from the `StatisticsService` MBean.

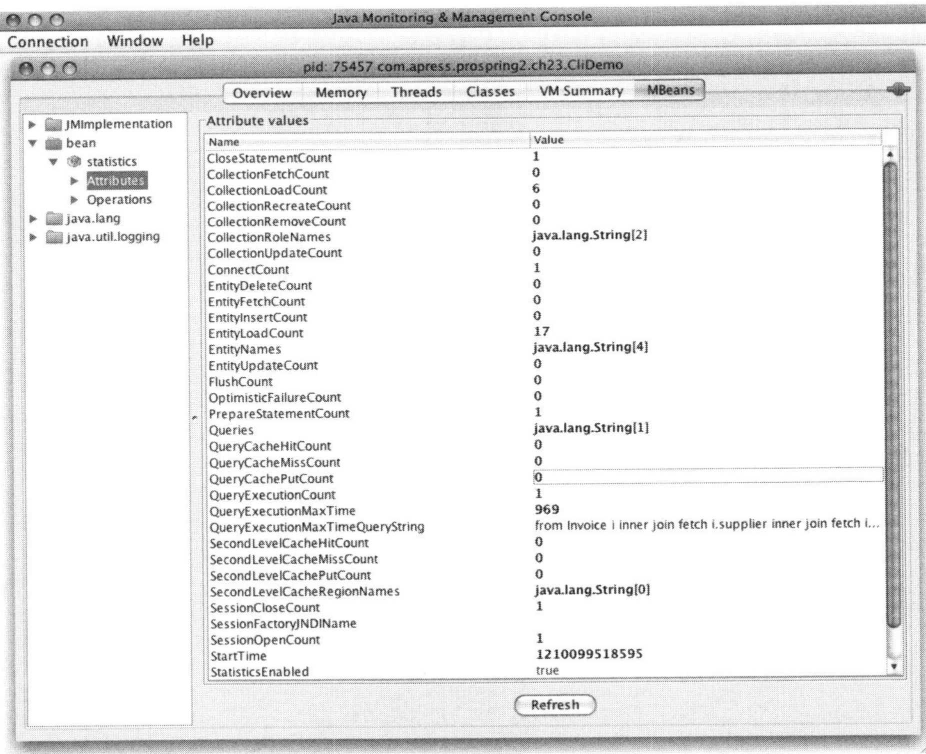

Figure 22-7. *Hibernate StatisticsService MBean*

Figure 22-7 shows the attributes of the `StatisticsService` MBean after running the `i 14000` command in the CLI application. We can see that Hibernate has executed one query (`QueryExecutionCount`) and loaded 17 entities (`EntityLoadCount`). We can also see that the longest query took 969 milliseconds to complete (MBean property `QueryExecutionMaxTime`) and its text was `"from Invoice i inner join fetch i.supplier inner join fetch i.lines il inner join fetch il.discounts where id=?"` (MBean property `QueryExecutionMaxTimeQueryString`). Using this MBean, you can quickly find out the performance of the ORM.

Next, you should consider implementing the performance and health-monitoring AOP infrastructure. We explain this in full detail in Chapter 6.

More Resources on Performance Tuning

Performance tuning is a vast topic; we have only covered the aspects that are closest to the Spring Framework and Java EE applications. After you have optimized all your Java code, you may want to consider tuning your JVM (see Sun's *Java Performance Guides* at `http://java.sun.com/docs/performance`). In particular, tuning the garbage collector can bring significant performance benefits to your application.

We have touched on the topic of SQL tuning, for much more information, take a look at Thomas Kyte's "Runstats.sql" article at `http://asktom.oracle.com/tkyte/`.

To create complete integration tests, you should consider Apache JMeter (`http://jakarta.apache.org/jmeter`) and Selenium (`http://selenium.openqa.org/`). Both of these tools allow you to measure the performance of the entire application by interacting with the web tier.

Finally, to keep an eye on your application in a production environment, take a look at JAMon (`http://jamonapi.sourceforge.net`).

Summary

In this chapter, you have learned how to improve your Spring application's performance. In our experience, most performance (and memory) problems are centered on the data access layer, and we have dedicated the larger part of this chapter to identifying and improving the performance of the DAO tier, in particular the object-relational mapping.

You also know how XA transactions can slow down a Java EE application. Staying in the Java EE domain, you know how to deal with remote calls; because of Spring's easy-to-use remoting infrastructure (see Chapter 15), you can experiment with your application's remoting protocols until you find the best compromise between interoperability and performance. Finally, you have learned how great an impact XML processing can have, particularly when dealing with views.

You also know how to write tests that evaluate the performance of your application. If you include these tests in your test suite, you can be confident that your application's speed fits the requirements.

Finally, we discussed ways of monitoring your application once it is deployed in the production environment.

There are other aspects of performance tuning—JVM tuning (particularly related to garbage collection strategies), SQL tuning, load balancing, and many, many more—but they are beyond the scope of this chapter and this book. To get you started, though, we've offered some suggested resources for further reading.

Index

Special Characters

A

B

C

J

N

O

P

S

T

U

X

Y